D1556321

DISCARD

Ladies and Gentlemen in the Box Seats

The Audience in the Pit

BRITISH PLAYS
OF THE
NINETEENTH
CENTURY

An Anthology to Illustrate the Evolution of the Drama

J. O. BAILEY
University of North Carolina

THE ODYSSEY PRESS · INC · NEW YORK

Frontispiece illustrations by courtesy of the Mansell Collection, 42 Linden Gardens, London, W.2.
R. C. Maturin's *Bertram* and J. B. Buckstone's *Luke the Labourer* are reproduced by permission
of The Huntington Library, San Marino, California.

PREFACE

It is the intention of this anthology to present plays that illustrate the evolution of the English drama in the nineteenth century from the legitimate verse drama of 1800 into the new drama of the 1890's. An Introduction sketches the constantly changing environment to which the drama had to adapt. Not intended to be a history of the Victorian theatre, this Introduction is condensed from the detailed studies listed in the Bibliography. But perhaps it offers the information needed to explain the phenomena evident in the plays.

Mr. Allardyce Nicoll's lists of nineteenth-century plays indicate the intense dramatic activity of this period. The lists give the names of about thirty thousand plays, and these are not all, for American and other foreign plays appeared on the London stages (the centers of dramatic activity), other plays were produced briefly and died in "provincial" theatres, and doubtless no records remain of hundreds of melodramas, extravaganzas, and dramatic entertainments, performed for a few evenings and thrown away. Though no anthology of seventeen plays can illustrate everything that happened in all this bustle, the plays chosen show the major types and main lines of development. Such plays are not necessarily the best of the period. Judged by any high standard of dramatic art, *Luke the Labourer* is a poor play, but it illustrates a significant development. Boucicault's *After Dark* is hardly his best play, but it exhibits the effort of melodrama to thrill audiences with sensation scenes. *East Lynne* is wretched as dramatic art, but it holds up a mirror to public taste in the years when this play was almost universally acclaimed.

To some extent, plays available in recent anthologies are not included. Mr. Montrose Moses's *Representative British Dramas, Victorian and Modern* (still available in many bookstores) contains twelve plays produced between 1820 and 1900, and Mr. George Rowell's *Nineteenth Century Plays* presents ten plays between 1829 and 1890. The plays in these volumes are briefly mentioned in the Introduction and are listed in the Bibliography with the idea that the student may supplement his reading from these collections. Tom Robertson's *Caste* is included even though it appears in both collections, for it perfectly illustrates a significant mutation. To sample the new drama of the 1890's I have chosen Shaw's first play, *Widowers' Houses*, rather than a far better play, *Candida* or *Caesar and Cleopatra*, because *Widowers' Houses* illustrates a transition as Shaw felt his way from a melodramatic plot William Archer gave him toward the drama of significant ideas. Pinero's *The Second Mrs. Tanqueray* is a finer play than *The Notorious Mrs. Ebbsmith*, but I have chosen *Mrs. Ebbsmith* because *Mrs. Tanqueray* appears in nearly every Victorian anthology that includes plays. The comments introducing each play are not intended to be exhaustive critiques. In varying degrees they summarize opinions in standard books, express my own reactions, and point out the role of each play in the evolution of the drama.

Comparison of the dramas here reprinted with texts available in libraries may show some startling variations. There are no "definitive" editions for many of these plays. They were printed "as produced at" this theatre or that one, in this or that acting version. For example, I have examined four printings of Maturin's *Bertram*, each different in many details from the others, and chosen what seems to me the best to exhibit the essential play. Plays printed from actors' copies usually included abbreviated directions for production: "L. H., U. E.," etc. I have taken the liberty of editing out directions that might impede reading. In short, the present anthology is intended not for close textual study, but for reading to understand the plays.

It is hoped that the dramas chosen will be of interest, partly even for qualities that thrilled our great-grandparents — for these plays were popular in America as well as in England. Even if the forms are old-fashioned, the basic substance of the old dramas can be gripping, as the melodramas on television demonstrate. Beyond this interest these plays throw light on Victorian life and thought, not on the high levels where Carlyle and George Eliot expounded, but among the common people. The drama was, from the Restoration almost to 1800, the art of a somewhat sophisticated upper class, but after 1800 it became the entertainment of an increasingly democratic society. That is why it clearly exhibits the manners, moral "ideals," prejudices, sentiments, and values of the English people under Victoria. And that is why it had to adapt and evolve.

In the Introduction I have here and there quoted a sentence or two from an author who is listed in the Bibliography and who phrased an idea perfectly. In this summary I have not thought it necessary to provide footnote references.

J. O. Bailey

CONTENTS

Introduction   1

THE THEATRES OF LONDON   2

The Theatres Royal before 1843   2

The Minor Theatres in Uncertain Bondage   4

Freeing of the Theatres   5

The Stage and the Auditorium   5

Actors and Acting   8

Reformers and Reforms   11

THE AUDIENCE   13

AUTHORS   16

ROMANTIC VERSE DRAMA   20

The Traditional Modes   20

The Gothic Thriller   23

The Historical Play   24

The Domestic Play   25

The Closet Drama   26

COMEDY   27

The Comedy of Manners   27

The Burletta   28

MELODRAMA   30

THE RISE OF THE NEW DRAMA   35

Romantic Verse Drama   39

The Traditional Modes

CHARLES ROBERT MATURIN, *1780-1824:*
Bertram; *or*, The Castle of St. Aldobrand (1816)   41
EDWARD BULWER-LYTTON, *1803-1873:*
Richelieu; *or*, The Conspiracy (1839)   70

Experimentation and the Closet Drama

JOHN WESTLAND MARSTON, *1819-1890:*
The Patrician's Daughter (1842)   110
ROBERT BROWNING, *1812-1889:*   Pippa Passes (1841)   132

Comedy   157

Comedy of Manners

DION BOUCICAULT, *1820?-1890:*   London Assurance (1841)   159

Farce

TOM TAYLOR, *1817-1880:*   Our American Cousin (1858)   192

Melodrama   221

THOMAS HOLCROFT, *1745-1809:*   A Tale of Mystery (1802)   223
JOHN BALDWIN BUCKSTONE, *1802-1879:*
Luke the Labourer; *or*, The Lost Son (1826)   238
DOUGLAS WILLIAM JERROLD, *1803-1857:*   The Rent-Day (1832)   258

DION BOUCICAULT, *1820?-1890:*   After Dark (1868)   281

MRS. HENRY WOOD, *1814-1887:*   East Lynne (1862)   303

HENRY ARTHUR JONES, *1851-1929:*   The Silver King (1882)   328

The Rise of the New Drama   371

Transitional Plays: Comedy-Drama and Burlesque

THOMAS WILLIAM ROBERTSON, *1829-1871:*   Caste (1867)   373

WILLIAM SCHWENK GILBERT, *1836-1911:*   Engaged (1877)   405

The New Drama

GEORGE BERNARD SHAW, *1856-1950:*   Widowers' Houses (1892)   431

HENRY ARTHUR JONES, *1851-1929:*   The Masqueraders (1894)   460

ARTHUR WING PINERO, *1855-1934:*
The Notorious Mrs. Ebbsmith (1895)   493

Bibliography   532

INTRODUCTION

Though the nineteenth century English drama is generally regarded as a desert stretching from Sheridan to Wilde and Shaw, an evolution of first importance took place during this period. This evolution parallels the Darwinian processes of adaptation for survival. Briefly, a well-developed species found itself in a changing environment; it struggled to adapt, failed, declined, and died. The traditional "legitimate" drama inherited from Elizabethan and Restoration times was moribund by 1800. The tragedies or histories of this drama were in verse; they treated themes reminiscent of Shakespeare or Otway, or the heroic love-and-honor themes of Dryden's theatre. Legitimate comedies were in prose, but they presented the old situations of Congreve, Steele, and Sheridan with little reference to anything observable in nineteenth-century society. Plays like Bulwer-Lytton's *Richelieu*, Marston's *The Patrician's Daughter*, and Boucicault's *London Assurance* sought to please their audiences by adding some popular, democratic subject matter, still expressed in the old aristocratic forms, but this compromise was not enough to save the legitimate drama. It was virtually dead by about 1850. Tennyson's *Becket* and Jones's *The Tempter*, late in the century, represent a final gasp in the death agony of the species.

An "illegitimate" mutation of the drama, the melodrama, came into existence in response to popular taste; as this taste changed, it changed, in step-by-step processes of adaptation. Without binding traditions or inhibitions, it provided audacious spectacles, songs, and dances; it treated the domestic interests of middle- and lower-class audiences in plays like Jerrold's *The Rent-Day*; it took over the French formula of the "well-made" play; it presented the local plumber, Sam Gerridge, and "natural" dialogue in Robertson's *Caste*. During the 1890's a final mutation of the melodrama produced the species called the new drama—the plays of Jones, Pinero, and Shaw. The following sketches indicate the environment to which the drama adapted.

THE THEATRES OF LONDON

The Theatres Royal before 1843

When "the immortal Siddons" first entered the Theatre Royal, Drury Lane, she looked quietly around the vast building and then said with a sigh, "Behold the tomb of the drama!" Drury Lane was one of the three legitimate theatres in London; the other two were Covent Garden and the Haymarket, which was chiefly devoted to opera. The term "legitimate" means that these theatres were licensed by royal patents and by law (Acts of 1737 and later) to produce plays of any kind, though the Haymarket might produce dramas only during the summer months when the other "patent houses" might be closed. In the seventeenth century and through much of the eighteenth, three theatres royal were adequate for their somewhat aristocratic audiences; not many members of the middle and lower classes, still influenced by Puritan antagonism to the theatre, attended plays. As London grew in size and as Puritanism relaxed, however, the ever-more-prosperous lower classes swarmed into the theatres. Whenever a theatre burned — as often happened — it was rebuilt larger than ever to admit more and more of the common people. After being rebuilt in 1794, Drury Lane Theatre burned down in 1809. It was rebuilt by 1812, with more attention to ornate columns and statuary than to the needs of the drama. It held an audience of more than three thousand. Likewise, Covent Garden, rebuilt in 1792, burned in 1808, and was again rebuilt, with an enormous stage (sixty-eight feet deep and eighty-two feet wide) and a magnificent auditorium (including four tiers of twenty-six boxes each) to seat three thousand. In these coliseums many members of the audience could not see the faces of the actors or hear lines that might be spoken in a natural tone of voice. The vast size of the theatres royal, where drama had to be presented as pomp and spectacle, thus helped to fulfill Mrs. Siddons's prophetic words.

Since the theatres royal were intended to foster the drama as art (originally the concern of a small, sophisticated upper class), these theatres were obligated to produce dramas from a repertory of Shakespeare and other time-tested, standard dramatists. Yet to attract audiences they had to offer a miscellany of several plays on an evening's bill and to change the program frequently. This required a large company, with a separate corps of actors for tragedy, comedy, and musical plays, an orchestra, soloists, and choral singers, not to mention scene painters, property men, etc. These people were hired by the season. An evening's receipts had to support not only the performers seen on the stage, but performers not then acting and a great deal of "overhead." For example, during the week ending December 26,

1840, when Madame Vestris and Charles Mathews were managing Covent Garden, six hundred and eighty-four persons were on the payroll.

The monarch of such a theatrical company was ordinarily an actor-manager, the star in whatever Shakespearean or other traditional play might be on the bill. At least in the early years of the century this star was chiefly occupied with his own roles; supporting actors played in the background as they pleased. Charles Kemble, managing Covent Garden from 1803 to 1817, had some idea of stately, perfected presentations; he arranged his actors on the stage for pictorial effects, though always to focus attention on the star. This, with the absence of ensemble acting and other conditions in the theatre, encouraged impassioned elocution more than naturalness of performance. When William Charles Macready, who managed Covent Garden from 1837 to 1839 and Drury Lane from 1841 to 1843, demanded rehearsals for unified effects and the harmony of scenery and stage action with the dramatic text, his innovations earned him the title "Sergeant Macready" and a newspaper comment that on a "drill-day" he "takes his recruits, rehearses for and with them, making them all speak in his own peculiar manner, conceive, read, and execute the parts his way."

These facts — the obligation to produce standard dramas of the past, vast auditoriums, huge expenses, and the star system — partly account for the decline of the traditional drama, the desperate efforts of the theatres royal to meet the competition of the minor theatres, and the headway the minor theatres were able to make against the patent houses. The minor theatres could ignore tradition and produce the entertainment their audiences wanted — burlettas, melodramas, extravaganzas, spectacles, and "the horses." Though responsible for upholding the dignity of Shakespearean and other verse plays as *the* drama, the legitimate theatres were forced to appeal to audiences by producing the popular shows of the minor theatres as curtain raisers or afterpieces. The theatres royal found audiences respectful to Shakespeare, but thrilled by such a melodramatic, equestrian spectacle as *Timour the Tartar*, produced at Covent Garden with real horses in 1814. In fact, they had produced such pieces in the eighteenth century, and the first English play labeled "mélodrame," Holcroft's *A Tale of Mystery* (1802), was produced at Covent Garden. Increasingly through the early nineteenth century they presented spectacles to compete with performances at, for instance, the Adelphi: "a Chinese giant, Indian dancers, a legless acrobat who got himself up with spreading wings as a monstrous fly," and the like.

Consequently, though the theatres royal continued to support traditional dramas, their performances by the 1830's scarcely differed from those at the minor theatres. For example, the program at Drury Lane for May 2, 1832, was: *The Tyrolese Peasant*, a domestic opera; *The Rent-Day*, a domestic melodrama; and *The Beggar's Opera*. The playbill at Covent Garden for March 13, 1840, lists: Sheridan Knowles's *Love*, a "new, original play"; Charles Mathews's *Patter v. Clatter*, a burletta; and anonymous, *The Fortunate Isles; or, The Triumphs of Britannia*, a "grand allegorical and nautical masque." When W. C. Macready, resolute champion of the traditional drama, gave up the management of Drury Lane in 1843, this theatre turned avidly to novelty and spectacle. It had found, as F. B. Chatterton said later, that "Shakespeare spells ruin, Byron bankruptcy." In this year the minor theatres were "freed," and the monopoly of the legitimate drama by the theatres royal came to an end.

The Minor Theatres in Uncertain Bondage

The Act of 1737 that established the monopoly of the legitimate drama in the theatres royal intended to prohibit the presentation of plays anywhere else in London; but it permitted other places of public entertainment to present music, singing, dancing, and animal shows. Gradually such entertainments came to include songs with connecting recitative, and then full-length recitations with connecting songs. The term "burletta" was coined to describe such pieces. The Lord Chamberlain and even magistrates licensed theatres to produce burlettas, but as these grew more and more elaborate it became hard to distinguish between a burletta and a play with music. Songs were added to versions of standard tragedies and comedies so that they might be presented as burlettas; a melodrama with musical accompaniment might be called a burletta. Required to define the term, the Lord Chamberlain ruled that a burletta must have six songs. To get their plays licensed for production, managers of the minor theatres would send him manuscripts accompanied by six songs — whatever was handy — but in production they might "forget" the songs. Ordinarily there was some pretense, at least, that a play was a musical entertainment; a few lines might be recited to a piano accompaniment, or a few chords struck from time to time without a recitation. Generally, by 1832 violations of the law tended to be ignored; in any case the minor theatres were thriving on kinds of drama that featured music, dancing, and pantomine.

The term "minor theatre" used in relation to the theatres royal does not necessarily refer to a small, insignificant playhouse. Some of the early minor theatres rivaled the theatres royal in size and splendor. Though theatres had come and gone, apparently six minor theatres were producing in London in 1800; eleven new ones were built before 1832, but four were destroyed and not rebuilt. Between 1832 and 1843 fifteen more were built, though seven were destroyed. When the theatres were freed in that year, apparently enough were already in existence, for no new theatre was built for some time. A few of these theatres were even larger and more elaborate than the theatres royal; the Coburg, for instance, held nearly four thousand, and was decorated with gold-braided mirrors and a looking-glass curtain in which every member of the audience could see himself and his fellows. The Surrey had gold and velvet decorations.

During the first decade of the century the minor theatres, besides spectacles, acrobatic exhibitions, and animal shows, chiefly presented plays that could be called burlettas: extravaganzas, nautical pieces (singing and dancing sailors, with some dialogue), and melodramas. By the 1830's some of the minor theatres were producing plays that attracted the better actors and challenged the art of the theatres royal. Indeed, an article in the *Theatrical Observer* for May 28, 1831, ironically commented upon this situation: "At the theatre royal, Drury Lane, we have *Timour the Tartar* and the horses. At the theatre royal, Covent Garden, we have the *Life and Death of Buonaparte*, as a mere spectacle accompanied by every kind of catchshilling gee-gaw, and some horses, while, on the other hand, we find at Sadler's Wells, *Romeo and Juliet, Katharine and Petruchio*; at the Surrey, *Richard III*, several other of Shakespeare's plays and Cumberland's *Jew*, with Elliston; and finally at the new City Theatre in Milton Street (alias Grub) the *Merchant of Venice;* Shylock, Mr. Kean!!!"

Some theatres developed specialties for particular audiences: the Olympic was noted for burlesque and the Adelphi for melodrama. Charles Rice's manuscript, written in the 1830's, gives a typical program at the New Strand Theatre for August 13, 1836: *The Bride of Ludgate*, a comedy by Douglas Jerrold; *The Bill Sticker*, a burletta "attributed to a Mr. Brownrigg" (in fact, Douglas Jerrold); *Hercules*, a burletta; and *Othello (According to Act of Parliament)*, an "inimitable burlesque extravaganza." The manuscript comments: "In *Hercules* the whole of the interest is centered in Mr. Hammond, who sings a song, and throws the Grecian Statues, with equal ability. . . . I think there was hardly enough of the burlesque in Miss Daly's Desdemona to well accord with a Duke sitting in council with a pipe in his mouth, a pot of hevy [*sic*, strong ale] before him, and attended by policemen."

Freeing of the Theatres

An effort to remove the legal restrictions on the minor theatres was made in 1832, when a bill to free the theatres, largely framed by Edward Bulwer, was introduced into Parliament. This bill, which included provisions to check the censorship of the Lord Chamberlain and to provide for the copyright of plays, passed the Commons, but was defeated by the Lords. Perhaps the strong sentiment in favor of the bill accounted for the laxity in enforcing the monopoly between 1832 and 1843. At any rate, a bill ending the monopoly and permitting any properly licensed theatre to produce spoken drama was passed in 18__. But the expected surge forward in the erection of theatres and the production of traditional plays did not take place. By this time, no doubt, members of the upper class who might support the traditional drama formed only a small proportion of the audience. So for some twenty years the existing theatres continued to produce what they had been producing, often with a melodrama as the serious part of the program. If freeing the theatres had any immediate effect, it was chiefly to justify the theatres royal in attempting to please large audiences by producing more melodramas and spectacles; they were, in fact, the right size for these productions. When effective reforms came at last, they came from the smaller, more intimate stages. No new theatre was built in London until the 1860's, though, for reasons to be discussed later, twelve new playhouses were erected between 1866 and 1880.

The Stage and the Auditorium

The stage inherited from the eighteenth century had a large apron that extended in front of the proscenium doors and over the pit — a relic of the Elizabethan platform stage. In the traditional manner actors advanced upon the apron to speak their lines to the audience: an actor far back on the stage might not be heard. As new stages were built, and old ones rebuilt, this apron receded, becoming smaller and smaller until it was at last a slight bulge in front of the proscenium doors. Efforts to remove these incongruous doors, one on each side of the stage, were made in the first decade of the century, and they were removed from Drury Lane in 1822. The traditional setting for the stage consisted of a painted curtain at the back and painted wings at the sides. Madame Vestris, who then managed the Olympic, in 1832 introduced the box set, with side walls and a ceiling instead of wings with a curtain to cut off their tops. A similar box set appeared at Drury Lane in 1834, and the team of Mathews and Vestris used box sets in producing Boucicault's *London Assurance* at Covent Garden in 1841. Yet many theatres continued to use wings and back cloths, and it was not until the 1870's that the box set became standard. In other features of scenery, progress was much more rapid and sensational. For one thing, spectacles and tableaux became standard theatrical fare, and for another, the developing melodrama, with somewhat monotonous plots, structures, and sentiments, found its lifeblood in ever more sensational scenery.

In the traditional drama of the early nineteenth century a minimum of scenery and properties was used: there would be only two chairs on the stage if only two people were to sit down. The great theatres had stock scenery for a city square, a street, a room, and a mountain pass, and re-used the same backdrop and wings for play after play. A repertory theatre, presenting several plays an evening for short runs, had to use stock sets or go bankrupt. As late as 1843, Robert Browning was annoyed with W. C. Macready for setting the stage for *A Blot in the 'Scutcheon* with parts of old, often-seen sets. Producers of traditional drama made little effort to use fresh, suitable scenery until Charles Kean, in mid-century, produced Shakespeare with historically accurate settings and costumes.

But the melodrama, its life dependent on thrills, used scenery to make the spectators gasp. A multiple-room effect, two cells separated by a partition, appeared in Lewis's *Venoni* at Drury Lane in 1808. Fitzball's *Jonathan Bradford*, at the Surrey in 1833, presented an interior of four rooms. Melodramas exhibited grand outdoor spectacles from the time of *A Tale of Mystery* (1802) onward. *The Siege of Gibraltar* at Sadler's Wells in 1804 presented "a grand Naval Spectacle . . . with real Men of War and Floating Batteries . . . in a receptacle containing nearly 8000 cubic feet of real water." In the same play, a town burns, floating batteries take fire and blow up, and drowning Spaniards flounder in the water till British Jack Tars plunge in to rescue them. *Bertram* (1816) presents a storm, a sinking ship, monks with torches at night, processions, and wild woods and caverns. Using a diorama, Moncrieff's *Zoroaster* (1824) presented a succession of scenes: "The Great Desert by Twilight; a Caravan of Merchants; the Pyramids" and on to "the Destruction of Babylon" and beyond. The domestic melodrama brought widows' cottages, village merrymakings, and factory scenes to the stage. Fitzball's *Paul Clifford* (1835) required "a stage coach, and six *real* horses."

Scenes had to become more thrilling as the century advanced in order to hold audiences jaded by the repetitions of melodrama. In the 1870's a Professor Pepper invented an arrangement of glass, black cloth, and light to bring onto the stage ghosts that "materialized" and faded away — a novelty used in *Hamlet*. Mists (made of gauze), agitated seas, waterfalls, raging fires (of gas, lycopodium, and blowers), snow storms, fire engines, and railroad engines were a few of the spectacular features of the late melodrama. W. S. Gilbert cynically observed: "Every play which contains a house on fire, a sinking steamer, a railway accident, and a dance in a casino, will (if it is liberally placed on the stage) succeed in spite of itself. In point of fact, nothing could wreck such a piece but carefully written dialogue and strict attention to probability." Sensation, that kept the melodrama alive, demanded a kind of fresh reality in scenic effect, and this reality was basic in plays that at last rejected mere spectacle and depended upon "carefully written dialogue and strict attention to probability."

Lighting was important in scenic effects. At the opening of the century theatres were still lighted by candles, but gas began to be used in the second decade. Covent Garden and Drury Lane installed gas lighting in 1817 — though odors were so offensive that in 1828 they returned for a while to candles and oil. In 1825 the limelight was invented, and Macready used it in staging *Richelieu* at Covent Garden in 1839 — though it did not come into general use until the late 1850's. Color screens could be used with limelight.

The auditoriums were usually lit by chandeliers and wall brackets. For most of the period before 1850 lights were kept burning in the auditorium during a play, but by mid-century houselights were generally dimmed during the performance. The Savoy, producing Gilbert and Sullivan's *Patience* in 1881, was the first English theatre to light both stage and auditorium with electricity.

At the beginning of the nineteenth century, though a curtain was raised to begin and lowered to end a play, the stage was often bare till actors came on, and many a play closed with "Exeunt." Ordinarily the curtain was not lowered to mark the end of a scene or an act. Scenery was shifted and properties were dragged on and off in full view of the audience. During the first decade, here and there, curtains began to be lowered between acts, and instead of leaving the stage bare actors began to group themselves in picturesque poses or tableaux. Yet it was not until the 1880's that the practice of lowering the curtain between scenes became general.

Costuming in 1800 was a kind of rummage — neither accurate nor consistent. Each actor was responsible for "finding" his costume. Stars ordinarily found something reasonably appropriate, but lesser actors in a Roman scene, for instance, might appear in something more appropriate to the Elizabethan age. The actor John Philip Kemble, staging *King John* and *Henry IV* in 1824, conceived the idea of costuming these plays accurately. J. R. Planché, under Kemble's direction, undertook the task of researching the proper costumes — and advertisements for the plays proudly listed "Authorities for the Costumes." The example was followed here and there. When Mathews and Vestris produced *London Assurance* in 1841, they were careful to dress the actors in elegant contemporary clothing instead of the grotesque outfits usual to comedy. In general, after mid-century costumes were reasonably appropriate to the characters.

The auditorium of a theatre in 1800 consisted of the pit, tiers of boxes, and a gallery. The pit occupied the entire ground floor from the orchestra to the back of the house. It was furnished with hard benches without backs; there was no aisle down the center. "Pittites" paid an entrance fee and scrambled for whatever seats they could find. Boxes were comfortably furnished; the gallery was pretty much what it is today, but farther from the stage in the larger theatres. Changes took place gradually. The Haymarket announced in 1843 that "For the comfort of those visiting the pit, backs have been placed to all the seats." Yet Clement Scott recorded that when he first visited Drury Lane in 1849 he saw "the faithful pittities sitting on hard benches, and constantly disturbed between the acts by women with huge and clumsy baskets filled with apples, oranges, nuts, ginger beer, bottled stout, and bills of the play." After 1840 reserved stalls (cushioned seats) began to occupy the area just in front of the stage and to push the pit back. Stalls and reserved seats became general after the Bancrofts introduced them at the Prince of Wales's Theatre in the 1860's. By the 1880's the old pit had either been pushed under the dress circle or abolished altogether. This change is significant in relation to the behavior of the audience.

As programs mentioned above illustrate, theatres through much of the nineteenth century performed more than one play in an evening. Before 1817, the curtain at Covent Garden and Drury Lane usually went up at 6:30 o'clock, but in that year curtain time was changed to 7:00. Opera, catering to the upper class, began at 8:00. The minor theatres continued to open to suit their varied audiences: the Coburg at 6:15, the Surrey at 6:30, and the Adelphi at 6:45. The theatres sought to entertain until midnight or sometimes 1:00. The custom of performing a single play, opening at 8:30, was instituted by the Bancrofts at the Prince of Wales's Theatre in the 1860's. The Bancrofts also began matinee performances, but these did not become general until the 1890's.

Prices of admission varied. In the early part of the century those at the theatres royal were nearly double the prices at the minor theatres. The famous "Old Price" riots at Covent Garden occurred when, reopening after the expense of rebuilding, the management raised prices from six shillings to seven for the boxes and from three shillings to four for the pit. The riots continued for months, with the carrying of banners, throwing of garbage, war dances, and howls during performances, until the management cut sixpence from the price for the pit. These riots indicate the popularity of the theatre and the growing "democracy" of the audiences. The custom of "half-price at 9:00 o'clock" is perhaps more important than a list of prices. Whatever might be going on — tragedy, comedy, or melodrama — the pit filled then, in a noisy scramble for seats. The system continued, in general, until the 1870's and the reforms at the Prince of Wales's Theatre.

Actors and Acting

Acting styles through the first half of the nineteenth century reflect the personalities of a few famous players and their interpretations of legitimate drama. We can understand the stylized action of the melodrama (and the play scripts that specify this action) if we observe John Philip Kemble and Edmund Kean in traditional verse plays. Flashes of truth to life in Macready's art paralleled growing naturalness in domestic plays and helped these plays toward greater realism. Then the evolving drama broke away from the Shakespearean tradition, and the chief influences of acting upon the drama (and vice versa) came from the Bancrofts and Tom Robertson.

The famous actors played verse drama at Covent Garden and Drury Lane. The size of these theatres demanded exaggerated acting, for the players had to move to tears or rage spectators in the abysm of a candle-lit immensity. Acting styles from Kemble to the 1860's rest upon this simple fact. In the theory of the day, acting was not supposed to imitate nature. It was art — sublime poetry expressed in gesture, tone, and declamatory power. This concept shaped the would-be exalted verse drama of the early 1800's. The opposite concept began to shape the plays of the 1880's, written to be acted naturally because acting is properly imitation of nature. We see the gulf between these concepts if we try to imagine a successful production today of Maturin's *Bertram*. The lines could not be played as they were written (in an inflated and ranting style) without producing laughter; they could not be played quietly and make sense. It is equally unthinkable to imagine Edmund Kean in Wilder's *Our Town*. (The Victorians knew their acting styles were absurd; the poems quoted below describing Kemble and Kean make this clear. The popular Victorian burlesque rested on something like the effort to imagine Kean in *Our Town*.)

The actor-manager system in the early years had much to do with acting styles. As one road to performance and success, a playwright would study a star and write a play to give this actor scope for his particular style, as Bulwer-Lytton wrote *Richelieu* for Macready, or, looking through play scripts, a star would choose the play he might act to best advantage. A star might refuse any part he held to be beneath his genius. Macready included in his contract with manager Alfred Bunn a clause allowing him to refuse any part "such as he, W. C. Macready, may deem as partaking of a melo-dramatic character, and . . . he is to have the choice of characters on all occasions." In short, as the public demanded, a play was performed to exhibit the star actor.

Under this system there was little question of teamwork in production. The ordinary actor was expected to appear, stand in his proper place, and feed cues to the star. He had little incentive to rehearse, for all eyes would be on the star. For example, when Kemble starred in *The Iron Chest*, Colman recorded: ". . . there never was one fair rehearsal of the play, wherein one, two or more of the performers, very essential to the piece, were not absent; and all the rehearsals which I attended, so slovenly and irregular, that the ragged master of a theatrical barn might have blushed for the want of discipline."

Nearly all depended, then, upon the star. In the theatres royal, where half the audience could hardly see or hear, the star had to *act*, in the artificial sense: to pose, to gesture, to stamp, to rave, to shout, to menace, to plead. Each great star rose to that mad eminence through qualities of appearance, voice, or gesture that took the public fancy, and maintained his position by displaying these qualities in a hundred roles.

John Philip Kemble was the star at Drury Lane and Covent Garden (which he managed successively) from the late eighteenth century to 1817. He liked to play classic roles — Brutus, Cato, Coriolanus, as well as Hamlet — and his acting style was a relic from the Attic attitude of the eighteenth century. His toga-wrapping gestures were modeled less upon classical life than upon classical statuary. He posed and declaimed, with "outbursts of excitement at a climax." Alan Downer quotes a contemporary description — none too friendly — of Kemble's style:

> Stiff, pompous, stern, each haggard feature gloom'd;
> Each step predestin'd, and each look foredoom'd;
> Precise in passion, cautious e'en in rage,
> Lo! Kemble comes, the Euclid of the stage;

Who moves in given angles, squares a start,
And blows his Roman beak by rules of art;
Writhes with a grace to agony unknown,
And gallops half an octave in a groan.
His solemn voice, like death-bell heard afar,
Or death-watch clicking in an old crackt jar,
He measures out, monotonous and slow,
In-one-long-sing-song-to-joy-or-woe.

Kemble's successor as England's leading actor, Edmund Kean, was more romantic. After being a strolling player in country towns, Kean played Shylock at Drury Lane in 1814, interpreting this character as "a swarthy fiend with a huge butcher's knife in his grasp and blood-lust in his eyes." He played, with impassioned frenzy, the roles of evil men — for instance, the outrageous villain of Maturin's *Bertram*. He specialized in an "hysterical sob under powerful emotion" that threw the ladies in the boxes into fainting postures. A contemporary realist wrote of him:

Holding in high disdain all sort of action
That does not evidence complete distraction;
His locks, his legs, his arms, his all, he scatters,
And tears a passion into very tatters. . . .
His conduct on the whole the keenest satire
On all that's natural — he christens nature.

Perhaps, to audiences tired of Kemble's classic poses and now thrilled by Gothic romances and Lord Byron's bleeding heart, Kean's style seemed a return to nature. He spanned the romantic era, acting until his death in 1835.

Kemble and Kean set the pattern for portraying the type characters of the melodrama: chiefly the hero, the villain, and the orphan-ingénue. Because early melodramas were performed by nondescript actors for noisy audiences, some formula for easily understood acting was necessary. The simplest formula was exaggeration of Kemble's stately poses and gestures and Kean's passionate rant. The hero stalked in attitudes à la Kemble, and the villain scowled and writhed like Kean; the ingénue was inclined to weep and faint. These actions became as stylized as the movements in ballet. Thomas Erle summed up the action of a melodrama as late as 1880. A midnight assassin tiptoes across the stage to find his victim asleep: "He looks at him — starts — recoils — then turns to the audience, and in a whisper fraught with tremendous significance puts them in possession of a circumstance which they have already had abundant opportunity of observing for themselves, namely that 'he sleeps!' He then proceeds to execute a series of brisk, but elaborate manoeuvres about the body, comprising . . . tactics sufficient to carry a small army through an ordinary campaign." The melodrama did not evolve into the new drama because it was acted naturally; rather, when a melodramatic piece was acted naturally, it ceased to that extent to be melodrama.

William Charles Macready rose to stardom during Kean's life, rivalled Kean in popularity, and after Kean's death dominated the London stage until he retired in 1851. To some extent Macready combined Kemble's classic style and Kean's emotional fervor. Macready was a scholar and an associate of cultured gentlemen, writers, and poets, among them Browning. He spoke the great speeches of his heroic roles with rhetorical passion and a peculiar jerk in his voice, but in less important passages he acted with some subtlety and variety based on an understanding and appreciation of the poetry he recited. He sought to give a measure of naturalness, tones of tenderness, and everyday gestures, to many human reactions.

As actor-manager Macready sought to improve staging; he rehearsed his companies with unusual care; and he subordinated himself to the meaning of a play. Distressed at the decline in quality and popularity of the verse drama — to him *the* drama — Macready struggled to elevate it. For his Shakespearean roles he discarded corrupt acting versions (common since the eighteenth century) and restored original texts. He labored hard with Bulwer-Lytton to make *Richelieu* a great play; he urged Browning to write for the theatre and did all he could to help Browning understand the needs of the stage. However, Macready was mistaken in one passionately held belief, that the future of the drama lay in a return to the traditional verse play and in original, new dramas of that kind.

No actor of similar stature followed Macready immediately, but, coming up through stock parts, acting for Boucicault, and at last creating a sensation in Lewis's *The Bells* (1871), Henry Irving dominated the English stage during the last thirty years of the century. Irving's characteristic power was revealed in *The Bells*. His role of a guilty man tortured by remorse that he must not show demanded variety, flashing change, and a subtle, hinting quality in his voice and facial expressions. In this and other roles the roughnesses and impediments in his speech actually helped Irving convey the impressions of passion and tenderness which were difficult to express. He seemed not so much to recite lines as, haltingly (with an effect of naturalness), to think them. Acting of this kind was possible on the quieter stages of the 1870's. When performing in Shakespeare and, later, in the new drama, Irving staged his plays carefully and imaginatively; whatever may be said of Tennyson's *Becket* as drama, Irving's production was a splendid spectacle. He was created Sir Henry Irving in 1895, the first English actor to be knighted for the quality of his work on the stage.

The new drama developed with the aid of an even more natural kind of acting. Increasingly through the century naturalness in acting advanced; in comedy because it was in prose, and in domestic melodrama because it exhibited something like everyday situations. No eminent actor led the way, though Macready's intelligent interpretations of character were suggestive. Naturalness accompanied a new vision of the drama — of the play as the thing (not the star), of ensemble acting, and of dialogue like normal human speech. The reforms of Madame Vestris and the Bancrofts did as much as anything else to advance the cause of quiet, rational modern acting.

Reformers and Reforms

The most ardent reformer of theatrical conditions in the first half of the nineteenth century was Madame Lucy Eliza Vestris, a singer, dancer, and burlesque performer who, in 1830, took over the management of a dingy little theatre in Wych Street — a slum area. Determined to make this theatre, the Olympic, the most fashionable rendezvous in town, she redecorated it in a gorgeous style, with a painted ceiling, a crystal chandelier, real curtains, a Brussels carpet; etc. In 1832 she constructed the first box set seen on a London stage — solidly made, papered, decorated, and ceiled. Abandoning makeshift properties, she furnished the stage with elegant pieces of solid carved oak. She abolished grotesque costumes and silly comic acting, and tried, at least, for naturalness. She prospered, for the Olympic did become fashionable.

In 1839 she and her husband, Charles Mathews, took over the management of Covent Garden, carrying some of her reforms into that citadel, and successfully producing *London Assurance*. Later, in 1847, managing the Lyceum, Vestris and Mathews abolished half-price tickets there. But these reforms did not have the influence they deserved to have. For Madame Vestris specialized in farce and burlesque, Charles Mathews was a light comedy star, and they were not aided (as the Bancrofts were) by a talented playwright who shared their aims.

Marie Wilton, also a singer and dancer in burlesque, in 1865 took over the management of a run-down and generally unsuccessful theatre commonly called the "Dust Hole" — though officially named the Queen's Theatre in Tottenham Street. Together with her partner at the time, H. J. Byron, she requested permission to change the name of the theatre to the Prince of Wales's, and was informed that "his Royal Highness the Prince of Wales . . . signified his consent to the proposed change." Without much money, Miss Wilton repainted and redecorated the theatre with "Curtain, carpets, in fact all the appointments . . . of the cheapest kind, but in good taste." She abolished much of the pit, filled the area near the stage with comfortable stalls, and decorated their seats with white lace antimacassars. She placed the musicians out of sight and filled their place with rockwork, running water, and a fernery.

Marie Wilton married an intelligent comedy actor, Sir Squire Bancroft, and discovered a playwright, Tom Robertson, with ideas similar to her own. She and her husband played in roles Robertson wrote for them. This team staged Robertson's epoch-making series of comedy dramas with the utmost attention to naturalness and realism. For *Caste* they built box sets with great care, and all of the plays were costumed with equal attention to detail. Mrs. Bancroft abolished the theatrical wardrobe and paid for suitable dresses for her actresses, while Sir Squire "cast his careful and critical eye over the clothes of the men." Most radically, the Bancrofts abandoned the custom of offering a medley of plays; they raised the curtain at 8:30 and produced one play. They also raised prices. In 1868 they advanced the price from eighteen pence to two shillings for the pit and from six to seven shillings for the stalls, and in 1873 to ten shillings for the stalls. In a sense, they selected their audience. The Prince of Wales was proud of the transformation of the old Dust Hole into the theatre that bore his name. He and the Princess frequently attended performances and attracted other royal persons there. On November 23, 1874, when Robertson's *Society* was enjoying a successful revival, the Prince attended in the company of the Duke of Edinburgh, the Cesarewitch who became the Emperor of Russia, his brother the Grand Duke Alexis, and Prince Louis of Battenburg. After the play the Prince brought the royal visitors to the greenroom to meet the Bancrofts. Sir Squire stated with modest pride, "I only mention the circumstance, as I doubt if any little greenroom ever received so large a contingent of royalty at the same time."

To justify their prices, the Bancrofts produced Robertson's plays as no plays had ever before been produced in London. Robertson, with his eye on the company of actors, provided roles to fit the peculiar talents of Marie and Sir Squire Bancroft and each of the others. He wrote plays to discourage — indeed, to destroy — the star system: he spread the action all over the stage, with two or more conversations going on simultaneously, and he invented stage business to force actors to speak quietly and naturally. It was impossible to indulge in rhetoric and grand gestures while balancing a teacup and saucer in one hand and a plate of sandwiches in the other. He wrote detailed stage directions, and then he himself rehearsed the productions. He demanded ensemble playing that focused on the play — not the star. Sir Squire Bancroft was proud of this reform and wrote: "No attempt is made by any one . . . to eclipse his fellows, or to monopolize either the space on the boards, or the attention of the audience. No piece is presented in such a state of unpreparedness that the first dozen performances are no better than rehearsals; no slovenliness in the less important accessories of the play is permitted."

In earlier days stars had visited the "provincial" theatres in other English cities, performing there with whatever local "stock" might be on hand. The Bancrofts sent out an entire company, carefully rehearsed, to present Robertson's *Caste* on a national tour. It was not the first such company, for Boucicault had taken companies on tour, but it was the first to tour with a single play fully equipped and thoroughly rehearsed. By the 1890's London companies were touring all over England with well-rehearsed plays. Successful in their little theatre, in 1879 the Bancrofts took over the Haymarket. There they abolished the apron and gave the stage a picture frame by running a gold border two feet wide all around it. Again they were successful. They chose to retire in 1885.

The reforms of the Bancrofts and Robertson had lasting influence. W. S. Gilbert declared that Robertson "invented stage management," and in his own plays, including the Savoy operas, he followed Robertson's example, becoming "probably the most dreaded director in London," meticulous in attention to "the scenery, the lighting . . . the groupings of the chorus . . . practically every inflection of the voice and every gesture of the actors." Arthur W. Pinero, whose *Lords and Commons* the Bancrofts produced in 1883, so admired Robertson and his methods that he wrote a play, *Trelawny of the "Wells,"* about Robertson. The Bancrofts and Robertson set the stage, so to speak, for the Independent Theatre and the new drama generally.

THE AUDIENCE

In *The Old Drama and the New* William Archer wrote: "In the survey of the English dama, old and new, which we are now undertaking, I propose to begin by enquiring whether we can discover in the history of the drama as a whole any guiding principle of evolution." Perhaps the principle is simply that of adaptation to the demands of changing society. In a time of social change the melodrama appeared as a mutation and became so popular that it threatened the legitimate drama. The drama of the theatres royal fought for life: Shakespearean plays returned to the original texts and were acted in elaborate settings with authentic period costumes; authors tried to make new romantic verse plays more popular by adding exciting material from the melodrama and by using blank verse to portray contemporary life. Meanwhile the melodrama improved in technique and structure, and became more realistic in settings and action. Taken to be a serious portrayal of life, this new species usurped the proper role of the verse drama by the 1850's. In this evolution, growth to maturity depended upon improvements in methods of staging and acting styles. Continuing to improve in these areas from the 1860's onward, the melodrama developed into the new drama of the 1890's. It now seems that the process was inevitable, but it was no more planned than a biological mutation. Tom Robertson did not know and might have been shocked to imagine that in his comedies at the Prince of Wales's he was preparing the way for Pinero's *The Second Mrs. Tanqueray.*

The introduction to an anthology of plays offers no room for a survey of nineteenth-century social history. But a few facts may call to mind the social changes to which the drama had to adapt. England's population nearly quadrupled during the nineteenth century, from 8,892,536 in 1801 to 32,527,843 in 1901. It became increasingly democratic. The Reform Bill of 1832 defined the ruling class to be the upper-middle class; the Bill of 1867 extended the right to vote to all literate males except day laborers and farm laborers. In the early part of the century illiteracy was common, though there were dame schools and charity schools for the more fortunate members of the lower class, governesses and tutors for the well-to-do middle class, and a classical education at Eton and Oxford for the aristocracy. In 1870, to educate the voters, England established a system of universal elementary education. A third Reform Bill in 1884 granted the right to vote to all literate male citizens. Agitation for woman suffrage began in the 1860's and extended through the 1890's, resulting in the enfranchisement of women in the twentieth century.

These facts underlie England's change from a semi-feudal to a democratic society. Patterns of living evolved from those suggested by knee breeches and powdered wigs in the age of Samuel Johnson to those suggested by motion pictures and motor cars in the age of H. G. Wells. The aristocratic taste for Byron and Carlyle early in the century evolved into the democratic taste for the daily newspaper in the 1890's. Problems of adjustment to social and intellectual change had long agitated the leaders of the country; these problems were stated for playgoers in the new drama of the 1890's.

The drama developed in London, where population increased even faster than in the country at large, from 959,310 in 1800 to 4,536,267 in 1900. The audiences in the London theatres changed with the basic changes mentioned above. The most important mutation in the evolution of the drama was the appearance of the melodrama, which continually adapted to a lower and middle class increasing in numbers, power, and education throughout the century.

In this period, for the first time since the Puritans closed the theatres in 1642, large numbers of the common people went to see plays. In the early decades of the century literacy in this group was low and taste was depraved, and yet, as Allardyce Nicoll remarks, audiences were "constantly thirsting, thirsting, thirsting," not only for entertainment, but for some interpretation of their own lives that would seem true, real, and natural. They could not find (or at least did not perceive) much truth and reality in the traditional verse dramas; they admired and applauded, but could not understand plays about life outside their experience or beyond their education. Democracy advanced and literacy increased, but for most people not to that point of a classical education where a play like Talfourd's *Ion* (on a Greek subject) could seem real. But the domestic melodrama, evolving into the better constructed and staged mid-century play, seemed almost a mirror of life — if not everyday life, at least a comprehensible life and one possible for members of the audience themselves. It is worth noting that not only sensational scenes and actions, but any touch of recognizable reality — a realistic lamppost, for instance, or the name of an actual street — sent a thrill through the audience and insured the success of the melodrama. Boucicault knew that trick — it was the foundation for *The Streets of London* — and Robertson's dramas at the Prince of Wales's seemed to audiences of the 1860's the last word in realism.

The pittites who conducted the Old Price riots at Covent Garden in 1809 established in the theatres a kind of mob rule that lasted for half a century, until the popularity of music halls lured away the rowdies, the rising standards of literacy sobered the remainder, stalls pushed the pit back from the stage, and more solid citizens joined the audience. To an unusual extent the pittites were members of the lower class, with incomes just sufficient to enable them to spend three or four shillings on the theatre. No doubt they included respectable, middle-class people, but many of these stayed away, still influenced by the Puritan prejudice against the theatre as a hangout of libertines, where wives and daughters might be insulted and God-fearing men disdained by perfumed dandies, and where the citizen who could not afford a box might (at best) rub elbows with ruffians.

There was good reason for this view. In the early decades of the century theatres were something like public brothels, for prostitutes and their gallants made up a sizable part of the audience. In the 1830's areas were provided for prostitutes to make their solicitations; at Covent Garden certain rooms were allotted to them. W. C. Macready did not like this situation and all that it implied — the immorality and low social status of actors and actresses, for instance — as well as the discredit it cast upon the drama. When he became manager of Covent Garden in 1837, he excluded "women of the town" from the two lowest tiers of boxes. In 1841, becoming manager of Drury Lane, he limited them to a gallery, which they "could reach . . . only by a separate pay-box, and by passing through a dismantled and unseated lobby, unpainted and unpapered, and patrolled constantly by a policeman." Apparently this partial reform led to discussion in the newspapers, for in 1842 he tried to exclude prostitutes altogether, ordering that the money of " 'all persons of supposed improper character' should be refused at the door." The *Times* congratulated him. But at least until mid-century most of the theatres were regarded, with some justice, as hot-beds of vice.

Besides prostitutes, their clients, and workingmen looking for entertainment, the pit attracted gay blades of the upper class out for a night on the town, drunkards, practical jokers, and bullies of every sort. These people were usually noisy and often rowdy. During five hours or more on hard, backless benches they required refreshment, and it was furnished by women hawking apples, oranges, nuts, and ginger beer between acts or even during performances: it was difficult to enact high-flown tragedy for an audience cracking nuts and popping corks. Yet the profits from the hawking were important. About 1850 the Grecian Theatre even provided little shelves for the pies, sandwiches, and bottles of the audience. When those in the pit or the gallery did not like an actor, a play, or a scene, they rained apples, orange peels, and other missiles upon the stage to support their shouts, hisses, catcalls, and whistles. The half-price system added to the turmoil. Even if the spectators who came at 7:00 o'clock were intent upon a play being performed, there was an uproar at 9:00 when newcomers (perhaps fresh from a tap room) stormed the benches. If the members of the audience in the pit were rowdy and illiterate, and if some were depraved, they were also generally simple-minded and sentimental. They loved the melodrama and apparently accepted its blacks and whites for life itself.

The audience included, of course, people of the class that had formed the total audience in the Restoration period and through much of the eighteenth century. These aristocrats occupied the boxes, viewing from an elevation the stage below and the doings in the pit — or perhaps not viewing, but lolling, courting, showing themselves in silks and evening dress. Later, as prosperity became more general and stalls began to push the pit toward the back, citizens of the middle class made up a larger proportion of the audience. Perhaps Macready, in his struggle to elevate the drama, had the people of the boxes and the stalls in mind. He supposed (naturally, for the dramatic critics generally agreed) that these people wanted traditional drama in verse — surely not absurd melodramas. The idea seemed reasonable, for by the 1850's the social level and the level of literacy among playgoers was higher than it had been earlier in the century.

Even so, it would seem, Macready's efforts were in the wrong direction. Not only the members of the working class, but also citizens of a middle class emerging from this populace preferred drama about life as they understood it. Queen Victoria's visits to the theatre had made playgoing respectable. At last the Bancrofts, who, like Macready, wished to elevate the drama, sought reform in the right direction. They took the road toward the new drama by producing Robertson's plays for and about a rising middle class, the people in the stalls. By the 1890's the typical audience at the theatre was quiet, decorous, well-mannered — and thirsting for drama as real and significant as the Victorian novel.

AUTHORS

The drama lagged behind other forms of literature in the nineteenth century not only because of conditions in the theatre and the audience, but also because of conditions hampering dramatic authorship. Through much of the century playwriting was poorly paid. At first, payments were not unreasonably low. Allardyce Nicoll states that Frederic Reynolds received three hundred to seven hundred pounds each for plays produced between 1800 and 1810. George Colman the younger received five hundred and fifty pounds each for two plays, "this being the customary price for a five-act comedy at the rate of 300 pounds for the first nine nights, 100 pounds on the twentieth night, and 150 pounds for the copyright." There were other methods of payment. An author might be "given the receipts, after expenses, of the third, sixth, ninth, and twentieth nights." However, in a few years prices began to fall sharply. Augustin Filon recorded that about 1835 "a well-known author was glad to sell a drama to Frederick Yates, manager of the Adelphi, for the sum of 70 pounds, plus 10 pounds for provincial rights." Managers found it even cheaper to select successful plays from the Paris stage and employ clever hacks to translate and adapt them. Boucicault for a time was house dramatist, so to speak, for the Princess's, MacDermott for the Grecian, Hazlewood for the Britannia, and so on.

It was Boucicault, successful in his own plays, who began a revolution in rates of pay to dramatic authors. In 1860 he took *The Colleen Bawn* to Webster at the Haymarket and proposed that instead of payment he should have a share of the proceeds. In this manner, says Ernest Watson, "he inaugurated an era of prosperity for dramatists — greater, perhaps, than that enjoyed by any other class of intellectual workers. For a play such as would have brought only 60 or 100 pounds in 1850, Boucicault in 1866 received 6,500 pounds." The practice of selling plays on a royalty basis became general in the 1880's. It made playwriting worth the toil, and it undergirded the distinguished dramatic writing of the 1890's. The royalty system was also important in another way. When a play was sold outright, the author had nothing more to say about it: his meaning or intention could be changed, his lines or scenes doctored or omitted, and his tragedy played as a farce. Under the royalty system the author had a right to demand that his play be competently produced without mutilation.

As suggested above, a great many nineteenth-century plays were simply translations or adaptations of successful French pieces. Development of a native English drama was of little interest to the typical manager: if a play was successful in Paris, he felt it would succeed in London. Until late in the century no copyright law protected the French playwright; a play might be purchased for a few pounds or even filched from a French theatre. For a few pounds more it could be translated and adapted. The effect upon authorship in England is suggested in Boucicault's brag: "I sold a work for 100 pounds that took me six months' hard work to compose, and accepted a commission to translate three French plays for 50 pounds apiece. The work afforded me child's play for a fortnight." English dramatists had either to labor for low wages or copy the French.

They copied the French. The first English play to be labeled a melodrama, Holcroft's *A Tale of Mystery*, was simply a hashed-up translation of Pixérécourt's *Cœlina, ou l'Enfant du Mystère*. As it helped establish the popularity of melodrama, it also pointed toward more adaptations. Mr. Nicoll estimates that "Fully one-half the plays written between 1800 and 1850 must have been suggested by Parisian models, and many were literally adapted by English authors." A large number of Boucicault's melodramas are translations of French plays, often adroitly doctored with striking scenes from other plays.

Yet, in the evolution of melodrama into drama, adaptation from the French played a helpful role. Through the 1820's English melodramas were generally formless or episodic. Jerrold's *Black-Eyed Susan* is a good example, with its two nearly unrelated plots laid end to end. There was no future for the melodrama as a mere sprawl of sensations. In France the dramatist Eugène Scribe, head of something like a syndicate of playwrights that turned out four hundred plays, developed a formula for melodramatic materials: the "pièce bien faite," the well-made play. This formula demanded unity, balance, a constant seesaw of conflict between hero and villain, rapid action, and economy, the omission of irrelevance. It was French logic — apparently alien to the English genius, at least to the writers of melodramas. Adapting plays by Scribe and his associates, English writers learned to write prose dramas.

Many plays were adapted from novels. From the beginning of the century a successful novel was at once adapted for the stage. *Frankenstein*, of course, was dramatized; Scott's romances and Dickens's novels appeared on the stage in dozens of versions (often several versions of a Dickens novel would appear at the same time in various theatres). At least through the 1860's adapting novels had a bad effect upon playwrights. They selected sensational material, strung together episodes, and scrawled details quickly to get a play on the stage ahead of one another. When playwriting became more careful, however, it is probable that dramatists learned something about characterization from their study of novels. Hazlewood's *Lady Audley's Secret* (1877), adapted from a novel by Mary Elizabeth Braddon, is generally considered the best of his one hundred and eighteen plays.

The absence of effective copyright protection for plays discouraged dramatic authorship. At least before 1833, dramatic piracy was common. Planché, seeing Colman's *The Actor of All Work* produced at the Haymarket in 1817, wrote it out for produciotn by another company. Any play that was in print might be produced by any theatre. In 1833 Parliament passed an Act intended to define a play as the playwright's property for his lifetime or twenty-eight years, whichever was the longer; it stated that a manager must have an author's permission in writing before producing a play, and specified damages if a play were otherwise performed. Managers soon found loopholes in the law: when prosecuted for unauthorized production, the manager and the owner of a theatre would each disclaim responsibility, and booksellers who had purchased printing rights claimed production rights as well and were upheld by the courts. Furthermore, the law did not entitle a playwright who sold his play to any control over its performance or mutilation in production.

Foreign plays were considered common property until an Act of 1852 guaranteed foreign authors copyright for five years. The right applied only to translation, not to adaptation. It was common practice for English authors to evade the law by shifting scenes and adding comic characters. Boucicault did this frequently. In 1875 the law was tightened to include adaptation, but it was not until after the Treaty of Berne in 1887 that an Order in Council gave full copyright protection to French and other European damatists.

Laxity in copyright cut both ways. Throughout most of the century an English play might be produced by any American who could get hold of a script, just as American plays could be produced in England. For this reason authors hesitated to allow plays to be printed. Congress in 1890 passed a copyright law protecting English dramatists. Immediately Henry Arthur Jones, the first English dramatist to take advantage of the American copyright law, published *Saints and Sinners* for general reading.

Through most of the century, most playwrights did not bother to publish their plays. Indeed, before 1833 a manager who had purchased the right to produce a play sought to prevent publication, for then any theatre could produce it without payment. In fact, publishers often sent shorthand writers to the theatres. In 1832 Douglas Jerrold testified bitterly to a Parliamentary Committee: "Mr. Kenneth, at the corner of Bow-Street, will supply any gentleman with any manuscript on the lowest terms." After 1833 many successful plays were published, though publication meant that American managers could perform the plays without payment. The best works were printed in various collections of "Standard Plays," but often the text varied greatly from collection to collection. A collected play was commonly published "as presented at" this or that theatre, English or American, with all the cuts, transpositions, and even additions of the production, and whatever errors were in the prompt book or shorthand copy taken from the performance. Presumably authors had little control over these publications.

Full copyright protection by the 1890's undoubtedly had a maturing effect upon the literary quality of the drama. Henry Arthur Jones proclaimed in these years that the ultimate test of a play was whether it could be read and appreciated in the library. For this it had to be written with care; it had to be literary to match the high standard of the novel.

A rigid and irrational censorship was another millstone that bent down the neck of the dramatic author through most of the century. Everyone is familiar with the lines of the Captain of the *Pinafore* in Gilbert and Sullivan's opera:

> Though "bother it," I may
> Occasionally say,
> I never use a big, big D——.

These lines both satirize the censorship of the drama and illustrate a method of evading it.

The Licensing Act of 1737 to curb political satire on the stage established the Lord Chamberlain (or his delegate) as "Examiner of all Plays, Tragedies, Comedies, Operas, Farces, Interludes, or any other entertainment of the stage, of what denomination soever." It required that every manager intending to produce a stage entertainment submit the piece to the Examiner fourteen days before performance. The playwright might not appear before the Examiner or make any objection or appeal to him. Upon reading the play the Examiner might forbid its performance altogether, or he might direct that "any profaneness, immorality, or anything political" be omitted from performances. For reading each play the Examiner received a fee of one or two pounds, according to the number of acts. A manager producing an unlicensed play might be fined fifty pounds and have his theatre closed and his license forfeited. The Examiners of plays in the first half of the nineteenth century were John Larpent to 1824, George Colman to 1836, Charles Kemble to 1840, and John Mitchell Kemble. These men exercised their duties with an excess of prudery. Larpent and Colman especially insisted on such decency, piety, and loyalty that a play could say nothing to bring a blush to the cheek of a child or an unconventional thought to the mind of anyone.

Larpent, a strict Methodist, would allow a play to make no reference to religion except in a pious context. He would permit no discussion of politics. The situation during Colman's reign may be illustrated in a memorandum he sent to Douglas Jerrold: "23rd January, 1832. Please to omit the following underlined words in the representation of the drama called *The Rent-Day*. Act I. Scene I. 'The blessed little babes, God bless 'em!' Scene III. 'Heaven be kind to us, for I've almost lost all other hope.' Ditto. 'Damn him.' Scene IV. 'Damn business.' 'No, don't damn business. I'm very drunk, but I can't damn business — it's profane.' Ditto. 'Isn't that an angel?' 'I can't tell; I've not been used to such company.' Scene V. 'Oh, Martin, husband, for the love of heaven!' Ditto. 'Heaven help us, Heaven help us!' Act III. Scene III. 'Heaven forgive you, can you speak it?' 'I leave you, and may heaven pardon and protect you!' Scene last. 'Farmer, neighbours, heaven bless you — let the landlord take all the rest.' Ditto. 'They have not the money, and <u>heaven</u> prosper it with them.' " Colman refused to let a lover call his sweetheart an angel, for the term meant "a character in Scripture, and not to be profaned on the stage by being applied to a woman." He forbade "O lud" and "demme" as evasions for "O Lord" and "Damn me." He would not even allow the inclusion of nuns chanting a prayer. After Colman, censorship became a little less rigid, but as late as 1879 the Examiner refused to license Jones's *Welcome, Little Stranger* because, according to Doris Jones, "The opening scene of this play was a corridor — a nurse crossed the stage, the servant opened a door for a doctor carrying a bag, one or two other characters came on, and, after a certain amount of *va et vient*, the nurse entered and said, 'It is a fine boy.' "

Naturally authors and actors sought to evade censorship of this kind. Where "damned" was not permitted in Fitzball's *The Pilot*, the comic actor Cooke would say, "No, if I do I'm d——d." When the Examiner (Colman) attended the play, Cooke said, "No, if I do I'm ——," placed his thumb on his nose, and looked so comic that even Colman burst out laughing. It was common for writers adapting French plays to replace the word "cocotte" with "actress," and "adultery" with "flirtation." The actor usually supplied winks and nods to make the terms clear. On the other hand, censorship was sometimes irregular, careless, and arbitrary; words cut out of some plays were apparently spoken in others. Printed versions restored phrases that were not spoken on the stage. *The Rent-Day*, for example, includes the phrases that Colman censored for its performance.

Besides evasion, some struggle against the censorship went on throughout the century. Bulwer's efforts in 1832 to free the theatres included a motion for Parliament to investigate the censorship. Parliamentary committees then and in 1843, 1866, and 1892 found that the censorship had not been vexatiously exercised. However, censorship greatly relaxed toward the end of the nineteenth century. Until this time, though, along with other liabilities, censorship discouraged authors with any message for their times from turning to drama.

ROMANTIC VERSE DRAMA

The Traditional Modes

As pointed out above, the theatres royal were expected, as a kind of patriotic duty, to support legitimate drama: chiefly histories or tragedies in the verse tradition of Marlowe, Shakespeare, Dryden, Otway, and Addison. At least in the early part of the century, seventeenth- and eighteenth-century plays in this tradition appeared regularly on the stage; the cultivated part of an audience considered a performance of a play like Otway's *Venice Preserved* a theatrical event. Shakespeare remained a part of the living repertory of the London theatres throughout the century. But in the 1840's Macready lamented the decline of the legitimate drama, especially the failure of poets to match the power of the great dramas of the past. Original verse drama was in fact declining, and it is interesting to look at some of the reasons for this.

One reason was bardolatry, or reverence for Shakespeare. A talented actor reached his coveted goal when he thrilled audiences with his interpretation of Shylock, Othello, or Hamlet. Interpretations of Shakespeare fixed patterns of acting in plays of all kinds. In spite of what Shakespeare might have intended, Kemble and Kean delivered stylized orations on the apron in front of the stage. Custom and reverence demanded this kind of performance in verse drama, but it placed a burden upon playwrights of a more democratic age who sought to write great plays in verse. For, unable to create genuine characters the size of Lear and Othello, they had to blow up their heroes with rhetoric or bombast. This may explain the straining for grandeur in such a play as Bulwer-Lytton's *Richelieu*. As time passed the pattern-setting stars disappeared and the apron receded, but the custom of writing heroic rhetoric for the platform stage was carried on. Thus the old aristo-cratic forms prevented new dramatic poets from developing the substance of a living drama for an increasingly democratic time.

In other ways bardolatry laid a deadening hand upon the verse drama. In earlier periods actors had felt free to adapt Shakespeare to the demands of the time; the acting texts were corrupted. But the philosophic critics of literature — Coleridge Lamb, Hazlitt — reversed that current. They exalted Shakespeare to a godlike eminence, and turning to the minor Elizabethans, the Jacobeans, and even the playwrights of the Restoration, submitted them to criticism that placed them on pedestals only a little lower than the master's. Macready's earnest efforts to elevate the drama centered on restoring Shakespeare's original texts in the acting versions. In 1843 Macready's admirers gave a dinner commemorating his management of Covent Garden, and testified that "his personation of the characters, his restora-tions of the text, and his illustration of the best intellectual aids of the historical facts and poetical creations of the plays of Shakespeare, formed an epoch in the-atrical annals." At another dinner when Macready retired in 1851, John Forster read a sonnet by Tennyson with these lines:

> Thine it is that our drama did not die,
> > Nor flicker down to brainless pantomime,
> > And those gilt gauds men-children swarm to see.
> Farewell, Macready; moral, grave, sublime;
> Our Shakespeare's bland and universal eye
> > Dwells pleased, through twice a hundred years, on thee.

The lines disdain the very idea that the drama might adapt itself to what audiences "swarm to see."

In themselves the scholarly study of Shakespeare and the restoration of his text were good, but such an excessive emphasis was deadly to original playwriting. As Augustin Filon put it, actors "saw no reason why they, their successors, and the general public should not continue until the end of time to carp over an entry of Macbeth or an exit of Othello!" Bardolatry killed invention. It defined what great drama ought to be and what the writers of serious verse drama in the nineteenth century hoped to make it. It defined the drama not as an imitation of life, but an imitation of art, an emulation of Shakespeare, Dryden, or Otway. Nicoll comments on the result: "The poetic dramas of the time are literally filled with Shakespearian and Elizabethan imagery. Often does Patience sit melancholy upon a monument; often do characters look in a moved sort as if they were dismayed. This wholesale borrowing is accompanied by slavish imitation of plot and character. . . . Many dramatists, 'thouing' through five acts, seem physically incapable of penning a 'you.' Blank verse unimaginatively follows the cadences of a Shakespeare or a Fletcher."

Shakespeare's plays were sufficiently constant fare at the theatres that audiences with a taste for the master could see the originals, those plays that presented subjects from all times and places with the heightened vision of the Renaissance. But when dramatists of the nineteenth century drew themes for new plays from heroic ages far removed from modern ways and thought, they seldom tried to give these themes modern significance. Without Shakespeare's scope or depth of insight into human nature, and compromising their own insight with worn-out language, they copied the old concepts in the old familiar imagery. The plays of Sheridan Knowles and Bulwer-Lytton, the most successful of the age, display their heroes in grand postures and provide them with versified rhetoric, but these heroes sound off like braggarts.

Certainly a lack of poets was no reason for the decline of verse drama, for Wordsworth, Coleridge, Shelley, Byron, and Browning all wrote plays. The romantic poets failed as dramatists not because they wrote for a noisy, rowdy audience — Shakespeare's pit was crowded with the common people — but because they wrote for the applause of the educated part of the audience, and, perhaps, because their gifts were lyric, not dramatic, and they were more interested in passions than in people. In this connection we might observe the theories of Joanna Baillie, who, between 1800 and 1836, wrote several series of Plays on the Passions, each play a study of the operation on the mind of a particular passion: fear, love, hate, jealousy, and so on. She said that in her plays "it is attempted to delineate the stronger passions of the mind, each passion being the subject of a tragedy and a comedy." She theorized that tragedy is more powerful the more it concerns the life common to many people: "A king driven from his throne will not move our sympathy so strongly as a private man torn from the bosom of his family." But her practice belied her theory. She did not treat the common *man*, but personified abstractions. Like Joanna Baillie the romantic poets seemed to fix upon a passion, embody it in a character, and invent action to illustrate the passion. This tendency is evident in the Gothic drama and in the general tendency of romantic verse plays to exhibit heroes possessed by a single passion, like the Count's Satanism in Shelley's *The Cenci* and Richelieu's passion for France in Bulwer-Lytton's play.

Romantic verse dramas in the traditional modes were of three types according to subject: the Gothic thriller and play of the passions, dominant from 1800 to about 1820; the history play, from 1820 to Bulwer-Lytton's *Richelieu*, 1839; and, overlapping the historical, the domestic play, from 1830 to about 1850. The closet drama was a fourth type of verse drama that flourished throughout the century.

The Gothic Thriller

As Bertrand Evans has shown in *Gothic Drama from Walpole to Shelley*, not only the Gothic novel and the so-called Byronic hero, but also the play of terror originated in the eighteenth century. The stimulus to drama of this type was the novel of terror, beginning with Horace Walpole's *The Castle of Otranto* in 1764 and reaching a peak of popularity in the works of Anne Radcliffe and Matthew Gregory ("Monk") Lewis in the 1790's. Shortly after the success of *The Castle of Otranto*, Walpole privately printed and distributed in 1767 among his friends a Gothic play, *The Mysterious Mother*, which was not produced because it dealt with incest. Robert Jephson dramatized *The Castle of Otranto* in a play called *The Count of Narbonne* (1781). The villain of this play anticipates the Byronic hero; wrapped in mysterious gloom and filled with hatred for the human race, he is nonetheless to be pitied as the victim of some terrible and nameless wrong. Perhaps a more influential play was Lewis's *The Castle Spectre* of 1797. Though not so titled, it was a melodrama, and it demonstrated the possibilities of terror on the stage. Lewis's *Adelmore, The Outlaw* in 1801 was important in establishing the theme of the innocent hero, remorseful because he believes himself guilty — a theme still found in Jones's *The Silver King* toward the end of the nineteenth century. Another element that appears in some Gothic plays stems from the German Friedrich Schiller's *Die Räuber* (*The Robbers*) of 1781. This play was imitated in England in Henry Siddons's *A Sicilian Romance*, a play about a band of robbers with a secret tribunal that wrought justice not in terms of conventional law, but of eternal right.

These plays established a pattern followed by the Gothic drama in romantic verse. The aim of a Gothic play was to provide thrills by creating terror through suggestions of the supernatural. Setting and atmosphere played an important part in creating the proper mood. Usually the setting was a barbarous medieval castle, or a ruined abbey, or a church, or convent, presumably haunted by ancient curses or other mysterious evil forces. This castle or abbey was usually in a Roman Catholic country, preferably southern Italy, where horrors of the Inquisition might have been committed in its dungeons. The play had to have a heroine persecuted by a villain and defended by a hero; but the hero of a Gothic drama is a passive character who does little to defeat the villain. The villain is the dynamic character, self-defeated at last, often a suicide, when his own evil deeds return to crush him. He is a man of strangely intense and uncontrollable passions. In some mysterious way he has been wronged by a tyrannical and heartless society and forced to become an outlaw. He is solitary and gloomy, for past crimes have taken him beyond the mercy of Heaven. Impetuous, raging, fitful, he stalks the stage in an agony of remorse. The wrong he has endured and his remorse engage pity, and he is, though a villain, the real hero of the play. He is the so-called Byronic hero, created before Byron touched up the portrait. Romantic theories of the passions argued that the result of this pity would be a true Aristotelian catharsis, enabling the spectator to save himself from destruction "in checking and subduing those visitations of the soul."

Whatever the theories, the seeds of its collapse were present in the excesses of the Gothic drama. *Bertram* was the most successful play of its time; its true hero was not the virtuous Aldobrand, but Bertram, a man of unmitigated evil — most shocking of all, a seducer and adulterer during the course of the play. The attempt to thrill audiences with such plays came to an end when excesses like those exhibited in *Bertram* exhausted the capacity to be thrilled, and revolted the sensitivities, of people who were moving toward Victorian patterns of morality.

Important verse dramas treating Gothic subjects include Joanna Baillie's *Orra* (1812, not produced), Samuel Taylor Coleridge's *Remorse* (1813), Henry Hart Milman's *Fazio* (1816), Charles Robert Maturin's *Bertram* (1816), Richard Lalor Sheil's *The Apostate* (1817), and Percy Bysshe Shelley's *The Cenci* (1819, not produced at the time).

The Historical Play

When interest in the Gothic play declined, playwrights of romantic verse turned to history. The play that set the fashion was James Sheridan Knowles's *Virginius* (1820). It tells a somewhat domestic story based upon the well-known Roman legend, accepted as history, of Appius, a lustful tyrant, and Virginia, whose father, Virginius, slays her rather than let her be dishonored. Like the historical plays of Shakespeare, the play was partly in prose, but the grand and emotional speeches were in verse. The play had some contemporary interest in this year when senile George III died and the somewhat immoral George IV became king. In a necessarily veiled way, it cast aspersions upon tyranny, defended the rights of the middle-class liberal Virginius, and hinted at rebellion.

Knowles's *Virginius* was hailed as a revival of the older tradition in tragedy, but censorship would not allow dramatists to revive vital treatment of English history. Questions of democracy were alive, but they could not be discussed on the stage, and audiences found it hard to sustain interest in the history of other countries. Immensely popular, *Virginius* was followed the next year by Byron's *Marino Faliero*, also somewhat political in implication — and set in a foreign land. The style and the plot of this tragedy, though certainly reflecting Byron's genius and energy, strongly suggest Otway's *Venice Preserved*. Other notable plays of this type include C. E. Walker's *Wallace* (1820), Sir Walter Scott's *Halidon Hill* (1822), Mrs. Felicia Hemans's *The Vespers of Palermo* (1823), Mary Russell Mitford's *Rienzi* (1828), Robert Browning's *Strafford* (1837), and Edward Bulwer-Lytton's *Richelieu* (1839). The history play remained popular till about 1840 and then declined.

In the later years of the century ambitious and idealistic playwrights and poets, sharing some of Macready's feeling that the triumphing prose drama was a debased form, sought to revive history plays. Having succeeded in melodrama and farce, Tom Taylor, in his old age, wrote history plays in verse, notably *'Twixt Axe and Crown* (1870). Alfred Lord Tennyson, with the expressed ambition to fill in the historical gaps in Shakespeare's treatment of English history, wrote *Queen Mary* (1873) and *Becket* (1884). *Becket* achieved a startling success when Henry Irving staged it in 1893, but Augustine Filon, who witnessed it, said that "three-fourths of the success was due to Irving." These attempts did not succeed in reviving this dead form, but simply added museum pieces to dramatic libraries.

The Domestic Play

Knowles's *Virginius*, though it treats an historical subject, exhibits many features of the domestic play. The heroine is a helpless, simple girl who innocently reveals her love for Icilius to her doting father. She is completely passive throughout the play, a model daughter — innocent to the point of being childishly naïve. The plot of the play turns upon the father's protection of his daughter's honor. An interest in domestic material runs through many of the historical dramas, as in the relationship of the simple Julie and the great Richelieu in Bulwer-Lytton's play.

Eighteenth-century sentimentalism and the early nineteenth-century trend toward the patriarchal Victorian family helped turn romantic verse dramatists (as well as the writers of melodrama) toward domestic subjects. The domestic drama had a message: prescriptive morality. As distinguished from the moral issues explored in plays of the 1890's and later, this was the morality prescribed by convention, sentiment, and contemporary manners. It was, so to speak, Sunday School morality taught to make children docile and obedient. The plays presented idealized patterns of feminine marital behavior, Victorian Christian gentlemanly sentiments, and family virtues. They idealized the relationship between the all-wise, ever-loving father and the dutiful daughter or son. Mr. Disher, discussing this point, quotes from Prince Hoare's play *Indiscretion* of 1800: "To quit the roof of a parent is the most alarming indiscretion of which a female can be guilty; she forfeits the regard of the author of her being; and is thus too apt to supply the loss, by accepting a protection which brings with it dishonour and ruin." Eighteenth-century sentiments regarding female virtue had made the rebellious daughter "the equivalent of the defaulting solicitor." Besides affirming the virtues of the home, domestic dramas expressed the concepts that inherent worth is not dependent on birth or rank, and that the lowborn may rise. The heroes of Bulwer-Lytton's *The Lady of Lyons* and Marston's *The Patrician's Daughter* fall in love above their rank. These plays examine pride of rank and show it to be artificial and vicious: the lowborn lover may be in every respect except title the equal of the highborn beloved. Important domestic dramas in verse include Sheridan Knowles's *The Wife* (1833), Sir Thomas Noon Talfourd's *Ion* (1836), Edward Bulwer-Lytton's *The Lady of Lyons* (1838), John Westland Marston's *The Patrician's Daughter* (1842), and Robert Browning's *A Blot in the 'Scutcheon* (1843).

The Patrician's Daughter is unusual among romantic verse dramas; it is experimental in its effort to give new vitality to the play in blank verse. It is set in a contemporary time, "in modern dress," and it explores contemporary social and domestic problems. Except that the people occupy exalted positions in political and social life, the play parallels the discussion of democracy and rank found in the domestic melodrama. But the realism of contemporary life seems a bit absurd when it is expressed in romantic verse. Ladies in silks carrying parasols and speaking in blank verse caused some laughter.

In *A Blot in the 'Scutcheon* Browning tried to bring verse drama reasonably close to modern life; he even stated an unconventional theme which challenged Victorian prudery. His interest in the complexities of personality had possibilities, but he could not work out a way to project these complexities on the stage. The introspective self-analysis of his characters was nearly impossible for his audience to follow. Browning turned to the closet drama and achieved greatness there, like many other dramatists either unable or unwilling to write verse plays for the stage of the 1850's. The great tradition stemming from Marlowe and Shakespeare had failed to adapt to the age of Darwin, where it produced no significant play.

The Closet Drama

The most radical experimentation with the romantic verse play occurred in the closet drama. The closet drama was not entirely unique in the nineteenth century, but it was then more prevalent than ever before or since. It was, so to speak, a third contender in the struggle for survival between the verse drama and the evolving melodrama.

The term "closet drama" is properly applied to a poem (or possibly a piece of prose) written in the form of a drama but neither intended for performance nor professionally staged. Shelley's *The Cenci*, for instance, is not a closet drama, for it was written to be staged. It was not performed when written both because the taste for Gothic horrors was fading and the Examiner of Plays would not have allowed its presentation of incest. It was staged in 1886 by the Shelley Society, but even at that time the censor would not permit a public performance (it has been performed at various times and places in the twentieth century). On the other hand, Thomas Hardy's *The Dynasts* is a closet drama; though Hardy enthusiasts have performed portions of it, it was written to be read.

To some extent the popularity of this form may be explained by conditions in the theatre. Robert Browning tried to write for the stage, but could not write a play that would both explore the minds and hearts of his characters as subtly as he wished and also succeed. Other authors wishing to write in dramatic forms were reluctant to write for a stage that seemed given to vulgarity, melodrama, farce, and spectacle. They believed their material too precious to be cast before the audiences they saw in the pit. Other writers who wrote closet plays to express social, political, or unconventional moral views were deterred by the censorship from writing for the stage.

In tone, treatment, and subject, many closet dramas continued the Elizabethan-Jacobean-Caroline tradition. They contain elements of mysticism borrowed from the Gothic writers, many are historical, and some contain domestic material. George Gordon Lord Byron's *Manfred* (1817), published with the subtitle "A Dramatic Poem," evidently was not intended for stage performance; its mystical elements, allegorical spirits, and phantom voices belong more properly to poetry than to the theatre. Its production at Covent Garden in 1834 was perhaps more a *tour de force* to capitalize on the great name of Byron than a normal choice. Percy Bysshe Shelley's *Prometheus Unbound* (1820) is a complex allegory of the soul, with tremendous, shadowy, symbolic characters, difficult if not impossible to put on the stage. Walter Savage Landor wrote a number of closet dramas, including the trilogy of *Andrea of Hungary*, *Giovanna of Naples*, and *Fra Rupert*, published in 1839–1840. These plays tell a semi-historical story from the fourteenth century, but in difficult verse unsuited for the stage. Robert Browning's *Pippa Passes* (1841) and his dramatic monologues exhibit imaginative experimentation in the dramatic form, but they were never adapted for performance in the theatre. Thomas Lovell Beddoes's *Death's Jest Book, or The Fool's Tragedy* (1850) is a mystic, macabre, semi-Gothic poem in dramatic form with allegorical and symbolic figures. Matthew Arnold's *Empedocles on Etna* (1852) is a dramatic poem that discusses social, religious, and philosophic questions. Alfred Lord Tennyson's *Maud* (1855) has the subtitle "A Monodrama," in which, as Tennyson carefully explained, the various moods of the single speaker perform the function of various characters in the ordinary play. Algernon Charles Swinburne's *Atalanta in Calydon* (1865) is, in subject, theme, and structure, a Greek play, too elaborately poetized for stage production, even if its anti-religious sentiments could have passed the censorship. Though Thomas Hardy's *The Dynasts* was published in 1904–1908, it is essentially a late-Victorian historical drama, not to be staged as a whole because of its length and complexity in presenting both the Napoleonic wars and simultaneous philosophic comments by allegorical spirits.

Perhaps if these and other writers had used as much imagination and ingenuity in writing plays for the stage as they did in writing for the reader, the verse drama could have survived.

COMEDY

The Comedy of Manners

The traditional comedy of manners was in prose, which in the plays of Congreve and Sheridan had been witty, sophisticated, and artificial — in repartee as patterned as blank verse. In the nineteenth century the comedy of manners was more feebly represented than the verse drama, and the genuine fun of the Victorian drama was expressed in the burletta.

The two forces which hampered high comedy were sentimentality and censorship. As George Meredith theorized later, the essence of high comedy is thoughtful laughter at pretensions, follies, and vices. In Restoration times foppery and a sexual game as mannered as a minuet amused the lords and ladies of King Charles's court; they could laugh at these follies presented on the stage as violations of good sense. But to the sentimental mood and to Victorian morality or prudishness, folly and vice seemed subjects more for sermons than for comedy. Also, strict censorship forbade the sexual diversions which characterized Restoration comedy. With its foundations thus undermined, high comedy had to be meretriciously witty without liberty to provoke laughter at the real follies of the time.

Three of the most nearly successful attempts at comedy of manners up through mid-century were Edward Bulwer-Lytton's *Money* (1840), Dion Boucicault's *London Assurance* (1841), and Tom Taylor and Charles Reade's *Masks and Faces; or, Before and Behind the Curtain* (1852). *Money* is basically a comedy of manners portraying the fashionable world of contemporary London, with the satiric intention of holding a mirror up to its follies. It presents a gambling scene and fops, and it rails at social vices. But it omits a typical ingredient of Restoration comedy, the duel of the sexes leading toward a victorious seduction. The times themselves were perhaps not too moral for this theme, but the stage was. Instead the play offers material from sentimental drama: a happy ending with a marriage depending on the hero's discovery of the modest heroine's goodness of heart. Some of the characters are drawn from the comedy of humors and some devices (like the unexpected inheritance) from the melodrama. The dialogue and stagecraft are unusually natural for the 1840's. *London Assurance*, discussed in the introduction to the play, likewise bows to Victorian morality. *Masks and Faces*, set in the eighteenth century, tells a sentimental story of the famous actress Peg Woffington. It exhibits a mixture of various types of comedy, with less material drawn from the comedy of manners than from sentimental drama, domestic melodrama, and farce. Allardyce Nicoll calls it a comedy drama, with its mixture of wit and pathos in a serious theme treated sentimentally. The play daringly presents its heroine as the immoral woman Peg Woffington was known to be, but provides her with a generous heart. The characterization and dialogue are natural and approach that of Tom Robertson's later comedy dramas.

When comic art moved toward the high comedies of Oscar Wilde and other playwrights of the 1890's, it developed more from the burletta or the melodrama than from the earlier comedy of manners. Tom Robertson's *Society* (1865), for example, was transitional between the melodrama and high comedy; W. S. Gilbert's comedies and comic operas evolved chiefly from burlesques and extravaganzas; and *The Importance of Being Earnest* imitated Gilbert's burlesques. Like them, it is a mock play, mocking the melodrama from which it partly evolved. In doing so, it achieved the tones of true high comedy for the first time since Sheridan.

The Burletta

As pointed out in the sketch of the minor theatres, the term "burletta" was coined for a musical entertainment that might be presented at a minor theatre because it was not a play. The term was stretched to mean almost anything. Mr. Nicoll has this comment on the spring season at the Surrey Theatre in 1810: "... the managers ... present, as burlettas, both Farquhar's *The Beaux Stratagem* (May 21) and Shakespeare's *Antony and Cleopatra* (May 28), following up the production of these two plays with another of Mrs. Centlivre's *A Bold Stroke for a Wife* (August 27). Nothing could have been more 'legitimate' than these dramas, yet the burletta conception [sounding of a musical chord now and then] could allow of their free performance."

Yet, as the Examiners of Plays attempted over and over again to define the burletta, their emphasis was always on comic entertainment, as in this definition by Examiner George Colman: ". . . a drama in rhyme . . . which is entirely musical; a short comic piece, consisting of recitative and singing, wholly accompanied, more or less, by the Orchestra." This emphasis on something both comic and with public appeal encouraged every imaginable kind of dramatic fun, and scrambled mixtures of all the genres together. For example, Thomas John Dibdin's *Don Giovanni; or, A Spectre on Horseback!* (1817) is printed with this descriptive subtitle: "A Comic, heroic, operatic, tragic, pantomimic, burletta-spectacular extravaganza." It is difficult to characterize the burlettas announced in a program at Sadler's Wells in 1825: "The amusements will consist of a romantic tale of mysterious horror and broad grin, never acted, called the *Enchanted Girdles, or Winki the Witch and the Ladies of Samarkand.* A most whimsical burletta which sends people home perfectly exhausted from uninterrupted risibility, called *The Lawyer, the Jew and the Yorkshireman* with, by request of 75 distinguished families, and a party of 5, that never to be sufficiently praised pantomine, called *Magic in Two Colours, or Fairy Blue and Fairy Red, or Harlequin and the Marble Rock.*" In this mélange, *Enchanted Girdles* would seem to be partly a Gothic melodrama and partly a burlesque. The words "broad grin" promise the comic action found in most melodramas. The pantomime suggests the popularity of spectacle that became an important part of the developing melodrama.

Insofar as types can be isolated, the most popular was the farce. Farces were lively plays with broad humor, bustling action, horseplay or slapstick, contretemps, mistaken identities, and ridiculous situations — like farces today. Other qualities of the farce were perhaps more appreciated on the Victorian stage than they would be on ours. Atrocious puns that today would make an audience jeer were greeted with loud laughter, and in the smaller theatres where facial expressions could be seen, comic actors built reputations upon grimaces, smirks, and other distortions of the countenance. Clever caricature of some well-known person or type was sure to get a laugh. Lessons learned from Scribe's formula for the well-made play gave mid-century farces an interestingly tight, complex structure, as in Tom Taylor's *Our American Cousin* (1858). This play illustrates the union of comic action and well-made structure typical of farce. It was written as a somewhat comic melodrama, but actor E. A. Sothern's development of the character of Lord Dundreary turned it into farce. Such comedy dramas of the 1890's as Pinero's *The Gay Lord Quex* (1900) exhibit lessons apparently learned from the farce.

The burlesque ran a close second to the farce in popularity. The nineteenth-century burlesque was not a "girlie" show. It was a parody full of jokes and puns mocking something solemn. A favorite subject for a burlesque might be such a serious play as *Romeo and Juliet*, or a stilted grand opera, or, by mid-century, an especially stereotyped melodrama. Acting styles were also ridiculed, best-selling sensational novels were caricatured, and classical mythology and medieval legends were parodied. In short, the Victorian theatre, employing exuberant exaggeration, made hilarious fun of the very stuffiness that people of the twentieth century are apt to think characteristic of the Victorians. A number of W. S. Gilbert's early plays are burlesques, and indeed the Gilbert and Sullivan operas are developments from this form.

Gilbert also wrote extravaganzas, like *The Palace of Truth* (1870). J. R. Planché, who specialized in writing extravaganzas, defined this type of play as "a whimsical treatment of a poetical subject as distinguished from the broad caricature of a tragedy or serious opera which was correctly described as burlesque." Presenting prettily costumed dancing elves, gnomes, or fairies, the extravaganza tells a fairy tale respectfully, so that the charm of the story, rather than the parody and the humor, hold the interest. The fantasy, the spectacle, and the singing and dancing of the extravaganza still give us as much pleasure in the Savoy operas as in Walt Disney's recent creations.

MELODRAMA

In Mark Twain's *Huckleberry Finn* the Duke is a strolling "theater-actor — tragedy, you know!" The stratagem he uses to gain special privileges shows that the "tragedy" he acted was melodrama. Revealing "the secret of my birth," he says: "My great-grandfather, eldest son of the Duke of Bridgewater, fled to this country about the end of the last century, to breathe the pure air of freedom; married here, and died, leaving a son, his own father dying about the same time. The second son of the late duke seized the titles and estates — the infant real duke was ignored. I am the lineal descendant of that infant — I am the rightful Duke of Bridgewater; and here am I, forlorn, torn from my high estate, hunted of men, despised by the cold world, ragged, worn, heartbroken, and degraded to the companionship of felons on a raft!" In the Duke's fantastic tale of injustices, his inflated language, and his pathos, Twain summarized and satirized the mid-century melodrama. Revelation of his secret of high birth was the expected "surprise" ending for hundreds of these plays, English and American alike.

The underlying emotional attitudes of melodrama probably developed from the eighteenth-century cult of sensibility as formulated by Rousseau, meditated by educated people, and in various seepages (sentimental novels, for instance) filtered down into popular feeling. This feeling underlies the identification of virtue with poverty and simplicity and the naïve faith in poetic justice.

Earlier plays suggested themes that became standard in the melodrama. George Lillo's *The London Merchant* (1731) and Edward Moore's *The Gamester* (1753) offered moral lessons to inculcate honesty in apprentices and warn against the dangers of gambling. The German playwright A. F. F. Von Kotzebue wrote plays upon the theme of *The London Merchant*, and these plays poured into England. Bertrand Evans says that "There were no fewer than sixty-five translations and adaptations of Kotzebue's works between 1797 and 1802." The sources of the Gothic drama, discussed above, also provided material for melodramas.

But the most immediate stimulus for melodrama probably came from the French stage. Before 1800, plays with sensational action were scrappily adapted from the French for the minor theatres. Thomas Holcroft's *A Tale of Mystery* (1802), adapted from the French, may reasonably be regarded as the first full-fledged English melodrama; it was the first to call itself by this name. Details of the play that helped establish the melodrama formula include dialogue stripped to essential exposition; rapid, violent, and unmotivated action accompanied by music to heighten the

excitement; songs, dances, and some comedy; somewhat Gothic settings and atmosphere; a passive but perfect hero; a helpless orphan heroine (whose father is discovered during the play); a dynamic vil.ain with remorseful speeches when trapped;
and a happy ending with virtue triumphant.

Jolly Jack Tars, singing and dancing sailors, soon entered the melodrama. In the
eighteenth century sailors went singing from tavern to tavern, and ballads of sea-
faring life were popular. Isaac Bickerstaffe's *Thomas and Sally; or, The Sailor's
Return* appeared on the stage of Covent Garden in 1760. Thomas, after singing of a
sailor's life, rescues Sally from a tyrannical squire. Skits featuring Jack Tars were
popular in music halls after Nelson's victory at Trafalgar. The combination of
sailors, songs, and the domestic theme of melodrama insured the success of Jerrold's
Black-Eyed Susan in 1829, and it was revived frequently thereafter. The singing
sailors appeared at last in W. S. Gilbert's *Pinafore*, climaxing a long development.

The common factor in the mélange of melodrama was the taste of the people.
Melodrama satisfied their desire to escape monotony through the vicarious excitement of thrilling entertainment, and yet to see their lives portrayed on the stage.
There was, of course, an idealizing tendency with a sentimental faith in poetic
justice. The play of threats and dangers that reaches a happy ending through lucky
accident scrambles tragic possibility and comic outcome, but naïve audiences liked
this mixture.

Every melodrama presents a conflict between virtue and vice. In a sense, all
serious drama exhibits the clash of good and evil, but the peculiarity of this theme
in melodrama is that virtue is overt conformity to the image of conduct fostered
by the Sunday Schools: honesty, industry, thrift, purity of life, goodness of heart,
and horror of sin. There is never any question in a melodrama about virtue; it is
what everybody knows it to be. It is without alloy. The same is true of vice. A
villain's vices are evident: greed, lust, cruelty, and indulgence in expensive dissipa-
tions. Melodrama teaches that in the conflict between virtue and vice, virtue is
always rewarded, here and now. Vice is always punished. The reward is always
material: an inheritance, a wealthy marriage, a business success; the hero and the
heroine will live happily ever after. The villain (if not changed of heart and remorseful) is crushed beyond recovery.

The characters of melodrama were chiefly symbols of virtue and vice, personified
moral qualities rather than complex people. The definitions were clear-cut, unmistakable at a glance. Ordinarily the conflict between the hero and the villain was a
tug of war for the possession of the heroine, who was helpless between the two.
The hero often had a comic friend who might play jokes on the villain, and the
heroine a confidante. The hero might be an ambitious young man, a bank clerk, a
sailor, a farmer, a laborer. The villain might be a squire, a banker, a rich curmudgeon,
or a criminal. Sometimes there was even a villainess. The heroine was nearly always
a motherless orphan. (Amazingly few mothers appear in melodrama.)

Except for some early melodramas using Gothic materials, and some historical
plays, the conflict of virtue and vice occurred in the immediate present. Motifs
included stories of the long-lost son (a sailor perhaps), supposed to be drowned,
and almost disinherited by the trickery of a villain; of the helpless heroine trapped
into choosing between disaster for her father and unwelcome marriage to the
villain; of a hero unjustly accused by the real perpetrator of a crime; of the grasping cheat who manipulated legacies or other legal papers; of true love in danger

through libels and misunderstandings; of true love across class lines (solved when the secret of high birth is revealed); of the villainous employer's oppression of his workmen; of a virtuous youth tricked into apparent crime and hounded till saved by a detective; of the evils of strong drink and gambling. Varied as the themes are, the melodrama does not bring accepted values into question. Though attacking a grasping landlord, it does not discuss land tenure. In *Black-Eyed Susan*, for instance, no question of injustice is raised in sailor William's punishment for striking his captain, even though the drunken captain was about to attack William's wife, Susan.

To place the hero in direst danger and yet rescue him in a happy ending, melodrama ignored the laws of cause and effect. It did not physically lower the medieval *deus ex machina* from the loft, but the principle was the same: Providence always came to the rescue in the nick of time. In *Black-Eyed Susan* the noose is around William's neck when word arrives that he did not strike his captain after all, for his discharge from the Navy was signed before he struck the blow. Many a hero is saved by just such a technicality. A secret is disclosed, a birthmark is found, a Jack Tar arrives (or perhaps a squad of marines!) to save the hero, or, more miraculously, a marble heart softens to thwart the villain's designs.

The subject matter of melodramas through the first half of the century paralleled that of the verse drama. *A Tale of Mystery* was romantic, with Gothic touches in the scenery, for at that time melodramas followed the fashion for Gothic plays. With greater freedom to mix forms and moods, they were even wilder than those plays. Mr. Nicoll cites William Moncrieff's *Giselle; or, The Phantom Night Dancers* (1841) as typical: "A Domestic, Melo-dramatic, Choreographic, Fantastique, Traditionary Tale of Superstition." Some melodramas treated history, like Isaac Pocock's *Alfred the Great; or, The Enchanted Standard* (1827), but it was in dealing with domestic materials that melodrama achieved greatest popularity. Domestic melodramas expressed the attitudes of domestic plays in verse, though melodramas were even more narrowly prescriptive in their morality. In addition, these domestic melodramas about and for the people were mainly concerned with the daily life of the common man and his family. They dealt with sons or daughters tempted to go astray and with the problem of drunkenness and its effect upon wives and children. They expanded their scope to include the trouble of tenants with landlords and of factory workers with unjust employers.

These plays for the people were naturally democratic, echoing the sentiment behind the Reform Bill of 1832, and afterwards the sentiments of the Chartist Movement, but with only here and there a hint of rebellion, as in *Luke the Labourer*, with its protest against injustice, and in *Slave Life* (1852), by Tom Taylor and Mark Lemon, one of several dozen plays adapted from *Uncle Tom's Cabin* that portrayed the evils of slavery in America. Melodramas later in the century portrayed cross sections of life among the poor in a dingy great city, as in Boucicault's *The Streets of London* (1864). Though realistic in some ways, as in scenery, and suggestive of social evils, these plays made no clear, effective social protest.

The situations in melodrama were the most exciting the playwrights could invent. Madame Celeste, manager of the Adelphi, which specialized in melodrama, demanded "mystery, villainy, comic business, smugglers, caves, crossing of swords, firing of guns, lost daughters mysteriously recovered, shrieking their way into their fathers' arms, hair-breadth perils, executions, reprieves."

Perhaps the audiences did not believe the melodramas were true, but they responded to them as if they did. In twentieth-century revivals, actors stand in exaggeratedly stylized poses, gesture broadly, eavesdrop with hand to ear, and twist mustaches with a smirk, apparently under the impression that melodrama was written to mock naturalness. Actually, there is nothing new about ridiculing melodramas. In the nineteenth century burlesque after burlesque mocked these plays, using grotesque exaggeration, horseplay, and puns to parody scenes of peril and pathos. But melodramas had a power that neither words like "trash" nor ridicule could destroy. Ernest Watson visualizes the audience at a mid-century theatre just after it has witnessed respectfully a performance of Shakespeare. With a melodrama next on the bill, the audience becomes alert and eager. It "fairly vibrates to the thrills of the pulsing music, and the bursts of heroic music to carry entrenchment after entrenchment of injustice. Oh, the joy of suffering the agonies of the dumb and helpless father, and of the abused maid of snow-white innocence! But oh, the still greater joy of seeing the villain brother's retribution!" Whatever the logic or the art, the stimulus to feeling was real.

Action in the melodrama was vigorous. It demanded relevant dialogue. Verbal patterns developed for repeated situations — "Unhand me, villain!" — and heroes (or villains) in different plays talked like one another. Perhaps, as Nicoll says, authors wrote action to save themselves the trouble of writing dialogue: "Naturally, as the writers of melodramas had to turn out scores of these pieces to make a living, and as stage directions are easier to write than dialogue, this action-element was increased. . . . Whenever a Pocock or a Fitzball comes to a really difficult situation he switches off his dialogue and turns to . . . stage directions." As time passed and the melodrama developed toward realism, playwrights wrote better dialogue. Tom Taylor's *The Ticket-of-Leave Man*, for instance, exhibits interesting dialogue that has a Dickensian flavor.

Though melodramas were often lively with a great deal of singing and dancing, much of the comedy was a kind of clowning. The role of Gnatbrain in *Black-Eyed Susan* is perhaps typical. Besides hiding in a cupboard and beating Jacob with a rolling pin, he makes love to Dolly by saying, "Won't you be the summer cabbage of my heart, and let me cultivate you?"

Long after the minor theatres were no longer compelled to use music in a play, the orchestra accompanied the action and heightened the emotions of melodrama. Certain chords marked slow or rapid action, expressed joy or sorrow, heralded the hero, or thundered the entrance of the villain.

Melodrama constantly required more spectacular scenery, supplied by ingenious stage machinery: ghosts, storms, waterfalls, horse-races, fires with fire engines, and even trains. Melodramas drew material from every corner of modern life, including workhouses, prisons, and city slums. Most sensational when most realistic, this scenery led the melodrama toward realism.

Early melodramas tended to be episodic in structure, loosely tying two or more plot incidents end to end. Adaptations from the novels of Scott, Ainsworth, and Dickens increased this fault as writers found grist for the mill in quite unrelated scenes. Gradually the structures of melodramas were tightened and unified through the influence of Scribe's formula for the well-made play. Perhaps the plays written for the Olympic by Tom Taylor in the 1850's best define the technique. Winton Tolles states the formula this way: "Two human forces, A and B, are opposed to each other in a struggle to be decided by brains and chance. . . . The action then leads the opposing forces through a series of artfully contrived crises, each more exciting and piquant than the last. Suspense is constantly present, and surprise occurs repeatedly as first A and then B gains the supremacy through the amazing influence of some apparently trivial factor. The most common device to throw the weight first on one side and then the other is the shifting possession of some material object, preferably a letter. As the play develops the pace with which the commanding position changes accelerates, until in a whirlwind climax one force attains final victory." Taylor's most famous play, *The Ticket-of-Leave Man* (1863), excellently illustrates the technique. The plot presents a struggle between the detective Hawkshaw on the one hand, and the thieves Moss and Dalton on the other, for the soul, so to speak, of Bob Brierly. The action sways back and forth, with comic scenes and even a love story, but no letup of tension, until finally Hawkshaw has handcuffs on the criminals and Bob is restored to his employment and has his May in his arms. The sensation scenes, with fires, duels, or drownings, supplemented the well-made structure. But at last this structure, along with deepened characterization, made the sensation scene unnecessary. For instance, no scene dependent upon stage machinery is needed in Jones's well-made melodrama *The Silver King* (1882).

By the 1860's melodramas were simply better written than they had been earlier. Characters remained types, but touches of subtlety and complexity appeared in characterization. Slapstick was replaced by witty repartee. Restrained sentiment now and then replaced tear-jerking sentimentality. Hazlewood's famous *Lady Audley's Secret* (1877), for instance, is a melodrama adapted from a novel; the villainess Lady Audley does not at first seem evil, but only misunderstood. Alicia does not like Lady Audley, but she does not quite know why. Thus a sense of mystery and foreboding is established more subtly than in melodramas where the obvious villain is announced. This well-made "Society melodrama" (as Mr. Rowell calls it) has an aristocratic setting; it is adapted to its audience of 1877, more largely middle class than audiences earlier in the century.

While the finer art of the verse drama died, melodrama was able to survive and at last to develop into a more mature form because it expressed a vital force in the common people. Its sentimentality rested upon their simple idealism. Its humanitarian message had a strong appeal for audiences who understood and felt poverty and injustice. Its happy ending, however naïve, expressed the hope that springs eternal in people who find the present weary. It had the vitality to experiment and to become natural in performance, and, finally, it had the strength to live on in the product of its own evolution.

A public better educated than ever before had begun to ridicule the sensational features of melodrama by the 1880's, and they enjoyed Gilbert and Sullivan's popular burlesques of the form. The branch of the melodrama that remained old-fashioned — the Boucicault branch — died out in the 1890's. A more vigorous branch evolved into the new drama.

THE RISE OF THE NEW DRAMA

The branch of the melodrama that lived evolved into the new drama in a series of adaptations to the social and intellectual status of the audiences of 1865 to the 1890's. The splitting of the melodrama into two branches took place in 1865 when the Bancrofts produced Tom Robertson's *Society*. Robertson shared the desire of the Bancrofts to produce plays as lifelike as possible. Though using types drawn from the melodrama, Robertson deepened the personality of each character by adding realistic traits and attempting to make dialogue perfectly natural. If the action called for sentiment, he was careful to avoid sentimentality. He not only wrote stage directions to forbid sentimental tones, but also provided comic lines or situations to deflate pathos: George returning from the "dead," in *Caste*, brings in the milk. Where the typical melodrama inserted jokes, gags, and scenes of song-and-dance for comedy, Robertson incorporated unforced comedy in character and event. He wrote detailed stage directions, not to call for more action, but to describe little, significant movements. Finally, to secure performances harmonious in all their parts, Robertson directed his own plays. For perhaps the first time in the nineteenth century, the author's personal vision of his play was produced on the stage. Though the messages in Robertson's plays are not far in advance of the prescriptive morality of most domestic melodramas, the plays seem to be exploring problems from a liberal point of view, as *Caste* treats marriage across class lines. The very titles of his major plays, one-word titles each naming the subject for discussion, indicate his intention to treat a theme: *Society*, *Play* (gambling), *Home*, *School*, *Progress*, *War*.

The increased naturalness of Robertson's plays and the reforms of the Bancrofts led many playwrights of the 1870's and 1880's toward careful craftsmanship in structure and naturalness in characterization and dialogue. The influence of Robertson is evident in James Albery's *Two Roses* (1870), the play in which Henry Irving, as Digby Grant, first became famous. Though the play retains some melodramatic devices, it is primarily a comedy of character revealed in quietly realized ironies. It discards bustle and spectacle and offers a study of an egoist who is unconsciously a hypocrite; it exhibits the contrapuntal dialogue of Robertson's comedies, with the drama developing in the interplay of person upon person. The heroines (like Robertson's) are no longer weak, pathetic creatures to be rescued, but are fresh, athletic girls.

Leopold Lewis's *The Bells* (1871), though an adaptation from the French and somewhat Gothic in its setting and its theme of a murderer's remorse, advances far beyond the older melodrama, especially in its use of irony. The play presents a murderer with great subtlety of psychological analysis. Mathias is a respected citizen whose prosperity rests upon a murder he has long concealed. Fears arise from his subconscious, creating a terror of the soul that is not expressed in the old way of the villain's rhetoric, but is suggested in little delusions and involuntary reactions that he attempts to ignore, suppress, and conceal. But at last when he sleeps and can no longer will away his fantasies, the reason for his inner struggle is staged in an eerie sequence of stylized, ballet-like dreams. Presentation of Mathias's conflicts thus leaps across the realism toward which the drama was moving to some of the devices of twentieth-century plays.

Sydney Grundy's *A Pair of Spectacles* (1890) also shows naturalness of characterization and symbolism. The play is a well-constructed comic farce based on a French original, presenting the fairly obvious theme that conduct springs from temperament. Two brothers, one stingy and one generous, inadvertently exchange spectacles, symbolizing each man's view of human nature. The play exhibits heart-warming sentiments expressed in crisp, natural dialogue.

These plays by Albery, Lewis, and Grundy are particular examples of the widespread influence of Robertson and the Bancrofts upon dramatic craftsmanship through the 1880's. Yet one ingredient essential to the new drama was lacking — a significant theme or problem to provoke thought and discussion among educated adults. Two other playwrights, W. S. Gilbert and Arthur W. Pinero, provided this ingredient.

Gilbert supervised the production of his own plays and the Savoy operas with the careful attention to every detail of production that he had learned from his close friend Tom Robertson. He also brought to the stage something Robertson did not have, an innate passion for seeing into the soul of society. In plays like *The Palace of Truth* (1870) and *Engaged* (1877) Gilbert stripped veils of sentimentality, convention, and hypocrisy from his characters and revealed self-delusion and self-interest; and in his operas, as all the world knows, he mocked the melodramas that helped create these veils. Pinero was too young to know Robertson (whose plays he greatly admired), but the Bancrofts produced one of Pinero's early plays, *Lords and Commons* (1883), and he learned stagecraft from them. He lacked Gilbert's mordant cynicism and for some years wrote only farces with bright, brisk dialogue. Apparently with no reforming purpose he wrote a play, *The Profligate* (1889), that bared the double standard of sexual morality. To get it produced he had to change his original ending to a happy one. But he had it printed with his logical, tragic ending. The experience led him to reflect further upon both the double standard and the hypocrisy of the stage. Consequently he wrote *The Second Mrs. Tanqueray* (1893) and insisted (against much resistance) that it be performed with his true, bitter ending. In these different ways, Gilbert and Pinero added adult themes to Robertsonian craftsmanship.

While these playwrights were approaching the new drama in practice, a few dramatic critics and another playwright, Henry Arthur Jones, were calling for it in theory. The leader of the critics was William Archer, supported by Arthur B. Walkley and Bernard Shaw (not yet a playwright). Praising the Robertsonian-Gilbertian branch of the drama and condemning the branch that continued to present melodramas in the older formula, Archer called for a drama more deeply true to life and significant in its message, and he even sought to herald Ibsen and make his plays known to English readers.

In the 1880's the playwright Henry Arthur Jones, who had written melodramas and was later to write problem plays, started a vigorous crusade for a new drama free to discuss living ideas and sensible of some responsibility to do so. In 1884 he wrote a somewhat melodramatic play, *Saints and Sinners*, that included among the characters a pair of hypocritical Baptist deacons. Performance was possible because of the relaxed state of the censorship, but the play raised a furor. For a hundred years the stage had not dared portray a man of religion as a hypocrite. In the *Nineteenth Century* for January, 1885, Jones answered his critics. He said: "It is for those who would deny to the dramatist the right to depict religious life on the stage, to show either that religion has become a quite unessential and useless portion of human life, and is effete and defunct and has no bearing upon character in England today . . . or it is for them to show why religion should not occupy the same part in the dramatist's scheme and view of human life as it is supposed to do in the outer world around him." He wrote again: "The real knot of the question is in the method of treating the great passions of humanity. If the English public sticks to its present decision that these passions are not to be handled at all, then no drama is possible. We shall continue our revels of wax dolls, and our theatres will provide entertainments, not drama." Jones, however, would go no further than serious, realistic presentation of modern problems. He opposed the more radical "Ibsenite" drama.

Ibsen's plays were not widely known in England until 1891, when J. T. Grein's Independent Theatre company produced *Ghosts* and *Hedda Gabler*. Ibsen's subjects offended many people, and the newspapers poured abuse upon him, but William Archer and Bernard Shaw defended him. Shaw said: "What really interests [cultured] people on the stage is . . . stories of lives, discussion of conduct, unveiling of motives, conflicts of character in talk, laying bare of souls, discovery of pitfalls — in short, *illumination of life*." In the work of Gilbert, Pinero, and Jones, the new drama was in process of development before 1891, but Ibsen's plays helped define the goal toward which the drama was moving.

The time was ripe for the new drama. For at least two decades after the death of Robertson social and intellectual changes had been preparing the new audience, without which the new drama would have been a first-night failure. Dickens, England's favorite novelist until his death, had died in 1870. The novelists of the 1870's and 1880's, George Eliot, George Meredith, George Gissing, and Thomas Hardy, had begun shaping the minds of their readers to more philosophic points of view. Some intellectuals were reading the thought-provoking novels of the French naturalist writer Zola. In this period the advanced ideas of Darwin, Huxley, and Spencer in science and philosophy, and of Karl Marx and Henry George in economics, became subjects of popular discussion. Many people who were aware of the ideas expressed by these authors were growing impatient with the melodrama and hoped to find something more provocative on the stage.

Although these forces created the new drama, it did not enjoy a sudden triumph that immediately banished the older plays from the stage. Many people still preferred plays with plots they easily understood and with messages they would have agreed with before entering the theatre. Melodramas drained away these people who attended the theatre for mere entertainment (much as moving pictures and television drain a portion of the audience away from serious drama today); the reflective people who remained were numerous enough to support the new drama.

To appeal to this audience playwrights sought to write dramatic literature and to make the stage a tribunal for the exploration, illustration, and discussion of vital ideas. They wrote on domestic themes, but to question conventional morality rather than to prescribe it. Discarding the obvious heroes and villains of melodrama, they sought to discover what heroism and villainy are. Shaw's *Arms and the Man* (1894), for example, brings Bluntschli upon the stage as a coward and a villain, and Sergius as the romantic hero. Then the action of the play explores the nature of heroism and reverses the roles, exhibiting Bluntschli as a brave, resourceful man with common sense and Sergius as an empty poseur.

Instead of stock villains, the new drama presented mistaken people, idealists who wrecked their own and others' lives through lack of common sense, or narrow or prejudiced characters brought through experience to more enlightened views. Generally, instead of the old conflict between obvious right and wrong, the new dramatists opposed two rights each represented in a character honest and just from his own point of view — as in Jones's *The Notorious Mrs. Ebbsmith* both Agnes and the Duke are sincere in their conflicting views. Or, instead of a conflict between two human beings, the new drama presented a struggle between man and circumstance or man and hostile forces in society.

The purpose of action in the new drama was not to make the audience feel good about a happy outcome manipulated by the playwright. Dramatists sought to make the audience feel that what happened in the end of a play *had* to happen as the inevitable solution to the problem posed in the situation. They were not always successful; nothing gave the new dramatist more trouble than ending his play. The radical Shaw had answers, but the more conservative Jones, writing to question rather than answer, sometimes lacked the strength of conviction to follow the logic of his presentation to its rational conclusion; one feels uncertain and unconvinced by the ending of a play like Jones's *Michael and His Lost Angel* (1896).

In the new drama the emphasis was not on what happened to the characters; it was on what happened inside them. Because honest men may be mistaken, the playwrights could make new use of the old Greek dramatic irony; the audience, sympathizing with the just man, could see his mistake in Act I and throughout the play observe the slow, agonizing discovery of its consequences. For example, in *The Second Mrs. Tanqueray*, because he wishes to trust and be merciful, Aubrey throws Paula's written confession into the fire. The consequences of this idealistic generosity are realized in Paula's suicide. Because the purpose of the new drama was illumination rather than prescription, a play might end quietly with a character staring out into the night. Members of the audience knew what he was pondering, pondered it themselves, and took it home for discussion.

Some of the new dramas were called problem plays, for, questioning accepted orthodoxies, they asked "What is truth?" about social classes, religion, domestic relationships, woman's place in society, the double standard of morality, justice to the criminal, relations between capital and labor, the necessity of poverty, and so on. The drama undertook to examine society and its accepted values. If for later generations the problem plays of the 1890's are somewhat dated, perhaps this is because they contributed toward the solution of the problems they presented.

ROMANTIC VERSE DRAMA

The Traditional Modes

CHARLES ROBERT MATURIN

Bertram;

or,

The Castle of St. Aldobrand (1816)

EDWARD BULWER-LYTTON

Richelieu; or, The Conspiracy (1839)

Experimentation and the Closet Drama

JOHN WESTLAND MARSTON

The Patrician's Daughter (1842)

ROBERT BROWNING

Pippa Passes (1841)

CHARLES ROBERT MATURIN
1780-1824

Bertram;

or,

The Castle of St. Aldobrand

(1816)

Charles Robert Maturin is known in the twentieth century for his novel *Melmoth the Wanderer*, although in his own age he was famous for his dramas as well. Born in Dublin in 1780 and educated at Trinity College, he took holy orders and served as a curate in the country town of Longhrea until he was promoted to the curacy of St. Peter's in Dublin, a position he held until his death. With a growing family and a taste for elegance and luxury, he turned to literature to supplement his income, writing in the popular mode of Gothic fiction and drama. When his successes brought fame and money, which he spent on entertainments and extravagant furnishings for his house, some of his parishioners (perhaps moved by envy) deplored his demonic writing; but others expressed pride in having a famous literary man in their pulpit.

Maturin's early novels include *The Fatal Revenge* (1807), *The Wild Irish Boy* (1808), and *The Milesian Chief* (1811). He turned to playwriting with *Bertram* (1816), *Manuel* (1817), and *Fredolfo* (1819). *Bertram*, a tremendous success on the stage, marked a climax in the craze for Gothic drama, though ironically this craze was to some extent sobered by the excesses of *Bertram*. *Manuel* and *Fredolfo*, with characters still more depraved than Bertram, failed. Among his later novels, Maturin did his best work in *Melmoth the Wanderer* (1820).

In both novels and plays Maturin used every device he could command to satisfy the taste for tales of terror. In line with Joanna Baillie's theories of the passions, his characters are more projections of pride, despair, and vengeance than credible human beings. Yet his novels and plays seem natural expressions of his temperament. He said, "If I possess any talent, it is that of darkening the gloomy, and of deepening the sad; of painting life in extremes, and representing those struggles of passion when the soul trembles on the verge of the unlawful and the unhallowed."

Maturin first offered *Bertram* to the Crow Street Theatre in Dublin, but it was rejected. He then asked the advice of Sir Walter Scott, who forwarded the manuscript to the actor John Philip Kemble. When Kemble also refused the play, Scott recommended it to Lord Byron, then on the managerial committee for Drury Lane. Byron called the play to Edmund Kean's attention; the character of Bertram seemed made for Kean's acting talents, and on May 9, 1816, Kean produced the play. It created a sensation.

Bertram illustrates nearly every trait typical of nineteenth-century Gothicism. The settings are a bleak coast in southern Italy, a castle, a monastery, and wild woods and caverns. The play opens with the scenic climax of a violent storm and shipwreck, described by terror-stricken holy men who fear the storm is the work of fiends. Later scenic effects include the appearance of monks at midnight with flaring torches, processions of knights and monks, and the solemn chanting of a hymn. The story follows the sentimental conventions of Gothicism. Love is presented as a mystic, sacred, overpowering force of nature that inexorably moves its victims to defy all vows, duties, and reason. This amoral world is symbolized in a turmoil of nature that manifests the anger of Heaven. The action is conventional, with a hero-villain, a figure of inordinate pride and cruelty, motivated by his vaguely stated past injuries; a persecuted heroine who was driven to wed where she did not love and who, yielding to the villain, becomes his partner in guilt; remorse that leads the heroine to madness and the hero-villain to suicide; and a completely passive hero-victim. There are sentimental soliloquies on the state of the soul, and a somewhat irrelevant band of robbers. With some inflation, in evident imitation of Byron's Eastern tales, the poetry of the play achieves a somber and melancholy grandiloquence.

Bertram is the epitome of the Gothic hero-villain. At first sight he is a wild man of mysterious woe, raving insanely, and tormented even in his sleep. Apparently, he suffers because of the tradition in which he was created; the hero-villain must suffer; and no cause is necessary. But some reasons are suggested: at first a loyal but overly ambitious subject of his king, Bertram came to be distrusted, and Aldobrand, who took his place as the king's favorite, married his beloved. Moved by a mixture of pride and revenge, he is contemptuous of petty men and the laws of common life. He seems to disdain riches, but has become the chief of a band of robbers. Though his imposing qualities rest on his own declamations and Imogine's idealizations, he impresses even the Prior, of all people, as something like a fallen archangel or Miltonic Satan. But to a rational view, he acts like a paranoid ruffian, who, trapped, kills himself, exulting in his "warrior's soul."

Imogine is a development from the Gothic tradition of the heroine as the innocent victim. At first she is not the victim of the villain, but, in her marriage, the victim of the king (hardly of her kind-hearted husband?): some lines suggest that she married to save her father from penury, but others that she was hypnotized and married in a trance. At any rate, she has loved Bertram from girlhood. She adores his picture before he arrives, and in his presence she is completely pliant. She seems to share Bertram's passionate nature until after the adultery. Then she becomes more like the usual Gothic heroine — a victim hysterically frightened by the villain and frantic to save her husband. At this point she indulges in remorse that becomes dementia. Apparently (the point is not clear) she murders her child, and she dies shortly afterwards (of no stated physical cause).

The Prior was probably intended to help shape the admiration of the audience for Bertram as a wicked but somehow noble and grand character. He is represented as a saintly man (perhaps spokesman for the author, a minister of the Church) who finds Bertram sublime even in guilt — beyond good and evil. When Bertram makes clear his intention to destroy Aldobrand, the Prior will not betray Bertram's designs even to save the life of his generous and hospitable friend.

Aldobrand is the passive hero and victim, the symbol in the play of law and order, as opposed to Bertram's Satanic role. Aldobrand is zealous in the service of his king. In private life he is considerate, kind, and loved by all — even his faithless wife. It is Bertram's original intention to kill Aldobrand; he relents when he has injured him by seducing Imogine, but commits the murder in a fury when he learns that Aldobrand has been charged to hunt down Bertram and his outlaws. Perhaps the aroused audience, sympathetic with Bertram's fury, is supposed to feel that the deed is justified.

This is only one of several flaws in the play if it is viewed rationally. It is made fairly clear in Act I that Bertram alone was saved from the shipwreck. But in later acts both sailors and Bertram's robbers appear. Just how they were saved when the Prior saw the ship go down and declared "All, all did perish . . . every soul did perish" is not clear. They play no essential role in the action. Perhaps, familiar with the bandits in the Gothic plays influenced by Schiller's *Die Räuber*, Maturin tucked in this item because it was part of the formula. Also, when Aldobrand starts for the monastery he cannot cross a swollen stream even on horseback; but shortly after, Imogine crosses on foot with her child. It would seem that Maturin put his characters where he wanted them without attention to probabilities.

However, it was not on these grounds that critics judged the play. *Bertram* was very popular and was printed in eight editions within a year. The editor's introduction to the second edition (the version printed in this text) speaks of the high moral value of the play: it proclaims the justice and omnipotence of Heaven. Others did not agree. The adultery seemed both revolting and unnecessary to complete Bertram's revenge. In his *Biographia Literaria* S. T. Coleridge attacked the amoral hero and the public that admired him. He called Bertram "this *felo de se*, and thief captain, this loathsome and leprous confluence of robbery, adultery, murder, and cowardly assassination." He said of the audience, "I want words to describe the mingled horror and disgust with which I witnessed the opening of the fourth act, considering it as a melancholy proof of the depravation of the public mind." Richard Mears's comment is a just modern estimate: "*Bertram* is known today through the criticism of it that became part of *Biographia Literaria*, but it is more than an insect in amber: it is the example, par excellence, of amoral Gothicism in the drama."

BERTRAM

or,

THE CASTLE OF ST. ALDOBRAND

A Tragedy In Five Acts

by

CHARLES ROBERT MATURIN

First performed at the Theatre Royal, Drury Lane, May 9, 1816.

Cast of Characters

St. Aldobrand	Imogine
Bertram, *at first a* Stranger	Clotilda
Prior of St. Anselm	Teresa
Hugo	Knights, Monks, Soldiers,
Pietro	Sailors, Banditti, etc.
Child *of* Imogine	

Act I.

Scene 1.

Night. A gallery in a convent. A large Gothic window in the extremity, through which lightning is seen flashing. Two Monks enter in terror.

1st Monk. Heaven for its mercy! — what a night is here —
Oh! didst thou hear that peal?
2d Monk. The dead must hear it. — (*A pause — thunder*) Speak! speak, and let me hear a human voice.
1st Monk. While the dark terror hurtled distantly,
Lapt in the skirts of the advancing clouds,
I cower'd with head full low upon my pallet,
And deem'd that I might sleep — till the strong light

Did, clear as noonday, show each object round me.
Relic, and rosary, and crucifix
Did rock and quiver in the bickering glare —
Then forth I rushed in agony of fear.
2d Monk. Among the tombed tenants of the cloister
I walked and told my beads,
But, by the momently gleams of sheeted blue,
Did the pale marbles glare so sternly on me
I almost deemed they lived, and fled in horror.
1st Monk. There is much comfort in a holy man
In such an hour as this. (*Knocking at a door*)
Ho, wake thee, prior.
2d Monk. Oh! come forth, holy prior, and pray for us.

Enter the Prior.

Prior. All peace be with you! — 'tis a fearful hour.
1st Monk. Hath memory a parallel to this?

44

2d Monk. How hast thou fared in this most
  awful time?
Prior. As one whom fear did not make
  pitiless:
I bowed me at the cross for those whose heads
Are naked to the visiting blasts of Heav'n
In this its hour of wrath —
For the lone traveller on the hill of storms,
For the tossed shipman on the perilous deep;
Till the last peal that thundered o'er mine
  head
Did force a cry of — mercy for myself.
  1st Monk. (*Eagerly*) Think'st thou these
  rock-based turrets will abide?
  2d Monk. Think'st thou they will not
  topple o'er our heads?
  Prior. The hand of Him who rules the
  storm is o'er us.
  1st Monk. Oh, holy prior, this is no earthly
  storm.
The strife of fiends is on the battling clouds,
The glare of hell is in these sulphurous light-
  nings, —
This is no earthly storm.
  Prior. Peace, peace — thou rash and un-
  advised man;
Oh! add not to this night of nature's horrors
The darker shadowing of thy wicked fears.
The hand of Heaven, not man, is dealing with
  us,
And thoughts like thine do make it deal thus
  sternly.

Enter a Monk pale and breathless.

Speak, thou hast something seen.
  3d Monk. A fearful sight.
  Prior. What hast thou seen?
  3d Monk. A piteous, fearful sight —
A noble vessel labouring with the storm
Hath struck upon the rocks beneath our
  walls,
And by the quivering gleams of livid blue
Her deck is crowded with despairing souls,
And in the hollow pauses of the storm
We heard their perishing cries —
  Prior. Now haste ye forth,
Haste all —
  3d Monk. It cannot be, it is too late;
For many a fathom doth the beetling rock
Rise o'er the breaker's surge that dashes o'er
  them —
No help of human hand can reach them
  there —
One hour will hush their cries — and by the
  morn
Thou wilt behold the ruin — wreck and corse
Float on the weltering wave.
  Prior. Almighty power,

Can nought be done? All things are possi-
  ble —
Wave high your torches on each crag and
  cliff —
Let many lights blaze on our battlements —
Shout to them in the pauses of the storm,
And tell them there is hope —
And let our deep-toned bell its loudest peal
Send cheerly o'er the deep —
'Twill be a comfort to the wretched souls
In their extremity — All things are possible;
Fresh hope may give them strength, and
  strength deliverance —
I'll hie me forth with you.
  3d Monk. Wilt thou go forth —
Hardly the vigorous step of daring youth
May hold its footing on those wave-washed
  crags:
And how wilt thou abide?
  1st Monk. 'Tis tempting Heaven.
  Prior. To succour man, not tempt my God,
  I go;
He will protect his servant.   *Exeunt.*

Scene 2.

*The rocks. The sea. A storm. The convent illu-
minated in the background. The bell tolls at
intervals. A group of Monks on the rocks with
torches. A vessel in distress in the offing.*

Enter the Prior and Monks below.

  Prior. (*Clasping his hands*) Holy St.
  Anselm — what a sight is here!
  1st Monk. Pray for their souls — their
  earthly part is doomed —
  Prior. Oh! that a prayer could hush the
  elements! —
Hold, I do espy a hope, a blessed hope —
That wave hath heaved her from the rock she
  struck on.
Lo, every arm on board is plied for safety —
Now, all the saints to speed. —
  1st Monk. No saint doth hear.
Lo, the recoiling surge drives fiercely o'er
  her —
In, holy prior, or ere their drowning shrieks
Do rive the sense; in, in, and tell thy beads —
  Prior. I will not in, while to that hopeless
  wreck
One arm doth cling; while o'er the roaring
  waste
One voice be raised for help — I will not
  hence.
  Monks. (*Above*) She sinks — she sinks —
  Oh hour of woe and horror!
    *The vessel sinks. The Prior falls into
    the arms of the Monks. The scene
    shuts.*

Scene 3.

The gallery.

Enter the first Monk and the Prior.

1st Monk. Now rest you, holy prior, you
  are much moved —
Prior. (*Not heeding him*) All, all did
  perish —
1st Monk. Change those drenched weeds —
Prior. I wist not of them — every soul did
  perish —

Enter third Monk hastily.

3d Monk. No, there was one did battle
  with the storm
With careless, desperate force; full many
  times
His life was won and lost, as though he recked
  not —
No hand did aid him, and he aided none —
Alone he breasted the broad wave, alone
That man was saved —
Prior. Where is he? lead him hither.

The Stranger is led in by Monks.

Raise to St. Anselm, thou redeemed soul,
Raise high thy living voice in prayer and
  praise;
For wonderous hath his mercy been to
  thee —
2d Monk. He hath not spoken yet —
Stranger. Who are those round me?
Where am I?
Prior. On the shore of Sicily —
The convent of St. Anselm this is called —
Near is the castle of Lord Aldobrand —
A name far known, if, as thy speech imports,
Thou'rt of Italian birth —

> *At the name of Aldobrand, the
> Stranger makes an effort to break
> from the Monks, but falls through
> weakness.*

Tell us thy name, sad man —
Stranger. A man of woe —
Prior. What is thy woe, that Christian love
  may heal it —
Hast thou upon the pitiless waters lost
Brother, or sire, or son? did she thou lovest
Sink in thy straining sight! —
Or have the hoardings of thy worldly thrift
Been lost with yonder wreck? —

> *To these questions the Stranger gives
> signs of dissent.*

Why dost thou then despond?
Stranger. Because I live —
Prior. Look not so wild — can we do aught
  for thee?
Stranger. Yes, plunge me in the waves
  from which ye snatched me;

So will the sin be on your souls, not mine —
Prior. I'll question not with him — his
  brain is wrecked —
For ever in the pauses of his speech
His lip doth work with inward mutterings,
And his fixed eye is riveted fearfully
On something that no other sight can spy.
Food and rest will restore him — lead him
  in —
Stranger. (*Dashing off the monks as they
approach*) Off — ye are men — there's poison
  in your touch — (*Sinking back*)
But I must yield, for this hath left me
  strengthless.   *Exeunt.*

Scene 4.

A hall in the Castle of Aldobrand.

Enter Pietro and Teresa meeting.

Piet. Hah! Teresa waking! Was ever such a
  tempest?
Teres. The Lady Imogine would watch all
  night. —
And I have tended on her. What roused thee?
Piet. Would you could tell me what would
give me sleep in such a night. I know of but
one remedy for fear and wakefulness; that
is a flagon of wine. I hoped the thunder would
have waked old Hugo to open the cellar-door
for me.
Teres. He hath left his bed. E'en now I
  passed him
Measuring the banquet-hall with restless
  steps
And moody fretful gestures. He approaches.

Enter Hugo.

Piet. Hugo, well met. Does e'en thy age
bear memory of so terrible a storm?
Hugo. They have been frequent lately.
Piet. They are ever so in Sicily.
Hugo. So it is said. But storms when I was
  young
Would still pass o'er like Nature's fitful fevers
And render'd all more wholesome. Now their
  rage
Sent thus unseasonable and profitless
Speaks like the threats of Heaven.
Teres. Heaven grant its wrath visit not my
  kind Lady!
Hugo. Heaven grant, Teresa,
She may be still as happy in these halls,
As when she tripp'd the green a rural maid
And carol'd light of heart — ere her good
  father's ruin;
Or our Lord saw and loved her!
Piet. See, if Madam Clotilda be not roused.
Teres. I'm glad, for she's our lady's loved
  companion

And most esteemed attendant.

Enter Clotilda.

Clo. Is the Lady Imogine risen?
Teres. She hath not rested through the night.
Long ere the storm arose, her restless gestures
Forbade all hope to see her bless'd with sleep.
Clo. Since her lord's absence it is ever thus.
But soon he will return to his loved home,
And the gay knights and noble wassailers
Banish her lonely melancholy.

          Horn heard without.

Monk. (*Without*) What, ho.
Hugo. There's someone at the gate.
My fears presage unwelcome messengers
At such untimely hours.
   Clo. Attend the summons, Hugo.
I seek the Lady Imogine. If 'tis aught
Concerns her or our Lord, follow me thither.

          Exeunt.

Scene 5.

A Gothic apartment. Imogine discovered sitting at a table, looking at a picture.

Imo. Yes,
The limner's art may trace the absent feature,
And give the eye of distant weeping faith
To view the form of its idolatry;
But oh! the scenes 'mid which they met and parted —
The thoughts, the recollections sweet and bitter —
Th' Elysian dreams of lovers, when they loved —
Who shall restore them?
Less lovely are the fugitive clouds of eve,
And not more vanishing — if thou couldst speak,
Dumb witness of the secret soul of Imogine,
Thou might'st acquit the faith of womankind —
Since thou wast on my midnight pillow laid
Friend hath forsaken friend — the brotherly tie
Been lightly loosed — the parted coldly met —
Yea, mothers have with desperate hands wrought harm
To little lives from their own bosoms lent.
But woman still hath loved — if that indeed
Woman e'er loved like me.

Enter Clotilda.

Clo. The storm seems hushed — wilt thou to rest, Lady?
Imo. I feel no lack of rest —

Clo. Then let us stay —
And watch the last peal murmuring on the blast.
I will sit by the while, so thou wilt tell
Some pleasant story to beguile the time.
Imo. I am not in the mood.
Clo. I pray thee, tell me of some shadowy thing
Crossing the traveller on his path of fear
On such a night as this —
Or shipwrecked seaman clinging to a crag
From which some hand of darkness pushes him.
Imo. Thou simple maid —
Thus to enslave thy heart to foolish fears.
Clo. Far less I deem of peril is in such
Than in those tales women most love to list to,
The tales of love — for they are all untrue.
Imo. Lightly thou say'st that woman's love is false,
The thought is falser far —
For some of them are true as martyrs' legends,
As full of suffering faith, of burning love,
Of high devotion — worthier heaven than earth —
Oh, I do know a tale.
Clo. Of knight or lady?
Imo. Of one who loved — She was of humble birth
Yet dared to love a proud and noble youth.
His sovereign's smile was on him — glory blazed
Around his path — yet did he smile on her —
Oh then, what visions were that blessed one's!
His sovereign's frown came next —
Then bowed the banners on his crested walls
Torn by the enemies' hand from their proud height,
Where twice two hundred years they mocked the storm.
The stranger's step profaned his desolate halls,
An exiled outcast, houseless, nameless, abject,
He fled for life, and scarce by flight did save it.
No hoary beadsman bid his parting step
God speed — No faithful vassal followed him;
For fear had withered every heart but hers,
Who amid shame and ruin lov'd him better.
Clo. Did she partake his lot?
Imo. She burned to do it,
But 'twas forbidden.
Clo. How proved she then her love?
Imo. Was it not love to pine her youth away?

In her lone bower she sat all day to hearken
For tales of him, and — soon came tales of
    woe.
High glory lost, he recked not what was
    saved —
With desperate men in desperate ways he
    dealt —
A change came o'er his nature and his heart
Till she that bore him had recoiled from him,
Nor known the alien visage of her child.
Yet still she loved, yea, still loved hopeless
    on.
  Clo. Hapless lady! What hath befallen her?
  Imo. Full many a miserable year hath
    passed —
She knows him as one dead, or worse than
    dead;
And many a change her varied life hath
    known,
But her heart none.
In the lone hour of tempest and of terror
Her soul was on the dark hill's side with
    Bertram,
Yea, when the launched bolt did sear her
    sense
Her soul's deep orisons were breathed for
    him.
Was this not love? yea, thus doth woman
    love.
  Clo. I would I had beheld their happier
    hours,
Hast thou e'er seen the dame? I pray thee,
    paint her.
  Imo. They said her cheek of youth was
    beautiful
Till withering sorrow blanched the bright
    rose there —
And I have heard men swear her form was
    fair;
But grief did lay his icy finger on it,
And chilled it to a cold and joyless statue.
Methought she caroled blithely in her youth,
As the couched nestling trills his vesper lay,
But song and smile, beauty and melody,
And youth and happiness are gone from her.
Perchance — even as she is — *he* would not
    scorn her
If he could know her — for, for him she's
    changed;
She is much altered — but her heart — her
    heart.
  Clo. I would I might behold that wretched
    lady
In all her sad and waning loveliness.
  Imo. Thou would'st not deem her wretched
    — outward eyes
Would hail her happy.
They've decked her form in purple and in
    pall.

When she goes forth, the thronging vassals
    kneel,
And bending pages bear her footcloth well —
No eye beholds that lady in her bower,
That is her hour of joy, for then she weeps,
Nor does her husband hear.
  Clo. Sayst thou her husband? —
How could she wed, she who did love so well?
  Imo. How could she wed! What could I do
    but wed —
Hast seen the sinking fortunes of thy
    house —
Hast felt the gripe of bitter shameful want —
Hast seen a father on the cold cold earth,
Hast read his eye of silent agony,
That asked relief, but would not look re-
    proach
Upon his child unkind —
I would have wed disease, deformity,
Yea, griped Death's grisly form to 'scape
    from it —
And yet some sorcery was wrought on me,
For earlier things do seem as yesterday,
But, I've no recollection of the hour
They gave my hand to Aldobrand.
  Clo. Blessed saints —
And was it thou indeed?
  Imo. I am that wretch —
The wife of a most noble, honoured lord —
The mother of a babe whose smiles do stab
    me —
But *thou* art Bertram's still, and Bertram's
    ever! (*Striking her heart*)
  Clo. Hath time no power upon thy hope-
    less love?
  Imo. Yea, time hath power, and what a
    power I'll tell thee,
A power to change the pulses of the heart
To one dull throb of ceaseless agony,
To hush the sigh on the resigned lip
And lock it in the heart — freeze the hot tear
And bid it on the eyelid hang for ever —
Such power hath time o'er me.
  Clo. And has not then
A husband's kindness —
  Imo. Mark me, Clotilda.
And mark me well, I am no desperate wretch
Who borrows an excuse from shameful pas-
    sion
To make its shame more vile —
I am a wretched, but a spotless wife,
I've been a daughter but too dutiful —
But, oh! the writhings of a generous soul
Stabb'd by a confidence it can't return,
To whom a kind word is a blow on th' heart —
I cannot paint thy wretchedness.
                   Bursts into tears.
  Clo. Nay, nay,
Dry up your tears, soon will your lord return,

Let him not see you thus by passion shaken.

Imo. Oh wretched is the dame, to whom
the sound
"Your lord will soon return" — no pleasure
brings.

Clo. Some step approaches — 'tis St.
Anselm's Monk.

Imo. Remember — now, what wouldst
thou reverend father?

Enter first Monk.

Monk. St. Anselm's benison on you,
gracious dame.
Our holy prior by me commends him to
you —
The wreck that struck upon our rocks i' th'
storm
Hath thrown some wretched souls upon his
care.
(For many have been saved since morning
dawned)
Wherefore he prays the wonted hospitality
That the free noble usage of your castle
Doth grant to ship-wreck'd and distressed
men —

Imo. Bear back my greetings to your holy
prior —
Tell him the lady of St. Aldobrand
Holds it no sin, although her lord be absent,
To ope her gates to wave-tossed mariners —
Now Heaven forefend your narrow cells were
cumbered
While these free halls stood empty — tell
your prior
We hold the custom of our castle still.

Exeunt.

End of the First Act.

ACT II.

Scene 1.

*An apartment in the convent. The Stranger lies
sleeping on a couch. The Prior watching him.*

Prior. He sleeps, if it be sleep; this starting
trance
Whose feverish tossings and deep muttered
groans,
Do prove the soul shares not the body's
rest — (*Hanging over him*)
How the lip works, how the bare teeth do
grind —
And beaded drops course down his writhen
brow —
I will awake him from this horrid trance,
This is no natural sleep — ho, wake thee,
stranger —

Stranger. What wouldst thou have, my
life is in thy power —

Prior. Most wretched man, whose fears
alone betray thee —
What art thou? — speak.

Stranger. Thou sayest I am a wretch —
And thou sayest true — these weeds do wit-
ness it —
These wave-worn weeds — these bare and
bruised limbs,
What wouldst thou more? — I shrink not
from the question.
I am a wretch, and proud of wretchedness,
'Tis the sole earthly thing that cleaves to me.

Prior. Lightly I deem of outward wretched-
ness,
For that hath been the lot of blessed saints —
But in their dire extreme of outward
wretchedness
Full calm they slept in dungeons and in dark-
ness —
Such hath not been thy sleep —

Stranger. Didst watch my sleep —
But thou couldst glean no secret from my
ravings. —

Prior. Thy secrets, wretched man, I reck
not of them —
But I adjure thee by the church's power
(A power to search man's secret heart of sin),
Show me thy wound of soul —
Weep'st thou, the ties of nature or of passion
Torn by the hand of Heaven —
Oh no! full well I deemed no gentler feeling
Woke the dark lightning of thy withering
eye —
What fiercer spirit is it tears thee thus?
Show me the horrid tenant of thy heart —
Or wrath, or hatred, or revenge, is there —

Stranger. (*Suddenly starting from his couch,
falling on his knees, and raising his clasped
hands*) I would consort with mine eternal
enemy,
To be revenged on him. —

Prior. Art thou a man, or fiend, who
speakest thus?

Stranger. I was a man, I know not what I
am —
What others' crimes and injuries have made
me —
Look on me — What am I? — (*Advancing*)

Prior. I know thee not.

Stranger. I marvel that thou say'st it —
For lowly men full oft remember those
In changed estate, whom equals have for-
gotten:
A passing beggar hath remembered me,
When with strange eyes my kinsmen looked
on me —
I wore no sullied weeds on that proud day

When thou a barefoot monk didst bow full
  low
For alms, my heedless hand hath flung to
  thee —
Thou dost not know me. — (*Approaching
  him*)
  Prior. Mine eyes are dim with age — but
    many thoughts
Do stir within me at thy voice.
  Stranger. List to me, monk, it is thy trade
    to talk,
As reverend men do use in saintly wise,
Of life's vicissitudes and vanities —
Hear one plain tale that doth surpass all
  saws —
Hear it from me — *Count Bertram* — aye —
  Count Bertram —
The darling of his liege and of his land,
The army's idol, and the council's head —
Whose smile was fortune, and whose will was
  law —
Doth bow him to the prior of St. Anselm
For water to refresh his parched lip,
And this hard-matted couch to fling his limbs
  on. —
  Prior. Good Heaven and all its saints! —
  Ber. Wilt thou betray me? —
  Prior. Lives there the wretch beneath these
    walls to do it?
Sorrow enough hath bowed thy head already
Thou man of many woes. —
Far more I fear lest thou betray thyself.
Hard by do stand the halls of Aldobrand
(Thy mortal enemy and cause of fall),
Where ancient custom doth invite each
  stranger
Cast on this shore to sojourn certain days,
And taste the bounty of the castle's lord —
If thou goest not, suspicion will arise,
And if thou dost (all changed as thou art),
Some desperate burst of passion will betray
  thee
And end in mortal scathe —
What dost thou gaze on with such fixed eyes?
  Ber. What sayest thou?
I dreamed I stood before Lord Aldobrand
Impenetrable to his searching eyes —
And I did feel the horrid joy men feel
Measuring the serpent's coil whose fangs
  have stung them;
Scanning with giddy eye the air-hung rock
From which they leapt and live by miracle;
Following the dun skirt of the o'erpast storm
Whose bolt did leave them prostrate —
To see that horrid spectre of my thoughts
In all the stern reality of life —
To mark the living lineaments of hatred,
And say, this is the man whose sight should
  blast me;

Yet in calm dreadful triumph still gaze on: —
It is a horrid joy.
  Prior. Nay, rave not thus —
Thou wilt not meet him, many a day must
  pass
Till from Palermo's walls he wend him home-
  ward —
Where now he tarries with St. Anselm's
  knights. —
His dame doth dwell in solitary wise —
Few are the followers in his lonely halls —
Why dost thou smile in that most horrid
  guise? —
  Ber. (*Repeating his words*) His dame doth
    dwell alone — perchance his child —
Oh, no, no, no — it was a damned thought.
  Prior. I do but indistinctly hear thy words,
But feel they have some fearful meaning in
  them. —
  Ber. Oh, that I could but mate him in his
    might,
Oh, that we were on the dark wave together,
With but one plank between us and destruc-
  tion,
That I might grasp him in these desperate
  arms,
And plunge with him amid the weltering
  billows —
And view him gasp for life — and —
  Prior. Horrible — horrible — I   charge
    thee cease —
The shrines are trembling on these sainted
  walls —
The stony forms will start to life and answer
  thee.
  Ber. Ha ha — I see him struggling —
I see him — ha, ha, ha! (*A frantic laugh*)
  Prior. Oh horrible —
Help, help — to hold him — for my strength
  doth fail —

Enter first Monk.

  1st Monk. The lady of St. Aldobrand sends
    greeting —
  Prior. Oh, art thou come, this is no time
    for greeting —
Help — bear him off — thou see'st his fear-
  ful state.   *Exeunt bearing him off.*

Scene 2.

Hall in the Castle of St. Aldobrand.

*Enter Hugo showing in Bertram's comrades,
  Clotilda following.*

  Hugo. This way, friends, this way, good
    cheer awaits you.
  1st Sailor. Well then, good cheer was never
    yet bestowed
On those who need it more.

Hugo. To what port bound,
Did this fell storm o'ertake you?
    1st Sailor. No matter
So we find here a comfortable haven.
    Hugo. Whence came you?
    1st Sailor. Psha, I cannot answer fasting.
    Hugo. Roughness, the proverb says, speaks
        honesty,
I hope the adage true.
    Clo. Lead them in, Hugo,
They need speedy care — which is your
        leader?
    1st Sailor. He will be here anon — what ye
        would know,
Demand of him.
    2d Sailor. (*Advancing*) He's here.
    Clo. I fain would learn
Their country and their fortunes.

*Enter Bertram, with a sullen air, but
        scrutinizing all around.*

Is that him?
His looks appal me, I dare not speak to him.
                    All pause at his appearance.
    Hugo. Come, come, the feast's prepared
        within, this way.
            Bertram passes on sullenly and exits.
    Clo. The grief that clothes that leader's
        woeworn form,
The chilling awe his ruin'd grandeur wears
Is of no common sort — I must observe him.
                            Exit Clotilda.
    1st Sailor. Now, comrades, we will honour
        our host's bounty
With jovial hearts, and gay forgetfulness
Of perils past and coming.
                    Glee.
We be men escaped from dangers,
Sweet to think of o'er our bowls; —
Wilds have ne'er known hardier rangers,
Hall shall ne'er see blither souls. *Exeunt.*

Scene 3.

*Moonlight; a terraced rampart of the castle; a
part of the latter is seen, the rest concealed by
woods. Imogine alone. She gazes at the moon
for some time, and then advances slowly.*

    Imo. Mine own loved light,
That every soft and solemn spirit worships,
That lovers love so well — strange joy is
        thine,
Whose influence o'er all tides of soul hath
        power,
Who lend'st thy light to rapture and de-
        spair; —
The glow of hope and wan hue of sick fancy
Alike reflect thy rays: alike thou lightest
The path of meeting or of parting love —
Alike on mingling or on breaking hearts

Thou smil'st in thronèd beauty. — Bertram
        — Bertram.
How sweet it is to tell the listening night
The name beloved — it is a spell of power
To wake the buried slumberers of the heart,
Where memory lingers o'er the grave of
        passion
Watching its trancèd sleep! —
The thoughts of other days are rushing on
        me,
The loved, the lost, the distant, and the dead
Are with me now, and I will mingle with them
Till my sense fails, and my raised heart is
        wrapt
In secret suspension of mortality.

Enter Clotilda.

    Clo. Why dost thou wander by this mourn-
        ful light,
Feeding sick fancy with the thought that
        poisons? —
    Imo. I will but weep beneath the moon
        awhile. —
Now do not chide my heart for this sad
        respite,
The thoughts it most doth love do visit it
        then,
And make it feel like heaven —
    Clo. Nay, come with me, and view those
        storm 'scaped men
A-feasting in thy hall; 'twill cheer thy
        heart —
Of perils 'scaped by flood and fire they tell,
And many an antique legend wild they know
And many a lay they sing — hark, their deep
        voices
Come faintly on the wind.
            Noise of singing and revelry without.
    Imo. Their wild and vulgar mirth doth
        startle me.
This clamorous wassail in a baron's hall
Ill suits the state of rescued fearful men: —
But as I passed the latticed gallery
One stood alone; — I marked him where he
        stood,
His face was veiled, — faintly a light fell on
        him;
But through soiled weeds his muffled form
        did show
A wild and terrible grandeur.
    Clo. I marked him too. He mixed not with
        the rest,
But o'er his wild mates held a stern control —
Their rudest burst of riotous merriment
Beneath his dark eye's stilling energy
Was hushed to silence.
    Imo. He never spoke?
    Clo. No, he did nought but sigh,
If I might judge by the high-heaving **vesture**

Folded so deep on his majestic breast; —
Of sound I heard not —
   Imo. Call him hither. —
There is a mystery of woe about him
That strongly stirs the fancy.
   Clo. Wilt thou confer alone, at night, with
     one
Who bears such fearful form?
   Imo. Why therefore send him —
All things of fear have lost their power o'er
   me —
       Exit Clotilda. Imogine appears to be
       debating with herself how to receive
       him, at length she says:
If he do bear, like me, a withered heart
I will not mock him with a sound of com-
   fort —
       Bertram enters slowly from the end of
       the stage; his arms folded, his eyes
       fixed on the earth, she does not know
       him.
A form like that hath broken on my dreams
So darkly wild, so proudly stern,
Doth it rise on me waking?
       Bertram comes to the end of the stage,
       and stands without looking at her.
Stranger, I sent for thee, for that I deemed
Some wound was thine, that yon free band
   might chafe, —
Perchance thy worldly wealth sunk with yon
   wreck —
Such wound my gold can heal — the castle's
   almoner —
   Ber. The wealth of worlds were heaped on
   me in vain.
   Imo. Oh then I read thy loss — Thy heart
   is sunk
In the dark waters pitiless; some dear friend,
Or brother, loved as thine own soul, lies
   there —
I pity thee, sad man, but can no more —
Gold I can give, but can no comfort give
For I am comfortless —
Yet if I could collect my faltering breath
Well were I meet for such sad ministry,
For grief hath left my voice no other
   sound —
   Ber. (*Striking his heart*) No dews give
   freshness to this blasted soil. —
   Imo. Strange is thy form, but more thy
   words are strange —
Fearful it seems to hold this parley with thee.
Tell me thy race and country —
   Ber. What avails it?
The wretched have no country: that dear
   name
Comprises home, kind kindred, fostering
   friends,
Protecting laws, all that binds man to man —

But none of these are mine; — I have no
   country —
And for my race, the last dread trump shall
   wake
The sheeted relics of mine ancestry,
Ere trump of herald to the armed lists
In the bright blazon of their stainless coat,
Calls their lost child again. —
   Imo. I shake to hear him —
There is an awful thrilling in his voice, —
The soul of other days comes rushing in
   them. —
If nor my bounty nor my tears can aid thee,
Stranger, farewell; and 'mid thy misery
Pray, when thou tell'st thy beads, for one
   more wretched.
   Ber. Stay, gentle lady, I would somewhat
with thee. (*Imogine retreats terrified. Detaining*
her) — Thou shalt not go —
   Imo. Shall not! — Who art thou? speak —
   Ber. And must I speak? —
There was a voice which all the world, but
   thee,
Might have forgot, and been forgiven, —
   Imo. My senses blaze — between the dead
   and living
I stand in fear — oh God! — It cannot be —
Those thick black locks — those wild and
   sun-burnt features
He looked not thus — but then that voice —
It cannot be — for he would know my name.
   Ber. Imogine.
       She has tottered towards him during
       the last speech, and when he utters her
       name, shrieks and falls into his arms.
Imogine — yes,
Thus pale, cold, dying, thus thou art most fit
To be enfolded to this desolate heart —
A blighted lily on its icy bed —
Nay, look not up, 'tis thus I would behold
   thee.
That pale cheek looks like truth — I'll gaze
   no more —
That fair, that pale, dear cheek, these helpless
   arms,
If I look longer they will make me human.
   Imo. (*Starting from him*) Fly, fly, the vas-
   sals of thine enemy wait
To do thee dead.
   Ber. Then let them wield the thunder,
Fell is their dint, who're mailed in despair.
Let mortal might sever the grasp of Bertram.
   Imo. Release me — I must break from him
   — he knows not —
Oh God!
   Ber. Imogine — madness seizes me —
Why do I find thee in mine enemy's walls?
What dost thou do in halls of Aldobrand?
Infernal light doth shoot athwart my mind —

Swear thou art a dependent on his bounty,
That chance, or force, or sorcery, brought
    thee hither;
Thou canst not be — my throat is swoln with
    agony —
Hell hath no plague — Oh no, thou couldst
    not do it.
  Imo. (*Kneeling*) Mercy.
  Ber. Thou hast it not, or thou wouldst
    speak —
Speak, speak! (*With frantic violence*)
  Imo. I am the wife of Aldobrand, —
To save a famishing father did I wed.
  Ber. I will not curse *her* — but the hoarded
    vengeance —
  Imo. Aye — curse, and consummate the
    horrid spell,
For broken-hearted, in despairing hour
With every omen dark and dire I wedded —
Some ministering demon mocked the robed
    priest,
With some dark spell, not holy vow they
    bound me,
Full were the rites of horror and despair.
They wanted but — the seal of Bertram's
    curse.
  Ber. (*Not heeding her*) — Talk of her
    father — could a father love thee
As I have loved? — the veriest wretch on
    earth
Doth cherish in some corner of his heart
Some thought that makes that heart a sanc-
    tuary
For pilgrim dreams in midnight-hour to
    visit,
And weep and worship there.
— And such thou wert to me — and thou art
    lost.
— What was her father? could a father's love
Compare with mine? — in want, and war, and
    peril,
Things that would thrill the hearer's blood to
    tell of,
My heart grew human when I thought of
    thee —
Imogine would have shuddered for my
    danger —
Imogine would have bound my leechless
    wounds —
Imogine would have sought my nameless
    corse,
And known it well — and she was wedded —
    wedded —
Was there no name in hell's dark catalogue
To brand thee with, but mine immortal
    foe's? —
And did I 'scape from war, and want, and
    famine
To perish by the falsehood of a woman?

  Imo. Oh spare me, — Bertram — oh pre-
    serve thyself —
  Ber. A despot's vengeance, a false coun-
    try's curses,
The spurn of menials whom this hand had
    fed —
In my heart's steeled pride I shook them off,
As the bayed lion from his hurtless hide
Shakes his pursuers' darts — across their
    path —
One dart alone took aim, thy hand did barb it.
  Imo. He did not hear my father's cry —
    Oh heaven —
Nor food, nor fire, nor raiment, and his child
Knelt madly to the hungry walls for succour
Ere her wrought brain could bear the horrid
    thought —
Or wed with him — or — see my father
    perish.
  Ber. Thou tremblest lest I curse thee,
    tremble not —
Though thou hast made me, woman, very
    wretched —
Though thou hast made me — but I will not
    curse thee —
Hear the last prayer of Bertram's broken
    heart,
That heart which thou hast broken, not his
    foes! —
Of thy rank wishes the full scope be on
    thee —
May pomp and pride shout in thine addered
    path
Till thou shalt feel and sicken at their
    hollowness —
May he thou'st wed, be kind and generous to
    thee
Till thy wrung heart, stabb'd by his noble
    fondness
Writhe in detesting consciousness of false-
    hood —
May thy babe's smile speak daggers to that
    mother
Who cannot love the father of her child,
And in the bright blaze of the festal hall,
When vassals kneel, and kindred smile
    around thee,
May ruined Bertram's pledge hiss in thine
    ear —
Joy to the proud dame of St. Aldobrand —
While his cold corse doth bleach beneath her
    towers.
  Imo. (*Detaining him*) Stay.
  Ber. No.
  Imo. Thou hast a dagger.
  Ber. Not for woman. —
  Imo. (*Flinging herself on the ground*) It was
    my prayer to die in Bertram's presence,
But not by words like these —

Ber. (Turning back) — On the cold earth!
— I do forgive thee from my inmost soul —
The child of Imogine rushes in and clings to her.
Child. Mother.
Ber. (Eagerly snatching up the child) God
    bless thee, child — Bertram hath kissed
    thy child.

> *He rushes out. Clotilda enters gazing*
> *after him in terror, and goes to afford*
> *relief to Imogine.*
>
> *End of the Second Act.*

ACT III.

Scene 1.

A wood. The stage darkened. St. Aldobrand
speaking to a Page behind the scenes.

Ald. Hold thou my good steed, page; the
    moon is down,
We've far outstript the knights, but slacker
    speed
Hath found a surer road — where, think'st
    thou, are we?

> *Enter St. Aldobrand and a Page.*

Vainly I listen through the night so still
For bell that tells of holy convent near,
Or warder's bugle from the battlement,
Or horn of knight returning from the
    chase —
All is dark, still, and lorn; where deemest
    thou are we?
Page. Oh, we are nigh a fell and fearful
    spot,
For by the last gleams of the sunken moon
I saw the towers —
Ald. What towers are those, boy?
Page. The ruined towers that 'tis said are
    haunted —
Dimly they rose amid the doubtful gloom,
But not one star-beam twinkled on their
    summits.
Ald. Then, not four leagues divide me
    from mine home. —
Mine home — it is a pleasant sound — there
    bide
My dame and child — all pleasant thoughts
    dwell there —   *A bell tolls.*
Hark! 'tis the convent bell, forego thy tale —
The blessed thoughts of home are in that
    sound
That near my castle's gallant walls doth
    float —

> *Chorus of knights heard faintly from*
> *the forest.*

What voices swell upon the midnight air?

Page. St. Anselm's knights.
Ald. Yes, 'tis their pious wont,
When journeying near the sound of convent-
    bell
'Mid flood or fire, to raise the holy hymn
That chaunts the praise of their protecting
    saint —
List to the solemn harmony —
Guided by that we may rejoin their company.

> *Exeunt. Chorus heard again, and con-*
> *tinues drawing nearer till the scene*
> *changes.*

Scene 2.

The convent. The Prior reading; Bertram views
him with the attention of one who envies him,
then speaks.

Ber. How many hours have passed since
    matin-bell?
Prior. I know not, till it sound again to
    vespers.
Time passes o'er us with a noiseless lapse:
Our hours are marked alone by prayer and
    study,
And know no change but by their mute suc-
    cession —
Ber. Yea — thus they live, if this may life
    be called
Where moving shadows mock the parts of
    men.
Prayer follows study, study yields to
    prayer —
Bell echoes bell, till wearied with the sum-
    mons
The ear doth ache for that last welcome peal
That tolls an end to listless vacancy —
Aye — when the red swol'n stream comes
    roaring down —
Full many a glorious flower, and stately tree,
Floats on the ruthless tide, whose unfelt
    sway
Moves not the mire that stagnates at the
    bottom.
The storm for Bertram — and it hath been
    with me,
Dealt with me branch and bole, bared me to
    th' roots,
And where the next wave bears my perished
    trunk
In its dread lapse, I neither know, nor reck
    of —
Prior. Thou desperate man, whom mercy
    woos in vain,
Although with miracles she pleads —
Forbear, I say, to taint these holy echoes
With the fell sounds of thy profane de-
    spair. —
Ber. Good monk, I am beholden to your
    patience.

Take this from one, whose lips do mock at
  praise; —
Thou art a man, whose mild and reverend
  functions
Might change the black creed of misanthropy,
And bid my better angel half return. —
But — 'tis impossible — I will not trouble
  thee —
The wayward Bertram and his moody mates
Are tenants all unmeet for cloistered walls —
We will find fitter home.
  Prior. Whither wilt thou resort?
  Ber. Is there no forest
Whose shades are dark enough to shelter us;
Or cavern rifted by the perilous lightning,
Where we must grapple with the tenanting
  wolf
To earn our bloody lair? — there let us bide,
Nor hear the voice of man, nor call of
  heaven. —
  Prior. Wend not, I charge thee, with those
  desperate men.
Full well I wot who are thy fearful mates —
In their stern strife with the incensed deep,
That dashed them bruised and breathless on
  our shores,
When their drenched hold forsook both gold
  and gear,
They griped their daggers with a murderer's
  instinct.
— I read thee for the leader of a band
Whose trade is blood. —
  Ber. Well then, thou knowest the worst —
And let the worst be known, I am their
  leader —
  Prior. Mark what I read, renounce that
  horrid league —
Flee to the castle of St. Aldobrand,
His power may give thee safety, and his dame
May plead for thee against the law's stern
  purpose —
All as thou art unknown —
  Ber. His dame plead for me! —
When my cold corse, torn from some felon
  wheel,
Or dug from lightless depth of stony dungeon,
Welters in the cold gaze of pitiless strangers,
Then fling it at his gate, whose cursed stones
My living foot treads never, — yet beware
Lest the corse burst its cerements stark, and
  curse thee —
  Prior. Hush, hush these horrid sounds;
  where wilt thou bide?
Near us nor knight nor baron holds his keep,
For far and wide thy foeman's land extends.
  Ber. The world hath ample realms beyond
  his power.
There must I dwell — I seek my rugged
  mates —

The frozen mountain, or the burning sand
Would be more wholesome than the fertile
  realm
That's lorded o'er by Aldobrand.
                                    Exit Bertram.
  Prior. High-hearted man, sublime even in
  thy guilt,
Whose passions are thy crimes, whose angel-
  sin
Is pride that rivals the star-bright apos-
  tate's. —
Wild admiration thrills me to behold
An evil strength, so above earthly pitch —
Descending angels only could reclaim thee —
            Enter second Monk.
  2d Monk. The lady of St. Aldobrand in
  haste
Craves swift admittance to your sacred cell.
  Prior. She is a gracious, and a pious dame,
And doth our cell much honour by her
  presence.
        Enter Imogine. She kneels to him.
The blessings of these sainted walls be on
  thee.
Why are thou thus disturbed, what moves
  thee, daughter?
  Imo. Nay, do not raise me with those
  reverend hands,
Nor benison of saint greet mine approach,
Nor shadow of holy hand stretched forth to
  bless me. —
I am a wretched, soul-struck, guilty woman.
  Prior. Thou dost amaze me; by mine holy
  order
I deemed no legends of our cloistered saints
Held holier records of pure sanctity
Than the clear answer of thy stainless life
To shrift's most piercing search —
  Imo. Oh holy prior, no matron proud and
  pure,
Whose dreams ne'er wandered from her
  wedded lord,
Whose spoused heart was plighted with her
  hand,
Kneels for thy prayer of power — I am a
  wretch,
Who, pale and withering with unholy love,
Lay a shrunk corse in duty's fostering arms,
And with cold smiles belied her heart's
  despair.
I've nursed a slumbering serpent till it stung
  me,
And from my heart's true guardian, hid its
  foulness.
  Prior. Thou'st done an evil deed —
For sin is of the soul, and thine is tainted —
But most I blame thee, that from thy soul's
  guardian

Thou hiddest thy secret guilt.
 Imo. I knew it not —
Last night, oh! last night told a dreadful
 secret —
The moon went down, its sinking ray shut
 out
The parting form of one beloved too well. —
The fountain of my heart dried up within
 me, —
With nought that loved me, and with nought
 to love
I stood upon the desert earth alone —
I stood and wondered at my desolation —
For I had spurned at every tie for him,
And hardly could I beg from injured hearts
The kindness that my desperate passion
 scorned —
And in that deep and utter agony,
Though then, than ever most unfit to die,
I fell upon my knees, and prayed for death.
 Prior. And did deserve it, wert thou meet
 for it —
Art thou a wife and mother, and canst speak
Of life rejected by thy desperate passion —
These bursting tears, wrung hands, and burn-
 ing words,
Are these the signs of penitence or passion?
Thou comest to me, for to my ear alone
May the deep secret of thy heart be told,
And fancy riot in the luscious poison —
Fond of the misery we paint so well,
Proud of the sacrifice of broken hearts,
We pour on Heav'n's dread ear, what man's
 would shrink from —
Yea, make a merit of the impious insult,
And wrest the functions of mine holy office
To the foul ministry of earthly passion.
 Imo. Why came I here, I had despair at
 home —
Where shall the wretch resort whom Heaven
 forsakes?
 Prior. Thou hast forsaken Heaven.
Speed to thy castle, shut thy chamber door,
Bind fast thy soul by every solemn vow
Never to hold communion with that object —
If still thy wishes contradict thy prayers,
If still thy heart's responses yield no har-
 mony —
Weary thy saint with agonies of prayer;
On the cold marble quench thy burning
 breast;
Number with every bead a tear of soul;
Press to thy heart the cross, and bid it banish
The form that would usurp its image there —
 Imo. (*Kneeling*) One parting word —
 Prior. No, not one parting look —
One parting thought, I charge thee on thy
 soul.
 Imo. (*Turning away*) He never loved. —

 Prior. Why clingest thou to my raiment?
Thy grasp of grief is stronger on my heart —
For sterner oft our words than feelings are.
   Enter first Monk and Page.
 1st Monk. Hail, holy prior, and hail thou
 noble dame,
With joyful heart I break upon your pri-
 vacy —
St. Aldobrand before his own good gates
Doth rein his war-steed's pride; the warder's
 horn
Full merrily rings his peal of welcome
 home —
I hied me onward with the joyful tidings
To greet his happy dame.
 Imo. My thanks await them. —
 Prior. Now, by my beads the news is
 wond'rous welcome —
Hath thy brave lord in safety reached his
 home —
Praise to St. Anselm who ne'er leaves his
 servants.
My rosary hath been well told for him —
(Clear thy dimmed brow, for shame! hie to
 thy lord,
And show a dame's true duty in his welcome.)
Came with thy lord the knights of good St.
 Anselm
Bearing the banner of their guardian saint
Safe from the infidel scathe? —
 Page. They come with speed —
Though lated in the forest's wildering maze;
Last night their shelter was the broad brown
 oak —
 Prior. High praise be given — haste, sum-
 mon all our brethren;
Th' occasion, noble dame, doth call me from
 thee —
So Benedicite — *Exeunt except Imogine.*
 Imo. (*Alone*) That word should mean —
A blessing rest on me — I am not blest —
I'm weary of this conflict of the heart —
These dying struggles of reluctant duty —
These potent throes of wild convulsive
 passion.
Would I were seared in guilt, or strong in
 innocence —
I dare not search my heart; some iron vow
Shall bind me down in passive wretchedness,
And mock the force of my rebellious heart
To break its riveting holds —
  As she kneels, enter Bertram.
Ha! art thou there? —
Come kneel with me, and witness to the vow
I offer to renounce thee, and to die —
 Ber. Nay, it is meet that we renounce each
 other —
Have we not been a miserable pair?

Hath not our fatal passion cursed, not blessed
    us? —
Had we not loved, how different were our
    fates;
For thou hadst been a happy honoured dame,
And I had slept the sleep of those that dream
    not —
But life was dear, while Imogine did love.
    Imo. Witness my vow — while I have
      breath to speak it —
    Ber. Then make it thus — why dost thou
      shrink from me?
Despair hath its embrace as well as passion —
May I not hold thee in these folded arms?
May I not clasp thee to this blasted heart?
When the rich soil teemed with youth's
    generous flowers —
I felt thee sunshine — now thy rayless light
Falls like the cold moon on a blasted heath
Mocking its desolation — speak thy vow —
I will not chide thee if the words should kill
    me —
    Imo. (*Sinking into his arms*) I cannot utter
      it —
    Ber. Have we not loved, as none have ever
      loved,
And must we part as none have ever parted?
I know thy lord is near; I know his towers
Must shut thee from my sight — the curfew-
    hour
Will send me on a far and fearful journey —
Give me one hour, nor think thou givest too
    much,
When grief is all the boon. —
    Imo. One hour to *thee*?
    Ber. When the cold moon gleams on thy
      castle walls,
Wilt thou not seek the spot where last we
    met?
That be our parting spot — Oh Imogine —
Heaven that denies the luxury of bliss
Shall yield at least the luxury of anguish,
And teach us the stern pride of wretched-
    ness —
That hour shall light my parting step of
    darkness —
Imogine's form did gleam on my last glance,
Imogine's breath did mix with my last sigh,
Imogine's tear doth linger on my cheek,
But ne'er must dew my grave —
    Imo. I am desperate
To say I'll meet thee, but I will, will meet
    thee;
No future hour can rend my heart like this
Save that which breaks it. —

The child runs in, and clings to Imogine.

    Child. My father is returned, and kissed
      and blessed me —

    Imo. (*Falling on the child's neck*) What
      have I done, my child; forgive thy
      mother.
    Ber. (*Surveying her with stern contempt*)
Woman, oh woman, and an urchin's kiss
Rends from thy heart thy love of many
    years —
Go, virtuous dame, to thy most happy lord,
And Bertram's image taint your kiss with
    poison.   *Exit Bertram.*
    Imo. (*Alone*) 'Tis but the last — and I have
      sworn to meet him.
My boy, my boy, thy image will protect me.
    End of the Third Act.

ACT IV.

Scene 1.

*A dark night under the castle walls. Bertram
appears in a state of the utmost agitation; he
extends his arms towards a spot where the
moon has disappeared.*

    Ber. Thou hidest away thy face, and wilt
      not view me,
All the bright lights of heaven are dark above
    me —
Beneath the black cope of this starless night
There lurks no darker soul —
My fiend-like glory hath departed from me —
Bertram hath nought above the meanest
    losel —
I should have bearded him in halls of pride —
I should have mated him in fields of death —
Not stol'n upon his secret bower of peace,
And breathed a serpent's venom on his
    flower.
      *He looks up at the casement of the
      tower, at which a light appears; he
      gazes on it.*
She is there —
She weeps — no husband wipes her tears
    away —
She weeps — no babe doth cheer the guilty
    mother.
Aldobrand — No — I never will forgive thee,
For I am sunk beneath thee — Who art
    thou?
      Enter two of Bertram's band.

    1st Robber. Why dost thou wander in the
      woods alone,
Leaving thy mates to play with idle hilts,
Or dream with monks o'er rosary and relic?
Give us a deed to do.
    Ber. Yes, ye are welcome,
Your spirits shall be proud — ho! hear ye,
    villains,

I know ye both — ye are slaves that for a
 ducat
Would rend the screaming infant from the
 breast
To plunge it in the flames;
Yea, draw your keen knives cross a father's
 throat,
And carve with them the bloody meal ye
 earned;
Villains, rejoice, your leader's crimes have
 purged you,
You punished guilt — I preyed on innocence —
Ye have beheld me fallen — begone — begone.
   1st Robber. Why then, Heaven's benison
 be with you,
Thou'lt need it if thou tarriest longer here.
   Ber. How, slave, what fear you?
   2d Robber. Fly; this broad land hath not
 one spot to hide thee,
Danger and death await thee in those walls.
   Ber. They'd fell a blasted tree — well —
 let it fall —
But though the perished trunk feel not the
 wound;
Woe to the smiting hand — its fall may
 crush him.
   1st Robber. Lord Aldobrand
Holds high commission from his sovereign
 liege
To hunt thy outlaw'd life through Sicily.
   Ber. (*Wildly*) Who — what — ?
   2d Robber. We mingled with the men at
 arms
As journeying home. Their talk was of Count
 Bertram,
Whose vessel had from Manfredonia's coast
Been traced towards this realm.
   1st Robber. And if on earth his living form
 were found,
Lord Aldobrand had power to seal his doom.
Some few did pity him.
   Ber. (*Bursting into ferocity*) Villain, ab-
 horred villain.
Hath he not pushed me to extremity?
Are these wild weeds, these scarred and
 scathed limbs,
This wasted frame, a mark for human malice?
There have been those who from the high
 bark's side
Have whelmed their enemy in the flashing
 deep;
But who hath watch'd to see his struggling
 hands,
To hear the sob of death? — Fool — idiot —
 idiot —
'Twas but e'en now, I would have knelt to
 him

With the prostration of a conscious villain;
I would have crouched beneath his spurning
 feet;
I would have felt their trampling tread, and
 blessed it —
For I had injured him — and mutual injury
Had freed my withered heart — Villain — I
 thank thee.
   1st Robber. Wilt thou fly?
   Ber. Never — on this spot I stand
The champion of despair — this arm my
 brand —
This breast my panoply — and for my gage —
(Oh thou hast reft from me all knightly
 pledge)
Take these black hairs torn from a head that
 hates thee —
Deep be their dye, before that pledge is
 ransomed —
In thine heart's blood or mine — why
 strivest thou with me?
(*Wild with passion*) Lord Aldobrand, I brave
 thee in thy halls,
Wrecked, famished, wrung in heart, and
 worn in limb —
For bread of thine this lip hath never
 stained —
I bid thee to the conflict — aye, come on —
Coward — hast armed thy vassals? — come
 then all —
Follow — ye shall have work enough —
 Follow.   *Exeunt.*

Scene 2.

*Imagine in her apartment. A lamp burning on
the table. She walks some time in great agitation and then pushes the light away.*

   Imo. Away, thou glarest on me, thy light is
 hateful;
Whom doth the dark wind chide so hollowly?
The very stones shrink from my steps of
 guilt,
All lifeless things have come to life to curse
 me:
Oh! that a mountain's weight were cast on
 me;
Oh! that the wide, wild ocean heaved o'er
 me;
Oh! that I could into the earthy centre
Sink and be nothing.
Sense, memory, feeling, life extinct and
 swallowed,
With things that are not, or have never been,
Lie down and sleep the everlasting sleep —
          She sinks on the ground.
If I run mad, some wild word will betray me,
Nay — let me think — what am I? — no,
 what was I?

(*A long pause*) I was the honoured wife of
Aldobrand;
I am the scorned minion of a ruffian.

Enter Clotilda.

Who art thou that thus comest on me in
darkness?
Clo. The taper's blaze doth make it bright
as noon.
Imo. I saw thee not, till thou wert close to
me.
So steal the steps of those who watch the
guilty;
How darest thou gaze thus earnestly upon
me;
What see'st thou in my face?
Clo. A mortal horror.
If aught but godless souls at parting bear
The lineaments of despair, such face is thine.
Imo. See'st thou despair alone?
Nay, mock me not, for thou hast read more
deeply,
Else why that piercing look.
Clo. I meant it not —
But since thy lonely walk upon the ram-
part —
Strange hath been thy demeanour, all thy
maidens
Do speak in busy whispers of its wildness —
Imo. Oh hang me shuddering on the base-
less crag —
The vampire's wing, the wild-worm's sting be
on me,
But hide me, mountains, from the man I've
injured —
Clo. Whom hast thou injured?
Imo. Whom doth woman injure?
Another daughter dries a father's tears;
Another sister claims a brother's love;
An injured husband hath no other wife,
Save her who wrought him shame.
Clo. I will not hear thee.
Imo. We met in madness, and in guilt we
parted —
Oh! I see horror rushing to thy face —
Do not betray me, I am penitent —
Do not betray me, it will kill my Lord —
Do not betray me, it will kill my boy,
My little one that loves me.
Clo. Wretched woman —
Whom guilt hath flung at a poor menial's
feet —
Rise, rise, how canst thou keep thy fatal
secret?
Those fixt and bloodshot eyes, those wringing
hands —
Imo. And were I featureless, inert, and
marble —
Th' accuser *here* would speak —

Clo. Wilt thou seek comfort from the holy
prior?
Imo. When I was innocent, I sought it of
him —
For if his lip of wrath refused my pardon,
My heart would have absolved me —
Now when that heart condemns me, what
avails
The pardon of my earthly erring judge?
Clo. Yet, hie from hence, upon their lady's
bower
No menial dares intrude.
Imo. That seat of honour —
My guilty steps shall never violate —
What fearful sound is that?
Clo. Alas, a feller trial doth abide thee;
I hear thy lord's approach.
Madness is in thy looks, he'll know it all —
Imo. Why, I am mad with horror and
remorse —
He comes, he comes in all that murderous
kindness;
Oh Bertram's curse is on me.

Enter Aldobrand.

Ald. How fares my dame? give me thy
white hand, love.
Oh it is pleasant for a war-worn man
To couch him on the downy lap of comfort —
And on his rush-strewn floors of household
peace
Hear his doffed harness ring — Take thou
my helmet; (*To page who goes out*)
Well may man toil for such an hour as
this.
Imo. (*Standing timidly near him*) Yea,
happier they, who on the bloody field
Stretch when their toil is done —
Ald. What means my love?
Imo. Is there not rest among the quiet
dead;
But is there surely rest in mortal dwellings?
Ald. Deep loneliness hath wrought this
mood in thee,
For like a cloistered votaress, thou hast kept,
Thy damsels tell me, this lone turret's
bound —
A musing walk upon the moonlight ramparts,
Or thy lute's mournful vespers all thy cheer-
ing —
Not thine to parley at the latticed casement
With wandering wooer, or —
Imo. (*Wildly*) For mercy's sake forbear —
Ald. How farest thou?
Imo. (*Recovering*) Well — well — a sud-
den pain o' th' heart.
Ald. Knowest thou the cause detained me
hence so long,
And which again must call me soon away?

Imo. (Trying to recollect herself) Was it not war?

Ald. Aye, and the worst war, love —
When our fell foes are our own countrymen.
Thou knowest the banished Bertram — why, his name
Doth blanch thy altered cheek, as if his band,
With their fierce leader, were within these towers —

Imo. Mention that name no more — on with thy tale —

Ald. I need not tell thee, how his mad ambition
Strove with the crown itself for sovereignty —
The craven monarch was his subject's slave —
In that dread hour my country's guard I stood,
From the state's vitals tore the coiled serpent,
First hung him writhing up to public scorn,
Then flung him forth to ruin.

Imo. Thou need'st not tell it —

Ald. Th' apostate would be great even in his fall —
On Manfredonia's wild and wooded shore
His desperate followers awed the regions round —
Late from Taranto's gulf his bark was traced
Right to these shores. Perchance the recent storm
Hath spared me further search, but if on earth
His living form be found —

Imo. Think'st thou he harbours here —
Go, crush thy foe — for he is mine and thine —
But tell me not when thou hast done the deed.

Ald. Why art thou thus, my Imogine, my love?
In former happier hours thy form and converse
Had, like thy lute, that gracious melancholy
Whose most sad sweetness is in tune with joy —
Perchance I've been to thee a rugged mate —
My soldier's mood is all too lightly chafed —
But when the gust hath spent its short-liv'd fury,
I bowed before thee with a child's submission,
And wooed thee with a weeping tenderness.

Imo. (After much agitation) Be generous, and stab me —

Ald. Why is this?
I have no skill in woman's changeful moods,
Tears without grief and smiles without a joy —
My days have passed away 'mid war and toil —

The grinding casque hath worn my locks of youth;
Beshrew its weight, it hath ploughed furrows there,
Where time ne'er drove its share — mine heart's sole wish
Is to sit down in peace among its inmates —
To see mine home for ever bright with smiles,
'Mid thoughts of past, and blessed hopes of future,
Glide through the vacant hours of waning life —
Then die the blessed death of aged honour,
Grasping thy hand of faith, and fixing on thee
Eyes that, though dim in death, are bright with love.

Imo. Thou never wilt — thou never wilt on me —
Ne'er erred the prophet heart that grief inspired
Though joy's illusions mock their votarist —
I'm dying, Aldobrand, a malady
Preys on my heart, that medicine cannot reach,
Invisible and cureless — look not on me
With looks of love, for then it stings me deepest —
When I am cold, when my pale sheeted corse
Sleeps the dark sleep no venomed tongue can wake
List not to evil thoughts of her whose lips
Have then no voice to plead —
Take to thine arms some honourable dame,
(Blessed will she be within thine arms of honour)
And — if he dies not on his mother's grave —
Still love my boy as if that mother lived.

Ald. Banish such gloomy dreams —
'Tis solitude that makes thee speak thus sadly —
No longer shalt thou pine in lonely halls.
Come to thy couch, my love —

Imo. Stand off — unhand me. —
Forgive me, oh my husband;
I have a vow — a solemn vow is on me —
And black perdition gulf my perjured soul
If I ascend the bed of peace and honour
Till that —

Ald. Till what?

Imo. My penance is accomplished.

Ald. Nay, Heav'n forefend I should disturb thy orisons —
The reverend prior were fittest counsellor —
Farewell! — but in the painful hour of penance
Think upon me, and spare thy tender frame.

Imo. And dost thou leave me with such stabbing kindness?

Ald. (*To Clotilda who goes out*) Call to my page
To bring the torch and light me to my chamber —
Imo. (*With a sudden impulse falling on her knees*) Yet, ere thou goest, forgive me, oh my husband —
Ald. Forgive thee! — What? —
Imo. Oh, we do all offend —
There's not a day of wedded life, if we
Count at its close the little, bitter sum
Of thoughts, and words, and looks unkind and froward,
Silence that chides and woundings of the eye —
But prostrate at each other's feet, we should
Each night forgiveness ask — then what should I? —
Ald. (*Not hearing the last words*) Why take it freely;
I well may pardon, what I ne'er have felt.
Imo. (*Following him on her knees, and kissing his hand*) Dost thou forgive me from thine inmost soul —
God bless thee, oh, God bless thee —
Ald. Farewell — mine eyes grow heavy, thy sad talk
Hath stolen a heaviness upon my spirits —
I will unto my solitary couch — Farewell.
                                        Exit Aldobrand.
Imo. There is no human heart can bide this conflict —
All dark and horrible, — Bertram must die —
But oh, within these walls, before mine eyes,
Who would have died for him, while life had value; —
He shall not die, — Clotilda, ho, come forth —
He yet may be redeemed, though I am lost —
Let him depart, and pray for her he ruin'd.
Hah! was it fancy's work — I hear a step —
It hath the speech-like thrilling of *his* tread:
It is himself.

Enter Bertram.

It is a crime in me to look on thee —
But in whate'er I do there now is crime —
Yet wretched thought still struggles for thy safety —
Fly, while my lips without a crime may warn thee —
Would thou hadst never come, or sooner parted.
Oh God — he heeds me not;
Why comest thou thus, what is thy fearful business?
I know thou comest for evil, but its purport
I ask my heart in vain.

Ber. Guess it, and spare me.
        A long pause, during which she gazes at him.
Canst thou not read it in my face?
Imo. I dare not;
Mixt shades of evil thought are darkening there;
But what my fears do indistinctly guess
Would blast me to behold — (*Turns away, a pause*)
Ber. Dost thou not hear it in my very silence?
That which no voice can tell, doth tell itself.
Imo. My harassed thought hath not one point of fear,
Save that it must not think.
Ber. (*Throwing his dagger on the ground*)
Speak thou for me, —
Show me the chamber where thy husband lies,
The morning must not see us both alive.
Imo. (*Screaming and struggling with him*)
Ah! horror! horror! off — withstand me not,
I will arouse the castle, rouse the dead,
To save my husband. (*Falling at his feet*)
I am a wretch — but — who hath made me so?
I'm writhing like a worm, beneath thy spurn.
Have pity on me, I have had much wrong.
Ber. My heart is as the steel within my grasp.
Imo. (*Still kneeling*) Thou hast cast me down from light,
From my high sphere of purity and peace,
Where once I walked in mine uprightness, blessed —
Do not thou cast me into utter darkness.
Ber. (*Looking on her with pity for a moment*) Thou fairest flower —
Why didst thou fling thyself across my path,
My tiger spring must crush thee in its way,
But cannot pause to pity thee.
Imo. Thou must,
For I am strong in woes — I ne'er reproached thee —
I plead but with my agonies and tears —
Kind, gentle Bertram, my beloved Bertram,
For thou wert gentle once, and once beloved,
Have mercy on me — Oh thou couldst not think it —
        Looking up, and seeing no relenting in his face, she starts up wildly.
By heaven and all its host, he shall not perish.
Ber. By hell and all its host, he shall not live.
This is no transient flash of fugitive passion —
His death hath been my life for years of misery —

Which else I had not lived —
Upon that thought, and not on food, I fed,
Upon that thought, and not on sleep, I
    rested —
I come to do the deed that must be done —
Nor thou, nor sheltering angels, could pre-
    vent me.
    Imo. But man shall — miscreant — help!
    Ber. Thou callest in vain —
The armed vassals all are far from succour —
Following St. Anselm's votarists to the con-
    vent —
My band of blood are darkening in their
    halls —
Wouldst have him butchered by their ruffian
    hands
That wait my bidding?
    Imo. (*Falling on the ground*) — Fell and
    horrible
I'm sealed, shut down in ransomless perdi-
    tion.
    Ber. Fear not, my vengeance will not
    yield its prey,
He shall fall nobly, by my hand shall fall —
But still and dark the summons of its fate,
So winds the coiled serpent round his victim.
                A horn sounds without.
Whence was that blast? those felon slaves
    are come —
He shall not perish by their ruffian hands.
                Exit Bertram.
    Imo. (*Gazing round her, and slowly recover-
ing recollection, repeats his last words*) — He
    shall not perish —
Oh! it was all a dream — a horrid dream —
He was not here — it is impossible —
        Tottering towards the door.
I will not be alone another moment
Lest it do come again — where, where art
    thou? —

        Enter Clotilda.

    Clo. Didst thou not call me? — at thy
    voice of anguish
I hasten, though I cannot hear thy words —
    Imo. Let me lean on thee, let me hold thee
    fast —
They have been with me in my loneliness.
    Clo. What hath been with thee?
    Imo. Something the thought doth try in
    vain to follow —
Through mist and twilight —
    Clo. Woe is me! methought
I saw the form of Bertram as I entered —
    Imo. (*Starting with sudden recollection*) Oh
God — it was no vision then, thou sawest
    him —
Give me my frenzy back — one moment's
    thought —

'Tis done, by Heaven, 'tis done —
I will fall down before his injured feet,
I'll tell him all my shame, and all my guilt,
My wrongs shall be a weapon in his hand,
And if it fail, this tainted frame of sin
Shall fall a shield before my husband's
    breast —
I'll wake the castle — wake the faithful
    vassals
I'll — (*Going, she stops suddenly*)
I cannot be the herald of my shame,
Go thou, and tell them what I cannot
    utter.
    Clo. Oh, yet forgive me, through that
    gloomy passage
I dare not venture, lest that dark form meet
    me.
    Imo. Nay, thou must go, 'tis I that dare not
    venture —
For, if I see him in his holy sleep
Resting so calmly on the bed I've wronged,
My heart will burst, and he must die
    warned —   *Exit Clotilda.*
(*Listening after her*) How long she lingers —
    aye — he knows my guilt
Even from this untold summons — aye —
    my boy
They'll clothe thee with *my* shame.
Hush — look — all's still within — an hor-
    rid stillness —
Perchance, that she, even she is bribed to
    aid —
Woe's me, who now can trust a menial's
    faith,
When that his wedded wife hath done him
    wrong —

        Enter Clotilda.

    Clo. All's safe — all's well —
    Imo. What meanest thou by those
    words? —
For sounds of comfort to my blasted ear
Do ring a death-peal —
    Clo. Heardest thou not the horn?
    Imo. I heard no horn, I only heard a voice
That menaced murder —
    Clo. Oh! the horn did sound —
And with it came a blessed messenger.
St. Anselm's knights within their patron's
    walls
Do hold a solemn feast, and o'er his shrine
They hang the holy banner of his blessing —
Full swiftly came the summons to thy lord
To join them in their solemn ceremony —
Lord Aldobrand with few attendants gone,
Though late the hour, and dark the way, ere
    this
Hath measured half the distance —
    Imo. (*Throwing herself vehemently on her*

knees) Thank God, thank God — Heaven bless the gallant knights!
Then he is safe until the morning's dawn.

Enter Page.

Speak — who art thou?
Page. Dost thou not know me, lady?
Imo. Well, well, I reck not — wherefore art thou come?
Page. So fierce the mountain-stream comes roaring down,
The rivulet that bathes the convent walls
Is now a foaming flood — upon its brink
Thy lord and his small train do stand appalled —
With torch and bell from their high battle-ments
The monks do summon to the pass in vain;
He must return to-night.
Imo. 'Tis false, he must not — Oh, I shall run mad —
Go thou, and watch upon the turret's height — (*To Clotilda*)
The flood must fall — the bright moon must shine forth;
Go, go and tell me so — why stayest thou here? (*To Page*)
Begone, and do not heed, and do not watch me. *Exit Page.*
I've lost the courage of mine innocence,
And dare not have the courage of despair —
The evil strength that gave temptation danger,
Yet cannot give remorse its energy.

Enter Clotilda.

Clo. The night is calm and clear, and o'er the plain
Nor arms do glimmer on my straining sight,
Nor through the stilly air, did horseman's tramp
Ring in faint echo from the hollow hill,
Though my fixed ear did list to giddiness —
Be comforted, he must have passed the stream —
Imo. Yea, I am comforted, 'tis blessed comfort —
He must have passed the stream — Oh pity-ing Heaven,
Accept these tears, these are not sinful tears —
Tell me again that he will not return.
Clo. I soothly say, he must have passed the stream.
The horn is heard without, announc-ing Aldobrand's return.
'Tis Aldobrand, he's lost — we all are lost —
Imo. (*Without*) Now Heaven have mercy on thy soul, my husband,

For man hath none — Is there no hope — no help? —
Looking towards the door, across which the band of Bertram march silently and range themselves.
None, none — his gathering band are dark around me —
I will make one last effort for their mercy —
If they be human, they will listen to me —
Rushing towards them, they step for-ward and point their swords to resist her.
Oh, there is nothing merciful in their looks;
Oh, there is nothing human in their hearts;
They are not men — Hell hath sent up its devils.
There is no hope — I'll hear his dying groan —
I'll hear his last cry for that help that comes not —
I'll hear him call upon his wife and child —
I will not hear it. — (*Stopping her ears*)
Oh that my tightened heart had breath for prayer —
Mercy, oh mercy, Bertram.
Another horn heard without, she starts and staggers towards the door; — a noise of swords within.
Ald. (*Within*) Off, villain, off —
Ber. Villain, to thy soul — for I am Bertram.
Aldobrand retreating before Bertram rushes on the stage, and falls at Imogine's feet.
Ald. Let me die at her feet, my wife, my wife —
Wilt thou not staunch the life-blood stream-ing from me?
Wilt thou not look at me? — Oh save my boy. *Dies.*
Imogine, at the name of her son, rushes off; — Bertram stands over the body holding the dagger with his eyes fixed on it. — The band fill up the back.

End of the Fourth Act.

Act V.

Scene 1.

The chapel in the Convent of St. Anselm, the shrine splendidly illuminated and decorated. The Prior rising from before the altar.

Enter first Monk.

1st Monk. Lo, where the knights approach.

Enter the Knights in solemn procession with the consecrated banner. The Prior advances to meet them.

Prior. Hail! champions of the church and of the land,
The banner of our holy saint in fight
Full bravely have ye borne, and scatheless back,
From unblessed weapon and from arm unholy,
Restored it to the power whose might struck for you —

> *The music commences, the Knights and Monks advance in procession, the Prior bearing the banner, which he has received from the principal Knight.*

Hymn.

Guardian of the good and brave
Their banner o'er thy shrine we wave —
Monk, who counts the midnight bead —
Knight, who spurs the battle steed, —
He, who dies 'mid clarion's swelling
He, who dies 'mid requiem's knelling —
Alike thy care, whose grace is shed
On cowled scalp and helmed head —
Thy temple of the rock and flood
For ages 'mid their wrath has stood —
Thy midnight bell, through storm and calm
Hath shed on listening ear its balm. —

The hymn is interrupted by the third Monk rushing in distractedly.

3d Monk. Forbear — forbear —
Prior. Why comest thou thus with voice of desperate fear,
Breaking upon our solemn ceremony?
3d Monk. Despair is round our walls, a wailing spirit.
Yea, the mixt wailings of the infernal host
Burst deafeningly amid the shuddering blast —
No earthly lip might utterance give to such —
Prior. Thou'rt wild with watching, fear and loneliness,
In thy sole turret that o'erhangs the flood.
Of winds and waves, the strangely-mingled sounds
Ride heavily the night-wind's hollow sweep,
Mocking the sounds of human lamentation —
3d Monk. Hush, look, it comes again.
                                        A scream.
Prior. Defend us, heaven,
'Twas horrible indeed — 'tis in our walls —
Ha, through the cloister there doth something glide
That seems in truth not earthly —

Imogine rushes in with her child, her hair dishevelled, her dress stained with blood.

Imo. Save me — save me —
Prior. Save thee, from what?
Imo. From earth, and heaven, and hell,
All, all are armed, and rushing in pursuit —

Prior, Monks and Knights gathering around, and speaking together.

All. Who — what — what hath befallen thee? Speak.
Imo. Oh wait not here to speak, but fly to save him,
For he lies low upon the bloody ground —
Knight. She speaks in madness, ask the frighted boy,
Hath aught befallen his father? —
Imo. Ask him not —
He hath no father — we have murdered him —
Traitress and murderer — we have murdered him —
They'll not believe me for mine agony —
Is not his very blood upon my raiment?
Reeks not the charnel-stream of murder from me?
Prior and Monks. (*Vehemently*) Impossible.
Imo. Aye, heaven and earth do cry impossible,
The shuddering angels round th' eternal throne,
Veiling themselves in glory, shriek impossible,
But hell doth know it true —
Prior. (*Advancing to her solemnly*) Spirits of madness, that possess this woman
Depart I charge you, trouble her no more,
Till she do answer to mine adjuration —
Who did the deed?

> *Imogine sinks gradually from his fixed eye, till hiding her face, she falls on the ground in silence.*

Knight. I do believe it, horrid as it seems —
1st Monk. I'd not believe her words, I do her silence.
Prior. (*Who has fallen back in horror into the arms of the monks, rushes forward*) Oh!
draw your swords, brave knights, and sheathe them not —
Arise, pursue, avenge, exterminate.

> *Exeunt tumultuously Knights, Monks, and attendants; the Prior is following them. Imogine still kneeling grasps him by the robe. Prior, with mixed emotion— turns on her.*

Thou art a wretch, I did so love and honour thee —
Thou'st broke mine aged heart — that look again —
Woman, let go thy withering hold —

Imo. I dare not —
I have no hold but upon heaven and thee.
Prior. (*Tearing himself from her*) I go, yet
ere mine aged feet do bear me
To the dark chase of that fell beast of blood —
Hear thou, and — hope not — if by word or
deed
Yea, by invisible thought, unuttered wish
Thou hast been ministrant to this horrid
act —
With full collected force of malediction
I do pronounce unto thy soul — despair —
Exit.
Imo. (*Looking round on the chapel, after a
long pause*) They've left me — all things
leave me — all things human —
Follower and friend — last went the man of
God —
The last — but yet he went —
Child. I will not leave thee —
Imo. My son, my son, was that thy voice —
When heaven and angels, earth and earthly
things
Do leave the guilty in their guiltiness —
A cherub's voice doth whisper in a child's.
There is a shrine within thy little heart
Where I will hide, nor hear the trump of
doom —
Child. Dear mother, take me home —
Imo. Thou hast no home —
She, whom thou callest mother, left thee
none —
We're hunted from mankind — (*Sinking
down*)
Here will we lie in darkness down together,
And sleep a dreamless sleep — what form is
that —
Why have they laid him there? (*Recoiling*)
Plain in the gloomy depth he lies before me
The cold blue wound whence blood hath
ceased to flow,
The stormy clenching of the bared teeth —
The gory socket that the balls have burst
from —
I see them all — (*Shrieking*)
It moves — it moves — it rises — it comes
on me —
'Twill break th' eternal silence of the grave —
'Twill wind me in its creaking marrowless
arms.
Hold up thy hands to it, it was thy father —
Ah, it would have thee too; off — save me —
off — *Rushes out with the child.*

Scene 2.

The castle — Prior enters alone.

Prior. His halls are desolate — the lonely
walls
Echo my single tread — through the long
galleries —
The hurrying knights can trace nor friend
nor foe —
The murderer hath escaped — the saints
forgive me,
I feel mine heart of weakness is come back.
Almost I wish he had — ha, here is blood—
Mine ebbing spirits lacked this stirring im-
pulse —
Ho — haste ye here — the shedder must be
near —

*Enter the Knights, Monks, etc., supporting
Clotilda.*

Knight. We found this trembling maid,
alone, concealed —
Prior. Speak — tell of Bertram — of thy
lord — the vassals —
Clo. Oh, give me breath, for I am weak
with fear —
Short was the bloody conflict of the night —
The few remaining vassals fled in fear —
The bandits loaded with the castle's spoil —
Are gone — I saw them issue from the
walls —
But yet I dared not venture forth, while
Bertram —
All. Go on — go on —
Clo. He bore the murdered body —
Alone into yon chamber. (*Pointing*)
I heard the heavy weight trail after him —
I heard his bloody hands make fast the
door —
There hath he sat in dread society,
The corse and murderer are there together.
*The Knights draw their swords, and
rush towards the door.*
Prior. (*Interposing*) Hold, champions hold,
this warfare is for me.
The arm of flesh were powerless on him
now —
Hark how the faltering voice of feeble age
Shall bow him to its bidding. Ho, come forth
(*Striking the door*)
Thou man of blood, come forth, thy doom
awaits thee.
*Bertram opens the door, and advances
slowly, his dress is stained with blood,
and he grasps the hilt of a dagger in
his hand — his look is so marked and
grand, that the knights, etc., make
room for him, and he advances to the
front of the stage untouched.*
All. Who art thou?
Ber. I am the murderer — Wherefore are
ye come? —
Prior. — This majesty of guilt doth awe my
spirit —

Is it th' embodied fiend who tempted him
Sublime in guilt?
   Ber. Marvel not at me — Wist ye whence
     I come?
The tomb — where dwell the dead — and I
    dwelt with him —
Till sense of life dissolved away within me —
    (*Looking round ghastlily*)
I am amazed to see ye living men,
I deemed that when I struck the final blow
Mankind expired, and we were left alone,
The corse and I were left alone together,
The only tenants of a blasted world
Dispeopled for my punishment, and changed
Into a penal orb of desolation —
   Prior. Advance and bind him, are ye men
    and armed? —
What, must this palsied hand be first on
    him? —
Advance, and seize him, ere his voice of
    blasphemy
Shall pile the roof in ruins o'er our heads —
   Ber. — Advance, and seize me, ye who
    smile at blood —
For every drop of mine a life shall pay —
I'm naked, famished, faint, my brand is
    broken —
Rush, mailed champions, on the helpless
    Bertram —   *They sink back.*
Now prove what fell resistance I shall make.
    Throws down the hilt of his dagger.
There — bind mine arms — if ye do list to
    bind them —
I came to yield — but not to be subdued —
   Prior. Oh thou, who o'er thy stormy
    grandeur flingest
A struggling beam that dazzles, awes, and
    vanishes —
Thou, who dost blend our wonder with our
    curses —
Why didst thou this?
   Ber. He wronged me, and I slew him —
To man but thee I ne'er had said even this —
To man but thee, I ne'er shall utter more —
Now speed ye swift from questioning to
    death —   *They surround him.*
One prayer, my executioners, not con-
    querors —
Be most ingenious in your cruelty —
Let rack and pincer do their full work on
    me —
'Twill rouse me from that dread unnatural
    sleep,
In which my soul hath dreamt its dreams of
    agony —
This is my prayer, ye'll not refuse it to me —
    *As they are leading him off, the Prior
    lays hold of him.*

   Prior. Yet bend thy steeled sinews, bend
    and pray —
The corse of him thou'st murdered, lies
    within —   *A long pause.*
   Ber. I have offended Heaven, but will not
    mock it —
Spare me your racks and pincers, spare me
    words.   *Exeunt.*

Scene 3.

*A dark wood, in the back scene a cavern, rocks
and precipices above. Imogine comes forward.*

   Imo. (*Sighing heavily after a long pause*) If
    I could waft away this low-hung mist
That darkens o'er my brow —
If I could but unbind this burning band
That tightens round my heart —
Or night or morning is it?
I wist not which, a dull and dismal twilight
Pervading all things, and confounding all
    things,
Doth hover o'er my senses and my soul —
    (*Comes forward shuddering*)
The moon shines on me, but it doth not light
    me;
The surge glides past me, but it breathes not
    on me.
My child, my child, where art thou; come to
    me —
I know thou hidest thyself for sport to mock
    me —
Yet come — for I am scared with loneli-
    ness —
I'll call on thee no more, lo, there he glides —
And there, and there — he flies from me —
    he laughs —
I'll sing thee songs the church-yard spirits
    taught me —
I'll sit all night on the grey tombs with thee,
So thou wilt turn to me — he's gone — he's
    gone.

Enter Clotilda, Prior and Monks surrounding.

   Clo. She's here — she's here — and is it
    thus I see her?
   Prior. All-pitying Heaven — release her
    from this misery.
   Imo. Away, unhand me, ye are execu-
    tioners —
I know your horrible errand — who hath
    sent you?
This is false Bertram's doing — God — oh,
    God,
How I did love — and how am I requited —
Well, well, accuse me of what crime you will,
I ne'er was guilty of not loving thee —
Oh, spare the torture — and I will confess.

Nay, now there needs it not — his look's
enough —
That smile hath keener edge than many
daggers. *She sinks into Clotilda's arms.*
Clo. How could this wasted form sustain
the toils —
Bearing her helpless child.
Imo. (*Starting up*) I was a mother — 'twas
my child I bore —
The murderer hung upon my flying steps —
The winds with all their speed had failed to
match me.
Oh! how we laughed to see the baffled fiend
Stamp on the shore, and grind his iron
teeth —
While safe and far, I braved the wave
triumphant,
And shook my dripping locks like trophied
banner.
I was a mother then.
Prior. Where is thy child?
Clo. (*Pointing to the cave into which she has
looked*) Oh, he lies cold within his cavern-
tomb —
Why dost thou urge her with the horrid
theme?
Prior. It was to wake one living chord o'
th' heart,
And I will try — though mine own breaks at
it —
Where is thy child?
Imo. (*With a frantic laugh*) The forest fiend
hath snatched him —
He rides the night-mare through the wizard
woods.
Prior. Hopeless and dark — even the last
spark extinct.

Enter third Monk hastily.

3d Monk. Bertram — the prisoner Ber-
tram —
Prior. Hush — thou'lt kill her —
Haste thee, Clotilda, — holy brethren, haste;
Remove her hence — aye, even to that sad
shelter —(*Pointing to the cave*)
I see the approaching torches of the guard,
Flash their red light athwart the forest's
shade —
Bear her away — oh my weak eye doth fail
Amid these horrors —
*Imogine is borne to the cave, the Prior
follows. A gleam of torch-light falls
on the rocks. Bertram, Knights, and
Monks are seen winding down the
precipices, the clank of Bertram's
chains the only sound heard. They
enter; Bertram is between two Monks,
who bear torches.*

1st Monk. Leave him with us, and seek the
Prior, I pray you.
Knight. (*Aside to Monk*) He yet may try
escape. We'll watch concealed.
*Exeunt all but Bertram and the two
Monks.*
1st Monk. Brief rest is here allowed thee —
murderer, pause —
How fearful was our footing on those cliffs,
Where time had worn those steep and rocky
steps —
I counted them to thee as we descended,
But thou for pride wast dumb —
Ber. I heard thee not —
2d Monk. Look round thee, murderer,
drear thy resting place —
This is thy latest stage — survey it well —
Lo, as I wave my dimmed torch aloft,
Yon precipice crag seems as if every tread
(Yea, echoed impulse of the passing foot)
Would loose its weight to topple o'er our
heads —
Those cavities hollowed by the hand of
wrath —
Those deepening gulfs, have they no horrible
tenant?
Dare thine eye scan that spectred vacancy?
Ber. I do not mark the things thou tell'st
me of. —
1st Monk. Wretch, if thy fear no spectred
inmate shapes —
Ber. (*Starting from his trance*) Cease,
triflers, would you have *me* feel remorse?
Leave me alone — nor cell, nor chain, nor
dungeon,
Speaks to the murderer with the voice of
solitude.
1st Monk. Thou sayest true —
In cruelty of mercy will we leave thee —
Exeunt Monks.
Ber. If they would go in truth — but what
avails it?
*He meditates in gloomy reflection for
some minutes, and his countenance
slowly relaxes from its stern expression. The Prior enters unobserved, and
stands opposite him in an attitude of
supplication. Bertram resumes his
sternness.*
Why art thou here? — There was an hover-
ing angel
Just lighting on my heart — and thou hast
scared it —
Prior. Yea, rather, with my prayers I'll woo
it back.
In very pity of thy soul I come
To weep upon that heart I cannot soften —
(*A long pause*)

Oh! thou art on the verge of awful death —
Think of the moment, when the veiling scarf
That binds thine eyes, shall shut out earth
    for ever —
When in thy dizzy ear, hurtles the groan
Of those who see the smiting hand upreared,
Thou canst but feel — that moment comes
    apace —   *Bertram smiles.*
But terrors move in thee a horrid joy,
And thou art hardened by habitual danger
Beyond the sense of aught but pride in death.
             Bertram turns away.
Can I not move thee by one power in nature?
There have been those whom Heaven hath
    failed to move,
Yet moved they were by tears of kneeling age.
    (Kneels)
I waive all pride of ghostly power o'er thee —
I lift no cross, I count no bead before thee —
By the locked agony of these withered hands,
By these white hairs, such as thy father bore,
(Whom thou could'st ne'er see prostrate in
    the dust)
With toil to seek thee here my limbs do fail,
Send me not broken-hearted back again —
Yield, and relent, Bertram, my son, my son.
    (Weeping)
(Looking up eagerly) Did not a gracious drop
    bedew thine eye?
    Ber. Perchance a tear had fallen, hadst
thou not marked it.
    Prior. *(Rising with dignity)* Obdurate soul
— then perish in thy pride —
Hear in my voice thy parting angel speak,
Repent — and be forgiven —
    Bertram turns towards him in strong
    emotion; when a shriek is heard from
    the cavern, Bertram stands fixed in
    horror. The Prior stretches out his
    hands towards the cavern.
Plead *thou* for me — thou, whose wild voice
of horror
Has pierced the heart my prayers have failed
to touch —
    Ber. *(Wildly)* What voice was that — yet
do not dare to tell me,
Name not her name, I charge thee.
    Prior. Imogine —
A maniac through these shuddering woods
    she wanders,
But in her madness never cursed thy name.
    Bertram attempts to rush towards the
    cave, but stands stupefied on hearing
    a shriek from the cavern. Imogine
    rushes from it in distraction, bursting
    from the arms of Clotilda; the Monks
    and Knights follow, and remain in
    the background.

    Imo. Away, away, away, no wife — no
    mother —
    She rushes forward till she meets
    Bertram, who stands in speechless
    horror.
Give me my husband, give me back my
    child —
Nay, give me back myself —
They say I'm mad, but yet I know thee well —
Look on me — They would bind these wasted
    limbs —
I ask but death — death from thy hand —
    that hand
Can deal death well — and yet thou wilt not
    give it.
    Ber. *(Gazing on her for a moment, then*
rushing to the Prior, and sinking at his feet)
Who hath done this? Where are the racks I
    hoped for?
Am I not weak? am I not humbled now?
    Grovelling at the Prior's feet, and then
    turning to the Knights.
Hast thou no curse to blast — no curse for
    me —
Is there no hand to pierce a soldier's heart?
Is there no foot to crush a felon's neck?
    Imo. *(Raising herself at the sound of his*
voice) Bertram.
    He rushes towards her, and first re-
    peats Imogine *feebly; as he ap-*
    proaches, he utters her name again
    passionately, but as he draws nearer
    and sees her look of madness and
    desperation, he repeats it once more in
    despair, and does not dare to ap-
    proach her, till he perceives her falling
    into Clotilda's arms, and catches her
    in his.
Have I deserved this of thee? —
    She dies slowly, with her eyes fixed on
    Bertram, who continues to gaze on
    her, unconscious of her having
    expired.
    Prior. 'Tis past — remove him from the
    corse —
    The Knights and Monks advance; he
    waves them off with one hand still
    supporting the body.
(To the Monks) — Brethren, remove the
    corse —
    Ber. She is not dead —   *Starting up.*
She must not, shall not die, till she forgives
    me —
Speak — speak to me —
             Kneeling to the corse.
(Turning to the Monks) — Yes — she will
    speak anon —
        A long pause; he drops the corse.

She speaks no more — Why do ye gaze on
  me —
I loved her, yea, I love, in death I loved
  her —
I killed her — but — I loved her —
What arm shall loose the grasp of love and
  death?
  The Knights and Monks surround,
  and attempt to tear him from the
  body. He snatches a sword from one
  of the Knights, who retreats in terror,
  as it is pointed towards him. Bertram,
  resuming all his former previous
sternness, bursts into a disdainful
  laugh.
Thee — against thee — oh, thou art safe —
  thou worm —
Bertram hath but one fatal foe on earth —
And *he is here* —   *Stabs himself.*
  Prior. (Rushes forward) He dies, he dies.
  Ber. (Struggling with the agonies of death)
I know thee holy Prior — I know ye, brethren.
Lift up your holy hands in charity.
(With a burst of wild exultation) I died no
  felon death —
A warrior's weapon freed a warrior's soul —

THE END.

EDWARD BULWER-LYTTON
1803-1873

Richelieu; *or,* The Conspiracy
(1839)

The most important dramatist writing for the legitimate stage in the first half of the nineteenth century was Edward Bulwer-Lytton, and *Richelieu* was his most ambitious play. He was born Edward Bulwer in 1803, the son of General William Bulwer and his wife Elizabeth, a wealthy woman in her own right. Romantic and literary in temperament and a great admirer of Lord Byron, Bulwer had already published a volume of verse before he entered Trinity College, Cambridge. On leaving the university he entered social life as a dandy and engaged in dueling, fashionable flirtation, and intrigue. When he married an Irish beauty against his mother's wishes and she withdrew his ample allowance, Bulwer began to publish. He had already collected material for several novels, and in 1827 and 1828 *Falkland* and *Pelham* appeared. He wrote best-selling novels and poetry the rest of his life. Elected to Parliament in 1831, he also had a distinguished career in the House of Commons. (To inherit a fortune under the terms of his mother's will, he added her maiden name to his when she died, and became Edward Bulwer-Lytton.) As a consequence of his performing many services for the English government, in 1866 he was created the first Baron Lytton.

While a young man he was much interested in the theatre. Aware of the legal disabilities that hampered dramatic development, he was the leader of a Parliamentary effort in 1832 to free the theatres from the monopoly of the patent houses, to establish effective copyright for plays, and to abolish censorship by the Lord Chamberlain. The movement failed in 1832, but it stimulated the sentiment that freed the theatres in 1843. Already famous as a novelist, Bulwer turned his facile hand to the drama. His first play, *The Duchess de la Vallière*, performed at Covent Garden in 1837, was not a success, but Bulwer learned from the experience. He became a friend of London's leading actor, W. C. Macready, who was earnestly seeking to elevate the legitimate drama. Working in close cooperation with Macready, Bulwer wrote (among other pieces) three plays that were great successes and that were performed regularly, as part of the standard repertory, for forty years. These plays represent his contribution to romantic verse drama and traditional comedy. Since Bulwer also wished his plays to be popular, they exhibit an interesting compromise, for he sought to give life to his legitimate plays by including material from the melodrama.

The first of these plays, *The Lady of Lyons* (1838), a romantic comedy-drama partly in verse, develops the quasi-democratic theme of a noble-hearted commoner tricked into marriage with an aristocratic lady who (also tricked) scorns him, till the hero wins fame and wealth in his country's service. After his next play, *Richelieu*, Bulwer wrote *Money* (1840), briefly discussed in the Introduction as a comedy of manners.

He turned to the plays of the French romantic poets for help in this attempt to elevate the English drama; *The Lady of Lyons* and *Richelieu* are set in France. Working with Macready on the production, he planned scenery, costumes, and stage business in great detail. But in spite of Bulwer's admirable effort to give new life to the declining traditional drama and his apparent success at the time, the plays today seem cosmetic in sentiment, one-dimensional in characterization, and rhetorical in tone.

Richelieu is an historical play that pays more attention to the romantic idealization of its central character than it does to historical accuracy or the movement of social forces in the formation of modern France. Bulwer industriously read history, but sources named in his preface and notes to the published play include pieces of fiction: Santine's romantic novel *Une Maîtresse de Louis XIII* and De Vigny's *Cinq Mars*. Scholarship, especially an article by Mr. Charles Qualia, has demonstrated that Bulwer drew also upon Victor Hugo's play *Cromwell*, Nepomucène Lemercier's play *Richelieu, ou La Journée des Dupes*, and other pieces. Insofar as Bulwer's play uses history, it puts together several events that occurred in different periods of Richelieu's career. It even has Richelieu, who died in 1642, make references to Cromwell, at that time only the unknown leader of a small band of cavalry.

Bulwer's preface rationalizes his treatment of history: "The historical drama is the concentration of historical events. In the attempt to place upon the stage the picture of an era, that license with dates and details which Poetry permits . . . has been, though not unsparingly, indulged. The conspiracy of the Duc de Bouillon is, for instance, amalgamated with the *dénouement* of *The Day of Dupes;* and circumstances connected with the treason of Cinq Mars . . . are identified with the fate of the earlier favourite Baradas." The question, of course, is whether the license taken helps to fulfil the stated aim of placing "upon the stage the picture of an era," and whether including purely fictional material taken from romances is justifiable. As Mr. Qualia points out, "Richelieu had no daughter of his own, but Bulwer gave him an adopted daughter, Julie," and the plot to kill the Cardinal in his sleep is taken from the story of Cromwell. These and other incidents are not historical facts. Nor do these fictions serve to illustrate Richelieu's role in building France. The French critic Augustin Filon, who witnessed a late nineteenth-century production of the play, called it a "mixture of tragedy and melodrama . . . of historical documents and . . . ignorance of what is essential in history."

Interested chiefly in creating the character of Richelieu, the playwright chose the hero-villain of the Gothic drama (or the Byronic hero) as his model. Richelieu as the hero is on the right side, but he is like a villain in being, as he calls himself, both lion and fox. His passion for grandeur is presented as passion for France, but it is stated in the vainglorious tones of Gothic drama, and is not entirely justified in the action of the play. There is a suggestion of terrible, supernatural power when he draws about Julie an "awful circle" and would upon the head of any entering it "launch the curse of Rome." (It is a grand, theatrical scene: Richelieu towering in his blood-red robes!) The long melancholy speech ringing with "I am not happy" is pure Byronism, and so is the emphasis upon Richelieu's isolation, the lion bayed by jackals. The portrait of Richelieu is theatrically powerful, but it is hardly credible as historical or psychological truth.

To contrast with this grandeur, Bulwer added domestic interest which centers in great Richelieu's doting fondness for the orphan Julie, who is, after France, the second passion of his life. To create pathos Julie must be an orphan, but to create displays of fond affection, paternal authority, and filial duty, Richelieu must be her father — as for all sentimental purposes he is: "May I say 'Father'?" — "Now and ever!" The domestic morality is exemplary: Julie is a simple, clinging, helpless ingénue to be protected. She suspects no evil: "As well have placed a doll about the Queen." She is, in a phrase fondly spoken, a "senseless puppet." But it is her simplicity, perhaps, that gives her enough virtuous indignation to drive the King of France from her bedchamber like a whipped dog.

Aside from being fascinated with the red-robed Cardinal, the audience found most of their excitement in the devices taken from melodrama. Richelieu as the grand Byronic hero is surrounded by petty villains; the straw men are sure to fall — there is no real antagonist. In spite of threats of disaster all will end happily. The document that bears the names of the conspirators disappears mysteriously, passes from hand to hand, but at last reaches Richelieu in the nick of time. There is no logic in the chase, for surely the governor of the Bastille would have searched a prisoner's pockets. The eavesdropping of Huguet and his change of sides, the gullibility of conspirators who do not examine the body of Richelieu, the comedy of De Beringhen, who must "discuss the paté," Richelieu's stale jokes about Joseph's poetry, the revival of a feeble Richelieu at the word "France" — all have the flavor of melodrama.

The play as a whole is artificial and full of somewhat hackneyed poetic sentiments. Bulwer sought to write a great play, but without anything to say, he merely distorted history into theatrical Byronism, and then added domestic materials for sentiment and melodramatic materials for action and excitement. *Richelieu* excellently illustrates an effort to save the declining romantic verse drama by keeping the traditional form, but, for popular interest, incorporating materials from the melodrama Macready and the intellectuals despised.

RICHELIEU;

or,

THE CONSPIRACY

A Drama In Five Acts

by

EDWARD BULWER-LYTTON

To the
Marquis of Landsdowne, K.G., &c., &c.
This Drama
Is Inscribed in Tribute
To the Talents which Command
and
The Qualities which Endear
Respect

First performed at the Theatre Royal, Covent Garden, March 7, 1839.

Cast of Characters

LOUIS THE THIRTEENTH
GASTON, DUKE OF ORLEANS, *brother to Louis XIII*
BARADAS, *favourite of the King, first gentleman of the Chamber, Premier, Ecuyer, etc.*
CARDINAL RICHELIEU
THE CHEVALIER DE MAUPRAT
THE SIEUR DE BERINGHEN, *in attendance on the King as First Valet de Chambre, one of the Conspirators*
JOSEPH, *a Capuchin, Richelieu's confidant*
HUGUET, *an officer of Richelieu's guard — a spy*
FRANÇOIS, *first Page to Richelieu*
CLERMONT
GOVERNOR OF THE BASTILLE
GAOLER
JULIE DE MORTEMAR, *an orphan, ward to Richelieu*
MARION DE LORME, *Mistress to Orleans, but in Richelieu's pay*
COURTIERS, PAGES, CONSPIRATORS, OFFICERS, SOLDIERS, ETC.

Act I.

Scene 1.

First day. A room in the house of Marion de Lorme; a table towards the front of the stage (with wine, fruits, etc.), at which are seated Baradas, four Courtiers, splendidly dressed in the costume of 1641–42; the Duke of Orleans reclining on a large fauteuil; Marion de Lorme, standing at the back of his chair, offers him a goblet, and then retires. At another table, De Beringhen, De Mauprat, playing at dice; other Courtiers, of inferior rank to those at the table of the Duke, looking on.

Orl. (*Drinking*) Here's to our enterprise! —

Bar. (*Glancing at Marion*) Hush, Sir! —

Orl. (*Aside*) Nay, Count,
You may trust her; she dotes on me; no house
So safe as Marion's.

Bar. Still, we have a secret,
And oil and water — woman and a secret —
Are hostile properties.

Orl. Well — Marion, see
How the play prospers yonder.

　　　　*Marion goes to the next table, looks
　　　　on for a few moments, then exits.*

Bar. (*Producing a parchment*) I have now
All the conditions drawn; it only needs
Our signatures upon receipt of this,
(Whereto is joined the schedule of our treaty
With the Count-Duke, the Richelieu of the Escurial,)
Bouillon will join his army with the Spaniard,
March on to Paris, — there, dethrone the King:
You will be Regent; I, and ye, my Lords,
Form the new Council. So much for the core
Of our great scheme.

Orl. But Richelieu is an Argus:
One of his hundred eyes will light upon us,
And then — good-bye to life.

Bar. To gain the prize
We must destroy the Argus: — ay, my Lords,
The scroll the core, but blood must fill the veins
Of our design; — while this despatched to Bouillon,
Richelieu despatched to Heaven! — The last
my charge.
Meet here to-morrow night. *You*, Sir, as first
In honour and in hope, meanwhile select

Some trusty knave to bear the scroll to Bouillon;
Midst Richelieu's foes *I'll* find some desperate hand
To strike for vengeance, while we stride to power.

Orl. So be it; — to-morrow, midnight. —
Come, my Lords.

　　　　*Exeunt Orleans, and the Courtiers in
　　　　his train. Those at the other table rise,
　　　　salute Orleans, and re-seat them-
　　　　selves.*

De B. Double the stakes.

De M. Done.

De B. Bravo; faith it shames me
To bleed a purse already *in extremis*.

De M. Nay, as you've had the patient to yourself
So long, no other doctor should despatch it.

　　　　De Mauprat throws and loses.

Omnes. Lost! Ha, ha, — poor De Mauprat!

De B. One throw more?

De M. No, I am bankrupt. (*Pushing gold*)
There goes all — except
My honour and my sword.　　　　*They rise.*

De B. Long cloaks and honour
Went out of vogue together, when we found
We got on much more rapidly without them;
The sword, indeed, is never out of fashion, —
The Devil has care of *that*.

First Gamester. Ay, take the sword
To Cardinal Richelieu — he gives gold for steel,
When worn by brave men.

De M. Richelieu!

De B. (*To Baradas*) At that name
He changes colour, bites his nether lip.
Ev'n in his brightest moments whisper "Richelieu,"
And you cloud all his sunshine.

Bar. I have mark'd it,
And I will learn the wherefore.

De M. The Egyptian
Dissolved her richest jewel in a draught:
Would I could so melt time and all its treasures,
And drain it thus. (*Drinking*)

De B. Come, gentlemen, what say ye,
A walk on the Parade?

Omnes. Ay, come, De Mauprat.

De M. Pardon me; we shall meet again, ere nightfall.

Bar. I'll stay and comfort Mauprat.

De B. Comfort! — when
We gallant fellows have run out a friend
There's nothing left — except to run him through!
There's the last act of friendship.

De M. Let me keep
That favour in reserve; in all beside
Your most obedient servant.
   Exeunt De Beringhen, etc., manent
   De Mauprat and Baradas.
Bar. You have lost —
Yet are not sad.
De M. Sad! — Life and gold have wings
And must fly one day: — open, then, their
  cages
And wish them merry.
Bar. You're a strange enigma: —
Fiery in war — and yet to glory lukewarm;
All mirth in action — in repose all gloom —
These are extremes in which the unconscious
  heart
Betrays the fever of deep-fix'd disease.
Confide in me! our young days roll'd together
In the same river, glassing the same stars
That smile i' the heaven of hope; — alike we
  made
Bright-winged steeds of our unform'd
  chimeras,
Spurring the fancies upward to the air,
Wherein we shaped fair castles from the
  cloud.
Fortune of late has sever'd us, and led
Me to the rank of Courtier, Count, and
  Favourite —
You to the titles of the wildest gallant
And bravest knight in France; — are you
  content?
No; — trust in me — some gloomy secret —
De M. Ay: —
A secret that doth haunt me, as, of old,
Men were possess'd of fiends? Where'er I
  turn,
The grave yawns dark before me! I *will* trust
  you; —
Hating the Cardinal, and beguiled by Orleans,
You know I join'd the Languedoc revolt —
Was captured — sent to the Bastile —
Bar. But shared
The general pardon, which the Duke of
  Orleans
Won for himself and all in the revolt,
Who but obey'd his orders.
De M. Note the phrase: —
"Obey'd his orders." Well, when on my way
To join the Duke in Languedoc, I (then
The down upon my lip — less man than
  boy)
Leading young valours — reckless as myself,
Seized on the town of Faviaux, and displaced
The Royal banners for the Rebel. Orleans
(Never too daring) when I reach'd the camp,
Blamed me for acting — mark — *without his
  orders:*

Upon this quibble Richelieu razed my name
Out of the general pardon.
Bar. Yet released you
From the Bastile —
De M. To call me to his presence,
And thus address me: — "You have seized a
  town
Of France, without the orders of your leader,
And for this treason, but one sentence
  — DEATH."
Bar. Death!
De M. "I have pity on your youth and
  birth,
Nor wish to glut the headsman; — join your
  troop,
Now on the march against the Spaniards;
  — change
The traitor's scaffold for the Soldier's
  grave; —
Your memory stainless — they who shared
  your crime
Exil'd or dead, — your king shall never learn
  it."
Bar. O tender pity! — O most charming
  prospect!
Blown into atoms by a bomb, or drill'd
Into a cullender by gunshot! — Well? —
De M. You have heard if I fought bravely.
  — Death became
Desired as Daphne by the eager Day-god.
Like him I chas'd the nymph — to grasp the
  laurel!
I could not die!
Bar. Poor Fellow!
De M. When the Cardinal
Review'd the troops — his eye met mine;
  — he frown'd,
Summon'd me forth — "How's this?" quoth
  he; "you have shunn'd
The sword — beware the axe! — 'twill fall
  one day!"
He left me thus — we were recalled to
  Paris,
And — you know all!
Bar. And, knowing this, why halt you,
Spell'd by the rattlesnake, — while in the
  breasts
Of your firm friends beat hearts, that vow the
  death
Of your grim tyrant? — wake! — Be one of
  us;
The time invites — the King detests the
  Cardinal,
Dares not disgrace, — but groans to be
  deliver'd
Of that too great a subject — join your
  friends,
Free France and save yourself.

De M. Hush! Richelieu bears
A charmed life: — to all who have braved
his power,
One common end — the block.
  Bar. Nay, if he live,
The block your doom!
  De M. Better the victim, Count,
Than the assassin — France requires a
Richelieu,
But does not need a Mauprat. Truce to
this; —
All time one midnight, where my thoughts
are spectres.
What to me fame? — What love? —
  Bar. Yet dost thou love *not?*
  De M. Love? — I am young —
  Bar. And Julie fair! (*Aside*) It is so,
Upon the margin of the grave — his hand
Would pluck the rose that I would win and
wear!
  De M. (*Gaily*) No more! —
I love! — Your breast holds both my secrets;
— Never
Unbury either! — Come, while yet we may,
We'll bask us in the noon of rosy life: —
Lounge through the gardens, — flaunt it in
the taverns, —
Laugh, — game, — drink, — feast; — If so
confine my days,
Faith, I'll enclose the nights. — Pshaw! not
so grave;
I'm a true Frenchman! — *Vive la bagatelle!*

*As they are going out enter Huguet and four
Arquebusiers.*

  Hug. Messire De Mauprat, — I arrest
you! — Follow
To the Lord Cardinal.
  De M. You see, my friend,
I'm out of my suspense — The tiger's play'd
Long enough with his prey. — Farewell!
— Hereafter
Say, when men name me, "Adrien de
Mauprat
Lived without hope, and perished without
fear!"
        Exeunt De Mauprat, Huguet, etc.
  Bar. Farewell! — I trust forever! I de-
sign'd thee
For Richelieu's murderer — but, as well his
martyr!
In childhood you the stronger — and I
cursed you;
In youth the fairer — and I cursed you still;
And now my rival! While the name of Julie
Hung on thy lips — I smiled — for then I
saw
In my mind's eye, the cold and grinning
Death

Hang o'er thy head the pall! — Ambition,
Love,
Ye twin-born stars of daring destinies,
Sit in my house of Life! — By the King's aid
I will be Julie's husband — in despite
Of my Lord Cardinal — By the King's aid
I will be minister of France — in spite
Of my Lord Cardinal; — and then — what
then?
The King loves Julie — feeble prince —
false master —
      *Producing and gazing on the parch-
      ment.*
Then, by the aid of Bouillon and the Span-
iard,
I will dethrone the King; and all — ha! —
ha! —
All, in despite of my Lord Cardinal.   *Exit.*

Scene 2.

*A room in the Palais Cardinal, the walls hung
with arras. A large screen in one corner. A
table covered with books, papers, etc. A rude
clock in a recess. Busts, statues, bookcases,
weapons of different periods, and banners
suspended over Richelieu's chair. Richelieu
and Joseph.*

  Rich. And so you think this new con-
spiracy
The craftiest trap yet laid for the old fox? —
Fox! — Well, I like the nickname! What did
Plutarch
Say of the Greek Lysander?
  Jos. I forget.
  Rich. That where the lion's skin fell short,
he eked it
Out with the fox's. A great statesman, Joseph,
That same Lysander?
  Jos. Orleans heads the traitors.
  Rich. A very wooden head then! Well?
  Jos. The favourite,
Count Baradas —
  Rich. A weed of hasty growth,
First gentleman of the chamber, — titles,
lands,
And the King's ear! — it cost me six long
winters
To mount as high, as in six little moons
This painted lizard — But I hold the ladder,
And when I shake — he falls! What more?
  Jos. A scheme
To make your orphan-ward an instrument
To aid your foes. You placed her with the
Queen,
One of the royal chamber, — as a watch
I' th' enemy's quarters —
  Rich. And the silly child
Visits me daily, — calls me "Father,"
— prays

Kind heaven to bless me — And for all the
rest,
As well have placed a doll about the Queen!
She does not heed who frowns — who smiles;
with whom
The King confers in whispers; notes not when
Men who last week were foes, are found in
corners
Mysteriously affectionate; words spoken
Within closed doors she never hears; — by
chance
Taking the air at keyholes — Senseless
puppet!
No ears — nor eyes! — and yet she says —
"She loves me!"
Go on —
Jos. Your ward has charm'd the King.
Rich. Out on you!
Have I not, one by one, from such fair shoots
Pluck'd the insidious ivy of his love?
And shall it creep around my blossoming tree
Where innocent thoughts, like happy birds,
make music
That spirits in Heaven might hear? They're
sinful too,
Those passionate surfeits of the rampant
flesh,
The Church condemns them; and to us, my
Joseph,
The props and pillars of the Church, most
hurtful.
The King is weak — whoever the King loves
Must rule the King; the lady loves another,
The other rules the lady — thus we're balked
Of our own proper sway — The King must
have
No Goddess but the State: — the State —
That's Richelieu!
Jos. This not the worst; — Louis, in all
decorous,
And deeming you her least compliant
guardian,
Would veil his suit by marriage with his
minion,
Your prosperous foe, Count Baradas.
Rich. Ha! ha!
I have another bride for Baradas!
Jos. You, my lord?
Rich. Ay — more faithful than the love
Of fickle woman: — when the head lies low-
liest,
Clasping him fondest; — Sorrow never knew
So sure a soother, — and her bed is stainless!
Jos. (*Aside*) If of the grave he speaks I do
not wonder
That priests are bachelors!

Enter François.

Fran. Mademoiselle De Mortemar.

Rich. Most opportune — admit her.
                              Exit François.
In my closet
You'll find a rosary, Joseph; ere you tell
Three hundred beads, I'll summon you.
— Stay, Joseph;
I did omit an Ave in my matins, —
A grievous fault; — atone it for me, Joseph;
There is a scourge within; I am weak, you
strong,
It were but charity to take my sin
On such broad shoulders. Exercise is health-
ful.
Jos. I! guilty of such criminal presumption
As to mistake myself for you. — No, never!
Think it not. — (*Aside*) Troth, a pleasant
invitation!   *Exit Joseph.*

Enter Julie De Mortemar.

Rich. That's my sweet Julie! why, upon
this face
Blushes such daybreak, one might swear the
Morning
Were come to visit Tithon.
Julie. (*Placing herself at his feet*) Are you
gracious?
May I say "Father?"
Rich. Now and ever!
Julie. Father!
A sweet word to an orphan.
Rich. No; not orphan
While Richelieu lives; thy father loved me
well;
My friend, ere I had flatterers (now, I'm
great,
In other phrase, I'm friendless) — he died
young
In years, not service, and bequeathed thee to
me;
And thou shalt have a dowry, girl, to buy
Thy mate amidst the mightiest. Drooping? —
sighs? —
Art thou not happy at the Court?
Julie. Not often.
Rich. (*Aside*) Can she love Baradas? —
Ah! at thy heart
There's what can smile and sigh, blush and
grow pale,
All in a breath! — Thou art admired — art
young;
Does not his Majesty commend thy beauty —
Ask thee to sing to him? and swear such
sounds
Had smooth'd the brows of Saul? —
Julie. He's very tiresome,
Our worthy King.
Rich. Fie; kings are never tiresome,
Save to their ministers. — What courtly
gallants

Charm ladies most? De Sourdiac, Longue-
 ville, or
The favourite Baradas?
 Julie. A smileless man —
I fear, and shun him.
  Rich. Yet he courts thee?
 Julie. Then
He is more tiresome than his Majesty.
  Rich. Right, girl, shun Baradas. — Yet of
 these flowers
Of France, not one, in whose more honied
 breath
Thy heart hears Summer whisper?

   Enter Huguet.

 Hug. The Chevalier
De Mauprat waits below.
 Julie. (*Starting up*) De Mauprat!
 Rich. Hem!
He has been tiresome, too. — Anon.
      Exit Huguet.
 Julie. What doth he? —
I mean — I — Does your Eminence — that
 is —
Know you Messire de Mauprat?
 Rich. Well! — and you —
Has he address'd you often?
 Julie. Often! No, —
Nine times; — nay, ten! — the last time, by
 the lattice
Of the great staircase. (*In a melancholy tone*)
 The Court sees him rarely.
 Rich. A bold and forward royster?
 Julie. He? — nay, modest,
Gentle, and sad methinks.
 Rich. Wears gold and azure?
 Julie. No; sable.
 Rich. So you note his colours, Julie?
Shame on you, child, look loftier. By the
 mass
I have business with this modest gentleman.
 Julie. You're angry with poor Julie.
 There's no cause.
 Rich. No cause — you hate my foes?
 Julie. I do!
 Rich. Hate Mauprat!
 Julie. Not Mauprat. No, not Adrien,
 father?
 Rich. Adrien!
Familiar! — Go, child; no, — not *that* way;
 — wait
In the tapestry chamber; I will join you —
 go.
 Julie. His brows are knit; — I dare not
 call him father!
But I *must* speak — Your Eminence —
 Rich. (*Sternly*) Well! girl!
 Julie. Nay

Smile on me — one smile more; there, now
 I'm happy.
Do not rank De Mauprat with your foes; he
 is not,
I know he is not, he loves France too well.
 Rich. Not rank De Mauprat with my foes?
 So be it.
I'll blot him from that list.
 Julie. That's my own father. *Exit Julie.*
 Rich. (*Ringing a small bell on the table*)
Huguet!

   Enter Huguet.

De Mauprat struggled not, nor murmur'd?
 Hug. No; proud and passive.
 Rich. Bid him enter. — Hold:
Look that he hide no weapon. Humph, despair
Makes victims sometimes victors. When he
 has enter'd,
Glide round unseen; — place thyself yonder
 (*Pointing to the screen*); watch him;
If he show violence — (let me see thy carbine;
So, a good weapon) — if he play the lion,
Why — the dog's death.
 Hug. I never miss my mark.
   Exit Huguet; Richelieu seats himself
   at the table, and slowly arranges the
   papers before him. Enter De Mauprat,
   preceded by Huguet, who then retires
   behind the screen.
 Rich. Approach, Sir. — Can you call to
 mind the hour,
Now three years since, when in this room,
 methinks,
Your presence honour'd me?
 De M. It is, my Lord,
One of my most —
 Rich. (*Airily*) Delightful recollections.
 De M. (*Aside*) St. Denis! doth he make a
 jest of axe
And headsman?
 Rich. (*Sternly*) I did then accord you
A mercy ill requited — you still live?
Messire de Mauprat
Doom'd to sure death, how hast thou since
 consumed
The time allotted thee for serious thought
And solemn penitence?
 De M. (*Embarrassed*) The time, my Lord?
 Rich. Is not the question plain? I'll answer
 for thee:
Thou hast sought nor priest nor shrine; no
 sackcloth chafed
Thy delicate flesh. The rosary and the
 death's-head
Have not, with pious meditation, purged
Earth from the carnal gaze. What thou hast
 not done

Brief told; what done, a volume! Wild debauch,
Turbulent riot: — for the morn the dice-box —
Noon claim'd the duel — and the night the wassail:
These, your most holy, pure preparatives
For death and judgment. Do I wrong you, Sir?
De M. I was not always thus: — if chang'd my nature
Blame that which changed my fate. — Alas, my Lord,
Were you accursed with that which you inflicted
By bed and board, dogg'd by one ghastly spectre —
The while within you youth beat high, and life
Grew lovelier from the neighbouring frown of death —
The heart no bud, nor fruit — save in those seeds
Most worthless, which spring up, bloom, bear, and wither
In the same hour — Were this your fate, perchance
You would have err'd like me!
Rich. I might, like you,
Have been a brawler and a reveller; — not,
Like you trickster and a thief. —
De M. (*Advancing threateningly*) Lord Cardinal! —
Unsay those words!
Huguet deliberately raises his carbine.
Rich. (*Waving his hand*) Not quite so quick, friend Huguet;
Messire de Mauprat is a patient man,
And he can wait! —
You have outrun your fortune; —
I blame you not, that you would be a beggar —
Each to his taste! — But I do charge you, Sir,
That, being beggar'd, you would coin false monies
Out of that crucible, called DEBT. — To live
On means not yours — be brave in silks and laces,
Gallant in steeds — splendid in banquets; — all
Not *yours* — ungiven — unherited — unpaid for; —
This is to be a trickster; and to filch
Men's art and labour, which to them is wealth,
Life, daily bread — quitting all scores with — "Friend,
You're troublesome!" — Why this, forgive me,

Is what — when done with a less dainty grace —
Plain folks call *"Theft!"* You owe eight thousand pistoles,
Minus one crown, two liards! —
De M. (*Aside*) The old conjuror! —
'Sdeath, he'll inform me next how many cups
I drank at dinner! —
Rich. This is scandalous,
Shaming your birth and blood. — I tell you, Sir,
That you must pay your debts. —
De M. With all my heart,
My Lord. — Where shall I borrow, then, the money?
Rich. (*Aside and laughing*) A humorous dare-devil! — The very man
To suit my purpose — ready, frank, and bold!
(*Rising and earnestly*)
Adrien de Mauprat, men have called me cruel; —
I am not; — I am *just!* — I found France rent asunder, —
The rich men despots, and the poor banditti; —
Sloth in the mart, and schism within the temple;
Brawls festering to Rebellion; and weak Laws
Rotting away with rust in antique sheaths. —
I have re-created France; and, from the ashes
Of the old feudal and decrepit carcase,
Civilization on her luminous wings
Soars, phoenix-like, to Jove! What was my art?
Genius, some say — some, Fortune, — Witchcraft, some.
Not so; — my art was JUSTICE! Force and Fraud
Misname it cruelty — you shall confute them!
My champion YOU! You met me as your foe,
Depart my friend. — You shall not die.
— France needs you.
You shall wipe off all stains — be rich, be honour'd,
Be great
*De Mauprat falls on his knee,
Richelieu raises him.*
I ask, Sir, in return, this hand,
To gift it with a bride, whose dower shall match,
Yet not exceed, her beauty.
De M. I, my Lord, (*Hesitating*)
I have no wish to marry.
Rich. Surely, Sir,
To die were worse.

De M. Scarcely; the poorest coward
Must die, — but knowingly to march to
  marriage —
My Lord, it asks the courage of a lion!
  Rich. Traitor, thou triflest with me! — I
  know *all!*
Thou hast dared to love my ward — my
  charge.
  De M. As rivers
May love the sunlight — basking in the
  beams,
And hurrying on! —
  Rich. Thou hast told her of thy love?
  De M. My Lord, if I had dared to love a
  maid,
Lowliest in France, I would not so have
  wrong'd her
As bid her link rich life and virgin hope
With one, the deathman's gripe might, from
  her side
Pluck at the nuptial altar.
  Rich. I believe thee;
Yet since she knows not of thy love, renounce
  her;
Take life and fortune with another! —
  Silent?
  De M. Your fate has been one triumph.
  — You know not
How bless'd a thing it was in my dark hour
To nurse the one sweet thought you bid me
  banish.
Love hath no need of words; — nor less
  within
That holiest temple — the heaven-builded
  soul —
Breathes the recorded vow — Base knight,
  — false lover
Were he, who barter'd all, that brighten'd
  grief
Or sanctified despair, for life and gold.
Revoke your mercy; — I prefer the fate
I look'd for!
  Rich. Huguet! To the tapestry chamber
Conduct your prisoner.
(*To Mauprat*) You will there behold
The executioner: — your doom be private —
And Heaven have mercy on you!
  De M. When I'm dead,
Tell her, I loved her.
  Rich. Keep such follies, Sir,
For fitter ears; — go —
  De M. Does he mock me?
           Exeunt De Mauprat and Huguet.
  Rich. Joseph,
Come forth.

        Enter Joseph.

Methinks your cheek hath lost its rubies;

I fear you have been too lavish of the flesh;
The scourge is heavy.
  Jos. Pray you, change the subject.
  Rich. You good men are so modest! —
  Well, to business!
Go instantly — deeds — notaries! bid my
  stewards
Arrange my house by the Luxembourg — *my*
  house
No more! — a bridal present to my ward,
Who weds to-morrow.
  Jos. Weds, with whom?
  Rich. De Mauprat.
  Jos. Penniless husband!
  Rich. Bah! the mate for beauty
Should be a man, and not a money-chest!
When her brave sire lay on his bed of death,
I vow'd to be a father to his Julie; —
And so he died — the smile upon his lips! —
And when I spared the life of her young
  lover,
Methought I saw that smile again! Who else,
Look you, in all the Court — who else so
  well,
Brave, or supplant the favourite; — balk the
  King —
Baffle their schemes? — I have tried him: —
  He has honour
And courage; — qualities that eagle plume
Men's souls — and fit them for the fiercest
  sun,
Which ever melted the weak waxen minds
That flutter in the beams of gaudy Power!
Besides, he has taste, this Mauprat: — When
  my play
Was acted to dull tiers of lifeless gapers,
Who had no soul for poetry, I saw him
Applaud in the proper places; trust me,
  Joseph,
He is a man of an uncommon promise!
  Jos. And yet your foe.
  Rich. Have I not foes enow? —
Great men gain doubly when they make foes
  friends.
Remember my grand maxims: — First em-
  ploy
All methods to conciliate.
  Jos. Failing these?
  Rich. (*Fiercely*) All means to crush; as
  with the opening, and
The clenching of this little hand, I will
Crush the small venom of these stinging
  courtiers,
So, so we've baffled Baradas.
  Jos. And when
Check the conspiracy?
  Rich. Check, check? Full way to it.
Let it bud, ripen, flaunt i' the day, and burst

To fruit, — the Dead Sea's fruit of ashes;
ashes
Which I will scatter to the winds.
Go, Joseph;
When you return, I have a feast for you:
The last great act of my great play; the verses
Methinks are fine, — ah, very fine. — *You*
write
Verses! — (*Aside*) *such* verses! — You have
wit, discernment.
   Jos. (*Aside*) Worse than the scourge!
Strange that so great a statesman
Should be so bad a poet.
   Rich. What dost say?
   Jos. That it is strange so great a statesman
should
Be so sublime a poet.
   Rich. Ah, you rogue;
Laws die, Books never. Of my ministry
I am not vain; but of my muse, I own it.
Come, you shall hear the verses now.
                   Takes up a MS.
   Jos. My Lord,
The deeds, the notaries!
   Rich. True, I pity you;
But business first, then pleasure.
                   Exit Joseph.
(*Seats himself, and reading*) Ah sublime!

Enter De Mauprat and Julie.

   De M. Oh, speak, my Lord — I dare not
think you mock me,
And yet —
   Rich. Hush, hush — this line must be
considered!
   Julie. Are we not both your children?
   Rich. What a couplet!
How now! Oh, sir — you live! —
   De M. Why, no, methinks,
Elysium is not life!
   Julie. He smiles! — you smile,
My father! From my heart for ever, now,
I'll blot the name of orphan!
   Rich. Rise, my children,
For ye are mine — mine both; — and in your
sweet
And young delight — your love — (life's
first-born glory)
My own lost youth breathes musical!
   De M. I'll seek
Temple and priest henceforward; — were it
but
To learn Heaven's choicest blessings.
   Rich. Thou shalt seek
Temple and priest right soon; the morrow's
sun
Shall see across these barren thresholds pass
The fairest bride in Paris. Go, my children:

Even *I* loved once. — Be lovers while ye may.
How is it with you, Sir? You bear it bravely;
You know, it asks the courage of a lion.
            Exeunt De Mauprat and Julie.
Oh, godlike Power! Woe, Rapture, Penury,
Wealth, —
Marriage and Death, for one infirm old man
Through a great empire to dispense — with-
hold —
As the will whispers! And shall things — like
motes
That live in my daylight — lackies of court
wages,
Dwarf'd starvelings — manikins, upon whose
shoulders
The burthen of a province were a load
More heavy than the globe on Atlas — cast
Lots for my robes and sceptre? France, I love
thee!
All Earth shall never pluck thee from my
heart!
My mistress France — my wedded wife —
sweet France,
Who shall proclaim divorce for thee and me!
                  Exit Richelieu.

End of the First Act.

Act II.

Scene 1.

*Second day. A splendid apartment in De
Mauprat's new house. Casements opening to
the gardens, beyond which the domes of the
Luxembourg Palace.*

Enter Baradas.

   Bar. Mauprat's new home: — too splendid
for a soldier!
But o'er his floors — the while I stalk —
methinks
My shadow spreads gigantic to the gloom
The old rude towers of the Bastile cast far
Along the smoothness of the jocund day.
Well, thou hast 'scaped the fierce caprice of
Richelieu;
But art thou farther from the headsman, fool?
Thy secret I have whisper'd to the King; —
Thy marriage makes the King thy foe. Thou
stand'st
On the abyss — and in the pool below
I see a ghastly, headless phantom mirror'd:
Thy likeness ere the marriage moon hath
waned.
Meanwhile — meanwhile — ha, ha — if thou
art wedded
Thou art not wived.

Enter De Mauprat, splendidly dressed.

De M. Was ever fate like mine?
So blest, and yet so wretched!
Bar. Joy, de Mauprat!
Why, what a brow, man, for your wedding-
    day!
De M. Jest not. — Distraction!
Bar. What, your wife a shrew
Already? Courage, man — the common lot!
De M. Oh, that she were less lovely, or
    less loved!
Bar. Riddles again!
De M. You know what chanced between
The Cardinal and myself.
Bar. This morning brought
Your letter — a strange account! I laugh'd
And wept at once for gladness.
De M. We were wed
At noon — the rite performed, came hither
    — scarce
Arrived, when —
Bar. Well? —
De M. Wide flew the doors, and lo,
Messire de Beringhen, and this epistle!
Bar. 'Tis the King's hand! — the royal
    seal!
De M. Read — read!
Bar. (*Reading*) "Whereas, Adrien de
Mauprat, Colonel and Chevalier in our
armies, being already guilty of high treason,
by the seizure of our town of Faviaux, has
presumed, without our knowledge, consent,
or sanction, to connect himself by marriage
with Julie de Mortemar, a wealthy orphan attached to the person of Her Majesty, without
our knowledge or consent — We do hereby
proclaim and declare the said marriage contrary to law. On penalty of death, Adrien de
Mauprat will not communicate with the said
Julie de Mortemar by word or letter, save in
the presence of our faithful servant, the Sieur
de Beringhen, and then with such respect and
decorum as are due to a Demoiselle attached
to the Court of France, until such time as it
may suit our royal pleasure to confer with the
Holy Church on the formal annulment of the
marriage, and with our Council on the punishment to be awarded to Messire de Mauprat,
who is cautioned for his own sake to preserve
silence as to our injunction, more especially
to Mademoiselle de Mortemar. Given under
our hand and seal at the Louvre. LOUIS."
                    (*Returning the letter*)
Amazement! — Did not Richelieu say, the
    King
Knew not your crime?
De M. He said so.
Bar. Poor de Mauprat!

See you the snare, the vengeance worse than
    death,
Of which you are the victim?
De M. Ha!
Bar. (*Aside*) It works!
        *Julie and De Beringhen in the gar-
        dens.*
You have not sought the Cardinal yet, to —
De M. No!
Scarce yet my sense awaken'd from the
    shock;
Now I will seek him.
Bar. Hold — beware! Stir not
Till we confer again.
De M. Speak out, man!
Bar. Hush!
Your wife! — De Beringhen! — Be on your
    guard.
Obey the royal orders to the letter.
I'll look around your palace. By my troth,
A princely mansion!
De M. Stay —
Bar. So new a bridegroom
Can want no visitors. — Your Servant,
    Madam.
Oh, happy pair — oh, charming picture!
                Exit through a side door.

Julie. Adrien,
You left us suddenly — are you not well?
De M. Oh, very well — that is — ex-
    tremely ill.
Julie. Ill, Adrien?   *Taking his hand.*
De M. Not when I see thee.
        *He is about to lift her hand to his lips,
        when De Beringhen coughs, and pulls
        his mantle. De Mauprat drops the
        hand, and walks away.*

Julie. Alas!
Should he not love me?
De B. (*Aside*) Have a care, I must
Report each word, each gesture to his
    Majesty.
De M. Sir, if you were not in his Majesty's
    service,
You'd be the most officious, impudent,
Damn'd busy-body ever interfering
In a man's family affairs.
De B. But as
I do belong, Sir, to his Majesty —
De M. You're lucky! — Still, were we a
    story higher,
'Twere prudent not to go too near the
    window.
Julie. Adrien, what have I done? Say, am
    I changed
Since yesterday? — or was it but for wealth,
Ambition, life — that — that — you swore
    you loved me?

De M. I shall go mad! I do, indeed I do —
De B. (*Aside*) Not love her! that were
highly disrespectful.
Julie. You do — what, Adrien?
De M. Oh! I do, indeed —
I do think, that this weather is delightful!
A charming day! the sky is so serene!
And what a prospect! — (*To De Beringhen*)
Oh! you Popinjay!
Julie. He jests at me! — he mocks me! —
yet I love him,
And every look becomes the lips we love!
Perhaps I am too grave? — You laugh at
Julie;
If laughter please you, welcome be the music!
Only say, Adrien, that you love me.
De M. (*Kissing her hand*) Ay;
With my whole heart I love you! — Now,
Sir, go,
And tell that to his Majesty! Whoever
Heard of its being a state-offence to kiss
The hand of one's own wife?
Julie. He says he loves me,
And starts away, as if to say "I love you"
Meant something *very* dreadful. — Come, sit
by me, —
I place your chair! — fie on your gallantry!
*They sit down; as he pushes his chair
back, she draws hers nearer.*
Why must this strange Messire de Beringhen
Be always here? He never takes a hint.
Do you not wish him gone?
De M. Upon my soul
I do, my Julie! — Send him for your *bouquet*,
Your glove, your — anything —
Julie. Messire de Beringhen,
I dropp'd my glove in the gardens by the
fountain,
Or the alcove, or — stay — no, by the
statue
Of Cupid; may I ask you to —
De B. To send for it?
Certainly. (*Ringing a bell on the table*) André,
Pierre, (you rascals, how
Do ye call them?)

Enter Servants.

Ah — *Madame* has dropp'd her glove
In the gardens, by the fountain, or the
alcove;
Or — stay — no, by the statue — eh? — of
Cupid.
Bring it.
De M. Did ever now one pair of shoulders
Carry such waggon-loads of impudence
Into a gentleman's drawing-room? Dear Julie,
I'm busy — letters — visitors — the devil!
I do beseech you leave me — I say — leave
me.

Julie. (*Weeping*) You are unkind.   *Exit.*
*As she goes out, De Mauprat drops on
one knee, and kisses the hem of her
mantle, unseen by her.*
De B. Ten millions of apologies —
De M. I'll not take one of them. I have,
as yet,
Withstood all things — my heart — my love
— my rights.
But Julie's tears! — When is this farce to
end?
De B. Oh! when you please. His Majesty
requests me,
As soon as you infringe his gracious orders,
To introduce you to the Governor
Of the Bastile. I should have had that
honour
Before, but, gad, my foible is good nature.
One can't be hard upon a friend's infirmities.
De M. I know the King can send me to the
scaffold.
Dark prospect! — but I'm used to it; and if
The Church and Council, by this hour to-
morrow,
One way or other settle not the matter,
I will —
De B. What, my dear Sir?
De M. Show you the door,
My dear, dear Sir; talk as I please, with whom
I please, in my own house, dear Sir, until
His Majesty shall condescend to find
A stouter gentleman than you, dear Sir,
To take me out: and now you understand me,
My dear, most dear — Oh, damnably dear
Sir!
De B. What! almost in a passion! you will
cool
Upon reflection. Well, since *Madame's*
absent,
I'll take a small refreshment. Now, don't stir;
Be careful; — how's your burgundy? — I'll
taste it —
Finish it all before I leave. Nay,
No form; — you see. I make myself at home.
Exit De Beringhen.

De M. (*Going to the door, through which
Baradas had passed*) Baradas! Count!

Enter Baradas.

You spoke of snares — of vengeance
Sharper than death — be plainer.
Bar. What so clear?
Richelieu has but two passions —
De M. Richelieu!
Bar. Yes!
Ambition and revenge — in you both
blended.
First for ambition — Julie is his ward,
Innocent — docile — pliant to his will —

He placed her at the Court — foresaw the
   rest —
The King loves Julie!
   De M. Merciful Heaven! The King!
   Bar. Such Cupids lend new plumes to
   Richelieu's wings:
But the Court etiquette must give such
   Cupids
The veil of Hymen — (Hymen but in name).
He looked abroad — found you his foe; —
   thus served
Ambition — by the grandeur of his ward.
And vengeance — by dishonour to his foe!
   De M. Prove this.
   Bar. You have the proof — The royal
   Letter: —
Your strange exemption from the general
   pardon,
Known but to me and Richelieu; can you
   doubt
Your friend to acquit your foe? The truth is
   glaring —
Richelieu alone could tell the princely lover
The tale which sells your life, — or buys
   your honour!
   De M. I see it all! Mock pardon — hurried
   nuptials!
False bounty! — all! — the serpent of that
   smile!
Oh! it stings home!
   Bar. You yet shall crush his malice;
Our plans are sure: — Orleans is at our head;
We meet to-night; join us, and with us
   triumph.
   De M. To-night? — Oh Heaven! — my
   marriage night! — Revenge!
   Bar. (*Unheeding him*) As yet the Fiend
   that serves hath saved his power
From every snare; and in the epitaphs
Of many victims dwells a warning moral
That preaches caution. Were I not assured
That what before was hope is ripen'd now
Into most certain safety, trust me, Mauprat,
I still could hush my hate and mark my
   wrongs,
And say "Be patient!" — *Now*, the King
   himself
Smiles kindly when I tell him that his peers
Will rid him of his Priest. You knit your
   brows,
Noble impatience! — Pass we to our scheme!
'Tis Richelieu's wont, each morn, within his
   chapel,
(Hypocrite worship ended) to dispense
Alms to the Mendicant friars, — in that
   guise
A band (yourself the leader) shall surround
And seize the despot.
   De M. But the King? but Julie?

   Bar. The King, infirm in health, in mind
   more feeble,
Is but the plaything of a Minister's will.
Were Richelieu dead — his power were mine;
   and Louis
Soon shall forget his passion and your crime.
But whither now?
   De M. I know not; I scarce hear thee;
A little while for thought anon I'll join thee;
But now, all air seems tainted, and I loathe
The face of man!
         *Exit De Mauprat, through the
         gardens.*
   Bar. Start from the chase, my prey,
But as thou speed'st the hell-hounds of
   Revenge
Pant in thy track and dog thee down.

*Enter De Beringhen, his mouth full, a napkin
        in his hand.*

   De B. Chevalier,
Your cook's a miracle — what, my Host
   gone?
Faith, Count, my office is a post of danger —
A fiery fellow, Mauprat! — touch and go, —
Match and saltpetre, — pr-r-r-r!
   Bar. You
Will be released ere long. The King resolves
To call the bride to Court this day.
   De B. Poor Mauprat!
Yet, since *you* love the lady why so careless
Of the King's suit!
   Bar. Because the lady's virtuous,
And the King timid. Ere he win the suit
He'll lose the crown, — the bride will be a
   widow —
And I — the Richelieu of the Regent Orleans.
   De B. Is Louis still so chafed against the
   Fox,
For snatching yon fair dainty from the Lion?
   Bar. So chafed that Richelieu totters.
   Yes, the King
Is half conspirator against the Cardinal.
Enough of this. I've found the man we
   wanted, —
The man to head the hands that murder
   Richelieu —
The man, whose name the synonym for
   daring.
   De B. He must mean me! No, Count, I am
   — I own,
A valiant dog — but still —
   Bar. Whom can I mean
But Mauprat? — Mark, to-night we meet at
   Marion's,
There shall we sign: — thence send this
   scroll (*Showing it*) to Bouillon.
You're in that secret (*Affectionately*) one
   of our new Council.

De B. But to admit the Spaniard —
France's foe —
Into the heart of France, — dethrone the
King, —
It looks like treason, and I smell the heads-
man.
Bar. Oh, Sir, too late to falter: when we
meet
We must arrange the separate — coarser
scheme,
For Richelieu's death. Of this despatch
Mauprat
Must nothing learn. He only bites at ven-
geance,
And he would start from treason. — We must
post him
Without the door at Marion's — as a sentry.
(*Aside*) — So, when his head is on the block
— his tongue —
Cannot betray our more august designs!
De B. I'll meet you, if the King can spare
me. — (*Aside*) — No!
I am too old a goose to play with foxes,
I'll roost at home. Meanwhile in the next
room
There's a delicious pâté, let's discuss it.
Bar. Pshaw! a man fill'd with a sublime
ambition
Has no time to discuss your pâtés.
De B. Pshaw!
And a man fill'd with as sublime a pâté
Has no time to discuss ambition. — Gad,
I have the best of it!

Enter Julie hastily with first Courtier.

Julie. (*To Courtier*) A summons, Sir,
To attend the Louvre? — On *this* day, too?
Courtier. Madame,
The royal carriage waits below. — Messire
(*To De Beringhen*),
You will return with us.
Julie. What can this mean? —
Where is my husband?
Bar. He has left the house
Perhaps till nightfall — so he bade me tell
you.
Alas, were I the Lord of such fair treasure —
Julie. (*Impatiently*) Till nightfall? —
Strange — my heart misgives me!
Courtier. Madame,
My orders will not brook delay.
Julie. (*To Baradas*) You'll see him —
And you will tell him!
Bar. From the flowers of Hybla
Never more gladly did the bee bear honey,
Than I take sweetness from those rosiest lips,
Though to the hive of others!
Courtier. (*To De Beringhen*) Come, Mes-
sire.

De B. (*Hesitating*) One moment, just to —
Courtier. Come, Sir.
De B. I shall not
Discuss the pâté after all. 'Ecod,
I'm puzzled now. I don't know who's the best
of it!

*Exeunt Julie, De Beringhen, and
Courtier.*

Bar. Now will this fire his fever into
madness!
All is made clear! Mauprat *must* murder
Richelieu —
Die for that crime; — I shall console his
Julie —
This will reach Bouillon! — from the wrecks
of France
I shall carve out — who knows — perchance
a throne!
All in despite of my Lord Cardinal.

Enter De Mauprat from the Gardens.

De M. Speak! can it be? — Methought,
that from the terrace
I saw the carriage of the King — and Julie!
No, — no, — my frenzy peoples the void air
With its own phantoms!
Bar. Nay, too true. Alas!
Was ever lightning swifter or more blasting,
Than Richelieu's forked guile?
De M. I'll to the Louvre —
Bar. And lose all hope! — The Louvre! —
the sure gate
To the Bastile!
De M. The King —
Bar. Is but the wax,
Which Richelieu stamps! Break the malig-
nant seal
And I will rase the print! Come, man, take
heart!
Her virtue well could brave a sterner trial
Than a few hours of cold imperious court-
ship.
Were Richelieu *dust* — no danger!
De M. Ghastly Vengeance!
To thee and thine august and solemn sister
The unrelenting Death! I dedicate
The blood of Armand Richelieu. When Dis-
honour
Reaches our hearths Law dies, and Murther
takes
The angel shape of Justice!
Bar. Bravely said!
At midnight, — Marion's! — Nay, I cannot
leave thee
To thoughts that —
De M. Speak not to me! — I am yours! —
But speak not! There's a voice within my
soul,

Whose cry could drown the thunder! — Oh,
    if men
Will play dark sorcery with the heart of man,
Let them, who raise the spell, beware the
    Fiend!   *Exeunt.*

Scene 2.

*A room in the Palais Cardinal (as in the First
Act).*

*Richelieu and Joseph. François, writing at a
    table.*

Jos. Yes, — Huguet, taking his accustom'd
    round, —
Disguised as some plain burgher, — heard
    these rufflers
Quoting your name: — he listen'd, —
    "Pshaw!" said one.
"We are to seize the Cardinal in his palace
To-morrow!" — "How?" the other ask'd —
    "You'll hear
The whole design to-night; the Duke of
    Orleans
And Baradas have got the map of action
At their fingers' end." — "So, be it," quoth
    the other,
"I will be there, — Marion de Lorme's — at
    midnight!"
    Rich. I have them, man, I have them!
    Jos. So they say
Of you, my Lord; — believe me, that their
    plans
Are mightier than you deem. You must
    employ
Means no less vast to meet them.
    Rich. Bah! in policy
We foil gigantic danger, not by giants,
But dwarfs. — The statues of our stately
    fortune
Are sculptured by the chisel — not the axe!
Ah, were I younger — by the knightly heart
That beats beneath these priestly robes, I
    would
Have pastime with these cutthroats! Yea —
    as when,
Lured to the ambush of the expecting foe, —
I clove my pathway through the plumèd sea!
Reach me yon falchion, François, — not
    that bauble
For carpet-warriors — yonder — such a blade
As old Charles Martel might have wielded,
    when
He drove the Saracen from France.
    *François brings him one of the long
    two-handed swords worn in the mid-
    dle ages.*
With this
I, at Rochelle, did hand to hand engage
The stalwart Englisher — no mongrels, boy,

Those island mastiffs — mark the notch — a
    deep one —
His casque made here, — I shore him to the
    waist!
A toy — a feather — then! (*Tries to wield,
    and lets it fall*) You see a child could
Slay Richelieu now.
    Fran. (*His hand on his hilt*) But *now*, at
    your command
Are other weapons, my good Lord.
    Rich. (*Who has seated himself as to write,
    lifts the pen*) True, THIS!
Beneath the rule of men entirely great
The pen is mightier than the sword. Behold
The arch-enchanter's wand! — itself a noth-
    ing!
But taking sorcery from the master hand
To paralyse the Caesars — and to strike
The loud earth breathless! — Take away the
    sword;
States can be saved without it! (*Looking on the
    clock*) 'Tis the hour!
Retire, sir.   *Exit François.*
    *A knock — A door concealed in the
    arras opens cautiously.*

Enter Marion De Lorme.

Jos. (*Amazed*) Marion de Lorme!
    Rich. Hist! — Joseph,
Keep guard.
    *Joseph retires to the principal en-
    trance.*
My faithful Marion!
    Mar. Good my Lord,
They meet to-night in my poor house. The
    Duke
Of Orleans heads them.
    Rich. Yes; go on.
    Mar. His Highness
Much question'd if I knew some brave, dis-
    creet,
And vigilant man, whose tongue could keep a
    secret,
And who had those twin qualities for service,
The love of gold, the hate of Richelieu.
    Rich. You —
    Mar. Made answer, "Yes, my brother; —
    bold and trusty:
Whose faith, my faith could pledge;" — the
    Duke then bade me
Have him equipp'd and arm'd — well
    mounted — ready
This night to part for Italy.
    Rich. Aha! —
Has Bouillon too turn'd traitor? — So me-
    thought!
What part of Italy?
    Mar. The Piedmont frontier,
Where Bouillon lies encamp'd.

Rich. Now there is danger!
Great danger! If he tamper with the Spaniard,
And Louis list not to my council, as,
Without sure proof he will not, France is
lost.
What more?
  Mar. Dark hints of some design to seize
Your person in your palace. Nothing clear —
His Highness trembled while he spoke — the
words
Did choke each other.
  Rich. So! — Who is the brother
You recommended to the Duke?
  Mar. Whoever
Your Eminence may father!
  Rich. Darling Marion!
    Goes to the table, and returns with a
    large bag of gold.
There — pshaw — a trifle! What an eye you
have!
And what a smile, child! — (*Kisses her*)
  — Ah! you fair perdition —
'Tis well I'm old!
  Mar. (*Aside and seriously*) What a great
man he is!
  Rich. You are sure they meet? — the
hour?
  Mar. At midnight.
  Rich. And
You will engage to give the Duke's despatch
To whom I send?
  Mar. Aye, marry!
  Rich. (*Aside*) Huguet? No;
He will be wanted elsewhere. Joseph? —
  zealous,
But too well known — too much the *elder*
brother!
Mauprat? — alas, it is his wedding-day!
François? — the Man of Men! — unnoted —
  young,
Ambitious — (*Goes to the door*) François!

    Enter François.

Follow this fair lady:
(Find him the suiting garments, Marion;)
  take
My fleetest steed; arm thyself to the teeth;
A packet will be given you, with orders,
No matter what! The instant that your hand
Closes upon it, clutch *it*, like your honour,
Which Death alone can steal, or ravish: set
Spurs to your steed — be breathless, till you
  stand
Again before me. Stay, Sir! — You will find
  me
Two short leagues hence — at Ruelle, in my
  castle.
Young man, be blithe! for — note me —
  from the hour

I grasp that packet, think your guardian star
Rains fortune on you!
  Fran. If I fail —
  Rich. Fail — fail?
In the lexicon of youth, which Fate reserves
For a bright manhood, there is no such word
As — *fail!* — (You will instruct him further,
  Marion.)
Follow her — but at distance; — speak not
to her,
Till you are housed — Farewell, boy! Never
  say
"*Fail*" again.
  Fran. I will not!
  Rich. (*Patting his locks*) There's my young
hero! —   *Exeunt François and Marion.*
So they would seize my person in this
  palace?
I cannot guess their scheme: — but my
  retinue
Is here too large! A single traitor could
Strike impotent the faith of thousands; —
  Joseph,
Art sure of Huguet? — Think — we hang'd
  his father?
  Jos. But you have bought the son; —
heap'd favours on him!
  Rich. Trash! — favours past — that's
nothing; in his hours
Of confidence with you, has he named the
favours
To *come* he counts on?
  Jos. Yes: — a Colonel's rank,
And Letters of Nobility.
  Rich. What, Huguet! —
    Here Huguet enters, as to address the
    Cardinal, who does not perceive him.
  Hug. My own name, soft —
    Glides behind the screen.
  Rich. Colonel and Nobleman!
My bashful Huguet — that can never be! —
We have him not the less — we'll *promise* it!
And see the King withholds! — Ah, Kings
are oft
A great convenience to a minister!
No wrong to Huguet either! — Moralists
Say, Hope is sweeter than Possession! Yes —
We'll count on Huguet! Favours *past* do
  gorge
Our dogs; leave service drowsy — *dull* the
  scent,
Slacken the speed; — favours *to come*, my
  Joseph,
Produce a lusty, hungry gratitude,
A ravenous zeal, that of the commonest cur
Would make a Cerberus. — You are right,
  this treason
Assumes a fearful aspect; — but once
  crush'd,

Its very ashes shall manure the soil
Of power: and ripen such full sheaves of
greatness,
That all the summer of my fate shall seem
Fruitless beside the autumn!

*Huguet holds up his hand menacingly
and creeps out.*

Jos. The saints grant it!
Rich. (*Solemnly*) Yes — for sweet France,
Heaven grant it! — O my country,
For thee — thee only — though men deem
it not —
Are toil and terror my familiars! — I
Have made thee great and fair — upon thy
brows
Wreath'd the old Roman laurel; — at thy feet
Bow'd nations down. — No pulse in my
ambition
Whose beatings were not measured from thy
heart!
We Priests, to whom the Church forbids in
youth
The plighted one — to manhood's toil denies
The soother helpmate — from our wither'd
age
Shuts the sweet blossoms of the second spring
That smiles in the name of Father — We are
yet
Not holier than Humanity and must
Fulfil Humanity's condition — Love!
Debarr'd the Actual, we but breathe a life
To the chill Marble of the Ideal — Thus,
In thy unseen and abstract Majesty,
My France — my Country, I have bodied
forth
A thing to love. What are these robes of
state,
This pomp, this palace? perishable baubles!
In this world two things only are immortal:
Fame and a People!

Enter Huguet.

Hug. My Lord Cardinal,
Your Eminence bade me seek you at this
hour.
Rich. Did I? — True, Huguet. — So —
you overheard
Strange talk amongst these gallants? Snares
and traps
For Richelieu? — Well — we'll balk them;
let me think, —
The men-at-arms you head — how many?
Hug. Twenty,
My Lord.
Rich. All trusty?
Hug. Yes, for ordinary
Occasions — if for great ones, I would
change
Three-fourths at least!

Rich. Ay, what are great occasions?
Hug. Great bribes!
Rich. (*To Joseph*) Good lack, he knows
some paragons
Superior to great bribes!
Hug. True Gentlemen
Who have transgress'd the Laws — and value
life
And lack not gold; your Eminence alone
Can grant them pardon. *Ergo* you can trust
them!
Rich. Logic! — So be it — let this *honest*
twenty
Be arm'd and mounted. — (*Aside*) So they
meet at midnight,
The attempt on me to-morrow. Ho! we'll strike
'Twixt wind and water. — (*Aloud*) Does it
need much time
To find these ornaments to Human Nature?
Hug. My Lord — the trustiest of them are
not birds
That love the daylight. — I do know a haunt
Where they meet nightly.
Rich. Ere the dawn be grey,
All could be arm'd, assembled, and at Ruelle
In my own hall?
Hug. By one hour after midnight.
Rich. The castle's strong. You know its
outlets, Huguet?
Would twenty men, well posted, keep such
guard
That no one step (and Murther's step is
stealthy)
Could glide within — unseen?
Hug. A triple wall,
A drawbridge and portcullis — twenty
men —
Under my lead, a month might hold that
castle
Against a host.
Rich. They do not strike till morning,
Yet I will shift the quarter — Bid the grooms
Prepare the litter — I will to Ruelle
While daylight last — and one hour after
midnight
You and your twenty saints shall seek me
thither!
You're made to rise! — You are, Sir —
Eyes of lynx,
Ears of the stag, a footfall like the snow;
You are a valiant fellow; — yea, a trusty,
Religious, exemplary, incorrupt,
And precious jewel of a fellow, Huguet!
If I live long enough — ay, mark my words —
If I live long enough, you'll be a Colonel, —
Noble, perhaps! — One hour, Sir, after mid-
night.
Hug. You leave me dumb with gratitude,
my lord;

I'll pick the trustiest (*Aside*) Marion's house
    can furnish!   *Exit Huguet.*
Rich. How like a spider shall I sit in my
    hole,
And watch the meshes tremble.
    Jos. But, my Lord,
Were it not wiser still to man the palace,
And seize the traitors in the act?
    Rich. No; Louis,
Long chafed against me—Julie stolen from him,
Will rouse him more, — He'll say I hatch'd
    the treason,
Or scout my charge — He half desires my
    death:
But the despatch to Bouillon, some dark
    scheme
Against *his* crown — there is our weapon,
    Joseph!
With that all safe — without it, all is peril!
Meanwhile to my old castle; *you* to Court,
Diving with careless eyes into men's hearts
As ghostly churchmen should do! See the
    King,
Bid him pursue that sage and holy treatise,
Wherein 'tis set forth how a Premier should
Be chosen from the Priesthood — how the
    King
Should never listen to a single charge
Against his servant, nor conceal one whisper
That the rank envies of a Court distill
Into his ear — to fester the fair name
Of my — I mean his Minister! — Oh! Joseph,
A most convincing treatise.
Good! all favours,
If François be but bold, and Huguet hon-
    est. —
Huguet — I half suspect — he bow'd too
    low —
'Tis not his way.
    Jos. This is the curse, my Lord,
Of your high state; — suspicion of all men.
    Rich. (*Sadly*) True; — true; — my leeches
    bribed to poisoners; — pages
To strangle me in sleep. — My very King
(This brain the unresting loom, from which
    was woven
The purple of his greatness) leagued against
    me.
Old — childless — friendless — broken —
    all forsake —
All — all — but —
    Jos. What?
    Rich. The indomitable heart
Of Armand Richelieu!
    Jos. Nought beside?
    Rich. Why, Julie,
My own foster-child, forgive me! — yes;
This morning, shining through their happy
    tears,

Thy soft eyes bless'd me! and thy Lord, — in
    danger
He would forsake me not.
    Jos. And Joseph —
    Rich. (*After a pause*) You —
Yes, I believe you — yes — for all men fear
    you —
And the world loves you not. — And I,
    friend Joseph,
I am the only man who could, my Joseph,
Make you a Bishop — Come, we'll go to
    dinner,
And talk the while of methods to advance
Our Mother Church — Ah, Joseph — *Bishop
Joseph!*   *Exeunt.*

End of the Second Act.

Act III.

Scene 1.

Second day (*midnight*). *Richelieu's castle at
Ruelle. A Gothic chamber. Moonlight at the
window, occasionally obscured.*
    Rich. (*Reading*) "In silence, and at night,
    the Conscience feels
That life should soar to nobler ends than
    Power."
So sayest thou, sage and sober moralist!
But wert thou tried? Sublime Philosophy,
Thou art the Patriarch's ladder, reaching
    heaven,
And bright with beck'ning angels — but,
    alas!
We see thee, like the Patriarch, but in
    dreams,
By the first step — dull-slumbering on the
    earth.
I am not happy! — with the Titan's lust,
I woo'd a goddess, and I clasp a cloud.
When I am dust, my name shall, like a star,
Shine through wan space, a glory — and a
    prophet
Whereby pale seers shall from their aery
    towers
Con all the ominous signs, benign or evil,
That make the potent astrologue of kings.
But shall the Future judge me by the ends
That I have wrought — or by the dubious
    means
Through which the stream of my renown
    hath run
Into the many-voiced unfathomed Time?
Foul in its bed lie weeds — and heaps of
    slime,
And with its waves — when sparkling in the
    sun,

Oft times the secret rivulets that swell
Its might of waters — blend the hues of
    blood.
Yet are my sins not those of CIRCUMSTANCE,
That all-pervading atmosphere wherein
Our spirits like the unsteady lizard, take
The tints that colour, and the food that
    nurtures?
Oh! ye, whose hour-glass shifts its tranquil
    sands
In the unvex'd silence of a student's cell;
Ye, whose untempted hearts have never
    toss'd
Upon the dark and stormy tides where life
Gives battle to the elements, — and man
Wrestles with man for some slight plank,
    whose weight
Will bear but one — while round the desper-
    ate wretch
The hungry billows roar — and the fierce
    Fate,
Like some huge monster, dim-seen through
    the surf,
Waits him who drops; — ye safe and formal
    men,
Who write the deeds, and with unfeverish
    hand
Weigh in nice scales the motives of the
    Great,
Ye cannot know what ye have never tried!
History preserves only the fleshless bones
Of what we are — and by the mocking skull
The would-be wise pretend to guess the
    features!
Without the roundness and the glow of life
How hideous is the skeleton! Without
The colourings and humanities that clothe
Our errors, the anatomists of schools
Can make our memory hideous! I have
    wrought
Great uses out of evil tools — and they
In the time to come may bask beneath the
    light
Which I have stolen from the angry gods,
And warn their sons against the glorious
    theft,
Forgetful of the darkness which it broke.
I have shed blood — but I have had no foes
Save those the State had — if my wrath was
    deadly,
'Tis that I felt my country in my veins,
And smote her sons as Brutus smote his own.
And yet I am not happy — blanch'd and
    sear'd
Before my time — breathing an air of hate,
And seeing daggers in the eyes of men,
And wasting powers that shake the thrones of
    earth
In contest with the insects — bearding kings

And braved by lackies — murder at my bed;
And lone amidst the multitudinous web,
With the dread Three — that are the fates
    who hold
The woof and shears — the Monk, the Spy,
    the Headsman.
And this is Power! Alas! I am not happy.
    (After a pause)
And yet the Nile is fretted by the weeds
Its rising roots not up: but never yet
Did one least barrier by a ripple vex
My onward tide, unswept in sport away.
Am I so ruthless then that I do hate
Them who hate me? Tush, tush! I do not
    hate;
Nay, I forgive. The Statesman writes the
    doom,
But the Priest sends the blessing. I forgive
    them,
But I destroy; forgiveness is my own,
Destruction is the State's! For private life,
Scripture the guide — for public, Machiavel.
Would Fortune serve me if the Heaven were
    wroth?
For chance makes half my greatness. I was
    born
Beneath the aspect of a bright-eyed star,
And my triumphant adamant of soul
Is but the fix'd persuasion of success.
Ah! — here! — that spasm! — Again! How
    Life and Death
Do wrestle for me momently! And yet
The King looks pale. I shall outlive the King!
And then, thou insolent Austrian — who
    didst gibe
At the ungainly, gaunt, and daring lover,
Sleeking thy looks to silken Buckingham, —
Thou shalt — no matter! I have outlived
    love.
O! beautiful — all golden — gentle Youth!
Making thy palace in the careless front
And hopeful eye of man — ere yet the soul
Hath lost the memories which (so Plato
    dream'd)
Breath'd glory from the earlier star it dwelt
    in —
O! for one gale from thine exulting morning,
Stirring amidst the roses, where of old
Love shook the dew-drops from his glancing
    hair!
Could I recall the past — or had not set
The prodigal treasures of the bankrupt soul
In one slight bark upon the shoreless sea;
The yoked steer, after his day of toil,
Forgets the goad and rests — to me alike
Or day or night — Ambition has no rest!
Shall I resign — who can resign himself?
For custom is ourself; — as drink and food
Become our bone and flesh — the aliments

Nurturing our nobler part, the mind —
  thoughts, dreams,
Passions, and aims, in the revolving cycle
Of the great alchemy — at length are made
Our mind itself; and yet the sweets of lei-
  sure —
An honour'd home — far from these base
  intrigues —
An eyrie on the heaven-kiss'd heights of
  wisdom.   (*Taking up the book*)
Speak to me, moralist! I will heed thy
  counsel.
Were it not best —

Enter François, hastily and in part disguised.

  (*Flinging away the book*) Philosophy, thou
  liest!
Quick — the despatch! — Power — Empire!
  Boy — the packet!
  Fran. Kill me, my Lord.
  Rich. They knew thee — they suspected —
They gave it not —
  Fran. He gave it — *he* — the Count
De Baradas — with his own hand he gave
  it!
  Rich. Baradas! Joy! out with it!
  Fran. Listen,
And then dismiss me to the headsman.
  Rich. Ha!
Go on.
  Fran. They led me to a chamber — There
Orleans and Baradas — and some halfscore
Whom I knew not — were met —
  Rich. Not more!
  Fran. But from
The adjoining chamber broke the din of
  voices,
The clattering tread of armed men; — at
  times
A shriller cry, that yell'd out, "Death to
  Richelieu!"
  Rich. Speak not of *me:* thy *country* is in
  danger!
The adjoining room. — So, so — a *separate*
  treason!
The one thy ruin, France! — the meaner
  crime,
Left to their tools, my murder!
  Fran. Baradas
Questioned me close — demurr'd — until,
  at last,
O'erruled by Orleans, — gave the packet —
  told me
That life and death were in the scroll — this
  gold —
  Rich. Gold is no proof —
  Fran. And Orleans promised thousands,
When Bouillon's trumpets in the streets of
  Paris

Rang out shrill answer; hastening from the
  house,
My footstep in the stirrup, Marion stole
Across the threshold, whispering "Lose no
  moment
Ere Richelieu have the packet: tell him too —
Murder is it the winds of Night, and Orleans
Swears, ere the dawn the Cardinal shall be
  clay."
She said, and trembling fled within; when,
  lo!
A hand of iron griped me; thro' the dark
Gleam'd the dim shadow of an armed man:
Ere I could draw — the prize was wrested
  from me,
And a hoarse voice gasp'd — "Spy, I spare
  thee, for
This steel is virgin to thy Lord!" — with
  that
He vanish'd. — Scared and trembling for thy
  safety,
I mounted, fled, and, kneeling at thy feet,
Implore thee to acquit my faith — but not,
Like him, to spare my life.
  Rich. Who spake of *life?*
I bade thee grasp that treasure as thine
  honour —
A jewel worth whole hecatombs of lives!
Begone — redeem thine honour — back to
  Marion —
Or Baradas or Orleans — track the robber —
Regain the packet — or crawl on to Age —
Age and grey hairs like mine — and know,
  thou hast lost
That which had made thee great and saved
  thy country.
See me not till thou'st bought the right to
  seek me.
Away! — Nay, cheer thee — thou hast not
  fail'd yet —
There's no such word as "fail!"
  Fran. Bless you, my Lord,
For that one smile! I'll wear it on my heart
To light me back to triumph.   *Exit.*
  Rich. The poor youth!
An elder had ask'd life! I love the young!
For as great men live not in their own
  time
But the next race, — so in the young, my
  soul
Makes many Richelieus. He will win it yet.
François! He's gone. My murder! Marion's
  warning!
This bravo's threat! O for the morrow's
  dawn!
I'll set my spies to work — I'll make all space
(As does the sun) an Universal Eye —
Huguet shall track — Joseph confess — ha!
  ha!

Strange, while I laugh'd I shudder'd, and
ev'n now
Thro' the chill air the beating of my heart
Sounds like a death-watch by a sick man's
pillow;
If Huguet *could* deceive me — hoofs with-
out —
The gates unclose — steps near and nearer!

Enter Julie.

Julie. Cardinal!
My father!   *Falls at his feet.*
  Rich. Julie at this hour! — and tears!
What ails thee?
  Julie. I am safe; I am with thee! —
  Rich. Safe! why in all the storms of this
wild world
What wind would mar the violet?
  Julie. That man —
Why did I love him? — clinging to a breast
That knows no shelter? Listen — late at
noon —
The marriage-day — ev'n then no more a
lover —
He left me coldly, — well, — I sought my
chamber
To weep and wonder — but to hope and
dream.
Sudden a mandate from the King — to attend
Forthwith his pleasure at the Louvre.
  Rich. Ha! —
You did obey the summons; and the King
Reproach'd your hasty nuptials. —
  Julie. Were that all!
He frown'd and chid; — proclaim'd the bond
unlawful:
Bade me not quit my chamber in the palace,
And there at night — alone — this night —
all still —
He sought my presence — dared — thou
read'st the heart,
Read mine! — I cannot speak it!
  Rich. He a king, —
You — woman; well, you yielded!
  Julie. Cardinal —
Dare you say "yielded"? — Humbled and
abash'd,
He from the chamber crept — this mighty
Louis;
Crept like a baffled felon! — yielded! Ah!
More royalty in woman's honest heart
Than dwells within the crowned majesty
And sceptred anger of a hundred kings!
Yielded! — Heavens! — yielded!
  Rich. To my breast, — close — close!
The world would never need a Richelieu, if
Men — bearded, mailed men — the Lords of
Earth —
Resisted flattery, falsehood, avarice, pride,

As this poor child with the dove's innocent
scorn
Her sex's tempters, Vanity and Power! —
He left you — well!
  Julie. Then came a sharper trial!
At the King's suit the Count de Baradas
Sought me to soothe, to fawn, to flatter, while
On his smooth lip insult appear'd more hate-
ful
For the false mask of pity: letting fall
Dark hints of treachery, with a world of sighs
That heaven had granted to so base a Lord
The heart whose coldest friendship were to
him
What Mexico to misers! Stung at last
By my disdain, the dim and glimmering sense
Of his cloak'd words broke into bolder light,
And THEN — ah, then, my haughty spirit
fail'd me!
Then I was weak — wept — oh! such bitter
tears!
For (turn thy face aside, and let me whisper
The horror to thine ear) then did I learn
That he — that Adrien — that my husband
— knew
The King's polluting suit, and deemed it
honour!
Then all the terrible and loathsome truth
Glared on me; — coldness — waywardness
— reserve —
Mystery of looks — words — all unravell'd,
— and
I saw the impostor, where I had loved the
God! —
  Rich. I think thou wrong'st thy husband
— but proceed.
  Julie. Did you say "wrong'd" him? —
Cardinal, my father,
Did you say "wrong'd"? Prove it, and life
shall grow
One prayer for thy reward and his forgive-
ness.
  Rich. Let me know all.
  Julie. To the despair he caused
The courtier left me; but amid the chaos
Darted one guiding ray — to 'scape — to
fly —
Reach Adrien, learn the worst — 'twas then
near midnight:
Trembling I left my chamber — sought the
Queen —
Fell at her feet — reveal'd the unholy
peril —
Implored her aid to flee our joint disgrace.
Moved, she embraced and soothed me; nay,
preserved;
Her word sufficed to unlock the palace-gates:
I hasten'd home — but home was desolate, —
No Adrien there! Fearing the worst, I fled

To thee, directed hither. As my wheels
Paused at thy gates — the clang of arms
    behind —
The ring of hoofs —
    Rich. 'Twas but my guards, fair trembler.
(So Huguet keeps his word, my omens
    wrong'd him.)
    Julie. Oh, in one hour what years of
    anguish crowd!
    Rich. Nay, there's no danger now. Thou
    need'st rest.
Come, thou shalt lodge beside me. Tush!
    be cheer'd,
My rosiest Amazon — thou wrong'st thy
    Theseus.
All will be well — yes, yet all well.
        Exeunt through a side door.

Scene 2.

The moonlight obscured at the casement.

Enter Huguet, De Mauprat, in complete armour,
    his vizor down.

    Hug. Not here!
    De M. Oh, I will find him, fear not. Hence,
    and guard
The galleries where the menials sleep —
    plant sentries
At every outlet. Chance should throw no
    shadow
Between the vengeance and the victim! Go!
Ere yon brief vapour that obscures the moon,
As doth our deed pale conscience, pass away,
The mighty shall be ashes.
    Hug. Will you not
A second arm?
    De M. To slay one weak old man?
Away! No lesser wrongs than mine can make
This murder lawful. — Hence!
    Hug. A short farewell!   *Exit.*
Re-enter Richelieu, not perceiving De Mauprat.

    Rich. How heavy is the air! the vestal lamp
Of the sad moon, weary with vigil, dies
In the still temple of the solemn heaven!
The very darkness lends itself to fear —
To treason —
    De M. And to death!
    Rich. My omens lied not!
What art thou, wretch?
    De M. Thy doomsman!
    Rich. Ho, my guards!
Huguet! Montbrassil! Vermont!
    De M. Ay, thy spirits
Forsake thee, wizard; thy bold men of mail
Are *my confederates.* Stir not! but one step,
And know the next — thy grave!
    Rich. Thou liest, knave!
I am old, infirm — most feeble — but thou
    liest!

Armand de Richelieu dies not by the hand
Of man — the stars have said it — and the
    voice
Of my own prophetic and oracular soul
Confirms the shining Sibyls! Call them all —
Thy brother butchers! Earth has no such
    fiend —
No! as one parricide of his father-land,
Who dares in Richelieu murder France!
    De M. Thy stars
Deceive thee, Cardinal; thy soul of wiles
May against kings and armaments avail,
And mock the embattled world; but powerless
    now
Against the sword of one resolved man,
Upon whose forehead thou hast written
    shame!
    Rich. I breathe; — he is not a hireling.
Have I wronged thee?
Beware surmise — suspicion — lies! I am
Too great for men to speak the truth of
    me!
    De M. Thy *acts* are thy accusers, Cardinal.
In his hot youth, a soldier, urged to crime
Against the State, placed in your hands his
    life; —
You did not strike the blow, — but, o'er his
    head,
Upon the gossamer thread of your caprice,
Hovered the axe. — His the brave spirit's
    hell,
The twilight terror of suspense; — your
    death
Had set him free. — He purposed not, nor
    prayed it.
One day you summoned — mocked him with
    smooth pardon —
Showered wealth upon him — bade an
    Angel's face
Turn earth to paradise —
    Rich. Well!
    De M. Was this mercy?
A Caesar's generous vengeance? — Cardinal,
    no!
Judas, not Caesar, was the model! You
Saved him from death for shame; reserved to
    grow
The scorn of living men — to his dead sires
Leprous reproach — scoff of the age to
    come —
A kind convenience — a Sir Pandarus
To his own bride, and the august adulterer!
Then did the first great law of human hearts,
Which with the patriot's, not the rebel's
    name
Crowned the first Brutus, when the Tarquin
    fell,
Make Misery royal — raise this desperate
    wretch

Into thy destiny! Expect no mercy!
Behold De Mauprat! *Lifts his visor.*
Rich. To thy knees, and crawl
For pardon; or, I tell thee, thou shalt live
For such remorse, that, did I hate thee, I
Would bid thee strike, that I might be
    avenged!
It was to save my Julie from the King,
That in thy valour I forgave thy crime; —
It was, when thou — the rash and ready
    tool —
Yea of that shame thou loath'st — did'st
    leave thy hearth
To the polluter — in these arms thy bride
Found the protecting shelter thine withheld.
Goes to the side door.
Julie de Mauprat — Julie!

Enter Julie.

Lo, my witness!
    De M. What marvel's this? I dream. My
    Julie — *thou!*
This, thy belovèd hand?
    Julie. Henceforth all bond
Between us twain is broken. Were it not
For this old man, I might, in truth, have
    lost
The right — now mine — to scorn thee!
    Rich. So, you hear her!
    De M. Thou with some slander hast her
    sense infected!
    Julie. No, Sir; he did excuse thee in
    despite
Of all that wears the face of truth. Thy
    friend —
Thy *confidant* — familiar — *Baradas* —
Himself revealed thy baseness.
    De M. Baseness!
    Rich. Ay;
That *thou* didst *court* dishonour.
    De M. Baradas!
Where is thy thunder, Heaven? — Duped! —
    snared! — undone!
Thou — thou could'st not believe him! Thou
    dost love me!
Love cannot feed on falsehood!
    Julie. (*Aside*) Love him! Ah!
Be still, my heart! Love you I did: — how
    fondly,
Woman — if women were my listeners
    now —
Alone could tell! — For ever fled my dream.
Farewell — all's over!
    Rich. Nay, my daughter, these
Are but the blinding mists of day-break love
Sprung from its very light, and heralding
A noon of happy summer. — Take her hand
And speak the truth, with which your heart
    runs over —

That this Count Judas — this Incarnate
    Falsehood —
Never lied more, than when he told thy Julie
That Adrien loved her not — except, indeed,
When he told Adrien, Julie could betray him.
    Julie. (*Embracing De Mauprat*) You love
    me, then! you love me! — and they
    wrong'd you!
    De M. Ah, could'st thou doubt it?
    Rich. Why, the very mole
Less blind than thou! Baradas loves thy
    wife; —
Had hoped her hand — aspired to be that
    cloak
To the King's will, which to thy bluntness
    seems
The Centaur's poisonous robe — hopes even
    now
To make thy corpse his footstool to thy
    bed!
Where was thy wit, man? Ho, these schemes
    are glass!
The very sun shines through them.
    De M. O, my Lord,
Can you forgive me?
    Rich. Ay, and save you!
    De M. Save! —
Terrible word! — O, save *thyself*; these halls
Swarm with thy foes; already for thy blood
Pants thirsty murder!
    Julie. Murder!
    Rich. Hush! put by
The woman. Hush! a shriek — a cry — a
    breath
Too loud, would startle from its horrent
    pause
The swooping Death! Go to the door, and
    listen!
Now for escape!
    De M. None, — none! Their blades shall
    pass
This heart to thine.
    Rich. (*Airily*) An honourable outwork,
But much too near the citadel. I think
That I can trust you now (*Slowly, and gazing
    on him*) — yes; I can trust you.
How many of my troop league with you?
    De M. All! —
We *are* your troop!
    Rich. And Huguet? —
    De M. Is our captain.
    Rich. A retributive Power! This comes of
    spies.
All? then the lion's skin too short tonight, —
Now for the fox's! —
    Julie. A hoarse gathering murmur! —
Hurrying and heavy footsteps! —
    Rich. Ha, the posterns?
    De M. No egress where no sentry!

Rich. Follow me —
I have it! to my chamber — quick! Come,
　Julie!
Hush! Mauprat, come!
　　Murmur at a distance "Death to the
　　　Cardinal!"
Bloodhounds, I laugh at ye!
Ha! ha! we will baffle them yet! Ha! ha!
　　Exeunt Julie, De Mauprat, Richelieu.
Hug. (*Without*) This way — this way!

Scene 3.

Enter Huguet, and the Conspirators.

Hug. De Mauprat's hand is never slow in
　battle; —
Strange, if it falter now! Ha! gone!
First Conspirator. Perchance
The fox had crept to rest! and to his lair
Death, the dark hunter, tracks him.

*Enter De Mauprat, throwing open the doors of
the recess, in which a bed, whereon Richelieu
lies extended.*

De M. Live the King!
Richelieu is dead!
　Hug. (*Advancing towards the recess; De
　Mauprat following, his hand on his dag-
　ger*) Are his eyes open?
De M. Ay.
As if in life!
　Hug. (*Turning back*) I will not look on him.
You have been long.
De M. I watched him till he slept.
Heed me. No trace of blood reveals the
　deed; —
Strangled in sleep. His health hath long been
　broken —
Found breathless in his bed. So runs our tale,
Remember! Back to Paris — Orleans gives
Ten thousand crowns, and Baradas a lord-
　ship,
To him who first gluts vengeance with the
　news
That Richelieu is in Heaven! Quick, that all
　France
May share your joy.
　Hug. And you?
De M. Will stay to crush
Eager suspicion — to forbid sharp eyes
To dwell too closely on the clay; prepare
The rites, and place him on his bier — this
　my task.
I leave to you, Sirs, the more grateful lot
Of wealth and honours. Hence!
　Hug. I shall be noble!
De M. Away!
First Conspirator. Five thousand crowns!
Omnes. To horse! to horse!
　　　　　Exeunt Conspirators.

Scene 4.

*Still night. — A room in the house of Count de
Baradas, lighted, etc.*

Orleans and De Beringhen.

De B. I understand. Mauprat kept guard
　without:
Knows nought of the despatch — but heads
　the troop
Whom the poor Cardinal fancies his pro-
　tectors.
Save us from such protection!
Orl. Yet if Huguet,
By whose advice and proffers we renounced
Our earlier scheme, should still be Riche-
　lieu's minion,
And play us false —
De B. The fox must then devour
The geese he gripes. I'm out of it, thank
　Heaven!
And you must swear you smelt the trick, but
　seem'd
To approve the deed to render up the doers.

Enter Baradas.

Bar. Julie is fled — the King, whom now
　I left
To a most thorny pillow, vows revenge
On her — on Mauprat — and on Richelieu!
　Well;
We loyal men anticipate his wish
Upon the last — and as for Mauprat —
　　　　　(*Showing a writ*)
De B. Hum!
They say the devil invented printing! Faith,
He has some hand in writing parchment —
　eh, Count?
What mischief now?
Bar. The King at Julie's flight
Enraged will brook no rival in a subject —
So on this old offence — the affair of Fa-
　viaux —
Ere Mauprat can tell tales of *us*, we build
His bridge between the dungeon and the
　grave.
Orl. Well; if our courier can but reach the
　army,
The cards are ours! and yet I own, I tremble.
Our names are in the scroll — discovery,
　death!
Bar. Success, a crown!
De B. (*Apart to Baradas*) Our future
　regent is
No hero.
Bar. (*To De Beringhen*) But his rank
　makes others valiant;
And on his cowardice I mount to power.
Were Orleans Regent — what were Baradas?

Oh! by the way — I had forgot, your Highness,
Friend Huguet whisper'd me, "Beware of Marion:
I've seen her lurking near the Cardinal's palace."
Upon that hint — I've found her lodgings elsewhere.
　　Orl. You wrong her, Count: — Poor Marion! she adores me.
　　Bar. (*Apologetically*) Forgive me, but —

Enter Page.

Page. My Lord, a rude, strange soldier,
Breathless with haste, demands an audience.
　　Bar. So!
The Archers!
　　Page. In the ante-room, my Lord,
As you desired.
　　Bar. 'Tis well, admit the soldier.
　　　　　　　　　　　　　　Exit Page.
Huguet! I bade him seek me here!

Enter Huguet.

　　Hug. My Lords,
The deed is done. Now Count, fulfil your word,
And make me noble!
　　Bar. Richelieu dead? — art sure?
How died he?
　　Hug. Strangled in his sleep: — no blood,
No tell-tale violence.
　　Bar. Strangled? monstrous villain!
Reward for murder! Ho, there!　　(*Stamping*)

Enter Captain with five Archers.

　　Hug. No, thou durst not!
　　Bar. Seize on the ruffian — bind him — gag him! Off
To the Bastile!
　　Hug. Your word — your plighted faith!
　　Bar. Insolent liar! — ho, away!
　　Hug. Nay, Count;
I have that about me, which —
　　Bar. Away with him!
　　　　　　　　　　　Exeunt Huguet and Archers.
Now, then, all's safe; Huguet must die in prison,
So Mauprat: — coax or force the meaner crew
To fly the country. Ha, ha! thus your Highness,
Great men make use of little men.
　　De B. My Lords,
Since our suspense is ended — you'll excuse me;
'Tis late, and, *entre nous*, I have not supp'd yet!
I'm one of the new Council now, remember;
I feel the public stirring here already;

A very craving monster. *Au revoir!*
　　　　　　　　　　　Exit De Beringhen.
　　Orl. No fear, now Richelieu's dead.
　　Bar. And could he come
To life again, he could not keep life's life —
His power — nor save De Mauprat from the scaffold, —
Nor Julie from these arms — nor Paris from
The Spaniard — nor your Highness from the throne!
All ours! all ours! in spite of my Lord Cardinal!

Enter Page.

　　Page. A gentleman, my Lord, of better mien
Than he who last —
　　Bar. Well, he may enter.　　*Exit Page.*
　　Orl. Who
Can this be?
　　Bar. One of the conspirators:
Mauprat himself, perhaps.

Enter François.

　　Fran. My Lord —
　　Bar. Ha, traitor!
In Paris still?
　　Fran. The packet — the despatch —
Some knave play'd spy without, and reft it from me,
Ere I could draw my sword.
　　Bar. Play'd spy *without!*
Did he wear armour?
　　Fran. Ay, from head to heel.
　　Orl. One of our band. Oh, heavens!
　　Bar. Could it be Mauprat?
Kept guard at the *door* — knew *naught of the despatch* —
How HE? — and yet, who other?
　　Fran. Ha, De Mauprat
The night was dark — his visor closed.
　　Bar. 'Twas he!
How could he guess? — 'sdeath! if he should betray us.
His hate to Richelieu dies with Richelieu — and
He was not great enough for treason. Hence!
Find Mauprat — beg, steal, filch, or force it back,
Or, as I live, the halter —
　　Fran. By the morrow
I will regain it, (*Aside* and redeem my honour!　　　　*Exit François.*
　　Orl. Oh! we are lost —
　　Bar. Not so! But cause on cause
For Mauprat's seizure — silence — death!
Take courage.
　　Orl. Should it once reach the King, the Cardinal's arm
Could smite us from the grave.

Bar. Sir, think it not!
I hold De Mauprat in my grasp. Tomorrow
And France is ours! Thou dark and fallen
Angel,
Whose name on earth's AMBITION — thou
that mak'st
Thy throne on treasons, stratagems, and
murder —
And with thy fierce and blood-red smile canst
quench
The guiding stars of solemn empire — hear
us —
(For we are thine) — and light us to the
goal!   *Exeunt.*

End of the Third Act.

ACT IV.

Scene 1.

Third day. The gardens of the Louvre.

Orleans, Baradas, De Beringhen, Courtiers, etc

Orl. How does my brother bear the Cardi-
nal's death?
Bar. With grief, when thinking of the
toils of State;
With joy, when thinking on the eyes of
Julie: —
At times he sighs, "Who now shall govern
France?"
Anon exclaims — "Who now shall baffle
Louis?"

Enter Louis and other Courtiers. They uncover.

Orl. Now my Liege, now, I can embrace a
brother.
Louis. Dear Gaston, yes. I do believe you
love me; —
Richelieu denied it — sever'd us too long.
A great man, Gaston! Who shall govern
France?
Bar. Yourself, my Liege. That swart and
potent star
Eclipsed your royal orb. He serv'd the
country,
But did he *serve*, or seek to *sway* the *King*?
Louis. You're right — he was an able
politician,
That's all. — Between ourselves, Count, I
suspect
The largeness of his learning — specially
In falcons — a poor huntsman, too!
Bar. Ha — ha!
Your Majesty remembers —
Louis. Ay, the blunder
Between the *greffier* and the *souillard* when —
(*Checks and crosses himself*)
Alas! poor sinners that we are! we laugh

While this great man — a priest, a cardinal,
A faithful servant — out upon us!
Bar. Sire,
If my brow wear no cloud, 'tis that the
Cardinal
No longer shades the King.
Louis. (*Looking up at the skies*) Oh,
Baradas!
Am I not to be pitied? — what a day
For —
Bar. Sorrow? — No, Sire!
Louis. Bah! for *hunting*, man,
And Richelieu's dead; 'twould be an in-
decorum
Till he is buried (*Yawns*) — life is very
tedious.
I made a madrigal on life last week:
You do not sing, Count? Pity; you should
learn.
Poor Richelieu had no ear — yet a great man.
Ah! what a weary weight devolves upon me!
These endless wars — these thankless Parlia-
ments —
The snares in which he tangled States and
Kings,
Like the old fisher of the fable, Proteus,
Netting great Neptune's wariest tribes, and
changing
Into all shapes when Craft pursued himself:
Oh, a great man!
Bar. Your royal mother said so,
And died in exile.
Louis. (*Sadly*) True: I loved my mother!
Bar. The Cardinal dies. Yet day revives
the earth;
The rivers run not back. In truth, my Liege,
Did your high orb on others shine as him,
Why, things as dull in their own selves as
I am
Would glow as brightly with the borrowed
beam.
Louis. Ahem! He was too stern.
Orl. A very Nero.
Bar. His power was like the Capitol of
old
Built on a human skull.
Louis. And, had he lived,
I know another head, my Baradas,
That would have propp'd the pile: I've seen
him eye thee
With a most hungry fancy.
Bar. (*Anxiously*) Sire, I knew
You would protect me.
Louis. Did you so: of course!
And yet he had a way with him — a some-
thing
That always — But no matter, he is dead.
And, after all, men called his King "The
Just,"

And so I am. Dear Count, this silliest Julie,
I know not why, she takes my fancy. Many
As fair, and certainly more kind; but yet
It is so. Count, I am no lustful Tarquin,
And do abhor the bold and frontless vices
Which the Church justly censures: yet 'tis
    sad
On rainy days to drag out weary hours,
Deaf to the music of a woman's voice —
Blind to the sunshine of a woman's eyes.
It is no sin in kings to seek amusement;
And that is all I seek. I miss her much.
She has a silver laugh — a rare perfection.
   Bar. Richelieu was most disloyal in that
    marriage.
   Louis. (*Querulously*) He knew that Julie
    pleased me — a clear proof
He never loved me!
   Bar. Oh, most clear! — But now
No bar between the lady and your will!
This writ makes all secure: a week or two
In the Bastile will sober Mauprat's love,
And leave him eager to dissolve a hymen
That brings him such a home.
   Louis. See to it, Count;   *Exit Baradas.*
I'll summon Julie back. A word with you.
    Takes aside First Courtier and De
    Beringhen, and passes, conversing
    with them, through the gardens.

    Enter François.

   Fran. All search, as yet, in vain for
    Mauprat! Not
At home since yesternoon — a soldier told
    me
He saw him pass this way with hasty strides;
Should he meet Baradas — they'd rend it
    from him —
And then — benignant Fortune smiles upon
    me —
I am thy son! — if thou desert'st me now,
Come Death and snatch me from disgrace.
    But, no,
There's a great Spirit ever in the air
That from prolific and far-spreading wings
Scatters the seeds of honour — yea, the walls
And moats of castled forts — the barren
    seas —
The cell wherein the pale-eyed student holds
Talk with melodious science — all are sown
With everlasting honours, if our souls
Will toil for fame as boors for bread —

    Enter De Mauprat.

   De M. Oh, let me —
Let me but meet him foot to foot — I'll dig
The Judas from his heart; — albeit the King
Should o'er him cast the purple!
   Fran. Mauprat! hold: —
Where is the —

   De M. Well! What would'st thou?
   Fran. The despatch!
The packet. — Look on me — I serve the
    Cardinal —
You know me. Did you not keep guard last
    night
By Marion's house?
   De M. I did: — no matter now! —
They told me, *he* was *here!* —
   Fran. O joy! quick — quick —
The packet thou didst wrest from me?
   De M. The packet? —
What, art thou he I deem'd the Cardinal's
    spy
(Dupe that I was) — and overhearing
    Marion —
   Fran. The same — restore it! haste!
   De M. I have it not:
Methought it but reveal'd our scheme to
    Richelieu,
And, as we mounted, gave it to —

    Enter Baradas.

Stand back!
Now, villain! now — I have thee!
(*To François*) — Hence, Sir. *Draw!*
   Fran. Art mad? — the King's at hand!
    leave *him* to Richelieu!
Speak — the despatch — to whom —
   De M. (*Dashing him aside, and rushing to*
    Baradas) Thou triple slanderer!
I'll set my heel upon thy crest!
         A few passes.
   Fran. Fly — fly!
The King! —

Enter at one side Louis, Orleans, De Beringhen,
Courtiers, etc. At the other, the Guards hastily.

   Louis. Swords drawn — before our very
    palace!
Have our laws died with Richelieu?
   Bar. Pardon, Sire, —
My crime but self-defence. (*Aside to King*)
    It is De Mauprat!
   Louis. Dare he thus brave us?
    Baradas goes to the Guard and gives
    the writ.
   De M. Sire, in the Cardinal's name —
   Bar. Seize him — disarm — to the Bastile!
    De Mauprat seized, struggles with the
    Guard. — François restlessly endeav-
    ouring to pacify and speak to him —
    when the gates open.

Enter Richelieu and Joseph, followed by
    arquebusiers.

   Bar. The Dead
Return'd to life!
   Louis. What a *mock* death! this tops
The Infinite of Insult.

De M. (*Breaking from Guards*) Priest and Hero!

For you are both — protect the truth! —

Rich. What's this? (*Taking the writ from the Guard*)

De B. Fact in Philosophy. Foxes have got Nine lives as well as cats!

Bar. Be firm, my Liege.

Louis. I have assumed the sceptre — I will wield it!

Jos. The tide runs counter — there'll be shipwreck somewhere.

> *Baradas and Orleans keep close to the King — whispering and prompting him when Richelieu speaks.*

Rich. High treason. — Faviaux! still that stale pretence!

My Liege, bad men (ay, Count, most *knavish* men!)

Abuse your royal goodness. For this soldier, France hath none braver, and his youth's hot folly,

Misled (by whom *your Highness* may conjecture!),

Is long since cancell'd by a loyal manhood.

I, Sire, have pardoned him.

Louis. And we do give Your pardon to the winds. Sir, do your duty!

Rich. What, Sire? you do not know — Oh, pardon me —

You know not yet, that this brave, honest heart

Stood between mine and murder! — Sire, for my sake —

For your old servant's sake — undo this wrong.

See, let me rend the sentence.

Louis. At your peril!

This is too much: — Again, Sir, do your duty!

Rich. Speak not, but go: — I would not see young Valour

So humbled as grey Service!

De M. Fare you well!

Save Julie and console her.

Fran. (*Aside to De Mauprat*) The despatch! Your fate, foes, life, hang on a word! to whom?

De M. To Huguet.

Fran. Hush! — keep counsel! silence — hope!   *Exeunt De Mauprat and Guard.*

Bar. (*Aside to François*) Has he the packet?

Fran. He will not reveal —

(*Aside*) Work, brain! beat, heart!

"There's no such word as fail."
Exit François.

Rich. (*Fiercely*) Room, my Lords, room! — the Minister of France

Can need no intercession with the King.
They fall back.

Louis. What means this false report of death, Lord Cardinal?

Rich. Are you then anger'd, Sire, that I live still?

Louis. No; but such artifice —

Rich. Not mine: — look elsewhere!

Louis — my castle swarm'd with the assassins.

Bar. (*Advancing*) We have punish'd them already. Huguet now

In the Bastile. Oh! my Lord, *we* were prompt To avenge you, *we* were.

Rich. We? Ha! ha! you hear,

My Liege! What page, man, in the last court grammar

Made you a plural? Count, you have seized the *hireling:* —

Sire, shall I name the *master?*

Louis. Tush! my Lord, The old contrivance: — ever does your wit Invent assassins, — that ambition may Slay rivals —

Rich. Rivals, Sire! in what?

Service to France? *I have none!* Lives the man

Whom Europe, paled before your glory, deems

Rival to Armand Richelieu?

Louis. What so haughty!

Remember, he who made, can unmake.

Rich. Never!

Never! Your anger can recall your trust, Annul my office, spoil me of my lands, Rifle my coffers, — but my name — my deeds,

Are royal in a land beyond your sceptre!

Pass sentence on me, if you will; from kings, Lo, I appeal to Time!
Louis appears irresolute.

Bar. (*Passing him, whispers*) But Julie, Shall I not summon her to Court?

Louis. (*Motions to Baradas and turns haughtily to the Cardinal*) Enough!

Your Eminence must excuse a longer audience.

To your own palace: — For our conference, this

Nor place — nor season.

Rich. Good my Liege, for *Justice*

All place a temple, and all season, summer!

Do you deny me justice? Saints of Heaven!

He turns from me! *Do you deny me justice?*

For fifteen years, while in these hands dwelt Empire,

The humblest craftsman -- the obscurest vassal —

The very leper shrinking from the sun,

Tho' loathed by Charity, might ask for
 justice! —
Not with the fawning tone and crawling mien
Of some I see around you — Counts and
 Princes —
Kneeling for *favours;* but, erect and loud,
As men who ask man's rights! my Liege, my
 Louis,
Do you refuse me justice — audience even —
In the pale presence of the baffled Murder?
 Louis. Lord Cardinal — one by one you
 have sever'd from me
The bonds of human love. All near and dear
Mark'd out for vengeance — exile or the
 scaffold.
You find me now amidst my trustiest friends,
My closest kindred; — you would tear them
 from me;
They murder *you* forsooth, since *me* they
 love.
Eno' of plots and treasons for one reign!
Home! Home! And sleep away these phan-
 toms!
 Rich. Sire!
I — patience, Heaven! sweet Heaven! —
 Sire, from the foot
Of that Great Throne, these hands have
 raised aloft
On an Olympus, looking down on mortals
And worshipp'd by their awe — before the
 foot
Of that high throne — spurn you the grey-
 hair'd man,
Who gave you empire — and now sues for
 safety?
 Louis. No: — when we see your Eminence
 in truth
At the *foot* of the throne — we'll listen
 to you.   *Exit Louis.*
 Orl. Saved!
 Bar. For this deep thanks to Julie and to
 Mauprat.
 Rich. My Lord de Baradas, I pray your
 pardon —
You are to be my successor! your hand,
 Sir!
 Bar. (*Aside*) What can this mean?
 Rich. It trembles, see! it trembles!
The hand that holds the destinies of nations
Ought to shake less! poor Baradas! poor
 France!
 Bar. Insolent —
    Exeunt Baradas and Orleans.
 Rich. Joseph — Did you hear the King?
 Jos. I did, — there's danger! Had you been
 less haughty —
 Rich. And suffer'd slaves to chuckle —
 "see the Cardinal —
How meek his Eminence is to-day." tell thee

This is a strife in which the loftiest look
Is the most subtle armour —
 Jos. But —
 Rich. No time
For ifs and buts. I will accuse these traitors!
François shall witness that De Baradas
Gave him the secret missive for De Bouillon,
And told him life and death were in the scroll.
I will — I will —
 Jos. Tush! François is your creature;
So they will say and laugh at you! — *your
 witness
Must be that same Despatch.*
 Rich. Away to Marion!
 Jos. I have been there — she is seized —
 removed — imprisoned —
By the Count's orders.
 Rich. Goddess of bright dreams,
My Country — shalt thou lose me now, when
 most
Thou need'st thy worshipper? My native
 land!
Let me but ward this dagger from thy heart,
And die — but on thy bosom.

    Enter Julie.

 Julie. Heaven! I thank thee!
It cannot be, or this all-powerful man
Would not stand idly thus.
 Rich. What dost *thou* here? Home!
 Julie. Home! is *Adrien there?* — you're
 dumb — yet strive
For words; I see them trembling on your
 lip,
But choked by pity. It *was* truth — all truth!
Seized — the Bastile — and in your presence
 too!
Cardinal, where is Adrien? Think — he
 saved
Your life: — your name is infamy, if wrong
Should come to his!
 Rich. Be sooth'd, child.
 Julie. Child no more;
I love, and I am woman! Hope and suffer —
Love, suffering, hope, — what else does make
 the strength
And majesty of woman? Where is Adrien?
 Rich. (*To Joseph*) Your youth was never
 young — you never loved;
Speak to her —
 Jos. Nay, take heed — the King's com-
 mand,
'Tis true — I mean — the —
 Julie. (*To Richelieu*) Let thine eyes meet
 mine;
Answer me but one word — I am a wife —
I ask thee for my *home* — my FATE — my
 ALL!
Where is my *husband?*

Rich. You are Richelieu's ward,
A soldier's bride: they who insist on truth
Must out-face fear; you ask me for your
husband!
There — where the clouds of heaven look
darkest, o'er
The domes of the Bastile!
Julie. I thank you, father,
You see I do not shudder. Heaven forgive you
The sin of this desertion!
Rich. (*Detaining her*) Whither would'st
thou?
Julie. Stay me not. Fie; I should be there
already.
I am thy ward, and haply he may think
Thou'st taught *me* also to forsake the
wretched!
Rich. I've fill'd those cells — with many
— traitors all.
Had *they* wives too? Thy memories, Power,
are solemn!
Poor sufferer! think'st thou that yon gates of
woe
Unbar to love? Alas! if love once enter,
'Tis for the last farewell; between those walls
And the mute grave — the blessed household
sounds
Only heard once — while hungering at the
door,
The headsman whets the axe.
Julie. O, mercy, mercy!
Save him, restore him, father! Art thou not
The Cardinal-King? — the Lord of life and
death —
Beneath whose light as deeps beneath the
moon,
The solemn tides of Empire ebb and flow? —
Art thou not Richelieu?
Rich. Yesterday I was! —
To-day a very weak old man! Tomorrow,
I know not what!
Julie. Do you conceive his meaning?
Alas! I cannot. But, methinks, my senses
Are duller than they were!
Jos. The King is chafed
Against his servant. Lady, while we speak,
The lackey of the ante-room is not
More powerless than the Minister of France.

Enter First Courtier.

First Courtier. Madame de Mauprat!
Pardon, your Eminence — even now I seek
This lady's home — commanded by the King
To pray her presence.
Julie. (*Clinging to Richelieu*) Think of my
dead father! —
Think, how, an infant, clinging to your knees,
And looking to your eyes, the wrinkled
care

Fled from your brow before the smile of
childhood,
Fresh from the dews of heaven! Think of this,
And take me to your breast.
Rich. To those who sent you! —
And say, you found the virtue they would
slay
Here — couch'd upon this heart, as at an
altar,
And sheltered by the wings of sacred Rome!
Be gone!
First Courtier. My Lord, I am your friend
and servant —
Misjudge me not; but never yet was Louis
So roused against you: — shall I take this
answer? —
It were to be your foe.
Rich. All time my foe
If I a Priest could cast this holy Sorrow
Forth from her last Asylum!
First Courtier. He is lost! *Exit.*
Rich. God help thee, child! — she hears
not! Look upon her!
The storm that rends the oak, uproots the
flower.
Her father loved me so! and in that age
When friends are brothers! She has been to
me
Soother, nurse, plaything, daughter. Are
these tears?
Oh! shame, shame! — dotage!
Jos. Tears are not for eyes
That rather need the lightning, which can
pierce
Through barred gates and triple walls, to
smite
Crime, where it cowers in secret! The
Despatch!
Set every spy to work; the morrow's sun
Must see that written treason in your hands,
Or rise upon your ruin.
Rich. Ay — and close
Upon my corpse! I am not made to live —
Friends, glory, France, all reft from me;
— my star
Like some vain holiday mimicry of fire,
Piercing imperial heaven, and falling down
Rayless and blacken'd to the dust — a thing
For all men's feet to trample! Yea! to-morrow
Triumph or death! Look up, child! — Lead
us, Joseph.

*As they are going out, enter Baradas and De
Beringhen.*

Bar. My Lord, the King cannot believe
your Eminence
So far forgets your duty, and his greatness,
As to resist his mandate! Pray you, Madam,
Obey the King — no cause for fear!

Julie. My father!

Rich. She shall not stir!

Bar. You are not of her kindred —
An orphan —

Rich. And her country is her mother!

Bar. The country is the King!

Rich. Ay, is it so?
Then wakes the power which in the age of
   iron
Burst forth to curb the great, and raise the
   low.
Mark, where she stands, around her form I
   draw
The awful circle of our solemn Church!
Set but a foot within that holy ground,
And on thy head — yea, though it wore a
   crown —
I launch the curse of Rome!

Bar. I dare not brave you!
I do but speak the orders of my King.
The Church, your rank, power, very word,
   my Lord,
Suffice you for resistance: — blame yourself,
If it should cost you power!

Rich. That *my* stake. Ah!
Dark gamester! *what is thine?* Look to it
   well! —
Lose not a trick. By this same hour to-morrow
Thou shalt have France, or I thy head!

Bar. (*Aside to De Beringhen*) He cannot
Have the despatch?

De B. No: were it so, your stake
Were lost already.

Jos. (*Aside*) Patience is your game:
Reflect you have not the Despatch!

Rich. O monk!
Leave patience to the saints — for *I* am
   human!
Did not thy father die for France, poor
   orphan?
And now they say thou hast *no* father! Fie!
Art thou not pure and good? if so, thou art
A part of that — the Beautiful, the Sacred —
Which in all climes, men that have hearts
   adore,
By the great title of their mother country!

Bar. (*Aside*) He wanders!

Rich. So cling close unto my breast,
Here where thou droop'st — lies France! I
   am very feeble —
Of little use it seems to either now.
Well, well — we will go home.

Bar. In sooth, my Lord,
You do need rest — the burthens of the
   State
O'ertask your health!

Rich. (*To Joseph*) I'm patient, see?

Bar. (*Aside*) His mind
And life are breaking fast!

Rich. (*Overhearing him*) Irreverent ribald!
If so, beware the falling ruins! Hark!
I tell thee, scorner of these whitening hairs,
When this snow melteth there shall come a
   flood!
Avaunt! my name is Richelieu — I defy thee!
Walk blindfold on; behind thee stalks the
   headsman.
Ha! ha! — how pale he is! Heaven save my
   country!

> *Falls back in Joseph's arms. Exit*
> *Baradas followed by De Beringhen,*
> *betraying his exultation by his ges-*
> *tures.*
> *End of the Fourth Act.*

ACT V.

Scene 1.

Fourth day. The Bastile — a corridor. In the
background, the door of one of the con-
demned cells.

> *Enter Joseph and Gaoler.*

Gaoler. Stay, father, I will call the governor.   *Exit Gaoler.*

Jos. He has it, then — this Huguet; — so
   we learn
From François — Humph! Now if I can but
   gain
One moment's access, all is ours! The
   Cardinal
Trembles 'tween life and death. His life is
   power: —
Smite one — slay both! No Aesculapian
   drugs,
By learned quacks baptised with Latin jargon,
E'er bore the healing which that scrap of
   parchment
Will medicine to Ambition's flagging heart.
France shall be saved — and Joseph be a
   bishop!

> *Enter Governor and Gaoler.*

Gov. Father, you wish to see the prisoners
   Huguet
And the young knight De Mauprat?

Jos. So my office,
And the Lord Cardinal's order warrant, son!

Gov. Father, it cannot be: Count Baradas
Has summon'd to the Louvre Sieur De
   Mauprat.

Jos. Well, well! But Huguet —

Gov. Dies at noon.

Jos. At noon!
No moment to delay the pious rites

Which fit the soul for death — quick, quick
— admit me!
Gov. You cannot enter, monk! Such are
my orders!
Jos. Orders! vain man! — the Cardinal
still is minister.
His orders crush all others!
Gov. (*Lifting his hat*) Save his King's!
See, monk, the royal sign and seal affix'd
To the Count's mandate. None may have
access
To either prisoner, Huguet or De Mauprat,
Not even a priest, without the special pass-
port
Of Count de Baradas. I'll hear no more!
Jos. Just Heaven! and are we baffled thus!
— Despair!
Think on the Cardinal's power — beware his
anger.
Gov. I'll not be menaced, Priest! Besides,
the Cardinal
Is dying and disgraced — all Paris knows it.
You hear the prisoner's knell. (*Bell tolls*)
Jos. I do beseech you —
The Cardinal is *not* dying — But one moment,
And — hist! — five thousand pistoles! —
Gov. How! a bribe,
And to a soldier, grey with years of honour?
Begone! —
Jos. Ten thousand — twenty! —
Gov. Gaoler — put
This monk without our walls.
Jos. By those grey hairs,
Yea, by this badge (*Touching the Cross of St.
Louis worn by the Governor*) — the
guerdon of your valour —
By all your toils, hard days and sleepless
nights —
Borne in your country's service, noble son —
Let me but see the prisoner! —
Gov. No! —
Jos. He hath
Secrets of state — papers in which —
Gov. (*Interrupting*) I know,
Such was his message to Count Baradas.
Doubtless the Count will see to it.
Jos. The Count!
Then not a hope! — You shall —
Gov. Betray my trust!
Never — not one word more — you heard
me, gaoler?
Jos. What can be done? — distraction! —
Richelieu yet
Must — what? — I know not — thought,
nerve, strength, forsake me.
Dare you refuse the Church her holiest
rights?
Gov. I refuse nothing — I obey my
orders —

Jos. And sell your country to her par-
ricides!
Oh, tremble yet! — Richelieu —
Gov. Begone!
Jos. Undone! *Exit Joseph.*
Gov. A most audacious shaveling, inter-
dicted
Above all others by the Count —
Gaoler. I hope, Sir,
I shall not lose my perquisites. The Sieur
De Mauprat will not be reprieved?
Gov. Oh, fear not.
The Count's commands by him who came for
Mauprat
Are to prepare headsman and axe by noon;
The Count will give you perquisites enough;
Two deaths in one day!
Gaoler. Sir, may Heaven reward him!
Oh, by the way, that troublesome young
fellow,
Who calls himself the prisoner Huguet's son,
Is here again — implores, weeps, raves, to
see him.
Gov. Poor youth, I pity him!

Enter De Beringhen, followed by François.

De B. (*To François*) Now, prithee, friend,
Let go my cloak; you really discompose
me.
Fran. No, they will drive me hence; my
father! Oh!
Let me but see him once — but once — one
moment!
De B. (*To Governor*) Your servant, Mes-
sire, — this poor rascal, Huguet,
Has sent to see the Count de Baradas
Upon state secrets, that afflict his conscience.
The Count can't leave his Majesty an instant:
I am his proxy.
Gov. The Count's word is law!
Again, young scapegrace! How com'st thou
admitted?
De B. Oh, a most filial fellow: Huguet's
son!
I found him whimpering in the court below.
I pray his leave to say good-bye to father,
Before that very long unpleasant journey
Father's about to take. Let him wait here
Till I return.
Fran. No; take me with you.
De B. Nay;
After *me*, friend — the Public first!
Gov. The Count's
Commands are strict. No one must visit
Huguet
Without his passport.
De B. Here it is! Pshaw! nonsense!
I'll be your surety. See, my Cerberus,
He is no Hercules!

Gov. Well, you're responsible.
Stand there, friend. If, when you come out,
  my Lord,
The youth slip in, 'tis *your* fault.
    De B. So it is!
        Exit through the door of the cell fol-
        lowed by the Gaoler.
    Gov. Be calm, my lad. Don't fret so. I had
  once
A father too! I'll not be hard upon you,
And so stand close. I must not see you enter:
You understand. Between this innocent
  youth
And that intriguing monk there is, in truth,
A wide distinction.
        Re-enter Gaoler.
Come, we'll go our rounds;
I'll give you just one quarter of an hour;
And if my Lord leave first, make my excuse.
Yet stay, the gallery's long and dark; no
  sentry
Until he reach the grate below. He'd best
Wait till I come. If he should lose the way,
We may not be in call.
    Fran. I'll tell him, Sir —
        Exeunt Governor and Gaoler.
He's a wise son that knoweth his own father.
I've forged a precious one! So far, so well!
Alas, what then? this wretch has sent to
  Baradas —
Will sell the scroll to ransom life. Oh,
  Heaven!
On what a thread hangs hope!
        Listens at the door.
Loud words — a cry!
        Looks through the key-hole.
They struggle! Ho! — the packet!!!
    (Tries to open the door) Lost! He has it —
The courtier has it — Huguet, spite his
  chains,
Grapples! — well done! Now, now!
        Draws back.
The gallery's long! And this is left us!
    Drawing his dagger, and standing
    behind the door.
Re-enter De Beringhen, with the packet.
Victory! Yield it, robber — Yield it — or
  die —   *A short struggle.*
De B. Off! ho! — there!
Fran. (Grappling with him) Death or
  honour!   *Exeunt struggling.*

Scene 2.

The King's closet at the Louvre. A suite of
rooms in perspective at one side.

Baradas and Orleans.

Bar. All smiles! the Cardinal's swoon of
  yesterday

Heralds his death to-day; could he sur-
  vive,
It would not be as minister — so great
The King's resentment at the priest's
  defiance.
All smiles! and yet, should this accurs'd De
  Mauprat
Have given our packet to another. — 'Sdeath!
I dare not think of it!
    Orl. You've sent to search him?
    Bar. Sent, Sir, to search? — that hireling
  hands may find
Upon him, naked, with its broken seal,
That scroll, whose every word is death! No —
  no —
These hands alone must clutch that awful
  secret.
I dare not leave the palace, night or day,
While Richelieu lives — his minions —
  creatures — spies —
Not one must reach the King!
    Orl. What hast thou done?
    Bar. Summon'd De Mauprat hither!
    Orl. Could this Huguet,
Who pray'd thy presence with so fierce a
  fervour,
Have thieved the scroll?
    Bar. Huguet was housed with us,
The very moment we dismiss'd the courier.
It cannot be! a stale trick for reprieve.
But, to make sure, I've sent our trustiest
  friend
To see and sift him — Hist! here comes the
  King.
How fare you, Sire?

Enter Louis.

Louis. In the same mind, I have
Decided! yes, he would forbid your presence,
My brother, — yours, my friend, then Julie,
  too;
Thwarts — braves — defies — *(Suddenly turn-*
  ing to Baradas) We make you minister.
Gaston, for you — the baton of our armies.
You love me, do you not?
    Orl. Oh, love you, Sire?
(Aside) Never so much as now.
    Bar. May I deserve
Your trust *(Aside)* — until you sign your
  abdication!
My Liege, but one way left to daunt De
  Mauprat,
And Julie to divorce. — We must prepare
The death-writ; what, tho' sign'd and seal'd?
  we can
Withhold the enforcement.
    Louis. Ah, you may prepare it;
We need not urge it to effect.
    Bar. Exactly!

No haste, my Liege. (*Looking at his watch and
aside*) He may live one hour longer.

Enter Courtier.

Courtier. The Lady Julie, Sire, implores an
audience.
Louis. Aha! repentant of her folly! —
Well,
Admit her.
Bar. Sire, she comes for Mauprat's pardon,
And the conditions —
Louis. You are minister,
We leave to you our answer.
   *As Julie enters, the Captain of the
   Archers enters by another door and
   whispers to Baradas.*
Captain. The Chevalier
De Mauprat waits below.
Bar. (*Aside*) Now the despatch!
               Exit with Officer.

Enter Julie.

Julie. My Liege, you sent for me. I come
where Grief
Should come when guiltless, while the name
of King
Is holy on the earth! — Here, at the feet
Of Power, I kneel for mercy.
Louis. Mercy, Julie,
Is an affair of state. The Cardinal should
In this be your interpreter.
Julie. Alas!
I know not if that mighty spirit now
Stoop to the things of earth. Nay, while I
speak,
Perchance he hears the orphan by the throne
Where kings themselves need pardon; O, my
Liege,
Be father to the fatherless; in you
Dwells my last hope!

Enter Baradas.

Bar. (*Aside*) He has not the despatch;
Smiled, while we search'd, and braves me.
— Oh!
Louis. (*Gently*) What would'st thou?
Julie. A single life. — You reign o'er mil-
lions. — What
Is *one man's* life to you? — and yet to *me*
'Tis France, — 'tis earth, — 'tis everything!
— a life —
A human life — my husband's.
Louis. (*Aside*) Speak to her,
I am not marble, — give her hope — or —
Bar. Madam,
Vex not your King, whose heart, too soft for
justice,
Leaves to his ministers that solemn charge.
         Louis walks up the stage.
Julie. You *were* his friend.

Bar. I *was* before I loved thee.
Julie. Loved me!
Bar. Hush, Julie: could'st thou misinter-
pret
My acts, thoughts, motives, nay, my very
words,
Here — in this palace?
Julie. Now I know I'm mad,
Even that memory fail'd me.
Bar. I am young,
Well-born and brave as Mauprat: — for thy
sake
I peril what he has not — fortune — power;
All to great souls most dazzling. I alone
Can save thee from yon tyrant, now my
puppet!
Be mine; annul the mockery of this marriage,
And on the day I clasp thee to my breast
De Mauprat shall be free.
Julie. Thou durst not speak
Thus in *his* ear. (*Pointing to Louis*) Thou
double traitor! — tremble.
I will unmask thee.
Bar. I will say thou ravest,
And see this scroll! its letters shall be blood!
Go to the King, count with me word for word;
And while you pray the life — I write the
sentence!
Julie. Stay, stay. (*Rushing to the King*)
You have a kind and princely heart,
Tho' sometimes it is silent: you were born
To *power* — it has not flushed you into mad-
ness,
As it doth meaner men. Banish my hus-
band —
Dissolve our marriage — cast me to the
grave
Of human ties, where hearts congeal to
ice,
In the dark convent's everlasting winter —
(Surely eno' for justice — hate — re-
venge —)
But spare this life, thus lonely, scathed, and
bloomless;
And when thou stand'st for judgment on
thine own,
The deed shall shine beside thee as an angel.
Louis. (*Much affected*) Go, go, to Baradas:
and annul thy marriage,
And —
Julie. (*Anxiously, and watching his coun-
tenance*) Be his bride!
Louis. A form, a mere decorum.
Thou know'st I love thee.
Julie. O thou sea of shame,
And not one star.
     *The King goes up the stage and
     passes through the suite of rooms at
     the side in evident emotion.*

Bar. Well, thy election, Julie;
This hand — his grave!
    Julie. His grave! and I —
    Bar. Can save him.
Swear to be mine.
    Julie. That were a bitterer death!
Avaunt, thou tempter! I did ask his life
A boon, and not the barter of dishonour.
The heart can break, and scorn you: wreak
    your malice;
Adrien and I will leave you this sad earth,
And pass together hand in hand to Heaven!
    Bar. You have decided. (*Withdraws to the
side scene for a moment and returns*)   Listen
    to me, Lady;
I am no base intriguer. I adored thee
From the first glance of those inspiring eyes;
With thee entwined ambition, hope, the
    future.
I will not lose thee! I can place thee nearest —
Ay, to the throne — nay, on the throne,
    perchance;
My star is at its zenith. Look upon me;
Hast thou decided?
    Julie. No, no; you can see
How weak I am, be human, Sir — one
    moment.
    Bar. (*Stamping his foot. De Mauprat ap-
pears at the side of the stage guarded*)
Behold thy husband! — Shall he pass to
    death,
And know thou could'st have saved him?
    Julie. Adrien, speak!
But say you wish to *live!* — if not your wife,
Your slave, — do with me as you will!
    De M. Once more! —
Why, this is mercy, Count! Oh, think, my
    Julie,
Life, at the best, is short, — but love im-
    mortal!
    Bar. (*Taking Julie's hand*) Ah, loveliest —
    Julie. Go, that touch has made me iron.
We have decided — death!
    Bar. (*To De Mauprat*) Now, say to whom
Thou gavest the packet, and thou yet shalt
    live.
    De M. I'll tell thee nothing!
    Bar. Hark, — the rack!
    De M. Thy penance
For ever, wretch! — What rack is like the
    conscience?
    Julie. I shall be with thee soon.
    Bar. (*Giving the writ to the Officer*) Hence,
    to the headsman.

*The doors are thrown open. The Hussier an-
nounces "His Eminence the Cardinal Duke de
Richelieu." Enter Richelieu, attended by
Gentlemen, Pages, etc., pale, feeble, and leaning
on Joseph, followed by Secretaries of State,
attended by three Sub-secretaries with papers,
etc.*

    Julie. (*Rushing to Richelieu*) You live —
    you live — and Adrien shall not die!
    Rich. Not if an old man's prayers, himself
    near death,
Can aught avail thee, daugher! Count, you
    now
Hold what I held on earth: — one boon, my
    Lord,
This soldier's life.
    Bar. The stake — my head! — you said it.
I cannot lose one trick. Remove your
    prisoner.
    Julie. No! — No! —

    Enter Louis from the rooms beyond.

    Rich. (*To Officer*) Stay, Sir, one moment.
    My good Liege,
Your worn-out servant, willing, Sire, to spare
    you
Some pain of conscience, would forestall
    your wishes.
I do resign my office.
    De M. You?
    Julie. All's over!
    Rich. My end draws near. These sad ones,
    Sire, I love them,
I do not ask his life; but suffer justice
To halt, until I can dismiss his soul,
Charged with an old man's blessing.
    Louis. Surely!
    Bar. Sire —
    Louis. Silence — small favour to a dying
    servant.
    Rich. You would consign your armies to
    the baton
Of your most honour'd brother. Sire, so be
    it!
Your minister, the Count de Baradas;
A most sagacious choice! — Your Secretaries
Of State attend me, Sire, to render up
The ledgers of a realm. — I do beseech you,
Suffer these noble gentlemen to learn
The nature of the glorious task that waits
    them,
Here, in my presence.
    Louis. You say well, my Lord. (*To Secre-
taries as he seats himself*) Approach, Sirs.
    Rich. I — I — faint! — air — air.
        *Joseph and a Gentleman assist him to
        a sofa, placed beneath a window.*
I thank you —
Draw near, my children.
    Bar. He's too weak to question,
Nay, scarce to speak; all's safe.

Scene 3.

Manent Richelieu, De Mauprat and Julie, the last kneeling beside the Cardinal; the Officer of the Guard behind De Mauprat. Joseph near Richelieu, watching the King. Louis. Baradas at the back of the King's chair, anxious and disturbed. Orleans at a greater distance, careless and triumphant. The Secretaries. As each Secretary advances in his turn, he takes the portfolios from the Sub-secretaries.

First Secretary. The affairs of Portugal,
Most urgent, Sire — One short month since the Duke
Braganza was a rebel.
Louis. And is still!
First Secretary. No, Sire, *he has succeeded!* He is now
Crown'd King of Portugal — craves instant succour
Against the arms of Spain.
Louis. We will not grant it
Against his lawful King. Eh, Count?
Bar. No, Sire.
First Secretary. But Spain's your deadliest foe; whatever
Can weaken Spain must strengthen France. The Cardinal
Would send the succours; — (*Solemnly*) — balance, Sire, of Europe!
Louis. The Cardinal! — balance! — We'll consider — Eh, Count?
Bar. Yes, Sire; — fall back.
First Secretary. But —
Bar. Oh, fall back, Sir!
Jos. Humph!
Second Secretary. The affairs of England, Sire, most urgent; Charles
The First has lost a battle that decides
One half his realm — craves moneys, Sire, and succour.
Louis. He shall have both. — Eh, Baradas?
Bar. Yes, Sire.
(Oh, that despatch! — my veins are fire!)
Rich. (*Feebly, but with great distinctness*) My Liege —
Forgive me — Charles' cause is lost. A man,
Named Cromwell, risen, — a great man! — your succour
Would fail — your loans be squander'd!
Pause — reflect.
Louis. Reflect — Eh, Baradas?
Bar. Reflect, Sire.
Jos. Humph!
Louis (*Aside*) I half repent! No successor to Richelieu!
Round me thrones totter! dynasties dissolve!

The soil he guards alone escapes the earth-quake!
Jos. Our star not yet eclipsed! — you mark the King?
Oh! had we the despatch!
Rich. Ah! Joseph! Child —
Would I could help thee.

Enter Gentleman, whispers to Joseph, they exeunt hastily.

Bar. (*To Secretary*) Sir, fall back!
Second Secretary. But —
Bar. Pshaw, Sir!
Third Secretary. (*Mysteriously*) *The secret correspondence*, Sire, most urgent —
Accounts of spies — deserters — heretics —
Assassins — poisoners — schemes against yourself!
Louis. Myself! — most urgent! (*Looking on the documents*)

Re-enter Joseph with François, whose pourpoint is streaked with blood. François passes behind the Cardinal's attendants, and sheltered by them from the sight of Baradas, etc., falls at Richelieu's feet.

Fran. O! my Lord!
Rich. Thou art bleeding!
Fran. A scratch — I have not fail'd!
Gives the packet.
Rich. Hush! (*Looking at the contents*)
Third Secretary. (*To King*) Sire, the Spaniards
Have reinforced their army on the frontiers.
The Duc de Bouillon —
Rich. (*To Secretary, giving an open parchment*) Hold! In this department —
A paper — here, Sire — read yourself — then take
The Count's advice in 't.

Enter De Beringhen hastily, and draws aside Baradas.

Bar. (*Bursting from De Beringhen*) What! and reft it from thee!
Ha! — hold!
Jos. Fall back, son, — it is your turn now!
Bar. Death! — the Despatch!
Louis. (*Reading*) To Bouillon — and sign'd Orleans! —
Baradas, too! — league with our foes of Spain! —
Lead our Italian armies — what! to Paris! —
Capture the King — my health require repose —
Make me subscribe my proper abdication —
Orleans, my brother, Regent! — Saints of Heaven!
These are the men I loved!

Baradas draws, — attempts to rush out, — is arrested. Orleans, endeavouring to escape more quickly, meets Joseph's eye and stops short. Richelieu falls back.

Jos. See to the Cardinal.

Bar. He's dying! — and I yet shall dupe the King.

Louis. (*Rushing to Richelieu*) Richelieu! — Lord Cardinal! — 'tis *I* resign!
Reign thou!

Jos. Alas! too late! — he faints!

Louis. Reign, Richelieu!

Rich. (*Feebly*) With absolute power?

Louis. Most absolute! Oh, live! If not for me — for France!

Rich. FRANCE!

Louis. Ah! this treason!
The army — Orleans — Bouillon! Heavens! — the Spaniard!
Where will they be next week?

Rich. (*Starting up*) There, — at my feet! (*To First and Second Secretaries*)
Ere the clock strike! — The Envoys have their answer! (*To Third Secretary, with a ring*)
This to De Chavigny — he knows the rest —
No need of parchment here — he must not halt
For sleep — for food — In *my* name — MINE — he will
Arrest the Duc de Bouillon at the head
Of his army! Ho! there, Count de Baradas.
Thou hast lost the stake. — Away with him!

As the Guards open the folding doors, a view of the ante-room beyond, lined with Courtiers. Baradas passes thro' the line.

Ha! — ha! — (*Snatching De Mauprat's death warrant from the Officer*) See here, De Mauprat's death-writ, Julie! —
Parchment for battledores! — Embrace your husband!
At last the old man blesses you!

Julie. Oh, joy!
You are saved, you live — I hold you in these arms!

De M. Never to part —

Julie. No — never, Adrien — never!

Louis. (*Peevishly*) One moment makes a startling cure, Lord Cardinal.

Rich. Ay, Sire; for in one moment there did pass
Into this wither'd frame the might of France! —
My own dear France. — I have thee yet —
I have saved thee!
I clasp thee still! it was thy voice that call'd me

Back from the tomb! What mistress like our country?

Louis. For Mauprat's pardon — well! But Julie, — Richelieu,
Leave me one thing to love!

Rich. A subject's luxury!
Yet, if you must love something, Sire — *love me!*

Louis. (*Smiling in spite of himself*) Fair proxy for a fresh young Demoiselle!

Rich. Your heart speaks for my clients: — Kneel, my children —
And thank your King —

Julie. Ah, tears like these, my Liege,
Are dews that mount to Heaven.

Louis. Rise — rise — be happy!

Retires. Richelieu beckons to De Beringhen.

De B. (*Falteringly*) My Lord — you are most — happily recover'd.

Rich. But you are pale, dear Beringhen: — this air
Suits not your delicate frame — I long have thought so:
Sleep not another night in Paris: — Go, —
Or else your precious life may be in danger.
Leave France, dear Beringhen!

De B. I shall have time,
More than I ask'd for, — to discuss the pâté.
Exit.

Rich. (*To Orleans*) For you, repentance — absence, and confession! (*To François*)
Never say *fail* again. Brave Boy! (*To Joseph*)
He'll be —
A Bishop first.

Jos. Ah, Cardinal —

Rich. Ah, Joseph! (*To Louis, as De Mauprat and Julie converse apart*)
See, my Liege — see thro' plots and counterplots —
Thro' gain and loss — thro' glory and disgrace —
Along the plains, where passionate Discord rears
Eternal Babel — still the holy stream
Of human happiness glides on!

Louis. And must we
Thank for *that* also — our prime minister?

Rich. No — let us own it: — there is ONE above
Sways the harmonious mystery of the world
Ev'n better than prime ministers. Alas!
Our glories float between the earth and heaven
Like clouds that seem pavilions of the sun,
And are the playthings of the casual wind;
Still, like the cloud which drops on unseen crags

The dews the wild flower feeds on, our
    ambition
May from its airy height drop gladness down

On unsuspected virtue; — and the flower
    May bless the cloud when it hath pass'd
    away!

THE END.

JOHN WESTLAND MARSTON
1819-1890

The Patrician's Daughter
(1842)

Dr. John Westland Marston is remembered as a playwright who, during his lifetime, was held in high esteem as a serious dramatist. Thomas Purnell in 1871 called him "with the possible exception of Lord Lytton, the sole living representative of the legitimate drama." In two experimental plays, *The Patrician's Daughter* and *Anne Blake* (1852), he sought to give new vitality to the traditional verse drama by treating modern subjects in blank verse. In other plays, written in prose, he sought a credible realism in characterization and theme. Allardyce Nicoll says that "In Marston's plays clearly another step is being taken towards that union of popular and literary elements out of which the new drama was to grow." Marston avoided melodramatic sensationalism by placing all violent action offstage, for his interest was rather in literary excellence and psychological reality.

London's leading actor of the 1840's, W. C. Macready, was seeking to give traditional verse plays enough vitality to survive the competition of the melodrama he despised. Macready's production of *The Patrician's Daughter*, with himself in the role of Mordaunt, was an experiment toward this end. Verse dramas were usually costume pieces set in the historical past. It was felt that the drab humdrum of Victorian life lacked the poetic elevation and color essential for a play in verse. When Macready read *The Patrician's Daughter* he was doubtful that it could succeed, yet the idea, the chance that a treatment of modern life might be the needed stimulant, excited him — he decided to risk it. In a prologue to define the intention of the play and prepare the audience to accept it, Charles Dickens wrote and Macready declaimed:

> Awake the Present! Shall no scene display
> The tragic passion of the passing day?
> . . . . .
> Learn from the lessons of the present day.
> Not light its import and not poor its mien;
> Yourselves the actors and your homes the scene.

Within the play lines defended the idea that modern times as well as ancient may have the charm of romance. When Mabel wishes she had lived in ancient days and asks, "Do you not think / I should have been a heroine?" Mordaunt replies, "Why not be one now?" Marston's and Macready's effort was both to raise the subject matter of everyday life to a universal and poetic level by presenting it in verse, and to give vitality to verse drama by infusing it with everyday realism.

Aside from these purposes, *The Patrician's Daughter* is a serious domestic play. In the opening scene between Mabel and her father the Victorian family relationship is prescriptive: the good daughter will obey her father. The central theme is the domestic question of interclass marriage. Marston, in a preface written for his collected dramas, said that his intention was "simply to exhibit, as impartially as might be, the conflict between the pride of Aristocracy and that of Democracy, with the evils resulting from their collision." These subjects were intended to make the message of the play seem significant to every member of the audience.

But the audience did not like the play, and it ran at Drury Lane for only eleven performances. Accustomed to think of blank verse in connection with Elizabethan or Roman settings and costumes, the audience found verse and modern dress absurdly incongruous. Mrs. Warner, the actress who played Lady Lydia, pointed out this incongruity while the play was in rehearsal. As the season in the play was summer, Macready, to make the scene seem real, directed the actresses to carry parasols. "Blank verse and parasols!" said Mrs. Warner. "Is not that quite a new combination?" Except in the Society of Friends, "thee" and "thou" were sacred to prayer or poetry. The poetic language of the play was meant to elevate scenes in a library or a drawing room, but instead the furniture deflated the verse.

Perhaps the theme also failed to reach the audience — at least the audience in the pit. The conflict could not seem much like a treatment of aristocratic pride versus anything the Chartists of these years, for instance, would call democratic. The democrats in the play were not common people, but "swells" who occupied high places in the government and vacationed on yachts in the Mediterranean. No doubt, following Shakespeare's practice, Marston meant Mordaunt's stooping to revenge to be a "fatal flaw" in his character. But members of the audience accustomed to melodrama probably assumed that Mordaunt was the hero, identified themselves with him, and felt a lapse in decent manners when he jilted Mabel in a public ceremony. Finally, the death of Mabel for no physical cause, just at the moment when she discovers she is truly loved and might be happy, probably made no sense to people who expected a reconciliation, an embrace, and happiness ever after. In any case, the ending has more of pathos than the inevitability of tragedy.

THE PATRICIAN'S DAUGHTER

A Tragedy In Five Acts

by

J. WESTLAND MARSTON

First performed at the Drury Lane Theatre, December 10, 1842

Cast of Characters

LYNTERNE	DEANCOURT
PIERPONT	COLVILLE
HEARTWELL	LADY LYDIA
LISTER	LADY MABEL
MORDAUNT	SERVANTS, NOTARY, PHYSICIAN

ACT I.

Scene 1.

Library in Lynterne Castle. The Earl and Lady Mabel discovered, with a book.

Mabel. Yes, my lord.
But have you read this scene?
Earl. I have not.
But the point in hand, dear Mabel!
Mabel. 'Tis full of mirth and sprightly incident,
And keen, bright satire, through all which the heart
Breathes truth and sympathy! O, how I love
To track a noble soul in masquerade!
Earl. If it so please you, Mabel, that I wait
Until your raptures shall expend themselves,
I am content.

> *He arranges papers. Mabel, after a pause, rises and gives book to Earl, stands by side of Earl, who is seated by table.*

Mabel. You think, dear father, that I trifle. No!
You question of a lover; I reply
By comment on a book — themes separate,
As it may seem to you, but in my mind
Blended together; for the qualities
This book discloses I would have inspire
The man to whom my tributary soul
Should render its allegiance.
Earl. (*Taking the book*) Poor child! the author of the book you laud,
This limner of the mind's fantastic dreams,
Long ere old age found his art profitless,
Forswore his troth to fancy, — and died rich.
Mabel. His book is henceforth sealed to eyes of mine.
O, how degraded is the venal soul
Chartered by its Creator to be free,
Yet putting on the great world's livery,
Not the less menial for its golden fringe!
Earl. Thou art enthusiastic, my fair girl!
I blame thee not; those who aspire too high
Rest nearer heaven than those who ne'er aspired.
I love thee, Mabel.
Thou summest up for me all human ties
Save those which link me to my country's weal.
Thy mother lives in thee, and in some sort
Thou art my age's *bride* as well as *daughter;*
To lose thee were a second widowhood.
My only child! sole tenant of the heart

Thy brothers, did they live, would share with
  thee.
Mabel. (*Embracing him*) O, my dear lord
  and father, well I know
Your love, your patient and forgiving love,
To your oft wayward Mabel! Sir, your will
Shall guide me in this matter; but command,
And I will wed Sir Everard.
Earl. At no command unsanctioned by thy
  heart
Would I require thee wed; yet would I speak
Of poor Sir Everard a word or two,
And leave to time and thy own heart the
  judgment.
He loves thee well, is generous and kind.
Mabel. He is most kind; he is most
  generous.
Earl. And though he be no genius, hath
  fine taste
In arts that charm a woman's eye and ear;
Hath an accomplished mind and graceful
  bearing.
Mabel. That all who know Sir Everard
  will confess.
Earl. Is rich.
Mabel. He has the broadest lands in War-
  wickshire.
Earl. And has the one great requisite —
  high birth.
Mabel. Most true; and yet I hope, pos-
  sessing these,
He has no more than I; for generous,
I trust, I am, and riches and descent
I know we have, surpassing even his own.
Earl. And holdest thou these things of
  light account!
Methinks they should be potent arguments.
Mabel. True; but the heart ne'er guides its
  choice by logic.
There is nought *rational* in love; it hath,
Above all reason, high prerogative.
Who is there that hath loved because he
  ought?
The meet, the proper, and the dutiful
Belong to the head's lore; above all rule
Is the heart's passion, gushing like a stream,
In its exuberant nature finding law
For all it doth, and pouring oft, alas!
Its unblessed course along the wilderness
Which reason would have taught it to avoid.
Earl. Then Mabel is in love; for never,
  sure,
Was one who valued reason less than she.
            Earl rises, comes forward.
Mabel. Not so; for, although reason makes
  not love,
Love may consist with reason; am I right?
Now, if you grant me audience, I will
Possess you of my secret thoughts, till now

Nursed in the solitude of my own heart.
He whom my will shall for its king elect
Must bring me something more than that I
  have;
Women who marry seldom act but once;
Their lot is, ere they wed, obedience
Unto a father; thenceforth to a husband;
But in the *one* election which they make,
Choice of a mate for life and death, and
  heaven,
They may be said to *act*. The man they wed
Is as the living record of the deed,
Their one momentous deed. If he be base,
It veils their deed with shame; if he be great,
Encircles it with glory; and if good,
Haloes it with religion. Wouldst thou know
Whom I would have to be *my* husband, sire?
In brief terms I will sketch him. He shall be
High born; handsome, I'd rather, but at least
With features lit up by the sacred light
Which marks the elect band of noble men,
Whose history is the world's; and whose high
  names,
Linked close with empires, sound their
  synonyms;
With eye that quails not in the war; with voice
That thrills the popular ear, and o'erawes
  senates;
And of a wide, ceaseless benevolence,
Bounded but by the walls of the great world;
And O, whene'er affection breathed his name,
Or mind did homage to it, should my heart
Rush back to the bright hour when first I
  chose him,
Saying it was *my act!*
    Earl. Well, well, my sweet one! all I would
  require
Is, that the proffered love you cannot take,
You should put back with thoughtful gentle-
  ness.
I censure not your nature. Some there be,
Of a romantic spirit like your own,
Have thought all decencies chimerical,
And plighted faith to rude, plebeian swains,
That they might thereby show contempt of
  station,
And all that wisdom holds inviolate:
But this from you I fear not; you have been
Nurtured too well; you are too much my
  daughter.
    Mabel. You do me justice, sir; nor think
  that I
Will e'er disgrace our lineage; whom I wed
High in descent, noble in mind, shall be.
    Earl. Thou art my best beloved; but leave
  me now —
        *Earl goes to chair at table; Mabel
        prepares to go off through centre
        doors.*

Stay, Mabel; one word more with thee! To-
morrow
A visitor named Mordaunt tarries here;
Perchance a week or twain, as it may be.
Show him all kindness; though of obscure
birth,
He is no common man — may serve me
much.
  Mabel. (*By Earl's side*) Mean you *the*
  Mordaunt?
  Earl. I did not know his fame had risen so
  high
As to make him *the* Mordaunt; but I think
We mean the same man; he whose eloquence
Hath stirred the commons so.
  Mabel. My Mordaunt is a poet.
  Earl. True! he has
That failing, I believe, and 'tis a great one
In public men; but time will cure him on't.
  Mabel. Fie, fie, my lord! Do we not mourn
  when time
Plants wrinkles on the brow? and shall we joy
When his touch chills the freshness of the
heart?
For such is poetry.
  Earl. Be it so, chit! (*Rises and comes for-
  ward*)
I'll not contest the point; as to this stranger,
Let his reception be most courteous;
I would we could persuade aunt Lydia
To doff her stateliness for some few days;
It must be looked to, let us seek her, sweet.
  Mabel. With all my heart; — *the* Mor-
  daunt! I am ready.   *Exeunt.*

Scene 2.

*Mordaunt's House. Enter Colville, Deancourt,
Mordaunt, Heartwell, and Lister.*

  Dean. Decide for one of us.
  Col. My yacht's the thing!
After your labors you need change of
scene —
Almost of element, which you shall have
When, the dull land forgotten, our light
skiff
The Mediterranean skims.
  Dean. There's nothing beats
A good old English house — the morning
rides;
A sweep, perchance, o'er hill and hedge to
sound
Of the enlivening bugle; then at night,
The merry party, and the bright fireside;
The good old games and stories.
  Heart. Gentlemen,
Duties are sometimes pleasures. Perhaps
Mordaunt
May hold the cares of public life too dear
To wish a respite, though it be recess.

  Lister. We cannot spare him from us.
  Col. I will take no answer but his own.
  Dean. Nor I!
  Mor. Good friends,
Hold me excused, I pray you. Were my *will*
To arbitrate this matter, I would go
Delightedly with both; but, as it is,
I stand engaged already to Heartwell. That
reminds me
To ask your eye for this. (*Presenting a letter
which Heartwell reads apart*)
  Dean. If it be so
There's nothing left but to regret your
absence,
And wish you well in ours. Farewell till
spring.
  Col. Adieu, dear Mordaunt.
  Mor. Heaven be with you, friends.
  Lister. I'll walk with you.
  Mor. What! all take flight together?
  Heart. No; I'll stay in very pity to your
solitude.
(*To the others*) I trust ere you leave London
we shall meet.
          *Exeunt Lister, Colville, and Dean-
          court. Heartwell carelessly folds up
          and returns the letter. Mordaunt
          brings down chairs.*
I had expected this; you are a prize
To him who shall have wit to capture
you;
But who is he? Not this complacent earl!
This sleek and courteous earl! You must have
smiled,
My Edgar, at each gracious period.
He has a high esteem for you, forsooth!
Admires your views, your mind's great
scope!
And though he sees in all your daring plans
Unsoundness, here and there temerity,
He has a marvellous respect for them,
And being at this moment respited
From cares of state, some portion of his
leisure
He'd have your sweet society engross!
Well, in what terms was your denial couched?
  Mor. Denial! On what grounds should I
  refuse
Such kindly tendered courtesy?
  Heart. I did not think thine eye, so quick
  to pierce
Public hypocrisy through all the glare
With which convention decks it, could have
been
Dazzled by one man's hollow compliment;
I charge thee, spurn this specious show of
friendship.
  Mor. Why call it specious, ere you prove
  it so?

Heart. If you seek evidence that would
convict,
According to the strictest forms of law,
This man of guile, why, I have none to give;
But on plain likelihood and inference
My censure rests. Mark me! two years ago
Had any to another breathed thy name,
His fellow had made question, "Of whom
speak you?
What hath he writ, said, done, or in what
way
Approved himself?" and had he been in-
formed
Of thy capacity, not then confirmed
By the world's attestation, he had cried,
Less in encouragement than mockery,
"One of your rising men! Town's full of
them."
But now thou art a theme of public talk —
A name not only metropolitan,
But known in every district of the isles.
Mor. Thanks for your eulogy; but whither
tends it?
Heart. Faith! to this:
Minds of thine order come not every year,
Nor are they grown in clusters; instruments
Of power! if they be true, of destiny!
Apostles to their age! the virtuous
Hail them as saviours, while the common
herd
Of coward knaves grow paralyzed with fear,
Expectant that their day is passing hence!
Now, while the issues undetermined hang
Between the just and base, if one step forth,
Wily, and smooth of speech, and can arrest
The great man's march a moment, turn his
eye
Upon the glitter of some costly bribe,
It may be that he spurns it, and it *may* be
That he becomes Iscariot to his cause.
Mor. Nay; speak out, if you would call me
traitor!
Heart. I mean not so to name you. I do but
say
Beware the subtle courtier.
Mor. The grounds
Of your suspicion? Why do you condemn
him?
Heart. Is he not the sworn foe of our
party?
Mor. I have no party.   *Both rise.*
Heart. Rapidly the poison works; and yet
it is not strange
That one so loving to his party's foe
Should soon disclaim his old associates.
Mor. Where is your warrant, sir,
To bait me thus? I say I have no party.
You and your friends of late have striven
hard

For certain end which I approved; 'twas fit
That I should aid you — so far travel with
you,
As one road served us both. Therefore have I
Entered in league with you? or am I bound
To follow where your trumpet blows, and
fight
With whom you list to bid me? Have I sworn
To shut my eyes to all the greatness grows
In one half of the empire? That's the oath
Ta'en by the partisan. (*Crosses*)
Heart. You speak right loftily. Perchance
your speech
May couch itself in humbler tones when
meant
For the earl's ear.
Mor. Sir, I have known you long; re-
spected you;
And it may be have served you heretofore;
And not on slight occasion would I wear
The stranger's carriage to you; but take heed.
You speak as if I were a parasite,
A hireling, an apostate: had my *father*
Broached such surmise of me, it had gone far
In recollection of that one dishonor,
To merge all kinder memory.
Heart. I seek your love
No longer than pure friendship's elements
Are fruitful in your nature. Let me ask
If it be meet if one like you should wait
For an occasional condescending smile
From this proud nobleman; or haply make,
Through ignorance of unaccustomed forms,
Mirth for his haughty daughter. But your
pardon —
Perchance you aim at greatness, and will
deign
Honor the Lady Mabel with your hand.
Mor. Peace, sir. Your language holds not
with my mood.
By all report upon the face of earth,
No fairer nor more noble creature moves
Than this same Lady Mabel; for the rest,
The man who hath credentials in his soul,
Avouching its immortal ancestry,
Presumes but little, even if he seek
Alliance with the proudest of the earth.
Is it your creed, sir, that in righteous scales
The name outweighs the man? Shame on
such doctrine.
Heart. Nay, shame on thee, who dar'st
thus to upbraid
An age 'tis fit that thou shouldst venerate!
Farewell, sir! Should we ever meet again,
It will be in that deepest of all strangeness
Which grows 'twixt those who have loved
once, and love not.   *Exit Heartwell.*
Mor. So friendship passes. Well, I will not
seek

A heart to rule in, if affection's sway
Depend on paying dues to interest.
I'll not believe that Heartwell judged aright.
This noble means me fairly — will not dare
To use me for his tool. Yet, if he do —
O, if he do! — my heart heaves at the
    thought,
So that I fear and quake before myself.
There is within me that quick sense of shame
Which, being stung, would spur me on to
    vengeance,
Although the path were fire! And I have, too,
That in my nature which would make me
    slave
To genuine kindness. I'll deal with the world
As the world deals with me, — if well, its
    friend, —
If otherwise, — but for the day, 'tis said,
Sufficient is the evil.   *Exit.*

End of the First Act.

ACT II.

*Handsome drawing room in Lynterne Castle.
Mordaunt discovered.*

Mor. Rumor has not o'erdrawn her. She
    is rich
In beauty, and in that which passeth beauty,
Or is, perchance, its source — a glorious
    soul.
I've known her but a month, and yet she
    seems,
As their own light, familiar to mine eyes.
Would that I
Were sprung of lofty lineage. That's un-
    worthy.
Was not my father tender, constant, upright?
And shall I wrong his homely, honest virtues
By vain repinings at my humble lot?
Heaven sees not with our eyes. That's well
    at least.

*Enter Mabel in a fashionable morning dress,
        with fancy work.*

Mabel. Bright morrow to you, sir! 'Tis a
    fair change
From last eve's tempest.
            *About to take chair; Mordaunt puts it
            forward; Mabel seated; Mordaunt
            stands.*
Mor. 'Twas a stormy eve.
Mabel. And yet I never knew a briefer one.
For that I must thank you, and the sweet tale,
In listening which the hours like minutes
    sped.
Mor. Thank you lady.

Mabel. Yet I somewhat marvel
That you, whose life is chiefly dedicate
To grave *state policy*, should yet beguile
Your leisure with the poet's simple art.
Mor. What is the end of all true policy,
    if it be not
To work out poetry in act? to feel
A deep and constant love for human kind;
A sense of beauty's presence, not alone
In lofty show, but in its latent haunts,
Which few investigate — the humble hut
And bosom meanly clad; worship of justice;
The warm emotions of an unchecked nature,
Which rises, as by instinct, against wrong:
These are the elements of poetry.
Is that man fit to be a statesman, think you,
Whose heart is stranger to them?
Mabel. After I retired,
Your tale dwelt on my mind, moved me to
    tears —
Those sweet and tender tears that speak not
    pain,
But soothe whoever sheds them. In my
    dreams
The maid whose fate you told was present
    still.
O, would that I had lived in ancient days,
The times of old romance! Do you not think
I should have been a heroine?
Mor. Why not be one now?
Mabel. There is no scope for it.
O, would that I had been the worshipped one
Of some devoted Troubadour, half knight,
Half minstrel. My sire, a baron,
Irascible and proud, perchance commands
That I forswear my troth. I cannot do it.
Straight in some chamber, tapestried and
    lone,
I am confined, armed guards before my door.
I pen a *billet*. O, sweet traveller,
Into whose care these tidings, from the hand
Of an unhappy maid, shall come, haste thee
To Sieur — "De Lacy," — that shall be his
    name, —
And tell him in this castle's eastern tower
His Eleanora lies a prisoner —
For his dear love. I drop my scroll; its words
Are borne to my brave Troubadour. Some
    night,
While I sit gazing at the placid moon,
Soft music floats
Around my lattice — quick I open it!
O, joy! 'tis he! — he scales the wall, secures,
Fast by the casement, his elastic stair
Which straightway I descend — I'm on the
    earth —
I'm on my steed: away! away we fly!
I and my Troubadour, and in the morn
My hand rewards my brave deliverer!

What think you, sir, is not my tale well told?
It is my first attempt. You do not smile!
 Mor. Alas, sweet lady! mournful thoughts
  were mine.
 Mabel. Why mournful?
 Mor. Your tale is blithe, and goes off
  trippingly:
I make no question of your constancy,
Your enterprise, your courage; but methinks
You scarce had borne the part you paint so
 well.
 Mabel. Wherefore not? O for one year
Of the romantic past, that I might prove
Myself, in your despite, a heroine.
 Mor. I have known heroines in this mod-
  ern time, —
Ay, there are homesteads which have wit-
 nessed deeds
That battle fields, with all their bannered
 pomp,
Have little to compare with. Life's great play
May, so it have an actor great enough,
Be well performed upon a humble stage.
 Mabel. Your discourse goes far to make me
  look with kinder eyes
Upon the present time.
 Mor. The *forms* of the heroic change from
  age to age;
The *spirit of the forms* remains the same:
Your heroine of old, in love's behalf,
Would dare imprisonment and venture flight,
Though near her files of lances were arrayed.
Your modern heroine, in love's behalf,
Will often dare hostility as dread.
Not seldom you will meet a maiden whose
 heart
Was pledged to one of lowly heritage,
But of high qualities, that well atoned
The churlish lot of Fortune. Enmity
From haughty parents, exile from the sphere
Had been her own from birth, chill penury,
And other ills as weighty, have conspired
Against her love, and yet she has avowed it,
And cherished it as life. O Lady Mabel —
 Mabel. Why do you pause?
 Mor. I fear I weary you.
 Mabel. O, no, for such a heroine —
 Mor. What would you say of her?
 Mabel. That albeit she had acted indis-
  creetly;
For the high love that caused her so to act,
She should be gently censured — not cast
 out.
 Mor. And her lover?
 Mabel. Nay, I know not what to say of him.
 Mor. I knew a lover once (*Takes chair*)
Whose heart had poured its riches at the
 shrine
Of one whose lot ranked higher than his own,

In the wise world's esteem; and this he knew,
Yet could he not recall to his lone breast
The feelings thence allured. She was their
 home,
And — all beside was foreign.
 Mabel. And she loved him?
 Mor. His love was silent, and dared scarce
  intrude
Upon her sight. He prayed for her — he
 blessed her —
He wept for her; but she heard not his words,
Nor saw his tears; for they were breathed
 and shed
In sacred solitude. He thought of angels
Who nightly to the sleeper's couch repair,
But vanish ere he wakens.
 Mabel. Did he not lay his heart open to
  her?
 Mor. As I said, he was of lower rank than
  she, and feared
That she might scorn him.
 Mabel. Scorn such fervent worship?
Had she so done, *she* were the thing to
 scorn.
 Mor. *You* had not spurned him, then?
 Mabel. I cannot dream
What I have said to move you. O, this friend!
'Tis like you loved him as a very brother,
And own a debt to all who pity him.
Your story interests. How ended it?
And was this long since?
 Mor. It is very strange.
I cannot call the time to mind. I know
The truth of what I tell, but nothing more.

   Enter the Earl and Lady Lydia.

 Lydia. Not out yet, Mabel? Should you
  thus permit
The freshness of the morning to escape?
It counts three hours since noon.
 Mabel. Is it so late? — (*To Mordaunt*) Do
  you ride with us, sir?
(*To the Earl*) And you? You must;
I know you will; these are your holidays.
 Earl. I may not, sweetest.
 Mabel. No! — (*To Mordaunt*) You then
  will be
Our single cavalier.
 Earl. I fear, dear Mabel,
I must assert a prior claim to Mordaunt.
We've themes of pressing import to discuss.
 Mabel. 'Tis very late. I will not ride to-day.
 Lydia. You will.
 Mabel. I think you said that it was late.
 Lydia. (*Aside to Mabel*) Go for my sake.
 Mabel. Well, if it please you, aunt.
 Earl. Adieu! (*Going*)
 Mor. A pleasant morning.
 Lydia. Thank you, thank you.

Exeunt Earl and Mordaunt. Lady Lydia walks after them, and then advances to Mabel, who is seated in centre.

Lydia. Mabel, you love that man!

Mabel. Love whom? Sir Everard?

Lydia. This is evasion.
I know you have refused Sir Everard;
I say you love this Mordaunt.

Mabel. I fail to comprehend you.

Lydia. Wilt deny it?

Mabel. (*Haughtily rises from chair*) It doth
not need denial. Edgar Mordaunt!

Lydia. Pardon me!
I did but jest. I knew you loved him not;
It was impossible, for he hath nought
In station, fortune, or in qualities
That can excite esteem, far less affection.

Mabel. O, now methinks you are somewhat
harsh.

Lydia. Harsh! would you have me patient
in my speech?
I am beside myself to see a man
Whose birth had fitted well a servitor
Thus licensed to invade patrician's bounds,
And wearing in them the familiar air
Of one inured to dignity!

Mabel. Good aunt, men three relations
hold to dignity:
By gradual use some grow inured to it,
And some are born to it; but there be those
Born *of it*, nurtured of its elements;
With them nobility is personal,
And they must die ere it can.

Lydia. In which rank place you Mordaunt?

Mabel. In the last.

Lydia. What fantasy hath sealed thine
eyelids close!
Canst thou not read the obvious history
Of an ambitious and time-serving man?
What doth he here who was thy father's foe
Upon all public questions? Trust me, Mabel,
He is of those who, by exciting speech
And persevering effort, make their names
Of value in the mart of policy,
And sell them to the man who offers most.

Mabel. Madam, 'tis false — his heart is
virtue's home,
His deeds her witnesses — O, foully false!

Lydia. This is unmaidenly and insolent!
Does no shame flush thy cheek? or where-
fore is it
Thou shouldst forget all deference to me
In favor of a stranger?

Mabel. Because *he is a stranger*,
And has no friend to spurn back calumny,
When those whose guest he is forget the
rights

Owing to hospitality and justice.
(*Throws herself into chair*)

Lydia. Under pretence of what is due to
justice
Your passion flaunts it bravely:
Henceforth suit your bearing
More to the decent, less to the fantastic,
Or I will to your father, and require
His comment on your conduct.

Mabel. Do you threaten? (*Rises*)

Lydia. Ay! threaten. Wherefore not?

Mabel. I am amazed you can, so strange it
seems
That you, whose words suffice to show what
you are,
Should dare rebuke what I am.
I wonder not you value station so:
It is but a poor treasure in itself,
Yet becomes rich when 'tis the sole posses-
sion.

Lydia. (*Aside*) I have gone too far. Mabel,
could you have looked
Into my heart, you would have spared me
this.

Mabel. Could you have sounded mine, I
do not think
You would have ventured to this length of
insult. (*Retires to table*)

Lydia. Insult! Mabel! And is your father's
sister's love so strange,
That when it would advise you, guard you,
save you,
You should miscall it thus? Perhaps my zeal
Took an impatient tone, but did not need
The deep rebuke it suffered.

Mabel. (*Coming to her*) I have been wrong,
dear aunt! but still I say,
You judge poor Mordaunt harshly.

Lydia. I think he is ambitious.

Mabel. What's he that is not so? Ambition,
aunt,
Is instinct in great minds, even as to soar
Is nature to the eagle.

Lydia. This plausible and general reason-
ing, however just,
Meets not the special instance; beside all
which, but note
How much he adds, by glances, motions,
sighs,
Smiles, even casts of visage, to his words,
Which, as I lately said, your eyes reward
With interest more than maidenly.

Mabel. Nay, gentle aunt,
I am not carved from stone, and cannot hear
Music without emotion, nor unmoved
Look on a flower, or aught that's beautiful;
And must I, when a glowing sentiment
Or noble thought finds utterance, emulate

The barren rock that never pays the sun
With produce for his smiles? O, blame me
    not,
If at discourse on themes magnificent
My eyes light up with joy! They testify
Love to the speaker's *thoughts*, not to *himself*.
    Lydia. The speaker will not make that
        nice distinction;
And, to be plain, he has sufficient cause
To augur that.
    Mabel. That I esteem, admire him;
I will not wrong him so as to surmise
He would aspire to more. He knows my rank;
But let us hasten, 'tis so *very* late.
I trust we're friends again. You'll follow me.
                                Exit Lady Mabel.
    Lydia. Esteem and admiration! likely
        terms
To cozen me, forsooth! No; this is love,
And has gone further than I thought. This
    Mordaunt
Is a right skilful player on the heart:
That praise I'll give him. He must read suc-
    cess —
Success in the girl's face, which, like a mirror,
    shows
The image of his thoughts. Should this
    proceed,
No motives, counsel, prayer, threat, in-
    fluence,
Will stand between her and her love. Well,
    then,
I and this schemer are at war! I'll watch
His demonstrations one more week; if then
He purpose longer stay, I'll in plain terms
Urge his departure; if he still remain,
I'll move him to disclosure of his end
Before it ripen further, and thus shake,
In spring, the blossoms autumn had seen
    fruit.   *Exit.*
        End of the Second Act.

ACT III.

Scene 1.

*A terrace in front of Lynterne Castle. Evening;
    half dark. Enter Mordaunt.*
    Mor. How beautiful are all things when
        we love!
She I love is human; and through Nature's
    wide extent
All that is human, for her sake, I love.
Our planet earth is her abode; for her sake I
    love earth,
And for earth's sake love all that earth con-
    tains.

O, it is great, and wise, and good to love!
What joy it is to love! And loves she me?
She listens to my words, and seldom speaks.
First it was otherwise; her repartee,
Quick wit, and lively sallies flashed all day;
Her answers now are few and brief, as though
The task of ordering her thoughts for speech
Woke her from blissful dreams; my soul
    itself
Seemed suffused in her presence, bathed in
    light,
As plants beneath the solemn, tender moon,
Which gilds their life with beauty, as she
    mine,
And joys in heaven to see their silvered
    leaves,
Unknowing 'tis her smile that makes their
    brightness,
Which fades from earth whene'er she wanes
    in heaven.

            Enter Lady Lydia.

A cloud comes over mine. Lo! Lady Lydia!
I trust you find the evening breeze refresh
    you.
    Lydia. A debtor to your wishes, sir! I
        thank you.
(*Aside*) I'll not delay, for opportunity,
Once slighted, oft escapes. When do you
    leave us?
    Mor. Shortly. Perhaps within a week or
        two,
Provided for that time my sojourn prove
No inconvenience here.
    Lydia. I fear it will.
    Mor. Had I thought so, you had not seen
        me now.
    Lydia. I will be plain, sir.
Plainness is always the best courtesy,
Where truths are to be told. You still are
    young,
And want not personal grace; your air, your
    words
Are such as captivate. You understand me.
    Mor. I do not; for these things most men
        seek to harbor guests.
    Lydia. True, except sometimes
When they are fathers. You are honorable,
And what has passed will leave us straight.
    Mor. I scarcely dare presume to give your
        words
Their nearest meaning.
    Lydia. Yet you may do so.
    Mor. The Lady Mabel!
    Lydia. Yes.
    Mor. Looks not on me indifferently.
    Lydia. That you will join me in regretting,
        sir.

Mor. And have you certain warrant for
    your thought?
Lydia. She has confessed it.
Mor. In your hearing?
Lydia. You are minute, I see, and well
    may doubt,
Except on surer witness than surmise,
So strange a tale. Alas! the evidence
Courts sight and touch. I hold it in my
    hand —
This letter! (*Mordaunt regards her inquiringly*)
    Nothing — (*As with a sudden impulse*)
I dare trust your honor.
This letter, then, — sweet patience! — by
    my niece
Addressed to me, doth full disclosure bear
Of her hid passion.
Mor. Writ to you?
Lydia. You doubt. (*Showing the address*)
Her lips refused allegiance to her will,
Which made her hand its deputy. Behold!
    (*Extending the letter*)
Mor. Her love for me! The glory on the
    page
Dazzles mine eyes.
Lydia. (*Withdrawing it*) Forgive me: 'tis
    too much. (*Tears it*)
Thus let the winds disperse the signs of
    shame. (*Throws it off*)
'Twould be most happy, were its memory
As easily effaced.
Mor. Your hand hath rent
The *record*; but your voice transfers its
    purport
To the more lasting tablet of my heart!
I'll seek her on the instant. (*Going*)
Lydia. (*Aside*) That, indeed,
Would mar my plan. No; silence is your
    course:
It is most delicate, least painful, too.
No word were well, save farewell, and that
    said
As those who have no long acquaintance
    say it.
Mor. I will not say it so to the Lady Mabel,
    now,
Or ever, unless it be her will.
Lydia. You would not surely take
Advantage of her weakness. Do not, sir,
Let it be thought that we, in welcoming you,
Shook hands with an adventurer.
Mor. (*Indignantly*) Madam! (*With con-
strained courtesy*) you are her relative,
and I am dumb. (*Going*)
Lydia. Stay. Think you the earl's voice
    will not crush your plan
The moment that surprise permitted speech?
Mor. Why should it?
Lydia. Must I speak outright?

Mor. Surely.
Lydia. The house of Lynterne
Dates from the time that he of Normandy
O'erthrew the Saxon sway; since then, its
    lords,
In war or peace, have held the foremost rank
In conflict or in council. Sir, our house
Is noble — must remain so till its *end*.
Mor. Is not yon sunset splendid?
Lydia. Yes.
But we may see that often, and it bears
Not now on our discourse.
Mor. Indeed it does.
However proud, or great, or wise, or valiant
The Lady Mabel's ancestors, that sun,
From age to age, has watched their honors
    end,
As man by man fell off; and centuries hence
Yon light unto oblivion may have lit
As many stately trains as now have passed.
And yet my soul, orb of eternity,
When yonder globe is ashes, as your sires,
Shall shine on undecaying. When men know
What their own natures are, and feel what
    God
Intended them to be, they are not awed
By pomps the sun outlives.
Lydia. Think of me, as your friend, when
    you are gone.
You have a towering spirit. Had the rank
And blood of Lady Mabel been as yours,
I had not said a word to spite your wish.
Mor. You see this ring?
Lydia. I have admired it oft. Would you
    thus hint
That you are rich?
Mor. Is not the setting precious?
Lydia. The diamond is magnificent!
Mor. True, madam! But the setting —
Lydia. The diamond is the treasure.
Mor. No! the setting!
Lydia. The setting is but silver, worthless,
    base,
Contrasted with the stone.
Mor. True, Lady Lydia!
Then when I treat for merchandise would
    buy
All stars of heaven up, were they diamond
    worlds, —
A peerless woman's love, — why runs your
    phrase,
"You might have had that unmatched gem
    for nought
Had it not been so *set*" in ancestry,
Or some such silver rim? But enough —
Enough — now to Lady Mabel. (*Going*)
Lydia. Let me advise.
If you persist in this strange scheme, seek,
    first,

An audience of the earl; if he consent,
The which is most unlikely, Mabel's love
Is honorably yours; if he refuse,
You incur no disgrace, as you would do
Luring his daugher's heart unknown to him.
   Mor. I take your counsel. The earl is in the
   library even now.
I'll learn his thoughts at once.
   Lydia. I pity you. It will be a hard task for
   your high spirit
To sue the earl in such a humble strain as
   will be requisite.
   Mor. Humble! I — Mordaunt!
   Lydia. Your ground is delicate; you must
   be cautious;
Confess your low estate, and own the prize
You seek to gain far beyond your desert;
You must put by your recent haughty tone
And kingly glances; plead with downcast eye
And hesitating voice; all this, I say, must
   keenly
Gall your nature; therefore I pity you.
   Mor. I were indeed a slave,
And needing pity, could I so forget
My manhood; but enough, methinks, is said
To one who knows me not.   *Exit.*
   Lydia. O, this is well!
He'll to my brother in a haughty mood —
The very one I wished for. 'Twill arouse
All the earl's latent pride. And now for Mabel.
Upon the wish she comes.   *Retires up stage.*

*Enter Lady Mabel, with bonnet, scarf, and
parasol; comes on with eyes bent on ground,
slowly, in thought.*

   Mabel. Why have not noble natures noble
   names?
Or why are names of import? O world! world!
With many a captious custom dost thou bind
The heart that seeks enlargement! What is
   birth!
Even my father
Seeks his alliance. What is this to me?
A line invisible divides our fates!
O, would that he had rank! The day may
   come
When he will *earn* nobility, and men
Of prouder birth may court his smile; and
   then,
Perchance, (for love is strong), I might
   descend
A few steps from my pinnacle. Fool! fool!
This is a dream of summer and of youth.
I know not my own soul; 'tis ardent now,
But years may chill it into apathy.
Why not? 'Tis thus with others; I could weep.
   Lydia. So, you've been secret, Mabel!
'Twas hardly kind; but I waive all displeasure;
I trust you may be happy.

   Mabel. This is strange language, aunt.
   Lydia. I might reply, yours is strange con-
   duct, niece,
But let that pass. The earl was silent too,
   but I
Surmise he understood it all; perhaps had
Planned it before his guest arrived.
   Mabel. Tax not my patience thus, but in
   one word
Explain your meaning.
   Lydia. Why counterfeit surprise? Know
   you not well
Mordaunt is with the earl this very hour?
   Mabel. Well, what is that to me?
   Lydia. Much, I should say,
Were I now young, in love, and knew what
   boon
The man I loved was seeking from my sire.
   Mabel. You jest.
   Lydia. I am in earnest. He had your con-
   sent,
Doubtless, to back his prayer.
   Mabel. No; never.
   Lydia. Not in strict, formal terms, per-
   haps, but still
By such expressions as the timid use
To help the lip's checked utterance by the
   eye.
   Mabel. I never spoke the word Presump-
   tion's self
Could torture to a pledge of love for him.
   Lydia. I am amazed! it is not half an hour
Since his own lips assured me that the earl
Must needs confirm his choice.
   Mabel. Presuming arrogance!
   Lydia. He spoke in easy strain,
His air, half buoyancy, half carelessness,
As though success were slave to him, and
   came
Without the pains of calling.
   Mabel. What sanction have I given him
   thus to boast?
   Lydia. I warned you once to guard, lest
   what you meant
For courtesy he should interpret love.
   Mabel. In word or look I never passed the
   bound of courtesy.
   Lydia. Did you not tell me, Mabel, that
   the earl
Requested special kindness for this man?
   Mabel. What *man?* (*With sudden indigna-
   tion*)
   Lydia. This gentleman, this Mordaunt, at
   whose hands
The earl looked for some service. Am I right?
   Mabel. Yes! so he said.
   Lydia. Nothing is more plain than
That your father seeks some grace of Mor-
   daunt

Which he intends to sell — the price, your
  hand.
How now! you shiver!
  Mabel. The earl shall spurn him. (*Crosses*)
Buy my hand, said you?
  Lydia. You may depend he means it.
  Mabel. Why is your tone so measured, and
    your brow
So clear on this occasion? Where's the fire
That should be in your eyes? Your temper's
  sweet;
But now I like it not, I like it not. (*Weeps*)
  Lydia. I cannot chide, if under quick
    excitement at your
Wrong, you are unjust to me. A step!

        Enter Servant.

  What now?
  Ser. Madam, my lord would see you and
    the Lady
Mabel; he waits you in the library.   *Exit.*
  Lydia. Come, Mabel; take heart, sweet.
  Mabel. What is there that I should fear?
Let us be going, aunt.   *Exeunt.*

        Scene 2.

*Library, as before. The Earl and Mordaunt
discovered.*

  Mor. Is love a crime?
Can we prevent its coming? or when come,
Can we command it from us?
  Earl. We may, at least, curb its expression,
When disgrace and grief are like to follow it.
  Mor. Disgrace! Your daughter's noble, fair,
    and good;
I shall not feel disgraced in taking her.
  Earl. Sir! You are insolent. (*Takes chair*)

    Enter Lady Mabel and Lady Lydia.

Mabel, my child, have I not loved you truly,
Shown all kindness that is a daughter's due?
  Mabel. Indeed, my lord, you have.
  Earl. Have you done well
In making stranger to a father's heart
The dearest wish of yours? — in plighting
  faith
For life, unknown to him who gave you life?
  Mabel. This have I never done. (*Leaning
    on her father's shoulder*)
  Mor. Speak frankly; have you not, Lady
    Mabel, given me proof
Of favor in your sight will justify
The boon I have entreated of the earl —
Permission to be ranked as one who looks
For closer union with you than a friend?
Answer, Mabel.
  Mabel. Mabel! the Lady Mabel, when *you*
    speak.
  Lydia. She utterly denies what you infer.
  Mabel. Yes, utterly.

  Mor. And Lady Lydia speaks thus; she
    whose words
Confirmed all I once hoped?
  Lydia. We think you but presumptuous;
    let your honor
Guard you from veiling shame by sin; nor
  strive
From loose discourse, spoken in pleasantry,
To justify your conduct.
  Mor. And the letter?
  Lydia. The letter! He's distraught.
  Mabel. (*Aside to Lydia*) The letter! Aunt!
  Lydia. Yes, love. (*Going to Mabel*)
  Mabel. No, no; I will not wrong her; it is
    plain
His folly has deceived him.
  Mor. May I then ask,
If you have never loved me, why you deigned
To speak in tones so soft, to let each glance
Be tempered with such sweetness; oftentimes
To sit mute by the hour, as if my words
Were music to your ear, and when I ceased,
To pay me with a smile, in which there
  seemed
A heart's whole volume writ?
  Mabel. This is too much. (*Sits in chair,
    centre*)
Whate'er my kindness meant, it did not mean
To foster your presumption, though, perhaps,
Suspecting it, and lacking at the time
Better employment, I allowed it scope,
Did not repress it harshly, and amused,
Rather than angered, failed to put a bound
To its extravagance.
  Mor. All, then, has been a jest; the thing
    resolves
Itself into a harmless *badinage!*
You had no other toy, so took my heart
To wile away an hour. The plaything *broke;*
But then it was *amusement!*
  Lydia. Well, you were honored
In thus assisting to beguile the hours
Of Lady Mabel's solitude.
  Mor. Honored, say you?
Men's hearts have leaped within them at my
  words.
The lowly have adored me, and the proud —
Ay, sir, the proud — have courted me; you
  know it.
  Lydia. All this would sound much to your
    credit, sir,
Were other lips to speak it.
  Mor. Understand me.
You deem me proud. I am so; and yet humble:
To you I would have been a slave; have
  moulded
Each wish to your desire; have laid my
  fame,
Though earth had ratified it, at your feet,

Nor deemed the offering worthy of your
    smile!
But when, admitting what I am, you scorn me
For what my father was, sport with me,
    trample
On the same hopes you fostered, then I
    claim
The patent which the Great Paternity
Of heaven assigns me as its elder born,
And walk before you in the march of time!
    Lydia. The stale, fond trick — to boast of
    honors stored
In ether, where no human eye can pierce.
You may be prince of several stars — possess
An empire in the ocean. But the meanest
    knighthood
Conferred by a real sword on real shoulders,
Beats fifty thousand dukedoms in the air.
The old, convenient trick!
    Earl. Nay, courtesy!
    Lydia. To check the signs of loathing, it
    were best
The eye should shun the object. May we go?
    Earl. Yes, leave me. (*Mabel rises, and they
    are going up centre*)
    Mor. Stay! Before we part, I have a word
    or two
For Lady Mabel's ear. (*Mabel returns to centre*)
I know right well
The world has no tribunal to avenge
An injury like mine; you may allure
The human heart to love, warm it with smiles,
To aspirations of a dream-like bliss,
From which to wake is madness;
And that very heart, brought to this pass,
You may spurn from your path, pass on in
    jest,
And the crowd will jest with you; you may
    glide,
With eye as radiant, and with brow as
    smooth,
And feet as light, through your charmed
    worshippers,
As though the angel's pen had failed to trace
The record of your crime; and every night,
Lulled by soft flatteries, you may calmly sleep
As do the innocent; but it is crime,
Deep crime, that you commit. Had you, for
    sport,
Trampled upon the earth a favorite rose,
Pride of the garden, or in wantonness
Cast in the sea a jewel not your own,
All men had held you guilty of offence.
    Lydia. Is't meet that longer you should
    brook this censure?
    Mor. And is it then not sin
To crush those flowers of life, our freshest
    hopes,
With all the incipient beauty in the bud,

Which knows no second growth? to cast our
    faith
In human kind, the only amulet
By which the soul walks fearless through the
    world,
Into those floods of memoried bitterness,
Whose awful depths no diver dares explore?
To paralyze the expectant mind, while yet
On the world's threshold, and existence' self
To drain of all save its inert endurance?
To do this unprovoked, I ask it of you,
Is it not sin? To the unsleeping eye of Him
Who sees all aims, and knows the wrongs
No laws, save his, redress, I make appeal
To judge between us. There's an hour will
    come,
Not of revenge, but of righteous retribution.
    Earl. Well, sir, our conference is ended.
    Mor. Yes; but its issues have yet to be
    revealed.   *Exit.*
    Mabel. He is deceived! He hears me not!
    He knows me not! He's gone!
    Earl. Why, what is this, dear Mabel?
    Mabel. (*With a forced smile*) Nothing, sir.
I am not used, you know, to witness strife.
It somewhat chafes my spirit.
    Earl. Hither, love!

    *Mabel reels forward, and falls into
    her father's arms.*

    End of the Third Act.

ACT IV.

Scene 1.

*The terrace, same as Act Three, Scene One —
An interval of five years is supposed to have
elapsed between the third and fourth acts.*

    Enter Lister and Heartwell.

    Lister. The marriage rites take place to-
    morrow morn!
    Heart. So the earl purposes. His prepara-
    tions
Are of such magnitude as to compete
Almost with royal nuptials. It will be
A gorgeous festival.
    Lister. I did not think to see it.
    Heart. For myself, I never looked within
    these ancient walls
For welcome as guest, far less as one
Summoned to Mordaunt's marriage.
    Lister. It is strange, after the rumors
    bruited of his suit,
And its vain issue, scarce five years ago,
He should now have renewed it with success.
Besides this, I had deemed his pride too great

To brook his chance of scorn a second time.
I well remember the affair was made
A theme of public jest.
   Heart. Yes. He became
The gibe of every lisping fool, whose wit
Had taught his lips to sneer, though scarce to
   speak.
Poor Mordaunt! They who envied his ascent
Gloried in his disgrace, and prudent mothers
Quoted his story to their heedless daugh-
   ters —
The moral of a fable meant to teach
The vulgar crime of loving plain, bare merit:
Scarce any one dared know him.
   Lister. For all this he was indebted much
   to Lady Lydia;
And, as you say, I took him for a man
Too proud to bear with insult. It amazed me
To see him subject thus to general scoff,
Calmly outbrave it, give his mind entire
To public duties, daily gathering friends,
Until his strength grew such, the earl pre-
   ferred
Concession rather than hostility,
Admitted all our claims, procured him rank,
Now takes him for his son. He showed no
   sign
Of pain at this contempt?
   Heart. Save once, I think;
And then I tented him. "Good friend," said
   he,
"That Edgar Mordaunt suffers wrong is little.
He is not the first injured man by thousands;
But when I think that all who rise, like me,
From lowly state, should be like me con-
   temned,
Whate'er their virtues be, I feel it there —
I feel it *there.*" He grasped my hand; his
   shook;
But this was for a moment. "Never, sir,
Renew this theme." He thus entreated me.
An instant served to banish every trace
Of past emotion. The clear, resolute brow,
The calm, yet searching eye, the lip just
   curved,
His usual look — you know it well — re-
   turned.
I probed the wound no more.

   Enter Lady Lydia and Captain Pierpont.

Let us pass on. The Lady Lydia and her
   nephew come.
Blithe weather for the festival, good madam.
   Lydia. Fair as our brightest hopes are,
   gentlemen.
          Exeunt Heartwell and Lister.
You know already these are the members of a
   factious clique,
Mordaunt has brought to notice of the earl.

   Pier. You bear this Mordaunt no better
   will, then, than I.
   Lydia. I hate him, nephew. I foiled him
   once.
I owe him
The hatred of the vanquished, besides that
Which springs from shame, in calling relative
A man without an ancestor.
   Pier. I am poor, yet had I rather starved
   on soldier's pay
Than thus disgraced my house, how great
   soe'er
The bribe might have been tendered; but,
   good aunt,
I should have held your wit too quick to lose
The conflict with this churl.
   Lydia. I did all I could — strove to in-
   sinuate that Mabel's hand
Rather obeyed her father's will than hers.
Since I am conquered, nothing now remains
Except to make the best on't.
We'll hasten to the castle: 'tis the hour
My brother named to read the marriage deed.
   (*About to go*)

   Enter Mabel.

Your pardon. I will follow you anon.
   *She advances to meet Mabel. Exit
   Pierpont.*
Nay, be of better cheer. Should one betrothed
Upon her bridal eve look downcast thus?
There dwells a settled sadness on your brow
I marked not ere this wooing. O my child!
Carry it gayly; go among your guests;
Be liberal of your smiles, free of your mirth,
As one should be upon the verge of bliss.
   Mabel. Believe me, I have striven to do my
   best,
Nor quite in vain; nay, heard you not your-
   self
Our sprightly jests, as I led forth the train
Through the wood's maze? O, we were gay!
   Lydia. I was not unobservant of your
   mirth;
It did not please me, Mabel; it was strained,
Abrupt — wanted tranquillity; your tones
Were quicker than belonged to quiet joy;
Your smiles not such as *peace* serenely wears,
But vanishing on sudden, as if hid
By the dark shadow on some inward cloud,
That would not be commanded to depart.
   Mabel. You are right; and I, it seems, am
   not so skilled
As I had thought in artifice. Yes, aunt!
There is a care lies heavy at my heart.
   Lydia. I knew there was: confide your grief
   to me.
   Mabel. I fear that time has changed him.
   Lydia. Changed Sir Edgar!

Mabel. Ay: 'tis even so.

Lydia. Despite of which your love still
perseveres?

Mabel. True love, though tender, is im-
mortal too —
Easy to wound, incapable of death.
Not that he has at any time been harsh,
At least in words; but that to me seems stern
Which others might not deem so. Public
cares
Leave him few hours for converse, and in
those
He speaks me formally. I know I'm blameful
To tell you this; but then I have no mother,
Whose voice might solace weakness or re-
prove it.

Lydia. Alas! Sweet niece, you merit better
fate.

Mabel. Why say so, aunt? I have in nought
accused him,
Except in change; such change as comes like
growth,
Sure, but unnoted.

Lydia. I trust you kept my counsel,
dearest child —
Avoided all recurrence to the past.

Mabel. We have not spoken of it. Much I
fear
It steals upon his memory, and clouds
The sunshine of his love.

Lydia. I would fain hope
The best, dear Mabel. You did well at least
In keeping silence; but we shall be late.
You know your father's wishes are to grace
Your nuptials with all ceremony, whence
This public reading of the marriage treaty.
Would I could bribe those lips to smile.
Come, love.

Exeunt Lady Mabel and Lydia.

Enter Mordaunt, looking after them.

Mor. 'Tis she. What sad reluctance in her
step!
The conscious victim in each gesture speaks.
True, true, confirmed by many a certain sign,
The Lady Lydia's tale. She loves me not,
And curbs her loathing at her sire's behest!
She turns within. What witchery of grace,
Less seen than felt! We know not where it
dwells,
Nor how it works; but it doth work to *mad-
ness!*
Bright fascination, wanting only heart
To make thee perfect. Thou that in the thrall
Of fatal beauty didst my spirit bind,
Delilah-like, to prostrate and betray;
Still, still there's magic to me in thy motions.
Still find thy sighs their echoes in my heart's
Reverberating ruins. Still thy voice
Wakes a wild music from these jarring
strings.
Proud scorner! I could love thee spite of
scorn.
Ill fits this mood the time. Hence, yielding
self!
No private interests now. The truth! the
right!
Yea, though each syllable were coined in fire,
And my own heart the furnace, I would speak
My message. Haughty lady, heart, take heart!
Fate yet may snatch thee from the base-born
Mordaunt.

Enter Servant.

Servant. My lord, sir, seeks your presence.

Mor. Does he so? I will attend him
instantly.
I come.   *Exeunt Mordaunt and Servant.*

Scene 2.

*Library, as before. Earl of Lynterne, Mordaunt,
Deancourt, Pierpont, Colville, Lady Lydia,
Mabel, Notary, and Wedding Guests dis-
covered.*

Earl. Good friends assembled here to con-
fer honor
Upon the near espousals, I beseech
Your kind attention while this gentleman
                    (*Notary rises*)
Reads in your hearing the accustomed deed
Determining the rights and property
Of such as stand affianced.

Mor. (*Rising*) My Lord Lynterne,
And guests who grace us with your presence
here,
I've that to say, which 'twere unseasonable
To broach at any later stage than this.
                    (*Notary sits*)
Deem you not me much honored, who have
sprung
From lineage obscure, in this alliance
With a most noble lady, who can trace
An ancestry which from the Conqueror's
time
Hath never mingled blood with churls before?

Lydia. What frantic scheme has this man
now to compass?
Nay, dear Sir Edgar, your modesty doth underrate your birth.

Mor. Not so. My father was a man of toil;
I mean real toil, such toil as makes the hand
Uncouth to sight, coarse, hard to the touch;
There are none here who would have clasped
that hand
Save at election contests, when all fingers
Grow marvellously pliant.

Lydia. How well this frankness becomes a
noble mind!

How great it is to rise by our desert from
    lowliness,
And blush not at its memory!
  Omnes. Most noble.
  Lister. (*To Heartwell, aside*) I understand
    not this.
  Heart. There's a deep meaning in it.
  Mor. You would do honor, then, good
    friends, to him
Who by his own endeavor should win his way
To eminence and power?
  Dean. Such men adorn their country.
  Col. Their merit doth distance praise!
  Lydia. They are earth's master spirits.
  Mor. Then had you known one such, in his
    first years
Of effort, you had aided him; at least
Given him your hand — showed him respect?
  Lydia. Respect most due.
  Heart. Decidedly! Who doubts it?
  Mor. You had been just, and had not
    plotted then
Against his peace, and baited with such smiles
As the heart loves to feed on, the dire poison
Of wanton, causeless scorn?
  Lydia. Why ask them this, knowing that
    they would not?
  Mor. But did such live, what should be
    their desert?
  Earl. You trespass, sir, too much upon the
    time
Of this high company. Methinks 'twere well
The notary should proceed.
  Mor. I am indifferent.
  Earl. Mean you to wed my daughter?
  Mor. NO! (*Turning upon him fiercely; all
    rise in surprise*)
  Pier. Malignant viper, you shall dearly pay
The debt of this disgrace.   *Exit Notary.*
  Mor. Yet hold a while;
If you accuse me, grant me the same rights
That all accused enjoy. Hear my defence;
That over, I will bide whatever shape
Your anger wills to take.
  Earl. Begone, sir; leave us while contempt
    stills wrath.
  Mabel. I do beseech you, hear him; I am
    curious
To hear what sins of my commission urged
To deed so pitiful. If I had wronged —
  Pier. Even then it was most pitiful
    revenge.
  Lydia. But still consistent with his char-
    acter.
  Omnes. O, yes, yes!
  Mor. Why, see how much your expecta-
    tions mock your acts!
You sow the heart with bitterness, and marvel

That it bears kindless fruit. The slave's treat-
    ment
Is what you give man, and the angel's meek-
    ness
Is what you demand from him. 'Tis five years
Since this same Lady Mabel lured my soul
With such soft praises, and such winning
    looks
As only leave the words "I love" unsaid.
'Twas not my vanity that thus construed
These signs of tenderness. The Lady Lydia
Noted their import; nay, with earnestness,
Not willing then our union, besought me
To quit the castle,
Avowed that Lady Mabel had confessed her
    love.
Encouraged thus, I straightway sought the
    earl,
Entreated his permission to be ranked
As Lady Mabel's suitor, when it pleased her
Smilingly to admit that she had toyed
With me to wile away an idle hour.
I hasted home; in a few days the tale
Of my crushed love was blazoned to the
    world,
Blown, published, chorused,
In the quick ear of scoffers! This low churl,
This foiled plebeian aspirant, supplied
Mirth to a thousand jesters. What presump-
    tion
In him to love thus! What effrontery
To have a heart! Now, for once be men
And women; or, if you can, be human.
Have you loved ever? known what 'tis to
    stake
Your heart's whole capital of blessedness
Upon one die — the chance of love returned;
To lose the cast; be beggared in your soul;
Then to be spurned, and made a public scorn
By those who tempted to the fatal throw
Which drained your heart of riches; and all
    this
Because your birth was lowly? Had you
    borne it?
  Earl. Enough, sir! You have had your
    vengeance. Hence!
  Mor. I have not sought for vengeance in
    this act.
My life, my energies, my talents, all
Did I task for the deed! Such apparatus
Was meant for nobler uses than belong
To a mere private feud; but I have fought
A battle for high principles, and taught
Convention, when it dares to tread down
    man,
Man shall arise in turn and tread it down!
As for this lady — she has never loved me,
Nor have I lately sought to win her love;

Nor shall I ever seek again to win her love.
I would not wreak on her such wretchedness
As she caused me for pastime. I have done.
My mission is fulfilled.   (*Going*)
   Pier. You shall not quit this house until
    you answer
For this indignity. (*Draws his sword. Mabel
   rushes forward and arrests his arm with
   great agitation*)
   Mabel. Upon your life injure him not;
Put up your sword, I say. (*Mordaunt regards
   her earnestly*)
   Mor. He is not worthy of it.   *Exit.*
     TABLEAU. Quick drop.
     End of the Fourth Act.

ACT V.

Scene 1.

*In the interval between the fourth and fifth acts
the season changes from summer to autumn.
Library in Lynterne Castle, as before.
Physician and Earl discovered.*

   Phy. Have you, my lord, of late received
    account
Of Lady Lydia's state?
   Earl. No recent news; poor sister Lydia!
When first suspicion dawned that my child's
   grief
Was wearing health away, her aunt, o'ercome
By daily witness of such touching woe,
Grew pale almost to wanness.
From Venice, where my sister purposes
Some few months to stay, I anxiously wait
   letters.
But say! how fares it with my blessed one?
Tell me the worst. — Nay, pause a mo-
   ment. — Now
I think I am man enough to hear you.
   Phy. The mind is our chief enemy;
And failing its alliance, all endeavor
Hastens the evil it would fain arrest.
   Earl. O, tax your whole resources; could I
   find
The healing drug would save her, I would
   buy it,
Though beggared by the purchase.
   Phy. Could we obliterate the past, efface
All memory of this wrong, whose double edge
Wounds both her love and pride, recall to life
Her hopes and her affections —
   Earl. Cease, sir, to torture me; 'tis
   mockery
To name specifics out of human grasp.

*Enter Servant announcing Lady Lydia, who
enters in traveling costume. Exit Servant.*

   Earl. (*Advancing to meet her*) My sister!
   Dearest Lydia! thou art changed.
   Lydia. Speak not of me. Mabel, is she
   much altered, brother?
   Earl. Alas! much altered, as yourself may
   see.

*Enter Mabel and attendant. They draw near
Mabel. Lydia keeping her eyes on the ground,
and suddenly raising them as she faces her
   niece.*

   Lydia. (*Trembling*) Ha! I need not sup-
   port; let us embrace.
No, no, it is forbidden.
   Mabel. Forbidden, sweetest kinswoman!
   Lydia. By CONSCIENCE.
Let me tell you, conscience can bow
Wills tyrants cannot move — extort deep
   groans
     *Physician wheels arm chair to Mabel
     in centre. Mabel seated and arranging
     herself in chair.*
From men mute on the rack — and from the
   lips
Of guilty pride, which the flames' agony
Cannot distort or open, wring the tale
Of sin and degradation.
   Earl. (*To Physician*) What can this mean?
   I fear her mind's disturbed.
   Lydia. (*Overhearing him*) True! but not in
   your sense; now, listen to me.
I am my niece's murderer! (*Mabel looks up*)
   Earl. Poor, poor unfortunate! (*Compas-
   sionately*)
   Lydia. I did not drug her drink
With poison, nor at night with unsheathed
   blade
Startle her chamber's darkness; but by arts
Born of infernal pride, I *poisoned hopes*
That outlive life in worth, and plunged my
   dart
Where it is mercy to stab mortally,
Such anguish follows where the wound is
   made.
   Mabel. O, mercy! mercy! Did you deceive
   me *there?*
   Lydia. When he who shall be nameless
   was our guest,
I prompted him at once to ask your hand,
Assured him of your love, which I declared
Yourself had owned to me. With sinful wiles
I taught you to believe that he had dared
To ask you of your father as the hire
For future service. I awoke your wrath,
Moved you to show him scorn.
   Mabel. Alas! Alas!

Lydia. With bitter raillery I told the tale
I had invented where I knew 'twould gain
Admission to his ear: the effect you know.

Mabel. Wake me! I cannot bear this dream.
  O, wake me!
Will none of you have pity?

Lydia. More remains. This letter will tell
  all. (*Gives letter. Mabel takes the letter
  mechanically*)
Mabel, my niece, in deep remorse, in guilty
  agony,
I pray you to forgive me. (*Kneeling to Mabel*)

Mabel. Hence! your presence (*Passionately*)
Tortures my eyes, as have your deeds my
  heart!

Lydia. Niece! child! turn not away. I will
  be heard!
I loved thee ever. When I wronged thee most,
My sin was born of love. So high my aims
And hopes for thee, I could not brook thee
  wed,
Save where to every human excellence
Was added all the world accounts most noble.
And now these tears, this soft and plenteous
  dew,
Speak not an arid soil — a stony heart.
After my long and weary pilgrimage,
I clasp thy feet, a humbled penitent.

Mabel. I — I — O God, send tears!

Lydia. (*With solemnity*) Ah, Mabel,
  think —
We both are dying women —
O, think that you
May need forgiveness too! (*Lydia kneels at
  Mabel's feet, and puts her arms round her
  neck*)

Mabel. You are forgiven. (*Falteringly*)

Lydia. Bless thee! Death will be gentler
  now. Farewell! (*Kisses Mabel's hand,
  then advances to Earl*)
Brother! (*Kneels*)

Earl. Yes, I will not add to other misery
That of repulsing penitence. Now go:
You need rest, and must take it.
                              Exit Lady Lydia.

Earl. The tale so long discredited was true.
Mordaunt is wronged.

Mabel. (*A pause*) I ruined and disgraced!

Earl. It shall be done. Avaunt, rebellious
  pride!
What though I grovel at a peasant's foot
To save my dear one's life. Give me the letter.
                      (*Takes letter from Mabel*)

Mabel. What mean you, for your air is
  strangely wild,
And your frame trembles?

Earl. No, no; the strife is passed. O God!
  that we,

Whom thy one breath can prostrate utterly
And sweep from earth our love's inheritance,
Should dare to foster pride!

Mabel. (*Starting to her feet*) You would see
  Mordaunt!

Earl. Yes, I will see him — supplicate his
  ear
For this most sad mischance. My prayers and
  tears
Will surely reach his heart. I'll bend my knee,
And wear a look so meek, so lowly!

Mabel. Never!

Earl. O, yes; and he will pardon all the
  past.

Mabel. My path of desolation nears the
  grave;
Yet can I turn my face to him once more,
And look on him forgivingly. I know
That he has been deceived, and I forgive him.
He might have pardoned *me;* but he chose
  vengeance,
And left the print of shame on my crushed
  heart;
Yet wrung not from its depths one sigh of
  pain.
My misery has been silent. O, dear father,
Torture it not to speech!

Earl. Be calm, my child.

Mabel. Then go you not. Bow not your
  reverend head
In unavailing shame, nor let *him* know
What cause hath sped me hence.
It shall not be. Your hand — a sudden weak-
  ness. (*Mabel sinks into a chair*)

Earl. Alas! emotion has o'ertaxed her
  strength!

Phy. I will attend her. Meanwhile, my
  dear lord,
If your good purpose hold, seek Mordaunt
  straight.
Show him the letter. His mind, once con-
  vinced,
May prompt him to contrition, and such signs
Of penitent affection as shall win
Your daughter's heart to love of life again.

Earl. And yet I fear I go on a vain errand;
For should *he* yield, to o'ercome *her* resolve
Will be a task yet harder.

Phy. We are in a strait
Of peril that admits no other hope.
I do conjure you go, and please you bid
Some one to attend to share with me my
  watch.

Earl. You counsel right, my friend. I go.
  Farewell.

Phy. Almighty aid be with you.
                                    Exit Earl.
Her eyelids open. She revives. Dear lady!

Mabel. Who speaks? Where am I?

Phy. 'Tis I, your faithful friend who watch
by you.

Enter Maid Servant.

Mabel. Thanks, sir. Where is my father?
Call him hither!

Phy. Affairs of moment took him hence a
while.

Mabel. Is he within? He has not left the
house?

Phy. Soon to return.

Mabel. 'Twas strange he did not wait till
I revived,
Nor stayed to say farewell. (*Weeps*) 'Tis not
his wont
To quit me thus abruptly. I remember
He spoke of seeing Mordaunt. (*Servant comes
down*)
Heard you the earl's command? Which way
went he?

Servant. Madam, I think to Richmond.

Mabel. (*Rises*) Go straight and order that
the fleetest steeds
Be harnessed instantly. Then wait a while
My coming, in my chamber. (*Exit Maid Ser-
vant*) Check surprise;
I must depart at once and seek the earl.

Phy. 'Tis madness! Think not that your
shattered frame
Could undergo such trial of its strength!

Mabel. The feelings that inspire the deep
resolve
Can grant the aid to execute. I must go.

Phy. You will forgive me if I countermand
Your order lately given.   (*Going*)

Mabel. Stay! stay! (*Rushing to him. During
this, catches at back of chair for support*)
'Tis to preserve my father and myself
From scorn, from ignominy, from repulse,
I venture on this errand. O, just Heaven!
It will be thought we have devised some
feint
To move this proud man's heart. In vain, in
vain
My father will abase himself.
Do you deny me? Think you that my life
Is not more perilled by your present act
Than by my own design? What, not moved
yet?
Behold me take the suppliant's attitude.
(*Kneels*)
I do implore you in all humbleness
To let me now depart. You will not yet?
(*Rises*)
I claim my right of motion — trample on
All counsel that prescribes subservience
From soul to its poor vassal. I command
You let me pass forthwith. You dare not
brave me.

Phy. What supernatural wrath illumes her
eye!
She speaks sooth; the greater peril lies
In opposition. Madam, your will has way.

Mabel. Thanks, thanks; *you are* my friend.
In a short space
I shall expect you join me. Thanks! No help.
Exeunt.

Scene 2.

Mordaunt's House. Sofa, table and two chairs.

Enter Mordaunt.

Mor. I know not whence or wherefore
there hath come
This woman's weakness o'er my yielding
soul!
My deed was nobly done; then wherefore is't
That I am not at peace? Why will the thought,
Perchance, she may have loved me thus
intrude?
Why should I rack my soul with phantom
fears
Bred out of my weak pity? Can it be
That I have sought revenge and called it
justice?
Beautiful stars! how once I gazed on ye!
Ye almost seem to justify ambition;
For ye, though throned in loftiest altitude,
Have yet preëminence in purity!
These fancies once were my realities.
All Nature, with a meaning eloquence,
Addressed me to encourage! That hath
passed,
Yet nature is the same in outward show;
Each man makes his own world or unmakes
it;
And there he exiles whom no kingly edict,
Nor voice of law, has banished.

Enter Servant.

Ser. The Earl of Lynterne. (*Enter the Earl*)
Exit Servant.

Earl. Pardon, Sir Edgar, that I venture
thus
To break on your retirement; but my cause
Is one that outruns all respect of forms.

Mor. A country's servant knows no
privacy
That bars consideration of her weal.
I pray you sit, my lord.

Earl. My errand is not public. 'Tis not
now
The minister, who claims your patient ear,
But a plain, sorrowing man, whose wounded
heart
Your skill alone can heal. To be brief,
I am a father; let that word tell all.

Mor. The father of a daughter! Is it well
We should discourse of her?
    Earl. Tell me that you permit it. May I
    speak?
    Mor. Of her, my lord, or any other
    stranger,
If mention of a name delight your ear.
    Earl. And you will bear with me — you
    will be patient?
    Mor. Why should I not? What man is
    there so well
Can bear the verbal history of wrong
As he who hath it written on his heart?
If you recite the past, you will not grave
The inward record deeper. And its trace
Endures, though you be silent.
    Earl. O sir, repulse me not, for love of
    mercy.
Say that you retain some gentle thought,
Some tender recollection —
    Mor. Of your daughter? My lord, she has
    my pity.
    Earl. What! No more?
Ah, sir, I watched Mabel many a time,
When accident has held you longer space
Than was your wont to tarry, quit her chair,
And by the hour watch in love's deep sus-
    pense,
Pale, fixed, and mute — a very statue;
But when the tramp of thy approaching steed
Broke on her ear — for that love-quickened
    sense
Anticipated sight — she woke to life,
As though thy safety gave her leave to be,
Rushed forth to meet thee, but stopped bash-
    fully
To wait thine entrance with downcast lids,
Which vainly tried to hide the lucid joy
Floating, like sunshine, in the orbs beneath.
    Mor. What is your story's sequel? What
    succeeds?
    Earl. You loved her once!
    Mor. I did; and since it pleases you, I
    speak.
It shall be to such purpose as to wring,
Even from your confession, that my act
Was one of justice, not of cruelty.
I loved her once! Ay, she was then to me
The incorporated spirit of all good.
My soul's once science was to study her;
Her eyes were all my light, her voice my
    music,
Her movements all I cared to know of grace.
Loved her! 'Twas worship! 'Twas idolatry!
And how was I repaid? The meanest man
Who has nor wealth, nor talent, nor dis-
    tinction,
Giving his *heart*, proffers the dearest gift
His Maker gave to him, and meriting,

Even when not accepted, gratitude!
I was not such a one; in the world's van
I stood distinguished and preëminent!
I gave my heart, my mind, unto your
    daughter,
Of which she feigned acceptance, not by
    words,
But by confession far more eloquent.
I pressed the love she favored; she repulsed
    it!
She trampled on it! It was glowing fire;
She trod it into ashes!
    Earl. It was not so; but hear me.
    Mor. It is too late.
    Earl. (*Rises*) I do implore you, then, to
    read this letter. (*Mordaunt takes letter,
    reads, and speaks*)
    Mor. If this be true, it does pronounce me
    guilty;
Yet may this not turn out a fine device?

    Mabel enters and rushes to the Earl.

    Mabel. My father!
    Earl. My child! Read *there* the answer to
    your doubt.
    Mor. 'Tis evidence that stabs, while it
    convicts.
Why knew I not this sooner?
O Mabel, how I've wronged thee! (*Kneels to
    her*)
    Mabel. What words are these? I came here
    to forbid
Vain supplication to a haughty heart,
And lo! I find one meek and penitent.
And dost thou love me, Mordaunt?
    Mor. Love thee, Mabel!
My care-worn heart revives at sight of thee,
And hoards the life 'twas weariness to keep.
How now! thou tremblest, sweet!
    Mabel. Love! aid me to my chair;
My strength is failing fast; I am as one
Who has striven hard to distance grief, and
    gained
The goal before her, my strength but sufficing
To win the triumph. Mordaunt, I shall die
With thy love for my chaplet, and in peace!
    Mor. And thou wilt *live* in peace for many
    years!
What demon gives my fear-struck heart the lie!
    Mabel. I've much to say, and but brief
    time to speak it.
Thou knowest *now* I love thee; but thou
    canst not,
Thou canst not tell how deeply. That our lips
Should so belie our hearts! Couldst thou read
    mine —
    Mor. Or thou read mine; the thoughts of
    agony
Remorse sears on it with a brand of fire!

Mabel. O, couldst thou know how often in my walks
My soul drank gladness from the thought that thou
Wouldst share them with me, and the beautiful
Grow brighter as thy voice interpreted
Its hidden loveliness; and our fireside!
How I should greet thee from the stormy war
Of public conflict, kneel beside thy chair,
And cause thee bend thine eyes on mine, until
Thy brow expanded, and thy lips confessed
The blessedness of home!
Mor. Home, sayest thou? *Home!*
Home! That means *Grave.*
Mabel. My fate is gentler, love,
Than I had dared to hope. I shall not *live*
Encircled by thine arms; but I may die so.
Mor. I cannot bear it; O, I cannot bear it.
Fool! fool! Not to know the vengeance of forgiveness!

Earl. You see, sir, that the wound is deep enough.
Mabel. Nay, speak not harshly; for in noble minds
Error is suffering, and we should soothe
The breast that bears its punishment within.
Tell him that you forgive him. Do not pause.
Think not thy affluent affection now,
That hitherto outran my need in granting —
Dimness floats before me. While I yet
Can hear your voice, tell me that you forgive
him. (*Mabel has now raised herself, and stands erect*)
Earl. I do, I do!
Mabel. Now take him to your arms,
And call him son. (*She staggers to Edgar*)
Earl. I do, I do! My son, my son!
Mor. My father!
Mabel. I am happy — very, very happy!
Dies.

THE END.

ROBERT BROWNING
1812-1889

Pippa Passes
(1841)

If anyone had the intellectual, emotional, and intuitive equipment to rescue the declining verse drama, it was Robert Browning. He was the greatest dramatic *poet* of the nineteenth century; he was willing to present modern scenes in verse, and he had sufficient creative power and originality to elevate material of any place or time to exhibit the universal traits of human nature. Or, at least, this is what W. C. Macready thought.

On May 26, 1836, Browning attended a dinner given to celebrate the opening of Sir Thomas Noon Talfourd's play *Ion*. Macready, who was present, knew Browning's poems "Pauline" and "Paracelsus" and recognized in them authentic poetry. He said to Browning, "Will you write me a tragedy and save me from going to America?" As historical plays were then fashionable, Browning replied, "Shall it be historical or English? What do you say to Strafford?" Macready agreed, and Browning immediately set to work on a play about Sir Thomas Wentworth, Earl of Strafford, and the struggle between Charles I and the Puritans. Macready produced the play at Covent Garden on May 1, 1837, but since the action dragged and the lines were too obscure for the audience to follow, the play had to close after five nights. During the following years Browning wrote other plays for stage performance, including *King Victor and King Charles* (1842), which was not produced, and *A Blot in the 'Scutcheon*, which was produced by Macready at Drury Lane on February 11, 1843.

A Blot in the 'Scutcheon might have given new life to the verse drama, for it contained a number of vital ingredients. A domestic drama, written to appeal to the taste of the 1840's, it had a deeper message than the conventional prescriptive morality. Instead of merely presenting a pure heroine and an honorable hero, it undertook to discover the essence of purity and honor. Like the problem plays of the 1890's, it opposed one apparent right against another, and sought to find the truth in the motives of the characters. There was also more action than in *Strafford*. In part this was due to Macready's help, for he labored over the play, cut lines, and made suggestions. That he particularly suggested more action and less talk is clear in a note from Browning: "There is ACTION in it, drabbing, stabbing, et autres gentillesses." He trusted that he had reached a successful "compromise between my own notion and yours — as I understand it, at least." Browning does have a good deal of romantic action. An attractive young nobleman loves an orphan girl, and climbs a yew tree to her bower when a signal light appears there. At the climax there is dueling, a suicide, and death of a broken heart. The usual pathos of the melodrama appears in the heroine's repeated lines, "I was so young, I loved him so, I had / No mother, God forgot me, and I fell."

In spite of all this the play ran only three nights. To the audience and Macready the idea that a fallen woman might be pure of heart seemed incredible. When Mertoun in the yew tree sang to Mildred, "There's a woman like a dew-drop, she's so purer than the purest," the audience laughed. Macready had wished to give Browning's tragedy a happy ending with Tresham's retreat to a monastery instead of his death. Frictions during the production and the failure of the play in performance led Browning and Macready into a quarrel.

But perhaps the real reason for the play's failure lay in what might have been a source of strength, success, and revival of the verse drama. Instead of presenting one-dimensional characters, Browning analyzed mental and emotional states. Besides the conflict between one man and another, he sought to exhibit conflicts of impulse, emotion, and reason within the individual. As Browning himself put it, he conceived of drama as "Action in Character, rather than Character in Action." He insisted upon this characterization in depth, but did not know how to project it for the nineteenth-century stage. A quotation from *A Blot in the 'Scutcheon* will illustrate this weakness. Guendolen, having come to Mildred's chamber for a serious talk, feels that she is coolly received. In order to say, "I came up here to talk with you about Lord Mertoun and your brother. Why are you reluctant to talk about them?" she says:

> Now, Mildred, spare those pains. I have not left
> Our talkers in the library, and climbed
> The wearisome ascent to this your bower
> In company with you, — I have not dared . . .
> Nay, worked such prodigies as sparing you
> Lord Mertoun's pedigree before the flood,
> Which Thorold seemed in very act to tell
> — Or bringing Austin to pluck up that most
> Firm-rooted heresy — your suitor's eyes,
> He would maintain, were gray instead of blue —
> I think I brought him to contrition! — Well,
> I have not done such things, (all to deserve
> A minute's quiet cousin's talk with you,)
> To be dismissed so coolly.

Browning felt it essential to make every flicker of Guendolen's feelings clear. But the audience in a large and often noisy theatre could not follow the involved sentences. Apparently Browning could not discover how to adapt the analysis he felt essential to the conditions of the theatre. After *A Blot in the 'Scutcheon*, self-defensively perhaps, Browning said, "I conceived a disgust for play-writing, and never attempted it again." Meanwhile, he was working in a type of drama that gave scope to his genius — the closet drama.

Pippa Passes was not intended for performance, but as a play it exhibits imaginative experimentation in every feature except the dialogue; luminous when studied, it remains too intricate for the immediate clarity needed on the stage. The drama consists of four one-act plays within the envelope of a fifth action, Pippa's passing, which penetrates each of the four inner plays at its crisis and determines its outcome. According to Mrs. Sutherland Orr, "Mr. Browning was walking alone, in a wood near Dulwich, when the image flashed upon him of someone walking thus alone through life; one apparently too obscure to leave a trace of his or her passage, yet exercising a lasting though unconscious influence at every step of it; and the image shaped itself into the little silk winder of Asolo, Felippa, or Pippa." Within this enveloping frame, Browning gave unity to the four inner plays by treating the meaning of love on four levels: illicit passion, married love, mother's love, and God's love.

The dramatic conflict in each inner play is an internal spiritual struggle between conscience and desire, pride, fear, or self-interest. Just as each struggle reaches a crisis, Pippa passes by, unintentionally singing a song appropriate to touch the heart of the hearer. That she passes at just the right moment, singing the right song, is quite contrived. But Mr. W. C. De Vane calls this fact a "legitimate poetic extension of the idea that the casual spoken word may have a tremendous effect upon the lives of men." To some extent, Pippa is symbolic; carrying God's message, she is God's whisper, an objective symbol of the conscience of each hearer. Externally the characters and situations are stock, even melodramatic, but internally each simple "villain" is the baser in conflict with the better self. The whisper recalls each to his better self and changes his course of action. Pippa herself, unaware of any effect upon others, is not affected within the play; beyond it, perhaps, Monsignor may restore her inheritance.

In connecting passages between the plays Browning presents as a general setting a realistic cross-section of Asolo, an Italian mill town he had visited in 1838. Many of the town characters appear: the Austrian police seeking to trap patriotic Italian "subversives," art students from France, Germany, and England, and a group of prostitutes. In incidental references the plays cast further light on the town and on the Church, and social criticism is implied in the picture of Pippa's hard life in the silk mills.

The plays and their interrelationships display many complex ironies. Browning's meaning in some details is left incomplete, perhaps to let the insight of the reader complete the drama. But interpretation of the problems in this closet drama (for instance, whether Sebald kills Ottima and himself) belongs more to the study of Browning's poetry than to this introduction.

PIPPA PASSES

A Drama In Four Scenes
by
ROBERT BROWNING

I dedicate my best intention in this poem,
admiringly to the author of "Ion,"
affectionately to Mr. Sergeant Talfourd. R.B.

A closet drama, not performed. London, 1841.

Cast of Characters

PIPPA	PHENE
OTTIMA	AUSTRIAN POLICE
SEBALD	BLUPHOCKS
FOREIGN STUDENTS	LUIGI AND HIS MOTHER
GOTTLIEB	POOR GIRLS
SCHRAMM	MONSIGNOR AND HIS ATTENDANTS
JULES	

Introduction

New Year's Day at Asolo in the Trevisan. A
large, mean, airy chamber. A girl, Pippa,
from the silk-mills, springing out of bed.

DAY!
Faster and more fast,
O'er night's brim, day boils at last:
Boils, pure gold, o'er the cloud-cup's brim
Where spurting and suppressed it lay,
For not a froth-flake touched the rim
Of yonder gap in the solid gray
Of the eastern cloud, an hour away;
But forth one wavelet, then another, curled,
Till the whole sunrise, not to be suppressed,
Rose, reddened, and its seething breast
Flickered in bounds, grew gold, then over-
flowed the world.

Oh, Day, if I squander a wavelet of thee,
A mite of my twelve hours' treasure,
The least of thy gazes or glances.
(Be they grants thou art bound to or gifts
above measure)
One of thy choices or one of thy chances,
(Be they tasks God imposed thee or freaks at
thy pleasure)
— My Day, if I squander such labor or
leisure,
Then shame fall on Asolo, mischief on me!

Thy long blue solemn hours serenely flowing,

Whence earth, we feel, gets steady help and
  good —
Thy fitful sunshine-minutes, coming, going,
As if earth turned from work in gamesome
  mood —
All shall be mine! But thou must treat me not
As prosperous ones are treated, those who
  live
At hand here, and enjoy the higher lot,
In readiness to take what thou wilt give,
And free to let alone what thou refusest;
For, Day, my holiday, if thou ill-usest
Me, who am only Pippa, — old-year's sorrow,
Cast off last night, will come again to-morrow:
Whereas, if thou prove gentle, I shall borrow
Sufficient strength of thee for new-year's
  sorrow.
All other men and women that this earth
Belongs to, who all days alike possess,
Make general plenty cure particular dearth,
Get more joy one way, if another, less:
Thou art my single day, God lends to leaven
What were all earth else, with a feel of
  heaven, —
Sole light that helps me through the year,
  thy sun's!
Try now! Take Asolo's Four Happiest Ones —
And let thy morning rain on that superb
Great haughty Ottima; can rain disturb
Her Sebald's homage? All the while thy rain
Beats fiercest on her shrub-house window-
  pane,
He will but press the closer, breathe more
  warm
Against her cheek; how should she mind the
  storm?
And, morning past, if mid-day shed a gloom
O'er Jules and Phene, — what care bride and
  groom
Save for their dear selves? 'Tis their marriage-
  day;
And while they leave church and go home
  their way,
Hand clasping hand, within each breast
  would be
Sunbeams and pleasant weather spite of thee.
Then, for another trial, obscure thy eve
With mist, — will Luigi and his mother
  grieve —
The lady and her child, unmatched, forsooth,
She in her age, as Luigi in his youth,
For true content? The cheerful town, warm,
  close
And safe, the sooner that thou art morose,
Receives them. And yet once again, outbreak
In storm at night on Monsignor, they make
Such stir about, — whom they expect from
  Rome
To visit Asolo, his brothers' home,

And say here masses proper to release
A soul from pain, — what storm dares hurt
  his peace?
Calm would he pray, with his own thoughts
  to ward
Thy thunder off, nor want the angels' guard.
But Pippa — just one such mischance would
  spoil
Her day that lightens the next twelvemonth's
  toil
At wearisome silk-winding, coil on coil!
  And here I let time slip for naught!
Aha, you foolhardy sunbeam, caught
With a single splash from my ewer!
You that would mock the best pursuer,
Was my basin over-deep?
One splash of water ruins you asleep,
And up, up, fleet your brilliant bits
Wheeling and counterwheeling,
Reeling, broken beyond healing:
Now grow together on the ceiling!
That will task your wits.
Whoever it was quenched fire first, hoped to
  see
Morsel after morsel flee
As merrily, as giddily . . .
Meantime, what lights my sunbeam on,
Where settles by degrees the radiant cripple?
Oh, is it surely blown, my martagon?
New-blown and ruddy as St. Agnes' nipple,
Plump as the flesh-bunch on some Turk bird's
  poll!
Be sure if corals, branching 'neath the ripple
Of ocean, bud there, — fairies watch unroll
Such turban-flowers; I say, such lamps dis-
  perse
Thick red flame through that dusk green
  universe!
I am queen of thee, floweret!
And each fleshy blossom
Preserve I not — (safer
Than leaves that embower it,
Or shells that embosom)
— From weevil and chafer?
Laugh through my pane then; solicit the bee;
Gibe him, be sure; and, in midst of thy
  glee,
Love thy queen, worship me!

— Worship whom else? For am I not, this
  day,
Whate'er I please? What shall I please to-
  day?
My morn, noon, eve and night — how spend
  my day?
To-morrow I must be Pippa who winds silk,
The whole year round, to earn just bread and
  milk:
But, this one day, I have leave to go,

And play out my fancy's fullest games;
I may fancy all day — and it shall be so —
That I taste of the pleasures, am called by the
names
Of the Happiest Four in our Asolo!

See! Up the hill-side yonder, through the
morning,
Some one shall love me, as the world calls
love:
I am no less than Ottima, take warning!
The gardens, and the great stone house above,
And other house for shrubs, all glass in front,
Are mine; where Sebald steals, as he is wont,
To court me, while old Luca yet reposes:
And therefore, till the shrub-house door
uncloses,
I . . . what now? — give abundant cause for
prate
About me — Ottima, I mean — of late,
Too bold, too confident she'll still face down
The spitefullest of talkers in our town.
How we talk in the little town below!
  But love, love, love — there's better love,
  I know!
This foolish love was only day's first offer;
I choose my next love to defy the scoffer:
For do not our Bride and Bridegroom sally
Out of Possagno church at noon?
Their house looks over Orcana valley:
Why should not I be the bride as soon
As Ottima? For I saw, beside,
Arrive last night that little bride —
Saw, if you call it seeing her, one flash
Of the pale snow-pure cheek and black bright
tresses,
Blacker than all except the black eyelash;
I wonder she contrives those lids no dresses!
— So strict was she, the veil
Should cover close her pale
Pure cheeks — a bride to look at and scarce
touch,
Scarce touch, remember, Jules! For are not
such
Used to be tended, flower-like, every feature,
As if one's breath would fray the lily of a
creature?
A soft and easy life these ladies lead:
Whiteness in us were wonderful indeed.
Oh, save that brow its virgin dimness,
Keep that foot its lady primness,
Let those ankles never swerve
From their exquisite reserve,
Yet have to trip along the streets like me,
All but naked to the knee!
How will she ever grant her Jules a bliss
So startling as her real first infant kiss?
Oh, no — not envy, this!
— Not envy, sure! — for if you gave me

Leave to take or to refuse,
In earnest, do you think I'd choose
That sort of new love to enslave me?
Mine should have lapped me round from the
beginning;
As little fear of losing it as winning:
Lovers grow cold, men learn to hate their
wives,
And only parents' love can last our lives.
At eve the Son and Mother, gentle pair,
Commune inside our turret: what prevents
My being Luigi? While that mossy lair
Of lizards through the winter-time is stirred
With each to each imparting sweet intents
For this new-year, as brooding bird to bird —
(For I observe of late, the evening walk
Of Luigi and his mother, always ends
Inside our ruined turret, where they talk,
Calmer than lovers, yet more kind than
friends)
— Let me be cared about, kept out of harm,
And schemed for, safe in love as with a
charm;
Let me be Luigi! If I only knew
What was my mother's face — my father,
too!
  Nay, if you come to that, best love of all
Is God's; then why not have God's love befall
Myself as, in the palace by the Dome,
Monsignor? — who to-night will bless the
home
Of his dead brother; and God bless in turn
That heart which beats, those eyes which
mildly burn
With love for all men! I, to-night at least,
Would be that holy and beloved priest.

Now wait! — even I already seem to share
In God's love: what does New-year's hymn
declare?
What other meaning do these verses bear?

All service ranks the same with God:
If now, as formerly he trod
Paradise, his presence fills
Our earth, each only as God wills
Can work — God's puppets, best and worst,
Are we; there is no last nor first.
Say not "a small event!" Why "small"?
Costs it more pain that this, ye call
A "great event," should come to pass,
Than that? Untwine me from the mass
Of deeds which make up life, one deed
Power shall fall short in or exceed!

And more of it, and more of it! — oh yes —
I will pass each, and see their happiness,
And envy none — being just as great, no
doubt,
Useful to men, and dear to God, as they!

A pretty thing to care about
So mightily, this single holiday!
But let the sun shine! Wherefore repine?
— With thee to lead me, O Day of mine,
Down the grass path gray with dew,
Under the pine-wood, blind with boughs
Where the swallow never flew
Nor yet cicala dared carouse —
No, dared carouse! *She enters the street.*

Scene 1.

MORNING

*Up the hill-side, inside the shrub-house. Luca's
wife, Ottima, and her paramour, the German
Sebald.*

Sebald. (Sings)
  Let the watching lids wink!
  Day's a-blaze with eyes, think!
  Deep into the night, drink!
Ottima. Night? Such may be your Rhine-
    land nights perhaps;
But this blood-red beam through the shutter's
    chink
— We call such light, the morning: let us see!
Mind how you grope your way, though! How
    these tall
Naked geraniums straggle! Push the lattice
Behind that frame! — Nay, do I bid you? —
    Sebald,
It shakes the dust down on me! Why, of
    course
The slide-bolt catches. Well, are you content,
Or must I find you something else to spoil?
Kiss and be friends, my Sebald! Is't full
    morning?
Oh, don't speak then!
Sebald. Ay, thus it used to be.
Ever your house was, I remember, shut
Till mid-day; I observed that, as I strolled
On mornings through the vale here; country
    girls
Were noisy, washing garments in the brook,
Hinds drove the slow white oxen up the hills:
But no, your house was mute, would ope no
    eye.
And wisely: you were plotting one thing
    there,
Nature, another outside. I looked up —
Rough white wood shutters, rusty iron bars,
Silent as death, blind in a flood of light.
Oh, I remember! — and the peasants laughed
And said, "The old man sleeps with the
    young wife."
This house was his, this chair, this window —
    his.
Ottima. Ah, the clear morning! I can see
    St. Mark's;
That black streak is the belfry. Stop: Vicenza

Should lie . . . there's Padua, plain enough,
    that blue!
Look o'er my shoulder, follow my finger!
Sebald. Morning?
It seems to me a night with a sun added.
Where's dew, where's freshness? That
    bruised plant, I bruised
In getting through the lattice yestereve,
Droops as it did. See, here's my elbow's mark
I' the dust o' the sill.
Ottima. Oh, shut the lattice, pray!
Sebald. Let me lean out. I cannot scent
    blood here,
Foul as the morn may be. There, shut the
    world out!
How do you feel now, Ottima? There, curse
The world and all outside! Let us throw off
This mask: how do you bear yourself? Let's
    out
With all of it.
Ottima. Best never speak of it.
Sebald. Best speak again and yet again of it,
Till words cease to be more than words. "His
    blood,"
For instance — let those two words mean
    "His blood"
And nothing more. Notice, I'll say them now,
"His blood."
Ottima. Assuredly if I repented
The deed—
Sebald. Repent? Who should repent, or
    why?
What puts that in your head? Did I once say
That I repented?
Ottima. No, I said the deed.
Sebald. "The deed" and "the event" —
    just now it was
"Our passion's fruit" — the devil take such
    cant!
Say, once and always, Luca was a wittol,
I am his cut-throat, you are . . .
Ottima. Here's the wine;
I brought it when we left the house above,
And glasses too — wine of both sorts. Black?
    White then?
Sebald. But am not I his cut-throat? What
    are you?
Ottima. There trudges on his business
    from the Duomo
Benet the Capuchin, with his brown hood
And bare feet; always in one place at church,
Close under the stone wall by the south entry.
I used to take him for a brown cold piece
Of the wall's self, as out of it he rose
To let me pass — at first, I say, I used:
Now, so has that dumb figure fastened on me,
I rather should account the plastered wall
A piece of him, so chilly does it strike.
This, Sebald?

Sebald? No, the white wine — the white
wine!
Well, Ottima, I promised no new year
Should rise on us the ancient shameful way;
Nor does it rise. Pour on! To your black eyes!
Do you remember last damned New Year's
day?
Ottima. You brought those foreign prints.
We looked at them
Over the wine and fruit. I had to scheme
To get him from the fire. Nothing but saying
His own set wants the proof-mark, roused
him up
To hunt them out.
Sebald. 'Faith, he is not alive
To fondle you before my face.
Ottima. Do you
Fondle me then! Who means to take your life
For that, my Sebald?
Sebald. Hark you, Ottima!
One thing to guard against. We'll not make
much
One of the other — that is, not make more
Parade of warmth, childish officious coil,
Than yesterday: as if, sweet, I supposed
Proof upon proof were needed now, now first,
To show I love you — yes, still love you —
love you
In spite of Luca and what's come to him
— Sure sign we had him ever in our thoughts,
White sneering old reproachful face and all!
We'll even quarrel, love, at times, as if
We still could lose each other, were not tied
By this: conceive you?
Ottima. Love!
Sebald. Not tied so sure.
Because though I was wrought upon, have
struck
His insolence back into him — am I
So surely yours? — therefore forever yours?
Ottima. Love, to be wise, (one counsel pays
another)
Should we have — months ago, when first we
loved,
For instance that May morning we two stole
Under the green ascent of sycamores —
If we had come upon a thing like that
Suddenly . . .
Sebald. "A thing" — there again — "a
thing!"
Ottima. Then, Venus' body, had we come
upon
My husband Luca Gaddi's murdered corpse
Within there, at his couch-foot, covered
close —
Would you have pored upon it? Why persist
In poring now upon it? For 'tis here
As much as there in the deserted house:
You cannot rid your eyes of it. For me,

Now he is dead I hate him worse: I hate . . .
Dare you stay here? I would go back and hold
His two dead hands, and say, "I hate you
worse,
Luca, than . . ."
Sebald. Off, off — take your hands off
mine,
'Tis the hot evening — off! oh, morning is it?
Ottima. There's one thing must be done;
you know what thing.
Come in and help to carry. We may sleep
Anywhere in the whole wide house to-night.
Sebald. What would come, think you, if
we let him lie
Just as he is? Let him lie there until
The angels take him! He is turned by this
Off from his face beside, as you will see.
Ottima. This dusty pane might serve for
looking-glass.
Three, four — four gray hairs! Is it so you
said
A plait of hair should wave across my neck?
No — this way.
Sebald. Ottima, I would give your neck,
Each splendid shoulder, both those breasts of
yours,
That this were undone! Killing! Kill the world
So Luca lives again! — ay, lives to sputter
His fulsome dotage on you — yes, and feign
Surprise that I return at even to sup,
When all the morning I was loitering here —
Bid me despatch my business and begone.
I would . . .
Ottima. See!
Sebald. No, I'll finish. Do you think
I fear to speak the bare truth once for all?
All we have talked of, is, at bottom, fine
To suffer; there's a recompense in guilt;
One must be venturous and fortunate:
What is one young for, else? In age we'll
sigh
O'er the wild reckless wicked days flown over;
Still, we have lived: the vice was in its place.
But to have eaten Luca's bread, have worn
His clothes, have felt his money swell my
purse —
Do lovers in romances sin that way?
Why, I was starving when I used to call
And teach you music, starving while you
plucked me
These flowers to smell!
Ottima. My poor lost friend!
Sebald. He gave me
Life, nothing less: what if he did reproach
My perfidy, and threaten, and do more —
Had he no right? What was to wonder at?
He sat by us at table quietly:
Why must you lean across till our cheeks
touched?

Could he do less than make pretence to
   strike?
'Tis not the crime's sake — I'd commit ten
   crimes
Greater, to have this crime wiped out,
   undone!
And you — O how feel you? Feel you for me?
   Ottima. Well then, I love you better now
   than ever,
And best (look at me while I speak to you) —
Best for the crime; nor do I grieve, in truth,
This mask, this simulated ignorance,
This affectation of simplicity,
Falls off our crime; this naked crime of ours
May not now be looked over: look it down!
Great? let it be great; but the joys it brought,
Pay they or no its price? Come: they or it!
Speak not! The past, would you give up the
   past
Such as it is, pleasure and crime together?
Give up that noon I owned my love for you?
The garden's silence: even the single bee
Persisting in his toil, suddenly stopped,
And where he hid you only could surmise
By some campanula chalice set a-swing.
Who stammered — "Yes, I love you"?
   Sebald. And I drew
Back; put far back your face with both my
   hands
Lest you should grow too full of me — your
   face
So seemed athirst for my whole soul and
   body!
   Ottima. And when I ventured to receive
   you here,
Made you steal hither in the mornings —
   Sebald. When
I used to look up 'neath the shrub-house
   here,
Till the red fire on its glazed windows spread
To a yellow haze?
   Ottima. Ah — my sign was, the sun
Inflamed the sere side of yon chestnut-tree
Nipped by the first frost.
   Sebald. You would always laugh
At my wet boots: I had to stride thro' grass
Over my ankles.
   Ottima. Then our crowning night!
   Sebald. The July night?
   Ottima. The day of it too, Sebald!
When heaven's pillars seemed o'erbowed
   with heat,
Its black-blue canopy suffered descend
Close on us both, to weigh down each to each,
And smother up all life except our life.
So lay we till the storm came.
   Sebald. How it came!
   Ottima. Buried in woods we lay, you
   recollect;

Swift ran the searching tempest overhead;
And ever and anon some bright white shaft
Burned thro' the pine-tree roof, here burned
   and there,
As if God's messenger thro' the close wood
   screen
Plunged and replunged his weapon at a
   venture,
Feeling for guilty thee and me: then broke
The thunder like a whole sea overhead —
   Sebald. Yes!
   Ottima. — While I stretched myself upon
   you, hands
To hands, my mouth to your hot mouth, and
   shook
All my locks loose, and covered you with
   them —
You, Sebald, the same you!
   Sebald. Slower, Ottima!
   Ottima. And as we lay —
   Sebald. Less vehemently! Love me!
Forgive me! Take not words, mere words, to
   heart!
Your breath is worse than wine! Breathe
   slow, speak slow!
Do not lean on me!
   Ottima. Sebald, as we lay,
Rising and falling only with our pants,
Who said, "Let death come now! 'Tis right
   to die!
Right to be punished! Naught completes such
   bliss
But woe!" Who said that?
   Sebald. How did we ever rise?
Was't that we slept? Why did it end?
   Ottima. I felt you
Taper into a point the ruffled ends
Of my loose locks 'twixt both your humid
   lips.
My hair is fallen now: knot it again!
   Sebald. I kiss you now, dear Ottima, now
   and now!
This way? Will you forgive me — be once
   more
My great queen?
   Ottima. Bind it thrice about my brow;
Crown me your queen, your spirit's arbitress,
Magnificent in sin. Say that!
   Sebald. I crown you
My great white queen, my spirit's arbitress,
Magnificent . . .
       From without is heard the voice of
       Pippa, singing —

       The year's at the spring
       And day's at the morn;
       Morning's at seven;
       The hill-side's dew-pearled;
       The lark's on the wing;

The snail's on the thorn:
God's in his heaven —
All's right with the world!

Pippa passes.

Sebald. God's in his heaven! Do you hear
that? Who spoke?
You, you spoke!
Ottima. Oh — that little ragged girl!
She must have rested on the step: we give
them
But this one holiday the whole year round.
Did you ever see our silk-mills — their in-
side?
There are ten silk-mills now belong to you.
She stoops to pick my double heartsease . . .
Sh!
She does not hear: call you out louder!
Sebald. Leave me!
Go, get your clothes on — dress those
shoulders!
Ottima. Sebald?
Sebald. Wipe off that paint! I hate you.
Ottima. Miserable!
Sebald. My God, and she is emptied of it
now!
Outright now! — how miraculously gone
All of the grace — had she not strange grace
once?
Why, the blank cheek hangs listless as it
likes,
No purpose holds the features up together,
Only the cloven brow and puckered chin
Stay in their places: and the very hair,
That seemed to have a sort of life in it,
Drops, a dead web!
Ottima. Speak to me — not of me!
Sebald. — That round great full-orbed
face, where not an angle
Broke the delicious indolence — all broken!
Ottima. To me — not of me! Ungrateful,
perjured cheat!
A coward too: but ingrate's worse than all.
Beggar — my slave — a fawning, cringing
lie!
Leave me! Betray me! I can see your drift!
A lie that walks and eats and drinks!
Sebald. My God!
Those morbid olive faultless shoulder-
blades —
I should have known there was no blood
beneath!
Ottima. You hate me then? You hate me
then?
Sebald. To think
She would succeed in her absurd attempt,
And fascinate by sinning, show herself
Superior — guilt from its excess superior
To innocence! That little peasant's voice
Has righted all again. Though I be lost,

I know which is the better, never fear,
Of vice or virtue, purity or lust,
Nature or trick! I see what I have done,
Entirely now! Oh I am proud to feel
Such torments — let the world take credit
thence —
I, having done my deed, pay too its price!
I hate, hate — curse you! God's in his
heaven!
Ottima. — Me!
Me! no, no, Sebald, not yourself — kill me!
Mine is the whole crime. Do but kill me —
then
Yourself — then — presently — first   hear
me speak!
I always meant to kill myself — wait, you!
Lean on my breast — not as a breast; don't
love me
The more because you lean on me, my own
Heart's Sebald! There, there, both deaths
presently!
Sebald. My brain is drowned now — quite
drowned: all I feel
Is . . .is, at swift-recurring intervals,
A hurry-down within me, as of waters
Loosened to smother up some ghastly pit:
There they go — whirls from a black fiery sea!
Ottima. Not me — to him, O God, be
merciful!

*Talk by the way, while Pippa is passing from
the hill-side to Orcana. Foreign Students of
painting and sculpture, from Venice, assembled opposite the house of Jules, a young
French statuary, at Possagno.*

1st Student. Attention! My own post is
beneath this window, but the pomegranate
clump yonder will hide three or four of you
with a little squeezing, and Schramm and his
pipe must lie flat in the balcony. Four, five —
who's a defaulter? We want everybody, for
Jules must not be suffered to hurt his bride
when the jest's found out.
2nd Student. All here! Only our poet's
away — never having much meant to be
present, moonstrike him! The airs of that
fellow, that Giovacchino! He was in violent
love with himself, and had a fair prospect of
thriving in his suit, so unmolested was it, —
when suddenly a woman falls in love with
him, too; and out of pure jealousy he takes
himself off to Trieste, immortal poem and all:
whereto is this prophetical epitaph appended
already, as Bluphocks assures me, — *"Here a
mammoth-poem lies, Fouled to death by butter-
flies."* His own fault, the simpleton! Instead
of cramp couplets, each like a knife in your
entrails, he should write, says Bluphocks,
both classically and intelligibly. — *Aescula-*

pius, an Epic. Catalogue of the drugs: Hebe's plaister — One strip Cools your lip. Phoebus' emulsion — One bottle Clears your throttle. Mercury's bolus — One box Cures . . .

3rd Student. Subside, my fine fellow! If the marriage was over by ten o'clock, Jules will certainly be here in a minute with his bride.

2nd Student. Good! — only, so should the poet's muse have been universally acceptable, says Bluphocks, *et canibus nostris* . . . and Delia not better known to our literary dogs than the boy Giovacchino!

1st Student. To the point, now. Where's Gottlieb, the new-comer? Oh, — listen, Gottlieb, to what has called down this piece of friendly vengeance on Jules, of which we now assemble to witness the winding-up. We are all agreed, all in a tale, observe, when Jules shall burst out on us in a fury by and by: I am spokesman — the verses that are to undeceive Jules bear my name of Lutwyche — but each professes himself alike insulted by this strutting stone-squarer, who came alone from Paris to Munich, and thence with a crowd of us to Venice and Possagno here, but proceeds in a day or two alone again — oh, alone indubitably! — to Rome and Florence. He, forsooth, take up his portion with these dissolute, brutalized, heartless bunglers! — so he was heard to call us all: now, is Schramm brutalized, I should like to know? Am I heartless?

Gottlieb. Why, somewhat heartless; for, suppose Jules a coxcomb as much as you choose, still, for this mere coxcombry, you will have brushed off — what do folks style it? — the bloom of his life. Is it too late to alter? These love-letters now, you call his — I can't laugh at them.

4th Student. Because you never read the sham letters of our inditing which drew forth these.

Gottlieb. His discovery of the truth will be frightful.

4th Student. That's the joke. But you should have joined us at the beginning: there's no doubt he loves the girl — loves a model he might hire by the hour!

Gottlieb. See here! "He has been accustomed," he writes, "to have Canova's women about him, in stone, and the world's women beside him, in flesh; these being as much below, as those above, his soul's aspiration: but now he is to have the reality." There you laugh again! I say, you wipe off the very dew of his youth.

1st Student. Schramm! (Take the pipe out of his mouth, somebody!) Will Jules lose the bloom of his youth?

Schramm. Nothing worth keeping is ever lost in this world: look at a blossom — it drops presently, having done its service and lasted its time; but fruits succeed, and where would be the blossom's place could it continue? As well affirm that your eye is no longer in your body, because its earliest favorite, whatever it may have first loved to look on, is dead and done with — as that any affection is lost to the soul when its first object, whatever happened first to satisfy it, is superseded in due course. Keep but ever looking, whether with the body's eye or the mind's, and you will soon find something to look on! Has a man done wondering at women? — there follow men, dead and alive, to wonder at. Has he done wondering at men? — there's God to wonder at: and the faculty of wonder may be, at the same time, old and tired enough with respect to its first object, and yet young and fresh sufficiently, so far as concerns its novel one. Thus . . .

1st Student. Put Schramm's pipe into his mouth again! There, you see! Well, this Jules . . . a wretched fribble — oh, I watched his disportings at Possagno, the other day! Canova's gallery — you know: there he marches first resolvedly past great works by the dozen without vouchsafing an eye: all at once he stops full at the *Psiche-fanciulla* — cannot pass that old acquaintance without a nod of encouragement — "In your new place, beauty? Then behave yourself as well here as at Munich — I see you!" Next he posts himself deliberately before the unfinished *Pietà* for half an hour without moving, till up he starts of a sudden, and thrusts his very nose into — I say, into — the group; by which gesture you are informed that precisely the sole point he had not fully mastered in Canova's practice was a certain method of using the drill in the articulation of the knee-joint — and that, likewise, has he mastered at length! Good-bye, therefore, to poor Canova — whose gallery no longer needs detain his successor Jules, the predestinated novel thinker in marble!

5th Student. Tell him about the women: go on to the women!

1st Student. Why, on that matter he could never be supercilious enough. How should we be other (he said) than the poor devils you see, with those debasing habits we cherish? He was not to wallow in that mire, at least: he would wait, and love only at the proper time, and meanwhile put up with the *Psiche-fanciulla.* Now, I happened to hear of a young Greek — real Greek girl at Malamocco; a true Islander, do you see, with

Alciphron's "hair like sea-moss" — Schramm knows! — white and quiet as an apparition, and fourteen years old at farthest, — a daughter of Natalia, so she swears — that hag Natalia, who helps us to models at three *lire* an hour. We selected this girl for the heroine of our jest. So first, Jules received a scented letter — somebody had seen his Tydeus at the Academy, and my picture was nothing to it: a profound admirer bade him persevere — would make herself known to him ere long. (Paolina, my little friend of the *Fenice*, transcribes divinely.) And in due time, the mysterious correspondent gave certain hints of her peculiar charms — the pale cheeks, the black hair — whatever, in short, had struck us in our Malamocco model: we retained her name, too — Phene, which is, by interpretation, sea-eagle. Now, think of Jules finding himself distinguished from the herd of us by such a creature! In his very first answer he proposed marrying his monitress: and fancy us over these letters, two, three times a day, to receive and despatch! I concocted the main of it: relations were in the way — secrecy must be observed — in fine, would he wed her on trust, and only speak to her when they were indissolubly united? St — st — Here they come!

6th Student. Both of them! Heaven's love, speak softly, speak within yourselves!

5th Student. Look at the bridegroom! Half his hair in storm and half in calm, — patted down over the left temple, — like a frothy cup one blows on to cool it: and the same old blouse that he murders the marble in.

2nd Student. Not a rich vest like yours, Hannibal Scratchy! — rich, that your face may the better set it off.

6th Student. And the bride! Yes, sure enough, our Phene! Should you have known her in her clothes? How magnificently pale!

Gottlieb. She does not also take it for earnest, I hope?

1st Student. Oh, Natalia's concern, that is! We settle with Natalia.

6th Student. She does not speak — has evidently let out no word. The only thing is, will she equally remember the rest of her lesson, and repeat correctly all those verses which are to break the secret to Jules?

Gottlieb. How he gazes on her! Pity — pity!

1st Student. They go in: now, silence! You three, — not nearer the window, mind, than that pomegranate: just where the little girl, who a few minutes ago passed us singing, is seated!

Scene 2.

NOON

Over Orcana. The house of Jules, who crosses its threshold with Phene: she is silent, on which Jules begins —

Do not die, Phene! I am yours now, you
Are mine now; let fate reach me how she likes,
If you'll not die: so, never die! Sit here —
My work-room's single seat. I over-lean
This length of hair and lustrous front; they turn
Like an entire flower upward: eyes, lips, last
Your chin — no, last your throat turns: 'tis their scent
Pulls down my face upon you. Nay, look ever
This one way till I change, grow you — I could
Change into you, beloved! You by me,
And I by you; this is your hand in mine,
And side by side we sit: all's true. Thank God!
I have spoken: speak you!
 O my life to come!
My Tydeus must be carved that's there in clay;
Yet how be carved, with you about the room?
Where must I place you? When I think that once
This room-full of rough block-work seemed my heaven
Without you! Shall I ever work again,
Get fairly into my old ways again,
Bid each conception stand while, trait by trait,
My hand transfers its lineaments to stone?
Will my mere fancies live near you, their truth —
The live truth, passing and repassing me,
Sitting beside me? Now speak! Only first,
See, all your letters! Was't not well contrived?
Their hiding-place is Psyche's robe; she keeps
Your letters next her skin: which drops out foremost?
Ah, — this that swam down like a first moonbeam
Into my world! Again those eyes complete
Their melancholy survey, sweet and slow,
Of all my room holds; to return and rest
On me, with pity, yet some wonder too:
As if God bade some spirit plague a world,
And this were the one moment of surprise
And sorrow while she took her station, pausing
O'er what she sees, finds good, and must destroy!
What gaze you at? Those? Books, I told you of;

Let your first word to me rejoice them, too:
This minion, a Coluthus, writ in red
Bistre and azure by Bessarion's scribe —
Read this line . . . no, shame — Homer's be
    the Greek
First breathed me from the lips of my Greek
    girl!
This Odyssey in coarse black vivid type
With faded yellow blossoms 'twixt page and
    page,
To mark great places with due gratitude;
"He said, and on Antinous directed
A *bitter shaft"* . . . a flower blots out the rest!
Again upon your search? My statues, then!
— Ah, do not mind that — better that will
    look
When cast in bronze — an Almaign Kaiser,
    that,
Swart-green and gold, with truncheon based
    on hip.
This, rather, turn to! What, unrecognized?
I thought you would have seen that here you
    sit
As I imagined you, — Hippolyta,
Naked upon her bright Numidian horse.
Recall you this then? "Carve in bold re-
    lief" —
So you commanded — "carve, against I
    come,
A Greek, in Athens, as our fashion was,
Feasting, bay-filleted and thunder-free,
Who rises 'neath the lifted myrtle-branch.
'Praise those who slew Hipparchus!' cry the
    guests,
'While o'er thy head the singer's myrtle
    waves
As erst above our champion: stand up, all!' "
See, I have labored to express your thought.
Quite round, a cluster of mere hands and
    arms,
(Thrust in all senses, all ways, from all sides,
Only consenting at the branch's end
They strain toward) serves for frame to a
    sole face,
The Praiser's, in the centre: who with eyes
Sightless, so bend they back to light inside
His brain where visionary forms throng up,
Sings, minding not that palpitating arch
Of hands and arms, nor the quick drip of wine
From the drenched leaves o'erhead, nor
    crowns cast off,
Violet and parsley crowns to trample on —
Sings, pausing as the patron-ghosts approve,
Devoutly their unconquerable hymn.
But you must say a "well" to that — say
    "well!"
Because you gaze — am I fantastic, sweet?
Gaze like my very life's-stuff, marble —
    marbly

Even to the silence! Why, before I found
The real flesh Phene, I inured myself
To see, throughout all nature, varied stuff
For better nature's birth by means of art:
With me, each substance tended to one form
Of beauty — to the human archetype.
On every side occurred suggestive germs
Of that — the tree, the flower — or take the
    fruit, —
Some rosy shape, continuing the peach,
Curved beewise o'er its bough; as rosy limbs,
Depending, nestled in the leaves; and just
From a cleft rose-peach the whole Dryad
    sprang.
But of the stuffs one can be master of,
How I divined their capabilities!
From the soft-rinded smoothening facile
    chalk
That yields your outline to the air's embrace,
Half-softened by a halo's pearly gloom;
Down to the crisp imperious steel, so sure
To cut its one confided thought clean out
Of all the world. But marble! — 'neath my
    tools
More pliable than jelly — as it were
Some clear primordial creature dug from
    depths
In the earth's heart, where itself breeds
    itself,
And whence all baser substance may be
    worked;
Refine it off to air, you may, — condense it
Down to the diamond; — is not metal there,
When o'er the sudden speck my chisel trips?
— Not flesh, as flake off flake I scale, ap-
    proach,
Lay bare those bluish veins of blood asleep?
Lurks flame in no strange windings where,
    surprised
By the swift implement sent home at once,
Flushes and glowings radiate and hover
About its track? Phene? what — why is this?
That whitening cheek, those still dilating
    eyes!
Ah, you will die — I knew that you would
    die!

Phene begins, on his having long remained
    silent.
Now the end's coming; to be sure, it must
Have ended sometime! Tush, why need I
    speak
Their foolish speech? I cannot bring to mind
One half of it, beside; and do not care
For old Natalia now, nor any of them.
Oh, you — what are you? — if I do not try
To say the words Natalia made me learn,
To please your friends, — it is to keep myself
Where your voice lifted me, by letting that

Proceed: but can it? Even you, perhaps,
Cannot take up, now you have once let fall,
The music's life, and me along with that —
No, or you would! We'll stay, then, as we are:
Above the world. You creature with the eyes!
If I could look forever up to them,
As now you let me, — I believe, all sin,
All memory of wrong done, suffering borne,
Would drop down, low and lower, to the
    earth
Whence all that's low comes, and there touch
    and stay
— Never to overtake the rest of me,
All that, unspotted, reaches up to you,
Drawn by those eyes! What rises is myself,
Not me the shame and suffering; but they
    sink,
Are left, I rise above them. Keep me so,
Above the world! But you sink, for your eyes
Are altering — altered! Stay — "I love you,
    love" . . .
I could prevent it if I understood:
More of your words to me: was't in the tone
Or the words, your power? Or stay — I will
    repeat
Their speech, if that contents you! Only
    change
No more, and I shall find it presently
Far back here, in the brain yourself filled up.
Natalia threatened me that harm should
    follow
Unless I spoke their lesson to the end,
But harm to me, I thought she meant, not
    you.
Your friends, — Natalia said they were your
    friends
And meant you well, — because, I doubted
    it,
Observing (what was very strange to see)
On every face, so different in all else,
The same smile girls like me are used to bear,
But never men, men cannot stoop so low;
Yet your friends, speaking of you, used that
    smile,
That hateful smirk of boundless self-conceit
Which seems to take possession of the world
And make of God a tame confederate,
Purveyor to their appetites . . . you know!
But still Natalia said they were your friends,
And they assented though they smiled the
    more.
And all came round me, — that thin English-
    man
With light lank hair seemed leader of the rest;
He held a paper — "What we want," said he,
Ending some explanation to his friends —
"Is something slow, involved and mystical,
To hold Jules long in doubt, yet take his taste
And lure him on until, at innermost

Where he seeks sweetness' soul, he may find
    — this!
— As in the apple's core, the noisome fly:
For insects on the rind are seen at once,
And brushed aside as soon, but this is found
Only when on the lips or loathing tongue."
And so he read what I have got by heart:
I'll speak it, — "Do not die, love! I am
    yours."
No — is not that, or like that, part of words
Yourself began by speaking? Strange to lose
What cost such pains to learn! Is this more
    right?
I am a painter who cannot paint;
In my life, a devil rather than saint;
In my brain, as poor a creature too:
No end to all I cannot do!
Yet do one thing at least I can —
Love a man or hate a man
Supremely: thus my lore began.
Through the Valley of Love I went,
In the lovingest spot to abide,
And just on the verge where I pitched my
    tent,
I found Hate dwelling beside.
(Let the Bridegroom ask what the painter
    meant,
Of his Bride, of the peerless Bride!)
And further, I traversed Hate's grove,
In the hatefullest nook to dwell;
But lo, where I flung myself prone, couched
    Love
Where the shadow threefold fell.
(The meaning — those black bride's-eyes
    above,
Not a painter's lip should tell!)
"And here," said he, "Jules probably will ask,
'You have black eyes, Love, — you are, sure
    enough,
My peerless bride, — then do you tell indeed
What needs some explanation! What means
    this?'"
— And I am to go on, without a word —
So, I grew wise in Love and Hate,
From simple that I was of late.
Once, when I loved, I would enlace
Breast, eyelids, hands, feet, form and face
Of her I loved, in one embrace —
As if by mere love I could love immensely!
Once, when I hated, I would plunge
My sword, and wipe with the first lunge
My foe's whole life out like a sponge —
As if by mere hate I could hate intensely!
But now I am wiser, know better the fashion
How passion seeks aid from its opposite pas-
    sion:
And if I see cause to love more, hate more
Than ever man loved, ever hated before —
And seek in the Valley of Love,

The nest, or the nook in Hate's Grove,
Where my soul may surely reach
The essence, naught less, of each,
The Hate of all Hates, the Love
Of all Loves, in the Valley or Grove, —
I find them the very warders
Each of the other's borders.
When I love most, Love is disguised
In Hate; and when Hate is surprised
In Love, then I hate most: ask
How Love smiles through Hate's iron casque,
Hate grins through Love's rose-braided
mask, —
And how, having hated thee,
I sought long and painfully
To reach thy heart, nor prick
The skin but pierce to the quick —
Ask this, my Jules, and be answered straight
By thy bride — how the painter Lutwyche
can hate!

Jules interposes.

Lutwyche! Who else? But all of them, no
doubt,
Hated me: they at Venice — presently
Their turn, however! You I shall not meet:
If I dreamed, saying this would wake me. Keep
What's here, the gold — we cannot meet
again,
Consider! and the money was but meant
For two years' travel, which is over now,
All chance or hope or care or need of it.
This — and what comes from selling these,
my casts
And books and medals, except . . . let them
go
Together, so the produce keeps you safe
Out of Natalia's clutches! If by chance
(For all's chance here) I should survive the
gang
At Venice, root out all fifteen of them,
We might meet somewhere, since the world
is wide.

From without is heard the voice of
Pippa, singing —

Give her but a least excuse to love me!
When — where —
How — can this arm establish her above me,
If fortune fixed her as my lady there,
There already, to eternally reprove me?
("Hist!" — said Kate the Queen;
But "Oh!" — cried the maiden, binding
her tresses,
"'Tis only a page that carols unseen,
Crumbling your hounds their messes!")

Is she wronged? — To the rescue of her honor,
My heart!

Is she poor? — What costs it to be styled a
donor?
Merely an earth to cleave, a sea to part.
But that fortune should have thrust all this
upon her!
("Nay, list!" — bade Kate the Queen;
And still cried the maiden, binding her
tresses,
"'Tis only a page that carols unseen,
Fitting your hawks their jesses!")

Pippa passes.

Jules resumes.

What name was that the little girl sang forth?
Kate? The Cornaro, doubtless, who re-
nounced
The crown of Cyprus to be lady here
At Asolo, where still her memory stays,
And peasants sing how once a certain page
Pined for the grace of her so far above
His power of doing good to, "Kate the
Queen —
She never could be wronged, be poor," he
sighed,
"Need him to help her!" Yes, a bitter thing
To see our lady above all need of us;
Yet so we look ere we will love; not I,
But the world looks so. If whoever loves
Must be, in some sort, god or worshipper,
The blessing or the blest one, queen or page,
Why should we always choose the page's
part?
Here is a woman with utter need of me, —
I find myself queen here, it seems! How
strange!
Look at the woman here with the new soul,
Like my own Psyche, — fresh upon her lips
Alit, the visionary butterfly,
Waiting my word to enter and make bright,
Or flutter off and leave all blank as first.
This body had no soul before, but slept
Or stirred, was beauteous or ungainly, free
From taint or foul with stain, as outward
things
Fastened their image on its passiveness:
Now, it will wake, feel, live — or die again!
Shall to produce form out of unshaped stuff
Be Art — and further, to evoke a soul
From form be nothing? This new soul is
mine!

Now, to kill Lutwyche, what would that do?
— save
A wretched dauber, men will hoot to death
Without me, from their hooting. Oh, to hear
God's voice plain as I heard it first, before
They broke in with their laughter! I heard
them

Henceforth, not God. To Ancona — Greece
— some isle!
I wanted silence only; there is clay
Everywhere. One may do whate'er one likes
In Art: the only thing is, to make sure
That one does like it — which takes pains to
know.
    Scatter all this, my Phene — this mad
dream!
Who, what is Lutwyche, what Natalia's
friends,
What the whole world except our love —
my own,
Own Phene? But I told you, did I not,
Ere night we travel for your land — some isle
With the sea's silence on it? Stand aside —
I do but break these paltry models up
To begin Art afresh. Meet Lutwyche, I —
And save him from my statue meeting him?
Some unsuspected isle in the far seas!
Like a god going through his world, there
stands
One mountain for a moment in the dusk,
Whole brotherhoods of cedars on its brow:
And you are ever by me while I gaze
— Are in my arms as now — as now — as
now!
Some unsuspected isle in the far seas!
Some unsuspected isle in far-off seas!

*Talk by the way, while Pippa is passing from
Orcana to the Turret. Two or three of the
Austrian Police loitering with Bluphocks,
an English vagabond, just in view of the
Turret.*
Bluphocks. So, that is your Pippa, the
little girl who passed us singing? Well, your
Bishop's Intendant's money shall be honestly
earned: — now, don't make me that sour
face because I bring the Bishop's name into
the business; we know he can have nothing
to do with such horrors: we know that he is a
saint and all that a bishop should be, who is a
great man beside. *Oh were but every worm a
maggot, Every fly a grig, Every bough a
Christmas faggot, Every tune a jig!* In fact, I
have abjured all religions; but the last I
inclined to, was the Armenian: for I have
travelled, do you see, and at Koenigsberg,
Prussia Improper (so styled because there's
a sort of bleak hungry sun there), you might
remark over a venerable house-porch, a
certain Chaldee inscription; and brief as it is,
a mere glance at it used absolutely to change
the mood of every bearded passenger. In they
turned, one and all; the young and lightsome,
with no irreverent pause, the aged and decrepit, with a sensible alacrity: 'twas the
Grand Rabbi's abode, in short. Struck with

curiosity, I lost no time in learning Syriac —
(these are vowels, you dogs, — follow my
stick's end in the mud — *Celarent, Darii,
Ferio!*), and one morning presented myself,
spelling-book in hand, a, b, c, — I picked it
out letter by letter, and what was the purport
of this miraculous posy? Some cherished
legend of the past, you'll say — "*How Moses
hocuspocussed Egypt's land with fly and lo-
cust,*" — or, "*How to Jonah sounded harshish,
Get thee up and go to Tarshish,*" — or, "*How
the angel meeting Balaam, Straight his ass
returned a salaam.*" In no wise! "*Shackabrack
— Boach — somebody or other — Isaach, Re-
cei-ver, Pur-cha-ser and Ex-chan-ger of —
Stolen Goods!*" So, talk to me of the religion
of a bishop! I have renounced all bishops
save Bishop Beveridge — mean to live so —
and die — *As some Greek dog-sage, dead and
merry, Hellward bound in Charon's wherry,
With food for both worlds, under and upper,
Lupine-seed and Hecate's supper, And never an
obolus* ... (Though thanks to you, or this
Intendant through you, or this Bishop
through his Intendant — I possess a burning
pocketful of *zwanzigers*) ... *To pay the
Stygian Ferry!*
1st Policeman. There is the girl, then; go
and deserve them the moment you have
pointed out to us Signor Luigi and his
mother. (*To the rest*) I have been noticing a
house yonder, this long while: not a shutter
unclosed since morning!
2nd Policeman. Old Luca Gaddi's, that
owns the silk-mills here: he dozes by the
hour, wakes up, sighs deeply, says he should
like to be Prince Metternich, and then dozes
again, after having bidden young Sebald, the
foreigner, set his wife to playing draughts.
Never molest such a household, they mean
well.
Bluphocks. Only, cannot you tell me something of this little Pippa, I must have to do
with? One could make something of that
name. Pippa — that is, short for Felippa —
rhyming to *Panurge consults Hertrippa —
Believest thou, King Agrippa?* Something
might be done with that name.
2nd Policeman. Put into rhyme that your
head and a ripe muskmelon would not be dear
at half a *zwanziger!* Leave this fooling, and
look out; the afternoon's over or nearly so.
3rd Policeman. Where in this passport of
Signor Luigi does our Principal instruct you
to watch him so narrowly? There? What's
there beside a simple signature? (That
English fool's busy watching.)
2nd Policeman. Flourish all round — "Put
all possible obstacles in his way;" oblong dot

at the end — "Detain him till further advices reach you;" scratch at bottom — "Send him back on pretence of some informality in the above;" ink-spirt on right-hand side (which is the case here) — "Arrest him at once." Why and wherefore, I don't concern myself, but my instructions amount to this: if Signor Luigi leaves home to-night for Vienna — well and good, the passport deposed with us for our *visa* is really for his own use, they have misinformed the Office, and he means well; but let him stay over to-night — there has been the pretence we suspect, the accounts of his corresponding and holding intelligence with the Carbonari are correct, we arrest him at once, to-morrow comes Venice, and presently Spielberg. Bluphocks makes the signal, sure enough! That is he, entering the turret with his mother, no doubt.

Scene 3.

EVENING

Inside the Turret on the hill above Asolo. Luigi and his Mother entering.

Mother. If there blew wind, you'd hear a
   long sigh, easing
The utmost heaviness of music's heart.
Luigi. Here in the archway?
Mother. Oh no, no — in farther,
Where the echo is made, on the ridge.
Luigi. Here surely, then.
How plain the tap of my heel as I leaped up!
Hark — "Lucius Junius!" The very ghost of
   a voice
Whose body is caught and kept by . . . what
   are those?
Mere withered wallflowers, waving overhead?
They seem an elvish group with thin bleached
   hair
That lean out of their topmost fortress —
   look
And listen, mountain men, to what we say,
Hand under chin of each grave earthy face.
Up and show faces all of you! — "All of
   you!"
That's the king dwarf with the scarlet comb;
   old Franz,
Come down and meet your fate? Hark —
   "Meet your fate!"
Mother. Let him not meet it, my Luigi —
   do not
Go to his City! Putting crime aside,
Half of these ills of Italy are feigned:
Your Pellicos and writers for effect,
Write for effect.
Luigi. Hush! Say A. writes, and B.
Mother. These A.s and B.s write for effect,
   I say.

Then, evil is in its nature loud, while good
Is silent; you hear each petty injury,
None of his virtues; he is old beside,
Quiet and kind, and densely stupid. Why
Do A. and B. not kill him themselves?
   Luigi. They teach
Others to kill him — me — and, if I fail,
Others to succeed; now, if A. tried and failed,
I could not teach that: mine's the lesser task.
Mother, they visit night by night . . .
   Mother. — You, Luigi?
Ah, will you let me tell you what you are?
   Luigi. Why not? Oh, the one thing you
   fear to hint,
You may assure yourself I say and say
Ever to myself! At times — nay, even as now
We sit — I think my mind is touched, sus-
   pect
All is not sound: but is not knowing that,
What constitutes one sane or otherwise?
I know I am thus — so, all is right again.
I laugh at myself as through the town I walk,
And see men merry as if no Italy
Were suffering; then I ponder — "I am rich,
Young, healthy; why should this fact trouble
   me,
More than it troubles these?" But it does
   trouble.
No, trouble's a bad word; for as I walk
There's springing and melody and giddiness,
And old quaint turns and passages of my
   youth,
Dreams long forgotten, little in themselves,
Return to me — whatever may amuse me:
And earth seems in a truce with me, and
   heaven
Accords with me, all things suspend their
   strife,
The very cicala laughs "There goes he, and
   there!
Feast him, the time is short; he is on his
   way
For the world's sake: feast him this once, our
   friend!"
And in return for all this, I can trip
Cheerfully up the scaffold-steps. I go
This evening, mother!
   Mother. But mistrust yourself —
Mistrust the judgment you pronounce on
   him!
   Luigi. Oh, there I feel — am sure that I
   am right!
   Mother. Mistrust your judgment then, of
   the mere means
To this wild enterprise. Say, you are right, —
How should one in your state e'er bring to
   pass
What would require a cool head, a cold heart,
And a calm hand? You never will escape.

Luigi. Escape? To even wish that, would
    spoil all.
The dying is best part of it. Too much
Have I enjoyed these fifteen years of mine,
To leave myself excuse for longer life:
Was not life pressed down, running o'er with
    joy,
That I might finish with it ere my fellows
Who, sparelier feasted, make a longer stay?
I was put at the board-head, helped to all
At first; I rise up happy and content.
God must be glad one loves his world so much.
I can give news of earth to all the dead
Who ask me: — last year's sunsets, and
    great stars
Which had a right to come first and see ebb
The crimson wave that drifts the sun away —
Those crescent moons with notched and
    burning rims
That strengthened into sharp fire, and there
    stood,
Impatient of the azure — and that day
In March, a double rainbow stopped the
    storm —
May's warm slow yellow moonlit summer
    nights —
Gone are they, but I have them in my soul!
Mother. (He will not go!)
Luigi. You smile at me? 'Tis true, —
Voluptuousness, grotesqueness, ghastliness,
Environ my devotedness as quaintly
As round about some antique altar wreathe
The rose festoons, goats' horns, and oxen's
    skulls.
Mother. See now: you reach the city, you
    must cross
His threshold — how?
Luigi. Oh, that's if we conspired!
Then would come pains in plenty, as you
    guess —
But guess not how the qualities most fit
For such an office, qualities I have,
Would little stead me, otherwise employed,
Yet prove of rarest merit only here.
Every one knows for what his excellence
Will serve, but no one ever will consider
For what his worst defect might serve: and
    yet
Have you not seen me range our coppice
    yonder
In search of a distorted ash? — I find
The wry spoilt branch a natural perfect bow.
Fancy the thrice-sage, thrice-precautioned
    man
Arriving at the palace on my errand!
No, no! I have a handsome dress packed up —
White satin here, to set off my black hair;
In I shall march — for you may watch your
    life out

Behind thick walls, make friends there to
    betray you;
More than one man spoils everything. March
    straight —
Only, no clumsy knife to fumble for.
Take the great gate, and walk (not saunter) on
Thro' guards and guards — I have rehearsed
    it all
Inside the turret here a hundred times.
Don't ask the way of whom you meet, ob-
    serve!
But where they cluster thickliest is the door
Of doors; they'll let you pass — they'll never
    blab
Each to the other, he knows not the favorite,
Whence he is bound and what's his business
    now.
Walk in — straight up to him; you have no
    knife:
Be prompt, how should he scream? Then,
    out with you!
Italy, Italy, my Italy!
You're free, you're free! Oh mother, I could
    dream
They got about me — Andrea from his exile,
Pier from his dungeon, Gualtier from his
    grave!
Mother. Well, you shall go. Yet seems this
    patriotism
The easiest virtue for a selfish man
To acquire: he loves himself — and next, the
    world —
If he must love beyond, — but naught be-
    tween:
As a short-sighted man sees naught midway
His body and the sun above. But you
Are my adored Luigi, ever obedient
To my least wish, and running o'er with
    love:
I could not call you cruel or unkind.
Once more, your ground for killing him! —
    then go!
Luigi. Now do you try me, or make sport
    of me?
How first the Austrians got these prov-
    inces . . .
(If that is all, I'll satisfy you soon)
— Never by conquest but by cunning, for
That treaty whereby . . .
Mother. Well?
Luigi. (Sure, he's arrived,
The tell-tale cuckoo: spring's his confidant,
And he lets out her April purposes!)
Or . . . better go at once to modern time,
He has . . . they have . . . in fact, I under-
    stand
But can't restate the matter; that's my boast:
Others could reason it out to you, and prove
Things they have made me feel.

Mother. Why go to-night?
Morn's for adventure. Jupiter is now
A morning-star. I cannot hear you, Luigi!
   Luigi. "I am the bright and morning-star,"
     saith God —
And, "to such an one I give the morning-
     star,"
The gift of the morning-star! Have I God's
     gift
Of the morning-star?
   Mother. Chiara will love to see
That Jupiter an evening-star next June.
   Luigi. True, mother. Well for those who
live through June!
Great noontides, thunder-storms, all glaring
     pomps
That triumph at the heels of June the god
Leading his revel through our leafy world.
Yes, Chiara will be here.
   Mother. In June: remember,
Yourself appointed that month for her com-
     ing.
   Luigi. Was that low noise the echo?
   Mother. The night-wind.
She must be grown — with her blue eyes
     upturned
As if life were one long and sweet surprise:
In June she comes.
   Luigi. We were to see together
The Titian at Treviso. There, again!

From without is heard the voice of Pippa,
     singing —

   A king lived long ago,
   In the morning of the world,
   When earth was nigher heaven than now:
   And the king's locks curled,
   Disparting o'er a forehead full
   As the milk-white space 'twixt horn and
     horn
   Of some sacrificial bull —
   Only calm as a babe new-born:
   For he was got to a sleepy mood,
   So safe from all decrepitude,
   Age with its bane, so sure gone by,
   (The gods so loved him while he dreamed)
   That, having lived thus long, there seemed
   No need the king should ever die.

   Luigi. No need that sort of king should
ever die!

   Among the rocks his city was:
   Before his palace, in the sun,
   He sat to see his people pass,
   And judge them every one
   From its threshold of smooth stone.
   They haled him many a valley-thief
   Caught in the sheep-pens, robber-chief

   Swarthy and shameless, beggar-cheat,
   Spy-prowler, or rough pirate found
   On the sea-sand left aground;
   And sometimes clung about his feet,
   With bleeding lip and burning cheek,
   A woman, bitterest wrong to speak
   Of one with sullen thickset brows:
   And sometimes from the prison-house
   The angry priests a pale wretch brought,
   Who through some chink had pushed and
     pressed
   On knees and elbows, belly and breast,
   Worm-like into the temple, — caught
   He was by the very god,
   Who ever in the darkness strode
   Backward and forward, keeping watch
   O'er his brazen bowls, such rogues to
     catch!
   These, all and every one,
   The king judged, sitting in the sun.

   Luigi. That king should still judge sitting
in the sun!

   His councillors, on left and right,
   Looked anxious up, — but no surprise
   Disturbed the king's old smiling eyes
   Where the very blue had turned to white.
   'Tis said, a Python scared one day
   The breathless city, till he came,
   With forky tongue and eyes on flame,
   Where the old king sat to judge alway;
   But when he saw the sweepy hair
   Girt with a crown of berries rare
   Which the god will hardly give to wear
   To the maiden who singeth, dancing bare
   In the altar-smoke by the pine-torch lights,
   At his wondrous forest rites, —
   Seeing this, he did not dare
   Approach that threshold in the sun,
   Assault the old king smiling there.
   Such grace had kings when the world
     begun!
          Pippa passes.

   Luigi. And such grace have they, now that
the world ends!
The Python at the city, on the throne,
And brave men, God would crown for slaying
     him,
Lurk in bye-corners lest they fall his prey.
Are crowns yet to be won in this late time,
Which weakness makes me hesitate to reach?
'Tis God's voice calls: how could I stay?
     Farewell!

Talk by the way, while Pippa is passing from
   the Turret to the Bishop's Brother's House,
   close to the Duomo S. Maria. Poor Girls
   sitting on the steps.

1st Girl. There goes a swallow to Venice —
 the stout seafarer!
Seeing those birds fly, makes one wish for
 wings.
Let us all wish; you wish first!
2nd Girl. I? This sunset
To finish.
3rd Girl. That old — somebody I know,
Grayer and older than my grandfather,
To give me the same treat he gave last
 week —
Feeding me on his knee with fig-peckers,
Lampreys and red Breganze-wine, and mum-
 bling
The while some folly about how well I fare,
Let sit and eat my supper quietly:
Since had he not himself been late this morning
Detained at — never mind where, — had he
 not . . .
"Eh, baggage, had I not!" —
2nd Girl. How she can lie!
3rd Girl. Look there — by the nails!
2nd Girl. What makes your fingers red!
3rd Girl. Dipping them into wine to write
 bad words with
On the bright table: how he laughed!
1st Girl. My turn.
Spring's come and summer's coming. I would
 wear
A long loose gown, down to the feet and
 hands,
With plaits here, close about the throat, all
 day;
And all night lie, the cool long nights, in
 bed;
And have new milk to drink, apples to eat,
Deuzans and junetings, leather-coats . . . ah,
 I should say,
This is away in the fields — miles!
3rd Girl. Say at once
You'd be at home: she'd always be at home!
Now comes the story of the farm among
The cherry orchards, and how April snowed
White blossoms on her as she ran. Why,
 fool,
They've rubbed the chalk-mark out, how tall
 you were,
Twisted your starling's neck, broken his cage,
Made a dung-hill of your garden!
1st Girl. They, destroy
My garden since I left them? well — perhaps!
I would have done so: so I hope they have!
A fig-tree curled out of our cottage wall;
They called it mine, I have forgotten why,
It must have been there long ere I was born:
Cric — cric — I think I hear the wasps o'er-
 head
Pricking the papers strung to flutter there

And keep off birds in fruit-time — coarse
 long papers,
And the wasps eat them, prick them through
 and through.
3rd Girl. How her mouth twitches! Where
 was I? — before
She broke in with her wishes and long gowns
And wasps — would I be such a fool! — oh,
 here!
This is my way: I answer every one
Who asks me why I make so much of him —
(If you say, "you love him" — straight "he'll
 not be gulled!")
"He that seduced me when I was a girl
Thus high — had eyes like yours, or hair like
 yours,
Brown, red, white," — as the case may be:
 that pleases!
See how that beetle burnishes in the path!
There sparkles he along the dust: and,
 there —
Your journey to that maize-tuft spoiled at
 least!
1st Girl. When I was young, they said if
 you killed one
Of those sunshiny beetles, that his friend
Up there, would shine no more that day nor
 next.
2nd Girl. When you were young? Nor are
 you young, that's true.
How your plump arms, that were, have
 dropped away!
Why, I can span them. Cecco beats you still?
No matter, so you keep your curious hair.
I wish they'd find a way to dye our hair
Your color — any lighter tint, indeed,
Than black: the men say they are sick of
 black,
Black eyes, black hair!
4th Girl. Sick of yours, like enough.
Do you pretend you ever tasted lampreys
And ortolans? Giovita, of the palace,
Engaged (but there's no trusting him) to
 slice me
Polenta with a knife that had cut up
An ortolan.
2nd Girl. Why, there! Is not that Pippa
We are to talk to, under the window, —
 quick, —
Where the lights are?
1st Girl. That she? No, or she would sing,
For the Intendant said . . .
3rd Girl. Oh, you sing first!
Then, if she listens and comes close . . . I'll
 tell you. —
Sing that song the young English noble made,
Who took you for the purest of the pure,
And meant to leave the world for you —
 what fun!

2nd Girl. (*Sings*)

> You'll love me yet! — and I can tarry
> Your love's protracted growing:
> June reared that bunch of flowers you
>   carry,
> From seeds of April's sowing.

> I plant a heartful now: some seed
>   At least is sure to strike,
> And yield — what you'll not pluck indeed,
>   Not love, but, may be, like.

> You'll look at least on love's remains,
>   A grave's one violet:
> Your look? — that pays a thousand pains.
>   What's death? You'll love me yet!

3rd Girl. (*To Pippa, who approaches*) Oh,
you may come closer — we shall not eat you!
Why, you seem the very person that the great
rich handsome Englishman has fallen so
violently in love with. I'll tell you all about it.

Scene 4.

NIGHT

*Inside the Palace by the Duomo. Monsignor,
dismissing his Attendants.*

Monsignor. Thanks, friends, many thanks!
I chiefly desire life now, that I may recompense every one of you. Most I know something of already. What, a repast prepared?
Benedicto benedicatur ... ugh, ugh! Where
was I? Oh, as you were remarking, Ugo, the
weather is mild, very unlike winter-weather:
but I am a Sicilian, you know, and shiver in
your Julys here. To be sure, when 'twas full
summer at Messina, as we priests used to
cross in procession the great square on
Assumption Day, you might see our thickest
yellow tapers twist suddenly in two, each
like a falling star, or sink down on themselves
in a gore of wax. But go, my friends, but go!
(*To the Intendant*) Not you, Ugo! (*The others
leave the apartment*) I have long wanted to
converse with you, Ugo.

Intendant. Uguccio —

Monsignor. . . . 'guccio Stefani, man! of
Ascoli, Fermo and Fossombruno; — what I
do need instructing about, are these accounts
of your administration of my poor brother's
affairs. Ugh! I shall never get through a third
part of your accounts: take some of these
dainties before we attempt it, however. Are
you bashful to that degree? For me, a crust
and water suffice.

Intendant. Do you choose this especial
night to question me?

Monsignor. This night, Ugo. You have
managed my late brother's affairs since the
death of our elder brother: fourteen years
and a month, all but three days. On the Third
of December, I find him . . .

Intendant. If you have so intimate an
acquaintance with your brother's affairs, you
will be tender of turning so far back: they
will hardly bear looking into, so far back.

Monsignor. Ay, ay, ugh, ugh, — nothing but
disappointments here below! I remark a considerable payment made to yourself on this
Third of December. Talk of disappointments!
There was a young fellow here, Jules, a
foreign sculptor I did my utmost to advance,
that the Church might be a gainer by us both:
he was going on hopefully enough, and of a
sudden he notifies to me some marvellous
change that has happened in his notions of
Art. Here's his letter, — "He never had a
clearly conceived Ideal within his brain till
to-day. Yet since his hand could manage a
chisel, he has practised expressing other
men's Ideals; and, in the very perfection he
has attained to, he foresees an ultimate failure: his unconscious hand will puruse its
prescribed course of old years, and will re-
produce with a fatal expertness the ancient
types, let the novel one appear never so
palpably to his spirit. There is but one method
of escape: confiding the virgin type to as
chaste a hand, he will turn painter instead of
sculptor, and paint, not carve, its charac-
teristics," — strike out, I dare say, a school
like Correggio: how think you, Ugo?

Intendant. Is Correggio a painter?

Monsignor. Foolish Jules! and yet, after
all, why foolish? He may — probably will —
fail egregiously; but if there should arise a
new painter, will it not be in some such way,
by a poet now, or a musician (spirits who
have conceived and perfected an Ideal
through some other channel), transferring it
to this, and escaping our conventional roads
by pure ignorance of them; eh, Ugo? If you
have no appetite, talk at least, Ugo!

Intendant. Sir, I can submit no longer to
this course of yours. First, you select the
group of which I formed one, — next you
thin it gradually, — always retaining me with
your smile, — and so do you proceed till you
have fairly got me alone with you between
four stone walls. And now then? Let this
farce, this chatter end now: what is it you
want with me?

Monsignor. Ugo!

Intendant. From the instant you arrived,
I felt your smile on me as you questioned me
about this and the other article in those

papers — why your brother should have given me this villa, that *podere*, — and your nod at the end meant, — what?

Monsignor. Possibly that I wished for no loud talk here. If once you set me coughing, Ugo! —

Intendant. I have your brother's hand and seal to all I possess: now ask me what for! what service I did him — ask me!

Monsignor. I would better not: I should rip up old disgraces, let out my poor brother's weaknesses. By the way, Maffeo of Forli (which, I forgot to observe, is your true name), was the interdict ever taken off you, for robbing that church at Casena?

Intendant. No, nor needs be: for when I murdered your brother's friend, Pasquale, for him . . .

Monsignor. Ah, he employed you in that business, did he? Well, I must let you keep, as you say, this villa and that *podere*, for fear the world should find out my relations were of so indifferent a stamp? Maffeo, my family is the oldest in Messina, and century after century have my progenitors gone on polluting themselves with every wickedness under heaven: my own father . . . rest his soul! — I have, I know, a chapel to support that it may rest: my dear two dead brothers were, — what you know tolerably well; I, the youngest, might have rivalled them in vice, if not in wealth: but from my boyhood I came out from among them, and so am not partaker of their plagues. My glory springs from another source; or if from this, by contrast only, — for I, the bishop, am the brother of your employers, Ugo. I hope to repair some of their wrong, however; so far as my brother's ill-gotten treasure reverts to me, I can stop the consequences of his crime: and not one *soldo* shall escape me. Maffeo, the sword we quiet men spurn away, you shrewd knaves pick up and commit murders with; what opportunities the virtuous forego, the villainous seize. Because, to pleasure myself apart from other considerations, my food would be millet-cake, my dress sackcloth, and my couch straw, — am I therefore to let you, the offscouring of the earth, seduce the poor and ignorant by appropriating a pomp these will be sure to think lessens the abominations so unaccountably and exclusively associated with it? Must I let villas and *poderi* go to you, a murderer and thief, that you may beget by means of them other murderers and thieves? No — if my cough would but allow me to speak!

Intendant. What am I to expect? You are going to punish me?

Monsignor. — Must punish you, Maffeo. I cannot afford to cast away a chance. I have whole centuries of sin to redeem, and only a month or two of life to do it in. How should I dare to say . . .

Intendant. "Forgive us our trespasses"?

Monsignor. My friend, it is because I avow myself a very worm, sinful beyond measure, that I reject a line of conduct you would applaud perhaps. Shall I proceed, as it were, a-pardoning? — I? — who have no symptom of reason to assume that aught less than my strenuousest efforts will keep myself out of mortal sin, much less keep others out. No: I do trespass, but will not double that by allowing you to trespass.

Intendant. And suppose the villas are not your brother's to give, nor yours to take? Oh, you are hasty enough just now!

Monsignor. 1, 2 — N° 3! — ay, can you read the substance of a letter, N° 3, I have received from Rome? It is precisely on the ground there mentioned, of the suspicion I have that a certain child of my late elder brother, who would have succeeded to his estates, was murdered in infancy by you, Maffeo, at the instigation of my late younger brother — that the Pontiff enjoins on me not merely the bringing that Maffeo to condign punishment, but the taking all pains, as guardian of the infant's heritage for the Church, to recover it parcel by parcel, howsoever, whensoever, and wheresoever. While you are now gnawing those fingers, the police are engaged in sealing up your papers, Maffeo, and the mere raising my voice brings my people from the next room to dispose of yourself. But I want you to confess quietly, and save me raising my voice. Why, man, do I not know the old story? The heir between the succeeding heir, and this heir's ruffianly instrument, and their complot's effect, and the life of fear and bribes and ominous smiling silence? Did you throttle or stab my brother's infant? Come now!

Intendant. So old a story, and tell it no better? When did such an instrument ever produce such an effect? Either the child smiles in his face; or, most likely, he is not fool enough to put himself in the employer's power so thoroughly: the child is always ready to produce — as you say — howsoever, wheresoever, and whensoever.

Monsignor. Liar!

Intendant. Strike me? Ah, so might a father chastise! I shall sleep soundly to-night at least, though the gallows await me to-morrow; for what a life did I lead! Carlo of Cesena reminds me of his connivance, every time I pay his annuity; which happens commonly thrice a year. If I remonstrate, he will confess all to the good bishop — you!

Monsignor. I see through the trick, caitiff! I would you spoke truth for once. All shall be sifted, however — seven times sifted.

Intendant. And how my absurd riches encumbered me! I dared not lay claim to above half my possessions. Let me but once unbosom myself, glorify Heaven, and die!

Sir, you are no brutal dastardly idiot like your brother I frightened to death: let us understand one another. Sir, I will make away with her for you — the girl — here close at hand; not the stupid obvious kind of killing; do not speak — know nothing of her nor of me! I see her every day — saw her this morning: of course there is to be no killing; but at Rome the courtesans perish off every three years, and I can entice her thither — have indeed begun operations already. There's a certain lusty blue-eyed florid-complexioned English knave, I and the Police employ occasionally. You assent, I perceive — no, that's not it — assent I do not say — but you will let me convert my present havings and holdings into cash, and give me time to cross the Alps? 'Tis but a little black-eyed pretty singing Felippa, gay silk-winding girl. I have kept her out of harm's way up to this present; for I always intended to make your life a plague to you with her. 'Tis as well settled once and forever. Some women I have procured will pass Bluphocks, my handsome scoundrel, off for somebody; and once Pippa entangled! — you conceive? Through her singing? Is it a bargain?

From without is heard the voice of Pippa, singing —

Overhead the tree-tops meet,
Flowers and grass spring 'neath one's feet;
There was naught above me, naught below,
My childhood had not learned to know:
For, what are the voices of birds
— Ay, and of beasts, — but words, our words,
Only so much more sweet?
The knowledge of that with my life begun.
But I had so near made out the sun,
And counted your stars, the seven and one,
Like the fingers of my hand:
Nay, I could all but understand
Wherefore through heaven the white moon ranges;
And just when out of her soft fifty changes
No unfamiliar face might overlook me —
Suddenly God took me.

Pippa passes.

Monsignor. (*Springing up*) My people — one and all — all — all within there! Gag this villain — tie him hand and foot! He dares . . . I know not half he dares — but remove him — quick! *Miserere mei, Domine!* Quick, I say!

Scene — Pippa's chamber again. She enters it.

The bee with his comb,
The mouse at her dray,
The grub in his tomb,
Wile winter away;
But the fire-fly and hedge-shrew and lob-worm, I pray,
How fare they?
Ha, ha, thanks for your counsel, my Zanze!
"Feast upon lampreys, quaff Breganze" —
The summer of life so easy to spend,
And care for to-morrow so soon put away!
But winter hastens at summer's end,
And fire-fly, hedge-shrew, lob-worm, pray,
How fare they?
No bidding me then to . . . what did Zanze say?
"Pare your nails pearlwise, get your small feet shoes
More like" . . . (what said she?) — "and less like canoes!"
How pert that girl was! — would I be those pert
Impudent staring women! It had done me,
However, surely no such mighty hurt
To learn his name who passed that jest upon me:
No foreigner, that I can recollect,
Came, as she says, a month since, to inspect
Our silk-mills — none with blue eyes and thick rings
Of raw-silk-colored hair, at all events.
Well, if old Luca keep his good intents,
We shall do better, see what next year brings.
I may buy shoes, my Zanze, not appear
More destitute than you perhaps next year!
Bluph . . . something! I had caught the uncouth name
But for Monsignor's people's sudden clatter
Above us — bound to spoil such idle chatter
As ours: it were indeed a serious matter
If silly talk like ours should put to shame
The pious man, the man devoid of blame,
The . . . ah but — ah but, all the same,
No mere mortal has a right
To carry that exalted air;
Best people are not angels quite:
While — not the worst of people's doings scare
The devil; so there's that proud look to spare!
Which is mere counsel to myself, mind! for
I have just been the holy Monsignor:

And I was you too, Luigi's gentle mother,
And you too, Luigi! — how that Luigi started
Out of the turret — doubtlessly departed
On some good errand or another,
For he passed just now in a traveller's trim,
And the sullen company that prowled
About his path, I noticed, scowled
As if they had lost a prey in him.
And I was Jules the sculptor's bride,
And I was Ottima beside,
And now what am I? — tired of fooling.
Day for folly, night for schooling!
New Year's day is over and spent,
Ill or well, I must be content.
    Even my lily's asleep, I vow:
Wake up — here's a friend I've plucked you:
Call this flower a heart's-ease now!
Something rare, let me instruct you,
Is this, with petals triply swollen,
Three times spotted, thrice the pollen;
While the leaves and parts that witness
Old proportions and their fitness,
Here remain unchanged, unmoved now;
Call this pampered thing improved now!
Suppose there's a king of the flowers
And a girl-show held in his bowers —
"Look ye, buds, this growth of ours,"
Says he, "Zanze from the Brenta,
I have made her gorge polenta
Till both cheeks are near as bouncing
As her . . . name there's no pronouncing!
See this heightened color too,
For she swilled Breganze wine
Till her nose turned deep carmine;
'Twas but white when wild she grew.
And only by this Zanze's eyes
Of which we could not change the size,
The magnitude of all achieved
Otherwise, may be perceived."

Oh what a drear dark close to my poor day!
How could that red sun drop in that black
    cloud?

Ah Pippa, morning's rule is moved away,
Dispensed with, never more to be allowed!
Day's turn is over, now arrives the night's.
Oh lark, be day's apostle
To mavis, merle and throstle,
Bid them their betters jostle
From day and its delights!
But at night, brother howlet, over the woods,
Toll the world to thy chantry;
Sing to the bat's sleek sisterhoods
Full complines with gallantry:
Then, owls and bats,
Cowls and twats,
Monks and nuns, in a cloister's moods,
Adjourn to the oak-stumped pantry!
                    After she has begun to undress herself.
Now, one thing I should like to really know:
How near I ever might approach all these
I only fancied being, this long day:
— Approach, I mean, so as to touch them, so
As to . . . in some way . . . move them — if
    you please,
Do good or evil to them some slight way.
For instance, if I wind
Silk to-morrow, my silk may bind
                    Sitting on the bedside.
And border Ottima's cloak's hem.
Ah me, and my important part with them,
This morning's hymn half promised when I
    rose!
True in some sense or other, I suppose.
                    As she lies down.
God bless me! I can pray no more to-night.
No doubt, some way or other, hymns say
    right.
All service ranks the same with God —
With God, whose puppets, best and worst,
Are we: there is no last nor first.
                    She sleeps.

THE END.

COMEDY

Comedy of Manners

DION BOUCICAULT

London Assurance (1841)

Farce

TOM TAYLOR

Our American Cousin (1858)

DION BOUCICAULT

1820?-1890

London Assurance

(1841)

Dion Boucicault was the master of melodrama, the supreme showman and dramatic wizard of the mid-century stage. Montrose Moses and Maurice Disher both state that Boucicault turned out "more than four hundred plays," though Allardyce Nicoll's hand-lists give data about only ninety-odd, some of them under several names. In any case Boucicault wrote plays "as a hen lays eggs," but "wrote" means translated, adapted, doctored, or put together with scissors and paste.

Fittingly, the life of Boucicault (what is known of it) has all the sensational elements of melodrama. He was born in Dublin in either 1820 or 1822. He was apparently the natural son of Dr. Dionysius Lardner and Mrs. Samuel Boursiquot, who had been for some time separated from her husband. Boucicault was sent to various schools at Dr. Lardner's expense, but according to Boucicault's own anecdotes, he was more lively than studious and found nothing interesting in school until the boys at Brentford put on a play, *Pizarro*. "Then," said Boucicault, "for the first time, my mind seemed to soar. I wanted to play every part in the piece, but had to content myself by teaching all the rest how their parts should be given." Dr. Lardner tried to put the boy to work, but in 1839, with a few pounds of pocket money, Boucicault ran away to the theatres of Cheltenham, Gloucester, Bristol, Hull, and Brighton, finding engagements to act in small parts. In the spring of 1840 he arrived in London penniless, but with a "portmanteau chiefly filled with hopes" — play scripts. Using the name Lee Moreton, Boucicault offered his plays to Charles Mathews and Madame Vestris, then managing Covent Garden. "Lee Moreton's" *London Assurance* was accepted and produced on March 4, 1841. After its success he changed his name to Dionysius Lardner Bourcicault (with an r) for some years, before he became Dion Boucicault. He produced other comedies in the style of Congreve and Farquhar, but without the success of his first and best one. Up to about 1843, Boucicault dreamed of glory, read the great dramas of the past, and wrote original plays on these models. Then he decided to crib from the French as the short and easy way to success. He stated the creed that governed the rest of his life: "I am an emperor and take what I think best for Art, whether it be a story from a book, a play from the French, or an actor from a rival company."

The story of Boucicault's career as "emperor" is the saga of a somewhat irresponsible genius. He went to Paris and lived there until 1848 under the self-assumed title of Viscount Boucicault. He married a well-to-do French woman older than he and went with her on a wedding journey to Switzerland. When he came back alone, he let it be known that she had fallen over a precipice. He returned to London in 1848 and took a position at the Princess's Theatre to provide plays which he translated and adapted from the French. He was attracted to a beautiful and talented actress at this theatre, Miss Agnes Robertson. In 1853 Miss Robertson sailed to Montreal and then to New York; Boucicault sailed straight to New York and met Miss Robertson there. Letting it be understood that they were married, the couple toured America together, lecturing and performing in melodramas, many written by Boucicault. But as war loomed in America, the Boucicaults returned to England in 1860. Making fortune after fortune on successful plays, Boucicault spent extravagant sums. In partnership with Lord Londesborough, he staged a recklessly costly spectacle, *Babil and Bijou*, at Covent Garden in 1872, but then mysteriously disappeared on the opening night, August 29. He turned up in New York, but after a while went back to England. His eldest son, Willie, was killed in a railway accident at Huntingdon, England, in 1876. Boucicault, again wealthy, built a splendid grammar school on the market place there in memory of his son. Back in New York in 1879, the Boucicaults played together in *The Colleen Bawn* at Booth's Theatre. Shortly afterward, Miss Robertson returned to England alone. Boucicault barnstormed America with his company, playing in San Francisco with Miss Louise Thorndike. From there Boucicault and Miss Thorndike took passage to Australia and were married in Sydney on September 9, 1885. Agnes Robertson, hearing the news, brought suit for divorce. Apparently she and Boucicault had never married, but she wished to establish the legitimacy of her children. The court granted the divorce on the ground that Queen Victoria had addressed communications to "Mr. and Mrs. Boucicault." Returning to New York, Boucicault remarried Miss Thorndike.

He was now an old man in a world that had changed. He turned out play after play that did not please new audiences. Baffled, he was at last employed by A. M. Palmer of Palmer's Theatre to teach acting at a salary of fifty dollars a week. After a life of wealth that he had flung to the winds, of barnstorming and living mostly from suitcases, and of writing and producing plays and throwing the scripts away, he died on September 18, 1890, still full of faith that the old days and the old ways on the stage were the best.

Boucicault firmly believed that melodrama was the vital drama. Playwright, actor, and producer on every kind of stage from those of New York (better than the English then, he said) to the barns of American frontier towns, Boucicault knew his theatre and his audience and wrote for them. Much of his writing was hack work, ingenious adaptations shamelessly plagiarized, but nearly always touched with his extraordinary sense of what would thrill his audiences.

He had no message. He wrote on every subject that offered sentiment, pathos, and the flavor of romance. His subjects included tales of terror (*The Vampire*, 1852), duels, horse-races, history (*Genevieve; or, The Reign of Terror*, 1853), current events (*Jessie Brown; or, The Relief of Lucknow*, 1858), slavery (*The Octoroon*, 1859), and labor problems (*The Long Strike*, 1865, with a seduction and a murder to make the play a melodrama). He followed the formula, with nick-of-time rescues and happy endings with virtue triumphant, but he always included bold theatrical effects, a flamboyant style, and broad wit and humor. He relied much upon richness of spectacle and "sensation" scenes: exploding steamboats, burning tenements, ocean caverns, and locomotives on the stage. And yet he aided the drama in its approach to realism. He kept his eyes open for whatever in actual life might provide sensation, as in his play on the slavery question in 1859 in which he used a camera (a new invention then) to solve a mystery. Producing his own plays, he sought for a heightened naturalness in acting combined with theatrical effect.

Certain plays well illustrate these features of Boucicault's work. Townsend Walsh states that the idea for *The Poor of New York* (1857) came to Boucicault as he looked at a picture in a current magazine portraying events of the financial panic of 1857, and "thought it might be worth while to take the events of the day into partnership with him." He found a plot in a French play by MM. E. Brisbane and Eugène Nus, *Les Pauvres de Paris*, and adapted it to New York localities: a snow storm in Union Square and "The exterior of a tenement house, No. 19½ Cross Street, Five Points," to be burned in a great fire. Besides the fire, the events of financial panic and a murder provided thrills that made the play a great success in New York. In 1864 Boucicault was in Liverpool, England, at loose ends, but with the script of *The Poor of New York* in his trunk. He dug it out, changed local allusions (including even an allusion to the theatre that would produce it), and offered it as *The Poor of Liverpool*. He took it to London with appropriate changes as *The Streets of London*. Sure that it would succeed, he demanded of London managers payment by the unheard-of method of royalties. His own opinion of the play and a statement of his attitude toward the drama are contained in a bragging letter Boucicault wrote to a man named Stirling. He said:

> I introduced "The Poor of Liverpool" — a bobtail piece — with local scenery. . . . I share after thirty pounds a night, and I am making a hundred pounds a week on the —— thing.
> I localize it for each town, and hit the public between the eyes; so they see nothing but fire. *Et voilà!*
> I can spin out these rough-and-tumble dramas as a hen lays eggs. It's a degrading occupation, but more money has been made out of guano than out of poetry.

The Octoroon; or, Life in Louisiana, produced in New York in 1859, treated the inflammatory subject of slavery and racial intermarriage. It contrasted the magnolia South and the shrewd Yankee North, kindly slaveholders and mistreated slaves, all in a sensational plot with a slave-auction, a chase by night through a bayou, murder, a steamship afire, and an automatic camera to record villainy. Sympathies were so adroitly balanced that both Northerners and Southerners cheered the performance. *The Colleen Bawn; or, The Brides of Garryowen* (1860), "Founded on a true history First told by an Irishman and now Dramatized by an Irishman," avoided the older stock Irish-butt of English comedy and created a new image of the Irishman as happy-go-lucky and irresponsible, but witty, loyal, and lovable — in scenes on the Lake of Killarney, by the fireside of a thatched cottage (with Irish whiskey), in— castle, and in a sea cavern. In this play Boucicault established a picture of the

Irishman that he exploited in half a dozen later plays, that became a stock image, that delighted "wearers of the green," and that infuriated the later playwrights of the Abbey Theatre. Though details are not entirely clear in conflicting accounts, Boucicault touched a failing American play with his magic. Joseph Jefferson had faith in his version of *Rip Van Winkle*, but the play dragged in performance. Jefferson, visiting London in 1865, brought the play to Boucicault, who "doctored" it. Then, when produced at the Adelphi, it ran for a hundred and seventy nights. Jefferson brought it back to America, where it held the stage for the next thirty years. In this way, from the 1850's through the 1870's, Boucicault altered whatever he found to suit his audiences. When he did not then change his formula, he found it impossible to please audiences of the 1880's. The new drama was on the way, and the old man could not adapt to meet a challenge he did not even understand.

But Boucicault's first great success, *London Assurance*, belongs to the comedy of manners developed during the Restoration and the eighteenth century. Treated as legitimate drama, it was brilliantly produced at Covent Garden by Mathews and Vestris, with a realistic box set, well-furnished interiors, smart costumes, and careful rehearsals. Just as the historic verse tragedies are reminiscent of Shakespeare, this play echoes Farquhar, Congreve, Sheridan, and Goldsmith. In a sense, it has the traditional comic theme of the sexual game played for money and rank; but it lacks the hardness and true cynicism of that game in Restoration comedy. It has the form of the comedy of manners, but not the foundation in a true picture of a contemporary society. The characters are types from the older drama: the aging foppish beau, Sir Harcourt Courtly; the bluff, fox-hunting squire, Max Harkaway; the profligate son who pretends to all the virtues, Charles Courtly; the faithless wife (modified to suit Victorian morality), Lady Gay; the witless husband who is duped, Dolly Spanker; the pettifogging lawyer, Meddle; the brazen servant, Cool; and importunate tradesmen to be hoodwinked. Charles and Dazzle engage in the bell-pulling games of eighteenth-century Mohocks, but not in their more vicious amusements. Though the dialogue flows easily, the traditional cynicism sounds insincere, and the clever epigrams seem shopworn.

Clearly, in *London Assurance*, the really rakish comedy of manners ("rakehellish" it was in Restoration days) is inhibited. Boucicault's play is not, as it was hailed, a "modern comedy," but an imitation comedy. It did not satirize the significant follies of society in 1841, and it was inhibited by Victorian manners from presenting the picture of any real past. It had to pretend to be immoral, but actually be moral and end with a moral tag — a pedantic definition of the gentleman. The seduction and the duel are sheer make-believe.

The closest approaches to reality in the play are in the characters of Lady Gay and Dazzle. It is interesting that Lady Gay is the only character Boucicault created with a real person in mind. His roving eye had taken a fancy to a vivacious actress, Mrs. Nisbett, but when the play was cast the only two female parts went to Madame Vestris and Mrs. Humby. Boucicault asked to borrow his script, rushed to his rooms, and in a few days returned the play with the added characters of Spanker and Lady Gay, the latter written for Mrs. Nisbett. The part had her vivacity, and it made the play. When Lady Gay came in, cracking her whip and hallooing the hunt, she conquered. Up to this point the play had dragged, but now it seemed to race all the way to the climax in Dazzle's equally unexpected, "I have not the remotest idea."

With the possible exception of Bulwer-Lytton's *Money, London Assurance* is the best comedy of manners between Sheridan and Oscar Wilde. Like the verse drama, this traditional form died in the nineteenth century, to live again only when it again satirized something real in the life of its time.

LONDON ASSURANCE

A Comedy In Five Acts

by

DION BOUCICAULT

To
Charles Kemble
This Comedy
(with his Kind Permission)
Is Dedicated
By his Fervent Admirer and Humble Servant
Dion. L. Boucicault

First performed at the Theatre Royal, Covent Garden, March 4, 1841.

Cast of Characters

Sir Harcourt Courtly	Cool, *valet*
Max Harkaway	Simpson, *butler*
Charles Courtly	Martin
Mr. Spanker	Lady Gay Spanker
Dazzle	Grace Harkaway
Mark Meddle	Pert

Act I.

An ante-room in Sir Harcourt Courtly's house in Belgrave Square.

Enter Cool.

Cool. Half-past nine, and Mr. Charles has **not yet returned**. I am in a fever of dread. If his father happen to rise earlier than usual on any morning, he is sure to ask first for Mr. Charles. Poor deluded old gentleman — he little thinks how he is deceived.

Enter Martin, lazily.

Well, Martin, he has not come home yet!

Martin. No; and I have not had a wink of sleep all night — I cannot stand this any longer; I shall give warning. This is the fifth night Mr. Courtly has remained out, and I'm obliged to stand at the hall window to watch for him.

Cool. You know, if Sir Harcourt was aware that we connived at his son's irregularities, we should all be discharged.

Martin. I have used up all my common excuses on his duns. — "Call again," "Not at home," and "Send it down to you," won't serve any more; and Mr. Crust, the wine merchant, swears he will be paid.

Cool. So they all say. Why, he has arrests out against him already. I've seen the fellows watching the door — (*Loud knock and ring heard*) — There he is, just in time — quick, Martin, for I expect Sir William's bell every moment — (*Bell rings*) — and there it is. (*Exit Martin, slowly*) Thank heaven! he will return to college to-morrow, and this heavy responsibility will be taken off my shoulders. A valet is as difficult a post to fill properly as that of prime minister.   *Exit.*

Court. (*Without*) Hollo!

Dazzle. (*Without*) Steady!

Enter Young Courtly and Dazzle.

Court. Hollo-o-o!

Dazzle. Hush! what are you about, howling like a Hottentot. Sit down there, and thank heaven you are in Belgrave Square, instead of Bow Street.

Court. D—n — damn Bow Street.

Dazzle. Oh, with all my heart! — you have not seen as much of it as I have.

Court. I say — let me see — what was I going to say? — oh, look here — (*Pulls out a large assortment of bell-pulls, knockers, etc., from his pocket*) There! dam'me! I'll puzzle the two-penny postmen, — I'll deprive them of their right of disturbing the neighbourhood. That black lion's head did belong to old Vampire, the moneylender; this bell-pull to Miss Stitch, the milliner.

Dazzle. And this brass griffin —

Court. That! oh, let me see — I think — I twisted that off our own hall-door as I came in, while you were paying the cab.

Dazzle. What shall I do with them?

Court. Pack 'em in a small hamper, and send 'em to the sitting magistrate with my father's compliments; in the mean time, come into my room, and I'll astonish you with some Burgundy.

Re-enter Cool.

Cool. Mr. Charles —

Court. Out! out! not at home to any one.

Cool. And drunk —

Court. As a lord.

Cool. If Sir Harcourt knew this, he would go mad, he would discharge me.

Court. You flatter yourself: that would be no proof of his insanity. — (*To Dazzle*) This is Cool, sir, Mr. Cool; he is the best liar in London — there is a pungency about his invention, and an originality in his equivocation, that is perfectly refreshing.

Cool. (*Aside*) Why, Mr. Charles, where did you pick him up?

Court. You mistake, he picked *me* up.

(*Bell rings*)

Cool. Here comes Sir Harcourt — pray do not let him see you in this state.

Court. State! what do you mean? I am in a beautiful state.

Cool. I should lose my character.

Court. That would be a fortunate epoch in your life, Cool.

Cool. Your father would discharge me.

Court. Cool, my dad is an old ass.

Cool. Retire to your own room, for heaven's sake, Mr. Charles.

Court. I'll do so for my own sake. (*To Dazzle*) I say, old fellow, (*Staggering*) just hold the door steady while I go in.

Dazzle. This way. Now, then! — take care! (*Helps him into the room*)

Enter Sir Harcourt Courtly in an elegant dressing-gown, and Greek scull-cap and tassels, etc.

Sir H. Cool, is breakfast ready?

Cool. Quite ready, Sir Harcourt.

Sir H. Apropos. I omitted to mention that I expect Squire Harkaway to join us this morning, and you must prepare for my departure to Oak Hall immediately.

Cool. Leave town in the middle of the season, Sir Harcourt? So unprecedented a proceeding!

Sir H. It is! I confess it: there is but one power could effect such a miracle — that is divinity.

Cool. How!

Sir H. In female form, of course. Cool, I am about to present society with a second Lady Courtly; young — blushing eighteen; — lovely! I have her portrait; rich! I have her banker's account; — an heiress, and a Venus!

Cool. Lady Courtly could be none other.

Sir H. Ha! ha! Cool, your manners are above your station. — Apropos, I shall find no further use for my brocade dressing-gown.

Cool. I thank you, Sir Harcourt; might I ask who the fortunate lady is?

Sir H. Certainly: Miss Grace Harkaway, the niece of my old friend, Max.

Cool. Have you never seen the lady, sir?

Sir H. Never — that is, yes — eight years ago. Having been, as you know, on the continent for the last seven years, I have not had the opportunity of paying my devoirs. Our connexion and betrothal was a very extraordinary one. Her father's estates were contiguous to mine; — being a penurious, miserly, *ugly* old scoundrel, he made a market of my indiscretion, and supplied my extravagance with large sums of money on mortgages, his great desire being to unite the two properties. About seven years ago, he died — leaving Grace, a girl, to the guardianship of her uncle, with this will: — if, on attaining the age of nineteen, she would consent to marry me, I should receive those deeds, and all his property, as her dowry. If she refused to comply with this condition, they should revert to my heir-presumptive or apparent. — She consents.

Cool. Who would not?

Sir H. I consent to receive her 15,000*l.* a year.

Cool. (*Aside*) Who would not?

Sir H. So prepare, Cool, prepare; — but where is my boy, where is Charles?

Cool. Why — oh, he is gone out, Sir Harcourt; yes, gone out to take a walk.

Sir H. Poor child! A perfect child in heart — a sober, placid mind — the simplicity and verdure of boyhood, kept fresh and unsullied by any contact with society. Tell me, Cool, at what time was he in bed last night?

Cool. Half-past nine, Sir Harcourt.

Sir H. Half-past nine! Beautiful! What an original idea! Reposing in cherub slumbers, while all around him teems with drinking and debauchery! Primitive sweetness of nature! No pilot-coated, bear-skinned brawling!

Cool. Oh, Sir Harcourt!

Sir H. No cigar-smoking —

Cool. Faints at the smell of one.

Sir H. No brandy and water bibbing.

Cool. Doesn't know the taste of anything stronger than barley-water.

Sir H. No night parading —

Cool. Never heard the clock strike twelve, except at noon.

Sir H. In fact, he is my son, and became a gentleman by right of paternity. He inherited my manners.

Enter Martin.

Martin. Mr. Harkaway!

Enter Max Harkaway.

Max. Squire Harkaway, fellow, or Max Harkaway, another time. (*Martin bows, and exit*) Ah! Ha! Sir Harcourt, I'm devilish glad to see you! Gi' me your fist. Dang it, but I'm glad to see ye! Let me see: six — seven years, or more, since we have met. How quickly they have flown!

Sir H. (*Throwing off his studied manner*) Max, Max! Give me your hand, old boy. — (*Aside*) Ah! he *is* glad to see me: there is no fawning pretence about that squeeze. Cool, you may retire. *Exit Cool.*

Max. Why, you are looking quite rosy.

Sir H. Ah! ah! rosy! Am I too florid?

Max. Not a bit; not a bit.

Sir H. I thought so. — (*Aside*) Cool said I had put too much on.

Max. How comes it, Courtly, that you manage to retain your youth? See, I'm as grey as an old badger, or a wild rabbit; while you are — are as black as a young rook. I say, whose head grew your hair, eh?

Sir H. Permit me to remark that all the beauties of my person are of home manufacture. Why should you be surprised at my youth? I have scarcely thrown off the giddiness of a very boy — elasticity of limb — buoyancy of soul! Remark this position — (*Throws himself into an atittude*) I held that attitude for ten minutes at Lady Acid's last *réunion*, at the express desire of one of our first sculptors, while he was making a sketch of me for the Apollo.

Max. (*Aside*) Making a butt of thee for their gibes.

Sir H. Lady Sarah Sarcasm started up, and, pointing to my face ejaculated, "Good gracious! Does not Sir Harcourt remind you of the countenance of Ajax, in the Pompeian portrait?"

Max. Ajax! — humbug.

Sir H. You are complimentary.

Max. I'm a plain man, and always speak my mind. What's in a face or figure? Does a Grecian nose entail a good temper? Does a waspish waist indicate a good heart? Or, do oily perfumed locks necessarily thatch a well-furnished brain?

Sir H. It's an undeniable fact, — *plain* people always praise the beauties of the *mind*.

Max. Excuse the insinuation; I had thought the first Lady Courtly had surfeited you with beauty.

Sir H. No; she lived fourteen months with me, and then eloped with an intimate friend. Etiquette compelled me to challenge the seducer; so I received satisfaction — and a bullet in my shoulder at the same time. However, I had the consolation of knowing that he was the handsomest man of the age. She did not insult me, by running away with a d—d ill-looking scoundrel.

Max. That, certainly, was flattering.

Sir H. I felt so, as I pocketed the ten thousand pounds damages.

Max. That must have been a great balm to your sore honour.

Sir H. It was — Max, my honour would have died without it; for on that year the wrong horse won the Derby — by some mistake. It was one of the luckiest chances — a thing that does not happen twice in a man's life — the opportunity of getting rid of his wife and his debts at the same time.

Max. Tell the truth, Courtly! Did you not feel a little frayed in your delicacy — your honour, now? Eh?

Sir H. Not a whit. Why should I? I married *money*, and I received it — virgin gold! My delicacy and honour had nothing to do with hers. The world pities the bereaved husband, when it should congratulate. No: the affair made a sensation, and I was the object. Besides, it is vulgar to make a parade of one's feelings, however acute they may be: impenetrability of countenance is the sure sign of your highly-bred man of fashion.

Max. So, a man must, therefore, lose his wife and his money with a smile, — in fact, every thing he possesses but his temper.

Sir H. Exactly, — and greet ruin with *vive la bagatelle!* For example, — your modish beauty never discomposes the shape of her features with convulsive laughter. A smile rewards the *bon mot*, and also shows the whiteness of her teeth. She never weeps impromptu — tears might destroy the economy of her cheek. Scenes are vulgar, — hysterics obsolete; she exhibits a calm, placid, impenetrable lake, whose surface is reflexion, but of unfathomable depth, — a statue, whose life is hypothetical, and not a *prima facie* fact.

Max. Well, give me the girl that will fly at your eyes in an argument, and stick to her point like a fox to his own tail.

Sir H. But etiquette! Max, — remember etiquette!

Max. Damn etiquette! I have seen a man who thought it sacrilege to eat fish with a knife, that would not scruple to rise up and rob his brother of his birthright in a gambling-house. Your thorough-bred, well-blooded heart will seldom kick over the traces of good feeling. That's my opinion, and I don't care who knows it.

Sir. H. Pardon me, — etiquette is the pulse of society, by regulating which the body politic is retained in health. I consider myself one of the faculty in the art.

Max. Well, well; you are a living libel upon common sense, for you are old enough to know better.

Sir H. Old enough! What do you mean? Old! I still retain all my little juvenile indiscretions, which your niece's beauties must teach me to discard. I have not sown my wild oats yet.

Max. Time you did, at sixty-three.

Sir H. Sixty-three! Good God! — forty, 'pon my life! forty, next March.

Max. Why, you are older than I am.

Sir H. Oh! you are old enough to be my father.

Max. Well, if I am, I am; that's etiquette, I suppose. Poor Grace! how often I have pitied her fate! That a young and beautiful creature should be driven into wretched splendour, or miserable poverty!

Sir H. Wretched! wherefore? Lady Courtly wretched! Impossible!

Max. Will she not be compelled to marry you, whether she likes you or not? — a choice between you and poverty. (*Aside*) And hang me if it isn't a tie! But why do you not introduce your son Charles to me? I have not seen him since he was a child. You would never permit him to accept any of my invitations to spend his vacation at Oak Hall, — of course, we shall have the pleasure of his company now.

Sir H. He is not fit to enter society yet. He is a studious, sober boy.

Max. Boy! Why, he's five-and-twenty.

Sir H. Good gracious! Max, — you will permit me to know my own son's age, — he is not twenty.

Max. I'm dumb.

Sir H. You will excuse me while I indulge in the process of dressing. — Cool!

Enter Cool.

Prepare my toilet. (*Exit Cool*) That is a ceremony, which, with me, supersedes all others. I consider it a duty which every gentleman owes to society — to render himself as agreeable an object as possible: and the least compliment a mortal can pay to nature, when she honours him by bestowing extra care in the manufacture of his person, is to display her taste to the best possible advantage; and so, *au revoir.*   *Exit.*

Max. That's a good soul — he has his faults, and who has not? Forty years of age! Oh, monstrous! — but he does look uncommonly young for sixty, spite of his foreign locks and complexion.

Enter Dazzle.

Dazzle. Who's my friend, with the stick and gaiters, I wonder — one of the family — the governor, may be?

Max. Who's this? Oh, Charles — is that you, my boy? How are you? (*Aside*) This is the *boy*.

Dazzle. He knows me — he is too respectable for a bailiff. (*Aloud*) How are you?

Max. Your father has just left me.

Dazzle. (*Aside*) The devil he has! He has been dead these ten years. Oh! I see, he thinks I'm young Courtly. (*Aloud*) The honour you would confer upon me, I must unwillingly disclaim, — I am not Mr. Courtly.

Max. I beg your pardon — a friend, I suppose?

Dazzle. Oh, a most intimate friend — a friend of years — distantly related to the family — one of my ancestors married one of his. (*Aside*) Adam and Eve.

Max. Are you on a visit here?

Dazzle. Yes. Oh! yes. (*Aside*) Rather a short one, I'm afraid.

Max. (*Aside*) This appears a dashing kind of fellow — as he is a friend of Sir Harcourt's, I'll invite him to the wedding. (*Aloud*) Sir, if you are not otherwise engaged, I shall feel honoured by your company at my house, Oak Hall, Gloucestershire.

Dazzle. Your name is —

Max. Harkaway — Max Harkaway.

Dazzle. Harkaway — let me see — I ought to be related to the Harkaways, somehow.

Max. A wedding is about to come off — will you take a part on the occasion?

Dazzle. With pleasure! any part, but that of the husband.

Max. Have you any previous engagement?

Dazzle. I was thinking — eh! why, let me see. (*Aside*) Promised to meet my tailor and his account to-morrow; however, I'll postpone that. (*Aloud*) Have you good shooting?

Max. Shooting! Why, there's no shooting at this time of the year.

Dazzle. Oh! I'm in no hurry — I can wait till the season, of course. I was only speaking precautionally — you have good shooting?

Max. The best in the country.

Dazzle. Make yourself comfortable! — Say no more — I'm your man — wait till you see how I'll murder your preserves.

Max. Do you hunt?

Dazzle. Pardon me — but will you repeat that? (*Aside*) Delicious and expensive idea!

Max. You ride?

Dazzle. Anything! Everything! From a blood to a broomstick. Only catch me a flash of lightning, and let me get on the back of it, and dam'me if I wouldn't astonish the elements.

Max. Ha! ha!

Dazzle. I'd put a girdle round about the earth, in very considerably less than forty minutes.

Max. Ah! ha! We'll show old Fiddlestrings how to spend the day. He imagines that Nature, at the earnest request of Fashion, made summer days long for him to saunter in the Park, and winter nights, that he might have good time to get cleared out at hazard or at whist. Give me the yelping of a pack of hounds, before the shuffling of a pack of cards. What state can match the chase in full cry, each vying with his fellow which shall be most happy? A thousand deaths fly by unheeded in that one hour's life of ecstasy. Time is outrun, and Nature seems to grudge our bliss by making the day so short.

Dazzle. No, for then rises up the idol of my great adoration.

Max. Who's that?

Dazzle. The bottle — that lends a lustre to the soul! — When the world puts on its night-cap, and extinguishes the sun — then comes the bottle! Oh, mighty wine! Don't ask me to apostrophise. Wine and love are the only two indescribable things in nature; but I prefer the wine, because its consequences are not entailed, and are more easily got rid of.

Max. How so?

Dazzle. Love ends in matrimony, wine in soda water.

Max. Well, I can promise you as fine a bottle as ever was cracked.

Dazzle. Never mind the bottle, give me the wine. Say no more; but, when I arrive, just shake one of my hands, and put the key of the cellar into the other, and, if I don't make myself intimately acquainted with its internal organization — well, I say nothing — time will show.

Max. I foresee some happy days.

Dazzle. And I some glorious nights.

Max. It mustn't be a flying visit.

Dazzle. I despise the word — I'll stop a month with you.

Max. Or a year or two.

Dazzle. I'll live and die with you!

Max. Ha! ha! Remember Max Harkaway, Oak Hall, Gloucestershire.

Dazzle. I'll remember — fare ye well. (*Max is going*) I say, holloa! — Tallyho-o-o-o!

Max. Yoicks! — Tallyho-o-o-o! *Exit.*

Dazzle. There I am — quartered for a couple of years, at the least. The old boy wants somebody to ride his horses, shoot his game, and keep a restraint on the morals of the parish; I'm eligible. What a lucky accident to meet young Courtly last night! Who could have thought it? — Yesterday, I could not make certain of a dinner, except at my own proper peril; to-day, I would flirt with a banquet.

Enter Young Courtly.

Court. What infernal row was that? Why, (*Seeing Dazzle*) are you here still?

Dazzle. Yes. Ain't you delighted? I'll ring, and send the servant for my luggage.

Court. The devil you will! Why, you don't mean to say you seriously intend to take up a permanent residence here? (*He rings the bell*)

Dazzle. Now, that's a most inhospitable insinuation.

Court. Might I ask your name?

Dazzle. With a deal of pleasure — Richard Dazzle, late of the Unattached Volunteers, vulgarly entitled the Dirty Buffs.

Enter Martin.

Court. Then, Mr. Richard Dazzle, I have the honour of wishing you a very good morning. Martin, show this gentleman the door.

Dazzle. If he does, I'll kick Martin out of it. — No offence. (*Exit Martin*) Now, sir, permit me to place a dioramic view of your conduct before you. After bringing you safely home this morning — after indulgently waiting, whenever you took a passing fancy to a knocker or bell-pull — after conducting a retreat that would have reflected honour on Napoleon — you would kick me into the street, like a mangy cur; and that's what you call gratitude. Now, to show you how superior I am to petty malice, I give you an unlimited invitation to my house — my country house — to remain as long as you please.

Court. Your house!

Dazzle. Oak Hall, Gloucestershire, — fine old place! — for further particulars see road-book — that is, it *nominally* belongs to my old friend and relation, Max Harkaway; but I'm privileged. Capital old fellow — say, shall we be honoured?

Court. Sir, permit me to hesitate a moment. (*Aside*) Let me see: I go back to college to-morrow, so I shall not be missing; tradesmen begin to dun —

Enter Cool.

I hear thunder; here is shelter ready for me.

Cool. Oh, Mr. Charles, Mr. Solomon Isaacs is in the hall, and swears he will remain till he has arrested you!

Court. Does he! — sorry he is so obstinate — take him my compliments, and I will bet him five to one he will not.

Dazzle. Double or quits, with my kind regards.

Cool. But, sir, he has discovered the house in Curzon Street; he says he is aware the furniture, at least, belongs to you, and he will put a man in immediately.

Court. That's awkward — what's to be done?

Dazzle. Ask him whether he couldn't make it a woman.

Court. I must trust that to fate.

Dazzle. I will give you my acceptance, if it will be of any use to you — it is of none to me.

Court. No, sir; but in reply to your most generous and kind invitation, if you be in earnest, I shall feel delighted to accept it.

Dazzle. Certainly.

Court. Then off we go — through the stables — down the Mews, and so slip through my friend's fingers.

Dazzle. But, stay, you must do the polite; say farewell to him before you part. Damn it, don't cut him!

Court. You jest!

Dazzle. Here, lend me a card. (*Courtly gives him one*) Now, then, (*Writes*) "Our respects to Mr. Isaacs — sorry to have been prevented from seeing him." — Ha! ha!

Court. Ha! ha!

Dazzle. We'll send him up some game.

Court. (*To Cool*) Don't let my father see him.   *Exeunt Young Courtly and Dazzle.*

Cool. What's this? "Mr. Charles Courtly, P.P.C., returns thanks for obliging inquiries."   *Exit.*

End of the First Act.

ACT II.

The lawn before Oak Hall, a fine Elizabethan mansion; a drawing-room is seen through large French windows at the back. Statues, urns, and garden chairs about the stage.

Enter Pert and James.

Pert. James, Miss Grace desires me to request that you will watch at the avenue, and let her know when the squire's carriage is seen on the London road.

James. I will go to the lodge.   *Exit.*

Pert. How I do long to see what kind of a man Sir Harcourt Courtly is! They say he is sixty; so he must be old, and consequently ugly. If I was Miss Grace, I would rather give up all my fortune and marry the man I liked, than go to church with a stuffed eel-skin. But taste is everything, — she doesn't seem to care whether he is sixty or sixteen; jokes at love; prepares for matrimony as she would for dinner; says it is a necessary evil, and what can't be cured must be endured. Now, I say this is against all nature; and she is either no woman, or a deeper one than I am, if she prefers an old man to a young one. Here she comes! looking as cheerfully as if she was going to marry Mr. Jenks! my Mr. Jenks! whom nobody won't lead to the halter till I have that honour.

Enter Grace from the drawing-room.

Grace. Well, Pert? any signs of the squire yet?

Pert. No, Miss Grace; but James has gone to watch the road.

Grace. In my uncle's letter, he mentions a Mr. Dazzle, whom he has invited; so you must prepare a room for him. He is some friend of my husband that is to be, and my uncle seems to have taken an extraordinary predilection for him. Apropos! I must not forget to have a bouquet for the dear old man when he arrives.

Pert. The dear old man! Do you mean Sir Harcourt?

Grace. Law, no! my uncle, of course. (*Plucking flowers*) What do I care for Sir Harcourt Courtly?

Pert. Isn't it odd, Miss, you have never seen your intended, though it has been so long since you were betrothed?

Grace. Not at all; marriage matters are conducted now-a-days in a most mercantile manner; consequently, a previous acquaintance is by no means indispensable. Besides, my *prescribed* husband has been upon the continent for the benefit of his — property! They say a southern climate is a great restorer of consumptive estates.

Pert. Well, Miss, for my own part, I should like to have a good look at my bargain before I paid for it; 'specially when one's life is the price of the article. But why, ma'am, do you consent to marry in this blind-man's-buff sort of manner? What would you think if he were not quite so old?

Grace. I should think he was a little younger.

Pert. I should like him all the better.

Grace. That wouldn't I. A young husband might expect affection and nonsense, which 'twould be deceit in me to render; nor would he permit me to remain with my uncle. — Sir Harcourt takes me with the incumbrances on his estate, and I shall beg to be left among the rest of the live stock.

Pert. Ah, Miss! but some day you might chance to stumble over *the* man, — what could you do then?

Grace. Do! beg *the* man's pardon, and request *the* man to pick me up again.

Pert. Ah! you were never in love, Miss?

Grace. I never was, nor will be, till I am tired of myself and common sense. Love is a pleasant scape-goat for a little epidemic madness. I must have been inoculated in my infancy, for the infection passes over poor me in contempt.

Enter James.

James. Two gentlemen, Miss Grace, have just alighted.

Grace. Very well, James. (*Exit James*) Love is pictured as a boy; in another century they will be wiser, and paint him as a fool, with cap and bells, without a thought above the jingling of his own folly. Now, Pert, remember this as a maxim, — A woman is always in love with one of two things.

Pert. What are they, Miss?

Grace. A man, or herself — and I know which is the most profitable. *Exit.*

Pert. I wonder what my Jenks would say, if I was to ask him. Law! here comes Mr. Meddle, his rival contemporary solicitor, as he calls him, — a nasty, prying, ugly wretch — what brings him here? He comes puffed with some news. *Retires.*

Enter Meddle, with a newspaper.

Meddle. I have secured the only newspaper in the village — my character, as an attorney-at-law, depended on the monopoly of its information. — I took it up by chance, when this paragraph met my astonished view: (*Reads*) "We understand that the contract of marriage so long in abeyance on account of the lady's minority, is about to be celebrated, at Oak Hall, Gloucestershire, the well-known and magnificent mansion of Maximilian Harkaway, Esq., between Sir Harcourt Courtly, Baronet, of fashionable celebrity, and Miss Grace Harkaway, niece to the said Mr. Harkaway. The preparations are proceeding in the good old English style." Is it possible! I seldom swear, except in a witness box, but, damme, had it been known in the village, my reputation would have been lost; my voice in the parlour of the Red Lion mute, and Jenks, a fellow who calls himself a lawyer, without more capability than a broomstick, and as much impudence as a young barrister after getting a verdict by mistake; why, he would actually have taken the Reverend Mr. Spout by the button, which is now my sole privilege. Ah! here is Mrs. Pert: couldn't have hit upon a better person. I'll cross-examine her — Lady's maid to Miss Grace, — confidential purloiner of second-hand silk — a *nisi prius* of her mistress — Ah! sits on the woolsack in the pantry, and dictates the laws of kitchen etiquette. — Ah! Mrs. Pert, good morning; permit me to say, — and my word as a legal character is not unduly considered — I venture to affirm, that you look a — quite like the — a —

Pert. Law! Mr. Meddle.

Meddle. Exactly like the law.

Pert. Ha! indeed; complimentary, I confess; like the law; tedious, prosy, made up of musty paper. You shan't have a long suit of me. Good morning. (*Going*)

Meddle. Stay, Mrs. Pert; don't calumniate my calling, or dissimulate vulgar prejudices.

Pert. Vulgar! you talk of vulgarity to me! you, whose sole employment is to sneak about like a pig, snouting out the dust-hole of society, and feeding upon the bad ends of vice! you, who live upon the world's iniquity; you miserable specimen of a bad six-and-eightpence!

Meddle. But, Mrs. Pert —

Pert. Don't but me, sir; I won't be butted by any such low fellow.

Meddle. This is slander; an action will lie.

Pert. Let it lie; lying is your trade. I'll tell you what, Mr. Meddle; if I had my will, I would soon put a check on your prying propensities. I'd treat you as the farmers do the inquisitive hogs.

Meddle. How?

Pert. I would ring your nose. *Exit.*

Meddle. Not much information elicited from that witness. Jenks is at the bottom of this. I have very little hesitation in saying, Jenks is a libellous rascal; I heard reports that he was undermining my character here, through Mrs. Pert. Now I'm certain of it. Assault is expensive; but, I certainly will put by a small weekly stipendium, until I can afford to kick Jenks.

Dazzle. (*Outside*) Come along; this way!

Meddle. Ah! whom have we here? Visitors; I'll address them.

Enter Dazzle.

Dazzle. Who's this, I wonder; one of the family? I must know him. (*To Meddle*) Ah! how are ye?

Meddle. Quite well. Just arrived? — ah! — um! — Might I request the honour of knowing whom I address?

Dazzle. Richard Dazzle, Esquire; and you —

Meddle. Mark Meddle, attorney-at-law.

Enter Young Courtly.

Dazzle. What detained you?

Court. My dear fellow, I have just seen such a woman!

Dazzle. (*Aside*) Hush! (*Aloud*) Permit me to introduce you to my very old friend, Meddle. He's a capital fellow; know him.

Meddle. I feel honoured. Who is your friend?

Dazzle. Oh, he? What, my friend? Oh! Augustus Hamilton.

Court. How d'ye do? (*Looking off*) There she is again!

Meddle. (*Looking off*) Why, that is Miss Grace.

Dazzle. Of course, Grace.

Court. I'll go and introduce myself.
Dazzle stops him.

Dazzle. (*Aside*) What are you about? Would you insult my old friend, Puddle, by running away? (*Aloud*) I say, Puddle, just show my friend the lions, while I say how d'ye do to my young friend, Grace. (*Aside*) Cultivate his acquaintance.

Exit. Young Courtly looks after him.

Meddle. Mr. Hamilton, might I take the liberty?

Court. (*Looking off*) Confound the fellow!

Meddle. Sir, what did you remark?

Court. She's gone! Oh, are you here still, Mr. Thingomerry Puddle?

Meddle. Meddle, sir, Meddle, in the list of attorneys.

Court. Well, Muddle, or Puddle, or whoever you are, you are a bore.

Meddle. (*Aside*) How excessively odd! Mrs. Pert said I was a pig; now I'm a boar! I wonder what they'll make of me next.

Court. Mr. Thingamy, will you take a word of advice?

Meddle. Feel honoured.

Court. Get out.

Meddle. Do you mean to — I don't understand.

Court. Delighted to quicken your apprehension. You are an ass, Puddle.

Meddle. Ha! ha! another quadruped! Yes; beautiful — (*Aside*) I wish he'd call me something libellous: but that would be too much to expect. — (*Aloud*) Anything else?

Court. Some miserable, pettifogging scoundrel!

Meddle. Good! ha! ha!

Court. What do you mean by laughing at me?

Meddle. Ha! ha! ha! excellent! delicious!

Court. Mr. — are you ambitious of a kicking?

Meddle. Very, very—Go on—kick—go on.

Court. (*Looking off*) Here she comes! I'll speak to her.

Meddle. But, sir — sir —

Court. Oh, go to the devil! *He runs off.*

Meddle. There, there's a chance lost — gone! I have no hesitation in saying that, in another minute, I should have been kicked; literally kicked — a legal luxury. Costs, damages, and actions rose up like sky-rockets in my aspiring soul, with golden tails reaching to the infinity of my hopes. (*Looking*) They are coming this way; Mr. Hamilton in close conversation with Lady Courtly that is to be. Crim. Con. — Courtly versus Hamilton — damages problematical — Meddle, chief witness for plaintiff — guinea a day — professional man! I'll take down their conversation verbatim. (*He retires behind a bush*)

Enter Grace, followed by Young Courtly.

Grace. Perhaps you would follow your friend into the dining-room; refreshment after your long journey must be requisite.

Court. Pardon me, madam; but the lovely garden and the loveliness before me is better refreshment than I could procure in any dining-room.

Grace. Ha! Your company and compliments arrive together.

Court. I trust that a passing remark will not spoil so welcome an introduction as this by offending you.

Grace. I am not certain that anything you could say would offend me.

Court. I never meant —

Grace. I thought not. In turn, pardon me, when I request you will commence your visit with this piece of information: — I consider compliments impertinent, and sweetmeat language fulsome.

Court. I would condemn my tongue to a Pythagorean silence if I thought it could attempt to flatter.

Grace. It strikes me, sir, that you are a stray bee from the hive of fashion; if so, reserve your honey for its proper cell. A truce to compliments. — You have just arrived *from town*, I apprehend.

Court. This moment I left mighty London, under the fever of a full season, groaning with the noisy pulse of wealth and the giddy whirling brain of fashion. Enchanting, busy London! how have I prevailed on myself to desert you! Next week the new ballet comes out, — the week after comes Ascot. — Oh!

Grace. How agonizing must be the reflection.

Court. Torture! Can you inform me how you manage to avoid suicide here? If there was but an opera, even, within twenty miles! We couldn't get up a rustic ballet among the village girls? No? — ah!

Grace. I am afraid you would find that difficult. How I contrive to support life I don't know — it is wonderful — but I have not precisely contemplated suicide yet, nor do I miss the opera.

Court. How can you manage to kill time?

Grace. I can't. Men talk of killing time, while time quietly kills them. I have many employments — this week I devote to study and various amusements — next week to being married — the following week to repentance, perhaps.

Court. Married!

Grace. You seem surprised; I believe it is of frequent occurrence in the metropolis. — Is it not?

Court. Might I ask to whom?

Grace. A gentleman who has been strongly recommended to me for the situation of husband.

Court. What an extraordinary match! Would you not consider it advisable to see him, previous to incurring the consequences of such an act?

Grace. You must be aware that fashion says otherwise. The gentleman swears eternal devotion to the lady's fortune, and the lady swears she will outvie him still. My lord's horses and my lady's diamonds shine through a few seasons, until a seat in Parliament, or the continent, stares them in the face; then, when thrown upon each other for resources of comfort, they begin to quarrel about the original conditions of the sale.

Court. Sale! No! that would be degrading civilization into Turkish barbarity.

Grace. Worse, sir, a great deal worse; for there at least they do not attempt concealment of the barter; but here, every London ball-room is a marriage mart — young ladies are trotted out, while the mother, father, or chaperone plays auctioneer, and knocks them down to the highest bidder — young men are ticketed up with their fortunes on their backs, — and Love, turned into a dapper shopman, descants on the excellent qualities of the material.

Court. Oh! that such a custom could have ever emanated from the healthy soil of an English heart!

Grace. No. It never did — like most of our

literary dandyisms and dandy literature, it was borrowed from the French.

Court. You seem to laugh at love.

Grace. Love! why, the very word is a breathing satire upon man's reason — a mania, indigenous to humanity — nature's jester, who plays off tricks upon the world, and trips up common sense. When I'm in love, I'll write an almanac, for very lack of wit — prognosticate the sighing season — when to beware of tears — about this time, expect matrimony to be prevalent! Ha! ha! Why should I lay out my life in love's bonds upon the bare security of a man's word?

Enter James.

James. The Squire, madam, has just arrived, and another gentleman with him.

Grace. (*Aside*) My intended, I suppose.
                                    Exit James.

Court. I perceive you are one of the railers against what is termed the follies of high life.

Grace. No, not particularly; I deprecate all folly. By what prerogative can the west-end mint issue absurdity, which, if coined in the east, would be voted vulgar?

Court. By a sovereign right — because it has Fashion's head upon its side, and that stamps it current.

Grace. Poor Fashion, for how many sins hast thou to answer! The gambler pawns his birth-right for fashion — the *roué* steals his friend's wife for fashion — each abandons himself to the storm of impulse, calling it the breeze of fashion.

Court. Is this idol of the world so radically vicious?

Grace. No; the root is well enough, as the body was, until it had outgrown its native soil; but now, like a mighty giant lying over Europe, it pillows its head in Italy, its heart in France, leaving the heels alone its sole support for England.

Court. Pardon me, madam, you wrong yourself to rail against your own inheritance — the kingdom to which loveliness and wit attest your title.

Grace. A mighty realm, forsooth, — with milliners for ministers, a cabinet of coxcombs, envy for my homage, ruin for my revenue — my right of rule depending on the shape of a bonnet or the sit of a pelisse, with the next grand noodle as my heir-apparent. Mr. Hamilton, when I am crowned, I shall feel happy to abdicate in your favour.
                              Curtseys and exit.

Court. What did she mean by that? Hang me if I can understand her — she is evidently not used to society. Ha! — takes every word I say for infallible truth — requires the solution of a compliment, as if it were a problem in Euclid. She said she was about to marry, but I rather imagine she was in jest. 'Pon my life, I feel very queer at the contemplation of such an idea — I'll follow her. (*Meddle comes down*) Oh! perhaps this booby can inform me something about her. (*Meddle makes signs at him*) What the devil is he at!

Meddle. It won't do — no — ah! um — it's not to be done.

Court. What do you mean?

Meddle. (*Points after Grace*) Counsel retained — cause to come off!

Court. Cause to come off!

Meddle. Miss Grace is about to be married.

Court. Is it possible?

Meddle. Certainly. If *I* have the drawing out of the deeds —

Court. To whom?

Meddle. Ha! hem! Oh, yes! I dare say — Information being scarce in the market, I hope to make mine valuable.

Court. Married! married!

Meddle. Now I shall have another chance.

Court. I'll run and ascertain the truth of this from Dazzle.   *Exit.*

Meddle. It's of no use: he either dare not kick me, or he can't afford it — in either case, he is beneath my notice. Ah! who comes here? — can it be Sir Harcourt Courtly himself? It can be no other.

Enter Cool.

Sir, I have the honour to bid you welcome to Oak Hall and the village of Oldborough.

Cool. (*Aside*) Excessively polite. (*Aloud*) — Sir, thank you.

Meddle. The township contains two thousand inhabitants.

Cool. Does it! I am delighted to hear it.

Meddle. (*Aside*) I can charge him for that — ahem — six and eightpence is not much — but it is a beginning. (*Aloud*) If you will permit me, I can inform you of the different commodities for which it is famous.

Cool. Much obliged — but here comes Sir Harcourt Courtly, my master, and Mr. Harkaway — any other time I shall feel delighted.

Meddle. Oh! (*Aside*) Mistook the man for the master.   *He retires up.*

Enter Max and Sir Harcourt.

Max. Here we are at last. Now give ye welcome to Oak Hall, Sir Harcourt, heartily!

Sir H. (*Languidly*) Cool, assist me.
          Cool takes off his furred cloak and gloves; gives him white gloves and a handkerchief.

Max. Why, you require unpacking as carefully as my best bin of port. Well, now you are decanted, tell me what did you think of my park as we came along?

Sir H. That it would never come to an end. You said it was only a stone's throw from your infernal lodge to the house; why, it's ten miles, at least.

Max. I'll do it in ten minutes any day.

Sir H. Yes, in a steam carriage. Cool, perfume my handkerchief.

Max. Don't do it. Don't! perfume in the country! why, it's high treason in the very face of Nature; 'tis introducing the robbed to the robber. Here are the sweets from which your fulsome essences are pilfered, and libelled with their names; — don't insult them, too.

Sir H. (*To Meddle*) Oh! cull me a bouquet, my man!

Max. (*Turning*) Ah, Meddle! how are you? This is Lawyer Meddle.

Sir. H. Oh! I took him for one of your people.

Meddle. Ah! naturally — um — Sir Harcourt Courtly, I have the honour to congratulate — happy occasion approaches. Ahem! I have no hesitation in saying this *very* happy occasion approaches.

Sir H. Cool, is the conversation addressed towards me?

Cool. I believe so, Sir Harcourt.

Meddle. Oh, certainly! I was complimenting you.

Sir H. Sir, you are very good; the honour is undeserved; but I am only in the habit of receiving compliments from the fair sex. Men's admiration is so damnably insipid.

Meddle. I had hoped to make a unit on that occasion.

Sir H. Yes, and you hoped to put an infernal number of cyphers after your unit on that and any other occasion.

Meddle. Ha! ha! very good. Why, I did hope to have the honour of drawing out the deeds; for, whatever Jenks may say to the contrary, I have no hesitation in saying —

Sir H. (*Putting him aside — To Max*) If the future Lady Courtly be visible at so unfashionable an hour as this, I shall beg to be introduced.

Max. Visible! Ever since six this morning, I'll warrant ye. Two to one she is at dinner.

Sir H. Dinner! Is it possible? Lady Courtly dine at half-past one P.M.!

Meddle. I rather prefer that hour to peck a little my —

Sir H. Dear me! who was addressing you?

Meddle. Oh! I beg pardon.

Max. Here, James! (*Calling*)

Enter James.

Tell Miss Grace to come here directly. (*Exit James*) Now prepare, Courtly, for, though I say it, she *is* — with the exception of my bay mare, Kitty — the handsomest thing in the country. Considering she is a biped, she is a wonder! Full of blood, sound wind and limb, plenty of bone, sweet coat, in fine condition, with a thorough-bred step, as dainty as a pet greyhound.

Sir H. Damme, don't compare her to a horse!

Max. Well, I wouldn't, but she's almost as fine a creature, — close similarities.

Meddle. Oh, very fine creature! Close similarity, amounting to identity.

Sir H. Good gracious, sir! What can a lawyer know about women!

Meddle. Everything. The consistorial court is fine study of the character, and I have no hesitation in saying that I have examined more women than Jenks, or —

Sir H. Oh, damn Jenks!

Meddle. Sir, thank you. Damn him again, sir, damn him again!

Enter Grace.

Grace. My dear uncle!

Max. Ah, Grace, you little jade, come here.

Sir H. (*Eyeing her through his glass*) Oh, dear! she is a rural Venus! I'm astonished and delighted.

Max. Won't you kiss your old uncle?

(*He kisses her*)

Sir H. (*Draws an agonizing face*) Oh! — ah — um! — *N'importe!* — my privilege in embryo — hem! It's very tantalizing, though.

Max. You are not glad to see me, you are not. (*Kissing her*)

Sir H. Oh; no, no! (*Aside*) that is too much. I shall do something horrible presently, if this goes on. (*Aloud*) I should be sorry to curtail any little ebullition of affection; but — ahem! May I be permitted?

Max. Of course you may. There, Grace, is Sir Harcourt, your husband that will be. Go to him, girl.

Sir H. Permit me to do homage to the charms, the presence of which have placed me in sight of Paradise.

Sir Harcourt and Grace retire.

Enter Dazzle.

Dazzle. Ah! old fellow, how are you?

Max. I'm glad to see you! Are you comfortably quartered, yet, eh?

Dazzle. Splendidly quartered! What a place you've got here! Here, Hamilton.

Enter Young Courtly.

Permit me to introduce my friend, Augustus Hamilton. Capital fellow! drinks like a sieve, and rides like a thunder-storm.

Max. Sir, I'm devilish glad to see you. Here, Sir Harcourt, permit me to introduce to you —

Court. The devil!

Dazzle. (*Aside*) What's the matter?

Court. (*Aside*) Why, that is my governor, by Jupiter!

Dazzle. (*Aside*) What, old Whiskers? you don't say that!

Court. (*Aside*) It is: what's to be done now?

Max. Mr. Hamilton, Sir Harcourt Courtly — Sir Harcourt Courtly, Mr. Hamilton.

Sir H. Hamilton! Good gracious! God bless me! — why, Charles, is it possible? — why Max, that's my son!

Court. (*Aside*) What shall I do!

Max. Your son!

Grace. Your son, Sir Harcourt! have you a son as old as that gentleman!

Sir H. No — that is — a — yes, — not by twenty years — a — Charles, why don't you answer me, sir?

Court. (*Aside to Dazzle*) What shall I say?

Dazzle. (*Aside*) Deny your identity.

Court. (*Aside*) Capital! (*Aloud*) What's the matter, sir?

Sir H. How came you down here, sir?

Court. By one of Newman's — best fours — in twelve hours and a quarter.

Sir H. Isn't your name Charles Courtly?

Court. Not to my knowledge.

Sir H. Do you mean to say that you are usually called Augustus Hamilton?

Court. Lamentable fact — and quite correct.

Sir H. Cool, is that my son?

Cool. No, sir — it is not Mr. Charles — but is very like him.

Max. I cannot understand all this.

Grace. (*Aside*) I think I can.

Dazzle. (*Aside to Young Courtly*) Give him a touch of the indignant.

Court. Allow me to say, Sir What-d'ye-call-'em Hartly —

Sir H. Hartly, sir! Courtly, sir! Courtly!

Court. Well, Hartly, or Court-heart, or whatever your name may be, I say your conduct is — a — a —, and were it not for the presence of this lady, I should feel inclined — to — to —

Sir H. No, no, that can't be my son, — he never would address me in that way.

Max. (*Coming down*) What is all this?

Sir H. Sir, your likeness to my son Charles is so astonishing, that it, for a moment —

the equilibrium of my etiquette — 'pon my life, I — permit me to request your pardon.

Meddle. (*To Sir Harcourt*) Sir Harcourt, don't apologize, don't — bring an action. I'm witness.

Sir H. Some one take this man away.

Enter James.

James. Luncheon is on the table, sir.

Sir H. Miss Harkaway, I never swore before a lady in my life — except when I promised to love and cherish the late Lady Courtly, which I took care to preface with an apology, — I was compelled to the ceremony, and consequently not answerable for the language — but to that gentleman's identity I would have pledged — my hair.

Grace. (*Aside*) If that security were called for, I suspect the answer would be — no effects.   *Exeunt Sir Harcourt and Grace.*

Meddle. (*To Max*) I have something very particular to communicate.

Max. Can't listen at present.   *Exit.*

Meddle. (*To Dazzle and Young Courtly*) I can afford you information, which I —

Dazzle. Oh, don't bother!

Court. Go to the devil!   *Exeunt.*

Meddle. Now, I have no hesitation in saying that is the height of ingratitude. — Oh — Mr. Cool — can you oblige me? (*Presents his account*)

Cool. Why, what is all this?

Meddle. Small account *versus* you — to giving information concerning the last census of the population of Oldborough and vicinity, six and eightpence.

Cool. Oh, you mean to make me pay for this, do you?

Meddle. Unconditionally.

Cool. Well, I have no objection — the charge is fair — but remember, I am a servant on board wages, — will you throw in a little advice gratis — if I give you the money?

Meddle. Ahem! — I will.

Cool. A fellow has insulted me. I want to abuse him — what terms are actionable?

Meddle. You may call him anything you please, providing there are no witnesses.

Cool. Oh, may I? (*Looks around*) — then you rascally, pettifogging scoundrel!

Meddle. Hallo!

Cool. You mean — dirty — disgrace to your profession.

Meddle. Libel — slander —

Cool. Aye, but where are your witnesses?

Meddle. Give me the costs — six and eighteen pence.

Cool. I deny that you gave me information at all.

Meddle. You do!

Cool. Yes, where are your witnesses?

Exit.

Meddle. Ah — damme! *Exit.*

End of the Second Act.

ACT III.

A morning-room in Oak Hall, French windows opening to the lawn. Max and Sir Harcourt seated on one side, Dazzle on the other; Grace and Young Courtly are playing chess at back. All dressed for dinner.

Max. (Aside to Sir Harcourt) What can I do?

Sir H. Get rid of them civilly.

Max. What, turn them out, after I particularly invited them to stay a month or two?

Sir H. Why, they are disreputable characters; as for that young fellow, in whom my Lady Courtly appears so particularly absorbed, — I am bewildered — I have written to town for my Charles, my boy — it certainly is the most extraordinary likeness —

Dazzle. Sir Harcourt, I have an idea —

Sir H. Sir, I am delighted to hear it. — *(Aside)* That fellow is a swindler.

Max. I met him at your house.

Sir H. Never saw him before in all my life.

Dazzle. (Crossing to Sir Harcourt) I will bet you five to one that I can beat you three out of four games at billiards, with one hand.

Sir H. No, sir.

Dazzle. I don't mind giving you ten points in fifty.

Sir H. Sir, I never gamble.

Dazzle. You don't! Well, I'll teach you — easiest thing in life — you have every requisite — good temper.

Sir H. I have not, sir.

Dazzle. A long-headed, knowing old buck.

Sir H. Sir! *(They go up conversing with Max)*

Grace. Really, Mr. Hamilton, you improve. — A young man pays us a visit, as you half intimate, to escape inconvenient friends — that is complimentary to us, his hosts.

Court. Nay, that is too severe.

Grace. After an acquaintanceship of two days, you sit down to teach me chess, and domestic economy at the same time. — Might I ask where you graduated in that science — where you learned all that store of matrimonial advice which you have obliged me with?

Court. I imbibed it, madam, from the moment I beheld you, and having studied my subject *con amore*, took my degrees from your eyes.

Grace. Oh, I see you are a Master of Arts already.

Court. Unfortunately, no — I shall remain a bachelor — till you can assist me to that honour. *(Sir Harcourt comes down — aside to Dazzle)* Keep the old boy away.

Dazzle. (Aside) How do you get on?

Court. (Aside) Splendidly!

Sir H. Is the conversation strictly confidential? — or might I join?

Dazzle. (Taking his arm) Oh, not in the least, my dear sir — we were remarking that rifle shooting was an excellent diversion during the summer months.

Sir H. (Drawing himself up) Sir, I was addressing —

Dazzle. And I was saying what a pity it was I couldn't find any one reasonable enough to back his opinion with long odds — come out on the lawn, and pitch up your hat, and I will hold you ten to one I put a bullet into it every time, at forty paces.

Sir H. No, sir — I consider you —

Max. Here, all of you — look, here is Lady Gay Spanker coming across the lawn at a hard gallop!

Sir H. (Running to the window) Bless me, the horse is running away!

Max. Look how she takes that fence! there's a seat.

Sir H. Lady Gay Spanker — who may she be?

Grace. Gay Spanker, Sir Harcourt? My cousin and dearest friend — you *must* like her.

Sir H. It will be my devoir, since it is your wish — though it will be a hard task in your presence.

Grace. I am sure she will like you.

Sir H. Ha! ha! I flatter myself.

Court. Who, and what is she?

Grace. Glee, glee made a living thing — Nature, in some frolic mood, shut up a merry devil in her eye, and spiting Art, stole joy's brightest harmony to thrill her laugh, which peals out sorrow's knell. Her cry rings loudest in the field — the very echo loves it best, and, as each hill attempts to ape her voice, earth seems to laugh that it made a thing so glad.

Max. Ay, the merriest minx I ever kissed.

(Lady Gay laughs without)

Lady G. (Without) Max!

Max. Come in, you mischievous puss.

Enter James.

James. Mr. Adolphus and Lady Gay Spanker.

Enter Lady Gay, fully equipped in riding habit, etc.

Lady G. Ha! ha! Well, Governor, how are ye? I have been down five times, climbing up your stairs in my long clothes. How are you, Grace, dear? (*Kisses her*) There, don't fidget, Max. And there — (*Kisses him*) there's one for you.

Sir H. Ahem!

Lady G. Oh, gracious, I didn't see you had visitors.

Max. Permit me to introduce — Sir Harcourt Courtly, Lady Gay Spanker. Mr. Dazzle, Mr. Hamilton — Lady Gay Spanker.

Sir H. (*Aside*) A devilish fine woman!

Dazzle. (*Aside to Sir Harcourt*) She's a devilish fine woman.

Lady G. You mustn't think anything of the liberties I take with my old papa here — bless him!

Sir H. Oh, no! (*Aside*) I only thought I should like to be in his place.

Lady G. I am so glad you have come, Sir Harcourt. Now we shall be able to make a decent figure at the heels of a hunt.

Sir H. Does your ladyship hunt?

Lady G. Ha! I say, Governor, does my ladyship hunt? I rather flatter myself that I do hunt! Why, Sir Harcourt, one might as well live without laughing as without hunting. Man was fashioned expressly to fit a horse. Are not hedges and ditches created for leaps? Of course! And I look upon foxes to be one of the most blessed dispensations of a benign Providence.

Sir H. Yes, it is all very well in the abstract: I tried it once.

Lady G. Once! Only once?

Sir H. Once, only once. And then the animal ran away with me.

Lady G. Why, you would not have him walk?

Sir H. Finding my society disagreeable, he instituted a series of kicks, with a view to removing the annoyance; but aided by the united stays of the mane and tail, I frustrated his intentions. His next resource, however, was more effectual, for he succeeded in rubbing me off against a tree.

Max and Lady G. Ha! ha! ha!

Dazzle. How absurd you must have looked with your legs and arms in the air, like a ship-wrecked tea-table.

Sir H. Sir, I never looked absurd in my life. Ah, it may be very amusing in relation, I dare say, but very unpleasant in effect.

Lady G. I pity you, Sir Harcourt; it was criminal in your parents to neglect your education so shamefully.

Sir H. Possibly; but be assured I shall never break my neck awkwardly from a horse, when it might be accomplished with less trouble from a bed-room window.

Court. (*Aside*) My dad will be caught by this she-Bucephalus tamer.

Max. Ah! Sir Harcourt, had you been here a month ago, you would have witnessed the most glorious run that ever swept over merry England's green cheek — a steeple-chase, sir, which I intended to win, but my horse broke down the day before. I had a chance, notwithstanding, and but for Gay here, I should have won. How I regretted my absence from it! How did my filly behave herself, Gay?

Lady G. Gloriously, Max! gloriously! There were sixty horses in the field, all mettle to the bone: the start was a picture — away we went in a cloud — pell-mell — helter-skelter — the fools first, as usual, using themselves up — we soon passed them — first your Kitty, then my Blueskin, and Craven's colt last. Then came the tug — Kitty skimmed the walls — Blueskin flew over the fences — the Colt neck and neck, and half a mile to run — at last the Colt baulked a leap and went wild. Kitty and I had it all to ourselves — she was three lengths ahead, as we breasted the last wall, six feet, if an inch, and a ditch on the other side. Now, for the first time, I gave Blueskin his head — ha! ha! — Away he flew like a thunderbolt — over went the filly — I over the same spot, leaving Kitty in the ditch — walked the steeple, eight miles in thirty minutes, and scarcely turned a hair.

All. Bravo! Bravo!

Lady G. Do you hunt?

Dazzle. Hunt! I belong to a hunting family. I was born on horseback and cradled in a kennel! Aye, and I hope I may die with a whoo-whoop!

Max. (*To Sir Harcourt*) You must leave your town habits in the smoke of London: here we rise with the lark.

Sir H. Haven't the remotest conception when that period is.

Grace. The man that misses sunrise loses the sweetest part of his existence.

Sir H. Oh, pardon me; I have seen sunrise frequently after a ball, or from the windows of my travelling carriage, and I always considered it disagreeable.

Grace. I love to watch the first tear that glistens in the opening eye of morning, the silent song the flowers breathe, the thrilling choir of the woodland minstrels, to which the modest brook trickles applause: — these swelling out the sweetest chord of sweet creation's matins, seem to pour some soft and merry tale into the daylight's ear, as if the waking world had dreamed a happy thing, and now smiled o'er the telling of it.

Sir H. The effect of a rustic education! Who could ever discover music in a damp foggy morning, except those confounded waits, who never play in tune, and a miserable wretch who makes a point of crying coffee under my window just as I am persuading myself to sleep; in fact, I never heard any music worth listening to, except in Italy.

Lady G. No? then you never heard a well-trained English pack, full cry?

Sir H. Full cry!

Lady G. Aye! there is harmony, if you will. Give me the trumpet-neigh; the spotted pack just catching scent. What a chorus is their yelp! The view-hallo, blent with a peal of free and fearless mirth! That's our old English music, — match it where you can.

Sir H. (*Aside*) I must see about Lady Gay Spanker.

Dazzle. (*Aside to Sir Harcourt*) Ah, would you —

Lady G. Time then appears as young as love, and plumes as swift a wing. Away we go! The earth flies back to aid our course! Horse, man, hound, earth, heaven! — all — all — one piece of glowing ecstasy! Then I love the world, myself, and every living thing, — my jocund soul cries out for very glee, as it could wish that all creation had but one mouth that I might kiss it!

Sir H. (*Aside*) I wish I were the mouth!

Max. Why, we will regenerate you, Baronet! But Gay, where is your husband? — Where is Adolphus!

Lady G. Bless me, where is my Dolly?

Sir H. You are married, then?

Lady G. I have a husband somewhere, though I can't find him just now. Dolly, dear! (*Aside to Max*) Governor, at home I always whistle when I want him.

Enter Spanker.

Spanker. Here I am, — did you call me, Gay?

Sir H. (*Eyeing him*) Is that your husband?

Lady G. (*Aside*) Yes, bless his stupid face, that's my Dolly.

Max. Permit me to introduce you to Sir Harcourt Courtly.

Spanker. How d'ye do? I — ah! — um! (*Appears frightened*)

Lady G. Delighted to have the honour of making the acquaintance of a gentleman so highly celebrated in the world of fashion.

Spanker. Oh, yes, delighted, I'm sure — quite — very, so delighted — delighted! (*Gets confused, draws on his glove, and tears it*)

Lady G. Where have you been, Dolly?

Spanker. Oh, ah, I was just outside.

Max. Why did you not come in?

Spanker. I'm sure I didn't — I don't exactly know, but I thought as — perhaps — I can't remember.

Dazzle. Shall we have the pleasure of your company to dinner?

Spanker. I always dine — usually — that is, unless Gay remains.

Lady G. Stay dinner, of course; we came on purpose to stop three or four days with you.

Grace. Will you excuse my absence, Gay?

Max. What! what! Where are you going? What takes you away?

Grace. We must postpone the dinner till Gay is dressed.

Max. Oh, never mind,—stay where you are.

Grace. No, I must go.

Max. I say you shan't! I will be king in my own house.

Grace. Do, my dear uncle; — you shall be king, and I'll be your prime minister, — that is, I will rule, and you shall have the honour of taking the consequences. *Exit.*

Lady G. Well said, Grace; have your own way; it is the only thing we women ought to be allowed.

Max. Come, Gay, dress for dinner.

Sir H. Permit me, Lady Gay Spanker.

Lady G. With pleasure, — what do you want?

Sir H. To escort you.

Lady G. Oh, never mind, I can escort myself, thank you, and Dolly too; — come, dear! *Exit.*

Sir H. Au revoir!

Spanker. Ah, thank you!

Exit awkwardly.

Sir H. What an ill-assorted pair!

Max. Not a bit! She married him for freedom, and she has it; he married her for protection, and he has it.

Sir H. How he ever summoned courage to propose to her, I can't guess.

Max. Bless you, he never did. She proposed to him! She says he would, if he could; but as he couldn't, she did it for him.

Exeunt, laughing.

Enter Cool with a letter.

Cool. Mr. Charles, I have been watching

to find you alone. Sir Harcourt has written to town for you.

Court. The devil he has!

Cool. He expects you down to-morrow evening.

Dazzle. Oh! he'll be punctual. A thought strikes me.

Court. Pooh! Confound your thoughts! I can think of nothing but the idea of leaving Grace, at the very moment when I had established the most —

Dazzle. What if I can prevent her marriage with your Governor?

Court. Impossible!

Dazzle. He's pluming himself for the conquest of Lady Gay Spanker. It will not be difficult to make him believe she accedes to his suit. And if she would but join in the plan —

Court. I see it all. And do you think she would?

Dazzle. I mistake my game if she would not.

Cool. Here comes Sir Harcourt!

Dazzle. I'll begin with him. Retire, and watch how I'll open the campaign for you.

Young Courtly and Cool retire.

Enter Sir Harcourt.

Sir H. Here is that cursed fellow again.

Dazzle. Ah, my dear old friend!

Sir H. Mr. Dazzle!

Dazzle. I have a secret of importance to disclose to you. Are you a man of honour? Hush! don't speak; you are. It is with the greatest pain I am compelled to request you, as a gentleman, that you will shun studiously the society of Lady Gay Spanker!

Sir H. Good gracious! Wherefore, and by what right do you make such a demand?

Dazzle. Why, I am distantly related to the Spankers.

Sir H. Why, damme, sir, if you don't appear to be related to every family in Great Britain!

Dazzle. A good many of the nobility claim me as a connexion. But, to return — she is much struck with your address; evidently, she laid herself out for display.

Sir H. Ha! you surprise me!

Dazzle. To entangle you.

Sir H. Ha! ha! why, it did appear like it.

Dazzle. You will spare her for my sake; give her no encouragement; if disgrace come upon my relatives, the Spankers, I should never hold up my head again.

Sir H. (*Aside*) I shall achieve an easy conquest, and a glorious. Ha! ha! I never remarked it before; but this is a gentleman.

Dazzle. May I rely on your generosity?

Sir H. Faithfully. (*Shakes his hand*) Sir, I honour and esteem you; but, might I ask, how came you to meet our friend, Max Harkaway, in my house in Belgrave Square?

Re-enter Young Courtly. Sits on sofa at back.

Dazzle. Certainly. I had an acceptance of your son's for one hundred pounds.

Sir H. (*Astonished*) Of my son's? Impossible!

Dazzle. Ah, sir, fact! he paid a debt for a poor, unfortunate man — fifteen children — half-a-dozen wives — the devil knows what all.

Sir H. Simple boy!

Dazzle. Innocent youth, I have no doubt; when you have the hundred convenient, I shall feel delighted.

Sir H. Oh! follow me to my room, and if you have the document, it will be happiness to me to pay it. Poor Charles! good heart!

Dazzle. Oh, a splendid heart! I dare say. (*Exit Sir Harcourt*) Come here; write me the bill.

Court. What for?

Dazzle. What for? why, to release the unfortunate man and his family, to be sure, from jail.

Court. Who is he?

Dazzle. Yourself.

Court. But I haven't fifteen children!

Dazzle. Will you take your oath of that?

Court. Nor four wives.

Dazzle. More shame for you, with all that family. Come, don't be obstinate; write and date it back.

Court. Ay, but where is the stamp?

Dazzle. Here they are, of all patterns. (*Pulls out a pocketbook*) I keep them ready drawn in case of necessity, all but the date and acceptance. Now, if you are in an autographic humour, you can try how your signature will look across half a dozen of them; — there — write — exactly — you know the place — across — good — and thank your lucky stars that you have found a friend at last, that gives you money and advice.   *Takes paper and exit.*

Court. Things are approaching to a climax; I must appear *in propriâ personâ* — and immediately — but I must first ascertain what are the real sentiments of this riddle of a woman. Does she love me? I flatter myself — By Jove, here she comes — I shall never have such an opportunity again!

Enter Grace.

Grace. I wish I had never seen Mr. Hamilton. Why does every object appear robbed of the charm it once presented to me? Why do I shudder at the contemplation of this marriage, which, till now, was to me a subject of indifference? Am I in love? In love! if I am, my past life has been the work of raising up a pedestal to place my own folly on — I — the infidel — the railer!

Court. Meditating upon matrimony, madam?

Grace. (*Aside*) He little thinks he was the subject of my meditations! (*Aloud*) No.

Court. (*Aside*) I must unmask my battery now.

Grace. (*Aside*) How foolish I am — he will perceive that I tremble — I must appear at ease. (*A pause*)

Court. Eh? ah! um!

Grace. Ah! (*They sink into silence again. Aside*) How very awkward!

Court. (*Aside*) It is a very difficult subject to begin. (*Aloud*) Madam — ahem — there was — is — I mean — I was about to remark — a — (*Aside*) Hang me if it is not a very slippery subject. I must brush up my faculties; attack her in her own way. (*Aloud*) Sing! oh, muse! (*Aside*). Why, I have made love before to a hundred women!

Grace. (*Aside*) I wish I had something to do, for I have nothing to say.

Court. Madam — there is — a subject so fraught with fate to my future life, that you must pardon my lack of delicacy, should a too hasty expression mar the fervent courtesy of its intent. To you, I feel aware, I must appear in the light of a comparative stranger.

Grace. (*Aside*) I know what's coming.

Court. Of you — I know perhaps too much for my own peace.

Grace. (*Aside*) He *is* in love.

Court. I forget all that befell before I saw your beauteous self; I seem born into another world — my nature changed — the beams of that bright face falling on my soul, have, from its chaos, warmed into life the flowrets of affection, whose maiden odours now float toward the sun, pouring forth on their pure tongue a mite of adoration, midst the voices of a universe. (*Aside*) That's something in her own style.

Grace. Mr. Hamilton!

Court. You cannot feel surprised —

Grace. I am more than surprised. (*Aside*) I am delighted.

Court. Do not speak so coldly.

Grace. You have offended me.

Court. No, madam; no woman, whatever her state, can be offended by the adoration even of the meanest; it is myself whom I have offended and deceived — but still I ask your pardon.

Grace. (*Aside*) Oh! he thinks I am refusing him. (*Aloud*) I am not exactly offended, but —

Court. Consider my position — a few days — and an insurmountable barrier would have placed you beyond my wildest hopes — you would have been my mother.

Grace. I should have been your mother! (*Aside*) I thought so.

Court. No — that is, I meant Sir Harcourt Courtly's bride.

Grace. (*With great emphasis*) Never!

Court. How! never! may I then hope? — you turn away — you would not lacerate me by a refusal?

Grace. (*Aside*) How stupid he is!

Court. Still silent! I thank you, Miss Grace — I ought to have expected this — fool that I have been — one course alone remains — farewell!

Grace. (*Aside*) Now he's going.

Court. Farewell forever! (*Sits*) Will you not speak one word? I shall leave this house immediately — I shall not see you again.

Grace. Unhand me, sir, I insist.

Court. (*Aside*) Oh! what an ass I've been! (*Rushes up to her, and seizes her hand*) Release this hand? Never! never! (*Kissing it*) Never will I quit this hand! it shall be my companion in misery — in solitude — when you are far away.

Grace. Oh! should any one come! (*Drops her handkerchief; he stoops to pick it up*) For heaven's sake do not kneel.

Court. (*Kneels*) Forever thus prostrate, before my soul's saint, I will lead a pious life of eternal adoration.

Grace. Should we be discovered thus — pray, Mr. Hamilton — pray — pray.

Court. Pray! I am praying; what more can I do?

Grace. Your conduct is shameful.

Court. It is. (*Rises*)

Grace. And if I do not scream, it is not for your sake — that — but it might alarm the family.

Court. It might — it would. Say, am I wholly indifferent to you? I entreat one word — I implore you — do not withdraw your hand — (*She snatches it away — he puts his round her waist*) You smile.

Grace. Leave me, dear Mr. Hamilton!

Court. Dear! Then I am dear to you; that word once more; say — say you love me!

Grace. Is this fair? (*He catches her in his arms, and kisses her*)

Enter Lady Gay Spanker.

Lady G. Ha! oh!

Grace. Gay! destruction!   *Exit.*

Court. Fizgig! The devil!

Lady G. Don't mind me — pray, don't let me be any interruption!

Court. I was just —

Lady G. Yes, I see you were.

Court. Oh! madam, how could you mar my bliss, in the very ecstasy of its fulfilment?

Lady G. I always like to be in at the death. Never drop your ears; bless you, she is only a little fresh — give her her head, and she will outrun herself.

Court. Possibly; but what am I to do?

Lady G. Keep your seat.

Court. But in a few days she will take a leap that must throw me — she marries Sir Harcourt Courtly.

Lady G. Why, that is awkward, certainly; but you can challenge him, and shoot him.

Court. Unfortunately, that is out of the question.

Lady G. How so?

Court. You will not betray a secret, if I inform you?

Lady G. All right — what is it?

Court. I am his son.

Lady G. What — his son? But he does not know you?

Court. No. I met him here, by chance, and faced it out. I never saw him before in my life.

Lady G. Beautiful! — I see it all — you're in love with your mother, that should be — your wife, that will be.

Court. Now, I think I could distance the old gentleman, if you will but lend us your assistance.

Lady G. I will, in anything.

Court. You must know, then, that my father, Sir Harcourt, has fallen desperately in love with you.

Lady G. With me! — (*Utters a scream of delight*) — That is delicious!

Court. Now, if you only could —

Lady G. Could! — I will. Ha! ha! I see my cue. I'll cross his scent — I'll draw him after me. Ho! ho! won't I make love to him? Ha!

Court. The only objection might be Mr. Spanker, who might —

Lady G. No, he mightn't, — he's no objection. Bless him, he's an inestimable little character — you don't know him as well as I do. I dare say — ha! ha! (*Dinner-bell rings*) Here they come to dinner. I'll commence my operations on your Governor immediately. Ha! ha! how I shall enjoy it.

Court. Be guarded!

Enter Max Harkaway, Sir Harcourt, Dazzle, Grace, and Spanker.

Max. Now, gentlemen — Sir Harcourt, do you lead Grace.

Lady G. I believe Sir Harcourt is engaged to me. (*Takes his arm*)

Max. Well, please yourselves.

They file out, Max first, Young Courtly and Grace, Sir Harcourt coquetting with Lady Gay, leaving Dazzle, who offers his arm to Spanker.

End of the Third Act.

ACT IV.

A handsome drawing-room in Oak Hall, chandeliers, tables with books, drawings, etc. Grace and Lady Gay discovered. Servant handing coffee.

Grace. If there be one habit more abominable than another, it is that of the gentlemen sitting over their wine: it is a selfish, unfeeling fashion, and a gross insult to our sex.

Lady G. We are turned out just when the fun begins. How happy the poor wretches look at the contemplation of being rid of us.

Grace. The conventional signal for the ladies to withdraw is anxiously and deliberately waited for.

Lady G. Then I begin to wish I were a man.

Grace. The instant the door is closed upon us, there rises a roar!

Lady G. In celebration of their short-lived liberty, my love; rejoicing over their emancipation.

Grace. I think it very insulting, whatever it may be.

Lady G. Ah! my dear, philosophers say that man is the creature of an hour — it is the dinner hour, I suppose. (*Loud noise. Cries of "A song, a song"*)

Grace. I am afraid they are getting too pleasant to be agreeable.

Lady G. I hope the squire will restrict himself; after his third bottle, he becomes rather voluminous. (*Cries of "Silence"*) Some one is going to sing. (*Jumps up*) Let us hear! (*Spanker is heard to sing*)

Grace. Oh, no, Gay, for heaven's sake!

Lady G. Oho! ha! ha! why, that is my Dolly. (*At the conclusion of the verse*) Well, I never heard my Dolly sing before! Happy wretches, how I envy them!

Enter James, with a note.

James. Mr. Hamilton has just left the house for London.

Grace. Impossible! — that is, without see-ing — that is —

Lady G. Ha! ha!

Grace. He never — speak, sir!

James. He left, Miss Grace, in a desperate hurry, and this note, I believe, for you. (*Presenting a note on a salver*)

Grace. For me!

She is about to snatch it, but re-straining herself, takes it coolly. Exit James.

(*Reads*) "Your manner during dinner has left me no alternative but instant departure; my absence will release you from the oppres-sion which my society must necessarily inflict on your sensitive mind. It may tend also to smother, though it can never extinguish, that indomitable passion, of which I am the passive victim. Dare I supplicate par-don and oblivion for the past? It is the last request of the self-deceived, but still loving

AUGUSTUS HAMILTON."

Puts her hand to her forehead and appears giddy.

Lady G. Hallo, Grace! what's the matter?

Grace. (*Recovering herself*) Nothing — the heat of the room.

Lady G. Oh! what excuse does he make? particular unforeseen business, I suppose?

Grace. Why, yes — a mere formula — a — a — you may put it in the fire. (*She puts it in her bosom*)

Lady G. (*Aside*) It is near enough to the fire where it is.

Grace. I'm glad he's gone.

Lady G. So am I.

Grace. He was a disagreeable, ignorant person.

Lady G. Yes; and so vulgar!

Grace. No, he was not at all vulgar.

Lady G. I mean in appearance.

Grace. Oh! how can you say so; he was very *distingué.*

Lady G. Well, I might have been mis-taken, but I took him for a forward, intru-sive —

Grace. Good gracious, Gay! he was very retiring — even shy.

Lady G. (*Aside*) It's all right. *She* is in love, — blows hot and cold in the same breath.

Grace. How can you be a competent judge? Why, you have not known him more than a few hours, — while I — I —

Lady G. Have known him two days and a quarter! I yield — I confess, I never was, or

will be so intimate with him as you appeared to be! Ha! ha!

Loud noise of argument. The folding-doors are thrown open. Enter the whole party of gentlemen apparently engaged in warm discussion. They assemble in knots, while the Servants hand coffee, etc. Max, Sir Harcourt, Dazzle, and Spanker, together.

Dazzle. But, my dear sir, consider the position of the two countries under such a constitution.

Sir H. The two countries! What have they to do with the subject?

Max. Everything. Look at their two legislative bodies.

Spanker. Ay, look at their two legislative bodies.

Sir H. Why, it would inevitably establish universal anarchy and confusion.

Grace. I think they are pretty well es-tablished already.

Spanker. Well, suppose it did, what has anarchy and confusion to do with the sub-ject?

Lady G. Do look at my Dolly: he is arguing — talking politics — 'pon my life he is. (*Calling*) Mr. Spanker, my dear!

Spanker. Excuse me, love, I am discussing a point of importance.

Lady G. Oh, that is delicious; he must discuss that to me. — (*She goes up and leads him down; he appears to have shaken off his gaucherie; she shakes her head*) Dolly! Dolly!

Spanker. Pardon me, Lady Gay Spanker, I conceive your mutilation of my sponsorial appellation derogatory to my *amour propre.*

Lady G. Your what? Ho! ho!

Spanker. And I particularly request that, for the future, I may not be treated with that cavalier spirit which does not become your sex, nor your station, your ladyship.

Lady G. You have been indulging till you have lost the little wit nature dribbled into your unfortunate little head — your brains want the whipper-in — you are not yourself.

Spanker. Madam, I am doubly myself; and permit me to inform you, that unless you voluntarily pay obedience to my commands, I shall enforce them.

Lady G. Your commands!

Spanker. Yes, madam; I mean to put a full stop to your hunting.

Lady G. You do! ah! (*Aside*) I can scarcely speak from delight. (*Aloud*) Who put such an idea into your head, for I am sure it is not an original emanation of your genius?

Spanker. Sir Harcourt Courtly, my friend; and now, mark me! I request, for your own sake, that I may not be compelled to assert my a — my authority, as your husband. I shall say no more than this — if you persist in this absurd rebellion —

Lady G. Well!

Spanker. Contemplate a separation.

He looks at her haughtily, and retires.

Lady G. Now I'm happy! My own little darling, inestimable Dolly, has tumbled into a spirit, somehow. Sir Harcourt, too! Ha! ha! he's trying to make him ill-treat me, so that his own suit may thrive.

Sir H. (*Advances*) Lady Gay!

Lady G. Now for it.

Sir H. What hours of misery were those I passed, when, by your secession, the room suffered a total eclipse.

Lady G. Ah! you flatter.

Sir H. No, pardon me, that were impossible. No, believe me, I tried to join in the boisterous mirth, but my thoughts would desert to the drawing-room. Ah! how I envied the careless levity and cool indifference with which Mr. Spanker enjoyed your absence.

Dazzle. (*Who is lounging in a chair*) Max, that Madeira is worth its weight in gold; I hope you have more of it.

Max. A pipe, I think.

Dazzle. I consider a magnum of that nectar, and a meerschaum of kanaster, to consummate the ultimatum of all mundane bliss. To drown myself in liquid ecstasy, and then blow a cloud on which the enfranchised soul could soar above Olympus. — Oh!

Enter James.

James. Mr. Charles Courtly!

Sir H. Ah, now, Max, you must see a living apology for my conduct.

Enter Young Courtly, dressed very plainly.

Well, Charles, how are you? Don't be afraid. There, Max, what do you say now?

Max. Well, this is the most extraordinary likeness.

Grace. (*Aside*) Yes — considering it is the original. I am not so easily deceived!

Max. Sir, I am delighted to see you.

Court. Thank you, sir.

Dazzle. Will you be kind enough to introduce me, Sir Harcourt?

Sir H. This is Mr. Dazzle, Charles.

Court. Which? (*Looking from Mr. Spanker to Dazzle*)

Sir H. (*To Lady Gay*) Is not that refreshing? Miss Harkaway — Charles, this is your mother, or rather will be.

Court. Madam, I shall love, honour, and obey you punctually. (*Takes out a book, sighs, and goes up reading*)

Enter James.

Sir H. You perceive? Quite unused to society — perfectly ignorant of every conventional rule of life.

James. The Doctor and the young ladies have arrived. *Exit.*

Max. The young ladies — now we must to the ball — I make it a rule always to commence the festivities with a good old country dance — a rattling Sir Roger de Coverley; come, Sir Harcourt.

Sir H. Does this antiquity require a war-whoop in it?

Max. Nothing but a nimble foot and a light heart.

Sir H. Very antediluvian indispensables! Lady Gay Spanker, will you honour me by becoming my preceptor?

Lady G. Why, I am engaged — but (*Aloud*) on such a plea as Sir Harcourt's, I must waive all obstacles.

Max. Now, Grace, girl — give your hand to Mr. Courtly.

Grace. Pray, excuse me, uncle — I have a headache.

Sir H. (*Aside*) Jealousy! by the gods. — Jealous of my devotions at another's fane! (*Aloud*) Charles, my boy! amuse Miss Grace during our absence. *Exit with Lady Gay.*

Max. But don't you dance, Mr. Courtly!

Court. Dance, sir! — I never dance — I can procure exercise in a much more rational manner — and music disturbs my meditations.

Max. Well, do the gallant. *Exit.*

Court. I never studied that Art — but I have a Prize Essay on a Hydrostatic subject, which would delight her — for it enchanted the Reverend Doctor Pump, of Corpus Christi.

Grace. (*Aside*) What on earth could have induced him to disguise himself in that frightful way! — I rather suspect some plot to entrap me into a confession.

Court. (*Aside*) Dare I confess this trick to her? No! Not until I have proved her affection indisputably. — Let me see — I must concoct. (*He takes a chair, and, forgetting his assumed character, is about to take his natural free manner. — Grace looks surprised. — He turns abashed*) Madam, I have been desired to amuse you.

Grace. Thank you.

Court. "The labour we delight in, physics pain." I will draw you a moral, ahem! Subject, the effects of inebriety! — which, according to Ben Jonson — means perplexion of the intellects, caused by imbibing spirituous liquors. — About an hour before my arrival, I passed an appalling evidence of the effects of this state — a carriage was overthrown — horses killed — gentleman in a helpless state, with his neck broken — all occasioned by the intoxication of the postboy.

Grace. That is very amusing.

Court. I found it edifying — nutritious food for reflection — the expiring man desired his best compliments to you.

Grace. To me?

Court. Yes.

Grace. His name was —

Court. Mr. Augustus Hamilton.

Grace. Augustus! Oh! (*Affects to faint*)

Court. (*Aside*) Huzza!

Grace. But where, sir, did this happen?

Court. About four miles down the road.

Grace. He must be conveyed here.

Enter Servant.

Servant. Mr. Meddle, madam.

Enter Meddle.

Meddle. On very particular business.

Grace. The very person. My dear sir!

Meddle. My dear madam!

Grace. You must execute a very particular commission for me immediately. Mr. Hamilton has met with a frightful accident on the London road, and is in a dying state.

Meddle. Well! I have no hesitation in saying, he takes it uncommonly easy — he looks as if he was used to it.

Grace. You mistake: that is not Mr. Hamilton, but Mr. Courtly, who will explain everything, and conduct you to the spot.

Court. (*Aside*) Oh! I must put a stop to all this, or I shall be found out. — (*Aloud*) Madam, that were useless; for I omitted to mention a small fact which occurred before I left Mr. Hamilton — he died.

Grace. Dear me! Oh, then we needn't trouble you, Mr. Meddle. (*Music heard*) Hark! I hear they are commencing a waltz — if you will ask me — perhaps your society and conversation may tend to dispel the dreadful sensation you have aroused.

Court. (*Aside*) Hears of my death — screams out — and then asks me to waltz! I am bewildered! Can she suspect me? I wonder which she likes best — me or my double? Confound this disguise — I must retain it — I have gone too far with my dad to pull up now. — At your service, madam.

Grace. (*Aside*) I will pay him well for this trick! *Exeunt, all but Meddle.*

Meddle. Well, if that is not Mr. Hamilton, scratch me out with a big blade, for I am a blot — a mistake upon the rolls. There is an error in the pleadings somewhere, and I will discover it. I would swear to his identity before the most discriminating jury. By the bye, this accident will form a capital excuse for my presence here. I just stepped in to see how matters worked, and — stay — here comes the bridegroom elect — and, oh! in his very arms, Lady Gay Spanker! (*Looks round*) Where are my witnesses? Oh, that some one else were here! However, I can retire and get some information, eh — Spanker versus Courtly — damages — witness. (*Gets into an arm-chair, which he turns round*)

*Enter Sir Harcourt, supporting
Lady Gay.*

Sir H. This cool room will recover you.

Lady G. Excuse my trusting to you for support.

Sir H. I am transported! Allow me thus ever to support this lovely burden, and I shall conceive that Paradise is regained. (*They sit*)

Lady G. Oh! Sir Harcourt, I feel very faint.

Sir H. The waltz made you giddy.

Lady G. And I have left my salts in the other room.

Sir H. I always carry a flacon, for the express accommodation of the fair sex. (*Producing a smelling-bottle*)

Lady G. Thank you — ah! (*She sighs*)

Sir H. What a sigh was there!

Lady G. The vapour of consuming grief.

Sir H. Grief? Is it possible! Have you a grief? Are you unhappy? Dear me!

Lady G. Am I not married?

Sir H. What a horrible state of existence!

Lady G. I am never contradicted, so there are none of those enlivening, interesting little differences, which so pleasingly diversify the monotony of conjugal life, like spots of verdure — no quarrels, like oases in the desert of matrimony — no rows.

Sir H. How vulgar! what a brute!

Lady G. I never have anything but my own way; and he won't permit me to spend more than I like.

Sir H. Mean-spirited wretch!

Lady G. How can I help being miserable?

Sir H. Miserable! I wonder you are not in a lunatic asylum, with such unheard-of barbarity!

Lady G. But worse than all that!

Sir H. Can it be out-Heroded?

Lady G. Yes, I could forgive that — I do — it is my duty. But only imagine — picture to yourself, my dear Sir Harcourt, though I, the third daughter of an Earl, married him out of pity for his destitute and helpless situation as a bachelor with ten thousand a year — conceive, if you can — he actually permits me, with the most placid indifference, to flirt with any old fool I may meet.

Sir H. Good gracious! miserable idiot!

Lady G. I fear there is an incompatibility of temper, which renders a separation inevitable.

Sir H. Indispensable, my dear madam! Ah! had I been the happy possessor of such a realm of bliss — what a beatific eternity unfolds itself to my extending imagination! Had another man but looked at you, I should have annihilated him at once; and if he had the temerity to speak, his life alone could have expiated his crime.

Lady G. Oh, an existence of such a nature is too bright for the eye of thought — too sweet to bear reflection.

Sir H. My devotion, eternal, deep —

Lady G. Oh, Sir Harcourt!

Sir H. (*More fervently*) Your every thought should be a separate study, — each wish forestalled by the quick apprehension of a kindred soul.

Lady G. Alas! how can I avoid my fate?

Sir H. If a life — a heart — were offered to your astonished view by one who is considered the index of fashion — the vane of the *beau monde*, — if you saw him at your feet, begging, beseeching your acceptance of all, and more than this, what would your answer —

Lady G. Ah! I know of none so devoted!

Sir H. You do! (*Throwing himself upon his knees*) Behold Sir Harcourt Courtly!

(*Meddle jumps up in the chair*)

Lady G. (*Aside*) Ha! ha! Yoicks! Puss has broken cover.

Sir H. Speak, adored, dearest Lady Gay! — speak — will you fly from the tyranny, the wretched misery of such a monster's roof, and accept the soul which lives but in your presence!

Lady G. Do not press me. Oh, spare a weak, yielding woman, — be contented to know that you are, alas! too dear to me. But the world — the world would say —

Sir H. Let us be a precedent, to open a more extended and liberal view of matrimonial advantages to society.

Lady G. How irresistible is your argument! Oh! pause!

Sir H. I have ascertained for a fact, that every tradesman of mine lives with his wife, and thus you see it has become a vulgar and plebeian custom.

Lady G. Leave me; I feel I cannot with-stand your powers of persuasion. Swear that you will never forsake me.

Sir H. Dictate the oath. May I grow wrinkled, — may two inches be added to the circumference of my waist, — may I lose the fall in my back, — may I be old and ugly the instant I forego one tithe of adoration!

Lady G. I must believe you.

Sir H. Shall we leave this detestable spot — this horrible vicinity?

Lady G. The sooner the better: to-morrow evening let it be. Now let me return; my absence will be remarked. (*He kisses her hand*) Do I appear confused? Has my agitation rendered me unfit to enter the room?

Sir H. More angelic by a lovely tinge of heightened colour.

Lady G. To-morrow, in this room, which opens on the lawn.

Sir H. At eleven o'clock.

Lady G. Have your carriage in waiting, and four horses. Remember, please be particular to have four; don't let the affair come off shabbily. Adieu, dear Sir Harcourt! *Exit.*

Sir H. Veni, vidi, vici! Hannibal, Caesar, Napoleon, Alexander never completed so fair a conquest in so short a time. She dropped fascinated. This is an unprecedented example of the irresistible force of personal appearance combined with polished address. Poor creature! how she loves me! I pity so prostrating a passion, and ought to return it. I will: it is a duty I owe to society and fashion. *Exit.*

Meddle. (*Turns the chair round*) "There is a tide in the affairs of men, which, taken at the flood, leads on to fortune." This is my tide — I am the only witness. "Virtue is sure to find its own reward." But I've no time to contemplate what I shall be — something huge. Let me see — Spanker *versus* Courtly — Crim. Con. — Damages placed at 150,000*l.*, at least, for juries always decimate your hopes.

Enter Mr. Spanker.

Spanker. I cannot find Gay anywhere.

Meddle. The plaintiff himself — I must commence the action. Mr. Spanker, as I have information of deep, vital importance to impart, will you take a seat? (*They sit solemnly. Meddle takes out a note-book and pencil*) Ahem! You have a wife?

Re-enter Lady Gay behind.

Spanker. Yes, I believe I —

Meddle. Will you be kind enough, without any prevarication, to answer my questions?

Spanker. You alarm — I —

Meddle. Compose yourself and reserve

your feelings; take time to consider. You have a wife?

Spanker. Yes —

Meddle. He has a wife — good — a *bona-fide* wife — bound morally and legally to be your wife, and nobody else's in effect, except on your written permission —

Spanker. But what has this —

Meddle. Hush! allow me, my dear sir, to congratulate you. (*Shakes his hand*)

Spanker. What for?

Meddle. Lady Gay Spanker is about to dishonour the bond of wedlock by eloping from you.

Spanker. (*Starting*) What?

Meddle. Be patient — I thought you would be overjoyed. Will you place the affair in my hands, and I will venture to promise the largest damages on record.

Spanker. Damn the damages! — I want my wife. Oh, I'll go and ask her not to run away. She may run away with me — she may hunt — she may ride — anything she likes. Oh, sir, let us put a stop to this affair.

Meddle. Put a stop to it! do not alarm me, sir. Sir, you will spoil the most exquisite brief that was ever penned. It must proceed — it shall proceed. It is illegal to prevent it, and I will bring an action against you for wilful intent to injure the profession.

Spanker. Oh, what an ass I am! Oh, I have driven her to this. It was all that damned brandy punch on the top of Burgundy. What a fool I was!

Meddle. It was the happiest moment of your life.

Spanker. So I thought at the time; but we live to grow wiser. Tell me, who is the vile seducer?

Meddle. Sir Harcourt Courtly.

Spanker. Ha! he is my best friend.

Meddle. I should think he is. If you will accompany me — here is a verbatim copy of the whole transaction in short-hand — sworn to by me.

Spanker. Only let me have Gay back again.

Meddle. Even that may be arranged: — this way.

Spanker. That ever I should live to see my wife run away. Oh, I will do any thing — keep two packs of hounds — buy up every horse and ass in England — myself included — oh! *Exit with Meddle.*

Lady G. Ha! ha! ha! Poor Dolly! I'm sorry I must continue to deceive him. If he would kindle up a little — So, that fellow overheard all — well, so much the better.

Enter Young Courtly.

Court. My dear madam, how fares the plot? does my Governor nibble?

Lady G. Nibble! he is caught, and in the basket. I have just left him with a hook in his gills, panting for very lack of element. But how goes on your encounter?

Court. Bravely. By a simple ruse, I have discovered that she loves me. I see but one chance against the best termination I could hope.

Lady G. What is that?

Court. My father has told me that I return to town again to-morrow afternoon.

Lady G. Well, I insist you stop and dine — keep out of the way.

Court. Oh, but what excuse shall I offer for disobedience? What can I say when he sees me before dinner?

Lady G. Say — say Grace.

Enter Grace, who gets behind the window curtains.

Court. Ha! ha!

Lady G. I have arranged to elope with Sir Harcourt myself to-morrow night.

Court. The deuce you have!

Lady G. Now, if you could persuade Grace to follow that example — his carriage will be waiting at the Park — be there a little before eleven, and it will just prevent our escape. Can you make her agree to that?

Court. Oh, without the slightest difficulty, if Mr. Augustus Hamilton supplicates.

Lady G. Success attend you. (*Going*)

Court. I will bend the haughty Grace.

(*Going*)

Lady G. Do. *Exeunt severally.*

Grace. Will you?

End of the Fourth Act.

ACT V.

A drawing-room in Oak Hall.

Enter Cool.

Cool. This is the most serious affair Sir Harcourt has ever been engaged in. I took the liberty of considering him a fool when he told me he was going to marry: but voluntarily to incur another man's incumbrance is very little short of madness. If he continues to conduct himself in this absurd manner, I shall be compelled to dismiss him.

Enter Sir Harcourt, equipped for travelling.

Sir H. Cool!

Cool. Sir Harcourt.

Sir H. Is my chariot in waiting?

Cool. For the last half hour at the park wicket. But, pardon the insinuation, sir; would it not be more advisable to hesitate a little for a short reflection before you undertake the heavy responsibility of a woman?

Sir H. No: hesitation destroys the romance of a *faux pas*, and reduces it to the level of a mere mercantile calculation.

Cool. What is to be done with Mr. Charles?

Sir H. Ay, much against my will, Lady Gay prevailed on me to permit him to remain. You, Cool, must return him to college. Pass through London, and deliver these papers: here is a small notice of the coming elopement for the *Morning Post;* this, by an eye-witness, for the *Herald;* this, with all the particulars, for the *Chronicle;* and the full and circumstantial account for the evening journals — after which, meet us at Boulogne.

Cool. Very good, Sir Harcourt. (*Going*)

Sir H. Lose, no time. Remember — Hotel Anglais, Boulogne-sur-Mer. And, Cool, bring a few copies with you, and don't forget to distribute some amongst very particular friends.

Cool. It shall be done.   *Exit Cool.*

Sir H. With what indifference does a man of the world view the approach of the most perilous catastrophe! My position, hazardous as it is, entails none of that nervous excitement which a neophyte in the school of fashion would feel. I am as cool and steady as possible. Habit, habit! Oh! how many roses will fade upon the cheek of beauty, when the defalcation of Sir Harcourt Courtly is whispered — then hinted — at last, confirmed and bruited. I think I see them. Then, on my return, they will not dare to eject me — I am their sovereign! Whoever attempts to think of treason, I'll banish him from the West End — I'll cut him — I'll put him out of fashion!

Enter Lady Gay.

Lady G. Sir Harcourt!

Sir H. At your feet.

Lady G. I had hoped you would have repented.

Sir H. Repented!

Lady G. Have you not come to say it was a jest? — say you have!

Sir H. Love is too sacred a subject to be trifled with. Come, let us fly! See, I have procured disguises —

Lady G. My courage begins to fail me. Let me return.

Sir H. Impossible!

Lady G. Where do you intend to take me?

Sir H. You shall be my guide. The carriage waits.

Lady G. You will never desert me?

Sir H. Desert! Oh, heavens! Nay, do not hesitate — flight, now, alone is left to your desperate situation! Come, every moment is laden with danger. (*They are going*)

Lady G. Oh! gracious!

Sir H. Hush! what is it?

Lady G. I have forgotten — I must return.

Sir H. Impossible!

Lady G. I must! I must! I have left Max — a pet staghound, in his basket — without whom life would be unendurable — I could not exist!

Sir H. No, no. Let him be sent after us in a hamper.

Lady G. In a hamper! Remorseless man! Go — you love me not. How would you like to be sent after me — in a hamper? Let me fetch him. Hark! I hear him squeal! Oh! Max — Max!

Sir H. Hush! for heaven's sake. They'll imagine you're calling the Squire. I hear footsteps; where can I retire?

*Enter Meddle, Spanker, Dazzle, and Max.
Lady Gay screams.*

Meddle. Spanker *versus* Courtly! — I subpoena every one of you as witnesses! — I have 'em ready — here they are — shilling a-piece. (*Giving them round*)

Lady G. Where is Sir Harcourt?

Meddle. There! — bear witness! — call on the vile delinquent for protection!

Spanker. Oh! his protection!

Lady G. What? ha!

Meddle. I'll swear I overheard the whole elopement planned — before any jury! — where's the book?

Spanker. Do you hear, you profligate?

Lady G. Ha! ha! ha! ha!

Dazzle. But where is this wretched Lothario?

Meddle. Ay, where is the defendant?

Spanker. Where lies the hoary villain?

Lady G. What villain?

Spanker. That will not serve you! — I'll not be blinded that way!

Meddle. We won't be blinded any way!

Max. I must seek Sir Harcourt, and demand an explanation! Such a thing never occurred in Oak Hall before! — It must be cleared up!   *Exit.*

Meddle. (*Aside to Spanker*) Now, take my advice; remember your gender. Mind the notes I have given you.

Spanker. (Aside) All right! Here they are! Now, madam, I have procured the highest legal opinion on this point.

Meddle. Hear! hear!

Spanker. And the question resolves itself into a — into — What's this? (*Looks at notes*)

Meddle. A nutshell!

Spanker. Yes, we are in a nutshell. Will you, in every respect, subscribe to my requests — desires — commands — (*Looks at notes*) — orders — imperative — indicative — injunctive — or otherwise?

Lady G. (Aside) 'Pon my life, he's actually going to assume the ribbons, and take the box-seat. I must put a stop to this. I will! It will all end in smoke. I know Sir Harcourt would rather run than fight!

Dazzle. Oh! I smell powder! — command my services. My dear madam, can I be of any use?

Spanker. Oh! a challenge! — I must consult my legal adviser.

Meddle. No! impossible!

Dazzle. Pooh! the easiest thing in life! Leave it to me: What has an attorney to do with affairs of honour? — they are out of his element.

Meddle. Compromise the question! Pull his nose! — we have no objection to that.

Dazzle. (Turning to Lady Gay) Well, we have no objection either — have we?

Lady G. No! — pull his nose — that will be something.

Meddle. And, moreover, it is not exactly actionable!

Dazzle. Isn't it! — thank you — I'll note down that piece of information — it may be useful.

Meddle. How! cheated out of my legal knowledge.

Lady G. Mr. Spanker, I am determined! — I insist upon a challenge being sent to Sir Harcourt Courtly! — and — mark me — if you refuse to fight him — I will.

Meddle. Don't. Take my advice — you'll incapacit —

Lady G. Look you, Mr. Meddle, unless you wish me to horsewhip you, hold your tongue.

Meddle. What a she-tiger — I shall retire and collect my costs.   *Exit.*

Lady G. Mr. Spanker, oblige me by writing as I dictate.

Spanker. He's gone — and now I am defenceless! Is this the fate of husbands? — A duel! — Is this the result of becoming master of my own family?

Lady G. "Sir, the situation in which you

were discovered with my wife, admits neither of explanation nor apology."

Spanker. Oh, yes! but it does — I don't believe you really intended to run quite away.

Lady G. You do not; but I know better, I say I did! and if it had not been for your unfortunate interruption, I do not know where I might have been by this time. Go on.

Spanker. "Nor apology." I'm writing my own death-warrant, — committing suicide on compulsion.

Lady G. "The bearer will arrange all preliminary matters, for another day must see this sacrilege expiated by your life, or that of
Yours very sincerely,
DOLLY SPANKER."

Now, Mr. Dazzle. (*Gives it over his head*)

Dazzle. The document is as sacred as if it were a hundred-pound bill.

Lady G. We trust to your discretion.

Spanker. His discretion! Oh, put your head in a tiger's mouth, and trust to his discretion!

Dazzle. (Sealing letter, etc., with Spanker's seal) My dear Lady Gay, matters of this kind are indigenous to my nature, independently of their pervading fascination to all humanity; but this is more especially delightful, as you may perceive I shall be the intimate and bosom friend of both parties.

Lady G. Is it not the only alternative in such a case?

Dazzle. It is a beautiful panacea in any, in every case. (*Going — returns*) By the way where would you like this party of pleasure to come off? Open air shooting is pleasant enough, but if I might venture to advise, we could order half a dozen of that Madeira and a box of cigars into the billiard-room, so make a night of it; take up the irons every now and then; string for first shot, and blaze away at one another in an amicable and gentleman-like way; so conclude the matter before the potency of the liquor could disturb the individuality of the object, or the smoke of the cigars render the outline dubious. Does such an arrangement coincide with your views?

Lady G. Perfectly.

Dazzle. I trust shortly to be the harbinger of happy tidings.   *Exit.*

Spanker. (Coming forward) Lady Gay Spanker, are you ambitious of becoming a widow?

Lady G. Why, Dolly, woman is at best but weak, and weeds become me.

Spanker. Female! am I to be immolated on the altar of your vanity?

Lady G. If you become pathetic, I shall laugh.

Spanker. Farewell — base, heartless, unfeeling woman! *Exit.*

Lady G. Ha! well, so I am. I am heartless, for he is a dear, good little fellow, and I ought not to play upon his feelings: but 'pon my life he sounds so well up at concert pitch, that I feel disinclined to untune him. Poor Dolly, I didn't think he cared so much about me. I will put him out of pain.

Exit. Sir Harcourt comes down.

Sir H. I have been a fool! a dupe to my own vanity. I shall be pointed at as a ridiculous old coxcomb — and so I am. The hour of conviction is *arrived.* Have I deceived myself? — Have I turned all my senses inward — looking towards self — always self? — and has the world been ever laughing at me? Well, if they have, I will revert the joke; — they may say I am an old ass; but I will prove that I am neither too old to repent my folly, nor such an ass as to flinch from confessing it. A blow half met is but half felt.

Enter Dazzle.

Dazzle. Sir Harcourt, may I be permitted the honour of a few minutes' conversation with you?

Sir H. With pleasure.

Dazzle. Have the kindness to throw your eye over that. (*Gives the letter*)

Sir H. (*Reads*) "Situation — my wife — apology — expiate — my life." Why, this is intended for a challenge.

Dazzle. Why, indeed, I am perfectly aware that it is not quite *en règle* in the couching, for with that I had nothing to do; but I trust that the irregularity of the composition will be confounded in the beauty of the subject.

Sir H. Mr. Dazzle, are you in earnest?

Dazzle. Sir Harcourt Courtly, upon my honour I am, and I hope that no previous engagement will interfere with an immediate reply *in propriâ personâ.* We have fixed upon the billiard-room as the scene of action, which I have just seen properly illuminated in honour of the occasion; and, by-the-bye, if your implements are not handy, I can oblige you with a pair of the sweetest things you ever handled — hair-triggered — saw grip; heir-looms in my family. I regard them almost in the light of relations.

Sir H. Sir, I shall avail myself of one of your relatives. (*Aside*) One of the hereditaments of my folly — I must accept it. (*Aloud*) Sir, I shall be happy to meet Mr. Spanker at any time or place he may appoint.

Dazzle. The sooner the better, sir. Allow me to offer you my arm. I see you understand these matters; — my friend Spanker is wofully ignorant — miserably uneducated.

Exeunt.

Re-enter Max, with Grace.

Max. Give ye joy, girl, give ye joy. Sir Harcourt Courtly must consent to waive all title to your hand in favour of his son Charles.

Grace. Oh, indeed! Is that the pith of your congratulation — humph! the exchange of an old fool for a young one? Pardon me if I am not able to distinguish the advantage.

Max. Advantage!

Grace. Moreover, by what right am I a transferable cipher in the family of Courtly? So, then, my fate is reduced to this, to sacrifice my fortune, or unite myself with a worm-eaten edition of the Classics!

Max. Why, he certainly is not such a fellow as I could have chosen for my little Grace; but consider, to retain fifteen thousand a-year! Now, tell me honestly — but why should I say *honestly?* Speak, girl, would you rather not have the lad?

Grace. Why do you ask me?

Max. Why, look ye, I'm an old fellow; another hunting season or two, and I shall be in at my own death — I can't leave you this house and land, because they are entailed, nor can I say I'm sorry for it, for it is a good law; but I have a little box with my Grace's name upon it, where, since your father's death and miserly will, I have yearly placed a certain sum to be yours, should you refuse to fulfil the conditions prescribed.

Grace. My own dear uncle! (*Clasping him round the neck*)

Max. Pooh! pooh! what's to do now? Why, it was only a trifle — why, you little rogue, what are you crying about?

Grace. Nothing, but —

Max. But what? Come, out with it: Will you have young Courtly?

Re-enter Lady Gay.

Lady G. Oh! Max, Max!

Max. Why, what's amiss with you?

Lady G. I'm a wicked woman!

Max. What have you done?

Lady G. Everything — oh, I thought Sir Harcourt was a coward, but now I find a man may be a coxcomb without being a poltroon. Just to show my husband how inconvenient it is to hold the ribands sometimes, I made him send a challenge to the old fellow, and he, to my surprise, accepted it, and is going to blow my Dolly's brains out in the billiard-room.

Max. The devil!

Lady G. Just when I imagined I had got my whip hand of him again, out comes my linch-pin — and over I go — oh!

Max. I will soon put a stop to that — a duel under my roof! Murder in Oak Hall! I'll shoot them both! *Exit.*

Grace. Are you really in earnest?

Lady G. Do you think it looks like a joke? Oh! Dolly, if you allow yourself to be shot, I will never forgive you — never! Ah, he is a great fool, Grace! but I can't tell why, but I would sooner lose my bridle hand than he should be hurt on my account.

Enter Sir Harcourt Courtly.

Tell me — tell me — have you shot him — is he dead — my dear Sir Harcourt? You horrid old brute — have you killed him? I shall never forgive myself. *Exit.*

Grace. Oh! Sir Harcourt, what has happened?

Sir H. Don't be alarmed, I beg — your uncle interrupted us — discharged the weapons — locked the challenger up in the billiard-room to cool his rage.

Grace. Thank heaven!

Sir H. Miss Grace, to apologise for my conduct were useless, more especially as I am confident that no feelings of indignation or sorrow for my late acts are cherished by you; but still, reparation is in my power, and I not only waive all title, right, or claim to your person or your fortune, but freely admit your power to bestow them on a more worthy object.

Grace. This generosity, Sir Harcourt, is most unexpected.

Sir H. No, not generosity, but simply justice, justice!

Grace. May I still beg a favour?

Sir H. Claim anything that is mine to grant.

Grace. You have been duped by Lady Gay Spanker, I have also been cheated and played upon by her and Mr. Hamilton — may I beg that the contract between us may, to all appearances, be still held good?

Sir H. Certainly, although I confess I cannot see the point of your purpose.

Enter Max, with Young Courtly.

Max. Now, Grace, I have brought the lad.

Grace. Thank you, uncle, but the trouble was quite unnecessary — Sir Harcourt holds to his original contract.

Max. The deuce he does!

Grace. And I am willing — nay, eager, to become Lady Courtly.

Court. (*Aside*) The deuce you are!

Max. But, Sir Harcourt —

Sir H. One word, Max, for an instant.

They retire.

Court. (*Aside*) What can this mean? Can it be possible that I have been mistaken — that she is not in love with Augustus Hamilton?

Grace. Now we shall find how he intends to bend the haughty Grace.

Court. Madam — Miss, I mean, — are you really in love with my father?

Grace. No, indeed I am not.

Court. Are you in love with any one else?

Grace. No, or I should not marry him.

Court. Then you actually accept him as your real husband?

Grace. In the common acceptation of the word.

Court. (*Aside*) Hang me if I have not been a pretty fool! (*Aloud*) Why do you marry him, if you don't care about him?

Grace. To save my fortune.

Court. (*Aside*) Mercenary, cold-hearted girl! (*Aloud*) But if there be any one you love in the least — marry him; — were you never in love?

Grace. Never!

Court. (*Aside*) Oh! what an ass I've been! (*Aloud*) I heard Lady Gay mention something about a Mr. Hamilton.

Grace. Ah, yes, a person who, after an acquaintanceship of two days, had the assurance to make love to me, and I —

Court. Yes, — you — Well?

Grace. I pretended to receive his attentions.

Court. (*Aside*) It was the best pretence I ever saw.

Grace. An absurd, vain, conceited coxcomb, who appeared to imagine that I was so struck with his fulsome speech, that he could turn me round his finger.

Court. (*Aside*) My very thoughts!

Grace. But he was mistaken.

Court. (*Aside*) Confoundedly! (*Aloud*) Yet you seemed rather concerned about the news of his death?

Grace. His accident! No, but —

Court. But what?

Grace. (*Aside*) What can I say? (*Aloud*) Ah! but my maid Pert's brother is a post-boy, and I thought he might have sustained an injury, poor boy.

Court. (*Aside*) Damn the post-boy! (*Aloud*) Madam, if the retention of your fortune be the plea on which you are about to bestow your hand on one you do not love, and whose very actions speak his carelessness for that inestimable jewel he is incapable of appreciating — Know that I am devotedly, madly attached to you.

Grace. You, sir? Impossible!

Court. Not at all, — but inevitable, — I have been so for a long time.

Grace. Why, you never saw me till last night.

Court. I have seen you in imagination — you are the ideal I have worshipped.

Grace. Since you press me into a confession, — which nothing but this could bring me to speak, — know, I did love poor Augustus Hamilton —

Re-enter Max and Sir Harcourt.

but he — he is — no — more! Pray, spare me, sir.

Court. (*Aside*) She loves me! And, oh! what a situation I am in! — if I own I am the man, my Governor will overhear, and ruin me — if I do not, she'll marry him. — What is to be done?

Enter Lady Gay.

Lady G. Where have you put my Dolly? I have been racing all round the house — tell me, is he quite dead!

Max. I'll have him brought in.   *Exit.*

Sir H. My dear madam, you must perceive this unfortunate occurrence was no fault of mine. I was compelled to act as I have done — I was willing to offer any apology, but that resource was excluded, as unacceptable.

Lady G. I know — I know — 'twas I made with him that letter — there was no apology required — 'twas I that apparently seduced you from the paths of propriety, — 'twas all a joke, and here is the end of it.

Enter Max, Mr. Spanker, and Dazzle.

Oh! if he had but lived to say, "I forgive you, Gay!"

Spanker. So I do!

Lady G. (*Seeing him*) Ah! he is alive!

Spanker. Of course I am!

Lady G. Ha! ha! ha! (*Embraces him*) I will never hunt again — unless you wish it. Sell your stable —

Spanker. No, no — do what you like — say what you like for the future! I find the head of a family has less ease and more responsibility than I, as a member, could have anticipated. I abdicate!

Enter Cool.

Sir H. Ah! Cool, here! (*Aside to Cool*) You may destroy those papers — I have altered my mind, — and I do not intend to elope at present. Where are they?

Cool. As you seemed particular, Sir Harcourt, I sent them off by mail to London.

Sir H. Why, then, a full description of the whole affair will be published to-morrow.

Cool. Most irretrievably!

Sir H. You must post to town immediately, and stop the press.

Cool. Beg pardon — they would see me hanged first, Sir Harcourt; they don't frequently meet with such a profitable lie.

Servant. (*Without*) No, sir! no, sir!

Enter Simpson.

Simpson. Sir, there is a gentleman, who calls himself Mr. Solomon Isaacs, insists upon following me up.

Enter Mr. Solomon Isaacs.

Isaacs. Mr. Courtly, you will excuse my performance of a most disagreeable duty at any time, but more especially in such a manner. I must beg the honour of your company to town.

Sir H. What! — how! — what for?

Isaacs. For debt, Sir Harcourt.

Sir H. Arrested? — impossible! Here must be some mistake.

Isaacs. Not the slightest, sir. Judgment has been given in five cases, for the last three months; but Mr. Courtly is an eel rather too nimble for my men. — We have been on his track, and traced him down to this village, with Mr. Dazzle.

Dazzle. Ah! Isaacs! how are you?

Isaacs. Thank you, sir. (*Speaks to Sir Harcourt*)

Max. Do you know him?

Dazzle. Oh, intimately! Distantly related to his family — same arms on our escutcheon — empty purse falling through a hole in a — pocket: motto, "Requiescat in pace" — which means, "Let virtue be its own reward."

Sir H. (*To Isaacs*) Oh, I thought there was a mistake! Know, to your misfortune, that Mr. Hamilton was the person you dogged to Oak Hall, between whom and my son a most remarkable likeness exists.

Isaacs. Ha! ha! Know, to your misfortune, Sir Harcourt, that Mr. Hamilton and Mr. Courtly are one and the same person!

Sir H. Charles!

Court. Concealment is in vain — I am Augustus Hamilton.

Sir H. Hang me, if I didn't think it all along! Oh, you infernal, cozening dog!

Isaacs. Now, then, Mr. Hamilton —

Grace. Stay, sir — Mr. Charles Courtly is under age — ask his father.

Sir H. Ahem! — I won't — I won't pay a shilling of the rascal's debts — not a sixpence!

Grace. Then, I will — you may retire.
Exit Isaacs.

Court. I can now perceive the generous point of your conduct towards me; and, believe me, I appreciate, and will endeavour to deserve it.

Max. Ha! ha! Come, Sir Harcourt, you have been fairly beaten — you must forgive him — say you will.

Sir H. So, sir, it appears you have been leading, covertly, an infernal town life?

Court. Yes, please, father. (*Imitating Master Charles*)

Sir H. None of your humbug sir! (*Aside*) He is my own son — how could I expect him to keep out of the fire? (*Aloud*) And you, Mr. Cool! — have you been deceiving me?

Cool. Oh! Sir Harcourt, if your perception was played upon, how could I be expected to see?

Sir H. Well, it would be useless to withhold my hand. There, boy! (*He gives his hand to Young Courtly. Grace comes down on the other side, and offers her hand; he takes it*) What is all this? What do you want?

Court. Your blessing, father.

Grace. If you please, father.

Sir H. Oho! the mystery is being solved. So, so, you young scoundrel, you have been making love — under the rose.

Lady G. He learnt that from you, Sir Harcourt.

Sir H. Ahem! What would you do now, if I were to withhold my consent?

Grace. Do without it.

Max. The will says, if Grace marries any one but you, — her property reverts to your heir-apparent — and there he stands.

Lady G. Make virtue of necessity.

Spanker. I married from inclination; and see how happy I am. And if ever I have a son —

Lady G. Hush! Dolly, dear!

Sir H. Well! take her, boy! Although you are too young to marry. *They retire with Max.*

Lady G. Am I forgiven, Sir Harcourt?

Sir H. Ahem! Why — a — (*Aside*) Have you really deceived me?

Lady G. Can you not see through this?

Sir H. And you still love me?

Lady G. As much as I ever did.

Sir H. (*Is about to kiss her hand, when Spanker interposes between*) A very handsome ring, indeed.

Spanker. Very. (*Puts her arm in his, and they go up*)

Sir H. Poor little Spanker!

Max. (*Coming down, aside to Sir Harcourt*) One point I wish to have settled. Who is Mr. Dazzle?

Sir H. A relative of the Spankers, he told me.

Max. Oh, no, a near connexion of yours.

Sir H. Never saw him before I came down here, in all my life. (*To Young Courtly*) Charles, who is Mr. Dazzle?

Court. Dazzle, Dazzle, — will you excuse an impertinent question? — but who the deuce are you?

Dazzle. Certainly. I have not the remotest idea.

All. How, sir?

Dazzle. Simple question as you may think it, it would puzzle half the world to answer. One thing I can vouch — Nature made me a gentleman — that is, I live on the best that can be procured for credit. I never spend my own money when I can oblige a friend. I'm always thick on the winning horse. I'm an epidemic on the trade of a tailor. For further particulars, inquire of any sitting magistrate.

Sir H. And these are the deeds which attest your title to the name of gentleman? I perceive that you have caught the infection of the present age. Charles, permit me, as your father, and you, sir, as his friend, to correct you on one point. Barefaced assurance is the vulgar substitute for gentlemanly ease; and there are many who, by aping the *vices* of the great, imagine that they elevate themselves to the rank of those, whose faults alone they copy. No, sir! The title of gentleman is the only one *out* of any monarch's gift, yet within the reach of every peasant. It should be engrossed by *Truth* — stamped with *Honour* — sealed with *good-feeling* — signed *Man* — and enrolled in every true young English heart.

THE END.

TOM TAYLOR
1817-1880

Our American Cousin
(1858)

As the audiences of the nineteenth century preferred melodrama to tragedy, they preferred farce to comedy of manners. Tom Taylor (christened Tom, not Thomas) wrote plays of many types, but perhaps his most popular farce will serve to illustrate this type, some of his qualities as a playwright, and the influence of the nineteenth-century audience upon the drama.

Taylor was born near Sunderland in the north of England on October 19, 1817. As a boy he liked the theatre, writing plays at home that he and his brothers and sisters staged in a stable loft, and presenting marionette shows at school in which he played the role of master of revels. Taylor was also an excellent student. Besides winning scholastic honors at the Sunderland Grange School, he was awarded three gold medals and other prizes during two terms at the University of Glasgow. Taylor spent three years at Trinity College, Cambridge, and was awarded his B.A. in 1840, with honors in all fields of study. He became a Fellow and tutor for undergraduates at Cambridge in 1842, and earned a Master of Arts degree in 1843. Still fascinated by the theatre, he attended any play performed at Cambridge and when he could afford it went to London to see Macready act Shakespeare. Taylor was one of the founders of the Cambridge Old Stagers, an amateur group that sponsored dramatic festivals.

The need to earn his living and the impulse to take an active part in civic life caused Taylor to treat playwriting as an avocation. He moved to London in 1844 to study law. At the same time he began to write for newspapers and magazines; in 1848 he joined the staff of the *Times* as critic of drama, literature, and art, and kept this post the rest of his life. He was chosen Professor of English Language and Literature at University College (now the University of London), a post he held for two years. He also began to practise law. He had published a series of articles on bad conditions of sanitation in London, and when a Board of Health was created, he gave up his law practice to become an assistant secretary for this Board. He continued this work during most of his life.

In spite of all this activity, Taylor did not lose interest in the theatre, but was constantly writing plays. His first play to be professionally produced was the farcical *A Trip to Kissingen* in 1848. His first big success was the production in 1852 of the sentimental comedy-drama *Masks and Faces*, written in collaboration with the novelist Charles Reade. Fame as a playwright inspired him to more earnest efforts, including *Slave Life; or, Uncle Tom's Cabin* (1852, in collaboration with Mark Lemon) and other melodramas with some seriousness of social purpose. He also wrote history plays, including *Plot and Passion* (1853) which treated episodes at the court of Napoleon.

Taylor was happily married in 1855, and he and his wife set up a home noted for its genial hospitality and distinguished literary guests like Alfred Tennyson. But he continued to write plays as the leading dramatist for the Haymarket and the Olympic. Popular successes of this period were *Our American Cousin* (1858) and his important melodrama *The Ticket-of-Leave Man* (1863). Taylor's dramatic development was a steady progression from early farces to serious melodramas and history plays, with increasing elements of realism, more skilful characterization, and suggestions of social purpose. He stood on the threshold of the new drama. But instead of continuing to advance in these directions, he turned back toward the defunct verse drama with *'Twixt Axe and Crown; or, The Lady Elizabeth* (1870), which relates in verse the events in the life of Princess Elizabeth when "Bloody Mary" was Queen of England. His *Joan of Arc* (1871) and *Anne Boleyn* (1877) were also in verse.

Taylor was seriously interested in language (he was chosen to teach English philology at University College), and this interest is evident in his plays. He was careful not only of dialogue, but of dialect — Cockneys, Americans, and characters from various parts of England speak in typical forms of speech. In fact, a sizable dictionary of slang, thieves' argot, and Americanisms could be compiled from Taylor's plays. This interest in language is especially evident in *The Ticket-of-Leave Man* and *Our American Cousin*.

The Ticket-of-Leave Man is based upon the French play *Léonard* by Édouard Brisebarre and Eugène Nus, but Taylor thoroughly and realistically assimilated into it London scenes and varied English types of characters. It is the detective play that created the best-known fictional detective before Sherlock Holmes — Hawkshaw, a man of gumshoes and disguises rather than deductive genius like Holmes. The play opens with an unprecedentedly realistic crowd scene in an open-air restaurant. It sets in conflict a naïve young man, whose realistic dialect betrays his Lancashire origin, and a pair of clever "con men," who speak in thieves' argot and deceive the young man into passing counterfeit bills. The story tells of the hero's arrest, his term in prison, and his efforts to lead an upright life although he is continually thwarted by the thieves until they are captured by Hawkshaw. Taylor included in the play a street singer, a song-and-dance man and his wife (a burlesque queen) down on their luck, a fascinatingly garrulous keeper of lodgings, and her grandson — a good-hearted, would-be tough. Perhaps Taylor's interest in linguistic curiosities made him overdo the display of humorous slang, but the dialogue flows with extraordinary naturalness. Treating the difficulties that face an ex-convict who wishes to live honestly, *The Ticket-of-Leave Man* approaches the problem play, but melodramatic excitement and a happy ending obscure this serious theme.

In these ways Taylor advanced to the threshold of the new drama in the decade when Tom Robertson stepped across it. He was equipped to go forward — in education, knowledge of the theatre, curiosity about people of all classes, and consciousness of evils in his society. Although he used the stereotyped characters of melodrama, he individualized them. It is evident that he was ambitious to give the drama literary depth, and at the peak of his powers he sought to move toward that goal — but he moved in the wrong direction, to the verse drama. Farce though it is, *Our American Cousin* illustrates some of these elements of strength — for example, the exaggerated but informed use of cockneyisms and Americanisms.

Winton Tolles has suggested that Taylor got the idea for *Our American Cousin* by observing and listening to the American tourists who visited London for the Crystal Palace Exhibition of 1851. Englishmen generally found Americanisms like "guess" and "calculate" for "suppose," and the American taste for peanuts and pumpkin pie, quaint, amusing, and somehow backwoodsy. Since he was interested in linguistics, no doubt Taylor made notes. It would seem that he intended some comedy, for although he wrote the play as a melodrama, he slightly exaggerated and burlesqued the language and manners that caricature both the English characters and the American Asa. Perhaps some wordplay and puns appeared in the original — though the wilder, more farcical jokes and riddles were added later. It is worth noting that where the action is straight and no humor is intended, the dialogue is natural.

The title and the action indicate that Taylor intended Asa to be both the hero and, to an English audience, a quaintly comic character. Asa is a type — the "Nathan Yank" who had developed in American drama and had appeared on English stages (as in Mrs. Anna Cora Mowatt's *Fashion*, where the genuine, blunt farmer Trueman exposes the pretences of high society). The only scenes in *Our American Cousin* that promised much excitement were the crisis when Asa, all for love of a sound-hearted dairymaid, lights his cigar with a paper worth a fortune, and the scene where the villain Coyle is made drunk in the wine cellar. A producer, Webster, purchased the play, but decided not to perform it.

This apparently dull melodrama, comic only in its caricatures of British and American speech, was developed by the comedian Edward Askew Sothern into the most hilarious farce of the mid-century theatre. Webster entrusted the play to an American actor temporarily in England for marketing in this country. After some time and neglect, it came into the hands of Miss Laura Keene of New York, whose theatrical company included Joseph Jefferson, a "Yankee character" actor. Miss Keene did not value the play highly, but she decided to produce it while she was waiting for scene painters to prepare the sets for *Midsummer Night's Dream*. When she cast the play she assigned the part of Dundreary to Sothern. The part was minor, with only forty-odd lines. Sothern rebelled, and was persuaded to play the role only when Miss Keene told him he might "gag" it as he pleased. Sothern then set about making Dundreary the center of attention. He dressed the character in a claret-colored frock coat that came to his heels, peg top plaid trousers, and a flowing tie. He wore a monocle and whiskers with a melancholy droop. He invented a lisp and stutter. Stamping about the stage to keep warm on a chill day, Sothern broke into a jig taken from the blackface minstrel shows then popular. Perhaps sarcastically, Miss Keene asked whether he intended to include that shuffle in his act. He did, and it became the famous Dundreary hop. The sum of these mannerisms, acted to exhibit well-bred, obtuse eccentricity, so caricatured the popular image of an English lordling that audiences went wild. Sothern, listening to their laughter, adapted his antics to it by adding fatuous lines, puns, twisted proverbs ("Dundrearyisms"), and riddles. Thus he made a minor role in a slightly comic melodrama into the life of a roaring farce. Sothern played Lord Dundreary in more than eight hundred performances all over America. Then the play ran for four hundred nights at the Haymarket in 1861. Dundreary's eccentricities set the London fashion for Dundreary whiskers, dressing gowns, shoes, hats, and monocles. *Our American Cousin*, constantly revived, was the play being performed at Ford's Theatre in Washington when Abraham Lincoln was shot — presumably during one of Asa's soliloquies in the second scene of the third act.

The text of the play presented here is slightly edited from an acting text that includes Sothern's additions.

OUR AMERICAN COUSIN

A Drama In Three Acts

by

TOM TAYLOR

First performed at Laura Keene's Theatre, New York, October 15, 1858.

Cast of Characters

LORD DUNDREARY	JOHN WICKENS
ASA TRENCHARD	MRS. MOUNTCHESSINGTON
SIR EDWARD TRENCHARD	FLORENCE TRENCHARD
CAPT. DE BOOTS	MARY
HARRY VERNON	AUGUSTA
ABEL MURCOTT	GEORGINA
MR. COYLE	SHARPE
MR. BUDDICOMBE	SKILLET
MR. BINNY	

ACT I.

Scene 1.

Drawing room in Trenchard Manor, discovering table with luncheon spread. Large French window, through which a fine English park is seen. Open archway. Set balcony behind. Table, books and papers on it. Work basket containing wools and embroidery frame. A fashionable arm chair, sofa, and small table. Stage handsomely set, costly furniture, carpet down, chairs, etc. Buddicombe discovered on sofa reading newspaper. Skillet and Sharpe busily arranging furniture as curtain rises.

Sharpe. I don't know how you may feel as a visitor, Mr. Buddicombe, but I think this is a most uncomfortable family.

Bud. Very uncomfortable, I have no curtain to my bed.

Skil. And no wine at the second table.

Sharpe. And meaner servants I never seed.

Bud. I'm afraid Sir Edward is in a queer strait.

Skil. Yes, for only this morning, Mr. Binny, Mrs. Skillet says he —

Enter Binny.

Binny. Mind your hown business instead hof your betters. I'm disgusted with you lower servants. When the wine merchant presents his bills, you men, hear me, say he's been pressing for the last six months, do you?

Skil. Not I, that the last year's milliner's bills have not been paid.

Sharpe. Nor I, that Miss Florence has not had no new dresses from London all winter.

Bud. And I can solemnly swear that his lordship's hair has been faithfully bound in this bosom.

Binny. That'll do, that'll do; but to remember to check hidle curiosity is the first duty of men hin livery. Ha, 'ere hare the letters.

Enter John Wickens, with green baize bag. Binny takes bag, takes out letters and reads addresses.

Binny. Hah! bill, of course, Miss Augusta, Mrs. Mountchessington, Lord Dundreary, Capt. De Boots, Miss Georgina Mountchessington, Lieut. Vernon, ah! that's from the admiralty. What's this? Miss Florence Trenchard, via. Brattleboro', Vermont.

Bud. Where's that, Mr. Binny?

John. Why that be hin the United States of North Hamerica, and a main good place for poor folks.

Binny. John Wickens, you forget yourself.

John. Beg pardon, Mr. Binny.

Binny. John Wickens, leave the room.

John. But I know where Vermont be tho'.

Binny. John Wickens, get hout.

Exit John.

Bud. Dreadful low fellow, that.

Binny. Halways himpudent.

Bud. (*Looking at letter in Binny's hand*) Why, that is Sir Edward's hand, Mr. Binny, he must have been sporting.

Binny. Yes, shooting the wild helephants and buffalos what abound there.

Bud. The nasty beasts. (*Looking off*) Hello, there comes Miss Florence tearing across the lane like a three year old colt.

Sharp and Skil. Oh, Gemini.

Run off. Buddicombe runs off.

Enter Florence.

Flo. (*As if after running*) Oh! I'm fairly out of breath. Good morning, Binny, the letter bag I saw coming, Wickens coming with it. I thought I could catch him before I reached the house. (*Sits*) So off I started, I forgot the pond, it was in or over. I got over, but my hat got in. I wish you'd fish it out for me, you won't find the pond very deep.

Binny. Me fish for an 'at? Does she take me for an hangler?

Flo. Give me the letters. (*Takes them*) Ah, blessed budget that descends upon Trenchard Manor, like rain on a duck pond. Tell papa and all, that the letters have come, you will find them on the terrace.

Binny. Yes, Miss. (*Going*)

Flo. And then go fish out my hat out of the pond, it's not very deep.

Binny. (*Aside*) Me fish for 'ats? I wonder if she takes me for an hangler.

Exit disgusted.

Flo. (*Reading directions*) Lieut. Vernon. (*This is a large letter with a large white envelope, red seal*) In Her Majesty's service. Admiralty. R. N. Ah, that's an answer to Harry's application for a ship. Papa promised to use his influence for him. I hope he has succeeded, but then he will have to leave us, and who knows if he ever comes back. What a foolish girl I am, when I know that his rise in the service will depend upon it. I do hope he'll get it, and, if he must leave us, I'll bid him good bye as a lass who loves a sailor should.

Enter Sir Edward, Mrs. Mountchessington, Augusta, Capt. De Boots, Vernon.

Flo. Papa, dear, here are letters for you, one for you, Mrs. Mountchessington, one for you, Capt. De Boots, and one for you, Harry. (*Hiding letter behind her*)

Ver. Ah, one for me, Florence?

Flo. Now what will you give me for one?

Ver. Ah, then you have one?

Flo. Yes, there, Harry. (*Gives it*)

Ver. Ah, for a ship. (*Opens and reads*)

Flo. Ah! Mon ami, you are to leave us. Good news, or bad?

Ver. No ship yet, this promises another year of land lubbery. (*Goes up*)

Flo. I'm so sorry. (*Aside*) I'm so glad he's not going away. But where's Dundreary? Has anybody seen Dundreary?

Enter Dundreary.

Dun. Good morning, Miss Florence.

Flo. (*Comes down*) Good morning, my Lord Dundreary. Who do you think has been here? What does the postman bring?

Dun. Well, sometimes he brings a bag with a lock on it, sometimes newspapers, and sometimes letters, I suppothe.

Flo. There.

> *Gives letter. Dundreary opens letter, knocks knees against chair, turns round, knocks shins, and at last is seated.*

Dun. Thank you. (*Reads letter*)

De B. (*Reading paper*) By Jove, old Soloman has made a crop of it.

Dun. A — what of it?

De B. I beg pardon, an event I am deeply interested in, that's all. I beg pardon.

Aug. Ah! Florence, dear, there's a letter of yours got among mine. (*Gives it*)

Flo. Why papa, it's from dear brother Ned.

Sir E. From my boy! Where is he? How is he? Read it.

Flo. He writes from Brattleboro', Vt. (*Written letter*) "Quite well, just come in from a shooting excursion, with a party of Crows, splendid fellows, six feet high."

Dun. Birds six feet high, what tremendous animals they must be.

Flo. Oh, I see what my brother means; a tribe of Indians called Crows, not birds.

Dun. Oh, I thought you meant those creatures with wigs on them.

Flo. Wigs!

Dun. I mean those things that move, breathe and walk, they look like animals with those things. (*Moving his arms like wings*)

Flo. Wings.

Dun. Birds with wings, that's the idea.

Flo. (*Reading written letter*) "Bye-the-bye, I have lately come quite hap-hazard upon the other branch of our family, which emigrated to America at the Restoration. They are now thriving in this State, and discovering our relationship, they received me most hospitably. I have cleared up the mysterious death of old Mark Trenchard."

Sir E. Of my uncle!

Flo. (*Reading written letter*) "It appears that when he quarreled with his daughter on her marriage with poor Meredith, he came here in search of this stray shoot of the family tree, found them and died in their house, leaving Asa, one of the sons, heir to his personal property in England, which ought to belong to poor Mary Meredith. Asa is about to sail for the old country, to take possession. I gave him directions to find you out, and he should arrive almost as soon as this letter. Receive him kindly for the sake of the kindness he has shown to me, and let him see some of our shooting.

Your affectionate brother, Ned."

Sir E. An American branch of the family.

Mrs. M. Oh, how interesting!

Aug. (*Enthusiastically*) How delightfully romantic! I can imagine the wild young hunter. An Apollo of the prairie.

Flo. An Apollo of the prairie; yes, with a strong nasal twang, and a decided taste for tobacco and cobblers.

Sir E. Florence, you forget that he is a Trenchard, and no true Trenchard would have a liking for cobblers or low people of that kind.

Flo. I hate him, whatever he is, coming here to rob poor cousin Mary of her grandmother's guineas.

Sir E. Florence, how often must I request you not to speak of Mary Meredith as your cousin?

Flo. Why, she is my cousin, is she not? Besides she presides over her milk pail like a duchess playing dairymaid. Ah! Papa won't hear me speak of my poor cousin, and then I'm so fond of syllabubs. Dundreary, do you know what syllabubs are?

Dun. Oh, yeth, I know what syllabubs is — yeth — yeth.

Flo. Why, I don't believe you do know what they are.

Dun. Not know what syllabubs are? That's a good idea. Why, they are — syllabubs are — they are silly babies, idiotic children; that's a good idea, that's good. (*Bumps head against Florence*)

Flo. No, it's not a bit like the idea. What you mean are called cherubims.

Dun. What, those things that look like oranges, with wings on them?

Flo. Not a bit like it. Well, after luncheon you must go with me and I'll introduce you to my cousin Mary and syllabubs.

Dun. I never saw Mr. Syllabubs, I am sure.

Flo. Well, now, don't forget.

Dun. I never can forget — when I can recollect.

Flo. Then recollect that you have an appointment with me after luncheon.

Dun. Yeth, yeth.

Flo. Well, what have you after luncheon?

Dun. Well, sometimes I have a glass of brandy with an egg in it, sometimes a run 'round the duck-pond, sometimes a game of checkers — that's for exercise, and perhaps a game of billiards.

Flo. No, no; you have with me after luncheon, an ap — an ap —

Dun. An ap — an ap —

Flo. An ap — an appoint — appointment.

Dun. An ointment, that's the idea. (*Knocks against De Boots as they go up stage*)

Mrs. M. (*Aside*) That artful girl has designs upon Lord Dundreary. Augusta, dear, go and see how your poor, dear sister is this morning.

Aug. Yes, mamma. *Exit.*

Mrs. M. She is a great sufferer, my dear.

Dun. Yeth, but a lonely one.

Flo. What sort of a night had she?

Mrs. M. Oh, a very refreshing one, thanks to the draught you were kind enough to prescribe for her, Lord Dundreary.

Flo. What! has Lord Dundreary been prescribing for Georgina?

Dun. Yeth. You see I gave her a draught that cured the effect of the draught, and that draught was a draft that didn't pay the doctor's bill. Didn't that draught —

Flo. Good gracious! what a number of draughts. You have almost a game of draughts.

Dun. Ha! ha! ha!

Flo. What's the matter?

Dun. That wath a joke, that wath.

Flo. Where's the joke? (*Dundreary screams and turns to Mrs. Mountchessington*)

Mrs. M. No.

Dun. She don't see it. Don't you see — a game of drafts — pieces of wound wood on square pieces of leather. That's the idea. Now, I want to put your brains to the test. I want to ask you a whime?

Flo. A whime, what's that?

Dun. A whime is a widdle, you know.

Flo. A widdle!

Dun. Yeth; one of those things, like — why is so and so or somebody like somebody else?

Flo. Oh, I see, you mean a conundrum.

Dun. Yeth, a drum, that's the idea. What is it gives a cold in the head, cures a cold, pays the doctor's bill and makes the homeguard look for substitutes? (*Florence repeats it*) Yeth, do you give it up?

Flo. Yes.

Dun. Well, I'll tell you — a draught. Now, I've got a better one than that: When is a dog's tail not a dog's tail? (*Florence repeats*) Yeth, that's a stunner. You've got to give that up.

Flo. Yes, and willingly.

Dun. When it's a cart. (*They look at him enquiringly*)

Flo. Why, what on earth has a dog's tail to do with a cart?

Dun. When it moves about, you know. A horse makes a cart move, so does a dog make his tail move.

Flo. Ah, I see what you mean — when it's a wagon. (*Wags the letter in her hand*)

Dun. Well, a wagon and a cart are the same thing, ain't they! That's the idea — it's the same thing.

Flo. They are not the same. In the case of your conundrum there's a very great difference.

Dun. Now I've got another. Why does a dog waggle his tail!

Flo. Upon my word, I never inquired.

Dun. Because the tail can't waggle the dog. Ha! Ha!

Flo. Ha! ha! Is that your own, Dundreary?

Dun. Now I've got one, and this one is original.

Flo. No, no, don't spoil the last one.

Dun. Yeth; but this is extremely interesting.

Mrs. M. Do you think so, Lord Dundreary?

Dun. Yeth. Miss Georgina likes me to tell her my jokes. Bye-the-bye, talking of that lonely sufferer, isn't she an interesting invalid? They do say that's what's the matter with me. I'm an interesting invalid.

Flo. Oh, that accounts for what I have heard so many young ladies say — "Florence, dear, don't you think Lord Dundreary's extremely interesting?" I never knew what they meant before.

Dun. Yeth, the doctor recommends me to drink donkey's milk.

Flo. (*Hiding laugh*) Oh, what a clever man he must be. He knows we generally thrive best on our native food. (*Goes up*)

Dun. (*Looking first at Florence and then at Mrs. Mountchessington*) I'm so weak, and that is so strong. Yes, I'm naturally very weak, and I want strengthening. Yes, I guess I'll try it.

Enter Augusta. Signals to Dundreary, who finally exits and brings on Georgina.

Dun. Look at this lonely sufferer. (*Bringing on Georgina, seats her on sofa*) There, repothe yourself.

Geo. (*Fanning herself*) Thank you, my lord. Everybody is kind to me, and I am so delicate.

Aug. (*At table*) Capt. De Boots, do help to unravel these wools for me, you have such an eye for color.

Flo. An eye for color! Yes, especially green.

Dun. (*Screams*) Ha! ha! ha!

All. What's the matter?

Dun. Why, that wath a joke, that wath.

Flo. Where was the joke?

Dun. Especially, ha! ha!

Sir E. Florence, dear, I must leave you to represent me to my guests. These letters will give me a great deal of business to-day.

Flo. Well, papa, remember I am your little clerk and person of all work.

Sir E. No, no; this is private business — money matters, my love, which women know nothing about. (*Aside*) Luckily for them. I expect Mr. Coyle to-day.

Flo. Dear papa, how I wish you would get another agent.

Sir E. Nonsense, Florence, impossible. He knows my affairs. His father was agent for the late Baronet. He's one of the family almost.

Flo. Papa, I have implicit faith in my own judgment of faces. Depend upon it, that man is not to be trusted.

Sir E. Florence, you are ridiculous. I could not get on a week without him. (*Aside*) Curse him, I wish I could! Coyle is a most intelligent agent, and a most faithful servant of the family.

Enter Binny.

Binny. Mr. Coyle and hagent with papers.

Sir E. Show him into the library. I will be with him presently.   *Exit Binny.*

Flo. Remember the archery meeting, papa. It is at three.

Sir E. Yes, yes, I'll remember. (*Aside*) Pretty time for such levity when ruin stares me in the face. Florence, I leave you as my representative. (*Aside*) Now to prepare myself to meet my Shylock.   *Exit.*

Flo. Why will papa not trust me? (*Vernon comes down*) Oh, Harry! I wish he would find out what a lot of pluck and common sense there is in this feather head of mine.

Dun. Miss Florence, will you be kind enough to tell Miss Georgina all about that American relative of yours.

Flo. Oh, about my American cousin; certainly. (*Aside to Harry*) Let's have some fun. Well, he's about seventeen feet high.

Dun. Good gracious! Seventeen feet high!

Flo. They are all seventeen feet high in America, ain't they, Mr. Vernon?

Ver. Yes, that's about the average height.

Flo. And they have long black hair that reaches down to their heels; they have dark copper-colored skin, and they fight with — What do they fight with, Mr. Vernon?

Ver. Tomahawks and scalping knives.

Flo. Yes; and you'd better take care, Miss Georgina, or he'll take his tomahawk and scalping knife and scalp you immediately. (*Georgina screams and faints*)

Dun. Here, somebody get something and throw over her; a pail of water; no, not that, she's pale enough already. (*Fans her with handkerchief*) Georgina, don't be afraid. Dundreary's by your side, he will protect you.

Flo. Don't be frightened, Georgina. He will never harm you while Dundreary is about. Why, he could get three scalps here. (*Pulls Dundreary's whiskers. Georgina screams*)

Dun. Don't scream, I won't lose my whiskers. I know what I'll do for my own safety. I will take this handkerchief and tie the roof of my head on. (*Ties it on*)

Flo. (*Pretending to cry*) Good bye, Dundreary. I'll never see you again in all your glory.

Dun. Don't cry, Miss Florence, I'm ready for Mr. Tommy Hawk.

Enter Binny.

Binny. If you please, Miss, 'ere's a gent what says he's hexpected.

Flo. What's his name? Where's his card?

Binny. He didn't tell me his name, Miss, and when I haxed him for his card 'e said 'e had a whole pack in his valise and if I 'ad a mine 'e'd play me a game of seven hup. He says he has come to stay, and he certainly looks as if he didn't mean to go.

Flo. That's him. Show him in, Mr. Binny.   *Exit Binny.*
That's my American cousin, I know.

Aug. (*Romantically*) Your American cousin. Oh, how delightfully romantic, isn't it, Capt. De Boots? (*Comes down*) I can imagine the wild young hunter, with the free step and majestic mien of the hunter of the forest.

Asa. (*Outside*) Consarn your picture, didn't I tell you I was expected? You are as obstinate as Deacon Stumps' forelock, that wouldn't lie down and couldn't stand up. Wouldn't pint forward and couldn't go backward. (*Enter Asa, carrying a valise*) Where's the Squire?

Flo. Do you mean Sir Edward Trenchard, sir?

Asa. Yes.

Flo. He is not present, but I am his daughter.

Asa. Well, I guess that'll fit about as well if you tell this darned old shoat to take me to my room.

Flo. What does he mean by shoat?

Binny. (*Taking valise*) He means me, mum; but what he wants —

Asa. Hurry up, old hoss!

Binny. He calls me a 'oss, Miss, I suppose I shall be a hox next, or perhaps an 'ogg.

Asa. Wal, darn me, if you ain't the consarnedest old shoat I ever did see since I was baptised Asa Trenchard.

Flo. Ah! then it is our American cousin. Glad to see you — my brother told us to expect you.

Asa. Wal, yes, I guess you do b'long to my family. I'm Asa Trenchard, born in Vermont, suckled on the banks of Muddy Creek, about the tallest gunner, the slickest dancer, and generally the loudest critter in the state. You're my cousin, be you? Wal, I ain't got no objections to kiss you, as one cousin ought to kiss another.

Ver. Sir, how dare you?

Asa. Are you one of the family? Cause if you ain't, you've got no right to interfere, and if you be, you needn't be alarmed, I ain't going to kiss you. Here's your young man's letter. (*Gives letter and attempts to kiss her*)

Flo. In the old country, Mr. Trenchard, cousins content themselves with hands, but our hearts are with them. You are welcome, there is mine. (*Gives her hand, which he shakes heartily*)

Asa. That'll do about as well. I won't kiss you if you don't want me to; but if you did, I wouldn't stop on account of that sailor man. (*Business of Vernon threatening Asa*) Oh! now you needn't get your back up. What an all-fired chap you are. Now if you'll have me shown to my room, I should like to fix up a bit and put on a clean buzzom. (*All start*) Why, what on earth is the matter with you all? I only spoke because you're so all-fired go-to-meeting like.

Flo. Show Mr. Trenchard to the red room, Mr. Binny, that is if you are done with it, Mr. Dundreary.

Dun. Yeth, Miss Florence. The room and I have got through with each other, yeth.

  Asa and Dundreary see each other
   for the first time.

Asa. Concentrated essence of baboons, what on earth is that?

Dun. He's mad. Yes, Miss Florence, I've done with that room. The rooks crowed so that they racked my brain.

Asa. You don't mean to say that you've got any brains?

Dun. No, sir, such a thing never entered my head. The wed Indians want to scalp me. (*Holding hands to his head*)

Flo. The red room, then, Mr. Binny.

Asa. (*To Binny*) Hold on! (*Examines him*) Wal, darn me, but you keep your help in all-fired good order here. (*Feels of him*) This old shoat is fat enough to kill. (*Hits Binny in stomach. Binny runs off*) Mind how you go up stairs, old hoss, or you'll bust your biler.
           Exit.

Dun. Now he thinks Binny's an engine, and has got a boiler.

Flo. Oh, what fun!

Mrs. M. Old Mark Trenchard died very rich, did he not, Florence?

Flo. Very rich, I believe.

Aug. He's not at all romantic, is he, mamma?

Mrs. M. (*Aside to her*) My dear, I have no doubt he has solid good qualities, and I don't want you to laugh at him like Florence Trenchard.

Aug. No, mamma, I won't.

Flo. But what are we to do with him?

Dun. Ha! ha! ha!

All. What is the matter?

Dun. I've got an idea.

Flo. Oh! let's hear Dundreary's idea.

Dun. It's so seldom I get an idea that when I do get one it startles me. Let us get a pickle bottle.

Flo. Pickle bottle!

Dun. Yeth; one of those things with glass sides.

     Enter Asa.

Flo. Oh! you mean a glass case.

Dun. Yeth, a glass case, that's the idea, and let us put this Mr. Thomas Hawk in it, and have him on exhibition. That's the idea.

Asa. (*Overhearing*) Oh! that's your idea, is it? Wal, stranger, I don't know what they're going to do with me, but wherever they do put me, I hope it will be out of the reach of a jackass. I'm a real hoss, I am, and I get kinder riley with those critters.

Dun. Now he thinks he's a horse. I've heard of a great jackass, and I dreampt of a jackass, but I don't believe there is any such insect.

Flo. Well, cousin, I hope you made yourself comfortable.

Asa. Well, no, I can't say as I did. You see there was so many all-fired fixins in my room I couldn't find anything I wanted.

Flo. What was it you couldn't find in your room?

Asa. There was no soft soap.

De B. Soft soap!

Aug. Soft soap!

Ver. Soft soap!

Mrs. M. Soft soap!

Flo. Soft soap!

Geo. (*On sofa*) Soft soap!

Dun. Thoft thoap?

Asa. Yes, soft soap. I reckon you know what that is. However, I struck a pump in the kitchen, slicked my hair down a little, gave my boots a lick of grease, and now I feel quite handsome; but I'm everlastingly dry.

Flo. You'll find ale, wine and luncheon on the side-table.

Asa. Wal, I don't know as I've got any appetite. You see comin' along on the cars I worried down half a dozen ham sandwiches, eight or ten boiled eggs, two or three pumpkin pies and a string of cold sausages — and — Wal, I guess I can hold on till dinner-time.

Dun. Did that illustrious exile eat all that? I wonder where he put it.

Asa. I'm as dry as a sap-tree in August.

Binny. (*Throwing open door*) Luncheon!

Asa. (*Goes hastily up to table*) Wal, I don't want to speak out too plain, but this is an awful mean set out for a big house like this.

Flo. Why, what's wrong, sir?

Asa. Why, there's no mush!

Dun. No mush?

Asa. Nary slapjack.

Dun. Why, does he want Mary to slap Jack?

Asa. No pork and beans!

Dun. Pork's been here, but he's left.

Asa. And where on airth's the clam chowder?

Dun. Where *is* clam chowder? He's never here when he's wanted.

Asa. (*Drinks and spits*) Here's your health, old hoss. Do you call that a drink? See here, cousin, you seem to be the liveliest critter here, so just hurry up the fixins, and I'll show this benighted aristocratic society what real liquor is. So hurry up the fixins.

All. Fixins?

Flo. What do you mean by fixins?

Asa. Why, brandy, rum, gin and whiskey. We'll make them all useful.

Flo. Oh, I'll hurry up the fixins. What fun! *Exit.*

Dun. Oh! I thought he meant the gas fixins.

Asa. Say, you, you Mr. Puffy, you run out and get me a bunch of mint and a bundle of straws; hurry up, old hoss. (*Exit Binny, indignantly*) Say, Mr. Sailor man, just help me down with this table. Oh! don't you get riley, you and I ran against each other when I came in, but we'll be friends yet. (*Vernon helps him with table*)

Enter Florence, followed by servants in livery; they carry a case of decanters and water, on which are seven or eight glasses, two or three tin mixers and a bowl of sugar. Binny enters with a bunch of mint and a few straws.

Flo. Here, cousin, are the fixins.

Asa. That's yer sort. Now then, I'll give you all a drink that'll make you squeal. (*To Binny*) Here, Puffy, just shake that up, faster. I'll give that sick gal a drink that'll make her squirm like an eel on a mud bank.

Dun. (*Screams*) What a horrible idea. (*Runs about stage*)

Flo. Oh, don't mind him! That's only an American joke.

Dun. A joke! Do you call that a joke? To make a sick girl squirm like a mud bank on an eel's skin.

Asa. Yes, I'll give you a drink that'll make your whiskers return under your chin, which is their natural location. Now, ladies and gentlemen, what'll you have, Whiskey Skin, Brandy Smash, Sherry Cobbler, Mint Julep or Jersey Lightning?

Aug. Oh, I want a Mint Julep.

De B. Give me a Gin Cocktail.

Flo. I'll take a Sherry Cobbler.

Ver. Brandy Smash for me.

Mrs. M. Give me a Whiskey Skin.

Geo. I'll take a Lemonade.

Dun. Give me a Jersey Lightning.

Asa. Give him a Jersey Lightning. (*As Dundreary drinks*) Warranted to kill at forty rods.

> *Dundreary falls back on Mrs. Mount-chessington and Georgina.*

Scene 2.

Library in Trenchard Manor. Oriel window, with curtains. Two chairs and table brought on at change.

Enter Binny and Coyle.

Binny. Sir Hedward will see you directly, Mr. Coyle.

Coyle. Very well. House full of company, I see, Mr. Binny.

Binny. Cram full, Mr. Coyle. As one of the first families in the country we must keep up our position.

Coyle. (*Rubbing his hands*) Certainly, certainly, that is, as long as we can, Mr. Binny. Tell Murcott, my clerk, to bring my papers in here. You'll find him in the servant's hall, and see that you keep your strong ale out of his way. People who serve me must have their senses about them.

Binny. (*Aside*) I should say so, or 'e'd 'ave hevery tooth hout in their 'eds, the wiper. *Exit.*

Coyle. And now to show this pompous baronet the precipice on which he stands. (*Enter Murcott, with green bag and papers*) Are you sober, sirrah?

Mur. Yes, Mr. Coyle.

Coyle. Then see you keep so.

Mur. I'll do my best, sir. But, oh! do tell them to keep liquor out of my way. I can't keep from it now, try as I will, and I try hard enough, God help me!

Coyle. Pshaw! Get out those mortgages and the letters from my London agent. (*Murcott takes papers from bag and places them on table. Coyle looks off*) So; here comes Sir Edward. Go, but be within call. I may want you to witness a signature.

Mur. I will sir. (*Aside*) I must have brandy, or my hand will not be steady enough to write. *Exit.*

Enter Sir Edward. Coyle bows.

Sir E. Good morning, Coyle, good morning. (*With affected ease*) There is a chair, Coyle. (*They sit*) So you see those infernal tradepeople are pretty troublesome.

Coyle. My agent's letter this morning announces that Walter and Brass have got judgment and execution on their amount for repairing your town house last season. (*Refers to papers*) Boquet and Barker announce their intention of taking this same course with the wine account. Handmarth is preparing for a settlement of his heavy demand for the stables. Then there is Temper for pictures and other things, and Miss Florence Trenchard's account with Madame Pompon, and —

Sir E. Confound it, why harass me with details, these infernal particulars. Have you made out the total?

Coyle. Four thousand, eight hundred and sixty pounds, nine shillings and sixpence.

Sir E. Well, of course we must find means of settling this extortion.

Coyle. Yes, Sir Edward, if possible.

Sir E. If possible?

Coyle. I, as your agent, must stoop to detail, you must allow me to repeat, if possible.

Sir E. Why, you don't say there will be any difficulty in raising the money?

Coyle. What means would you suggest, Sir Edward?

Sir E. That, sir, is your business.

Coyle. A foretaste in the interest on the Fanhille and Ellenthrope mortgages, you are aware both are in the arrears, the mortgagees in fact, write here to announce their intentions to foreclose. (*Shows papers*)

Sir E. Curse your impudence, pay them off.

Coyle. How, Sir Edward?

Sir E. Confound it, sir, which of us is the agent? Am I to find you brains for your own business?

Coyle. No, Sir Edward, I can furnish the brains, but what I ask of you is to furnish the money.

Sir E. There must be money somewhere, I came into possession of one of the finest properties in Hampshire only twenty-six years ago and now you mean to tell me I cannot raise 4,000 pounds.

Coyle. The fact is distressing, Sir Edward, but so it is.

Sir E. There's the Ravensdale property unencumbered.

Coyle. There, Sir Edward, you are under a mistake. The Ravensdale property is deeply encumbered, to nearly its full value.

Sir E. (*Springing up*) Good heavens.

Coyle. I have found among my father's papers a mortgage of that very property to him.

Sir E. To your father! my father's agent?

Coyle. Yes, bearing date the year after the great contested election for the county, on which the late Sir Edward patriotically spent sixty thousand pounds for the honor of not being returned to Parliament.

Sir E. A mortgage on the Ravensdale estate. But it must have been paid off. Mr. Coyle, (*Anxiously*) have you looked for the release or the receipt?

Coyle. Neither exists. My father's sudden death explains sufficiently. I was left in ignorance of the transaction, but the seals on the deed and the stamps are intact, here it is, sir. (*Shows it*)

Sir E. Sir, do you know that if this be true I am something like a beggar, and your father something like a thief.

Coyle. I see the first plainly, Sir Edward, but not the second.

Sir E. Do you forget sir, that your father was a charity boy, fed, clothed by my father?

Coyle. Well, Sir Edward?

Sir E. And do you mean to tell me, sir, that your father repaid that kindness by robbing his benefactor?

Coyle. Certainly not, but by advancing money to that benefactor when he wanted it, and by taking the security of one of his benefactor's estates, as any prudent man would under the circumstances.

Sir E. Why, then, sir, the benefactor's property is yours.

Coyle. Pardon me, to keep the estate you have your equity of redemption. You have only to pay the money and the estate is yours as before.

Sir E. How dare you, sir, when you have just shown me that I cannot raise five hundred pounds in the world. Oh! Florence, why did I not listen to you when you warned me against this man?

Coyle. (*Aside*) Oh! she warned you, did she? (*Aloud*) I see one means, at least, of keeping the Ravensdale estate in the family.

Sir E. What is it?

Coyle. By marrying your daughter to the mortgagee.

Sir E. To you?

Coyle. I am prepared to settle the estate on Miss Trenchard the day she becomes Mrs. Richard Coyle.

Sir E. (*Springing up*) You insolent scoundrel, how dare you insult me in my own house, sir. Leave it, sir, or I will have you kicked out by my servants.

Coyle. I never take an angry man at his word, Sir Edward. Give a few moments' reflection to my offer; you can have me kicked out afterwards.

Sir E. (*Pacing stage*) A beggar, Sir Edward Trenchard a beggar, see my children reduced to labor for their bread, to misery perhaps; but the alternative, Florence detests him, still the match would save *her*, at least, from ruin. He might take the family name, I might retrench, retire to the continent for a few years. Florence's health might serve as a pretence. Repugnant as the alternative is, yet it deserves consideration.

Coyle. (*Who has watched*) Now, Sir Edward, shall I ring for the servants to kick me out?

Sir E. Nay, Mr. Coyle, you must pardon my outburst, you know I am hasty, and —

Flo. (*Without*) Papa, dear (*Enters gaily, starts on seeing Coyle*) papa, pardon my breaking in on business, but our American cousin has come, such an original — and we are only waiting for you to escort us to the field.

Sir E. I will come directly, my love. Mr. Coyle, my dear, you did not see him.

Flo. (*Disdainfully*) Oh! yes, I saw him, papa.

Sir E. Nay, Florence, your hand to Mr. Coyle. (*Aside*) I insist.

Flo. Papa.

> Frightened at his look, gives her hand. Coyle attempts to kiss it, she snatches it away.

Sir E. Come, Florence. Mr. Coyle, we will join you in the park. Come, my love, take my arm. *Hurries her off.*

Coyle. Shallow, selfish fool. She warned you of me, did she? And you did not heed her; you shall both pay dearly. She, for her suspicions, and you that you did not share them. (*Walks up and down*) How lucky the seals were not cut from that mortgage, when the release was given. 'Tis like the silly security of the Trenchards'. This mortgage makes Ravensdale mine, while the release that restores it to its owner lies in the recess of the bureau, whose secret my father revealed to me on his death bed.

Enter Murcott.

Write to the mortgagee of the Fanhille and Ellenthrope estates, to foreclose before the week is out, and tell Walters and Brass to put in execution to-day. We'll prick this windbag of a Baronet. Abel, we have both a bone to pick with him and his daughter. (*Murcott starts*) Why, what's the matter?

Mur. Nothing, the dizziness I've had lately.

Coyle. Brandy in the evening, brandy in the morning, brandy all night. What a fool you are, Murcott?

Mur. Who knows that as well as I do?

Coyle. If you would but keep the money out of your mouth, there's the making of a man in you yet.

Mur. No, no, it's gone too far, it's gone too far, thanks to the man who owns this house, you know all about it. How he found me a thriving, sober lad, flogging the village children through their spelling book. How he took a fancy to me as he called it, and employed me here to teach his son and Miss Florence. (*His voice falters*) Then remember how I forgot who and what I was, and was cuffed out of the house like a dog. How I lost my school, my good name, but still hung about the place, they all looked askance at me, you don't know how that kills the heart of a man, then I took to drink and sank down, down, till I came to this.

Coyle. You owe Sir Edward revenge, do you not? You shall have a rare revenge on him, that mortgage you found last week puts the remainder of the property in my reach, and I close my hand on it unless he will consent to my terms.

Mur. You can drive a hard bargain. I know.

Coyle. And a rare price I ask for his forbearance, Abel — his daughter's hand.

Mur. Florence?

Coyle. Yes, Florence marries Richard Coyle. Richard Coyle steps into Sir Edward's estates. There, you dog, will not that be a rare revenge? So follow me with those papers. And now to lay the mine that will topple over the pride of the Trenchards. *Exit.*

Mur. He marry Florence! Florence Trenchard! My Florence. Mine! Florence *his wife.* No, no, better a thousand times she had been mine, low as I am, when I dreampt that dream, but it shan't be, it shan't be. (*Tremblingly putting papers in bag*) If I can help her, sot though I am. Yes, I can help her, if the shock don't break me down. Oh! my poor muddled brain, surely there was a release with it when I found it. I must see Florence to warn her and expose Coyle's villainy. Oh! how my poor head throbs when I try to. I shall die if I don't have a drop of brandy, yes, brandy. *Exit.*

Scene 3.

Chamber at Trenchard Manor. Large shower bath, toilet table with drawer. Small bottle in drawer with red sealing wax on cork. Asa discovered seated, with foot on table, smoking a cigar. Valise on floor in front of him. Binny discovered standing by his side.

Asa. Wal, I guess I begin to feel kinder comfortable here in this place, if it wan't for this tarnal fat critter. He don't seem to have any work to do, but swells out his big bosom like an old turkey-cock in laying time. I do wonder what he's here for. Do they think I mean to absquatulate with the spoons? (*Binny attempts to take valise — Asa puts his foot on it*) Let that sweat. That's my plunder.

Bin. Will you have the kindness to give me your keys, hif you please, sir?

Asa. What do you want with my keys?

Bin. To put your things away in the wardrobe, sir.

Asa. Wal, I calculate if my two shirts, three bosoms, four collars, and two pair of socks were to get into that everlasting big bunk, they'd think themselves so all-fired small I should never be able to crawl into them again.

Bin. Will you take a bawth before you dress.

Asa. Take a bawth?

Bin. A bawth.

Asa. I suppose you mean a bath. Wal, man, I calkalate I ain't going to expose myself to the shakes by getting into cold water in this cruel cold climate of yours, so make tracks.

Bin. Make what?

Asa. Vamoose!

Bin. Make vamoose!

Asa. Absquatulate.

Bin. Ab — what sir?

Asa. Skedaddle.

Bin. Skedaddle?

Asa. Oh! get out.

Bin. Oh! (*Going*) If you are going to dress you'll want some hassistance.

Asa. Assistance! what to get out of my unmentionables and into them again? Wal, 'spose I do, what then?

Bin. Just ring the bell, hi'll hattend you.

Asa. All right, come along. (*Binny going*) Hold on, say, I may want to yawn presently and I shall want somebody to shut my mouth. (*Binny hurries off*) Wal, now I am alone, I can look about me and indulge the enquiring spirit of an American citizen. What an everlasting lot of things and fixins there is to be sure. (*Opens table drawer*) Here's a place will hold my plunder beautifully. (*Sees bottle*) Hallo, what's this? (*Comes down*) Something good to drink. (*Smells bottle*) It smells awful bad. (*Reads label*) Golden Fluid, one application turns the hair a beautiful brown, several applications will turn the hair a lustrous black. Well, if they keep on it may turn a pea green. I reckon this has been left here by some fellow who is ashamed of the natural color of his top knot. (*Knock*) Come in.

Enter Binny.

Bin. Mr. Buddicombe, sir, my lord's hown man.

Asa. Roll him in. (*Binny beckons, enter Buddicombe*) Turkey cock number two, what is it?

Bud. My Lord Dundreary's compliments and *have* you seen a small *bottle* in the toilet table drawer?

Asa. Suppose I had, what then?

Bud. My lord wants it particly.

Asa. Was it a small bottle?

Bud. A small bottle.

Bin. Bottle small.

Asa. Blue label?

Bin. Label blue.

Asa. Red sealing wax on the top?

Bud. Red sealing wax.

Bin. Wax red.

Asa. Nice little bottle?

Bin. Little bottle nice.

Asa. Wal, I ain't seen it. (*Aside*) If my lord sets a valley on it, guess it must be worth something.

Bud. Sorry to trouble you, sir.

Bin. (*Aside to Buddicombe*) What his hit?

Bud. My lord's hair dye, the last bottle, and he turns red to-morrow. *Exit in haste.*

Bin. Orrable, what an hawful situation, to be sure.

Asa. (*Aside*) So I've got my ring on that lord's nose, and if I don't make him dance to my tune it's a pity.

Bin. Miss Florence begged me to say she had borrowed a costume for you, for the harchery meeting, sir.

Asa. Hain't you dropped something?

Bin. Where?

Asa. What do you mean by the harchery meeting?

Bin. Where they shoot with bows and harrows.

Asa. There goes another of them, oh! you needn't look for them; you can't find 'em when you want 'em. Now you just take my compliments to Miss Trenchard; when I goes out shooting with injurious weapons I always wears my own genuine shooting costume. That's the natural buff tipped off with a little red paint.

Bin. Good gracious, he'd look like Hadam and Heve, in the garden of Eden.

Exit Binny.

Asa. Wal, there's a queer lot of fixings. (*Sees shower bath*) What on airth is that? looks like a 'skeeter net, only it ain't long enough for a feller to lay down in unless he was to coil himself up like a woodchuck in a knot hole. I'd just like to know what the all-fired thing is meant for. (*Calls*) Say Puffy, Puffy, oh! he told me if I wanted him to ring the bell. (*Looks round room*) Where on airth is the bell. (*Slips partly inside shower bath, pulls rope, water comes down*) Murder! help! fire! water! I'm drown.

Enter Skillet, Sharpe, Binny, and Buddicombe, seeing Asa, all laugh, and keep it up till curtain falls.

End of the First Act.

Act II.

Scene 1.

Oriel Chamber, as in Act One. Enter Mrs. Mountchessington and Augusta, dressed for archery meeting.

Mrs. M. No, my dear Augusta, you must be very careful. I don't by any means want you to give up De Boots, his expectations are excellent, but pray be attentive to this American savage, as I rather think he will prove the better match of the two, if what I hear of Mark Trenchard's property be correct.

Aug. (*Disdainfully*) Yes, ma.

Mrs. M. And look more cheerful, my love.

Aug. I am so tired, ma, of admiring things I hate.

Mrs. M. Yes, my poor love, yet we must all make sacrifices to society. Look at your poor sister, with the appetite.

Aug. What am I to be enthusiastic about with that American, ma?

Mrs. M. Oh! I hardly know yet, my dear. We must study him. I think if you read up Sam Slick a little, it might be useful, and just dip into Bancroft's History of the United States, or some of Russell's Letters; you should know something of George Washington, of whom the Americans are justly proud.

Aug. Here he comes, ma. What a ridiculous figure he looks in that dress, ha! ha!

Mrs. M. Hush, my dear!

Enter Asa, in archery dress.

Aug. Oh, Mr. Trenchard, why did you not bring me one of those lovely Indian's dresses of your boundless prairie?

Mrs. M. Yes, one of those dresses in which you hunt the buffalo.

Aug. (*Extravagantly*) Yes, in which you hunt the buffalo.

Asa. (*Imitating*) In which I hunt the buffalo. (*Aside*) Buffaloes down in Vermont. (*Aloud*) Wal, you see, them dresses are principally the nateral skin, tipped off with paint, and the Indians object to parting with them.

Both. Ahem! ahem!

Asa. The first buffalo I see about here I shall hunt up for you.

Mrs. M. Oh, you Americans are so clever, and so acute.

Aug. Yes, so 'cute.

Asa. Yes, we're 'cute, we are; know soft solder when we see it.

Aug. (*Aside*) Ma, I do believe he's laughing at us.

Mrs. M. Oh, no, my dear, you are mistaken. Oh! I perceive they are appearing for the archery practice. I suppose we shall see you on the ground, Mr. Trenchard.

Asa. Yes, I'll be there like a thousand of brick.

Aug. A thousand of brick!

Mrs. M. Hush, my dear! that is doubtless some elegant American expression. Au revoir, Mr. Trenchard.

Asa. Which?

Mrs. M. Au revoir.   *Exit with Augusta.*

Asa. No, thank you, don't take any before dinner. No use their talking Dutch to me. Wal, I never seed an old gal stand fire like that, she's a real old bison bull. I feel all-fired tuckered out riding in those keers. I'd like to have a snooze if I could find a place to lay down in. (*Sees curtains on recess*) Oh, this might do! (*Pulls curtain, then starts back*) No you don't! One shower bath a day is enough for me. (*Cautiously opens them*) No, I guess this is all right, I shall be just as snug in here as in a pew at meeting, or a private box at the Theatre. Hello! somebody's coming. (*Goes into recess*)

Enter Dundreary and Buddicombe.

Bud. My lord —

Dun. (*Business*)

Bud. My lord!

Dun. (*Business*)

Bud. Your lordship!! (*Louder*)

Dun. There, now you've spoiled it.

Bud. Spoiled what, my lord?

Dun. Spoiled what, my lord; why, a most magnificent sneeze!

Bud. I am very sorry, my lord.

Dun. Now that I can speak alone with you, tell me about that hair dye. Have you found it?

Bud. Not a trace of it, my lord.

Dun. If you don't find it, I'll discharge you.

Bud. Very well, my lord. *Bows and exits.*

Dun. Very well, my lord! He's gone and lost my hair dye, and my hair turns red to-morrow, and when I ask him to find it for me or I'll discharge him, he says, "Very well, my lord." He's positively idiotic, he is — Ah! here comes Miss Georgina, that gorgeous creature — that lovely sufferer. *Exit.*

Asa. (*Looking out*) What's the price of hair dye? Hallo! he's coming again with that sick girl.

Re-enter Dundreary and Georgina.

Dun. Will you try and strengthen your limbs with a gentle walk in the garden!

Geo. No, thank you, my lord. I'm so delicate. Oh, my lord, it is so painful to walk languidly through life, to be unable, at times, to bear the perfumes of one's favorite flowers. Even those violets you sent me yesterday I was compelled to have removed from my room, the perfume was too strong for me. I'm *so* delicate.

Dun. Yes, Miss Georgina; but they're very strengthening flowers, you know.

Geo. Yes, my lord, you are always right.

Dun. Do you know I'm getting to be very robust?

Geo. Would I could share that fault with you; but I am so delicate.

Dun. If you were robust I should not love you as I do. It would deprive you of that charm which enchains me to your lovely side which — which —

Geo. Oh, my lord, my lord! I'm going to faint.

Dun. And I'm going to sneeze, you faint while I sneeze.

Geo. (*Taking his arm*) Oh! my lord.

Dun. Do you know what a sneeze is?

Geo. No, my lord.

Dun. Did you ever sneeze?

Geo. No, my lord.

Dun. She never sneezed. I'll tell you what a sneeze is. Imagine a very large spider.

Geo. (*Screams*) Where, my lord?

Dun. No, no, I don't mean a real spider, only an imaginary one, a large spider getting up your nose, and all of a sudden, much to his disgust, he discovers he has put his foot in it and can't get it out again.

Geo. That must be very distressing.

Dun. For the spider, yes, and not very pleasant for the nose.

Geo. Oh! my lord, do take me to mamma.

Dun. No, you lovely sufferer, let's walk a little more.

Geo. I can't my lord, I'm *so* delicate.

Dun. Well, then, exercise, imitate that little hop of mine. (*Hops*) It isn't a run, it's a —

Geo. What is it?

Dun. No, it isn't a what is it. Well, let me suppose I get you an oyster. (*Georgina shakes her head*) Oh! then suppose I get you an oyster.

Geo. No, my lord, I'm too delicate.

Dun. How would you like the left wing of a canary bird?

Geo. No, my lord, it's too strong for me.

Dun. Let me ask you a widdle — why does a duck go under water? for divers reasons. Now I'll give you another — why does a duck come out of the water? for sundry reasons. No! No! see, you live on suction, you're like that bird with a long bill, they call doctor, no, that's not it, I thought it was a doctor, because it has a long bill — I mean a snipe — yes, you're a lovely snipe.

Exeunt.

Asa. (*Looking after them*) There goes a load of wooden nutmegs. Hello, here comes somebody else.

Enter Florence, with paper.

Flo. (*Reads*) "One who still remembers what he ought long since to have forgotten, wishes to speak with Miss Trenchard" — Florence scratched out — "on matters of life and death, near the oriel, in the west gallery." Written upon a dirty sheet of paper, in a hardly legible hand. What does this mean? It opens like one of Mrs. Radcliffe's romances. Well, here I am, and now for my correspondent.

Enter Murcott.

Mur. Oh! for one minute's clear head, Miss Florence.

Flo. I presume you are the writer of this?

Mur. Yes, I am.

Flo. You address me as an old acquaintance, but I do not recognize you.

Mur. So much the better. So much the better.

Flo. I hate mystery, sir; but you see I have come to rendezvous. I must know to whom I am speaking.

Mur. As frank as ever. I am Abel Murcott.

Flo. (*Starting back*) You?

Mur. Do not be ashamed, I have not the strength to injure you, if I had the evil. In this shabby, broken down drunkard you need not fear the madman, who years ago forgot in his frantic passion the gulf that lay between your station and his own. I am harmless except to my self.

Flo. Speak on, sir; I hear you.

Mur. I need not tell you by what steps I came to this; you don't know, maybe you never knew, what a maddening thing a passion is when it turns against itself. After being expelled from my tutorship in this house, I lost my employment, self respect, hope. I sought to drown recollection and draw courage from drink. It only embittered remembrances, and destroyed the little courage I had left. That I have bread to eat, I owe to Mr. Coyle; he employed me as his clerk. You know he has been with your father this morning. I have come to tell you my errand; are you as brave as you used to be when I knew —

Flo. I fear nothing.

Mur. I come to tell you of your father's ruin, his utter ruin.

Flo. My father's ruin. What? What?

Mur. His estates are mortgaged, his creditors clamorous. The Bailiffs will be in Trenchard Manor to-day, disguised as your own servants. This much Mr. Coyle has conceded to your father's respect for appearances.

Flo. Then beggary stares him in the face. Poor father, what a sad blow for him. Is that all, sir?

Mur. No; the worst remains.

Flo. Go on, sir.

Mur. Coyle knows your father's weakness and as a means of escape from ruin to the verge of which he has brought him, he has this day proposed for your hand.

Flo. Mine!

Mur. On consideration of settling on you the Ravensdale Estate.

Flo. And my father, how did he listen to such insolence?

Mur. You know as well as I do how he would hear such a proposal, at first a torrent of rage, then the strong ebb of selfishness set in, and he consented to listen to the terms, to view them as something to be considered, to consider them.

Flo. Good Heavens, can this be true? No, I will not believe it of my father, and from such lips.

Mur. You have full right to think this and to say it, but mark your father and Coyle to-day. You will then see if I speak truth or not.

Flo. Forgive my distrust, Mr. Murcott.

Mur. I am past taking offence or feeling scorn, I have carried more than can be heaped upon me, but I did not come only to give you warning of your danger.

Flo. Can you avert it?

Asa. (*Coming down between them*) Wal, stranger, that's just the question I was going to ask.

Flo. You here, sir, and listening.

Asa. Wal, it wasn't purpose, I went in there to take a snooze, I heard you talking and I thought it wouldn't be polite of me not to listen to what you had to say, I'm a rough sort of a customer, and don't know much about the ways of great folks, I've got a cool head, a stout arm, and a willing heart, and I think I can help you, just as one cousin ought to help another.

Flo. Well, I do think you are honest.

Mur. Shall I go on?

Flo. Yes, we will trust him, go on.

Mur. I found the Ravensdale mortgage while rumaging in an old deed box of Coyle's father's, there was a folded paper inside the deed. I took both to Coyle unopened, like a besotted fool that I was. My belief is strong that the paper was the release of the mortgage, that the money had been paid off, and the release executed without the seals having been cut from the original mortgage. I have known such things happen.

Asa. Have ye, now? Well, if a Yankee lawyer had done such a thing he would have Judge Lynch after him in no time.

Mur. You can but find that release, we may unmask this diabolical fiend and save you.

Flo. But, surely, a villain of Coyle's stability wou'd have destroyed the paper, the very keystone of his fraud.

Mur. I fear so.

Asa. Do you, now, wal, you're wrong, you're both wrong. I guess you ain't either on you done much cyphering human nature. The keystone of their fraud is just the point your mighty cute rascals always leave unsecured. Come along with me, stranger, and we'll just work up this sum a little, two heads are better than one. Yours is a little muddled, but mine's pretty clear, and if I don't circumvent that old sarpint, Coyle —

Flo. Well?

Asa. Say I am a skunk, that's all, and that's the meanest kind of an animal.

Exit.

Flo. I owe you much, Mr. Murcott, more than I can ever repay.

Mur. No, no, no, if you did but know the hope of seeing you has roused all the manhood that drink and misery has left me. God bless you, Miss Florence.

Flo. No, you don't call me Florence as you did when I was the truant pupil and you the indulgent tutor. (*Offers her hand*)

Mur. No, no; for heaven's sake do not call back that time or I shall go mad! mad! mad.

Rushes off, followed by Florence.

Scene 2.

Park. Rural cottage, adjoining which, and projecting on stage an inside view, a dairy with sloping roof, with milk pans. The whole scene should have a picturesque appearance. Garden fence runs across back; ornamental gate or archway at the right. Pigeon house on pole near dairy. Spinning wheel inside cottage door. One or two rustic benches. Enter John, with two milk pails on a yoke, puts them down near dairy, then looks off.

John. There they go, that's a bull's eye, I warrant. Dang me though, if I wouldn't rather see Miss Mary than this cock robin sports yonder; here she comes. Good morning, Miss Mary.

Enter Mary from cottage.

Mary. Oh, Wickens, you are there. How kind of you to help me with the milk pails to-day, when all the lads and lasses have given themselves a holiday to see the shooting.

John. Ah, Miss Mary, you ought to be among them, with a green hat and feather, if all had their rights.

Mary. (*Laughing*) Nay, ladies without a farthing in the world ought to put aside their ladyships and be themselves; besides I'm proud of my dairy here, just help me with this troublesome fellow, steady, don't shake it, the cream is foaming so beautifully. There. (*John carries pan into cottage and returns*)

John. Now, Miss Mary, what can I do for you?

Mary. Let me see; well, really, I do believe, Wickens, I've nothing to do but amuse myself.

John. Dang it, Miss, that's a pity, cos I can't help you at that, you see.

Mary. Oh! yes, bring me out dear old Welsh nurse's spinning wheel (*Exit John into cottage*) by the side of which I have stood so

often, a round eyed baby wondering at its whirring wheel. (*Re-enter John with wheel, places it near cottage*) There, that will do famously. I can catch the full scent of the jessamines.

John. Anything more, Miss Mary?

Mary. No, thank you, Wickens!

John. (*Going*) Good morning, Miss Mary.

Mary. Good morning, Wickens.

John. (*Returning*) Is there anything I can get for you, Miss Mary?

Mary. (*Spinning*) Nothing, thank you.

John. Dang me if I wouldn't like to stop all day, and watch her pretty figure and run errands for her.   *Exit behind fence.*

Mary. Poor Wickens is not the only one who thinks I am a very ill-used young body. Now I don't think so. Grandfather was rich, but he must have had a bad heart, or he never could have cast off poor mamma; had he adopted me, I should never have been so happy as I am now, uncle is kind to me in his pompous, patronizing way, and dear Florence loves me like a sister, and so I am happy. I am my own mistress here, and not anybody's humble servant, I sometimes find myself singing as the birds do, because I can't help it. (*Song, "Maid with the milking pail"*)

Enter Florence and Asa through gate.

Flo. Come along, cousin, come along. I want to introduce you to my little cousin. (*Kisses Mary*) Miss Mary Meredith, Mr. Asa Trenchard, our American cousin. (*They shake hands*) That will do for the present. This young gentleman has carried off the prize by three successive shots in the bull's eye.

Mary. I congratulate you, sir, and am happy to see you.

Asa. (*Shakes hands again*) Thank you, Miss.

Flo. That will do for a beginning.

Asa. (*Aside*) And so that is Mark Trenchard's grandchild.

Mary. Why have you left the archery, Florence?

Flo. Because, after Mr. Asa's display, I felt in no humor for shooting, and I have some very grave business with my cousin here.

Mary. You, grave business, why I thought you never had any graver business than being very pretty, very amiable, and very ready to be amused.

Asa. Wal, Miss, I guess the first comes natural round these diggins. (*Bows*)

Mary. You are very polite. This is my domain, sir, and I shall be happy to show you, that is, if you understand anything about a dairy.

Flo. Yes, by the way, do you understand anything about dairies in America?

Asa. Wal, I guess I do know something about cow juice. (*They turn to smother laugh*) Why, if it ain't all as bright and clean as a fresh washed shirt just off the clover, and is this all your doin's, Miss?

Mary. Yes, sir, I milk the cows, set up the milk, superintend the churning and make the cheese.

Asa. Wal, darn me if you ain't the first raal right down useful gal I've seen on this side the pond.

Flo. What's that, sir? Do you want to make me jealous?

Asa. Oh, no, you needn't get your back up, you are the right sort too, but you must own you're small potatoes, and few in a hill compared to a gal like that.

Flo. I'm what?

Asa. Small potatoes.

Flo. Will you be kind enough to translate that for me, for I don't understand American yet.

Asa. Yes, I'll put it in French for you, "petite pommes des terres."

Flo. Ah, it's very clear now; but, cousin, do tell me what you mean by calling me small potatoes.

Asa. Wal, you can sing and paint, and play on the pianner, and in your own particular circle you are some pumpkins.

Flo. Some pumpkins, first I am small potatoes, and now I'm some pumpkins.

Asa. But she, she can milk cows, set up the butter, make cheese and, darn me, if them ain't what I call raal downright feminine accomplishments.

Flo. I do believe you are right cousin, so Mary, do allow me to congratulate you upon not being small potatoes.

Mary. Well, I must look to my dairy or all my last week's milk will be spoiled. Good bye, Florence, dear. Good bye, Mr. Trenchard. Good morning, sir. *Exit into cottage.*

Asa. (*Following her to door*) Good morning, miss, I'll call again.

Flo. Well, cousin, what do you think of her?

Asa. Ain't she a regular snorter?

Flo. A what?

Asa. Wal, perhaps I should make myself more intelligible if I said a squeeler, and to think I'm keepin' that everlasting angel of a gal out of her fortune all along of this bit of paper here. (*Takes paper from pocket*)

Flo. What is that?

Asa. Old Mark Trenchard's will.

Flo. Don't show it to me, I don't want to look at it; the fortune should have come to Mary, she is the only relation in the direct line.

Asa. Say, cousin, you've not told her that darned property was left to me, have you?

Flo. Do you think I had the heart to tell her of her misfortune?

Asa. Wal, darn me, if you didn't show your good sense at any rate. (*Goes up to dairy*)

Flo. Well, what are you doing, showing *your* good sense?

Asa. Oh, you go long.

Flo. Say, cousin, I guess I've got you on a string now, as I heard you say this morning.

Asa. Wal, what if you have, didn't I see you casting sheep's eyes at that sailor man this morning? Ah, I reckon I've got you on a string now. Say, has he got that ship yet?

Flo. No, he hasn't, though I've used all my powers of persuasion with that Lord Dundreary, and his father has so much influence with the admiralty.

Asa. Wal, didn't he drop like a smoked possum.

Flo. There you go, more American. No, he said he was very sorry, but he couldn't.

Asa. (*Taking bottle out*) Oh, he did, did he? Wal, I guess he'll do his best all the same.

Flo. I shall be missed at the archery grounds. Will you take me back?

Asa. Like a streak of lightning. (*Offers arm and takes her to dairy*)

Flo. That's not the way.

Asa. No, of course not. (*Takes her round stage back to dairy*)

Flo. Well, but where are you going now?

Asa. I was just going round. I say, cousin, don't you think you could find your way back alone?

Flo. Why, what do *you* want to do?

Asa. Wal, I just wanted to see how they make cheese in this darned country.

Exit into dairy.

Flo. (*Laughing*) And they call that man a savage; well, I only wish we had a few more such savages in England.

Dun. (*Without*) This way, lovely sufferer.

Flo. Ah, here's Dundreary.

Dundreary enters with Georgina, places her in rustic chair.

Dun. There, repothe yourself.

Geo. Thank you, my lord; you are so kind to me, and I am so delicate.

Flo. Yes, you look delicate, dear; how is she this morning, any better?

Dun. When she recovers, she'll be better.

Flo. I'm afraid you don't take good care of her, you are so rough.

Dun. No, I'm not wruff, either. (*Sings*)
   I'm gentle and I'm kind,
   I'm — I forget the rest.

Flo. Well, good morning, dear — do take care of her — good day, Dundreary.
                               Exit through gate.

Dun. Now, let me administer to your wants. How would you like a roast chestnut.

Geo. No, my lord, I'm too delicate.

Dun. Well, then, a peanut; there is a great deal of nourishment in peanuts.

Geo. No, thank you.

Dun. Then what can I do for you?

Geo. If you please, ask the dairy maid to let me have a seat in the dairy. I am afraid of the draft, here.

Dun. Oh! you want to get out of the draft, do you? Well, you're not the only one that wants to escape the draft. Is that the dairy on top of that stick? (*Points to pigeon house*

Geo. No, my lord, that's the pigeon house.

Dun. What do they keep in pigeon houses? Oh! pigeons, to be sure; they couldn't keep donkeys up there, could they? That's the dairy, I suppothe?

Geo. Yes, my lord.

Dun. What do they keep in dairies?

Geo. Eggs, milk, butter and cheese.

Dun. What's the name of that animal with a head on it? No, I don't mean that, all animals have heads. I mean those animals with something growing out of their heads.

Geo. A cow?

Dun. A cow growing out of his head?

Geo. No, no, horns.

Dun. A cow! well, that accounts for the milk and butter; but I don't see the eggs; cows don't give eggs; then there's the cheese — do you like cheese?

Geo. No, my lord.

Dun. Does your brother like cheese?

Geo. I have no brother. I'm so delicate.

Dun. She's so delicate, she hasn't got a brother. Well, if you had a brother do you think he'd like cheese?

Geo. I don't know; do please take me to the dairy.

Dun. Well, I will see if I can get you a broiled sardine.   *Exit into dairy.*

Geo. (*Jumps up*) Oh! I'm so glad he's gone. I am so dreadful hungry. I should like a plate of corn beef and cabbage, eggs and bacon, or a slice of cold ham and pickles.

Dun. (*Outside*) Thank you, thank you.

Geo. (*Running back to seat*) Here he comes. Oh! I am so delicate.

Enter Dundreary.

Dun. I beg you pardon, Miss Georgina, but I find upon enquiry that cows don't give sardines. But I've arranged it with the dairy maid so that you can have a seat by the window that overlooks the cow house and the pig sty, and all the pretty things.

Geo. I'm afraid I'm very troublesome.

Dun. Yes, you're very troublesome, you are. No, I mean you're a lovely sufferer, that's the idea. (*They go up to cottage door. Enter Asa, running against Dundreary*) There's that damned rhinoceros again.
            Exit into cottage, with Georgina.

Asa. There goes that benighted aristocrat and that little toad of a sick gal. (*Looks off*) There he's a-settling her in a chair and covering her all over with shawls. Ah! it's a caution, how these women do fix our flint for us. Here he comes. (*Takes out bottle*) How are you, hair dye? (*Goes behind dairy*)

Enter Dundreary.

Dun. That lovely Georgina puts me in mind of that beautiful piece of poetry. Let me see how it goes. The rose is red, the violet's blue. (*Asa tips Dundreary's hat over his eyes. Dundreary repeats the verse, and Asa again tips his hat over his eyes in mockery. Dundreary comes down, takes off hat, looking in it*) There must be something alive in that hat. (*Goes up, and commences again*) The rose is red, the violet's blue, sugar is sweet, and so is somebody, and so is somebody else. (*Asa puts yoke on Dundreary's shoulders gently. Dundreary comes down with pails*) I wonder what the devil that is? (*Lowers one, then the other, they trip him up*) Oh, I see, somebody has been fishing and caught a pail. (*Goes hopping up stage, stumbling over against spinning wheel. Looks at yarn on stick*) Why, what a little old man. (*Sees Asa*) Say, Mr. Exile, what the devil is this?

Asa. That is a steam engine, and will bust in about a minute.

Dun. Well, I haven't a minute to spare, so I'll not wait till it busts. (*Crosses, knocks against private box, apologizes*)

Asa. Say, whiskers, I want to ask a favor of you.

Dun. (*Attempts to sneeze*) Now I've got it.

Asa. Wal, but say. (*Dundreary sneezes again. Asa takes his hand*) How are you? (*Squeezes it*)

Dun. There, you've spoiled it.

Asa. Spoiled what?

Dun. Spoiled what! why a magnificent sneeze.

Asa. Oh! was that what you was trying to get through you!

Dun. Get through me; he's mad.

Asa. Wal, now, the naked truth is — (*Leans arm on Dundreary's shoulder*) Oh, come, now, don't be putting on airs. Say, do you know Lieutenant Vernon?

Dun. Slightly.

Asa. Wal, what do you think of him, on an average?

Dun. Think of a man on an average?

Asa. Wal, I think he's a real hoss, and he wants a ship.

Dun. Well, if he's a real hoss, he must want a carriage.

Asa. Darn me, if that ain't good.

Dun. That's good.

Asa. Yes, that is good.

Dun. Very good.

Asa. Very good, indeed, *for you.*

Dun. Now I've got it. (*Tries to sneeze*)

Asa. Wal, now, I say. (*Dundreary trying to sneeze*) What, are you at that again?

> *Dundreary business. Asa bites his finger. Dundreary goes up, stumbles against chair and comes down again.*

Dun. I've got the influenza.

Asa. Got the what?

Dun. He says I've got a wart. I've got the influenza.

Asa. That's it exactly. I want your influence, sir, to get that ship.

Dun. That's good.

Asa. Yes, that's good, ain't it?

Dun. Very good.

Asa. Yes, darn me, if that ain't good.

Dun. For you. Ha! ha! One on that Yankee.

Asa. Well done, Britisher. Wal, now, about that ship?

Dun. I want all my influence, sir, for my own w — w — welations. (*Stammering*)

Asa. Oh! you want it for your own w — w — weltions. (*Mimicking*)

Dun. I say, sir.

Asa. Eh? (*Asa pretends deafness*)

Dun. He's hard of hearing, and thinks he's in a balloon. Mister.

Asa. Eh?

Dun. He thinks he can hear with his nose. I say —

Asa. Eh?

> *Dundreary turns Asa's nose around with his thumb. Asa puts his two hands up to Dundreary's.*

Dun. Now he thinks he's a musical instrument. I say —

Asa. What?

Dun. You stutter. I'll give you a k — k — k —

Asa. No you won't give me a kick.

Dun. I'll give you a c — c — card to a doctor and he'll c — c — c —

Asa. No he won't kick me, either.

Dun. He's idiotic. I don't mean that, he'll cure you.

Asa. Same one that cured you?

Dun. The same.

Asa. Wal, if you're cured I want to stay sick. He must be a mighty smart man.

Dun. A very clever man, he is.

Asa. Wal, darn me, if there ain't a physiological change taking place. Your whiskers at this moment —

Dun. My whiskers!

Asa. Yes, about the ends they're as black as a nigger's in biling time, and near the roots they're all speckled and streaked.

Dun. (*Horror struck*) My whiskers speckled and streaked?

Asa. (*Showing bottle*) Now, this is a wonderful invention.

Dun. My hair dye. My dear sir.

Asa. (*Squeezing his hand*) How are you?

Dun. Dear Mr. Trenchard. (*Puts arm on shoulder. Asa repeats Dundreary business, putting on eye glass, hopping round stage and stroking whiskers*) He's mad, he's deaf, he squints, he stammers and he's a hopper.

Asa. Now, look here, you get the lieutenant a ship and I'll give you the bottle. It's a fine swap.

Dun. What the devil is a swap?

Asa. Well, you give me the ship, and I'll give you the bottle to boot.

Dun. What do I want of your boots? I haven't got a ship about me.

Asa. You'd better make haste or your whiskers will be changed again. They'll be a pea green in about a minute.

Dun. Pea green!

> *Exits hastily into house.*

Asa. I guess I've got a ring in his nose now. I wonder how that sick gal is getting along. Wal, darn me, if the dying swallow ain't pitching into ham and eggs and home-made bread, wal, she's a walking into the fodder like a farmer arter a day's work rail splitting. I'll just give her a start. How de do, Miss, allow me to congratulate you on the return of your appetite. (*Georgina screams*) Guess I've got a ring in her pretty nose now. (*Looks off*) Hello! here comes the lickers and shooters, it's about time I took my medicine, I reckon.

Enter Sir Edward, Mrs. Mountchessington, Florence, Vernon, Augusta, De Boots, Wickens, Coyle, Sharpe, Binny, Skillet, Buddicombe, two servants in livery, carrying tray and glasses, a wine basket containing four bottles to represent champagne, knife to cut strings, some powerful acid in one bottle for Asa — pop sure.

Sir E. Now to distribute the prizes, and drink to the health of the winner of the golden arrow.

Flo. And there stands the hero of the day. Come, kneel down.

Asa. Must I kneel down?

Flo. I am going to crown you Captain of the Archers of Trenchard Manor.

Asa. (*Aside to Florence*) I've got the ship.

Flo. No; have you?

Sir E. Come, ladies and gentlemen, take from me. (*Takes glasses. Starts on seeing men in livery*) Who are these strange faces?

Coyle. (*In his ear*) Bailiffs, Sir Edward.

Sir E. Bailiffs! Florence, I am lost.

Florence supports her father. At the same moment Dundreary enters. Georgina appears at dairy door as Dundreary comes down. Asa cuts string of bottle, cork hits Dundreary. General commotion as drop descends.

End of the Second Act.

Act III.

Scene 1.

Dairy set as before in Act Two, Scene Two. Asa discovered on bench, whittling stick. Mary busy with milk pans in dairy.

Asa. Miss Mary, I wish you'd leave off those everlasting dairy fixings, and come and take a hand of chat along with me.

Mary. What, and leave my work? Why, when you first came here, you thought I could not be too industrious.

Asa. Well, I think so yet, Miss Mary, but I've got a heap to say to you, and I never can talk while you're moving about so spry among them pans, pails and cheeses. First you raise one hand and then the other, and well, it takes the gumption right out of me.

Mary. (*Brings sewing down*) Well, then, I'll sit here — (*Sits on bench with Asa, vis-à-vis*) Well now, will that do?

Asa. Well, no, Miss Mary, that won't do, neither; them eyes of yourn takes my breath away.

Mary. What will I do, then?

Asa. Well, I don't know, Miss Mary, but, darn me, if you could do anything that wasn't so tarnal neat and handsome, that a fellow would want you to keep on doing nothing else all the time.

Mary. Well, then, I'll go away. (*Rises*)

Asa. (*Stopping her*) No, don't do that, Miss Mary, for then I'll be left in total darkness. (*She sits*) Somehow I feel kinder lost, if I haven't got you to talk to. Now that I've got the latitude and longitude of all them big folks, found out the length of every lady's foot, and the soft spot on everybody's head, they can't teach me nothing; but here, (*Whittling*) here I come to school.

Mary. Then throw away that stick, and put away your knife, like a good boy. (*Throws away stick up stage*) I must cure you of that dreadful trick of whittling.

Asa. Oh, if you only knew how it helps me to keep my eyes off you, Miss Mary.

Mary. But you needn't keep your eyes off me.

Asa. I'm afraid I must, my eyes are awful tale-tellers, and they might be saying something you wouldn't like to hear, and that might make you mad, and then you'd shut up school and send me home feeling about as small as a tadpole with his tail bobbed off.

Mary. Don't be alarmed, I don't think I will listen to any tales that your eyes may tell unless they're tales I like and ought to hear.

Asa. If I thought they'd tell any others, Miss Mary, I'd pluck them right out and throw them in the first turnip patch I came to.

Mary. And now tell me more about your home in America. Do you know I've listened to your stories until I'm half a backwoodsman's wife already.

Asa. (*Aside*) Wouldn't I like to make her a whole one.

Mary. Yes, I can shut my eyes and almost fancy I see your home in the backwoods. There are your two sisters running about in their sunbonnets.

Asa. Debby and Nab? Yes!

Mary. Then I can see the smoke curling from the chimney, then men and boys working in the fields.

Asa. Yes.

Mary. The girls milking the cows, and everybody so busy.

Asa. Yes.

Mary. And then at night, home come your four big brothers from the hunt laden with game, tired and foot sore, and covered with snow.

Asa. That's so.

Mary. Then how we lasses bustle about to prepare supper. The fire blazes on the hearth, while your good old mother cooks the slapjack.

Asa. (*Getting very excited*) Yes.

Mary. And then after supper the lads and lasses go to a corn husking. The demijohn of old peach brandy is brought out and everything is so nice.

Asa. I shall faint in about five minutes. Miss Mary, you're a darned sight too good for this country. You ought to make tracks.

Mary. Make what?

Asa. Make tracks, pack up, and emigrate to the roaring old state of Vermont, and live 'long with mother. She'd make you so comfortable, and there would be sister Debby and Nab, and well, I reckon I'd be there, too.

Mary. Oh! I'm afraid if I were there your mother would find the poor English girl a sad incumbrance.

Asa. Oh, she ain't proud, not a mite, besides they've all seen Britishers afore.

Mary. I suppose you allude to my cousin, Edward Trenchard?

Asa. Well, he wan't the only one, there was the old Squire, Mark Trenchard.

Mary. (*Starting. Aside*) My grandfather!

Asa. Oh! he was a fine old hoss, as game as a bison bull, and as gray as a coon in the fall; you see he was kinder mad with his folks here, so he came over to America to look after the original branch of the family, that's our branch. We're older than the Trenchards on this side of the water. Yes, we've got the start of the heap.

Mary. Tell me, Mr. Trenchard, did he never receive any letters from his daughter?

Asa. Oh yes, lots of them, but the old cuss never read them, though; he chucked them in the fire as soon as he made out who they come from.

Mary. (*Aside*) My poor mother.

Asa. You see, as nigh as we could reckon it up, she had gone and got married again his will, and that made him mad, and well, he was a queer kind of a rusty fusty old coon, and it appeared that he got older, and rustier, and fustier, and fustier and coonier every fall, you see it always took him in the fall, it was too much for him. He got took down with the ague, he was so bad the doctors gave him up, and mother she went for a minister, and while she was gone the old man called me in his room, 'come in, Asa, boy,' says he, and his voice rang loud and clear as a bell, 'come in,' says he. Well I comed in; 'sit down,' says he; well, I sot down. You see I was always a favorite with the old man. 'Asa, my boy,' says he, takin' a great piece of paper, 'when I die, this sheet of paper makes you heir to all my property in England.' Well, you can calculate I pricked up my ears about that time, bime-by the minister came, and I left the

room, and I do believe he had a three days' fight with the devil, for that old man's soul, but he got the upper hand of Satan at last, and when the minister had gone the old man called me into his room again. The old Squire was sitting up in his bed, his face as pale as the sheet that covered him, his silken hair flowing in silvery locks from under his red cap, and the tears rolling from his large blue eyes down his furrowed cheek, like two mill streams. Will you excuse my lighting a cigar? For the story is long, awful moving, and I don't think I could get on without a smoke. (*Strikes match*) Wal, says he to me, and his voice was not as loud as it was afore — it was like the whisper of the wind in a pine forest, low and awful. 'Asa, boy,' said he, 'I feel that I've sinned in hardening my heart against my own flesh and blood, but I will not wrong the last that is left of them; give me the light,' says he. Wal I gave him the candle that stood by his bedside, and he took the sheet of paper I was telling you of just as I might take this. (*Takes will from pocket*) And he twisted it up as I might this, (*Lights will*) and he lights it just this way, and he watched it burn slowly and slowly away. Then, says he, 'Asa, boy that act disinherits you, but it leaves all my property to one who has a better right to it. My own daughter's darling child, Mary Meredith,' and then he smiled, sank back upon his pillow, drew a long sigh as if he felt relieved, and that was the last of poor old Mark Trenchard.

Mary. Poor Grandfather. (*Buries her face and sobs*)

Asa. Wal, I guess I'd better leave her alone. (*Sees half burned will*) There lies four hundred thousand dollars, if there's a cent. Asa, boy, you're a hoss. (*Starts off*)

Mary. To me, all to me. Oh, Mr. Trenchard, how we have all wronged poor grandfather. (*Asa goes*) What, gone? He felt after such tidings, he felt I should be left alone — who would suspect there was such delicacy under that rough husk, but I can hardly believe the startling news — his heiress — I, the penniless orphan of an hour ago, no longer penniless, but, alas, an orphan still,

Enter Florence.

with none to share my wealth, none to love me.

Flo. (*Throwing arms around Mary's neck*) What treason is this, Mary, no one to love you, eh, what's the matter? You've been weeping, and I met that American Savage coming from here. He has not been rude to you?

Mary. Oh, no, he's the gentlest of human beings, but he has just told me news that has moved me strangely.

Flo. What is it, love?

Mary. That all grandfather's property is mine, mine, Florence, do you understand?

Flo. What! he has popped, has he? I thought he would.

Mary. Who do you mean?

Flo. Who? Asa Trenchard, to be sure.

Mary. Asa Trenchard, why, what put that in your head?

Flo. Why how can Mark Trenchard's property be yours, unless you marry the legatee.

Mary. The legatee? Who?

Flo. Why, you know Mark Trenchard left everything to Asa.

Mary. No, no, you have been misinformed.

Flo. Nonsense, he showed it to me, not an hour ago on a half sheet of rough paper just like this. (*Sees will*) Like this. (*Picks it up*) Why, this is part of it, I believe.

Mary. That's the paper he lighted his cigar with.

Flo. Then he lighted his cigar with 80,000 pounds. Here is old Mark Trenchard's signature,

Mary. Yes, I recognize the hand.

Flo. And here are the words "Asa Trenchard, in consideration of sole heir" — etc. — etc. — etc.

Mary. Oh, Florence, what does this mean?

Flo. It means that he is a true hero, and he loves you, you little rogue. (*Embraces her*)

Mary. Generous man. (*Hides face in Florence's bosom*)

Flo. Oh, won't I convict him, now. I'll find him at once.   *Runs off.*

Mary. (*Runs after her, calling*) Florence!!! Florence!!!

Scene 2.

Chamber as before.

Enter Mrs. Mountchessington and Augusta.

Mrs. M. Yes, my child, while Mr. De Boots and Mr. Trenchard are both here, you must ask yourself seriously, as to the state of your affections, remember, your happiness for life will depend on the choice you make.

Aug. What would you advise, mamma? You know I am always advised by you.

Mrs. M. Dear, obedient child. De Boots has excellent expectations, but then they are only expectations after all. This American is rich, and on the whole I think a well regulated affection ought to incline to Asa Trenchard.

Aug. Very well, mamma.

Mrs. M. At the same time, you must be cautious, or in grasping at Asa Trenchard's solid good qualities, you may miss them, and De Boots's expectations into the bargain.

Aug. Oh, I will take care not to give up my hold on poor De Boots till I am quite sure of the American.

Mrs. M. That's my own girl.

Enter Asa.

Ah, Mr. Trenchard, we were just talking of your archery powers.

Asa. Wal, I guess shooting with bows and arrows is just about like most things in life, all you've got to do is to keep the sun out of your eyes, look straight — pull strong — calculate the distance, and you're sure to hit the mark in most things as well as shooting.

Aug. But not in England, Mr. Trenchard. There are disinterested hearts that only ask an opportunity of showing how they despise that gold, which others set such store by.

Asa. Wal, I suppose there are, Miss Gusty.

Aug. All I crave is affection.

Asa. Do you, now? I wish I could make sure of that, for I've been cruelly disappointed in that particular.

Mrs. M. Yes, but we are old friends, Mr. Trenchard, and you needn't be afraid of us.

Asa. Oh, I ain't afraid of you — both on you together.

Mrs. M. People sometimes look a great way off, for that which is near at hand. (*Glancing at Augusta and Asa alternatively*)

Asa. You don't mean Miss Gusta. (*Augusta casts sheep's eyes at him*) Now, don't look at me in that way. I can't stand it. If you do, I'll bust.

Mrs. M. Oh, if you only knew how refreshing this ingenuousness of yours is to an old woman of the world like me.

Asa. Be you an old woman of the world?

Mrs. M. Yes, sir.

Aug. Oh, yes.

Asa. Well, I don't doubt it in the least. (*Aside*) This gal and the old woman are trying to get me on a string. (*Aloud*) Wal, then, if a rough spun fellow like me was to come forward as a suitor for your daughter's hand, you wouldn't treat me as some folks do, when they find out I wasn't heir to the fortune.

Mrs. M. Not heir to the fortune, Mr. Trenchard?

Asa. Oh, no.

Aug. What, no fortune?

Asa. Nary red, it all comes to their barkin' up the wrong tree about the old man's property.

Mrs. M. Which he left to you.

Asa. Oh, no.

Aug. Not to you?

Asa. No, which he meant to leave to me, but he thought better on it, and left it to his granddaughter, Miss Mary Meredith.

Mrs. M. Miss Mary Meredith! Oh, I'm delighted.

Aug. Delighted?

Asa. Yes, you both look tickled to death. Now, some gals and mothers would go away from a fellow when they found that out, but you don't valley fortune, Miss Gusty?

Mrs. M. (*Aside, crosses to Augusta*) My love, you had better go.

Asa. You crave affection, *you* do. Now I've no fortune, but I'm biling over with affections, which I'm ready to pour out all over you like apple sass over roast pork.

Mrs. M. Mr. Trenchard, you will please recollect you are addressing my daughter, and in my presence.

Asa. Yes. I'm offering her my heart and hand just as she wants them, with nothing in 'em.

Mrs. M. Augusta, dear, to your room.

Aug. Yes, ma, the nasty beast. *Exit.*

Mrs. M. I am aware, Mr. Trenchard, you are not used to the manners of good society, and that, alone, will excuse the impertinence of which you have been guilty.

Asa. Don't know the manners of good society, eh? Well, I guess I know enough to turn you inside out, old gal — you sock-dologizing old man-trap. Wal, now, when I think what I've thrown away in hard cash to-day I'm apt to call myself some awful hard names, 400,000 dollars is a big pile for a man to light his cigar with. If that gal had only given me herself in exchange, it wouldn't have been a bad bargain. But I dare no more ask that gal to be my wife, than I dare ask Queen Victoria to dance a Cape Cod reel.

Enter Florence.

Flo. What do you mean by doing all these dreadful things?

Asa. Which things?

Flo. Come here, sir. (*He does so*)

Asa. What's the matter?

Flo. Do you know this piece of paper? (*Showing burnt paper*)

Asa. Well, I think I have seen it before. (*Aside*) It's old Mark Trenchard's will that I left half burned up like a lunkhead that I am.

Flo. And you're determined to give up this fortune to Mary Meredith.

Asa. Well, I couldn't help it if I tried.

Flo. Oh, don't say that.

Asa. I didn't mean to do it when I first came here — hadn't the least idea in the world of it, but when I saw that everlasting angel of a gal moving around among them dairy fixings like a sunbeam in a shady place; and when I pictured her without a dollar in the world — I — well, my old Adam riz right up, and I said, "Asa do it" — and I did it.

Flo. Well, I don't know who your old Adam may be, but whoever it is, he's a very honest man to consult you to do so good an action. But how dare you do such an outrageous thing? you impudent — you unceremonious, oh! you unselfish man! you! you, you!

Smothers him with kisses, and runs off.

Asa. Well, if that ain't worth four hundred thousand dollars, I don't know what is; it was sweeter than sweet cider right out of the bung hole. Let me see how things stand round here. Thanks to old whiskers I've got that ship for the sailor man, and that makes him and Miss Florence all hunk. Then there's that darned old Coyle. Well, I guess me and old Murcott can fix his flint for him. Then there's — (*Looks off*) Christopher Columbus, here comes Mary.

Enter Mary.

Mary. Mr. Trenchard, what can I say to you but offer you my lifelong gratitude.

Asa. Don't now, Miss, don't —

Mary. If I knew what else to offer. Heaven knows there is nothing that is mine to give that I would keep back.

Asa. Give me yourself. I know what a rude, ill-mannered block I am; but there's a heart inside of me worth something, if it's only for the sake of your dear little image, that's planted right plump in the middle of it.

Mary. Asa Trenchard, there is my hand, and my heart is in it.

Asa. (*Seizes her hand, then drops it suddenly*) Miss Mary, I made what folks call a big sacrifice for you, this morning. Oh! I know it, I ain't so modest, but that I know it. Now, what's this you're doing? Is this sacrifice you are making out of gratitude for me? Cause if it is, I wouldn't have it, though not to have it would nigh break my heart, tough as it is.

Mary. No, no, I give myself freely to you — as freely as you, this morning, gave my grandfather's property to me.

Asa. Say it again, last of hope and blessed promise. (*Clasps her in his arms*) Mary, there's something tells me that you'll not repent it. I'm rough, Mary, awful rough, but you needn't fear that I'll ever be rough to you. I've camped out in the woods, Mary, often and often, and seen the bears at play with their cubs in the moonlight; the glistening teeth, that would tear the hunter, was harmless to them; the big strong claws that would peel a man's head, as a knife would a pumpkin, was as soft for them as velvet cushions, and that's what I'll be with you, my own little wife; and if ever harm does come to you, it must come over the dead body of Asa Trenchard.

Mary. I know it, Asa; and if I do not prove a true and loving wife to you, may my mother's bright spirit never look down to bless her child.

Asa. Wal, if I don't get out in the air, I'll bust.   *Exit hastily, pulling Mary after him.*

Enter Binny, drunk.

Binny. (*Calling*) Mr. H'Asa, Mr. H'Asa! Oh, he's gone; well, I suppose he'll come back to keep his happointment. Mr. Coyle's quite impatient. It isn't hoften that han Hamerican has the run of the wine cellars of Trenchard Manor, and in such company, too. There's me and Mr. Coyle, which is a good judge of old port wine, and he knows it when he drinks; and his clerk, Mr. Murcott, which I don't hexactly like sitting down with clerks. But Mr. H'Asa wished it and Mr. Coyle hadn't any objections, so in course I put my feelings in my pocket, besides, Murcott is a man of hedication, though unfortunately taken to drink. Well, what of that, it's been many a man's misfortune, though I say it, what shouldn't say it, being a butler. But now to join my distinguished party.   *Exit.*

Scene 3.

Wine cellar. Coyle, Murcott and Binny discovered. Table with two cups and bottles. Coyle seated. Binny back of table. Murcott sitting on barrel. Door with staircase, dark. Stage half dark. Candles on table, lighted.

Coyle. A capital glass of wine, Mr. Binny, and a capital place to drink it.

Asa. (*Without*) Bring a light here, can't you. I've broken my natural allowance of shins already.

Asa enters down stairs.

Asa. (*To Murcott*) Is he tight yet?

Mur. Histered, but not quite gone yet.

Coyle. Oh, Mr. Trenchard, glad to see you, to welcome you to the vaults of your ancestors.

Asa. Oh! these are the vaults of my ancesters, are they? Wal, you seem to be punishing their spirits pretty well.

Binny. Wines, Mr. Asa? The spirits are in the houter cellar.

Coyle. Oh, Mr. Asa, there is no place like a wine cellar for a hearty bout. Here you might bawl yourself hoarse beneath these ribs of stone, and nobody hear you. (*He shouts and sings very loud*)

Asa. Oh, wouldn't they hear you? (*Aside*) That's worth knowing.

Binny. (*Very drunk — rising*) That's right, Mr. Coyle, make as much noise as you like, you are in the cellars of Trenchard Manor, Mr. Coyle. Mr. Coyle, bless you, Mr. Coyle. Mr. Coyle, why his hit Mr. Coyle, I am sitting at the present time, in this present distinguished company? I will tell you, Mr. Coyle, hit his because Hi always hacts and conducts myself has becomes a gentleman, hand Hi knows what's due to manners. (*Falls in chair*)

Asa. Steady, old hoss, steady.

Binny. Hi'm steady. Hi always was steady. (*Staggers*) Hi'm going to fetch clean glasses.   *Exit.*

Asa. Now, Mr. Coyle, suppose you give us a song.

Coyle. (*Very drunk*) I can't sing, Mr. Trenchard, but I sometimes join in the chorus.

Asa. Wal, give us a chorus.

Coyle. Will you assist in the vocalization thereof?

Asa. (*Mimicking*) Will do the best of my endeavors thereunto.

Coyle. (*Sings*) "We won't go home till morning". (*Repeats. Falls off chair, senseless*)

Asa. (*Finishing the strain*) I don't think you'll go home at all. Now, then, quick, Murcott, before the butler comes back, get his keys. (*Murcott gets keys from Coyle's pocket and throws them to Asa.*) Is this all?

Mur. No; the key of his private bureau is on his watch chain, and I can't get it off.

Asa. Take watch and all.

Mur. No; he will accuse us of robbing him.

Asa. Never mind, I'll take the responsibility. (*Coyle moves*)

Mur. He is getting up.

Asa. Well, darn me, knock him down again.

Mur. I can't.

Asa. Can't you? Well, I can.

Pulls Murcott away. Knocks Coyle down; is going towards door, meets Binny with tray and glasses; kicks it, knocks Binny down and exits up staircase, followed by Murcott, carrying candle. Dark stage. Binny rises, Coyle ditto. Blindly encounter each other and pummel soundly till curtain falls.

Scene 4.

Chamber, same as Scene Two. Enter Dundreary and Vernon. Dundreary stops, and is seized with an inclination to sneeze. Motions with his hand to Vernon.

Ver. My lord! (*Dundreary sneezes*) Your lordship! (*Dundreary sneezes again. Louder*) My lord!

Dun. There you go; now you've spoiled it.

Ver. Spoiled what, my lord?

Dun. Spoiled what? why, a most magnificent sneeze.

Ver. I'm very sorry to interrupt your lordship's sneeze, but I merely wanted to express my gratitude to you for getting me a ship.

Dun. Sir, I don't want your gratitude, I only want to sneeze.

Ver. Very well, my lord, then I will leave you, and thus give you an opportunity for sneezing. But in return for what you have done for me, should you ever want a service a sailor can offer you, just hail Harry Vernon, and you'll find he'll weigh anchor and be alongside. *Hitches up breeches and exits.*

Dun. Find him alongside? What does he mean by a long side? and he always wants to weigh anchor. What funny fellows the sailors are. Why the devil don't they keep a memorandum of the weight of their anchor? What's the matter with the sailor's side! (*Imitates Vernon*) Oh, I see, he's got the stomach ache.
Exit.

Scene 5.

Library in Trenchard Manor. Enter Buddicombe, following Lord Dundreary.

Bud. A letter, my lord.

Dun. (*Takes letter*) You may go. (*Exit Buddicombe. Opens letter*) "My dear Frederick." He calls me Frederick because my name is Robert. "I wrote you on my arrival." Why, I never heard from him. "But I am afraid you didn't get the letter, because I put no name on the envelope." That's the reason why I didn't get it, but who did get it? It must have been some fellow without any name. "My dear brother, the other day a rap came to my door, and some fellows came in and proposed a quiet game of poker." A quiet game of poker, why, they wanted to kill him with a poker. "I consented and got stuck —" Sam's dead, I've got a dead lunatic for a brother — "for the drinks." He got on the other side of the paper, why couldn't he get stuck all on one side. "P. S. — If you don't get this letter let me know, for I shall feel anxious." He's a mad lunatic. *Exit.*

Scene 6.

Coyle's Office, high desk, stool and cabinet. Asa discovered looking over papers on box. Murcott looking in desk.

Asa. Have you found it?

Mur. No, Mr. Trenchard. I've searched all the drawers but can find no trace of it.

Asa. What's this?

Mur. That's a cabinet where his father kept old deeds, the key he always carries about him.

Asa. Oh, he does, does he? Well, I reckon I saw a key as I came in that will open it. *Exit.*

Mur. Key, oh, my poor muddled brain, what can he mean!

Asa. (*Re-enters with axe*) Here's a key that will open any lock that Hobb ever invented.

Mur. Key? what key?

Asa. What key, why, Yankee.

(*Shows axe, begins to break open Cabinet*)

Enter Coyle.

Coyle. Villains! would you rob me?

Mur. Stand off, Mr. Coyle, we are desperate. (*Now seizes him*)

Asa. Here it is as sure as there are snakes in Virginia. Let the old cuss go, Murcott.

Coyle. Burglars! oh, you shall dearly pay for this.

Asa. Yes, I'll pay — but I guess you'll find the change.

Coyle. The law — the law shall aid me.

Asa. Wal, perhaps it would be as well not to call in the law just yet. It might look a little further than might be convenient.

Mur. It's no use to bluster, Mr. Coyle, you are harmless to us now, for we have that, that will crush you.

Coyle. Well, what are your conditions? money, how much?

Asa. Wal, we warn't thinking of coming down on your dollars. But you have an appointment with Sir Edward at two, haven't you?

Coyle. Well?

Asa. Well, I want you to keep that appointment.

Coyle. Keep it?

Asa. Yes, and that's all I do want you to keep of his, and instead of saying you have come to foreclose the mortgage, I want you to say you have found the release which proves the mortgage to have been paid off.

Coyle. I accept. Is that all?

Asa. Not quite. Then I want you to pay off the execution debts.

Coyle. What, I pay Sir Edward's debts?

Asa. Yes, with Sir Edward's money that stuck to your fingers naturally while passing through your hands.

Coyle. (*To Murcott*) Traitor!

Mur. He knows all, Mr. Coyle.

Coyle. Is there anything more!

Asa. Yes, I want you to apologize to Miss Florence Trenchard, for having the darned impudence to propose for her hand.

Coyle. What more?

Asa. Then you resign your stewardship in favor of your clerk, Abel Murcott.

Coyle. What, that drunkard vagabond?

Asa. Well, he was, but he's going to take the pledge at the first pump he comes to.

Mur. Yes, I *will* conquer the demon drink, or die in the struggle with him.

Coyle. Well, anything more?

Asa. Yes, I think the next thing will be to get washed. You're not a handsome man at the best, and now you're awful. (*Coyle makes a dash at Murcott. Asa catches him and turns him round*) Mr. Coyle, in your present state of mind, you had better go first.

Coyle. (*Bitterly*) Oh, sir, it is your turn now.

Asa. Yes, it is my turn, but you can have the first wash. Come along, Murcott.

Exeunt.

Scene 7.

Library in Trenchard Manor. Sir Edward discovered seated at table.

Sir E. The clock is on the stroke of two, and Coyle is waiting my decision. In giving her to him, I know I shall be embittering her life to save my fortune, but appearances — no, no, I will not sacrifice her young life so full of promise, for a few short years of questionable state for myself, better leave her to the mercy of chance (*Enter Florence*) than sell her to this scoundrel; as to myself, I will not survive the downfall of my house, but end it thus.

Raises pistol to his head. Florence seizes his arm and screams.

Flo. Father, dear father, what despair is this? (*Sir Edward buries his face in his hands*) If it is fear of poverty, do not think of me, I will marry this man if I drop dead in my bridal robes.

Enter Binny.

Binny. Mr. Coyle, sir, who has come by happointment.

Sir E. I will not see him.

Flo. Yes, yes, show him up, Mr. Binny.

Exit Binny.

Sir E. Florence, I will not consent to this sacrifice.

Enter Asa, Coyle and Murcott.

Sir E. How is this Mr. Coyle, you are not alone?

Asa. No, you see, squire, Mr. Coyle wishes me and his clerk to witness the cutting off the seals from the mortgage, which he has been lucky enough to find the release of.

Sir E. Heavens, is it so?

Coyle. Yes, Sir Edward, there is the release executed by my father, which had become detached.

Asa. (*To him*) Accidentally.

Sir E. Saved, saved at last from want!

Coyle. Meanwhile I have paid the execution debts out of a fine which has just fallen in.

Asa. Accidentally. It's astonishing how things have fallen in and out to-day.

Sir E. But your demand here? (*Points to Florence*)

Coyle. I make none, Sir Edward. I regret that I should have conceived so mad a thought; it is enough to unfit me for longer holding position as your agent, which I beg humbly to resign —

Asa. (*Aside to him*) Recommending as your successor —

Coyle. Recommending as my successor Abel Murcott, whose knowledge of your affairs, gained in my office, will render him as useful as I have been.

Asa. Yes, just about.

Sir E. Your request is granted, Mr. Coyle.

Asa. And now, my dear Mr. Coyle, you may a-b-s-q-u-a-t-u-l-a-t-e.

Coyle. I go, Sir Edward, with equal good wishes for all assembled here.

Darts a look at Murcott and exits.

Asa. That's a good man, Sir Edward.

Sir E. Yes.

Asa. Oh, he's a very good man.

Sir E. Yes, he is a good man.

Asa. But he can't keep a hotel.

Sir E. Mr. Murcott, your offence was heavy.

Flo. And so has been his reparation. Forgive him, papa. Mr. Murcott, you saved me; may Heaven bless you.

Mur. Yes, I saved her, thank Heaven. I had strength enough for that.   *Exit.*

Flo. You'll keep your promise and make Mr. Murcott your clerk, papa?

Sir E. Yes, I can refuse nothing; I am so happy; I am so happy, I can refuse none anything to-day.

Asa. Can't you, Sir Edward? Now, that's awful lucky, for there's two gals want your consent mighty bad.

Sir E. Indeed; for what?

Asa. To get hitched.

Sir E. Hitched?

Asa. Yes, to get spliced.

Sir E. Spliced?

Asa. Yes, to get married.

Sir E. They have it by anticipation. Who are they?

Asa. There's one on 'em. (*Points to Florence*)

Sir E. Florence! and the other?

Asa. She's right outside.   *Exit, hastily.*

Sir E. Well, and who is the happy man, Lord Dun —

Flo. Lord Dundreary! No, papa — but Harry Vernon. He's not poor now, though; he's got a ship.

Re-enter Asa, with Mary.

Asa. Here's the other one, Sir Edward.

Sir E. Mary? Who is the object of your choice?

Mary. Rough-spun, honest-hearted Asa Trenchard.

Sir E. Ah! Mr. Trenchard you win a heart of gold.

Flo. And so does Mary, papa, believe me. (*Crosses to Asa. Mary and Sir Edward go up*) What's the matter?

Asa. You make me blush.

Flo. I don't see you blushing.

Asa. I'm blushing all the way down my back.

Flo. Oh, you go long.

Asa. Hello! here's all the folks coming two by two, as if they were pairing for Noah's ark. Here's Mrs. Mountchestnut and the Sailor man. (*Enter as Asa calls them off*) Here's De Boots and his gal, and darn me, if here ain't old setidy fetch it, and the sick gal, how are you, buttons? (*Dundreary knocks against Asa*)

Dun. There's that damned rhinocerous again. (*Crosses with Georgina, and seats her*)

Asa. Here comes turkey cock, number two, and his gal, and, darn me, if here ain't Puffy and his gal.

Sir E. Mr. Vernon, take her, she's yours, though Heaven knows what I shall do without her.

Mrs. M. (*Rising*) Ah, Sir Edward, that is just my case; but you'll never know what it is to be a mother. Georgina, Augusta, my dears, come here. (*They come down each side of her*) You'll sometimes think of your poor mamma, bless you. (*Aside to them*) Oh, you couple of fools.

Bumps their foreheads. Dundreary has business with Georgina, then leads her to a seat.

De B. (*To Dundreary*) Why, Fred, we're all getting married!

Dun. Yes, it's catching, like the cholera.

Binny. I 'ope, Sir Edward, there's no objections to my leading Miss Sharpe to the hymenial halter.

Sir E. Certainly not, Mr. Binny.

Bud. (*To Dundreary*) And Skillet and I have made so bold, my lord —

Dun. Yes, you generally do make bold — but bless you, my children — bless you.

Asa. Say, you, lord, buttons, I say, whiskers.

Dun. Illustrious exile? (*Comes down*)

Asa. They're a nice color, ain't they?

Dun. Yes, they're all wight now.

Asa. All wight? no, they're all black.

Dun. When I say wight I mean black.

Asa. Say, shall I tell that sick gal about that hair dye?

Dun. No, you needn't tell that sick gal about that hair dye!

Asa. Wal, I won't, if you don't want me to.

Dun. (*Aside*) That man is a damned rattlesnake.

Goes up, sits in Georgina's lap — turns to apologize, sits in Augusta's lap — same business with Mrs. Mountchessington, then goes back to Georgina.

Asa. Miss Georgina. (*She comes down*) How's your appetite? Shall I tell that lord about the beefsteak and onions I saw you pitching into?

Geo. Please don't, Mr. Trenchard, I'm so delicate.

Asa. Wal, I won't, if you don't want me to.

Geo. Oh, thank you. (*Backs up stage and sits in Dundreary's lap, who has taken her seat*)

Asa. Miss Gusty. (*Augusta comes down*) Got your boots, hain't you?

Aug. Yes, Mr. Trenchard.

Asa. How do they fit you? Say, shall I tell that fellow you were after me first?

Aug. (*Extravagantly*) Not for the world, Mr. Trenchard.

Asa. (*Mimicking*) Wal, I won't, if you don't want me to.

Asa. Mrs. Mountchestnut.

Dun. (*Coming down*) Sir, I haven't a chestnut to offer you, but if you'd like some of your native food, I'll order you a doughnut?

Asa. I dough not see it.

Dun. (*Laughs*) That's good.

Asa. Yes, very good.

Dun. For you.

Asa. Oh, you get out, I mean the old lady.

Dun. Mrs. Mountchessington, this illustrious exile wishes to see you. (*Mrs. Mountchessington comes down*)

Asa. Wal, old woman?

Mrs. M. Old woman, sir?

Asa. Got them two gals off your hands, haven't you?

Mrs. M. I'm proud to say, I have.

Asa. Shall I tell them fellows you tried to stick them on me first!

Mrs. M. You'll please not mention the subject.

Asa. Wal, I won't, if you don't want me to. (*Backs up; — curtseying; — knocks against Dundreary, who is stooping to pick up handkerchief. They turn and bump foreheads*) Say, Mr. Puffy. (*Binny comes down*) Shall I tell Sir Edward about your getting drunk in the wine cellar?

Binny. You need not — not if you don't like unto.

Asa. Wal, I won't, if you don't want me to.

Binny. Remember the hold hadage. "A still tongue shows a wise 'ead."

Asa. X Q's me.

Binny. O, I, C. (*Goes up*)

Flo. (*Comes down*) Well cousin, what have you to say to us?

Asa. (*Mary comes down*) Wal, I ain't got no ring, to put in your noses, but I's got one to put on your finger. (*To Mary*) And I guess the sailor man has one to put on yours, and I guess you two are as happy as clams at high water.

Flo. I am sure you must be very happy.

Asa. Wal, I am not so sure about my happiness.

Flo. Why, you ungrateful fellow. What do you want to complete it?

Asa. (*To Audience*) My happiness depends on you.

Flo. And I am sure you will not regret your kindness shown to Our American Cousin. But don't go yet, pray — for Lord Dundreary has a word to say. (*Calls Dundreary*)

Dun. (*Sneezes*) That's the idea.

THE END.

MELODRAMA

THOMAS HOLCROFT

A Tale of Mystery (1802)

JOHN BALDWIN BUCKSTONE

Luke the Labourer; or, The Lost Son (1826)

DOUGLAS WILLIAM JERROLD

The Rent-Day (1832)

DION BOUCICAULT

After Dark (1868)

MRS. HENRY WOOD

East Lynne (1862)

HENRY ARTHUR JONES

The Silver King (1882)

THOMAS HOLCROFT
1745-1809

A Tale of Mystery
(1802)

Although Thomas Holcroft lived to write nine plays in the nineteenth century, most of his life and literary work belong to the eighteenth. To some extent a hack writer, he is remembered in literary history primarily as the author of four popular novels and two influential plays, *The Road to Ruin* (1792) and *A Tale of Mystery* (1802). *The Road to Ruin* was a popular domestic comedy treating middle-class characters and embodying features later assimilated into countless melodramas. (A prodigal son is eventually saved through a change of heart, an awakened sense of duty, and the discovery of a long-lost will.) *A Tale of Mystery* has the distinction of being the first English play to be labeled a melodrama.

The experiences of Holcroft's life aptly fitted him to establish the drama of the people. He had been a shoemaker, school teacher, translator, book reviewer for magazines, musician, novelist, minor poet, strolling actor, and playwright. His literary works set forth doctrines that associate him with the radical William Godwin: the perfectibility of human nature and the need for paternalistic benevolence in the aristocracy until the education of the poor might make a basis for democracy.

But these experiences and doctrines do not appear in *A Tale of Mystery*, except as they may be implied in the sentimental attitudes of the characters. This work was neither an original play nor a serious expression of Holcroft's views. It was a somewhat slipshod adaptation from a play by Guilbert de Pixérécourt, hack writer and "father of the melodrama" on the French stage. Pixérécourt's play was *Cœlina; ou, L'Enfant du Mystère*. In his preface to the published *A Tale of Mystery* Holcroft acknowledged his source, saying, "I cannot forget the aid I received from the French Drama from which the principal incidents, many of the thoughts, and much of the manner of telling the story, are derived." In fact, *A Tale of Mystery* is not even a good rendition of Pixérécourt's drama. Maurice Disher calls it a "scrawled version, such as a [play] pirate might scribble from memory over his supper after the performance." Holcroft kept some names from the original — for instance, the meaningless name Exempt — but changed the heroine Cœlina to Selina; and he cut dialogues and soliloquies to the barest essentials, in favor of vigorous pantomimic action. Aware that his play was not developed drama, he placed on the title page a word invented in France to describe such a play: "Mélodrame." It was not the first English play to exhibit the features of melodrama, for earlier burlettas had stripped the stories of the traditional drama of everything but essential action, but it was the first to announce this fact.

To some extent *A Tale of Mystery* echoes the increasingly popular Gothic drama. It creates terror with storms, an Italian setting, and especially the scene in "wild mountainous country . . . with pines and massy rocks." The villain is a Gothic stereotype, with his crime in the past, his remorse when trapped, and the change of heart that leads him to offer his life nobly to his wronged brother.

A reviewer in the *Times* expressed an interesting reaction to this new type of play. Calling the dialogue "natural and characteristic," he said: "There is no extravagance of idea — no laborious research after simile and metaphor, no display of pomp and inflated expression: the thought seems to arise from the moment, and the words appear to be suggested by the circumstances which pass under the eye of the spectator." With the hindsight of the historian one may interpret "natural and characteristic" to mean direct and immediate in identifying the hero and the villain, and the comments upon "laborious research after simile and metaphor" to express weariness at the efforts of the verse drama to give poetic grandeur to characters and emotional depth to their motives. Apparently the reviewer and the audience were tired of words that many of them could not understand. They wanted action, with just enough words to explain what was going on. In *A Tale of Mystery* the dialogue drives always forward; except for some wordplay for laughs, the dialogue exhibits no subtlety, irony, side thrusts, or discussion of motives and states of mind.

The play is almost a pantomime. Stage directions tell the actors to express meanings in poses, stares, grimaces, and gestures. When Montano enters and recognizes the villain, music, grimaces, and gestures define the situation: "Music loud and discordant at the moment the eye of Montano catches the figure of Romaldi; at which Montano starts with terror and indignation. He then assumes the eye and attitude of menace, which Romaldi returns. The music ceases." Then Montano expresses in rather feeble speech the feelings that have just been revealed in action: "Can it be possible!" A noisy audience in the pit could follow this play without hearing the lines.

The play was produced at Covent Garden, where the law did not require music; but in the burlettas at the minor theatres playwrights had discovered uses for the music they were forced to include. *A Tale of Mystery* uses music to create the mood of the play; music expresses "discontent and alarm" before the characters enter the scene. It accompanies all actions throughout the play to guide and heighten the feelings of the audience. Music "to express pain and disorder" accompanies the entrance of the villain; "Music of doubt and terror" accompanies his soliloquy when Bonamo's suspicions are aroused. When Selina shrieks, the music "likewise shrieks." Perhaps the orchestra was trusted to strike the proper chords for such emotions. Scenic devices work with music to take the place of poetry in creating gaiety or terror. As the play approaches its climax, "The increasing storm of lightning, thunder, hail, and rain, becomes terrible. Suitable music." Perhaps this storm was intended also to suggest Providence in pursuit of justice; at the climax, the villain enters "with terror, pursued, as it were, by heaven and earth."

These and other features of the play became standard in melodrama. The characters are so simplified that they are entirely white or black, heroic or villainous. There is a "straight" hero, Stephano, who is simple, handsome, and stalwart, but he takes little part in the action except as a suitable match for Selina. The active hero is Francisco, upright, spotless, compassionate, wronged and pitiful, but romantically generous. Romaldi and his accomplice, Malvoglio, stand for ruthless villainy, until it is time for Romaldi, trapped and in terror, to express remorse. The moods of the play are likewise white or black, sentimental expressions of innocence, pity, and remorse, or violent expressions of rage, revenge, and menace. The heroine is a helpless orphan, dependent upon her uncle; she discovers the "secret of her birth" and a father during the play, but she has no mother. As an aid to pathos, nearly all later heroines of melodramas are orphans. Domestic themes appear in Stephano's and Selina's duty to Bonamo and their defiance of this duty only in the name of love. Preparations for the wedding include the broad humor of puns and clowning. Virtue triumphant in a happy ending, in spite of seemingly certain disaster, became an essential feature in the flood of melodramas that followed *A Tale of Mystery*.

A TALE OF MYSTERY

A Mélo-Drame In Two Acts
by
THOMAS HOLCROFT

First performed at the Theatre Royal, Covent Garden, November 13, 1802.

Cast of Characters

BONAMO	PIERO
ROMALDI	EXEMPT
FRANCISCO	SELINA
STEPHANO	FIAMETTA
MONTANO	GARDENERS, PEASANTS, MUSICIANS,
MICHELLI	DANCERS, ARCHERS
MALVOGLIO	

ACT I.

A hall in the house of Bonamo, with two side doors, and folding doors in the back scene: a table, pen, ink, and paper, chairs, etc. Music to express discontent and alarm.

Enter Selina and Fiametta.

Sel. You seem hurried, Fiametta.

Fiam. Hurried, truly! Yes, yes, and you'll be hurried too.

Sel. I?

Fiam. Fine news!

Sel. Of what kind?

Fiam. A very bad kind. The Count Romaldi—

Sel. (*Alarmed*) What of him?

Fiam. Is coming.

Sel. When?

Fiam. This evening.

Sel. Heavens! What can he want?

Fiam. Want? He wants mischief. We all know he wants you to marry his son, because you're a rich heiress.

Sel. Surely, my uncle will never consent?

Fiam. Your uncle and all Savoy fear him.

Bona. (*Calling without*) Fiametta!

Fiam. I am here, sir.

Bona. But I want you here.

Fiam. Lord, sir, I am busy.

Sel. Go, run to my uncle.

Fiam. It's a shame that he should not think of marrying you to his own son, when he knows how dearly you love each other.

Sel. It is the excellence of my dear uncle's heart, that disdains the appearance of self-interest.

Fiam. So, rather than be blamed himself, he'll make you and I and everybody miserable! But I'll talk to him.

Bona. (*Without*) Fiametta, I say!

Fiam. Coming! (*Going*) He shall hear of it. I'm in the proper cue. He knows I'm right, and I'll not spare him. *Exit, talking.*

Hunting music. Enter Stephano, with his fowling-piece, net, and game.

Sel. Why are you so late, Stephano? I had a thousand alarms.

Steph. Forgive me, dear Selina. The pursuit of game led me too far among the mountains.

Sel. Do you know — ?

Steph. What?

Sel. I almost dread to tell you. Count Romaldi is coming.

Steph. Romaldi!

Sel. I shudder, when I recollect the selfishness of his views, and the violence of his character.

Steph. Add, the wickedness of his heart.

Music, to express chattering contention.
Enter Bonamo and Fiametta.

Fiam. I tell you again, sir, it is uncharitable, it is cruel, it is hard-hearted in you to give any such orders.

Bona. And I tell you they shall be obeyed. Have not I a right to do as I please in my own house?

Fiam. No, sir, you have no right to do wrong anywhere.

Steph. What is the dispute, sir?

Fiam. He has ordered me to turn the poor Francisco out of doors, because, forsooth, the house is not large enough to hold this Count Romaldi.

Sel. Think, my dear uncle, how grateful and kind is his heart.

Steph. And that he is a man of misfortune.

Bona. Folly and misfortune are twins: nobody can tell one from the other. He has got footing here, and you seem all determined he shall keep it.

Sel. I own I am interested in his favor. His manners are so mild!

Steph. His eye so expressive!

Sel. His behaviour so proper!

Fiam. I'll be bound he is of genteel parentage!

Bona. Who told you so?

Fiam. Not he, himself, for certain, because, poor creature, he is dumb. But only observe his sorrowful looks. What it is I don't know, but there is something on his mind so —

Bona. You are a fool!

Fiam. Fool or not, I have served you faithfully these three-and-twenty years; so you may turn me out of doors at last, if you please.

Bona. I?

Fiam. Yes; for if you turn Francisco out, I'll never enter them again.

Bona. You certainly know more concerning this man?

Fiam. Since it must be told, I do.

Bona. Then speak.

Fiam. It is quite a tragedy!

Bona. Indeed! Let us hear.

Fiam. It is now seven or eight years ago, when, you having sent me to Chamberry, I was coming home. It was almost dark; everything was still; I was winding along the dale, and the rocks were all as it were turning black. Of a sudden, I heard cries! A man was murdering! I shook from head to foot! Presently the cries died away; and I beheld two bloody men, with their daggers in their hands, stealing off under the crags at the foot of the mill. I stood like a stone, for I was frightened out of my wits! So I thought I heard groans; and, *afeared* as I was, I had the sense to think they must come from the poor murdered creature. So I listened, and followed my ears, and presently I saw this very man —

Sel. Francisco?

Fiam. Weltering in his blood! To be sure I screamed and called loud enough; for what could I do by myself? So presently my cries *was* heard; and honest Michelli, the miller, with his man, came running.

Bona. I now remember the tale. The poor man recovered, and everybody praised Michelli.

Fiam. So they ought; he is an honest good soul! What then, sir, can you suppose I thought, when about a week ago, I again saw Francisco's *apparition* standing before me, making signs that he was famished with hunger and thirst? I knew him at once, and he soon bethought himself of me. If you had *seen* his clasped hands, and his thankful looks, and his dumb notes, and his signs of joy at having found me! — While I have a morsel, he shall never want. I'll hire him a cottage; I'll wait upon him; I'll work for him; so turn him out of doors, if you have the heart.

Steph. Fiametta, you wrong my father.

Bona. I'll hear his story from himself.

Fiam. He can't speak.

Bona. But he can write.

Fiam. I'll warrant him. I'm sure he's a gentleman.

Bona. Bring him here: if he prove himself an honest man, I am his friend.

Fiam. I know that, or you should be no master of mine. *Exit.*

Steph. His kind attentions to Selina are singular.

Sel. Every morning I find him waiting for me with fresh gathered flowers, which he offers with such modest yet affectionate looks!

Fiametta returns with Francisco, the latter poor in appearance, but clean, with a reserved, placid, and dignified air.

Bona. Come near, friend. You understand his gestures, Fiametta; so stay where you are.

Fiam. I intend it.

Bona. (*To himself*) He has a manly form! a

benevolent eye! (*Aloud*) Sit down, sir. Leave us, my children. (*Francisco suddenly rises, as Stephano and Selina offer to go, brings them back, and intreats they may remain*) Since he desires it, stay. — There is pen, ink, and paper: when you cannot give answer by signs, write, but be strict to the truth. (*Francisco, with dignity, points to heaven and his heart*) Who are you? (*Francisco writes; and Stephano, standing behind him, takes up the paper and reads the answers*)

Fran. "A noble Roman!"

Bona. Your family? —

Fran. (*Gives a sudden sign of Forbear! and writes*) "Must not be known."

Bona. Why?

Fran. "It is disgraced."

Bona. By you? (*Francisco gesticulates*)

Fiam. (*Interpreting*) No, no, no!

Bona. Who made you dumb?

Fran. "The Algerines."

Bona. How came you in their power?

Fran. "By treachery."

Bona. Do you know the traitors? (*Francisco gesticulates*)

Fiam. (*Eagerly*) He does! he does!

Bona. Who are they?

Fran. "The same who stabbed me among the rocks." (*A general expression of horror*)

Bona. Name them.

Fran. (*Gesticulates violently, denoting painful recollection; then writes*) "Never!"

Bona. Are they known by me?

Fiam. (*Interpreting*) They are! They are!

Bona. Are they rich?

Fran. "Rich and powerful."

Bona. Astonishing! Your refusal to name them gives strange suspicions. I must know more; tell me all, or quit my house.

Music to express pain and disorder. Enter Piero.

Pier. Count Romaldi, sir. (*Francisco starts up, struck with alarm*)

Steph. So soon!

Bona. Show him up.

Pier. He's here.

Similar music. Romaldi suddenly enters, as Francisco is attempting to pass the door: they start back at the sight of each other. Romaldi recovers himself; and Francisco, in an agony of mind, leaves the room.

Bona. What is all this! — Where is he gone? — Call him back, Fiametta.

Exeunt Fiametta and Stephano, both regarding Romaldi with dislike.

Rom. (*With forced ease*) At length, my good friend, I am here. I have long promised myself the pleasure of seeing you. Your hand. How hearty you look! And your lovely niece! Her father's picture!

Bona. Rather her mother's.

Rom. My son will adore her. In two days I expect him here. I have serious business to communicate.

Sel. (*To her uncle*) Permit me to retire, sir.

Bona. (*Tenderly*) Go, my child; go.

Sel. (*Aside*) Grant, oh merciful Heaven, I may not fall a sacrifice to avarice.   *Exit.*

Bona. And now your pleasure, Count?

Rom. Nay, I imagine, you can guess my errand. You know my friendship for my son, who, let me tell you, is your great admirer. The care you have bestowed upon your niece, her education, mind and manners, and the faithful guardian you have been, both of her wealth and person, well deserve praise.

Bona. If I have done my duty, I am greatly fortunate.

Rom. She is a lovely young lady, and you are not ignorant of my son's passion; to which your duty towards your niece must make you a friend. I therefore come, with open frankness, to propose their union.

Bona. And I, with equal candor, must tell you, I can give no answer.

Rom. (*Haughtily affecting surprise*) No answer?

Bona. Your rank and wealth make the proposal flattering; but there is a question still more serious.

Rom. (*In the same tone*) What can that be?

Bona. One which my niece only can resolve.

Rom. Inexperience like hers should have no opinion.

Bona. How, my lord? Drag the bride, by force, to that solemn altar, where, in the face of Heaven, she is to declare her choice is free?

Rom. Mere ceremonies!

Bona. Ceremonies! Bethink yourself; lest marriage become a farce, libertinism a thing to laugh at, and adultery itself a finable offence!

Rom. Ay, ay; you are a moralist, a conscientious man. Your son is reported to have designs on Selina.

Bona. My lord!

Rom. No anger: I speak as a friend. Her fortune is tempting; but you disdain to be influenced. The wealth and rank of our family —

Bona. Surpass mine. True; still my niece, I say, must be consulted.

Rom. Indeed! (*Sternly*) Then my alliance, it seems, is refused?

Bona. By no means: I have neither the right to refuse nor to accept. If Selina —

Re-enter Selina with a letter.

Sel. (*Presenting it to Bonamo*) From the unfortunate Francisco.

Rom. What, that strange fellow I met as I came in?

Sel. (*Aside*) He knows his name!

Rom. I forgot to ask you how he got admittance here?

Sel. (*With marked displeasure*) I should hope, my lord, there would always be some charitable door open to the unfortunate!

Rom. (*With courteous resentment*) I address your uncle, lovely lady.

Bona. When you came in, he was relating his adventures, which have been strange.

Rom. (*Retaining himself*) And are you, my friend, simple enough to believe such tales?

Sel. What tales, my lord?

Bona. The proofs are convincing! The mutilations he has suffered; the wounds he received, not a league from hence; the —

Rom. (*Alarmed*) Did he name — ?

Bona. Who? The monsters that gave them? — No; but they are not unknown to him.

Rom. That — that is fortunate.

Bona. I was amazed to learn —

Sel. That they are rich and powerful. But I forget: the story can have no interest for you.

Rom. (*Eagerly*) You mistake: I — (*Recollecting himself*) my feelings are as keen as yours.

Bona. But what has he written? (*Offers to open the letter*)

Rom. If you will take my advice, you will not read. Doubtless he has more complaints, more tales, more favors to request. Be kind and hospitable; but do not be a dupe.

Bona. Of which, I own, there is danger.

Rom. (*Seizing the letter, which Bonamo carelessly holds*) Then let me guard you against it.

Sel. (*After continually watching and suspecting Romaldi, snatches the letter back; while he, remarking her suspicions, is confused*) This letter, my lord, was given in charge to me; I promised to bring an answer, and I respectfully intreat my uncle will read it.

Bona. Well, well. (*Reads*) "Friend of humanity, should I remain, the peace of your family might be disturbed. I therefore go; but earnestly intreat you will neither think me capable of falsehood nor ingratitude. — Wherever I am, my wishes and my heart will be here. — Farewell." He shall not go.

Rom. Why not? He owns the peace of your family may be disturbed.

Bona. Fly, Selina; tell him I require, I request, him to sleep here to-night, that I may speak with him to-morrow.

Rom. (*Aside*) That must not be.

Sel. Thanks, my dear uncle! you have made me happy. *Exit in haste.*

Confused music. Enter Piero.

Bona. What now, Piero?

Pier. Signor Montano is below.

Rom. (*Alarmed and aside*) Montano!

Bona. I'm very glad of it, for I wanted his advice. (*To Romaldi*) The best of men!

Pier. Please to come up, sir.

Rom. With your permission, I will retire.

Enter Montano. Music plays alarmingly, but piano when he enters and while he stays.

Mon. I beg pardon, good sir, but —
> *Music loud and discordant at the moment the eye of Montano catches the figure of Romaldi; at which Montano starts with terror and indignation. He then assumes the eye and attitude of menace, which Romaldi returns. The music ceases.*

Can it be possible!

Rom. (*Returning his threatening looks*) Sir!

Mon. You here!

Rom. Not having the honor of your acquaintance, I know not why my presence should please or displease you.

Mon. (*After a look of stern contempt at Romaldi, and addressing Bonamo*) Good night, my friend; I will see you to-morrow.
> *Exit suddenly. Hurrying music, but half piano.*

Bona. (*Calling*) Nay, but signor! Signor Montano! Are the people all mad? Fiametta!

Fiam. (*Without*) Sir!

Bona. Run, overtake him; and say I must speak with him. (*Music ceases*) Excuse me for going. (*To Romaldi*)

Rom. Why in such haste? I have heard of this Montano: a credulous person, a relator of strange stories.

Bona. Signor Montano credulous! There is not in all Savoy a man of sounder understanding. Good night, my lord; I will send your servant: that door leads to your bedroom. Call for whatever you want; the house is at your command.
> *Exit with looks of suspicion. Music of doubt and terror.*

Rom. What am I to think? How act? — The arm of Providence seems raised to strike! — Am I become a coward? Shall I betray, rather than defend myself? I am not yet an idiot.

Threatening music. Enter the Count's servant, Malvoglio, who observes his master. Music ceases.

Mal. Your lordship seems disturbed.
Rom. Francisco is here.
Mal. I saw him.
Rom. And did not your blood freeze?
Mal. I was sorry.
Rom. For what?
Mal. That my dagger had missed its aim.
Rom. We are in his power.
Mal. He is in ours.
Rom. What are your thoughts?
Mal. What are yours, my lord?
Rom. Guess them.
Mal. Executioners!
Rom. Infamy!
Mal. Racks!
Rom. Maledictions!
Mal. From all which a blow may yet deliver us.

Selina, entering and hiding behind the door, opposite to the chamber of Romaldi, overhears them.

Rom. 'Tis a damning crime!
Mal. Were it the first.
Rom. Where is he to sleep?
Mal. There! (*Pointing to the chamber opposite to Romaldi's*)
Sel. (*Behind the door*) They mean Francisco!
Rom. Obstinate fool! Since he will stay —
Mal. He must die.
Sel. The monsters!
Rom. I heard a noise.
Mal. (*Looking towards the folding doors*) He's coming.
Rom. Let us retire and concert —
Mal. Then, at midnight—
Rom. When he sleeps —
Mal. He'll wake no more!
Exeunt to the chamber of the Count.

The stage dark: soft music, but expressing first pain and alarm, then the successive feelings of the scene. Fiametta enters, with Francisco and a lamp, which she places on the table. She regards him with compassion, points to his bedroom, then curtsies with kindness and respect, and retires; he returning her kindness. He seats himself as if to write, rises, takes the lamp, looks round with apprehension, goes to the chamber-door of Romaldi, starts away with horror, recovers himself, again places the lamp on the table, and sits down to write. The door of Romaldi opens; Malvoglio half appears, watching Francisco; but, as he turns, again retires.

Enter Selina, who gently pulls the sleeve of Francisco: he starts, but seeing her, his countenance expands with pleasure. Music pauses on a half close.

Sel. (*In a low voice*) Dare not to sleep! I will be on the watch! Your life is in danger!
Exit. Music continues tremendous.

Francisco, greatly agitated, draws a pair of pistols, lays them on the table, and seats himself to consider if he should write more. Romaldi and Malvoglio appear. Music suddenly stops.

Rom. (*To Malvoglio*) Watch that entrance. (*To Francisco*) Wretched fool! Why are you here?

> *Music: terror, confusion, menace, command. Francisco starts up, seizes his pistols, points them towards Romaldi and Malvoglio, and commands the former, by signs, to read the paper that lies on the table. Music ceases.*

Rom. (*Reads*) "Repent; leave the house. Oblige me not to betray you. Force me not on self-defence." Fool! Do you pretend to command? (*Throws him a purse*) We are two. Take that, and fly. (*Music. Francisco, after a look of compassionate appeal, spurns it from him, and commands them to go. After which, sudden pause of music. — Aside to Malvoglio*) I know him; he will not fire.

Music. They draw their daggers; he at first avoids them; at length they each seize him by the arm, and are in the attitude of threatening to strike, when the shrieks of Selina, joining the music, which likewise shrieks, suddenly brings Bonamo, Stephano, and Servants, through the folding doors.

Sel. Uncle! Stephano! Murder!
> *Romaldi and Malvoglio, at hearing the noise behind, quit Francisco, and feign to be standing on self-defence. — Music ceases.*

Bona. What mean these cries? What strange proceedings are here?
Sel. They are horrible.
Bona. Why, my lord, are these daggers drawn against a man under my protection?
Rom. Self-defence is a duty. Is not his pistol levelled at my breast?
Bona. (*To Francisco*) Can it be? (*Francisco inclines his head*) Do you thus repay hospitality?
Sel. Sir, you are deceived: his life was threatened.
Rom. (*Sternly*) Madam —
Sel. I fear you not! I watched, I overheard you!

Bona. Is this true?

Rom. No.

Sel. By the purity of heaven, yes! Behind that door, I heard the whole; Francisco must quit the house, or be murdered.

Rom. (*To Bonamo sternly*) I expect, sir, my word will not be doubted.

Bona. My lord, there is one thing of which I cannot doubt: the moment you appeared, terror was spread through my house. Men's minds are troubled at the sight of you: they seem all to avoid you. Good seldom accompanies mystery; I therefore now decidedly reply to your proposal, that my niece cannot be the wife of your son; and must further add, you oblige me to decline the honor of your present visit.

Rom. (*With threatening haughtiness*) Speak the truth, old man, and own you are glad to find a pretext to colour refusal, and gratify ambition. Selina and Stephano; you want her wealth, and mean in that way to make it secure. But beware! Dare to pursue your project, and tremble at the consequences! To-morrow, before ten o'clock, send your written consent; or dread what shall be done.

 Exeunt Romaldi and Malvoglio: appropriate music.

Bona. Dangerous and haughty man! But his threats are vain; my doubts are removed; Selina shall not be the victim of mean precaution, and cowardly fears. I know your wishes, children. Let us retire. (*To his Servants*) Make preparations for rejoicing: early to-morrow, Stephano and Selina shall be affianced. (*Music of sudden joy, while they kneel*)

Steph. My kind father!

Sel. Dearest, best of guardians! (*Music pauses*)

Bona. Francisco shall partake the common happiness.

Fiam. (*As they are all retiring*) Dear, dear! I shan't sleep to-night.

 Exeunt: Bonamo expressing friendship to all, which all return, Francisco with joy equal to that of the lovers. Sweet and cheerful music, gradually dying away.

 End of the First Act.

Act II.

Scene 1.

A beautiful garden and pleasure grounds, with garlands, festoons, love devices and every preparation for a marriage festival. Joyful music. First and Second Gardeners, Piero and his Companions, all busy.

Pier. Come, come; bestir yourselves! The company will soon be here.

First Gard. Well; let them come: all is ready.

Pier. It has a nice look, by my fackins!

First Gard. I believe it has! thanks to me.

Pier. Thanks to *you?*

Second Gard. And me.

Pier. And *you?* Here's impudence! I say it is thanks to me.

First and Second Gard. You, indeed!

Pier. Why, surely, you'll not have the face to pretend my incapacity?

First Gard. Yours?

Second Gard. Yours?

Pier. Mine! mine!

 Enter Stephano.

Steph. What is the matter, my honest friends?

First Gard. Why, here's Mr. Piero pretends to dispute his claim to all that has been done.

Second Gard. Yes; and says everything is owing to his incapacity.

First Gard. Now I maintain the incapacity was all my own. (*To Stephano*) Saving and excepting yours, sir.

Second Gard. And mine.

First Gard. Seeing you gave the first orders.

Pier. But *wasn't* they given to me, sir? Didn't you say to me, Piero, says you —

Steph. (*Interrupting*) Ay, ay; each man has done his part: all is excellent, and I thank you kindly. Are the villagers invited?

Pier. Invited! They no sooner heard of the wedding than they were half out of their wits! There will be such dancing and sporting! Then the music! Little Nanine, with her hurdy-gurdy; her brother, with the tabor and pipe; the blind fiddler, the lame piper, I and my jew's harp! such a band!

Steph. Bravo! Order everything for the best.

Pier. But who is to order? Please to tell me that, sir?

Steph. Why, you.

Pier. There! (*To his companions*) Mind! I am to order! Mark that!

Steph. You shall be major-domo for the day.

Pier. You hear. I am to be — do — drum-major for the day!

Steph. Selina is coming. To your posts.

Music. They hurry each to his garland, and conceal themselves by the trees and bushes.

Enter Bonamo, Selina, and Fiametta. Music ceases.

Bona. (*Looking round*) Vastly well, upon my word!

Sel. (*Tenderly*) I fear, Stephano, you have slept but little?

Bona. (*Gaily*) Sleep indeed! He had something better to think of. Come, come; we'll breakfast here in the bower. Order it, Fiametta.

Fiam. Directly, sir. (*She goes, and returns with the Servants; aiding them to arrange the breakfast table*)

Bona. How reviving to age is the happiness of the young! And yet — (*Sighs*) — thou hast long been an orphan, Selina; it has more than doubled thy fortune, which was great at my brother's sudden death. Would thou hadst less wealth, or I more!

Sel. And why, my dear uncle?

Bona. Evil tongues — this Romaldi —

Steph. Forget him.

Sel. Would that were possible! his menace — before ten o'clock — oh! that the hour were over!

Bona. Come, come; we'll not disturb our hearts with fears. To breakfast, and then to the notary. I forgot Francisco; why is he not here?

Sel. Shall I bring him?

Bona. Do you go, Fiametta.

Fiam. Most willingly.

Bona. Come, sit down. (*They seat themselves. Sweet music. Piero peeps from behind a shrub. Stephano gives a gentle clap with his hands, and the Peasants all rise from their hiding-places, and suspend their garlands in a picturesque group, over Bonamo, Selina, and Stephano. Music ceases*)

Pier. What say you to that, now?

Bona. Charming! charming!

Pier. I hope I am not made a major for nothing.

Bona. (*To Francisco, who enters with Fiametta*) Come, sir, please to take your seat.

Pier. (*To Stephano*) Shall the sports begin? (*Stephano gives an affirmative sign*) Here! dancers! pipers! strummers! thrummers! to your places. This bench is for the band of music — mount.

Here the dancing, which should be of the gay, comic, and grotesque kind; with droll attitudes, gesticulations, and bounds, in imitation of the mountaineers, the goats they keep, etc., that is, the humorous dancing of the Italian peasants. In the midst of the rejoicing the clock strikes; the dancing suddenly ceases; the changing music inspires alarm and dismay. Enter Malvoglio. He stops in the middle of the stage; the

company start up; Francisco, Stephano, Selina, and Bonamo, all with more or less terror. The Peasants, alarmed and watching: the whole, during a short pause, forming a picture. Malvoglio then presents a letter to Bonamo, with a malignant assurance, and turns away, gratified by the consternation he has occasioned: with which audacious air and feeling, he retires. While Bonamo opens the letter and reads with great agitation, the music expresses confusion and pain of thought; then ceases.

Bona. Oh, shame! dishonor! treachery!

Steph. My father! —

Sel. My uncle!

Fiam. What treachery? (*Francisco is in an attitude of despair*)

Bona. No more of love or marriage! no more of sports, rejoicing, and mirth.

Steph. Good Heavens!

Sel. My guardian! my friend! my uncle!

Bona. (*Repelling her*) I am not your uncle.

Sel. Sir!

Steph. Not?

Bona. She is the child of crime! of adultery. (*A general stupefaction: the despair of Francisco at its height*)

Steph. 'Tis malice, my father.

Bona. Read.

Steph. The calumny of Romaldi!

Bona. (*Seriously*) Read.

Steph. (*Reads*) "Selina is not your brother's daughter. To prove I speak nothing but the truth, I send you the certificate of her baptism."

Bona. 'Tis here — authenticated. Once more read.

Steph. (*Reads*) "May the 11th, 1584, at ten o'clock this evening was baptized Selina Bianchi, the daughter of Francisco Bianchi." (*Francisco utters a cry, and falls on the seat*)

Sel. Is it possible! my father! (*Francisco opens his arms, and Selina falls on his neck*)

Steph. Amazement!

Bona. Sinful man! Not satisfied with having dishonored my brother, after claiming my pity, would you aid in making me contract a most shameful alliance? Begone! you and the offspring of your guilt.

Steph. Selina is innocent. (*Francisco confirms it*)

Bona. Her father is — a wretch! Once more, begone. (*Francisco during this dialogue had held his daughter in his arms; he now rises with a sense of injury and is leading her away*) Hold, miserable man. (*To himself*) Houseless — penniless — without bread — without asylum — must she perish because her father has been wicked? (*To Francisco*) Take this purse, conceal your shame, and, when 'tis empty, let me know your hiding place. (*Francisco expresses gratitude, but rejects the purse*)

Sel. (*With affection*) Spare your benefits, sir, till you think we deserve them.

Bona. Poor Selina!

Steph. (*Eagerly*) What say you, sir?

Bona. Nothing — let them begone.

Sel. Stephano! farewell.

Steph. She shall not go! or — I will follow.

Bona. And forsake your father! ungrateful boy! (*To Francisco*) Begone, I say. Let me never see you more. (*To the Peasants*) Confine that frantic youth.

> *Violent distracted music. Stephano endeavours to force his way to Selina. Fiametta passionately embraces her; and by gesture reproaches Bonamo, who persists, yet is tormented by doubt. Stephano escapes, and suddenly hurries Selina forward, to detain her; after violent efforts, they are again forced asunder; and, as they are retiring on opposite sides, with struggles and passion, the Scene closes.*

Scene 2.

The house of Bonamo. Bonamo; Stephano, brought on by the Peasants, who then leave the room.

Bona. Disobedient, senseless boy!

Steph. (*Exhausted*) Selina! give me back Selina, or take my life!

Bona. Forbear these complaints.

Steph. She is the woman I love.

Bona. Dare you —

Steph. None but she shall be my wife.

Bona. Your wife!

Steph. To the world's end I'll follow her!

Bona. And quit your father? Now, when age and infirmity bend him to the grave?

Steph. We will return to claim your blessing.

Bona. Stephano! I have loved you like a father; beware of my malediction.

Steph. When a father's malediction is unjust, Heaven is deaf.

Enter Fiametta, retaining her anger

Fiam. Very well! It's all very right! But you will see how it will end!

Bona. (*To Stephano*) I no longer wonder Count Romaldi should advise me to drive such a wretch from my house.

Fiam. Count Romaldi is himself a wretch.

Bona. Fiametta! —

Fiam. (*Overcome by her passion*) I say it again: a vile wicked wretch! and has written —

Bona. (*Imperiously*) The truth. The certificate is incontestable.

Fiam. I would not for all the world be guilty of your sins.

Bona. Woman!

Fiam. I don't care for you. I loved you this morning; I would have lost my life for you, but you are grown wicked.

Bona. Will you be silent?

Fiam. Is it not wickedness to turn a sweet innocent helpless young creature out of doors, one who has behaved with such tenderness, and leave her at last to starve? Oh, it is abominable!

Bona. Once more, hold your tongue.

Fiam. I won't! I can't! Poor Stephano! And do you think he'll forbear to love her? If he did, I should hate him! But he'll make his escape. You may hold him to-day, but he'll be gone to-morrow. He'll overtake and find his dear forlorn Selina; and they will marry, and live in poverty: but they will work, and eat their morsel with a good conscience; while you will turn from your dainties with an aching heart!

Bona. For the last time, I warn you —

Fiam. I know the worst: I have worked for you all the prime of my youth; and now you'll serve me as you have served the innocent wretched Selina; you'll turn me out of doors. Do it! But I'll not go till I've said out my say: so I tell you again, you are a hard-hearted uncle, an unfeeling father, and an unjust master! Everybody will shun you! You will dwindle out a life of misery, and nobody will pity you, because you don't deserve pity. So now I'll go, as soon as you please.

Enter Signor Montano, hastily. Fiametta and Stephano eagerly attentive.

Mon. What is it I have just heard, my friend? Have you driven away your niece?

Bona. She is not my niece.

Mon. 'Tis true.

Fiam. How?

Mon. But where did you learn that?

Bona. From these papers.

Mon. Who sent them?

Bona. Count Romaldi.

Mon. Count Romaldi is — a villain.

Fiam. There! There!

Steph. You hear, Sir!

Fiam. I hope I shall be believed another time.

Bona. (*Greatly interested*) Silence, woman! — By a man like you such an accusation cannot be made without sufficient proofs.

Mon. You shall have them. Be attentive.

Fiam. I won't breathe! A word shan't escape my lips. (*They press round Montano*)

Mon. Eight years ago, before I had the honor to know you, returning one evening after visiting my friends, I was leisurely ascending the rock of Arpennaz.

Fiam. So, so! The rock of Arpennaz! You hear! But I'll not say a word.

Mon. Two men, wild in their looks and smeared with blood, passed hastily by me, with every appearance of guilt impressed upon their countenances.

Fiam. The very same! Eight years ago! The rock of Arpennaz! The —

Bona. Silence!

Fiam. I'll not say a word. Tell all, sir, I am dumb.

Mon. They had not gone a hundred paces before he, who appeared the master, staggered and fell. I hastened to him: he bled much, and I and his servant supported him to my house. They said they had been attacked by banditti, yet their torn clothes, a deep bite, which the master had on the back of his hand, and other hurts appearing to be given by an unarmed man, made me doubt. Their embarrassment increased suspicion, which was confirmed next day by Michelli, the honest miller of Arpennaz, who, the evening before, near the spot from which I saw these men ascend, had succoured a poor wretch, dreadfully cut and mangled.

Fiam. It's all true! 'Twas I! I myself! My cries made Michelli come! Eight years —

Bona. Again?

Fiam. I've done.

Mon. I no longer doubted I had entertained men of blood, and hastened to deliver them up to justice; but, when I returned, they had flown, having left a purse, and this letter.

Bona. (*Having seen it*) 'Tis the hand of Romaldi.

Mon. Imagine my surprise and indignation, yesterday evening, when I here once more beheld the assassin! I could not disguise my emotion; and I left you with such abruptness to give immediate information. The archers are now in pursuit: I have no doubt they will soon secure him, as they already have secured his accomplice.

Steph. Malvoglio?

Mon. Yes, who has confessed —

Steph. What?

Mon. That the real name of this pretended Romaldi is Bianchi.

Bona. Just heaven! Francisco's brother!

Mon. Whose wife this wicked brother loved. Privately married, and she pregnant, Francisco put her under the protection of his friend here in Savoy.

Steph. My uncle! His sudden death occasioned the mystery.

Mon. But the false Romaldi decoyed Francisco into the power of the Algerines, seized his estates, and, finding he had escaped, attempted to assassinate him.

Fiam. Now are you convinced! He would not 'peach his brother of abomination! (*Raising her clasped hands*) I told you Francisco was an angel! but, for all you know me so well, I'm not to be believed.

Bona. You are not to be silenced.

Fiam. No; I'm not. Francisco is an angel, Selina is an angel, Stephano is an angel: they shall be married, and all make one family, of which, if you repent, you shall be received into the bosom.

Bona. (*Slowly, earnestly*) Pray, good woman, hold your tongue.

Fiam. Repent, then! Repent! (*Here the distant thunder is heard, and the rising storm perceived*)

Bona. (*To Montano and Stephano*) I do repent!

Fiam. (*Affectionately*) Then I forgive you. (*Sobs*) I won't turn away. You're my master again. (*Kisses his hand and wipes her eyes*)

Bona. But where shall we find Selina, and — ?

Fiam. Oh, I know where!

Steph. (*Eagerly*) Do you?

Fiam. Why, could you think that — (*her heart full*) Follow me! Only follow me.

Exeunt hastily. Thunder heard, while the Scene changes. Music.

Scene 3.

The wild mountainous country called the Nant of Arpennaz; with pines and massy rocks. A rude wooden bridge on a small height thrown from rock to rock; a rugged mill stream a little in the background; the miller's house on the right; a steep ascent by a narrow path to the bridge; a stone or bank to sit on, on the right-hand side. The increasing storm of lightning, thunder, hail, and rain, becomes terrible. Suitable music. Enter Romaldi from the rocks, disguised like a peasant, with terror, pursued, as it were, by heaven and earth.

Rom. Whither fly? Where shield me from pursuit, and death, and ignominy? My hour is come! The fiends that tempted me now tear me. (*Dreadful thunder*) The heavens shoot their fires at me! Save! Spare! Oh spare me. (*Falls on the bank*)

Music, hail, etc. continue; after a pause, he raises his head. More fearful claps of thunder are heard, and he again falls on his face. The storm gradually abates. Pause in the music. A very distant voice is heard: Holloa! *Music continues. He half rises, starts, and runs from side to side, looking and listening. Music ceases. Voice again:* Holloa!

Rom. They are after me! Some one points me out! No den, no cave, can hide me! (*Looks the way he came*) I cannot return that way, I cannot. It is the place of blood! A robbed and wretched brother! 'Tis his blood, by which I am covered! Ay! There! There have I been driven for shelter! Under those very rocks! Oh, that they would open! Cover me, earth! Cover my crimes! Cover my shame!

Falls motionless again. Music of painful remorse; then changes to the cheerful pastorale, etc. Michelli is seen coming toward the bridge, which he crosses, stopping to look round and speak; then speaks as he descends by the rugged narrow path, and then in the front of the stage.

Mich. (*On the bridge*) 'Tis a fearful storm! One's very heart shrinks! It makes a poor mortal think of his sins — and his danger.

Rom. (*After listening*) Danger! What? — Is it me? (*Listening*)

Mich. (*Descending*) Every thunder clap seems to flash vengeance in his face!

Rom. I am known; or must be! — Shall I yield; or shall I — (*Points his pistol at Michelli, then shrinks*) More murder!

Mich. (*In the front of the stage*) At such terrible times, a clear conscience is better than kingdoms of gold mines.

Rom. (*In hesitation whether he shall or shall not murder*) How to act?

Mich. (*Perceiving Romaldi, who conceals his pistol*) Now, friend!

Rom. Now, miller!

Mich. (*Observing his agitation*) You look —

Rom. How do I look? (*Fearing, and still undetermined*)

Mich. I — What have you there?

Rom. Where?

Mich. Under your coat.

Rom. (*Leaving the pistol in his inside pocket, and showing his hands*) Nothing.

Mich. Something is the matter with you.

Rom. (*Sudden emotion to shoot: restrained*) I am tired.

Mich. Come in, then, and rest yourself.

Rom. Thank you! (*Moved*) Thank you!

Mich. Whence do you come?

Rom. From — the neighbourhood of Geneva.

Mich. (*As if with meaning*) Did you pass through Sallancha?

Rom. (*Alarmed*) Sallancha? Why do you ask?

Mich. You have heard of what has happened?

Rom. Where?

Mich. There! At Sallancha! One Count Romaldi —

Rom. What of him?

Mich. (*Observing*) Do you know him?

Rom. I — How should a poor — ?

Mich. Justice is at his heels. He has escaped: but he'll be taken. The executioner will have him.

Rom. (*Shudders*) Ay?

Mich. As sure as you are here.

Rom. (*Aside*) All men hate me! Why should I spare him?

Mich. I saved the good Francisco.

Rom. (*Gazing steadfastly at him*) You! Was it you?

Mich. I.

Rom. Then — live.

Mich. Live?

Rom. To be rewarded.

Mich. I'd have done the same for you.

Rom. Live — live!

Mich. I will, my friend, as long as I can; and when I die, I'll die with an honest heart.

Rom. Miserable wretch!

Mich. Who?

Rom. That Count Romaldi.

Mich. Why ay! Unless he is a devil, he is miserable indeed. (*Music, quick march*) He'll be taken; for, look, yonder are the archers. (*They cross the bridge*)

Rom. (*Fearing Michelli knows him*) What then? Where is Romaldi?

Mich. How should I know?

Rom. (*Aside*) Does he dissemble? They are here! I am lost! (*Retires. Music. The Archers come forward*)

Mich. Good day, worthy Sirs.

Exempt. Honest miller, good day. We are in search of Count Romaldi, whom we are to take, dead or alive. Do you know his person?

Mich. No.

Rom. (*Aside, and out of sight of the Archers*) Thanks, merciful heaven!

Exempt. (*Reads*) "Five feet eight" (*The description must be that of the actor's voice, size and person: to which add:*) "with a large scar on the back of the right hand."

Rom. (*Thrusting his hand in his bosom*) 'Twill betray me!

Exempt. 'Twas a bite! The wretch Malvoglio has deposed that good Francisco is the brother of the vile Romaldi.

Mich. How!

Exempt. And that Francisco, tho' robbed,

betrayed and mutilated, has endured every misery, and lived in continual dread of steel or poison, rather than bring this monster to the scaffold.

Mich. But he'll come there at last!

Exempt. We are told, he is among these mountains.

Mich. Oh, could I catch him by the collar!

Exempt. Should you meet him, beware: he's not unarmed.

Mich. There is no passing for him or you by this valley after the storm; the mountain torrents are falling. You must go back.

Exempt. Many thanks. We must lose no time.

Mich. Success to you.

Archers re-ascend the hill. Music. Quick march, as when they entered.

Rom. Death! Infamy! Is there no escaping?

Mich. The day declines, and you look —

Rom. How?

Mich. Um — I wish you looked better. Come in; pass the evening here: recover your strength and spirits.

Rom. (*With great emotion, forgetting and holding out his hand*) You are a worthy man.

Mich. I wish to be. (*Feeling Romaldi's hand after shaking*) Zounds! What? Hey?

Rom. (*Concealing his confusion*) A scar —

Mich. On the back of the right hand!

Rom. I have served. A hussar with his sabre gave the cut.

Mich. (*After considering*) Humph! It may be.

Rom. It is.

Mich. At least it *may* be; and the innocent —

Rom. Ay! Might suffer for the guilty.

Mich. (*After looking at him*) Rather than that — I will run all risks. I am alone; my family is at the fair, and cannot be home to-night. But you are a stranger; you want protection —

Rom. (*With great emotion*) I do, indeed!

Mich. You shall have it. Come. Never shall my door be shut against the houseless wretch.   *Exeunt to the house.*

Music expressing dejection. Francisco and Selina approaching the bridge, he points to the Miller's house. Cheerful music; she testifies joy, and admiration of the Miller. They descend, he carefully guiding and aiding her. The Miller, supposed to hear a noise, comes to inquire, sees Francisco, and they run into each other's arms.

Mich. Welcome! A thousand times welcome!

Sel. Ten thousand thanks to the saviour of my father!

Mich. Your father, sweet lady?

Sel. Oh yes! discovered to me by his mortal enemy.

Mich. The monster Romaldi!

Sel. (*Dejectedly*) Alas!

Mich. For your father's sake, for your own sake, welcome both.

Rom. (*Half from the door*) I heard my name!

Mich. (*Leading them to the door, just as Romaldi advances a step*) Come. I have a stranger —

Sel. (*Seeing Romaldi, shrieks*) Ah! (*Francisco falls back and covers his eyes, with agony*)

Mich. How now? (*Romaldi retires*)

Sel. 'Tis he!

Music of hurry, terror, etc. Francisco, putting his hand towards her mouth, enjoins her silence with great eagerness. Michelli, by making the sign of biting his right hand, asks Francisco if it be Romaldi. Francisco turns away without answering. Michelli denotes his conviction it is Romaldi, and hastily ascends to cross the bridge in search of the Archers; Francisco intreats him back in vain. Romaldi, in terror, enters from the house presenting his pistol. Francisco opens his breast for him to shoot if he pleases. Selina falls between them. The whole scene passes in a mysterious and rapid manner. Music suddenly stops.

Rom. No! Too much of your blood is upon my head! Be justly revenged: take mine!

Music continues as Romaldi offers the pistol; which Francisco throws to a distance, and intreats him to fly by the valley. — Romaldi signifies the impossibility, and runs distractedly from side to side: then after Francisco and Selina's intreaties, ascends to cross the bridge. Met at the edge of the hill by an Archer, he is driven back; they struggle on the bridge. The Archer's sword taken by Romaldi; who, again attempting flight, is again met by several Archers. Romaldi maintains a retreating fight. Fiametta, Bonamo, Stephano, Montano, and Peasants follow the Archers. Francisco and Selina, in the greatest agitation, several times throw themselves between the assailants and Romaldi. When the combatants have descended the hill, Romaldi's foot slips, he falls, and Francisco intervenes to guard his body. By this time all the principal characters are near the front. The Archers appear prepared to shoot, and strike with their sabres; when the intreaties and efforts of Francisco and Selina are renewed. The Archers forbear for a moment; and Francisco shields his brother. The music ceases.

Sel. Oh, forbear Let my father's virtues plead for my uncle's errors!

Bon. We will all intreat for mercy; since of mercy we all have need: for his sake, and for our own, may it be freely granted!

The Curtain falls to slow and solemn music.

THE END.

JOHN BALDWIN BUCKSTONE
1802-1879

Luke the Labourer; *or*, The Lost Son
(1826)

John Baldwin Buckstone began his preparation for a career as an apprentice to a lawyer, but, fascinated by the stage, gave up this study to become a strolling player of comedy roles. He first appeared in London in 1827 at the Coburg and the Adelphi, where he played in his own successful melodrama, *Luke the Labourer*. (In previous performances another famous comedian, T. P. Cooke, had played the role of Philip.) He became actor-manager of the Haymarket in 1853 for a period of five years and for various periods afterwards. Because of his taste for melodrama he made up his company with players skilled in the stereotyped roles of this genre, and he was so opposed to departures from the old ways that when Tom Robertson submitted his epoch-making *Society* in 1865 Buckstone rejected it with one word — written across the script — "Rubbish."

Buckstone's career as a playwright began in 1825 with *The Bear-Hunters; or, The Fatal Ravine*, and during the rest of his life he turned out a total of about two hundred plays of various types — chiefly melodramas and farces. Buckstone sometimes based his plays on French originals, as did other writers of farces and melodramas, but he prided himself on the fact that his plays were more than slightly-doctored translations. He sought to make them thoroughly English, and in his prefaces to his published plays discussed his adaptations to native situations. Yet his melodramas follow the formula — with ample stage directions for thrilling action.

Luke the Labourer is a domestic melodrama which exhibits both those features of the melodrama observed in the prototype, *A Tale of Mystery*, and new features that belong to the domestic subtype Buckstone helped establish. In general, the characters are stereotypes. Charles is the "straight" hero who wins Clara in the end; while Clara, of course, is the persecuted heroine (though not an orphan as usual in melodrama). Philip is the active hero whose appearance in the nick of time saves Clara from the Squire, and whose revelation that he is the long-lost son of Wakefield — the typical "secret of his birth!" — insures a happy ending. Philip's nautical lingo is characteristic of the Jolly Jack Tar who dressed in pigtail, blouse, and sailor hat and sang, danced, and performed skits in music halls. To balance the two heroes there are two villains. The Squire is the model villain of melodramas for years to come. That he typifies what Carlyle called the "idle, game-preserving" gentry is clear in his occupation of partridge shooting. Of course, he poses as a kind-hearted landlord to cover his intention of abducting Clara. Luke is the more obvious villain, so identified when he first appears by Clara's shrieks and her explanation that he has a "bad heart." The minor characters Bobby Trot and Jenny are introduced to provide a comic subplot of clowning and singing. Besides the interspersed songs, instrumental music marks important entrances and accompanies the action at stirring moments. When Wakefield returns from jail and rushes into his wife's arms and when Luke enters on "noa business particular," the orchestra is instructed to define their characters; when Luke climbs in the window to murder Philip the music heightens the thrill of danger. Scenic effects also heighten emotion: when the Squire attempts to abduct Clara thunder and lightning make the night scene lurid.

To give length and complexity to a play made up of simple situations and stock characters, Buckstone laid two somewhat episodic plots end to end. The first presents the Squire's attempt to abduct Clara with Philip's entry at its climax; the second treats the long-lost Philip's return, revelation of his identity, and Luke's attempted revenge. Luke's participation in the Squire's plot helps link the two episodes, but with its two climaxes, the play still exhibits the loose structure of early melodramas.

Thus, as Winton Tolles says, *Luke the Labourer* "cut the pattern for native melodrama." The setting in an English village, the local characters (including the gypsies, often seen in England), other features typically English (the song of harvest home, the Squire, Bobby's longing to see London, the ducking of Michael, and Philip as a Jack Tar), and the dialectal forms of speech, all support Buckstone's statement in his preface: "It is *not* taken from the French, but is entirely original."

Furthermore, the play presents some criticism of social conditions in England in 1826. During this period of social turmoil preceding the Reform Bill of 1832, *Luke the Labourer* voiced a protest against injustice to the poor. By implication the play attacks the system of debtors' prisons — for Luke is able to imprison Wakefield for a debt, and the latter has no hope of being released until someone outside the prison pays the amount due. Wakefield, though an honest, hard-working farmer, is nearly destitute. Besides these suggestions, Luke makes a forthright protest against injustice in the most moving speech of the play. Beginning "I ha' summut to say, summut at my tongue's end — it must come out," Luke tells a pitiful story. He was dismissed for drunkenness — though remorseful, repentant, and willing to labor — and was prevented by prejudice from earning a living and by his wife's pride from begging, with the result that his wife died of starvation in his arms. This speech is stark and direct and carries the emotional power of fact — like something Buckstone himself had heard. Perhaps, in working on this section of the play, he was writing from memory, rather than filling in a dramatic pattern. But the mood passed. The author returned to his formula. Luke was the villain, and Buckstone had to make the audience despise him as a drunkard and trouble maker capable of abducting Clara and murdering Philip. Possibly the human quality in Luke's speech stirred the audience for a moment, but in the hurly-burly of performance at the Adelphi and the excitement of two climaxes this "touch of nature" was blurred.

LUKE THE LABOURER;

or,

THE LOST SON

A Domestic Melodrama In Two Acts

by

JOHN BALDWIN BUCKSTONE

First performed at the Adelphi Theatre, Strand, October 17, 1826.

Cast of Characters

SQUIRE CHASE, *lord of the manor*
WAKEFIELD, *a decayed farmer*
CHARLES MAYDEW, *a young farmer*
LUKE THE LABOURER
PHILIP, *a sailor*
BOBBY TROT, *a country lad*
MICHAEL, *an old Gipsy*

DICK, *a postilion*
THOMAS, *landlord of the "King's Head"*
DAME WAKEFIELD
CLARA, *her daughter*
JENNY, *a country girl*
VILLAGERS, SERVANTS, GIPSIES, ETC.

ACT I.

Scene 1.

A village, with distant view of the city of York. — Harvest-carts in the background; a group of villagers discovered, celebrating the Harvest Home. — An alehouse at the side, and Luke seated at the door, smoking, and disregarding their actions.

Chorus.

OUR last load of corn is now in, boys,
'Tis time that our mirth should begin, boys;
For grief would be worse than a sin, boys,
At this our harvest home.
Our labours have now a relief, boys,

So there's bacon and cabbage, and beef, boys;
But a barrel of ale is the chief, boys,
To rule o'er a harvest home.

Enter Charles.

Char. This is all as it should be, my lads; everything is prepared for you in my cottage; but, as I am a bachelor, you must elect the prettiest lass among you to preside; so away with you, and be as happy as you ought.

The villagers go off, singing the burden of the chorus: enter Clara, hastily; on perceiving Charles, she stops.

You appear to be travelling post haste, Clara. I was in hopes we should have had you with us at our harvest home; your absence has disappointed many who have been expecting you anxiously.

Clara. I have to attend to duties, Sir, which should be considered before pleasures, however I might wish to indulge in them.

Char. Sir! — You speak very coolly to me, Clara; have I not known you long enough to be called Charles?

Clara. Superiors should have that distinction, Char——Sir.

Char. Superiors, Clara! — But I see how it is, you are rather ironical to-day.

Clara. Nay, Sir, indeed I did not mean to — to — say anything, Sir; but you are now growing rich, and, I hear, likely to become our landlord — so I thought — I thought — nothing more, indeed, Sir.

Char. Be assured, Clara, it is not through pride that I have offered to purchase your father's cottage of 'Squire Chase: 'tis true, I wish so to do, but I have my reasons for it; and, though I have been so fortunate as to raise myself from a poor farmer's boy to what I now am, I shall never forget that the first week's wages I earned, were paid me by Farmer Wakefield.

Clara. Ah, Sir, my poor father has been sadly unfortunate since that time: it is a bitter thing for an old man to meet misfortunes, when he has known prosperity in his youth; but I am now old enough to assist, and it must be something worse than sickness that shall prevent my striving to bring comfort to that heart which administered to mine in its helplessness.

Char. You are a good girl, Clara; I always said you were. But how is my old master, Farmer Wakefield? I have not seen him for some weeks.

Clara. (*Dejectedly*) He is very well, Sir.

Char. Tell him to call on me this evening, and take a jug of ale to the memory of old times.

Clara. He has not been out for some time, Sir.

Char. Indeed — not ill, I hope.

Clara. Only in mind, Sir.

Char. He should take some exercise; it would assist in driving away thought. Why don't he join us now in the evening, as he used to do?

Clara. Oh, Sir — (*Bursting into tears*) — don't, don't ask me.

> *Luke rises, and comes forward.*
> *Clara, on perceiving him, utters a*
> *faint shriek.*

Luke. Eh, wench, what's the matter wi' ye; there be naught about me, I hope, to scare you so.

Clara. There is that about you, enough to scare any one, could they but see it.

Luke. What be that?

Clara. A bad heart.

Luke. A bad heart. — It an't a bad heart, but a heart that has been stung through and through.

Char. What is the meaning of this — what have you done, Luke, to cause this alarm?

Luke. Why, you see her feyther owed me a bit o' money, and when I wanted it, he wouldn't pay it, and so I thought —

Char. You'd put him in gaol for it, eh?

Luke. If you'd ha' been a witch, you could not ha' guessed better.

Char. (*Aside*) It is as I suspected — but why didn't you tell me of this before, Clara?

Clara. I couldn't, sir; I often thought of telling you, but when the words came to my tongue's end, I felt as if I could die, and had no power to speak them.

Char. How much is the debt?

Clara. Oh, sir, a very great sum.

Char. Indeed! I'm sorry for that.

Luke. (*Aside*) Yes, and that's all *you'll* do.

Char. But tell me the amount?

Clara. Nineteen pounds, sir.

Luke. Nineteen pound, six shilling —

Char. Well, Luke, you need not be so exact.

Luke. Some folk ha' been exact enough with me, before this time, and now it be my turn; I've had measters to teach me, and I'll show that I've larned my lesson.

Char. Luke, I know you to be a needy man — How could Farmer Wakefield become your debtor in that sum?

Luke. Why — for vally received.

Char. In what?

Luke. Why, for a stack o' wheat. Ah, you may stare — poor Luke, who never owned an acre, measter of a stack o' wheat — you see some folk can get as well as other folk.

Char. Well, well —

Luke. Yes, it would ha' been well for me if I hadn't sold it to a beggar.

Char. What? — Remember, Luke, the misfortunes of a ruined man are not to be insulted.

Luke. Aye, we be all ruin'd in turn — I ha' been — ruin'd — goods — body — character — all ruin'd. But now I can hold my head as high as you, Measter Charles, and defy you to say as I ever wrong'd my neighbour.

Char. It is the luck of some men to have good friends.

Luke. Aye, aye — you be right.

Char. And sometimes for bad purposes.

Luke. What! — dom thee, I — no, I'll not be in a passion now — another time — yes, another time. (*A shot heard without*) Here comes 'Squire, — he be at work among the partridges already.

Clara. The 'Squire? — Good day to ye, Mr. Charles. (*Crossing*)

Char. Nay, Clara, do not go yet; I wish to speak with you, alone.

Enter Squire Chase and Gamekeeper.

Luke. A dutiful good day to ye, 'Squire — you ha' just bagg'd summat, I suppose?

Squire. Ha! the pride of the village here! the very lass I wish'd to meet — and Mr. Charles, too — glad to see you, my honest fellow. (*Charles slightly bows*) Well, Clara, and how is your father?

Clara. He's very — that is, but poorly, sir.

Squire. Come hither, Clara; let me speak to you alone. (*The rest retire*) Your father is in difficulties, I understand.

Clara. He is, indeed, sir.

Squire. I'm very sorry; but if you will come to the manor house, this evening, I shall be at leisure, and will give you my assistance and advice.

Clara. Ah, sir! assistance and advice have long been needed.

Squire. Keep up your spirits, Clara, and fail not to come.

Clara. At what time, sir?

Squire. About half-past eight, or nine — say nine.

Clara. It will be dark before I can return; and I am very timid since I saw my father taken to — can't you make it earlier, sir?

Squire. Not very conveniently; but a servant shall see you safe home. Luke?

Luke. Here, 'Squire. (*Coming down*)

Squire. Follow me, I want you. (*Aside*) You'll not fail? (*To Clara*)

Clara. No, sir, and thank you.

Squire. I shall expect you; and, depend upon it, nothing that can be done to alleviate your distress shall be wanting. At nine o'clock.

Clara. I shall be punctual, sir.

Squire. (*Aside*) Now, Luke, we shall accomplish it.

Exit, followed by Luke and Gamekeeper.

Clara. The Squire's freedom with that man is very strange.

Char. (*Coming forward*) Clara, I — that is — I hope — do not think me too curious if I ask you a question.

Clara. No, indeed, Charles.

Char. Will you answer me?

Clara. If I can, sir.

Char. What was it the Squire said to you?

Clara. He wishes me to go this evening to the manor house.

Char. For what purpose?

Clara. He has promised to assist my father in his difficulties.

Char. Then he has only *promised* you?

Clara. That is all, Sir.

Char. Take my advice, Clara, and don't go.

Clara. Why should I not?

Char. Umph! — Here is a pocket-book that I have no particular use for; and, as I know you are fond of reading, and making memorandums, will you accept it?

Clara. Nay, Charles, I do not wish to —

Char. But as a keep-sake.

Clara. You are very kind. (*Taking the book timidly*)

Char. When I am gone, open it; it contains nothing but what you are freely welcome to: I know its contents — all is yours; and I am convinced your own heart will tell you, better than I can, how to dispose of it.

Clara. Nay, Charles, I — (*Offering to return it*)

Char. I insist upon it. *Exit.*

Clara. What can he mean? The contents are mine. No, Charles, I guess your object; how! gone: yet he insisted on my acceptance of it, and I was not to open it till he had left me — how my hand trembles. (*Opens the book*) There's nothing here — no — only some poetry. "How to dye green." (*Reading*) "Verses to Betsey Jones." March — April — May. Ha! pockets — papers in them — Bank notes! One, two, three, four, five — another five — that's five and five is ten — and ten's twenty. Twenty pounds! Kind, generous Charles; yes, my heart indeed tells me how to dispose of it. But for me to be so mean as to take it! No, I'll — I'll return it to him. But my father is in prison, and this would make him happy — what shall I do? I'll borrow it — I'll but borrow it, and I'll work night and day to get it together again. Oh my poor father! I'll fly immediately to the gaol, and will not return home, but with him. Father, father, let me not speak till I rush into your arms and tell you, that your prison doors are open. *Exit.*

Enter Bobby Trot, singing, with a bundle on a stick at his back.

Bob. Well, here I be, once more, ready to start for Lunnun: this makes the fourth time as I've had my Sunday clothes on, and my bundle at my back, when, somehow, summut have always happened to make I turn whoame again; but now I wool go, come what may. All's snug about, nobody have seen me, and I ha' gotten three half-crowns, two silver sixpences, and a penny halfpenny in copper, to pay my way there, which be 187 miles;

and, as to coming back again, that must take care of itself. Perhaps I may never come back; who knows but some grand lady, wi' a coach and a blackamoor servant, may say, Bobby, thee be'st a pretty lad, wool't come and be my husband? He, he, there be noa telling; for I be told there be wonderfuller things come aboot in Lunnun than in any other town out o' Yorkshire. So here goes, once more.

Enter Luke, hastily, with a letter.

Luke. Bobby, lad, come hither: I want thee.

Bob. Eh? Oh!

Luke. The work ha' now begun, and this will complete it. (*Aside*) I ha' been looking for thee, Bobby.

Bob. Dang it, I shall be stopp'd again — I be going, mun.

Luke. Going — Where?

Bob. To Lunnun, sure.

Luke. Why, what be'st thee going there for?

Bob. Oh, summut.

Luke. Nonsense; I've a job for thee to do.

Bob. I thought so: it be vary cruel, so it be, that a poor lad canna run away when he ha' legs o' his own, without being beholden to any body.

Luke. What ha' put going to Lunnun in your head? Why, a lad like you will be ruined and killed in such a place.

Bob. Eh! How?

Luke. Why, there be so many wenches and temptations loike.

Bob. Noa, be there tho'? Dom if I doan't go. (*Aside*)

Luke. How much money has't got?

Bob. Oh, a power! Three half-crowns, two silver sixpences, and a penny halfpenny in copper. I sav'd it all up in a flower-pot.

Luke. Be that all? Come, lad, listen to me: you know Measter Charles.

Bob. What, young Farmer Charles?

Luke. Yes — you go look for him, and give him this letter.

Bob. Vary well.

Luke. You know Ripley, twenty miles off, where his brother James do live.

Bob. Ees, I do.

Luke. Doan't you tell him I gave you this letter, but say you be just come from Ripley, and brought it from his brother there, who be vary ill, and like to die.

Bob. I doan't know as I wool.

Luke. Why not?

Bob. Because it be nataral the letter should be post paid.

Luke. Thee be'st a bit cutish, Bobby.

Bob. I be getting cuterer every day, do you know.

Luke. Well, well, thee shalt go to Lunnun, if this job be done cleverly; so, when you ha' found un, come to me, and you shall be paid double postage.

Bob. Shall I tho'? But where shall I find ye, Measter Luke, 'cause I be determined to go to-day, if I start at night; shall you be at this alehouse?

Luke. Alehouse — noa — at the 'Squire's.

Bob. What, wi' the sarvants in the kitchen?

Luke. Sarvants — pish! wi' his worship up stairs.

Bob. You doan't say so — what, be you hired to sit up stairs wi' his worship?

Luke. Don't ask questions, but mind your business. Eh — somebody be coming — it be he for sartin — now, lad, mind thy P's and Q's, and you're a made man! *Exit.*

Bob. Wi' his worship up stairs! Oh, I'll go to Lunnun now, for sartin; if a great ugly chap loike Measter Luke do keep company wi' 'squires, what shall a smart lad loike I do, when I get among lords and dukes.

Enter Charles.

Sarvant, Measter Charles.

Char. Well, Bobby, what news?

Bob. Very bad, zur — I ha' gotten a letter.

Char. For me?

Bob. Ees, zur.

Char. Who sent you with it?

Bob. Somebody.

Char. (*Reading*) "Dear Brother. This comes hoping you are in good health, which I be not at present. I be very ill, and doctor do say I be dying. Dear brother, do come without fail, when you get this letter from your loving brother till death,

JAMES MAYDEW.

Postscript. — A neighbour ha' wrote this, I be so bad."

Poor fellow — have you just come from there, Bobby?

Bob. Here be my bundle, you see.

Char. Did you see my brother?

Bob. Noa.

Char. Who gave you this?

Bob. A mon.

Char. My brother's man, I suppose.

Bob. He — he — wasn't a woman.

Char. What's to be done? I wish'd to have seen Clara this evening, but this certainly demands the first attention. Here, Bobby, here's sixpence for you; and should you see Farmer Wakefield's daughter, tell her what has happened, but say I shall return early in the morning, if possible, and call at her father's in my way home. *Exit.*

Bob. Oh sly! I see how things do stand — if Measter Charles bean't her sweetheart, I know nowt o' the matter. Well, I think that job were done quite neatish and clever, and without a bit o' lie ony way. Oh, I be a main cute lad, and, if Lunnun doan't make my fortin, she doan't know how to vally a genus. (*Jenny is heard without, crying violently*) My stars! here be a stoppage now for sartin — I'd better run for it.

Enter Jenny; she runs up to Bobby, and catches him by the collar.

Jen. I've cotch'd you at last, have I now, — bean't you a sad parjury fause lovier? and you be resolute bent on going away?

Bob. Ees, I be. Here's a rumpus.

Jen. Haven't you said, over and over again, that I were the girl of your heart; and, if ever you had a wife, nobody but I should be Mistress Trot.

Bob. Ees, but I said *if,* you know; moind that.

Jen. Then what did you make me fall in love for?

Bob. That be no fault o' mine; you couldn't help it.

Jen. Then you don't care about breaking my heart, I suppose? But harkye, Bobby, — if you go to Lunnun, I'll follow you, if I walk every step o' th' way barefoot.

Bob. Now, don't ye be a fool, Jenny.

Jen. You shan't make one o' me, I can tell ye, Bobby.

Bob. You make one o' yourself — I be only going to see the curiosities; I shall come back, mun.

Jen. But I be so afraid o' thee; for, when a young man gets there fra' the country as knows summut, he'll never get away again till he knows summut more than that summut.

Bob. You doan't say so. Dom if I doan't go! (*Aside*) Now, Jenny, listen to me: it be no use your taking on so; I've told you, often and often, I was determined to see Lunnun some day, so hadn't I better go now I be a single man and you a single 'oman, than walk away some time when you ha' gotten a dozen young 'uns: besides, what I see, I can tell you all about, and then you'll be as wise as me every bit.

Jen. That will na' better me, Bobby; for most things that are larn'd in Lunnun had better never be know'd at all.

Bob. But, bless ye, I needn't know more than wad be proper.

Jen. But you would not rest there, Bobby; if you get to know a little, you'll never be quiet till you know every thing. Now, I tell thee what, Bobby, — if thee woan't go, you shall come to my mother's, and have as much cold pudding for supper as ever you can eat.

Bob. You don't keep cold pudding, do ye?

Jen. Oh, plenty.

Bob. Well, now, I never do.

Jen. Why, thee doesn't throw't away.

Bob. No — I eat it all, when it be hot.

Jen. But woan't you come, Bobby? (*Coaxing him*)

Bob. He! he! he! I — I think I wool.

Jen. (*Pulling him along gently*) Come.

Bob. He! he! he! you know how to do't.

Jen. (*Chucking him under the chin*) I know you wool, Bobby.

Bob. He! he! he! I'll be shot if Lunnun temptation be ony thing to this.

Duet. Air, "Le Saboteire."

Bobby.
Lunnun's curiosities tempt me away, —
Fortune may smile, and pay well for the trip.
Jenny.
Nay, Bobby, pray let me persuade thee to stay,
There's many a slip 'twixt the cup and the lip.
Bobby.
Talents and person be sure o' promotion,
So that, you see, I've two strings to my bow.
Jenny.
The proverb do say, "twixt two stools," I've a notion,
Plump on the ground you will sartainly go:
Bobby.
Odds! bobbs! both be so 'ticing,
Lunnun and Jenny — I can't get away.
Jenny.
You look like the donkey who stood, over nice, in
Choosing between two fine bundles of hay,
Fal, lal, lal! etc.
Bobby.
Your coaxing and wheedling I cannot resist,
And the thought o' cold pudding do alter my plan.
Jenny.
Why, Bobby, I know you've a nation good twist,
And a rare gaping mouth for a sop in the pan.
Bobby.
Ah! Jenny, my roaming ambition
Be melting to love, just like kitchen fat.
Jenny.
If you be so warm wi' your loving condition,
A lump of cold pudding will soon settle that.

Bobby.

Legs! fegs! to Lunnun shou'd carry me,
Where I be sure to get brass in my purse.

Jenny.

You don't want for brass in your face, —
    stay and marry me;
Further you'll travel, and, maybe, fare worse.
         Fal, lal, lal! etc.
         Exeunt.

Scene 2.

*A kitchen. Enter Dame Wakefield, placing the
chairs and table.*

Dame. Where can my poor girl be? I be
sore afraid when she do stay so long away; a
fair flower hazards the plucking of every
hand, and she ha' now no protector but her
old mother: my poor husband in prison, and
the young hope of our days fled from us when
he wur but ten years old! But that grief I can
never speak of to my husband, it do almost
turn his brain, — but many and many a night
ha' found me waking and thinking what ha'
been his fate. Hey, bless me, this is a sad
world for the helpless and unfriended!

Clara. (Without) Mother! Mother!

Dame. My child's voice, — bless us, what
can be the matter?

Music. She opens the door, and Clara rushes in.

Clara. He's coming! He's coming!

Dame. Who, child?

Clara. My father!

*Music. Farmer Wakefield enters, and rushes
into his wife's arms.*

Wake. (After a pause) My warm, my comfortable fireside, do I again see thee? Oh,
dame, dame! no man truly knows the blessings of his home but he who has been shut
out from it.

Dame. George! — I've look'd for this day,
but never expected to see it. — I've dream'd
of it, but the morning always found your
chair vacant; but now sit down, George.

Clara. Sit, father, sit. How pale and
changed you look, — shall I get you anything, father?

Wake. Not yet, child — not yet.

Dame. But who have done this?

Clara. A friend, mother.

Wake. He is, indeed, a friend.

Dame. Bless us, what friend?

Clara. Charles.

Dame. What, Charles Maydew?

Clara. He drew from me what I never intended should be known, but where it could
not be avoided: he asked me questions, many
questions, and put them so kindly, that they
seemed to charm an answer from me; and,
when I at length confess'd our distress, he
gave me a pocket-book, told me the contents
were mine, and my own heart would direct
me what to do.

Wake. Grateful boy, — if ever it be in my
power to return thy kindness, — but what
are hopes to me — am I not ruin'd? — No
farm, no land! Blight, distemper, and misfortune, have swept all away, and I am now a
bereft and comfortless old man.

Clara. Father, I hope you have one comfort left. *(Embracing him with affection)*

Wake. Bless thee girl, bless thee, — I
wrong'd thee in saying so; thou art indeed a
blessing, and, if any thing should tear thee
from me, there then remains but one thing
to be done. *(A knock at the cottage door)*

Wake. (Starting) Who's there?

Clara. Nay, father, don't stir; sit still, sit
quiet, — I'll open the door — it's nobody of
consequence: some friend, perhaps.

Dame. Mayhap, Mr. Charles.

*Music. — Clara opens the door cautiously —
Luke walks in, but stops suddenly on perceiving Wakefield, and remains fixed with surprise.
— Clara comes down, Wakefield still keeping his
seat, while the Dame views him with anxiety.*

Wake. Well, sir, your business here?

Luke. I ha' noa business particular, I ha'
noa — only a — how came you out o' gaol?

Wake. That be no affair o' yours: the
keeper of the prison will answer that.

Luke. Well, well — I suppose it be all
right; but, but — who'd ha' thought it, —
you arn't paid t' money?

Wake. It be paid; and now your business.

Luke. Why, you see I be com'd fra' Squire
— he heard you were misfortunate, and
wish'd your daughter to come to him, when
he were at whome this evening, and consult
wi' him upon the business.

Clara. Yes, father, he saw me this afternoon, and desired me to go to the manor-
house this evening.

Wake. The Squire be very good, certainly;
but it be all settled now, and things may take
a better turn wi' me.

Luke. Well, I hope they may; but, Miss
Clara, as t' Squire said he would do summut
for thee, mayhap it may be better for you to
see him — he be very civil, and who knows
but he may set thy feyther on his legs.

Wake. I should think it be of little consequence to you whether I stand or fall.

Luke. Oh, I only speak out o' pity.

Wake. Curse your pity!

Luke. Nay, not so; I be a friend o' the

family, bless you — I bears no malice. No, no — noa malice, — noa malice!

Wake. Then why be so hard upon me, when I couldn't pay you at the time promised?

Luke. Why, you see I wanted t' money, and I thought, as you had been a thriving man, you might ha' some about thee that you didn't just like to touch, you see.

Wake. (*Rises*) And why did you tempt me to buy it, wi' your false words of "any time would do to pay"? But I see through you — you be a scoundrel!

Luke. What? Be quiet! be quiet!

Clara. (*Crossing to Wakefield*) Nay, father, — dear father, say no more. Luke, go, leave the house; my father is passionate, and he may say that which at another time he would be sorry for.

Luke. I ha' summut to say, summut at my tongue's end — it must come out. Farmer, do you recollect when you sent me away fra' your sarvice? Do you recollect when I were starving for want o' work, and, because I were at times given to drink, you turn'd your back upon me? I ha' never been a man since that time.

Wake. What, do you wish to rake up old affairs that ha' been gone by mony a day?

Luke. If it had been gone by a hundred years, and I alive, I should never ha' forgotten it; and I must and I will tell thee on't. I never had the chance 'afore; but now it do all come fresh upon my brain, my heart do seem ready to burst wi' summut buried in it, and I cannot keep it down. You turn'd me away, and I had no character, because you said I were a drunkard. I were out o' work week after week, till I had not a penny in the world, nor a bit o' bread to put in mine nor my wife's mouth. I then had a wife, but she sicken'd and died — yes, died — all — all along o' you.

Wake. You never came to me in a right way.

Luke. She wouldn't let me go to parish, because she were daughter of as good a man as you were then; so we crept on little by little, and bad enough it were — but at last all things went cross; and at one time, when a bit hadn't been in my mouth for two days, I sat thinking, wi' my wife in my arms — she were ill, very ill — I saw her look at me wi' such a look as I shall never forget — she laid hold o' this hand, and, putting her long thin fingers all round it, said, "Luke, would na' the farmer give you sixpence if he thought I were dying o' want?" I said I'd try once more — I got up, to put her in a chair, when she fell, stone dead, down at my feet.

Clara. Oh, Luke! Luke! — for mercy's sake, no more — forgive him.

Luke. (*After a pause*) I were then quite ruin'd. I felt alone in the world. I stood looking on her white face near an hour, and did not move from the spot an inch; but, when I *did* move, it were wi' my fist clench'd in the air, while my tongue, all parch'd and dry, curs'd a curse, and swore that, if I had not my revenge, I wish'd I might fall as stiff and as dead as she that lay before me.

Clara. Oh, Luke! — I beseech you — I implore you — forgive my father! (*Falling at Luke's feet*)

Luke. Ha! ha! ha! — this is a great sight — the daughter at my feet.

Wake. Get up, Clara, I'll not see it — I'll not see thee beg to any man — obey me, girl.

Luke. My eyes are wet — 'tis ten years and more since they were so — it were but a drop, and now they're dry as dust again.

Wake. Tell me, Luke — did you not bring all your troubles on yourself; did you not drink, and swear, and be idle, for whole days?

Luke. (*Not heeding him*) I'll have it yet — if I die for't, I'll have it. Yes, yes — you arn't the man you were once. You are not that Farmer Wakefield that stood almost as high as t' 'Squire — noa! noa! — Luke ha' seen that which has been bread to him.

Wake. Villain, leave the house! Don't you hold me, dame — he shan't bide in this place a moment — leave my house, I say.

Luke. I arn't yet had my full o' what pleases me — here's a little alteration here.

Wake. Do you abuse me on my own hearth? Now, Luke, heed me — if you don't instantly go out, I'll lay hold o' thee by the neck, and send you forth quicker than you came in.

Luke. Touch me, and I'll —

Wake. Stand off, dame — Clara, be you quiet — let me come at him.

> *Music. — Wakefield seizes Luke, but is grappled in return by the throat — Luke dashes him on the ground, and rushes out of the cottage, with a loud laugh — Clara screams, the Dame sinks senseless in the chair, Clara is endeavouring to raise her Father, and the scene closes.*

Scene 3.

An apartment at the Squire's. Enter Bobby, cautiously looking about him.

Bob. Measter Luke! Measter Luke! — I can't find him any where. I popp'd up stairs so snug, when sarvant's back wur turned, because they do say he be often here wi' Squire; if I could but find him, I'd ax for t' letter job money, and go; for Jenny do so come over I wi' her little bits of love, and great bits of pudding, that it do quite puzzle I what to do. What a grand parlour surely — but this be naught to what I shall see in Lunnun — for the 'Squire there be so big, they ha' built a large hall o' purpose for his corporation. Here be somebody coming! — Dickens and daisies, it be 'Squire himsel'! — He musn't see me, by gum — I shall meake such a clatter if I run down stairs: here be a cupboard-door open — I'll pop in here till he be gone — gently, Bobby — gently. (*Conceals himself in closet*)

Enter Squire and Dick.

Squire. How far can we get on the road without changing horses?

Dick. Why, your honour, with four good cattle, we may run a matter o' twenty miles.

Squire. That will do; now attend to me — clap four of my best horses to the light chaise, and be at the Three Oaks, near the main road, by a quarter to nine.

Dick. And spank along in the old way, your honour?

Squire. As hard as you can go; but make no noise in getting ready, and drive quietly to the place, without saying a word about it to anybody — keep the steps down and the door open.

Dick. I know, sir.

Squire. And, understand — (*Gives him money*)

Dick. Oh, sir, perfectly — your honour intends to go to London, I suppose?

Squire. Ask no questions, but obey me.

Dick. It shall be done; anything else, your honour?

Squire. Get your horses ready immediately.

Dick. In the cracking of a whip, your honour. *Exit.*

Squire. It may be necessary to make these preparations, for have the girl I will. She has given me a little trouble, certainly — perhaps more than I intended to take; but a genuine man of gallantry should never flinch while there remains a chance of obtaining his object.

Enter Luke.

Luke. It be all out now — I've had it laying up here for mony a day, but it would burst out at last. I could ha' put my foot upon his neck, had na' the women screech'd so

deadly; but I've given him earnest o' what's to come.

Squire. Why, Luke, you appear ruffled — nothing wrong, I hope?

Luke. Eh! — I didn't see your worship. Oh, no, bless ye — I've only been talking a bit o' my mind. Who do you think be out o' gaol?

Squire. Wakefield?

Luke. Yes, sure. I know who's done it.

Squire. Charles, I suppose?

Luke. Aye, sure; but he ha' gone on his fool's errand — that be all correct.

Squire. Then my rival has swallow'd the bait?

Luke. Oh, yes, and is now on the road to Ripley.

Enter Servant.

Serv. Farmer Wakefield has sent to speak with you, sir.

Squire. Sent! whom?

Serv. His daughter, sir.

Squire. Desire her to come up.
Exit Servant.

Luke. Hush, hush — it be all right yet — I know what she be come for.

Squire. The puss breaks cover. Away, lad, take the back stairs, and be at your station; it is getting dark, and we shall run her down as she returns home. Keep your scent good, my lad, and you'll be the best hound in my pack. (*Exit Luke*) Here she comes.

Enter Clara.

Well, Clara, you come to your time, like a good woman of business — sit down.

Clara. I'd rather stand, if you please, sir.

Squire. Well, as you please; but don't be timid, — come nearer to me; have you seen your father today?

Clara. Yes, sir.

Squire. And how is he?

Clara. Better than he has been for many a day. He's at home, sir.

Squire. At home!

Clara. Yes, sir; a good friend has done what you were thinking about, sir.

Squire. That's a home thrust, however. (*Aside*) Oh, I understand, — well, I'm rejoiced to hear it; I hoped I should have had that pleasure.

Clara. But you can do as good an action, sir; if not to serve my father, at least to — to — please me, sir.

Squire. Indeed; believe me, Clara, I would rather have that office than the former.

Clara. My father did not wish me to come, but I am disobedient for once; I should not have slept if I had not. That villain, Luke, sir, has insulted my father, shamefully insulted him!

Squire. Indeed, insulted him!

Clara. Struck him, sir; struck an old man to the ground, whose grey hairs alone should have been his protection; and I come to you, 'Squire Chase, as lord of the manor and a magistrate, instantly to secure the ruffian, for my father's life is in danger while he is at liberty.

Squire. Where is Luke to be found?

Clara. It has been said that he is in your service.

Squire. In mine — Oh, no, the steward, I believe, employs him on the grounds.

Clara. If you are inclined to serve the oppressed, sir, you will not let this matter rest; pardon my boldness, sir, but my poor father is a ruined and a broken man, with no one to stand up for him but his daughter.

Squire. Well, I — that is, my dear girl — my dear Clara —

Clara. Sir!

Squire. Damn it — I haven't a word to say for myself. (*Aside*) You have it in your power to place yourself and your family above insult from any one.

Clara. I — I do not understand.

Squire. There is one who takes more than common interest in your situation, — one who has felt the expression of those eyes, and admired charms he is convinced were never intended to be obscured in a village.

Clara. Sir, I — you amaze me — frighten me — what is it you mean?

Squire. It is myself, Clara, that admires you, loves you.

Clara. Do not forget yourself; unhand me, sir, or I will call for help. Let me depart.

A loud crash is heard in the closet, — the 'Squire starts amazed, and Clara rushes out. — The 'Squire runs to the closet, and drags out Bobby, with a broken basin in his hand.

Bob. Oh, your Worship, I didn't mean to do it.

Squire. Who are you, Sirrah?

Bob. I be Bobby Trot, Sir.

Squire. How came you in that closet?

Bob. I didn't go to steal any thing, zur — I wonted to speak to Measter Luke, zur — and I got in there, zur — and a great basin fell upon me, zur, without ony body touching it.

Squire. How long have you been there, Sirrah?

Bob. All the while you have been here, Sir.

Squire. He may have overheard what has been said; but I'll secure him, whoever he is.

(*Still holding him*) Have you heard what has pass'd in this room?

Bob. He, he, — you be going to Lunnun in a shay.

Squire. That's quite enough. (*Holding him*) Here, Thomas! William! James! (*Calling*)

Bob. Oh, zur, I be innocent; indeed I be!

Enter Servants.

Squire. This fellow has been concealed in my closet, no doubt with an intention to rob the house; take him to the constable, and lock him up in the cage till morning.

Bob. Oh, zur, doan't — I'll never do so ony more.

Squire. Away with him instantly!

Bob. I be innocent, indeed I be. — Oh dear, this be a stoppage — I shall never go to Lunnun. *Exit, dragged by Servants.*

Squire. That booby might have destroyed my plan, but Luke must see after him; he is, no doubt, at his post. The sky looks rather dark; no storm coming, I hope. No matter — Jupiter enjoyed his Semele in a storm, and surely a poor mortal need not stand upon trifles. *Exit.*

Scene 4.

A cut wood. Low thunder. Enter Phillip through the centre, with a large bundle, and a cudgel.

Phil. Holloa! Anybody a-hoy? Nobody within hail? I want a pilot here: the wind has shifted four points, and brought the ebb-tide slap on my broadside; shall drift out, I'm thinking, and lose my way. Let me see, here's a track of some sort; I'll follow it, must reach port at last. (*Lightning*) The clouds are preparing for action: splice my old shoes, but I must take care of my cargo. Now, messmate, keep you tight in my fist, and, if a pirate dare board a king's ship, damme but we'll set her keel upwards, and leave her to founder. Steady she goes! *Exit.*

Enter Luke, cautiously.

Luke. I thought I heard summut. No, it be all right; Dick ha' gotten the shay ready, and t' lass be coming across t'other meadow. But where be 'Squire? I suppose I must manage t' job mysel'. Who's there?

Enter Squire, through centre.

Squire. Luke!

Luke. Be that you, 'Squire?

Squire. She's coming. I've had a steeple chase to be up with you.

Luke. All be ready, zur! (*Thunder*) Hush! keep thee back. (*They retire back*)

Enter Clara.

Clara. If I can but get home before the storm increases! That treacherous Squire — this is a sad world. (*A flash of lightning makes her start back*) Bless me, what a flash! I must put my hands before my eyes; I was always afraid of the lightning!

A clap of thunder — music — Luke rushes forward, and seizes her in his arms: she screams, and struggles with him: the Squire is taking her from him, when Philip re-enters. Lightning.

Phil. What ship ahoy! Sheer off, there! (*He knocks Luke down with his cudgel, who falls senseless; then grapples the Squire by the throat*) Slip your cable, my girl, and stand out to sea! the lubbers shan't grapple you.

Clara exits; the Squire struggles with Philip, and runs off, pursued by him. The thunder continues, and the curtain falls.

End of the First Act.

ACT II.

Scene 1.

The interior of a village alehouse. Three reapers discovered sitting at a table, drinking; another small table, chairs, etc.

Glee.

1st Reap. We three be farmer lads,
And yeomen every one,
Ploughtail Thomas,
2nd Reap. Sickle James,
3rd Reap. And I be flail John.
1st Reap. I drive the plough,
2nd Reap. I reap the corn,
3rd Reap. And I thrash the sheaves
Till the wheat be gone.
All. We three be farmer lads,
And yeomen every one.
1st Reap. Thomas loves cherry-cheek
Kate o' the vale,
2nd Reap. James loves the lass with the milking pail,
3rd Reap. Flail John loves nothing but nut-brown ale.
All. We three be farmer lads,
And yeomen every one.

Enter Luke, with a handkerchief bound round his head; crosses the stage, and sits at the table.

1st Reap. Fine morning, Master Luke.
Luke. Yes, I see it be.
1st Reap. Capital weather for the squire to shoot.

Luke. Yes, dom him. (*Half aside*) Thomas! (*Calling*) I want a jug of ale.

Enter Thomas.

Thos. Jug of ale, Luke — what be the matter with your head?
Luke. It do ache, Thomas.
Thos. What, too jolly at the harvest-home, I reckon? I hear farmer Charles left all the lads to shift for themselves, and went over to Ripley.
Luke. Did he? Doan't thee talk, Thomas, but bring th' ale. *Exit Thomas.*
1st Reap. You seem out of sorts, Master Luke.
Luke. Be that my affair, o' yours?
1st Reap. I only made a civil remark.
Luke. When I be ill, I'll let thee know.

Enter Thomas, with ale.

Thos. Fine day, after the storm last night.
Luke. Yes. (*Sullenly*)
Thos. You were not out in it, I suppose?
Luke. No. (*Quickly*)
Thos. Some folks grow mighty grand in a little time. *Exit.*
Luke. Just as it were all right — just as I were in the very nick o' the job, to be stunned to the ground by a blow that came from nobody knows where; and the 'Squire too, to run away, and leave me to get up as I could: and, when I came to myself, I could see nothing, and hear nothing; but I could feel summut. Well, well — it ha' been twenty years about, and, if it be twenty more, I'll have my ends at last. (*Going to drink*)
Phil. (*Without*) Landlord ahoy! anybody aboard the King's Head?
Luke. (*Starting up and dropping his jug*) That be the vary voice.
1st Reap. Master Luke, you have spilt t' ale, man.

Enter Philip, singing.

What argufies snivelling and piping your eye?
Why, what a damn'd fool you must be.
Luke turns his chair, and sits with his back to Philip.

Phil. All hands are asleep, I think — a messmate or two here I see — holloa! (*To the reapers*) What cheer, my hearties?
1st Reap. We be very well, hope you're the same.
Phil. That's right, my boys — we shal! soon know one another — here, landlord! (*Enter Thomas*) Bring a good allowance of grog alongside, and hand us something to stow in the bed-room. (*Exit Thomas*) Well, my boys, how are you off for lasses in this port!

1st Reap. Very well for that matter; only, if you are too sharp after the lasses, you must keep prepared for the lads.

Phil. You're a bit of a weather-beaten old hand, but you know how to use your speaking trumpet. I'm a stranger in this channel, you see, and want a little information; is it the custom of the natives here to overhaul a young woman whether she's willing or no?

1st Reap. I don't know about that, without the lasses will say "no," when they mean "yes."

Phil. Hark ye, my lad — I was steering into port last night, as well as the breakers ahead and contrary winds would allow, and, while tacking about, I heard the cry of a ship in distress, pip'd all hands, bore up to the spot, and found a tight little brig grappled by a couple of Algerines — all dark — not a lantern to be seen — except the flash now and then of the great guns in the air — saw how it was — bore slap upon the enemy — tipp'd him a broadside — boarded him on his lee quarter — drubb'd him about his upper-works till his daylights danc'd again — fell to work yard-arm and yard-arm with t'other — he lower'd his top-sails, slipp'd under my stern, and got clear off — gave chase, but lost him in the dark — hail'd the little brig, but found she had set all sheets to the wind, and put out to sea — gave three skips and a huzza for the victory — steer'd my course again, till I got safely harbour'd in the King's Head.

1st Reap. Have you been talking Greek all this time?

Phil. Greek, you swab — but what's the use of talking the king's English to a Hottentot — harkye!

1st Reap. Beg pardon, master sailor, it is our time for work again — you have done yours, and have plenty o' time to talk, but we have none to listen. (*Going*)

Phil. Avast now — don't sheer off till I've ask'd a question or two. I shan't veer out much more jaw, as you've no gumption. Tip us a few of the farmers' names in this port.

1st Reap. Names? — There be Farmer Jones, and Farmer Gosling, and Farmer May-dew, and Farmer Holly, and — there's no more.

Phil. No more, you lubber! (*Laying hold of the 1st Reaper*) Tell me there's no more, and I'll pitch you to Davy Jones in the twinkling of a handspike.

1st Reap. Oh, yes, I'd forgot — one more — but he's no farmer now.

Phil. His name, swab; his name.

1st Reap. His name is Wakefield.

Phil. (*Sinking on his seat*) Splice my old shoes — the name sure enough — quite upsets me — strike my topmast, that name sets my head singing like a teakettle on the galley fire.

2nd Reap. Come, lad, come — he be drunk.

Phil. Stay, my lads — bring to a bit — give me some account of him — no palaver, on the word of a sailor — he's no farmer now, you say? — overhaul his affairs, and let me know how he stands in the world.

1st Reap. If you want to learn the particulars, ask him in the corner — he can tell you more than I can.

> *Exeunt Reapers. Luke still sits with his back towards Philip, but, during this scene, has taken the handkerchief from his head.*

Phil. I haven't felt so queer since the Neptune's jolly-boat upset with me in the Baltic. Ask him in the corner — who's he, I wonder — an exciseman, perhaps — service to you, mate. (*Drinking to Luke*)

Luke. Same to you.

Phil. Come, don't clap a stopper on your cable end, my friend — hoist your colours, and return the salute — can you tell me of one Farmer Wakefield in these parts?

Luke. (*Turning half round to Philip*) Do you want to know about him?

Phil. Come, come, lad — let's have no sauerkraut when we can drink good flip. What, though I am a stranger, this is one of the friendly islands, and if I've put in for fresh water, you won't send me away with empty buckets. It's some time since I anchored in this channel, and then Farmer Wakefield was master of a tight bit of land or so, didn't spare the grog and biscuits, and could keep up a Saturday night like an admiral — so, you see, I should like to learn how the good soul thrives in the sea of life.

Luke. Very poorly, I can tell thee.

Phil. Poor soul.

Luke. He's been many a day growing poor, and now ha' gotten quite down — bad crops, distemper among the cattle, bad debts, misfortune, and rack and ruin more and more every day. I ha' seen it — I ha' seen it. (*With self-satisfaction*)

Phil. Well, thank heaven, he's alive.

Luke. Oh, yes, he do live.

Phil. And his wife?

Luke. Yes.

Phil. And — and his children?

Luke. Yes; that is, he had two, you see, but now he ha' gotten but one.

Phil. That's a girl.

Luke. Yes; t'other were a boy.

Phil. He's dead, I suppose.

Luke. Very like — very like.

Phil. You don't know for certain?

Luke. Why, you see he were a lost a long time ago; kidnapp'd away, it be thought, by gipsies.

Phil. True — true, I recollect now.

Luke. You be too young to recollect the boy.

Phil. Yes, yes, and the old farmer is very poor?

Luke. Deadly poor, indeed.

Phil. I'm glad of it — I'm glad of it.

Luke. (*Rising eagerly, and looking earnestly at Philip*) No, be you tho'?

Phil. Holloa, brother, you've a smart bump on your forecastle.

Luke. (*Confused*) Have I? Oh yes — I know, I know.

Phil. Where did you get it?

Luke. Get it — why — I ha' gotten it on my head, you see.

Phil. I think I know you. (*Significantly*)

Luke. What? Know me.

Phil. Are you fond of young women?

Luke. (*Endeavouring to laugh*) Mayhap I be.

Phil. Did you get that blow last night?

Luke. No — no — not last night.

Phil. You lie.

Luke. What?

Phil. (*Seizing him*) You were grappling with a young woman last night; you and another.

Luke. If thee doesn't loose th' grip, I'll dash thy brains out.

Phil. I see how the land lies: here, landlord, you've got among the breakers. — Landlord. (*Calling*) All hands ahoy!

Enter Thomas and Charles.

Thos. What's the matter?

Phil. I'll fathom it to the bottom. — I've got you in tow, and splice my old shoes if you go till I'm satisfied.

Char. Luke, what is the cause of this?

Phil. Your honour, I sav'd a young woman from being ill-treated last night, and I could swear this is one of the crew that had his grappling irons aboard of her.

Char. Where was the place?

Phil. I don't know, your honour. I was steering without rudder or compass, and had lost my way, but it was in some woody place leading out of a meadow.

Char. It is as Clara suspected: — you *did* save a young woman last night, my friend. Hark ye, Luke, I have heard of your conduct, and be assured that proper authorities shall interfere; if justice cannot be procured here, there are means to obtain it elsewhere.

Phil. What, we've caught a mutineer, eh? Beg pardon, your honour, is the young woman your wife?

Char. No — no — not my wife; she is Farmer Wakefield's daughter.

Phil. Shiver my topmast. Say it again, your honour.

Char. I repeat it.

Phil. Handspikes and buntlines, but I'll know who you are. (*Seizes Luke with both hands, who trembles violently*) I value not your looks a rope's end. (*Drags him to the front of the stage, and looks at him earnestly*) It is — no it an't: snatch my bowlines, but it is. Hark ye, I think I've seen your ugly mug before: if it's the same, you'll go to the devil with a flowing sail, I can tell you; you are set adrift now, but, when I grapple you again, I'll send such a broadside into you, as shall sink you in a jiffy. — Noble captain, steer me to Farmer Wakefield's, and you shall swim in grog for a month.

Char. I am returning there this instant.

Phil. Say you so: not a word more, on your life — heave ahead, landlord, and pitch my cargo out of the hold. Now, your honour, seize the rudder — wind and weather all right. Clap on all your canvas — leave this half-timber'd pirate to founder as he will, and spank away to the farmer's.

Exeunt, Philip, followed by Charles and Thomas. Luke remains fixed with astonishment, mingled with fear.

Luke. Summut do pass to and fro upon my brain; but no, it cannot be, it cannot be — he were fair-hair'd, and, beside, it be twenty year ago, and nothing ever heard — I'll not think it; but, if it be, what then? I'll do that which shall outdo all I've ever done — I'll not be baulk'd. — My heart ha' been rent in twain; and, tho' fate and devils do stand afore me, I'll burst through them all, but I'll have my hands full o' what they do long for. Landlord — Thomas, I say?

Enter Thomas.

Bring me a whole pint o' brandy; no water, not a drop: doan't thee stand there, I'll pay thee for't. Stop, I'll go with thee myself — thee shan't stint me of a drop — I'm stone cold — my finger ends do feel like flakes of ice. — Come, Thomas, come?

Exit, dragging Thomas after him.

Scene 2.

Wakefield's cottage. Enter Jenny and Clara.

Clara. He has something particular to tell me?

Jenny. Very, — and he won't say a word to anybody, while they do keep him lock'd up in the cage, not even to me.

Clara. Mr. Charles threatens to punish him severely, for bringing a letter, which stated his brother to be ill, and was the cause of keeping him from home all night.

Jenny. He says summut about that too, and that somebody gave it him to give somebody; but he won't tell nobody till he be out of the cage.

Clara. Don't they intend to take him before the Squire?

Jenny. I don't know; he be shut up there for all the world like a bird; I ha' been to his uncle Peter, but he says, belike he desarves it, so he must abide by it; and, if I hadn't given him some breakfast through the iron bars, he would have been starved to death.

Clara. Well, Jenny, be you here again in an hour; perhaps Mr. Charles may return.

Jenny. Yes, madam; for it be a hard thing, so it be, for a poor young man to lose his character, because 'Squire do choose to say a thing that be false; but he does just as he likes — I wish I were a queen, or an emperor, for his sake: I'd see whether a 'Squire should not go in the cage as well as a poor man, when he deserved it. Good day, madam.

Clara. Good day, Jenny.

As Jenny is going out, Farmer Wakefield enters — Jenny drops a curtsey, and exits.

Wake. Who be that?

Clara. She came to inquire for Mr. Charles, respecting the lad who gave him the false letter yesterday.

Wake. Did Charles say he would be here again?

Clara. Yes, father; perhaps in an hour.

Wake. Oh! — Get me my chair.

Clara. Yes, father. (*Clara brings the Farmer his chair; he sits*)

Wake. Put my stick in the corner.

Clara. Yes, father.

Wake. Where be your mother?

Clara. Gone to market.

Wake. Where do she get money to go to market? I have none.

Clara. Has not Charles been our friend?

Wake. True, I ha' borrow'd a pound of him — I might as well say begg'd it; for I know not when I shall have another shilling to call my own.

Clara. Nay, father, let us hope for the best.

Wake. Hope! — don't talk to me of hope! what have I to look forward to? Nothing but a pauper's life; and then I shall break my heart; and, when I be nail'd down, to be carried to my grave, no one will care, no one will know about it; there will be no passing-bell — nothing to let folks know, there goes poor Farmer Wakefield.

Clara. Father, dear father, do not encourage such gloomy thoughts; there is no man so clouded by misfortune, but a star *will* glimmer through the darkness, which, pale as it may be, is the light that bids us live, and look forward — 'tis the light of hope, father.

Wake. Don't thee prate, don't thee prate; thy father knows what has pass'd, and he knows full well what's to come — (*Rises*) — The workhouse.

Clara. (*Almost overpowered by her feelings*) Not while I have health, and hands to work.

Wake. Come hither, girl — I can't see thee just now, my old eyes are dimmer than usual. — (*Taking her in his arms*) — Bless thee, bless thee.

Enter Charles.

Charles, be that you? Do not stand away from us; I be only pressing my only link of life to my heart.

Char. I should not have come in so suddenly, but I have an impatient friend without, who has a desire to be introduced here.

Wake. I don't want him; he can't come in, whoever he be. (*Pettishly*)

Clara. Not a friend of *your* friend, father?

Wake. You see, Charles, I can't help a little old pride. I were once glad to see as many about me as would come; but I have nothing now to make friends welcome with; and it do cut me to the heart to seem as poor as I be.

Char. This is a friend I know you will be glad to see; and, if you do not, you will be sorry when he is gone, and you are told who he was.

Wake. Where is he?

Char. You shall hear. (*Goes to the door, calling*) Neptune ahoy!

Phil. (*Without*) Hillioh! — Is the captain aboard?

Clara. Heavens! my preserver's voice!

Wake. What, the man that fought for thee last night? — Let him come in — let him come in.

Enter Philip.

Welcome, my friend, welcome; I'm glad to see thee, indeed I am; and thank thee for my poor girl's protection.

Phil. What cheer, my old master? — Glad

to see you — avast, don't slip your cable yet — Lord love your old heart. — What the devil am I about? — I beg your pardon, your honour, only you see I — that is — I suppose that's the tight little vessel that fell in with the enemy last night — split my binnacle, if she an't as handsomely built, and prettily rigg'd, as e'er a frigate in the service.

Wake. I'm very sorry, my good fellow, that it be not in my power to reward you as you deserve; but, if a father's hearty thanks —

Phil. Now, no palaver; only rate me on your good books, and I'm satisfied. Glad I've found you, tho' — I'm but a young man, you see, tho' I've sailed the salt seas twelve years — east, west, north, and south — aloft and below. Have work'd my way through, as hard as any man, from a powder-monkey and cook-shifter to a foremast station; and, split my snatchblock, if e'er a porpoise-fac'd land-lubber in the world shall fall foul of a young woman against her will, when I'm within hail.

Wake. Come, friend, sit you down; the dame will soon be home.

Phil. The dame! — Your wife, I suppose — odds buntlines, but I'll stay to see her — poor old creature — Lord love her heart. (*Half aside*)

Wake. She will make you as welcome as our means will allow; for I am but a poor man now, tho' I have known better days.

Phil. Bless your old soul, don't mention it. (*Aside*) Pitch me overboard, if I can stand it much longer. And that's your daughter? Splice my old shoes, I must fire a salute. (*Crosses to Clara*) Beg pardon, my lass, if I am somewhat too racketified; but we sailors never see a pretty girl, but, somehow, we want to — to — damn it, give us a buss.

Char. What?

Wake. Eh?

Phil. Shiver me, if I know what I'm about. You must excuse me, you see, if I've sprung a leak in my manners. I'm a little outlandish at present — lost the helm of my conduct, as it were. But a word with you, commodore — I must put upon another tack; never mind my lingo — a man that's been half his life at sea, can't help smelling of old junk.

Wake. Bring a chair, girl. (*To Clara*)

Phil. Not for me, your honour — avast now — I've something to say, something to overhaul that concerns you.

Wake. Concerns me.

Phil. Bring up alongside, here — a-hem. — Didn't you lose a son?

Wake. What, what! — speak not of it —

say not a word. Do you wish to make me go mad in your sight? (*Turning away*)

Clara. (*Crossing to Philip*) Oh, Sir, as you value my father's feelings, avoid that subject; he has forbidden it ever to be mentioned; my mother dares not name it.

Phil. I see how it is; my pumps will be at work in a minute. (*Aside*) Lord love your heart, I can't help it — I — I — don't be alarmed — I've news of him.

Wake. (*Rushing between them*) News of whom?

Phil. Of your son.

Wake. Of my boy? — Speak — does he live?

Phil. Tight and hearty.

Wake. Thank heaven! Come hither, Clara — I be so agitated — let me hold thee. My boy, my poor boy — tell me — tell me. Now, don't thee hurry — tell me coolly — you see I be cool.

Phil. I was his messmate, you see —

Wake. Well — go on — but don't thee hurry.

Phil. Many a taut gale we've weather'd together — so you see, poor fellow —

Wake. Poor fellow! — What, be there anything the matter? — But go on.

Phil. Strike my topmast, I shall run aground. (*Aside*) He's anchor'd in foreign parts.

Clara. Then he's not in England?

Wake. But he's alive — go on — go on. Shall I see him again before I die?

Phil. Here goes at once. (*Aside*) I left him in the Indies, you see, safely stow'd in a snug berth; and he desired me, if I was cruizing in these parts, to find you out, and let you know he was still on deck in the ship of life; that, tho' he had a sweetheart in every port, he couldn't steer clear of a wife; so got reev'd in the block of matrimony, and can man his jolly-boat with a couple of young tars, that know how to splice a rope already. (*Aside*) Split my capstan, but that's a whistler.

Wake. Clara! Charles! — Run, look for the dame; this news must not be kept — fly — you'll find her on the road home from market; but, be careful, tell her slowly at first — and stop, Clara — tell her to bring home something good for the stranger; and, hark ye, (*Aside to her*) let her spend every farthing, before we appear to be stinted. Mind that now, mind that.

Clara. Yes, father; and I'll tell her to hasten home.

Wake. Do, girl, do. (*Exit Clara*) After her, Charles, after her; you'll manage better between you.

Char. (*Aside to Wakefield*) Excuse me, Farmer; but this man must be made welcome, so pray accept. —

Wake. No, no; I won't hear of it. No more, no more. Nay, nay; now go after the girl, and take care of her. — I won't, I tell you. (*Putting Charles out at the door*) My poor boy — how I should like to see him.

Phil. Should you? — Should you? (*Aside*) No, I won't — not yet — not yet.

Wake. But I shall hear from him, I hope. How came he to turn sailor? Where did he go to? Who took him away from me?

Phil. That is all duly entered in his log-book, and will be shipped home the first opportunity.

Wake. If I could but see him once before I die — but I never shall be so happy. Do you know when he were lost? I were next to a madman for a whole fortnight — no sleep, no rest. I were then a prosperous man, with acres of land, and full barns; but the loss of my boy made me neglect everything: I did not care what came — bad luck followed bad luck — and misfortunes did then begin, which ended in my ruin.

Phil. Very molloncholy. (*Wiping his eyes*) But cheer up, my worthy master — you'll be well-timbered yet.

Wake. No, no, want have griped me too hard.

Phil. Now what should you think if I was to say — (*A loud shout without*) Holloa! Is that your Yorkshire warwhoop?

Wake. (*Going to the door*) As I live, the lads have gotten an old gipsy, and are ducking him in Prickle's Pond.

Phil. A gipsy! — stand aside — no — yes — start my timbers — split my binnacle if they shall touch a hair of his head. I know him, Farmer — I know him. Belay there, belay. — Let me come alongside. — Hilloah.
Exit.

Wake. (*Calling after him*) Come back to see the dame.

Phil. (*Without*) Oy, oy, master.

Scene 3.

A view of the country. A shout without. —

Enter villagers, dragging on Michael.

Mich. For the love of heaven, no more: you'll kill me, you'll kill me.

1st Vil. Away with him again!

2nd Vil. Throw him into the mill-stream.

All. The mill-stream — the mill-stream!

They are proceeding to drag him off — Philip enters.

Phil. Hilloah! — Avast, ye cannibals! —

Sea room, sea room, here. — (*Philip drives them off with his cudgel — Michael sinks on the ground — Philip raises him up*) — Cheerly, old Triton, cheerly. How do you feel in your hold?

Mich. Blessings on you.

Phil. What were they doing with your old hull?

Mich. Another dip would have killed me — they were drowning me — I'm a poor old gipsy.

Phil. I know you are — Where's the crew?

Mich. About a mile off, in a meadow.

Phil. Just the very thing. — Now, Beelzebub, we shall be a match for you.

Mich. They wanted to drown me for only looking into a henroost — a murrain seize every mother's son of 'em.

Phil. I understand — the old tricks, Michael.

Mich. Who told you my name?

Phil. I know the trim of your vessel well — but mum for the present — the coast is clear, so make the best of your way to the gang; here's some shot to put in your locker. (*Giving money*)

Mich. Blessings on you.

Phil. Go back to the tent, and bring a few of your lads to Farmer Wakefield's, in this port.

Mich. What for?

Phil. I want you to overhaul an affair of consequence.

Mich. But tell me — is Farmer Wakefield still alive?

Phil. You'll see him without a telescope, if you obey my orders; but say — will you come this evening?

Mich. It must be after dark, then. I know Farmer Wakefield well enough by name; perhaps I know a matter concerning him too.

Phil. I shall be on the look-out for you; don't let your memory start a timber.

Mich. But, Master Sailor, tell me if —

Phil. I can't stand palavering here; I must push off to the King's Head for my cargo. Now, belay, clap a stopper on your tongue, and be mum till you see me at the Farmer's; anybody will direct you — obey orders, and I'll make you an admiral; mutiny, and I'll blow you to the Devil.

Mich. But, Master Sailor —

Phil. I shall look out for you, old Mike.
Exit.

Mich. Old Mike! How should he know my name? — Well, I must hear what the lads say to this business — Old Mike's very cold — duck-ponds and mill-streams don't agree with old limbs — lucky I should meet with that sailor — he's given me five shillings. I'll try and scrape up a halfpenny more.

Enter Luke.

Spare a halfpenny for the love of charity — poor old man — seventy odd — spare a halfpenny.

Luke. (*Crossing*) Doan't thee bother, doan't thee bother.

Mich. Ah — let me look at you — let me look at ye. (*Aside*) I know you — know you well — won't you spare a halfpenny to an old acquaintance?

Luke. Dom thee, be quiet — I ha' nothing about me.

Mich. You won't, not a farthing?

Luke. If thee doesn't budge, I'll put thee in the stocks for a vagram!

Mich. You will put me in the stocks! Then evil betide you, ill luck blight you. Put me in the stocks! Hark ye — I could ruin you, vagram as I am; you may look, man. Come hither, let me whisper in your ear. (*Laying hold of his arm*) Don't thee flinch and shake at my cold hand — but it is chilly with the water: bend down your ear, and I'll make you tremble from head to foot.

Luke. Be you mad — why dost thee grip me so hard — I doan't know thee.

Mich. You don't — (*Michael whispers in Luke's ear*)

Luke. (*In great terror*) Toads and serpents! (*Aside*) Be it you? I thought you had been dead and buried — have you brought *him* here?

Mich. Him! — *him*, you say? — You remember that too? Wilt put me in the stocks now?

Luke. (*Aside*) It be all out now, for sartin — here be money for you; so be quiet about *that*, not a word —

Mich. Money! — I won't touch it — when the poor old gipsy ask'd for charity, you had nothing about you; but, now he can tread you to dust, you can find silver in your pockets: but I won't touch it — no, not if it were gold. You'll forget an old acquaintance, will you? — I won't have it — not a halfpenny — not a farthing — not a mite. *Exit.*

Luke. Now I do know the worst — now I be more comfortable than I ha' been for mony a day; because I be fix'd what to do. Ere this week be out, the turf may be on my head; but I shall have a neighbour in the same plight, and then I shall rest content. (*Bobby heard without, singing*) That be the lad's voice — Squire ha' let him out, I suppose, now it be all over about the girl.

Enter Bobby.

Bob. Tol de rol lol — Tol de rol lol. I be

out — I be out. Ah, Measter Luke bean't you ashamed to look me in the feace? I might ha' been kept i' the cage till Christmas, for what you'd ha' cared. Dickens and daisies, how deadly white you be.

Luke. I know it — I know it. (*Turning away*)

Bob. I see how it be — conscience ha' flung her flour-sack in your face; but it do sarve thee right, for I ha' lost my good character through being your postman, and I'm sure you can't help me to another; so the sooner I get to Lunnun, the better for I. (*Looking out*) Eh! — sure and sure, there be a shay going along the road like the wind.

Luke. A shay! (*Looking out*)

Bob. Oh dear, I wish I had my bundle, I'd run after it and jump up behind — I'm sure it be going to Lunnun.

Luke. (*Looking out with astonishment*) It be Squire's — yes it be, and there he sits inside, sure enough. Then he ha' run away, and left me to fight it out by myself.

Bob. Oh, my bundle! — I wish I had my bundle.

Luke. A chicken-hearted coward! he couldn't stay and face it out as I do; but let him go, I shall manage it better now. I must clean up my pistols — my heart be already fix'd, and I feel as bold as a lion. A drop more brandy; a look at my wife's grave; a good long think of what ha' passed, and then for the finish of my long, long day's work. *Exit.*

Bob. What a cruel pity it be I hadn't my bundle — I can't go without it, because there be my new shoes, and clean stockings, and a waistcoat that cost me a matter o' two shillings, all pack'd up in it. But stop — canna Measter Luke send it after me, directed Mister Robert Trot, Lunnun? — To be sure he can. Dang it if I don't go, then: the shay must stop to change horses, so I'll run till I overtake it. Now for it — nothing shall stop me; — good bye, every body, and now for Lunnun.

As he is running off, two villagers enter, and seize him.

1st Vil. So we have caught you at last, my little tom tit.

Bob. What, be I stopped again?

1st Vil. Farmer Charles has a word to say to you.

Bob. Now doan't — let me go — let me go — and I give you two shilling.

1st Vil. No, Master Bobby, that won't answer; so come quietly.

Bob. (*Lying down*) I'll be shot if I wool.

2nd Vil. Come, no obstinacy.

Bob. Oh, dear! Oh, dear! — caged, horse-whipped, and killed — I shall never get to Lunnun.

> *They drag him off, kicking and struggling.*

Scene 4.

Interior of Wakefield's cottage. A table set out for supper — Philip, Wakefield, Dame Wakefield, Charles, and Clara discovered — Philip's bundle is on a stool near him.

Dame. Don't thee say no, Master Sailor.

Phil. No more, dame, I thank you; I've stow'd away enough for the night. Come, Farmer, cheer up, don't be down-hearted. What, though you be somewhat founder'd, who knows but the next breeze may send you spanking along with wind and weather.

Wake. And be all that so valuable?

Phil. What, my cargo? Don't say a word — only wait till morning, and I'll show you the stuff in a box here, that shall set your heart afloat in a sea of joy; — talk of bank notes — ropes-end and old junk to this; — but wait till a friend calls here for me, and, if you don't dance a hornpipe on the quarter deck, I'm no seaman. — Where's old Mike, I wonder? I suppose it must rest till the morning. (*Aside*) Come, my lass, — Lord love you, I like to look at you; you do mount a smile and cheer us a bit — what say you to joining with me in a ditty? "Poor Jack," "Black-Ey'd Susan," or "The Old Commodore"?

Wake. No, no; no singing — I be tired, and —

Phil. Belay, belay, don't run foul of my inclination. Come, come, pipe all hands for fun; sew up old care in a blanket, and pitch him to Davy Jones. Nothing like a ditty — aloft in a storm, on deck at the mid-watch, or buffeting with the billows of misfortune, what cheers the heart like a good old song; when the deck has been clearing for action, what could make us fight better than "Rule Britannia, Britannia rules the Waves"; or, "Stand to your Guns, my Hearts of Oak"; and, when wounded, in the cockpit, what could better teach us to bear our misfortunes like men, than "Here, a sheer Hulk, lies poor Tom Bowling"?

Wake. Well, well, do as you will. Come, girl, do thy best.

Phil. That's your sort; that's tight and hearty.

Clara sings.

Young Susan had lovers so many, that she
  Hardly knew upon which to decide;
They all spoke sincerely and promised to be
  So worthy of such a sweet bride.

In the morning she'd gossip with William, and then
The noon would be spent with young Harry,
The evening with John; so, among all the men,
  She never could tell which to marry.
      Heigho! heigho!
      I'm afraid,
That too many lovers will puzzle a maid.

William grew jealous, and so went away,
  Young Harry got tired of wooing;
While John, having teazed her to fix on the day,
  Received but a frown for so doing.
So, among all her lovers, quite left in the lurch,
  She wept every night on her pillow;
And meeting, one day, a pair going to church,
  Turned away and died under a willow.
      Heigho! heigho!
      I'm afraid,
That too many lovers will puzzle a maid.

Phil. That's the sort of thing — splice me — what d'ye think o' that pipe, my commodore? — well, here's wishing you may be a captain's wife — no offence, I hope; I see how the land lies; excuse me if I've lost the steerage of my tongue.

Dame. But I want you to talk about my poor boy.

Wake. Silence, Dame — have I not told thee not to speak on't at present! Be quiet, I say: I'm thinking how the sailor may be accommodated here; Dame Hillock said you could sleep at her cottage? (*To Clara*)

Clara. Yes, father; she will come for me before she goes to rest.

Phil. What, turn the lass out of her hammock; no, that won't do. Yet I *should* like to rest here too: I should sleep so comfortable.

Wake. Hark ye, Master Sailor, you shall have my bed.

Phil. Now — now — commodore.

Wake. I insist upon it: 'tis the best bed in my poor home, and you shall sleep in it.

Phil. Huzza! (*Cuts a caper*) I could jump over the moon. (*Aside*) Where can old Mike be?

Wake. Come, girl, get ready. Charles will go with you, but there be no fear of any more such work as happened last night.

Clara. Good night, father. Charles, you might stay with my father, to amuse him for half an hour, and advise for the best. I have only a few yards to go, and shall not be out of hearing.

Char. I can return immediately.

Wake. No, no; I do not wish to sit up late to-night; I be fatigued, and do want rest: so kiss me, girl, and go — there, good night. Good night, Charles, and thank thee for your kindness.

Phil. Avast there — are you going without noticing me?

Clara. Good night, my friend.

Phil. Give me your hand: good night, my lass, Lord love you. *Exit Clara and Charles.* (*Aside*) It's no use waiting for old Mike, he won't come to-night — so I'll surprise 'em all to-morrow: I am very sorry to put you about in this way, but —

Wake. Say no more, my friend. Dame, take a light, and show the sailor up stairs.

Phil. What, so soon! Well, just as you please — take care of my cargo tho'. (*Gives his bundle to Wakefield*) Good night, noble captain: pipe all hands at five o'clock, for I've a day's work to do. We'll jig it to-morrow, to the piping of goldfinches; heave ahead, Dame. Good night, old Commodore.

The Dame precedes Philip up the stairs with a light; the Farmer is shaking hands with them, and the scene shuts them in.

Scene 5.

The back part of Wakefield's cottage. A light is seen through a window in the flat. Enter Luke, with a brace of pistols in his hand.

Luke. There be a light in the place where the Farmer sleeps; I'll watch here till it be out, and then he'll be in bed. I must get round the garden, climb up the gate at the side, and get in at the window. (*The light seen through the window goes out*) Ah, he ha' put out the candle: now to make all ready for climbing — this shall do it. — I'll take my aim steady and sure; then I'll snap the trigger; then there'll be a stunning sound, a cry of death, a flooding o' blood on the floor, and Luke's revenge finished. Ha! ha! this will be one of the merriest nights I ha' passed for mony a year — I ha' been drinking, too, all day, but, instead of getting drunk, it ha' made me fierce and bold. (*He places the pistols in a belt under his frock*) Now for it — gently, be quiet, don't thee be scared, or my hand will shake — lay still, lay still. (*Striking his breast*) Now I be right again, — 'twere but a little fit, and now I be firm as oak. *Exit.*

Music. — Enter Michael, followed by two Gipsies. They advance a few paces, as if watching Luke.

Mich. There he goes — hush lad — I know he's after something; going to rob the house, maybe; we'll teach him to spurn a poor old gipsy: hush.

1st Gip. He's climbing up the fence.

Mich. Follow him, lads, — follow him, — see what he be about; and then for the sailor, — now, gently — no noise.

Music and exeunt.

Scene 6.

A bed-room in the cottage. — Bed in the corner — Philip is discovered lying asleep. — A window, through which the moon is seen shining — a door in flat. Music. — Luke is at the window, in the act of climbing up — he opens it gently, and advances one leg in, and, resting on the side, looks towards the bed — he speaks in a whisper.

Luke. He sleeps — and alone, I think. Now, Farmer, we shall be even. (*He cocks the pistol, and levels it at Philip; at that moment the first Gipsy appears at the window*) My hand do shake so, I shall miss him.

1st Gip. Aye, that thee shalt.

Music. — The Gipsy dislodges Luke from his seat, and throws him into the room — the pistol goes off in the air — in the act, Philip springs from the bed, seizes Luke, and drags him to the front of the stage.

1st Gip. Hold him tight — hold him tight.

The Gipsy enters at the window.

Phil. Holloa! Farmer, Farmer Wakefield, we're boarded by pirates — I'll grapple you — what — Luke!

Music. — The Dame enters with a light, followed by the Farmer, Clara, Charles, Michael, and the other Gipsy, at the door.

Wake. Luke, what be the meaning of this?

Mich. Stop — hear old Gipsy Mike: — Master Luke stole away your boy, and sold him to me; I took care of him till one day —

Phil. He ran away, and went to sea — I am that boy.

Mike, Farmer, Dame, Clara, Charles. You!

Wake. You my boy Philip!

Phil. Aye, old Mike will soon know me.

Luke struggles with Philip, and succeeds in drawing another pistol from his belt, and is levelling it at the Farmer, when Philip thrusts back his arm, and Luke, receiving the fire, falls dead.

Wake. My boy! My boy! Your old Father's arms are open to receive you.

Philip runs into Wakefield's arms; then the Dame is warmly embraced by him; Wakefield kneels; Philip takes Clara round the waist, and occupies the centre of the stage; the Gipsies fill up one side, and Michael and Charles the other.

THE END.

DOUGLAS WILLAM JERROLD
1803-1857

The Rent-Day
(1832)

Douglas Jerrold is best remembered today as a contributer to *Punch*, a friend of
Dickens and Thackeray, and the author of *Black-Eyed Susan*. He found the materials
for this popular nautical melodrama in the experiences of his childhood and youth.
Douglas's father was a strolling player in country towns, and the boy's schooling
was limited to occasional lessons from his grandmother and a man named Wilkinson
in the theatrical troupe, and a few seasons in school in the towns where his father
was acting. Now and then Douglas appeared on the stage when a play called for a
child's part. But in 1813, when he was ten and the English Navy needed sailors for
the struggle with Napoleon, Douglas went aboard the *Namur* as a "first-class volun-
teer." He and other boys on shipboard amused themselves with getting up amateur
theatrical shows. In 1815 he was transferred to the brig *Earnest*, which was engaged
in carrying military supplies to Ostend just before the battle of Waterloo. In
October, after the battle, Jerrold was discharged from the Navy, joined his family
in London, and was articled to a printer. Resolved to educate himself in spite of
long hours in the print shop, he rose early to study Latin, French, and Italian and
to read a good deal, especially Shakespeare and Sir Walter Scott.

After marrying in 1824, Jerrold became a newspaperman. He had begun to con-
tribute dramatic criticism to the *Mirror of the Stage* in 1823, and by 1830 he was
writing essays and articles for numerous newspapers and magazines, including *The
Athenaeum* and *Blackwood's*. He started a humor magazine, *Punch in London*, in
1832; it anticipated the more famous *Punch*, founded in 1841, to which Jerrold contributed for some years. In 1845 he established *Douglas Jerrold's Shilling Magazine*
to provide popular reading at a low price; and in 1846 *Douglas Jerrold's Weekly
Newspaper*. Both these journals, successful for a while, ceased publication by 1849.
In 1852 he became editor of *Lloyd's Illustrated Weekly Newspaper* and continued in
this position until his death in 1857.

In spite of all this busy journalistic activity Jerrold found time to write more than sixty plays of various types. He began with *More Frightened than Hurt* (1821), when he was eighteen years old. Its mild success, and that of others within the next few years, led Manager Davidge of the Coburg to employ Jerrold as playwright for the theatre — a post that Jerrold held for some years. His first widely popular success was *Black-Eyed Susan*, based on a sentimental song, "Sweet William's Farewell to Black-Eyed Susan," and produced at the Surrey in 1829. Besides the materials of domestic melodrama (the landlord who would evict a widow unless the rent is paid), the play includes a simple sailor lad as hero, a troupe of Jolly Jack Tars (singing and dancing sailors), smugglers, a drunken Captain's assault upon Susan, William's sentence to death for striking his Captain, and a last-minute reprieve. Jerrold's experience on shipboard enabled him to sprinkle William's lines with an amazing patter of nautical terms. Rapid action, British pride in the Navy, the arrival of marines to overpower the villains, and domestic love passages perhaps account for the popularity of this play, which became standard in every repertory for the next fifty years — and more.

In 1829 Jerrold contributed to the stream of history plays with *Thomas à Becket*, a serious play, but in prose. His *Mutiny at the Nore; or, British Sailors in 1797* (1830) sympathetically set forth the grievances that underlay the mutiny. Jerrold tried blank verse in *The Devil's Ducat* of 1830, a fanciful drama laid in Naples. The play was produced at the Adelphi for the Christmas season, but verse was not Jerrold's forte. In 1832, with *The Rent-Day* and *The Factory Girl* Jerrold produced melodramas that contained some social criticism.

In his playwriting Jerrold prided himself upon originality and his use of English materials. He bitterly opposed the vogue for translations from the French, and when asked to adapt a French play for Drury Lane, replied: "I will come into this theatre as an original dramatist or not at all." Even if Jerrold's plays seem to twentieth-century readers scrappy or mere "bubbles of the day" (the title of one of Jerrold's comedies), serious intentions are apparent in them. A close friend of Dickens, Thackeray, Tom Taylor, and other literary men, Jerrold had something of their spirit of reform. In newspapers and magazines he opposed capital punishment, the hawking of the dying speeches of executed criminals through the streets, and the scandalous conditions of the slaughterhouse at Smithfield Market. He founded the Whittington Club to provide some social life for apprentices and clerks, and agitated mildly for other liberal and humanitarian reforms. Some of his feeling may be seen in *The Rent-Day*, even if any reforming purpose is overshadowed by the action of this melodrama.

Jerrold's inspiration for *The Rent-Day* was two well-known paintings by Sir David Wilkie. Jerrold proudly represented these paintings in stage tableaux: the picture entitled "The Rent-Day" in the opening scene, and "Distraining for Rent" in the opening and closing scenes of Act II. Walter Jerrold reports that the audience greeted the opening scene with "rapturous applause . . . as an exact reproduction of Wilkie's popular picture." Sir David Wilkie wrote to Jerrold that his "inventive fancy has created . . . all the living characters and progressive events of real life" suggested by the pictures.

The farmer's annual rent, paid to his landlord's steward, was drawn from the farmer's subsistence; the play portrayed both the hardships of farm life that follow poor crops, and the suffering of wives and children when a wastrel Squire may demand his rent whatever the human cost. The prescriptive morality of the domestic play is evident in the portrayal of Martin's home life, the relations between Martin and Rachel, their love for their children, and the woeful threat of a broken home. Rachel's scorn for her would-be seducer exhibits the domestic ideal. Perhaps the audience thought Martin's hasty and unjust suspicions of his spotless wife a lesson in the need for conjugal faith and trust. Jerrold intended the play to exhibit "strong human . . . emotion of that universal kind which the untaught pauper understands." He intended his play to stir the audience in the pit. He may also have intended a lesson for the audience in the boxes.

The drama of realistic social protest, implicit in Jerrold's subject, had not been invented; and Jerrold, unlike Bernard Shaw, was not equipped to invent it. Jerrold turned to the materials of melodrama for the action in his play and forced his scenes into a complex of manipulated plots, absurd incidents, incredible villainies, and nick-of-time rescues, including the farfetched motivation for Crumbs's extortions, the fragmentary plot to blackmail him, the attempt to rob and perhaps murder Squire Grantley, Rachel's arrival in the nick of time to prevent the deed, Martin's arrival in time to be cozened into suspicion of his wife, the discovery of grandfather's gold hidden in a chair, and the revelation that the stranger is the Squire. Instead of developing a plot with adequate motivation and characterization, Jerrold filled out his pages with irrelevant bits and pieces — the comic scenes between Bullfrog and Polly, for instance, serve no purpose in the plot and lead us away from the unprepared revelation that Polly will marry Toby.

An interesting fact about the published play is that it restored lines that George Colman, Examiner of Plays, ordered omitted from the performance as profane, including "The blessed little babes, God bless 'em!" "Heaven help us!" and "Isn't that an angel?"

The play does exhibit some originality and perhaps one conscious departure from the pattern of melodrama. In the opening of the play it is assumed, on the basis of apparent evidence, that Squire Grantley is the typical wastrel, gambler, and heartless oppressor of the poor usual in the melodramatic pattern. Martin easily assumes that the stranger is also a seducer. But in the revelation scene, Squire Grantley turns out to be a kindhearted landlord, who hereafter will live on his estate and deal generously with his tenants. The year was 1832, when the first Reform Bill was passed; and there were high hopes that a triumphant reforming spirit in the land might remedy old injustices. *The Rent-Day* reflected the hope that landlords might assume their responsibilities and treat their tenants with justice and generosity. The play would not reform a system (nor would *Widowers' Houses* in 1892), but it might reform the men who administered the system. Touches of such humanitarian doctrine throughout Jerrold's life support the possibility that he intended his play to touch the hearts of the gentlemen in the theatre's box seats.

THE RENT-DAY

A Domestic Drama In Three Acts

by

DOUGLAS JERROLD

First performed at the Theatre Royal, Drury Lane, January 25, 1832.

Cast of Characters

MARTIN HEYWOOD	STEPHEN
GRANTLEY	BURLY
OLD CRUMBS	SAILOR
TOBY HEYWOOD	RACHEL HEYWOOD
BULLFROG	POLLY BRIGGS
SILVER JACK	DAME BEANSTALK
HYSSOP	FARMERS, FARMERS' WIVES,
BEANSTALK	CHILDREN, ETC.

ACT I.

Scene 1.

An apartment in Grantley Hall. Discovered, Crumbs (the steward), Beanstalk, farmers, their wives and children, servants, etc. The characters and stage so arranged as to form, on the rising of the curtain, a representation of Wilkie's picture of "Rent-Day." A large archway in front, and a door beyond.

Crumbs. By my heart! there's naught so pleasant as a rent-day.

Bean. Thee be'st right, master Crumbs; naught; — when the corn's in the barn and the money in the bag; but rent-day, wi' bad crops and low pockets, be an awful thing.

1st Far. It be, indeed. See what it ha' brought Phil Jones to. That seizure, master Crumbs, ha' broke his heart. Warn't you a bit hasty like?

Crumbs. Ha, friends! it's a sad task to be steward! I often seize with tears in my eyes. What then? we must keep a clear book. I never turn out a family but — (*To one of the farmers*) — you don't drink your ale, master Stoke — with the greatest reluctance. Last week, when Miles and his children went to the workhouse; it — (*To another farmer*) — help your dame to some pie — it made me really uneasy. Yet one's feelings must suffer. One must keep a clear book.

Bean. Where be Martin Heywood, I wonder? Ha! things ha' ne'er gone right since the old man died of a sudden. I had hopes to see Martin here.

Crumbs. I've had hopes, some time past. But here's a toast: (*Fills a glass*) Here's punctuality to all tenants. (*They drink — looking significantly at each other*)

Bean. Come, I'll gi' thee another. Here be mercy and liberality to all landlords!

All — except Crumbs. Well said. Mercy all landlords! (*Drinking*)

Bean. Why, Master Crumbs, be there a spider in the glass? — thee dost not drink. Come, "mercy," man. There be few on us, I fear, would be worse for a little more on't. Tak' another sup.

Crumbs. No more. There, Master Beanstalk, is your receipt—there, friend Thomas, (*Giving various papers to farmers*) is yours. As for that matter about the tithes, Master

261

Hodge, we must talk on't. All our business is now despatched, and I'll drain another glass to our next merry meeting. (*All rise, having filled their glasses*)

Bean. Stay. I'll clap a tail to that toast: so drink "Good fortune to Master Heywood!"

All. Ay! ay!

Bean. Stop: and his wife, Rachel — not yet — and all his darling little babes — God bless 'em! (*All drink*) Why, Master Crumbs, what makes thee look so blank! It be a bad sign, if a man make wry faces when he hears luck wished to another.

Crumbs. Wry faces! you mistake. But you take a good deal of interest in Martin Heywood.

Bean. Naturally. I ha' known him ever since he could ha' lain in my hat. My dame, here, stood for his wife, Rachel; and a blessed little blossom she was. If it hadn't been for bad times, — but I won't brag. (*Retires amongst farmers*)

2d Far. (*Comes down to Crumbs*) Now, good master steward, you'll give me time, I hope?

Crumbs. Time isn't in my gift, if I would.

2d Far. I have a wife and eight children.

Crumbs. A marvellous pity; but I must make up my book.

2d Far. Give me but two months.

Crumbs. You shall have two weeks. Don't reckon on an hour more. Two weeks, and then I sell every stick.

2d Far. Have you no heart?

Crumbs. I must make up my book! — Two weeks.

> *Farmer retires. Beanstalk, who, with others, has filled his glass, comes down and forces a glass on Crumbs.*

Bean. I say, Master Crumbs, the old toast at parting "Here's mercy to all landlords!"

Crumbs. (*Unwillingly drinking*) "Mercy — landlords!" — Farewell, farewell! — (*All exeunt but Crumbs*) They're gone; now to sort the money. (*Employs himself sorting papers, notes, etc.*) Heywood must pack. The farm must come into my hands. Let me reckon. Another twelvemonth, — the landlord still away, and my fortune is complete. I have scraped, and scratched, and wrung! — 'Tis very well. Such another year, and farewell, England.

> *Silver Jack and Hyssop look in.*

Jack. (*Pointing out Crumbs to Hyssop*) 'Tis he! I'll swear it!

Crumbs. Who's there?

> *Jack and Hyssop disappear.*

> *Enter Stephen, with letters.*

Is it you, Stephen, talking to yourself!

Ste. Talking, sir? not I. Here be letters: this, from London; it has our master's crest. (*Retires*)

Crumbs. Master! Humph! (*Reads*) 'Tis from young Spendthrift. The old style: more money. He shall have it.

Toby. (*Without*) No, no; I'll walk in. When he sees me, he'll be sure I'm here.

> *Enter Toby Heywood — Stephen comes down.*

Servant, Master Crumbs.

Crumbs. Servant; I had hoped to see your brother, Martin. (*To Stephen, half aside*) Stephen, go to Bullfrog. Tell him to come to me to-night; I shall have business for him. Ay, and call on Burly, too, and tell him the same.   *Exit Stephen.*

Toby. Bullfrog and Burly! What devil's feast's afoot, that they must have a spoon in?

Crumbs. All trades must be filled: Bullfrog's is an ugly one.

Toby. Ay; but the ugliest trades have their moments of pleasure. Now, if I were a grave-digger, or even a hang-man, there are some people (*Glancing at Crumbs*) I could work for with a great deal of enjoyment.

Crumbs. That Bullfrog's maxim; he's very merry.

Toby. The most jovial of brokers and appraisers. He levies a distress as though he brought a card of invitation; giggles himself into possession; makes out the inventory with a chuckle; and carts off chairs and tables to "Begone dull care!" or "How merrily we live who shepherds be."

Crumbs. True, in these matters he has a coolness.

Toby. Coolness! he'd eat oysters whilst his neighbour's house was in flames — always provided that his own was insured. Coolness! he's a piece of marble, carved into a broad grin!

Crumbs. Well, well, your business with me?

Toby. My brother, Martin, has been once more disappointed.

Crumbs. So have I.

Toby. That's lucky. You'll be better able to feel for him.

Crumbs. I want money.

Toby. So does he.

Crumbs. I'll give time, if there be any one to answer for him. Can't you assist him? have you nothing?

Toby. Yes: fifteen pounds a year, as principal usher to the town free-school. My goods and chattels are a volume of "Robinson Crusoe"; ditto "Pilgrim's Progress"; with "Plutarch's Morals," much like the morals of many other people, — a good deal dog's-eared. If my uncle had made me a plough-man, instead of a mongrel scholar, I might have a mouldy guinea or so.

Crumbs. But has your brother no one to speak for him?

Toby. Yes. There are two.

Crumbs. Where shall I find them?

Toby. In the church-yard. His grandfather and his father lie there. Go to the graves of the old men, and these are the words the dead will say to you: "We lived sixty years in Holly Farm. In all that time we never begged an hour of the Squire. We paid rent, tax, and tithe: we earned our bread with our own hands, and owed no man a penny when laid down here. Well, then, will ye be hard on young Heywood? will ye press upon our child, our poor Martin, when murrain has come upon his cattle, and blight fallen upon his corn?" This is what the dead will say. I should like to know what the living has to answer?

Crumbs. (*Handing over the Squire's letter*) This.

Toby. (*Opening it*) From the young Squire. (*Reads*) "Master Crumbs, use all despatch, and send me, on the receipt of this, £500: Cards have tricked me, and the devil cogged the dice. Get the money at all costs, and quickly. Robert Grantley." Ay, a right true letter from an absent landlord.

Crumbs. 'Tis hard to be steward to a wild youth, who looks not after his own estate. You see, he leaves me no discretion.

Toby. Oh, no! If the landlord lose at gaming, his tenants must suffer for't. The Squire plays a low card — issue a distress warrant! He throws deuce-ace — turn a family into the fields! 'Tis only awkward to lose hundreds on a card; but very rascally to be behind-hand with one's rent!

Crumbs. As you say — very true. — Good morning, Master Toby.

Toby. Good morning. Poor brother Martin wouldn't come himself, and so I thought I'd step up and speak to you. But I'll tell him that you'll give him all time, and that he's not to make himself uneasy, and all that. I'll comfort him, depend on't. And, I say; when you write back to the Squire, you can tell him, by way of postscript, if he must feed the gaming-table, not to let it be with money, wrung, like blood, from the wretched. Just tell him, whilst he shuffles the cards, to remember the aching hearts of his distressed tenants. And when he'd rattle the dice, let him stop and think of the knuckles of the bailiff and the tax-gatherer, knocking at the cottage doors of the poor. Good morning, Mr. Steward; good morning. *Exit.*

Crumbs. Now to give my instructions to the beadle and appraiser, and out he goes. *Exit.*

Scene 2.

A rustic view. Enter Jack and Hyssop.

Hys. (*To Jack, who is looking back*) Come, come; why do you loiter?

Jack. Don't you see that woman still at the stile? — the prettiest creature I've looked on this many a day.

Hys. Tush! now we're on business. Go on with your story. Let me see, where did that wench's black eyes interrupt us? Oh! you were about to tell me how you knew that this steward, Crumbs, as he is called, was your master, when you took to live by your wits, and the nimbleness of your five fingers. Now, are you sure you know him?

Jack. Do I know my own hand? Thirty years ago, when but a boy, I ran away from my apprenticeship —

Hys. Ay, of rope-making: a fatal profession. Go on.

Jack. Pshaw! I fell in with John Harris — for that's his real name — in London. He was a knight of the road, of the first order; kept as pretty a blood, and shuffled a card better than any baronet of St. James's. Bless you! he gave the fashion to Hounslow and Finchley. Well, Newgate hath clipped many a brave fellow's wing! Captain Harris was taken, tried, and condemned for Tyburn.

Hys. Then he got a reprieve?

Jack. Yes, in the way of some files, sent to him in a pigeon-pie, and twenty fathom of cord, baked in a few loaves. He gave them the slip, and started for the Indies. There, I heard, he met with an Englishman, was brought back again, and here he is. Have you a mind to earn fifty pounds?

Hys. If't may be done with the leisure of a gentleman.

Jack. 'Tis but to open your mouth. See: (*Takes out a seal-skin tobacco pouch, and from it an old hand-bill. Gives it to Hyssop*) I have worn it about me for many a long day.

Hys. (*Reading the bill*) "Fifty pounds reward! Escaped from Newgate! John Harris, a convict. He is five feet ten; of darkish complexion; oval face; quick black eyes, with an eager look: his mouth large and restless; his hair a deep chestnut brown, in close curls. His voice is full, and his manner of speaking, rapid. His pace is short and hurried. Has a scar over the left eye; also a scar on the back of the left hand." This can never be the picture of that old man?

Jack. Why, 'tis seven-and-twenty years since he sat for it: that's some time for one who hasn't walked upon velvet. Why, even *I* am changed. I can remember when my mother used to call me her "lovely little Jack." As for Harris, 'twould have done you good to hear him cry "Stand!" — it came sharp upon you, like the click of a trigger. Step aside, Hyssop; here are two of the natives. (*They retire amongst the trees*)

Enter Polly Briggs, Bullfrog following her.

Pol. Now, Mr. Bullfrog, don't tease me.

Bul. I tease! I should like to know how a man with a freehold of twenty pounds per year, a pretty business, and a genteel figure, could tease, even if he would? It's only poor people who tease: we moneyed men delight!

Pol. Well, I'm very poor, Mr. Bullfrog.

Bul. You are: it's your only fault.

Pol. Fault! poverty's no crime.

Bul. Isn't it? well, it's so like, I don't know the difference. It's a pity poor girls have pretty faces; they lead us prudent capitalists into many false reckonings. Oh, Polly! if I should love you!

Pol. La! what should you see to love in me?

Bul. See! why, there's a beautiful face, with its streaks of red, and the blue veins running up and down the white skin, for all the world like the ruled pages of a new ledger!

Pol. White skin! Wouldn't you be better pleased if it were yellow?

Bul. La! why?

Pol. 'Twould remind you of your guineas, you know. And, I'm sure, you love nothing so well.

Bul. Yes, one thing — almost: that pretty little red mouth! Oh, Polly! if you had but a small annuity, or expectations from a sick aunt, or anything of that kind, you'd be a perfect woman. — But I must have a kiss.

Pol. A kiss! I never heard of such a thing!

Enter Toby Heywood.

Bul. What an ignorant young woman you must be. A kiss is — (*He is approaching her, when Toby comes down between them*)

Toby. She knows. I taught her long ago. And harkye, Master Bullfrog!

Bul. Now be cool. I'm always cool.

Toby. You'll still be meddling. Don't you remember that you were *once* kicked?

Bul. Yes. And wasn't I a picture of pa-tience? Did I fly into a rage? No: I flung my-self upon the laws. I made twenty pounds by that job, and that didn't make me conceited, either.

Toby. Take care, or I may kick, too!

Bul. No. Prudence won't let you.

Toby. Why not?

Bul. You can't afford to pay for luxuries!

Toby. Oh! on such an occasion, I'd not mind running in debt! (*To Polly*) But, Polly, go to the farm; run and comfort Rachel. Leave the appraiser to me. Go. (*Exit Polly*) What! waste your valuable time with a girl not worth a groat?

Bul. That's true. And I ought to be down at Brown's, the millwright.

Tobby. Ha! No use going there. I'm told they barricade doors and windows. You'll never get in there.

Bul. Ha! ha! You don't know my wit. I took possession this morning.

Toby. Why, how?

Bul. Such a scheme! About an hour after Brown had let himself out of the window, I got a little girl to go and knock at the door, and call for Mrs. Brown. I taught her her lesson; this was it: "Mrs. Brown, for Heaven's sake!" — I made her say "Heaven," because it sounded more real.

Toby. Yes, Heaven is a good word to lie under.

Bul. Bless you! I've found it so. "For Heaven's sake, come to your husband! he's chopped his leg clean through with an axe!" You should have heard Mrs. Brown scream! Out she ran, wringing her hands, her three children tumbling after her; and in I and the beadle walked.

Toby. Then 'twas all a lie?

Bul. Lord love you, only my wit. And so I told Mrs. Brown; and bade her wipe her eyes, and make herself comfortable, whilst I took down the goods. I shall sell on Thursday.

Toby. Sell! You are throwing away your time, knocking down tea-cups and wooden dishes. You should go to the colonies, and sell the blacks.

Bul. I certainly do pass off an article with a flourish.

Toby. Flourish! how capitally you'd dis-pose of a man, his wife, and six children!

Bul. I'm not conceited; but I think I should. Hem! "Ladies and gentlemen, the next lot consists of eight mortals." — Stop, are blacks mortals?

Toby. Why, with some, it's a matter of doubt, so let them have the benefit of it.

Bul. "Eight mortals. How much shall we say for the lot?"

Toby. Or you might ask, — "How much for the man? a strong-bodied labourer, a virtuous husband, and an affectionate father. He weighs fourteen stone, hasn't a single vice, stands five feet eleven, is very handsome, and is going at only a handful of dollars."

Bul. Must you talk about affection, and all that?

Toby. Of course. Virtue is especially marketable in the West Indies. There, it's worth while being a constant husband and a doting parent; for one sells for a few dollars extra. Go to Jamaica, by all means.

Bul. I think I should succeed.

Toby. Succeed! After your story to Mrs. Brown, if your own father were going by auction, you'd knock him down with the greatest grace in life.

Bul. Now you flatter!

Toby. Impossible. With you, there's no improving upon truth.

Bul. Well, that's really handsome. But I —

Enter Crumbs.

Good day, Master Crumbs. I was coming, by your order, about —

Crumbs. In good time. (*Seeing Toby*) He here!

Toby. Don't let me interrupt business. (*Crosses*) I'm going to the farm. Good by, Bullfrog; and, I say, if, in the course of auction matters, you've a lot of humanity to dispose of —

Bul. Well!

Toby. Think of Mrs. Brown, and buy it in for yourself! *Exit.*

Crumbs. A subtle, sneering rogue, that. Harkye, Bullfrog, you must this day seize on Heywood's goods. (*Silver Jack and Hyssop come down*) Strangers here!

Jack. (*Slapping Crumbs on back*) Your servant, old sir!

Crumbs. Old sir!

Jack. Ay. There's no shame in gray hairs, is there? even though they once were a chesnut brown. (*Sarcastically*) What then! hair will change.

Hys. Yes, and quick black eyes, with an eager look, will grow dim and dull.

Jack. A deep voice will lose something of its music: and five feet ten shrink into (*Measuring Crumbs with his eye*) five feet seven or eight.

Hys. A large and restless mouth *may* last.

Jack. Ay, and scars — (*Seizing the hand of Crumbs, who stands amazed and trembling*) Yes, scars will not rub out.

Crumbs. Villains! robbers! (*Passionately*)

Bul. Robbers! shall I call the constable?

Crumbs. Peace! away! (*Is hurrying off; Jack arrests him. Bullfrog goes up to them*)

Jack. Nay, nay, old gentleman; we are strangers, and ask a day's hospitality at the mansion. (*Follows him*)

Crumbs. (*Endeavouring to escape*) Away — away!

Jack. (*Holding him*) As you will not give us houseroom, will you tell me where I may find a printer? — I wish to distribute through the village some hundred copies of this little bill. (*Shows Crumbs handbill: he staggers back*)

Bul. A printer! My cousin Hairspace is the man. Does all my catalogues. Give me the bill. (*Is about to take the bill*)

Crumbs. Touch it not; touch it not, I say! Come, gentlemen! (*Inviting them on*)

Jack. Nay, we will not trouble you. (*To Bullfrog*) Your cousin, you say?

Bul. The best printer forty miles about. In black, blue, or red ink, plain or ornamental, — there is no printer who — (*Endeavouring to get the bill*)

Crumbs. The devil seize thee! peace! — (*Crosses to Jack and Hyssop*) Come, gentlemen; nay, you must with me to the mansion. We will have a brave dinner! Some wine! wine! I do entreat you not to stay, my good friends. — (*Anxiously endeavouring to lead them off*)

Jack. As you're so pressing — but we shall trouble you?

Crumbs. No, no; it gladdens me that I have met you. Come. (*Going*)

Bul. (*Comes between Crumbs and Jack. Gives Jack a card*) My cousin's card.

Crumbs. (*To Bullfrog*) What dost mutter?

Bul. Mutter! La! Mr. Crumbs! I only presented Timothy's card. Must always think of trade, you know.

Crumbs. (*In extreme passion*) Think of trade! would'st see me hanged?

Bul. No. I never neglect business for pleasure.

Crumbs. Beware! beware! and follow me! (*To Jack and Hyssop*) Come, gentlemen; come, my good friends! Nay, you first; I entreat.

Exit, bowing off Jack and Hyssop, who exchange looks.

Bul. Beware — beware — to a freeholder! I'll — no — I'm not yet rich enough to be in passion. When I've made my fortune, then I may indulge in the feelings of a gentleman. *Exit.*

Scene 3.

Stage a little dark. A rustic landscape. Evening. Rachel discovered, seated on the projecting step of a stile at the side.

Rach. The sun is almost set, and yet I see not Martin. Oh! my dear husband! my poor children! Heaven be kind to us, — for I've almost lost all other hope. — Ha! Martin! Martin!

Martin Heywood appears at the stile: — crosses it.

Mar. Rachel here! — Why did you leave the farm?

Rach. I could not stay there, and you away. Our children, Martin; they cried for you. I could not speak to them. I could not stay. Now, Martin, your friend?

Mar. (*With bitterness*) Friend!

Rach. Oh! do not look so — do not.

Mar. I have done that to-day I never did before; I have wished myself dead! ay, dead! that I might be quit of all.

Rach. And our children, Martin?

Mar. 'Twould be better for 'em. There's some spell upon me! Do what I will, it does not thrive! Why, 'tis certain there's some curse upon me!

Rach. Be patient, dear Martin!

Mar. Patient! I have been patient. Harvest after harvest's failed; — flock after flock has died; yet I have smiled upon't, and gone whistling 'bout the fields. I have been hunted by landlord — threatened by the taxman — yet I've put a stout heart upon't and never drooped. Rachel Heywood, you see me now without a shilling — without a home — my children with not a week's food before them — my wife starving — and yet I'm patient.

Rach. I never saw you so till now. Martin, what has happened?

Mar. I may sit down, and see my little ones pine day by day; I may feel their wasting limbs, and hear them scream for bread; and I may stare in their white faces, and tell them to be patient. Patient!

Rach. Look not so fiercely at me, Martin. Are they not my children — mine? Am I not their mother? Can your love be more than mine? But no; you did not mean that. Come, Martin, be not so hasty. What has happened?

Mar. No matter; let it rest with me.

Rach. But it must not, Martin. How many a time have you said that you could have no secret from Rachel?

Mar. I don't remember that.

Rach. Look there, Martin. (*Pointing to the stile*) How often have we met at yonder stile? how often have we waited there for hours, and talked of our wedding-day, and all our hopes? — then you have said —

Mar. Ay, those were gay days! Then, life seemed full of promise, as a field of ripened corn. Those were happy times!

Rach. They will come back; never fear it. Now tell me, Martin, have you been to your friend?

Mar. I have been to Harry Wilson. The same Harry Wilson to whom my grandfather lent good guineas to begin the world.

Rach. You asked him to lend you the money for a time?

Mar. I stammered it out somehow.

Rach. And did he?

Mar. Damn him!

Rach. Oh, Martin!

Mar. I thought I was talking to a brother. I told him all, Rachel, all! — And he heard me with a smile on his face, and said he was sorry!

Rach. Then he could not assist us?

Mar. No. His money was laid out in ventures, — he had lost by lending; — but he was very sorry!

Rach. And he offered nothing?

Mar. When I told him we had not a guinea, — not a home that we could call ours, — not a certain meal, — the tears came into my eyes, and I felt like a thief whilst I said all this, — well, he wouldn't lend me a farthing; but, kind soul! he bade me take a glass of wine, and hope for better days! I took the wine, and pouring it upon the floor, wished that my blood might be so poured out of my heart, if ever again I stood beneath his roof and so I left him.

Rach. And your other friend?

Mar. No: I asked no other. One denial was enough.

Rach. Then every hope is gone!

Mar. No; there is one hope yet. And yet I cannot bear to think of it. Rachel, our children must not starve. — What say you, shall we cross the sea?

Rach. What! leave the farm?

Mar. I am offered a place on an estate, far away in the Indies. What say you?

Rach. Leave this place?

Mar. Why not? We shall find sun, and sky, and green fields there.

Rach. But not our own fields, not our own sky, — not the friends who love us, not the neighbours who respect us. Oh! think not of it. Our children! they would die there! Die amongst strangers! Martin, would you quit our home?

Mar. Our home! where is it? — the workhouse! — Ha! ha! — Our home! Rachel, it shall be. We'll not be pointed at as beggars. We'll be no burden to the parish. We'll take our children in our arms, and leave this place for ever —

Enter Toby Heywood.

Toby. Leave this place! what for, Martin; have you got scent of a gold mine?

Rach. Oh, speak to him — persuade him!

He would go from here — go and die in some foreign place!

Toby. Nay, he has more wisdom than that. Thou'rt not such a fool, Martin. Come, I'll give you better advice.

Mar. Spare it for those who ask it: I want none.

Toby. Come, don't snub your younger brother. If you did enter the world ten months and a few seconds before me, you can hear reason. Go to foreign parts, eh?

Mar. Shall I stay here and starve?

Toby. Come, Martin, we never looked sulkily at one another when we were boys; now, 'twould be too late to begin; we should make no hand of it. Starve!

Mar. Ay. Will not the steward seize?

Toby. No, no. I have been and talked to him.

Mar. You didn't beg for? —

Toby. Beg? There's little of the beggar in my face. I talked reason to him. I said, a man who hadn't money couldn't well pay any. All you wanted was time; and he didn't refuse.

Rach. There, Martin, I told you not to be cast down. I knew we should yet be happy.

Mar. Still there is no certainty that —

Toby. I tell you what, brother; you are one of those people who are so very fond of ill-luck, that they run halfway to meet it. Old Crumbs will give you time — I know it. Go, Rachel; go to the farm. Wipe your eyes, kiss the babies, take down the bacon; draw a mug of nut-brown, and Martin and I will find appetites. There, away with you.

Rach. You will follow, Martin? There, look light again. That's well. We shall once more be happy — very happy! Fortune will change, be sure of it. *Exit.*

Toby. Change! to be sure she will: Fortune's a woman! Hang it, Martin, do muster up a laugh. There, now, — practise that fifty times a-day, and care would as soon be hanged as dare to look at you!

Clapping Martin on the shoulder, gradually rouses him into cheerfulness, and exeunt.

Scene 4.

The old Oak Room in Grantley's Mansion. — The panels elaborately carved in antique style. In one of the panels, a picture of a young female, richly habited. Enter Grantley, shown in by Bullfrog, who is slightly intoxicated.

Bul. Master Crumbs will be with you, sir, in the knocking down of a hammer. From London, sir?

Gran. I am. A fine old mansion this. *(Looks at pictures)*

Bul. Beautiful! Capital piece of oak-tree paneling, that: nice bold carving, sir. *(Pointing to figures)* Pretty cherubim's heads in the corners. That's a figure of Mercy. Should like to have the selling of the house and furniture.

Gran. The owner is indebted to your good wishes.

Bul. The owner? Oh! he's a wild fellow. He's never among us. No, sir; he's a London spark. His father left him abroad; and though the old man's been dead, and the young gentleman's been in England these two years, he has never paid us a visit.

Gran. Fond of a town life, I suppose?

Bul. Very fond. And then he's so lucky in his steward.

Gran. Indeed!

Bul. Oh! he's a jewel of a man! — so punctual with the tenants. There's no keeping a guinea from him, sir. He's a delightful man for our business.

Gran. And your profession is —

Bul. *(Giving card)* Appraiser and auctioneer. Happy to serve you. I made one seizure this morning; shall have another to-night. If you've thoughts of staying amongst us, and want to furnish, I can assist you to two or three good penn'orths. *(Grantley has been observing the picture)* What, sir! you are looking at that picture? I don't know the painter. It's not a —

Gran. No — *(Musing)*

Bul. No. And it's not by — by — *(Aside)* — I must get an Italian smatter, or I shall never be able to knock down the painters!

Gran. Is it a family portrait?

Bul. Why, sir, between ourselves, if I were to put it up for auction, I should call it a conundrum in an oak frame!

Gran. Why so?

Bul. Why, more than twice, I've caught Mr. Crumbs standing before it, looking at it; — and once (you'll hardly believe it, for nobody who knows him would) I caught him with the tears rolling down his cheeks. Nobody would believe it!

Gran. Then he is not generally given to strong emotion?

Bul. Bless you! no, sir. He's too much a man of business for that. Here he comes. Not a word.

Enter Crumbs.

Crumbs. Your servant, sir. Business must excuse me, that I made you wait. *(To Bullfrog)* Go you, and see that Burly is at hand. I seize within this hour. Go!

Bul. I will; — *(Aside)* — but first for the

other bottle with Captain Jack. I must better my taste in wines, if only in the way of trade.   *Exit.*

Gran. I shall tax your hospitality for some days. This (*Giving a letter*) from my friend, Grantley.

Crumbs. He's well, I trust? (*Aside*) Curses on it. (*Reads*) "*The bearer is my most special friend: treat him with all respect, as he were myself. He will stay to sport some week or two.*" I would, sir, we had had earlier notice. I fear me, you will find us ill provided.

Gran. Never fear it.

Crumbs. In truth, sir, 'tis a dull spot. Here we see no one — hear no one.

Gran. Indeed, it seems still enough.

Crumbs. You never hear a sound — not a sound; unless it be the birds in the rookery, or, at night, a mouse scratching in the wall.

> *Loud laughing and knocking within. Silver Jack sings in a loud voice, behind.*

"May corn never fail: for that makes good ale,
  But a blight to all hempseed, brave boys, brave boys,
  But a blight to all hempseed, brave boys."

Gran. Do the mice scratch thus early?

Crumbs. (*Confused*) I — I — (*More laughing and noise*)

Gran. The rooks are somewhat jovial.

Crumbs. It hath never happened until now. They are the richest of the Squire's tenants — devout, religious men; but to-day being rent-day —

Jack and Hyssop. (*Heard by the door*) Holloa, Master Crumbs.

Crumbs. I come — I — (*To Grantley*) Men of worth and reputation.

Jack. (*At door*) Master Crumbs! John Harris! Fifty pounds reward!

Crumbs. Damnation!

In extreme terror, rushes up, and opens folding doors. Silver Jack and Hyssop are seen, with Bullfrog, trying to keep them back. They come down, all flushed with wine, Jack holding a bottle.

Crumbs. (*Aside to them*) I am busy. I will return. Go.

Jack. Busy! Damn business!

Bul. No: don't damn business. I'm very drunk, but I can't damn business; it's profane.

Jack. To leave your company, and — (*Seeing Grantley*) Oh! a gentleman! Introduce us. You won't! — no? — I'll introduce myself. (*Crosses to Grantley, puts bottle upon the*

stage, which Bullfrog takes up, and retires to back; seats himself in a chair, and, during the following, drinks until he falls asleep) Servant, sir. Nice house, this. Capital wine; yes, and a civil steward. Sir, I beg your friendship. If you're for anything in this way, I — (*Taking from his pocket a pack of cards and shuffling them*)

Hys. Ay, sir; or if there be music in this — (*Rattling a dice box, crosses to Grantley. Crumbs endeavours to keep them back*)

Gran. (*Aside*) Devout, religious men!

Jack. We're not avaricious. We play for anything, from a marvedi to a thousand guineas.

Crumbs. (*Who has been vainly endeavoring to keep them back*) No, no; the gentleman does not play. (*Crosses over to Grantley*) Go in, my good friends.

Gran. (*To Crumbs*) With your leave, I'll look about the grounds. (*Going*)

Jack. Fine spot — nice house — good wine — ay, and (*Looking at portrait*) pretty pictures! Well, I say, (*To Hyssop*) isn't that an angel?

Hys. I can't say: I've not been used to such company.

Gran. It is, indeed, beautiful. (*To Crumbs*) Tell me, whose portrait is it? Did you know the lady?

Crumbs. (*With suppressed emotion*) She was a — a favourite of the late Squire's. She's long since dead.

Jack. A favourite, and dead! Ha! I suppose the Squire was fond of her, and so broke her heart.

Crumbs. (*With passion*) How dare you —

Jack. (*Coolly, and in an under-tone*) Come, come, John Harris; fifty pounds reward!

Crumbs. (*Recovering himself — to Grantley*) Come, sir, I will show you —

Gran. Do not quit your friends. With your leave, I'll go alone. Gentlemen, I'm the humblest of your servants. (*Aside*) Devout, religious men!   *Exit.*

Hys. A pretty spoken fellow.

Jack. And a rich one. Did you see the diamonds on his fingers? I warrant me his pockets are — umph! a prize? (*To Crumbs*) What say you?

Crumbs. I — I? —

Jack. I'd forgot — you only rob now as a steward. You're one of the regulars.

Crumbs. Rob! harkye! —

Jack. Come, come, John Harris; no big words. I've something here (*Showing bill*) wouldn't look so well framed as that red-lipped young lady. (*Pointing to picture*)

Crumbs. Well, well, we're friends; but be

cautious, I implore you. (*In great agitation*)
Come, you shall have more wine, wine!
(*Goes up and throws door open, still with his
back to Bullfrog*)

Jack. Wine! Ay, we will have more. And
then for our plans, old boy; then for our
plans. Why, how lucky it was we met one
another! You see, there were a few pressing
inquiries about us in London, so we thought
we'd take the benefit of country air until the
anxiety of our friends cooled a little. But
then, to think of the luck of our meeting!
Aren't you delighted? (*Embracing him*)

Crumbs. Yes, yes. But go in. You shall
have wine. I'll go see to it.

Jack. Wine, wine! Ha! ha! We drink courage with wine. Success to the grapes, —
(*Sings*)

"But a blight to all hempseed, brave
boys, brave boys;
A blight to all hempseed, brave boys!"

> *Crumbs forces them into room and
> comes down.*

Crumbs. The devil has forsaken me! To be
tracked out after so many years! This visitor,
too. No: my course is clear. But how to dispose of that ruffian? Ha! he has been prating
of some woman; — by the description, 'tis
Heywood's wife. — I'll put him in possession
of the farm, and thus rid me of him, whilst I
— let me see —

Bul. (*Still asleep*) What shall we say for
this wine, fifty years in bottle? Thank'e, sir;
it's going, — going, — gone. (*Lets the bottle
fall out of his hand*)

Crumbs. (*Who has remained in deep
thought, startled, rushes up to Bullfrog, and
seizes him*) Scoundrel! listening?

Bul. Dreaming — only dreaming. I just
knocked down the sweetest ten dozen! —

Crumbs. Up, or I strangle you! Is't thus
you mind your business?

Bul. Business! — that's enough. Cry business — and if I don't move, you may send
for the undertaker.

Crumbs. Hence.

Bul. I'm going. Business is business.
Capital wine (*Sings*) "And a blight to all
hempseed," etc.

Crumbs. Hence! Hence! — *Forces him off.*

> End of the First Act.

ACT II.

Scene 1.

*The interior of Heywood's Farm. The scene,
furniture, etc., as in Wilkie's picture of*

"*Distraining for Rent.*" *Martin and Rachel
seated at Table, with Toby, Beanstalk, his
Dame, and the children. Ale, jugs, etc., on
the table.*

Bean. Come, Martin, here be better
times. — So: we shall be jovial yet, man.

Rach. Ay, that we shall; and so I tell him,
farmer; but he will not heed me.

Mar. We have had naught but ill-luck
since the old man died.

Bean. Why, 'twas awfully sudden, to be
sure.

Mar. Here he was, one minute, as strong
and as lightsome as ever; when death fell
upon him like a bolt, and he lay upon that
bed, panting, like a run-down hare.

Toby. Odds, Martin! look into your ale:
you'll see something better than dying men.
Our grandfather's in heaven. Here's to the
memory of him! Let him rest.

Mar. I tell, you, I can't but think of him.
Abroad or at home, I see him. Sometimes,
when I'm falling into sleep, his eyes seem to
stare close at my face, and I start and gasp
again; and then I see him looking and pointing at that chair. (*To farmer*) You know,
farmer, he'd sit in it for hours, with one of
the youngsters on his knee. — Still I see him,
with his hand stretched forth, and his throat
working, as though the words were there, but
couldn't out; — and so he died. Depend on't,
there was something on the old man's mind.

Toby. Brother, shall I go to the church-
yard and bring you a skull and cross-bones?
for in your present humour, they're your
fittest company.

Mar. I'm a fool to think so. (*Fills horn*)
Come, farmer your hand; Toby, yours;
Rachel, lass, we'll be merry yet. Here's to
better times! (*Drinks; then takes two of the
children on his knees*)

Toby. Come, I warrant me, there's more
comfort in that than in ghost's eyes at midnight. Why, it's up in your cheek already,
man. Take another.

Mar. With all my heart. And again I'll
drink, "Here's better times!"

Enter Polly Briggs.

Pol. Oh, Farmer Heywood! Here comes
the steward, and that nasty appraiser, and
the beadle; and all the folks say they are
coming here to seize! —

Mar. (*Putting down the children*) Rachel,
stand aside! — that gun! — (*Is going to take
the gun from over the chimney piece; Rachel
prevents him*)

Rach. Oh, Martin! husband! for the love
of heaven!

Toby. What would you, Martin?

Mar. Shoot the first man who crosses yonder threshold.

Bean. Come, come, Martin, be not rash: thee's no reason to be so.

Mar. No reason! You have a wife and children, yet say I have no reason! — Are not here five — (*Pointing to Rachel and Children*) — five bitter reasons? The gun! (*Violently*)

Toby. Martin, Martin, are you mad?

Mar. (*Falling despairingly into a chair*) I am mad. God help me! — I am mad!

Enter Crumbs.

Crumbs. This is a disagreeable business.

Toby. I should know that by your looking so pleased.

Crumbs. I want my due.

Toby. You'll have it some day. I wish the law allowed me to give it you now.

Bean. Come, come, Master Crumbs, have compassion.

Toby. Compassion! — tell him to have three heads.

Rach. Do not anger him. (*To Crumbs*) Good sir, give us time: but a short time: have mercy. — Kneel, children, kneel! (*Children are about to kneel, when Martin starts up*)

Mar. Stand! if you're of my blood. They are the children of an honest man, and must not kneel before a villain!

Crumbs. Mighty well. You owe a twelvemonth's rent; and instead of money, you give blustering words. Rent-day passes lightly with you.

Mar. Lightly! (*To Beanstalk*) Farmer, as I am a man, I have lived a whole year in torment. Day has been all misery to me, and bed no bed. Still, as rent-day would come, I have lain awake whole nights, and every night was more dreadful than the past. Then I've tried to think no more, but dug my head into my pillow, and fixed my fingers tightly in my hair, and tried to stun myself to sleep; — but all would not do. — There appeared a something hanging over me — about me; heavy and stifling it seemed, — and my blood would run hot and cold; and so I've lain and watched, and prayed the daylight in. The next night worse; for it brought the time still nearer. And when at last the rent-day came, and I without one groat, I've crossed yon door, not with an English farmer's tread, but with a thief's pace, crawling to the gallows! — This is to pass rent-day lightly!

Crumbs. Why not give up the farm? Why not leave the house?

Mar. Why not? My father's father grew gray under this roof. And sooner should these beams fall and knock my brains out, than I would quit them. Here I was born, and here I will die. If you would take me through yon door, Master Crumbs, I tell you it must be heels foremost. Leave the house! I almost love it like a living thing.

Crumbs. All very fine. For my part, I can't see why one house shouldn't be as good as another.

Mar. Likely you cannot. But I have crawled a little child upon this floor: the very door-step is worn with my feet. I have seen my mother, father, die here! — I — I tell you, here I first saw the light, and here I'll close my eyes.

Rach. Dear Martin, be calm.

Crumbs. You'll not oppose the law?

Mar. I know not that. I tell you, don't provoke me. (*Taking the arm-chair*) Here I sit in my grandfather's chair: the chair of that old man, who, for forty years, paid rent and tithe to the last guinea. Here I sit! And I warn you, put not a hand upon a stick or thread!

Crumbs. (*Calling at door*) Come in, friends.

Enter Bullfrog and Burly.

Mar. I warn you back.

Burly. (*Showing a paper*) What say you to our warrant, Master Heywood?

Mar. I tell you not to tempt me. I cannot trust myself, for I am desperate! Leave the farm!

Crumbs. (*To Bullfrog and Burly*) You know your duties.   *Exit.*

Bul. (*Who has been looking over goods*) Business is business. (*Takes out pen, ink, and book*) One bedstead!

Mar. Let me come at them!

Toby. Nay, nay, brother!

Rach. Husband!

Children. Father! (*They all hang about Martin, keeping him from attacking Burly and Bullfrog*)

Mar. (*After a struggle, sinks into the chair*) Rachel! — my poor babes! — take all, take all.

Bul. (*Making out inventory*) One bedstead — one table!

Beanstalk and Neighbours. (*Who have entered, come down, some remaining behind*) Shame! Shame!

Toby. Blood-suckers!

Bul. One toasting-fork, one bird-cage, one baby's rattle!

Mar. God help us! God help us! (*Buries his face in his hands*)

       Bullfrog seats himself on bed; and

other characters so arrange themselves as to represent Wilkie's picture of "Distraining for Rent."

End of the Second Act.

Act III.

Scene 1.

The interior of Heywood's Farm. Day breaking. The furniture of the scene as at the conclusion of the first act. Polly Briggs discovered, seated at table, — a light burning.

Pol. Dear me! how heavily the time goes, — and the farm, — I declare, it doesn't look as it used to do. I'm so tired — yet I must keep my eyes open, for company's sake.

Enter Rachel.

Rach. They sleep soundly. Poor children! Heaven knows where they will rest another night. I stood and watched them; and they looked so innocent — so happy — they smiled, and my heart died within me.

Pol. Don't take on so. Martin will return with good news, never fear.

Rach. I'm so wretched, I have lost even hope. — My pretty babes, had we been always beggars, then you could have borne cold, nipping winds, rough words, uncertain food; — but now they'll pine, and so they'll die. Even our children will be taken from us.

Pol. Well, I never thought you could talk after this fashion.

Rach. Nor I. But then I had not seen my infants lying on a bed no longer theirs. — Is it not almost day-break? Had Martin been successful, he would surely have been back.

Pol. Now, why will you think the worst? I shouldn't wonder if he returned with a large bag of money. I'll go to the end of the lane, and see if either he or Toby be coming.

Rach. No, do not leave me — the stranger up stairs — Yet go; but do not stay. (*Exit Polly*) Sure the morning will never come. Oh, yes, 'twill come too soon! Then another, and another, and we are houseless beggars. I walk about the place like a restless ghost. — To know the worst were better than to remain thus. (*Sits*) I am worn and tired — even too tired to sleep. (*Fatigued, falls asleep*)

Enter Silver Jack, cautiously.

Jack. All quiet. Harris must have put some devil in that wine, or I had never slept so. Here am I in possession, — a watch-dog over spoons and platters, whilst Hyssop, I warrant me, is rarely plucking that new-comer. Jack, so it has ever run; a pair of bright eyes has been a will-o'-the-wisp to you, leading you through quagmires all your life. — Ha! (*Seeing Rachel*) she's here, and sleeping! How tired, pale, yet pretty, she seems! She looks good, and — pshaw! we all look good asleep. How still the place is; no one here but ourselves: — yes, the children. I just passed through their room, and saw them looking as fresh and as rosy — I felt as I hadn't felt for many a day. — 'Twas a fool's moment, and is gone, — (*Approaching her, she wakes*)

Rach. Martin, Martin! (*Sees Jack*) You here!

Jack. I couldn't well sleep, so I thought I'd come down and keep you company. This is a much pleasanter room.

Rach. It is at your service. I can go to my children's. (*Going.*)

Jack. (*Staying her*) They're all fast asleep. Bless their little hearts! I stood and looked at them just now till I quite loved them. They are very handsome.

Rach. And most unfortunate.

Jack. Why, this is an awkward business. But you may yet find friends.

Rach. Friendship!

Jack. We sometimes find it where we had least thoughts of it. Your children are very like you.

Rach. It has been remarked. (*Going.*)

Jack. (*Lingering*) Yes, full purses ought to go with full hearts.

Rach. 'Twould save much misery. I would your employer —

Jack. My employer! Why, to be sure, old Crumbs was once my master: but times are changed; we are now bosom friends. I am here only to oblige him.

Rach. Your task can hardly be a pleasant one.

Jack. Nay, 'tis very pleasant. Look you, I have been rolling these many years about the world, and this (*Displaying a purse*) has still been gathering. Those pretty babes of yours, — I'm mightily taken with them. Where is your husband?

Rach. Gone, as a last hope, to try to borrow. He should have been back by this.

Jack. I never found this purse so troublesome before. Will you lighten it for me? Come, no ceremony. You want money: I don't.

Rach. Oh! this is kind, most kind. Yet, from a stranger —

Jack. Pshaw! Ill-fortune, now and then, makes sudden acquaintances. (*Presses the money on her*)

Rach. Indeed, sir, I — I cannot.

Jack. Yet the poor babes must sleep some-where to-morrow. Come!

Rach. My husband will speedily be here; he, perhaps —

Jack. Nay, when I'm in the humour, I wouldn't be balked. Now or never! Hang it! take the purse. — (*Forces it into her hand*)

Rach. My husband will return it with a thousand thanks. My children are saved. Oh! you have made us most happy!

Jack. That's enough for me. As for return-ing the money, that may rest with yourself. 'Twould have been hard for you to see your husband in a jail; yourself and little ones without a home.

Rach. Only to hear you name it makes me tremble.

Jack. But there's no such hard fortune for you. No, you may stay in your farm, have your children about you, whilst all fears of beggary and the workhouse — why, you seem ill?

Rach. The sudden joy — 'tis nothing, and will pass.

Jack. Come, sit down — (*She sits*) — There, you are looking better whilst I speak. (*Hanging over the chair*) As for the money if you like to have it as a gift, 'tis a bargain be-tween us. So, to make it binding, just one kiss! — (*Throws his arms about her: she shrinks from him*) Why do you look so at me?

Rach. I was deceived! I thought I saw a friend: I was deceived! (*Rises*)

Jack. Tush! I am your friend. Come, one kiss.

Rach. There (*Drops the purse at his feet*) is your money. (*Going*)

Jack. Will you be blind to your own good? I tell you, the money shall be yours — all yours. — I care not for a penny of it.

Rach. Be silent, and let me go. (*Endeavours to pass*)

Jack. Think of your children — your husband — (*Seizes her*)

Rach. I do, and scorn you. (*Breaks away from him*)

Jack. Are you mad? — listen to my offer.

Rach. Had you made it when the world went well with us — when this roof sheltered a happy family — when every day brought its plenty, its content — when we had no fear of poverty or persecution — even then, the thought of that you propose, should have brought the blushes to your face, and made you dumb with shame; — but now, — with want at our hearth — a husband mad with sorrow — children unprotected — now to offer! — oh! you have a heart of stone, or you could ne'er have thought it.

Jack. Hear reason, and take the purse. I tell you, I do not mean —

Rach. You mean the worst. He who would destroy a happy fireside, is vile and infamous; but he who insults its wretchedness, is base indeed.

Jack. Base! Look you! — zounds! to be whipped by a woman's tongue! Come, don't let us part so. This is all very well, but, but, — hang it, can't we understand one another?

Rach. Oh! Martin! Martin!

Jack. (*Chinking the purse*) He may sleep in a prison tomorrow!

Rach. Let me pass. I must, will go to my children.

Jack. (*Throwing up the purse*) And they may want a breakfast.

Rach. Villain! though you insult the wife, have pity on the mother. (*Attempting to cross, he seizes her*) Let me go!

Jack. Not now — I have gone too far.

Rach. Oh! you will not! Mercy! Martin! (*Despairingly*) He comes not!

Jack. (*Passionately*) You may rave. You've roused me, and I'll not be trifled with.

Rach. Help! help! (*They struggle*) My hus-band! — he is here! — (*Jack, surprised, lets her go, and falls back. She rushes to the door, and seizes a woodcutter's bill that is lying on some wood near the wall*)

Jack. Tricked!

Rach. You see, a sound will make a coward of the wicked. Do not come near me; pray, do not. This, though you die, shall protect me.

Jack. Well, well, I own I've been wrong — I ask pardon. Come back. Put your trust —

Rach. In this! (*Lifting the bill*) I say again, stir not! Stay beneath this roof! Stay in the poor man's house you would have outraged! Stay, — blush, — and beg to be forgiven!
Exit.

Jack. Gone! what devil is it that cows me? Ha! (*Looking out*) She flies down the lane. That copse! — yes, though I ran to the gal-lows, I would follow her. *Exit.*

Bul. (*Putting his head from between the bed-curtains*) Run to the gallows! — you needn't hurry yourself; the gallows will wait for you. Well, this I call an adventure! Now, if this cause come to trial, I'm witness ready for either side. As I'm a sworn appraiser, it's almost day-light! — why, I must have been asleep these seven or eight hours, and nobody knew it. This all comes of the steward's wine. Eh? I hear a footstep. I must sleep and listen. (*Disappears*)

Enter Polly.

Pol. Why, Rachel! Oh! gone up stairs, I

suppose, to cry over the poor little things! Well, I've no good news for her. I went all down the lane, and came back over the fields, and saw no signs of Martin or Toby either. If these are the troubles that are to come upon the married, I am sure a poor girl is better single. There's nothing but vexation in this world! — and, dear me, I'm so sleepy! — I haven't had a single wink all night, and it's a shame, too; for there stood the bed, so inviting, as though it said, do come and lie down! There'll be no harm in sitting upon it. (*Sits upon the bed*) How I should like to lie down!

Bul. (*Putting his head through the curtains*) Well, there's plenty of room for two!

Pol. (*Screaming and running into corner*) Thieves! Murder! —

Toby appears at the door.

Toby. Polly! — Bullfrog!

Pol. Oh! the wretch!

Toby. (*Seizing him*) What's this? — speak!

Bul. How can I, with your fingers in my windpipe?

Toby. (*Drags him out of bed*) Answer me: what is all this?

Pol. Yes, explain, Mr. Bullfrog.

Bul. (*Half aside to Polly*) Don't be a fool, and nobody will be the wiser.

Pol. The wiser, sir? — the wiser!

Toby. Speak, I say!

Bul. (*Aside*) Now I'll talk nettles to him. Well, Mr. Heywood; the fact is, I — I am but a man.

Toby. Why, no; I never took you for an angel.

Bul. Perhaps not, Mr. Heywood; but the fair sex — (*Winking to Polly*) — the fair sex can discover modest merit.

Pol. Now, as I'm alive. I was here alone, — and never knowing that that wretch —

Bul. Fie! wretch! What, *now!* call me wretch now?

Pol. That monster! —

Bul. Come, no scandal. If you will tell the truth, I can't help it; but no scandal.

Pol. That — that —

Bul. There, don't press her: you see her feelings —

Toby. Master Bullfrog, you've had a marvellous escape.

Bul. How?

Toby. In not lighting on as great a fool as yourself: else, my life on't, your head had been broken.

Bul. A fool! And have you the audacity to call me a fool?

Toby. And not all fool: for the rogue is so equally mixed, that there is no saying where either begins or ends.

Bul. Fool! rogue! — The law will tell you this is slander.

Toby. I know it: I'm speaking the truth.

Bul. And the law shall mend my character.

Toby. The character that needs law to mend it, is hardly worth the tinkering. In one word, how came you here?

Pol. That's right. Make him tell you.

Bul. Tell? well, you're a courageous woman! What, then, (*To Toby*) you've no suspicion? — there's no making you unhappy?

Toby. No.

Bul. Mrs. Heywood will be a fortunate woman.

Toby. What put you into that bed?

Pol. Yes, what put you into that bed?

Bul. If you must know, — this. (*Producing a bottle from his pocket*) This put me to bed: it's done as much for many a man.

Toby. What do you mean?

Bul. Mean? — Didn't I attend here as sworn appraiser, and didn't I make the inventory? Yes. (*Producing it*) Here it is: "One cradle, one toasting-fork," — all right; move a stick, and I'll indict you! Well, there was a great noise in the family; one running one way — one another, — children crying— women fainting, a smell of burnt feathers; and your brother, swearing enough to shock any Christian who knows what virtue is, and pays his way. I had brought a little wine from the mansion, and all of a sudden, I found myself quite alone here, so I sat down upon the bed, and drank and drank. Then I got on the bed; then between the blankets, pulled-to the curtains, looked at my inventory — (some of the things will sell well) — said my prayers — droned a hymn, and went to sleep! Then — no, I pass over the rest — when you came in, you — but I musn't go any further.

Toby. Yes, you must.

Bul. I tell you, I can't.

Toby. I tell you, you must — you must go over that doorstep. If you remain here two minutes longer, 'twill not be on your legs, I promise you. (*Menacing him*)

Bul. I give you warning! Remember, I'm a sworn appraiser.

Toby. You're better able to judge for what you ought to be knocked down. — Come, pack!

Bul. I'm going. But only threaten me, and I'll call down the man from up stairs — he who's in possession — (*Aside*) They musn't know he's gone, or they'll block up the premises.

Toby. (*Still threatening him*) I've given you fair words.

Bul. Keep to 'em: you can't do better. Ha! drop your arm, or I'll call for the man. If you put me in bodily fear, it's no fault of mine! — Now, Mr. Toby! — here! my good man— (*Shrinking from Toby, and feigning to call down Silver Jack*) My good man!

Toby. Will you go?

Bul. I will, (*Aside*) to give Crumbs notice. Ha! I'll call! — I tell you, I'll call. As for that young woman, if you demand any satisfaction? — oh! you don't? well, it's very prudent of you. — Don't stir a step, or down he comes. And now — now (*Aside*) to put another man in. (*Gets to the door, stops, and calls, as to man up-stairs*) My good man, see that they don't move a stick! (*Toby runs to door, and Bullfrog makes his escape*)

Pol. If you'll believe me, my dear Toby, I never dreamt that that wretch — that villain — that —

Toby. I'm sure you must be intimate with him, by the correctness of your description. Let the fool go. Where's Rachel?

Pol. With the children. Have you seen nothing of Martin?

Toby. No. For once, I fear the worst. But my mind's made up. I'll go to London.

Pol. Mercy save us! to London!

Toby. To London; though I walk every inch of the way, and live upon blackberries. I'll see the young Squire himself.

Pol. But why go, — why not write?

Toby. No. A letter's but a scribbled bit of paper, to be tossed aside, and there's an end. No! he shall look in my face, and hear me talk; and if I don't bring the blood into his cheek, why, there's not a blush to be had from all London.

Pol. Don't be rash. Do but consider who the Squire is, and who you are.

Toby. That's what I intend to let him know. I shall tell him, if landlords are too proud or too idle to look after the comforts of their tenants, and to live upon their own lands, why, 'tis a great pity that Providence should have intrusted them with any. What! haven't we paid truly for sixty years? and now that a rascal should screw, and grind, and crush us. No! 'tis a good thought, tho' it's come so late. — I'll go to London.

Pol. Martin may yet bring good news.

Toby. He may; but I'll provide against the worst. You go to Rachel. I'll be hence soon. (*Exit Polly*) My luggage won't stop my speed upon the road. Yes, and now I have it: I'll once more to the mansion; and if old Crumbs be as deaf as ever, I'll see if the Squire himself be not less hard of hearing than his servant. *Exit.*

Scene 2.

A copse. Enter Rachel, in flight.

Rach. I hear his step. Yes, there again. 'Tis he. Could I but gain the main road; — I cannot stir. I am almost dead with grief and fear. (*Hides*)

Enter Silver Jack, in pursuit.

Jack. This was the place. I'm sure 'twas here.

Enter Hyssop, hastily.

Hys. Jack, is't you?

Jack. Ay: did you pass a woman in fast flight?

Hys. A woman! Will you never be serious? Come with me.

Jack. Stop till I have found my runaway.

Hys. And lost a golden prize. I was coming for you.

Jack. A prize! — What do you mean?

Hys. That visitor at the mansion! Why, he has heaps of guineas, rings, and a brilliant snuff-box, that alone would make us.

Jack. Well?

Hys. Well? — If you're the Silver Jack of yesterday, they must be ours.

Jack. How?

Hys. Easily. He is now in bed. I have left open all the doors. — (*Rachel shows herself through the trees, listening*) We can get into his chamber, and then —

Jack. But if he wake and resist?

Hys. A knife!

Jack. The booty is large?

Hys. I tell you, enough to set us up.

Jack. Where the devil can that woman have flown?

Hys. A woman! — It's a pity women aren't thief-catchers, for they'd only have to show you the darbies, and you'd run your hands into 'em. Will you join me, or shall I do the work alone?

Jack. I'm for you. But you're too much of a philosopher; you should consider one's little frailties. (*Taking out small pocket-pistols, and looking at the priming, etc.*) Man was born to love, and that's my weakness. If he stir, here are two bullets for his head! The doors are open, you say?

Hys. Every one. — (*Rachel expresses her resolution to give their victim notice, and glides off*) And now for the shiners. *Exeunt.*

Enter Martin Heywood.

Mar. Poor Rachel! — I hadn't the heart to go to the farm. For her — for my children's sake, I'll once more try to move the steward. It a'most chokes me to think of it; but it must be tried. Every one refuses me: 'tis my last hope. If that fail, too, 'tis needless to whimper about it, — good by, farm! — good by, England! I have promised to give my answer to-day: and it may be to-night we sleep upon the sea. Now for Master Crumbs, to beg, and pray, and be refused. He is an early riser, and I may now see him without fear of interruption. If he denies me, why, then, for a foreign home, for I have lost my own. *Exit.*

Scene 3.

An old gallery in the mansion. Door leading into apartment. Enter Hyssop and Jack. Rachel glides in and retires at back.

Hys. You see all the doors were open.

Jack. Yes; it's what I call house-breaking made easy. No one stirring, either. — Where's Crumbs?

Hys. Vanished in a blue flame, for what I know. I hope he means no mischief; but I've scarcely seen him since he went with you to the farm. Should he blow on us now! —

Jack. He dares not; 'twould cost him his neck.

Hys. Yet we'll not trust him. We'll do this piece of work on our own behalf. Then — for I've left nothing unprovided — there are a couple of horses, ready saddled, in the stable; we'll spare not the spur: and once off, let the steward settle the account as best he may.

Jack. Where does the spark sleep?

Hys. In yonder chamber. I have secured the key. The bird is nicely caged. Come! — *(Goes to the door, and opens it, leaving the key in. Jack pulls him back)*

Jack. Stay, Frank. I've been thinking of it: — there must be no blood in this.

Hys. That's at the option of the gentleman. I've no objection, if it can be made comfortable to him.

Jack. 'Twould make a stir that might be fatal to us. You must promise me.

Hys. As far as I can keep my temper, I do. Now, then; for there's no time to lose. *(At this moment Rachel, who has secured the key, glides into the room. She is seen by Hyssop, who staggers back)* Ha! trapped!

Jack. *(Clapping his hand to his pistols)* What do you mean?

Hys. A woman entered that room!

Jack. You dream! *(Rushes to the door, and looks through the key-hole)*

Hys. *(Listening)* There! I hear her footstep.

Jack. Why, no! yes; — it is the farmer's wife!

Hys. And there! *(Rachel is heard to turn the key in the lock)* She locks the door. — We're rarely gulled. Now there's but one plan. We'll force the way.

Jack. *(Stopping him, and pointing off with astonishment)* Her husband! *They retire.*

Enter Martin.

Mar. All the doors open, yet not a soul about! *(Sees them)* Is the steward? — Surely, *(Recognizing Jack)* 'tis he who was put into the farm. *(Aside)*

Jack. *(To Hyssop)* Peace! I have it. — You wanted the steward?

Mar. Yes. Did he not put you into my house?

Jack. Ay; but I've finished my errand there: 'twas not the pleasantest.

Mar. I come to beg for time. Had I any one to intercede for me —

Jack. You may be quite easy. You have a friend, depend on't.

Mar. I know not where.

Jack. *(Pointing to room)* There! In that room is a young London spark, the Squire's acquaintance — the door locked, and with him, — yes, you'll keep the farm: — 'twas he who sent me to your house.

Mar. He! for what?

Jack. You've a pretty wife, he has plenty of money — I delivered my message, and there your wife is.

Mar. My wife! villain! *(Seizes him)* Unsay the slander — on your knees unsay it — or, were you the father of all lies, I would not quit you.

Jack. Leave your hold! I say your wife.

Mar. My Rachel! *(Bewildered)* Why, how you look at me?

Jack. Knock at the door, perhaps she'll answer.

Mar. I am a wretched, ruined man; but do not play with me. Grief has worn me, but revenge will make me strong. If this be a lie! —

Jack. Knock at the door.

Mar. There seems blood before my eyes; and I feel of a sudden weak and old.

Jack. Knock at the door.

Mar. I'll tear his life out!

Hys. Why, that's manful. Here's that will help you. *(Cocks a pistol and forces it into his hand)*

Mar. *(Rushes to the door)* Come out, I say!

Enter Grantley, armed with a brace of pistols, Rachel following him.

Gran. *(Speaking as he enters)* Villains! I am armed!

Mar. Die!

Rach. (*Screams and runs before Grantley*)
Martin! what would you?

Mar. What! you cling to him, — before
my eyes? — Rachel Heywood, I forgive that
man! (*Drops the pistols — Jack and Hyssop
glide off*) Let him but send a bullet through
the heart you've broken, and I will thank him
with my last breath.

Gran. This your husband, — and leagued
with the robbers?

Rach. No, no; he knows not what he says.
Grief has distracted him.

Mar. Yes, grief. Falsehood, where I had
hoped for truth. Scorn, where I had looked
for love. Shame, where I had built my greatest pride.

Gran. Go, I pardon you — I spare you.

Mar. Pardon! Spare! I have at home four
motherless children;— what! do you spare
me them? Will you leave the poor man one
miserable comfort?

Rach. Husband!

Mar. Can your lips yet say that word? —
Heaven forgive you! — can you yet speak it?
Let it be for the last time! Never let us look
again upon each other's face. (*She clings to
him*) Away! (*Casts her off*) My heart sinks at
your touch! I leave you; and may God pardon
and protect you.　　　　　　　　*Rushes off.*

Rach. Martin! Martin! Oh! he is lost with
misery!

Gran. Fear not: for your sake I will not
accuse him.

Rach. Accuse!

Gran. Nay, I perceive and value your
motives. You would not suffer your husband
to become a criminal. You preserved, it may
be, my life. I thank you, and pardon him.

Rach. And was it for this I saved you? —
for this have endured the bitterest words that
wife can listen to? — for this have made him
mad? Sir, I never saw you till this hour. I
never heard of you till named by villains who
would have destroyed you. Then I flew to
give you warning — I saved you; — and you
give me this reward, — suspicion of my
husband.

Gran. Your eloquence, my good woman,
does not deceive me. The other villains shall
be pursued. For your husband, trust me, he
is safe.　　　　　　　　　　　　　　*Exit.*

Rach. 'Tis no matter. — I will go home.
Home! did he not forbid me? — Oh! he knew
not what he said. And yet he found me —
Oh! that he should harbour such a thought.
I will fly and explain all; for now I should go
mad to live one moment from him.　　*Exit.*

Enter Crumbs.

Crumbs. All is stored — all packed! — all
the harvest of my thrift and enmity. Ye
cursed walls, I leave ye to your owner, — to
him who I had vainly hoped to beggar — to
sink into the dust, a wretched, undone spendthrift! — May ye become the haunt of
gamesters, — of hungry, smooth-faced
knaves, who flatter and devour! May ye be
staked upon a card, and pass from him who
stakes ye! For ten years have I dwelt here,
nursing my revenge. For ten years has
vengeance been to me as a food — a nourishment. I have lived and gloated on it. May
others finish the ruin I've begun! Now I must
leave, ere my visitor — plagues light upon
him! — be stirring. That villain, Jack, is still
at Heywood's farm, his companion yet asleep.
I live within the gallows' foot whilst near
them. I have hid my treasure in the laurel
hedge. — I've bought the captain of the
vessel, and this night I leave the shore. I walk
'mongst pitfalls whilst I tread it.

Bullfrog runs in.

Bul. Oh! Master Crumbs! such an affair.

Crumbs. Peace, ye roaring fool! (*Going*)

Bul. Fool! Early as it is, you're the second
man who has called me fool this morning. I
come upon business.

Crumbs. To-night — to-morrow!

Bul. Not my maxim. Shut your door upon
business, and business will soon forget to
knock at it. Your friend, Captain Jack. —

Crumbs. What of him?

Bul. He might be a good hand to put in
possession if one were to distrain a nunnery;
but where a quick eye is to be kept on chairs
and tables, he's as blind as Cupid.

Crumbs. What jargon is this?

Bul. I only hope there'll not be an action;
but, if there should be, —

Crumbs. Speak out, or I'll throttle you.
(*Grasping him*)

Bul. There certainly is a conspiracy to
call me a fool and choke me. Don't stare at
me in that manner: it isn't business-like.

Crumbs. Speak, or begone.

Bul. Well, then, it's a serious truth that
the Heywoods might clear out the farm; for
nobody is there to prevent them.

Crumbs. Is that all!

Bul. All? what! where I have once seized?
what's to become of my reputation? I employ
nobody but respectable, steady men. The
fact is, Captain Jack was above his calling;
for he made love to the farmer's wife.

Crumbs. Well?

Bul. Not well, Mr. Crumbs. When a man's
on business, he should be above such trifles.

Crumbs. Where is he now?

Bul. Run off — left the premises in the most scandalous manner. I shouldn't wonder if he comes here.

Crumbs. (*Aside*) I must be gone.

Bul. You are not going? I must put another man in, you know? I say, I must —

Crumbs. Leave me.

Bul. Business! Who shall I put in? (*Follows him*)

Crumbs. (*Furiously*) Any one — no one — the devil! *Rushes off.*

Bul. I'll have nothing more to do with any of your acquaintance. Why, he's quite in a fury. I see it: I know he dabbles — stocks must have fallen. Nothing else could put a man in such a passion. (*Exit, and returns*) Here comes Stephen. Perhaps he may know the cause why old Crumbs is in such a fury. — Stephen! Stephen!

Enter Stephen.

Ste. I can't stop now — the whole place is in an uproar!

Bul. Well, they've kept it very quiet. What's the matter?

Ste. There's been robbery, and nearly —

Bul. Robbery?

Ste. Yes, and nearly murder.

Bul. Murder's very bad, but I hope there's no property lost?

Ste. We don't know what's lost yet. But for the two chaps you drank with and were such friends, the gentleman offers a reward for whoever seizes them.

Bul. A reward! — I'll put on my cricketing pumps, and run directly. Are they thieves, think you?

Ste. You've been more it their company than I have. There's Toby Heywood in the garden. Go and talk to him. Business, you know, —

Bul. Business! — right. Toby here! then I'll just run and put Nokes into the farm, and then after my friends. I say, what's happened to Master Crumbs?

Ste. Why, between you and me, the steward — but while I talk to you I may miss what the gentleman offers. *Runs off.*

Bul. Something wrong with the steward. If he should go out, I might come in. I'll run and show my activity. *Runs off.*

Scene 4.

The interior of Heywood's Farm. Martin discovered, seated in his arm-chair. His children grouped about him.

Mar. And this, then, is the end! All's gone! — I cannot carry with me even a hope of better days. Now, indeed, labour will be hard to me; for I shall work with a broken heart. Now, fortune cannot bless me; for she with whom I should have shared all good — But let me think no more of her. Think no more! Like a ghost she seems to haunt me. But she has shamed me — and may she ——! No, I cannot curse her, with her children looking in my face. I will not curse her. I must say farewell to the home where I was born — where I had hoped to die. — Oh! as I think of the long past days, — as I sit here staring my last at these walls, those who are now in their graves come gathering about me; — faces that seem a part of the place — that seem as they had never been away; — looks that take me back, and make me a child again. — All from then till now is like a dream; the things of my boyhood alone seem real: — all else is —

Rach. (*Without*) Martin! Martin!

Mar. (*Starting*) No no; that is real — would it were not! (*To children*) Go, bolt the door.

Boy. Why, it is my mother. I musn't bolt the door against my mother.

Mar. No. — I had forgot. A good child; you must not. (*Boy runs and opens the door*)

Rach. (*Running in*) Martin! dear Martin!

Mar. (*Rises*) Rachel, if you can look in my face, and do not sink with shame, can you look on these? (*Pointing to children*)

Rach. Shame! — You are deceived.

Mar. I have been: so deceived, that had a voice from the sky called you what it tears my heart to think of, I would not have listened to it. But, these eyes — these eyes — oh! that I had been blind!

Rach. You never loved me if you will not hear me.

Mar. Never loved you! It was that love that smoothed all trouble to me. It was that love, that, when all men, — fortune, — seemed set against me, cheered me on, and put a strength into my heart, — that made me smile as I would think — well, let all go, let all else fail me, there's one who'll never change; — there is one who is as good, as constant as the angels. Poverty came upon me: the blow was sudden and unkind. Still I thought, though we have but a crust, we'll share that crust together: though our bed be straw, that bed shall bear us both! — As you say, I am deceived.

Rach. But hear me, Martin; then judge me as you will.

Mar. That man — that devil whom they put here — would his blood were on my hearth! — did he not tempt you?

Rach. He did. —

Mar. With gold — filthy gold? — He came into the poor man's house — bought that which I thought worlds could never buy — robbed me of my wife, these children of their mother.

Rach. Martin, may you be pardoned that thought! — It is true, that man showed me gold — dared to speak — to seize me, — but casting his money in the dust, I tore myself from his arms. —

Mar. His arms! (*Passionately*) Woman! I would not kill you.

Rach. I fled and hid myself — listened to a plan of murder, and ran to the mansion.

Mar. I found you there, coming from his chamber.

Rach. I knew not the man! 'Twas to save his life. Upon my soul, I speak the truth!

Mar. (*With emotion*) A lie — a foul lie!

Rach. The truth, or may I die at your feet. Oh, Martin! can you think thus of me, — after the years — the happy years? — or am I become tiresome to you, and so with this excuse you'd —

Mar. Excuse! Are these tears an excuse, — these trembling limbs, these scalded eyes, this broken heart? (*Sinks into a chair*)

Enter Sailor.

Sailor. (*Speaking at door*) Now, Master, if you're for starting, we shall sail in an hour. Here's a whole crew of neighbours, too, coming to take leave of you.   *Disappears.*

Rach. Martin?

Mar. I have accepted the place abroad, to attend an estate, (*With suppressed disgust*) and overlook the slaves. I leave the farm — the country, this day.

Rach. The children?

Mar. They go with me.

Rach. And I, Martin — I?

Mar. Go where you will, may you be happy.

Rach. (*Wildly*) My children! Use me as you please, — but my babes! — Oh, Martin! what madness is upon you? (*Martin crosses and takes one of the children by the hand*) Hear me! — you shall hear me! If it must be so, think not of me as your wife; but have mercy on the mother of your children!

Mar. I love them, Rachel.

Rach. Dearly, very dearly; but not like a mother.

Mar. Bid them farewell, for they must go.

Rach. But not without me! Children, pray to your father — pray to him I must not call my husband? (*Kneeling to Martin*)

Mar. Rachel, this is wild and useless. Be calm, and give them up.

Rach. I tell you, I shall go mad — raving mad — to lose my children! Take me with them. I do not ask you to speak to me, to look at me; — let me work with the slaves you speak of; — let me die, so as I die not from my children! (*Faints, and falls over Martin's knee — the children surround her*)

Enter Farmer Beanstalk, Polly, Dame, Neighbours, and Sailor.

Bean. Why, Martin, and bee'st thee really going? (*Sees Rachel*) Why, what's the matter with thee wife?

Pol. Bless me, Rachel!

They bear her to the back.

Mar. Farmer, farewell; neighbours, heaven bless you! — let the landlord take all the rest, — this chair, — my grandfather's chair, — I'll bear with me.

Enter Bullfrog and Burly.

Bul. Not a splinter of it, as I'm a sworn appraiser.

Mar. I do not wish to hurt you, man; but do not strive to prevent me.

Bul. Mustn't move a stick, Mr. Heywood. Business is business.

Mar. I tell you, this chair shall go with me. Let him who dares, lay a finger on it. (*Is about to lift the chair. Bullfrog advances*)

Bul. Business is business. I seize in the king's name.

Mar. Then you must fight for it.

Strikes Bullfrog, who seizes the chair with Burly. Neighbours assist Martin, exclaiming, "Down with them!" In the struggle, the back of the chair is pulled off when out fall loose gold, money-bags, and a paper.

All. Gold! Money!

Bul. I seize it in the king's name.

Far. (*Throwing him aside*) What be this? (*Taking up paper*) Your grandfather's name. (*Bullfrog is going to seize the will. Martin rushes across and keeps him back*)

Mar. Read, read!

Far. (*Reads*) "Should any sudden accident light upon me, so that I be not able to tell my last wishes, let this certify, that the three hundred guineas hidden, with this paper, in my walnut chair, be the rightful property of Martin and Tobias Heywood, my grandsons.
Signed,
THOMAS HEYWOOD."

Mar. I shall keep the farm! — ha! ha! — I shall keep the farm! (*Sinks upon the neck of farmer. Neighbours shout*)

Enter Grantley.

Gran. Where is Master Heywood?

Mar. Come not here, man — come not here!

Gran. Be calm. I have injured you — in thought, I mean. All your neighbours praise you for an honest, upright man. I thought you the companion of scoundrels. But for your wife, whose devotedness I have wronged, I had fallen their victim. She came to save me —

Toby. (*Without*) Come along, rascal. Stand out of the way!

Enters, dragging in Crumbs, and throws him around. Servant following, carrying a box.

Crumbs. Villain! why am I thus used?

Toby. (*To Grantley*) Here is the rascal, sir. You know we found that box among the laurel trees. Luckily, you took my advice, and let it rest. We watched, and as I expected, the thief came creeping down to carry away the spoil. We pounced upon him, — here he is, and here's his plunder.

Gran. What answer make you to this?

Crumbs. None to you. I shall make a clear answer to Mr. Robert Grantley.

Gran. Then speak — Robert Grantley is before you. (*General surprise*) What! you shrink? — I had heard of your oppression. I wrote for further sums of money, and then, under a feigned character, came to witness the means you'd take to answer the demand. Fie upon you! My father left you to husband my estate: it was your duty to check my extravagance, not feed it. And now, you add to your iniquity by wholesale theft. What say you to this?

Crumbs. Robert Grantley, — since you are he, — listen. At the mansion you saw a certain picture. You remember you asked me whose it was — I'll tell you. It was the likeness of a young and once virtuous wife. A devil, a golden devil, dazzled her vain heart, and she left her husband and disgraced him. That husband plunged in vice to fly from thought. He gamed, robbed, and was devoted to the thief's reward — the gallows. He escaped and fled abroad. Years rolled away. In a foreign land he met his wife's destroyer, who, knowing not the man he had wronged, fostered him — took him to his heart — made him his man of trust, and brought him to England. He died, and left him to manage his estate for his wild and absent son, Robert Grantley. That man was your father; — the picture is the picture of his victim; — I — I was her wronged and broken-hearted husband!

Gran. Can it be?

Crumbs. My purpose was to beggar you — to revenge me on the father, in his dearest part, his darling son!

Gran. Your injuries were great; yet how could your malice survive the author of your wrongs?

Crumbs. That picture! I have stood and looked at it — in the still night I have gazed on it, until I have thought the devil himself looked from its eyes, and smiled upon my purpose. That picture, and the recollection that those cursed walls received my wife when she fled from her home, and left me to seek companions with the vile and infamous — Oh! I am an old man! — but there are injuries so graven in the heart, so burnt within the brain, that with the heart and brain they must live and die together! Enough. Now for my gaol.

Gran. No; I pardon you; nay, more; I will provide for you.

Crumbs. Never, I scorn and spit at you. — Am I free?

Stephen and others bring in Silver Jack and Hyssop, bound.

Ste. Here are the thieves! (*To Grantley*) I was told you were here, sir, and so here I've brought them. — Bob, the carter here, saw them on the road, and knowing our cattle, gave the cry; they were soon unhorsed, and here they are, ready trussed for the gibbet. We found these few matters on them. (*Shows dice, cards, picklocks, etc.*) And here's something folded up. (*Gives paper to Grantley*)

Gran. What is this? — (*Reading bill*) "Escaped from Newgate — John Harris!" — Who can this mean?

Crumbs. The man your father robbed! Read and see what time and he have made of him. I took ten guineas from a rich usurer, and was condemned for Tyburn. Your father stole the wife of my bosom, and lived a wealthy, charitable gentleman, — had the respect of all while on the earth, and a lying tombstone when under it! May I leave now?

Grantley bows, and Crumbs crosses. Jack and Hyssop give way, and retire a little. Crumbs looks fiercely around him, exchanges a look of contempt with Jack and Hyssop, who laugh, and rushes off.

Jack. Perhaps we're intruding: may we leave, too?

Gran. Away with them, and keep them for the present.

Ste. They deserve hanging, if it's only for the lies they told about Master Heywood's wife. Why, they've been laughing over it as a good joke — (*Jack and Hyssop laugh*) — that they tried to make Martin jealous, that he might save them the sin of blowing out your brains. (*They laugh*) Oh, you rascals! —

your hanging-day will be a rare holiday thirty miles round.

> *Stephen, etc., take Jack and Hyssop off, laughing.*

Mar. Rachel! can I be forgiven! I dare not look at you. (*Rachel throws herself into his arms*)

Toby. I don't wonder at that, he's a poor wizard whom every fool can drive mad. Suspect Rachel! why, if we weren't all made so happy with our grandfather's gold, I'd turn boy again, and thrash you myself. Here was Bullfrog trying to disturb me and my wife.

Bul. Wife!

Toby. Yes. I shall never know what to do with my part of the money, so I must have a wife to get her advice about it. (*Taking Polly's arm*) I hope (*To Bullfrog*) you've no objection?

Bul. None, (*Aside*) as the money's not on the other side. But business is business; you'll want furniture; I have the sweetest four-post bedstead you ever looked upon.

Mar. (*To Grantley*) I have now, sir, to ask your pardon. Can you excuse the passion of an oppressed —

Gran. Nay, it is I who have to ask forgiveness of you, and of all my tenants, that I have suffered them to be the victims of a mercenary agent. I will henceforth reside on my lands; and, by my future care, endeavour to remedy the injuries committed by my servant. To your wife, Heywood, I probably owe my existence. This farm has, I hear, been in your family for sixty years: may it remain so while the country stands! To-morrow shall give you a freeholder's right to it.

Neighbours, etc. Huzza! Huzza!

Bul. Well, this is capital. — I see. (*Aside*) I'm future steward to this young man. — But still I have to say one thing. Friendship and generosity are very well; but — (*To Martin*) now, it doesn't concern you, — you're a freeholder: all of us here aren't so lucky; therefore, as business is business, I trust nobody here will forget "THE RENT-DAY."

THE END.

DION BOUCICAULT

1820?-1890

After Dark

(1868)

Dion Boucicault, at the height of his powers in 1868, thrilled London theatregoers with *After Dark*. From a literary standpoint, it is not his best play; perhaps *The Octoroon* or *The Colleen Bawn* has that honor. But it is a typical play from this master of the melodrama.

With an unerring instinct for what his public wanted, Boucicault selected material for the play from a variety of sources. The playbill and printed version announced that the play was the "Authorized adaptation of MM. Grange and Dennery's 'Les Oiseaux de Proie' "; but probably the inspiration for the play was the success of Augustin Daly's *Under the Gaslight*, which was playing at the Whitechapel Pavilion in July of 1868 before *After Dark* opened at the Princess's Theatre on August 12. In the "sensation scene" of Daly's play the villain places a man bound hand and foot on the tracks in front of an approaching train. A girl locked in the railway station witnesses this act and tries frantically to escape; finding an axe, she breaks down the door just in time to untie the victim before the train arrives. Boucicault imitated Daly's scene, but doubled its eerie thrill. The first part of the London Metropolitan Underground Railway was opened in 1863, and it was still a novelty and a marvel in 1868. Instead of using an ordinary railroad, Boucicault placed his big scene in this subway; and instead of a girl's making the rescue in daylight, he has Old Tom frantically dig his way through the brick wall of a dark cellar as the train thunders down the adjoining tunnel.

To provide subsidiary thrills in a play full of constant motion, Boucicault included lurid scenes of London's criminal underworld: the roost of night birds under Blackfriars Bridge, beside the dark, corpse-haunted Thames; and a music hall and gambling den in full swing, with interesting revelations of the crooked tricks of such places. Perhaps the spectators were not familiar with these haunts, but other scenes thrilled them with such pictures of everyday actuality as the crowds at Victoria Station; the garrets and cellars of the poor and, for contrast,

Sir George's grand garden and villa, and the boudoir filled with wedding gifts. No doubt many a spectator gasped and nudged his neighbor when scenes located the action on well-known streets and even gave house numbers. The songs of the play were being sung in local music halls. In a sense Boucicault employed the techniques of realism and even of "slice of life" naturalism. But he was a showman, not a savant; the play exhibits none of the realist's or naturalist's sociological intention.

As these thrilling scenes gave new interest to the old formula of melodrama, the well-made plot gave the play unity. All the time-tested conventions of melodrama appear: the action is violent, with blackmail and attempted suicide and murder; the sinister villain appears with the equally sinister but somewhat comic villain; the "straight" hero (Chumley) appears with the broken old man who is the active hero. The play exhibits domestic affection, with danger for the faithful wife; regular doses of pathos, with moral lessons about drinking and gambling; and music to heighten moments of excitement. Even the lesser conventions of the form appear: incredible coincidences, secrets discovered through eavesdropping, soliloquies and asides to keep the audience informed, and, at the climax, revelations of identity that insure future happiness for all except the villains. But Boucicault knit these many parts and complications into the well-made pattern of one governing action that proceeds in a balanced alternation of threats, dangers, and rescues. He even integrated the comic elements, the singing and dancing, into the action. These features kept the play running at the Princess's Theatre for nine months.

Though more and more melodramas based on the old formula but enriched by increasingly lurid "sensation scenes" continued to be written through the century, *After Dark* was something like a climax. It nearly exhausted the possible thrills of sheer villainy, violence, and scenery — until moving pictures enabled producers to present perils impossible on the stage. Later melodramas, perhaps aided by the quasi-realism and well-made structure of plays like *After Dark*, began to grope toward greater reality of character and probability of action.

AFTER DARK

A Drama Of London Life In 1868 In Four Acts

by

DION BOUCICAULT

First performed at the Princess's Theatre, Wednesday, August 12, 1868.

Cast of Characters

OLD TOM, *a boardman*
CHANDOS BELLINGHAM, *man about town*
DICEY MORRIS, *gambling-house keeper*
SIR GEORGE MEDHURST
GORDON CHUMLEY, *captain of Dragoons*
POINTER, *a policeman*
CRUMPETS

AREA JACK, *a night bird*
THE BARGEE
MARKER
NICK
JEM AND JOSEY, *Negro minstrels*
ELIZA, *Sir George's wife*
ROSE EGERTON
POLICE, SERVANTS, RAILWAY PASSENGERS, BEGGARS, THIEVES, GAMBLERS, ETC.

ACT I.

Scene 1.

Exterior of Victoria Railway Station, London. Discover Gentlemen and Ladies passing on and off by the various entrances, separately, two by two, walking slowly or briskly, forming groups, etc. Man selling umbrellas and matches goes from party to party.

Match-Seller. Box o' lights! box o' lights, sir? cigar-lights! (*Repeats and goes about during opening*)

Common hand-bell rings. Commissionaries are called by Gentlemen and take notes or small parcels from them. Railway porters cross stage and exit. Policeman enters and exits. Enter from Station Chandos Bellingham, coming slowly. Enter Dicey Morris with a party of Girls and Men, whom he quits, they going off.

Boy. (*To Bellingham*) Box o' lights, sir? only one penny, sir.

Bel. What's that you say? (*Rouses himself*) Only one penny? Here, confound you! there's sixpence for you! (*Boy takes coin, touches his cap*) Be off with you! (*Aside*) That's my last sixpence — it shrank into a corner like a deer, in my pocket. (*Morris comes down towards Bellingham*) Well, it little matters when I'm so unlucky.

Mor. Ah! Mr. Bellingham!

Bel. Dicey Morris!

Mor. Down on your luck, Chandos, old friend?

Bel. Yes, I backed Lady Elizabeth, and she has let us all in. If I hadn't had my "return," I should have had to walk home.

Mor. So should I.

Bel. What did you back?

Mor. Blue Gown. Blue Petticuts! wager on the feminines, and you're sure to come to grief. So, Chandos, my boy, you are a broken man? Well, I'll mend you! I'll put you into a trick! I'll make your hair regularly stand up on end! (*Produces newspaper*) I wish I may die if I don't! Just throw your eye over that! The second column — the sensation column! (*Bellingham takes paper*)

Bel. (*Reads*) "George Medhurst. — Fifty pounds reward will be paid to anyone giving information of this gentleman. He is said to have emigrated for Canada or Australia, in 1856. Apply to G. C., Grosvenor Hotel, Pimlico." What does this mean, Dicey? Do you know of the man?

Mor. It means pounds sterling, and I can lay my hand on the man this blessed minute. Vy, I could have transported him three yearsh ago! and he knowsh it!

Bel. What has he done?

Mor. Forgery! He put his father's name to a bit of paper, sen' I may live if he didn't!

Bel. But may he not know of this?

Mor. Not likely! I'll show you him! (*All the other characters have gone off*) Hillo! here! hi, come here, hansom cabby! Come here!

Enter Medhurst, with whip in hand.

Med. Well, what do you want?

Mor. What do I want? Have you forgotten me, eh?

Med. Forgotten you, Dicey Morris! No! (*Sullenly*) Not since that day when you called me out of the rank in the Haymarket, and I came like a dog to your call! And now that you have got me, what do you want of me?

Mor. There ish gratitude for you! Just throw your eye over this! (*Offers paper*) Look at it! look at it!

Med. (*With newspaper*) "Fifty pounds reward — George Medhurst." Why, what does this mean?

Mor. It meansh that the police want to find out about that forgery business. But it won't work. You come to me tonight at my place in Little Rupert Street, and meanwhile I'll see the gent what holds the forged paper.

Med. I will come, don't doubt. (*Aside*) For I must!

Mor. By the way, where are you living now?

Med. 5½ Campton Mews.

Mor. Same place. And how ish Mrs. Hayward — pretty well?

Med. Yes.

Mor. That'sh right. (*Exit Medhurst*) That'sh right! (*Quickly, to Bellingham*) There! that'sh the heir to a barrowknightcy and five t'ousand a year, a-driving a night-cab and picking up hish living in the shtreets. There'sh not much fear of him going near "G. C." or the Grosvenor Hotel.

Bel. What are you going to do with me, Dicey? What do you want with me, when you have got him in your power? You wouldn't take me in as a partner, and show up the good

thing to me without security. Come, what's your game?

Mor. Well, Chandos, my boy, you know, eight year ago, when you wash transpor — I mean, when you emigrated to Australia, I called on you at your lodgings. You were living then in Pentonville, with such a fine lady and a little girl!

Bel. And I asked you, if anything should happen to me, to take care of that child!

Mor. I did take care of her — wish I may die if I didn't! I brought her up like a lady, like a lady, Bellingham — and, when she grew up, I made her one of my bar-maids —

Bel. Ah! what became of her?

Mor. Why that man you just saw fell in love with her at my place, and married her! (*Rubs his hands in glee*)

Bel. (*Startled*) Married *her*?

Mor. Yes, married your child, and he's heir to five t'ousand a year!

Bel. But she was not my child!

Mor. Not your child? Oh, then, it'sh all off — it'sh all off. I don't want you in the bishinessh at all.

Bel. What! You don't see your way to more than one thousand pounds? Pshaw! You hold in your hands the fair fame and honor of an old country family, and you cannot plan to squeeze more than a paltry one thousand pounds out of it? Dicey, you are a low, contemptible fellow.

Mor. I am, I am! I wish I may die if I ain't!

Bel. One thousand pounds; say five thousand!

Mor. Five t'ousand! You take my breath away.

Bel. Leave the game in my hands.

Mor. Yesh, yesh! You go see this "G. C." at the Grosvenor Hotel, Chandos, my dear. (*Walks with Bellingham*) I'll wait at the station here for you.   *Exit Bellingham.*

Morris writes in notebook, studying the newspaper. Music, lively. Laughter outside. Enter Old Tom, followed by Boys, laughing and hooting at him.

Boys. Ha, ha! only twig him, ha, ha!

1st Boy. I say, Tom, how does it feel in the high wind? (*Laughs*)

2nd Boy. He's been a-dining with the Lord Mayor! (*All laugh*)

1st Boy. Don't you know? He's sent out as a sample of the liquor they sell at the Elysium! (*Tom goes to lamp post*)

Mor. My establishment. (*He comes toward the group*) What's that about the Elysium? (*Sees Tom*) One of my bill-boards. This is the way my advertising is done.

Enter Pointer.

Pointer. (*Driving Boys*) Move on, move on, there, can't you!

1*st Boy.* You'd better keep your h'eye on him, "Robert"! he's going to make a hole in the water! (*All laugh*)

Pointer. You ought to be ashamed of yourselves to go and worry the poor old man so. (*Tom leans against lamp post and sings drunkenly to himself*)

1*st Boy.* You stick to him, bobby! and don't you let h'anybody touch him! Vy, he's sent out by the Temperance Society as a speciment of the Last Stage of 'Toxication. (*Pointer crosses to Boys. They run off, but he seizes one*)

Boy. (*Seized by Pointer, crying*) It wasn't me! it was the other boys. (*Pointer goes off after Boys, they laughing and shouting*)

Mor. I'll report this fellow for disgracing my bill-boards! (*To Tom*) What's your name?

Tom. I ain't got a name!

Mor. Come, drop it! drop it! That won't do with me. Why thosch boysh just now called you Old Tom.

Tom. Because I live on Old Tom! Old Tom for breakfast, Old Tom for dinner, Old Tom for supper, ha, ha! It keeps the rain out and I don't feel hungry. Gin, gin! give us the coppers for half a quartern!

Mor. Poor fellow, poor old fellow! I pities him — I pities him, I actually does!

Tom. (*Starts*) You pity me? You? You, Dicey Morris, that keeps the Silver Hell in Rupert Street and the Elysium Music Hall over the water! Oh, I know you! I lost my last sovereign over your tables, and my last sixpence over your pewter-bar. And *you* pity *me!* You, who picked me up out of the gutter, and clothed me in the rags that you keep for your customers — the livery of sin and degradation! I must be the meanest wretch in all the town to deserve pity from *you.*

Mor. (*Testily*) Hold your row! What are you making such a row about? There's a shilling. (*Offers coin*) Go and drink it.

Tom. A shilling! a shilling taken over your tables may be the last drop of some poor devil's blood, or the only coin of some shop-boy, stolen from his master's till to feed one of the painted jades of your Elysium! Ah! take it from you, Dicey Morris? No! it would choke me!   *Goes.*

Mor. Refuse a shilling! It's shocking what intemperance will bring a fellow to! I can't make him out! I never come across such a strange fellow.

He starts to go, meeting Bellingham, Gordon Chumley, and Rose Egerton, who enter.

Bel. I beg to present to you my friend, Mr. Morris — one who has been a friend to Mr. Medhurst in adversity. (*To Morris*) These are friends of our dear George.

Mor. (*Salutes Rose vulgarly*) Ah, ah, a friend of Mr. Medhurst — dear me!

Rose. (*Simply*) Oh! yes, we are cousins, and were brought up together in childhood.

Mor. I might have known it by the likeness! (*Bellingham pushes him*)

Bel. (*Aside*) Don't make a fool of yourself! (*Aloud to Morris*) And this is Captain Gordon Chumley. (*Chumley salutes, and Morris lifts his hat awkwardly*)

Chum. (*Aside*) He looks like a Jew horse-dealer. As for the other, I cannot make him out; I have seen his face somewhere before. (*Aloud*) I think, Mr. Bellingham, that we have met. Was it in India or the Crimea?

Bel. (*As if surprised*) Neither.

Chum. Then were you ever in Australia?

Mor. (*Aside*) Rather! something like seven years!

Bel. Never!

Chum. Ah, it's very odd. I beg your pardon.

Bel. Don't mention it. But we are forgetting our friend Medhurst.

Rose. I bring news to him. Poor old Sir John has died.

Mor. Died! Then he has come in for the money! (*Bellingham silences him with a look*)

Rose. Yes, Sir John at the last has forgiven him.

Chum. But conditionally. Remembering the wildness of his youth, he imposes upon him a proviso. He must marry to gain the estate.

Mor. I call that very unkind for a forgiving father.

Bel. (*Aside to Morris*) Hold your tongue! (*Aloud to Chumley*) On that condition, eh?

Chum. That he marries his cousin. If he refuses, all the property goes to her. A most painful position for the young lady, very painful.

Mor. I don't see it, not for her. She ish safe to have her share anyhow.

Bel. (*Aside to Morris*) Will you keep quiet!

Chum. It is not probable that Mr. Medhurst will rebel against the condition.

Bel. (*To Rose*) They say that there is no husband like the reformed rake. I trust that George will prove no exception to the rule. Madam, your servant! We will go and be the first to break the good fortune to George. (*Takes Morris aside*)

Mor. (*To Bellingham*) Now it's all up!

Bel. Better than I hoped.

Mor. But he is already married.

Bel. His wife must disappear.

Mor. I wish she may die if she don't!

      Exit with Bellingham.

Chum. Ah, it's awfully hard on me, Rose, to have to see you for the last time and say good-bye. (*Tom goes to sleep at foot of lamp post*)

Rose. You are not going to leave me all alone in London?

Chum. George will soon come to claim his bride.

Rose. Oh, when we tell him all, that I — I —

Chum. You love me? I feared as much, while I hoped. You might have spared me that, my task — our task — was hard enough before. But his father has pointed out the only way to restore him to his true position in the world. There can be no one to aid him like you. (*Tom rises and staggers down to Chumley's right during the following*) Ask me to help you in what is so right, and not to turn from you till all that is done. So much is duty — and pleasant so far. To part from you will be so hard, now that I know that you love me. (*Sees Tom*) What do you want?

Tom. (*Very drunkenly*) I saw you talking with them — them! (*Jerks his hand toward the right*) Don't have nothing to do with them! nothing to do!

Chum. Why, the man's drunk.

Tom. (*Starts*) Eh? (*Sobered somewhat*) It's Gordon Chumley.

Chum. (*Amazed*) You know me!

Tom. (*Aside*) He has forgotten me. No wonder! I have almost forgotten myself. (*Pathetically*) Never mind, never mind!

    Enter Pointer.

Pointer. Come, move on; this won't do. (*Pushing Tom*)

Tom. (*Whining*) I wasn't begging.

Chum. (*To Rose*) Stay! I know him now. He was an old brother-officer of mine.

Pointer. (*To Tom*) Come, be off.

Chum. Stay! (*Chumley crosses to Tom*) I know you, don't I? You are —

Tom. (*Screams*) Ah, don't speak it, don't speak it! Don't say my name. (*Whining*) I am Old Tom, Old Tom. (*Music*)

Pointer. Be off with you! (*Pushes Tom and follows him off*)

Chum. Poor old Frank; has he come to this? What a depth of misery. Look, Rose, he used to be the handsomest and gayest in the regiment, the pride of the mess. It is to save George from a fate like that we are working! For his sake we must keep our word.

      Scene closes in.

    Scene 2.

A garret interior, with semi-darkness. Music throughout, hurried music. Enter Medhurst.

Med. Eliza, Eliza!

  Enter Eliza, with lighted candle.

Has no one been here?

Eliza. No. What brings you home so early? (*Puts candles on shelf*)

Med. I have had an accident with the cab.

Eliza. An accident! You are not hurt, George?

Med. Come here, Eliza. I am compelled to leave London this night. Even now there may be hunters on my track. I am going to see Morris, who will assist me in my escape.

Eliza. Morris! my old employer, Morris? Oh, George, don't trust him!

Med. I must! I have no choice!

Eliza. Oh, what have you done?

Med. What I never had heart to tell to you. That's why I have been forced to go creeping out after dark, driving a night cab for fear that I would be seen — leading a dog's life, which you consented to share!

Eliza. What better have I ever known? You found me a nameless child! and I never asked more than to have you my own! and you are my own, George. (*Embraces him*)

Med. In the depth of my misery there was a deeper still which I have forborne to confide to you. Pardon me for having deceived you.

Eliza. You have not deceived me in your love! What do I care for the rest!

Med. I hear steps by the door. You do not expect anyone at this hour?

Eliza. No! Shade the light! (*Medhurst covers the candle and Eliza goes to the window*) There are men below who seem to be looking up here.

Med. I must escape by the other way. (*The following spoken very hurriedly*) Gain what time you can. Put out the light! (*Eliza puts out the candle*) Footsteps on the stairs! (*He embraces her*) Farewell! This may be our parting kiss. Good-bye, good-bye. (*He rushes off, and there is a knock at the door*)

Eliza. Ah! (*She goes slowly to the door and opens it*)

    Enter Bellingham.

Bel. Where is your husband?

Eliza. He has not yet returned from work.

Bel. That is false, for he was here not ten minutes ago. I will see if he is concealed on the premises. (*He blows a whistle at the window. A whistle outside replies*) He has escaped by the back yard and will soon be at Morris's. You can light the candle again.

He's safe enough. You see that I know more of your husband's doings than you do.

Eliza. Who are you? Friend or foe? (*She lights the candle*)

Bel. Look and see.

Eliza. Richard Knatchbull! (*A chord of music*)

Bel. No longer Dick Knatchbull, but Chandos Bellingham. I see you have not forgotten me.

Eliza. No, I have not forgotten the man who left my mother to die in the workhouse.

Bel. And not forgiven me?

Eliza. She forgave you, long since, but I never will.

Bel. This is dutiful language to hear from a daughter.

Eliza. You are not my father!

Bel. Ah! you know that? Then why did you not marry George Medhurst under your father's name? (*Aside*) If you knew who that father was!

Eliza. Because my mother had implored me with her latest breath not to bear the name which you had tried to disgrace.

Bel. It would be well if George Medhurst had not succeeded with a similar experiment on his own.

Eliza. What do you mean?

Bel. That he has committed a crime and may be forced to fly. What would you do to save him?

Eliza. He is my husband. I would lay down my life for him.

Bel. Less would do. Give me your hand. (*She offers her right hand*) The other — the left. (*She holds out her left hand*) Would you lay down this ring — this wedding-ring for his sake? He has committed forgery. The money can be obtained, but to secure his safety, you must sacrifice yourself.

Eliza. I do not understand.

Bel. It is necessary that he should marry again. Your marriage was made under false names; you need only go abroad and forget him.

Eliza. Forget him!

Bel. Oh, you can name your own terms. As long as you live he will be at your mercy.

Eliza. I see it all now. You want him to deceive some innocent girl, to induce me to join you to commit a bigamy! Has George agreed to this?

Bel. He had no choice. The man whose head is in the jaws of Newgate is not particular to a shade.

Eliza. (*Aside*) This is the depth of infamy which he was afraid to confide in me. (*Wrings her hands*)

Bel. You consent?

Eliza. No. Whatever he may have done — he is my husband. I will share with him, but I will not help him to commit a new crime!

Bel. And this is what you call love? You would rather see the man you love consigned to a convict cell than let another woman make him happy.

Eliza. (*Sobbing*) I would die for him, but I will not live in guilt.

Bel. Ahem! he has no alternative.

Eliza. But I have.

Bel. Will you be silent, at least?

Eliza. He has cast me off! I shall be silent as the grave.

Bel. He does not ask for your approval. He will be content with your silence.

Eliza. My silence! (*Aside, bitterly*) My silence! (*Dashes to open the door*) There's your way. Good night.

Bel. (*Goes to Eliza and looks her in the eyes*) Good night. *Exit, with hat on.*

Eliza. Merciful Heavens, what have I done? He said that might be our parting kiss. No, I cannot part from him like that. I cannot aid him to commit a wrong, but I can remove the consequences of his fault. I will go to Morris's and wait for him till I see him. Oh, I must see him again. Where is my bonnet and shawl? (*Takes candle, goes through door, gets hat and shawl, and returns*) Yes, I shall see him again, and then — oh, George! (*Sobs repeatedly*) Oh, George! oh, George! *Exit.*

Scene 3.

A gambling house interior. Discover Dicey Morris, apparently in impatience. Gamblers throwing dice around table. Doorkeeper seated, Waiter by sideboard.

Marker. Seven's the main!

2nd Gam. Five!

1st Gam. Six!

Mor. (*Aside*) Not here yet. What is Bellingham up to? He's almost as close as I am, wish he may die if he ain't! And the cabman, he's to come at eleven! and no signs of him yet.

Marker. Ten's the nick.

Mor. (*Aside*) What's he about? Is he going back on an old friend?

Marker. (*Comes down to Morris*) By the way, sir, I've lent Charley three pounds on this half of a five-pound note — he can't wait till the rest comes up by post.

Mor. What? Why, he's borrowed three pounds of me on the other half. He's pulled a clear pound off by the double transaction. (*Marker goes up to speak with Gamblers, who laugh at the trick*) That's the worst of my customers — there's nothing honorable about them.

Marker. (*Comes to Morris, aside*) That fellow's still winning; we've lost thirty pounds.

Mor. Bring out the loaded dice. What are you doing? Do you want to ruin me?

The Marker goes. Enter Medhurst.

Med. (*To Morris*) I am followed!

Mor. Of course you are. It's all right; it shows how much you are looked after since you've come into your fortune. (*Calls*) Waiter, waiter! bring a glass of champagne for this gentleman. (*Waiter brings glass, and Medhurst drinks*)

Med. It's so long since I drank champagne, I scarcely know the taste of it.

Mor. Well, I've been to the city and seen the gentleman — oh, he's very reasonable — he seesh that I was right when I said — you'll pay him; only give him time — give him time.

Med. Come into my fortune? Then my father is dead?

Mor. Yes, you are Sir George now! As good a name as ever wash known, and six t'ousand pounds a year!

Med. I see now what you want with me! What is your price for that paper?

Mor. The gentleman that holdsh it has the conscience to ask half the income —

Med. Three thousand pounds?

Mor. Three t'ousand pounds! Isn't it perfectly disgraceful! So I tells him; but then what would be the use of the whole if he brought you to trial? Better half the fortune than all, and you go to Newgate!

Med. I believe you hold the document yourself!

Mor. Ish it me?

Med. Then why don't your friend come forward for himself?

Mor. That would be compounding a felony! And he ish a shentlemans, moves in the same society as myself, a man of high prinshiples! high prinshiples, I tell you! high prinshiples!

Med. I suppose I must consent.

Mor. Of course, of course, there'sh no other way out of it. After all, you've got the other half — I calls it downright generous of him, downright generous.

Med. (*Aside*) I am in their power. Oh, then I will be free! free from these villains, and that will be the best of all. (*Aloud*) You are not deceiving me?

Mor. Sen' I may live! I look like deceiving a baronet! What'll you have — some money?

Five pounds — ten — fifty? Here, Marker, give this gentleman fifty pounds. (*Takes Medhurst to the table*) Renew the acquaintance of the bones!

Marker. Eight's the main. Here's the fifty, sir.

Med. (*Aside*) Fifty pounds! fifty devils! (*Puts notes on the corner of the table*)

Mor. That's right, George, my boy. Go in! you're sure to win! (*Music*)

Med. (*Somewhat drunk*) How's the game, gentlemen?

Mor. (*Aside*) It's all right. If Bellingham has only done his bit as well. Where can he be? (*Aloud to Medhurst*) That's the way, that's the way, George, my boy, to enjoy yourself! Ah, I hope to see you in another day or two tooling a phaeton in the Park with a pair of high-steppers, and with that lovely girl by your side.

Med. What do you mean?

Mor. I mean Miss Egerton, your cousin. You can't have your property unless you marry her!

Med. Then it was left on condition? (*Falls in chair*)

Mor. There's fatherly affection for you! actually a-spreading sugar over the butter!

Marker. (*To Medhurst*) Luck's turned. Does your money stand, sir?

Med. (*Impatiently*) Yes, yes! (*To Morris*) Then I can't have it. I am already married to Eliza.

Mor. Oh, that was when you made a fool of yourself when a boy. Done under false names — it won't hold in law. I'll get you a lawyer's opinion, a — a — a doctor's certificate, anything you like! But you've not had a fair taste yet! Here, waiter, give the gentleman some more champagne! (*Waiter brings glass to Medhurst, who drinks*) That's right! you'll see the thing in the right light now!

Marker. That gentleman's. He still wins.

Mor. (*Pushes Medhurst up to table*) Stick to it, George, my boy, it's all right! depend upon it, it'll all come right! (*Walking away*) What keeps Bellingham — oh, here he is.

Enter Bellingham.

Bel. (*To Morris*) You have him here? (*Looks at Medhurst gambling at table, glass in hand*) He seems sprung.

Mor. A little! I didn't give him too much till you would be here, to see how you got on with the woman.

Bel. I have seen Eliza. She will hold her tongue. (*Coming to Medhurst*) Good evening, Sir George! Allow me to congratulate you on coming into your title.

Med. Who is this gentleman?

Mor. The friend who holds the forged paper. (*Introduces them*) Sir George, Mr. Bellingham.

Bel. I've explained your position to your wife, and she recognizes the necessity of her secrecy. She consents to disappear and trouble you no more.

Med. Disappear?

Bel. That is, go abroad.

Med. She consents to go from me?

Bel. Yes. You see, I know her better than you do.

Mor. There! ain't you ashamed of yourself? I knew she would act right. She was sure to, or else she hadn't got any principles.

Bel. She sees the difference in your stations. How would you like to have her pointed at in your lordly mansion by her swell friends of the Elysium? It is all for the best; you could never have lived happy with her. Of course, you'll pay her liberally, and she'll live very happily without any annoyance to you.

Marker. (*To Medhurst*) Now, again, sir, at the game.

Med. (*Half aside*) I shall never love anyone like her.

Mor. Here, waiter, some more champagne. *Music: "Won't go home till Morning." Scene closes in.*

Scene 4.

A street at night. Enter Eliza in bonnet and shawl.

Eliza. He has not come out yet. (*Two Gamblers enter and exit*) Patience, patience!

First Gambler enters, shakes his fist through open door.

1st Gam. You are a gang of thieves! Curse me, if I ever set foot within your accursed den again. It's regular robbery.

Exit furiously.

Enter Medhurst drunk.

Med. I'll get a bed at some hotel for the night, see a tailor in the morning, pass my head through Truefitt's hands, and emerge in the Parks as a new man, leading a new life.

Eliza. George! (*Chord of music*) Don't be angry at my being here. I could not think of parting from you as I did. But is it true, what they have told me? Must I go away from you?

Med. Yes — for a time. You shall have everything you require — money, jewels —

Eliza. George, not money; do not pay me for my love. George, take me to your arms and ask me to lay down my life for your happiness and I will do it. Your embrace will give

me strength, and your kiss will seal my lips forever.

Med. (*Embraces her*) I do ask you, Eliza, dear, to save me from a felon's fate. I shall never care for anyone but you.

Eliza. I never loved you more, George, than now, when we must part forever.

Med. Not forever.

Eliza. Yes, forever! I do not forget our bond, "Till death do us part." Farewell; kiss me — kiss me, George; it is for the last time.

Med. (*Kisses her*) How cold your lips are.

Eliza. (*Half aside, going*) They will be colder before morning. God bless you, God bless you!

Med. How strange her manner is. I didn't think she would have taken it so kindly. She never said a hard word to me. Ah, no one can ever love me as she has done.

Exit. Scene closes in.

Scene 5.

A street at night. Enter Gordon Chumley.

Chum. I cannot rest till I have seen Frank. What can have brought him to such a pitch of misery? I appointed to meet a policeman at Temple Bar — and here he comes.

Enter Pointer.

Pointer. (*Touches hat to Chumley*) He lives, sir, at the Dry Arches, but he is to be found under the bridge. He works on the river by night.

Chum. Can you guide me there?

Pointer. Well, sir, it's hardly the place to take a gentleman. The night-birds of London roost there.

Chum. I don't care.

Pointer. Well, sir, put your watch-chain in your pocket; button up your coat; if you have anything in your coat-pockets, take it out.

Chum. All right. Will that do? (*Pointer nods*)

Enter Eliza, her hat off her head, hanging by the ribbons behind.

Eliza. Which is the way, please, to Blackfriars Bridge?

Pointer. Fifth turning on the right. We're going that way. Will you have our protection?

Eliza. Not for the world! (*Runs off*)

Pointer. I don't like the look of that girl!

Chum. Do you know her?

Pointer. No, sir. She's not an unfortunate —you can see that by her face. She is after no good. Come on, sir. Step out, sir.

Exit with Chumley.

Scene 6.

Arch of bridge with view of the River Thames and St. Paul's by moonlight. Discover Men, Girls, and Children asleep in different spots. Crumpet in the center reckoning a handful of money.

Crump. I can't make it out. Let's see — woman and two children, that's — one and two is three — no. (*Scratches his head*) Children is half price! That's all right.

Enter Area Jack and the Bargee, coming down steps.

Jack. Have you got comfortable lodgings for two gentlemen tonight?

Crump. Yes, mate.

Jack. How much is it?

Crump. A brown a nob! only think, ven it's a tizzy and tuppence h'outside!

Jack. And a bath gratis in the morning.

Crump. No, you don't have any bath gratis in the morning! The Police have warned me that the first time they catch any of my lodgers in the water they'll have me h'up for polluting the Thames!

Enter Jem and Josey.

Jem. Hab yer got accommerdation for two gen'lemens as is down on their luck tonight? (*Comes down steps with Josey*)

Jack. Hello! here's the h'ambassadors from the Theatre Ryal, b'Abyssinia.

Crump. Hain't been lucky today?

Jem. Not worth a punch in the head! Who'll paytronize the intellectual amusement when they can go into the music hall and get rough-and-tumble with a song over their swipes and pipes?

Jack. Why, for thruppence me an' the Bargee went h'into the Elysium, and we had three ballets, a selection from Il Trovytory, and we heard the great Muggings sing A-Walking in the Zoo!

Jem. Ah, yah, yah! A-Walking in the Zoo! (*Sings, the others gradually joining in the chorus of "Walking in the Zoo," and gives a few steps, finish of a break-down*) I say, that's what we shall come to, some of these days. I say, Crumpets, will you give us credit for the night?

Crump. No! Sleep's a cash article here. We don't do that business on tick here!

Jem. (*Shoulders his banjo*) Well, then, we must try the work'us!

Jack. Oh, I say, don't do that! Here, here's tuppence I got for running for carriages at the Adelphi.

Jem. You're a trump! I'll give you a season

ticket for our entertainment. Pass him always, Josey.

Crump. (*Receiving coin from Jack*) All right. Hullo! here's a ha'penny too much! it's only a penny.

Jack. A penny a head, and a ha'penny for the chambermaid.

Crump. Here's your beds. (*Gives Jem and Josey beds from a pile*)

Enter Pointer and Chumley, Pointer's lantern lit and in his belt.

Pointer. This is the place, sir. I don't see that girl, though it's sure she passed us. She must have given us the slip.

Chum. Perhaps gone over the bridge.

Pointer. Not likely, sir. (*They come down the steps*) I'll try and find the person you seek.

Jack. I say, pals! here's a lark! here's a broken-down swell come to beg a night's doss of old Crumpets.

Pointer. No, he don't, he's a gentleman, only come down to have a look around.

Jack. Well, then, the gentleman ought to stand something for his footing!

All. That's the ticket!

Pointer. (*To Chumley*) You'd better give them a little something, sir.

Chum. Do people live here?

Jack. Rayther! should think they does! Vy, this is Bankside Hotel, unlimited; airy rooms and the water always laid on.

Pointer. Have any of you seen Old Tom?

Crump. He went along the foreshore a moment ago.

Pointer. All right.   *Exit.*

Crump. You'll find him in the boat.

Jack. More like at the bottom of it, drunk. (*All laugh*)

Chum. (*To Jack*) Here's half a crown for you. Here comes Dalton. I want to speak with Old Tom — an old friend of mine. If you'll keep it quiet down here while we have our talk, there'll be another half crown for you.

Jack. Werry good, sir.

> *Tries coin between his teeth. Whispers to others, and All go off, except Woman and Children, who remain asleep.*

Pointer enters.

Pointer. Here he is, sir!   *Exit up stairs.*

Enter Old Tom.

Chum. Dalton!

Tom. (*Savagely*) Ah! is it for this I have been brought here? to be insulted by your commiseration? Well, you see how low I have sunk. You have seen what I do by day; at night I sell bills at the doors of the theatres, and eke out my living after midnight by helping a man who trawls for the dead — when I am sober enough to think of such things!

Chum. Have you no friends?

Tom. I don't want any!

Chum. You know what true comrades we were to one another. We shared the same meals, the same tent, and when I lay for dead under the cannon on the field, it was you who flew to lift me up and carry me back to our lines, where we arrived, you dripping with blood from a shot in your shoulder. Dalton, do you think I forget?

Tom. No! but I must! Oh, Gordon, don't harrow me with memories of the past; don't rouse up the devil within me, that I try to drown with drink.

Chum. Would you leave me if you found me in the mire without a helping hand? You had a wife — what has become of her?

Tom. What! you have not heard what became of the lovely Fanny Dalton? ha, ha!

Chum. I see. She died!

Tom. You remember how she clung round my neck when we were ordered off to the Crimea; and how I used to weep at her letters, and the postscript that she guided our little child's hand to write to me? You called me a fool, and laughed at me. You were right. For even then she was the prey of a designing villain. When I returned home, I found that she had fled with him. He was a convicted felon, and when justice seized upon him, she was left in the work-house.

Chum. And your child?

Tom. No one knows what became of it — no one but that villain, whom the care of the Government keeps from my vengeance. Oh! my bitterest curses light on every letter in the name of Richard Knatchbull!

Chum. Knatchbull! why that is the name of a convict that I met in Van Dieman's Land. (*Aside*) Ah, that face I saw at the railway station today. Impossible? Oh, if he may have come back?

Tom. (*Agitated*) Well, you have had your say, and I thank you. I will go back to my work — though — (*Looks at his shaking hands*) I am unfit for any work tonight.

Chum. Good-bye, Frank.

Tom. Good-bye.

Exit, hanging his head in thought.

Chum. I was afraid to offer him money. He might have been offended. It was better not.

Enter Jack, Crumpets, and the Others, as before. Enter Pointer.

(*To Jack*) Here's the half-crown I promised you. (*To Pointer*) Have you found her?

Pointer. No, she must have crossed the bridge. (*Chumley at foot of steps*) Mr. Crumpets, mind you look after your lodgers. If any of the workmen's tools are missing, we shall have to break up your nest!

Crump. (*Lighting a pipe*) All right, Sergeant! There's nobody frequents my establishment but members of the h'upper ten!

All. Good-bye, Sergeant! Good night, Sergeant! (*Laughter. Music, piano, long sustenuto chords on violin during the following*)

Jack. What a h'orful draft comes in here! Crumpets, you r'ally oughter hang up curtings in the arch! you'll spile my woice next! (*Lies down on steps, sings drowsily air of "All Round My Hat"*) All round the squares, I lugs a pair of babbies; all round the squares, of a quiet arternoon; when I sees the people passing by I pinches them fe-ro-ciously! which makes them blessed babbies cry, and (*Sleepily*) sympathy is riz! (*Asleep, mumbles*) Sympathy is riz.

All are asleep. Moonlight rises. Enter Eliza suddenly.

Eliza. Oh, merciful heavens, forgive me for what I am doing! farewell, George! farewell, wicked world, it is for his sake! his sake!

Leaps down and exit unseen.

Jem. (*Rises*) What's that?

Crump. (*Rises*) Where? What? (*All wake up. Lively music*)

Jack. Something in the water. (*All are up, grouped picturesquely*) It's a woman!

Enter Tom in boat.

Crump. Hunt up a rope somewhere.

Tom. It's all right. I am here! (*All cheer*)

Quick Curtain. If Curtain is called up, discover Eliza fainted in Tom's arms in boat.

End of the First Act.

Act II.

Scene 1.

Arched vault under a street. Discover Eliza sleeping on bed in vault, Tom seated by barrel, drinking.

Tom. I wonder who she is? She is not a servant girl, her hands do not show signs of work. She is not a seamstress, her fingers show no marks of the needle. I wonder what made her do it?

Eliza. (*In her sleep*) George! Farewell, George!

Tom. Ah! that's it! George is at the bottom of it, whoever he is. Ever since nine days ago when I picked her out of the Thames, nothing save that name "George" has passed her lips.

Enter Chumley.

Chum. Dalton, I received your message, and I have come.

Tom. (*Rises*) You are come to my mansion.

Chum. Do you live here?

Tom. Now that they let me. At first I was worried out of it by the overseer of the parish, but whenever I came out of prison, I came back to here. I told him he would get tired of it before I did. So here I am.

Chum. Well, you want me to assist you?

Tom. No, not me! It's that poor girl there. Nine days ago I fished her out of the Thames, and she has lain there ever since. It was not love that drove her to it, for there is her wedding-ring on her finger; it was not want, for she had one pound seven odd in her pockets.

Chum. What can I do with her?

Tom. I don't know. I thought that you might know of some situation for her.

Chum. Without a character? I have no knowledge of her but such as you give.

Tom. I'm a nice looking article to recommend anybody!

Chum. Stay! now I think of it, I do know a lady who is in want of a person; she is about to be married.

Tom. Not to you, I hope.

Chum. No!

Tom. That's right.

Chum. I wish she was, for I love her!

Tom. And do you think she will take her?

Chum. Yes, I shall see her today, and if your charge will come to her — here's her address —(*Puts card on barrel-head*) I am pretty sure she will not have to return. And now, Dalton, can I do nothing for you?

Tom. No! I have nothing to live for.

Chum. Not even your daughter?

Tom. I have buried my last hope of ever finding her.

Chum. Then I will dig it up — and revive it! (*Tom shows interest in what follows*) I have not been idle since I last saw you. I remembered that I had seen a convict of the name of your wronger in Australia. I inquired about him and found that he escaped. I traced him from place to place till I found that he was in New Orleans, where he joined the Confederate Army in '63. The record

says that he fell among the killed at the battle of Harper's Ferry.

Tom. (*Bitterly*) Ah! he died like a brave soldier — while I — shall perish like a dog.

Chum. No, he was not killed. Among the Southern officers who sought refuge in London, I know one General Freemantle. I went to him. He remembered Knatchbull, who had been in his corps, attached to him. In the action, the two had been thrown down by the explosion of the same shell, but both rose unhurt, save that Knatchbull lost a portion of his left ear!

Tom. Fate set the felon's mark on him after all.

Chum. If I am not much mistaken he is at this moment in London. If so, do not fear, I am in the same cage as the reptile, and he cannot escape. Leave him to me, and I'll give you a good account of him. *Exit.*

Tom. Knatchbull alive! Knatchbull here! here? I may have passed him on the street, looked him in the face! Oh, if I had his throat within the grip of these fingers as now (*Takes up pewter pot*) I grasp this pewter measure, I would — (*Squeezes pot out of shape*) No, I didn't mean to spoil you, old fellow. (*Sets down the pot*) Pah! a gorilla could have done as much. Can you take the demon in that pot and strangle him? Yes, I can. I'll — I'll give up drink. (*Eliza gradually wakes, pushes her hair from her eyes, presses her forehead, etc.*) I — I mean I will try. I'll —I'll do it! I will, by degrees. (*About to drink*)

Eliza. (*Rises*) Oh, sir! don't. (*Seizes bottle*)

Tom. (*Rises*) Leave go! (*Struggle*) I must have it.

Eliza. Don't, you hurt me. (*Tom lets go bottle. She flings it away*)

Tom. (*Falls into seat, shaking fearfully*) I am a brute.

Eliza. No!

Tom. I am a brute.

Eliza. No, you are not. You have a good heart under these rags. I esteem you now, but I should love you if — if —

Tom. If I did not drink?

Eliza. I cannot feel for you all the interest that you deserve; but I hope to see you worthy of more than my gratitude some day, soon. After Dark the light will come.

Tom. I was speaking to a friend about you, my girl; and he has given me this address as one useful to you.

Eliza. (*Takes card*) "Miss Egerton, the Lilacs."

Tom. That lady will take you into her

service, I hope. There you will find a home. This place is not for such as you — I did not pick you up out of the Thames to make you the drudge of a drunken beggar. Pack up your things, my girl; it is a good way off, and you must be there this afternoon. (*After Eliza gets shawl, etc., to make a bundle, Tom closes the sailcloth over the arch. Eliza, kneeling, packs bundle*) You will write to me sometimes?

Eliza. Oh, often!

Tom. What name will you go by?

Eliza. It little matters, now that he has deprived me of the one he gave me. You! You can call me Fanny Dalton.

Tom. (*Starts excitedly*) Fanny Dalton! What! is that your name?

Eliza. It seems familiar to me. It must have been that of one that I held dear in my childhood.

Tom. (*With emotion*) Your mother — does she live?

Eliza. No; she died in the St. Pancras Work-house, ten years ago.

Tom. And your father — your father?

Eliza. I never knew him. I only know the man who stole my mother from him only to let her die in misery.

Tom. How was he called?

Eliza. Richard Knatchbull.

Tom. (*Aside*) Richard Knatchbull! It is my own child!

Eliza. (*Rising*) Why do you look at me like that?

Tom. (*Aside*) My child! and I feel ashamed to own who I am. I am afraid to ask her to come to the arms of this drunkard, clothed in rags! Ashamed, ashamed!

Eliza What is the matter?

Tom. Oh, don't be frightened, I shall not hurt you *again!* Go on your way; I will follow you — but at a distance; you shall not be disgraced by the company of me.

Eliza. Oh, never!

Tom. Some day, when I shall have other clothes, if I come to you, you will see me sometimes? You have pity for me now, but in time you will learn something better — you will learn to love me — as if I were indeed your father?

Eliza. You deserve that name!

Tom. Not yet, not yet! but by the help of Heaven I will work to gain it. (*Suddenly kisses Eliza's hand*) Don't be alarmed. Go on — I will follow you! go on, go on! (*Exit Eliza*) Oh! (*He sobs*) She was right. After Dark the light *has* come. *Exit.*

Scene 2.

Villa and garden. A bell rings. Enter Bellingham and Morris.

Bel. This is the place.

Mor. And a fine place it ish. (*Servant enters from the house*)

Bel. Is Sir George Medhurst at home? (*Servant bows*) Take in my card. (*Exit Servant with card, into house*)

Mor. I say, don't he live in clover here? Such a beautiful garden! Why, Cremorne is not a figure to it.

Bel. Ah, I was born to this sort of thing. I feel at home here. I expand with each breath of the air.

Mor. Well, I don't! It's too much for me — I'm taken with a pain in the stomach, like I had been out riding.

Bel. Give me such a place and the money to keep it up!

Mor. Ah, I should like some one else to keep it up for me!

Enter, at the door in the house, Medhurst.

Med. So you have penetrated to this place of peace? You have come to me. What do you want?

Bel. We come now because we did not like to wait longer. It is best to see you on the eve of your marriage.

Med. I know what you would say, but go on.

Bel. Here is (*Produces paper*) an order for your banker to sell out the stock he has in his hands to the amount of your indebtedness to us.

Med. (*Takes paper*) I cannot give you the answer now —

Bel. Oh, any time before the ceremony. We are in no hurry. Besides, we can take advantage of the interval to make the acquaintance of your charming bride.

Med. Never! There is some excuse for your accosting me in my own house; but there is none to pollute by your presence the lady who is to be my bride.

Bel. What! madness makes you speak like this!

Med. No! it is remorse that makes me speak.

Bel. Remorse! that's the word of a fool. What has remorse to do with a man who has had all the obstacles swept from his path?

Mor. Remorse! (*Aside*) When he was poor, he was ready for anything, but now he is rich, he is getting pertickler!

Bel. Well, as you please. There is the paper — sign it and be free of us.

Med. Yes, I shall be free from you, but how can I be free from *her?* She is dead — she died as much murdered by us as though our own hands had thrust her into the grave. In the night I see her again, and I hear from her icy lips, in a cold breath like that of the dead: "For your sake, George, for your sake!" Poor Eliza!

Bel. (*Sneering*) "Poor Eliza!" Pah! are you going to hang her round your neck like a chaplet, forever? Pshaw, man, it's the change in your living! (*Medhurst falls seated on a garden chair, his face in his hand*) It's your digestion out of order!

Mor. Yesh, yesh, it'sh not the mind, it'sh the stomach!

Bel. You are behind the age; science has done away with all that ancient delicateness. You must not think of remorse; it is simply nausea.

Med. (*Rises*) I am in no mood to speak with you. Leave me now. I will meet you in the shrubbery.

Mor. (*To Bellingham*) What ish the matter with him?

Bel. (*To Morris*) He is a whining cur, and we'll be lucky to have done with him. (*To Medhurst*) We will expect your coming.

Exit with Morris.

Med. I have made my own taskmasters, and heavy as is the debt, alas, it must be paid.

Enter from the house Rose Egerton.

Rose. Dear George, you look sad. You are not displeased with me? I wish I could be more kind.

Med. You unkind, Rose?

Rose. You seem to see the approach of our marriage with regret. Might it not be arranged that I should not be your wife?

Med. No, no! I do not shrink from it. On the contrary, I wish you to be my wife. Love me, Rose, love me even more, and (*Aside*) perhaps she whom I have wronged will forgive me for your sake.

Enter Chumley.

I must — I will try to throw off my gloominess. (*Embraces Rose*)

Chum. (*Aside*) There they are. I asked Rose to be more kind to him, but she is carrying out my instructions with more fidelity than I could wish. (*Approaches*) I am not intruding?

Med. Certainly not.

Chum. I have obeyed you, and brought that bracelet. (*Gives Rose jewel-case*) You will see what a good likeness of George it contains.

Rose. (*Opens case*) Oh, how beautiful! (*To Medhurst*) Oh, have I again to thank you for something? (*To Chumley*) Now, you never give me anything.

Chum. (*Sadly, aside*) Have I not? (*Aloud*) Well, I will give you something. You were in need of a servant. Has anybody in the neighborhood made an application?

Rose. No.

Chum. Then there will be one come today whom I will leave to your kind heart.

Rose. What is she?

Chum. I know nothing of her, except her misfortunes, which must have been great.

Rose. Oh, George, can we take such a person into our house?

Med. What, Rose? A poor creature has lost her way in the storm, and comes to our door, and shall we refuse to let her in because the night is too dark, and she is too poor to enter our splendid house? No, take her in; and we shall not repent it.

Chum. Then she may depend upon having the situation?

Rose. Yes, and I shall be glad of her services. My rooms are so overcrowded with wedding finery that it has overflowed into the parlor, and thence to the library (*Going into into the house, laughingly*), from which places you are duly warned, under penalty of crushing a crinoline or sitting down on a bonnet.

Exit into house.

Chum. I wanted to speak with you, George. There were two men passed me at the railway station. They came this way. Have they called? (*Medhurst nods*) I hope you have shaken them off.

Med. I cannot. I am in their power.

Chum. I feared as much. May I be so bold as to inquire?

Med. You may know all. Tempted by Dicey Morris, in his gambling-house, in a fit of drunken desperation, I forged my father's name.

Chum. And these rascals hold the forgery?

Med. Yes. Here is a paper which I have but to sign to have that evidence of my guilt restored to me.

Chum. (*Takes paper*) You shall do no such thing.

Med. Eh?

Chum. Leave me to deal with these rascals. You shall not be ruined by them.

Med. What have I done to deserve your interest?

Chum. You? Nothing. But I wish her life to be shared with a man whom no one will be able to reproach. I wish her unclouded happiness — for I love her!

Med. You!

Chum. Yes, George, I love her, and with a love so pure that no better proof of its spotlessness can be given than my fearlessness to tell it to you. We are rivals!

Med. Rivals! and yet you would save me from the consequences of my own crime?

Chum. Yes. She says that "I gave her nothing." But I shall give her your name, cleared forever from disgrace.

Med. Oh! it shall never be disgraced again!

Chum. For her sake, George, I expect you to keep your word! (*They shake hands*) Goodbye, George.   *Exit George into house.*
Now, how am I to deal with these villains?

Enter Eliza.

Eliza. I beg your pardon, sir, but I found the garden-gate open, and I came in. Can I see Miss Egerton?

Chum. (*Aside*) This is she. It is an honest, suffering face. (*Aloud*) The lady will see you at once. I beg you to be seated.

Eliza. I beg pardon, sir, I am not the person that you take me for.

Chum. Nay, I never make mistakes in such things, I hope. I always recognize the gentlewoman, however misfortune may disguise her. (*He goes to the house and speaks to Servant within, who goes off*)

Enter Rose from the house.

This is the person of whom I spoke. (*To Eliza*) This is the lady.   *Exit into house.*

Rose. Poor girl! (*Takes seat*) You look very wearied and dusty.

Eliza. (*Faintly*) I have walked all the way from Waterloo Bridge. I have been ill and am not yet strong.

Rose. You wish to enter my service. What can you do?

Eliza. I can be faithful, obedient, and grateful.

Rose. (*Smiles*) You have evidently not been accustomed to service.

Eliza. No, madam. I — I never was — ah! I am faint. (*Hand to forehead*)

Rose. (*Rises*) Oh! (*Supports Eliza*) how thoughtless I am. (*Places Eliza in seat*) Don't cry! There is something in your manner that assures me that you will be invaluable to me — oh! do not give way to tears thus.

Eliza. How can I thank you? Such kindness from the hands of strangers makes the coldness of those who were dear to me in times past seem all the more painful by contrast.

Rose. Dry your tears. Come with me — you must not be seen in this dress.

Eliza. (*Rises*) I have no other.

Rose. Oh, I beg your pardon. Never mind; we'll find some of my dresses to replace those poor garments of yours.

> *Music. Eliza, leaning on Rose, goes into house. Scene closes in.*

Scene 3.

Garden and garden-wall. Enter Old Tom.

Tom. I have seen her in. Bless her that took her to her. I followed her all the way down here. And now to work — to work! till I can feel like her father. What a nice place! how good it smells! How I envy the birds that flit about from tree to tree, and even the vermin that lie out under the shade. (*Turning to the left*) Eh? I see two figures coming this way. Surely that can't be Morris! Dicey Morris here. (*Hides himself*)

Bellingham and Morris enter.

Bel. He seems a long time about that paper.

Mor. I am not inquisitive, Mr. Bellingham, but how is it to be managed?

Bel. I see no difficulty; I present the check and get the money.

Mor. Look here! It's not that I don't trust you — wish you may die if I do! but five thousand pounds is an awful hatful of money to be in one man's pocket. It might dazzle his eyesh and make him forget he had a partner.

Bel. Pshaw!

Mor. I'll tell you how to do it. Just tear the check in half — each keep a piece, and paste it together when we want it cashed — you understand?

Bel. Where in the geological formation of my character do you see any evidence of the vein of green that you are apparently in the thought of working?

Mor. (*Passionately*) See here, Mr. Bellingham, you are putting on airsh! and I won't shtand them — wish I may die if I do! I hold the capital — that ish the forgery, don't I? Well then!

Bel. Then allow me to open your eyes, Mr. Morris. *You* hold the forgery? (*Produces paper*) I beg your pardon; here is the document. (*Keeps it out of Morris's reach*)

Mor. (*Amazed*) What ish that? Sen' I may live. Look here; why, I put that in the hands of my banker for safety.

Bel. Exactly. By *my* suggestion.

Mor. Ye — yesh! it *was* by your suggestion. Chandos, my boy, you have not been robbing the bank, have you?

Bel. No.

Mor. That'sh a consolation.

Bel. I simply presented myself at the

banker's, said I was Sir John Medhurst, and wanted to pay an overdue bill of mine. I paid the money and obtained the bill — quite in the regular way of business. You called me the junior partner. Why, damme! I constitute the whole firm.

Mor. To be sure! That'sh quite right, quite right. Chandos, my dear, you wouldn't go back on an old friend, would you?

Bel. Go to the station; I'll meet you there to leave for London.

Mor. All right, all right! I'm to wait for you at the station?

Bel. Yes. Go, for I see him coming.
Exit Morris.

Enter Chumley.

Chum. Good day, sir.

Bel. I expected to see Sir George Medhurst.

Chum. I know it. But you see me instead.

Bel. It was a matter private and important.

Chum. I know that; but still I believe Sir George will not lose by my intermediation.

Bel. (*Carelessly*) I should say not.

Chum. I act just as if it were himself. Can you spare me five minutes?

Bel. Five minutes? No more, for I must catch the train that leaves for town in ten minutes.

Chum. I will be as brief as I can. Sir George has told me by what means he is in the power of Mr. Morris and yourself.

Bel. (*Half aside*) The more fool he!

Chum. Perhaps we shall alter our opinion on that point before our conversation is finished.

Bel. You know the terms?

Chum. Yes; but we will only pay double what is on the face of the note.

Bel. Mr. Morris would never listen to such a proposition.

Chum. Then Mr. Morris mistakes the value of the paper. I rely upon you to undeceive him.

Bel. Upon me? Your confidence does me honor!

Chum. You flatter me.

Bel. Not at all; I listen to you.

Chum. I do not forget your perspicuity as shown on other occasions.

Bel. "On *other* occasions?" I beg your pardon.

Chum. Yes; seven years ago I was stationed at Melbourne. (*Bellingham is at first uneasy, then smiles, and afterwards listens coolly*) I was ordered out to assist the constabulary in the arrest of a notorious bushranger, one Richard Knatchbull!

Bel. *Richard* Knatchbull? Ah! and you — a — caught him?

Chum. Yes — Yes! we caught him. And while we held him in custody, curiosity impelled me to inspect the wild beast!

Bel. And I suppose you think him like me?

Chum. Yes; very like you! The first time that I met you since, at the railway station, I recognized —

Bel. His features on my face? Ah, poor Dick! (*Chumley is amazed*) my elder brother, sir. He has been my ruin; his reputation has blasted mine; and caused me to live under a false name. So you caught him? You hung him, of course!

Chum. No, he escaped.

Bel. Did he, indeed! Ah, he has as many lives as a cat.

Chum. I beg your pardon, Mr. Bellingham. I really thought you were the fellow, and meant to use that belief as a weapon on you.

Bel. I saw you did! But never mind apologies. It is my misfortune, not your fault!

Chum. I am very sorry that you are not the other scoundrel!

Bel. Don't mention it.

Chum. But to business. Sir George will give five thousand pounds to be released.

Bel. My partner would never think of such an idea!

Chum. Six thousand?

Bel. It is hopeless!

Chum. Eight thousand?

Bel. It is useless to mention it!

Chum. As a last sum, ten thousand?

Bel. You are losing time, and I shall miss the train. I have (*Watch out*) but five minutes to reach the station.

Chum. (*Watch out*) You have lost it. Your watch is stopped.

Bel. (*Puts watch to right ear*) No.

Chum. Why do you test it by your right ear? Because Richard Knatchbull lost his left ear at Harper's Ferry.

Bel. Checkmate! the game is yours! You have mistaken your profession.

Chum. I am a soldier.

Bel. Nature has richly endowed you for that of a detective officer. Well, I think you mentioned ten thousand pounds.

Chum. Sir George would never think of such an idea.

Bel. Eight thousand?

Chum. It is useless to mention it.

Bel. Six thousand?

Chum. Quite hopeless, I assure you.

Bel. Then what are your terms?

Chum. Double that on the face of the note.

Bel. If I accept them, you will make no use of the secret in your hands?

Chum. Safety for safety! When and where shall I have the pleasure to see you?

Bel. At the Elysium Music Hall, in the Broadway, Westminster, tonight.

Chum. I will come. *Exit.*

Morris enters.

Bel. Ah! you here? You have overheard?

Mor. Every blessed word!

Bel. He will come to the Elysium — he will bring the money with him. You can have nobody within your doors but those you can depend upon.

Mor. I know, a private benefit — no one without a ticket. All right. *Exit.*

Bel. And till then, Mr. Gordon Chumley, I'll not lose sight of you. *Exit.*

Enter Tom.

Tom. And I of you, Richard Knatchbull! *Exit.*

Scene 4.

Interior. Discover Rose seated at dressing table.

Rose. She has told me all. And what a story! What are my sorrows compared to hers? Poor soul! so unused to kindness that one gentle word melts her to tears.

Enter Eliza. Rose rises.

Oh, Eliza! what a change. Who could make a servant of that? Why, you look as much of a lady as I do — a good deal more, I dare say.

Eliza. I shall try to be more humble.

Rose. I don't mean that.

Eliza. I am not accustomed to this life, madam.

Rose. Any one can see that. Do you write a good hand?

Eliza. I believe so. I used to copy music when I was employed in a French printing office.

Rose. Do you speak French?

Eliza. Yes, madam.

Rose. And to copy music you must understand it?

Eliza. I have not practised for a long while.

Rose. And, pray, have you any other accomplishments?

Eliza. I can read a little Italian.

Rose. Dear me! I can't have one for servant who would smile at my attempts to murder Mendelssohn, and who is, I dessay, more familiar with Molière and Dante than I am with Marshall and Snellgrove! Oh, what am I to do with her? Where am I to put her? (*She walks up and down, wringing her hands in playful distress*)

Eliza. Oh, don't send me away.

Rose. (*Goes to her*) Send you away! Oh, you great goose! No, you shan't be my servant, except to the household in appearance; but when we are together, as now, you shall be my friend. Yes, we shall be friends, shan't we? (*Makes Eliza take chair; she kneels beside her*) In the first place (*Pretending to cry*) I am going to be married. Isn't it dreadful?

Eliza. I wish you much joy.

Rose. And my husband — I hope you'll like him. I think you will, for he is much like you — I mean in manner; he is so grave and reserved. He's my cousin, and we have been betrothed almost since childhood. Poor George!

Eliza. (*Starts*) Is his name George?

Rose. Yes, George. Don't you like it? Oh, he's so generous to me. Only look at all the things I have! See here! (*She takes up necklace*) I wonder how you would look in it. (*Puts necklace on Eliza*) Oh, beautiful! the diamonds look like petrified tears! that! off again? You are crying. Oh! Look at this — nice bracelet, isn't it? (*Gives bracelet to Eliza while she arranges veil upon her*) There's his likeness in that; see if you can find the secret spring.

Eliza. No, I cannot find it.

Rose. Do you see that ruby heart? Press on that, and the loving giver will appear. (*Eliza starts up, opening bracelet*) Well?

Eliza. Oh! Who is this?

Rose. My husband, Sir George Medhurst! (*Eliza hangs her head*)

Enter Servant.

Servant. Captain Chumley wishes to speak to you, ma'am, before he leaves for London.

Rose. Tell him that I will be with him presently. *Exit Servant.*

Stay here, dear. I shall not be gone long. *Exit.*

Eliza. (*Rises*) My husband here! I am under his roof! And she, for whom I have been discarded — she has been kind to me. (*Tears off veil and necklace and throws them*) Oh, I must leave this place at once. I will go and change this dress for my old clothes, and — Is this window open? Yes. I — ah! some one approaches. Oh! (*Staggers to chair by table, as before*) my husband. (*Falls, seated, sobbing throughout the following*) Oh, oh!

Enter by window Medhurst; comes down, keeping his shadow on Eliza till she rises.

Med. (*With feeling*) Oh, Rose, dear Rose! I have come to tell you what I can keep hidden no longer. You were right when you said that I saw the approach of our wedding-day with aversion. I do not love you — for another has possession of my heart. I ask forgiveness of you — but, oh! I can never ask forgiveness of her. She is gone — I have murdered her.

Eliza. (*Faintly*) Spare me, oh, spare me!

Med. And not till that time did I know how she loved me. How did she love me? To the greatest, for she died for me. Oh, can you forgive me?

Enter Rose.

Rose. George!

Med. Rose! you here? Who is this, then? (*Eliza rises, and he retreats to let the light fall on her*) Oh, my wife!

End of the Second Act.

ACT III.

Scene 1.

Interior of Music Hall. Discover Audience, Marker, and Party playing billiards, Morris, Crumpets at front table with pack of cards. Jem and Josey, dancing on miniature stage, Negro breakdown. Dance ends; Jem and Josey make comic exit.

Audience. Order! encore! 'core, 'core! order!

Chairman. Ladies and gentlemen: the rules and regulations of this establishment is that there is no ang-cores. (*Sits down; takes a Girl on his knee, and she drinks out of his glass*)

Audience. (*Murmuring*) Oh, oh! (*Waiter goes round*)

Waiter. Give your orders, gen'lemen.

Marker. Are they all let? No! here you are! who's in for the dark blue?

Enter Area Jack.

Jack. Stop a bit! How are you playing?

Marker. Pool — it's two shilling'; tuppence a life.

Jack. Tuppence a life! Vy, I wouldn't give tuppence for the life of anybody in the room. (*Takes hold of his cravat and imitates hanging by it*) Well, what's for me? Dark blue? I'll take three to one on dark blue. (*Sings*) "Oh, the dark girl dressed in blue; the girl dressed in dark blue — oo — oo!"

Mor. Hold your row, hold your row, can't you? Do you think you are in a public house?

Crump. Here, who'll take a hand?

Jack. (*Cue in hand, crosses*) Want one, old pal? Take me! (*Sits at Crumpets's table and they shuffle cards*)

Mor. (*Comes down to pack*) Here, here! this sort of thing won't do — it won't do, I tell you — I can't allow games of chance!

Jack. (*Playing*) Game of chance! it ain't no game of chance! Why, Crumpets's play reduces it to certainty!

Marker. Now then, whose turn?

1st Player. Here you are, dark blue!

Marker. Oh, he ain't satisfied unless he's playing pool and cribbage at the same time.

Jack. (*Rises, goes to billiard table*) Dark blue wanted? Make way for indigo! Where am I? Poor thing. Hold open your pockets till I take my play. (*Plays his ball*) Oh, what have I done! (*Comic distress*) I've hopped myself over the pocket.

Chairman. (*Rises*) Ladies and Gentlemen, — — will have the honor of appearing before you as the original —. (*Introduces song in character. All join in chorus, pounding on table with billiard cues, glasses, and fists*)

Morris. What's Bellingham about — what's he about? I can't make him out. I wonder where he is.

Enter Bellingham.

Ah, Chandos, my boy! Here you are at last.

Bel. Are you sure of these people?

Mor. Of every one of them. They're all picked men; they've all been "in trouble." (*Jack goes to billiard table*) Look here, Bellingham, I am not inquisitive, but I don't understand what's going on.

Bel. There's no need for you to understand.

Mor. You have asked Mr. Chumley to come here. He'll bring the police at his heelsh.

Bel. No, he will not let the police into the secret; that would be betraying Medhurst.

Mor. What do you mean to do?

Bel. Chumley will bring the money with him. He shall have the paper, and yet he shall not go away with it.

Mor. It's a puzzle.

Bel. Last year you concealed Jem Morgan on these premises when the police were hot after him.

Mor. Yes.

Bel. How?

Mor. There was a hole in the wall that led out on the tunnel of the underground railway. It only needed a little work to make it large enough for him to creep out.

Bel. Is that hole there still?

Mor. Not likely. I bricked it all up again.

Bel. It must be opened once more!

Marker. Dark blue goes!

Jack. Let me in. Oh, I pass. (*Pretends to faint in Crumpets's arms*)

Marker. You can make a star.

Jack. (*Hopefully*) A star! Oh, oh! my own, my gee-yding star!

Bel. What's the game, Jack? Playing for coppers! Pah! There! (*Throws gold coin on billiard table*) there's a pool for you!

All. Thank'ee, sir.

Bel. Waiter, two glasses; my friend is to come yet. And take glasses round behind the scenes. Gentlemen, while I remain here, nobody shall pay for anything!

Crump. (*At table*) Waiter, a bottle of the best brandy and a box of cigars!

> *Waiter gets things and goes off with tray of glasses, and returns during following. Man goes to door as Doorkeeper. The Girls and some Men go out gradually, after business of taking leave of their friends. Crumpets goes to center. Bellingham takes up a glass from table and pours from a vial into it, then turns the glass around to coat the inside with the liquid.*

Mor. What are you doing?

Bel. This is a solution of morphine — you see these ten drops?

Mor. I can't say as I do.

Bel. I have spread it over the inside of the tumbler.

Mor. Have you, indeed?

Bel. He will have a glass with me before parting. In an instant the drug will set to work, and he will be benumbed and fall insensible into our power.

Mor. Then what will we do with him?

Bel. Little, yet much. There will appear in the newspaper tomorrow an account of the fatal accident on the Metropolitan Railway: a gentleman who had wandered from the street, in a state of intoxication, was found dead on the line.

Mor. Don't! You put me in a cold shiver.

Tom opens door. Doorkeeper stops him.

Tom. Who won't let me in? (*Drunkenly*) I will come in. (*Scuffle. Tom enters*) Now, then, who's going to stop me going into a public house? Who'll turn me out?

Mor. (*Excited, to Bellingham*) Look at that! What will we do with this fellow? What will we *do* with him? What *will* we do?

Bel. Is he one of us?

Mor. No, not exactly. (*Tom is caught by Jack and Crumpets, who carry him to seat*)

Bel. Give him some liquor, waiter. (*Goes up, looks at Tom, who mutters drunkenly to himself*) Oh, he's more than half drunk already; another glass will make him put his shutters up. He won't be in the way.

Chumley opens door and speaks with Doorkeeper.

Mor. (*To Doorkeeper*) It's quite right — quite right. Let the gentleman come in. You might have known that. (*Chumley enters*)

Bel. (*To Jack*) Go round and tell your comrades that there is a detective in the room who is in want of one of them. (*Jack and Crumpets and Morris speak with others, who nod and display signs of uneasiness*)

Chum. This is rather a curious place for an appointment.

Bel. Yes; but it belongs to my friend Morris, who refuses to let the document out of his possession. By the way, it's the custom for strangers to spend something for the good of the house. I can't recommend the wine, but the brandy is prime. Waiter, clean glasses. (*Waiter clears the front table, but replaces a glass with the one which Bellingham poisoned. Bellingham and Chumley take seats at the front of the table*) There is the document. (*Produces paper*)

Chum. May I examine it?

Bel. Certainly.

Mor. (*To Doorkeeper*) Mind, don't let anybody in without a ticket. (*Bellingham and Chumley drink. Chumley coughs several times during the following, as if the liquor hurt his throat*)

Bel. You see it is all regular.

Chum. It looks genuine enough. (*Cough*) Ah! All right. There is your money. (*Gives notes, which Bellingham counts. Chumley gets sleepy, drinks again, hangs his head, lifts it with an effort, presses his forehead*)

Bel. (*Aside*) So far, so well. (*Puts up notes. Chumley puts the paper in pocketbook, and then in coat breast pocket slowly. Bellingham drinks*) To our next merry meeting.

Chum. I hope not.

Bel. As you please. Let Sir George Medhurst know at once; don't deprive him of the news that he is free.

Chum. (*Rises*) I think I must — I think I mus' — I go! I — I feel queer — give me a glass of water. (*Supports himself by chair*)

Bel. Waiter, glass of ice-water for this gentleman. (*Waiter brings glass; Chumley hardly drinks. Waiter takes away glass; Chumley falls down into chair, his hat rolling under table*) Cover me, Dicey. (*Bends over Chumley to take his pocketbook, Morris on his left, before him*)

Marker. Round on your player. Play on the red ball.

Bel. (*Flourishes book*) All right; it is safe in my possession.

Tom. (*Starts up, snatches book from Bel-*

lingham) Safer in mine! (*Bellingham and Morris strike attitude of astonishment*)

Mor. What does this mean?

Tom. It means that I have frustrated your villainy.

Bel. Are you mad?

Tom. You must be.

Mor. What are you doing?

Tom. This is one of the crimes so frequent now; not the open robbery in the day, but done in some hidden den, after dark. But I have spoilt your work.

Bel. Will you give up that pocketbook or not?

Tom. I will hand it over to the police. (*Morris motions Jack and Crumpets to go to door*) Would you undertake to detain me in a public place? (*Goes to door*) Stand aside! (*Jack jerks his thumb over his left shoulder significantly; Crumpets winks*) Ah! I see you would keep me a prisoner. (*Staggers to center*)

Bel. Will you return that book?

Tom. Never! (*To Players*) Friends, these men would have committed a robbery — you will help me.

Marker. Round on your player.

Tom. (*Aside*) They don't heed me; they disregard me. Oh, where am I?

Bel. Are you satisfied now? Return that property.

Tom. No. There are houses close by; my voice will attract notice. Help, help! police, police! (*Jack and others sing "Not for Joseph" chorus, very noisily, and hammer on floor with cues, drowning Tom's cries*)

Bel. You will have it! (*Tom grapples him. Jack and Crumpets put bag over Tom's head and carry him off. Chumley has fallen under table, insensible. Knocking at the door*)

All. (*In a whisper*) The police!

Mor. (*To Waiter*) Take these glasses away. (*Waiter does so. Morris signs for Doorkeeper to open door. Police enter*)

1st Policeman. What's all the row about?

Bel. (*Looking down on Chumley at his feet*) Ha, ha, nothing! only my friend here has been dining out and — ha, ha, wanted to fight, but he's quiet now.

Mor. Oh, it's quite right, officer, it's a benefit for a benevolent object. Depend upon it, it's all right!   *Exit Police.*

All. (*Sneeringly*) Good night, Sergeant. (*Laughing*) Ha, ha, ha!

Jack. All's serene. (*All dance "Not for Joseph"*)

Scene 2.

A dark cellar. Enter Tom.

Tom. Caged, trapped by the villains! Oh,

Gordon Chumley, what have they done with him, since they dragged me here? Where am I? Oh, that fiend Knatchbull. After I had dogged him to this place, and then to lose him at the hour of triumph. Is there no means of escape from this place? (*Whistle, sound of train approaching*) What's that? (*Tom sees air hole in cellar wall. Noise of train passing*) I may be able to climb up and look out. (*Looks out of hole*) It looks like a long dark street with green and red lights in the distance. Oh, I know it, I know it now. It is the underground railway. (*Comes down from steps. Light shows at left*) What's that? A light in the adjoining cellar. A door! some one is in the next cellar. Surely that is Dicey's voice. I may hear what he says. Ah! a keyhole! Morris and Knatchbull. What are they carrying between them? The body of a man! Oh, it is Gordon, Gordon Chumley. They have murdered him and brought him here to bury him. What is it they are saying? "Is the hole large enough?" And Morris says, "Yes." Knatchbull speaks: "Is the line clear?" I hear footsteps returning. Ah, what do they say? "Brick up the hole again!" Ah! they have thrown the insensible man into some hole or blind well! (*Light moves away*) I must escape from this. What's this under my hand? a bar! a fastening to the door. (*Seizes bar*) Come on, come on! (*Through his set teeth as he breaks the bar away*) Ah! With this I can make the hole larger and escape. To work, Frank Dalton, to work! I must first find a barrel, or something to stand on to work. Here, here!

Exit, groping with bar before him.

Scene 3.

Discover Tom at hole in wall, working with bar to widen it, Chumley on railroad track.

Tom. I have got the bricks out — nearly room enough to squeeze through. (*Suddenly*) What's that lying on the line? It does not move, yet it looks like a man. Ah, it is Gordon Chumley! (*Bell rings faintly, then loudly; whistle sounds. The sound of train approaching begins and is continued till end. Music to accompany action*) I must be free now. Gordon, I am here, I am here! Oh, God, they have placed him there to die. Gordon, Gordon! I will save you. Oh, the train! the coming train! Good heart, courage, Gordon! (*He jumps down, falls upon Chumley, and rolls him off the tracks.*) You are saved. (*The train runs on, as a quick Curtain falls*)

End of the Third Act.

ACT IV.

Villa and garden, as in Scene Two, Act Two. Discover Eliza and Medhurst, Rose and Chumley.

Chum. Yes, they thought to obliterate all evidence of their crime by placing me in the way of a passing train.

Med. They must not go free after such a climax of villainy.

Chum. Old Tom is on their track, and has promised not to lose sight of them.

Enter Pointer.

Pointer. We have Mr. Morris, gentlemen.

Med. Chumley, suppose you step aside. *Chumley goes off.* You can show him in.

Two Police bring in Morris.

Mor. I tell you, it's some mistake. There'll be a row about thish, see if there don't. It's a mistake. I am as innocent as the baby that ish never born, wish I may die if I ain't. What, Eliza!

Med. Yes, Lady Medhurst.

Mor. Why, they told me, that is, they said as how she was dead.

Med. Murdered!

Mor. How'd — do you do, ma'am? Railly, you looked so much like your ghost that — that I took you for it, at first.

Med. You were not satisfied with one victim, but you must try to have another crime to your charge.

Mor. Me! me! that'sh a mistake; never set eyes on the gentleman.

Med. Of whom do you speak?

Mor. Mr. Gordon Chumley, of course.

Med. I never mentioned his name.

Mor. (*Eagerly*) That'sh just what I say; you never mentioned the gentleman's name. That'sh quite right.

Med. Mr. Gordon Chumley.

Enter Chumley.

Mor. (*Aghast*) Oh, take me away — on a charge.

Chum. I am not dead, though you and your villainous accomplice made me drugged and insensible. You see, I have survived to convict you.

Mor. To conwict me! conwict me! How will you do it! If you were drugged and insensible, how do you know I had anything to do with it?

Chum. That's true; and on my evidence alone perhaps it would be hard to bring it home to you.

Med. (*To Pointer*) Was anything found on him?

Pointer. No, sir.

Mor. (*Eagerly*) You see that! and they s'arched me — they s'arched my boots, and the wery roots of my hair, they did; but I came out of the inwestigation as innocent as a child; wish I may die if I didn't.

Chum. I cannot swear positively that you had a hand in the actual offence.

Enter Tom, leaning on cane.

Mor. Of course, you can't swear to it. You see that the gentleman can't swear to me! wish he may die if he can!

Tom. Then I can! There was nothing found on him because the stolen property is in the possession of his confederate.

Med. and Chum. Of Bellingham?

Tom. I followed him and Morris to his lodgings. I squared their cabman and rode on behind, and through the trapdoor I heard all their plans.

Mor. Oh! You know, going on like this is not good manners! Is a respectable householder to be run down in this way? I won't stand it! Wish I may die if I do. I'm a payer of rates and taxes, and a member of the westry. I won't stand it!

Tom. I overheard him and Morris agree to keep an appointment here to "put the screw" on Sir George. You will soon have him here! You can't deny it! If I press the charge against you, you will run a chance of dying in fetters.

Mor. Oh, don't press the charge! I'll swear to anything! (*Bell rings outside*)

Tom. Here he is.

Enter Bellingham. Police close in behind him.

Bel. (*Looks around*) Ah!

Pointer. Happy to see you, sir!

Bel. (*Sternly*) I cannot return the compliment! What! Eliza!

Med. Lady Medhurst!

Chum. Mr. Bellingham, you recognize your position?

Bel. Perfectly. I know all is up. That cringing hound has betrayed me!

Pointer. Yes, he has made a clean breast of it. And I'll trouble you to do the same, unless you fear it can be used against you.

Bel. I have nothing to say.

Pointer. Well, sir, I'll expect you to come to Bow Street. We shall require your presence, Mr. Chumley.

Bel. (*To Chumley, drawing him to the front*) If you appear against me, you will consign me to death. You pledged your word that you would not use the secret in your hands. Do as you please, but I relied on your honor.

Chum. You tried to kill me last night, but you have my word. We are quits.

Bel. (*Relieved*) Right! Then there is no one to appear against me.

Tom. I will!

Bel. Who are you?

Tom. Frank Dalton! the husband of your victim and the father of this girl! (*Embraces Eliza*)

Eliza. Father!

Tom. Yes, my child, you may call me so now.

Mor. Let ush take adwantage of a moment of excitement to forget and forgive everything! I'm sure I bear to malice to no one! I wish I may die if I do — there.

Bel. Dalton, there is that between us, which you can never forget or forgive.

Eliza. My father is not your judge.

Bel. No, he is my executioner. Thank you, Mr. Chumley, though your kindness is useless. Officer, I am Richard Knatchbull, escaped convict. There is five hundred pounds reward offered for my capture, by the authorities at Hobartstown. Take it, it is yours, on one condition, that you expend half of it in sending out that cowardly cur there.

Pointer. I will do my best, sir. Now, Mr. Morris, come along.

Mor. (*Dragged*) Oh, where are we going to?

Tom. You are going to the end of that crooked lane, where the guilty find their steps barred by the gates of justice.

Music. Characters form picture for Slow Curtain.

THE END.

MRS. HENRY WOOD

1814-1887

East Lynne

(1862)

The sentimental melodramas adapted from Mrs. Henry Wood's *East Lynne* were widely popular in England and America from the 1860's through the 1880's. An ardent churchwoman with strongly conservative ideas, Mrs. Wood was the author of numerous short stories and more than thirty romantic novels. The popularity of her fiction lay in its reflection of the lives, habits, and dreams of the middle class to which she belonged. Her books were welcomed for their lessons in domestic morality. *Danesbury House* (1860), her first novel, won a prize of a hundred pounds offered by the Scottish Temperance League for a tale on the evils of drink. Her *East Lynne* ran as a serial in *The New Monthly Magazine* in 1861, and appeared as a book in the autumn of that year. A best seller, with a mystery story, melodramatic plot, and abundant pathos, it invited adaptation for the stage.

Apparently the first adaptation was made in America. The actress Lucille Western, attracted to the role of the pathetic heroine, paid Clifton W. Tayleure one hundred dollars to prepare a stage version, which was first presented at matinees in January, 1862. The success of this venture led to its regular production at the Winter Garden Theatre in New York in March, 1863, with Miss Western as Isabel. Maurice Disher says that "the appeal of the heroine with the cry of 'To be for ever an outcast from society,' was so strong that . . . the management signed a contract that bestowed half the gross receipts upon the leading lady."

Other versions appeared in both England and America. Apparently the first stage version performed in London was *The Marriage Bells; or, The Cottage on the Cliff*, produced at the Effingham Theatre in 1864. The author of this version is listed by Allardyce Nicoll as unknown, but by Maurice Disher as a W. Archer — not William Archer the critic. The first London production with the title *East Lynne* was a version by John Oxenford given at the Surrey Theatre in February, 1866. Another version appeared at the Holburn Theatre in 1873; T. A. Palmer's well-known version appeared in Nottingham in November, 1874, with Madge Robertson (Tom Robertson's sister, Mrs. William Kendal) in the role of Isabel; and a version appeared at the Strand Theatre in 1878. Something like a public obsession with *East Lynne* began in 1879, when three London theatres, the Olympic, the Standard, and Astley's, all billed versions of the play. The American version (perhaps a doctored version of Tayleure's) was produced at the Standard in 1883. Mr. Nicoll lists nine English adaptations by unknown authors, performed under the title *East Lynne* between 1866 and 1899, besides versions by known authors under other titles.

The play reprinted in this anthology is the popular American version. Perhaps it is not the best of the adaptations, but its text is among the closest to the novel; it was popular in England as well as in America; and it is well-suited to exhibit the relationship between public taste and the dramatic fare this taste demanded. It held the stage in countless performances through the 1880's — and later.

Examination of *East Lynne* in relation to its popularity throws an interesting light on dramatic development. The play is a well-made melodrama in plot, structure, sentiments, and adherence to other features of the formula. The characters, in most respects, are extraordinarily good or bad. Isabel is a woman who makes one mistake, in a fit of jealousy, for which she must pay the rest of her life; and another good woman, Cornelia, is oppressively prim and demanding. (She is intended to be slightly comic, perhaps, with her red petticoat — a spinster sister playing the jealous mother-in-law.) The theme concerns Isabel's mistake and remorse, but a somewhat irrelevant murder mystery provides suspense and fills out the plot. Improbabilities and manipulations are evident — the villain is also the hero's rival for public office; Isabel's former husband does not penetrate her simple disguise, even though her former maid does so at a glance. The play also abounds in domestic pathos, heartbreak, and torrents of tears. Its moral lesson is entirely prescriptive, and the play is even more than usually didactic. Isabel's soliloquy which opens the second scene of Act III is a sermon on the virtue and necessity of a wife's humility and conjugal fidelity: "Oh, lady, wife, mother!" she addresses the audience, "whatever trials may be the lot of your married life. . . . Fall down on your knees and pray for patience. . . . Bear them unto death, rather than forget your good name and your good conscience." This domestic prescription is presented with tears, piety, and the hope of salvation; and, as the curtain falls, the words "Until eternity," spoken to soft music, provide a tearfully happy ending.

Critics attacked the play, blaming its weaknesses in dialogue on its close adherence to the diction of the novel. William Winter said, "But close adherence to the original is close adherence to trash. . . . There is the same fatal defect in the plot, which dramatic art only renders more prominent." He spoke of the "customary jargon of the sated libertine, and the stereotyped lamentations of the remorseful wife . . . forgiven because she dies."

These faults are obvious. The explanation for the popularity of *East Lynne* must lie in the audiences. In the 1870's they were quieter than they had been. Comfortable seats and carpeting were replacing the benches of the old pit. To a larger extent than ever before, audiences were respectable, decorous, middle-class people — the good, limited people described by Matthew Arnold in 1869 as Philistines. They were not well-educated, but they were literate. They believed in the patriarchal Victorian family, the necessity for a married woman's obedience and fidelity, and religious piety. In their theatregoing (and reading of sentimental novels) they had formed patterns of thought and images of the world like those long presented in melodrama. But they were beginning to disdain the rough-and-tumble melodrama of low life, physical violence, and sensational scenic effects. *East Lynne*, perhaps, seemed to be a faithful portrait of society in a class just above them, the upper-middle class overlapping into the aristocracy. The dialogue is just as artificial as that in other melodramas, but with a different kind of artificiality. It is the literary dialogue of sentimental novels by well-bred lady novelists. The speeches are reminiscent of copybooks with their prissy sentiments. Perhaps the audiences thought this language was elegant or at least "proper." Certainly, the pathos of the play echoed the sentimental and pious elements in the Philistine concept of culture.

It is likely that *East Lynne* seemed just the opposite of melodrama to these audiences. Perhaps, indeed, they were yearning for real drama, the true and provocative play — if not the problem play. Apparently these audiences considered *East Lynne* provocative. Had it not dared to present a woman who left her husband? There was something for them to think and feel deeply about in the picture of her punishment, remorse, and forgiveness. Apparently it occurred to very few that the only lesson the play taught was a conventional one. Few could realize the difference between this "serious" drama and the problem play — until the new drama of analysis and revelation arrived.

EAST LYNNE

A Drama In Five Acts

Adapted from the novel East Lynne, written by

MRS. HENRY WOOD

First performed in America at the Brooklyn Academy of Music, January 26, 1862

Cast of Characters

SIR FRANCIS LEVISON	LADY ISABEL, *alias* MADAME VINE
ARCHIBALD CARLYLE	BARBARA HARE
LORD MOUNT SEVERN	MISS CORNELIA CARLYLE
JUSTICE HARE	JOYCE
RICHARD HARE	WILSON
JOHN DILL	WILLIAM

ACT I.

Scene 1.

A Chamber, with a table and two chairs. Enter Miss Cornelia and Dill.

Dill. And so, Miss Corney, Mr. Carlyle will be here to-day, and bring home his bride.

Miss C. His bride, indeed! A pretty bride for him to take, an earl's daughter! And I've no doubt she'll prove as idle and extravagant as her worthless father. She'll waste his means and bring him to beggary.

Dill. I trust not, Miss Corney. But do you know I had a notion when Mr. Carlyle left home he went to be married?

Miss C. You did, eh? And Archibald never to tell me! I, who have been like a mother to him! But I always thought he loved that girl a great deal better than he should; for when he first took possession of East Lynne she left some gold-fish in his care, and when they died he made such a fuss about them — oh, I was so disgusted with such silly nonsense! However, I am glad that silly Barbara Hare hasn't got him, after all the years she's been fishing for him. A woman has no business to be always running after a man — it ain't decent.

But I've made up my mind to make East Lynne my home for the future. There's no use in keeping up the expense of two establishments. Besides, here I can watch over his interests, for I know she'll bring him to beggary.

Dill. Well, I must go now, and prepare myself to meet Mr. Carlyle and his lovely bride.

Exit.

Miss C. Lovely, indeed! Beauty is but skin deep. Here — Joyce, Joyce!

Enter Joyce.

Joyce, is everything prepared in Mr. Carlyle's apartment?

Joyce. Yes, ma'am, we've made everything look as tidy and as cheerful as possible.

Miss C. Cheerful, indeed! and for her? Well, there — do get along about your business, for I expect them here every minute now. I'm sure I'd as soon see Archibald hanged as married.

Enter Dill.

What an old fool! Why, what on earth has taken you? Why, you are decked out like a young buck!

Dill. I hope I am not too fine, Miss Corney?

Miss C. Fine? I don't know what you call it, but I wouldn't make such a spectacle of myself for untold gold. Why, all the boys in the street will be taking you for the bridegroom.

Dill. Well, now, really, Miss Corney, I thought this coat quite plain.

Miss C. Plain! and what would you have it, I should like to know? Perhaps you would like a wreath of embroidery around it — gold leaves and scarlet flowers, and a swan's-down collar. Pray, do you know your age?

Dill. I do; and I'm just turned sixty.

Miss C. You just are! And do you consider it decent for an old man of sixty to be decked out as you are now? Take care the boys don't tie a tin kettle to your coat-tails.

Dill. Well, now, Miss Corney, pray don't get excited about the matter. I'll go and change it to please you. Hush! I hear the carriage wheels now. (*Goes and looks off*) And here comes Mr. Carlyle and his bride.

Miss C. Well, I know one thing certain, I never will forgive *him* or tolerate *her*. (*Gets in corner*)

Enter Archibald Carlyle and Lady Isabel.

Arch. Welcome to East Lynne — to your childhood's home, Isabel! (*To Dill*) Ah, Dill! my old friend, I hope you are well? (*Shakes hands with him, and crosses to Miss Cornelia*) Ah, Cornelia! my dear sister, this is kind in you to meet me here. (*Shakes hands with her*) This is my wife — the Lady Isabel. Isabel, this is my sister Cornelia. (*Isabel bows*)

Miss C. (*Snappishly*) I hope you are well, madame?

Arch. This is my old friend and confidential clerk, Mr. John Dill.

Isabel. I hope I see you well, sir?

Miss C. Would you like to go up-stairs and take off your things before supper?

Isabel. I will go to my room, if you please, but Archibald and I have dined. I don't require anything, thank you.

Arch. Isabel, I have some private matters to talk over with Dill. I'm sure you will excuse me for a little time.

Isabel. Oh, yes; to be sure I will. I will remain here and talk to your sister.

Arch. Do so, then, if you like. I'll not be long absent. Come, Dill. *Exit with Dill.*

Miss C. What would you like to take?

Isabel. I would like some tea, if you please. I am very thirsty.

Miss C. Tea? so late as this? You'd never sleep a wink all night.

Isabel. Oh, well then, don't trouble yourself. I don't think I want anything. I'll just stay and talk to you about Archibald. He has often spoken to me about you, and I feel certain I shall like you.

Miss C. I hope you will be contented at East Lynne.

Isabel. Contented! why, of course I shall. The dear old place! I was very happy here when a child; and it was here that poor papa died, too. And then Archibald came, and bought the place, and he was very kind to me, too. I do believe it was that which first made me learn to love him!

Miss C. Archibald has a very kind and generous nature.

Isabel. He has indeed; and I shall try and be a good wife to him, and render him as happy as possible; and so, you know, I've been thinking how I can be of service to him, and I mean to try and persuade him to let me ride to town with him every morning, and assist him in his business affairs, and be his confidential clerk. Don't you think he will let me?

Miss C. He'd be a fool if he would.

Isabel. And then we'd all be so happy together; and you'll let me love you too, won't you, Miss Corney? Oh, do let me love you a little! (*Goes up and puts her arm around Cornelia, and kisses her*)

Miss C. (*Pushes her off*) She's really a most extraordinary girl. *Exit.*

Isabel. Why, she acts very strangely. I hope I haven't done anything wrong.

Re-enter Archibald.

Oh, Archibald, I'm so glad you've come! I am quite at a loss to know how to act. I think your sister is a very queer person. Do you know I kissed her just now, and she seemed quite frightened. I don't believe she was ever kissed before.

Arch. My sister is not over-pleasant in her manner, but she is a very upright and just person. You'll like her better when you come to know her. Now, Isabel, if you like, I'll walk with you through the grounds. *Exeunt.*

Scene 2.

Landscape. Enter Richard Hare, disguised in a ploughman's suit, with heavy black whiskers, carrying a large whip in one hand.

Rich. Here I am at length, after my absence of nearly two years, once more in sight of my dear old home. But, alas! I dare not enter even for a moment. I am a fugitive from justice, and even now the lynx-eyed officers of the law may be on my track, and discover me in spite of my disguise. Would I could see my dear mother, if only for a moment! Ah! the garden gate is open, and I see my sister Barbara standing in the door.

I'll venture to speak and call her out. Hist, Barbara! Barbara, come out! Don't you know me? it is I ! Richard!

Enter Barbara.

Barb. Oh, Richard, my dear brother; is it indeed you? What brings you here? How could you run such a risk? If you are discovered it is certain death upon — you know.

Rich. Upon the gibbet! I *do* know, Barbara.

Barb. Then why risk it by coming here? Should mamma see you it would kill her outright.

Rich. I can't live as I am living. I have been working in London ever since.

Barb. In London, Richard? How are you working — what at?

Rich. In a stable-yard.

Barb. In a stable-yard! Oh, Richard! you —

Rich. Did you expect it would be as a merchant or a banker? or that I was a gentleman living at large on my fortune? I get twelve shillings a week, Barbara, and that has to find me in everything.

Barb. Oh, Richard! my poor brother!

Rich. I could do no better. I was brought up to no kind of labor, and I did understand about horses. Besides, a man that the police-runners were after would be more safe in such obscurity than if he were a gentleman in fine clothes.

Barb. Poor Richard! what a miserable night that was for you, and for all of us! Our only comfort is, Richard, that you must have committed the deed in madness.

Rich. I did not commit the deed at all, Barbara. I swear to you that I am innocent of the crime. I was not even in the cottage at the time of the murder. The man who really did the deed was Thorn.

Barb. Thorn! Who was Thorn?

Rich. I don't know. I wish I did. I wish I could unearth him. He was a friend of Afy's.

Barb. Richard, you forget yourself when you mention her name in my presence.

Rich. Well, it was not to discuss such topics as these that I have put my life in jeopardy by coming here to-night, and to assert my innocence can do no good. It cannot set aside the coroner's verdict of willful murder against Richard Hare the younger. If I had not fled like a coward I might have stood some chance; but that flight, you know, looked like guilt. Is my father as bitter as ever against me?

Barb. Quite; he never mentions your name, or even suffers it to be spoken by the servants in his presence. After the delivery of the verdict, he took an oath in the justice's room, in the presence of his brother magistrates, that if he could find you, though it might not be for ten years, he would deliver you up to justice. You know his disposition; therefore you may be sure he will keep his word.

Rich. I know he never treated me as he ought. Had my home been made happier for me, I should not have sought the society I did elsewhere. Barbara, I must be allowed an interview with my mother.

Barb. It is impossible to think of that to-night. Papa has only gone on an errand, and may return at any moment. I don't see how it can be managed.

Rich. Why can she not come out to me as you have done?

Barb. Because she is ill, and has retired for the night. This separation from you has nearly killed her.

Rich. It is hard, after so long an absence, to go back without seeing her. What I want, Barbara, is a hundred pounds, and I think she can let me have it. If I can get that sum, I have an opportunity for doing better for myself than I have done. That was what I came to ask for. Do you think she can let me have it?

Barb. You must be here to-morrow night again. The money can no doubt be yours. But if, as you say, you *are* innocent, why not try and prove it?

Rich. Who is to prove it? The evidence was strong against me; besides, no one at West Lynne knew anything about Thorn but myself. He only came over on certain nights to see Afy, and he took precious good care to keep out of the way in the day-time.

Barb. Richard, why not tell the whole truth to Archibald Carlyle? If any one can help you, or take measures to establish your innocence, he can; and you know he is true as steel.

Rich. Well, perhaps you are right. He is the only person who ought to be entrusted with the secret of my being here. Where is it generally supposed that I am?

Barb. Some think that you are dead, others that you are in America or Australia. This very uncertainty has nearly killed mamma. But come again to-morrow night, at this same hour, and meanwhile I'll see what can be done about the money.

Justice Hare. (*Outside*) Barbara! Barbara!

Barb. Hark! there's papa returned. I dare not remain another instant. You must go now, Richard. Good night.

Rich. (*Going*) Barbara, you did not seem to believe my assertion of innocence; but we are standing here alone in the still night, with Him above us, and as truly as that I must one day meet Him face to face, I have told you the truth. It was not I who committed the murder. I swear it — there! (*Points to heaven*) Good night, sister.   *Exit hastily.*

Enter Justice Hare.

Justice. (*Speaking as entering*) Barbara! Barbara! I say. Hello! young lady, what brings you here this time of night?

Barb. I went down to the gate to meet you, and had strolled over the side path, and so I suppose that was how I missed you.

Justice. Come into the house, then. You ought to have been in bed an hour ago.
Both exit.

Scene 3.

Chamber, same as Scene 1. Enter Joyce, meeting Wilson.

Wilson. Oh, Joyce, did you see who is come? A whole carriage-load of visitors, and she among them. I watched her get out.

Enter Isabel, and listens.

Joyce. Watched *her.* Who?

Wilson. Why, Miss Barbara Hare, to be sure. Only fancy her coming to pay a wedding visit here! My lady had better take care she don't get a bowl of poison mixed for her. Master's out, or else I'd have given a shilling to have seen the interview between them.

Joyce. Wilson, you had better take care what you say here. Go and attend to the company.   *Exit Wilson.*

Isabel. (*Advancing*) Joyce, what was that I overheard you and Wilson gossiping about just now — about Miss Hare giving me a bowl of poison? Something in the dramatic line, I should fancy. Please tell her to keep her whispers to herself in future.

Joyce. It was merely a bit of nonsense, my lady. These stupid, ignorant servants will talk, and every one in West Lynne knew that Miss Barbara was in love with Mr. Carlyle; but I do not think she was the one to make him happy, with all her love.

Isabel. Joyce, how would you like the situation of lady's maid? that is, if Miss Carlyle will consent to the transfer.

Joyce. Oh, my lady, you are very kind. I should so like it; and I would serve you faithfully to the best of my ability.

Isabel. Well, then, if Miss Carlyle consents, you shall have it. I'll speak to her about it to-day. Now leave me, Joyce.
Exit Joyce.

Who is this Barbara Hare, of whom I hear so much, and whom East and West Lynne are busy associating with the name of my husband? Oh, I remember now: I noticed her at the church door the first day we came to East Lynne; and Mr. Carlyle said, as he pointed her out, "That is Miss Barbara Hare. Don't you think her a very pretty girl?" Perhaps he has loved her; perhaps he loves her still, and only married me out of sympathy. Oh! if I only thought that, it would drive me frantic! But no — no — no! I will not harbor a thought so foolish as that. Mr. Carlyle is an honorable man; he loves me truly — he has told me so, and he would not deceive me.

Enter Miss Cornelia.

Miss C. Lady Isabel, they are waiting for the order for dinner.

Isabel. Order a dinner, Miss Corney? (*Aside*) What shall I say? I never ordered a dinner in all my life. I must say something. She's evidently waiting for an answer. (*To Miss Corney*) Well, then, Miss Corney, you may tell them we'll have something to roast and something to boil.

Miss C. Something to roast and something to boil! Are you aware that such an order would puzzle the butcher to know whether you desired a few pounds of meat or a whole cow?

Isabel. A whole cow! Oh, bless me, Miss Corney, we never could eat a whole cow! (*Aside*) I've evidently made a mistake this time. I'll try again. What shall I say? I wish I dared to ask her; but she looks so cross and severe, and she would despise me for my ignorance. I'll venture again. (*Aloud*) Well, then, Miss Corney, order as much meat as you think Archibald and yourself will require. I don't want any.

Miss C. Lady Isabel, if you desire it, I will give the necessary orders myself.

Isabel. Oh! do, if you please, Miss Corney. I wanted to ask you to do it all the while, but I didn't want to trouble you. I don't think I know much about housekeeping.

Miss C. I don't think you do. (*Aside*) Poor Archibald! so much for marrying against my will.   *Exit.*

Isabel. I wish Archibald would come. The time hangs heavily when he is from my side.

Enter Lord Mount Severn; advances and bows stiffly.

Lord M. What is the meaning of this, Isabel? You are married, it seems.

Isabel. Yes; some days ago.

Lord M. And to Mr. Carlyle, the lawyer. How did this come about? And why was I kept in ignorance of the affair?

Isabel. I did not know you were kept in

ignorance of it. Mr. Carlyle wrote to you at the time, as also did Lady Mount Severn.

Lord M. I suppose this comes of your father having allowed him to visit daily at East Lynne, and so you fell in love with him.

Isabel. Oh, no, indeed! I never thought of such a thing as falling in love with Mr. Carlyle; but he came to Castle Marling at Easter; he proposed to me, and I accepted him. I like him very well, he, is so good to me.

Lord M. How comes it you are so nice in your distinctions between liking and loving? It cannot be that you love any one else. Who has been staying at Castle Marling during my absence?

Isabel. (*Confused*) Only Francis Levison.

Lord M. Francis Levison! You surely have not been foolish enough to fall in love with him! Isabel, Francis Levison is not a good man. If ever you were inclined to think him one, dispossess your mind of that idea, drop his acquaintance, encourage no intimacy.

Isabel. I have dropped it already, sir. But Lady Mount Severn must think well of him, or she would not have him there so often.

Lord M. (*Surprised*) She thinks none too well of him. None can of Francis Levison.

Enter Archibald. Offers his hand to Lord Mount Severn, who refuses it.

Isabel, I am sorry to turn you out of the room, but I must say a few words to Mr. Carlyle.

Isabel. Oh, certainly, sir, I'll retire. *Exit.*

Lord M. (*Severely*) Mr. Carlyle, sir, do you possess so little honor that, taking advantage of my absence, you must intrude yourself upon my family and clandestinely espouse Lady Isabel Vane, my ward?

Arch. Sir, there has been nothing clandestine in my conduct towards Lady Isabel Vane, nor shall there be anything but honor in my conduct towards Lady Isabel Carlyle, my wife. Your lordship has been misinformed.

Lord M. I have not been informed at all. I was allowed to learn this through the public journal — I, the *only* relative of Lady Isabel!

Arch. My first action after Isabel accepted me was to write to your lordship, asking your consent.

Lord M. And pray, sir, where did you direct your letter?

Arch. Lady Mount Severn could not give me your address, as you were then traveling; but she said if I would entrust my letter to her care, she would forward it to you with others she was then writing. I did so, and in a few days received a message from her lady-ship, that, as you had returned no answer, you of course approved of the match.

Lord M. Mr. Carlyle, is that a fact?

Arch. My lord, whatever may be my defects in your eyes, I am at least a man of truth. Until this moment the thought that you were ignorant of this transaction never occurred to me.

Lord M. So far, then, I ask your pardon. But how came the ceremony to be hurried on in this unseemly fashion? You made the offer at Easter, and were married three weeks after.

Arch. Business took me to Castle Marling on Good Friday. I called at your house. I found Lady Isabel ill-treated and miserable; far from enjoying a home in your house.

Lord M. What, sir? Ill-treated and miserable?

Arch. Ill-treated even to blows, my lord. I learned all this through the chattering revelations of your little son. Isabel, of course, would not have told me; but when he had spoken she could not deny it. In short, she was too completely bowed in spirit to deny it. It aroused all my feelings of indignation; it excited in me an irresistible desire to release her from the thraldom that this cruel life had thrown around her, and take her where she would find affection, and, I hope, happiness. There was only one way in which I could do so. I risked all, and asked her to become my wife, and return with me to East Lynne.

Lord M. Then I am to understand that when you called at my house you had no intention of proposing to Isabel?

Arch. Not any. It was an impromptu step, the circumstances under which I found her calling it forth.

Lord M. May I inquire if you love her, sir?

Arch. I do love her passionately and sincerely. I learned to love her at East Lynne; but I could have carried my love silently within me to the end of my life, and never have betrayed it, and probably should have done so, had it not been for that unexpected visit to Castle Marling. If the idea of making her my wife had ever previously entered my mind, the reason why I did not urge my suit was that I deemed her rank incompatible with my own.

Lord M. And so it was.

Arch. Country solicitors have married peers' daughters before to-day. I only add another to the list.

Lord M. But you cannot keep her as a peer's daughter, I presume.

Arch. East Lynne will be our home. Our establishment will be small and quiet to what it was in her father's time. I explained all this to Isabel at the first, so that she might have retracted had she chosen to have done so. Your lordship now perceives, I hope, that there has been nothing clandestine in my conduct towards Lady Isabel.

Lord M. Sir, I refused you my hand when you came in; perhaps you will refuse me yours now, though I should be proud to take it. When I find myself in the wrong I'm not above acknowledging my fault, and I must say that, in my opinion, you have acted most kindly and honorably. (*They shake hands*) Of course I cannot be ignorant that, in speaking of Isabel's ill-treatment, you allude to my wife. Has this transpired beyond yourselves?

Arch. Sir, you may be sure that neither Isabel nor myself will ever mention it. Let it be as though you never heard it; it is past and gone.

Re-enter Isabel.

Lord M. Isabel, I came here to-day almost prepared to strike your husband. I go away honoring him. Be a good, faithful wife to him, for he deserves it.

Isabel. Oh, of course I shall — never fear.

Lord M. And now, with your permission, I'll take a look about the grounds.

Isabel. We will accompany you.

All exeunt.

Enter Miss Cornelia and Barbara Hare.

Barb. Papa was out on business, mamma was too ill to come, so I have ventured here alone.

Miss C. I am glad you have come. I thought perhaps you would not be pleased with Archibald's selection of a wife.

Barb. Not pleased, Miss Corney? Why, what have I to do with his choice of a wife?

Miss C. Oh, nothing; only there are so many ladies in East and West Lynne that seemed to take such an interest in Archibald's welfare, that I thought they might be disappointed in his marriage — that's all.

Barb. On the contrary, I wish him all the happiness possible. He has ever treated me most kindly, and I sincerely hope he has found a wife worthy of him.

Miss C. Well, I like her better than I thought I should. I expected to find her full of airs and graces, but I must say she is perfectly free from them, and she seems quite wrapped up in Archibald; she watches for his coming as a cat would watch for a mouse.

Barb. That is quite natural, I suppose.

Miss C. I suppose it is very absurd. I give them very little of my company; they go strolling out together, or she sings to him,

while he hangs over her as if she were made of gold. Oh, dear! I have no patience with such silly nonsense.

Barb. You must make some allowance for the fervor of youth.

Miss C. Fervor of fiddlesticks! Shall I tell you what I saw last night? Well, Archibald had a severe headache after dinner, and went into the next room and lay upon the sofa. She took him in a cup of tea, and never came back again, leaving her own until it was perfectly cold. I went to say so to her, and there was my lady's fine cambric handkerchief, soaked in cologne, lying on his face, and she kneeling beside him. Now, Miss Barbara, don't you regard that as the height of nonsense?

Barb. I must say that I cannot agree with you in that respect.

Miss C. Well, I know this much. If he had a headache before he was married, I gave him a good dose of senna and salts, and sent him to bed to sleep the pain off. *Exit.*

Barb. And she is happy with him — the only man I ever loved, or ever can love. Why did he pass me by for a baby-faced girl like that? It cannot be that she is capable of loving him with the deep affection I might have bestowed on him. Ah! they are coming this way. I will retire into the conservatory. I could not endure a meeting now. *Retires.*

Re-enter Archibald and Isabel.

Arch. You are fatigued, are you not?

Isabel. Oh, no, not in the least! You say you have been intimate with this Hare family for a long time?

Arch. Quite so. Cornelia, my half-sister, is related to them.

Isabel. Don't you think Miss Barbara is very pretty?

Arch. Yes, very pretty.

Isabel. Then, intimate as you are, I wonder you never fell in love with her. Did you, Archibald — oh! did you?

Arch. Did I what, Isabel?

Isabel. You never loved Barbara Hare — did you?

Arch. Loved her? Why, Isabel, what is your mind running on? I never loved but *one* — and *that one* I have made my own, my cherished wife.

Isabel. Oh! I believe you, my dear husband.

Arch. Well, now you must sing to me, and then I'll pay you with a kiss.

Isabel. With all my heart. What shall it be?

Arch. Oh, you know my favorite song.

Isabel. Yes. Alas! that was poor papa's favorite, too.

*She sings song, "You'll Remember
Me." Archibald gets chair, and
places it; gets on left hand of her,
taking one hand in his, leans tenderly over her. At end of song kisses
her on the forehead. Barbara at back,
listening. Picture.*

End of the First Act.

ACT II.

Scene 1.

*Several years later. Chamber with table and
two chairs, books on table, vases, etc., etc.
Enter Lady Isabel and Levison.*

Lev. Do you remember the evening, Lady
Isabel — such a one as this — we all passed
at Richmond — your father, Mrs. Vane, you,
I, and the others?

Isabel. Yes, I remember it well. We passed
a very pleasant day. The two Miss Challoners
were with us. You drove Mrs. Vane home,
and I went with poor papa. You drove recklessly, I recollect, and Mrs. Vane declared
you should never drive her again.

Lev. Which meant, not till next time. Of
all capricious, vain, exacting women, Emma
Vane was the worst. She was a systematic
flirt — nothing better. I drove her recklessly
on purpose, to put her in a fright and pay her
off.

Isabel. Pay her off! Why, what had she
done?

Lev. Put me in a rage; saddled herself on
me when she knew I desired another companion.

Isabel. Oh, yes! I know — Blanche Challoner.

Lev. Blanche Challoner! What did I care
for her? No, Lady Isabel, it was not Blanche;
you might have made a better guess at that
time.

Isabel. I do not understand you, sir.

Lev. The past is gone and cannot be recalled. We have both played our cards like
simpletons. If ever two beings were formed
to love each other, you and I were. I sometimes thought you read my feelings.

Isabel. Francis Levison — sir!

Lev. I must speak, Lady Isabel; but a few
words, and then I am silent forever. I would
have declared myself then; but my debts, my
uncertain position, my inability to keep a
wife as your taste and style demanded,
crushed my hopes, and so I suffered you to
escape me.

Isabel. I will not listen to this language, sir.
(*Crosses*)

Lev. One single moment yet, I pray you. I
have long wished you to know why I lost
you — a loss that tells upon me yet; but I
knew not how passionately I loved you until
you became the wife of another. Isabel, I
love you still!

Isabel. How dare you presume to address
me thus?

Lev. What I have said can do no harm
now; the time has gone by. We have each
chosen our part in life and must abide by it.
The gulf between us is impassable, but the
fault was mine. I ought to have avowed my
affection for you, and not to have suffered
you to throw yourself away on Mr. Carlyle.

Isabel. Do I hear aright? Throw myself
away on Mr. Carlyle, my husband — beloved,
honored and esteemed by all who know him?
Why, I married him of my own choice, and
have never since regretted it. Look at his
manly bearing, his noble mind, his generous
nature! What are you in comparison? You
forget yourself, Francis Levison.   (*Crosses*)

Lev. No, I do not. I pray you forget and
forgive what has escaped me, and suffer me
to be, as heretofore, the kind friend, the
anxious brother, endeavoring to be of service
to you in the absence of Mr. Carlyle.

Isabel. It is what I have suffered you to be,
looking upon you in the light of a friend, I
might say, relative; not otherwise would I
have permitted your incessant companionship; and thus it is you have repaid me. My
husband, and whom you would depreciate in
my eyes, has sheltered you, and screened you
from the law. He has thanked you for your
attention to me. Could he have read what
was in your false heart, he would have offered
you thanks of a different sort, I fancy.

Lev. I ask your pardon, Lady Isabel. I have
acknowledged my fault; I can do no more.
I shall not offend you again. But there are
moments when our heart's dearest feelings
break through the conventionalities of life,
and betray themselves in spite of our sober
judgment. But I see that I must leave you
now; so, adieu — not adieu, but au revoir.
Exit.

Isabel. Oh, how can I ever tell my husband
that this man, whom he has befriended and
sheltered from the law, has thus dared to
speak to me of love? Heaven only knows
what the consequences would be — a duel,
perhaps. No, no, I cannot tell him; yet I feel
I ought to tell him all. I will seek him instantly — my kind, my good, my noble husband.   *Exit.*

Enter Joyce, meeting Wilson.

Wilson. I say, Joyce, don't you think she looks very ill? — my lady, I mean. She looks just as if she'd never get over it. My goodness! wouldn't somebody's hopes be raised again if anything was to happen?

Re-enter Isabel, and listens.

Joyce. Oh, nonsense! what stuff!

Wilson. You may cry out nonsense as much as you like, but they would; she'd snap him up to a dead certainty; she'd never let him escape her a second time; she is just as much in love with him as ever.

Joyce. That's all rubbish — all talk and fancy! Mr. Carlyle never cared for her, at all events.

Wilson. That's more than you know. I've seen him *kiss* her; and he gave her that locket and chain which she wears about her neck: she hardly lets it off, either; and I do believe she sleeps with it.

Joyce. How thoroughly stupid she must be!

Wilson. And that's not all. I saw them one evening, many months ago, when I lived at Miss Hare's house. She always steals out to the gate when she thinks it is about time for Mr. Carlyle to pass on his way from his office, on purpose to have a sly chat with him. Well, this evening I crept down behind the hedges, and then I heard all they were saying; she was crying bitterly, and then I heard Mr. Carlyle tell her that in future he could only be a dear brother to her; and then I saw him kiss her.

Joyce. Then she's a downright fool to go on crying for a man that never cared for her.

Wilson. But she does do it yet; and so I say if anything was to happen now, Miss Barbara, as sure as fate, would step into her shoes. I mean, if Mr. Carlyle should ever get tired of my lady.

Joyce. Wilson, have the goodness to recollect yourself.

Wilson. Well, what have I said now? Nothing but the truth. Men are shamefully fickle; husbands are worse than sweethearts, too, and if anything was to happen now —

Joyce. I tell you what it is, Wilson, if you think to pursue this sort of topic at East Lynne, I shall inform my lady that you are not fit for the situation.

Wilson. Oh, you were always one of the strait-laced sort; but I've had my say, and now I'm satisfied. *Exit Wilson and Joyce.*

Isabel. (*Advancing*) Oh, misery, misery! Oh, how palpable to all eyes must be that woman's love for my husband! Palpable, indeed, when all East and West Lynne are talking of it, and even my servants daily gossip over it, and extend their pity to me. Oh, I cannot bear it — the thought will drive me frantic!

Sees Archibald entering; rushes to him, and in a frantic manner.

Oh, Archibald, do not marry her! I could not rest in my grave if you did. She would draw your love from our children and from my memory. Archibald, you must not marry her.

Arch. Why, Isabel! you must be speaking under the influence of some terrible dream, and you are not awake. Be still awhile, and recollection will return to you. There, love, rest on me. (*Folds her to his breast*)

Isabel. Oh, no; I know perfectly well what I am saying. To think of her as your wife brings pain enough to kill me. Promise me you will not marry her.

Arch. I will promise anything in reason, my dear wife. But I do not know what you mean. There is no possibility of my marrying any one. You are my wife, are you not?

Isabel. I know I am now, but I might die. Indeed, I think I shall die. Oh! do not let her usurp my place.

Arch. Why, Isabel, what is your mind running on? Who is it that is thus troubling you? Of whom are you speaking?

Isabel. Of Barbara Hare.

Arch. Isabel, what notion you can possibly have picked up concerning Barbara Hare and myself I am unable to perceive. I never loved her, either before marriage or since.

Isabel. But she loved you.

Arch. If this was so she was more weak, reprehensibly foolish, than I could have thought her. I had given her credit for having better sense. A woman may almost as well love herself as suffer herself to love unsought. If, however, she did give her love to me, I can only say that I was entirely unconscious of it. Believe me, Isabel, you have as much cause to be jealous of my sister Cornelia as of Barbara Hare.

Isabel. Oh, I will believe you, Archibald; it was only a foolish thought. I will banish it forever from my mind. (*Aside*) I cannot tell him I was foolish enough to listen to the gossip of my servants; he would despise me for it. (*Aloud*) I will leave you now. I am fatigued; I will retire to my own room. (*Going*) Yes, I will trust him; if not, in whom can I trust? *Exit.*

Arch. What can have put this by-gone nonsense into my wife's head?

Enter Miss Cornelia.

Miss C. Archibald, I wish to speak to you in regard to that Francis Levison. I don't like either his appearance or his manners.

Arch. Cornelia, he is my guest, and as such must be treated with respect.

Miss C. (*Crossing*) With respect, indeed! He's a good-for-nothing villain, if I'm any judge of character, and I don't care how soon you tell him so.   *Exit.*

Arch. Poor Cornelia! she's hard to please; she's evidently annoyed at some trifling matter.

Enter Barbara.

Ah! good-morning, Barbara. I am glad to see you at my house. Did you come by yourself?

Barb. Yes, Archibald. You must pardon my intrusion at this hour, and regard me as a client. I came on some business for mamma, but it's of a private nature. Mamma was too ill to come out herself, so she has sent me. Can we converse without being overheard?

Arch. Be at ease, Barbara — this room is free from the intrusion of strangers. (*Gets chairs*) Pray be seated, Barbara. Come, what state secrets have you to disclose?

Barb. Richard is here.

Arch. Richard at East Lynne?

Barb. He appeared near the house last night, and made signs to me from the grove. You may imagine my surprise on finding it to be Richard in disguise. He has been in London all this time, working, half starving. I am almost ashamed to tell you, but working in a stable-yard; and oh, Archibald, he declares he is innocent. He says he was not even in the cottage at the time the murder was committed, but the man who really did the deed was a person by the name of Thorn.

Arch. Thorn? What Thorn can it be?

Barb. I don't know; some friend of Afy's, who used to ride over to the cottage in secret visits to her. Archibald, he swears to me in the most solemn manner, and I believe him as truly as that I am now speaking to you. I want you to see him yourself. He is coming to the grove again to-night. He will tell you all the circumstances of the terrible night, and perhaps you can find out a way in which his innocence can be made manifest. You are so clever, you can do anything.

Arch. Not quite everything, Barbara. But was this the purport of Richard's visit — to tell you this?

Barb. Oh, no; he thinks it would be of no use to assert his innocence, for nobody would believe him against the evidence already given. He came to ask for a hundred pounds. He says if he can get that sum he has an opportunity of doing better for himself than he has hitherto done. So mamma has sent me to you. She has not that sum by her at present, and, as it is for Richard, she dare not ask papa for it. She says if you can oblige her with the money, she will arrange with you about the repayment.

Arch. Do you want it now? If so, I must send Dill to the office. I have not that sum by me in the house.

Barb. Can you not bring it with you and see Richard at the same time?

Arch. It is hazardous — for him, I mean. Still, as he is to be in the grove, I may as well see him. What disguise is he in?

Barb. That of a farm laborer — the best he could adopt in these parts — also a heavy pair of black whiskers. He is to be there at ten precisely.

Arch. Well, then, I think I can come; but in order to do so I must disappoint a supper party to which we have been invited. However, my wife won't mind that when I tell her the business is so urgent. Yes, you can tell your mother I'll come.

Barb. Oh, Archibald, you are very kind to us! You have ever treated me like a dear sister, and mamma is grateful to you for all your attentions to her. I fear we can never repay you sufficiently. (*Rises to go*)

Arch. (*Rising*) I have only done what I felt to be my duty in the matter. (*Crosses*) Let me escort you to the gate. (*Exit with Barbara, arm in arm*)

At the same time enter Lady Isabel, and Levison, separately, in time to see them off.

Isabel. (*Looking after them*) That woman here — in privacy with my husband — under my very roof, too! Ah! then it is too true. My husband no longer loves me! (*Turns and sees Levison*) You here, sir? (*Sits at table*)

Lev. Who the deuce is that Barbara Hare? She's a devilish pretty girl. She seems to have a very good understanding with your husband. Several times I've encountered them together on the lawn enjoying moonlight walks and private confab.

Isabel. (*Coldly*) What did you say, sir?

Lev. Nothing. I only spoke of Monsieur, your husband. I meant not to offend.

                                        Retires.

Enter Joyce.

Joyce. If you please, my lady, little Isabel wishes to retire for the night, and she wants you to kiss her before going to sleep.

Isabel. (*Angrily*) Tell the nurse to put the child to bed, and leave me.

Joyce. (*Aside*) What! put the child to bed without even saying good night. There's something strange going on here. *Exit.*

Lev. (*Coming down*) By the bye, Lady Isabel, don't you think that Barbara Hare a devilish pretty girl?

Enter Miss Cornelia. Looks sharply at Levison. He crosses by her, bowing, and exits.

Miss C. Lady Isabel, I have taken the liberty of countermanding the order for little Isabel's new frock. I think she has quite enough already.

Isabel. (*Still at table*) Countermanding my orders, Miss Carlyle, is a liberty you have taken a great deal too often. Allow me to tell you that I am the most competent judge of what is best for my own children, and that for the future I will be mistress in my own house.

Enter Archibald.

Miss C. Archibald, what did Barbara Hare want with you just now?

Arch. Why, Cornelia, she merely wished to see me on some business, that's all.

Miss C. Why don't you say right out what she wanted, without making any mystery about it? She seems to be always wanting you now. Can it be that old affair is to be raked up again?

Arch. Cornelia, you will oblige me by never referring to that old affair again.

Miss C. Oh, indeed! Very well, very well; but I trust they will listen to me when they are brought to ruin through Lady Isabel's extravagance. Poor Archibald! he works like a horse now, and can hardly keep expenses down. *Exit.*

Isabel. (*Coming forward*) Archibald, what *did* that woman, that Barbara Hare, want here?

Arch. It is a private business, Isabel. She brings me messages from her mother.

Isabel. Must the business be kept secret from me?

Arch. It would not make you happier to know it, Isabel. There is a dark secret hanging over the Hare family; it is connected with that. I am summoned away on some urgent business this evening; therefore I cannot attend you to the supper party. You can use the carriage and go by yourself. I will endeavor to be there in time to escort you home. I am already late, and as I have to go to my office first, I must away at once. Good evening, and a pleasant party to you. *Exit.*

Isabel. What mystery can they have between them that he dares not reveal to me, his wife! Ah! he is deceiving me, I am certain of it. Oh! I am wretched, jealous, mad! (*Sits at table*)

Enter Levison.

Lev. (*Aside*) I wonder what the deuce that Hare girl can want with Carlyle! I followed them down to the gate and overheard them plan a meeting in the grove for this evening. Perhaps Lady Isabel would like to be present also. (*Aloud*) Ah! still alone, I see, Lady Isabel. I expected to find you so. I suspect Mr. Carlyle is more agreeably engaged.

Isabel. Engaged! in what manner, sir?

Lev. As I came up the lawn, a few minutes since, I saw a lady and gentleman enjoying a *tête-à-tête* by moonlight. I followed them to the gate, and overstepped the bounds of good manners so far as to listen to a part of their conversation. I heard them arrange a meeting in the grove for this evening, and unless I am very much mistaken the favored individual was Mr. Carlyle.

Isabel. (*Rising*) My husband! Oh, sir, you cannot mean that! Oh, if I thought him capable of such a falsehood to me, I would leave his roof at once!

Lev. That's right; be avenged on the false hound. He never was worthy of your love. Leave your home of misery, and come to one of happiness. Come, let me prove his perfidy to you.

Isabel. Only prove this, and I will quit his house forever.

Lev. With me, Isabel?

Isabel. Aye, with you. I care not who shall be the instrument of my vengeance. *Exeunt.*

Scene 2.

Landscape as in Act I. Enter Richard and Barbara.

Barb. Richard, we must not stand so near the house; papa is at home, you see, of all the nights in the world. You must wait till to-morrow night, and then perhaps you can see mamma.

Rich. I don't like waiting another night, Barbara, there's danger in every inch of ground this neighborhood contains.

Barb. You must wait, Richard, for other reasons. The man who caused all the mischief is at West Lynne; at least, there is a man staying there by the name of Thorn; so Bethel just told Mr. Carlyle as we stood by his gate, and Mr. Carlyle wishes you to see him. Should it prove to be the same, perhaps nothing can be done immediately towards discharging you, but it will be a great point ascertained. Are you sure that you should know him again?

Rich. Sure that I should know him? Should I know my own father? Should I know you? Is he not engraven on my brain in letters of blood? But how or when am I to see him?

Barb. I cannot tell you more till Mr. Carlyle comes. Poor Richard! I hope the time will soon come when you can walk forth in open day.

Enter Archibald.

Oh, Archibald, I am so glad that you have come! Our suspicion with regard to the man Thorn can now be set at rest. It seems to me Providence has directed his steps here at this very time. You must contrive that Richard shall see him.

Arch. (*Crossing to Richard*) Richard, your sister tells me that you wish to disclose to me the true history of that lamentable night. There is an old saying, and it is a sound advice, "Tell the whole truth to your doctor and your lawyer." If I am to judge whether anything can be attempted for you, you must tell me the whole truth without reserve; otherwise I would rather hear nothing. It shall be a sacred trust.

Rich. Well, if I must make a clean breast of it, I did love the girl, Afy, and would have made her my wife in time; but I could not do so then in the very face of my father's opposition. I went to the house on the evening in question to take my gun — Hallijohn had requested the loan of it; he was out at the time, so I handed it to Afy, who met me at the door. She would not allow me to go inside of it, as usual. I was mad with jealousy, for I felt sure that Thorn was in the cottage with her, although she strongly denied it; so I determined to wait and convince myself. I secreted myself in the shrubbery in the garden, where I could see all that passed within the cottage. Presently I saw Hallijohn come up the path by me and go into the house. Not long after, perhaps twenty minutes, I heard the gun fired, and at the same time saw Thorn leap from the cottage window and run wildly down the path, directly by me, to where his horse had been tied, jump in the saddle and gallop off.

Arch. Did you know where this Thorn lived?

Rich. I could never ascertain. Afy said he lived away ten miles distant. He used to ride over once or twice a week to see her. I always thought he came there under a false name. He appeared to be an aristocrat, though of very bad taste. He made a great display of jewelry, expensive, too — such as diamonds.

Arch. But you were afterwards seen with the gun in your hand coming from the cottage.

Rich. I went there to upbraid Afy for having deceived me. Mad with jealousy, I hardly knew what I did; but I had no idea that a murder had been committed. As I entered the door the first thing I stumbled over was Hallijohn's lifeless body. I saw my gun lying beside him. Some vague idea flashed across my brain that my gun ought not to be found there; so I seized it and rushed out just as people began to collect, and to my horror I was taken for the murderer; so I threw down my gun and fled.

Arch. And that act alone condemned you. You acted like a guilty man, and that line of conduct often entails as much trouble as real guilt.

Barb. And you do not believe him guilty?

Arch. I do not. I have little doubt of the guilt of Thorn; but I do not think, from your description of the man, that it is the same person who is now in the neighborhood. There is the money, Richard. (*Hands him notes*) You had better depart now, for fear of spies; but be here again to-morrow night at this hour, and in the mean time I'll decide what course you are to adopt, and how I can best serve you.

Rich. Good night, my more than friend; good night, my dear sister.   *Exit.*

Arch. And now, Barbara, I'll see you to your gate.

Barb. Never mind, Archibald; it is only a few steps. I can go by myself.

Arch. (*Crosses*) Nonsense, Barbara! Allow you to go by yourself along the high-road at this hour? Take my arm.   *Exeunt.*

Enter Lady Isabel and Levison, in time to see them off.

Lev. There, Lady Isabel, I told you what you might see — there is the proof.

Isabel. Take me away from this accursed place, Francis Levison. I am faint — ill — wretched — mad!   *Exeunt.*

Scene 3.

Chamber as in Scene 1. Enter Archibald; goes to table, and rings bell. Enter Joyce.

Arch. Joyce, where is your mistress?

Joyce. Is she not in her chamber, sir?

Arch. I have been looking everywhere. She is not in the house.

Joyce. Oh, heavens! I see it all now; her wild words to me — her strange look. Oh, master, she has destroyed herself, and she's been driven to it.

Arch. Destroyed herself! What do you mean?

Joyce. Master, she has destroyed herself as sure as we two are living. But a short time ago she called me to her — her face was like death — and exacted of me a solemn promise to stay here at East Lynne with the children, if anything happened to take her from them. I asked her if she was ill, and she said, "Yes, Joyce, ill and wretched!" Oh, sir, may Heaven support you in this dreadful trial!

Enter Miss Cornelia.

Miss C. What's all this? whatever's up? where's my lady?

Joyce. She has gone and taken the life that was not hers to take, and I say she has been driven to it by *you.* You've curbed her, you've snapped at her, and reproached her with extravagance — you know it, ma'am. All these years she's been crossed and put upon by you, and she's borne it all in silence like a patient angel. We all loved her, we all felt for her, and master's heart would have bled for her had he only known what she had to put up with from you day after day, year after year. Many and many's the time I've seen her coming from your reproaches with quivering lip and moistened eye, and her hands clasped meekly across her breast as though life was too heavy to bear. (*Goes up to table*)

Arch. (*Crosses to Cornelia*) Cornelia, if this be true, may Heaven forgive you for it!

Joyce. (*Finding letter on table; coming down*) Oh, master — see. Here is a letter she has left; it is my lady's handwriting; read it, master. (*Archibald takes the letter, opens it, reads it, and staggers to chair*) Oh! what does she say? Is she dead?

Arch. Worse than that! worse than that!

Miss C. Why, Archibald! what do you mean?

Arch. She has eloped with Francis Levison!

Miss C. Oh! the disgraceful, unworthy —

Arch. Hush, Cornelia! Not one word against her — no — not one!

> *Archibald in chair, overcome by deep grief; Joyce, appealing to heaven; Miss Cornelia bending over Archibald; Picture.*

End of the Second Act.

ACT III.

Scene 1.

Chamber. Enter Archibald, reading a letter.

Arch. "When years go on and my children ask where their mother is, and why she left them, tell them that you, their father, goaded her to it. If they inquire what she is, tell them also, if you will, but tell them at the same time that you outraged and betrayed her, driving her to the depths of desperation ere she quitted them in her despair." Oh, Isabel! I forgive you the injustice these words do my heart. May they never cause you the pangs of misery they have inflicted on me.

Enter Miss Cornelia.

Miss C. Archibald, what's the time, I wonder?

Arch. Just nine, Cornelia.

Miss C. Well, then, I think I'll go to bed, and after I'm in it I'll have a basin of arrowroot or gruel, or some slop of that sort. I'm sure I've been free enough all my life of wanting any such sick stuff.

Arch. Well, do so, if you think it will do you any good.

Miss C. Well, there's one thing I know of that's excellent for a cold in the head; and that is to take your red flannel petticoat and tie it on crosswise over your night-cap. I'll try it, too. (*Sneezes*)   *Exit.*

Arch. I'm uncommonly gloomy to-night; it's a bitter night out, too. I wonder if it's snowing yet. (*Goes to window*)

Rich. (*Speaks outside*) Oh, Mr. Carlyle! for the love of heaven let me come in. I'm nearly frozen; it is I, Richard!

Archibald opens door. Enter Richard Hare.

Arch. Richard, I'm thunderstruck! I fear you have done wrong in coming here.

Rich. What could I do better? The Bow Street officers were after me, set on by that wretch Thorn. I had to leave London at a moment's notice, without a thing belonging to me. Even now the officers may be in pursuit. I have walked all the way from London here. I had no money to pay for a lodging, or even to buy food. I waited outside the window till I saw you were alone; so I thought I would ask your advice.

Arch. Have you then discovered this man Thorn?

Rich. Yes; about a week ago, for the first time, I got a glimpse of him as he was passing by in a carriage. I tried to follow him then, but they drove too fast for me; but last evening I saw him again standing in front of one of the theatres. I went up and stood close at his elbow; he saw and in a moment recognized me, for he turned deadly pale. "What do you want, fellow?" said he, in an angry tone. "I want to know who you are," I replied. Then he flew into a fierce passion, and swore that if ever he caught me near him again he would hand me over to the nearest officer; "and remember," yelled he, as he walked away, "people are not given into custody for merely watching people!" That convinced me beyond all doubt that it was he. I tried to follow, but the great crowd of people in the street at that time kept me partially out of sight. At length he called a carriage, and as he rode away he pointed me out to an officer who had been standing near; but I managed to get among the crowd again, and fled as fast as possible. After that I knew I was no longer safe in London. Oh, Mr. Carlyle, is this life to go on with me forever?

Arch. I am deeply sorry for you, Richard; I wish I could remedy it.

Miss C. (*Outside*) Archibald! Who have you got in that room?

Arch. It's some person to see me on business, Cornelia. You cannot come in now. It's only my sister, Richard. Be a man, and shake off this fear. No harm shall come to you in my house. But you had better retire till I have spoken to my sister. (*Puts him off*)

Miss C. (*Outside*) Not come, indeed! Open the door, I say.

Archibald opens the door and Cornelia enters with a red petticoat tied on her head; looks round stage.

Where is she, I say? Oh! you ought to be ashamed of yourself — you, a married man, with children in the house, too! Oh! I'd rather believe anything wicked of myself than of you, Archibald.

Arch. Why, what do you mean? Are you crazy, Cornelia? There has been no woman here, but a man who fears the police are on his track; you ought to be able to guess his name.

Miss C. What! not Richard Hare? Let me see him.

Arch. Why, surely you would not present yourself to him in that guise?

Miss C. What? not show myself to Richard Hare in this guise? — he whom I have whipped ten times a day when he was a boy, and he deserves it now for getting into such a scrape. He looks no better than I do, I dare say. Where is he? (*Archibald brings him out*) Why, Richard, what on earth has brought you here? You must have been crazy.

Rich. The Bow Street officers were after me, and I had to cut away from London at a moment's notice. I had no money to pay for a lodging or to buy me food; so I came to Mr. Carlyle to befriend me.

Miss C. It just serves you right. You would go hunting after that brazen hussy, Afy Hallijohn.

Arch. Cornelia, this is no time for upbraidings. Do you go and prepare him some food, while I see after his lodgings.

Crosses and exits.

Miss C. Well, come along, Richard; I'll see what can be done for you; but you know you always was the greatest natural-born fool that was ever let loose out of leading-strings.

Exeunt.

Scene 2.

Chamber. Lady Isabel discovered seated at a table near fireplace, wrapped in a large shawl, very pale and very ill.

Isabel. Alas! what is to be the end of my sufferings? How much longer can I bear this torture of mind, this never-dying anguish of soul? From what a dream have I awakened! Oh, lady, wife, mother! whatever trials may be the lot of your married life, though they may magnify themselves to your crushed spirit as beyond the nature, the endurance of woman to bear, yet resolve to bear them. Fall down on your knees and pray for patience; pray for strength to resist that demon who would tempt you to flee them. Bear them unto death, rather than forget your good name and your good conscience. Oh! I have sacrificed husband, home, children, friends, and all that make life of value to woman — and for what? To be forever an outcast from society, to never again know a moment's peace. Oh! that I could die, and end my suffering and my misery. (*Sinks her head on table*)

Enter Levison. Isabel sees him and speaks coldly.

You here, sir? Why did you come now?

Lev. Why did I come? Are these all the thanks a fellow gets for traveling in this inclement weather? I thought, at least, that you would be glad to welcome me.

Isabel. I am glad, for one reason, to welcome you, that we may come to an understanding with each other. Let there be plain truth in this interview, if there never was before.

Lev. With all my heart. It is you who have thrown out the challenge, mind. (*Sits*)

Isabel. When you left me in July you gave

me your solemn promise to be back in time for our marriage. You well know what I mean when I say *in time*.

Lev. Oh, of course I meant to do so. I gave you the promise; but no sooner had I set foot in London than I found myself completely overwhelmed with business from which I could not extricate myself.

Isabel. You are breaking faith with me already; your words are not words of truth, but of deceit. You did not intend to be back in time for the marriage; otherwise you would have caused it to take place ere you went away.

Lev. Well, Isabel, you must be aware that it is an awful sacrifice for a man in my position to marry a divorced woman.

Isabel. When I wished or expected the sacrifice it was not for my own sake. I told you so then. It was for the sake of my child. But it is too late now, and his inheritance must be that of sin and shame.

Lev. Isabel, I am now the representative of an ancient and respected baronetcy, and to make you my wife would offend my family.

Isabel. (*Rising. At table*) Stay, sir! You need not trouble yourself to find new excuses now. Had you taken this journey on purpose to make me your wife — nay, were the clergyman standing by to perform the ceremony — I tell you, Francis Levison, I would not have you! I can imagine any fate in life better than being compelled to pass it with you. (*Sinks in seat, exhausted*)

Lev. Indeed! You made commotion enough once about my making you reparation.

Isabel. I know I did; but that time is over now. All the reparation in your power to make, all the reparation the whole world could invent, could not undo my sin — it and its effects must be upon me forever!

Lev. (*Laughing sarcastically*) Oh, sin! You ladies should think of that beforehand.

Isabel. I pray Heaven they may! May Heaven help all so to do who may be tempted as I was!

Lev. If you mean that as a reproach to me, it's rather out of place. The temptation to sin lay not in my persuasion half so much as in your ridiculous, jealous anger against your husband.

Isabel. Quite true! Quite true!

Lev. With regard to your husband and that Hare girl you were blindly, outrageously jealous. For my part, I don't believe Carlyle ever thought of the girl in the way you imagine he did. There was some disreputable secret connected with the Hare family, and Carlyle was acting in it *under the rose* for Mrs.

Hare. She was too ill to attend to the matter herself, so she sent the young lady.

Isabel. You told me a very different tale then, sir.

Lev. I know I did. That was merely my stratagem. All stratagems are fair in love and war. By the bye, what have you named the young article there? (*Points to cradle*)

Isabel. The name which ought to have been his by inheritance — Francis Levison.

Lev. What does he look like? Is he anything like my handsome self?

Isabel. If he did — if he were like you in thought or in spirit — I would pray to Heaven that he might die before he ever spoke!

Lev. Anything else? I would advise you to be careful how you deal out your small change, Lady Isabel. You may get it back with interest. Is my room prepared?

Isabel. You have no room here, sir. These apartments are rented to me in my own name now; they can no longer afford you shelter. I received these from you one month ago — (*Takes package of bank-notes from box on table*) forty pounds. Count them. Is all right? Because I wish to return them to you. I wish all to end between us.

Lev. If it be your wish that all relation between us should cease, why, so be it. Remember, though, it is your own doing, not mine. But you cannot suppose I will allow you to starve; a sum shall be placed at your banker's to your credit half-yearly.

Isabel. I beg you to cease. What do you take me for?

Lev. Take you for? Why, how can you live? You have no fortune — you must receive assistance from some one.

Isabel. But not from you — no, not from you. If the whole world denied me, if I could receive no help from strangers, or means of earning a livelihood, I'd go and ask my *husband* for bread, sooner than accept one farthing from you.

Lev. Bless us, how bitter! Oh, yes, I know, your husband — a very generous man. It's a pity you left him, though. Well, Isabel, since you will accept nothing for yourself, you must for the child. He, at any rate, falls to my share. I'll give you a few hundreds a year with him.

Isabel. Not a farthing now. Or even, sir, were you to send it, I would throw it into the nearest river. Whom do you take me for? If you have put me beyond the pale of the world, I am still Lord Mount Severn's daughter.

Lev. Well, Isabel, if you will persist in this

perverse resolution, of course I cannot amend it. In a little while, however, you may wish to recall it; if so, a line addressed to me at my banker's will always reach me.

Isabel. It will not be needed, sir. Your clothes, which you left here when you went to England, you will have the goodness to order Pierre to take away this afternoon. And now it is my wish that we part.

Lev. To remain as mortal enemies forever?

Isabel. To be as strangers, sir.

Lev. (*Rising, offering her his hand*) And will you not even shake hands at parting?

Isabel. I should prefer not, sir.

Lev. Oh, very well; just as you please. Da-da — ta-ta! *Exit.*

Isabel. And what is left me now but the deepest, blackest despair! I am bowed down by the weight of my own sin and shame. Why did I ever leave my home and my dear husband? Oh! would I could wake and find it all a terrible dream; that I could find myself once more at East Lynne, with my husband and children about me, a happy, contented mother. But no — no — it cannot be! and I must bear the consequences of my sin forever! (*Sinks her head on table*)

Enter Lord Mount Severn. Lady Isabel sees him and covers her head with the shawl.

Oh, go away, Lord Mount Severn, I beg! Why did you seek me out? I am not worth it. I have brought disgrace enough upon your name.

Lord M. And upon your husband and your children. Nevertheless, it is incumbent upon me, as your nearest blood relative, to look after you and see that you do not fall lower. You were one of the last I should have feared to trust. If ever a woman had a good husband, in every sense of the word, you had one in Mr. Carlyle. How could you so requite him?

Isabel. (*At table*) I believed that his love was no longer mine. I thought that he had deserted me for another.

Lord M. I had given you credit for having better sense, Isabel. But was that enough to hurl you on to the step you took? Surely not; you must have yielded to the persuasions of that bold, wicked man.

Isabel. It is all over now.

Lord M. Where do you intend to fix your future home?

Isabel. Wherever Heaven directs. I shall leave this place as soon as I am strong enough to travel.

Lord M. You were *here* with *him*, were you not?

Isabel. Yes; they think I am his wife.

Lord M. It is well. How many servants have you?

Isabel. Two; a maid and a — a nurse.

Lord M. A nurse! Isabel, is there then a *child?* Coward — sneak! may all good men shun him henceforth! O Isabel, you, an earl's daughter! How utterly you have lost yourself!

Isabel. Oh, spare me, I beseech you! You have been rending my heart ever since you came here. I am too weak to bear it.

Lord M. How do you propose to live?

Isabel. I have some money left.

Lord M. His money, Isabel?

Isabel. No, not his money. I am selling my trinkets one by one. Before they are all gone I shall look out for some means of earning a livelihood — by teaching, most probably.

Lord M. What sum will it take for you to live upon?

Isabel. I cannot accept anything from you.

Lord M. Absurd, Isabel. Do not add romantic folly to your other faults. Your father is gone, but I stand in his place.

Isabel. No — no — I do not desire it. I have forfeited all claim to assistance.

Lord M. But not to mine. I look upon this as a duty — an imperative one, too. On my return to England I will settle four hundred a year upon you, and you can draw it quarterly, and so, Isabel, I bid you farewell. May your future life be peaceful — for happy it can never be. (*Taking her hand kindly*) Farewell, Isabel. *Exit.*

Isabel. (*Rises and crosses to left of table*) And now I am alone forever! Why don't I die! — why don't I die!

> *Falls in chair — bows head on table, sobbing bitterly.*

> *End of the Third Act.*

ACT IV.

Scene 1.

Chamber. Enter Archibald and Dill.

Dill. Mr. Carlyle, who do you think has had the audacity to come to West Lynne, and set himself up as a candidate in opposition to you?

Arch. A second man? Let him come on; we shall have the satisfaction of knowing who wins in the end. Well, who is this formidable opponent?

Dill. Mr. Francis Levison. But you won't let that beast frighten you from the contest, will you?

Enter Barbara Hare, now Mrs. Carlyle.

Barb. Archibald, you will not suffer this insolent man's doings to deter you from your plans? You will not withdraw?

Arch. Certainly not, Barbara. He has thrust himself offensively upon me in this measure, amd I think my better plan will be to take no more notice of him than if he were the dirt under my feet.

Barb. Quite right, quite right, my husband.

Enter Miss Cornelia.

Miss C. Archibald, have you heard this disgraceful news?

Arch. I have heard it, Cornelia; and had I not, the very walls would have enlightened me.

Miss C. You will carry on the contest now? I was averse to it before; but now I withdraw all my objections. You will be no brother of mine if you yield the field to him.

Arch. I do not intend to yield it.

Miss C. Good! You will bear on upon your course, and let him crawl on his. Take no more notice of him than if he were a viper. Archibald, you must canvass now.

Arch. No, I shall be elected without canvassing. You'll see, Cornelia.

Miss C. I'll give you a thousand pounds myself for all of the electors.

Arch. Keep your money, sister, it will not be needed.

Miss C. Well, I've heard of a Lady Somebody that kissed a blacksmith to ensure her husband's election. Now I'm sure I'd kiss every man in East and West Lynne, blacksmiths included, to ensure your election.
Exit.

Dill. And I'm sure I'd kiss every woman.
Exit.

Barb. Archibald, I wish to say something to you. I fear I've done a foolish thing.

Arch. I fear we all do sometimes. Well, what is it?

Barb. It is something that I've had on my mind for months. You remember that night three years ago that Richard came to us in the grove. I mean that — that night that Lady Isabel quitted East Lynne. Richard came back to me again after he had left us in the grove. I was standing at the open window. He saw me, and motioned me out to him. He declared to me that he had just met the real Thorn in the lane. He described a peculiar motion of the hand as he constantly threw back the hair from his brow, and also spoke of the diamond ring, how it glittered in the moonbeams. Since that time

I have had a firm belief that Thorn and Levison are one and the same person.

Arch. Indeed! Why did you not mention this before?

Barb. I did not like to remind you of that night before; but to-day I saw Sir Francis Levison in the street, addressing a crowd of people who had assembled to hear him speak, and there was the old action of the hand that my brother had before described. I have therefore written to Richard to steal down here, and try, if possible, to discover the identity. The letter has gone.

Arch. Well, we must shelter him as best we can. I, myself, feel convinced that Thorn and Levison are one.

Barb. Indeed! how long have you thought so?

Arch. Not until to-day. I never suspected it before; but from many circumstances that I can now call to mind I am almost certain of it.

Barb. Archibald, dear husband, what can be done to clear him?

Arch. Being Levison, I cannot act.

Barb. Not act? — not act for Richard?

Arch. My dearest, how can I? You have not considered, Barbara — any one in the world but Levison. It would seem like my own revenge.

Barb. Forgive me. I did not think of it in that light. You are right, my husband, as you always are. Let us wait till Richard comes.

Arch. Spoken like my own wife. Now, Barbara, you must sing to me. (*She sings, "You'll Remember Me." Archibald in same situation with Barbara, as with Isabel at end of Act I*)

Enter Lady Isabel as Madame Vine, during song. At end of song she sighs deeply. Archibald and Barbara turn and see her.

Barb. Ah! This is Madame Vine, I believe, our new governess. Please to step this way, Madame Vine. I hope you are not overfatigued by your journey. Why, how pale you look! You are ill, are you not?

Mad. V. No, not ill, madame, only a little fatigued.

Arch. Barbara, you had better ring for a glass of wine and some lunch. I am sure Madame Vine must require some refreshment after her tiresome journey. And now I'll leave you to arrange matters between yourselves. (*Looks closely at Madame Vine as he goes out*) I've seen those features before, I'm certain of it; but where can it have been?
Exit slowly, as if in deep study.

Barb. Madame Vine, will you allow me to ring for some wine and a lunch?

Mad. V. Oh, no, madame, don't trouble yourself. I can't take anything just now.

Barb. You looked so pale I feared you might be ill.

Mad. V. I am generally pale, sometimes remarkably so; but my health is good.

Barb. Mrs. Latimer wrote us that you were a very estimable and worthy person, and that you would be sure to suit us. I hope you may, and that you may find your residence here agreeable. Have you lived much in England?

Mad. V. In the early portion of my life.

Barb. And you have lost your husband and your children. I think Mrs. Latimer mentioned children.

Mad. V. Madame, I've lost all — all!

Barb. Oh! it must be a terrible grief when our little ones die. I could not lose my babe for the world; it would kill me to part with him.

Mad. V. Terrible grief, indeed, and hard to bear; but it does not always kill.

Barb. You are no doubt aware that these children you will have charge of are not mine; they are the children of Mr. Carlyle's first wife.

Mad. V. And Mr. Carlyle's; yes, madame, I have heard so. She is dead, is she not?

Barb. Yes, she was killed by a railway accident in France some two years ago. She was the only daughter of the late Lord Mount Severn. She was very attractive and beautiful, but I do not think she cared much for her husband. Be that as it may, she ran away with Sir Francis Levison.

Mad. V. I have heard so, madame; it was very sad.

Barb. Sad? it was very wicked! it was infamous! Of all husbands in the world, of all men living, Mr. Carlyle least deserved such a requital; but the affair was a mystery throughout. Sir Francis Levison had been staying some time at East Lynne, but no one had ever detected any undue intimacy between them, not even Mr. Carlyle. To him, as to others, the cause must remain a mystery. But, of course the disgrace is inflicted on the children, and always will be — the shame of having a divorced mother.

Mad. V. But you say she is dead, madame.

Barb. Yes, true; but they will not be the less pointed at; the little girl especially. They allude to their mother now and then in conversation, Joyce tells me, but I would recommend you not to encourage them in that. They had better forget her altogether, if possible. Mr. Carlyle would naturally wish them to do so. I trust you may be able to instill such principles into the mind of the little girl, as shall keep her from a like fate.

Mad. V. I will, madame. But do they enjoy good health?

Barb. Quite so, all except the oldest boy, William. He has a slight cough, and the doctors think his lungs are affected. Mr. Carlyle also fears that he is not long for this world.

Mad. V. And how does Mr. Carlyle bear the thought of parting with him?

Barb. Bravely, madame. Mr. Carlyle is not the man to betray emotion, whatever his feelings may be. Even when Lady Isabel left him he made no outward sign of grief, although it must have wrung his very heart-strings.

Mad. V. Aye, madame, because he did not love her truly — his best love was given to another.

Barb. You are mistaken. She was his heart's sole idol. Mr. Carlyle is a man who always speaks the truth, and he told me, in his confidence, that he would never have married again during Lady Isabel's life-time.

Mad. V. But is it sure that she is dead?

Barb. Oh, yes, beyond all doubt. She was journeying with her nurse and infant child at the time of the shocking accident. Her uncle, the present Lord Mount Severn, wrote to the authorities of the little town where it happened, and they sent him word that the nurse and child were killed on the spot, and that the two ladies occupying the same compartment of the carriage had since died of their injuries, and that one of them was certainly the mother of the child. Besides, Lord Mount Severn had placed an annuity in the bank to be drawn by her quarterly, that has never been touched; so that proves, beyond all doubt, that she no longer lives.

Mad. V. Quite true, madame.

Barb. It was a shocking affair all through. Poor Lady Isabel! Could she have foreseen her fate she never would have taken such a rash step; or had she known what a villain Levison was. He was not only a bad man in principle, but he was a murderer!

Mad. V. Oh, no — no! not a murderer; a bad man, a very bad man; but not a murderer.

Barb. Oh! did you know him, then?

Mad. V. Oh, no; I did not know him, madame, but I have heard the story.

Barb. It has not been proved; but I feel confident, in my own mind, that it soon will be.

Enter William, followed by Joyce, Joyce goes up to the table.

This is the little sick boy I spoke of, Madame Vine — little William.

Mad. V. (Rushes to him and clasps him in her arms) Oh! my boy, my boy! Are you ill, my darling? *Are* you sick, William? *(To Barbara)* I beg your pardon, madame; but I have lately lost a little boy of his age, and when we have lost children of our own, we are apt to love fondly all we come near.

William. (With Madame Vine) Mamma, may I ride to town with you to-day?

Barb. My dear, I shall not go to town to-day; besides, you are not yet strong enough; you did wrong to leave the nursery to-day; this air is too chilly for you. Take him in, Joyce.

Joyce. (Gives Barbara letter) My lady, here's a letter the postman has just brought; I forgot it till now. Come, William.

Barb. Madame Vine, this is Joyce, who has had charge of the children ever since their mother left them. *(Joyce goes to take William from Madame Vine; recognizes her as Lady Isabel; makes a movement of surprise, as if to scream. Isabel puts a finger on her lips as a signal to be silent and not betray her. Joyce takes William and exits slowly. Barbara is busy reading the letter, and does not see this action. Aside)* Ah, this is from brother Richard, to inform me of his coming. I must go and see my husband at once. *(To Madame Vine)* Madame Vine, I must beg you to excuse me for the present. I am called away by some most important duties. Make yourself perfectly at home in my absence. East Lynne is small, and I've no doubt you'll soon become familiar with it. *Exit.*

Mad. V. Familiar with East Lynne! Did she but know how familiar East Lynne is to me! What will be my trials now! to see him, my husband once, caress the woman I hate; to be compelled to witness the thousand little proofs of affection that were once bestowed upon me; to see his love for her child, while I must teach my own children to forget my memory. Oh, why did I come here, why place myself in such daily torments? Oh, Isabel! patience, patience! Is it thus you bear your cross in life? *Retires up stage.*

Scene 2.

Landscape. Enter Sir Francis Levison, walking hurriedly about.

Lev. What a confounded fool I was to think of trying it on at East Lynne! Carlyle has, no doubt, double the friends I have; but since I've entered the list against him, I'll not back out. I'm determined to stand my ground.

Enter Miss Cornelia. She meets Levison face to face. He lifts his hat and bows.

Miss C. Did you intend that insult for me, Francis Levison?

Lev. That all depends upon how you are pleased to take it.

Miss C. You dare lift your hat to me? Have you forgotten that I am Miss Carlyle?

Lev. It would be a hard matter to forget the face, having once seen it.

Miss C. You contemptible worm, I despise you! Do you think I am to be insulted with impunity? Out upon you for a bold, bad man.

Enter Officer. Taps Levison on the shoulder.

Officer. Francis Levison, I arrest you — you are my prisoner.

Lev. (Pushing Officer's hand off him) Hands off, vermin! You are too familiar on short acquaintance. Of what crime am I accused?

Officer. That you will soon learn. You must come with me at once. *(Handcuffs Levison)*

Lev. Oh, certainly, sir, if you desire it. This is some ridiculous mistake — it will be set right in the morning. Good day, angelic Miss Carlyle, loveliest of your sex. I'm sorry this agreeable little confab was cut so short. I'll come back and renew it in the morning. Take care of your precious self, and look out for the naughty, naughty men — ta-ta — ta-ta. *Exit, followed by Officer.*

Miss C. (Calls after them) Here, officer, officer! Be sure you get his photograph taken. It will be an excellent picture for the rogues' gallery! Oh, dear, he's put me in such a fluster, that I must get home as fast as possible, and get some juniperberry tea to settle my nerves. *Exit.*

Scene 3.

Chamber. William discovered lying on couch. Madame Vine seated behind at head, bending over him.

William. Madame Vine, how long will it be before I die?

Mad. V. What makes you think you will die, William?

William. I am certain of it, Madame Vine; but it is nothing to die when our Saviour loves us; but why do you grieve so for me? I am not your child!

Mad. V. I know you are not my child, but I lost a little boy like you.

William. It will be so pleasant to go up there, and never be tired or ill any more.

Mad. V. Pleasant? Aye, William, would that time were come!

William. Madame Vine, do you think mamma will be there? I mean my own mamma that was.

Mad. V. Aye, child, ere long, I trust.

William. But how can I be sure that she will be there? You know she was not quite good to papa or to us, and I sometimes think she did not grow good and ask Heaven to forgive her.

Mad. V. Oh, William, her whole life after she left you was one long scene of repentance — of seeking forgiveness; but her sorrow was greater than she could bear, and her heart broke in its yearning for you.

William. What makes you think so?

Mad. V. Child, I know it — I know it.

William. Did you ever see her, Madame Vine? Did you know her abroad?

Mad. V. Yes, child, I knew her abroad.

William. Why did you not tell us before? What did she say to you?

Mad. V. That she was parted from her children here, but that she should meet them again in heaven, and be with them forever: there, where all the awful pain and sadness, all the guilt of this world will be washed out and He will wipe our tears.

William. How shall I know her there? You see I have nearly forgotten what she was like.

Mad. V. You will know her when you see her there, never fear, William.

Enter Archibald. Sits on foot of couch.

Arch. Well, Madame Vine, how is your little patient this evening?

Mad. V. He appears worse — more weak.

Arch. My little son, Madame Vine is an untiring nurse to you, is she not?

William. Papa, I want to see my sister Lucy, and Joyce, too.

Arch. Very well, my little son. I'll send them to you presently. Madame Vine, do you not perceive a change in his countenance?

Mad. V. Yes, he has looked like that since a strange fit of trembling that came over him this afternoon.

Arch. Oh! it is hard to lose him thus.

Mad. V. He will be better off. We can bear death; it is not the worst parting the earth knows. He will be quit of this cruel world and sheltered in heaven. It would be well for all of us if we could go there as pure as he is.

Arch. There, William, keep yourself quiet. I'll go and bring your sister Lucy and your mamma to see you. I'll not be gone many minutes.   *Exit.*

Mad. V. (*Rising*) Oh, Heaven! my punishment is more than I can bear. He has gone to bring that woman here, that she may mingle her shallow sympathy with his deep grief. Oh, if ever retribution came to woman, it has come to me now. I can no longer bear it.

I shall lose my senses. Oh, William! in this last, dying hour, try to think I am your mother.

William. Papa has gone for her now.

Mad. V. No, not that woman there, not that woman. (*Throws off cap and spectacles*) Look at me, William. I am your mother! (*Catches him in her arms. He says "Mother" faintly, and falls back dead in her arms*) Oh! he is dead! — he is dead! Oh, William! wake and call me mother once again! My child is dead! — my child is dead!

Enter Joyce.

Joyce. (*At foot of couch*) Oh, my lady, let me lead you from this room, they will discover you.

Mad. V. Oh, Joyce! leave me to my grief. See here — my child is dead! and never knew that I was his mother. I don't care what I've been, I am his mother still. Oh, my child — my child! my heart will break — my heart will break! (*Falls and sobs convulsively*)

End of the Fourth Act.

ACT V.

Scene 1.

Landscape. Enter Barbara and Joyce.

Joyce. But, my lady, will not Madame Vine's illness prevent you from making your usual trip to the seaside?

Barb. Oh, no. Miss Corney will look after the house in my absence, and Dill will be here to assist her. Richard's trial will be over today, and if he is cleared I shall prevail upon him to accompany me. I shall start on Monday; this, you know, is Friday; so you will have ample time to get everything in readiness.

Joyce. Very well, my lady. I'll attend to it.
                                        Exit.

Barb. My poor brother! If he were only free, my happiness would be complete. (*Shouts*) Hark! what mean those shouts?

Enter Miss Cornelia.

Miss. C. Well, it's all settled at last. Richard's free, at all events. I heard the news as I came along, and the very people who have been abusing him for the last seven years are the very ones who are cheering him. I saw that Afy Hallijohn as I came along — not that I'd condescend to notice such a creature, but she *was* decked out. She had on a green and white silk, flounced up to the waist, extended over a crinoline that would reach from here over yonder; a fancy bonnet stuck on the back part of her head, with a wreath and veil; delicate kid gloves, and swinging a handkerchief highly perfumed with musk. Oh, it was perfectly disgusting! (*Retires up*)

Enter Richard Hare; crosses to Barbara.

Rich. Barbara, my dear sister, I am free at last. Once more I can walk abroad without fear.

Barb. I thank Heaven my dear brother is restored to me at last.

Rich. Yes, the trial is over. Sir Francis Levison has been proved guilty, and has just received his sentence.

Miss C. What was it?

Rich. Transportation for life, for the murder of John Hallijohn.

Miss C. Only for life?

Barb. Oh, Miss Corney, you may depend upon it, his punishment is quite sufficient. The lingering torture of mind he will have to endure in the galleys is a thousand times worse than death. But see, Richard, here comes papa to welcome you.

Enter Justice Hare; crosses to Richard.

Justice H. Oh, Richard, my dear boy, I am now proud to own you. This is the happiest day of my life. (*Shouts and groans*) Hark! what's all that uproar and confusion? Oh, I see; it's that villain, Levison; they are taking him to prison, and the mob are after him. They are coming this way, too; let's be off. I'm so happy that I don't want to encounter that villain, for fear the sight of him would put me in a passion again. Come, my children. *All exeunt, except Miss Cornelia.*

Miss C. Well, *they* may all go; but I shall remain to have the pleasure of wishing Sir Francis Levison a pleasant journey to prison.

Enter Levison, followed by an Officer.

Lev. Thank fortune I have escaped the mob at last! They are on the wrong track, and I can now proceed in quietness. (*Turns and sees Miss Cornelia*) Oh! that hag here?

Miss C. Good day, *Sir* Francis Levison! those bracelets become you exceedingly well.

Lev. Yes, as you say, they are of a very choice pattern. The workmanship about them is very elaborate — truly fine. I'm sorry they've got such an affectionate hold on me, else I'd transfer them to you with the greatest pleasure. By the bye, Miss Corney, give my regards to your brother, the pettifogging lawyer at East Lynne, and tell him that should he want a lock of his first wife's hair, I have one, which I will give him, free gratis.

Miss C. Sir Francis Levison, you are utterly devoid of feeling or honor. But times are changed since last we met. What will you do for your diamonds, your kid gloves, your perfumed handkerchiefs, in the hulks?

Lev. Do? Why, I suppose I shall have to do without them, as many a man has done before me. There's one thing I shall have to console me, though — I shan't be bored with your ugly mug there. (*Officer taps him on the shoulder and points off*) Yes, I know, directly, sir. Don't interrupt me when you see I'm talking to a lady. (*To Miss Cornelia*) I hate to be severe upon you, *angelic* Miss Corney. Don't forget my advice about the naughty, naughty men; and take good care of yourself — your precious self; and also of your red flannel petticoat. Ta, la! ta, la!

Exit, with Officer.

Miss C. Well, I do declare! he's an out and out villain, and I do believe he'd try to practice his arts on me if he thought there was any chance of his succeeding. *Exit.*

Scene 2.

Chamber. Enter Archibald, meeting Joyce.

Arch. Well, Joyce, how is Madame Vine to-day? No worse, I hope.

Joyce. Oh, sir, I fear she is dying.

Arch. Dying! I'll see her myself. (*Attempts to go*)

Joyce (*Stopping him*) Oh, no, no, sir! do not go to her room, please, sir; don't think of going to her room.

Arch. What! let a lady die in my house and not look after her?

Enter Miss Cornelia.

Cornelia, Joyce tells me that she thinks Madame Vine is dying.

Miss C. Dying! I can't think what has come over Joyce. Lately she acts more like a simpleton than anything else. (*Crosses*) Move out of the way girl! (*Going*)

Joyce. Oh, no, no, ma'am! you must not enter her room.

Miss C. Well, I declare! what will you do next, I wonder? Archibald, do you go for a physician directly. *Exit Archibald.* Joyce, I think your brain must be softening. Move out of the way!

Throws Joyce round and exits.

Joyce. Oh, my poor lady! What will become of you now? They will discover all.

Exit.

Scene 3.

Chamber. Isabel discovered in bed.

Isabel. Oh, I am dying — dying alone! with no one to soothe and comfort me. Oh!

if I could but see Archibald and ask his forgiveness, I should die in peace.

Enter Miss Cornelia.

Miss C. Well, now, if that Joyce was a
drinking woman I should certainly say she
was frightfully boozy. (*Recognizing Isabel*)
Mercy be good! How came *you here?*

Isabel. Oh! do not reproach me, Miss
Corney. I am on my way to heaven, to answer
for all my sins and all my sorrows.

Miss C. (*At side of couch*) No, poor child,
I will not reproach you.

Isabel. I am glad to go. Our Saviour did
not come, you know, to save the good like
you, but for the sake of guilty wretches like
me. I have tried to take up my cross as He
bade me, and bear it bravely for His sake —
but its weight has killed me.

Miss C. Had I anything to do with sending
you from East Lynne?

Isabel. No; I was not very happy here
with you; but that was not the cause of my
going away. Forgive me, Miss Carlyle, but I
want to see Archibald and ask him to forgive
me before I die. I have prayed to Joyce to
bring him to me; but she said it could not be.
Oh, Miss Carlyle, do let me see him, only for
one little minute, and I will die blessing you.

Miss C. Poor child! You shall see him.
(*Goes and calls*) Here, Joyce, Joyce!

Enter Joyce.

Go and request your master to come up to me.

Joyce. Oh, ma'am, do you think it will do
— I mean, would it be well?

Miss C. Go and do as I bid you. Are you
the mistress here, or am I? Go!   *Exit Joyce.*
Now, poor child, I will leave you. You shall
see Archibald alone.

Isabel. Oh, bless you, Miss Corney; you
have taken a load from my soul; you are too
kind. (*Miss Cornelia kisses her*) And you have
kissed me, *too*, and I thank you for that.

Miss C. (*Going*) Well, I believe I did kiss
her; but it was all the fault of that Joyce,
she has flustered me so.   *Exit.*

Isabel. And I shall see my dear husband
once more — ask him to forgive me — and
then I shall have done with life.

Enter Archibald.

Arch. I am deeply grieved, Madame Vine
— (*Recognizes Isabel*) Great heavens! Isabel
— here!

Isabel. Archibald, I could not die till I had
your forgiveness. Oh, do not turn away from
me — bear with me one little minute — only
say that you will forgive me, and I can rest
in peace.

Arch. Why did you come here?

Isabel. I could not stay away from you and
my children. The longing for the sight of
them was killing me. I never knew one
moment's peace after the mad act I was
guilty of in quitting you. Not an hour had I
departed ere repentance set in. Even then I
would have come back, but I did not know
how. My sin was great, and my punishment
has been greater; it has been one long scene
of mental agony.

Arch. Why did you go away?

Isabel. Did you not know why?

Arch. No; it was always a mystery to me.

Isabel. I went out of love for you. Oh, do
not look at me in that reproachful way! I
loved you dearly, and I grew suspicious of
you. I thought you false and deceitful to me;
that your love was given to her who is now
your wife, and, in my sore jealousy, I listened
to the temptations of that bold, bad man, who
whispered of revenge. But it was not so —
was it, Archibald?

Arch. Can you ask me that, knowing me
as you did then, and as you must have known
me since? I never was false to you in word,
in thought or in deed.

Isabel. I know it now, but I was mad. I
never could have committed the act in anything but madness. Oh, say that you will forget all and forgive me!

Arch. I cannot *forget* — I have forgiven
already.

Isabel. Think what it has been for me to live
in the same house with her who is now
your wife; to watch the envied caresses which
once were mine, to see your great love for
her; think what it was for me to watch by
the death-bed of my own child, to see his de-
caying strength, to be alone with him in his
dying hour, and not be able to tell him *I* was
his mother. And then, to see you soothe her
petty grief, and I, his *mother*, standing by.
Oh, it has been to me as the bitterness of
death!

Arch. You were wrong to come back.

Isabel. I know it was all wrong; but you
were *my* husband once. Oh, that the fearful
past could be blotted out; that I could wake
and find this all a hideous dream! Archibald,
let your thoughts go back to the time when
you first knew me, when I was a happy girl
here, and my dear old father's petted child;
and after, in the happy days when I was your
wife, and our little ones were about us. Do
you not wish that all this dark fact had never
been? Do you not wish it, Archibald?

Arch. Yes, Isabel, for your sake I wish it.

Isabel. I am going to William, but my other

children will be left with you. Do not, in your love for your later children — do not lose your love for *them*.

Arch. Isabel, *they* are as dear to me as *you* once were.

Isabel. As I once was, and might have been now. Archibald, I am now on the very threshold of the other world; will you not say one word of love to me before I pass it? Let what I am be blotted for the moment from your memory. Will you not bless me? Only a word of love — my heart is breaking for it!

Arch. You nearly broke mine when you left me, Isabel. (*Goes to her and takes her hand*) May He so deal with you as I fully and freely forgive you. May He bless you, and take you to His rest in heaven.

Isabel. To His rest in heaven! Archibald, you are leaving me.

Arch. (*Gets back at head of couch*) You are growing faint, Isabel. Let me call assistance. (*Takes her head in his arms*)

Isabel. No, do not stir — it is not faintness — it is — death! Oh, but it is hard to part so! Farewell, my once dear husband — until eternity!

Arch. Until eternity.

> *Soft music. She falls back in his arms and dies. He lays her gently down, and stands in attitude of deep grief, as if invoking the blessing of Heaven for her soul.*

THE END.

HENRY ARTHUR JONES
1851-1929

The Silver King
(1882)

Henry Arthur Jones wrote the play that is generally considered the finest melo-drama of the nineteenth century, *The Silver King*. The great success of this play in 1882 encouraged Jones to bring to the stage of the later 1880's plays designed to do more than entertain. He was a serious-minded young man, who had painfully edu-cated himself in the economic, social, scientific, and philosophic ideas that were stirring throughout the late-Victorian transition to the twentieth century. Aware that one of his idols, Matthew Arnold, had said, "The theatre is irresistible. Organize the theatre!" Jones dared to treat themes formerly forbidden on the stage. When he was denounced by angry audiences and respected critics alike, Jones replied by becoming not only a pioneer in writing the drama of serious ideas, but also an ardent crusader for this new drama of naturalness, truth to life, and literary worth.

Jones was born in the village of Grandborough, Buckinghamshire, in 1851, but the family soon moved to the town of Winslow. From the age of five to the age of twelve, Henry attended a small girls' school and later Grace's Commercial Academy. Then his father decided that Henry should go to work and "packed him off" (Jones's words) to the home and the draper's shop of an uncle in the town of Ramsgate. This uncle was a pious deacon of a Baptist chapel. Doris Jones, in the biography of her father, says: "Henry Arthur loathed and hated the work, and loathed and hated his uncle." After three and a half years, Henry went to a similar shop in Gravesend, run by a Mr. Bryant.

His education interrupted by these occupations, Henry determined to educate himself, as he said, "in my own way and at my own expense, by keeping up a con-stant and loving acquaintance with the English classics, and with some of the French and German masterpieces; by a close study of social and political economy; and by extensive foragings among the sciences."

At eighteen Jones found work in London, and there became interested in the drama. He took part in amateur theatricals, first appearing on a stage in 1871 as the second grave digger in *Hamlet*. He became a commercial traveller for a firm of textile manufacturers when he was twenty-one, and made his living travelling over the west of England until he had established himself as a playwright. In these years, riding the trains or sitting in hotel rooms, Jones read — or studied — in "All my spare time in the day and sometimes half the night." He read literature, including the drama; he wrestled with the revolutionary thought of the scientists, Darwin, Huxley, and Spencer. A letter states: "I am now approaching the end of Herbert Spencer's system of philosophy. It has been a hard nut to crack, but I wanted first of all to get a good groundwork of the latest science to build upon."

He brought this seriousness of thought to his playwriting. He began with melodramas because they were the current drama, but, in the effort to make his plays say something significant, he became a crusader for something more serious, and a leading playwright of the new drama. The rest of his career was that of a writer of plays so successful that in 1907 Harvard University conferred on him the degree of Honorary Master of Arts, citing him as "for twenty years a leader in the revival of the English Drama and its reunion with English literature." It was the first time a university ever conferred an honorary degree for playwriting. Jones died on January 7, 1929.

Jones's first play to be produced was *It's Only Round the Corner*, performed at Leeds in December, 1878, a melodrama on the evils of drunkenness. Other melodramas followed, with *The Silver King* of 1882 as the first big success. He became acquainted with Ibsen's *A Doll's House*, which he neither understood at the time nor liked, and adapted it as *Breaking a Butterfly* (1884), with an ending in which Nora repents her rebellion. But he did understand pettifogging merchants of small towns and Baptist deacons who were hypocrites. He broke theatrical precedent by presenting religious hypocrisy on the stage in *Saints and Sinners* (1884). The play roused a furor of criticism because it presented characters who quoted Scripture for selfish ends. Jones defended his right to portray religious hypocrisy on the stage, and in the process of this defense clearly defined his intention to write dramas that would treat the significant issues of the age with seriousness. The plays of the following years, especially *Judah* (1890) and *The Crusaders* (1893), raised provocative questions about accepted conventions. Jones experimented in the old form of blank verse tragedy with *The Tempter* (1893), telling a moral story of Chaucer's time, but the play was a failure on the stage. *The Masqueraders* of 1894, distinctly a problem play, was a success. *The Triumph of the Philistines* (1895) satirizes both British prudery and the esthetic Bohemianism of the 1890's. *Michael and His Lost Angel* (1896) presents a deeply religious man, a minister of the Anglican Church, who is led by circumstances into a passionate relationship with an adventuress; the minister, Michael, at last finds some refuge for his conscience in the Roman Catholic fold. The play, both hooted and applauded, split public opinion. Not Jones's solution, but the candor of his treatment, won the applause of Bernard Shaw. *The Liars* of 1897 was a sparkling and successful comedy of manners satirizing realities in English social life. Jones continued as a successful dramatist into the period of World War I.

Jones's crusade for a new drama had begun with "The Theatre and the Mob" in the September, 1883, issue of *The Nineteenth Century*. This essay set forth Jones's developing belief that the drama, in addition to providing relaxation and entertainment, ought to present and discuss serious ideas. His conviction was strengthened by the reception of his effort in *Saints and Sinners* to tear the veil of piety from the face of hypocrisy. Charles Spurgeon, a narrow, popular, thundering Baptist revivalist, in 1884 denounced the stage and declared that any theatregoer would be cast out of the fellowship of his tabernacle. *Saints and Sinners*, in answer to this puritanical onslaught, is largely a melodrama, with the exaggerations of this form. It convincingly portrays the alliance between the money-making spirit and pious bigotry — an alliance Matthew Arnold had pointed out in *Culture and Anarchy*. Attacks in the newspapers expressed the old opinion that religion was not a proper subject for the stage. Jones's reply, "Religion and the Stage," in the *Nineteenth Century* for January, 1885, stated just the opposite opinion and asserted it to be the proper business of drama to portray candidly "the whole of the nature, and heart, and passions, and conduct of man."

We must recall that in 1884 Jones also wrote *Breaking a Butterfly*, which takes issue with Ibsen's radicalism. Jones came to understand Ibsen better in later years, but his attitude was never that of an Ibsenite. The difference between Ibsen's surgical analysis and Jones's more conservative views may be seen in a passage from one of Jones's speeches. He said, "I have no desire to see the drama posing as the surgeon and dissector of moral and social disorders. I would rather see our national drama worthily likened to the shrewd, confidential adviser and companion, the family friend, rather than the doser and potion-monger." In short, Jones was more a conservative than a radical. He did not wish to destroy hallowed institutions, but to examine them and preserve the good in them. In a sense, he stood with the realistic novelists George Eliot and William Dean Howells, not with the naturalists Émile Zola and Frank Norris.

Jones crusaded for a frank, moral, and adult drama that would present the best thought of the age in every area of human interest. He conducted his crusade in letters, articles, and speeches, collected and published in 1895 as *The Renascence of the English Drama*. He asserted in these pieces that the drama might be what Matthew Arnold said poetry should be, a criticism of life; that it had the duty of examining and inculcating a broad, sane morality. Though intended for stage production, plays should be written as literature to be published and read as one reads novels or poems. Jones wished to abolish all censorship beyond public opinion and reform the copyright laws to give the playwright the status of a literary man.

From the later 1890's through 1912 Jones wrote and spoke for a National Theatre to be state supported on the same basis as the National Gallery of Art. It would not replace or seriously compete with commercial theatres that present entertainment, but it would provide a stage for provocative or experimental plays that would not have to rely upon the prospect of commercial success in order to be written or performed. Jones collected his arguments on this subject in *The Foundations of a National Drama*, published in 1913.

In his own playwriting Jones illustrates the transition from the melodrama to the new drama for which he crusaded. His early melodrama *The Silver King* was performed and printed as the joint work of Henry Arthur Jones and Henry Herman. Apparently there was some collaboration: the two men discussed plans for the play. Jones said that "Herman gave me the end of the second act, but he never wrote a line of it. But [Jones admitted] there were a few lines which he suggested upon my reading the different scenes to him — I think not forty lines in all; to be quite sure that I am quite well within the mark, I will allow him a hundred." After the play became famous the actor Wilson Barrett claimed some of the authorship, but apparently there was little basis for the claim. Doris Jones's biography of her father examines these claims in some detail.

The Silver King has been called the "classic melodrama of the nineteenth century," so well characterized and constructed that its improbabilities and coincidences are overlooked. It ran for two hundred and eighty-nine nights on its first production; it had a long run in New York. It has been revived several times in the twentieth century and has twice been adapted for moving pictures.

The essential features of the melodrama are evident: the characters divide into heroes, villains, and a pathetic heroine with her children; the chief villain, a thief and murderer, is also Nellie's landlord who threatens her with eviction; the incidents are sensational; asides and soliloquies explain motives and intentions to the audience; and virtue is triumphant with happiness ever after. The printed play calls for music on a few occasions; notations for the acting version indicate more music in performance. The structure follows the theory of the well-made play in a nearly perfect balance and seesaw of opposing forces.

The advance of *The Silver King* over plays like *After Dark*, on the one hand, and *East Lynne*, on the other, is in naturalness. Though the play has sensation scenes, it does not rely upon stage machinery for storms, fires, and explosions. Though it exhibits pathos and remorse, these have a rational basis in the action and are relatively restrained. Matthew Arnold's estimate, published in the *Pall Mall Gazette*, seems a just one. He said: "The critics are right, therefore, in thinking that in this work they have something new and highly praiseworthy. . . . They have a sensational drama in which the diction and sentiments do not overstep the modesty of nature. In general, in drama of this kind, the diction and sentiments, like the incidents, are extravagant, impossible, transpontine; here they are not." Though the characters are the old stock types, they talk like people. Jones's effort to deepen the psychology of his characters is illustrated in a letter to Wilson Barrett, who acted the role of Denver. At the end of Act I, where Denver babbles "I've done it! I've done it!" Barrett spoke the lines with the usual melodramatic emphasis. Jones wrote, "Permit me to explain to you that these words are the involuntary jabbering protest of a stupefied half drunken man, self-startled at the commission of a terrible crime, repugnant to his whole nature. They should be spoken in a horrified involuntary whisper." Even the startling line "Oh God! put back Thy universe and give me yesterday" has been praised as natural. William Archer said, "It is not what you would call a realistic remark; but it is a natural thought vigorously expressed." And the comedy of melodrama is toned down from slapstick to such character play as Tabby's proposal to Jaikes.

The character of Denver is most adroitly developed as both hero and detective. As hero he is Jones's modernization of the old remorseful Gothic hero-villain. The cause of his remorse is more substantial than dark hints of past crimes: Denver discovers the body of the man he thinks he killed. The drama is heightened by irony in the audience's knowledge that he is not guilty. As detective he is a Hawkshaw of disguises and eavesdropping, rather than a Sherlock Holmes. In yet other ways the role of Denver is a gift and a challenge for a versatile actor: he appears in five personalities — a young man drunk, a young man sobered and frightened, a sailor, a man prematurely aged, and deaf Dicky.

The Silver King represents the well-made melodrama wrought to near perfection. The formula could not promise anything more until the development of moving pictures. Jones's advance from this point to the new drama of serious social problems was rapid.

THE SILVER KING

A Drama In Five Acts

by

HENRY ARTHUR JONES and HENRY HERMAN

First performed at the Princess's Theatre, November 16, 1882

Cast of Characters

WILFRED DENVER
NELLIE DENVER, *his wife*
CISSY AND NED, *their children*
DANIEL JAIKES, *their servant*
FRANK SELWYN, *private secretary
to Mr. John Franklin*
GEOFFREY WARE, *an engineer*
SAMUEL BAXTER, *a detective*
CAPT. HERBERT SKINNER, *known
as "The Spider"*
HENRY CORKETT, *Geoffrey Ware's
clerk*
ELIAH COOMBE, *a marine store
dealer*
CRIPPS, *a locksmith*
MR. PARKYN, *parish clerk of
Gaddesden*

MESSRS. BINKS AND BROWNSON,
tradesmen
BILCHER AND TEDDY, *betting men*
TUBBS, *landlord of the "Wheat-
sheaf"*
GAFFER POTTLE
LEAKER, *a porter*
OLIVE SKINNER, *Capt. Skinner's
wife*
TABITHA DURDEN
SUSY, *waitress at the "Chequers"*
MRS. GAMMAGE
A CABMAN, A PORTER, SERVANTS,
RAILWAY OFFICIALS, CLERKS,
CHILDREN, PASSENGERS, DETEC-
TIVES

ACT I.

Scene 1.

*The skittle alley at "The Wheatsheaf," Clerken-
well. Discover Tubbs, Teddy, Bilcher, and
drinkers. Bilcher is in the midst of an excited
narrative, the others are grouped round him
at bar.*

Bil. And they kept like that, neck and
neck the three of 'em till just as they were
turning the corner drawing in home, and
then Marcher put on a bit of a spurt, and by
Jove, Blue Ribbon shot ahead like a flash of
greased lightning and won by a short head.
Never saw such a pretty finish in my life!

Enter Ware.

Ware. (*To Bilcher*) Well, what about
Denver?

Bil. (*To Ware*) Doubled up this time and
no mistake. Went a smasher on Patacake and
lost everything — owes me a hundred and
fifty pounds besides.

Ware. Ah! (*Aside*) It has come at last then.
(*To Bilcher*) You're sure you've cleaned him
out?

Bil. Oh yes, me and Braggins between us.
Much obliged to you for introducing him to
us.

Ware. How did he take it?

Bil. Oh, tried to laugh and joke it off. He's
as drunk as a fiddler; he was pretty mellow
when we started this morning, and we've
kept him well doctored up all day.

Ware. That's right. Keep him at it. Where is he?

Bil. We left him drinking at the bar at Waterloo Station; but he's promised to turn up here.

Ware. I'll run in and have a look at him by and by. (*Going, aside*) Ruined! Now, Nellie Hathaway, I think I'll show you that you made a slight mistake when you threw me over and married Wilfred Denver.

Exit Ware.

Tubbs. So poor young Denver came a cropper to-day?

Bil. Yes.

Tubbs. Poor fellow! I'm sorry for him. He's a downright good-hearted, jolly young fellow, Mr. Denver is.

Teddy. So he is, Tubbs, when he's sober.

Bil. And that ain't been the last six months — Tubbs takes care of that.

Enter Jaikes as if looking round for somebody.

Tubbs. (*In low voice to drinkers at bar*) Look! There's Mr. Denver's old servant — he's come to look after his master.

Jaikes. What cheer, Mr. Tubbs?

Tubbs. You must give him a little extry time to-night. There's a good many public houses between Epsom and here.

Jaikes. Ah, but he'll be home early to-night; he promised the missis he would; and I want to ketch him and pop him off to bed quiet afore she sets eyes on him, d'ye see?

Tubbs. Ah, I shouldn't wonder if he's a bit fresh, eh?

Jaikes. Anybody might happen to get a bit fresh on Derby Day, you know.

Tubbs. He's been going it a pretty pace lately, ain't he?

Jaikes. Well, he's a bit wild, but there ain't no harm in him. Bless you, it's the blood; he's got too much nature in him, that's where it is. His father was just like him when he was a young man. Larking, hunting, drinking, fighting, steeple-chasing — any mortal spree under the sun, out all night, and as fresh as a daisy in the morning! And his grandfather, old Squire Denver, just such another. There was a man for you if you like. The last ten years of his life he never went to bed sober one night. Yes, he did one night, when the groom locked him in the stable by mistake, and then he was ill for months afterwards.

Teddy. Oh, he could take his lotion pretty reg'lar, eh?

Jaikes. I believe you. Well, when I was a dozen years younger, I could take my whack, and a tidy whack it was too, but, bless you, I

wasn't in it with old Squire Denver, and Master Will's a chip of the old block. He'll make a man yet.

Bil. He'll make a madman if he doesn't leave off drinking.

Jaikes. You let him be! He's all right — Master Will's all right!

Denver rolls in gate.

Den. (*Very drunk*) Yes, I'm all right — I'm all right! I'm 's drunk as a fool, and I've lost every cursed ha'penny I've got in the world. I'm all right!

Tubbs. What, backed the wrong horse, Mr. Denver?

Den. No, Tubbs, no, I backed the right horse, and then the wrong horse went and won.

Teddy. That's a pity!

Den. Not a bit of it. I've lost, you've won — if there were no fools like me in the world, what would become of the poor rogues?

Bil. Well, you seem pretty merry over it.

Den. Yes, Bilcher. I've lost my money to-day and to-morrow I shall lose your acquaintance. I'm quite satisfied with the bargain.

Jaikes. What? Bad luck again, Master Will?

Den. The devil's own luck, Jaikes. I put everything on Patacake, and I'm ruined, Jaikes.

Jaikes. No, Master Will, don't say that!

Den. Well, say stumped, cleaned out, licked into a cocked hat. Bilcher, I owe you a hundred and fifty pounds.

Bil. Yes, and I should like to know how I'm to be paid.

Den. So should I, Bilcher!

Bil. Why didn't you take my advice? I told you that blackguard Braggins was doing you.

Den. Yes, and Braggins told me the same about you. Come, Bilcher, don't be greedy — you've had a good picking out of me, let the other blackguards have their turn.

Bil. I wash my hands of you.

Den. Very well, Bilcher, they won't be any the worse for a good wash.

Jaikes. Come Master Will, you'd better come home.

Den. Home! What should I go home for? To show my poor wife what a drunken brute she's got for a husband? To show my innocent children what an object they've got for a father? No, I won't go home, I've got no home. I've drunk it up.

Jaikes. For mercy's sake, Master Will, don't talk like that!

Den. (*Furiously*) Get home with you!

Jaikes. Yes I'll go home!

Den. (*Drops his voice*) Jaikes, don't let her come here and find me like this — tell her I haven't come back — tell her I'm not to be found — tell her any lie that comes handiest, but don't let her see me. Be off now, be off!

Jaikes. (*Going*) Poor Master Will! Ruined! What'll become of poor Missus and the dear little 'uns?　　　　　　　　　　　*Exit.*

Baxter has entered.

Den. (*Takes out revolver*) There's always one way out of it. If it wasn't such a coward's trick I'd do it.

Bax. (*In a low voice to Denver*) If you don't know what to do with that, I'll take care of it for you.

Den. (*Putting revolver in pocket again*) Thank you, I do know what to do with it, much obliged for your advice. (*Aside*) I may want it, to-night.

Baxter looks after him, shrugs his shoulders, goes to table and picks up newspaper. Coombe enters directly after Baxter. Enter Henry Corkett, a young cockney clerk, flushed, swaggering, cigar in mouth, hat on one side.

Cork. (*With patronising wave of hand to Tubbs*) Ha, Tubbs, how do?

Tubbs. How do, 'Arry?

Cork. 'Enery Corkett, Esquire, from you, Tubbs, if you please. What do you think of that, Tubbs, eh? (*Flourishing a roll of bank notes*) Backed Blue Ribbon for a win and a place, and landed five hundred pounds. Look there! (*Flourishing notes*)

Den. Biggest fools, best luck!

Cork. (*Turning round angrily*) What did you say?

Den. I said I wished I'd got no brains, because then I could make money at horse racing.

Cork. Oh, it's you, is it, Mr. Denver? I've seen you at my guv'nor's place in Hatton Garden. You know me. My name's Corkett — I'm Mr. Ware's clerk.

Coombe. (*Aside*) Mr. Ware's clerk!

Den. (*After staring at him a moment*) No, beg pardon, but I don't know you.

Bax. (*Aside, seeing Coombe*) Mr. Eliah Coombe! Any little game on to-night, I wonder? A glass of bitter.

Cork. Bitter be blowed! Have some champagne. Tubbs, it's my shout. Champagne for everybody.

Coombe. (*Aside, watching Corkett*) Mr. Ware's clerk. If I could get hold of him it would make our little job easy to-night. (*Rises and goes up to skittle alley with drink*)

Cork. Come, gentlemen all, drink my health!

Den. Certainly! (*Raising his glass*) Here's to the health of the beggars that win — put them on horseback and let them ride to the devil!

Tubbs. (*To Corkett*) Don't take any notice of him. He's been hard hit at the Derby to-day.

Cork. Look here, gentlemen, I'm fly! Hang the expense!

Bax. You young ass, put those notes in your pocket and go home to bed.

Cork. (*Turns sharply around*) Shan't! Who are you? Can you show as much money as that? No! Then you shut up and take a back seat. I've won my money fair and honest and I shall spend it how I like. Hang it, I shall light my pipe with it if I like. Give me a cigar, Tubbs. (*Tubbs gives him cigar. Corkett strikes match. To Baxter*) There! That's a five pound note. (*Lights the note with match and then lights cigar with note*) There, that'll show you what I'm made of? I'm a gentleman, I am. Money ain't no object to me.

Den. (*Aside*) That fool with five hundred pounds, and to-morrow my wife and children will be starving. (*To Corkett*) Look here, you! You've got more money than you know what to do with, I'll have you at any game you like — for any stake.

Cork. I don't want your money.

Den. But I want yours! If you've got the pluck of a rabbit, stake it, win or lose.

Cork. Very well, what shall it be?

Den. Cards — Billiards, I don't care.

Cork. Fifty up then — I'm ready!

Den. Come on, then. Hang it all, my luck must change! It shall change! I will win or the devil's in it!　　　　　　　　　　　*Exit.*

Cork. Come on, gentlemen, and see the fun!

Exit, followed by several of the drinkers, leaving only one or two at bar.

Coombe. (*Aside*) The Spider at last!

Enter Skinner. Very well dressed. Light summer overcoat and faultless evening dress.

Bax. (*Aside*) The Spider and Coombe. There's some big game on to-night.

Skin. (*Glancing round*) Baxter the detective! The deuce! (*Goes to him*) Anything fresh in the paper?

Bax. Blue Ribbon pulled it off to-day.

Skin. Ah, I don't bet.

Bax. They've caught the man who committed the jewel robbery at Lady Fairford's. (*Giving him paper and indicating paragraph*)

It may interest you, it seems he was quite a swell, as well dressed as you are!

Skin. Was he? The cheek of these fellows!

Bax. You're right — they are cheeky! (*Looks straight at Skinner for some moments. Skinner's face remains perfectly impassive. Aside*) A cucumber isn't in it with him.

Coombe. (*To Skinner*) My dear boy, I'm so glad you've come.

Skin. (*In a low voice without taking his eyes off the paper*) If you accost me again in a public place, I'll wring your neck for you, you old weasel!

Coombe. My dear boy, business is business, and it's a big fortune for us all — a sackful of diamonds in Hatton Garden — no risk — no danger, all as safe and easy as saying your prayers.

Skin. How do we get in?

Coombe. Cut through the wall of the next house. There's a young chap playing billiards inside —

Skin. Will you hold your infernal cackle? Don't you see that man watching us? It's Baxter the detective.

Coombe. (*Alarmed*) Baxter the detective?

Skin. Yes, you fool, don't look at him. He means to follow me up. I'll throw him off the scent directly.

Re-enter Corkett, followed by drinkers.

Cork. (*Elated*) Landed him proper, didn't I? Ha, Tubbs, pulled it off again, my boy!

Tubbs. What — have you won, 'Arry?

Cork. Rather! Why, he wasn't in it.

Coombe. (*Aside to Spider*) See that young sprig there — he sleeps in the house we want to get into — if we could get hold of him —

Skin. Will you shut up?

Cork. Now, gentlemen, let's be merry! Drink up! Look here, I've made my money like a gentleman and I'll spend it like a gentleman.

Skin. Just relieve him of those notes while I draw off Baxter's attention. You'll be able to get hold of him when he's cleaned out.

Coombe. You'll be there as soon as it's dusk — a hundred and fourteen, Hatton Garden.

Skin. Where's the Ancient Briton?

Coombe. He'll be on the spot.

Skin. Right! So you want to have a finger in our pie, do you, Sam Baxter? (*Seeing that Baxter is cautiously following him*) That's right! Follow me up! I'll lead you a pretty dance to-night. (*Shouts off*) Hi! Boy! Get me a hansom!

Exeunt Skinner and Baxter. Coombe has in the meantime picked Corkett's pocket.

Cork. Now, gentlemen, I'm blowed if I don't stand you another bottle of champagne. I've got money enough — (*Stops short suddenly*) Here, somebody's stole my money.

Tubbs. What? Nonsense! 'Enery, there ain't no thieves here. Feel again.

Cork. (*Feeling desperately in his pockets*) Yes, it's gone. It's gone. My money — I'm robbed, I'm ruined! I'm ruined! Give me my money, do you hear — give me my money or I'll — (*Seizes Bilcher, who happens to stand next to him, by the throat*)

Bil. (*Shaking him off roughly*) You hold off, youngster, or I'll smash you. I haven't got your money.

Cork. Somebody's got it! Somebody must have it!

Coombe. Come, gentlemen, no larks with the poor young fellow. If you've got his money give it back to him!

Cork. (*Crying piteously*) I'm ruined, you know, I'm ruined!

Coombe. (*Suddenly*) Why, of course, that man must have it.

Cork. Which? (*Runs to Coombe*)

Coombe. Why, the man with the billy-cock hat and check trousers! (*Describing Baxter*) I saw him sneaking round your elbow — he's got it.

Cork. Which way did he go?

Coombe. This way — come on! I'll help you catch him — I shall know the rascal again when I see him — come on!

Cork. Come on, gentlemen, and help me find him. I'm ruined. I'm ruined.

Crying piteously. Exit Coombe followed by Corkett.

Enter Denver.

Den. There's another man ruined. Cheer up! We'll go to the dogs together. Tubbs, give me some brandy.

Tubbs. You've had enough, Mr. Denver.

Den. I'm the best judge of that — it's a free country — anybody can drink himself to death that likes — I will have it, I will.

Enter Geoffrey Ware.

Ware. (*Watching Denver*) Ah, there you are, my fine fellow. I think my plan is working pretty well. I think Nelly had better have married me after all. Stick to it, I'll bring you to the gutter, I'll see you in the workhouse yet before I've done with you. (*Comes up to Denver, slaps him on the back cordially*) Well, Will, how are you?

Den. I'm three parts drunk and the rest mad, so keep out of my way, Geoffrey Ware.

Ware. Nonsense, Will, I never saw you

looking so bright and sober. I'm very glad for Nelly's sake.

Den. (*Fiercely rising*) Whose sake?

Ware. Mrs. Denver — excuse the slip of the tongue. She was once engaged to me, you know.

Den. She knew better than to marry you, didn't she?

Ware. It seems she did, for she married you.

Den. Yes, and she'll stick to me through thick and thin. Why, you sneaking cur, do you think my wife can't see through you? Do you think I don't know why you're always creeping and skulking about my house under pretence of being my friend? Now listen to me, I'm going to the dogs — I'm drinking myself to death as fast as I can. I shall be dead in no time, but she won't marry you, Geoffrey Ware. She'll marry a sweep sooner — you know, a sweep of the other sort I mean. Now you've got it straight, go and chew the cud of that, and then buy a rope and hang youself.

Ware. Come, Will, I don't bear you any grudge for taking away my sweetheart, I'm only too glad to see what a nice, kind, sober husband she's got.

Den. I've warned you once. Take a fool's advice, and keep out of my way. The devil's in me to-night, and he'll break out directly.

Ware. Ah, well, take care of yourself, dear boy, for my sake. Give my kindest regards to Nelly.

Denver rising, dashes the contents of his glass in Ware's face. Tubbs and Bilcher come down and seize Denver. Teddy gets Ware away.

Den. (*Held by Tubbs and Bilcher*) Take that man away! Take him away before I kill him.

Ware. Ta, ta, Will, don't forget my message to your better half.   *Exit.*

Tubbs. Now, Mr. Denver, you'd better go home, you know.

Den. No, no, let me stay here, Tubbs! Oh, my head! (*Let's his head fall on table*)

Tubbs. Come away, Mr. Bilcher, perhaps he'll drop off to sleep and then we can carry him home.

Den. Yes, carry me home, Tubbs, and sing "Here the conquering hero comes!" and then bury me and play the Dead March in Saul.

Tubbs has beckoned all off. Denver is alone. Nelly enters, comes down behind him very timidly; he starts, turns around and sees her.

Den. Nelly, you here! You in this place?

Nelly. Yes, isn't a wife's place by her husband's side?

Den. Not when he's such a husband as I am. You go home, my darling; you go home, I'll come by and by.

Nelly. No, my poor Will, come now!

Den. I've ruined you, Nell, I've lost every sixpence I've got in the world. To-morrow you and the chicks will be starving. Ah, Nell, my bonnie, bonnie girl, look at me — what made you marry me, a drunken brute like me?

Nelly. Because I loved you — I love you still. Never mind the past, dear, come home and make a fresh start to-morrow.

Den. I can't. I must go on. I can't stop. I'm going down, down as fast as I can go — I don't know where!

Nelly. (*Throwing her arms round him*) Oh, don't say that, dear. You must stop yourself for my sake — for your Nell's sake.

Den. (*Stroking her face*) The sweetest and truest wife a man ever had, and married to such a wretch as I am. (*Changing his tone*) Don't you come here! You only make me think what a brute I've been to you.

Nelly. Oh, Will, I have just put our little Cissy and Ned to bed and they have said "God bless dear father!"

Geoffrey Ware enters behind unperceived.

Den. (*Starting up maddened*) Ah! Don't teach them that! Don't teach them to pray for me. Teach them to curse and hate me. Go away, Nell — don't you see the people all staring at us? Go home, my girl! I'll come home when I'm sober. Go home, my girl, go home! (*Rushes to bar*) Tubbs, give me some brandy, don't keep me waiting! (*Nelly goes a step after him and then sinks into chair crying*)

Ware. (*To her in low voice*) Have you suffered enough?

Nelly. (*Hiding her tears*) Geoffrey Ware! (*Aside*) That he should see me here!

Ware. Has he dragged you deep enough into the mire or will you go deeper still, to rags, to the gutter, to starvation? Nelly, you once promised to be my wife.

Nelly. Yes, and I repented even before I promised. I never loved you and you know it. You worried me into a consent, and when I found out my mistake, I told you of it and married a better man!

Den. (*Whose back is towards them*) That hound back again, and talking to my wife.

Ware. Ah, there stands the better man! Look at him. A pattern husband — a pattern father, prosperous, happy, respectable, sober!

Nelly. Oh, this is manly of you. What harm have I ever done to you?

Ware. You married him. I swore that day

I'd ruin him, and I kept my word. Good evening, Mrs. Denver.

Den. (*Turning*) Stop, you cur, and answer to me.

Ware. (*Coolly*) My dear fellow, you're drunk, you know.

Exit laughing at Denver. Denver rushes at him. Nelly stops him.

Nelly. Ah, Will, he's not worth it.

Tubbs and Others enter from house. Jaikes enters from gate.

Den. Let me get at him! Let me go!

Jaikes. Master Will! Master Will!

Nelly. No, no! Will, he's not worth it.

Jaikes. What are you going to do, Master Will?

Den. I'm going to kill that man! I'll shoot him like a dog!

Breaks from them and rushes off.

Nelly. (*Calling after him*) Will! Will! Stop! Ah, will nobody stop him?

Jaikes and Nelly go off.

Scene 2.

A street in Clerkenwell. Enter Coombe and Corkett.

Coombe. You say you don't know the numbers of the notes?

Cork. No, I only took 'em off the bookmaker this afternoon and I never took the numbers.

Coombe. (*Aside*) That's lucky! (*Aloud*) Well, you see the man got off with them.

Cork. Yes, and I say, you won't split on me, will yer? I'd borrowed that money to put it on Blue Ribbon.

Coombe. Borrowed the money?

Cork. Yes, eighty pounds off my guv'nor, Mr. Ware.

Coombe. Oh, I see, without his knowing, that's awkward — that's very awkward.

Cork. I'd got the straight tip — I knew Blue Ribbon was a moral, and I meant to put the money back, honor bright I did.

Coombe. Of course you did. You was actuated by very honorable intentions.

Cork. And now I shall be found out to-morrow and have to go to quod.

Coombe. Ah, that's a pity, and the worst of it is the judges are so unfeeling to parties as borrow their guv'nor's money without mentioning it to their guv'nors.

Cork. Are they?

Coombe. Oh, brutal, especially to young men as borrow their guv'nor's money to put it on horses.

Cork. You don't say so. I say — how long do you think I shall get?

Coombe. Well, if you happen to get a nice, kind, feeling judge with his stomick in good working order, you may get off with say — seven years.

Cork. Seven years?

Coombe. Yes, but don't reckon on that. There was a young fellow tried at the Old Bailey a week or two since, for borrowing money as you've done, a handsome, pleasant young man he seemed to be, just like you.

Cork. Yes, and what did he get?

Coombe. Fourteen years.

Cork. (*Collapses*) Fourteen years!

Coombe. Yes, I felt quite sorry for him.

Cork. I say, what's it like in —

Coombe. Speaking from hearsay, it ain't likely to suit a young man of your constitution. It'll bottle you up in less than three months.

Cork. Think so?

Coombe. Sure of it. Skilly won't relish much after champagne, will it? And as for the treadmill, though it's a prime *exercise*, as a *game* it ain't to be compared to billiards.

Cork. What can I do?

Coombe. Well, I've took a bit of a fancy to you, and I'll tell you what I'll do. I'll lend you the eighty pounds.

Cork. (*Seizing his hand eagerly*) You will? You're a brick!

Coombe. Yes, providing you'll oblige me in a little matter.

Cork. I'll do anything for you. You're a jolly kind old man and no mistake.

Coombe. You live at a hundred and fourteen Hatton Garden, don't you?

Cork. Yes.

Coombe. Who sleeps in the house beside you?

Cork. Only my guv'nor and the old porter.

Coombe. Your guv'nor spends his evenings out, don't he?

Cork. Comes in about twelve as a rule.

Coombe. Well, a friend of mine wants to spend half an hour in your guv'nor's sitting-room to-night — he's a photographer and he's taking views of London. Could you let us into the house and keep the old porter out of the way?

Cork. I say, what's up?

Coombe. Never mind, will you help us or will you go to quod to-morrow?

Cork. I'll help you.

Coombe. There's a sensible young man.

Enter Jaikes excited.

Jaikes. (*Crossing*) I've lost my way in these courts and alleys and goodness knows what mischief's happening. (*Seeing Corkett*) Ah, you're Mr. Ware's clerk, aren't you?

Cork. Yes. Why, it's Mr. Denver's servant, ain't it?

Jaikes. Yes, come on with me to Mr. Ware's in Hatton Garden. Come on quick.

Coombe. (*Aside*) Hillo, I must stop this.

Cork. (*Exchanging a glance with Coombe*) What's the matter?

Jaikes. Murder'll be the matter if we don't stop it. My poor master's got the drink inside of him. He's beside himself, he's threatened to kill Mr. Ware. Come and help me get him away.

Coombe. I beg your pardon, are you looking for the young gentleman as was drinking in the "Wheatsheaf" just now?

Jaikes. Yes, have you seen anything of him?

Coombe. Yes, he came out of that public house not two minutes ago, and he took a cab and told the driver to go to Charing Cross Station, didn't he? (*To Corkett*)

Cork. Yes, 'ansom.

Jaikes. Are you sure it was my master?

Coombe. Oh, quite sure. (*To Corkett*) You're sure it was Mr. Denver, ain't you?

Cork. Oh yes, I'll take my oath of it.

Coombe. It's very lucky you met us. You'll find your master at Charing Cross Railway Station. Make haste.

Jaikes. Thank you, mate, thank you, I'll go there straight!   *Exit.*

Coombe. Yes, do, you old fool, and you won't find him. We shall have to look out and keep that tipsy fellow out of our way. (*To Corkett*) Now, my dear boy, you stroll on just in front of me. Don't get out of my sight — that's it!

Cork. No, and if I once get out of this mess I'll never get into another.   *Exit.*

Coombe. That's done neat and clean. Now if the Ancient Briton can't work in off the leads, this young gentleman will open the front door for us, and all we've got to do is to walk upstairs.   *Exit.*

Scene 3.

Geoffrey Ware's sitting room in Hatton Garden. Window right. Table with cloth centre, sideboard against right wall. Door at back. Discover Ware standing by table, with hat on, buttoning his gloves; also Leaker, an old porter, at door.

Ware. Leaker, I'm going out, leave the door on the latch.

Leaker. Yes, sir. Shall I wait up for you, sir?

Ware. No, I don't know what time I shall be back. I may come in in half an hour, or I may not come in at all. You can go to bed when you like. (*Going out at door*) Good night.

Leaker. Good night, sir.

> *Exit Ware at back. Leaker takes out light and exit after him.*

A pause. Stage dark. Cripps is seen at window, he lifts window noiselessly and enters very softly with dark lantern in his hand.

Cripps. Coast clear, that's all right! (*Moves away sideboard from wall*) This must be the spot. (*Listens — a short, faint, peculiar whistle is heard off. Cripps returns it and goes on lifting sideboard*)

> *Enter Skinner at back.*

Skin. All clear?

Cripps. Yes, Captain!

Skin. Light! (*Cripps turns lantern on Skinner, helps him off with coat, discovers faultless evening dress-suit. Skinner turns up his sleeves*) Give me my tools. You'll find them in that pocket. (*Cripps takes case out of pocket, hands it to Skinner, then puts coat on front of table. Skinner opens case and looks at tools*)

Cripps. Beauties, ain't they? I was a week making them jemmies.

Skin. Well, it was time well spent. What the plague did you want me for to-night? I was just starting for Lady Blanche Wynter's dinner party.

Cripps. (*Measuring along wall*) What the blazes has that got to do with me? If you're above your business, say so, and I'll crack the crib myself.

Skin. (*Takes from neat mahogany case a tool and lays it on table*) Give me the plan! (*Cripps gives him the plan — he studies it*)

Cripps. The safe's just the other side of this wall here. Thinks I when I was a-fixing up that there safe, "This'll be a splendid plant for us;" and the gents next door was extry particular about having it made strong. "Cause," says they, "there'll often be fifty pounds worth of diamonds in that there safe."

Skin. (*Who has been studying plan and not listening to Cripps*) Shut up! Not so much cackle. Now, Cripps, look alive, because I must be at Lady Blanche's dance at twelve.

Cripps. Blow Lady Blanche!

> *Skinner takes up instrument, comes to wall, is about to pierce it when noise of knocking and ringing is heard down stairs.*

Skin. What's that row?

> *Enter Coombe in great trouble.*

Coombe. My dear boy, here's that tipsy fellow down at the door, playing deuce and tommy, swears he'll pull the house down if we don't let him come up. (*Knocking and ringing continues*)

Skin. What's he want?

Coombe. Mr. Ware. He won't take our word he's out. What can we do?

Skin. Send him up here.

Coombe. What, here?

Skin. Yes, tell him Mr. Ware's at home and send him up. (*Exit Coombe*) Where's my chloroform pad? Oh, here it is. (*Pours chloroform on pad*) I'll soon quiet him. Cripps, out with that light. Stand there! (*Stage dark. They stand behind door*)

Coombe. (*Outside*) There he is — you'll find Mr. Ware in that room.

Enter Denver with revolver, followed by Coombe.

Den. Now, you hound, come out and settle accounts with me. Come out and show your face. Where are you?

    Skinner leaps out on him, and puts chloroform on pad over Denver's nose. Cripps helps him. Denver struggles but is overpowered; they lay him on rug by fireplace.

Skin. That revolver! Take it away from him, put it on the table. (*Cripps takes revolver*) Lie there, you brute! You won't trouble us any more. (*Cripps is examining revolver as Skinner crosses*) Put that revolver down, Cripps, anywhere on the table. Look alive! Show me a light. (*Getting to wall again*)

    Enter Corkett suddenly.

Cork. (*In a frightened whisper*) Here, where are you? I say, clear out of this all of you. Here's my guv'nor coming back — he's left something. Oh, crimes, here he is.

Enter Ware. He stands a moment in doorway — strikes match. Corkett tries to dodge by him.

Ware. (*Sees him*) Hillo? What are you doing here? Who are these men? What business have you here?

Skin. We are friends of your clerk — we met him at the Derby, and he insisted on our coming here to spend the evening with him, and so naturally as a matter of course — (*Coolly putting tools in box*) — excuse me, I have an appointment!

Ware. Wait a bit, I want this cleared up! (*Sees tools on table*) Ah! These are burglars' tools! A revolver! Help! Murder! Thieves!

Skin. (*Snatching up revolver and shooting Ware*) Take that, you fool, since you won't be quiet! (*Ware falls in front of table — a pause*)

Coombe. My dear boy, this is terrible.

Cork. He's killed him, he's killed him!

Skin. Cripps, back with the case sharp! Everybody off. (*They put back bookcase quickly*)

Cork. We shall all swing for this. (*Shows great fright*)

Skin. You will, if you don't keep your mouth shut.

Cripps. We must risk the leads — come on — we mustn't be seen coming out of the door. (*Gets out at window*)

Skin. (*Putting on coat and coolly pocketing tools*) Look alive, Coombe! Shake up that idiot! (*Indicating Corkett who is paralyzed with fright*)

Coombe. (*Shaking Corkett*) Come on, or else they'll collar you for this. (*Hurries him out of window and gets out himself*)

Skin. (*Looking at Ware*) I've gone a step too far this time. The fool! Why wouldn't he let me pass! (*Gets out of window and closes it down*)

Stage dark. A pause. Enter Leaker with candle, rubbing his eyes and yawning as if just wakened from sleep.

Leaker. (*Yawning*) I thought I heard a noise like a shot. I must have been dreaming. I wonder how long I've been asleep? Mr. Ware not come yet. (*Going a step or two and stumbling over Denver*) Hillo! Who's this? (*Stoops and looks down*) Why, it's Mr. Denver! How did he get in here? (*Kneels down and shouts at and shakes Denver*) Mr. Denver! Wake up, wake up! (*Denver mutters something and stirs*) Don't lay there, sir. Let me assist you into this chair. (*Shakes him*) Drunk again. D'ye hear, Mr. Denver, wake up! (*Shakes him and gets him into chair*)

Den. (*Rousing himself and opening his eyes*) Al'right! Don't be in a hurry. Where am I?

Leaker. You're in Mr. Ware's room at Hatton Garden, sir.

Den. (*In chair*) Of course I am. (*Passing his hand over his head, drops back into chair*)

Leaker. Shall I light you downstairs?

Den. No, I'll go soon. Who is it — Leaker?

Leaker. Yes, it's Leaker.

Den. You know me, Leaker?

Leaker. Yes, I know you, sir. (*Aside*) I'd better let him stay, he won't do any harm. (*To Denver*) I'll leave you the candle, sir, and you can go home when you've quite woke up. Well, good-night, sir, I'm going to bed. Mind you latch the street door when you go out. Good-night, sir.

Den. Latch street door — all right, Leaker.

(*Exit Leaker. Sits up and stares round him, tries to collect himself*) What's up? What's the matter? (*Shakes himself*) What am I doing here? This won't do! Get home! Get home, you drunken scoundrel! Aren't you ashamed of yourself, Will Denver? Keeping your poor wife sitting up half the night for you — get home, d'ye hear, get home. (*Raises himself with difficulty and stares round and staggers*) What's the matter with my head? I can't recollect! What place is this? (*With a sudden flash of recollection*) Ah! Geoffrey Ware's room, I remember — yes, yes, I said I'd kill him and — Oh, my head, I'd better get home. Where's my hat? (*Gets up, takes candle, staggers, steadies himself, comes round table, sees Ware*) What's that? It's Geoffrey Ware! What's he doing here? Get up, will you? (*Kneels down*) Ah, what's this? Blood! He's shot! My God, I've murdered him. No! No! Let me think. What happened? Ah yes, I remember now — I came in at that door, he sprang at me and then we struggled. (*Looking at revolver*) My revolver. — One barrel fired — I've murdered him. No, he's not dead. Geoffrey Ware! Is he dead? (*Eagerly feeling Ware's pulse*) No, it doesn't beat. (*Tears down Ware's waistcoat and shirt, puts his ear over Ware's heart*) No, no, quite still, quite still. He's dead! Dead! Dead! Oh, I've killed him — I've killed him. (*Rising frantically, takes up revolver and puts it in his pocket*) What can I do? (*With a great cry*) Don't stare at me like that! (*Snatching off table cover and throwing it over body, his eyes fixed and staring at it unable to take off his glance*) Close those eyes, Geoffrey — close them. Ah, yes, I murdered him — I've done it — I've done it — murdered him! (*Exit, his lips mechanically jabbering*) I've done it! I've done it! I've done it! I've done it! I've done it!　　　　　　*Exit.*

End of the First Act.

ACT II.

Scene 1.

A night passes between Acts One and Two. Interior of Denver's house. Window at back. Doors right and left. Small table centre of stage. Chairs right and left. The clock strikes six. Nelly discovered at window looking anxiously off.

Nelly. Six o'clock! Will he never come?

Enter Jaikes.

Well, Jaikes?

Jaikes. I can't see nothing of him, missus!

Nelly. You don't think he has carried out his threat?

Jaikes. Not he, missus, don't you fear. Mr. Will won't do no harm. Now don't you sit up any longer, missus.

Nelly. I'm used to it, Jaikes, I'm used to it.

Jaikes. This sitting up o' nights is making you quite pale and thin, and such bonny rosy cheeks as you used to have in the old days.

Nelly. Ah, the old days — the dear old Grange. The happy, happy times that will never come again.

Jaikes. Yes, it will, missus. I don't know how, but some'ut inside me prophesies as it will.

Nelly. Bless you, Jaikes, I don't know how I shall bear my troubles when you are gone.

Jaikes. When I'm what, missus?

Nelly. Gone — yes, we're ruined; we can't pay you the wages we owe you.

Jaikes. There'll be time enough for that when I asks you.

Nelly. Ah, but we can't afford to keep a servant any longer — you have clung to us all through, my old friend, but we shall have to part from you now.

Jaikes. Will you, though? You won't find me so easy to get rid of.

Nelly. Ah, Jaikes, we're a sinking ship, you'd better leave us before we go down.

Jaikes. No, missus, my voyage is pretty well over, and if you go down, I'll go down with you. I stuck to you in your prosperity — I took your wages when your purse was full, and your hand was free, and I ain't going to leave you now adversity's come and the cupboard's empty. No! No!

Nelly. Dear kind Jaikes, but you know you could go back to the Grange; they want a butler, and would be glad to have you.

Jaikes. I daresay they would, but they won't get me — I know when I'm well off.

Nelly. But I am forgetting, Jaikes, you must be very tired. Go and get some sleep.

Jaikes. I'd rather wait with you, missus.

Nelly. I'll call you, Jaikes, if I want any help. Go, Jaikes, go just to please me.

Jaikes. Very well, missus, if you wish it.

Nelly, There's a good Jaikes. Good night.

Jaikes. Not 'good night,' missus, it's 'good morning.'　　　　　　*Exit Jaikes.*

Nelly. Ah! if it were the dawn of a new and happy life!

Enter Denver.

Will!

Den. Don't touch me! You don't know what I am! Keep away from me!

Nelly. Ah, Will! Not that — not that! For mercy's sake, say it's not true!

Den. Ah, if I could! Yes it's true! I've killed him! Oh, if I could wipe it out! If I could bring back the past few hours! Fool! Fool! Fool!

Nelly. How did it happen?

Den. I don't know! I was mad — dazed. I went to his rooms, it was dark — I called out for him — he sprang upon me from behind the door — we struggled — I suppose my revolver must have gone off — and then — I — I — I don't know what happened. The next thing I remember was Leaker, the porter, woke me and left me — and I looked round the room — and — and — (*Picturing the scene*) there he was — dead — dead — shot by me. Look! Look! he's staring at me. Look! Look! He'll stare at me for ever. There! Don't you see him? (*Pointing to the floor*) Hide him — hide him from me!

Nelly. (*With a great cry of pity goes to him and covers his face with her hands*) Oh, my poor Will!

Den. Don't touch me, I say! There's blood upon my hands. Oh, my poor girl! Have I brought you to this?

Nelly. Don't think of me — think of yourself — you must hide!

Den. Hide! No! let them come and take me, you will be well rid of me. (*Nelly puts her arms round his neck*) Don't pity me. If there is a spark of love left in your breast for me, crush it out. Oh, I've been the maddest fool that was ever sent upon this earth to work mischief.

Nelly. What time was it when it happened?

Den. I don't know — a little before twelve, I think. I've been rushing about the streets ever since trying to get away from him and from myself.

Nelly. You mustn't stay here! This will be the first place they will search. You must go to one of the big railway stations and take a ticket for a long distance — do you see — make it appear you are trying to leave the country, and then you must leave the train at the first station, and so throw them off the scent. (*Puts her arms round Denver's neck*) You'll do as I tell you, won't you, Will?

Den. Oh, my wife! Why don't you hate me? Why don't you curse me?

Nelly. Because you never had so much need of my love and of my prayers as you have now. We're wasting time. What money have you? (*Denver feels in his pocket, takes out revolver*)

Den. Ah! this cursed thing! Take it away before I do any more mischief with it. (*Nelly takes it from him*)

Nelly. Never mind that now. I'll get rid of it when you are gone. (*Puts revolver on table*) What money have you?

Den. Not a shilling in the world.

Nelly. Nor I. Ah, you will be lost and all for the want of a few pounds. (*Jaikes has entered during the last speech*)

Jaikes. No, missus, he shan't. I've saved up a little money against a rainy day, and Master Will's as welcome to it as if it was his own. But what has happened?

Nelly. Oh, the worst! Out of pity don't ask. Only help us.

Jaikes. Aye, that I will. What can I do?

Nelly. Quick, get the money. Wait! Your master must have some disguise. Think what he can have.

Jaikes. Yes, missus. There's my poor brother Frank's things. They sent 'em to me when he died. How will they do?

Nelly. Sailor's clothes! They'll do. Quick! Get them and put them into the portmanteau — and, Jaikes, his top coat and hat. Hurry, it's life or death! (*Exit Jaikes. Goes to Denver and puts her arms around his neck*) Oh, Will, you must save yourself for my sake.

Den. I shan't escape — they'll soon run me down, Nell.

Nelly. Ah! no, no, no, you must escape! You shall! Oh, how I will pray for it this night, and you will do your utmost for my sake? You will find means of letting me know where you are?

Den. Yes, and the children — my little Ned and Cissy — dare I kiss them before I go?

Nelly. Yes — come, they are asleep.

Den. No! No! I'm not fit to kiss them! Oh, Nelly, when they grow up and ask for their father, what will you say? (*Bursts into tears*)

Enter Jaikes with overcoat, hat, portmanteau and purse.

Jaikes. Here you are, Master Will. You'll find poor Frank's clothes inside — he was about your figure. Here's the money — there's nearly forty pounds. (*Nelly helps Denver on with his overcoat*)

Den. I can't take your savings, Jaikes.

Jaikes. Don't say mine, Master Will. It all came from you — and if the last drop of blood in my old heart could save you, you should have that as well.

Nelly. Quick, dear! you must take it.

Den. Give me a few pounds and then I'll shift for myself. Here, you keep the rest — for her. You'll take care of her, won't you, Jaikes?

Jaikes. You needn't ask me that, Master Will.

Nelly. (Throwing her arms round Denver) Oh, Will! that ever we should part like this! *(Loud knock at door)* What's that?

Den. They have come for me.

Jaikes. (Goes to window and looks off) A chap with a billycock hat and check trousers.

Den. It must be a detective. What shall I do?

Nelly. This way — quick, we'll try to keep him.

Den. Good-bye! Oh, my wife, forgive me! Forgive me!

Nelly. Go for your life! *(Nelly hurries Denver off then turns to Jaikes)* Jaikes, quick to your room. Look out of your window. Ask the man to wait a few minutes. Keep him as long as you can. *(Hurries Jaikes off. Sinks exhausted into chair)* Oh, my husband! my husband! *(Baxter enters through window. Nelly hears him and turns with a shriek)* Ah, what do you want?

Bax. Mr. Wilfred Denver — is he at home?

Nelly. (Making a desperate effort to appear calm) Yes — of course he is — he is upstairs in bed. What do you want him for?

Bax. (Looking at her keenly) I think you know; but if you don't I'd rather not tell you. I must see him at once.

Nelly. Yes, on what business? Can't you tell me? I am his wife.

Bax. God help you then!

Nelly. Why — why? Tell me your business — I must — I will know.

Bax. Since you will know, I want him on a charge of murder.

Nelly. Murder! Oh, he is innocent, he'll be able to explain.

Bax. No doubt! I must see him at once.

Nelly. I'll tell him. Will you kindly sit down and wait a few minutes till he is dressed?

Bax. Mrs. Denver, forgive me, you are not telling me the truth — your husband is not in this house.

Nelly. Yes — yes, wait a few moments. What makes you think I am deceiving you? Wait — sit down, I will fetch him.

2nd Detective rushes in.

Detective. Here, Sam! Look alive! Our man's got away in a cab. Quick, we'll catch him!

> *Exit. Nelly throws up her arms in despair. Baxter is going, sees revolver on table, picks it up.*

Bax. Revolver! One barrel fired! We'll see if the bullet'll fit it.

Nelly. (At door, clinging to Baxter) No, no, you shan't go!

Bax. I must do my duty! Stand aside, Mrs. Denver, I must do my duty.

> *Exit Baxter, Nelly clinging to him and trying to stop him.*

Scene 2.

A London railway station. Inspector opens doors. During scene, passengers of all classes enter from left and pass off through doors at back. Enter Denver hurriedly with portmanteau; he glances behind him, looks furtively round.

Den. They're after me. Will they reach the station before the train starts? It's my last chance!

> *(Newspaper boy coming through door)*

Boy. Paper, sir?

Den. No!

Boy. Winner of the Derby, sir! Murder in Hatton Garden last night.

Den. (Starting slightly) Yes, give me one — any one will do. *(Gives coin to boy and takes paper)*

Inspector. (Coming just through doors) Now, sir, quick if you're going by this train. Your ticket? *(Denver shows ticket, Inspector looks at it)* Liverpool — front carriage next the engine. Make haste! *(Denver exits hurriedly through doors in flat)*

Boy. That cove's in a big hurry. Give me a tanner — penny for the paper, fivepence for the boy. *Exit.*

Enter a Tipsy Passenger.

Tipsy P. (Going up to Inspector) Excuse me, sir, I want to ask you a simple question.

Inspector. Well, what is it?

Tipsy P. I've got a third class ticket for Glasgow, guv'nor. *(Produces ticket)* Look there, you can see it's all square — what I wish to know is simply this — does that include refreshments on the road?

Inspector. (Angrily) No, it don't!

Tipsy P. All right, guv'nor, no 'fence, I hope — merely a suggestion on my part — Railway Companies pr'vide r'freshments on the road. Splendid idea, old f'low! Bring you in lots of traffic.

Enter well-dressed Lady. Inspector leaves Tipsy Passenger and goes up to her, touches his cap very respectfully.

Inspector. (Very servilely) Can I find you a carriage, madam?

Lady. Yes. First class to Manchester.

Inspector. Yes, madam. Allow me to take your rugs and umbrella. *(Lady gives up things to Inspector)* Thank you — this way, madam. *(Bows her off very respectfully)*

Tipsy P. That's because she's a first classer. They don't show me to my carriage.

Inspector. (*Coming to door at back, rings bell*) This way for Rugby, Stafford, Crewe, Manchester, Liverpool and the North. (*Goes off again*)

Tipsy P. (*With much tipsy dignity*) Will you kindly conduct me to a third class smoking carriage?

Inspector. (*Has returned*) Third class smoking — at end of the train.

Tipsy P. Kindly conduct me to my carriage and open the door for me.

Inspector. Get out! Go and find your carriage.

Tipsy P. No, I will not find my carriage. I will be escorted to my carriage. (*Inspector takes him by the scruff of the neck and runs him off*)

Baxter rushes on.

Bax. Express gone?

Inspector. Yes, three minutes ago.

Bax. Just my luck again. I missed the Spider last night, and now this man's missed me. (*To Inspector*) Did you happen to notice a gentleman in a brown overcoat, brown hat, with a portmanteau?

Inspector. Rather dark, with small beard and moustache?

Bax. Yes.

Inspector. The very man. Came through this door about three minutes ago — he caught the express. He's got a first class ticket for Liverpool. He's in the front carriage of the train.

Bax. Where does the train stop — the first place?

Inspector. Rugby — nine thirty-five.

Exit.

Bax. (*Takes out pocketbook and writes hurriedly*) "From Sam Baxter, Scotland Yard. To Police Station, Rugby. Meet nine thirty-five down express, detain Wilfred Denver — front carriage of train — about thirty, dark, small beard and moustache, brown hat, brown overcoat. Wanted for murder." I'll just nip across to the Telegraph Office, then to Scotland Yard. We shall nab him at Rugby. *Exit.*

Scene 3.

The exterior of "The Chequers," a wayside inn with deeply recessed porch towards right. Discovered seated in the porch drinking and smoking, Binks and Brownson, two tradesmen, and Parkyn, the Parish clerk. Parkyn is reading the "Daily Telegraph."

Binks. (*Politely*) When you're quite finished with that paper, Mr. Parkyn.

Park. When I've quite finished with it, Mr. Binks, I'll hand it over to you.

Brown. Yes, Parkyn don't be greedy. Let's all have benefit of the news.

Park. I'm reading about a murder as was committed in Hatton Garden, London, last night.

Brown. Ah, I like a good murder; it's very pretty reading.

Binks. Ah! it's wonderful how tastes differ. Now my wife, she's all for divorce and breach of promise cases.

Brown. So's my missus. It's my belief that women never look at a newspaper for anything except these spicy little bits.

Binks. Well, a divorce is all very well in its way, but I say, Give me a jolly good murder, one as ain't found out for a month or two, and puzzles judge and jury and everybody. That's what I like.

Brown. Ah! and where you ain't quite certain it's the right man till after he's hung, eh? (*Regretfully*) Ah! we don't get such murders nowadays.

Binks. Have they found out who done the murder as you're reading about, Mr. Parkyn?

Park. Oh yes, a party by the name of Denver. There ain't no doubt about that.

Brown. Ah, that's a pity. It takes away all the interest and excitement.

Binks. I don't wish to hurry you, Mr. Parkyn, but when you've *quite* finished with the paper. Excuse me.

Park. Don't mention it, Mr. Binks.

Binks. (*Aside to Brownson*) Parkyn gets more hoggish over the paper every day.

Brown. Read it out loud, Parkyn, and then we can all hear it.

Park. Very well, gentlemen, if it's the wish of the company.

Binks. I think it's my turn to read out loud to-night, Mr. Parkyn. You read out the "Horrible affair at Camberwell" last night, and the "Revolting Tragedy" the night before.

Park. Well, Mr. Binks, and if I did, am I not the clerk of this parish?

Binks. Yes, Mr. Parkyn, but because we're obliged to listen to you on Sundays when you've got us in church and we can't help ourselves, is no reason why you should bully-rag us a week-days when we've got the right of reply.

Park. Perhaps you are not aware, Mr. Binks, that the Lord Bishop of this diocese has particularly admired my reading of the psalms.

Binks. Very likely, Mr. Parkyn, but then

the psalms is one thing and "The Daily Telegraph" another.

Park. Gentlemen, I'm in your hands.

Brown. Go on, Mr. Parkyn, read out — let's hear all about this murder.

Park. Mr. Binks, you are in a minority. (*Coughs, adjusts his spectacles, looks severely at Binks and begins*) "A Downward Career."

Brown. Wait a bit, let's fill up our glasses and then we can start comfortable. (*Calls*) Susy! Susy, my dear!

Enter Susy from house.

Susy. Did you call, sir?

Brown. (*Giving her his glass*) As per usual, my dear. (*Susy takes glass and exits*)

Park. (*Reading*) "A downward career. Last night a shocking murder was committed at 114 Hatton Garden. The victim was a young engineer named Geoffrey Ware, who occupied the first and second floors of the house in question. It appears that a few minutes before eleven last night, James Leaker, the porter, and the housekeeper of the premises, went into Mr. Ware's room, and found there an acquaintance of the deceased, by name Wilfred Denver."

Enter Susy with glass of grog which she places in front of Brownson.

Susy. Hot or cold, Mr. Brownson?

Park. If you interrupt, Susy, it's impossible for me to read.

Denver limps on in travel-stained sailor's dress, haggard and lame — he is clean shaven and appears utterly prostrate and exhausted.

Den. (*Aside*) I can't drag a step further. Let them come and take me and end it. (*Gets to porch and sinks on seat*)

Park. (*Resuming*) "And found there an acquaintance of the deceased, by name Wilfred Denver."

Den. (*Starts up as if shot, glances fiercely round at all of them*) Well! (*They all stare round at him*)

Brown. What's the matter, mate?

Den. (*Recovering himself*) Nothing — I beg pardon, gentlemen — I was thinking of something else. Don't take any notice of me. (*Sits*)

Brown. Go on, Mr. Parkyn.

Park. (*Resuming*) "Wilfred Denver, a young fellow of good connections, who has lately been leading a life of gambling and dissipation and who had returned from the Derby in a drunken frenzy, aggravated it is said by heavy betting losses."

Den. (*Starting up fiercely and calls*) Waiter! Waiter!

Park. (*Looking at him severely over his spectacles*) I really cannot read, sir, if you interrupt.

Den. (*Savagely*) Who asked you to read? Keep your tongue quiet for a few minutes, can't you?

Parkyn puts down paper in disgust, Binks and Brownson snatch it up and read. Enter Susy from Inn.

Susy. Did you call, sir?

Den. Yes, something to eat. Anything there is in the house. Lay it in a private room.

Susy. Yes, sir.   *Exit into house.*

Brown. Have they caught the man? (*Denver listens attentively*)

Binks. No, but the police are after him. Here's a description of him. "About thirty, medium height, well built, clean cut features, with dissipated look, a small beard and moustache."

Park. Poor fellow, I wonder how he feels to-night.

Brown. Ah! I shouldn't like to be in his shoes.

Den. Are you talking about the Hatton Garden murder?

Park. Yes, sir, we are!

Den. Ah! I know Hatton Garden very well. Have they discovered anything fresh?

Binks. No, that's only the morning paper. The evening paper ain't come yet.

Den. It is to be hoped they'll catch the man before long.

Park. Oh, I expect they'll soon run him down.

Den. Yes, I expect so. (*Aside*) I shall betray myself in another moment.

Binks. (*To Denver*) Stranger in these parts, mate?

Den. Yes — no — I know them a little.

Binks. Sailor, eh? (*Noticing his clothes*)

Den. Yes.

Park. Where might you be making for, sir?

Den. I'm going to join my ship.

Brown. And where might that be, mate?

Den. She's at — at — at — (*Starting up furiously*) What the devil's that got to do with you? (*Shouts*) Waiter! Waiter!

Enter Susy from Inn.

Show me to a private room where these men can't pester me.

Exeunt Denver and Susy into house.

Park. (*Rises*) Pester him! Why, what's the matter with the man?

Binks. (*Rising*) Pester him indeed! I wonder who he is? (*Looking after him*)

Park. He's a madman, that's what he is. Did you notice how he stared at us?

Brown. Perhaps he has escaped from somewhere.

Binks. Let's go in and put Mrs. Buddens on her guard. He's a dangerous character to have about the house.

Brown. Yes, come on, Mr. Parkyn, we may find out something more about him.

Exeunt All into Inn.

Scene 4.

Room in "The Chequers." Discover Denver hanging cap on peg. Susy right of table laying cloth. Music to begin.

Susy. You look tired.

Den. (*Getting left of table*) Yes, my girl, I am.

Susy. What's the matter with your foot?

Den. Nothing.

Susy. That's a fib — you're quite lame.

Den. No, no, I've walked a good bit to-day and I'm dead beat.

Susy. Never mind, you'll be better to-morrow.

Den. Yes, I shall be better to-morrow. Bring me some water, will you?

Susy. Yes — anything else?

Den. You get the London evening paper here?

Susy. Yes; it generally comes about this time.

Den. Let me have it the moment it comes. (*Aside*) I can't help what they suspect, I must know. (*Susy is looking compassionately at him*) Don't look at me, there's a good girl, go out — shut the door, and don't let me be disturbed.

Susy. (*Going out, aside*) Poor fellow, I wonder who he is. *Exit leaving door open.*

Den. How long will it last? I wonder if anyone saw me jump from the train. What a fearful jump! What a mercy I wasn't dashed to pieces. I wonder what time it is. It must be about a quarter-past eight. A quarter-past eight. And yesterday at this time I was innocent! Yesterday he was alive — and I could laugh and play the fool, and now! Oh God! put back Thy universe and give me yesterday! Too late! Too late! Ah, my wife, how thoughtful she was. Shall I ever see her again — and my children — Ah, Heaven, work out some way of escape for me — not for my own sake, not to shield me from the just consequences of my crime, but for the sake of my dear wife and innocent children who have never done any wrong. Spare me till I have made atonement for the evil I have done. (*Looks round*) I wonder where I am? I must have dragged at least twenty miles

to-day. (*Sees Railway Time Table*) Ah, a Railway Time Table, then there is a station somewhere near. (*Crosses and gets Time Table and returns to table and sits*)

Enter Susy with water.

Susy. (*Pouring out water*) There you are!

Den. Thank you, my girl. (*Drinks*)

Susy. You ain't a bit like a sailor.

Den. Why not? What makes you think that?

Susy. Sailors are always hearty and jolly, and want to kiss me. (*Pauses*) I know you've hurt your foot — I wish you'd let John the ostler see it — he's as good as a doctor for sprains, and he'll tell you what to bathe it with.

Den. No — no — let me alone, that's all I want, and don't forget the Evening Paper.

Susy. Very well, you shall have it the moment it comes. *Exit leaving door open.*

Den. I can't eat, and yet I must — I must put some strength into me. I can't last out another day like this. (*Parkyn and Brownson talk outside. Denver sees the door open, limps up to it and is about to shut it when his attention is arrested*) Hark! What are they talking about in there?

Park. (*Voice heard outside*) I never heard sentence of death passed but once, and that was when I was a boy, but I shall never forget it.

Binks. (*Outside*) Tell us all about it, Mr. Parkyn.

Park. (*Outside*) Well! It was on James Beecroft, the Aylesbury murderer; and the jury had been over two hours deliberating and it was late at night, and the court was lighted with candles in them days. And one of the candles was burnt down to the socket and kept on drip, drip, drip on my shoulder; and I couldn't stir, for we was packed as tight as herrings in a barrel; and the jury came out and everybody was as quiet as death; and the foreman of the jury gave in the verdict, and that candle went out the very moment as he said "Guilty." And the man's wife was in court and she screamed out to the judge to save her husband, and they had to drag her out of court, and she was carried out shrieking like a mad thing. And the judge was sobbing like a baby and when the court had got quiet again, the judge took out the Black Cap — (*Denver slams the door furiously*)

Den. God! I can bear it no longer. Have mercy upon me, and end it now.

Enter Susy with paper.

(*He stares at her*) Well?

Susy. Paper, sir.

Denver takes paper from her mechanically and watches her out of room. She delays her exit a moment looking at him. The moment she has gone, he opens the paper and with feverish haste looks up and down it.

Den. What's this? "Terrible railway calamity. Seven thirty-five express from Euston —" That's the train I was in. (*Reading breathlessly*) "ascending an incline came into collision with some detached wagons of a goods train descending the incline on the same line of rail — one of the wagons was loaded with petroleum — the barrels burst with the shock, the vapour of the oil came in contact with the engine fire and in a moment the front part of the train was wrapped in fierce and inextinguishable flames. The three front carriages, with all their occupants, were burning for upwards of an hour and were unapproachable on account of the intense heat. Nothing was left of them but cinders. Amongst the ill-fated passengers was Wilfred Denver — who committed the murder in Hatton Garden last night —" What's this? — "and who has thus paid the last penalty of his crime in the very act of flying from justice." (*Reads again*) "Amongst the ill-fated passengers was Wilfred Denver —" Yes, it is here! — "paid the last penalty of his crime." Then I am dead — dead to all the world. Dead! Yes, dead! (*Kneels*) Merciful Father, Thou hast heard my prayer and given me my life. I take it to give it back to Thee. My wife! She will see this and think me dead. Ah! better so, better so than to be tied to a murderer! (*Rises*) Yes, my darling, I have done you harm enough! Now I will set you free.

Enter Susy.

How far is it to the station?

Susy. A mile, sir.

Den. There is a late train down to Bristol, is there not?

Susy. Yes, sir, the down night mail.

Den. Order a horse and conveyance to meet it at once.

Susy. Yes, sir.   *Exit.*

Den. I shall reach Bristol to-night — Wilfred Denver is dead! To-morrow I begin a new life!

End of the Second Act.

ACT III.

Scene 1.

Skinner's villa at Bromley. A very luxuriously furnished apartment. Door right, window at back showing a snowy landscape outside. Fireplace right, with large comfortable fire burning. Door left. Discover Olive Skinner at window looking out. Skinner is seated in a luxurious arm-chair near fire. He is reading a French novel.

Olive. More snow! Herbert, you don't really mean to turn that poor woman and her children out of that wretched cottage?

Skin. Yes, I do!

Olive. Why?

Skin. They are starving, one of the children is dying. I object to people starving and dying on my property.

Olive. But what will they do? Where will they go?

Skin. There's a nice comfortable workhouse about two miles off.

Olive. But surely, Herbert —

Skin. Now don't argue, Olive, the woman can't pay her rent — she must go!

Olive. But it isn't her fault she is poor.

Skin. Fault! It's no fault in England to be poor. It's a crime. That's the reason I'm rich.

Olive. Rich? When I think how our money is got, I grudge the poorest labourer's wife her crust of bread and drink of water.

Skin. Ah, that's foolish. My dear Olive, all living creatures prey upon one another. The duck gobbles up the worm, the man gobbles up the duck, and then the worm gobbles up the man again. It's the great law of nature. My profession is just as good as any other, till I'm found out.

Olive. When you talk like that I hate you. Your profession, indeed! Burglary — burglary and — (*In a whisper*) — murder!

Skin. (*Starts up with a frightened look and seizes her by wrist*) If you remind me of that cursed affair again I'll — I'll — (*Dropping her hand*) There, don't be a fool, Olive, don't do it again, there's a good girl.

Olive. You're not quite deaf to the voice of conscience, it seems.

Skin. I wish to goodness I could be deaf to your voice occasionally.

Olive. Herbert, can't you make some reparation, can you not do something to wipe the stain off that man's memory?

Skin. No, I can't! Shut up! What a fool I was to tell you.

Olive. Do you think I would have let you tell me if I had guessed what your secret was? I've not had one peaceful moment since.

Skin. No, and what's more, you haven't let me have one either. For Heaven's sake, Olive, don't look like that, or you'll be old and ugly in no time. Let's forget the cursed thing. (*Enter Servant. To Servant, his manner entirely changed*) They've come?

Servant. Yes, sir.

Skin. Send them up. (*Exit Servant. Olive rises and is going out*) You'd better stay — one must be polite to one's business acquaintance.

Enter Servant showing in Coombe and Cripps. Exit Servant.

Coombe. (*To Skinner*) My dear boy! (*To Olive*) How d'ye do, ma'am? (*He holds out his hand to Olive, she shrinks from taking it. Skinner throws her a look of command, she then shakes hands with Coombe*)

Cripps. (*Is smoking a short pipe, does not take off his hat, nods familiarly to Olive*) My respects, ma'am. (*Looks round the room*) Spider, this is a blazing snug crib you have got here.

Skin. Yes, pretty well. By the way, Cripps, I wish you'd be a little more careful in your selection of adjectives.

Cripps. What's the matter with my adjectives? Them as don't like my company can leave it.

Olive. Then there's no occasion for me to stay, I think.

Cripps. (*Seated in easy-chair stretching out his legs and smoking a short pipe*) Not a bit, ma'am. No offence to you, but I hates a parcel of women folk poking their noses where they ain't wanted. There! That's what I call business. There ain't no nonsense about me.

Skin. No, nor any superfluous politeness.

Cripps. I hates politeness. I hates folks as are civil and stuck up.

Skin. My dear fellow, consider the dignity of our profession. There's no reason why we shouldn't be gentlemen.

Cripps. Gentlemen! There's nothing of the gentleman about me.

Skin. Hush, don't tell us so, or we shall begin to believe it by and bye.

Coombe. Now, my dear boys, let's get to business.

Skin. Fire away, Father Christmas! I'm all attention; but before we set out for fresh woods and pastures new, let's square Lady Blanche's diamonds. Where are they?

Coombe. Down at my wharf by the river along with the other swag.

Skin. Who looks after that place now?

Coombe. It's locked up at present.

Skin. That won't do, you know — you must keep somebody there — somebody you know.

Coombe. You can't spare one of your people, I suppose?

Skin. No, I'm very comfortably suited just now. My coachman has just done eighteen months; my cook's a jewel — she's the one that stole Lord Farthinghoe's silver — I always like to encourage enterprise. My housemaid was born in Durham jail, and my footman I took out of charity when his father went to do his fourteen years. In fact, I haven't a soul about the place that I can't trust.

Enter Servant.

Servant. The Duke of New York's below, sir.

Skin. That fellow! Give him a bit of dinner and kick him out of the place.

Servant. He says he must see you, sir.

Skin. (*Shrugs his shoulders*) Send him up.

Servant. Here he is, sir.

Enter Corkett, seedy, half starved, dirty, shivering, unshorn, ragged, his hair cropped as if just out of prison. Exit Servant.

Coombe. Dear me! Why, it's our dear old friend, Mr. 'Enery Corkett.

Cork. Your old friend. A pretty hole you let your friends into.

Coombe. My dear boy, what was we to do? Why, it might have happened to any of us.

Cork. All my eye, Father Christmas. You were wide oh, you three, and you meant to let me in. There's Spider there. (*Goes to Skinner*) Now then, Mr. Spider, can't you speak to an old pal?

Skin. So! you're out again, are you?

Cork. Yes, I've just done the twelve months as you ought to have done.

Skin. Very well, don't brag about it, and perhaps you'll get another twelve months.

Cork. Oh no, I shan't, I'm going to turn honest.

Skin. Very well — you make an infernally bad rogue, Corkett — I don't know how you'll answer in the other line. My private opinion is you won't be a credit to either.

Cork. I ain't going to be your tool and cat's-paw any longer.

Skin. Very well.

Cork. Here you are living in bang up style, surrounded by every luxury.

Skin. The fruits of years of honourable industry.

Cork. While I ain't got the price of a glass of bitter.

Skin. Try a few bitter reflections.

Cork. No, I shan't! I shall try honesty.

Skin. Do — it's always the last resource of people who fail as rogues.

Cork. And mind you, Spider, once I do turn honest, I shall turn damned honest, and make it jolly hot for all of you.

Coombe. Come, come, you know what the Spider is, you must brush him the right way of the wool. Now we've got a splendid plant on, ain't we, Spider, and he shall stand in.

Skin. No, I'm d——d if he shall.

Coombe. (*Aside to Skinner*) My dear boy, we must keep his mouth shut or else he'll go and blab about that Hatton Garden affair.

Skin. Corkett! Corkett! I'm not to be bullied, but if you behave yourself, I don't mind doing something for you.

Cork. All right, I'm fly! Let's have some dinner to start with. I've got rats inside of me. What time do you dine, Spider?

Skin. Seven. But pray don't wait for me. (*Rings*)

Cork. I won't; I'll have some lunch now and then I'll dine with you by and bye.

Skin. We always dress for dinner. Mrs. Skinner makes a point of it.

Cork. Very sorry, Spider, I've left my dress togs with my uncle. You'll have to excuse morning dress this time.

Enter Servant.

Skin. Some lunch for this gentleman.

Cork. And some wine, Spider.

Skin. Some claret for the gentleman.

Cork. Claret be blowed. Let's have some champagne.

Skin. Some champagne for the gentleman.

Cripps. (*Rising*) I think I'll join the gentleman. I've had one dinner, but mine's a wonderful accommodating sort of stomach.

Exeunt Servant and Cripps.

Cork. Au revoir — (*Going*) — Spider — meet you at dinner. Seven, I think you said. (*Aside*) If I can't take it out of Spider, I'll take it out of his champagne.   *Exit.*

Skin. The brute! If he gets a spoonful of wine into him, it'll fly into the place where his brains ought to be, and he may open his mouth too wide. Coombe, you'd better go and look after him.

Coombe. All right, my dear boy. Anything for an honest living.   *Exit.*

Skin. That cursed Corkett turned up again! Am I always to be reminded of that? I wish they'd all die. I'll cut the whole gang after my next "coup," disappear, retire to some quiet country place, go to church regularly, turn churchwarden and set an example to all the parish.

Enter Olive showing in Nelly. She is haggard, pale and very poorly dressed.

Olive. (*To Nelly*) Come in. Here is my husband — you shall speak to him yourself.

Skin. What is it now? Do shut that door. (*Nelly shuts door*) What is it?

Olive. This is the poor woman who lives in the gardener's old cottage.

Nelly. Mercy, sir, mercy on a starving woman and a dying child.

Skin. My good woman, you'll be much better off in the workhouse. You will be provided with food and your child will be attended by a doctor.

Nelly. But he will die — it will kill him to move him this bitter weather. Have mercy, sir, have mercy!

Skin. Now please don't make a scene. I've made up my mind to pull down that cottage. It isn't fit for a dog to live in.

Nelly. Then let me live in it, and my children, only for a few days — only till my child is better — or dead.

Skin. Yes, that's just it! Your child may die — and I don't wish him to die on my property, a hundred yards from my door. I dislike death, it's a nuisance, and I don't wish to be reminded of it.

Nelly. Ah, but think of it, it's the last chance for my child. If you turn us out to-night, my boy will die.

Olive. Oh, Herbert, think what you are doing!

Nelly. Oh, thank you for that. Beg him to let me stay.

Olive. I have no influence over my husband.

Skin. (*To Nelly*) Have the goodness to believe I mean what I say. (*Nelly kneels to him*) Now get up, there's no need to kneel to me.

Nelly. Yes! yes! there is much need. You shall not say me "no." Oh, I'm sure you are good and kind at heart — you do not wish my boy, my brave, beautiful boy to die. Ah, you are listening — you will have mercy — yes, yes, yes!

Skin. (*After a pause*) Very well. If you don't bother me any more you can stay till your child gets better.

Nelly. (*Rises*) God bless you! God bless you!

Skin. Yes, we know all about that. Now go away and don't make any more fuss.

Nelly. Oh, but I can't help thanking you and — you too with my whole heart.

Skin. There, that'll do, Olive, show the woman out.

Olive. Will you come this way, Mrs. — I don't know your name.

Nelly. My name is — Nelly. (*To Skinner*) Thank you again and again. You have saved my child's life.   *Exeunt Olive and Nelly.*

Coombe enters almost instantaneously, looking scared.

Skin. What's the matter now?

Coombe. (*Pointing out after Nelly*) That woman! That woman!

Skin. Well, what of her? What's the matter, man? Have you seen a ghost?

Coombe. I knew her again in a moment.

Skin. Who is she?

Coombe. Denver's widow.

Skin. You must be mistaken. How do you know her?

Coombe. They pointed her out to me at the inquest on Ware's body. I'm not likely to forget her.

Skin. (*Aside*) That man's widow here at my door. (*Stands pale and speechless, for a few moments, then in a low, hoarse voice speaks to Coombe*) Coombe, you can do this job for me.

Coombe. What? What?

Skin. My wife has got a maggot in her brain about that Hatton Garden — accident. If she finds out that this woman is Denver's widow, she'll make my life a purgatory and the whole business'll leak out.

Coombe. What's to be done?

Skin. She's living in that old tumble-down cottage of mine — you know. She can't pay her rent — she's had notice to quit for the last fortnight — go and get some men and turn her and her belongings out of my place.

Coombe. All right, leave it to me.

Skin. Do it at once.

Coombe. It's done.   *Exit.*

Skin. Denver's widow! Lucky I found it out and can bundle them out. They can do their starving somewhere else — they shan't do it on my property.   *Exit.*

Scene 2.

Nelly Denver's home. Winter. Cottage interior and schoolhouse. Enter Nelly from inner room of cottage. She pauses at the door and looks in again, speaking as she looks.

Nelly. Sleep on, my darling boy! You are happier so. You do not feel you are hungry, and you do not tear your poor mother's heart by begging for the food she has not got to give.

Enter Jaikes through stile with bundle of sticks and some coal in an old sack. He is beating himself to keep warm.

Jaikes. This is a freezer and no mistake. (*Enters cottage*)

Nelly. (*Eagerly*) Well, Jaikes, any success?

Jaikes. Success, missus, rather! Things is looking up. What do you think? I've been and earned a shilling this afternoon.

Nelly. (*Joyfully*) A shilling, Jaikes?

Jaikes. Yes, a whole shilling, straight off!

Earned it all in a couple of hours. There it is! (*Puts shilling on table*)

Nelly. Oh, Jaikes, isn't that lucky! I was just wondering whether we should have anything to eat tonight.

Jaikes. Eat! Lor' bless you, we'll have a reg'lar Lord Mayor's banquet. What did the gentleman say about letting us stay on?

Nelly. At first he was very hard and cruel and said we must go, but I went down on my knees to him and begged so hard and wouldn't take "no," till he was obliged to say we might stay till Ned was better.

Jaikes. Bless your sweet, pale face, missus, he must have had a heart made of bricrbats if he could have said "no" to you.

Nelly. And so you see we haven't got to turn out after all, Jaikes. (*Jaikes begins to put sticks and lay fire*) You have brought some wood and some coals?

Jaikes. Yes; you see it gets a bit chilly towards the evening, and I thought a fire 'ud look cheerful.

Nelly. Where did you get the firing from, Jaikes?

Jaikes. I begged it off Bodgers the baker.

Nelly. Bodgers the baker — that dreadful hard-hearted man?

Jaikes. Oh, Bodgers is all right once you get the right side of him, though judging from Bodgers's squint you'd think he was capable of anything.

Nelly. And how did you manage to get the soft side of him?

Jaikes. Well, I went to work artful; you see, Bodgers's missus is a regular downright tartar.

Nelly. Is she?

Jaikes. Oh, yes, she leads Bodgers a dreadful life. It's no wonder he squints with such a wife as he's got. Well I hangs about the bakehouse and sympathises with Bodgers, and says all the hard things as I could invent about womenkind. Oh, I laid it on thick!

Nelly. But you didn't mean it, Jaikes?

Jaikes. Not I, missus. My private opinion of women is as they're angels, you in particular, missus. Well, I kept on helping Bodgers and a sympathising with him, and Bodgers, he says, "I know what you're after, you old vagabond," says he.

Nelly. He called you an old vagabond?

Jaikes. Yes, but I didn't take no notice of that.

Nelly. No, put it down to his ignorance.

Jaikes. Yes, that's what I did, "You're after a job, you old scarecrow," says he. "Now be off! Get out, 'cos I shan't employ you," and he takes a shilling out of the till and chucks it down at me, and I picks it up and I says, "I takes it, Mr. Bodgers, just to show the respect I've got for you, and 'cos I know you'd be offended if I didn't."

Nelly. That was clever of you, Jaikes, to earn a shilling in that way.

Jaikes. It was artful, wasn't it? And now, missus, what shall we do with it?

Nelly. Well, Jaikes, it's your money.

Jaikes. No, missus, I only earned it for you and the dear little master and missy.

Nelly. Well, what do you think, Jaikes?

Jaikes. Faggots is cheap and relishing.

Nelly. I don't think they like faggots.

Jaikes. No? What do you say to some nice red herrings — soft roe'd 'uns?

Nelly. Yes, red herrings are nice, but do you think, Jaikes, there is enough support in them for growing children?

Jaikes. Well, perhaps there ain't, but there's plenty of flavour. (*Suddenly*) I've got it, missus!

Nelly. Well, what, Jaikes?

Jaikes. Saveloys! After all, there's nothing like saveloys, is there? Talk about your partridge, your venison, and your 'are, why, I've tasted saveloys as 'ud give 'em all a start if it came to a question of game. But there, missus, you take the shilling and spend it how you think proper.

Nelly. You may be sure I shan't forget half an ounce of tobacco.

Jaikes. Tobacco — now don't you, missus, I've given up smoking.

Nelly. Given up smoking, Jaikes?

Jaikes. Yes; you see, missus, there's so many boys have took to it lately — I thought it was about time for men to leave off.

Nelly. Well, I shall insist on your having a good hearty meal with us.

Jaikes. Now don't you, missus. I ain't hungry. I've been smelling the dinners at Bodgers's all day, and what with his roast beef and Yorkshire pudding, his beefsteak and kidney pie, roast duck and stuffing, I sniffed and sniffed at them till I got a reg'lar attack of indigestion.

Nelly. Well, if you don't manage to find a great big appetite before I come back, there'll be such a to-do in this house as never was.

Jaikes. Don't I tell you, missus, I ain't hungry. Now you make haste and get something for Master Ned — by when he wakes.

Nelly. (*Going to inner door and looking off*) Look, Jaikes, how pretty he looks in his sleep.

Jaikes. (*Going to inner door*) Yes, bless his heart. How much he do remind me of — but I mustn't say that, must I?

Nelly. Yes, say it, Jaikes — I like to think

of him — my dear dead Will! Whatever his faults, he was always the best of husbands to me. (*Crying a little, then wiping away her tears*) But there, I mustn't cry today now we've been so fortunate. Oh, Jaikes, I feel so much happier. I think we shall weather the storm after all.

Jaikes. Why, of course we shall, now I can go and earn shillings off-hand like that.

Nelly. (*Taking Jaikes's hands and swinging them backwards and forwards in her own*) And the cruel winter will soon be over.

Jaikes. And the nice warm spring days will come.

Nelly. And darling Ned will get well and strong again.

Jaikes. And I shall get lots of work and earn heaps of money.

Nelly. How happy we shall be!

Jaikes. Lor' bless you, missus, we shall get on like a house afire now.

Nelly. Dear old Jaikes! Wait here, Jaikes, I'll be back soon, and then we'll have our Lord Mayor's Banquet all together.

Opens door, crossing stage. Exit.

Jaikes. Blow up, Bodgers! (*Poking up fire*) There! That's ablazing up beautiful. We shall soon have quite a Fifth of November. Master Ned's asleeping as sound as a top — Miss Cissy will be out of school soon and she'll take care of him. I wish I could earn another sixpence. We can't have much of a Lord Mayor's Banquet with a shilling, but with eighteen pence, what a treat we could have. (*Exit from cottage*) I'll try! I'll try! There's life in the old dog yet.

Exit running feebly and beating his arms.

Children in school sing the following hymn. After first verse enter Denver. He has changed very much, his hair is almost white, and his face worn, his manner grave and subdued. He enters listening to the children's voices. The hymn is sung to the accompaniment of an harmonium.

1st Verse.

What though my sins as mountains rise
    And reach and swell to Heaven,
Yet Mercy is above the skies.
    I may be still forgiven.

2nd Verse.

Then let me stay in doubt no more
    Since there is sure release,
For ever open stands the door,
    Repentance, Pardon, Peace.

Den. Repentance, Pardon, Peace! The old, old message! The sweet old message! That must be for me — yes, even for me. They are coming out. Perhaps I shall be able to get some news of my dear ones. I have tracked them so far, from one wretched home to another — Shall I ever find them, or find them only in the grave?

Children come out of school, skipping, shouting, laughing, etc. Cissy Denver comes out among the others; they are laughing, romping, and playing. She stands apart for a moment and then goes timidly up to them.

Cissy. Let me play with you!

Big Girl. No, come away from her, girls! Nobody is to speak to her. (*To Cissy*) Our fathers and mothers are respectable. Come on, girls!

Exeunt all the school-girls but one. Cissy is left sobbing when the little school-girl who has stayed behind goes up to her and offers Cissy a piece of cake.

Little Girl. There, Cissy, don't you cry. I've got a piece of cake. There — (*Giving cake*) don't you tell anybody — I love you if the others don't. (*Kisses Cissy and runs off*)

Den. Why are you crying, my dear?

Cissy. The girls won't play with me. They won't speak to me.

Den. Why how's that? What makes them so cruel? (*Cissy is silent*) Come, tell me all about it. You're not afraid of me, are you?

Cissy. (*Looking up into his face*) No, I like you.

Den. That's right. I thought we should get on together. Now tell me all your troubles — why won't they play with you?

Cissy. (*Looking cautiously round*) You won't tell anybody, will you?

Den. No, I promise you — it shall be a secret.

Cissy. (*In a whisper*) They say my father killed a man. (*Denver starts up stung with pain and turns away his face*) Ah! that makes you turn away from me.

Den. No! No, my dear, don't think that. Tell me quick — what is your name?

Cissy. Cissy Denver.

Den. (*Aside*) My own child! The sins of the father are visted upon the children. Oh, Heaven, is it just? What has this innocent lamb done that she should be hounded for my crime?

Cissy. Why are you crying?

Den. Never mind me! Never mind me! Where do you live?

Cissy. (*Points*) In here.

Den. In there?

Cissy. Yes, will you come in? (*Goes inside the cottage, leaves the door open. As soon as she sees the fire, she runs to it*)

Den. My own little Cissy that I left a toddling baby. (*Enters cottage*)

Cissy. (*Kneeling by fire and clapping hands*) Oh, look! A fire! A fire! We haven't had a fire for I don't know how long. (*Warms her hands*)

Den. (*At back of table — aside*) In this wretched hole and without a fire! (*Comes to Cissy — aloud*) Who else lives with you, Cissy?

Cissy. Mother and Ned, and our old Jaikes. You don't know our old Jaikes. I do love him!

Den. God bless him! Where are the others, Cissy?

Cissy. I daresay Jaikes has gone to get some work, and mother is in the next room nursing Ned, I'll tell her you're here.

Den. No, no, I must go — I have no business here.

Cissy. (*Who has been to inner door, opened it and looked in*) No — mother isn't at home. Oh, I know, we can't pay our rent, and she's gone to ask the gentleman to let us stop on for a few days.

Den. (*Aside*) To stay on here!

Cissy. (*Runs to door*) Ned's in there, he's asleep. (*Denver is going to door to look, Cissy closes door and comes away*) Hush! you mustn't wake him. He's been very ill.

Den. Ill! Not very ill? Not dangerously ill?

Cissy. (*Goes to him*) Yes, but he's getting better. Won't you sit down and warm yourself. There's only one chair, but you may have that.

Den. (*Sits*) May I? And will you come and sit on my knee? (*Holds out his arms*) Don't be afraid — come!

Cissy. (*Going to him*) Oh, I'm not a bit afraid of you.

Den. What has been the matter with your little brother?

Cissy. (*Sitting on Denver's knee*) The doctor says he has not had enough to eat. We have been so poor; sometimes we have scarcely had anything for days. Mother tried to get a living by teaching, but when people found out who my father was, they wouldn't let her teach any more.

Den. (*Aside*) The fiends! (*Aloud*) But your mother has had some money — some friends have sent her some, eh?

Cissy. No, she has no friends.

Den. Yes, Cissy, yes — think again. She has had some money sent her?

Cissy. No; who would send her money?

Den. (*Aside*) It has never reached her. (*Aloud*) And does the doctor think your little brother will get better?

Cissy. Yes; if he could have nice things to eat.

Den. So he shall! Everything that money can buy. (*Takes out purse*) Here, take this, you'll find plenty of money in that.

Cissy. Is that for mother? Oh, that is kind.

Den. No, my dear, don't say that. Wait a minute. I've got some more money loose in my pocket. (*Taking it out and putting it in purse*) There, now you've got all my money.

Cissy. And what will you do without it?

Den. Oh, I've got plenty more at home; and now — (*Looking hungrily at her and longing to embrace her*) I wonder if you'll give me a kiss?

Cissy. Yes, that I will.

Den. (*Takes her in his arms and kisses her hungrily*) Don't take any notice of me, dear — don't mind my kissing you. I had a little girl of my own once, and when I kiss you it seems as if she came back to me again.

Cissy. She is dead then?

Den. Yes, dead — (*Aside*) — to me. Suppose, Cissy, that you — I mean that I — (*Aside*) I can't say it!

Cissy. I know I should have been very fond of you if you had been my father.

Den. (*Clasps her in his arms eagerly and kisses her again and again*) God bless you, my darling; you mustn't mind when your school-fellows speak unkindly of your dead father.

Cissy. I won't — I don't believe it's true. I don't believe he was a bad man, because if he had been, Jaikes and mother wouldn't have been so fond of him.

Den. Always think that, my dear, always think that. How thin your clothes are, dear. (*He takes his muffler off and puts it round Cissy*) There, dear, that will keep a little of the cold out.

Cissy. Oh, isn't it pretty?

Den. There, now run and find your mother and give her that purse.

Cissy. And who shall I tell her gave it to me?

Den. Say somebody gave it to you who happened to see you and thought you were like a little girl he had lost, and say, too, that — (*Breaking down, aside*) Oh, my wife, if I could but send you one word from my living grave!

Cissy. Yes, what else shall I say?

Den. (*Rising*) I dare not! No, dear, there is no other message. Your mother does not know me. (*Kisses her*) Run along, dear, make haste and tell her of your good fortune.

Cissy. Yes, that I will! (*Coming out of cottage*) She's gone to Mr. Skinner's — that nice big house across the field.   *Exit.*

Den. (*Following her to door*) Run on then, my brave little queen. (*He watches her off and then looks carefully and cautiously round*) My boy, I must see my boy! (*Re-enters cottage cautiously*) Just one look, one kiss, nobody is about.

Denver goes into inner room, is absent a few moments then returns in tears. Jaikes enters rubbing his hands to warm them.

Jaikes. Artfulness ain't done it this time. Not a blessed ha'penny! Whew! it gets colder and colder. I wonder where the missy is?

Den. (*Coming out*) My little baby boy that I left, grown so thin, so pale, so wasted — is there no end to my sin, no end to its bitter fruit? (*Sees Jaikes — aside*) Jaikes!

Jaikes. Hillo! What are you doing in there?

Den. (*Turns away his face from Jaikes and muffles it partly with his cape so that Jaikes does not see his features*) Excuse my intrusion, I was passing your cottage and happened to come in. I take a great interest in the sick poor. There's a little boy in that room — he's dangerously ill — send for the doctor to see him at once. Have the best advice you can get and give him some nourishing food, the best of everything. (*Still keeping his face averted from Jaikes and speaking in slightly disguised tones*)

Jaikes. Oh, yes, that's all very well, but where's the money to come from?

Den. (*Aside*) Cissy has my purse. (*Aloud*) I will pay for whatever is required. I have just given away all the money I have about me, but you can have the bills sent in to me. John Franklin, Kensington Gardens, London.

Jaikes. Oh, yes, it's likely I can get tick on the strength o' that, ain't it? A pound of tea and a quartern loaf and put it down to Mr. John Franklin, Kensington Gardens, London.

Den. Do as I tell you — you will find it all right.

Jaikes. Who is Mr. John Franklin? If you want to help us, why don't you give us some money and let's have a look at your face? (*Peers round Denver's muffler and recognises him*) Master Will! (*Drops on his knees*) Master Will! God forgive me! It's Master Will come back from the dead. Say it's really you, Master Will!

Den. Yes, it is I, come back, as you say from the dead. My wife! Is she well? How is she? Has she suffered much? Does she ever speak of me?

Jaikes. Oh, Master Will, I can't tell you what she's had to go through. It's been a terrible hard fight for her, but she's borne up like a angel. Oh, sir, you've come back at the right time. We're nearly starving.

Den. Starving? That's all over now. I'm

rich, Jaikes, I'm rich! When I left England I went to the Silver Mines of Nevada — I had to struggle hard at first and could only send you a few dollars — I was almost starving myself, but one morning I struck a rich vein of silver; to-day I'm richer than I can count; and then I sent you a thousand dollars, and so — none of it reached you?

Jaikes. No, sir, you see we've changed our home so often and she always took care not to leave our address for fear —

Den. For fear my wretched story should follow you, I see.

Jaikes. Ah, sir, don't say any more about that — that's all past now. Oh, don't you mind my crying, sir; to see you come back like this is too much for me — I can't believe it, sir. (*Rises*) And Miss Nelly — she'll go mad with joy.

Den. She must not know, Jaikes.

Jaikes. Not know? Not tell her, Master Will?

Den. Not yet! Not yet. Listen, Jaikes, I have come back to England with one thought, with one resolve — to make her happy. Whatever happens to me, that I will do. Shall I ask her to share my nightmare of a life, put her on a ceaseless rack of anxiety and suspense, torture her as I am tortured? Heaven forbid!

Jaikes. But surely, Master Will, you are safe after all these years?

Den. I shall never be safe till I stand in the dock to answer for my crime — I shall be safe then. I've started a hundred times to give myself up, but I have always been held back by the thought that I was not myself that night; but it will come, Jaikes.

Jaikes. What will come, sir?

Den. Detection. It may be to-morrow, or it may not be for years, but it will come, and if I were to join her, suspicion would be aroused at once. I might be discovered, dragged from her side, tried, condemned and hanged.

Jaikes. Master Will! But if missus could but know. If she could but know.

Den. Not yet Jaikes. Listen, you shall take her from this poverty and put her in her old home with everything that money can buy, and then, when I have made her rich, cheerful, contented, I will ask myself whether I may dare to throw the shadow of my life across her happiness. In the meantime, promise me, swear to me that she shall not know.

Jaikes. Why, of course, Master Will, if you wishes it.

Den. Jaikes, I must see her — I am dying to look on her dear face, to hear one word from her lips — to see her without being seen.

Jaikes. That's easily managed. Stand here, you'll be able to see her and hear her and she'll never be none the wiser.

Den. God bless you, my dear old Jaikes, for all your kindness. God bless you, I shall never be able to repay you.

Jaikes. There now, don't you talk nothing about that, Master Will. Why, to see you come back like this pays me fifty times over. I allus said you would. (*Crying with joy*) I allus said — (*Looks off*) Here comes Miss Nelly.

Denver and Jaikes go up and get behind cottage. Enter Nelly, crosses stage and goes into cottage.

Den. (*Coming from behind*) My poor wife! (*Nelly in cottage puts her purchases on table*)

Nelly. There, my precious ones, you shall have a meal to-night at any rate. I wonder where Jaikes and Cissy are?

Den. My own Nell, the girl who left her own bright home to follow my cursed fortunes. Oh, if I look another moment I must rush to her and hold her in my arms!

Enter Olive, quickly crosses stage and enters cottage. Denver retires behind cottage and comes out again after she has entered.

Olive. I am the bearer of bad news. My husband has repented of his kindness. He will not let you stay here.

Nelly. Not let me stay here?

Olive. No — since you left him he has learned who you are. He has found out that you are the wife of a — (*Denver turns aside as if stabbed with pain*)

Nelly. (*Checks Olive*) Ah no, no, for pity's sake don't say it. I have heard the word so often. Yes, it is true — I am the widow of such a man, and for that I am to be punished, it seems. (*Sobbing*)

Olive. Who knows it is true? Who knows that your husband did really kill that man?

Den. (*Eagerly*) What's that?

Nelly. Why, what doubt can there be?

Olive. It was never proved. He was never tried. Who knows but that there might have been some terrible mistake?

Den. (*Outside*) Some terrible mistake?

Nelly. What do you mean? What do you know?

Olive. (*Recovering herself quickly*) Nothing — I thought it might comfort you to think your husband was innocent. It could do no harm now that he is dead; but I am forgetting my errand. I came here to help you and I dare not stay. (*Takes out purse. Coombe's voice heard off*)

Coombe. (Outside) You can wait here. Be ready if I want you. (*Coombe enters. As Denver hears and sees Coombe, he retires*) But we'll try persuasion first. (*Enters cottage*)

Den. The man who showed me into Geoffrey Ware's room that dreadful night. What does it mean?

Olive. There are three pounds five shillings. It is all I have. (*Takes money out of purse and shows it empty. Coombe, who has entered unseen by Nelly or Olive, gets to back of table and picks up money*)

Coombe. It won't be necessary, ma'am. I'll take it to your husband. Your husband wants you — you'd better go. (*Holds door of cottage open for Olive*)

Olive. Oh, if he were not my husband!
    *Exits quickly from cottage and crosses
        stage, going off.*

Coombe. (Calling after her) Ah! you shouldn't have took your place for life. (*Shuts door and turns to Nelly*)

Den. What now? If I stop this ruffian he'll call his men and there may be a disturbance, and I may be involved. What can I do?

Coombe. Now, my dear good lady, there's a pleasant way of doing things and a unpleasant, and I always try the pleasant way first.

Nelly. Oh, don't make any words about it. You have come to turn me out, is it not so?

Coombe. Oh, dear no. I've only come to ask you in the kindest manner possible to pay your rent. Three pounds five shillings.

Nelly. How can I pay it? I haven't a shilling in the world, and you know I haven't.

Den. (Outside) Where is Cissy? Where is the money?

Coombe. Ah, that's a pity! Because as you can't pay you must go.

Nelly. No, no! Let me stay to-night — only to-night. I will go to-morrow morning. My child is in that room very ill, and if he is moved in this bitter weather, it will kill him. Let me stay to-night, I will do no harm.

Coombe. Now look here, my dear good lady — it's no good your begging and praying to me, 'cos go you must.

Nelly. Oh, is there no tenderness, no pity on the earth!

Coombe. Now, look sharp! Are you going to pack up?

Nelly. Yes, yes, give me a little time, I will go. (*Goes into inner room, re-entering almost immediately very determinedly*) No, I will not go. My child is sleeping. He is getting better, I will not wake him and take him into the bitter cold to kill him. (*She bolts the door and stands with her back to it*)

Coombe. (Stands with his back to fire) Will you go quietly, or shall I have to send for my men to turn you out?

Nelly. I tell you I will not go. Go back and tell your master that here I stay — I and my children — till he drags our bodies out and flings them into the streets.

Coombe. Oh very well, we must try the unpleasant way then.

Nelly. Merciful Father, help me now!

Den. (Outside) I can bear it no longer. (*Comes to door, is about to open it when Cissy runs to him*) Quick, my child, give your mother the money! (*Pushes her through doorway. He has opened the door*)

Cissy. Mother, look what the kind gentleman gave me!

Nelly. (Seizes money eagerly) An angel from Heaven has sent it. (*To Coombe, as she throws money on the table*) Here, take your money! Now you go! (*Points to door*)
        Coombe baffled, picks up money.

        End of the Third Act.

ACT IV.

Scene 1.

A room in Denver's house, Kensington Gardens. Doors right and left. Window to left. Enter Frank Selwyn, showing in Baxter.

Bax. Mr. John Franklin not in, eh?

Sel. No. I am his private secretary.

Bax. (Looking at him keenly) Oh! you are his private secretary? (*Aside*) This is the young sprig I'm after.

Sel. Perhaps I might do.

Bax. No. I think not. When can I see Mr. Franklin?

Sel. It's uncertain. What's your business?

Bax. That's my business! I'll wait. (*Turns back to audience and stands looking at picture on wall, whistling*)

Sel. (Aside, looking at Baxter) Can he have come about that cursed cheque? It must come sooner or later. Mr. Franklin must find me out, find out that I have repaid his goodness by robbing him, returned his trust by forging his name!

Bax. (Turning round) I suppose you've got a nice comfortable berth as Mr. Franklin's private secretary?

Sel. Yes.

Bax. Very rich man, isn't he?

Sel. Very.

Bax. Made his money in Silver Mining, didn't he?

Sel. Yes.

Bax. Ah! so I've heard. Went to bed one night a common miner, and the next a millionaire.

Sel. I've heard so. They call him the Silver King.

Bax. Gives a lot of money away, doesn't he?

Sel. His whole life is spent in doing good. He's as noble and generous as he is rich.

Bax. Ah! employs you to look after the deserving cases — trusts you with his purse, and his cheque book occasionally, eh?

Sel. (*Wildly*) What do you mean?

Bax. Nothing, only you must take care he doesn't get imposed on. (*Aside*) It's all right — the young idiot.

Sel. (*Aside*) It must come!

Enter Denver.

Den. Somebody wishes to see me, Frank?

Bax. Mr. John Franklin? (*Looking at Denver*)

Den. Yes, I am John Franklin. What do you want?

Bax. I beg pardon. That is my card. (*Giving card*) Sam Baxter, Scotland Yard. (*Aside, as Denver takes card*) I've seen you before somewhere, my gentleman.

Den. (*Wincing under Baxter's steady gaze*) Well, what is your business? I must beg you to make haste as I have to catch a train into the country.

Bax. Then I'll come to the point at once. (*Opens his pocket-book, takes out papers. Selwyn is going, Baxter stops him*) Mr. Private Secretary, you needn't go. We may want you. (*Aside, looking at papers*) Now where have I seen you before, Mr. Franklin? (*Aloud, taking a cheque from pocket-book*) Oh, here it is!

Sel. (*Aside*) The cheque I forged!

Bax. You bank at the County and Metropolitan?

Den. Yes.

Bax. This cheque was presented yesterday for payment in the ordinary way. The clerk refused to cash it, detained the presenter and sent for you immediately. You were not at home, and so the affair was placed in my hands. (*Denver comprehends the situation, and as Selwyn makes a movement as if to speak, stops him with a look of caution and silences him*)

Den. (*To Baxter*) Give me the cheque. (*Baxter gives cheque, Denver looks at it*) Well?

Bax. That signature, sir?

Den. Well?

Bax. Is it in your handwriting, sir?

Den. Yes, it's quite right. (*Selwyn gives*

sigh and shows immense relief, and is about to blab out his gratitude. Denver stops him with a look) Yes, the signature is a little awkward. I must have been in a hurry. (*Baxter still looks incredulous*) Do you doubt me?

Bax. Oh, no, sir, if you say so, sir, of course it's all right — if you wrote the cheque — why, there's an end of the matter, isn't there, sir?

Den. I think so. You may take the cheque back to the bank, tell the cashier it is all right. If necessary I'll call at the bank to-morrow and make the matter right. Will you accept a five-pound note for your trouble?

Bax. Thank you, sir, and if ever you should want my assistance in any little matter of business, sir, I shall be happy to oblige you, sir, and to keep my mouth shut. (*In putting the note in his pocket he intentionally drops a piece of paper*)

Den. Thank you, I have your card.

Bax. (*Aside to Denver*) Keep your eye on that youngster — he's got mixed up with a bad lot. (*Aloud*) Good day, Mr. Franklin.

Den. Good day, Mr. Baxter. (*Turns to Selwyn*)

Bax. (*Glancing back at Denver, aside*) I've had you through my hands somewhere. *Exit.*

Den. Don't do it again, my boy, don't do it again!

Sel. I never will, sir! Oh, sir, your kindness breaks my heart! I've been such a bad fellow, sir! I don't deserve that you should forgive me. I shall be ashamed to meet you in the future, sir.

Den. I hope not. This was your first step downwards, pray that it may be your last.

Sel. It shall! It shall!

Den. Remember, I still trust you! *Exit.*

Sel. I'll make a fresh start to-day. God bless him! *Exit.*

Re-Enter Baxter.

Bax. I beg pardon, I must have dropped a paper here! Nobody here! (*Picks up the paper he had previously dropped, creeps to the window and looks out.*) There goes Mr. Franklin in a cab. Drives off! Now when and where have I had that man through my hands? Deuce take my memory! (*Comes slowly away from window*) Dear! Dear! (*Snaps his fingers and taps his forehead to aid his memory in crossing the stage, stops suddenly*) Good heavens! Yes! that's the man! Derby night four years ago! The Skittle Alley at the "Wheatsheaf" — the revolver, whew! Here's a find! John Franklin, millionaire, philanthropist and Silver King, an unhung murderer. The hair grown grey but the same face. By Jove! What a catch for me!

Exit very swiftly and with great animation.

Scene 2.

Exterior of The Grange. Discover Old Village People. Jaikes enters very respectably dressed.

Jaikes. Well, Gaffer Pottle! Mrs. Gammage! Hillo, Tabby!

Gaffer. (*An ancient decrepit villager*) My humble respects, Muster Jaikes. (*Turning to Tabby*) Curtsey, Tabitha! Curtsey! Curtsey, you old fool! Don't you know Muster Jaikes is Master of the Grange and Lord of the Manor?

Tabby. Ah, Daniel Jaikes and me was brought up together. I ain't going to curtsey to Dan'l Jaikes. I'm going to shake hands with him. Don't you remember how fond we was of one another when we was boy and girl together, eh, Dan'l dear?

Jaikes. No, I don't. It's too many years ago — and don't call me Dan'l. (*Aside*) Tabby's a setting her cap at me again, I must put a stop to that.

Gaffer. I hopes Miss Nelly is pretty tolerable?

Jaikes. Oh, she's all right! Your dinner ain't ready yet. You can wait here a few minutes, and mind you all behaves yourselves! (*Very severely to Tabby*) Tabby, let those flowers alone. I'll tell Mrs. Denver you have arrove.   *Exit Jaikes.*

Gaffer. Dan'l Jaikes seems to be rather 'igh and mighty now he's come into his fortin'!

Mrs. G. Ah! Fancy Dan'l Jaikes coming and buying the Grange and being Lord of the Manor, and bringing Miss Nelly back to live in it.

Gaffer. I can't make out who this here Uncle Samiwell was as has died and left Dan'l all this money.

Mrs. G. Aye, Dan'l never had no Uncle Samiwell as ever I heered on.

Tabby. Ah, you folks don't know nothin' about it. Dan'l's master of the Grange, ain't he? And I wouldn't say as I mightn't be missus afore long.

Gaffer. I wouldn't say as you mightn't, Tabby. Pigs might fly, but I've kep' pigs for up'ards of fifty years, and I never see 'm make a start.

Mrs. G. No, Tabby, Muster Jaikes didn't seem to be noways particler smit with you just now.

Gaffer. Aye, aye, Tabby, you've had three husbands and buried 'em all. You let well alone.

Enter from house Nelly well dressed, with Cissy and Ned clinging to her, one on each side, Jaikes following them. Old people bow and curtsey.

Nelly. Well, you have come, all of you, that's right. How do you do, all of you? (*Shaking hands with some of them*) How do you do, Tabby?

Tabby. We're all well and hearty, thank you kindly, and we be mortal glad to see you back at the Grange again, bain't we, Gaffer?

Gaffer. Aye, we didn't like they folks as come here when you and Muster Denver left.

Mrs. G. They was mean, they was.

Tabby. Aye, no beef and coals at Christmas, no pea soup, no blankets, no flannel petticoats, no nothing! (*Cissy runs off into shrubbery*)

Gaffer. Aye, we knowed when you come back, Miss Nelly, there'd be plenty for everybody.

Nelly. I hope so. You see, my friends, I have known what it is to be poor myself. Since I left you I have heard my children cry for bread, indeed, if it were not for the kindness of my old friend here — (*Indicating Jaikes, who shuffles about and looks very uncomfortable*)

Jaikes. Yes, yes, missus! We'll drop the subject.

Nelly. No, we will not. You know I owe everything to you. (*To the old people*) Go and have your dinner, all of you. You'll find it ready in the hall. It is Jaikes that provides it for you, not I. First thank the Giver of all good, and then thank our dear old Jaikes.

Jaikes. No, no, I won't be thanked! (*Hurries them into house*) Be off, you old vermints, be off! (*Tabby stops behind*) Now, Tabby!

Nelly. What do you want?

Tabby. (*Curtseying to Nelly*) Oh! if you please, Miss Nelly, we liked that bit of beef you sent us so much. The next time we hopes it'll be a little larger and not quite so fat. And I'm getting short o' tea and candles, and a little drop of gin is comforting after washing all day. And my best gown's wore out.

Jaikes. Good job too! I wish it was your tongue instead.

Nelly. Very well, Tabby, I won't forget you.

Jaikes. Now will you be off and get your dinner, or else you shan't have none! Be off! (*Hurries her off. Exit Tabby*) The old hussy! You mustn't let her impose on you, missus.

Nelly. Ah, Jaikes, it is for you to say — you are master here.

Jaikes. Yes, yes — of course, so I am — I forgot that! Still, you know, missus, all this money is, as you may say, yours.

Nelly. Mine, Jaikes?

Jaikes. Yes, you see my Uncle Samuel left particular instructions in his will — well, never mind my Uncle Samuel, we'll drop the subject. Ain't you 'appy now you're back in your old home, missus?

Nelly. Yes, Jaikes, I am happy! (*Sighs*)

Jaikes. Quite happy, Missus?

Nelly. (*Sighs*) Yes, Jaikes, happier than I ever hoped to be.

Jaikes. There's some'ut, missus! I can see — something you miss, now, ain't there? Tell the truth.

Nelly. Yes, Jaikes, there is.

Jaikes. What is it, missus? I've ordered 'em to lay out the garden just as it used to be and to plant a new chestnut tree where the old 'un was blown down —

Nelly. It isn't that, Jaikes.

Jaikes. The old fish-pond as they folks filled up — I'll have it dug out again?

Nelly. Ah, no, don't trouble about that.

Jaikes. Then what is it, missus? You shall have it if it costs a mint of money.

Nelly. Oh, Jaikes, can't you see what it is? I'm back in my old home without the man who made it all dear to me — without my Will! Oh, I love him still — yes, I love him as much to-day as the day I married him in the church yonder. It was under this tree I promised to be his wife. Oh, Jaikes, I remember it as if it were yesterday. Everything here, every tree, every brick in the old house, every little nook and corner brings back to me his dear handsome face until I can sometimes hardly stop myself from running all through the grounds and fields and calling out "Will! Will! come back to me, come back to me, if it were but for a moment!" Now you know what it is I miss in my old home, my husband's love — and you can't give that back to me, Jaikes, no, no, not that, not that! *Exit.*

Jaikes. (*Looking after her*) Can't I? Oh, yes, I can, and I will, too, this very day! I've wrote and told him I can't keep his secret no longer — he's on his way to you now as fast as the train can bring him! You wait a bit, missus, and I'll dry up them tears for you! You shall be the happiest woman in England afore this day's over, that you shall! Make haste, Master Will, make haste and come! (*Re-enter Tabby*) Hillo! what now, Tabby?

Tabby. (*Very affectionately*) Oh, Dan'l dear! I'm so glad you've come back again. Ain't you glad to be back among your old friends, Dan'l dear?

Jaikes. (*Cautiously edging from her*) Yes — yes — middling!

Tabby. Don't you remember when we used to go cowslipping, eh, Dan'l?

Jaikes. (*Resolutely*) No, I never went cowslippin' along of you, Tabby.

Tabby. Oh, yes, you did, Dan'l. And our games at hide and seek?

Jaikes. No!

Tabby. Oh, yes, Dan'l, I used to hide and you used to try and find me.

Jaikes. Oh, no, Tabby! I used to hide and you used to try and find me!

Tabby. Oh, Dan'l, you don't know how fond I've allays been of you, and now you're gettin' old and I'm gettin' old —

Jaikes. Yes, you are, Tabby, and precious ugly into the bargain!

Tabby. And I've been thinking how nice it 'ud be if we could end our days together.

Jaikes. I'm much obliged, Tabby, but I don't want to end my days just at present.

Tabby. Ah, but, Dan'l dear — me to take care of you and nurse you up, and you to take care of me and nurse me up — wouldn't that be nice?

Jaikes. (*Resolutely*) No, no, you might like it; but I ain't ambitious, Tabby, I'm very content as I am.

Tabby. Ah, Dan'l — you've never been married.

Jaikes. And you have — three times.

Tabby. And the best of wives I've made, I'm sure. Ask my three good men else.

Jaikes. It 'ud be a sin to disturb 'em now they've got a bit of peace.

Tabby. And I should make a better wife now than ever.

Jaikes. You ought, Tabby, you've had plenty of experience.

Tabby. (*Taking his arm affectionately*) Well, then, what do you say, lovey — when shall we be married?

Jaikes. (*Aghast*) Married! Me marry you! Why, you old Mormon, you old female Henry the Eighth! You old wolf in sheep's clothing! You — you, you old Bluebeard in petticoats! Me marry you! Never! Never! Be off with you! Be off! (*Frightens her off*) I've had a narrow squeak that time!

Enter Cissy with flowers.

Cissy. Look, Jaikes, for mamma! Aren't

they pretty? Oh, Jaikes, it was kind of you to bring us to this beautiful home!

Jaikes. Ah! it ain't me, little missy, it isn't me as is doing it at all!

Cissy goes off.

Denver appears at gate.

Den. Jaikes!

Jaikes. Master Will!

Den. Is anybody about? Can I come in?

Jaikes. Yes, come in, Master Will! Miss Nelly's gone to give her poor people their dinner and I'm all alone.

Den. You're sure I shan't be seen?

Jaikes. No fear, sir, I'll keep a good look out.

Den. How is she? Is she quite well and happy — and the children?

Jaikes. Yes, they're all quite well. Oh, Master Will, I'm so glad you've come. I can't hold out much longer! Uncle Samuel has got me into a dreadful mess! I wish we hadn't invented him. And then there's all that money as you sent her anenonymously from America.

Den. Yes?

Jaikes. Well, it didn't turn up while we was starving, but now we're rolling in money and it's a nuisance, it all turns up as bold as brass. Oh, Master Will, don't hide it from her no longer — tell her as you're alive — you wait here — I'll go and fetch her to you.

Den. Stop, Jaikes, you mustn't go!

Jaikes. Master Will, when you brought her back here and spent all that money to make the old place just like it used to be when she was a girl, you thought you was going to make her happy, didn't you?

Den. And have I not made her happy? What more can I do?

Jaikes. Why, sir, don't you see — home ain't four walls and the ceiling and the furniture — home's the place where them as loves us is — and it was you what made this place home for her, and she's breaking her heart 'cause it's her home no longer.

Den. Jaikes, I will tell you why my wife must not know that I am alive, and when I have told you never speak of it again. Last night I went down to the river to a place owned by that man Coombe.

Jaikes. What, the man as was going to turn the missus out?

Den. Yes, I've been following him up for the last six months, ever since I recognised him as the man that showed me into Geoffrey Ware's room that night. Just as drowning men catch at straws, I have caught at the straw of a hope that I might find out some-thing. I don't know what — something that might give me a right to believe that I did not shed that man's blood —

Jaikes. Ah, how happy it would make her!

Den. And so night after night I go to that place and watch, and watch, and watch. I've tried to get in, all in vain, it's a hopeless task. Well, when I got back last night, I found your letter waiting for me — begging me to make myself known to my wife. I read the letter again and again, and the more I tried to persuade myself that for her dear sake I must keep silence, the more my heart cried out "I must have her! I will have her! If I die for it, she shall be my own again!" And then I thought I would take her out to Nevada, to the city that I have built, where every man would shed his blood for me, and every child is taught to reverence the name of John Franklin. "There," I thought, "I shall be free from the past, safe from the law — there," I said, "we will live the rest of our days honored, happy, beloved, in peace with ourselves and all the world." And so I spent half the night planning out a happy future with her and my children. Oh, Jaikes, I was so happy — I couldn't sleep for joy of it, and when at last I put my head on my pillow, my one thought was "To-morrow I will tell her I am alive! To-morrow I will take her in my arms and call her my wife again!"

Jaikes. And so you shall, Master Will! Let me fetch her to you! Let me fetch her to you!

Den. Stay! I fell asleep, Jaikes — do you know what a murderer's sleep is? It's the waking time of conscience! It's the whipping-post she ties him to while she lashes and stings his poor helpless guilty soul! Sleep! It's a bed of spikes and harrows! It's a precipice over which he falls sheer upon the jags and forks of memory! It's a torchlight procession of devils, raking out every infernal sewer and cranny of his brain! It's ten thousand mirrors dangling round him to picture and re-picture to him nothing but himself. Sleep — oh! God, there is no hell like a murderer's sleep! That's what my sleep has been these four years past. I fell asleep last night and I dreamed that we were over in Nevada and we were seated on a throne, she and I; and it was in a great hall of Justice, and a man was brought before me charged with a crime; and just as I opened my mouth to pronounce sentence upon him, Geoffrey Ware came up out of his grave, with his eyes staring, staring, staring, as they stared at me on that night, and as they will stare at me till I die, and he said, "Come down! Come down! you whited sepulchre! How dare you sit in that place to judge men?" And he leapt up in his grave — close to the throne where I was — and seized me by the throat and dragged me down, and we struggled and fought like wild beasts — we seemed to be fighting for years — and at last I mastered him, and held him down and wouldn't let him stir. And then I saw a hand coming out of the sky, a long, bony hand with no flesh on it, and nails like eagle's claws, and it came slowly — out of the sky, reaching for miles it seemed, slowly, slowly it reached down to the very place where I was, and it fastened on my heart, and it took me and set me in the justice hall in the prisoner's dock, and when I looked at my judge, it was Geoffrey Ware! And I cried out for mercy, but there was none! And the hand gripped me again as a hawk grips a wren, and set me on the gallows, and I felt the plank fall from my feet, and I dropped, dropped, dropped — and I awoke!

Jaikes. For mercy's sake, Master Will —

Den. Then I knew that the dream was sent for a message to tell me that though I should fly to the uttermost ends of the earth — as high as the stars are above, or as deep as the deepest sea bed is below, there is no hiding-place for me, no rest, no hope, no shelter, no escape!

A pause. Cissy runs on.

Cissy. Jaikes, who's that? (*Denver looks up and strives to hide his tears*) Oh! it's you! (*She runs to him and sits on his left knee*) You've come to see us in our new home! But you are crying — what's the matter? Are you unhappy?

Den. (*Putting his arms round her*) Not now, Cissy — not now! Not now!

Cissy. Jaikes, do you know the kind gentleman?

Jaikes. (*Who has gone up stage and keeping watch looking off*) No, missy, no!

Cissy. I'm so glad you've come! You shall come and live with us, will you?

Den. What would you do with me?

Cissy. You shall play with Ned and me. We've got a rocking horse and soldiers, and lots of things.

Den. What games we could have, couldn't we?

Cissy. (*Clapping her hands*) Yes! Oh, do stay, will you! Do! Do!

Den. And your mother?

Cissy. Oh, I know she'd be glad to have you. She's always talking about you and wondering who you are. Who are you?

Den. Who am I?

Cissy. Yes, tell me — tell me true!

Den. Well, I'm a king.

Cissy. But what king are you?

Den. I'm the Silver King! At least that's what men call me.

Jaikes. (*Looking off*) The other way, Gaffer Pottle — this (*Calls out severely*) is private! (*Looking at Denver warningly*)

Den. (*Starting up*) I must go — good-bye, Cissy! (*Kisses her*)

Cissy. (*Holding Denver's hand*) No, no, you mustn't go! Mamma does want to see you so badly! Wait here! I'll go and fetch her. (*Runs off to house calling*) Mamma!

Jaikes. Master Will, won't you stay?

Den. No, Jaikes — let me go! Not a word, for her sake! Let me go!   *Exit quickly.*

Enter Cissy.

Cissy. Come on, mamma! (*Looks round*) Where is he, Jaikes?

Enter Nelly.

Nelly. Where is he?

Jaikes. Where's who, missus?

Nelly. The gentleman who was here who gave the purse to Cissy.

Jaikes. Oh, yes, missus, there was a gentleman here, but as — as he was rather pressed for time he had to go — to — to — catch his train.

Nelly. (*Going up towards gate*) Why did you let him go, Jaikes, when you knew how much I wanted to thank him? He can't have got far — I'll go after him. (*Is preparing to go after Denver, Jaikes goes before her*)

Jaikes. No, don't you go, missus! I'll run after him and bring him back. I shall catch him before he gets to the station.

Exit Jaikes after Denver.

Nelly. (*At gate, slowly comes down to seat*) Who can it be, this unknown friend, this silent, unseen protector, this guardian who is ever watching over my path? Cissy, what was the gentleman like?

Cissy. Oh, he was a very nice old gentleman!

Nelly. Old?

Cissy. Oh, yes, his hair was nearly white, and he was crying so much.

Nelly. Crying? Why should he cry? (*With sudden joy, aside*) Can it be? Oh, if it were he, if it could be, if it might be, if it were possible! (*Eagerly snatches locket from neck, opens it, shows it to Cissy very eagerly*) Cissy, was he like this?

Cissy. Why, that's my father's likeness, mamma!

Nelly. Yes, was he like that?

Cissy. (*After looking at it for a moment or*

two) Oh, no, mamma! The Silver King's hair is nearly white.

Nelly. But the face, Cissy, the face?

Cissy. (*Looking again*) No, my father's face is quite young and happy, and the Silver King's face is so sad and old. No, the Silver King isn't a bit like that. (*Kneels by Nelly*)

Nelly. (*Shutting up locket*) Of course not, I knew it was impossible! I was mad to dream of such a thing.

Cissy. Mamma, it wasn't true, was it, what the school girls used to say?

Nelly. What, dear?

Cissy. That my father had killed a man.

Nelly. (*Aside*) I can't tell her the truth, I will not tell her a lie!

Enter Jaikes at gate.

Jaikes. (*Panting breathless*) I couldn't catch him, missus. (*Cissy goes up to gate and looks off*) I followed him right up to the station and the train had just started! (*Whistle heard*)

Cissy. Oh, Jaikes, that is a story! The train's only just started, for I heard the whistle and I can see the smoke. (*Points off. Nelly goes up to gate, looks at Jaikes, who shuffles about and looks guilty and miserable*)

Nelly. Why are you playing me false? Why don't you tell me the truth?

Jaikes. (*Aside, very uncomfortable*) It'll come out — it'll come out!

Nelly. Who is this man? Your uncle who died? This gentleman who gave the purse to Cissy, this unknown friend who sent me all that money from America — who is he?

Jaikes. How should I know? I hates folks as sends anenonymous letters — I'd string 'em all to the nearest lamp-post without judge or jury!

Nelly. Jaikes, I will take no more money from you, no more food, no more shelter till I know where it comes from. As bare and helpless as we came into this Grange, I and my children will leave it this very day and go out again to starve unless I know who it is that is loading me with all this wealth and kindness. Who is he, Jaikes? Who is he? Who is he, I say?

Jaikes. Oh, missus, can't you guess?

Nelly. (*Frantically*) Ah, I know it! I knew it! He is alive! Take me to him! Make haste! I cannot wait a moment! (*Catching Cissy and Ned in her arms*) Ned! Cissy! My darlings, kiss me, kiss me — your father is alive! (*Kissing them eagerly, crying with joy*)

PICTURE.

Scene 3.

Front scene. The exterior of Coombe's Wharf, with gate leading into the wharf yard. Enter Cripps from yard looking round.

Cripps. Now I wonder whether Father Christmas intends to turn up or whether I'm to be kept here all the night?

Enter Coombe.

Oh, here you are!

Coombe. My dear boy, I hope I ain't kept you waiting very long, my dear boy.

Cripps. Yes, you 'ave, and the next time just you give me the straight tip and I'll go and get drunk instead of wasting my time.

Coombe. Where's the Spider?

Cripps. He's just gone, and he wanted to know why the blazes you don't get somebody to look after this crib and let us in instead of keeping us hangin' about the place as if we was suspicious characters.

Coombe. I wish I could get hold of a likely party.

Cripps. I thought you had got your heye upon a man —

Coombe. So I had, little Johnny Piper, the very man for the job.

Cripps. Well, why didn't you have him?

Coombe. He got the clinch only last week — eighteen months. You see it's no good having anybody here as ain't got a unblemished character. We don't want to have the bluebottles come sniffing round here, do we?

Cripps. Not likely!

Coombe. I suppose the Spider's comin' back?

Cripps. Yes, he didn't seem much to relish the prospect of spending his time with me in your back-yard here, so he's gone off to his club — he said he'd be back here at ten.

Coombe. Ah! the Spider always keeps Greenwich time.

Cripps. Yes, other folks' Greenwich time, when he can nobble 'em. Ah! the Spider's a deep 'un! He was never bred up on pidgin's milk, Spider wasn't.

Coombe. Spider's too grasping. We shall have to take him down a peg or two.

Cripps. It's that viller residence of his what swallows up all our hard won earnings. Why, you and me might take viller residences if we liked, couldn't we?

Coombe. Yes, of course.

Cripps. And we could keep our cooks and buttons, and 'arf a dozen 'osses, and mix with the gentry if we felt so disposed, couldn't we?

Coombe. Yes, to be sure we could — but we don't.

Cripps. No — 'cos why? 'Cos the less we mix with the gentry the better — except in the way of business.

Coombe. Yes, Master Spider's a flying too high for us. You back me up to-night and we'll clip his wings a bit.

Cripps. All right, I'll back you up. Come on inside. (*Going in*)

Denver enters dressed as a ragged, shabby old porter.

Den. Here's poor deaf Dicky. (*Grinning to Coombe*)

Coombe. No! nothing for you to-night, Dicky!

Den. Yes, guv'nor, find a job for Dicky. Poor deaf Dicky! Find a job for poor deaf Dicky, guv'nor!

Cripps. Who the blazes is this cove?

Coombe. Oh, he's been knocking about here on and off for the last six months. He's handy to run errands and take letters to the sea captains that want to buy my old iron, d'ye see? (*Winking and nudging Cripps*) He's as deaf as a post, and he ain't quite right in his upper storey.

Den. Don't be hard on poor deaf Dicky, guv'nor — give Dicky a job! Dicky run very fast and get back in no time. Find a job for poor deaf Dicky.

Coombe. (*Shaking his head vigorously*) No! no! no!

Den. Mr. Coombe shakes his head and says No! no! no! but Dicky says Yes! yes! yes! Poor Dicky, so hungry! Dicky hasn't had a job all day.

Coombe. (*Entering wharf*) No, no, I've got no jobs tonight.

Den. (*Imploringly, stopping him*) Dicky only wants a master to treat him kind and dry bread to eat and rags to wear — Dicky's so cold.

Cripps. Well, be off and get what you want at the workhouse, you forty horse power idiot!

Coombe. Oh, he's useful to me sometimes. (*Takes out money*) There's a sixpence. Go and get some supper; and don't make a beast of yourself.

Den. Thank you, guv'nor, thank you! Dicky do anything for you, guv'nor! Dicky very fond of you! Dicky likes —

Coombe. (*Pointing him off*) Be off with you!

Den. (*Running off*) Dicky's got a sixpence! Dicky's got a sixpence!

Cripps. (*Looking after him*) He's as daft as forty blessed hatters. Come in, Father Christmas!

Coombe and Cripps go into gate. The gate closes with a clang.

Den. Shut out! Shut out! Shall I never worm myself in? I must be mad to dream that ever I shall wring this man's secret from him; and yet he was in Geoffrey Ware's room that night! Let me think of that! Let me beat it into my brain. This man led me up those stairs — why? why? Oh, if I could but remember after that! No! no! All's dark! All's uncertain. To think that within a dozen yards of me, there is a man whose word might give me wife, children, home, all! All! And I stand here and can do nothing!

Enter Corkett loudly dressed.

Cork. (*Aside*) Now I wonder which is old Coombe's shanty? I know it's somewhere about here!

Den. (*Saunters by him in apparent carelessness and recognizes him*) Geoffrey Ware's old clerk! What has he to do with this man? Can this be another link in the chain?

Cork. (*Aside*) I can see their little dodge. They mean to cut 'Enery Corkett. Spider's never at home when I call, and when I met him in Regent's Street the other day, he wouldn't so much as give me a friendly nod; stared at me as if I was so much dirt. I ain't going to be treated like so much dirt, and I ain't going to be cut, or else I shall cut up rough. I'll just let master Spider see as 'Enery Corkett's as good as he is. Now I wonder where Father Christmas hangs out? (*Sees Denver*) Hillo! I say, my good fellow!

Den. (*Holding his hand to his ear*) Eh?

Cork. (*Aside*) He's deaf! (*Shouts*) Can you tell me where I can find a party by the name of Coombe — a marine store dealer? Coombe!

Den. Deaf Dicky got no home — got no friends.

Cork. (*Aside*) He's a blooming idiot! (*Shouts*) Well, find me a party by the name of Coombe. He lives in the Gray's Inn Road, and he's got a wharf somewhere down here — Coombe!

Den. (*Nodding*) Coombe! Dicky knows Mr. Coombe! White hair, red nose, spectacles, nice kind gentleman, good old gentleman!

Cork. That's him! A perfect beauty, old Coombe is. Where is he?

Den. Dicky mustn't tell. Dicky take message — give Dicky letter and sixpence and Dicky take it to Mr. Coombe — let Dicky take letter to Mr. Coombe.

Cork. Oh, I see — caution's the word! Father Christmas don't want to be smelt out. I'll go into a pub and write a letter to Coombe and give it to this daffy to take, and then I'll follow him up and see where he goes. (*Shouts*)

Well, come on, old dunderhead, I'll give you a letter to take to him.

Den. Thank you, thank you! Dicky take it to Mr. Coombe!   *Exit Corkett.*
At last! At last! At last!

Exit after Corkett.

Scene 4.

Interior and exterior of Coombe's Wharf. Discover Coombe and Cripps.

Cripps. I say, let's have some wet. (*Lights pipe*)

Coombe. Put a name on it.

Cripps. Oh, beer, gin, rum, whisky, brandy, anything as has got some taste in it.

Coombe. I'll give you a wee drop of prime Highland whisky, my dear boy.

Exit at inner door.

Cripps. (*Shouting after him*) Bring the jar while you are about it.

Skinner enters outside and whistles.

The Spider! (*Rises and goes to door, unlocks it, admits Spider, then closes door and relocks it*)

Skin. Well! (*Taking off gloves*) Where is the venerable Coombe?

Cripps. The venerable Coombe is getting this child some whisky.

Skin. (*Dropping his voice*) Between ourselves, I half suspect Mr. Coombe means to execute a double shuffle on his own account with those diamonds of Lady Blanche.

Cripps. He'd better not try it on.

Skin. Just so! You back me up and we'll get at the truth to-night.

Cripps. All right! I'll back you up.

Coombe re-enters with whisky jar and water jug and glass, which he sets down in front of Cripps, who helps himself largely.

Coombe. (*Cordially holding out his hand to Skinner*) My dear boy, I'm delighted to see you.

Skin. Reciprocated, Mr. Coombe — there's something magical in the grasp of your hand. It's horny and damned dirty — what of that? It's honest! The shake of an honest hand does me good. (*Takes out his handkerchief and wipes his hands behind his back*)

Enter Denver outside with letter. Knocks at door. Skinner puts out light.

Cripps. Who the blazes is that?

Coombe. (*Goes to door, calls out*) Who's there? Who's there?

Den. (*Knocks*) Poor deaf Dicky got letter for Mr. Coombe. Let Dicky in please.

Coombe. All right, Spider, it's only a deaf idiot that brings messages for me! (*Opens door. Skinner lights candle*)

Den. (*At door*) Letter, guv'nor. Gentleman wanted to know where Mr. Coombe lived. Dicky wouldn't tell him. Dicky wanted to bring letter and earn sixpence — gentleman give Dicky twopence, gentleman hadn't got any more. (*He has been trying to enter but Coombe stops him at the door*)

Coombe. All right! Give me the letter. Wait! (*Denver is coming inside. Coombe shoves him out*) No, outside! (*Shuts door in Denver's face*)

Den. (*Outside*) How long? How long?

Coombe. (*Opens letter*) From the Duke of New York.

Skin. Curse the fellow! To think how many good people die off every day, and yet that blackguard persists in living on.

Coombe. (*Reads letter*) "Dear Father Christmas: — I'm cleaned out and I want a little of the rhino. You ain't treating me fair. I must see you to-night, so send me back a message by the idiot who brings this."

Skin. (*Snatching letter*) Tell him to go to the devil! Now, Coombe, sharp's the word! Let's get to business.

Coombe. I'll send off Deaf Dicky first.

Cripps. (*Suddenly struck with an idea*) Boil me down into mock turtle soup!

Skin. What's the matter, Cripps?

Cripps. Why, the deaf chap would be just the man to keep this here crib.

Skin. We ought to have somebody here. What's the fellow like?

Coombe. He's deaf and an idiot. The police'd never be able to get anything out of him, and he could never tell any lies against us.

Skin. That's the sort of man we want. Bring him in! Let's have a look at him. (*Coombe opens the door and beckons Denver in. He comes in grinning and touching his cap to Skinner and Cripps*) What's your name? (*Denver touches his cap and grins*) What's your name?

Den. (*Nodding and grinning*) Yes, guv'nor!

Cripps. What's your confounded name, you thick-headed hoddy-dod?

Den. He's round at the public house. Dicky go and fetch him, guv'nor?

Skin. This man would be a perfect treasure in the witness box.

Den. Dicky go there if you like, guv'nor.

Skin. I should like to see him under cross-examination.

Den. Dicky take him an answer?

Skin. (*Shaking his head*) No answer. Listen! You want work — don't you — WORK! (*Shouting*)

Den. Work? Oh, yes, guv'nor! Dicky

work very hard, scrub the floor, run messages. Dicky do what you tell him.

Skin. Coombe, this man is like you. He'll do anything for an honest living.

Coombe. Shall we have him?

Den. Dicky be as faithful as a dog. Dicky follow you about everywhere and never leave you — never leave you.

Skin. The devil you won't! That would be rather awkward!

Den. Give poor Dicky a chance, guv'nor.

Skin. He's as safe as anybody we can get. All right, Coombe, give him a trial!

Den. What did you say, guv'nor?

Skin. (*Indicating Coombe*) No, he'll tell you. I can't shout any more.

Coombe. You can come here as porter and sleep on the premises. (*Takes a shilling and counts on his fingers*) Look! Fifteen shillings a week — fifteen shillings!

Den. Oh, thank you! thank you! Dicky so glad! so glad! so glad!

Coombe. (*Beckoning Denver*) Come this way, I'll show you where you've got to sleep. Sleep!

Den. Dicky stay here always — Dicky very fond of Mr. Coombe — Dicky stay here always! Thank you, Mr. Coombe — thank you, too, sir! Thank you, too!

Exit at inner door, after Coombe.

Skin. (*To Cripps, taking out moulds*) Cripps, I want you to make me some keys to fit these moulds. (*Explains to Cripps in dumb show*)

Enter Corkett outside.

Cork. That idiot's a long time gone. This was the place he went in at. (*Looks through the keyhole*) There's a light inside. (*Knocks*)

Skin. (*Puts out light*) Who the plague is that? (*Corkett knocks again, and whistles in peculiar manner*)

Cripps. It's that blessed Duke of New York.

Skin. (*Relighting*) You'd better let him in or else he'll kick up a row. (*Cripps goes to door, unlocks it, admits Corkett, who is very loudly dressed, outrageous tweed suit, eyeglass, crutch stick, white hat, light kid gloves. Cripps locks door, leaving key*)

Cork. How do, dear boys! Ah, Spider, old chummy! (*Waving his hand to Skinner*) Bless you, bless you!

Skin. Bless yourself! Pray for some brains. What do you want here?

Cork. L. s. d., especially the L.

Skin. What have you done with that last twenty pounds?

Cork. Blued it!

Skin. (*Looking at Corkett's clothes*) You've been to my tailor's again, I see.

Cork. Yes. Neat, ain't they? Told him to put 'em down to your account. Hope you don't mind it, dear boy!

Skin. (*Venomously*) Take care, you brute! You're nearly at the end of your tether!

Enter Coombe.

Coombe. (*Seeing Corkett, shakes hands with him*) Why, it's our young friend, 'Enery Corkett.

Cork. Dear old Father Christmas!

Skin. Now, Coombe, have you stowed away your March hare?

Coombe. Yes, I've took him up to the cockloft and give him some bread and cheese and left him. He seems happy enough.

Skin. Then business sharp. Where's the money-box? (*Coombe takes cash-box out of chimney, opens it and takes out money*)

Cripps. How much?

Coombe. A hundred and eighty.

Skin. Only a hundred and eighty for all that plate? I'd better have left it on Sir George's sideboard — I shall miss it the next time I dine with him.

Coombe. (*Giving money to Cripps and Skinner*) That clears Sir George's plate.

Skin. (*Pocketing money*) Right! (*To Coombe*) Now, my venerable chum, just one word with you about Lady Blanche's jewels — where are they?

Coombe. (*Uneasily*) Well, you see, my dear boy, I didn't like to leave them here and — and so I took 'em to my own place — my shop in the Gray's Inn Road. I thought they'd be safe there.

Skin. Now, Coombe, you're telling lies, you know. Lies! and setting a bad example to Cripps here!

Cripps. Yes. Father Christmas, don't you try any hanky panky tricks with this child. You know me. Handle me gentle, use me well, fair and square, I've got the temper of a sucking lamb, haven't I, Spider?

Skin. You have, Mr. Cripps, and also its playfulness and innocence.

Cripps. But rub me the wrong way — come any dodge, try to do me out of my fair share of the swag, and then —! (*Brings fist on table with tremendous force*)

Skin. Then you have the ferocity of the British lion in mortal combat with the apocryphal unicorn. Now, Coombe, once more, where are Lady Blanche's diamonds?

Coombe. My dear boy, I've got a gentleman coming to see 'em next week — a gentleman from Amsterdam.

Cripps. Damn Amsterdam!

Skin. Never mind that, I want my property!

Cork. (*Aside*) There's a reward of a thousand pounds offered for them jewels, I'll have a cut in here!

Denver creeps on and hides behind bales and listens with great interest.

Skin. Those jewels are worth six thousand pounds, and once more for the last time, where are they?

Coombe. Don't get into a temper, Spider! I tell you I may have a customer for 'em next week — we'll settle for 'em then!

Skin. No, we won't settle for them then, we'll settle for them now!

Cripps. Yes, we'll settle for 'em now!

Cork. (*Joining in*) Yes, we'll settle for 'em now!

Skin. (*Turning sharply on Corkett*) You infernal jackanapes, what business is it of yours?

Cork. Every business of mine, Mr. Spider, look there! (*Turns out his pockets, shows they are empty*) That's what business it is of mine! I mean to have fifty quid out of this!

Skin. Oh, you do, do you?

Cork. (*Promptly*) If you don't give it me I'll let on about Hatton Garden four year ago. (*Denver starts violently and shows great interest*)

Skin. (*With deadly rage*) If you say half a word more —

Cork. (*Promptly*) Half a word more! (*Skinner seizes him by the throat; Coombe seizes Skinner*)

Coombe. (*Alarmed*) Come, come, my dear boys, this won't do!

Cripps. (*Holding Corkett*) Stow it, Spider, stow it!

Skin. I've given you rope enough, Mr. Corkett!

Cork. (*Still held by Cripps*) Don't you talk about rope, Spider! If it comes to hanging, it won't be me, it'll be you! (*Denver shows great interest. Skinner tries to get at Corkett. Coombe interposes*)

Skin. Curse you, will you never give me peace till I kill you?

Cork. Yes, as you killed Geoffrey Ware! (*Denver, no longer able to restrain himself, leaps up with a terrific scream of joy*)

Den. Ah! innocent! Innocent! Thank God!

All. (*Turn round and see Denver*) Who is it? Who is it?

Den. Wilfred Denver! (*To Cripps and Corkett, who are in front of door*) Stand from that door! (*They do not move. Denver flourishes*

crowbar — *Cripps and Corkett retreat down stage*)

All. (*Overcome, helpless*) Stop him! Stop him!

Den. Stop me! The whole world shall not stop me now!

> *Gets through door and bangs it to.*
> PICTURE.
> *End of the Fourth Act.*

ACT V.

Scene 1.

Skinner's villa as in the first scene of Act III. Night. Moonlight. Enter Skinner with a lighted candle and bag by door.

Skin. Olive! (*Pause*) Olive! Olive!

Olive. (*Outside*) Yes!

Skin. Come down at once, I want you. (*Takes jewel case and cash-box out of bag*) Now, have I got everything? Yes, I think so, everything worth taking. Coombe's private cash-box. (*Takes a jemmy from his pocket and prys cash-box open, takes out jewels*) As I thought — Lady Blanche's jewels! The old fox! The old sweep! I knew he meant to rob me. (*Takes out a bag of money from cash-box*) Hillo, Mr. Coombe's private savings! That's lucky. They'll come in handy at a pinch. (*Puts bag in his pocket*)

Enter Olive. She is in a dressing gown and with her hair down as if newly aroused from sleep.

Olive. What do you want?

Skin. Shut the door.

Olive. Herbert! Something has happened. What is it?

Skin. The worst. That man Denver is alive.

Olive. Alive! No — Impossible!

Skin. Yes, and has got on our scent. Knows everything.

Olive. Have I not always said a day of retribution would come?

Skin. For Heaven's sake don't preach now. Listen to me, and if you make one mistake in carrying out my instructions, it's death and ruin to me. Now will you obey?

Olive. Oh, Herbert!

Skin. No sermons. Will you do as I tell you?

Olive. You know I will — if it's to save you.

Skin. You see all this? (*Opens cabinet — puts all the jewels, etc., into it*)

Olive. Yes.

Skin. While this is safe, I'm safe. If it's found, I'm ruined — you understand?

Olive. Yes.

Skin. (*Locking cabinet and giving the key to Olive*) There's the key. The moment I leave this house, take all that, sew it securely in your dress, walk to Lewisham, take the first train to Charing Cross and the morning express to Paris — go to the old address, I'll join you as soon as I can. Remember what's at stake. If you find yourself watched or followed, get rid of it — burn it, plant it on somebody else, for Heaven's sake, don't be found with it on you. Don't write to me. Now, is that all? Yes, that's all.

Olive. I shall not see you again?

Skin. Not for a week or two. Good-bye! (*Kisses her*)

Olive. Good-bye, Herbert. Take care!

Skin. It's you who must take care. I can trust you, Olive?

Olive. Yes, I will make no mistake. It shall not be found.

Skin. Good girl! I shall make something of you yet. (*Whistle heard off*) Coombe! (*To Olive*) Now be off. The moment the house is clear set to work. *Exit Skinner.*

Olive. Oh, Herbert, what am I doing for your sake? *Exit Olive.*

Enter Skinner followed by Coombe, Cripps and Corkett.

Coombe. My dear boy! What luck! Did you follow him up?

Skin. Yes, to a big place in Kensington Gardens; he's John Franklin, the millionaire. The Silver King!

Coombe. Well, what did you do, my dear boy?

Skin. Cheeked it out, went into the place and asked for him — gave my name and was shown up.

Cork. And what did he say, Spider?

Skin. He's just driven off into the country — Heaven knows why; but I got his address and I can put my hand on him when I choose.

Cripps. Yes, but can you stop his jaw?

Skin. Yes, I can stop his, if I can stop yours! Now look here, you three — we are perfectly safe while we hold our tongues. There's not a fraction of evidence against us, and there never will be if we keep quiet. But the moment one of us opens his mouth, it's transportation for all of us. Now, do we stick together?

Cripps. Yes, of course we will, Spider.

Skin. Right! Now there's not a moment to waste. Coombe, you go to your place in the Gray Inn's Road. You may get a visit from the police to-morrow — be ready for them; destroy every scrap that could tell a tale. Sharp's the word — off you go!

Coombe. But the swag at the wharf?

Skin. The swag is not at the wharf. It's safe. Now will you go? (*Hustles Coombe off*) Now you, Cripps, you go to the Lawn, Kensington, and watch the house.

Cripps. Whose house?

Skin. Denver's — Franklin's, or whatever he calls himself — take the Moucher with you and send him to the Carr Lane Crib to report every three hours.

Cripps. But the blessed swag — what about that?

Skin. Don't I tell you the swag is safe?

Cripps. Yes, but where is it? What do you call safe?

Skin. I call a thing safe, Cripps, when that thing is in my possession and its whereabouts is known only to myself. Now the swag is safe in that sense.

Cripps. That's all my eye!

Skin. You shall have your share when the time comes.

Cork. (*Aside*) Yes, and I'll have mine.

Skin. No words — (*To Cripps*) Bundle off!
  Shoves Cripps off.

Cork. And what am I to do, Spider?

Skin. You! It was your cursed blabbing that brought us into this infernal mess. Now I'll give you just one word of caution. If you ever open your mouth one single half inch, it's all up with you. If that Hatton Garden business comes to light — if it's ever known that Denver didn't do it, it will be known that Corkett did. We've made up our minds that if one of us has to swing for it, it'll be you. Now you're warned.

Cork. Oh, yes, Spider, I'll take my davy I'll never mention it again.

Skin. (*Taking money bag from pocket*) Now if I let you have a sufficient sum, do you think you can manage to make yourself scarce for three months?

Cork. I'll try, Spider. I should like to go on the Continent if I'd got coin enough. I've got a pal in Amsterdam.

Skin. Very well, I'll let you have fifty pounds.

Cork. Fifty pounds! Oh, come, Spider, don't be stingy! Three months and they're sure to cheat me. I can't speak a word of Dutch. Make it a hundred and I'll be off slick to-morrow morning.

Skin. I shall give you sixty and not a penny more. (*Begins to count out money — aside*) Coombe's money comes in handy.

Cork. (*Watching him, aside*) That's one of old Coombe's bags. How did Spider get that? He must have brought the swag here.

Skin. (*Giving him money*) There you are, and don't reckon on getting any more from me. I've had just as much of you as I can swallow. There's a train from Liverpool Street to Harwich at eight o'clock. You'd better go by it.

Cork. All right, Spider, I'm off. Ta, ta.

Exit.

Skin. I think I've shut his mouth for the time; but the moment he's spent the money he'll come back. Curse them, I won't trust any of them. Now let me see! Olive is safe! The swag is safe! Nothing can touch me. The Grange, Gardenhurst, Bucks. Now then for Mr. John Franklin. *Puts out light. Exit.*

A pause. Enter Baxter cautiously by window.

Bax. The light out. Which way did they go? He brought that stuff here. It must be in the house somewhere. Oh, if I could only nab you, Spider. To think that I know that that rascal has had his finger in every jewel robbery for the last ten years, and I've never been able to lay my hands on him. But I think I shall be one too many for you this time. There's some big swag about here to-night, and I don't leave this house till I've smelt it out. (*Hears footsteps and retreats to window*)

Enter Olive.

(*Aside*) The Spider's wife!

Olive. They have left the house — now is the time. (*Goes to cabinet and unlocks it*) Oh, how my heart beats. Courage — for Herbert's sake. Hark, who's that? Somebody at that window. Who can it be? (*Leaves cabinet open, stands back, touches Baxter — screams*) Who's there?

Bax. Silence for your life. (*Struggles with Olive, who would scream out, but that Baxter puts his hand over her mouth and hustles her off*) Who's this coming? Is it Spider? Steady, Sam, steady! (*Hides behind curtain*)

Re-Enter Corkett.

Cork. Spider's safe off. He's all right — the swag must be here. He couldn't have carted it nowhere else. Now where's he put it? All's quiet — if I can only collar it I will make myself scarce. I'll go to the continent and enjoy myself. (*Knocks against cabinet*) What's that? Why it's the blessed cabinet. Crimes! It's open! (*Feels inside*) These are the cases! Here's a lucky squeeze. (*Takes jewel cases out, etc.*) Golly, here's all the blessed lot of it. Why it'll be a perfect little gold mine to

me. (*Kneels down to look at jewels and stuffs them into his pockets quickly*) I can be honest now for the rest of my life. After all, honesty is the best policy. (*Stuffs one case under his waistcoat*) Won't old Spider be jolly mad when he finds it out. I'm off — my name's Walker!

During the latter part of Corkett's speech, Larkin, a detective, has sneaked round from window. As Corkett rises and is going off he confronts him. Tableau. Corkett then turns to escape right and is met by Baxter who pounces on him.

Bax. No, it isn't! It's Corkett! I know you, you young blackguard. (*To Larkin*) Turn on the light.

Cork. Nobbled — Baxter — fourteen years!

Bax. Now, my young friend, turn out. Let's see what's in your pockets.

Cork. I've only got my handkerchief.

Bax. Let's have a look at it.

Cork. And a bunch of keys!

Bax. Turn out — produce! (*Corkett begins to gingerly fumble about and produces nothing*) Now, will you hand over?

Cork. Yes, sir. (*Produces a jewel case*)

Bax. (*Opens it*) The Honourable Mrs. Farebrother's rings. Stolen from her maid while travelling.

Cork. I don't know neither her nor her maid.

Bax. Fire away! The next! (*Corkett produces another. Baxter looks at it*) Hunt and Gask. Bracelets! Bond Street robbery last Autumn.

Cork. I can prove an alibi. I was in quod at the time.

Bax. The next? Look alive! Here, I've got no time to waste. (*Taps Corkett's waistcoat where case is*) What's this? (*Takes out case and looks at it*) By Jove, Lady Blanche Wynter's jewels!

Cork. Yes, I was just agoing to take 'em to her.

Bax. I'll save you the trouble.

Cork. There's a reward of a thousand pounds offered for them jewels.

Bax. I'll save you the trouble of taking that too.

Cork. I say, you know, I'll just tell you how this happened — now it ain't my fault, it's my misfortune ——

Bax. Oh yes, you're a very much injured young man. Now, my sweet innocent, you just come along nicely with me.

Cork. Yes, so I will. I'll come like a lamb. But I say, you know, this ain't my swag — not a blessed bit of it. It's all Spider's.

Bax. We'll talk about Spider by and by.
Trot!   *Exeunt all through window.*

Scene 2.

The Grange, Gardenhurst. As in Act IV, Scene 2. Early Morning. Nelly discovered at gate looking anxiously off.

Nelly. Make haste, Jaikes, make haste and bring him to me. What if Jaikes could not find him — or if Will would not come? Oh yes, he will — the train is whirling him to me. He is coming — he is coming!

Denver and Jaikes enter. Denver sends Jaikes off.

Den. (*To Jaikes, as they enter*) Go round to the front and bring her to me. (*Exit Jaikes. At gate, sees Nelly*) Ah, there she is. (*Aloud. Nelly turning, sees him, does not recognise him for a minute — he holds out his arms and she drops gradually into them*)

Nelly. Is it — my Will? My Will — this face — this white hair — my Will alive?

Den. (*Clasping her*) Nell? (*Kisses her hungrily — a long embrace*)

Nelly. (*Hysterically*) Oh, Will — don't speak. Don't say a word. Only let me look at you. Oh, let me cry or else my heart will break. Don't stop me, Will. Ha, ha, ha! (*Sobbing and laughing in Denver's arms*)

Enter Jaikes.

Jaikes. (*Aside*) I can't find her nowhere — she ain't at home. (*Sees Nelly in Denver's arms*) Ah, yes, she's at home at last. (*Creeping quietly off on tiptoe*)

Den. (*To Jaikes*) Where are you going?

Jaikes. I'm going to have a look at the weather, Master Will!   *Exit Jaikes.*

Den. (*Sitting on seat, Nelly at his feet. Soothing her*) That's right, have a good cry and ease your heart. Oh, Nell! Nell! I've such news for you — the best news ever spoken. There is no other news — think of it — I never killed that man, I am innocent!

Nelly. Oh, Will, can it be so? Oh, Will, it seems to me as if I were dreaming. I can only look in this dear changed face and ask — "Is it true?"

Den. Yes, my own. Do you think I am changed?

Nelly. Yes, and no — changed and not changed — you are always the same to me — you are always my Will! You are not changed a bit.

Den. Nell, our children — our little Ned and Cissy — where are they?

Nelly. I was waiting for you to ask that, I've been watching them all night. Come, we'll go and wake them.

Enter Jaikes, with the two children, one on each side, dragging him by each hand.

Jaikes. Gently — gently, missy — gently, Master Ned! That's my old rheumaticky arm. Don't you pull it out of joint, you young Turk.

Den. (*Meeting children and taking them to seat, puts them on his knees*) Ned, Cissy, do you know me? I'm your father that was dead — I am alive again and I have come home to you, my brave boy, my dear little girl; put your arms round my neck, both of you. Quite, quite close — that's it, my darlings!

Cissy. I know who that little girl was that you lost!

Den. Well, tell me — who was she?

Cissy. Why me, wasn't she?

Den. Yes. I've found her now — I shall never lose her again.

Cissy. No, we shall never let you go away again, shall we, mamma?

Ned. But you are crying?

Cissy. And Jaikes, you too? What is there to cry for?

Jaikes. Don't you take no notice of me, missy. (*Blubbering*) I'm not crying — I'm only laughing the wrong way.

Nelly. Cissy, when you were a little baby and could just run about, you used to call somebody upstairs and down — all over the house — don't you remember? Who was it?

Cissy. (*Hugging Denver*) Daddy!

Jaikes. Yes, missy, and I can remember when your daddy used to go toddling acalling "Jaikes" all over the house. Ah, Master Will, I can just remember your great great-grandfather. I've seen five generations of you and I've never had a happier moment than this in all my life.

Enter Skinner looking anxiously round. His face is livid and his whole appearance betokens his intense anxiety.

Nelly. (*Sees Skinner*) Look, Will, that man!

Den. (*Starts up, sees Skinner — to Jaikes*) Jaikes, take my children away! (*Exit Jaikes with Children. To Nelly*) Go into the house, Nell. I will come to you when I have sent this man away.

Nelly. No, let me stay — I would rather stay!

Skin. (*Advancing*) Mr. John Franklin!

Den. Denver, sir. (*To Nelly*) Come, Nell, I have no business with this man!

Skin. Mrs. Franklin, I hold your husband's life in my hands. If you value it, beg him to hear what I have to say.

Nelly. Oh, Will, is it true? Are you in danger? Yes, let us hear what he has to say.

Skin. What I have to say must be said to him alone.

Nelly. Oh, Will, listen to him — for my sake!

Den. Remain within sight, within call. (*To Skinner*) Now, sir!

Skin. Look here, Mr. Franklin!

Den. Denver, sir!

Skin. I thought I had better not mention that name — I do not want to get you into trouble.

Den. I'll take care you don't do that!

Skin. (*Aside*) He seems calm — he means mischief. (*Aloud*) You appear to misunderstand me.

Den. Not at all! I understand you perfectly. I've watched you night and day for the last five months.

Skin. (*Whose self-confidence is shaken by Denver's coolness*) What do you know! What have you seen?

Den. Enough for my purpose.

Skin. And you mean to use it?

Den. I do.

Skin. Take care! I warn you, don't quarrel with me. I'll give you a chance — if you're wise, you'll take it before it's too late.

Den. Go on.

Skin. We are both in a devil of a mess. Why not make a mutual concession, silence for silence — you keep quiet on my affairs, I will keep quiet on yours — you allow me to pursue my business, I allow you to pursue yours.

Den. And the alternative?

Skin. You fight me — I fight you. You proclaim me a thief and get me a possible five or seven years — I proclaim you as a murderer and get you hanged. Take care, it's an edged tool we are playing with. It cuts both ways, but the handle is in my hands, and the blade towards you. You had better remain John Franklin — Wilfred Denver is dead — let him remain so.

Den. You lie! Down to your very soul, you lie! Wilfred Denver is alive, and to-day all the world shall know it. (*Calls*) Nell! (*Nelly comes to him*) There stands the murderer of Geoffrey Ware! He wants to bargain with me, shall I hide myself or shall I tell the truth to the world? Shall I make peace with him or shall I fight him? Give him his answer, Nell!

Nelly. You shall fight him!

Den. You have your answer — go!

Skin. I shall go straight from here and give information to the police that Wilfred Denver is alive.

Den. Nell, send Jaikes to me. *Exit Nelly.* (*Takes pocket-book and writes hurriedly,* speaking as he writes*) "From Wilfred Denver, The Grange, Gardenhurst, Bucks. To Superintendent, Criminal Investigation Department, Scotland Yard. I surrender myself to take my trial on the charge of the murder of Geoffrey Ware, of which I am innocent, and I know the whereabouts of the real murderer."

Enter Jaikes and Nelly from house.

Jaikes, take this telegram at once.

Baxter appears at gate, speaks as he enters garden.

Bax. I'll take that. (*Holds out his hand, takes the telegram from Jaikes, who is going towards gate*)

Den. Baxter!

Skin. (*Aside*) Baxter! Now for my chance! (*Aloud*) Mr. Baxter, do your duty and arrest the murderer of Geoffrey Ware! (*Pointing to Denver*)

Bax. (*Taking out handcuffs*) Very well, I will do my duty and arrest the murderer of Geoffrey Ware! (*Clasps the handcuffs on Skinner, who is much surprised and drops his stick. Two detectives walk on*)

Skin. (*Struggling*) What do you mean?

Bax. I mean that your dear friend Mr. Henry Corkett has turned Queen's evidence.

Skin. And you believe him?

Bax. Oh, yes, I always believe what's told me — especially when it's proved.

Skin. And what proof have you of this tale?

Bax. The evidence of your other friends, Mr. Coombe and Mr. Cripps. Thanks to Mr. Corkett, I've bagged the lot of 'em and they all tell the same tale. Is that enough, Spider?

Skin. The blackguards, hang the lot.

Bax. Well, no. I think that may happen to you, but I fancy they'll get off.

Jaikes. Oh, don't let 'em off, master. Hang the lot of 'em.

Bax. Mr. Wilfred Denver, I believe?

Den. That is my name.

Bax. I shall want you as a witness against this man.

Den. I shall be ready to come when called upon; but I've no desire for revenge — my only wish is to clear my name.

Bax. That is already done. (*Picks up Skinner's stick*) Come, Spider, I want to catch the up train — I've got a call to make on Lady Blanche Wynter in town this morning.

Skin. (*Glancing at handcuffs*) Is this necessary?

Bax. (*Giving him his walking-stick*) Well, yes, I think so, if you don't mind. (*To Detectives*) Take care of him, Bob. (*Turns to*

Denver) You've had a very narrow escape, sir. Good morning, sir.

> *Exit Skinner and Two Detectives followed by Baxter. They go off at gate.*

Den. (*As they go*) Good morning, Mr. Baxter! (*Jaikes goes off during the above and returns with the two children*) Come, let us kneel and give thanks on our own hearth in the dear old home where I wooed you, and won you in the happy, happy days of long ago. Come, Jaikes — Cissy, Ned, Nell — come in — Home at last!

THE END.

THE RISE
OF THE NEW DRAMA

Transitional Plays

COMEDY–DRAMA

THOMAS WILLIAM ROBERTSON

Caste (1867)

BURLESQUE

WILLIAM SCHWENK GILBERT

Engaged (1877)

The New Drama

GEORGE BERNARD SHAW

Widowers' Houses (1892)

HENRY ARTHUR JONES

The Masqueraders (1894)

ARTHUR WING PINERO

The Notorious Mrs. Ebbsmith (1895)

THOMAS WILLIAM ROBERTSON

1829-1871

Caste

(1867)

Tom Robertson has been called the Marlowe of the Victorian stage, the man who prepared the way for the new drama as the earlier playwright prepared the way for Shakespeare. Writing to some extent within the tradition of the melodrama, Robertson's dialogue was so natural that, to mid-century audiences, it sounded like the speech of real people. He wrote scenes that mocked melodramatic excesses of sentiment and pathos. Furthermore, he not only wrote stage directions to control each tone and gesture, but also, directing his own plays, insisted upon a style of acting either quiet or, when the situation demanded it, spontaneously lively. In short, he made the world of the stage seem natural, as it had to seem before the deeper realism of the new drama could develop.

Thomas William Robertson, born at Newark-on-Trent, January 9, 1829, came of a theatrical family. His father was a travelling actor in the Lincoln circuit, and Tom was "nursed in dressing rooms and cradled in costume trunks." While growing up he learned everything about the stage as he built, painted, and shifted scenery, prompted, acted, managed the stage, and finally wrote plays. He had a somewhat fragmentary education at Young's Academy in Spaulding and, from the age of twelve to fourteen, at Moore's School in Whittlesea. Then he returned to the circuit, keeping up his studies between odd jobs on the stage and acting. At nineteen Robertson went to London, where he helped Henry J. Byron adapt French plays. For a while, as prompter at the Lyceum, he observed the staging methods of Madame Vestris and Charles Mathews and wrote farces for them. He married the actress Elizabeth Burton in 1856 and with her acted in Irish cities. He wrote a novel, *David Garrick*, and then made it into a play which was produced at the Haymarket. With original ideas about naturalness in the drama, he wrote the play *Society*, which J. B. Buckstone, the manager to whom he submitted it, rejected as "Rubbish." He took it to the Bancrofts at the Prince of Wales's Theatre who produced it on May 8, 1865. This production made Robertson famous. His first wife having died, Robertson married Rosetta Feist during a trip to Germany in 1867. He continued to write plays for the Bancrofts until his early death on February 3, 1871.

Nicoll lists fifty-two plays by Tom Robertson. His plays that preceded *Society* are farces and melodramas that gave unusual attention to realism of characterization and costuming, and detail in stage directions. In these pieces he mastered the technique of the well-made play, but his contribution to the drama is chiefly in the "big six" plays written for the Bancrofts: *Society*, *Ours*, *Caste*, *Play*, *School*, and *M. P.*

Robertson knew the stage and audiences well enough to feel certain that *Society*, different as it was, would succeed. After Buckstone rejected the play, Robertson remarked to an acquaintance, "Look here, here is a capital play and these asses won't have it." It is fortunate that he took it to the Bancrofts, for they were interested in elevating the drama by producing plays which showed careful attention to naturalness and the minute details of performance. *Society* is by no means a great play, but characters in a club scene, the "Owl's Roost," were drawn from life, and the dialogue is carefully individualized. Produced in 1865, *Society* had a most unusual run of one hundred and fifty performances. (The Bancrofts' system of careful rehearsals demanded long runs. For a discussion of the Bancrofts see "Reformers and Reforms" in the Introduction.) In 1866 the Bancrofts produced Robertson's *Ours*, which tells a patriotic story of the Crimean War, a regiment of soldiers, jealous wives back home, and their trip to visit their heroes at war, with what Mr. Savin calls "a lawn party in the Crimea." The attention to naturalness of detail in these plays is carried still further in *Caste* (1867), written especially to fit the acting talents of Marie Wilton and her husband, Sir Squire Bancroft. *Play* (1868), a tale of romantic intrigue which takes place in a gambling resort, was also made to order for the Bancrofts. But in spite of its naturalness *Play* was the least successful of the six Robertsonian comedies. *School* (1869), a Cinderella tale of love in a girls' school, however, was a great success, running three hundred and eighty-one performances. The Bancrofts recorded that it "might, we truly believe, have been played for another year." *M. P.* (1870) treats political maneuvering, bribery, and crossed loves in a struggle for election to Parliament.

Robertson achieved the effects he wanted in these plays by directing them himself. Sir Squire Bancroft paid him high tribute by writing that his success in the role of Sidney Daryle in *Society* was "due to the encouragement and support I received from the author, who spared no pains with me, as with others, to have his somewhat novel type of characters understood and acted as he wished." In the composition of his plays Robertson visualized the action and wrote minutely-detailed stage directions; his directing then refined the acting toward a perfection previously unknown on the stage, often with two contrapuntal conversations going at the same time — a technique that made it impossible to act his scenes without ensemble playing. Robertson's anxiety to have his plays appear on the stage with just the finish he visualized is shown in his having the performers rehearse *M. P.* in his bedroom where he was slowly dying, so that he could direct the acting.

Robertson's plays were comedy dramas with features drawn from farce. Attempting mild satire, he sometimes achieved caricature, as in *Caste* with the Marquise de St. Maur and her quotations from Froissart. (Perhaps audiences used to the exaggerations of melodrama mistook her for a realistic creation.) But the audiences did observe in his plays little details that gave the scenes authenticity, and they experienced the illusion of eavesdropping rather than of sitting at a play. Standard melodrama thrilled audiences with real water in a waterfall or a faithfully imitated familiar street corner; Robertson thrilled them with bits of stage business that seemed real and commonplace — for instance, the broken candle in *Caste*. Such a detail might give shadowy depth to a feeling, for the candle is laughingly compared to Eccles. One trick that deepened the illusion of reality was continuation of the action after the curtain fell. When it rose in response to applause, the characters were not posed in a tableau or lined up to bow; they were in new positions that exhibited their continued action during the minute or two the curtain was down. Thinking of the mid-century painters who, in portraying a head, painted each individual hair, William Archer called Robertson "a pre-Raphaelite of the theatre."

Robertson's dramas anticipated the new drama and even, to some extent, the problem play. *Caste* beats down a bogey of straw, but it flattered the "liberal" views of the triumphant middle class. Robertson found the idea for *Caste* in a story, "The Poor Rate Unfolds a Tale," published in a Christmas miscellany, and perhaps he found details for characterization in the fiction of Dickens and Thackeray. The features in which the characters depart from the types of melodrama resemble those of mid-century fiction. Robertson sought to make his characters seem lifelike by placing them in lifelike rooms. His stage directions demanded convincing realistic properties. For instance, the opening description of the "little house in Stangate" uses the word "practicable" three times: no flimsy canvas-looking walls will do. The room described is one in which people live, with wallpaper "soiled," an "old piece of carpet," and a ballet shoe and a skirt thrown across a table. Before anyone enters, the handle of the door is shaken to show the audience that the door is real and will not sway. The same emphasis upon verisimilitude appears in the first action of the play. When Hawtree enters a room he has never before seen, he stands "back to audience, looking round," both breaking the old rule of "never turn a back to the audience" and acting like a stranger there. When the play was revived in 1897 Bernard Shaw raised the rhetorical question: "Where is there a touch of nature in 'Caste'?" and said, "I reply, 'In the windows, in the doors, in the walls, in the carpet, in the ceiling, in the kettle, in the fireplace, in the ham, in the tea, in the bread and butter, in the bassinet, in the hats and sticks and clothes, in the familiar phrases, the quiet, unpumped, everyday utterance.' " These touches of nature are evident in every scene of the play.

The structure of the play may seem artificial in days when a sprawling "slice of life" is frequently presented as a transcript of reality. Maynard Savin has pointed out that the play brings the well-made technique close to perfection. He suggests that the structure is like that of an isosceles triangle, with characters on each side balanced against one another: at the base, Eccles balanced against the Marquise; midway up, Gerridge against Hawtree; and at the apex, Esther and George. Within this grouping, Polly and Esther are "feminine foils." The movement of the action is likewise balanced, with contrapuntal contrasts throughout the scenes. The opening of the play is a little slow, and exposition is handled in a question-and-answer method that seems more contrived than natural. But after that, the pace of the dialogue is lively, and there is never a dragging moment.

The play is full of gaiety, song, and Polly's burlesque — she "sings, dances, boxes people's ears, plays the piano, pretends to blow a trumpet, puts on a forage cap, and imitates a squadron of cavalry." As Charles Dickens wrote, Polly is a one-girl imitation of the Christy minstrels. Yet these lively entertainments are not stuck into the play, as songs may be in melodrama; they are essential in it. For instance, Polly must find some way to tell Esther that George is alive without shocking her. It seems entirely natural that she should act out the ballet of "Jeanne la Folle" as

a means of breaking the news. While she sings, marches, pantomimes, and delightfully plays the roles of several people, the audience is poignantly aware that George
is waiting outside the door for his signal.

The play deliberately undermines the assumptions of domestic melodrama. The
girls, for example, feel a proper affection for old Eccles, but they know him to be
incorrigible, and that their own happiness will be marred so long as he remains
with them. When Eccles agrees to go to Jersey and drink himself to death, Esther
offers no objection, but turns to George and plays a love song on the piano. The
writing makes melodramatic acting by this or that star impossible. Toward the close
of Act I, for instance, Polly and Sam engage in lively, playful lovemaking, cavorting
in and out the door, while Esther and George at the same time make love in terms
of sentimental romance; this counterpoint not only distributes action all over the
stage, but Polly's "Nyer!" punctures any sentimentality in the audience's reaction
to George and Esther's kiss, and vice versa. Captain Hawtree tries to maintain his
dignity, but is reduced to a corporal and handed a teakettle; Polly "roars with
laughter" at his attempts to hold a pose. The melodramatic sensation of George's
entrance on his "return from the dead" is deflated when he appears with a milk
can in his hand. The play specifically mocks sentimentality and pathos. As usual in
the melodrama, the heroines are orphans; they have no mother, and they are the
responsible guardians of their father. But they do not whimper about it. When it
becomes necessary for Esther to tell George the story of her hard life, she does so
in a straightforward way, and Robertson, to make sure there will be no tearful over-
tones, writes the stage direction: "This speech is not to be spoken in a tone implying
hardship." Polly does much to destroy the stereotype of the heroine as a simple-
minded ingénue. She has a hard life, but she lives in high-spirited gaiety; a burlesque
actress, she burlesques the pathetic heroine. A spectator of 1867, after having seen
Caste, would have had some trouble in calling up tears for the typical helpless
heroine.

Henry Arthur Jones called Eccles a "great and vital tragi-comic figure." To some
extent he is a caricature of the idle labor-agitator, but he is more. He is a drunkard,
an alcoholic, but flashes of a former vitality remain in his nature. Like his daughter
Polly, he has the temperament of an actor. His soliloquy as he snitches his grandson's coral has the ring of a dramatized self-defense against a worn-down conscience.
He is properly loved, pitied, nominally consulted regarding Polly's marriage (where
he puts on an act), disciplined, and placed on an allowance — but he cannot be
helped. He is a broken candle. Throughout the play he darkly symbolizes the de-
pravities attributed to the working class; and he is sharply defined as a symbol at
the close of Act I. Polly has just agreed to marry George, and "Eccles reels in, very
drunk" to illustrate everything Hawtree has urged during the act.

The audience at the Prince of Wales's Theatre was small and quiet, sitting mostly
in stalls — and predominantly middle class. Caste is properly addressed to these
people. Its main theme, that an industrious, honest poor girl might marry an
aristocrat, pleased this audience and perhaps seemed important to them. Sam
Gerridge was not only amusing: as a man of energy and good will rising from the
working class to be a shopkeeper he was admirable. Hawtree behaved at last, shaking
Sam's hand, as a gentleman should. The theme is far from radical; it is stated in the
lines quoted from Tennyson. But the play expressed just enough advanced, liberal
thought to suit the audience, and, in total meaning, as well as in scenery, characterization, and acting, it prepared the way for the new drama.

CASTE

A Comedy In Three Acts
by
T. W. ROBERTSON

To
Miss Marie Wilton
(*Mrs. Bancroft*)
This Comedy is Dedicated
by
Her Grateful Friend
and
Fellow Labourer
The Author

First performed at the Prince of Wales's Theatre, April 6, 1867.

Cast of Characters

HON. GEORGE D'ALROY	DIXON
CAPTAIN HAWTREE	MARQUISE DE ST. MAUR
ECCLES	ESTHER ECCLES
SAM GERRIDGE	POLLY ECCLES

Act. I. The Little House in Stangate	COURTSHIP
Act II. The Lodgings in Mayfair	MATRIMONY
Act III. The Little House in Stangate	WIDOWHOOD

ACT I.

A plain set chamber, paper soiled. A window, with practicable blind; street backing and iron railings. Door practicable, when opened showing street door (practicable). Fireplace; two-hinged gas-burners on each side of mantelpiece. Sideboard cupboard, cupboard in recess; tea-things, teapot, tea-caddy, tea-tray, etc., on it. Long table, before fire; old piece of carpet and rug down; plain chairs; bookshelf, back; a small table under it with ballet-shoe and skirt on it; bunch of benefit bills hanging under book-shelf. Theatrical printed portraits, framed, hanging about; chimney glass clock; box of lucifers and ornaments on mantel-shelf; kettle on hob, and fire laid; door-mats on the outside of door. Bureau in lower right-hand corner. Rapping heard at door, the handle is then shaken as curtain rises. The door is unlocked. Enter George D'Alroy.

Geo. Told you so; the key was left under the mat in case I came. They're not back from rehearsal. (*Hangs up hat on peg near door as Hawtree enters*) Confound rehearsal! (*Crosses to fireplace*)

Haw. (*Back to audience, looking round*) And this is the fairy's bower!

Geo. Yes; and this is the fairy's fireplace; the fire is laid. I'll light it. (*Lights fire with lucifer from mantel-piece*)

Haw. (*Turning to George*) And this is the abode rendered blessed by her abiding. It is here that she dwells, walks, talks, — eats and drinks. Does she eat and drink?

Geo. Yes, heartily. I've seen her.

Haw. And you are really spoons! — case of true love — hit — dead.

Geo. Right through. Can't live away from her. (*With elbow on end of mantel-piece, down stage*)

Haw. Poor old Dal! and you've brought me over the water to —

Geo. Stangate.

Haw. Stangate — to see her for the same sort of reason that when a patient is in a dangerous state one doctor calls in another — for a consultation.

Geo. Yes. Then the patient dies.

Haw. Tell us about it — you know I've been away. (*Sits at table, leg on chair*)

Geo. Well then, eighteen months ago —

Haw. Oh cut that! you told me all about that. You went to a theatre, and saw a girl in a ballet, and you fell in love.

Geo. Yes, I found out that she was an amiable, good girl.

Haw. Of course; cut that. We'll credit her with all the virtues and accomplishments.

Geo. Who worked hard to support a drunken father.

Haw. Oh! the father's a drunkard, is he? The father does not inherit the daughter's virtues?

Geo. No. I hate him.

Haw. Naturally. Quite so! Quite so!

Geo. And she — that is, Esther — is very good to her younger sister.

Haw. Younger sister also angelic, amiable, accomplished, etc.

Geo. Um — good enough, but got a temper — large temper. Well, with some difficulty, I got to speak to her. I mean to Esther. Then I was allowed to see her to her door here.

Haw. I know — pastry-cooks — Richmond dinner — and all that.

Geo. You're too fast. Pastry-cooks — yes. Richmond — no. Your knowledge of the world, fifty yards round barracks, misleads you. I saw her nearly every day, and I kept on falling in love — falling and falling, until I thought I should never reach the bottom; then I met you.

Haw. I remember the night when you told me; but I thought it was only an amour-

ette. However, if the fire is a conflagration, subdue it; try dissipation.

Geo. I have.

Haw. What success?

Geo. None; dissipation brought me bad health and self-contempt, a sick head and a sore heart.

Haw. Foreign travel; absence makes the heart grow (*Slight pause*) — stronger. Get leave and cut away.

Geo. I did get leave, and I did cut away; and while away I was miserable and a gon-er coon than ever.

Haw. What's to be done? (*Sits cross-legged on chair, facing George*)

Geo. Don't know. That's the reason I asked you to come over and see.

Haw. Of course, Dal, you're not such a soft as to think of marriage. You know what your mother is. Either you are going to behave properly, with a proper regard for the world, and all that, you know; or you're going to do the other thing. Now, the question is, what do you mean to do? The girl is a nice girl, no doubt; but as to your making her Mrs. D'Alroy, the thing is out of the question.

Geo. Why? What should prevent me?

Haw. Caste! — the inexorable law of caste. The social law, so becoming and so good, that commands like to mate with like, and forbids a giraffe to fall in love with a squirrel.

Geo. But my dear Bark —

Haw. My dear Dal, all those marriages of people with common people are all very well in novels and plays on the stage, because the real people don't exist, and have no relatives who exist, and no connections, and so no harm's done, and it's rather interesting to look at; but in real life with real relations, and real mothers and so forth, it's absolute bosh; it's worse, it's utter social and personal annihilation and damnation.

Geo. As to my mother, I haven't thought about her. (*Sits on corner of table*)

Haw. Of course not. Lovers are so damned selfish; they never think of anybody but themselves.

Geo. My father died when I was three years old, and she married again before I was six, and married a Frenchman.

Haw. A nobleman of the most ancient families of France, of equal blood to her own. She obeyed the duties imposed on her by her station and by caste.

Geo. Still, it caused a separation and a division between us, and I never see my brother, because he lives abroad. Of course the Marquise de St. Maur is my mother, and

I look upon her with a sort of superstitious awe. (*Moves chair with which he has been twisting about during speech from table to left corner*)

Haw. She's a grand Brahmin priestess.

Geo. Just so; and I know I'm a fool. Now you're clever, Bark, — a little too clever, I think. You're paying your devoirs — that's the correct word, isn't it? — to Lady Florence Carberry, the daughter of a countess. She's above you — you've no title. Is she to forget *her* caste?

Haw. That argument doesn't apply. A man can be no more than a gentleman.

Geo.

"True hearts are more than coronets,
And simple faith than Norman blood."

Haw. Now, George, if you're going to consider this question from the point of view of poetry, you're off to No-Man's Land, where I won't follow you.

Geo. No gentleman can be ashamed of the woman he loves. No matter what her original station, once his wife he raises her to his rank.

Haw. Yes, he raises her; — *her;* but her connections — her relatives. How about them?

Eccles enters.

Eccles. (*Outside*) Polly! Polly! Polly! (*Enters*) Why the devil — (*George crosses to Hawtree, who rises. Eccles sees them and assumes a deferential manner*) Oh, Mr. De-Alroy! I didn't see you, sir. Good afternoon; the same to you, sir, and many on 'em. (*Puts hat on bureau and comes down*)

Haw. Who is this?

Geo. This is papa.

Haw. Ah! (*Turns up to book-shelf, scanning Eccles through eye-glass*)

Geo. Miss Eccles and her sister not returned from rehearsal yet?

Eccles. No, sir, they have not. I expect 'em in directly. I hope you've been quite well since I seen you last, sir?

Geo. Quite, thank you; and how have you been, Mr. Eccles?

Eccles. Well, sir, I have not been the thing at all. My 'elth, sir, and my spirits is both broke. I'm not the man I used to be. I am not accustomed to this sort of thing. I've seen better days, but they are gone — most like for ever. It is a melancholy thing, sir, for a man of my time of life to look back on better days that are gone most like for ever.

Geo. I daresay.

Eccles. Once proud and prosperous, now poor and lowly. Once master of a shop, I am

now, by the pressure of circumstances over which I have no control, driven to seek work and not to find it. Poverty is a dreadful thing, sir, for a man as has once been well off.

Geo. I daresay.

Eccles. (*Sighing*) Ah, sir, the poor and lowly is often 'ardly used. What chance has the working-man?

Haw. None when he don't work.

Eccles. We are all equal in mind and feeling.

Geo. (*Aside*) I hope not.

Eccles. I am sorry, gentlemen, that I cannot offer you any refreshment; but luxury and me has long been strangers.

Geo. I am very sorry for your misfortunes, Mr. Eccles. (*Looking round at Hawtree, who turns away*) May I hope that you will allow me to offer you this trifling loan? (*Giving him half a sovereign*)

Eccles. Sir, you're a gentleman. One can tell a real gentleman with half a sov — I mean half an eye — a real gentleman understands the natural emotions of the working-man. Pride, sir, is a thing as should be put down by the strong 'and of pecuniary necessity. There's a friend of mine round the corner as I promised to meet on a little matter of business; so if you will excuse me, sir —

Geo. With pleasure.

Eccles. (*Going up*) Sorry to leave you, gentlemen, but —

Geo. Don't stay on my account.

Haw. Don't mention it.

Eccles. Business is business. (*Goes up*) The girls will be in directly. Good afternoon, gentlemen, — good afternoon — (*Going out*) Good afternoon.

Exit. George sits in chair, corner of table, right.

Haw. (*Coming down left of table*) Papa is not nice, but — (*Sitting on corner of table down stage*)

"True hearts are more than coronets,
And simple faith than Norman blood."

Poor George! I wonder what your mamma — the Most Noble the Marquise de St. Maur — would think of Papa Eccles. Come, Dal, allow that there *is something* in caste. Conceive that dirty ruffian — that rinsing of stale beer — that walking tap-room, for a father-in-law. Take a spin to Central America. Forget her.

Geo. Can't.

Haw. You'll be wretched and miserable with her.

Geo. I'd rather be wretched with her than miserable without her. (*Hawtree takes out cigar case*) Don't smoke here!

Haw. Why not?

Geo. She'll be coming in directly.

Haw. I don't think she'd mind.

Geo. I should. Do you smoke before Lady Florence Carberry?

Haw. (*Closing case*) Ha! You're suffering from a fit of the morals.

Geo. What's that?

Haw. The morals is a disease, like the measles, that attacks the young and innocent.

Geo. (*With temper*) You talk like Mephistopheles, without the cleverness. (*Goes to the window and looks at watch*)

Haw. (*Arranging cravat at glass*) I don't pretend to be a particularly good sort of fellow, nor a particularly bad sort of fellow. I suppose I'm about the average standard sort of thing, and I don't like to see a friend go down hill to the devil while I can put the drag on. (*Turning, with back to fire*) Here is a girl of very humble station — poor, and all that, with a drunken father, who evidently doesn't care how he gets money so long as he don't work for it. Marriage! Pah! Couldn't the thing be arranged?

Geo. Hawtree, cut that! (*At window*) She's here! (*Goes to door and opens it*)

Enter Esther.

Geo. (*Flurried at sight of her*) Good morning. I got here before you, you see.

Esther. Good morning. (*Sees Hawtree — slight pause, in which Hawtree has removed his hat*)

Geo. I've taken the liberty — I hope you won't be angry — of asking you to let me present a friend of mine to you; Miss Eccles — Captain Hawtree. (*Hawtree bows. George assists Esther in taking off bonnet and shawl*)

Haw. (*Aside*) Pretty.

Esther. (*Aside*) Thinks too much of himself.

Geo. (*Hangs up bonnet and shawl on pegs*) You've had a late rehearsal. Where's Polly?

Esther. She stayed behind to buy something.

Enter Polly.

Polly. (*Head through door*) How de do, Mr. D'Alroy? Oh! I'm tired to death. Kept at rehearsal by an old fool of a stage manager. But stage managers are always old fools, — except when they are young. We sha'n't have time for any dinner, so I've brought something for tea.

Esther. What is it?

Polly. Ham. (*Showing ham in paper. Esther sits right, at window. Crossing. Seeing Hawtree*) Oh! I beg your pardon, sir. I didn't see you.

Geo. A friend of mine, Mary. Captain Hawtree — Miss Mary Eccles. (*George sits at window. Polly bows very low, to left, to right, and to front, half burlesquely, to Hawtree*)

Haw. Charmed.

Polly. (*Aside*) What a swell. Got nice teeth, and he knows it. How quiet we all are; let's talk about something. (*Hangs up her hat. She crosses to fire round table, front. Hawtree crosses and places hat on bureau*)

Esther. What can we talk about?

Polly. Anything. Ham. Mr. D'Alroy, do you like ham?

Geo. I adore her — (*Polly titters*) — I mean I adore it.

Polly. (*To Hawtree, who has crossed to table watching Polly undo paper containing ham. She turns the plate on top of the ham still in the paper, then throws the paper aside and triumphantly brings the plate under Hawtree's nose, Hawtree giving a little start back*) Do you like ham, sir? (*Very tragically*)

Haw. Yes.

Polly. Now that is very strange. I should have thought you'd have been above ham. (*Getting tea-tray*)

Haw. May one ask why?

Polly. You look above it. You look quite equal to tongue — glazed. (*Laughing*) Mr. D'Alroy is here so often that he knows our ways. (*Getting tea-things from sideboard and placing them on table*)

Haw. I like everything that is piquante and fresh, and pretty and agreeable.

Polly. (*Laying table all the time for tea*) Ah! you mean that for me. (*Curtseying*) Oh! (*Sings*) Tra, la, la, la, la, la. (*Flourishes cup in his face; he retreats a step*) Now I must put the kettle on. (*George and Esther are at window*) Esther never does any work when Mr. D'Alroy is here. They're spooning; ugly word, spooning, isn't it? — reminds one of red-currant jam. By the bye, love *is* very like red-currant jam — at the first taste sweet, and afterwards shuddery. Do you ever spoon?

Haw. (*Leaning across table*) I should like to do so at this moment.

Polly. I daresay you would. No, you're too grand for me. You want taking down a peg — I mean a foot. Let's see — what are you — a corporal?

Haw. Captain.

Polly. I prefer a corporal. See here. Let's change about. You be corporal — it'll do you good, and I'll be "my lady."

Haw. Pleasure.

Polly. You must call me "my lady," though, or you sha'n't have any ham.

Haw. Certainly, "my lady"; but I cannot

accept your hospitality, for I'm engaged to dine.

Polly. At what time?

Haw. Seven.

Polly. Seven! Why, that's halfpast tea-time. Now, Corporal, you must wait on me.

Haw. As the pages did of old.

Polly. "My lady."

Haw. "My lady."

Polly. Here's the kettle, Corporal. (*Holding out kettle at arm's length. Hawtree looks at it through eye-glass*)

Haw. Very nice kettle.

Polly. Take it into the back kitchen.

Haw. Eh!

Polly. Oh, I'm coming too.

Haw. Ah! that alters the case. (*He takes out handkerchief and then takes hold of kettle — crosses as George rises and comes down, slapping Hawtree on back. Hawtree immediately places kettle on the floor. Polly throws herself into chair by fireside up stage, and roars with laughter. George and Esther laugh*)

Geo. What are you about?

Haw. I'm about to fill the kettle.

Esther. (*Going to Polly*) Mind what you are doing, Polly. What will Sam say?

Polly. Whatever Sam chooses. What the sweetheart can't see the husband can't grieve at. Now then — Corporal!

Haw. "My lady!" (*Takes up kettle*)

Polly. Attention! Forward! March! and mind the soot don't drop upon your trousers.

  Exeunt Polly and Hawtree, Hawtree first.

Esther. What a girl it is — all spirits! The worst is that it is so easy to mistake her!

Geo. And so easy to find out your mistake. (*They cross down stage, Esther first*) But why won't you let me present you with a piano? (*Following Esther*)

Esther. I don't want one.

Geo. You said you were fond of playing.

Esther. We may be fond of many things without having them. (*Leaning against end of table. Taking out letter*) Now here is a gentleman says he is attached to me.

Geo. (*Jealous*) May I know his name?

Esther. What for? It would be useless, as his solicitations — (*Throws letter into fire*)

Geo. I lit that fire.

Esther. Then burn these, too. (*George crosses to fire*) No, not that. (*Taking one back*) I must keep that; burn the others.

  George throws letters on fire, crosses back of table quickly — takes hat from peg and goes to door as if leaving hurriedly. Esther takes chair from table and goes to centre of stage with

it, *noticing George's manner. George hesitates at door. Shuts it quickly, hangs his hat up again, and comes down to back of chair in which Esther has seated herself.*

Geo. Who is that from?

Esther. Why do you wish to know?

Geo. Because I love you, and I don't think you love me, and I fear a rival.

Esther. You have none.

Geo. I know you have so many admirers.

Esther. They're nothing to me.

Geo. Not one?

Esther. No. They're admirers, but there's not a husband among them.

Geo. Not the writer of that letter?

Esther. (*Coquettishly*) Oh, I like him very much.

Geo. (*Sighing*) Ah!

Esther. And I'm very fond of this letter.

Geo. Then, Esther, you don't care for me.

Esther. Don't I? How do you know?

Geo. Because you won't let me read that letter.

Esther. It won't please you if you see it.

Geo. I daresay not. That's just the reason that I want to. You won't?

Esther. (*Hesitates*) I will. There! (*Giving it to him*)

Geo. (*Reads*) "Dear Madam."

Esther. That's tender, isn't it?

Geo. "The terms are four pounds — your dresses to be found. For eight weeks certain, and longer if you should suit. (*In astonishment*) I cannot close the engagement until the return of my partner. I expect him back to-day, and I will write you as soon as I have seen him. Yours very," etc. Four pounds — find dresses. What does this mean?

Esther. It means that they want a Columbine for the Pantomime at Manchester, and I think I shall get the engagement.

Geo. Manchester; then you'll leave London?

Esther. I must. (*Pathetically*) You see this little house is on my shoulders. Polly only earns eighteen shillings a week, and father has been out of work a long, long time. I make the bread here, and it's hard to make sometimes. I've been mistress of this place, and forced to think ever since my mother died, and I was eight years old. Four pounds a week is a large sum, and I can save out of it. (*This speech is not to be spoken in a tone implying hardship*)

Geo. But you'll go away, and I sha'n't see you.

Esther. P'raps it will be for the best. (*Rises*

and crosses) What future is there for us? You're a man of rank, and I am a poor girl who gets her living by dancing. It would have been better that we had never met.

Geo. No.

Esther. Yes, it would, for I'm afraid that —

Geo. You love me?

Esther. I don't know. I'm not sure; but I think I do. (*Stops and turns half-face to George*)

Geo. (*Trying to seize her hand*) Esther!

Esther. No. Think of the difference of our stations.

Geo. That's what Hawtree says! Caste! caste! curse caste! (*Goes up*)

Esther. If I go to Manchester it will be for the best. We must both try to forget each other.

Geo. (*Comes down by table*) Forget you! no, Esther; let me — (*Seizing her hand*)

Polly. (*Without*) Mind what you're about. Oh dear! oh dear! (*George and Esther sit in window seat*)

Enter Polly and Hawtree.

Polly. You nasty, great clumsy Corporal, you've spilt the water all over my frock. Oh dear! (*Coming down. Hawtree puts kettle on ham on table*) Take it off the ham! (*Hawtree then places it on the mantel-piece*) No, no! put it in the fireplace. (*Hawtree does so*) You've spoilt my frock. (*Sitting*)

Haw. Allow me to offer you a new one. (*Crossing*)

Polly. No, I won't. You'll be calling to see how it looks when it's on. Haven't you got a handkerchief?

Haw. Yes.

Polly. Then wipe it dry. (*Hawtree bends almost on one knee, and wipes dress*)

Enter Sam, whistling. Throws cap into Hawtree's hat on drawers.

Sam. (*Sulkily*) Arternoon — yer didn't hear me knock! — the door was open. I'm afraid I intrude.

Polly. No, you don't. We're glad to see you if you've got a handkerchief. Help to wipe this dry. (*Sam pulls out handkerchief from slop, and dropping on one knee snatches skirt of dress from Hawtree, who looks up surprised*)

Haw. I'm very sorry. (*Rising*) I beg your pardon. (*Business; Sam stares Hawtree out*)

Polly. It won't spoil it.

Sam. The stain won't come out. (*Rising*)

Polly. It's only water.

Sam. (*To Esther*) Arternoon, Miss Eccles. (*To George*) Arternoon, sir! (*Polly rises. To Polly*) Who's the other swell?

Polly. I'll introduce you. Captain Hawtree — Mr. Samuel Gerridge.

Haw. Charmed, I'm sure. (*Staring at Sam through eye-glass. Sam acknowledges Hawtree's recognition by a "chuck" of the head over left shoulder; going up to George*) Who's this?

Geo. Polly's sweetheart.

Haw. Oh! Now if I can be of no further assistance, I'll go. (*Comes over back down to drawers*)

Polly. Going, Corporal?

Haw. Yaas! (*Business; taking up hat and stick from bureau he sees Sam's cap. He picks it out carefully, and coming down stage examines it as a curiosity, drops it on the floor and pushes it away with his stick, at the same time moving backwards, causing him to bump against Sam, who turns round savagely*) I beg your pardon. (*Crossing up stage*) George, will you — (*George takes no notice*) Will you —?

Geo. What!

Haw. Go with me?

Geo. Go? No!

Haw. (*Coming down to Polly*) Then, Miss Eccles — I mean "my lady." (*Shaking hands and going; as he backs away bumps against Sam, and business repeated, Hawtree close to door keeping his eye on Sam, who has shown signs of anger*)

Polly. Good-bye, Corporal!

Haw. (*At door*) Good-bye! Good afternoon, Mr. — Mr. — er — Pardon me.

Sam. (*With constrained rage*) Gerridge, sir — Gerridge.

Haw. (*As if remembering name*) Ah! Gerridge. Good-day. *Exit.*

Sam. (*Turning to Polly in awful rage*) Who's that fool? Who's that long idiot?

Polly. I told you; Captain Hawtree.

Sam. What's 'e want 'ere?

Polly. He's a friend of Mr. D'Alroy's.

Sam. Ugh! Isn't one of 'em enough!

Polly. What do you mean?

Sam. For the neighbours to talk about. Who's he after?

Polly. What do you mean by after? You're forgetting yourself, I think.

Sam. No, I'm not forgetting myself — I'm remembering you. What can a long fool of a swell dressed up to the nines within an inch of his life want with two girls of your class? Look at the difference of your stations! 'E don't come 'ere after any good. (*During the speech, Esther crosses to fire and sits before it in a low chair. George follows her and sits on her left*)

Polly. Samuel!

Sam. I mean what I say. People should stick to their own class. Life's a railway journey, and Mankind's a passenger — first class, second class, third class. Any person found riding in a superior class to that for which he has taken his ticket will be removed at the first station stopped at, according to the bye-laws of the company.

Polly. You're giving yourself nice airs! What business is it of yours who comes here? Who are you?

Sam. I'm a mechanic.

Polly. That's evident.

Sam. I ain't ashamed of it. I'm not ashamed of my paper cap.

Polly. Why should you be? I daresay Captain Hawtree isn't ashamed of his four-teen-and-sixpenny gossamer.

Sam. You think a deal of him 'cos he's a captain. Why did he call you "my lady"?

Polly. Because he treated me as one. I wish you'd make the same mistake.

Sam. Ugh! (*Sam goes angrily to bureau. Polly bounces up stage, and sits in window seat*)

Esther. (*Sitting with George, tête-à-tête, by fire*) But we must listen to reason.

Geo. I hate reason!

Esther. I wonder what it means?

Geo. Everything disagreeable. When people talk unpleasantly, they always say listen to reason.

Sam. (*Turning round*) What will the neighbours say?

Polly. I don't care! (*Coming down*)

Sam. What will the neighbours *think?*

Polly. They can't think. They're like you, they've not been educated up to it.

Sam. It all comes of your being on the stage. (*Going to Polly*)

Polly. It all comes of your not understanding the stage or anything else — but putty. Now, if you were a gentleman —

Sam. Why then, of course, I should make up to a lady.

Polly. Ugh! (*Polly flings herself into chair by table*)

Geo. Reason's an idiot. Two and two are four, and twelve are fifteen, and eight are twenty. That's reason!

Sam. (*Turning to Polly*) Painting your cheeks!

Polly. (*Rising*) Better paint our *cheeks* than paint *nasty old doors* as you do. How can you understand art? You're only a mechanic! You're not a professional! You're in trade. You are not of the same station as we are. When the manager speaks to you, you touch your hat, and say, "Yes, sir," because he's your superior. (*Snaps fingers under Sam's nose*)

Geo. When people love there's no such thing as money — it don't exist.

Esther. Yes, it does.

Geo. Then it oughtn't to.

Sam. The manager employs me same as he does you. Payment is good anywhere and everywhere. Whatever's commercial, is right.

Polly. Actors are not like mechanics. They wear cloth coats, and not fustian jackets.

Sam. (*Sneeringly in Polly's face*) I despise play actors.

Polly. I despise mechanics. (*Polly slaps his face*)

Geo. I never think of anything else but you.

Esther. Really?

Sam. (*Goes to bureau, misses cap, looks around, sees it on floor, picks it up angrily, and comes to Polly, who is sitting by the table*) I won't stay here to be insulted. (*Putting on cap*)

Polly. Nobody wants you to stay. Go! Go! Go!

Sam. I will go. Good-bye, Miss Mary Eccles. (*Goes off and returns quickly*) I sha'n't come here again! (*At door half-open*)

Polly. Don't! Good riddance to bad rubbish.

Sam. (*Rushing down stage to Polly*) You can go to your *captain!*

Polly. And you to your *putty.*
  Sam throws his cap down and kicks it — then goes up stage and picks it up. Polly turns and rises, leaning against table— facing him, crosses to door, and locks it. Sam, hearing click of lock, turns quickly.

Esther. And shall you always love me as you do now?

Geo. More.

Polly. Now you *sha'n't go.* (*Locking door, taking out key, which she pockets, and placing her back against door*) Nyer! Now I'll just show you my power. Nyer!

Sam. Miss Mary Eccles, let me out! (*Advancing to door*)

Polly. Mr. Samuel Gerridge, I sha'n't! (*Sam turns away*)

Esther. Now you two. (*Postman's knock*) The postman!

Sam. Now you must let me out. You must unlock the door.

Polly. No, I needn't. (*Opens window, looking out*) Here — postman. (*Takes letter from postman at window*) Thank you. (*Business; flicks Sam in the face with letter*) For you, Esther!

Esther (*Rising*) For me?

Polly. Yes. (*Gives it to her, and closes window, and returns to door triumphantly. Sam goes to window*)

Esther. (Going down) From Manchester!

Geo. Manchester? *(Coming down back of Esther)*

Esther. (Reading) I've got the engagement — four pounds a week.

Geo. (Placing his arm around her) You sha'n't go. Esther — stay — be my wife!

Esther. But the world — your world?

Geo. Hang the world! You're my world. Stay with your husband, *Mrs. George D'Alroy.*

> *During this Polly has been dancing up and down in front of the door.*

Sam. I *will* go out. *(Turning with sudden determination)*

Polly. You can't, and you sha'n't!

Sam. I can — I will! *(Opens window and jumps out)*

Polly. (Frightened) He's hurt himself. Sam — Sam, — dear Sam! *(Running to window. Sam appears at window. Polly slaps his face and shuts window down violently)* Nyer!

> *During this George has kissed Esther.*

Geo. My wife!

> *The handle of the door is heard to rattle, then the door is shaken violently. Esther crosses to door; finding it locked, turns to Polly sitting in window seat, who gives her the key. Esther then opens the door. Eccles reels in, very drunk, and clings to the corner of the bureau for support. George stands pulling his moustache. Esther, a little way up, looking with shame first at her father, then at George. Polly sitting in window recess.*

ACT DROP

For call. — George, hat in hand, bidding Esther good-bye. Eccles sitting in chair, nodding before fire. Sam again looks in at window. Polly pulls the blind down violently.

End of the First Act.

ACT II.

D'Alroy's lodgings in Mayfair. A set chamber. Folding doors opening on to drawing-room. Door on the right. Two windows, with muslin curtains. Loo-table. Sofa above piano. Two easy-chairs, on each side of table. Dessert — claret in jug; two wine-glasses half full. Box of cigarettes, vase of flowers, embroidered slipper on canvas, and small basket of coloured wools, all on table. Foot-stool by easy-chair. Ornamental gilt work-basket on stand in window. Easy-chair. Piano. Mahogany-stained easel with oil-painting of D'Alroy in full dragoon regimentals. Davenport with vase of flowers on it; a chair on each side; a water-colour drawing over it, and on each side of room. Half moonlight through window. Esther and George discovered. Esther at window. When curtain has risen she comes down slowly to chair right of table, and George sitting in easy-chair left of table. George has his uniform trousers and spurs on.

Esther. George, dear, you seem out of spirits.

Geo. (Smoking cigarette) Not at all, dear, not at all. *(Rallying)*

Esther. Then why don't you talk?

Geo. I've nothing to say.

Esther. That's no reason.

Geo. I can't talk about nothing.

Esther. Yes, you can; you often do. *(Crossing round back of table and caressing him)* You used to do before we were married.

Geo. No, I didn't. I talked about you, and my love for you. D'ye call that nothing?

Esther. (Sitting on stool left of George) How long have we been married, dear? Let me see; six months yesterday. *(Dreamily)* It hardly seems a week; it almost seems a dream.

Geo. (Putting his arm around her) Awfully jolly dream. Don't let us wake up. *(Aside and recovering himself)* How ever shall I tell her?

Esther. And when I married you I was twenty-two, wasn't I?

Geo. Yes, dear; but then, you know, you must have been some age or other.

Esther. No; but to think I lived two and twenty years without knowing you!

Geo. What of it, dear?

Esther. It seems such a dreadful waste of time.

Geo. So it was — awful.

Esther. Do you remember our first meeting? Then I was in the ballet.

Geo. Yes; now you're in the heavies.

Esther. Then I was in the front rank — now I am of high rank — the Honourable Mrs. George D'Alroy. You promoted me to be your wife.

Geo. No, dear, you promoted me to be your husband.

Esther. And now I'm one of the aristocracy; ain't I?

Geo. Yes, dear; I suppose that we may consider ourselves —

Esther. Tell me, George; are you quite sure that you are proud of your poor little humble wife?

Geo. Proud of you! Proud as the winner of the Derby.

Esther. Wouldn't you have loved me better if I'd been a lady?

Geo. You *are* a lady — you're my wife.

Esther. What will your mamma say when she knows of our marriage? I quite tremble at the thought of meeting her.

Geo. So do I. Luckily she's in Rome.

Esther. Do you know, George, I should like to be married all over again.

Geo. Not to anybody else, I hope?

Esther. My darling!

Geo. But why over again? Why?

Esther. Our courtship was so beautiful. It was like a novel from the library, only better. You, a fine, rich, high-born gentleman, coming to our humble little house to court poor me. Do you remember the ballet you first saw me in? That was at Covent Garden. "Jeanne la Folle; or, the Return of the Soldier." (*Goes up to piano*) Don't you remember the dance? (*Plays a quick movement*)

Geo. Esther, how came you to learn to play the piano? Did you teach yourself?

Esther. Yes. (*Turning on music-stool*) So did Polly. We can only just touch the notes to amuse ourselves.

Geo. How was it?

Esther. I've told you so often. (*Rises and sits on stool at George's feet*)

Geo. Tell me again. I'm like the children — I like to hear what I know already.

Esther. Well, then, mother died when I was quite young. I can only just remember her. Polly was an infant; so I had to be Polly's mother. Father — who is a very eccentric man (*George sighs deeply — Esther notices it and goes on rapidly — all to be simultaneous in action*) but a very good one when you know him — did not take much notice of us, and we got on as we could. We used to let the first floor, and a lodger took it — Herr Griffenhaagen. He was a ballet master at the Opera. He took a fancy to me, and asked me if I should like to learn to dance, and I told him father couldn't afford to pay for my tuition; and he said that (*Imitation*) he did not vant bayment, but dat he would teach me for noding, for he had taken a fancy to me, because I was like a leetle lady he had known long years ago in de far off land he came from. Then he got us an engagement at the theatre. That was how we first were in the ballet.

Geo. (*Slapping his leg*) That fellow was a great brick; I should like to ask him to dinner. What became of him?

Esther. I don't know. He left England. (*George fidgets and looks at watch*) You are restless, George. What's the matter?

Geo. Nothing.

Esther. Are you going out?

Geo. Yes. (*Looking at his boots and spurs*) That's the reason I dined in —

Esther. To the barracks?

Geo. Yes.

Esther. On duty?

Geo. (*Hesitatingly*) On duty. (*Rising*) And, of course, when a man is a soldier, he must go on duty when he's ordered, and where he's ordered — and — (*Aside*) — why did I ever enter the service? (*Crosses*)

Esther. (*Rises, crosses to George — and twining her arm round him*) George, if you must go out to your club, go; don't mind leaving me. Somehow or other, George, these last few days everything seems to have changed with me — I don't know why. Sometimes my eyes fill with tears, for no reason, and sometimes I feel so happy, for no reason. I don't mind being left by myself as I used to do. When you are a few minutes behind time I don't run to the window and watch for you, and turn irritable. Not that I love you less — no, for I love you more; but often when you are away I don't feel that I am by myself. (*Dropping her head on his breast*) I never feel alone. (*Goes to piano and turns over music*)

Geo. (*Watching Esther*) What angels women are! At least, this one is. I forget all about the others. (*Carriage-wheels heard off*) If I'd known I could have been so happy, I'd have sold my commission when I married. (*Knock at street door*)

Esther. (*Standing at table*) That for us, dear?

Geo. (*At first window*) Hawtree in a hansom. He's come for — (*Aside*) — me. I *must* tell her sooner or later. (*At door*) Come in, Hawtree.

Enter Hawtree, in regimentals.

Haw. How do? Hope you're well, Mrs. D'Alroy? (*Coming down*) George, are you coming to —

Geo. (*Coming down left of Hawtree*) No, I've dined — (*Gives a significant look*) — we dined early. (*Esther plays scraps of music at piano*)

Haw. (*Sotto voce*) Haven't you told her?

Geo. No, I daren't.

Haw. But you must.

Geo. You know what an awful coward I am. You do it for me.

Haw. Not for worlds. I've just had my own adieux to make.

Geo. Ah, yes, — to Florence Carberry. How did she take it?

Haw. Oh, (*Slight pause*) very well.

Geo. (*Earnestly*) Did she cry?

Haw. No.

Geo. Nor exhibit any emotion whatever?

Haw. No, not particularly.

Geo. (*Surprisedly*) Didn't you kiss her?

Haw. No; Lady Clardonax was in the room.

Geo. (*Wonderingly*) Didn't she squeeze your hand?

Haw. No.

Geo. (*Impressively*) Didn't she say anything?

Haw No, except that she hoped to see me back again soon, and that India was a bad climate.

Geo. Umph! It seems to have been a tragic parting (*Serio-comically*) — almost as tragic as parting — your back hair.

Haw. Lady Florence is not the sort of person to make a scene.

Geo. To be sure, she's not your wife. I wish Esther would be as cool and comfortable. (*After a pause*) No, I don't, — no, I don't. (*A rap at door*)

Enter Dixon.

Geo. (*Goes up to Dixon*) Oh, Dixon, lay out my —

Dix. I have laid them out, sir; everything is ready.

Geo. (*Going down to Hawtree — after a pause — irresolutely*) I must tell her — mustn't I?

Haw. Better send for her sister. Let Dixon go for her in a cab.

Geo. Just so. I'll send him at once. Dixon! (*Goes up and talks to Dixon*)

Esther. (*Rising and going to back of chair, left of table*) Do you want to have a talk with my husband? Shall I go into the dining-room?

Haw. No, Mrs. D'Alroy. (*Going to table and placing cap on it*)

Geo. No, dear. At once, Dixon. Tell the cabman to drive like — (*Exit Dixon*) — like a — cornet just joined.

Esther. (*To Hawtree*) Are you going to take him anywhere?

Haw. (*George comes down and touches Hawtree quickly on the shoulder before he can speak*) No. (*Aside*) Yes — to India. (*Crossing to George*) Tell her now.

Geo. No, no. I'll wait till I put on my uniform. (*Going up*)

Door opens and Polly peeps in.

Polly. How d'ye do, good people, — quite well? (*Polly gets back of table — kisses Esther*)

Geo. Eh? Didn't you meet Dixon?

Polly. Who?

Geo. Dixon — my man.

Polly. No.

Geo. Confound it! — he'll have his ride for nothing. How d'ye do, Polly! (*Shakes hands*)

Polly. How d'ye do, George.

Esther takes Polly's things and goes up stage with them. Polly places parasol on table. Esther returns left of Polly.

Polly. Bless you, my turtles. (*Blessing them, ballet fashion*) George, kiss your mother. (*He kisses her*) That's what I call an honourable brother-in-law's kiss. I'm not in the way, am I?

Geo. (*Behind easy-chair right of table*) Not at all. I'm very glad you've come.

Esther shows Polly the new music. Polly sits at piano and plays comic tune.

Haw. (*Back to audience, and elbow on easy-chair, aside to George*) Under ordinary circumstances she's not a very eligible visitor.

Geo. Caste again. (*Going up*) I'll be back directly. *Exit George.*

Haw. (*Looking at watch and crossing*) Mrs. D'Alroy, I —

Esther. (*Who is standing over Polly at piano*) Going?

Polly. (*Rising*) Do I drive you away, Captain?

Taking her parasol from table. Esther gets to back of chair left of table.

Haw. No.

Polly. Yes, I do. I frighten you, I'm so ugly. I know I do. You frighten me.

Haw. How so?

Polly. You're so handsome. (*Coming down*) Particularly in those clothes, for all the world like an inspector of police.

Esther. (*Half aside*) Polly!

Polly. I will! I like to take him down a bit.

Haw. (*Aside*) This is rather a wild sort of thing in sisters-in-law.

Polly. Any news, Captain?

Haw. (*In a drawling tone*) No. Is there any news with you?

Polly. (*Imitating him*) Yaas; we've got a new piece coming out at our theatre.

Haw. (*Interested*) What's it about?

Polly. (*Drawling*) I don't know. (*To Esther*) Had him there! (*Hawtree drops his sword from his arm; Polly turns round quickly, hearing the noise, and pretends to be frightened*) Going to kill anybody to-day, that you've got your sword on?

Haw. No.

Polly. I thought not.
(Sings)
"With a sabre on his brow,
    And a helmet by his side,
The soldier sweethearts servant-maids,
    And eats cold meat besides."
        *Laughs and walks about waving
        her parasol.*

*Enter George in uniform, carrying in his hand
his sword, sword-belt, and cap. Esther takes
them from him, and places them on sofa, then
comes half down. George goes down by
Hawtree.*

Polly. (Clapping her hands) Oh! here's a
beautiful brother-in-law! Why didn't you
come in on horseback as they do at Astley's?
— gallop in and say *(Imitating soldier on
horseback and prancing up and down stage
during the piece)*, Soldiers of France! the eyes
of Europe are a-looking at you! The Empire
has confidence in you, and France expects
that every man this day will do his — little
utmost! The foe is before you — more's the
pity — and you are before them — worse luck
for you! Forward! Go and get killed; and to
those who escape the Emperor will give a
little bit of ribbon! Nineteens, about! Forward! Gallop! Charge!
        *Galloping to right, imitating bugle,
        and giving point with parasol. She
        nearly spears Hawtree's nose. Haw-
        tree claps his hand upon his sword-
        hilt. She throws herself into chair,
        laughing, and clapping Hawtree's
        cap (from table) upon her head. All
        laugh and applaud. Carriage-wheels
        heard without.*
Polly. Oh, what a funny little cap, it's got
no peak. *(A peal of knocks heard at street door)*
What's that?
Geo. (Who has hastened to window) A car-
riage! Good heavens — my mother!
Haw. (At window) The Marchioness!
Esther. (Crossing to George) Oh, George!
Polly. (Crossing to window) A Marchioness!
A real, live Marchioness! Let me look! I never
saw a real live Marchioness in all my life.
Geo. (Forcing her from window) No, no,
no! She doesn't know I'm married. I must
break it to her by degrees. What shall I
do?
        *By this time Hawtree is at door right.
        Esther at door left.*
Esther. Let me go into the bedroom
until —
Haw. Too late! She's on the stairs.
Esther. Here, then! *(At centre doors, opens
them)*

Polly. I want to see a real, live March—
*George lifts her in his arms and places her
within folding-doors with Esther — then shutting doors quickly, turns and faces Hawtree,
who, gathering up his sword, faces George.
They then exchange places much in the fashion
of soldiers "mounting guard." As George opens
door and admits Marchioness, Hawtree drops
down to left.*

Geo. (With great ceremony) My dear
mother, I saw you getting out of the carriage.
Mar. My dear boy. *(Kissing his forehead)*
I'm so glad I got to London before you em-
barked. *(George nervous. Hawtree coming
down)* Captain Hawtree, I think. How do you
do?
Haw. (Coming forward a little) Quite well,
I thank your ladyship. I trust you are —
Mar. (Sitting in easy-chair) Oh, quite,
thanks. *(Slight pause)* Do you still see the
Countess and Lady Florence? *(Looking at him
through her glasses)*
Haw. Yes.
Mar. Please remember me to them —
*(Hawtree takes cap from table, and places
sword under his arm)* Are you going?
Haw. Yaas — Compelled. *(Bows, crossing
round back of table. To George who meets him)*
I'll be at the door for you at seven. We must
be at barracks by the quarter. *(George crosses
back of table)* Poor devil! This comes of a man
marrying beneath him.
        *Exit Hawtree. George comes down
        left of table.*
Mar. I'm not sorry that he's gone, for I
wanted to talk to you alone. Strange that a
woman of such good birth as the Countess
should encourage the attention of Captain
Hawtree for her daughter Florence. *(During
these lines D'Alroy conceals Polly's hat and
umbrella under table)* Lady Clardonax was one
of the old Carberrys of Hampshire — not the
Norfolk Carberrys, but the direct line. And
Mr. Hawtree's grandfather was in trade —
something in the City — soap, I think. Stool,
George! *(Points to stool. George brings it to her.
She motions that he is to sit at her feet. George
does so with a sigh)* He's a very nice person,
but parvenu, as one may see by his languor
and his swagger. My boy *(Kissing his forehead)* I am sure, will never make a mésal-
liance. He is a D'Alroy, and by his mother's
side Planta-genista. The source of our life
stream is royal.
Geo. How is the Marquis?
Mar. Paralysed. I left him at Spa with
three physicians. He is always paralysed at
this time of the year; it is in the family. The
paralysis is not personal, but hereditary. I

came over to see my steward; got to town last night.

Geo. How did you find me out here?

Mar. I sent the footman to the barracks, and he saw your man Dixon in the street, and Dixon gave him this address. It's so long since I've seen you. (*Leans back in chair*) You're looking very well, and I daresay when mounted are quite a "beau cavalier." And so, my boy (*Playing with his hair*), you are going ab road for the first time on active service.

Geo. (*Aside*) Every word can be heard in the next room. If they've only gone upstairs.

Mar. And now, my dear boy, before you go I want to give you some advice; and you mustn't despise it because I'm an old woman. We old women know a great deal more than people give us credit for. You are a soldier — so was your father — so was his father — so was mine — so was our royal founder; we were born to lead! The common people expect it from us. It is our duty. Do you not remember in the Chronicles of Froissart? (*With great enjoyment*) I think I can quote it word for word; I've a wonderful memory for my age. (*With closed eyes*) It was in the fifty-ninth chapter — "How Godefroy D'Alroy helde the towne of St. Amande duryng the siege before Tournay." It said "the towne was not closed but with pales, and captayne there was Sir Amory of Pauy — the Seneschall of Carcassoune — who had said it was not able to hold agaynste an hooste, when one Godefroy D'Alroy sayd that rather than he woulde depart, he woulde keepe it to the best of his power. Whereat the souldiers cheered and sayd, 'Lead us on, Sir Godefroy.' And then began a fierce assault; and they within were chased, and sought for shelter from street to street. But Godefroy stood at the gate so valyantly that the souldiers helde the towne until the commyng of the Earl of Haynault with twelve thousande men."

Geo. (*Aside*) I wish she'd go. If she once gets onto Froissart, she'll never know when to stop.

Mar. When my boy fights — and you will fight — he is sure to distinguish himself. It is his nature to — (*Toys with his hair*) — he cannot forget his birth. And when you meet these Asiatic ruffians, who have dared to revolt, and to outrage humanity, you will strike as your ancestor Sir Galtier of Chevrault struck at Poictiers. (*Changing tone of voice as if remembering*) Froissart mentions it thus: — "Sir Galtier, with his four squires, was in the front, in that battell, and there did marvels in arms. And Sir Galtier rode up to the Prince, and sayd to him — 'Sir, take your

horse and ryde forth, this journey is yours. God is this daye in your handes. Gette us to the French Kynge's batayle. I think verily by his valyantesse, he woll not fly. Advance banner in the name of God and of Saynt George!' And Sir Galtier galloped forward to see his Kynge's victory, and meet his own death."

Geo. (*Aside*) If Esther hears all this!

Mar. There is another subject about which I should have spoken to you before this; but an absurd prudery forbade me. I may never see you more. I am old — and you — are going into battle — (*Kissing his forehead with emotion*) — and this may be our last meeting. (*Noise heard within folding-doors*) What's that?

Geo. Nothing — my man Dixon in there.

Mar. We may not meet again on this earth. I do not fear your conduct, my George, with men; but I know the temptations that beset a youth who is well born. But a true soldier, a true gentleman, should not only be without fear, but without reproach. It is easier to fight a furious man than to forego the conquest of a love-sick girl. A thousand Sepoys slain in battle cannot redeem the honour of a man who has betrayed the confidence of a trusting woman. Think, George, what dishonour — what stain upon your manhood — to hurl a girl to shame and degradation! And what excuse for it? That she is plebeian? A man of real honour will spare the woman who has confessed her love for him as he would give quarter to an enemy he had disarmed. (*Taking his hands*) Let my boy avoid the snares so artfully spread; and when he asks his mother to welcome the woman he has chosen for his wife, let me take her to my arms and plant a motherly kiss upon the white brow of a lady. (*Noise of a fall heard within folding-doors. Rising*) What's that?

Geo. (*Rising*) Nothing.

Mar. I heard a cry.

> *Folding-doors open; discovering Esther with Polly, staggering in, fainting.*

Polly. George! George!

> *George goes up and Esther falls in his arms. George places Esther on sofa. George on her right, Polly on her left.*

Mar. (*Coming down*) Who are these women?

Polly. Women!

Mar. George D'Alroy, these persons should have been sent away. How could you dare to risk your mother meeting women of their stamp?

Polly. (*Violently*) What does she mean? How dare she call me a woman? What's she, I'd like to know?

Geo. Silence, Polly! You mustn't insult my mother.

Mar. The insult is from you. I leave you, and I hope that time may induce me to forget this scene of degradation. (*Turning to go*)

Geo. Stay, mother. (*Marchioness turns slightly away*) Before you go (*George has raised Esther from sofa in his arms*) let me present to you Mrs. George D'Alroy. *My wife!*

Mar. Married!

Geo. Married.

> *Marchioness sinks into easy-chair; George replaces Esther on sofa, but still retains her hand. Three hesitating taps at door heard. George crosses to door, opens it, discovers Eccles, who enters. George drops down back of Marchioness's chair.*

Eccles. They told us to come up. When your man came Polly was out; so I thought I should do instead. (*Calling at door*) Come up, Sam.

Enter Sam in his Sunday clothes, with short cane and smoking a cheroot. He nods and grins — Polly points to Marchioness — Sam takes cheroot from his mouth and quickly removes his hat.

Eccles. Sam had just called; so we three — Sam and I, and your man, all came in the 'ansom cab together. Didn't we, Sam? (*Eccles and Sam go over to the girls, and Eccles drops down to front of table — smilingly*)

Mar. (*With glasses up, to George*) Who is this?

Geo. (*Coming left of Marchioness*) My wife's father.

Mar. What is he?

Geo. A — nothing.

Eccles. I am one of nature's noblemen. Happy to see you, my lady — (*Turning to her*) — now. my daughters have told me who you are — (*George turns his back in an agony as Eccles crosses to Marchioness*) — we old folks, fathers and mothers of the young couples, ought to make friends. (*Holding out his dirty hand*)

Mar. (*Shrinking back*) Go away! (*Eccles goes back to table again, disgusted*) What's his name?

Geo. Eccles.

Mar. Eccles! Eccles! There never was an Eccles. He don't exist.

Eccles. Don't he, though? What d'ye call this? (*Goes up again to back of table as Sam*

drops down. He is just going to take a decanter when Sam stops him*)

Mar. No Eccles was ever born!

Geo. He takes the liberty of breathing notwithstanding. (*Aside*) And I wish he wouldn't.

Mar. And who is the little man? Is he also Eccles? (*Sam looks round. Polly gets close up to him, and looks with defiant glance at the Marchioness*)

Geo. No.

Mar. Thank goodness! What then?

Geo. His name is Gerridge.

Mar. Gerridge! It breaks one's teeth. Why is he here?

Geo. He is making love to Polly, my wife's sister.

Mar. And what is he?

Geo. A gasman.

Mar. He looks it. (*George goes up to Esther*) And what is she — the — the sister?

> *Eccles, who has been casting longing eyes at the decanter on table, edges towards it, and when he thinks no one is noticing, fills wine-glass.*

Polly. (*Asserting herself indignantly*) I'm in the ballet at the Theatre Royal, Lambeth. So was Esther. We're not ashamed of what we are. We have no cause to be.

Sam. That's right, Polly! pitch into them swells! — who are they?

> *Eccles by this time has seized wine-glass, and turning his back, is about to drink, when Hawtree enters. Eccles hides glass under his coat and pretends to be looking up at picture.*

Haw. (*Entering*) George! (*Stops suddenly, looking round*) So, all's known!

Mar. (*Rising*) Captain Hawtree, see me to my carriage; I am broken-hearted. (*Takes Hawtree's arm and is going up*)

Eccles. (*Who has tasted the claret, spits it out with a grimace, exclaiming*) Rot!

> *Polly goes to piano — sits on stool — Sam, back to audience, leaning on piano. Eccles exits through folding-doors.*

Geo. (*To Marchioness*) Don't go in anger. You may not see me again. (*Esther rises in nervous excitement, clutching George's hand. Marchioness stops. Esther brings George down*)

Esther. (*With arm round his neck*) Oh, George! must you go? (*They come to front of table*)

Geo. Yes.

Esther. I can't leave you. I'll go with you!

Geo. Impossible! The country is too unsettled.

Esther. May I come after you?

Geo. Yes.

Esther. (With her head on his shoulder) I mav.

Mar. (Coming down, Hawtree at door) It is his duty to go. His honour calls him. The honour of his family — *our* honour.

Esther. But I love him so! Pray don't be angry with me!

Haw. (Looking at watch and coming down) George!

Geo. I must go, love. *(Hawtree goes up to door again)*

Mar. (Advancing) Let me arm you, George — let your mother, as in the days of old. There is blood — and blood, my son. See, your wife cries when she should be proud of you!

Geo. My Esther is all that is good and noble. No lady born to a coronet could be gentler or more true. Esther, my wife, fetch me my sword, and buckle my belt around me.

Esther. (Clinging to him) No, no; I can't!

Geo. Try. *(Whispers to Esther)* To please my mother. *(To Marchioness)* You shall see. *(Esther totters up stage, Polly assisting her, and brings down his sword. As Esther is trying to buckle his belt, he whispers)* I've left money for you, my darling. My lawyer will call on you to-morrow. Forgive me! I tried hard to tell you we were ordered for India; but when the time came, my heart failed me, and I —

> *Esther, before she can succeed in fastening his sword-belt, reels, and falls fainting in his arms. Polly hurries to her. Sam standing at piano, looking frightened; Hawtree with hand upon handle of door; Marchioness looking on, at right of George.*

ACT DROP

For call — George and Hawtree gone. Esther in chair fainting; Polly and Sam each side of her, Polly holding her hands, and Sam fanning her with his red handkerchief. The folding-doors thrown open, and Eccles standing at back of table offering glass of claret.

End of the Second Act.

ACT III.

The room in Stangate (as in Act I). Same furniture as in Act I, with exception of piano, with roll of music tied up on it, in place of bureau. Map of India over mantel-piece. Sword with crape knot, spurs, and cap, craped, hanging over chimney-piece. Portrait of D'Alroy (large) on mantel-piece. Berceaunette, and child, with coral, in it. Polly's bonnet and shawl hanging on peg. Small tin saucepan in fender, fire alight, and kettle on it. Two candles (tallow) in sticks, one of which is broken about three inches from the top and hangs over. Slate and pencil on table. Jug on table, bandbox and ballet skirt on table. At rise of curtain Polly discovered at table, back of stage. Comes down and places skirt in bandbox. She is dressed in black.

Polly. (Placing skirt in box, and leaning her chin upon her hand) There — there's the dress for poor Esther in case she gets the engagement, which I don't suppose she will. It's too good luck, and good luck never comes to her, poor thing. *(Goes up to back of cradle)* Baby's asleep still. How good he looks — as good as if he were dead, like his poor father; and alive too, at the same time, like his dear self. Ah! dear me; it's a strange world. *(Sits in chair right of table, feeling in pocket for money)* Four and elevenpence. That must do for to-day and to-morrow. Esther is going to bring in the rusks for Georgy. *(Takes up slate)* Three, five — eight, and four — twelve, one shilling — father can only have twopence. *(This all to be said in one breath)* He must make do with that till Saturday, when I get my salary. If Esther gets the engagement, I sha'n't have many more salaries to take; I shall leave the stage and retire into private life. I wonder if I shall like private life, and if private life will like me. It will seem so strange being no longer Miss Mary Eccles — but Mrs. Samuel Gerridge. *(Writes it on slate)* "Mrs. Samuel Gerridge." *(Laughs bashfully)* La! to think of my being Mrs. Anybody! How annoyed Susan Smith will be! *(Writing on slate)* "Mrs. Samuel Gerridge presents her compliments to Miss Susan Smith, and Mrs. Samuel Gerridge requests the favour of Miss Susan Smith's company to tea, on Tuesday evening next, at Mrs. Samuel Gerridge's house." *(Pause)* Poor Susan! *(Beginning again)* "P.S. — Mrs. Samuel Gerridge —" *(Knock heard at room door; Polly starts)*

Sam. (Without) Polly, open the door.

Polly. Sam! come in.

Sam. (Without) I can't.

Polly. Why not?

Sam. I've got somethin' on my 'ead.

Polly rises and opens door. Sam enters, carrying two rolls of wall-paper, one in each hand, and a small table on his head, which he de-

posits down stage, then puts roll of paper on piano, as also his cap. Sam has a rule-pocket in corduroys.

Polly. (*Shuts door*) What's that?

Sam. (*Pointing to table with pride*) Furniture. How are you, my Polly? (*Kissing her*) You look handsomer than ever this morning. (*Dances and sings*) "Tid-dle-di-tum-ti-di-do."

Polly. What's the matter, Sam? Are you mad?

Sam. No, 'appy — much the same thing.

Polly. Where have you been these two days?

Sam. (*All excitement*) That's just what I'm goin' to tell yer. Polly, my pet, my brightest hatswing and most brilliant burner, what do yer think?

Polly. Oh, do go on, Sam, or I'll slap your face.

Sam. Well, then, you've 'eard me speak of old Binks, the plumber, glazier, and gasfitter, who died six months ago?

Polly. Yes.

Sam. (*Sternly and deliberately*) I've bought 'is business.

Polly. No!

Sam. (*Excitedly*) Yes, of 'is widow, old Mrs. Binks — so much down, and so much more at the end of the year. (*Dances and sings*)

> Ri-ti-toodle
> Roodle-oodle
> Ri-ti-tooral-lay.

Polly. La, Sam.

Sam. (*Pacing stage up and down*) Yes; I've bought the goodwill, fixtures, fittin's, stock, rolls of gas-pipe, and sheets of lead. (*Jumps on table, quickly facing Polly*) Yes, Polly, I'm a tradesman with a shop — a master tradesman. (*Coming to Polly seriously*) All I want to complete the premises is a missus. (*Tries to kiss her. She pushes him away*)

Polly. Sam, don't be foolish.

Sam. (*Arm round her waist*) Come and be Mrs. Sam Gerridge, Polly, my patent-safety-day-and-night-light. You'll furnish me completely.

> *Polly goes up, Sam watching her admiringly; he then sees slate, snatches it up and looks at it. She snatches it from him with a shriek, and rubs out the writing, looking daggers at him, Sam laughing.*

Sam. Only to think now. (*Putting arm round her waist. Polly pouting*)

Polly. Don't be a goose.

Sam. (*Going towards table*) I spent the whole of yesterday lookin' up furniture. Now I bought that at a bargain, and I brought it 'ere to show you for your approval. I've bought lots of other things, and I'll bring 'em all 'ere to show you for your approval.

Polly. I couldn't think what had become of you. (*Seated right of table*)

Sam. Couldn't yer? Oh, I say, I want yer to choose the new paper for the little back-parlour just behind the shop, you know. Now what d'yer think of this? (*Fetching a pattern from piano and unrolling it*)

Polly. No, I don't like that. (*Sam fetches the other, a flaming pattern*) Ah! that's neat.

Sam. Yes, that's neat and quiet. I'll new-paper it, and new-furnish it, and it shall all be bran-new. (*Puts paper on top of piano*)

Polly. But won't it cost a lot of money?

Sam. (*Bravely*) I can work for it. With customers in the shop, and you in the back-parlour, I can work like fifty men. (*Sits on table, beckons Polly to him; she comes left of table, Sam puts his arm round Polly, sentimentally*) Only fancy, at night, when the shop's closed, and the shutters are up, counting out the till together! (*Changing his manner*) Besides, that isn't all I've been doin'. I've been writin', and what I've written, I've got printed.

Polly. No!

Sam. True.

Polly. You've been writing — about me? (*Delighted*)

Sam. No — about the shop. (*Polly disgusted*) Here it is. (*Takes roll of circulars from pocket of his canvas slop*) Yer mustn't laugh — yer know — it's my first attempt. I wrote it the night before last; and when I thought of you the words seemed to flow like — red-hot solder. (*Reads*) Hem! "Samuel Gerridge takes this opportunity of informin' the nobility, gentry, and inhabitants of the Borough-road —"

Polly. The Borough-road?

Sam. Well, there ain't many of the nobility and gentry as lives in the Borough-road, but it pleases the inhabitants to make 'em believe yer think so (*Resuming*) — "of informin' the nobility, gentry and inhabitants of the Borough-road, and its vicinity" — and "its vicinity." (*Looking at her*) Now I think that's rather good, eh?

Polly. Yes. (*Doubtfully*) I've heard worse.

Sam. I first thought of saying neighbour'ood; but then vicinity sounds so much more genteel (*Resuming*) — "and its vicinity, that 'e has entered upon the business of the late Mr. Binks, 'is relict, the present Mrs. B., 'avin' disposed to 'im of the same" — now

listen, Polly, because it gets interestin' —
"S. G. —"

Polly. S. G. Who's he?

Sam. (*Looking at Polly with surprise*) Why,
me. S. G. — Samuel Gerridge — me, us.
We're S. G. Now don't interrupt me, or you'll
cool my metal, and then I can't work. "S. G.
'opes that, by a constant attention to business, and" — mark this — "by supplyin' the
best articles at the most reasonable prices, to
merit a continuance of those favours which
it will ever be 'is constant study to deserve."
There! (*Turning on table triumphantly*) Stop
a bit, — there's a little bit more yet. "Bell-
'angin', gas-fittin', plumbin', and glazin', as
usual." There! and it's all my own! (*Puts circular on mantel-piece, and crossing contemplates it*)

Polly. Beautiful, Sam. It looks very attractive from here, don't it?

Sam. (*Postman's knock*) There's the postman. I'll go. I shall send some of these out by
post. (*Goes off and returns with letter*)

Polly. (*Taking it*) Oh, for Esther. I know
who it's from. (*Places letter on mantel-piece.
At chair left of table. Sam sits corner of table,
reading circular. Seriously*) Sam, who do you
think was here last night?

Sam. Who?

Polly. Captain Hawtree.

Sam. (*Deprecatingly*) Oh, 'im! — Come
back from India, I suppose.

Polly. Yes, — luckily Esther was out.

Sam. I never liked that long swell. He was
a 'uppish, conceited —

Polly. (*Sitting at end of table*) Oh, he's
better than he used to be — he's a major
now. He's only been in England a fortnight.

Sam. Did he tell yer anything about
De Alroy?

Polly. (*Leaning against table end*) Yes; he
said he was riding out not far from the
cantonment, and was surrounded by a troop
of Sepoy cavalry, which took him prisoner,
and galloped off with him.

Sam. But about 'is death?

Polly. Oh! (*Hiding her face*) that he said
was believed to be too terrible to mention.

Sam. (*Crossing to Polly at table*) Did 'e tell
yer anything else?

Polly. No; he asked a lot of questions, and
I told him everything. How poor Esther had
taken her widowhood and what a dear good
baby the baby was, and what a comfort to us
all, and how Esther had come back to live
with us again.

Sam. (*Sharply*) And the reason for it?

Polly. (*Looking down*) Yes.

Sam. How your father got all the money
that 'e'd left for Esther?

Polly. (*Sharply*) Don't say any more about
that, Sam.

Sam. Oh! I only think Captain 'Awtree
ought to know where the money *did* go to,
and you shouldn't try and screen your
father, and let 'im suppose that you and
Esther spent it all.

Polly. I told him — I told him — I told
him. (*Angrily*)

Sam. Did you tell 'im that your father was
always at 'armonic meetin's at taverns, and
'ad 'arf cracked 'isself with drink and was
always singin' the songs and makin' the
speeches 'e 'eard there, and was always goin'
on about 'is wrongs as one of the workin'
classes? 'E's a pretty one for one of the
workin' classes, 'e is! 'Asn't done a stroke of
work these twenty year. Now, I *am* one of
the workin' classes, but I *don't* 'owl about it.
I work, I don't spout.

Polly. Hold your tongue, Sam. I won't
have you say any more against poor father.
He has his faults, but he's a very clever man.
(*Sighing*)

Sam. Ah! What else did Captain Hawtree
say?

Polly. He advised us to apply to Mr.
D'Alroy's mother.

Sam. What! the Marquissy? And what did
you say to that?

Polly. I said that Esther wouldn't hear of
it. And so the Major said that he'd write to
Esther, and I suppose this is the letter.

Sam. Now, Polly, come along and choose
the paper for the little back-parlour. (*Going
to table and taking it up to wall behind door*)

Polly. (*Rising*) Can't. Who's to mind
baby?

Sam. The *baby!* Oh, I forgot all about 'im.
(*Goes to cradle*) I see yer! (*Goes to window
casually*) There's your father comin' down
the street. Won't 'e mind 'im?

Polly. (*Going up*) I daresay he will. If I
promise him an extra sixpence on Saturday.
(*Sam opens window*) Hi! Father! (*Polly goes to
cradle*)

Sam. (*Aside*) 'E looks down in the mouth,
'e does. I suppose 'e's 'ad no drink this morning. (*Goes to Polly*)

*Enter Eccles in shabby black. Pauses on enter-
ing, looks at Sam, turns away in disgust, takes
off hat, places it on piano, and shambles across
stage. Taking chair, places it, and sits before
fire.*

Polly. (*Goes to Eccles*) Come in to stop a
bit, father?

Eccles. No; not for long. (*Sam comes down*)
Good morning, Samuel. Going back to work?

That's right, my boy, — stick to it. (*Pokes fire*) Stick to it — nothing like it.

Sam. (*Aside*) Now, isn't that too bad? No, Mr. Eccles. I've knocked off for the day.

Eccles. (*Waving poker*) That's bad, — that's very bad! Nothing like work — for the young. I don't work so much as I used to, myself, but I like to (*Polly sitting on corner of table up left*) see the young 'uns at it. It does me good, and it does them good, too. What does the poet say? (*Rising, impressively, and leaning on table*)

"A carpenter said tho' that was well spoke,
It was better by far to defend it with hoak.
A currier, wiser than both put together,
Said say what you will, there is nothing like *labour*.
For a' that and a' that,
Your ribbon, gown and a' that,
The rank is but the guinea stamp,
The working man's the gold for a' that."

(*Sits again, triumphantly wagging his head*)

Sam. (*Aside*) This is one of the public-house loafers, that wants all the wages and none of the work, an idle old — (*Goes in disgust to piano, puts on cap, and takes rolls of paper under his arm*)

Polly. (*To Eccles*) Esther will be in by-and-by. (*Persuasively*) Do, father.

Eccles. No, no, I tell you I won't!

Polly. (*Whispering, arm round his neck*) And I'll give you sixpence extra on Saturday. (*Eccles's face relaxes into a broad grin. Polly gets hat and cloak*)

Eccles. Ah! you sly little puss, you know how to get over your poor old father.

Sam. (*Aside*) Yes, with sixpence.

Polly. (*Putting on bonnet and cloak at door*) Give the cradle a rock if baby cries.

Sam. (*Crossing to Eccles*) If you should 'appen to want employment or amusement, Mr. Eccles, just cast your eye over this. (*Puts circular on table, then joins Polly at door*) Stop a bit, I've forgot to give the baby one.

Throws circular into cradle. Exeunt, Polly first. Eccles takes out pipe from pocket, looks into it, then blows through it making a squeaking noise, and finishes by tenderly placing it on table. He then hunts all his pockets for tobacco, finally finding a little paper packet containing a screw of tobacco in his waistcoat pocket, which he also places on table after turning up the corner of the tablecloth for the purpose of emptying the contents of his pocket of the few remnants of past screws of tobacco on to the bare table and mixing a little out of the packet

with it and filling pipe. He then brushes all that remains on the table into the paper packet, pinches it up, and carefully replaces it in waistcoat pocket. Having put the pipe into his mouth, he looks about for a light, across his shoulder and under table, though never rising from the chair; seeing nothing, his face assumes an expression of comic anguish. Turning to table he angrily replaces table-cloth and then notices Sam's circular. His face relaxes into a smile, and picking it up he tears the circular in half, makes a spill of it, and lighting it at fire, stands, with his back to fire-place, and smokes vigorously.

Eccles. Poor Esther! Nice market she's brought her pigs to — ugh! Mind the baby indeed! What good is he to me? That fool of a girl to throw away all her chances! — a *honourable-hess* — and her father not to have on him the price of a pint of early beer or a quartern of cool, refreshing gin! Stopping in here to rock a young honourable! Cuss him! (*Business, puffs smoke in baby's face, rocking cradle*) Are we slaves, are we working men? (*Sings savagely*) "Britons never, never, never shall be —" (*Nodding his head sagaciously, sits by table*) I won't stand this. I've writ to the old cat — I mean to the Marquissy — to tell her that her daughter-in-law and her grandson is almost starving. That fool Esther is too proud to write to her for money. I hate pride — it's *beastly!* (*Rising*) There's no beastly pride about me. (*Goes up, smacking his lips*) I'm as dry as a lime-kiln. (*Takes up jug*) Milk! — (*With disgust*) for this young aristocratic pauper. Everybody in the house is sacrificed for him! (*At foot of cradle, with arms on chair back*) And to think that a *working man*, and a member of the Committee of Banded Brothers for the Regeneration of Human Kind, by means of equal diffusion of intelligence and equal division of property, should be thusty, while this cub — (*Draws aside curtain, and looks at child. After a pause*) — That there coral he's got round his neck is gold, real *gold!* (*With hand on knob at end of cradle*) Oh, Society! Oh, Governments! Oh, Class Legislation! — *is this right?* Shall this mindless wretch enjoy himself, while sleeping, with a jewelled gawd, and his poor old grandfather want the price of half a pint? *No!* it shall not be! Rather than see it, I will myself resent this outrage on the rights of man! and in this holy crusade of class against class, of the weak and lowly against the *powerful and strong* — (*Pointing to child*)

— I will strike one blow for freedom! (*Goes to back of cradle*) He's asleep. It will fetch ten bob round the corner; and if the Marquissy gives us anything it can be got out with some o' that. (*Steals coral*) Lie still, my darling! — it's grandfather a-watchin' over you —

"Who ran to catch me when I fell,
And kicked the place to make it well?
                    My grandfather!"

Rocking cradle with one hand; leaves it quickly and as he takes hat off piano Esther enters. She is dressed as a widow, her face pale, and her manner quick and imperious. She carries a parcel and paper bag of rusks in her hand; she puts parcel on table, goes to cradle, kneels down and kisses child.

Eccles. My lovey had a nice walk? You should wrap yourself up well, — you are so liable to catch cold.

Esther. My Georgy? — Where's his coral? (*Eccles, going to door, fumbles with lock nervously, and is going out as Esther speaks*) Gone! — Father! (*Rising — Eccles stops*) The child's coral — where is it?

Eccles. (*Confused*) Where's what, duckey?

Esther. The coral! You've got it, — I know it! Give it me! (*Quickly and imperiously*) Give it me! (*Eccles takes coral from his pocket and gives it back*) If you dare to touch *my* child — (*Goes to cradle*)

Eccles. Esther! (*Going quickly to piano and banging hat on it*) Am I not your father? — (*Esther gets round to front of table*)

Esther. And I am his mother!

Eccles. (*Coming to her*) Do you bandy words with me, you pauper, you pauper!!! to whom I have given shelter — shelter to you and your brat! I've a good mind — (*Raising his clenched fist*)

Esther. (*Confronting him*) If you dare! I am no longer your little drudge — your frightened servant. When mother died — (*Eccles changes countenance and cowers beneath her glance*) — and I was so high, I tended you, and worked for you — and you beat me. That time is past. I am a woman — I am a wife — a widow — a *mother!* Do you think I will let you outrage *him?* Touch me if you dare! (*Advancing a step*)

Eccles. (*Bursting into tears and coming down*) And this is my own child, which I nussed when a babby, and sang "Cootsicum Coo" to afore she could speak. (*Gets hat from piano, and returns a step or two*) Hon. Mrs. De Alroy (*Esther drops down behind chair by table*) I forgive you for all that you have said. I forgive you for all that you have done. In everything that I have done I have acted with

the best intentions. May the babe in that cradle never treat you as you have this day *tret* a grey 'aired father. May he never cease to love and *honour* you, as you have ceased to love and *honour* me, after all that I have done for you, and the position to which I have raised you by my own *industry*. (*Goes to door*) May he never behave to you like the bad daughters of King Lear; and may you never live to feel how much more sharper than a serpent's (*Slight pause as if remembering quotation*) scale it is to have a thankless child!
                                        Exit.

Esther. (*Kneeling back of cradle*) My darling! (*Arranging bed and placing coral to baby's lips, then to her own*) Mamma's come back to her own. Did she stay away from him so long? (*Rises and looks at sabre, etc.*) My George! to think that you can never look upon his face or hear his voice. My brave, gallant, handsome husband! My lion and my love! (*Comes down, pacing stage*) Oh! to be a soldier, and to fight the wretches who destroyed him — who took my darling from me! (*Action of cutting with sabre*) To gallop miles upon their upturned faces. (*Crossing with action, breaks down sobbing at mantelpiece; sees letter*) What's this? Captain Hawtree's hand. (*Sitting in chair, reads, at left hand of table*) "My dear Mrs. D'Alroy, — I returned to England less than a fortnight ago. I have some papers and effects of my poor friend's, which I am anxious to deliver to you, and I beg of you to name a day when I can call with them and see you; at the same time let me express my deepest sympathy with your affliction. Your husband's loss was mourned by every man in the regiment. (*Esther lays the letter on her heart, and then resumes reading*) I have heard with great pain of the pecuniary embarrassments into which accident and imprudence of others have placed you. I trust you will not consider me, one of poor George's oldest comrades and friends, either intrusive or impertinent in sending the enclosed (*She takes out a cheque*), and in hoping that, should any further difficulties arise, you will inform me of them, and remember that I am, dear Mrs. D'Alroy, now, and always, your faithful and sincere friend, Arthur Hawtree." (*Esther goes to cradle and bends over it*) Oh, *his* boy, if you could read it! (*Sobs, with head on head of cradle*)

Enter Polly.

Polly. Father gone!

Esther. Polly, you look quite flurried. (*Polly laughs and whispers to Esther. Near head of table, taking Polly in her arms and kissing her*) So soon? Well, my darling, I hope you may be happy.

Polly. Yes. Sam's going to speak to father about it this afternoon. (*Crosses round table, putting rusks in saucepan*) Did you see the agent, dear?

Esther. (*Sits by table*) Yes; the manager didn't come—he broke his appointment again.

Polly. (*Sits opposite at table*) Nasty, rude fellow!

Esther. The agent said it didn't matter, he thought I should get the engagement. He'll only give me thirty shillings a week, though.

Polly. But you said that two pounds was the regular salary.

Esther. Yes, but they know I'm poor, and want the engagement, and so take advantage of me.

Polly. Never mind, Esther. I put the dress in that bandbox. It looks almost as good as new.

Esther. I've had a letter from Captain Hawtree.

Polly. I know, dear; he came here last night.

Esther. A dear, good letter — speaking of George, and enclosing a cheque for thirty pounds.

Polly. Oh, how kind! Don't you tell father. (*Noise of carriage-wheels without*)

Esther. I sha'n't.

Eccles enters, breathless. Esther and Polly rise.

Eccles. It's the Marquissy in her coach. (*Esther puts on the lid of bandbox*) Now, girls, do be civil to her, and she may do something for us. (*Places hat on piano*) I see the coach as I was coming out of the "Rainbow." (*Hastily pulls an old comb out of his pocket, and puts his hair in order*)

Esther. The Marquise! (*Esther comes down to end of table, Polly holding her hand*)

Eccles. (*At door*) This way, my lady — up them steps. They're rather awkward for the likes o' you; but them as is poor and lowly must do as best they can with steps and circumstances.

Enter Marquise. She surveys the place with aggressive astonishment.

Mar. (*Going down, half aside*) What a hole! And to think that my grandson should breathe such an atmosphere, and be contaminated by such associations! (*To Eccles, who is a little up*) Which is the young woman who married my son?

Esther. I am Mrs. George D'Alroy, widow of George D'Alroy. Who are you?

Mar. I am his mother, the Marquise de St. Maur.

Esther. (*With the grand air*) Be seated, I beg.

Eccles takes chair from right centre, which Esther immediately seizes as Sam enters with an easy chair on his head, which he puts down, not seeing Marquise, who instantly sits down in it, concealing it completely.

Sam. (*Astonished*) It's the Marquissy! (*Looking at her*) My eyes! These aristocrats are fine women — plenty of 'em — (*Describing circle*) quality and quantity!

Polly. Go away, Sam; you'd better come back.

Eccles nudges him and bustles him towards door. Exit Sam. Eccles shuts door on him.

Eccles. (*Coming down right of Marquise, rubbing his hands*) If we'd a-know'd your ladyship 'ad been a-coming we'd a' 'ad the place cleaned up a bit. (*With hands on chair-back, in lower right corner of stage. He gets round to right, behind Marquise, who turns the chair slightly from him*)

Polly. Hold your tongue, father! (*Eccles crushed*)

Mar. (*To Esther*) You remember me, do you not?

Esther. Perfectly, though I only saw you once. (*Seating herself en grande dame*) May I ask what has procured me the honour of this visit?

Mar. I was informed that you were in want, and I came to offer you assistance.

Esther. I thank you for your offer, and the delicate consideration for my feelings with which it is made. I need no assistance. (*Eccles groans and leans on piano*)

Mar. A letter that I received last night informed me that you did.

Esther. May I ask if that letter came from Captain Hawtree?

Mar. No — from this person — your father, I think.

Esther. (*To Eccles*) How dare you interfere in my affairs?

Eccles. My lovey, I did it with the best intentions.

Mar. Then you will not accept assistance from me?

Esther. No.

Polly. (*Aside to Esther, holding her hand*) Bless you, my darling. (*Polly standing beside her*)

Mar. But you have a child — a son — my grandson. (*With emotion*)

Esther. Master D'Alroy wants for nothing.

Polly. (*Aside*) And never shall. (*Eccles groans and turns on to piano*)

Mar. I came here to propose that my grandson should go back with me. (*Polly rushes up to cradle*)

Esther. (*Rising defiantly*) What! part with my boy! I'd sooner die!

Mar. You can see him when you wish. As for money, I —

Esther. Not for ten thousand million worlds — not for ten thousand million marchionesses!

Eccles. Better do what the good lady asks you, my dear; she's advising you for your own good, and for the child's likewise.

Mar. Surely you cannot intend to bring up my son's son in a place like this?

Esther. I do. (*Goes up to cradle*)

Eccles. It *is* a poor place, and we are poor people, sure enough. We ought not to fly in the faces of our pastors and masters — our pastresses and mistresses.

Polly. (*Aside*) Oh, hold your tongue, do! (*Up at cradle*)

Esther. (*Before cradle*) Master George D'Alroy will remain with his mother. The offer to take him from her is an insult to his dead father and to him.

Eccles. (*Aside*) He don't seem to feel it, stuck-up little beast.

Mar. But you have no money — how can you rear him? — how can you educate him? — how can you live?

Esther. (*Tearing dress from bandbox*) Turn columbine, — go on the stage again and dance.

Mar. (*Rising*) You are insolent — you forget that I am a lady.

Esther. You forget that I am a mother. Do you dare to offer to buy my child — *his* breathing image, *his* living memory — with money? (*Crosses to door and throws it open*) There is the door — go! (*Picture*)

Eccles. (*To Marquise, who has risen, aside*) Very sorry, my lady, as you should be tret in this way, which was not my wishes.

Mar. Silence! (*Eccles retreats, putting back chair. Marquise goes up to door*) Mrs. D'Alroy, if anything could have increased my sorrow for the wretched marriage my poor son was decoyed into, it would be your conduct this day to his mother.   *Exit.*

Esther. (*Falling into Polly's arms*) Oh, Polly! Polly!

Eccles. (*Looking after her*) To go away and not to leave a sov. behind her! (*Running up to open door*) Cat! Cat! Stingy old cat! (*Almost runs to fire, and pokes it violently; carriage-wheels heard without*)

Esther. I'll go to my room and lie down. Let me have the baby, or that old woman may come back and steal him.

Exit Esther, and Polly follows with baby.

Eccles. Well, women is the obstinatest devils as never wore horseshoes. Children? Beasts! Beasts!

Enter Sam and Polly.

Sam. Come along, Polly, and let's get it over at once. (*Sam places cap on piano, and goes to table. Polly takes bandbox from table, and places it up stage*) Now, Mr. Eccles (*Eccles turns suddenly, facing Sam*), since you've been talkin' on family matters, I'd like to 'ave a word with yer, so take this opportunity to —

Eccles. (*Waving his hand grandly*) Take what you like, and then order more (*Rising and leaning over table*), Samuel Gerridge. That hand is a hand that has never turned its back on a friend, or a bottle to give him. (*Sings, front of table*)
"I'll stand by my friend,
I'll stand by my friend,
I'll stand by my friend,
If he'll stand to me — me, gentlemen!"

Sam. Well, Mr. Eccles, sir, it's this —

Polly. (*Aside, coming down to Sam*) Don't tell him too sudden, Sam — it might shock his feelings.

Sam. It's this; yer know that for the last four years I've been keepin' company with Mary — Polly. (*Turning to her and smiling. Eccles drops into chair as if shot*)

Eccles. Go it! go it! strike home, young man! Strike on this grey head! (*Sings*) "Britons, strike home!" Here (*Tapping his chest*), to my heart! Don't spare me! Have a go at my grey hairs. Pull 'em — pull 'em out! A long pull, and a strong pull, and a pull all together! (*Cries, and drops his face on arm on table*)

Polly. Oh, father! I wouldn't hurt your feelings for the world. (*Patting his head*)

Sam. No, Mr. Eccles, I don't want to 'urt your feelin's, but I'm a-goin' to enter upon a business. Here's a circular. (*Offering one*)

Eccles. (*Indignantly*) Circ'lars. What are circ'lars? — compared to a father's feelings?

Sam. And I want Polly to name the day, sir, and so I ask you —

Eccles. This is 'ard, this is 'ard. One of my daughters marries a soger. The other goes a-gasfitting.

Sam. (*Annoyed*) The business which will enable me to maintain a wife is that of the late Mr. Binks, plumber, glazier, etc.

Eccles. (*Rising, sings. Air, "Lost Rosabelle"*)
"They have given thee to a plumber,

They have broken every vow,
They have given thee to a plumber,
And my heart, my heart is breaking now."
(*Drops into chair again*) Now, gentlemen!
> *Sam thrusts circulars into his pocket,
> and turns away angrily.*

Polly. You know, father, you can come
and see me. (*Leans over him*)

Sam. (*Sotto voce*) No, no. (*Motions to
Polly*)

Eccles. (*Looking up*) So I can, and that's a
comfort. (*Shaking her hand*) And you can
come and see me, and that's a comfort. I'll
come and see you often — very often —
every day (*Sam turns up stage in horror*), and
crack a fatherly bottle (*Rising*), and shed a
friendly tear. (*Wipes eyes with dirty pocket-
handkerchief, which he pulls from breast pocket*)

Polly. Do, father, do. (*Goes up and gets
tea-tray*)

Sam. (*With a gulp*) Yes, Mr. Eccles, do.
(*Goes to Polly and gesticulates behind tray*)

Eccles. I will. (*Goes to centre of stage*) And
this it is to be a father. I would part with any
of my children for their own good, readily —
if I was paid for it. (*Goes to right corner; sings*)
"For I know that the angels are whispering
to me" — me, gentlemen! (*Polly gets tea-
things*)

Sam. I'll try and make Polly a good husband, and anything that I can do to prove it
(*Lowering his voice*), in the way of spirituous
liquors and tobacco (*Slipping coin into his
hand, unseen by Polly*) shall be done.

Eccles. (*Lightening up and placing his left
hand on Sam's head*)
"Be kind to thy father,
    Wherever you be,
For he is a blessing
    And credit to thee, —
        thee, gentlemen."

(*Gets to centre of stage*) Well, my children —
bless you, take the blessing of a grey-'aired
father. (*Polly looking from one to the other*)
Samuel Gerridge, she shall be thine. (*Mock
heroically, looking at money*) You shall be his
wife (*Looking at Polly*) and you (*Looking at
Sam*) shall be her husband — for a husband
I know no fitter — no "gas-fitter" man.
(*Runs to piano and takes hat; goes to door,
looks comically pathetic at Sam and Polly, puts
on hat and comes towards centre of stage*) I've a
friend waiting for me round the corner,
which I want to have a word with; and may
you never know how much more sharper
than a serpent's tooth it is to have a mar-
riageable daughter. (*Sings*)
"When I heard she was married,
    I breathed not a tone,

The heyes of all round me
    Was fixed on my h'own;
I flew to my chamber
    To hide my despair,
I tore the bright circlet
    Of gems from my hair.
When I heard she was married,
When I heard she was married —"
> *Breaks down. Exit.*

Polly. (*Drying her eyes*) There, Sam. I
always told you that though father had his
faults, his heart was in the right place.

Sam. Poor Polly. (*Crosses to fireplace.
Knock at door*)

Polly. (*Top of table*) Come in.

> *Enter Hawtree.*

Major Hawtree.
> *Sam turns away as they shake hands.*

Haw. I met the Marquise's carriage on the
bridge. Has she been here?
> *Sam at fire, with back to it.*

Polly. Yes.

Haw. What happened?

Polly. Oh, she wanted to take away the
child. (*At head of table*)

Sam. In the coach.
> *Polly sets tea-things.*

Haw. And what did Mrs. D'Alroy say to
that?

Sam. Mrs. D'Alroy said that she'd see 'er
blowed first! (*Polly pushes Sam*) — or words
to that effect.

Haw. I'm sorry to hear this; I had hoped
— however, that's over.

Polly. (*Sitting at table*) Yes, it's over; and
I hope we shall hear no more about it. Want
to take away the child, indeed — like her
impudence! What next! (*Getting ready tea-
things*) Esther's gone to lie down. I sha'n't
wake her up for tea, though she's had nothing
to eat all day.

Sam. (*Head of table*) Shall I fetch some
shrimps?

Polly. No. What made you think of
shrimps?

Sam. They're a relish, and consolin' —
at least I always found 'em so. (*Check lights
gradually*)

Polly. I won't ask you to take tea with us,
Major, — you're too grand.
> *Sam motions approbation to Polly,
> not wanting Hawtree to remain.*

Haw. (*Placing hat on piano*) Not at all. I
shall be most happy. (*Aside*) 'Pon my word,
these are a very good sort of people. I'd no
idea —

Sam. (*Points to Hawtree*) He's a-goin' to
stop to tea, — well, I ain't. (*Goes up to win-*

dow and sits. Hawtree crosses and sits opposite Polly at table)

Polly. Sam! Sam! (*Pause — he says* Eh?) Pull down the blind and light the gas.

Sam. No, don't light up; I like this sort of dusk. It's unbusiness-like, but pleasant.

> *Sam cuts enormous slice of bread and hands it on point of knife to Hawtree. Cuts small lump of butter and hands it on point of knife to Hawtree, who looks at it through eye-glass, then takes it. Sam then helps himself. Polly meantime has poured out tea in two cups, and one saucer for Sam, sugars them, and then hands cup and saucer to Hawtree, who has both hands full. He takes it awkwardly and places it on table. Polly, having only one spoon, tastes Sam's tea, then stirs Hawtree's, attracting his attention by doing so. He looks into his tea-cup. Polly stirs her own tea, and drops spoon into Hawtree's cup, causing it to spurt in his eye. He drops eye-glass and wipes his eyes.*

Polly. (*Making tea*) Sugar, Sam! (*Sam takes tea and sits facing fire*) Oh, there isn't any milk — it'll be here directly, it's just his time.

Voice. (*Outside; rattle of milk-pails*) Miaoow.

Polly. There he is. (*Knock at door*) Oh, I know; I owe him four-pence. (*Feeling in her pocket*) Sam, have you got fourpence? (*Knock again, louder*)

Sam. No (*His mouth full*) — I ain't got no fourpence.

Polly. He's very impatient. Come in!

Enter George, his face bronzed, and in full health. He carries a milk-can in his hand, which, after putting his hat on piano, he places on table.

Geo. A fellow hung this on the railings, so I brought it in.

> *Polly sees him, and gradually sinks down under table on one side. Then Sam, with his mouth full, and bread and butter in hand, does the same on the other. Hawtree pushes himself back a space, in chair; remains motionless. George astonished. Picture.*

Geo. What's the matter with you?

Haw. (*Rising*) George!

Geo. Hawtree! You here?

Polly. (*Under table*) O-o-o-h! the ghost! the ghost!

Sam. It shan't hurt you, Polly. Perhaps it's only indigestion.

Haw. Then you are not dead?

Geo. Dead, no. Where's my wife?

Haw. You were reported killed.

Geo. It wasn't true.

Haw. Alive! My old friend alive!

Geo. And well. (*Shakes hands*) Landed this morning. Where's my wife?

Sam. (*Who has popped his head from under the tablecloth*) He ain't dead, Poll, — he's alive. (*Polly rises from under the table slowly*)

Polly. (*Pause; approaches him, touches him, retreats*) George! (*He nods*) George! George!

Geo. Yes! Yes!

Polly. Alive! My dear George! Oh, my brother! (*Looking at him intensely*) Alive! (*Going to him*) Oh, my dear, dear brother! (*In his arms*) — how could you go and do so? (*Laughs hysterically*)

> *Sam goes to Polly. George places Polly in Sam's arms. Sam kisses Polly's hand violently. Hawtree comes up, stares — business. Sam with a stamp of his foot moves away.*

Geo. Where's Esther?

Haw. Here, — in this house.

Geo. Here! — doesn't she know I'm back?

Polly. No, — how should she?

Geo. (*To Hawtree*) Didn't you get my telegram?

Haw. No; where from?

Geo. Southampton! I sent it to the Club.

Haw. I haven't been there these three days.

Polly. (*Hysterically*) Oh, my dear, dear, dear dead-and-gone, come-back-all-alive-oh, brother George! (*George passes her*)

Sam. Glad to see yer, sir.

Geo. Thank you, Gerridge. (*Shakes hands*) Same to you — but Esther?

Polly. (*Back to audience, and 'kerchief to her eyes*) She's asleep in her room. (*George is going; Polly stops him*)

Polly. You mustn't see her.

Geo. Not see her! — after this long absence! — why not?

Haw. She's ill to-day. She has been greatly excited. The news of your death, which we all mourned, has shaken her terribly.

Geo. Poor girl! Poor girl!

Polly. Oh, we all cried so when you died! — (*Crying*) — and now you're alive again, I want to cry ever so much more. (*Crying*)

Haw. We must break the news to her gently and by degrees. (*Crosses behind, to fire, taking his tea with him*)

Sam. Yes, if you turn the tap on to full pressure, she'll explode. (*Sam turns to Hawtree, who is just raising cup to his lips and brings it down on saucer with a bang; both annoyed*)

Geo. To return, and not to be able to see her — to love her — to kiss her! (*Stamps*)

Polly. Hush!

Geo. I forgot — I shall wake her!

Polly. More than that, — you'll wake the baby.

Geo. Baby! — what baby?

Polly. Yours.

Geo. Mine? — mine?

Polly. Yes, — yours and Esther's. Why, didn't you know there was a baby?

Geo. No!

Polly. La! the ignorance of these men!

Haw. Yes, George, you're a father. (*At fireplace*)

Geo. Why wasn't I told of this? Why didn't you write?

Polly. How could we when you were dead?

Sam. And 'adn't left your address. (*Looks at Hawtree, who turns away quickly*)

Geo. If I can't see Esther, I will see the child. The sight of me won't be too much for its nerves. Where is it?

Polly. Sleeping in its mother's arms. (*George goes to door — she intercepts him*) Please not! Please not!

Geo. I must! I will!

Polly. It might kill her, and you wouldn't like to do that. I'll fetch the baby; but, oh, please don't make a noise. (*Going up*) You won't make a noise — you'll be as quiet as you can, won't you? Oh! I can't believe it!

Exit Polly. Sam dances breakdown and finishes up by looking at Hawtree, who turns away astonished. Sam disconcerted; sits on chair by table; George at door.

Geo. My baby — my ba — It's a dream! (*To Sam*) You've seen it — What's it like?

Sam. Oh! it's like a — like a sort of — infant — white and — milky, and all that.

Enter Polly with baby wrapped in shawls; George shuts door and meets her.

Polly. Gently! gently, — take care! Esther will hardly have it touched.

Sam rises and gets near to George.

Geo. But I'm its father.

Polly. That don't matter. She's very particular.

Geo. Boy or girl?

Polly. Guess.

Geo. Boy! (*Polly nods. George proud*) What's his name?

Polly. Guess.

Geo. George? (*Polly nods*) Eustace? (*Polly nods*) Fairfax? Algernon? (*Polly nods; pause*) My names!

Sam. (*To George*) You'd 'ardly think there

was room enough in 'im to 'old so many names, would yer?

Hawtree looks at him — turns to fire. Sam disconcerted again. Sits.

Geo. To come back all the way from India to find that I'm dead, and that you're alive. To find my wife a widow with a new love aged — How old are you? I'll buy you a pony tomorrow, my brave little boy! What's his weight? I should say two pound nothing. My — baby — my — boy! (*Bends over him and kisses him*) Take him away, Polly, for fear I should break him. (*Polly takes child, and places it in cradle*)

Haw. (*Crosses to piano. Passes Sam, front — stares — business. Sam goes round to fireplace, flings down bread and butter in a rage and drinks his tea out of saucer*) But tell us how it is you're back — how you escaped? (*Hawtree leans against piano*)

Geo. (*Coming down*) By and by. Too long a story just now. Tell *me* all about it. (*Polly gives him chair*) How is it Esther's living here?

Polly. She came back after the baby was born, and the furniture was sold up.

Geo. Sold up? What furniture?

Polly. That you bought for her.

Haw. It couldn't be helped, George — Mrs. D'Alroy was so poor.

Geo. Poor! But I left her £600 to put in the bank!

Haw. We *must* tell you. She gave it to her father, who banked it in his own name.

Sam. And lost it in bettin' — every copper.

Geo. Then she's been in want?

Polly. No — not in want. Friends lent her money.

Geo. (*Seated*) What friends? (*Pause; he looks at Polly, who indicates Hawtree*) You?

Polly. Yes.

Geo. (*Rising and shaking Hawtree's hand*) Thank you, old fella. (*Hawtree droops his head*)

Sam. (*Aside*) Now who'd a thought that long swell 'ad it in 'im? 'e never mentioned it.

Geo. So Papa Eccles had the money! (*Sitting again*)

Sam. And blued it. (*Sits on corner of table*)

Polly. (*Pleadingly*) You see father was very unlucky on the race-course. He told us that if it hadn't been that all his calculations were upset by a horse winning who had no business to, he should have made our fortunes. Father's been unlucky, and he gets tipsy at times, but he's a very clever man, if you only give him scope enough.

Sam. I'd give 'im scope enough!

Geo. Where is he now?

Sam. Public-house.

Geo. And how is he?

Sam. Drunk!

> *Polly pushes him off table. Sam sits at fireplace up stage.*

Geo. (*To Hawtree*) You were right. There is "*something*" in caste. (*Aloud*) But tell us all about it. (*Sits*)

Polly. Well, you know, you went away; and then the baby was born. Oh! he was such a sweet little thing, just like — your eyes — your hair. (*Standing by George, who is sitting*)

Geo. Cut that!

Polly. Well, baby came; and when baby was six days old, your letter came, Major. (*To Hawtree*) I saw that it was from India, and that it wasn't in your hand (*To George*); I guessed what was inside it, so I opened it unknown to her, and I read there of your capture and death. I daren't tell her. I went to father to ask his advice, but he was too tipsy to understand me. Sam fetched the doctor. He told us that the news would kill her. When she woke up, she said she had dreamt there was a letter from you. I told her, No; and day after day she asked for a letter. So the doctor advised us to write one as if it came from you. So we did. Sam and I and the doctor told her — told Esther, I mean — that her eyes were bad and she mustn't read, and we read our letter to her; didn't we, Sam? But, bless you! she always knew it hadn't come from you! At last, when she was stronger, we told her all.

Geo. (*After a pause*) How did she take it?

Polly. She pressed the baby in her arms, and turned her face to the wall. (*A pause*) Well, to make a long story short, when she got up, she found father had lost all the money you had left her. There was a dreadful scene between them. She told him he'd robbed her and her child, and father left the house, and swore he'd never come back again.

Sam. Don't be alarmed, — 'e did come back. (*Sitting by fire*)

Polly. Oh, yes; he was too goodhearted to stop long from his children. He has his faults, but his good points, when you find 'em, are wonderful!

Sam. Yes, when you find 'em. (*Rises, gets bread and butter from table, and sits at corner of table*)

Polly. So she had to come back here to us, and that's all.

Geo. Why didn't she write to my mother?

Polly. Father wanted her to; but she was too proud — she said she'd die first.

Geo. (*Rising, to Hawtree*) There's a woman! Caste's all humbug. (*Sees sword over mantel-piece*) That's my sword (*Crossing round*) and a map of India, and that's the piano I bought her — I'll swear to the silk.

Polly. Yes; that was bought in at the sale.

Geo. (*To Hawtree*) Thank ye, old fella.

Haw. Not by me — I was in India at the time.

Geo. By whom, then?

Polly. By Sam. (*Sam winks to her to discontinue*) I shall! He knew Esther was breaking her heart about anyone else having it, so he took the money he'd saved up for our wedding, and we're going to be married now — ain't we, Sam?

Sam. (*Rushing to George and pulling out circulars from his pocket*) And hope by constant attention to business, to merit — (*Polly pushes him away*)

Polly. Since you died it hasn't been opened, but if I don't play it tonight, may I die an old maid!

> *Goes up. George crosses to Sam, and shakes his hand, then goes up stage, pulls up blind, and looks into street. Sam turns up and meets Polly by top of table.*

Haw. (*Aside*) Now who'd have thought that the little cad had it in him? He never mentioned it. (*Aloud*) Apropos, George, your mother — I'll go to the Square, and tell her of — (*Takes hat from piano*)

Geo. Is she in town? (*At cradle*)

Haw. Yes. Will you come with me?

Geo. And leave my wife? — and such a wife!

Haw. I'll go at once. I shall catch her before dinner. Good-bye, old fellow. Seeing you back again, alive and well, makes me feel quite — that I quite feel — (*Shakes George's hand. Goes to door, then crosses to Sam, who has turned Polly's tea into his saucer, and is just about to drink; seeing Hawtree, he puts it down quickly, and turns his back*) Mr. Gerridge, I fear I have often made myself very offensive to you.

Sam. Well, sir, yer 'ave.

Haw. (*At bottom of table*) I feared so. I didn't know you then. I beg your pardon. Let me ask you to shake hands — to forgive me, and forget it. (*Offering his hand*)

Sam. (*Taking it*) Say no more, sir; and if ever I've made myself offensive to you, I ask your pardon; forget it and forgive me. (*They shake hands warmly; as Hawtree crosses to door, recovering from Sam's hearty shake of the hand, Sam runs to him*) Hi, sir! When yer marry that young lady as I know you're engaged to, if you should furnish a house, and require anything in my way — (*He brings out circular; begins to read it. Polly comes down and pushes Sam away, against Hawtree. Sam goes and sits on low chair by fireplace, down stage, disconcerted— cramming circulars into his pocket)*

Haw. Good-bye, George, for the present. (*At door*) Bye, Polly. (*Resumes his Pall Mall manner as he goes out*) I'm off to the Square.
Exit Hawtree.

Geo. (*At cradle*) But Esther?

Polly. (*Meets George*) Oh, I forgot all about Esther. I'll tell her all about it.

Geo. How? (*By door*)

Polly. I don't know; but it will come. Providence will send it to me, as it has sent you, my dear brother. (*Embracing him*) You don't know how glad I am to see you back again! You must go. (*Pushing him. George takes hat off piano*) Esther will be getting up directly. (*At door with George, who looks through keyhole*) It's no use looking there; it's dark.

Geo. (*At door*) It isn't often a man can see his own widow.

Polly. And it isn't often that he wants to! Now, you must go. (*Pushing him off*)

Geo. I shall stop outside.

Sam. And I'll whistle for you when you may come in.

Polly. Now — hush!

Geo. (*Opening door wide*) Oh, my Esther, when you know I'm alive! I'll marry you all over again, and we'll have a second honeymoon, my darling.
Exit.

Polly. Oh, Sam, Sam! (*Commencing to sing and dance. Sam also dances; they meet in centre of stage, join hands, and dance around two or three times, leaving Sam on the left of Polly, near table. Polly going down*) Oh, Sam, I'm so excited, I don't know what to do. What shall I do — what shall I do?

Sam. (*Taking up Hawtree's bread and butter*) 'Ave a bit of bread and butter, Polly.

Polly. Now, Sam, light the gas; I'm going to wake her up. (*Opening door*) Oh, my darling, if I dare tell you! (*Whispering*) He's come back! He's alive! He's come back! He's come back! Alive! Alive! Alive! Sam, kiss me!
Sam rushes to Polly, kisses her, and she jumps off, Sam shutting the door.

Sam. (*Dances shutter-dance*) I'm glad the swells are gone; now I can open my safety-valve, and let my feelings escape. To think of 'is comin' back alive from India just as I am goin' to open my shop. Perhaps he'll get me the patronage of the Royal Family. It would look stunnin' over the door, a lion and a unicorn, a-standin' on their hind legs, doin' nothin' furiously, with a lozenge between 'em — thus. (*Seizes plate on table, puts his*

left foot on chair by table, and imitates the picture of the Royal arms) Polly said I was to light up, and whatever Polly says must be done. (*Lights brackets over mantel-piece, then candles; as he lights the broken one, says*) Why this one is for all the world like old Eccles! (*Places candles on piano and sits on music-stool*) Poor Esther! to think of my knowin' her when she was in the ballet line, — then in the 'onourable line; then a mother — no, honourables is "mammas", — then a widow, and then in the ballet line again! — and 'im to come back (*Growing affected*) — and find a baby, with all 'is furniture and fittin's ready for immediate use (*Crossing back of table during last few lines, sits in chair left of table*) — and she, poor thing, lyin' asleep with 'er eye-lids 'ot and swollen, not knowin' that that great big, 'eavy, 'ulkin', over-grown dragoon is prowlin' outside, ready to fly at 'er lips, and strangle 'er in 'is strong, lovin' arms — it — it — it — (*Breaks down and sobs, with his head on the table*)

Enter Polly.

Polly. Why, Sam! What's the matter?

Sam. (*Rises and crosses*) I dunno. The water's got into my meter.

Polly. Hush! Here's Esther.

Enter Esther. They stop suddenly. Polly down stage.

Sam. (*Singing and dancing*) "Tiddy-ti-tum," etc.

Esther. (*Sitting near fire, taking up costume and beginning to work*) Sam, you seem in high spirits to-night!

Sam. Yes; yer see Polly and I are goin' to be married — and — and 'opes by bestowing a merit — to continue the favour —

Polly. (*Who has kissed Esther two or three times*) What are you talking about?

Sam. I don't know, — I'm off my burner. (*Brings music-stool. Polly goes round to chair, facing Esther*)

Esther. What's the matter with you to-night, dear? (*To Polly*) I can see something in your eyes.

Sam. P'raps it's the new furniture! (*Sits on music-stool*)

Esther. Will you help me with the dress, Polly? (*They sit, Esther upper end, back of table, Polly facing her, at lower end*)

Polly. It was a pretty dress when it was new — not unlike the one Mdlle. Delphine used to wear. (*Suddenly clasping her hands*) Oh!

Esther. What's the matter?

Polly. A needle! (*Crosses to Sam, who examines finger*) I've got it!

Sam. What — the needle — in your finger?

Polly. No; an idea in my head!

Sam. (*Still looking at her finger*) Does it 'urt?

Polly. Stupid! (*Sam still sitting on stool. Aloud*) Do you recollect Mdlle. Delphine, Esther?

Esther. Yes.

Polly. Do you recollect her in that ballet that old Herr Griffenhaagen arranged? — Jeanne la Folle, or, the Return of the Soldier?

Esther. Yes; will you do the fresh hem?

Polly. What's the use? Let me see — how did it go? How well I remember the scene! — the cottage was on that side, the bridge at the back — then ballet of villagers, and the entrance of Delphine as Jeanne, the bride — tra-lal-lala-lala-la-la (*Sings and pantomimes, Sam imitating her*) Then the entrance of Claude, the bridegroom — (*To Sam, imitating swell*) How-de-do? how-de-do?

Sam. (*Rising*) 'Ow are yer? (*Imitating Polly, then sitting again*)

Polly. Then there was the procession to church — the march of the soldiers over the bridge — (*Sings and pantomimes*) — arrest of Claude, who is drawn for the conscription — (*Business; Esther looks dreamily*) and is torn from the arms of his bride, at the church-porch. *Omnes* broken-hearted. This is *Omnes* broken-hearted. (*Pantomimes*)

Esther. Polly, I don't like this; it brings back memories.

Polly. (*Going to table and leaning her hands on it. Looks over at Esther*) Oh, fuss about memories! — one can't mourn for ever. (*Esther surprised*) Everything in this world isn't sad. There's bad news — and there's good news sometimes — when we least expect it.

Esther. Ah! not for me.

Polly. Why not?

Esther. (*Anxiously*) Polly!

Polly. Second Act. (*This to be said quickly, startling Sam, who has been looking on the ground during last four or five lines*) Winter — the Village Pump. This is the village pump. (*Pointing to Sam, seated by piano, on music-stool; Sam turns round on music-stool, disgusted*) Entrance of Jeanne — now called Jeanne la Folle, because she has gone mad on account of the supposed loss of her husband.

Sam. The supposed loss?

Polly. The supposed loss!

Esther. (*Dropping costume*) Polly!

Sam. (*Aside to Polly*) Mind!

Polly. Can't stop now! Entrance of Claude, who isn't dead, in a captain's uniform — a cloak thrown over his shoulders.

Esther. Not dead!

Polly. Don't you remember the ballet? Jeanne is mad, and can't recognise her husband; and don't, till he shows her the ribbon she gave him when they were betrothed. A bit of ribbon! Sam, have you got a bit of ribbon? Oh, that crape sword-knot, that will do. (*Crosses down. Sam astonished*)

Esther. Touch that! (*Rising, coming down*)

Polly. Why not? — it's no use *now*.

Esther. (*Slowly, looking into Polly's eyes*) You have heard of George — I know you have — I see it in your eyes. You may tell me — I can bear it — I can indeed — indeed I can. Tell me — he is not dead? (*Violently agitated*)

Polly. No!

Esther. No?

Polly. No!

Esther. (*Whispers*) Thank Heaven! (*Sam turns on stool, back to audience*) You've seen him, — I see you have! — I know it! — I feel it! I had a bright and happy dream — I saw him as I slept! Oh, let me know if he is near! Give me some sign — some sound — (*Polly opens piano*) — some token of his life and presence!

> *Sam touches Polly on the shoulder, takes hat, and exit. All to be done very quickly. Polly sits immediately at piano and plays air softly — the same air played by Esther, Act II, on the treble only*)

Esther. (*In an ecstasy*) Oh, my husband! come to me! for I know that you are near! Let me feel your arms clasp round me! Do not fear for me! — I can bear the sight of you! — (*Door opens showing Sam keeping George back*) — it will not kill me! — George — love! husband — come, oh, come to me!

> *George breaks away from Sam, and coming down behind Esther places his hands over her eyes; she gives a faint scream, and turning, falls in his arms. Polly plays bass as well as treble of the air, forte, then fortissimo. She then plays at random, endeavouring to hide her tears. At last strikes piano wildly, and goes off into a fit of hysterical laughter to the alarm of Sam, who, rushing down as Polly cries "Sam! Sam!" falls on his knees in front of her. They embrace, Polly pushing him contemptuously away afterwards. George gets chair, sits, and Esther kneels at his feet — he snatches off Esther's cap, and throws it up stage. Polly goes left of George, Sam brings music-stool, and she sits.*

Esther. To see you here again — to feel

your warm breath upon my cheek — is it real, or am I dreaming?

Sam. (*Rubbing his head*) No; it's real.

Esther. (*Embracing George*) My darling!

Sam. My darling! (*Polly on music-stool, which Sam has placed for her. Sam, kneeling by her, imitates Esther — Polly scornfully pushes him away*) But tell us — tell us how you escaped.

Geo. It's a long story, but I'll condense it. I was riding out, and suddenly found myself surrounded and taken prisoner. One of the troop that took me was a fella who had been my servant, and to whom I had done some little kindness. He helped me to escape, and hid me in a sort of cave, and for a long time used to bring me food. Unfortunately, he was ordered away; so he brought another Sepoy to look after me. I felt from the first this man meant to betray me, and I watched him like a lynx, during the one day he was with me. As evening drew on, a Sepoy picket was passing. I could tell by the look in the fella's eyes, he meant to call out as soon as they were near enough; so I seized him by the throat, and shook the life out of him.

Esther. You strangled him?

Geo. Yes.

Esther. Killed him — dead?

Geo. He didn't get up again. (*Embraces Esther*)

Polly. (*To Sam*) You never go and kill Sepoys. (*Pushes him over*)

Sam. No! I pay rates and taxes.

Geo. The day after, Havelock and his Scotchmen marched through the village, and I turned out to meet them. I was too done up to join, so I was sent straight on to Calcutta. I got leave, took a berth on the P. & O. boat; the passage restored me. I landed this morning, came on here, and brought in the milk.

Enter the Marquise; she rushes to embrace George. All rise, Sam putting stool back.

Mar. My dear boy, — my dear, dear boy!

Polly. Why, see, she's crying! She's glad to see him alive and back again.

Sam. (*Profoundly*) Well! There's always some good in women, even when they're ladies. (*Goes up to window. Polly puts dress in box, and goes to cradle; then beside Sam*)

Mar. (*Crossing to Esther*) My dear daughter, we must forget our little differences. (*Kissing her*) Won't you? How history repeats itself! You will find a similar and as unexpected a return mentioned by Froissart in the chapter that treats of Philip Dartnell —

Geo. Yes, mother — I remember — (*Kisses her*)

Mar. (*To George, aside*) We must take her abroad, and make a lady of her.

Geo. Can't, mamma; — she's ready-made. Nature has done it to our hands.

Mar. (*Aside to George*) But I won't have the man who smells of putty — (*Sam, business at back. He is listening, and at the word "putty" throws his cap irritably on table. Polly pacifies him, and makes him sit down beside her on window*) — nor the man who smells of beer. (*Goes to Esther, who offers her chair, and sits in chair opposite to her. Marquise back to audience, Esther facing audience*)

Enter Hawtree, pale.

Haw. George! Oh, the Marchioness is here.

Geo. What's the matter?

Haw. Oh, nothing. Yes, there is. I don't mind telling you. I've been thrown. I called at my chambers as I came along and found this. (*Gives George a note. Sits on music-stool*)

Geo. From the Countess, Lady Florence's mother. (*Reads*) "Dear Major Hawtree, — I hasten to inform you that my daughter Florence is about to enter into an alliance with Lord Saxeby, the eldest son of the Marquis of Loamshire. Under these circumstances, should you think fit to call here again, I feel assured —" Well, perhaps it's for the best. (*Returning letter*) Caste! you know. Caste! And a marquis is a bigger swell than a major.

Haw. Yes, best to marry in your own rank of life.

Geo. If you can find *the* girl. But if ever you find *the* girl, marry her. As to her station, —

"True hearts are more than coronets,
And simple faith than Norman blood."

Haw. Ya-as. But a gentleman should hardly ally himself to a nobody.

Geo. My dear fella, Nobody's a mistake — he don't exist. Nobody's nobody! Everybody's somebody!

Haw. Yes. But still — Caste.

Geo. Oh, caste's all right. Caste is a good thing if it's not carried too far. It shuts the door on the pretentious and the vulgar; but it should open the door very wide for exceptional merit. Let brains break through its barriers, and what brains can break through love may leap over.

Haw. Yes. Why, George, you're quite inspired — quite an orator. What makes you so brilliant? Your captivity? The voyage? What then?

Geo. I'm in love with my wife!

Enter Eccles, drunk, a bottle of gin in his hand.

Eccles. (Crossing to centre of stage) Bless this 'appy company. May we 'ave in our arms what we love in our 'earts. *(Goes to head of table. Esther goes to cradle, back to audience. Polly and Sam, half amused, half angry. Marquise still sitting in chair, back to audience. Hawtree facing Eccles. George up stage, leaning on piano in disgust)* Polly, fetch wine-glasses — a tumbler will do for me. Let us drink a toast. Mr. Chairman *(To Marquise)*, ladies and gentlemen, — I beg to propose the 'ealth of our newly returned warrior, *my son-in-law. (Marquise shivers)* The Right Honourable George De Alroy. Get glasses, Polly, and send for a bottle of sherry wine for my ladyship. *My* ladyship! My ladyship! M' lad'ship! *(She half turns to him)* You and me'll have a drain together on the quiet. So delighted to see you under these altered circum — circum — circum — stangate. *(Polly, who has shaken her head at him to desist, in vain, very distressed)*

Sam. Shove 'is 'ead in a bucket!

Exit in disgust.

Haw. (Aside to George) I think I can abate this nuisance — at least, I can remove it. *(Rises and crosses to Eccles, who has got round to side of table, leaning on it. He taps Eccles with his stick, first on right shoulder, then on left, and finally sharply on right. Eccles turns round and falls on point of stick — Hawtree steadying him. George crosses behind, to Marquise, who has gone to cradle — puts his arm round Esther and takes her to mantelpiece)* Mr. Eccles, don't you think that, with your talent for liquor, if you had an allowance of about two pounds a week, and went to Jersey, where spirits are cheap, that you could drink yourself to death in a year?

Eccles. I think I could — I'm sure I'll try.

Goes up by table, steadying himself by it, and sits in chair by fire, with the bottle of gin. Hawtree standing by fire. Esther and Polly embracing. As they turn away from each other —

Geo. (Coming across with Esther) Come and play me that air that used to ring in my ears as I lay awake, night after night, captive in the cave — you know. *(He hands Esther to piano. She plays the air)*

Mar. (Bending over cradle, at end) My grandson!

Eccles falls off the chair in the last stage of drunkenness, bottle in hand. Hawtree, leaning one foot on chair from which Eccles has fallen, looks at him through eye-glass. Sam enters, and goes to Polly, behind cradle, and, producing wedding-ring from several papers, holds it up before her eyes. Esther plays until curtain drops.

THE END.

WILLIAM SCHWENK GILBERT
1836-1911

Engaged
(1877)

Perhaps the Gilbert and Sullivan operas belong to the new drama. At least they entertain our own age as well as the one they mirrored and mocked. That W. S. Gilbert also wrote plays bridging the gap between Tom Robertson and the new drama is less well known.

William Schwenk Gilbert was born in London on November 18, 1836. As a small child he travelled with his parents in Germany and Italy and had the adventure of being stolen by bandits in Naples and returned safely for a ransom of twenty-five pounds. "Bab," as he was called, went to school in Boulogne at seven, to the Great Ealing School at thirteen, and then to King's College, London, where he published his first verses in the college magazine. At nineteen he quit college to take part in the Crimean War, but the war ended before he could do so. He turned to the study of law and practised on the Northern Circuit; since this career did not satisfy him, he began writing humorous verses and other pieces for the magazine *Fun*, and joined its staff in 1861. He contributed stories, articles, and verses to other periodicals, including dramatic criticism for the *Illustrated Times* and news stories for a Russian newspaper, *Invalide Russe*. In 1861 he married Miss Lucy Turner. His famous illustrated comic poems, collected as *Bab Ballads*, began to appear in *Fun* on June 1, 1867, and became a regular feature. He was not merely amused at life, for satiric and critical ideas and even indignation at social injustice appear in his humor and in his articles. He penned, for instance, an indignant attack upon a fashionable milliner as the "murderer" of an employee who died of overwork and starvation.

Gilbert became a playwright through a recommendation by Tom Robertson. Miss Herbert, the manager of St. James's Theatre, asked Robertson if he knew anyone who could write a Christmas piece in a fortnight. Gilbert, recalling the event, said, "Robertson, who had often expressed to me his belief that I should succeed as a writer for the stage, advised Miss Herbert to entrust me with the work, and the introduction resulted in my first piece, a burlesque on *L'Elisir d'Amore*, called *Dulcamara; or, The Little Duck and the Great Quack.*" This piece, done in ten days, rehearsed in a week, and produced December 29, 1866, was a success. Gilbert wrote more plays and finally, in collaboration with Arthur Sullivan, *Trial by Jury* (1875), the first of the great comic operas. The rest of Gilbert's career is well known. He was knighted by King Edward VII in 1907. In a gallant attempt to save a child's life, he was drowned on May 29, 1911.

Gilbert's fame as the author of *Bab Ballads* and librettos for Sullivan's music has called attention away from his dramas. Besides the operettas, he wrote more than fifty plays. Perhaps they are not great, but they are part of the fresh, stimulating revolt against the older drama, and they point toward the plays of the 1890's. *The Palace of Truth* (1870) expresses Gilbert's view of life. Written in blank verse, it is a fantasy (an extravaganza) of a fairy world. But this fairy world is topsy-turvy. The fairy characters appear to be those of pretty ballets, and pretend all the generous, sentimental feelings of romance, but when they enter the palace they are forced by enchantment to tell the truth. They reveal their hidden thoughts and motives and exhibit the selfishness, egoism, lust, hypocrisy, and vanity that quite unconsciously they had rationalized as virtue, generosity, and romantic feeling. The play is not exactly bitter, for it is a comedy, but it is probing. *Pygmalion and Galatea* (1871) is an ironic fantasy. When the sculptor Pygmalion brings his marble Galatea to life, his jealous wife blinds him, until Galatea, shocked at what life means, returns to stone. *The Wicked World* (1873) is set in a fairyland on clouds above the earth. The fairies do not know what love is until their magic draws two cavaliers, Sir Ethias and Sir Phyllon, up from the earth. The fairies are delighted with love until its jealousies and cruelties wreck their happiness and the human beings are cast back to earth. *Charity* (1874) tells the story of a woman who had sinned and who redeemed herself by a lifetime of self sacrifice. The play is distinctly a problem play with a serious message. Gilbert's biographers, Sidney Dark and Rowland Grey, comment that "Gilbert preaches in *Charity*, deliberately preaches, for the jester, with whom all the world still laughs, was moved to the depths of his soul by cruelty either in individuals or institutions, and yearned, almost pathetically, to use his art to destroy the thing that he hated." *Broken Hearts* (1875) presents the fantasy of a tropical island where brokenhearted girls have fled in renunciation of the world. When Prince Florian arrives with a magic book that enables him to become invisible, love enters, with jealousies and disillusionment. Thus Gilbert's fantasies, delicate and whimsical in treatment, are not syllabub, any more than the great operas that followed these plays are, against their Victorian background, mere entertainment.

Gilbert's *Allow Me to Explain* (1867) and *Sweethearts* (1874) were produced at the Prince of Wales's Theatre. There Gilbert observed the methods of stage direction of Tom Robertson and the Bancrofts and emulated them in directing his own plays. Allardyce Nicoll, quoting Edmond Rickett, says that Gilbert was "the most dreaded director in London — for he invariably directed personally and autocratically the production of his own plays and operas. . . . He planned the scenery, the lighting, and ordered not only the groupings of the chorus but practically every inflection of the voice and every gesture of the actors."

Though his message was not a radical one, Gilbert intended his plays to say something to the audience. As Dark and Grey comment, "The Gilbert of the airy lyric and magical irresistible foolery was obsessed by the importance of being earnest. He wanted to preach." He could not escape from his private Palace of Truth. His fantasies and fairy worlds present a backdrop of sentimental idealism, but the action against this backdrop denies that it is real. The denial is not exactly cynical, for it is wry with compassion. But it effectively undercuts the pathos, pietisms, and other romantic assumptions of Victorian life and its beloved melo- drama. The method is that of topsy-turvydom, turning characters inside out to exhibit motives that are veiled by pretenses.

Engaged exhibits this topsy-turvydom. It is a burlesque, not of any particular play, but of the assumptions underlying domestic melodramas and romantic come- dies. It anticipates the operas (though not performed until after *Trial by Jury*), which likewise burlesque the assumptions of Victorian drama in general. To the extent that the Victorian world veiled itself in lilac and lavender-scented hypo- crisies, the play tore away the veil to reveal a mercenary Philistinism. The opening scene of *Engaged* presents the garden of an "humble but picturesque cottage . . . prettily filled with flowers," a girl singing at a spinning wheel, and a rustic lover with honest face and honest heart, "a prosperous, kirk-going man." But suddenly the lines reveal that Angus makes his "honest" living by poaching, operating a whiskey still, and wrecking trains. Cheviot Hill enters, sentimentally and eternally in love with Minnie. He palpitates with passion for her, an "Angel of Light, a perfect being, as innocent as a new-laid egg." She is "my whole life, my whole soul and body, my Past, my Present, and my To Come." But a few minutes later he has forgotten her and discovered several other Angels of Light and Destiny. The complex plot moves on, line by line mocking the honeyed covering on mercenary realities. Minnie is an ideally dutiful daughter, who thinks her father a fool, and the father would sell Minnie to the highest bidder.

The play has the complications of farce and the fortuitous events of melo- drama, exaggerated just enough to mock them. Sentimentally stated realisms deflate every romantic posture. Angus, in language that scorns gold, refuses to sell Maggie for thirty shillings, but nobly yields his "childhood's — boyhood's — manhood's love" for two pounds; after all "twa pound is twa pound" as (in Belinda's statement to Belvawney) "business is business." Symperson's advice to Minnie, to "be sure you have your own way in everything," inverts the ideal of the obedient, yielding wife of both domestic melodrama and the patriarchal Victorian family. The scene in Act II concerned with Belvawney's hypnotic eyes, to be played "with melodra- matic intensity," burlesques images of the Gothic hero-villain remaining in some melodramas. The plot device of an uncertain marriage on the Scottish border bur- lesques the revelation scene in comedies since Restoration times.

Some critics (even William Archer) found the play "extremely amusing," but also "repulsive, vulgar." No doubt, if it is taken literally. But Gilbert's method is exaggeration, both of the sentimental echoes from other plays and of the egoism and selfishness that underlie these pretenses. The play exhibits absurdity in both extremes; the audience may find the truth somewhere between.

Humorous inversions of sentimental attitudes had been the basis of most earlier burlesques, but the inversions were piecemeal, inserted wisecracks and puns, ironic flashes and references to particular absurdities. *Engaged* presents its inversions as part of a system, or an order of thought, or a view of the world. Gilbert's topsy-turvy is not mere playful nonsense, but an earnest attempt to laugh nonsense off the stage. His preliminary note to the actors indicates his intention: "It is absolutely essential to the success of this piece that it should be played with the most perfect earnestness and gravity throughout. There should be no exaggeration in costume, make-up or demeanour; and the characters, one and all, should appear to believe, throughout, in the perfect sincerity of their words and actions. Directly the actors show that they are conscious of the absurdity of their utterances the piece begins to drag."

Engaged paved the way for Oscar Wilde's more brilliant burlesque or mock play (as "The Rape of the Lock" is a mock epic), *The Importance of Being Earnest.* Several particular details are adapted into Wilde's play: the system of inversions, the "Bunburying" that resembles Cheviot Hill's love making, the gorging of food at solemn or sentimental moments, and the declarations of affection by ladies who would like to cut one another's throat. *Engaged* is the vigorous bud that blossomed into Wilde's world-famous play.

ENGAGED

An Entirely Original Farcical Comedy In Three Acts

by

W. S. GILBERT

First performed at the Haymarket Theatre, October 3, 1877.

Cast of Characters

CHEVIOT HILL, *a young man of property*
BELVAWNEY, *his friend*
MR. SYMPERSON
ANGUS MACALISTER, *a Lowland peasant lad*
MAJOR MCGILLICUDDY

BELINDA TREHERNE
MINNIE, *Symperson's daughter*
MRS. MACFARLANE, *a Lowland widow*
MAGGIE, *her daughter, a Lowland lassie*
PARKER, *Minnie's maid*

ACT I.

Garden of humble but picturesque cottage, near Gretna, on the border between England and Scotland. The cottage is covered with creepers, and the garden is prettily filled with flowers. The door faces audience. A wooden bridge leads off at the left. The whole scene is suggestive of rustic prosperity and content. Maggie Macfarlane, a pretty country girl, is discovered spinning at a wheel, and singing as she spins. Angus Macalister, a good-looking peasant lad, appears at the back, and creeps softly down to Maggie as she sings and spins, and places his hands over her eyes.

Ang. Wha is it?

Mag. Oh, Angus, ye frightened me sae! (*He releases her*) And see there — the flax is a' knotted and scrubbed — and I'll do naething wi' it!

Ang. Meg! My Meg! My ain bonnie Meg!

Mag. Angus, why, lad, what's wrang wi' ee? Thou hast tear-drops in thy bonnie blue een.

Ang. Dinna heed them, Meg. It comes fra glowerin' at thy bright beauty. Glowerin' at thee is like glowerin' at the noon-day sun!

Mag. Angus, thou'rt talking fulishly. I'm but a puir brown hill-side lassie. I dinna like to hear sic things from a straight honest lad like thee. It's the way the dandy toun-folk speak to me, and it does na come rightly from the lips of a simple man.

Ang. Forgive me, Meg, for I speak honestly to ye. Angus Macalister is not the man to deal in squeaming compliments. Meg, I love thee dearly, as thou well knowest. I'm but a puir lad, and I've little but twa braw arms and a straight hairt to live by, but I've saved a wee bit siller — I've a braw housie and a scrappie of gude garden-land — and it's a' for thee, lassie, if thou'll gie me thy true and tender little hairt!

Mag. Angus, I'll be fair and straight wi' ee. Thou askest me for my hairt. Why, Angus, thou'rt tall, and fair, and brave. Thou'st a gude, honest face, and a gude, honest hairt, which is mair precious than a' the gold on earth! No man has a word to say against Angus Macalister — no, nor any woman neither. Thou hast strong arms to work wi', and a strong hairt to help thee work. And wha am I that I should say that a' these blessings are not enough for me? If thou, gude, brave, honest man, will be troubled wi' sic a puir little, humble mousie as Maggie Macfarlane, why, she'll be just the proudest and happiest lassie in a' Dumfries!

Ang. My ain darling! (*They embrace*)

Enter Mrs. Macfarlane from cottage.

Mrs. Mac. Why, Angus — Maggie, what's a' this!

Ang. Mistress Macfarlane, dinna be fasht wi' me; dinna think worse o' me than I deserve. I've loved your lass honestly these fifteen years, but I never plucked up the hairt to tell her so until noo; and when she answered fairly, it wasna in human nature to do aught else but hold her to my hairt and place one kiss on her bonnie cheek.

Mrs. Mac. Angus, say nae mair. My hairt is sair at losing my only bairn; but I'm nae fasht wi' ee. Thou'rt a gude lad, and it's been the hope of my widowed auld heart to see you twain one. Thou'lt treat her kindly — I ken that weel. Thou'rt a prosperous, kirk-going man, and my Mag should be a happy lass indeed. Bless thee, Angus; bless thee!

Ang. (*Wiping his eyes*) Dinna heed the water in my ee — it will come when I'm ower glad. Yes, I'm a fairly prosperous man. What wi' farmin' a bit land, and gillieing [1] odd times, and a bit o' poachin' now and again; and what wi' my illicit whuskey still — and throwin' trains off the line, that the poor distracted passengers may come to my cot, I've mair ways than one of making an honest living — and I'll work them a' nicht and day for my bonnie Meg!

Mrs. Mac. D'ye ken, Angus, I sometimes think that thou'rt losing some o' thine auld skill at upsetting railway trains. Thou hast not done sic a thing these sax weeks, and the cottage stands sairly in need of sic chance custom as the poor delayed passengers may bring.

Mag. Nay, mither, thou wrangest him. Even noo, this very day, has he not placed twa bonnie braw sleepers across the up-line, ready for the express from Glaisgie, which is due in twa minutes or so?

Mrs. Mac. Gude lad! Gude thoughtfu' lad! But I hope the unfortunate passengers will na' be much hurt, puir unconscious bodies!

Ang. Fear nought, mither. Lang experience has taught me to do my work deftly. The train will run off the line, and the traffic will just be blocked for half a day, but I'll warrant ye that, wi' a' this, nae mon, woman, or child amang them will get sae much as a bruised head or a broken nose.

Mag. My ain tender-hearted Angus! He wadna hurt sae much as a blatherin' buzzin' bluebottle flee!

Ang. Nae, Meg, not if takin' care and thought could help the poor dumb thing! (*Wiping the eyes*) There, see, lass, (*Looking off*) the train's at a standstill, and there's nae harm done. I'll just go and tell the puir distraught passengers that they may rest them here, in thy cot, gin they will, till the line is cleared again. Mither, get thy rooms ready, and put brose [2] i' the pot, for mebbe they'll be hungry, puir souls. Farewell, Meg; I'll be back ere lang, and if I don't bring 'ee a full half-dozen o' well-paying passengers, thou may'st just wed the red-headed exciseman!

Exit Angus.

---

[1] Acting as a servant.

[2] A dish made of boiled oatmeal and a meat.

Mag. Oh, mither, mither, I'm ower happy! I've nae deserved sic a good fortune as to be the wife o' yon brave and honest lad!

Mrs. Mac. Meg, thine auld mither's hairt is sair at the thought o' losin' ye, for hitherto she's just been a' the world to 'ee; but now thou'lt cleave to thine Angus, and thou'lt learn to love him better than thy puir auld mither! But it mun be — it mun be!

Mag. Nay, mither, say not that. A gude girl loves her husband wi' one love and her mither wi' anither. They are not alike, but neither is greater nor less than the ither, and they dwell together in peace and unity. That is how a gude girl loves.

Mrs. Mac. And thou art a gude girl, Meg?

Mag. I am a varra gude girl indeed, mither — a varra, varra gude girl!

Mrs. Mac. I'm richt sure o' that. Well, the puir belated passengers will be here directly, and it is our duty to provide for them sic puir hospitality as our humble roof will afford. It shall never be said o' Janie Macfarlane that she ever turned the weary traveller fainting from her door.

Mag. My ain gentle-hearted mither!

Exeunt together into cottage.

Enter Angus with Belvawney and Miss Treherne. She is in travelling costume, and both are much agitated and alarmed.

Ang. Step in, sir — step in, and sit ye doun for a wee. I'll just send Mistress Macfarlane to ye. She's a gude auld bodie, and will see to your comforts as if she was your ain mither.

Bel. Thank you, my worthy lad, for your kindness at this trying moment. I assure you we shall not forget it.

Ang. Ah, sir, wadna any mon do as muckle? A dry shelter, a bannock[3] and a pan o' parritch is a' we can offer ye, but sic as it is ye're hairtily welcome.

Bel. It is well — we thank you.

Ang. For wha wadna help the unfortunate?

Bel. (*Occupied with Miss Treherne*) Exactly — every one would.

Ang. Or feed the hungry?

Bel. No doubt.

Ang. It just brings the tear drop to my ee to think —

Bel. (*Leading him off*) My friend, we would be alone, this maiden and I. Farewell!

Exit Angus, into cottage.

Belinda — my own — my life! Compose yourself. It was in truth a weird and gruesome accident. The line is blocked — your parasol is broken, and your butterscotch trampled in the dust, but no serious harm is done. Come, be cheerful. We are safe — quite safe.

Miss T. Safe! Ah, Belvawney, my own own Belvawney — there is, I fear, no safety for us so long as we are liable to be overtaken by that fearful Major to whom I was to have been married this morning.

Bel. Major McGillicuddy? I confess I do not feel comfortable when I think of Major McGillicuddy.

Miss T. You know his barbaric nature, and how madly jealous he is. If he should find that I have eloped with you he will most surely shoot us both!

Bel. It is an uneasy prospect. (*Suddenly*) Belinda, do you love me?

Miss T. With an impetuous passion that I shall carry with me to the tomb!

Bel. Then be mine to-morrow! We are not far from Gretna, and the thing can be done without delay. Once married, the arm of the law will protect us from this fearful man, and we can defy him to do his worst.

Miss T. Belvawney, all this is quite true. I love you madly, passionately; I care to live but in your heart, I breathe but for your love; yet, before I actually consent to take the irrevocable step that will place me on the pinnacle of my fondest hopes, you must give me some definite idea of your pecuniary position. I am not mercenary, Heaven knows; but business is business, and I confess I should like a little definite information about the settlements.

Bel. I often think that it is deeply to be deplored that these grovelling questions of money should alloy the tenderest and most hallowed sentiments that inspire our imperfect natures.

Miss T. It is unfortunate, no doubt, but at the same time it is absolutely necessary.

Bel. Belinda, I will be frank with you. My income is £1000 a year, which I hold on certain conditions. You know my friend Cheviot Hill, who is travelling to London in the same train with us, but in the third class?

Miss T. I believe I know the man you mean.

Bel. Cheviot, who is a young man of large property, but extremely close-fisted, is cursed with a strangely amatory disposition, as you will admit when I tell you that he has contracted a habit of proposing marriage, as a matter of course, to every woman he meets. His haughty father (who comes of a very old family — the Cheviot Hills had settled in this part of the world centuries before the Con-

[3] Bread of oatmeal or barley meal baked on a griddle.

quest) is compelled by his health to reside in Madeira. Knowing that I exercise an all but supernatural influence over his son, and fearing that his affectionate disposition would lead him to contract an undesirable marriage, the old gentleman allows me £1000 a year so long as Cheviot shall live single, but at his death or marriage the money goes over to Cheviot's uncle Symperson, who is now travelling to town with him.

Miss T. Then so long as your influence over him lasts, so long only will you retain your income?

Bel. That is, I am sorry to say, the state of the case.

Miss T. (*After a pause*) Belvawney, I love you with an imperishable ardour which mocks the power of words. If I were to begin to tell you now of the force of my indomitable passion for you, the tomb would close over me before I could exhaust the entrancing subject. But, as I said before, business is business, and unless I can see some distinct probability that your income will be permanent, I shall have no alternative but to weep my heart out in all the anguish of maiden solitude — uncared for, unloved, and alone!

Exit Miss Treherne into cottage.

Bel. There goes a noble-hearted girl, indeed! Oh, for the gift of Cheviot's airy badinage — oh, for his skill in weaving a net about the hearts of women! If I could but induce her to marry me at once before the dreadful Major learns our flight! Why not? We are in Scotland. Methinks I've heard two loving hearts can wed, in this strange country, by merely making declaration to that effect. I will think out some cunning scheme to lure her into marriage unawares.

Enter Maggie, from cottage.

Mag. Will ye walk in and rest a wee, Maister Belvawney? There's a room ready for ye, kind sir, and ye're heartily welcome to it.

Bel. It is well. Stop! Come hither, maiden.

Mag. Oh, sir! you do not mean any harm towards a puir, innocent, unprotected cottage lassie?

Bel. Harm! No! of course, I don't. What do you mean?

Mag. I'm but a puir, humble mountain girl; but let me tell you, sir, that my character's just as dear to me as the richest and proudest lady's in the land. Before I consent to approach ye, swear to me that you mean me no harm.

Bel. Harm? Of course, I don't. Don't be a little fool. Come here.

Mag. There is something in his manner

that reassures me. It is not that of the airy trifler with innocent hairts. (*Aloud*) What wad ye wi' puir, harmless Maggie Macfarlane, gude sir?

Bel. Can you tell me what constitutes a Scotch marriage?

Mag. Oh, sir, it's nae use asking me that; for my hairt is not my ain to give. I'm betrothed to the best and noblest lad in a' the bonnie Borderland. Oh, sir, I canna be your bride!

Bel. My girl, you mistake. I do not want you for my bride. Can't you answer a simple question? What constitutes a Scotch marriage?

Mag. Ye've just to say before twa witnesses, "Maggie Macfarlane is my wife"; and I've just to say, "Maister Belvawney is my husband," and nae mon can set us asunder. But, sir, I canna be your bride; for I am betrothed to the best and noblest —

Bel. I congratulate you. You can go.

Mag. Yes, sir.

Exit Maggie into cottage.

Bel. It is a simple process; simple, but yet how beautiful! One thing is certain — Cheviot may marry any day, despite my precautions, and then I shall be penniless. He may die, and equally I shall be penniless. Belinda has £500 a year; it is not much, but it would, at least, save me from starvation.

Exit Belvawney.

Enter Symperson and Cheviot Hill over bridge. They both show signs of damage — their hats are beaten in and their clothes disordered through the accident.

Symp. Well, here we are at last —

Ch. Yes; here we are at last, and a pretty state I'm in, to be sure.

Symp. My dear nephew, you would travel third class, and this is the consequence. After all, there's not much harm done.

Ch. Not much harm? What d'ye call that? (*Showing his hat*) Ten and ninepence at one operation! My gloves split — one and four! My coat ruined — eighteen and six! It's a coarse and brutal nature that recognizes no harm that don't involve loss of blood. I'm reduced by this accident from a thinking, feeling, reflecting human being, to a moral pulp — a mash — a poultice. Damme, sir, that's what I am! I'm a poultice!

Symp. Cheviot, my dear boy, at the moment of the accident you were speaking to me on a very interesting subject.

Ch. Was I? I forget what it was. The accident has knocked it clean out of my head.

Symp. You were saying that you were a man of good position and fortune; that you derived £2000 a year from your bank; that you thought it was time you settled. You then reminded me that I should come into Belvawney's £1000 a year on your marriage, and I'm not sure, but I rather think you mentioned, casually, that my daughter Minnie is an Angel of Light.

Ch. True, and just then we went off the line. To resume — Uncle Symperson, your daughter Minnie is an Angel of Light, a perfect being, as innocent as a new-laid egg.

Symp. Minnie is, indeed, all that you have described her.

Ch. Uncle, I'm a man of few words. I feel and I speak. I love that girl, madly, passionately, irresistibly. She is my whole life, my whole soul and body, my Past, my Present, and my To Come. I have thought for none but her; she fills my mind, sleeping and waking; she is the essence of every hope — the tree upon which the fruit of my heart is growing — my own To Come!

Symp. (*Who has sunk overpowered on to stool during this speech*) Cheviot, my dear boy, excuse a father's tears. I won't beat about the bush. You have anticipated my devoutest wish. Cheviot, my dear boy, take her, she is yours!

Ch. I have often heard of rapture, but I never knew what it was till now. Uncle Symperson, bearing in mind the fact that your income will date from the day of the wedding, when may this be?

Symp. My boy, the sooner the better! Delicacy would prompt me to give Belvawney a reasonable notice of the impending loss of his income, but should I, for such a mere selfish reason as that, rob my child of one hour of the happiness that you are about to confer upon her? No! Duty to my child is paramount!

Ch. On one condition, however, I must insist. This must be kept from Belvawney's knowledge. You know the strange, mysterious influence that his dreadful eyes exercise over me.

Symp. I have remarked it with astonishment.

Ch. They are much inflamed just now, and he has to wear green spectacles. While this lasts I am a free agent, but under treatment they may recover. In that case, if he knew that I contemplated matrimony, he would use them to prevent my doing so — and I cannot resist them — I cannot resist them! Therefore, I say, until I am safely and securely tied up, Belvawney must know nothing about it.

Symp. Trust me, Cheviot, he shall know nothing about it from *me.* (*Aside*) A thousand a year! I have endeavoured, but in vain, to woo Fortune for fifty-six years, but she smiles upon me at last! — she smiles upon me at last!

　　　　　　　Exit Symperson into cottage.

Ch. At length my hopes are to be crowned! Oh, my own — my own — the hope of my heart — my love — my life!

　　Enter Belvawney, who has overheard
　　　　　　　these words.

Bel. Cheviot! Whom are you apostrophizing in those terms? You've been at it again, I see!

Ch. Belvawney, that apostrophe was private; I decline to admit you to my confidence.

Bel. Cheviot, what is the reason of this strange tone of defiance? A week ago I had but to express a wish, to have it obeyed as a matter of course.

Ch. Belvawney, it may not be denied that there was a time when, owing to the remarkable influence exercised over me by your extraordinary eyes, you could do with me as you would. It would be affectation to deny it; your eyes withered my will; they paralyzed my volition. They were strange and lurid eyes, and I bowed to them. Those eyes were my Fate — my Destiny — my unerring Must — my inevitable Shall. That time has gone — for ever!

Bel. Alas for the days that are past and the good that came and went with them!

Ch. Weep for them if you will. I cannot weep with you, for I loved them not. But, as you say, they are past. The light that lit up those eyes is extinct — their fire has died out — their soul has fled. They are no longer eyes, they are poached eggs. I have not yet sunk so low as to be the slave of two poached eggs.

Bel. Have mercy. If any girl has succeeded in enslaving you — and I know how easily you are enslaved — dismiss her from your thoughts; have no more to say to her; and I will — yes, I will bless you with my latest breath!

Ch. Whether a blessing conferred with one's latest breath is a superior article to one conferred in robust health we need not stop to inquire. I decline, as I said before, to admit you to my confidence on any terms whatever. Begone!

　　　　　　　　Exit Belvawney.

Dismiss from my thoughts the only woman I ever loved! Have no more to say to the tree upon which the fruit of my heart is growing!

No, Belvawney, I cannot cut off my tree as if it were gas or water. I do not treat women like that. Some men do, but I don't. I am not that sort of man. I respect women; I love women. They are good; they are pure; they are beautiful; at least, many of them are.

Enter Maggie from cottage; he is much fascinated.

This one, for example, is very beautiful indeed!

Mag. If ye'll just walk in, sir, ye'll find a bannock and a pan o' parritch waitin' for ye on the table.

Ch. This is one of the loveliest women I ever met in the whole course of my life!

Mag. (*Aside*) What's he glowerin' at? (*Aloud*) Oh, sir, ye mean no harm to the poor Lowland lassie?

Ch. Pardon me; it's very foolish. I can't account for it — but I am arrested, fascinated.

Mag. Oh, gude sir, what's fascinated ye?

Ch. I don't know; there is something about you that exercises a most remarkable influence over me; it seems to weave a kind of enchantment around me. I can't think what it is. You are a good girl, I am sure. None but a good girl could so powerfully affect me. You *are* a good girl, are you not?

Mag. I am a varra gude girl indeed, sir.

Ch. I was quite sure of it. (*Gets his arm round her waist*)

Mag. I am a much better girl than nineteen out of twenty in these pairts. And they are all gude girls too.

Ch. My darling! (*Kisses her*)

Mag. Oh, kind sir, what's that for?

Ch. It is your reward for being a good girl.

Mag. Oh, sir, I did na look for sic a recompense; you are varra varra kind to puir little Maggie Macfarlane.

Ch. I cannot think what it is about you that fascinates me so remarkably.

Mag. Maybe it's my beauty.

Ch. Maybe it is. It is quite possible that it may be, as you say, your beauty.

Mag. I am remarkably pretty, and I've a varra neat figure.

Ch. There is a natural modesty in this guileless appreciation of your own perfection that is, to me, infinitely more charming than the affected ignorance of an artificial town-bred beauty.

Mag. Oh, sir, can I close my een to the picture that my looking-glass holds up to me twenty times a day? We see the rose on the tree, and we say that it is fair; we see the silver moon sailing in the braw blue heavens,

and we say that she is bright; we see the brawling stream purling over the smooth stanes i' the burn, and we say that it is beautiful; and shall we close our een to the fairest of nature's works — a pure and beautiful woman? Why, sir, it wad just be base ingratitude! No, it's best to tell the truth about a' things: I am a varra, varra, beautiful girl!

Ch. Maggie Macfarlane, I'm a plain, blunt, straightforward man, and I come quickly to the point. I see more to love in you than I ever saw in any woman in all my life before. I have a large income which I do not spend recklessly. I love you passionately; you are the essence of every hope; you are the tree upon which the fruit of my heart is growing — my Past, my Present, my Future — you are my own To Come. Tell me, will you be mine — will you join your life with mine?

Enter Angus, who listens.

Mag. Ah, kind sir, I'm sairly grieved to wound sae true and tender a love as yours, but ye're ower late, my love is nae my ain to give ye, it's given ower to the best and bravest lad in a' the bonnie Borderland!

Ch. Give me his address that I may go and curse him!

Mag. (*Kneels to Hill*) Ah, ye must not curse him. Oh, spare him, spare him, for he is good and brave, and he loves me, oh, sae dearly, and I love him, oh, sae dearly too. Oh, sir, kind sir, have mercy on him, and do not — do not curse him, or I shall die! (*Throwing herself at his feet*)

Ch. Will you, or will you not, oblige me by telling me where he is, that I may at once go and curse him?

Ang. (*Coming forward*) He is here, sir, but dinna waste your curses on me. Maggie, my bairn, (*Raising her*) I heard the answer ye gave to this man, my true and gentle lassie! Ye spake well and bravely, Meg — well and bravely! Dinna heed the water in my ee — it's a tear of joy and gratitude, Meg — a tear of joy and gratitude!

Ch. (*Touched*) Poor fellow! I will *not* curse him. (*Aloud*) Young man, I respect your honest emotion. I don't want to distress you, but I cannot help loving this most charming girl. Come, is it reasonable to quarrel with a man because he's of the same way of thinking as yourself?

Ang. Nay, sir, I'm nae fasht, but it just seems to drive a' the bluid back into my hairt when I think that my Meg is loved by anither! Oh, sir, she's a fair and winsome lassie, and I micht as justly be angry wi' ye for loving the blue heavens! She's just as far above us as they are! (*Wiping his eyes and kissing her*)

Ch. (*With decision*) Pardon me, I cannot allow that.

Ang. Eh?

Ch. I love that girl madly — passionately — and I cannot possibly allow you to do that — not before my eyes, I beg. You simply torture me.

Mag. (*To Angus*) Leave off, dear, till the puir gentleman's gone, and then ye can begin again.

Ch. Angus, listen to me. You love this girl?

Ang. I love her, sir, a'most as weel as I love mysel'!

Ch. Then reflect how you are standing in the way of her prosperity. I am a rich man. I have money, position, and education. I am a much more intellectual and generally agreeable companion for her than you can ever hope to be. I am full of anecdote, and all my anecdotes are in the best possible taste. I will tell you some of them some of these days, and you can judge for yourself. Maggie, if she married me, would live in a nice house in a good square. She would have wine — occasionally. She would be kept beautifully clean. Now, if you really love this girl almost as well as you love yourself, are you doing wisely or kindly in standing in the way of her getting all these good things? As to compensation — why, I've had heavy expenses of late — but if — yes, if thirty shillings —

Ang. (*Hotly*) Sir, I'm puir in pocket, but I've a rich hairt. It is rich in a pure and overflowing love, and he that hath love hath all. You canna ken what true love is, or you wadna dare to insult a puir but honest lad by offering to buy his treasure for money. (*Cheviot retires up*)

Mag. My ain true darling! (*They embrace*)

Ch. Now, I'll not have it! Understand me, I'll not have it. It's simple agony to me. Angus, I respect your indignation, but you are too hasty. I do not offer to buy your treasure for money. You love her; it will naturally cause you pain to part with her, and I prescribe thirty shillings, not as a cure, but as a temporary solace. If thirty shillings is not enough, why, I don't mind making it two pounds.

Ang. Nae, sir, it's useless, and we ken it weel, do we not, my brave lassie? Our hearts are one as our bodies will be some day; and the man is na born, and the gold is na coined, that can set us twain asunder!

Mag. Angus, dear, I'm varra proud o' sae staunch and true a love; it's like your ain

true self, an' I can say nae more for it than that. But dinna act wi'out prudence and forethought, dear. In these hard times twa pound is twa pound, and I'm nae sure that you're acting richtly in refusing sae large a sum. I love you varra dearly — ye ken that right weel — an' if ye'll be troubled wi' sic a poor little mousie I'll make ye a true an' loving wife, but I doubt whether, wi' a' my love, I'll ever be worth as much to ye as twa pound. Dinna act in haste, dear; tak' time to think before ye refuse this kind gentleman's offer.

Ang. Oh, sir, is not this rare modesty? Could ye match it amang your toun-bred fine ladies? I think not! Meg, it shall be as you say. I'll tak' the siller, but it'll be wi' a sair and broken hairt! (*Cheviot gives Angus money*) Fare thee weel, my love — my childhood's — boyhood's — manhood's love! Ye're ganging fra my hairt to anither, who'll gie thee mair o' the gude things o' this world than I could ever gie 'ee, except love, an' o' that my hairt is full indeed! But it's a' for the best; ye'll be happier wi' him — and twa pound is twa pound. Meg, mak' him a gude wife, be true to him, and love him as ye loved me. Oh, Meg, my poor bruised hairt is well nigh like to break!

Exit into cottage, in great agony.

Mag. (*Looking wistfully after him*) Puir laddie, puir laddie! Oh, I did na ken till noo how weel he loved me!

Ch. Maggie, I'm almost sorry I — poor lad, poor fellow! He has a generous heart. I am glad I did not curse him. (*Aside*) This is weakness! (*Aloud*) Maggie my own — ever and for always my own, we will be very happy, will we not?

Mag. Oh, sir, I dinna ken, but in truth I hope so. Oh, sir, my happiness is in your hands noo; be kind to the puir cottage lassie who loves ye sae weel; my hairt is a' your ain, and if ye forsake me my lot will be a sair one indeed! *Exit, weeping, into cottage.*

Ch. Poor little Lowland lassie! That's my idea of a wife. No ridiculous extravagance; no expensive tastes. Knows how to dress like a lady on £5 a year; ah, and does it too! No pretense there of being blind to her own beauties; she knows that she is beautiful, and scorns to lie about it. In that respect she resembles Symperson's dear daughter, Minnie. My darling Minnie. (*Looks at miniature*) My own darling Minnie. Minnie is fair, Maggie is dark. Maggie loves me! That excellent and perfect country creature loves me! She is to be the light of my life, my own to come! In some respects she is even prettier than Minnie — my darling Minnie, Symperson's dear daughter, the tree upon which the fruit of my heart is growing; my Past, my Present, and my Future, my own To Come! But this tendency to reverie is growing on me; I must shake it off.

Enter Miss Treherne.

Heaven and earth, what a singularly lovely girl!

Miss T. A stranger! Pardon me, I will withdraw! —

Ch. A stranger indeed, in one sense, inasmuch as he never had the happiness of meeting you before — but, in that he has a heart that can sympathize with another's misfortune, he trusts he may claim to be regarded almost as a friend.

Miss T. May I ask, sir, to what misfortunes you allude?

Ch. I — a — do not know their precise nature, but that perception would indeed be dull, and that heart would be indeed flinty, that did not at once perceive that you are very very unhappy. Accept, madam, my deepest and most respectful sympathy.

Miss T. You have guessed rightly, sir! I am indeed a most unhappy woman.

Ch. I am delighted to hear it — a — I mean I feel a pleasure, a melancholy and chastened pleasure, in reflecting that, if your distress is not of a pecuniary nature, it may perchance lie in my power to alleviate your sorrow.

Miss T. Impossible, sir, though I thank you for your respectful sympathy.

Ch. How many women would forego twenty years of their lives to be as beautiful as yourself, little dreaming that extraordinary loveliness can co-exist with the most poignant anguish of mind! But so, too often, we find it, do we not, dear lady?

Miss. T. Sir! this tone of address, from a complete stranger!

Ch. Nay, be not unreasonably severe upon an impassionable and impulsive man, whose tongue is but the too faithful herald of his heart. We see the rose on the tree, and we say that it is fair, we see the bonnie brooks purling over the smooth stanes — I should say stones — in the burn, and we say that it is beautiful, and shall we close our eyes to the fairest of nature's works, a pure and beautiful woman? Why, it would be base ingratitude, indeed!

Miss T. I cannot deny that there is much truth in the sentiments you so beautifully express, but I am, unhappily, too well aware that, whatever advantages I may possess, personal beauty is not among their number.

Ch. How exquisitely modest is this chaste insensibility to your own singular loveliness! How infinitely more winning than the bold-faced self-appreciation of under-bred country girls!

Miss T. I am glad, sir, that you are pleased with my modesty. It has often been admired.

Ch. Pleased! I am more than pleased — that's a very weak word. I am enchanted. Madam, I am a man of quick impulse and energetic action. I feel and I speak — I cannot help it. Madam, be not surprised when I tell you that I cannot resist the conviction that you are the light of my future life, the essence of every hope, the tree upon which the fruit of my heart is growing — my Past, my Present, my Future, my own To Come! Do not extinguish that light, do not disperse that essence, do not blight that tree! I am well off; I'm a bachelor; I'm thirty-two; and I love you, madam, humbly, truly, trustfully, patiently. Paralyzed with admiration, I wait anxiously, and yet hopefully, for your reply.

Miss T. Sir, that heart would indeed be cold that did not feel grateful for so much earnest, single-hearted devotion. I am deeply grieved to have to say one word to cause pain to one who expresses himself in such well-chosen terms of respectful esteem; but, alas! I have already yielded up my heart to one who, if I mistake not, is a dear personal friend of your own.

Ch. Am I to understand that you are the young lady of property whom Belvawney hopes to marry?

Miss T. I am, indeed, that unhappy woman!

Ch. And is it possible that you love him?

Miss T. With a rapture that thrills every fibre of my heart — with a devotion that enthralls my very soul! But there's some difficulty about his settlements.

Ch. A difficulty! I should think there was. Why, on my marrying, his entire income goes over to Symperson! I could reduce him to penury to-morrow. As it happens, I *am* engaged, I recollect, to Symperson's daughter; and if Belvawney dares to interpose between you and me, by George, I'll do it!

Miss T. Oh, spare him, sir! You say that you love me? Then, for my sake, remain single for ever — it is all I ask, it is not much. Promise me that you will never, never marry, and we will both bless you with our latest breath!

Ch. There seems to be a special importance attached to a blessing conferred with one's latest breath that I entirely fail to grasp. It seems to me to convey no definite advantage of any kind whatever.

Miss T. Cruel, cruel man!

Enter Belvawney, in great alarm.

Bel. We are lost! — we are lost!

Miss T. What do you mean?

Ch. Who has lost you?

Bel. Major McGillicuddy discovered your flight, and followed in the next train. The line is blocked through our accident, and his train has pulled up within a few yards of our own. He is now making his way to this very cottage! What do you say to that?

Miss T. I agree with you, we are lost!

Ch. I disagree with you; I should say you are found.

Bel. This man is a reckless fire-eater; he is jealous of me. He will assuredly shoot us both if he sees us here together. I am no coward — but — I confess I am uneasy.

Miss T. (*To Cheviot*) Oh, sir, you have a ready wit; help us out of this difficulty, and we will both bless you —

Bel. With our latest breath!

Ch. That decides me. Madam, remain here with me. Belvawney, withdraw. (*Belvawney retires*) I will deal with this maniac alone. All I ask is, that if I find it necessary to make a statement that is not consistent with strict truth, you, madam, will unhesitatingly endorse it?

Miss T. I will stake my very existence on its veracity, whatever it may be.

Ch. Good. He is at hand. Belvawney, go.

Exit Belvawney.

Now, madam, repose upon my shoulders, place your arms around me so — is that comfortable?

Miss T. It is luxurious.

Ch. Good.

Miss T. You are sure it does not inconvenience you?

Ch. Not at all. Go back, I like it. Now we are ready for him.

Enter McGillicuddy with two friends dressed as for a wedding, with white favours. McGillicuddy has pistols. All greatly excited.

McG. Where is the villain? I'll swear he is concealed somewhere. Search every tree, every bush, every geranium. Ha! they are here. Perjured woman! I've found you at last.

Miss T. (*To Cheviot*) Save me!

Belvawney appears at back, listening.

McG. Who is the unsightly scoundrel with whom you have flown — the unpleasant-looking scamp whom you have dared to prefer to me? Uncurl yourself from around the plain villain at once, unless you would share his fate.

Maggie and Angus appear from cottage.

Miss T. Major, spare him!

Ch. Now, sir, perhaps you will be so good as to explain who the deuce you are, and what you want with this lady?

McG. I don't know who you may be, but I'm McGillicuddy. I am betrothed to this lady; we were to have been married this morning. I waited for her at the church from ten till four, then I began to get impatient.

Ch. I really think you must be labouring under some delusion.

McG. Delusion? Ha! ha! (*Two friends produce large wedding cake*) Here's the cake!

Ch. Still I think there's a mistake somewhere. This lady is my wife.

McG. What! Belinda! oh, Belinda! Tell me that this unattractive man lies; tell me that you are mine and only mine, now and for ever!

Miss T. I cannot say that. This gentleman is my husband!

McGillicuddy falls sobbing on seat; Belvawney tears his hair in despair; Maggie sobs on Angus's shoulder.

End of the First Act.

ACT II.

Double Drawing-room in Symperson's House. Indications that a wedding is about to take place. A plate of tarts and a bottle of wine on table. Enter Minnie Symperson, in wedding dress, followed by Parker, her maid, holding her train.

Min. Take care, Parker — that's right. There! How do I look?

Par. Beautiful, miss; quite beautiful.

Min. (*Earnestly*) Oh, Parker, am I really beautiful? Really, *really* beautiful, you know?

Par. Oh, miss, there's no question about it. Oh, I do so hope you and Mr. Cheviot Hill will be happy.

Min. Oh, I'm sure we shall, Parker. He has often told me that I am the tree upon which the fruit of his heart is growing; and one couldn't wish to be more than *that*. And he tells me that his greatest happiness is to see me happy. So it will be my duty — my *duty*, Parker — to devote my life, my whole life, to making myself as happy as I possibly can.

Enter Symperson, dressed for wedding.

Symp. So, my little lamb is ready for the sacrifice. You can go, Parker. And I am to lose my pet at last; my little dickey-bird is to be married to-day! Well, well, it's for her good. I must try and bear it — I must try and bear it.

Min. And as my dear old papa comes into £1000 a year by it, I hope he won't allow it to distress him too much. He must try and bear up. He mustn't fret.

Symp. My child, I will not deny that £1000 a year is a consolation. It's quite a fortune. I hardly know what I shall do with it.

Min. I think, dear papa, you will spend a good deal of it on brandy, and a good deal more on billiards, and a good deal more on betting.

Symp. It may be so: I don't say it won't. We shall see, Minnie, we shall see. These simple pleasures would certainly tend to soothe your poor old father's declining years. And my darling has not done badly either, has she?

Min. No, dear papa; only fancy! Cheviot has £2000 a year from shares in the Royal Indestructible Bank.

Symp. And don't spend £200. By-the-bye, I'm sorry that my little bird has not contrived to induce him to settle anything on her; that, I think, was remiss in my tom-tit.

Min. Dear papa, Cheviot is the very soul of honour; he's a fine, noble, manly, spirited fellow, but if he *has* a fault, it is that he is very, oh very, *very* stingy. He would rather lose his heart's blood than part with a shilling unnecessarily. He's a noble fellow, but he's like that.

Symp. Still I can't help feeling that if my robin had worked him judiciously —

Min. Papa, dear, Cheviot is an all but perfect character, the very type of knightly chivalry; but he *has* faults, and among other things he's one of the worst tempered men I ever met in all my little life. Poor, simple, little Minnie thought the matter over very carefully in her silly childish way, and she came to the conclusion, in her foolish little noddle, that, on the whole, perhaps she could work it better after marriage, than before.

Symp. Well, well, perhaps my wren is right. (*Rises*)

Min. Don't laugh at my silly little thoughts, dear papa, when I say I'm sure she is.

Symp. Minnie, my dear daughter, take a father's advice, the last he will ever be entitled to give you. If you would be truly happy in the married state, be sure you have your own way in everything. Brook no con-

tradictions. Never yield to outside pressure. Give in to no argument. Admit no appeal. However wrong you may be, maintain a firm, resolute, and determined front. These were your angel mother's principles through life, and she was a happy woman indeed. I neglected those principles, and while she lived I was a miserable wretch.

Min. Papa dear, I have thought over the matter very carefully in my little baby-noddle, and I have come to the conclusion — don't laugh at me, dear papa — that it is my duty — my *duty* — to fall in with Cheviot's views in everything *before* marriage, and Cheviot's duty to fall into my views in everything *after* marriage. I think that is only fair, don't you?

Symp. Yes, I dare say it will come to that.

Min. Don't think me a very silly little goose when I say I'm sure it will. Quite, quite sure, dear papa. Quite.   *Exit Minnie.*

Symp. Dear child — dear child! I sometimes fancy I can see traces of her angel mother's disposition in her. Yes, I think — I *think* she will be happy. But, poor Cheviot! Oh, lor, poor Cheviot! Dear me, it won't bear thinking of!

Enter Miss Treherne, unobserved. She is dressed in stately and funereal black.

Miss T. Come here, man-servant. Approach. I'm not going to bite you. Can I see the fair young thing they call Minnie Symperson?

Symp. Well really, I can hardly say. There's nothing wrong, I hope?

Miss T. Nothing wrong? Oh, thoughtless, frivolous, light-hearted creature! Oh, reckless old butterfly! Nothing wrong! You've eyes in your head, a nose on your face, ears on each side of it, a brain of some sort in your skull, haven't you, butler?

Symp. Undoubtedly, but I beg to observe I'm not the —

Miss T. Have you or have you not the gift of simple apprehension? Can you or can you not draw conclusions? Go to, go to, you offend me.

Symp. (*Aside*) There *is* something wrong, and it's *here*. (*Touching his forehead*) I'll tell her you're here. Whom shall I say?

Miss T. Say that one on whose devoted head the black sorrows of a long lifetime have fallen, even as a funeral pall, craves a minute's interview with a dear old friend. Do you think you can recollect that message, butler?

Symp. I'll try, but I beg, I *beg* to observe, I'm not the butler. (*Aside*) This is a most surprising young person!   *Exit.*

Miss T. At last I'm in my darling's home, the home of the bright blythe carolling thing that lit, as with a ray of heaven's sunlight, the murky gloom of my miserable school-days. But what do I see? Tarts? Ginger wine? There are rejoicings of some kind afoot. Alas, I am out of place here. What have I in common with tarts? Oh, I am ill-attuned to scenes of revelry! (*Takes a tart and eats it*)

Enter Minnie.

Min. Belinda! (*They rush to each other's arms*)

Miss T. Minnie! My own long-lost lamb! This is the first gleam of joy that has lighted my darksome course this many and many a day! And in spite of the change that time and misery have brought upon me, you knew me at once! (*Eating the tart all this time*)

Min. Oh, I felt sure it was you, from the message.

Miss T. How wondrously fair you have grown! And this dress! Why, it is surely a bridal dress! Those tarts — that wine! Surely this is not your wedding-day?

Min. Yes, dear, I shall be married in half an hour.

Miss T. Oh, strange chance! Oh, unheard-of coincidence! Married! And to whom?

Min. Oh, to the dearest love — My cousin, Mr. Cheviot Hill. Perhaps you know the name.

Miss T. I have heard of the Cheviot Hills, somewhere. Happy — strangely happy girl! You, at least, know your husband's name.

Min. Oh yes, it's on all his pocket-handkerchiefs.

Miss T. It is much to know. I do not know mine.

Min. Have you forgotten it?

Miss T. No; I never knew it. It is a dark mystery. It may not be unfathomed. It is buried in the fathomless gulf of the Eternal Past. There let it lie.

Min. Oh, tell me all about it, dear.

Miss T. It is a lurid tale. Three months since I fled from a hated one, who was to have married me. He pursued me. I confided my distress to a young and wealthy stranger. Acting on his advice, I declared myself to be his wife; he declared himself to be my husband. We were parted immediately afterwards, and we have never met since. But this took place in Scotland; and by the law of that remarkable country we are man and wife, though I didn't know it at the time.

Min. What fun!

Miss T. Fun! Say, rather, horror — distraction — chaos! I am rent with conflicting doubts! Perhaps he was already married; in that case, I am a bigamist. Maybe he is dead; in that case, I am a widow. Maybe he is alive; in that case, I am a wife. What am I? Am I single? Am I married? Am I a widow? Can I marry? Have I married? May I marry? Who am I? Where am I? What am I? — What is my name? What is my condition in life? If I am married, to whom am I married? If I am a widow, how came I to be a widow, and whose widow came I to be? Why am I his widow? What did he die of? Did he leave me anything? if anything, how much, and is it saddled with conditions? — Can I marry again without forfeiting it? Have I a mother-in-law? Have I a family of step-children, and if so, how many, and what are their ages, sexes, sizes, names and dispositions? These are questions that rack me night and day, and until they are settled, peace and I are not on terms!

Min. Poor dear thing!

Miss T. But enough of my selfish sorrows. (*Goes up to table and takes a tart. Minnie is annoyed at this*) Tell me about the noble boy who is about to make you his. Has he any dross?[4]

Min. I don't know. (*Secretly removes tarts to another table close to door*) I never thought of asking — I'm such a goose. But papa knows.

Miss T. Have those base and servile things called settlements been satisfactorily adjusted? (*Eating*)

Min. I don't know. It never occurred to me to inquire. But papa can tell you.

Miss T. The same artless little soul!

Min. (*Standing so as to conceal tarts from Belinda*) Yes, I am quite artless — quite, quite artless. But now that you *are* here you will stay and see me married.

Miss T. I would willingly be a witness to my darling's joy, but this attire is, perhaps, scarcely in harmony with a scene of revelry.

Min. Well, dear, you're not a cheerful object, and that's the truth.

Miss T. And yet these charnel-house rags may serve to remind the thoughtless banquetters that they are but mortal.

Min. I don't think it will be necessary to do that, dear. Papa's sherry will make *that* quite clear to them.

Miss T. Then I will hie me home, and array me in garments of less sombre hue.

Min. I think it would be better, dear. Those are the very things for a funeral, but this is a wedding.

[4] Scum on metal, here apparently a pun meaning both "money" and "faults."

Miss T. I see very little difference between them. But it shall be as you wish, though I have worn nothing but black since my miserable marriage. There is breakfast, I suppose?

Min. Yes, at dear Cheviot's house.

Miss T. That is well. I shall return in time for it. Thank heaven I can still eat.

> *Takes a tart from table, and exit, followed by Minnie.*

> *Enter Cheviot Hill. He is dressed as for a wedding.*

Ch. Here I am at last — quite flurried and hot after the usual row with the cabman, just when I wanted to be particularly calm and self-contained. I got the best of it though. Dear me, this is a great day for me — a great day. Where's Minnie, I wonder? Arraying herself for the sacrifice, no doubt. Pouf! This is a very nervous occasion. I wonder if I'm taking a prudent step. Marriage is a very risky thing; it's like Chancery, once in it you can't get out of it, and the costs are enormous. There you are — fixed. Fifty years, hence, if we're both alive, there we shall both be — fixed. That's the devil of it. It's an unreasonably long time to be responsible for another person's expenses. I don't see the use of making it for as long as that. It seems greedy to take up half a century of another person's attention. Besides — one never knows — one might come across somebody else one liked better — that uncommonly nice girl I met in Scotland, for instance. No, no, I shall be true to my Minnie — quite true. I am quite determined that nothing shall shake my constancy to Minnie.

> *Enter Parker.*

What a devilish pretty girl!

Par. (*Aside*) He's a mean young man, but he ought to be good for half-a-crown to-day.

Ch. Come here, my dear; a — How do I look?

Par. Very nice indeed, sir.

Ch. What, really?

Par. Really.

Ch. What, tempting, eh?

Par. Very tempting indeed.

Ch. Hah! The married state is an enviable state, Parker.

Par. Is it, sir? I hope it may be. It depends.

Ch. What do you mean by "it depends"? You're a member of the Church of England, I trust? Then don't you know that in saying "it depends" you are flying in the face of the marriage service? Don't go and throw cold water on the married state, Parker. I know what you're going to say — it's expensive.

So it is, at first, very expensive, but with economy you soon retrench that. By a beautiful provision of Nature, what's enough for one is enough for two. This phenomenon points directly to the married state as our natural state.

Par. Oh, for that matter, sir, a tigress would get on with you. You're so liberal, so gentle, so — there's only one word for it — dove-like.

Ch. What, you've remarked that, eh? Ha! ha! But dove-like as I am, Parker, in some respects, yet (*Getting his arm round her*) in other respects —, (*Aside*) deuced pretty girl! — in other respects I am a man, Parker, of a strangely impetuous and headstrong nature. I don't beat about the bush; I come quickly to the point. Shall I tell you a secret? There's something about you, I don't know what it is, that — in other words, you are the tree upon which — no, no, damn it, Cheviot — not to-day, not to-day.

Par. What a way you have with you, sir!

Ch. What, you've noticed that, have you? Ha! ha! yes, I have a way, no doubt; it's been remarked before. Whenever I see a pretty girl (and you are a very pretty girl) I can't help putting my arm like that. (*Putting it round her waist*) Now, pleasant as this sort of thing is, and you find it pleasant, don't you? (*Parker nods*) Yes, you find it pleasant — pleasant as it is, it is decidedly wrong.

Par. It is decidedly wrong in a married man.

Ch. It is decidedly wrong in a married man. In a married man it's abominable, and I shall be a married man in half an hour. So, Parker, it will become necessary to conquer this tendency, to struggle with it, and subdue it — in half an hour. (*Getting more affectionate*) Not that there's any real harm in putting your arm round a girl's waist. Highly respectable people do it, when they waltz.

Par. Yes, sir, but then a band's playing.

Ch. True, and when a band's playing it don't matter, but when a band is *not* playing, why it's dangerous, you see. You begin with this, and you go from one thing to another, getting more and more affectionate, until you reach *this* stage. (*Kissing her*) Not that there's any real harm in kissing, either; for you see fathers and mothers, who ought to set a good example, kissing their children every day.

Par. Lor, sir, kissing's nothing; everybody does that.

Ch. That is your experience, is it? It tallies with my own. Take it that I am your father, you are my daughter — or take it even that I am merely your husband, and you my wife, and it would be expected of me. (*Kissing her*)

Par. But I'm not your wife, sir.

Ch. No, not yet, that's very true, and, of course, makes a difference. That's why I say I must subdue this tendency; I must struggle with it; I must conquer it — in half an hour.

Min. (*Without*) Parker, where's Mr. Cheviot?

Ch. There is your mistress, my dear — she's coming. Will you excuse me? (*Releasing her*) Thank you. Good day, Parker.

Par. (*Disgusted*) Not so much as a shilling; and that man's worth thousands!

Exit Parker.

Enter Minnie.

Ch. My darling Minnie — my own, own To Come! (*Kissing her*)

Min. Oh, you mustn't crush me, Cheviot, you'll spoil my dress. How do you like it?

Ch. It's lovely. It's a beautiful material.

Min. Yes; dear papa's been going it.

Ch. Oh, but you're indebted to me for that beautiful dress.

Min. To you! Oh, thank you — thank you!

Ch. Yes. I said to your papa, "Now do for once let the girl have a nice dress; be liberal; buy the very best that money will procure, you'll never miss it." So, thanks to me, he bought you a beauty. Seventeen and six a yard if it's a penny. Dear me! To think that in half an hour this magnificent dress will be *my* property!

Min. Yes. Dear papa said that as you had offered to give the breakfast at your house, he would give me the best dress that money could procure.

Ch. Yes, I *did* offer to provide the breakfast in a reckless moment; that's so like me. It was a rash offer, but I've made it, and I've stuck to it. Oh, then, there's the cake.

Min. Oh, tell me all about the cake.

Ch. It's a very pretty cake. Very little cake is eaten at a wedding breakfast, so I've ordered what's known in the trade as the three-quarter article.

Min. I see; three-quarters cake, and the rest wood.

Ch. No; three-quarters wood, the rest cake. Be sure, my dear, you don't cut into the wood, for it has to be returned to the pastrycook to be filled up with cake for another occasion. *I* thought at first of ordering a seven-eighths article; but one isn't married every day — it's only once a year — I mean it's only now and then. So I said, "Hang the

expense; let's do the thing well." And so it's a three-quarters.

Min. How good you are to me! We shall be very happy, shall we not?

Ch. I — I hope so — yes. I *hope* so. Playfully happy, like two little kittens.

Min. That will be delightful.

Ch. Economically happy, like two sensible people.

Min. Oh, we must be very economical.

Ch. No vulgar display; no pandering to a jaded appetite. A refined and economical elegance; that is what we must aim at. A simple mutton chop, nicely broiled, for you; and *two* simple mutton chops, *very* nicely broiled, for me —

Min. And some flowery potatoes —

Ch. A loaf of nice household bread —

Min. A stick of celery —

Ch. And a bit of cheese, and you've a dinner fit for a monarch.

Min. Then how shall we spend our evenings?

Ch. We'll have pleasant little fireside games. Are you fond of fireside games?

Min. Oh, they're great fun.

Ch. Then we'll play at tailoring.

Min. Tailoring? I don't think I know that game.

Ch. It's a very good game. You shall be the clever little jobbing tailor, and I'll be the particular customer who brings his own materials to be made up. You shall take my measure, cut out the cloth (real cloth, you know), stitch it together, and try it on; and then I'll find fault like a real customer, and you shall alter it until it fits, and when it fits beautifully that counts one to you.

Min. Delightful!

Ch. Then there's another little fireside game which is great fun. We each take a bit of paper and a pencil and try who can jot down the nicest dinner for ninepence, and the next day we have it.

Min. Oh, Cheviot, what a paradise you hold open to me!

Ch. Yes. How's papa?

Min. He's very well and very happy. He's going to increase his establishment on the strength of the £1000 a year, and keep a manservant.

Ch. I know. I've been looking after some servants for him; they'll be here in the course of the morning. A cook, a house-maid, and a footman. I found them through an advertisement. They're country people, and will come very cheap.

Min. How kind and thoughtful you are! Oh, Cheviot, I'm a very lucky girl!

Exit Minnie.

Ch. Yes, I think so too, if I can only repress my tendency to think of that tall girl I met in Scotland! Cheviot, my boy, you must make an effort; you are going to be married, and the tall girl is nothing to you!

Enter Parker.

Par. Please, sir, here's a gentleman to see you.

Ch. Oh, my solicitor, no doubt. Show him up.

Par. And please, some persons have called to see you about an advertisement.

Ch. Oh, Symperson's servants. To be sure. Show up the gentleman, and tell the others to wait. *Exit Parker.*

Enter Belvawney. He looks very miserable.

Ch. Belvawney! This is unexpected. (*Much confused*)

Bel. Yes, Cheviot. At last we meet. Don't, oh don't, frown upon a heartbroken wretch.

Ch. Belvawney, I don't want to hurt your feelings, but I will not disguise from you that, not having seen you for three months, I was in hopes that I had got rid of you for ever.

Bel. Oh, Cheviot, don't say that, I am so unhappy. And you have it in your power to make me comfortable. Do this, and I will bless you with my latest breath!

Ch. It is a tempting offer; I am not proof against it. We all have our price, and that is mine. Proceed.

Bel. Miss Treherne — Belinda — whom I love so dearly, won't have anything to say to me.

Ch. It does her credit. She's a very superior girl.

Bel. It's all through you, Cheviot. She declares that the mutual declaration you made to protect her from McGillicuddy amounts to a Scotch marriage.

Ch. What!!!

Bel. She declares she is your wife. She professes to love me as fondly as ever; but a stern sense of duty to you forbids her to hold any communication with me.

Ch. Oh, but this is absurd, you know!

Bel. Of course it is; but what's to be done? You left with Symperson immediately after making the declaration. As soon as she found you were gone she implored me to tell her your name and address. Of course I refused, and she quitted me, telling me that she would devote her life to finding you out.

Ch. But this is simple madness. I can't have it! This day, too, of all others! If she'd claimed me last week, or even yesterday, I

wouldn't have minded, for she's a devilish fine woman; but if she were to turn up now —! (*Aloud*) Belvawney, my dear friend, tell me what to do — I'll do anything.

Bel. It seems that there's some doubt whether this cottage, which is just on the border, is in England or Scotland. If it is in England, she has no case; if it is in Scotland, I'm afraid she has. I've written to the owner of the property to ascertain, and if, in the mean time, she claims you, you must absolutely decline to recognize this marriage for a moment.

Ch. Not for one moment!

Bel. It was a mere artifice to enable her to escape from McGillicuddy.

Ch. Nothing more!

Bel. It's monstrous — perfectly monstrous — that that should constitute a marriage. It's disgraceful — it's abominable. Damme, Cheviot, it's immoral.

Ch. So it is — it's immoral. That settles it in *my* mind. It's immoral.

Bel. You're quite sure you'll be resolute, Cheviot?

Ch. Resolute? I should think so! Why, hang it all, man, I'm going to be married in twenty minutes to Minnie Symperson!

Bel. What!

Ch. (*Confused at having let this out*) Didn't I tell you? I believe you're right; I did *not* tell you. It escaped me. Oh, yes, this is my wedding-day.

Bel. Cheviot, you're joking — you don't mean this! Why, I shall lose £1000 a year by it, every penny I have in the world! Oh, it can't be — it's nonsense!

Ch. What do you mean by nonsense? The married state is an honourable estate, I believe? A man is not looked upon as utterly lost to all sense of decency because he's got married, I'm given to understand! People have been married before this, and have not been irretrievably tabooed in consequence, unless I'm grossly misinformed? Then what the dickens do you mean by saying "nonsense" when I tell you that I'm going to be married?

Bel. Cheviot, be careful how you take this step. Beware how you involve an innocent and helpless girl in social destruction.

Ch. What do you mean, sir?

Bel. You cannot marry; you are a married man.

Ch. Come, come, Belvawney, this is trifling.

Bel. You are married to Miss Treherne. I was present, and can depose to the fact.

Ch. Oh, you're not serious.

Bel. Never more serious in my life.

Ch. But, as you very properly said just now, it was a mere artifice — we didn't mean anything. It would be monstrous to regard that as a marriage. Damme, Belvawney, it would be immoral!

Bel. I may deplore the state of the law, but I cannot stand tamely by and see it deliberately violated before my eyes.

Ch. (*Wildly*) But, Belvawney, my dear friend, reflect; everything is prepared for my marriage, at a great expense. I love Minnie deeply, devotedly. She is the actual tree upon which the fruit of my heart is growing. There's no mistake about it. She is my own To Come. I love her madly — rapturously. (*Going on his knees to Belvawney*) I have prepared a wedding breakfast at a great expense to do her honour. I have ordered four flys for the wedding party. I have taken two second-class Cook's tourists' tickets for Ilfracombe, Devon, Exeter, Cornwall, Westward Ho! and Bideford Bay. The whole thing has cost me some twenty or twenty-five pounds, and all this will be wasted — utterly wasted — if you interfere. Oh, Belvawney, dear Belvawney, let the recollection of our long and dear friendship operate to prevent your shipwrecking my future life. (*Sobbing hysterically*)

Bel. I have a duty to do. I must do it.

Ch. But reflect, dear Belvawney; if I am married to Miss Treherne, you lose your income as much as if I married Minnie Symperson.

Bel. No doubt, if you could prove your marriage to Miss Treherne. But you can't — (*With melodramatic intensity*)

Ch. Those eyes!

Bel. You don't know where she is — (*With fiendish exultation*)

Ch. Oh, those eyes!

Bel. The cottage has been pulled down, and the cottagers have emigrated to Patagonia —

Ch. Oh, those eyes!

Bel. I'm the only witness left. *I* can prove your marriage, if I like; but you can't. Ha! ha! ha! ha! (*With Satanic laugh*) It's a most painful and unfortunate situation for you; and, believe me, dear Cheviot, you have my deepest and most respectful sympathy.

Exit Belvawney.

Ch. This is appalling; simply appalling! The cup of happiness dashed from my lips just as I was about to drink a life-long draught. The ladder kicked from under my feet just as I was about to pick the fruit of my heart from the tree upon which it has been growing so long. I'm a married man! More than that, my honeymoon's past, and I never

knew it! Stop a moment, though. The bride can't be found; the cottage is pulled down, and the cottagers have emigrated; what proof is there that such a marriage ever took place? There's only Belvawney, and Belvawney isn't a proof. Corroborated by the three cottagers, his word might be worth something; uncorroborated, it is worthless. I'll risk it. He can do nothing; the bride is nowhere; the cottagers are in Patagonia, and —

At this moment Mrs. Macfarlane, Maggie, and Angus appear at the back. They stand bobbing and curtsying in rustic fashion to Cheviot (whom they do not recognise). He stares aghast at them for a moment, then staggers back to sofa.

Ch. The man, the woman, and the girl, by all that's infernal!

Mrs. Mac. Gude day, sir. We've just ca'd to see ye about the advertisement. (*Producing paper*)

Ch. I don't know you — I don't know you. Go away. (*Cheviot buries his head in a newspaper, and pretends to read on sofa*)

Mag. Ah, sir, ye said that we were to ca' on ye this day at eleven o'clock, and sae we've coom a' the way fra Dumfres ito see ye.

Ch. I tell you I don't know you. Go away. I'm not at all well. I'm very ill, and it's infectious.

Ang. We fear no illness, sir. This is Mistress Macfarlane, the gude auld mither, who'll cook the brose and boil the parritch, and sit wi' ye, and nurse ye through your illness till the sad day ye dee! (*Wiping his eye*)

Cheviot pokes a hole with his finger through newspaper, and reconnoitres unobserved.

Mrs. Mac. And this is Meg, my ain lass Meg!

Ch. (*Aside*) Attractive girl, very. I remember her perfectly.

Mrs. Mac. And this is Angus Macalister, who's going to marry her, and who'll be mair than a son to me!

Ang. Oh, mither, mither, dinna say it, for ye bring the tear drop to my ee; an' it's no canny for a strong man to be blithering and soughing like a poor weak lassie! (*Wiping his eye. Angus and Mrs. Macfarlane sit. Maggie advances to hole in newspaper and peeps through*)

Mag. Oh, mither, mither! (*Staggers back into Angus's arms*)

Mrs. Mac. What is it, Meg?

Ang. Meg, my weel lo'ed Meg, my wee wifie that is to be, tell me what's wrang wi' 'ee?

Mag. Oh, mither, it's him; the noble gentleman I plighted my troth to three weary months agone! The gallant English-man who gave Angus twa golden pound to give me up!

Ang. It's the coward Sassenach [5] who well nigh broke our Meg's heart!

Mrs. Mac. My lass, my lass, dinna greet, maybe he'll marry ye yet.

Ch. (*Desperately*) Here's another! Does anybody else want to marry me? Don't be shy. You. ma'am, (*To Mrs. Macfarlane*) you're a fine woman — perhaps *you* would like to try your luck?

Mag. Ah, sir! I dinna ken your name, but your bonnie face has lived in my twa een, sleeping and waking, three weary, weary months! Oh, sir, ye shouldna' ha' deceived a trusting, simple Lowland lassie. 'Twas na' weel done — 'twas na' weel done! (*Weeping on his shoulder; he puts his arm round her waist*)

Ch. (*Softening*) My good girl, what do you wish me to do? I remember you now per-fectly. I *did* admire you very much — in fact, I do still; you're a very charming girl. Let us talk this over, calmly and quietly. (*Maggie moves away*) No, you needn't go; you can stop there if you like. There, there, my dear! don't fret. (*Aside*) She *is* a very charming girl. I almost wish I — I really begin to think I — no, no! damn it, Cheviot! not to-day.

Mag. Oh! mither, he told me he loved me!

Ch. So I did. The fact is, when I fell in love with you — don't go my pretty bird — I quite forgot that I was engaged. There, there! I thought at the time that you were the tree upon which the fruit of my heart was growing; but I was mistaken. Don't go; you needn't go on that account. It was another tree —

Mag. Oh, mither, it was anither tree! (*Weeping on Cheviot's shoulder*)

Mrs. Mac. Angus, it was anither tree! (*Weeping on Angus's shoulder*)

Ang. Dinna, mither, dinna; I canna bear it! (*Weeps*)

Ch. Yes, it was another tree — you can remain there for the present — in point of fact, it was growing on both trees. I don't know how it is, but it seems to grow on a great many trees — a perfect orchard — and you are one of them, my dear. Come, come, don't fret, you are one of them!

Enter Minnie and Symperson.

Min. Cheviot!

[5] A Scotch term for an Englishman.

Symp. What is all this?

Ch. (*Rapidly referring to piece of paper given to him by Mrs. Macfarlane, as if going over a washerwoman's bill*) "Twenty-four pairs socks, two shirts, thirty-seven collars, one sheet, forty-four nightshirts, twenty-two flannel waistcoats, one white tie." Ridiculous — quite ridiculous — I won't pay it.

Min. Cheviot, who is this person who was found hanging on your neck? Say she is somebody — for instance, your sister or your aunt. Oh, Cheviot, say she is your aunt, I implore you! (*The three cottagers curtsy and bow to Minnie*)

Symp. Cheviot, say she is your aunt, I command you.

Ch. Oh, I beg your pardon. I didn't see you. These ladies are — are my washer-women. Allow me to introduce them. They have come — they have come for their small account. (*Maggie, who has been sobbing through this, throws herself hysterically on to Cheviot's bosom*) There's a discrepancy in the items — twenty-two flannel waistcoats are ridiculous, and, in short, some washerwomen are like this when they're contradicted — they can't help it — it's something in the suds; it undermines their constitution.

Symp. (*Sternly*) Cheviot, I should like to believe you, but it seems scarcely credible.

Mag. Oh, sir, he's na telling ye truly. I'm the puir Lowland lassie that he stole the hairt out of, three months ago, and promised to marry; and I love him sae weel — sae weel, and now he's married to anither!

Ch. Nothing of the kind. I —

Symp. You are mistaken, and so is your mith — mother. He is not yet married to anith — nother.

Mag. Why, sir, it took place before my very ain eyes, before us a', to a beautiful lady, three months since.

Min. Cheviot, say that this is not true. Say that the beautiful lady was somebody — for instance, your aunt. Oh, say she was your aunt, I implore you!

Symp. (*Sternly*) Cheviot, say she was your aunt, I command you!

Ch. Minnie, Symperson, don't believe them — it was no marriage. I don't even know the lady's name — I never saw her before — I've never seen her since. It's ridiculous — I couldn't have married her without knowing it — it's out of the ques-tion!

Symp. Cheviot, let's know exactly where we are. I don't much care whom you marry, so that you marry someone — that's enough for me. But please be explicit, for this is business, and mustn't be trifled with. Tell me all about it.

Ch. (*In despair*) I cannot.

Enter Belvawney.

Bel. I can.

Symp. Belvawney!

Bel. I was present when Cheviot and a certain lady declared themselves to be man and wife. This took place in a cottage on the Border — in the presence of these worthy people.

Symp. That's enough for me. It's a Scotch marriage! Minnie, my child, we must find you someone else. Cheviot's married. Belvawney, I am sorry to say, I deprive you of your income.

Bel. I beg your pardon, not yet.

Symp. Why not?

Bel. In the first place, it's not certain whether the cottage was in England or in Scotland; in the second place, the bride can't be found.

Symp. But she *shall* be found. What is her name?

Bel. That I decline to state.

Symp. But you shall be made to state. I insist upon knowing the young lady's name.

Enter Miss Treherne, in a light and cheerful dress.

Bel. (*Amazed*) Belinda Treherne!

Miss T. (*Rushing to Minnie*) Minnie, my own old friend!

Ch. 'Tis she!

Miss T. (*Turns and recognises Cheviot*) My husband!

Ch. My wife!

> *Miss Treherne throws herself at Cheviot's feet, kissing his hands rapturously. Belvawney staggers back. Minnie faints in her father's arms. Maggie sobs on Angus's breast.*

End of the Second Act.

Act III.

Same as Act II. Belvawney discovered with Miss Treherne and Minnie. He is singing to them. Miss Treherne is leaning romantically on piano. Minnie is seated on a stool.

Bel. (*Sings*)

Says the old Obadiah to the young Obadiah,
  "I am drier, Obadiah, I am drier."

Chorus.   "I am drier."

Bel.

Says the young Obadiah to the old Obadiah,
  "I'm on fire, Obadiah, I'm on fire."

Chorus.   "I'm on fire."

Min. Oh, thank you, Mr. Belvawney. How sweetly pretty that is. Where can I get it?

Miss T. How marvellous is the power of melody over the soul that is fretted and harassed by anxiety and doubt. I can understand how valuable must have been the troubadours of old, in the troublous times of anarchy. Your song has soothed me, sir.

Bel. I am indeed glad to think that I have comforted you a little, dear ladies.

Min. Dear Mr. Belvawney, I don't know what we should have done without you. What with your sweet songs, your amusing riddles, and your clever conjuring tricks, the weary days of waiting have passed like a delightful dream.

Miss T. It is impossible to be dull in the society of one who can charm the soul with plaintive ballads one moment, and the next roll a rabbit and a guinea-pig into one.

Bel. You make me indeed happy, dear ladies. But my joy will be of brief duration, for Cheviot may return at any moment with the news that the fatal cottage was in Scotland, and then — Oh, Belinda, what is to become of me?

Miss T. How many issues depend on that momentous question? Has Belvawney a thousand a year, or is he ruined? Has your father that convenient addition to his income, or has he not? May Maggie marry Angus, or will her claim on Cheviot be satisfied? Are you to be his cherished bride, or are you destined to a life of solitary maidenhood? Am I Cheviot's honoured wife, or am I but a broken-hearted and desolate spinster? Who can tell! Who can tell! (*Crosses to Minnie*)

Bel. (*Goes to window in second drawing-room*) Here is a cab with luggage — it is Cheviot! He has returned with the news! Ladies — one word before I go. One of you will be claimed by Cheviot, that is very clear. To that one (whichever it may be) I do not address myself — but to the other (whichever it may be), I say, I love you (whichever you are) with a fervour which I cannot describe in words. If you (whichever you are) will consent to cast your lot with mine, I will devote my life to proving that I love you and you only (whichever it may be) with a single-hearted and devoted passion, which precludes the possibility of my ever entertaining the slightest regard for any other woman in the whole world. I thought I would just mention it. Good morning! *Exit Belvawney.*

Miss T. How beautifully he expresses himself. He is indeed a rare and radiant being.

Min. (*Nervously*) Oh, Belinda, the terrible moment is at hand.

Miss T. Minnie, if dear Cheviot should prove to be my husband, swear to me that that will not prevent your coming to stop with us — with dear Cheviot and me — whenever you can.

Min. Indeed I will. And if it should turn out that dear Cheviot is at liberty to marry me, promise me that that will not prevent you looking on our house — on dear Cheviot's and mine — as your home.

Miss T. I swear it. We will be like dear, dear sisters.

Enter Cheviot, as from a journey, with bag and rug.

Miss T. Cheviot, tell me at once — are you my own — husband?

Min. Cheviot, speak — is poor, little, simple Minnie to be your bride?

Ch. Minnie, the hope of my heart, my pet fruit tree! Belinda, my Past, my Present, and my To Come! I have sorry news, sorry news.

Miss T. (*Aside*) Sorry news! Then I am *not* his wife.

Min. (*Aside*) Sorry news! Then she *is* his wife.

Ch. My dear girls — my very dear girls, my journey has been fruitless — I have no information.

Miss T. and Min. No information?

Ch. None. The McQuibbigaskie has gone abroad. (*Both ladies fall weeping*)

Miss T. More weary waiting! more weary waiting!

Min. Oh, my breaking heart; oh, my poor bruised and breaking heart!

Ch. We must be patient, dear Belinda. Minnie, my own, we must be patient. After all, is the situation so very terrible? Each of you has an even chance of becoming my wife, and in the mean time I look upon myself as engaged to both of you. I shall make no distinction. I shall love you both, fondly, and you shall both love me. My affection shall be divided equally between you, and we will be as happy as three little birds.

Miss T. (*Wiping her eyes*) You are very kind and thoughtful, dear Cheviot.

Min. I believe, in my simple little way, that you are the very best man in the whole world!

Ch. (*Deprecatingly*) No, no.

Min. Ah, but do let me think so: it makes me so happy to think so!

Ch. Does it? Well, well, be it so. Perhaps I am! And now tell me, how has the time passed since I left? Have my darlings been dull?

Miss T. We should have been dull indeed but for the airy Belvawney. The sprightly creature has done his best to make the lagging hours fly. He is an entertaining rattlesnake — I should say, rattletrap.

Ch. (*Jealous*) Oh, *is* he so? Belvawney has been making the hours fly, has he? I'll make *him* fly, when I catch him!

Min. His conjuring tricks are wonderful!

Ch. Confound his conjuring tricks!

Min. Have you seen him bring a live hen, two hair brushes, and a pound and a half of fresh butter out of his pocket-handkerchief!

Ch. No, I have not had that advantage!

Miss T. It is a thrilling sight.

Ch. So I should be disposed to imagine! Pretty goings on in my absence! you seem to forget that you two girls are engaged to be married to *me!*

Miss T. Ah, Cheviot! do not judge us harshly. We love you with a reckless fervour that thrills us to the very marrow — don't we, darling? But the hours crept heavily without you, and when, to lighten the gloom in which we were plunged, the kindly creature swallowed a live rabbit and brought it out, smothered in onions, from his left boot, we could not choose but smile. The good soul has promised to teach *me* the trick.

Ch. Has he! That's his confounded impudence. Now, once for all, I'll have nothing of this kind. One of you will be my wife, and until I know which, I will permit no Belvawneying of any kind whatever, or anything approaching thereto. When that is settled, the other may Belvawney until she is black in the face.

Miss T. And how long have we to wait before we shall know which of us may begin Belvawneying?

Ch. I can't say. It may be some time. The McQuibbigaskie has gone to Central Africa. No post can reach him, and he will not return for six years.

Miss T. Six years! Oh, I cannot wait six years! Why, in six years I shall be eight-and-twenty!

Min. Six years! Why, in six years the Statute of Limitations will come in, and he can renounce us both.

Miss T. True; you are quite right. (*To Cheviot*) Cheviot, I have loved you madly, desperately, as other woman never loved other man. This poor inexperienced child, who clings to me as the ivy clings to the oak, also loves you as woman never loved before. Even that poor cottage maiden, whose rustic heart you so recklessly enslaved, worships you with a devotion that has no parallel in the annals of the heart. In return for all this unalloyed affection, all we ask of you is that you will recommend us to a respectable solicitor.

Ch. But, my dear children, reflect — I can't marry all three. I am most willing to consider myself engaged to all three, and that's as much as the law will allow. You see I do all I can. I'd marry all three of you with pleasure, if I might; but, as our laws stand at present, I'm sorry to say — I'm very sorry to say — it's out of the question.
Exit Cheviot.

Miss T. Poor fellow. He has my tenderest sympathy; but we have no alternative but to place ourselves under the protecting ægis of a jury of our countrymen!

Enter Symperson, with two letters.

Symp. Minnie — Miss Treherne — the post has just brought me two letters; one of them bears a Marseilles post-mark, and is, I doubt not, from the McQuibbigaskie! He must have written just before starting for Central Africa!

Min. From the McQuibbigaskie? Oh, read, read!

Miss T. Oh, sir! how can you torture us by this delay? Have you no curiosity?

Symp. Well, my dear, very little on this point; you see it don't matter much to me whom Cheviot marries. So that he marries some one, that's enough for me. But, however, *your* anxiety is natural, and I will gratify it. (*Opens letter and reads*) "Sir, — In reply to your letter, I have to inform you that Evan Cottage is certainly in England. The deeds relating to the property place this beyond all question."

Min. In England!

Miss T. (*Sinking into a chair*) This blow is indeed a crusher. Against such a blow I cannot stand up! (*Faints*)

Min. (*On her knees*) My poor Belinda — my darling sister — love — oh forgive me — oh forgive me! Don't look like that! Speak to me, dearest — oh speak to me — speak to me.

Miss T. (*Suddenly springing up*) Speak to you? Yes, I'll speak to you! All is *not* yet lost! True, he is not married to me, but why should he not be? I am as young as you! I am as beautiful as you! I have more money than you! I will try — oh how hard will I try!

Min. Do, darling; and I wish — oh how I wish you may get him!

Miss T. Minnie, if you were not the dearest little friend I have in the world I could pinch you! *Exit Belinda.*

Symp. (*Who has been reading the other letter*) Dear me — how terrible!

Min. What is terrible, dear papa?

Symp. Belvawney writes to tell me the Indestructible Bank stopped payment yesterday, and Cheviot's shares are waste paper.

Min. Well, upon my word. There's an end of *him!*

Symp. An end of him. What do you mean? You are not going to throw him over?

Min. Dear papa, I am sorry to disappoint you, but unless your tom-tit is very much mistaken, the Indestructible was not registered under the Joint-Stock Companies Act of Sixty-two, and in that case the shareholders are jointly and severally liable to the whole extent of their available capital. Poor little Minnie don't pretend to have a business head; but she's not *quite* such a little donkey as *that,* dear papa.

Symp. You decline to marry him? Do I hear rightly?

Min. I don't know, papa, whether your hearing is as good as it was, but from your excited manner, I should say you heard me perfectly. *Exit Minnie.*

Symp. This is a pretty business! Done out of a thousand a year; and by my own daughter! What a terrible thing is this incessant craving after money! Upon my word, some people seem to think that they're sent into the world for no other purpose but to acquire wealth; and, by Jove, they'll sacrifice their nearest and dearest relations to get it. It's most humiliating — most humiliating!

Enter Cheviot, in low spirits.

Ch. (*Throwing himself into a chair; sobs aloud*) Oh Uncle Symperson, have you heard the news?

Symp. (*Angrily*) Yes, I *have* heard the news; and a pretty man of business *you* are to invest all your property in an unregistered company!

Ch. Uncle, don't *you* turn against me! Belinda is not my wife! I'm a ruined man; and my darlings — my three darlings, whom I love with a fidelity, which, in these easy-going days, is simply Quixotic — will have nothing to say to me. Minnie, your daughter, declines to accompany me to the altar. Belinda, I feel sure, will revert to Belvawney, and Maggie is at this present moment hanging round that Scotch idiot's neck, although she knows that in so doing she simply tortures me. Symperson, I never loved three girls as I loved those three — never! never! and now they'll all three slip through my fingers — I'm sure they will!

Symp. Pooh, pooh, sir. Do you think nobody loses but you? Why, I'm done out of a thousand a year by it.

Ch. (*Moodily*) For that matter, Symperson, I've a very vivid idea that you won't have to wait long for the money.

Symp. What d'you mean? Oh — of course — I understand.

Ch. Eh?

Symp. Mrs. Macfarlane! I have thought of her myself. A very fine woman for her years; a majestic ruin, beautiful in decay. My dear boy, my very dear boy, I congratulate you.

Ch. Don't be absurd. I'm not going to marry anybody.

Symp. Eh? Why, then how —? I don't think I quite follow you.

Ch. There is another contingency on which you come into the money. My death.

Symp. To be sure! I never thought of that! And, as you say, a man can die but once.

Ch. I beg your pardon. I didn't say anything of the kind — you said it; but it's true, for all that.

Symp. I'm very sorry; but, of course, if you have made up your mind to it —

Ch. Why, when a man's lost everything, what has he to live for?

Symp. True, true. Nothing whatever. Still —

Ch. His money gone, his credit gone, the three girls he's engaged to gone.

Symp. I cannot deny it. It is a hopeless situation. Hopeless, quite hopeless.

Ch. His happiness wrecked, his hopes blighted; the three trees upon which the fruit of his heart was growing — all cut down. What is left but suicide?

Symp. True, true! You're quite right. Farewell. (*Going*)

Ch. Symperson, you seem to think I *want* to kill myself. I don't want to do anything of the kind. I'd much rather live — upon my soul I would — if I could think of any reason for living. Symperson, can't you think of *something* to check the heroic impulse which is at this moment urging me to a tremendous act of self-destruction?

Symp. Something! Of course I can! Say that you throw yourself into the Serpentine[6] — which is handy. Well, it's an easy way of going out of the world, I'm told — rather pleasant than otherwise, I believe — quite

an agreeable sensation, I'm given to understand. But you — you get wet through; and your — your clothes are absolutely ruined!

Ch. (*Mournfully*) For that matter, I could take off my clothes before I went in.

Symp. True, so you could. I never thought of that. You could take them off before you go in — there's no reason why you shouldn't, if you do it in the dark — and *that* objection falls to the ground. Cheviot, my lion-hearted boy, it's impossible to resist your arguments, they are absolutely convincing.

Shakes his hand. Exit.

Ch. Good fellow, Symperson — I like a man who's open to conviction! But it's no use — all my attractions are gone — and I can *not* live unless I feel I'm fascinating. Still, there's one chance left — Belinda! I haven't tried her. Perhaps, after all, she loved me for myself alone! It isn't likely — but it's barely possible.

Enter Belvawney, who has overheard these words.

Bel. Out of the question; you are too late! I represented to her that you are never likely to induce any one to marry you now that you are penniless. She felt that my income was secure, and she gave me her hand and her heart.

Ch. Then all is lost; my last chance is gone, and the irrevocable die is cast! Be happy with her, Belvawney; be happy with her!

Bel. Happy! You shall dine with us after our honeymoon and judge for yourself.

Ch. No, I shall not do that; long before you return I shall be beyond the reach of dinners.

Bel. I understand — you are going abroad. Well, I don't think you could do better than try another country.

Ch. (*Tragically*) Belvawney, I'm going to try another world! (*Drawing a pistol from his pocket*)

Bel. (*Alarmed*) What do you mean?

Ch. In two minutes I die!

Bel. You're joking, of course?

Ch. Do I look like a man who jokes? Is my frame of mind one in which a man indulges in trivialities?

Bel. (*In great terror*) But my dear Cheviot, reflect —

Ch. Why should it concern you? You will be happy with Belinda. You will not be well off, but Symperson will, and I dare say he will give you a meal now and then. It will not be a nice meal, but still it will be a meal.

---

[6] A lake in Kensington, London.

Bel. Cheviot, you mustn't do this; pray reflect; there are interests of magnitude depending on your existence.

Ch. My mind is made up. (*Cocking the pistol*)

Bel. (*Wildly*) But I shall be ruined!

Ch. There is Belinda's fortune.

Bel. She won't have me if I'm ruined! Dear Cheviot, don't do it — it's culpable — it's wrong!

Ch. Life is valueless to me without Belinda. (*Pointing the pistol to his head*)

Bel. (*Desperately*) You shall have Belinda; she is much — very much to me, but she is not everything. Your life is very dear to me; and when I think of our old friendship —! Cheviot, you shall have anything you like, if you'll only consent to live!

Ch. If I thought you were in earnest; but no — no. (*Putting pistol to head*)

Bel. In earnest? of course I'm in earnest. Why, what's the use of Belinda to me if I'm ruined? Why, she wouldn't look at me.

Ch. But perhaps if I'm ruined, she wouldn't look at *me*.

Bel. Cheviot, I'll confess all, if you'll only live. You — you are *not* ruined!

Ch. Not ruined?

Bel. Not ruined. I — I invented the statement.

Ch. (*In great delight*) You invented the statement? My dear friend! My very dear friend! I'm very much obliged to you! Oh, thank you, thank you a thousand times! Oh, Belvawney, you have made me very, very happy! (*Sobbing on his shoulder, then suddenly springing up*) But what the devil did you mean by circulating such a report about me? How dare you do it, sir? Answer me that, sir.

Bel. I did it to gain Belinda's love. I knew that the unselfish creature loved you for your wealth alone.

Ch. It was a liberty, sir; it was a liberty. To put it mildly, it was a liberty.

Bel. It was. You're quite right — that's the word for it — it was a liberty. But I'll go and undeceive her at once.

Exit Belvawney.

Ch. Well, as I've recovered my fortune, and with it my tree, I'm about the happiest fellow in the world. My money, my mistress, and my mistress's money, all my own. I believe I could go mad with joy!

Enter Symperson, in deep black; he walks pensively, with a white handkerchief to his mouth.

Ch. What's the matter?

Symp. Hallo! You're still alive?

Ch. Alive? Yes; why, (*Noticing his dress*) is anything wrong?

Symp. No, no, my dear young friend, these clothes are symbolical; they represent my state of mind. After your terrible threat, which I cannot doubt you intend to put at once into execution —

Ch. My dear uncle, this is very touching; this unmans me. But, cheer up, dear old friend, I have good news for you.

Symp. (*Alarmed*) Good news? What do you mean?

Ch. I am about to remove the weight of sorrow which hangs so heavily at your heart. Resume your fancy check trousers — I have consented to live.

Symp. Consented to live? Why, sir, this is confounded trifling. I don't understand this line of conduct at all; you threaten to commit suicide; your friends are dreadfully shocked at first, but eventually their minds become reconciled to the prospect of losing you, they become resigned, even cheerful; and when they have brought themselves to this Christian state of mind, you coolly inform them that you have changed your mind and mean to live. It's not business, sir — it's not business.

Ch. But, my dear uncle, I've nothing to commit suicide for; I'm a rich man, and Belinda will, no doubt, accept me with joy and gratitude.

Symp. Belinda will do nothing of the kind. She has just left the house with Belvawney, in a cab, and under the most affectionate circumstances.

Ch. (*Alarmed*) Left with Belvawney? Where have they gone?

Symp. I don't know. Very likely to get married.

Ch. Married?

Symp. Yes, before the registrar.

Ch. I've been sold! I see that now! Belvawney has done me! But I'm not the kind of man who stands such treatment quietly. Belvawney has found his match. Symperson, they may get married, but they shall not be happy; I'll be revenged on them both before they're twenty-four hours older. She marries him because she thinks his income is secure. I'll show her she's wrong; I won't blow out my brains; I'll do worse.

Symp. What?

Ch. I'll marry.

Symp. Marry?

Ch. Anybody. I don't care who it is.

Symp. Will Minnie do?

Ch. Minnie will do; send her here.

Symp. In one moment, my dear boy — in one moment!

Exit Symperson, hurriedly.

Ch. Belinda alone in a cab with Belvawney! It's maddening to think of it! He's got his arm round her waist at this moment, if I know anything of human nature! I can't stand it — I cannot and I will not stand it! I'll write at once to the registrar and tell him she's married. (*Sits at writing table and prepares to write*) Oh, why am I constant by disposition? Why is it that when I love a girl I can think of no other girl but that girl, whereas, when a girl loves me she seems to entertain the same degree of affection for mankind at large? I'll never be constant again; henceforth I fascinate but to deceive!

Enter Minnie.

Min. Mr. Cheviot Hill, papa tells me that you wish to speak to me.

Ch. (*Hurriedly — writing at table*) I do. Miss Symperson, I have no time to beat about the bush; I must come to the point at once. You rejected me a short time since — I will not pretend that I am pleased with you for rejecting me — on the contrary, I think it was in the worst taste. However, let bygones be bygones. Unforeseen circumstances render it necessary that I should marry at once, and you'll do. An early answer will be esteemed, as this is business. (*Resumes his writing*)

Min. Mr. Hill, dear papa assures me that the report about the loss of your money is incorrect. I hope this may be the case, but I cannot forget that the information comes from dear papa. Now dear papa is the best and dearest papa in the whole world, but he has a lively imagination, and when he wants to accomplish his purpose, he does not hesitate to invent — I am not quite sure of the word, but I think it is "bouncers."

Ch. (*Writing*) You are quite right, the word is bouncers. Bouncers or bangers — either will do.

Min. Then forgive my little silly fancies, Mr. Hill; but, before I listen to your suggestion, I must have the very clearest proof that your position is, in every way, fully assured.

Ch. Mercenary little donkey! I will not condescend to proof. I renounce her altogether. (*Rings bell*)

Enter Maggie with Angus and Mrs. Macfarlane. Angus has his arm round her waist.

Ch. (*Suddenly seeing her*) Maggie, come here. Angus, do take your arm from round

that girl's waist. Stand back, and don't you listen. Maggie, three months ago I told you that I loved you passionately; to-day I tell you that I love you as passionately as ever; I may add that I am still a rich man. Can you oblige me with a postage-stamp? (*Maggie gives him a stamp from her pocket — he sticks it on his letter*) What do you say? I must trouble you for an immediate answer, as this is not pleasure — it's business.

Mag. Oh, sir, ye're ower late. Oh, Maister Cheviot, if I'd only ken'd it before! Oh, sir, I love ye right weel; the bluid o' my hairt is nae sae dear to me as thou. (*Sobbing on his shoulder*) Oh, Cheviot, my ain auld love! my ain auld love!

Ang. (*Aside*) Puir lassie, it just dra's the water from my ee to hear her. Oh, mither, mither! my hairt is just breaking. (*Sobs on Mrs. Macfarlane's shoulder*)

Ch. But why is it too late? You say that you love me. I offer to marry you. My station in life is at least equal to your own. What is to prevent our union?

Mag. (*Wiping her eyes*) Oh, sir, ye're unco guid to puir little Maggie, but ye're too late; for she's placed the matter in her solicitor's hands, and he tells her that an action for breach will just bring damages to the tune of a thousand pound. There's a laddie waiting outside noo, to serve the bonnie writ on ye! (*Turns affectionately to Angus*)

Ch. (*Falling sobbing on to sofa*) No one will marry me. There is a curse upon me — a curse upon me. No one will marry me — no, not one!

Mrs. Mac. Dinna say that, sir. There's mony a woman — nae young, soft, foolish lassie, neither; but grown women o' sober age, who'd be mair a mither than a wife to ye; and that's what ye want, puir laddie, for ye're no equal to takin' care o' yersel'.

Ch. Mrs. Macfarlane, you are right. I am a man of quick impulse. I see, I feel, I speak. I — you are the tree upon which — which — that is to say — no, no, d—n it, I can't; I can't! One must draw the line somewhere. (*Turning from her with disgust*)

Enter Miss Treherne and Belvawney. They are followed by Symperson and Minnie.

Ch. Belinda! Can I believe my eyes? You have returned to me, you have not gone off with Belvawney after all? Thank heaven, thank heaven!

Miss T. I thought that, as I came in, I heard you say something about a tree.

Ch. You are right. As you entered I was

remarking that I am a man of quick impulse. I see, I feel, I speak. I have two thousand a year, and I love you passionately. I lay my hand, my heart, and my income, all together, in one lot, at your feet!

Miss T. Cheviot, I love you with an irresistible fervour, that seems to parch my very existence. I love you as I never loved man before, and as I can never hope to love man again. But, in the belief that you were ruined, I went with my own adored Belvawney before the registrar, and that registrar has just made us one! (*Turns affectionately to Belvawney*)

Bel. (*Embraces Belinda*) Bless him for it — bless him for it.

Ch. (*Deadly calm*) One word. I have not yet seen the letter that blights my earthly hopes. For form's sake, I trust I may be permitted to cast my eye over that document? As a matter of business — that's all.

Bel. Certainly. Here it is. You will find the situation of the cottage described in unmistakable terms. (*Hands the letter to Cheviot*)

Ch. (*Reads*) "In reply to your letter I have to inform you that Evan Cottage is certainly in England. The deeds relating to the property place this beyond all question." Thank you; I am satisfied. (*Takes out pistol*)

Bel. Now, sir, perhaps you will kindly release that young lady. She is my wife! (*Cheviot's arm has crept mechanically round Miss Treherne's waist*)

Miss T. Oh, Cheviot! kindly release me — I am his wife!

Ch. Crushed! Crushed! Crushed!

Symp. (*Looking over his shoulder at letter, reads*) "Turn over."

Ch. (*Despairingly*) Why should I? What good would it do? Oh! I see. I beg your pardon. (*Turns over the page*) Halloa! (*Rises*)

All. What?

Ch. (*Reads*) "P. S. — I may add that the border line runs through the property. The cottage is undoubtedly in England, though the garden is in Scotland."

Miss T. And we were married in the garden!

Ch. Belinda, we were married in the garden. (*Belinda leaves Belvawney, and turns affectionately to Cheviot, who embraces her*)

Bel. Belinda, stop a bit! don't leave me like this!

Miss T. (*Crosses to Belvawney*) Belvawney, I love you with an intensity of devotion that I firmly believe will last while I live. But dear Cheviot is my husband now; he has a claim upon me which it would be impossible — nay, criminal — to resist. Farewell, Belvawney; Minnie may yet be yours! (*Belvawney turns sobbing to Minnie, who comforts him; Miss Treherne crosses back to Cheviot*) Cheviot — my husband — my own old love — if the devotion of a lifetime can atone for the misery of the last few days, it is yours, with every wifely sentiment of pride, gratitude, admiration, and love.

Ch. (*Embracing her*) My own! my own! Tender blossom of my budding hopes! Star of my life! Essence of happiness! Tree upon which the fruit of my heart is growing! My Past, my Present, my To Come!

Picture. — Cheviot embracing Miss Treherne. Belvawney is being comforted by Minnie. Angus is solacing Maggie, and Mrs. Macfarlane is reposing on Mr. Symperson's bosom.

THE END.

GEORGE BERNARD SHAW

1856-1950

Widowers' Houses

(1892)

George Bernard Shaw, as theatregoer and dramatic critic in the 1880's, was aware of the need for a vital drama. He said in the preface of his *Plays, Pleasant and Unpleasant:* "One of the worst privations of life in London for persons of intellectual and artistic interests is the want of a suitable theatre. The existing popular drama of the day is quite out of the question for cultivated people who are accustomed to use their brains. . . . Consequently, when I found myself coming across projects of all sorts for the foundation of the theatre which should be to the newly gathered intellectual harvest of the nineteenth century what Shakespeare's theatre was to the harvest of the Renascence, I was warmly interested." The plays and operas of W. S. Gilbert, the dramas of Henrik Ibsen, and the speeches of Henry Arthur Jones were evidence that the drama could treat this "intellectual harvest," which meant to Shaw the ideas of thinkers like Charles Darwin, J. S. Mill, Samuel Butler, Henry George, and Karl Marx, on biology, religion, economics, and sociology. Shaw determined to write plays that would throw the light of these ideas on problems of human nature and conduct, ignorance, folly, and poverty.

He saw in J. T. Grein's Independent Theatre group a chance to get such plays produced. In 1885, using a plot provided by the dramatic critic William Archer, Shaw had begun writing a play to be called *Rhinegold;* this told the story of a romantic hero who, on learning that the heroine's gold was tainted, idealistically threw it into the Rhine. After working on the play for some weeks Shaw told Archer he had used up all the plot and had completed only the first act. Archer had no more plot, and gave up the idea that Shaw could write a play. Shaw apparently gave up, too, until Grein's group was founded in 1891 to introduce London playgoers to Ibsen's dramas and to encourage vital dramatic writing. Shaw then hunted up his old beginning, completed the play, named it *Widowers' Houses*, and sent it to Grein, who produced it on December 9, 1892.

Though remnants of Archer's plot may remain in Shaw's first act, it is enlightening to note the parts of it that Shaw decided to throw away: Archer's romantic hero and his sentimental action at the climax. Shaw later laughed at people who regretted the loss and disliked *Widowers' Houses* "because its hero did not, when he learned that his income came from slum property, at once relinquish it, and go to the goldfields to dig out nuggets with his strong right arm, so that he might return and wed his Blanche after a shipwreck (witnessed by her in a vision), just in time to rescue her from beggary, brought upon her by the discovery that Lickcheese was the rightful heir to the property of Sartorious, who had dispossessed and enslaved him by a series of forgeries unmasked by the faithful Cokane." Shaw's first step toward a vital drama was to discard such foolish plots and visionary heroes. His real heroes in later plays — Bluntschli, Caesar, etc. — are quiet, effective, practical men.

Eric Bentley calls the last act of *Widowers' Houses* the "most revolutionary act in modern English drama." In this act Shaw rejects the essential feature of melodrama, virtue triumphant, and discovers an ending for the play in the realistically probable behavior of his characters. In actual life Dr. Harry Trench would not give up his seven hundred pounds, and he should not, for merely throwing money away solves no problems. Shaw repudiates the old pattern of the rich landlord as villain and the oppressed tenant as virtuous victim. He rejects also the solution of this problem offered in Jerrold's *The Rent-Day;* a landlord cannot be merciful toward his tenants if his real estate is mortgaged slum property. Sartorius is forced to squeeze his tenants for his rents in order to pay interest on his loan. The people in Sartorius's tenements probably do break up stair railings for firewood. The apparently pathetic Lickcheese proves himself as much a rascal as Sartorius when he has a chance. Shaw satirizes idealistic lip service to duty: Cokane, with unconscious hypocrisy, urges duty as a reason for repairing the tenements — and thus milking the public treasury. The play tells a love story, but with precious little romantic sentiment. The much stronger sexual drive replaces it. The introduction to *Plays, Pleasant and Unpleasant* says on this point: "Harry and Blanche are the natural products of their environment, and consummate their sordid, fleshly union without a vestige of illusion as to the baseness of their motives."

Widowers' Houses is a problem play with an implied solution: the problem of greed and consequent misery among the poor may be solved by changing the economic system that fosters them. Shaw intended to make people see clearly social evils which they had found it comfortable to ignore or smooth over with the mid-Victorian remedies of humanitarianism (baskets for the poor, as in Dickens's *A Christmas Carol*). In Shaw's thought, poverty is not to be pitied, but to be abolished. Perhaps to suggest that these radical ideas are Christian (if not respectable!) Shaw took his title from Jesus's words in Matthew 23:14: "Woe unto you, scribes and Pharisees, hypocrites! for ye devour widows' houses, and for a pretence make a long prayer. . . ." (He changed "widows" to "widowers" to fit the plot.) Shaw intended his play to bring about action as well as discussion. His preface says, "I must, however, warn my readers that my attacks are directed against themselves, not against my stage figures." The play "deals with a burning social question, and is deliberately intended to induce people to vote on the Progressive side at the next County Council elections in London." In short, Shaw believed some form of Socialism to be the only effective remedy for the horrors Lickcheese described, and he intended to move the people in the audience to the same conclusion.

The play also introduces Shaw's theory of the Life Force. From his reading in biology and philosophy Shaw was reaching the conclusion that the ultimate motive in lovemaking is propagation of the species and that the woman, not the man, as the primary vessel of the Life Force, is the real aggressor in love. He saw the sugary sentimentality of love in the melodramas as not only nonsense, but hypocrisy. To state this truth starkly, he created Blanche as a healthy, highly sexed, hot-tempered huntress. Her maneuvers to trap the man she wants are erotic; her lures are strong and amoral enough to make Trench throw away his scruples against hypocritically improving slum property so that he might sell it at a profit. (Blanche is a preliminary sketch of Ann Whitefield in *Man and Superman*, where the theory of the Life Force is presented fully.)

Grein's group produced *Widowers' Houses* at the Royalty Theatre. Grein, having produced some of Ibsen's plays, was expected to present something unusual and provocative. Therefore the audience was, in a sense, selected, an intellectual avant-garde; but few were prepared for anything as subversive as Shaw's play. Socialists and other radicals in the audience applauded loudly, but others hissed and hooted. Some were angered by the unveiling of unpleasant facts about slum landlordism and by Shaw's remedy of social reconstruction; others were outraged by Blanche's bad temper, treatment of her maid, and aggressive sexuality. The uproar at the end of the play included calls for the author. Shaw was ready and waiting. He told his audience that he was delighted with their reception of the play, for he intended to provoke discussion. He insisted that he had presented a faithful picture of what was then going on in London and that the people of the middle class, like those of the audience, were responsible; but he expressed the hope that the time would come when conditions would be so changed that the play would be meaningless. The next day, when Shaw found himself and his play subjects of vigorous discussion and execration, he decided that it was his destiny to be a great dramatist.

With *Widowers' Houses* the new drama had arrived. Problems of conduct, character, and social justice, stated with fidelity to fact, were its new subjects. The plays of this drama did not immediately push others from the stage, but, appearing alongside the melodramas, they presented the challenge of intellectual vitality.

WIDOWERS' HOUSES

An Original Didactic Realistic Play In Three Acts
by
GEORGE BERNARD SHAW

First performed by the Independent Theatre Society at the Royalty Theatre, December 9, 1892.

Cast of Characters

DR. HARRY TRENCH	BLANCHE
COKANE	ANNIE, *parlourmaid*
SARTORIUS	WAITER
LICKCHEESE	PORTER

ACT I.

In the garden restaurant of a hotel at Remagen on the Rhine, on a fine afternoon in August. Tables and chairs under the trees. The gate leading from the garden to the riverside is on the left. The hotel is on the right. It has a wooden annexe with an entrance marked Table d'Hôte. A waiter is in attendance. A couple of English tourists come out of the hotel. The younger, Dr. Harry Trench, is about 24, stoutly built, thick in the neck, with close-cropped and black hair, with undignified medical student manners, frank, hasty, rather boyish. The other, Mr. William de Burgh Cokane, is older — probably over 40, possibly 50 — an ill-nourished, scanty-haired gentleman, with affected manners, fidgety, touchy, and constitutionally ridiculous in uncompassionate eyes.

Cok. (On the threshold of the hotel, calling peremptorily to the waiter) Two beers for us out here. (*The waiter goes for the beer. Cokane comes down into the garden*) We have got the room with the best view in the hotel, Harry, thanks to my tact. We'll leave in the morning and do Mainz and Frankfurt. There is a very graceful female statue in the private house of a nobleman in Frankfurt — also a zoo. Next day, Nuremberg! finest collection of instruments of torture in the world.

Tren. All right. You look out the trains, will you? (*He takes out a Continental Bradshaw, and tosses it on one of the tables*)

Cok. (Baulking himself in the act of sitting down) Pah! the seat is all dusty. These foreigners are deplorably unclean in their habits.

Tren. (Buoyantly) Never mind: it don't matter, old chappie. Buck up, Billy, buck up. Enjoy yourself. (*He throws Cokane into the chair, and sits down opposite him, taking out his pipe, and singing noisily*)

Pass about the Rhine wine; let it flow
Like a free and flowing river —

Cok. (Scandalized) In the name of common decency, Harry, will you remember that you are a gentleman and not a coster on Hampstead Heath on Bank Holiday? Would you dream of behaving like this in London?

Tren. Oh, rot! I've come abroad to enjoy myself: so would you if you'd just passed an examination after four years in the medical school and walking the hospital. (*Sings*)

Cok. (Rising) Trench: either you travel as a gentleman, or you travel alone. This is what makes Englishmen unpopular on the

434

Continent. It may not matter before the natives; but the people who came on board the steamer at Coblentz are English. I have been uneasy all the afternoon about what they must think of us. Look at our appearance.

Tren. What is the matter with our appearance?

Cok. Negligé, my dear fellow, negligé. On the steamboat a little negligé was quite en règle; but here, in this hotel, some of them are sure to dress for dinner; and you have nothing but that Norfolk jacket. How are they to know that you are well connected if you do not show it by your manners?

Tren. Pooh! the steamboat people were the scum of the earth — Americans and all sorts. They may go hang themselves, Billy. I shall not bother about them. (*He strikes a match, and proceeds to light his pipe*)

Cok. Do drop calling me Billy in public, Trench. My name is Cokane. I am sure they were persons of consequence: you were struck with the distinguished appearance of the father yourself.

Tren. (*Sobered at once*) What! those people. (*He blows out the match and puts up his pipe*)

Cok. (*Following up his advantage triumphantly*) Here, Harry, h e r e —at this hotel. I recognized the father's umbrella in the stand in the hall.

Tren. (*With a touch of genuine shame*) I suppose I ought to have brought a change. But a lot of luggage is such a nuisance; and — (*Rising abruptly*) — at all events we can go and have a wash. (*He turns to go into the hotel, but stops in consternation, seeing some people coming up to the riverside gate*) Oh, I say. Here they are.

A lady and gentleman, followed by a porter with some light parcels, not luggage, but shop purchases, come into the garden. They are apparently father and daughter. The gentleman is 50, tall, well preserved and of upright carriage, with an incisive, domineering utterance and imposing style, which, with his strong aquiline nose and resolute clean-shaven mouth, give him an air of importance. He wears a light grey frock-coat with silk linings, a white hat, and a field-glass slung in a new leather case. A self-made man, formidable to servants, not easily accessible to any one. His daughter is a well-dressed, well-fed, good-looking, strong-minded young woman, presentably ladylike, but still her father's daughter. Nevertheless fresh and attractive, and none the worse for being vital and energetic rather than delicate and refined.

Cok. (*Quickly taking the arm of Trench, who is staring as if transfixed*) Recollect yourself, Harry; presence of mind, presence of mind! (*He strolls with him towards the hotel. The waiter comes out with the beer*) Kellner: ceci-là est notre table. Est-ce-que vous comprenez Français?

Waiter. Yes, zare. All right, zare.

The Gentleman. (*To his porter*) Place those things on that table. (*The porter does not understand*)

Waiter. (*Interposing*) Zese zhentellmen are using zis table, zare. Would you mind —

The Gentleman. (*Severely*) You should have told me so before. (*To Cokane, with fierce condescension*) I regret the mistake sir.

Cok. Don't mention it, my dear sir; don't mention it. Retain the place, I beg.

The Gentleman. (*Coldly turning his back on him*) Thank you. (*To the porter*) Place them on t h a t table. (*The porter makes no movement until the gentleman points to the parcels and peremptorily raps the table*)

Porter. Ja wohl, gnädige Herr. (*He puts down the parcels*)

The Gentleman. (*Taking out a handful of money*) Waiter.

Waiter. (*Awestruck*) Yes, zare.

The Gentleman. Tea. For two. Out here.

Waiter. Yes, zare. (*He goes into the hotel*) *The gentleman selects a small coin from his handful of money, and hands it to the porter, who receives it with a submissive touch to his cap, and goes out, not daring to speak. His daughter sits down and opens a parcel of photographs. The gentleman takes out a Baedeker; places a chair for himself; and then, instead of sitting down, looks truculently at Cokane, as if waiting for him to take himself off. Cokane, not at all abashed, resumes his place at the other table with an air of modest good breeding, and calls to Trench, who is prowling irresolutely in the background.*

Cok. Trench, my dear fellow, your beer is waiting for you. (*He drinks*)

Tren. (*Glad of the excuse to come back to his chair*) Thank you, Cokane. (*He also drinks*)

Cok. By the way, Harry, I have often meant to ask you — is Lady Roxdale your mother's sister or your father's? (*This shot tells immediately. The gentleman is perceptibly interested*)

Tren. My mother's, of course. What put that into your head?

Cok. Nothing — I was just thinking — hm! She will expect you to marry, Harry: a doctor ought to marry.

Tren. What has she got to do with it?

Cok. A great deal, dear boy. She looks forward to floating your wife in society in London.

Tren. What rot!

Cok. Ah, you are young, dear boy: you are young. You don't know the importance of these things — apparently idle ceremonial trifles, really the springs and wheels of a great aristocratic system. (*The waiter comes back with the tea things, which he brings to the gentleman's table. Cokane rises and addresses the gentleman*) My dear sir, excuse my addressing you; but I cannot help feeling that you prefer this table and that we are in your way.

The Gentleman. (*Graciously*) Thank you. Blanche, this gentleman very kindly offers us his table, if you would prefer it.

Blanche. Oh, thanks: it makes no difference.

The Gentleman. (*To Cokane*) We are fellow travellers, I believe, sir.

Cok. Fellow travellers and fellow countrymen. Ah, we rarely feel the charm of our own tongue until it reaches our ears under a foreign sky. You have no doubt noticed that?

The Gentleman. (*A little puzzled*) Hm! From a romantic point of view, possibly, very possibly. As a matter of fact, the sound of English makes me feel at home; and I dislike feeling at home when I am abroad. It is not precisely what one goes to the expense for. (*He looks at Trench*) I think this gentleman travelled with us also.

Cok. (*Rising to act as master of the ceremonies. The gentleman and Trench rise also*) My valued friend, Dr. Trench. Trench, my dear fellow, allow me to introduce you to — er —? (*He looks enquiringly at the gentleman, waiting for the name*)

The Gentleman. Permit me to shake your hand, Dr. Trench. My name is Sartorius; and I have the honour of being known to Lady Roxdale, who is, I believe, a near relative of yours. Blanche. (*She looks up*) My friend Dr. Trench. (*They bow*)

Tren. Perhaps I should introduce my friend Cokane to you, Mr. Sartorius — Mr. William de Burgh Cokane. (*Cokane makes an elaborate bow. Sartorius accepts it with dignity. The waiter meanwhile re-enters with teapot, hot water, etc.*)

Sar. (*To the waiter*) Two more cups.

Waiter. Yes, zare. (*He goes back into the hotel*)

Blanche. Do you take sugar, Mr. Cokane?

Cok. Thank you. (*To Sartorius*) This is really too kind. Harry: bring your chair around.

Sar. You are very welcome. (*Trench brings his chair to the tea table; and they all sit round it. The waiter returns with two more cups*)

Waiter. Table d'hôte at 'alf past zix, zhentellmenn. Anyzing else now, zare?

Sar. No. You can go. (*The waiter goes*)

Cok. (*Very agreeably*) Do you contemplate a long stay here, Miss Sartorius?

Blanche. We were thinking of going on to Rolandseck. Is it as nice as this place?

Cok. Harry: the Baedeker. Thank you. (*He consults the index, and looks out Rolandseck*)

Blanche. Sugar, Dr. Trench?

Tren. Thanks. (*She hands him the cup, and looks meaningly at him for an instant. He looks down hastily, and glances apprehensively at Sartorius, who is preoccupied with a piece of bread and butter*)

Cok. Rolandseck appears to be an extremely interesting place. (*He reads*) "It is one of the most beautiful and frequented spots on the river, and is surrounded with numerous villas and pleasant gardens, chiefly belonging to wealthy merchants from the Lower Rhine, and extending along the wooded slopes at the back of the village."

Blanche. That sounds civilized and comfortable. I vote we go there.

Sar. Quite like our place at Surbiton, my dear.

Blanche. Quite.

Cok. You have a place down the river? Ah, I envy you.

Sar. No: I have merely taken a furnished villa at Surbiton for the summer. I live in Bedford Square. I am a vestryman and must reside in the parish.

Blanche. Another cup, Mr. Cokane?

Cok. Thank you, no. (*To Sartorius*) I presume you have been round this little place. Not much to see here, except the Appollinaris Church.

Sar. (*Scandalized*) The what!

Cok. The Appollinaris Church.

Sar. A strange name to give a church. Very continental, I must say.

Cok. Ah, yes, yes, yes. That is where our neighbours fall short sometimes, Mr. Sartorius: taste — t a s t e is what they occasionally fail in. But in this instance they are not to blame. The water is called after the church, not the church after the water.

Sar. (*As if this were an extenuating circumstance, but not a complete excuse*) I am glad to hear it. Is the church a celebrated one?

Cok. Baedeker stars it.

Sar. (*Respectfully*) Oh, in that case I should like to see it.

Cok. (*Reading*) "— erected in 1839 by Zwirner, the late eminent architect of the cathedral of Cologne, at the expense of Count Furstenburg-Stammheim."

Sar. (*Much impressed*) We must certainly see that, Mr. Cokane. I had no idea that the architect of Cologne cathedral lived so recently.

Blanche. Don't let us bother about any more churches, papa. They're all the same; and I'm tired to death of them.

Sar. Well, my dear, if you think it sensible to take a long and expensive journey to see what there is to be seen, and then go away without seeing it —

Blanche. Not this afternoon, papa, please.

Sar. My dear: I should like you to see everything. It is part of your education—

Blanche. (*Rising, with a petulant sigh*) Oh, my education. Very well, very well: I suppose I must go through with it. Are you coming, Dr. Trench? (*With a grimace*) I'm sure the Johannis Church will be a treat for you.

Cok. (*Laughing softly and archly*) Ah, excellent, excellent: very good, indeed. (*Seriously*) But do you know, Miss Sartorius, there actually are Johannis churches here— several of them—as well as Appollinaris ones?

Sar. (*Sententiously taking out his field glass and leading the way to the gate*) There is many a true word spoken in jest, Mr. Cokane.

Cok. (*Accompanying him*) How true! How true!

> *They go out together, ruminating profoundly. Blanche makes no movement to follow them. She watches them till they are safely out of sight, and then posts herself before Trench, looking at him with an enigmatic smile, which he returns with a half sheepish, half conceited grin.*

Blanche. Well! So you have done it at last.

Tren. Yes. At least Cokane's done it. I told you he'd manage it. He's rather an ass in some ways; but he has tremendous tact.

Blanche. (*Contemptuously*) Tact! That's not tact: that's inquisitiveness. Inquisitive people always have a lot of practice in getting into conversation with strangers. Why didn't you speak to my father yourself on the boat? You were ready enough to speak to me without any introduction.

Tren. I didn't particularly want to talk to him.

Blanche. It didn't occur to you, I suppose, that you put me in a false position by that.

Tren. Oh, I don't see that, exactly. Besides your father isn't an easy man to tackle. Of course, now that I know him, I see that he's pleasant enough; but then you've got to know him first, haven't you?

Blanche. (*Impatiently*) Everybody is afraid of papa—I'm sure I don't know why. (*She sits down again, pouting a little*)

Tren. (*Tenderly*) However, it's all right now, isn't it? (*He sits near her*)

Blanche. (*Sharply*) I don't know. How should I? You had no right to speak to me that day on board the steamer. You thought I was alone, because (*With false pathos*) I had no mother with me.

Tren. (*Protesting*) Oh, I say! Come! It was you who spoke to me. Of course I was only too glad of the chance; but on my word I shouldn't have moved an eyelid if you hadn't given me a lead.

Blanche. I only asked you the name of a castle. There was nothing unladylike in that.

Tren. Of course not. Why shouldn't you? (*With renewed tenderness*) But it's all right now, isn't it?

Blanche. (*Softly—looking subtly at him*) Is it?

Tren. (*Suddenly becoming shy*) I—I suppose so. By the way, what about the Appollinaris Church? Your father expects us to follow him, doesn't he? (*He rises*)

Blanche. (*With suppressed resentment*) Don't let me detain you if you wish to see it.

Tren. Won't you come?

Blanche. No. (*She turns her face away moodily*)

Tren. (*Alarmed*) I say: you're not offended, are you? (*She looks round at him for a moment with a reproachful film on her eyes*) Blanche. (*She bristles instantly; and frightens him*) I beg your pardon for calling you by your name; but I—er— (*She corrects her mistake by softening her expression eloquently. He responds with a gush*) You don't mind, do you? I felt sure you wouldn't somehow. Well, look here. I have no idea how you will receive this: it must seem horribly abrupt; but the circumstances do not admit of—the fact is, my utter want of tact— (*He flounders more and more, unable to see that she can hardly contain her eagerness*) Now, if it were Cokane—

Blanche. (*Impatiently*) Cokane!

Tren. (*Terrified*) No, not Cokane. Though I assure you I was only going to say about him that—

Blanche. That he will be back presently with papa.

Tren. (*Stupidly*) Yes, they can't be very long now. I hope I am not detaining you.

Blanche. I thought you were detaining me because you had something to say.

Tren. (*Totally unnerved*) Not at all. At least nothing very particular. That is, I am afraid you would not think it very particular. Another time, perhaps—

Blanche. What other time? How do you know that we shall ever meet again? (*Desperately*) Tell me now. I w a n t you to tell me now.

Tren. Well, I was thinking that if we could make up our minds to—or not to—at least—er— (*He breaks down*)

Blanche. (*Giving him up as hopeless*) I do not think there is much danger of y o u r making up your mind, Dr. Trench.

Tren. (*Stammering*) I only thought— (*He stops and looks at her piteously. She hesitates a moment, and then puts her hands into his with calculated impulsiveness. He catches her in his arms with a cry of relief*) Dear Blanche! I thought I should never have said it. I believe I should have stood stuttering here all day if you hadn't helped me out with it.

Blanche. (*Trying to get away from him*) I d i d n ' t help you out with it.

Tren. (*Holding her*) I don't mean that you did it on purpose, of course. Only instinctively.

Blanche. (*Still a little anxious*) But you haven't said anything.

Tren. What more can I say — than this? (*He kisses her again*)

Blanche. (*Overcome by the kiss, but holding on to her point*) But Harry—

Tren. (*Delighted at the name*) Yes.

Blanche. When shall we be married?

Tren. At the first church we meet — the Appollinaris Church, if you like.

Blanche. No, but seriously. This is serious, Harry: you mustn't joke about it.

Tren. (*Looking suddenly round to the riverside gate and quickly releasing her*) So! Here they are back again. (*She mutters something not unlike a suppressed oath*)

The waiter appears on the steps of the hotel, with a bell on which he gives a long ring. Cokane and Sartorius are seen returning by the river gate.

Waiter. Table d'hôte in dwendy minutes, ladies and zhentellmenn. (*He goes into the hotel*)

Sar. (*Gravely*) I intended you to accompany us, Blanche.

Blanche. Yes, papa. We were just about to start.

Sar. We are rather dusty: we must make ourselves presentable at the table d'hôte. I think you had better come in with me, my child. Come. (*He offers Blanche his arm. The gravity of his manner overawes them all. Blanche silently takes his arm and goes into the hotel with him. Cokane, hardly less momentous than Sartorius himself, contemplates Trench with the severity of a judge*)

Cok. (*With reprobation*) No, my dear boy. No, no. Never. I blush for you — was never so ashamed in my life. You have been taking advantage of that unprotected girl.

Tren. (*Hotly*) Cokane!

Cok. (*Inexorable*) Her father seems to be a perfect gentleman. I obtained the privilege of his acquaintance; I introduced you: I allowed him to believe that he might leave his daughter in your charge with absolute confidence. And what did I see on our return? — what did her father see? Oh, Trench, Trench! No, my dear fellow, no, no. Bad taste, Harry, bad form!

Tren. Stuff! There was nothing to see.

Cok. Nothing to see! She, a perfect lady, a person of the highest breeding, actually in your arms; and you say there was nothing to see! — with a waiter there actually ringing a heavy bell to call attention to his presence. (*Lecturing him with redoubled severity*) Have you no principles, Trench? Have you no religious convictions? Have you no acquaintance with the usages of society? You actually kissed —

Tren. You didn't see me kiss her.

Cok. We not only saw but h e a r d it: the report positively reverberated down the Rhine. Don't condescend to subterfuge, Trench.

Tren. Nonsense, my dear Billy. You —

Cok. There you go again. D o n ' t use that low abbreviation. How am I to preserve the respect of fellow travellers of position and wealth, if I am to be Billied at every turn? My name is William — William de Burgh Cokane.

Tren. Oh, bother! There, don't be offended, old chap. What's the use of putting your back up at every trifle? It comes natural to me to call you Bill: it suits you, somehow.

Cok. (*Mortified*) You have no delicacy of feeling, Trench — no taste. I never mention it to any one; but nothing, I am afraid, will ever make a true gentleman of you.

Sartorius appears on the threshold of the hotel.

Here is my friend, Sartorius, coming, no

doubt, to ask you for an explanation of your conduct. I really should not have been surprised to see him bring a horsewhip with him. I shall not intrude on the painful scene. (*Going*)

Tren. Don't go, confound it. I don't want to meet him alone just now.

Cok. (*Shaking his head*) Delicacy, Harry, delicacy. Good taste! Savoir faire!

He walks away and disappears in the garden to the right. Trench tries to escape in the opposite direction by strolling off towards the garden entrance.

Sar. (*Mesmerically*) Dr. Trench.

Tren. (*Stopping and turning*) Oh, is that you, Mr. Sartorius? How did you find the church? (*Sartorius, without a word, points to a seat. Trench, half hypnotized by his own nervousness and the impressiveness of Sartorius, sits down helplessly*)

Sar. (*Also seating himself*) You have been speaking to my daughter, Dr. Trench?

Tren. (*With an attempt at ease of manner*) Yes: we had a conversation — quite a chat, in fact — whilst you were at the church with Cokane. How did you get on with Cokane, Mr. Sartorius? I always think he has such wonderful tact.

Sar. (*Ignoring the digression*) I have just had a word with my daughter, Dr. Trench; and I find her under the impression that something has passed between you which it is my duty as a father — the father of a motherless girl — to inquire into at once. My daughter, perhaps foolishly, has taken you quite seriously; and —

Tren. But —

Sar. One moment, if you will be so good. I have been a young man myself — younger, perhaps, than you would suppose from my present appearance. I mean, of course, in character. If you were not serious —

Tren. (*Ingeniously*) But I was perfectly serious. I want to marry your daughter, Mr. Sartorius. I hope you don't object.

Sar. (*Condescending to Trench's humility from the mere instinct to seize an advantage, and yet deferring to Lady Roxdale's relative*) So far, no. I may say that your proposal seems to be an honourable and straightforward one, and that is very gratifying to me personally.

Tren. (*Agreeably surprised*) Then I suppose we may consider the affair as settled. It's really very good of you.

Sar. Gently, Dr. Trench, gently. Such a transaction as this cannot be settled off-hand.

Tren. Not off-hand, no. There are settle-ments and things, of course. But it may be regarded as settled between ourselves, mayn't it?

Sar. Hm! Have you nothing further to mention?

Tren. Only that — that — no: I don't know that I have, except that I love —

Sar. (*Interrupting*) Anything about your family, for example? You do not anticipate any objection on their part, do you?

Tren. Oh, they have nothing to do with it.

Sar. (*Warmly*) Excuse me, sir: they have a great deal to do with it. (*Trench is abashed*) I am resolved that my daughter shall approach no circle in which she will not be received with the full consideration to which her education and her breeding (*Here his self-control slips a little; and he repeats, as if Trench had contradicted him*) — I say, her breeding — entitle her.

Tren. (*Bewildered*) Of course not. But what makes you think my family won't like Blanche? Of course my father was a younger son; and I've had to take a profession and all that; so my people won't expect us to entertain them: they'll know we can't afford it. But they'll entertain us: they always ask me.

Sar. That won't do for me, sir. Families often think it due to themselves to turn their backs on newcomers whom they may not think quite good enough for them.

Tren. But I assure you my people aren't a bit snobbish. Blanche is a lady: that'll be good enough for them.

Sar. (*Moved*) I am glad you think so. (*Offers his hand. Trench, astonished, takes it*) I think so myself. (*Sartorius presses Trench's hand gratefully and releases it*) And now, Dr. Trench, since you have acted handsomely, you shall have no cause to complain of me. There shall be no difficulty about money: you shall entertain as much as you please: I will guarantee all that. But I must have a guarantee on my side that she will be received on equal terms by your family.

Tren. Guarantee!

Sar. Yes, a reasonable guarantee. I shall expect you to write to your relatives explaining your intention, and adding what you think proper as to my daughter's fitness for the best society. When you can show me a few letters from the principal members of your family, congratulating you in a fairly cordial way, I shall be satisfied. Can I say more?

Tren. (*Much puzzled, but grateful*) No indeed. You are really very good. Many thanks. Since you wish it, I'll write to my people. But I assure you you'll find them as jolly as possible over it. I'll make them write by return.

Sar. Thank you. In the meantime, I must ask you not to regard the matter as settled.

Tren. Oh! Not to regard the — I see. You mean between Blanche and ——

Sar. I mean between you and Miss Sartorius. When I interrupted your conversation here some time ago, you and she were evidently regarding it as settled. In case difficulties arise, and the match — you see I call it a match — be broken off, I should not wish Blanche to think that she had allowed a gentleman to — to — (*Trench nods sympathetically*) — Quite so. May I depend on you to keep a fair distance, and so spare me the necessity of having to restrain an intercourse which promises to be very pleasant to us all?

Tren. Certainly; since you prefer it. (*They shake hands on it*)

Sar. (*Rising*) You will write to-day, I think you said?

Tren. (*Eagerly*) I'll write now, before I leave here — straight off.

Sar. I will leave you to yourself then. (*He hesitates, the conversation having made him self-conscious and embarrassed; then recovers himself with an effort and adds with dignity, as he turns to go*) I am pleased to have come to an understanding with you.

He goes into the hotel; and Cokane, who has been hanging about inquisitively, emerges from the shrubbery.

Tren. (*Excitedly*) Billy, old chap, you're just in time to do me a favour. I want you to draft a letter for me to copy out.

Cok. I came with you on this tour as a friend, Trench: not as a secretary.

Tren. Well, you'll write as a friend. It's to my Aunt Maria, about Blanche and me. To tell her, you know.

Cok. Tell her about Blanche and you! Tell her about your conduct! Betray you, my friend; and forget that I am writing to a lady? Never!

Tren. Bosh, Billy: don't pretend you don't understand. We're engaged — e n g a g e d, my boy: what do you think of that? I must write by to-night's post. You are the man to tell me what to say. Come, old chap (*Coaxing him to sit down at one of the tables*), here's a pencil. Have you a bit of — oh, here: this'll do: write it on the back of the map. (*He tears the map out of his Baedeker and spreads it face downwards on the table. Cokane takes the pencil and prepares to write*) That's right. Thanks awfully, old chap! Now fire away. (*Anxiously*) Be careful how you word it, though, Cokane.

Cok. (*Putting down the pencil*) If you doubt my ability to express myself becomingly to Lady Roxdale —

Tren. (*Propitiating him*) All right, old fellow, all right: there's not a man alive who could do it half so well as you. I only wanted to explain. You see, Sartorius has got it into his head, somehow, that my people will snub Blanche; and he won't consent unless they send letters and invitations and congratulations and the deuce knows what not. So just put it in such a way that Aunt Maria will write by return saying she is delighted, and asking us — Blanche and me, you know — to stay with her, and so forth. You know what I mean. Just tell her all about it in a chatty way; and —

Cok. (*Crushingly*) If you will tell me all about it in a chatty way, I daresay I can communicate it to Lady Roxdale with proper delicacy. What is Sartorius?

Tren. (*Taken aback*) I don't know: I didn't ask. It's a sort of question you can't very well put to a man — at least a man like him. Do you think you could word the letter so as to pass all that over? I really don't like to ask him.

Cok. I can pass it over if you wish. Nothing easier. But if you think Lady Roxdale will pass it over, I differ from you. I may be wrong: no doubt I am. I generally am wrong, I believe; but that is my opinion.

Tren. (*Much perplexed*) Oh, confound it! What the deuce am I to do? Can't you say he's a gentleman: that won't commit us to anything. If you dwell on his being well off, and Blanche an only child, Aunt Maria will be satisfied.

Cok. Henry Trench: when will you begin to get a little sense? This is a serious business. Act responsibly, Harry: act responsibly.

Tren. Bosh! Don't be moral!

Cok. I am not moral, Trench. At least I am not a moralist: that is the expression I should have used — moral, but not a moralist. If you are going to get money with your wife, doesn't it concern your family to know how that money was made? Doesn't it concern you — you, Harry? (*Trench looks at him helplessly, twisting his fingers nervously. Cokane throws down the pencil and leans back with ostentatious indifference*) Of course it is no business of mine: I only throw out the suggestion. Sartorius may be a retired burglar for all I know.

Sartorius and Blanche, ready for dinner, come from the hotel.

Tren. Sh! Here they come. Get the letter finished before dinner, like a good old chappie: I shall be awfully obliged to you.

Cok. (*Impatiently*) Leave me, leave me:

you disturb me. (*He waves him off and begins to write*)

Tren. (*Humbly and gratefully*) Yes, old chap. Thanks awfully. (*By this time Blanche has left her father and is strolling off toward the riverside. Sartorius comes down the garden, Baedeker in hand, and sits near Cokane, reading. Trench addresses him*) You won't mind my taking Blanche in to dinner, I hope, sir?

Sar. By all means, Dr. Trench. Pray do so.

He graciously waves him off to join Blanche. Trench hurries after her through the gate. The light reddens as the Rhenish sunset begins. Cokane, making wry faces in the agonies of composition, is disconcerted to find Sartorius' eye upon him.

Sar. I do not disturb you, I hope, Mr. Cokane.

Cok. By no means. Our friend Trench has entrusted me with a difficult and delicate task. He has requested me, as a friend of the family, to write to them on a subject that concerns you.

Sar. Indeed, Mr. Cokane. Well, the communication could not be in better hands.

Cok. (*With an air of modesty*) Ah, that is going too far, my dear sir, too far. Still, you see what Trench is. A capital fellow in his way, Mr. Sartorius, an excellent young fellow. But family communications like these require good manners. They require tact; and tact is Trench's weak point. He has an excellent heart, but no tact — none whatever. Everything depends on the way the matter is put to Lady Roxdale. But as to that, you may rely on me. I understand the sex.

Sar. Well, however she may receive it — and I care as little as any man, Mr. Cokane, how people may choose to receive me — I trust I may at least have the pleasure of seeing you sometimes at my house when we return to England.

Cok. (*Overwhelmed*) My d e a r sir! You express yourself in the true spirit of an English gentleman.

Sar. Not at all. You will always be most welcome. But I fear I have disturbed you in the composition of your letter. Pray resume it. I shall leave you to yourself. (*He pretends to rise, but checks himself to add*) Unless indeed I can assist you in any way? — by clearing up any point on which you are not informed, for instance; or even, if I may so far presume on my years, giving you the benefit of my experience as to the best way of wording the matter. (*Cokane looks a little surprised at this. Sartorius looks hard at him, and continues deliberately and meaningly*) I shall always be happy to

help any friend of Dr. Trench's, in a n y way, to the best of my ability and of my means.

Cok. My dear sir, you are really very good. Trench and I were putting our heads together over the letter just now; and there certainly were one or two points on which we were a little in the dark. (*Scrupulously*) But I would not permit Harry to question you. No. I pointed out to him that, as a matter of taste, it would be more delicate to wait until you volunteered the necessary information.

Sar. Hm! May I ask what you have said, so far?

Cok. "My dear Aunt Maria." That is, Trench's dear Aunt Maria, my friend Lady Roxdale. You understand that I am only drafting a letter for Trench to copy.

Sar. Quite so. Will you proceed; or would it help you if I were to suggest a word or two?

Cok. (*Effusively*) Your suggestions will be most valuable, my dear sir, most welcome.

Sar. I think I should begin in some such way as this. "In traveling with my friend Mr. Cokane up the Rhine —"

Cok. (*Murmuring as he writes*) Invaluable, invaluable. The very thing. "— my friend Mr. Cokane up the Rhine —"

Sar. "I have made the acquaintance of" — or you may say "picked up" or "come across," if you think that would suit your friend's style better. We must not be too formal.

Cok. "Picked up"! oh no: too dégagé, Mr. Sartorius, too dégagé. I should say, "had the privilege of becoming acquainted with."

Sar. (*Quickly*) By no means: Lady Roxdale must judge of that for herself. Let it stand as I said. "I have made the acquaintance of a young lady, the daughter of —" (*He hesitates*)

Cok. (*Writing*) "acquaintance of a young lady, the daughter of" — yes?

Sar. "of" — you had better say "a gentleman."

Cok. (*Surprised*) Of course.

Sar. (*With sudden passion*) It is not of course, sir. (*Cokane, startled, looks at him with dawning suspicion. Sartorius recovers himself somewhat shamefacedly*) Hm! "— of a gentleman of considerable wealth and position —"

Cok. (*Echoing him with a new note of coldness in his voice as he writes the last words*) "— and position."

Sar. "which, however, he has made entirely for himself." (*Cokane, now fully enlightened, stares at him instead of writing*) Have you written that?

Cok. (*Expanding into an attitude of pa-*

tronage and encouragement) Ah, indeed. Quite so, quite so. (*He writes*) "— entirely for himself." Just so. Proceed, Mr. Sartorius, proceed. Very clearly expressed.

Sar. "The young lady will inherit the bulk of her father's fortune, and will be liberally treated on her marriage. Her education has been of the most expensive and complete kind obtainable; and her surroundings have been characterized by the strictest refinement. She is in every essential particular —"

Cok. (*Interrupting*) Excuse the remark; but don't you think this is rather too much in the style of a prospectus of the young lady? I throw out the suggestion as a matter of taste.

Sar. (*Troubled*) Perhaps you are right. I am of course not dictating the exact words —

Cok. Of course not: of course not.

Sar. But I desire that there may be no wrong impression as to my daughter's — er — breeding. As to myself —

Cok. Oh, it will be sufficient to mention your profession, or pursuits, or — (*He pauses; and they look pretty hard at one another*)

Sar. (*Very deliberately*) My income, sir, is derived from the rental of a very extensive real estate in London. Lady Roxdale is one of the head landlords; and Dr. Trench holds a mortgage from which, if I mistake not, his entire income is derived. The truth is, Mr. Cokane, I am quite well acquainted with Dr. Trench's position and affairs; and I have long desired to know him personally.

Cok. (*Again obsequious, but still inquisitive*) What a remarkable coincidence! In what quarter is the estate situated, did you say?

Sar. In L o n d o n , sir. Its management occupies as much of my time as is not devoted to the ordinary pursuits of a gentleman. (*He rises and takes out his card case*) The rest I leave to your discretion. (*He puts a card upon the table*) That is my address at Surbiton. If it should unfortunately happen, Mr. Cokane, that this should end in a disappointment for Blanche, probably she would rather not see you afterwards. But if all turns out as we hope, Dr. Trench's best friends will then be our best friends.

Cok. (*Rising and confronting Sartorius confidently, pencil and paper in hand*) Rely on me, Mr. Sartorius. The letter is already finished h e r e (*Points to his brain*). In five minutes it will be finished t h e r e (*Points to the paper; nods to emphasize the assertion; and begins to pace up and down the garden, writing, and tapping his forehead from time to time as he goes, with every appearance of severe intellectual exertion*)

Sar. (*Calling through the gate after a glance at his watch*) Blanche.

Blanche. (*Replying in the distance*) Yes.

Sar. Time, my dear. (*He goes in to the table d'hôte*)

Blanche. (*Nearer*) Coming. (*She comes back through the gate, followed by Trench*)

Tren. (*In a half whisper, as Blanche goes towards the table d'hôte*) Blanche: stop — one moment. (*She stops*) We must be careful when your father is by. I had to promise him not to regard anything as settled until I hear from my people at home.

Blanche. (*Chilled*) Oh, I see. Your family may object to me; and then it will be all over between us. They are almost sure to.

Tren. (*Anxiously*) Don't say that, Blanche; it sounds as if you didn't care. I hope y o u regard it as settled. Y o u haven't made any promise, you know.

Blanche. (*Earnestly*) Yes, I have: I promised papa too. But I have broken my promise for your sake. I suppose I am not so conscientious as you. And if the matter is not to be regarded as settled, family or no family, promise or no promise, let us break it off here and now.

Tren. (*Intoxicated with affection*) Blanche: on my most sacred honour, family or no family, promise or no promise — (*The waiter reappears at the table d'hôte entrance, ringing his bell loudly*) Damn that noise!

Cok. (*As he comes to them, flourishing the letter*) Finished, dear boy, finished. Done to a turn, punctually to the second. C'est fini, mon cher garçon, c'est fini. (*Sartorius returns*)

Sar. Will you take Blanche in, Dr. Trench? (*Trench takes Blanche in to the table d'hôte*) Is the letter finished, Mr. Cokane?

Cok. (*With an author's pride, handing his draft to Sartorius*) There! (*Sartorius takes it, and reads it, nodding gravely over it with complete approval*)

Sar. (*Returning the draft*) Thank you, Mr. Cokane. You have the pen of a ready writer.

Cok. (*As they go in together*) Not at all, not at all. A little tact, Mr. Sartorius, a little knowledge of the world, a little experience of women —

The act drop descends and cuts off the rest of the speech.

End of the First Act.

ACT II.

In the library of a handsomely appointed villa at Surbiton on a sunny forenoon in September. Sartorius is busy at a writing table, littered with business letters, on the left. He sits facing the window, which is in the right wall. The fireplace, decorated for summer, is behind him. Between the table and the window Blanche, in her prettiest frock, sits reading "The Queen." The door, painted, like all the woodwork, in the blackest shade of red, with brass fittings, and moulded posts and pediment, is in the middle of the back wall. All the walls are lined with smartly tooled books, fitting into their places like bricks. A library ladder stands in the corner.

Sar. Blanche.

Blanche. Yes, papa.

Sar. I have some news here.

Blanche. What is it?

Sar. I mean news for you — from Trench.

Blanche. (*With affected indifference*) Indeed?

Sar. "Indeed?"! Is that all you have to say to me? Oh, very well. (*He resumes his work. Silence*)

Blanche. What do his people say, papa?

Sar. His people, I don't know. (*Still busy. Another pause*)

Blanche. What does he say?

Sar. He! He says nothing. (*He folds a lettter leisurely and looks for the envelope*) He prefers to communicate the result of his — where did I put that? — oh, here. Yes, he prefers to communicate the result in person.

Blanche. (*Springing up*) Oh, papa! When is he coming?

Sar. If he walks from the station, he may arrive in the course of the next half-hour. If he drives, he may be here any moment.

Blanche. (*Making hastily for the door*) Oh!

Sar. Blanche.

Blanche. Yes, papa.

Sar. You will of course not meet him until he has spoken to me.

Blanche. (*Hypocritically*) Of course not, papa. I shouldn't have thought of such a thing.

Sar. That is all. (*She is going, when he puts out his hand, and says with fatherly emotion*) My dear child. (*She responds by going over to kiss him. A tap at the door*) Come in.

Lickcheese enters, carrying a black hand-bag. He is a shabby, needy man, with dirty face and linen, scrubby beard and whiskers, going bald. A nervous, wiry, pertinacious sort of human terrier judged by his mouth and eyes, but miserably apprehensive and servile before Sartorius.

He bids Blanche "Good morning, miss"; and she passes out with a slight and contemptuous recognition of him.

Lick. Good morning, sir.

Sar. (*Harsh and peremptory*) Good morning.

Lick. (*Taking a little sack of money from his bag*) Not much this morning, sir. I have just had the honour of making Dr. Trench's acquaintance, sir.

Sar. (*Looking up from his writing, displeased*) Indeed?

Lick. Yes, sir. Dr. Trench asked his way of me, and was kind enough to drive me from the station.

Sar. Where is he, then?

Lick. I left him in the hall, with his friend, sir. I should think he is speaking to Miss Sartorius.

Sar. Hm! What do you mean by his friend?

Lick. There is a Mr. Cokane with him, sir.

Sar. I see you have been talking to him, eh?

Lick. As we drove along: yes, sir.

Sar. (*Sharply*) Why did you not come by the nine o'clock train?

Lick. I thought —

Sar. It cannot be helped now; so never mind what you thought. But do not put off my business again to the last moment. Has there been any further trouble about the St. Giles' property?

Lick. The Sanitary Inspector has been complaining again about number 13 Robbins's Row. He says he'll bring it before the vestry.

Sar. Did you tell him that I am on the vestry?

Lick. Yes, sir.

Sar. What did he say to that?

Lick. Said he supposed so. or you wouldn't dare to break the law so scand'lous. I only tell you what he said.

Sar. Hm! Do you know his name?

Lick. Yes, sir. Speakman.

Sar. Write it down in the diary for the day of the next vestry meeting. I will teach Mr. Speakman his duty — his duty to members of the vestry.

Lick. (*Doubtfully*) The vestry can't dismiss him, sir. He's under the Local Government Board.

Sar. I did not ask you that. Let me see the books. (*Lickcheese produces the rent book, and hands it to Sartorius; then makes the desired entry in the diary on the table, watching Sartorius with misgiving as the rent book is examined. Sartorius frowns and rises*) £1 : 4s. for repairs to No. 13. What does this mean?

Lick. Well, sir, it was the staircase on the third floor. It was downright dangerous: there weren't but three whole steps in it, and no handrail. I thought it best to have a few boards put in.

Sar. Boards! Firewood, sir, firewood! They will burn every stick of it. You have spent twenty-four shillings of my money on firewood for them.

Lick. There ought to be stone stairs, sir: it would be a saving in the long run. The clergyman says —

Sar. What! who says?

Lick. The clergyman, sir, only the clergyman. Not that I make much account of him; but if you knew how he has worried me over that staircase —

Sar. I am an Englishman; and I will suffer no clergyman to interfere in my business. (*He turns suddenly on Lickcheese*) Now look here, Mr. Lickcheese! This is the third time this year that you have brought me a bill of over a pound for repairs. I have warned you repeatedly against dealing with these tenement houses as if they were mansions in a West-end square. I have had occasion to warn you too against discussing my affairs with strangers. You have chosen to disregard my wishes. You are discharged.

Lick. (*Dismayed*) Oh, sir, don't say that.

Sar. (*Fiercely*) You are discharged.

Lick. Well, Mr. Sartorius, it is hard, so it is. No man alive could have screwed more out of them poor destitute devils for you than I have, or spent less in doing it. I have dirtied my hands at it until they're not fit for clean work hardly; and now you turn me —

Sar. (*Interrupting him menacingly*) What do you mean by dirtying your hands? If I find that you have stepped an inch outside the letter of the law, Mr. Lickcheese, I will prosecute you myself. The way to keep your hands clean is to gain the confidence of your employers. You will do well to bear that in mind in your next situation.

The Parlour Maid. (*Opening the door*) Mr. Trench and Mr. Cokane.

Cokane and Trench come in, Trench festively dressed and in the highest spirits, Cokane highly self-satisfied.

Sar. How do you do, Dr. Trench? Good morning Mr. Cokane. I am pleased to see you here. Mr. Lickcheese, you will place your accounts and money on the table: I will examine them and settle with you presently. (*Lickcheese retires to the table, and begins to arrange his accounts, greatly depressed*)

Tren. (*Glancing at Lickcheese*) I hope we're not in the way.

Sar. By no means. Sit down, pray. I fear you have been kept waiting.

Tren. (*Taking Blanche's chair*) Not at all. We've only just come in. (*He takes out a packet of letters and begins untying them*)

Cok. (*Going to a chair nearer the window, but stopping to look admiringly round before sitting down*) You must be happy here with all these books, Mr. Sartorius. A literary atmosphere.

Sar. (*Resuming his seat*) I have not looked into them. They are pleasant for Blanche occasionally when she wishes to read. I chose the house because it is on gravel. The death rate is very low.

Tren. (*Triumphantly*) I have any amount of letters for you. All my people are delighted that I am going to settle. Aunt Maria wants Blanche to be married from her house. (*He hands Sartorius a letter*)

Sar. Aunt Maria!

Cok. Lady Roxdale, my dear sir: he means Lady Roxdale. Do express yourself with a little more tact, my dear fellow.

Tren. Lady Roxdale, of course. Uncle Harry —

Cok. Sir Harry Trench. His godfather, my dear sir, his godfather.

Tren. Just so. The pleasantest fellow for his age you ever met. He offers us his house at St. Andrews for a couple of months, if we care to pass our honeymoon there. (*Handing Sartorius another letter*) It's the sort of house nobody can live in, you know; but it's a nice thing for him to offer. Don't you think so?

Sar. (*Preoccupied with the letters*) No doubt. These seem very gratifying, Dr. Trench.

Tren. Yes; aren't they? Aunt Maria has really behaved like a brick. If you read the postscript you'll see she spotted Cokane's hand in my letter. (*Chuckling*) He wrote it for me.

Sar. (*Glancing at Cokane*) Indeed? Mr. Cokane evidently did it with great tact.

Cok. (*Returning the glance*) Don't mention it.

Tren. (*Buoyantly*). Well, what do you say now, Mr. Sartorius? May we regard the matter as settled at last!

Sar. Quite settled. (*He rises and offers his hand. Trench, glowing with gratitude, rises and shakes it vehemently, unable to find words for his feelings*)

Cok. (*Coming between them*) Allow me to congratulate you both. (*Shakes hands with the two at the same time*)

Sar. And now, gentlemen, I have a word to say to my daughter. Dr. Trench, you will not, I hope, grudge me the pleasure of breaking this news to her: I have had to disappoint her more than once since I last saw you. Will you excuse me for ten minutes?

Cok. (*In a flush of friendly protest*) My dear sir, can you ask?

Tren. Certainly.

Sar. Thank you. (*He goes out*)

Tren. (*Still chuckling*) He won't have any news to break, poor old boy: she's seen all the letters already.

Cok. I must say your behaviour has been far from straightforward, Harry. You have been carrying on a clandestine correspondence.

Lick. (*Stealthily*) Gentlemen —

Tren., Cok. (*Turning — they had forgotten his presence*) Hallo!

Lick. (*Coming between them very humbly, but in mortal anxiety and haste*) Look here, gentlemen. (*To Trench*) You, sir, I address myself to more partic'lar. Will you say a word in my favour to the guv'nor? He's just given me the sack; and I have four children looking to me for their bread. A word from you sir, on this happy day, might get him to take me on again.

Tren. (*Embarrassed*) Well, you see, Mr. Lickcheese, I don't see how I can interfere. I'm very sorry, of course.

Cok. Certainly you cannot interfere. It would be in the most execrable taste.

Lick. Oh, gentlemen, you are young; and you don't know what loss of employment means to the like of me. What harm would it do you to help a poor man? Just listen to the circumstances, sir. I only —

Tren. (*Moved but snatching at an excuse for taking a high tone in avoiding the unpleasantness of helping him*) No: I had rather not. Excuse my saying plainly that I think Mr. Sartorius is not a man to act hastily or harshly. I have always found him very fair and generous; and I believe he is a better judge of the circumstances than I am.

Cok. (*Inquisitive*) I think you ought to hear the circumstances, Harry. It can do no harm. Hear the circumstances by all means.

Lick. Never mind, sir: it ain't any use. When I hear that man called generous and fair! — well, never mind.

Tren. (*Severely*) If you wish me to do anything for you, Mr. Lickcheese, let me tell you that you are not going the right way about it in speaking ill of Mr. Sartorius.

Lick. Have I said one word against him, sir? I leave it to your friend: have I said a word?

Cok. True, true. Quite true. Harry: be just.

Lick. Mark my words, gentlemen: he'll find what a man he's lost the very first week's rents the new man'll bring him. You'll find the difference yourself, Dr. Trench, if you or your children come into the property. I have got money when no other collector alive would have wrung it out. And this is the thanks I get for it! Why, see here, gentlemen! Look at that bag of money on the table. Hardly a penny of that but there was a hungry child crying for the bread it would have bought. But I got it for him — screwed and worried and bullied it out of them. I — look here, gentlemen: I'm pretty well seasoned to the work; but there's money there that I couldn't have taken if it hadn't been for the thought of my own children depending on me for giving him satisfaction. And because I charged him four-and-twenty shillin' to mend a staircase that three women have been hurt on, and that would have got him prosecuted for manslaughter if it had been let go much longer, he gives me the sack. Wouldn't listen to a word, though I would have offered to make up the money out of my own pocket — aye, and am willing to do it still if you will only put in a word for me, sir.

Tren. (*Aghast*) You took money that ought to have fed starving children! Serve you right! If I had been the father of one of those children, I'd have given you something worse than the sack. I wouldn't say a word to save your soul, if you have such a thing. Mr. Sartorius was quite right.

Lick. (*Staring at him, surprised into contemptuous amusement in the midst of his anxiety*) Just listen to this! Well, you are an innocent young gentleman. Do you suppose he sacked me because I was too hard? Not a bit of it: it was because I wasn't hard enough. I never heard him say he was satisfied yet — no, nor he wouldn't, not if I skinned 'em alive. I don't say he's the worst landlord in London: he couldn't be worse than some; but he's no better than the worst I ever had to do with. And, though I say it, I'm better than the best collector he ever done business with. I have screwed more and spent less on his properties than any one would believe that knows what such properties are. I know my merits, Dr. Trench, and will speak for myself if no one else will.

Tren. What sort of properties? Houses?

Lick. Tenement houses, let from week to week by the room or half-room — aye, or quarter-room — It pays when you know how to work it, sir. Nothing like it. It's been calculated on the cubic foot of space, sir, that you can get higher rents letting by the room than you can for a mansion in Park Lane.

Tren. I hope Mr. Sartorius hasn't much of that sort of property, however it may pay.

Lick. He has nothing else, sir; and he shows his sense in it too. Every few hundred pounds he could scrape together he bought old houses with — houses that you wouldn't hardly look at without holding your nose. He has 'em in St. Giles's: he has 'em in Marylebone: he has 'em in Bethnal Green. Just look how he lives himself, and you'll see the good of it to him. He likes a low death rate and a gravel soil for himself, he does. You come down with me to Robbins's Row; and I'll show you a soil and a death rate, so I will! And, mind you, it's me that makes it pay him so well. Catch him going down to collect his own rents! Not likely!

Tren. Do you mean to say that all his property — a l l his means — come from this sort of thing?

Lick. Every penny of it, sir. (*Trench, overwhelmed, has to sit down*)

Cok. (*Looking compassionately at him*) Ah, my dear fellow, the love of money is the root of all evil.

Lick. Yes, sir; and we'd all like to have the tree growing in our garden.

Cok. (*Revolted*) Mr. Lickcheese, I did not address myself to you. I do not wish to be severe with you; but there is something peculiarly repugnant to my feelings in the calling of a rent collector.

Lick. It's no worse than many another. I have my children looking to me.

Cok. True: I admit it. So has our friend Sartorius. His affection for his daughter is a redeeming point — a redeeming point, certainly.

Lick. She's a lucky daughter, sir. Many another daughter has been turned out upon the streets to gratify his affection for her. That's what business is, sir, you see. Come sir, I think your friend will say a word for me now he knows I'm not in fault.

Tren. (*Rising angrily*) I will not. It's a damnable business from beginning to end; and you deserve no better luck for helping in it. I've seen it all among the out-patients at the hospital; and it used to make my blood boil to think that such things couldn't be prevented.

Lick. (*His suppressed spleen breaking out*) Oh indeed, sir. But I suppose you will take your share when you marry Miss Blanche, all the same. (*Furiously*) Which of us is the worse, I should like to know — me that

wrings the money out to keep a home over my children, or you that spend it and try to shove the blame on to me?

Cok. A most improper observation to address to a gentleman, Mr. Lickcheese. A most revolutionary sentiment.

Lick. Perhaps so. But then, Robbins's Row ain't a school for manners. You collect a week or two there — you're welcome to my place if I can't keep it for myself — and you'll hear a little plain speaking, so you will.

Cok. (*With dignity*) Do you know to whom you are speaking, my good man?

Lick. (*Recklessly*) I know well enough who I'm speaking to. What do I care for you, or a thousand such? I'm poor; that's enough to make a rascal of me. No consideration for me — nothing to be got by saying a word for me! (*Suddenly cringing to Trench*) Just a word, sir. It would cost you nothing. (*Sartorius appears at the door unobserved*) Have some feeling for the poor.

Tren. I'm afraid you have shown very little, by your own confession.

Lick. (*Breaking out again*) More than your precious father-in-law, anyhow. I — (*Sartorius's voice, striking in with deadly calmness, paralyzes him*)

Sar. You will come here to-morrow not later than ten, Mr. Lickcheese, to conclude our business. I shall trouble you no further to-day.

> *Lickcheese, cowed, goes out amid dead silence. Sartorius continues, after an awkward pause.*

He is one of my agents, or rather was; for I have unfortunately had to dismiss him for repeatedly disregarding my instructions. (*Trench says nothing. Sartorius throws off his embarrassment, and assumes a jocose, rallying air, unbecoming to him under any circumstances, and just now almost unbearably jarring*) Blanche will be down presently, Harry (*Trench recoils*) — I suppose I must call you Harry now. What do you say to a stroll through the garden, Mr. Cokane? We are celebrated here for our flowers.

Cok. Charmed, my dear sir, charmed. Life here is an idyll — a perfect idyll. We were just dwelling on it.

Sar. (*Slyly*) Harry can follow with Blanche. She will be down directly.

Tren. (*Hastily*) No. I can't face her just now.

Sar. (*Rallying him*) Indeed! Ha, ha! (*The laugh, the first they have heard from him, sets Trench's teeth on edge. Cokane is taken aback, but instantly recovers himself*)

Cok. Ha! ha! ha! Ho! ho! —

Tren. But you don't understand.

Sar. Oh, I think we do, I think we do. Eh, Mr. Cokane? Ha! ha!

Cok. I should think we do. Ha! ha! ha!

> *They go out together, laughing at him. He collapses into a chair, shuddering in every nerve.*

Blanche appears at the door. Her face lights up when she sees that he is alone. She trips noiselessly to the back of his chair and clasps her hands over his eyes. With a convulsive start and exclamation he springs up and breaks away from her.

Blanche. (*Astonished*) Harry!

Tren. (*With distracted politeness*) I beg your pardon, I was thinking — won't you sit down.

Blanche. (*Looking suspiciously at him*) Is anything the matter? (*She sits down slowly near the writing table. He takes Cokane's chair*)

Tren. No. Oh no.

Blanche. Papa has not been disagreeable, I hope.

Tren. No: I have hardly spoken to him since I was with you. (*He rises; takes up his chair; and plants it beside hers. This pleases her better. She looks at him with her most winning smile. A sort of sob breaks from him; and he catches her hands and kisses them passionately. Then, looking into her eyes with intense earnestness, he says*) Blanche: are you fond of money?

Blanche. (*Gaily*) Very. Are you going to give me any?

Tren. (*Wincing*) Don't make a joke of it: I'm serious. Do you know that we shall be very poor?

Blanche. Is that what made you look as if you had neuralgia?

Tren. (*Pleadingly*) My dear: it's no laughing matter. Do you know that I have a bare seven hundred a year to live on?

Blanche. How dreadful!

Tren. Blanche: it's very serious indeed: I assure you it is.

Blanche. It would keep me rather short in my housekeeping, dearest boy, if I had nothing of my own. But papa has promised me that I shall be richer than ever when we are married.

Tren. We must do the best we can with seven hundred. I think we ought to be self-supporting.

Blanche. That's just what I mean to be, Harry. If I were to eat up half your £700, I should be making you twice as poor; but I am going to make you twice as rich instead. (*He shakes his head*) Has papa made any difficulty?

Tren. (*Rising with a sigh and taking his chair back to its former place*) No, none at all. (*He sits down dejectedly. When Blanche speaks again her face and voice betray the beginning of a struggle with her temper*)

Blanche. Harry, are you too proud to take money from my father!

Tren. Yes, Blanche: I am too proud.

Blanche. (*After a pause*) That is not nice to me, Harry.

Tren. You must bear with me Blanche. I — I can't explain. After all, it's very natural.

Blanche. Has it occurred to you that I may be proud, too?

Tren. Oh, that's nonsense. No one will accuse y o u of marrying for money.

Blanche. No one would think the worse of me if I did, or of you either. (*She rises and begins to walk restlessly about*) We really cannot live on seven hundred a year, Harry; and I don't think it quite fair of you to ask me merely because you are afraid of people talking.

Tren. It is not that alone, Blanche.

Blanche. What else is it, then?

Tren. Nothing. I —

Blanche. (*Getting behind him, and speaking with forced playfulness as she bends over him, her hands on his shoulders*) Of course it's nothing. Now don't be absurd, Harry: be good; and listen to me: I know how to settle it. You are too proud to owe anything to me; and I am too proud to owe anything to you. You have seven hundred a year. Well, I will take just seven hundred a year from papa at first; and then we shall be quits. Now, now, Harry, you know you have not a word to say against that.

Tren. It's impossible.

Blanche. Impossible!

Tren. Yes, impossible. I have resolved not to take any money from your father.

Blanche. But he will give the money to me: not to you.

Tren. It's the same thing. (*With an effort to be sentimental*) I love you too well to see any distinction. (*He puts up his hand half-heartedly: she takes it over his shoulder with equal indecision. They are both trying hard to conciliate one another*)

Blanche. That's a very nice way of putting it, Harry; but I am sure there is something I ought to know. H a s papa been disagreeable?

Tren. No: he has been very kind — to me, at least. It's not that. It's nothing you can guess, Blanche. It would only pain you — perhaps offend you. I don't mean, of course, that we shall live always on seven hundred a year. I intend to go at my profession in earnest, and work my fingers to the bone.

Blanche. (*Playing with his fingers, still over his shoulder*) But I shouldn't like you with your fingers worked to the bone, Harry. I must be told what the matter is. (*He takes his hand quickly away; she flushes angrily; and her voice is no longer even an imitation of the voice of a lady as she exclaims*) I hate secrets; and I don't like to be treated as if I were a child.

Tren. (*Annoyed by her tone*) There's nothing to tell. I don't choose to trespass on your father's generosity: that's all.

Blanche. You had no objection half an hour ago, when you met me in the hall, and showed me all the letters. Your family doesn't object. Do y o u object?

Tren. (*Earnestly*) I do not indeed. It's only a question of money.

Blanche. (*Imploringly, the voice softening and refining for the last time*) Harry: there's no use in our fencing in this way. Papa will never consent to my being absolutely dependent on you; and I don't like the idea of it myself. If you even mention such a thing to him you will break off the match: you will indeed.

Tren. (*Obstinately*) I can't help that.

Blanche. (*White with rage*) You can't help —! Oh, I'm beginning to understand. I will save you the trouble. You can tell papa that *I* have broken off the match; and then there will be no further difficulty.

Tren. (*Taken aback*) What do you mean, Blanche? Are you offended?

Blanche. Offended! How dare you ask me?

Tren. Dare!

Blanche. How much more manly it would have been to confess that you were trifling with me that time on the Rhine! Why did you come here to-day? Why did you write to your people?

Tren. Well, Blanche, if you are going to lose your temper —

Blanche. That's no answer. You depended on your family to get you out of your engagement; and they did not object: they were only too glad to be rid of you. You were not mean enough to stay away, and not manly enough to tell the truth. You thought you could provoke m e to break the engagement: that is so like a man — to try and put the woman in the wrong. Well, you have your way: I release you. I wish you had opened my eyes by downright brutality — by striking me — by anything rather than shuffling as you have done.

Tren. (*Hotly*) Shuffle! If I had thought you capable of turning on me like this, I should never have spoken to you. I have a good mind never to speak to you again.

Blanche. You shall not — not ever. I will take care of that. (*Going to the door*)

Tren. (*Alarmed*) What are you going to do?

Blanche. To get your letters — your false letters, and your presents — your hateful presents, to return them to you. I am very glad it is all broken off; and if —

As she puts her hand to the door it is opened from without by Sartorius, who enters and shuts it behind him.

Sar. (*Interrupting her severely*) Hush, pray, Blanche: you are forgetting yourself: you can be heard all over the house. What is the matter?

Blanche. (*Too angry to care whether she is overheard or not*) You had better ask h i m . He has some excuse about money.

Sar. Excuse! Excuse for what?

Blanche. For throwing me over.

Tren. (*Vehemently*) I declare I never —

Blanche. (*Interrupting him still more vehemently*) You did. You did. You are doing nothing else — (*Trench begins repeating his contradiction and she her assertion; so that they both speak angrily together*)

Sar. (*In desperation at the noise*) Silence. (*Still more formidably*) Silence. (*They obey. He proceeds firmly*) Blanche, you must control your temper: I will not have these repeated scenes within hearing of the servants. Dr. Trench will answer for himself to me. You had better leave us. (*He opens the door, and calls*) Mr. Cokane, will you kindly join us here.

Cok. (*In the conservatory*) Coming, my dear sir, coming. (*He appears at the door*)

Blanche. I am sure I have no wish to stay. I hope I shall find you alone when I come back.

An inarticulate exclamation bursts from Trench. She goes out, passing Cokane resentfully. He looks after her in surprise; then looks questioningly at the two men. Sartorius shuts the door with an angry stroke, and turns to Trench.

Sar. (*Aggressively*) Sir —

Tren. (*Interrupting him more aggressively*) Well, sir!

Cok. (*Getting between them*) Gently, dear boy, gently. Suavity, Harry, suavity.

Sar. (*Mastering himself*) If you have anything to say to me, Dr. Trench, I will listen to you patiently. You will then allow me to say what I have to say on my part.

Tren. (*Ashamed*) I beg your pardon. Of course, yes. Fire away.

Sar. May I take it that you have refused to fulfil your engagement with my daughter?

Tren. Certainly not: your daughter has refused to fulfil her engagement with me. But the match is broken off, if that is what you mean.

Sar. Dr. Trench: I will be plain with you. I know that Blanche has a strong temper. It is part of her strong character and her physical courage, which is greater than that of most men, I can assure you. You must be prepared for that. If this quarrel is only Blanche's temper you may take my word for it that it will be over before to-morrow. But I understood from what she said just now that you have made some difficulty on the score of money.

Tren. (*With renewed excitement*) It was Miss Sartorius who made that difficulty. I shouldn't have minded that so much, if it hadn't been for the things she said. She showed that she doesn't care t h a t (*Snapping his fingers*) for me.

Cok. (*Soothingly*) Dear boy —

Tren. Hold your tongue, Billy: it's enough to make a man wish he'd never seen a woman. Look here, Mr. Sartorius: I put the matter to her as delicately and considerately as possible, never mentioning a word of my reasons, but just asking her to be content to live on my own little income; and yet she turned on me as if I had behaved like a savage.

Sar. Live on your income! Impossible: my daughter is accustomed to a proper establishment. Did I not expressly undertake to provide for that? Did she not tell you I promised her to do so?

Tren. Yes, I know all about that, Mr. Sartorius; and I'm greatly obliged to you; but I'd rather not take anything from you except Blanche herself.

Sar. And why did you not say so before?

Tren. No matter why. Let us drop the subject.

Sar. No matter! But it d o e s matter, sir. I insist on an answer. Why did you not say so before?

Tren. I didn't know before.

Sar. (*Provoked*) Then you ought to have known your own mind before entering into such a very serious engagement. (*He flings angrily away across the room and back*)

Tren. (*Much injured*) I o u g h t to have known. Cokane: is this reasonable? (*Cokane's features are contorted by an air of judicial consideration; but he says nothing; and Trench, again addressing Sartorius, but with a marked diminution of respect, continues*) How the deuce could I have known? You didn't tell me.

Sar. You are trifling with me, sir. You say that you did not know your own mind before.

Tren. I say nothing of the sort. I say that I did not know where your money came from before.

Sar. That is not true, sir. I —

Cok. Gently, my dear sir. Gently, Harry, dear boy. Suaviter in modo: fort —

Tren. Let him begin, then. What does he mean by attacking me in this fashion?

Sar. Mr. Cokane: you will bear me out. I was explicit on the point. I said I was a self-made man; and I am not ashamed of it.

Tren. You are nothing of the sort. I found out this morning from your man — Lickcheese, or whatever his confounded name is — that your fortune has been made out of a parcel of unfortunate creatures that have hardly enough to keep body and soul together — made by screwing, and bullying, and driving, and all sorts of pettifogging tyranny.

Sar. (*Outraged*) Sir! (*They confront one another threateningly*)

Cok. (*Softly*) Rent must be paid, dear boy. It is inevitable, Harry, inevitable. (*Trench turns away petulantly. Sartorius looks after him reflectively for a moment; then resumes his former deliberate and dignified manner, and addresses Trench with studied consideration, but with a perceptible condescension to his youth and folly*)

Sar. I am afraid, Dr. Trench, that you are a very young hand at business; and I am sorry I forgot that for a moment or so. May I ask you to suspend your judgment until we have a little quiet discussion of this sentimental notion of yours? — if you will excuse me for calling it so. (*He takes a chair, and motions Trench to another on his right*)

Cok. Very nicely put, my dear sir. Come, Harry, sit down and listen; and consider the matter calmly and judicially. Don't be headstrong.

Tren. I have no objection to sit down and listen; but I don't see how that can make black white; and I am tired of being turned on as if I were in the wrong. (*He sits down. Cokane sits at his elbow, on his right. They compose themselves for a conference*)

Sar. I assume, to begin with, Dr. Trench, that you are not a Socialist, or anything of that sort.

Tren. Certainly not. I am a Conservative — at least, if I ever took the trouble to vote, I should vote for the Conservative and against the other fellow.

Cok. True blue, Harry, true blue!

Sar. I am glad to find that so far we are in perfect sympathy. I am, of course, a Conservative; not a narrow or prejudiced one, I hope, nor at all opposed to true progress, but still a sound Conservative. As to Lickcheese, I need say no more about him than that I have dismissed him from my service this morning for a breach of trust; and you will hardly accept his testimony as friendly or disinterested. As to my business. it is simply to provide homes suited to the small means of very poor people, who require roofs to shelter them just like other people. Do you suppose I can keep up these roofs for nothing!

Tren. Yes: that is all very fine; but the point is, what sort of homes do you give them for their money? People must live somewhere, or else go to jail. Advantage is taken of that to make them pay for houses that are not fit for dogs. Why don't you build proper dwellings, and give fair value for the money you take?

Sar. (*Pitying his innocence*) My young friend, these poor people do not know how to live in proper dwellings: they would wreck them in a week. You doubt me: try it for yourself. You are welcome to replace all the missing banisters, handrails, cistern lids and dusthole tops at your own expense; and you will find them missing again in less than three days — burnt, sir, every stick of them. I do not blame the poor creatures: they need fires, and often have no other way of getting them. But I really cannot spend pound after pound in repairs for them to pull down, when I can barely get them to pay me four and sixpence a week for a room, which is the recognized fair London rent. No, gentlemen: when people are very poor, you c a n n o t help them, no matter how much you may sympathize with them. It does them more harm than good in the long run. I prefer to save my money in order to provide additional houses for the homeless, and to lay by a little for Blanche. (*He looks at them. They are silent: Trench unconvinced, but talked down; Cokane humanely perplexed. Sartorius bends his brows; comes forward in his chair as if gathering himself together for a spring; and addresses himself, with impressive significance, to Trench*) And now, Dr. Trench, may I ask what y o u r income is derived from!

Tren. (*Defiantly*) From interest — not from houses. My hands are clean as far as that goes. Interest on a mortgage.

Sar. (*Forcibly*) Yes: a mortgage on m y property. When I, to use your own words, screw, and bully, and drive these people to pay what they have freely undertaken to pay me, I cannot touch one penny of the money they give me until I have first paid you your £700 out of it. What Lickcheese did for me, I do for you. He and I are alike intermediaries: y o u are the principal. It is because of the risks I run through the poverty of my tenants that you exact interest from me at the monstrous and exorbitant rate of seven per cent, forcing me to exact the uttermost farthing in my turn from the tenants. And yet, Dr. Trench, you have not hesitated to speak contemptuously of me because I have applied my industry and forethought to the management of o u r property, and am maintaining it by the same honourable means.

Cok. (*Greatly relieved*) Admirable, my dear sir, excellent! I felt instinctively that Trench was talking unpractical nonsense. Let us drop the subject, my dear boy: you only make an ass of yourself when you meddle in business matters. I told you it was inevitable.

Tren. (*Dazed*) Do you mean to say that I am just as bad as you are?

Cok. Shame, Harry, shame! Grossly bad taste! Be a gentleman. Apologize.

Sar. Allow me, Mr. Cokane. (*To Trench*) If, when you say you are just as bad as I am, you mean that you are just as powerless to alter the state of society, then you are unfortunately quite right. (*Trench does not at once reply. He stares at Sartorius, and then hangs his head and gazes stupidly at the floor, morally beggared, with his clasped knuckles between his knees, a living picture of disillusion. Cokane comes sympathetically to him and puts an encouraging hand on his shoulder*)

Cok. (*Gently*) Come, Harry, come! Pull yourself together. You owe a word to Mr. Sartorius.

Tren. (*Still stupefied, slowly unlaces his fingers; puts his hands on his knees, and lifts himself upright; pulls his waistcoat straight with a tug; and turns to Sartorius with an attempt to take his disenchantment philosophically*) Well, people who live in glass houses have no right to throw stones. But, on my honour, I never knew that my house was a glass one until you pointed it out. I beg your pardon. (*He offers his hand*)

Sar. Say no more, Harry: your feelings do you credit: I assure you I feel exactly as you do, myself. Every man who has a heart must wish that a better state of things was practicable. But unhappily it is not.

Tren. (*A little consoled*) I suppose not.

Cok. Not a doubt of it, my dear sir; not a doubt of it. The increase of the population is at the bottom of it all.

Sar. (*To Trench*) I trust I have convinced you that you need no more object to Blanche sharing my fortune, than I need object to her sharing yours.

Tren. (*With dull wistfulness*) It seems so. We're all in the same swim, it appears. I hope you will excuse my making such a fuss.

Sar. Not another word. In fact, I thank you for refraining from explaining the nature of your scruples to Blanche: I admire that in you, Harry. Perhaps it will be as well to leave her in ignorance.

Tren. (*Anxiously*) But I must explain now. You saw how angry she was.

Sar. You had better leave that to me. (*He looks at his watch, and rings the bell*) Lunch is nearly due: while you are getting ready for it I can see Blanche; and I hope the result will be quite satisfactory to us all. (*The parlour maid answers the bell; he addresses her with his habitual peremptoriness*) Tell Miss Blanche I want her.

Maid. (*Her face falling expressively*) Yes, sir. (*She turns reluctantly to go*)

Sar. (*On second thoughts*) Stop. (*She stops*) My love to Miss Blanche: and I am alone here and would like to see her for a moment if she is not busy.

Maid. (*Relieved*) Yes, sir. (*She goes out*)

Sar. I will show you your room, Harry. I hope you will soon be perfectly at home in it. You also, Mr. Cokane, must learn your way about here. Let us go before Blanche comes. (*He leads the way to the door*)

Cok. (*Cheerily, following him*) Our little discussion has given me quite an appetite.

Tren. (*Moodily*) It has taken mine away.

> They go out, Sartorius holding the door for them. He is following when the parlour maid reappears. She is a snivelling, sympathetic creature, and is on the verge of tears.

Sar. Well, is Miss Blanche coming?

Maid. Yes, sir. I think so, sir.

Sar. Wait here until she comes; and tell her that I will be back in a moment.

Maid. Yes, sir. (*She comes into the room. Sartorius looks suspiciously at her as she passes him. He half closes the door and follows her*)

Sar. (*Lowering his voice*) What is the matter with you?

Maid. (*Whimpering*) Nothing, sir.

Sar. (*At the same pitch, more menacingly*) Take care how you behave yourself when there are visitors present. Do you hear?

Maid. Yes, sir. (*Sartorius goes out*)

Sar. (*Outside*) Excuse me: I had a word to say to the servant.

> Trench is heard replying, "Not at all," Cokane "Don't mention it, my dear sir." The murmur of their voices passes out of hearing. The parlour maid sniffs; dries her eyes; goes to one of the bookcases; and takes some brown paper and a ball of string from a drawer. She puts them on the table and wrestles with another sob. Blanche comes in, with a jewel box in her hands. Her expression is that of a strong and determined woman in an intense passion. The maid looks at her with a mixture of abject wounded affection and bodily terror.

Blanche. (*Looking around*) Where's my father?

Maid. (*Tremulously propitiatory*) He left word he'd be back directly, miss. I'm sure he won't be long. Here's the paper and string all ready, miss. (*She spreads the paper on the table*) Can I do the parcel for you, miss?

Blanche. No. Mind your own business. (*She empties the box on the sheet of brown paper. It contains a packet of letters, a ring, and a set of gold bangles. At sight of them she has a paroxysm of passion, which she relieves by dashing the box to the floor. The maid submissively picks it up and puts it on the table, again sniffing and drying her eyes*) What are you crying for?

Maid. (*Plaintively*) You speak so brutal to me, Miss Blanche; and I do love you so. I'm sure no one else would stay and put up with what I have to put up with.

Blanche. Then go. I don't want you. Do you hear. Go.

Maid. (*Piteously, falling on her knees*) Oh no, Miss Blanche. Don't send me away from you: don't —

Blanche. (*With fierce disgust*) Agh! I hate the sight of you. (*The maid, wounded to the heart, cries bitterly*) Hold your tongue. Are those two gentlemen gone?

Maid. (*Weeping*) Oh, how could you say such a thing to me, Miss Blanche — me that —

Blanche. (*Seizing her by the hair and throat*) Stop that noise, I tell you, unless you want me to kill you.

Maid. (*Protesting and imploring, but in a carefully subdued voice*) Let me go, Miss Blanche: you know you'll be sorry: you always are. Remember how dreadfully my head was cut last time.

Blanche. (*Raging*) Answer me, will you? Have they gone?

Maid. Lickcheese has gone, looking dreadf— (*She breaks off with a stifled cry as Blanche's fingers tighten furiously on her*)

Blanche. Did I ask you about Lickcheese?

You beast: you know who I mean: you're doing it on purpose.

Maid. (*In a gasp*) They're staying to lunch.

Blanche. (*Looking intently into her face*) He? —

Maid. (*Whispering with a sympathetic nod*) Yes, miss. (*Blanche slowly releases her and stands upright with clenched fists and set face. The parlour maid, recognizing the passing of the crisis of passion and fearing no further violence, sits discomfitedly on her heels, and tries to arrange her hair and cap, whimpering a little with exhaustion and soreness*) Now you've set my hands all trembling; and I shall jingle the things on the tray at lunch so that everybody will notice me. It's too bad of you, Miss Bl— (*Sartorius coughs outside*)

Blanche. (*Quickly*) Sh! Get up.

The parlour maid hastily gets up, and goes out as demurely as she can, passing Sartorius on her way to the door. He glances sternly at her and comes to Blanche. The parlour maid shuts the door softly behind her.

Sar. (*Mournfully*) My dear: can you not make a little better fight with your temper?

Blanche. (*Panting with the subsidence of her fit*) No, I can't. I won't. I do my best. Nobody who really cares for me gives me up because of my temper. I never show my temper to any of the servants but that girl; and she is the only one that will stay with us.

Sar. But, my dear, remember that we have to meet our visitors at luncheon presently. I have run down before them to say that I have arranged that little difficulty with Trench. It was only a piece of mischief made by Lickcheese. Trench is a young fool; but it is all right now.

Blanche. I don't want to marry a fool.

Sar. Then you will have to take a husband over thirty, Blanche. You must not expect too much, my child. You will be richer than your husband, and, I think, cleverer too. I am better pleased that it should be so.

Blanche. (*Seizing his arm*) Papa.

Sar. Yes, my dear.

Blanche. May I do as I like about this marriage; or must I do as you like?

Sar. (*Uneasily*) Blanche —

Blanche. No, papa; you m u s t answer me.

Sar. (*Abandoning his self-control, and giving way recklessly to his affection for her*) You shall do as you like now and always, my beloved child. I only wish to do as my own darling pleases.

Blanche. Then I will not marry him. He has played fast and loose with me. He thinks us beneath him, he is ashamed of us; he

dared to object to being benefited by you — as if it were not natural for him to owe you everything; and yet the money tempted him after all. (*Suddenly throwing her arms hysterically about his neck*) Papa, I don't want to marry: I only want to stay with you and be happy as we have always been. I hate the thought of being married: I don't care for him: I don't want to leave you. (*Trench and Cokane return; but she can hear nothing but her own voice and does not notice them*) Only send him away: promise me that you will send him away and keep me here with you as we have always — (*Seeing Trench*) Oh! (*She hides her face on her father's breast*)

Tren. (*Nervously*) I hope we are not intruding.

Sar. (*Formidably*) Dr. Trench: my daughter has changed her mind.

Tren. (*Disconcerted*) Am I to understand —

Cok. (*Striking in in his most vinegary manner*) I think, Harry, under the circumstances, we have no alternative but to seek luncheon elsewhere.

Tren. But, Mr. Sartorius, have you explained —

Sar. (*Straight in Trench's face*) I have explained, sir. Good morning. (*Trench, outraged, advances a step. Blanche sinks away from her father into a chair. Sartorius stands his ground rigidly*)

Tren. (*Turning away indignantly*) Come on, Cokane.

Cok. Certainly, Harry, certainly. (*Trench goes out, very angry. The parlour maid, with a tray jingling in her hands, passes outside*) You have disappointed me, sir, very acutely. Good morning. (*He follows Trench*)

End of the Second Act.

ACT III.

The drawing-room in Sartorius's house in Bedford Square. Winter evening: fire burning, curtains drawn and lamps lighted. Sartorius and Blanche are sitting glumly near the fire. The Parlour Maid, who has just brought in coffee, is placing it on a small table between them. There is a large table in the middle of the room. The pianoforte, a grand, is on the left, with a photographic portrait of Blanche on a miniature easel on the top. Two doors, one on the right further forward than the fireplace, leading to the study; the other at the back, on the left, leading to the lobby. Blanche has her work basket at hand, and is knitting. Sartorius, closer to the fire, has a newspaper. The Parlour Maid goes out.

Sar. Blanche, my love.

Blanche. Yes.

Sar. I had a long talk to the doctor to-day about our going abroad.

Blanche. (*Impatiently*) I am quite well; and I will not go abroad. I loathe the very thought of the Continent. Why w i l l you bother me so about my health?

Sar. It was not about your health, Blanche, but about my own.

Blanche. (*Rising*) Yours! (*She goes anxiously to him*) Oh, papa, there is nothing the matter with you, I hope?

Sar. There will be — there must be, Blanche, long before you begin to consider yourself an old woman.

Blanche. But there is nothing the matter now?

Sar. Well, my dear, the doctor says I need change, travel, excitement —

Blanche. Excitement! Y o u need excitement! (*She laughs joylessly, and sits down on the rug at his feet*) How is it, papa, that you, who are so clever with everybody else, are not a bit clever with me? Do you think I can't see through your little plan to take me abroad? Since I will not be the invalid and allow you to be the nurse, you are to be the invalid and I am to be the nurse.

Sar. Well, Blanche, if you will have it that you are well and have nothing preying on your spirits, I must insist on being ill and have something preying on mine. And indeed, my girl, there is no use in our going on as we have for the last four months. You have not been happy; and I have been far from comfortable. (*Blanche's face clouds: she turns away from him and sits dumb and brooding. He waits in vain for some reply; then adds in a lower tone*) Need you be so inflexible, Blanche?

Blanche. (*Pained and rigid*) I thought you admired inflexibility: you have always prided yourself on it.

Sar. Nonsense, my dear, nonsense. I have had to give in often enough. And I could show you plenty of soft fellows who have done as well as I, and enjoyed themselves more, perhaps. If it is only for the sake of inflexibility that you are standing out —

Blanche. I am not standing out. I don't know what you mean. (*She tries to rise and go away*)

Sar. (*Catching her arm and arresting her on her knees*) Come, my child: you must not trifle with me as if I were a stranger. You are fretting because —

Blanche. (*Violently twisting herself free and speaking as she rises*) If you say it, papa, I will kill myself. It is not true. If he were here on his knees to-night, I would walk out of the house sooner than endure it.

She goes out excitedly. Sartorius, greatly troubled, turns again to the fire with a heavy sigh.

Sar. (*Gazing gloomily into the glow*) Now if I fight it out with her, no more comfort for months! I might as well live with my clerk or my servant. And if I give in now, I shall have to give in always. Well, I can't help it. I have stuck to having my own way all my life; but there must be an end to that drudgery some day. She is young: let her have her turn at it.

The parlour maid comes in.

Maid. Please sir, Mr. Lickcheese wants to see you very particular. On important business — y o u r business, he told me to say.

Sar. Mr. Lickcheese! Do you mean Lickcheese who used to come here on my business?

Maid. Yes, sir. But indeed, sir, you'd scarcely know him.

Sar. (*Frowning*) Hm! Starving, I suppose. Come to beg.

Maid. (*Intensely repudiating the idea*) O-o-o-o-h NO, sir. Quite the gentleman, sir! Sealskin overcoat, sir! Come in a hansom, all shaved and clean! I'm sure he's come into a fortune, sir.

Sar. Hm! Show him up.

Lickcheese, who has been waiting at the door, instantly comes in. The change in his appearance is dazzling. He is in evening dress, with an overcoat lined throughout with furs presenting all the hues of the tiger. His shirt is fastened at the breast with a single diamond stud. His silk hat is of the glossiest black; a handsome gold watch chain hangs like a garland on his filled out waistcoat; he has shaved his whiskers and grown a moustache, the ends of which are waxed and pointed. As Sartorius stares speechless at him, he stands, smiling, to be admired, intensely enjoying the effect he is producing. The parlour maid, hardly less pleased with her own share in this coup-de-théâtre, goes out beaming, full of the news for the kitchen. Lickcheese clinches the situation by a triumphant nod at Sartorius.

Sar. (*Bracing himself — hostile*) Well?

Lick. Quite well, Sartorius, thankee.

Sar. I was not asking after your health, sir, as you know, I think, as well as I do. What is your business?

Lick. Business that I can take elsewhere if I meet with less civility than I please to put up with, Sartorius. You and me is man and man now. It was money that used to be my master, and not you, don't think it. Now that I'm independent in respect of money —

Sar. (*Crossing determinedly to the door, and holding it open*) You can take your independence out of my house, then. I won't have it here.

Lick. (*Indulgently*) Come, Sartorius, don't be stiffnecked. I come here as a friend to put money in your pocket. No use in your lettin' on to me that you're above money. Eh?

Sar. (*Hesitates, and at last shuts the door, saying guardedly*) How much money?

Lick. (*Victorious, going to Blanche's chair and beginning to take off his overcoat*) Ah! there you speak like yourself, Sartorius. Now suppose you ask me to sit down and make myself comfortable.

Sar. (*Coming from the door*) I have a mind to put you downstairs by the back of your neck, you infernal blackguard.

Lick. (*Not a bit ruffled, takes off his overcoat and hangs it on the back of Blanche's chair, pulling a cigar case out of one of his pockets as he does so*) You and me is too much of a pair for me to take anything you say in bad part, Sartorius. 'Ave a cigar.

Sar. No smoking here: this is my daughter's room. However, sit down, sit down. (*They sit*)

Lick. I' bin gittin' orn a little since I saw you last.

Sar. So I see.

Lick. I owe it partly to you, you know. Does that surprise you?

Sar. It doesn't concern me.

Lick. So you think, Sartorius, because it never did concern you how *I* got on, so long as I got y o u on by bringing in the rents. But I picked up something for myself down at Robbins's Row.

Sar. I always thought so. Have you come to make restitution?

Lick. You wouldn't take it if I offered it to you, Sartorius. It wasn't money: it was knowledge — knowledge of the great public question of the Housing of the Working Classes. You know there's a Royal Commission on it, don't you?

Sar. Oh, I see. You've been giving evidence.

Lick. Giving evidence! Not me. What good would that do me! Only my expenses; and that not on the professional scale, neither. No: I gev no evidence. But I'll tell you what I did. I kep' it back, just to oblige one or two people whose feelings would have been hurt by seeing their names in a bluebook as keeping a fever den. Their Agent got so friendly with me over it that he put his name on a bill

of mine to the tune of — well, no matter: it gave me a start; and a start was all I ever wanted to get on my feet. I've got a copy of the first report of the Commission in the pocket of my overcoat. (*He rises and gets at his overcoat, from a pocket of which he takes a bluebook*) I turned down the page to show you: I thought you'd like to see it. (*He doubles the book back at the place indicated, and hands it to Sartorius*)

Sar. So blackmail is the game, eh? (*He puts the book on the table without looking at it, and strikes it emphatically with his fist*) I don't care t h a t for my name being in bluebooks. My friends don't read them; and I'm neither a Cabinet Minister nor a candidate for Parliament. There's nothing to be got out of me on that lay.

Lick. (*Shocked*) Blackmail! Oh, Mr. Sartorius, do you think I would let out a word about your premises? Round on an old pal! no: that ain't Lickcheese's way. Besides, they know all about you already. Them stairs that you and me quarrelled about, they was a whole afternoon examining the clergyman that made such a fuss — you remember? — about the women that was hurt on it. He made the worst he could of it, in an ungentlemanly, unchristian spirit. I wouldn't have that clergyman's disposition for worlds. Oh no: that's not what was in my thoughts.

Sar. Come, come, man: what w a s in your thoughts? Out with it.

Lick. (*With provoking deliberation, smiling and looking mysteriously at him*) You ain't spent a few hundreds in repairs since we parted, have you? (*Movement of impatience from Sartorius: Lickcheese goes on soothingly*) Now don't fly out at me. I know a landlord that owned as beastly a slum as you could find in London, down there by the Tower. By my advice that man put half the houses into first-class repair, and let the other half to a new Company — the North Thames Iced Mutton Depot Company, of which I held a few shares — promoters' shares. And what was the end of it, do you think?

Sar. Smash! I suppose.

Lick. Smash! not a bit of it. Compensation, Mr. Sartorius, compensation. Do you understand that?

Sar. Compensation for what?

Lick. Why, the land was wanted for an extension of the Mint; and the Company had to be bought out, and the buildings compensated for. Somebody has to know these things beforehand, you know, no matter how dark they're kept.

Sar. (*Interested, but cautious*) Well?

Lick. Is that all you have to say to me, Mr. Sartorius? "Well"! as if I was next door's dog! Suppose I'd got wind of a new street that would knock down Robbins's Row and turn Burke's Walk into a frontage worth thirty pounds a foot! — would you say no more to me than (*Mimicking*) "Well"? (*Sartorius hesitates, looking at him in great doubt: Lickcheese rises and exhibits himself*) Come, look at my get-up, Mr. Sartorius. Look at this watchchain! Look at the corporation I've got on me! Do you think all that came from keeping my mouth shut? No, it came from keeping my ears and eyes open.

Blanche comes in, followed by the parlour maid, who has a silver tray on which she collects the coffee cups. Sartorius, impatient at the interruption, rises and motions Lickcheese to the door of the study.

Sar. Sh. We must talk this over in the study. There is a good fire there, and you can smoke. Blanche: an old friend of ours.

Lick. And a kind one to me. I hope I see you well, Miss Blanche.

Blanche. Why it's Mr. Lickcheese! I hardly knew you.

Lick. I find you a little changed yourself, miss.

Blanche. (*Hastily*) Oh, I am the same as ever. How are Mrs. Lickcheese and the chil—

Sar. (*Impatiently*) We have business to transact, Blanche. You can talk to Mr. Lickcheese afterwards. Come on.

Sartorius and Lickcheese go into the study. Blanche, surprised at her father's abruptness, looks after them for a moment. Then, seeing Lickcheese's overcoat on her chair, she takes it up, amused, and looks at the fur.

Maid. Oh, we a r e fine, ain't we, Miss Blanche? I think Mr. Lickcheese must have come into a legacy. (*Confidentially*) I wonder what he can want with the master, Miss Blanche! He brought him this big book. (*She shows the bluebook to Blanche*)

Blanche. (*Her curiosity roused — taking the book*) Let me see. (*She looks at it*) There's something about papa in it. (*She sits down and begins to read*)

Maid. (*Folding the tea-table and putting it out of the way*) He looks ever so much younger, Miss Blanche, don't he? I couldn't help laughing when I saw him with his whiskers shaved off: it do look so silly when you're not accustomed to it. (*No answer from Blanche*) You haven't finished your coffee, miss: I suppose I may take it away? (*No answer*) Oh, you a r e interested in Mr. Lickcheese's book, miss. (*Blanche springs up. The parlour maid looks at her face, and instantly hurries out of the room on tiptoe with her tray*)

Blanche. So that was why he would not touch the money. (*She tries to tear the book across; but that is impossible; and she throws it violently into the fireplace. It falls into the fender*) Oh, if only a girl could have no father, no family, just as I have no mother! Clergyman! — beast! "The worst slum landlord in London." "Slum landlord." Oh! (*She covers her face with her hands and sinks shuddering into the chair on which the overcoat lies*)

The study door opens.

Lick. (*In the study*) You just wait five minutes. I'll fetch him. (*Blanche snatches a piece of work from her basket and sits erect and quiet, stitching at it. Lickcheese comes back, speaking to Sartorius, who follows him*) He lodges round the corner in Gower Street; and my private 'ansom's at the door. By your leave, Miss Blanche. (*Pulling gently at his overcoat*)

Blanche. (*Rising*) I beg your pardon. I hope I haven't crushed it.

Lick. (*With the coat on*) You're welcome to crush it again n o w , Miss Blanche. Don't say good evening to me, miss: I'm coming back, presently — me and a friend or two. Ta, ta, Sartorius: I shan't be long.

He goes out. Sartorius looks about for the bluebook.

Blanche. I thought we were done with Lickcheese.

Sar. Not quite yet, I think. He left a book here for me to look over — a large book in a blue paper cover. Has the girl put it away? (*He sees it in the fender; looks at Blanche; and adds*) Have you seen it!

Blanche. No. Yes. (*Angrily*) No, I have not seen it. What have I to do with it! (*Sartorius picks the book up and dusts it; then sits down quietly to read. After a glance up and down the columns, he nods assentingly, as if he found exactly what he expected*)

Sar. It's a curious thing, Blanche, that the Parliamentary gentlemen who write such books as these, should be so ignorant of practical business. One would suppose, to read this, that we are the most grasping, grinding, heartless pair in the world, you and I.

Blanche. Is it not true — about the state of the houses, I mean?

Sar. (*Calmly*) Oh, quite true.

Blanche. Then is it not our fault?

Sar. My dear, if we made the houses any better, the rents would have to be raised so much that the poor people would be unable to pay, and would be thrown homeless on the streets.

Blanche. Well, turn them out and get in a respectable class of people. Why should we have the disgrace of harbouring such wretches?

Sar. (*Opening his eyes*) That sounds a little hard on them, doesn't it, my child?

Blanche. Oh, I hate the poor. At least, I hate those dirty, drunken, disreputable people who live like pigs. If they must be provided for, let other people look after them. How can you expect any one to think well of us when such things are written about us in that infamous book?

Sar. (*Coldly and a little wistfully*) I see I have made a real lady of you, Blanche.

Blanche. (*Defiantly*) Well, are you sorry for that?

Sar. No, my dear, of course not. But do you know, Blanche, that my mother was a very poor woman, and that her poverty was not her fault?

Blanche. I suppose not; but the people we want to mix with now don't know that. And it was not my fault; so I don't see why *I* should be made to suffer for it.

Sar. (*Enraged*) Who makes you suffer for it, miss? What would you be now but for what your grandmother did for me when she stood at her wash-tub for thirteen hours a day and thought herself rich when she made fifteen shillings a week?

Blanche. (*Angrily*) I suppose I should have been down on her level instead of being raised above it, as I am now. Would you like us to go and live in that place in the book for the sake of grandmamma? I hate the idea of such things. I don't want to know about them. I love you because you brought me up to something better. (*Half aside, as she turns away from him*) I should hate you if you had not.

Sar. (*Giving in*) Well, my child, I suppose it is natural for you to feel that way, after your bringing up. It is the ladylike view of the matter. So don't let us quarrel, my girl. You shall not be made to suffer any more. I have made up my mind to improve the property, and get in quite a new class of tenants. There! does that satisfy you? I am only waiting for the consent of the ground landlord, Lady Roxdale.

Blanche. Lady Roxdale!

Sar. Yes. But I shall expect the mortgagee to take his share of the risk.

Blanche. The mortgagee! Do you mean — (*She cannot finish the sentence: Sartorius does it for her*)

Sar. Harry Trench. Yes. And remember, Blanche: if he consents to join me in the scheme, I shall have to be friends with him.

Blanche. And to ask him to the house?

Sar. Only on business. You need not meet him unless you like.

Blanche. (*Overwhelmed*) When is he coming?

Sar. There is no time to be lost. Lickcheese has gone to ask him to come round.

Blanche. (*In dismay*) Then he will be here in a few minutes! What shall I do?

Sar. I advise you to receive him as if nothing had happened, and then go out and leave us to our business. You are not afraid to meet him?

Blanche. Afraid! No, most certainly not. But — (*Lickcheese's voice is heard without*) Here they are. Don't say I'm here, papa.

She rushes away into the study. Lickcheese comes in with Trench and Cokane. Cokane shakes hands effusively with Sartorius. Trench, who is coarsened and sullen, and has evidently not been making the best of his disappointment, bows shortly and resentfully. Lickcheese covers the embarrassment of the position by talking cheerfully until they are all seated round the large table, Trench on the right, Cokane on the left; the other two between them, with Lickcheese next to Cokane.

Lick. Here we are, all friends round St. Paul's. You remember Mr. Cokane: he does a little business for me now as a friend, and gives me a help with my correspondence — sekketary we call it. I've no litery style, and that's the truth; so Mr. Cokane kindly puts it into my letters and draft prospectuses and advertisements and the like. Don't you, Cokane? Of course you do: why shouldn't you? He's been helping me tonight to persuade his old friend, Dr. Trench, about the matter we were speaking of.

Cok. (*Austerely*) No, Mr. Lickcheese, not trying to persuade him. No: this is a matter of principle with me. I say it is your duty, Henry — your d u t y — to put those abominable buildings into proper and habitable repair. As a man of science you owe it to the community to perfect the sanitary arrangements. In questions of duty there is no room for persuasion, even from the oldest friend.

Sar. (*To Trench*) I certainly feel, as Mr. Cokane puts it, that it is our duty: one which I have perhaps too long neglected out of regard for the poorest class of tenants.

Lick. Not a doubt of it, gents, a dooty. I can be as sharp as any man when it's a question of business; but dooty's another thing.

Tren. Well, I don't see that it is any more

my duty now than it was four months ago. I look at it simply as a question of so much money.

Cok. Shame, Harry, shame! Shame!

Tren. Oh, shut up, you fool. (*Cokane springs up. Lickcheese catches his coat and holds him*)

Lick. Steady, steady, Mr. Sekketary. Dr. Trench is only joking.

Cok. I insist on the withdrawal of that expression. I have been called a fool.

Tren. (*Morosely*) So you are a fool.

Cok. Then you are a damned fool. Now, sir!

Tren. All right. Now we've settled that. (*Cokane, with a snort, sits down*) What I mean is this. Don't let's have any nonsense about this job. As I understand it, Robbins's Row is to be pulled down to make way for the new street into the Strand; and the straight tip now is to go for compensation.

Lick. (*Chuckling*) That's so, Dr. Trench. That's it.

Tren. (*Continuing*) Well, it appears that the dirtier a place is, the more rent you get; and the decenter it is, the more compensation you get. So we're to give up dirt and go in for decency.

Sar. I should not put it exactly in that way; but —

Cok. Quite right, Mr. Sartorius, quite right. The case could not have been stated with worse taste or with less tact.

Lick. Sh-sh-sh-sh!

Sar. I do not quite go with you there, Mr. Cokane. Dr. Trench puts the case frankly as a man of business. I take the wider view of a public man. We live in a progressive age; and humanitarian ideas are advancing and must be taken into account. But my practical conclusion is the same as his. I should hardly feel justified in making a large claim for compensation under existing circumstances.

Lick. Of course not: and you wouldn't get it if you did. You see, it's like this, Dr. Trench. There's no doubt that the Vestries has legal powers to play old Harry with slum properties, and spoil the housenacking game if they please. That didn't matter in the good old times, because the Vestries used to be ourselves. Nobody ever knew a word about the election; and we used to get ten of us into a room and elect one another, and do what we liked. Well, that cock won't fight any longer; and, to put it short, the game is up for men in the position of you and Mr. Sartorius. My advice to you is, take the present chance of getting out of it. Spend a little money on the block at the Cribbs Market end — enough to make it look like a model dwelling; and let the other block to me on fair terms for a depot of the North Thames Iced Mutton Company. They'll be knocked down inside of two year to make room for the new north and south main thoroughfare; and you'll be compensated to the tune of double the present valuation, with the cost of the improvements thrown in. Leave things as they are; and you stand a good chance of being fined, or condemned, or pulled down before long. Now's your time.

Cok. Hear, hear! Hear, hear! Hear, hear! Admirably put from the business point of view! I recognize the uselessness of putting the moral point of view to you, Trench; but even you must feel the cogency of Mr. Lickcheese's business statement.

Tren. But why can't you act without me? What have I got to do with it? I am only a mortgagee.

Sar. There is a certain risk in this compensation investment, Dr. Trench. The County Council may alter the line of the new street. If that happens, the money spent in improving the houses will be thrown away — simply thrown away. Worse than thrown away, in fact; for the new buildings may stand unlet or half let for years. But you will expect your seven per cent as usual.

Tren. A man must live.

Cok. Je n'en vois pas la nécessité.

Tren. Shut up, Billy; or else speak some language you understand. No, Mr. Sartorius: I should be very glad to stand in with you if I could afford it; but I can't; so there's an end of that.

Lick. Well, all I can say is that you're a very foolish young man.

Cok. What did I tell you, Harry?

Tren. I don't see that it's any business of yours, Mr. Lickcheese.

Lick. It's a free country: every man has a right to his opinion. (*Cokane cries* Hear, hear!) Come, where's your feelings for them poor people, Dr. Trench? Remember how it went to your heart when I first told you about them. What! are y o u going to turn hard?

Tren. No: it won't do: you can't get over me that way. You proved to me before that there was no use in being sentimental over that slum shop of ours; and it's no good your turning round on the philanthropic tack now that you want me to put my capital into your speculation. I've had my lesson; and I'm going to stick to my present income. It's little enough for me as it is.

Sar. It really matters nothing to me, Dr. Trench, how you decide. I can easily raise the money elsewhere and pay you off. Then, since you are resolved to run no risks, you can invest your £10,000 in Consols and get £250 a year for it instead of £700. (*Trench, completely outwitted, stares at them in consternation. Cokane breaks the silence*)

Cok. This is what comes of being avaricious, Harry. Two thirds of your income gone at one blow. And I must say it serves you right.

Tren. That's all very fine; but I don't understand it. If you can do this to me, why didn't you do it long ago?

Sar. Because, as I should probably have had to borrow at the same rate, I should have saved nothing; whereas you would have lost over £400 — a very serious matter for you. I had no desire to be unfriendly; and even now I should be glad to let the mortgage stand, were it not that the circumstances mentioned by Mr. Lickcheese force my hand. Besides, Dr. Trench, I hoped for some time that our interests might be joined by closer ties even than those of friendship.

Lick. (*Jumping up, relieved*) There! Now the murder's out. Excuse me, Dr. Trench. Ex-cuse me, Mr. Sartorius: excuse my freedom. Why not Dr. Trench marry Miss Blanche, and settle the whole affair that way? (*Sensation. Lickcheese sits down triumphant*)

Cok. You forget, Mr. Lickcheese, that the young lady, whose taste has to be considered, decisively objected to him.

Tren. Oh! Perhaps you think she was struck with you.

Cok. I did not say so, Trench. No man of any delicacy would suggest such a thing. You have an untutored mind, Trench, an untutored mind.

Tren. Well, Cokane: I've told you my opinion of you already.

Cok. (*Rising wildly*) And I have told you m y opinion of y o u . I will repeat it if you wish. I am ready to repeat it.

Lick. Come, Mr. Sekketary: you and me, as married men, is out of the 'unt as far as young ladies is concerned. I know Miss Blanche: she has her father's eye for business. Explain this job to her; and she'll make it up with Dr. Trench. Why not have a bit of romance in business when it costs nothing? We all have our feelings: we ain't mere calculating machines.

Sar. (*Revolted*) Do you think, Lickcheese, that my daughter is to be made part of a money bargain between you and these gentlemen?

Lick. Oh, come, Sartorius: don't talk as if you was the only father in the world. I have

a daughter too; and my feelings in that matter is just as fine as yours. I propose nothing but what is for Miss Blanche's advantage and Dr. Trench's.

Cok. Lickcheese expresses himself roughly, Mr. Sartorius; but his is a sterling nature; and what he says is to the point. If Miss Sartorius can really bring herself to care for Harry, I am far from desiring to stand in the way of such an arrangement.

Tren. Why, what have you got to do with it?

Lick. Easy, Dr. Trench, easy. We want your opinion. Are you still on for marrying Miss Blanche if she's agreeable?

Tren. (*Shortly*) I don't know that I am. (*Sartorius rises indignantly*)

Lick. Easy one moment, Mr. Sartorius. (*To Trench*) Come, Dr. Trench: you say you don't know that you are. But do you know that you ain't: that's what we want to know?

Tren. (*Sulkily*) I won't have the relations between Miss Sartorius and myself made part of a bargain. (*He rises to leave the table*)

Lick. (*Rising*) That's enough: a gentleman could say no less. (*Insinuatingly*) Now, would you mind me and Cokane and the gov'nor steppin' into the study to arrange about the lease to the North Thames Iced Mutton Company?

Tren. Oh, *I* don't mind. I'm going home. There's nothing else to say.

Lick. No, don't go. Only just a minute: me and Cokane will be back in no time to see you home. You'll wait for us, won't you? there's a good fellow.

Tren. Well, if you wish, yes.

Lick. (*Cheerily*) Didn't I know you would!

Sar. (*At the study door, to Cokane*) After you, sir.

> Cokane bows formally and goes into the study.

Lick. (*At the door, aside to Sartorius*) You never 'ad such a managin' man as me, Sartorius.

> He goes into the study chuckling, followed by Sartorius.
> Trench, left alone, looks round carefully and listens a moment. Then he goes on tiptoe to the piano and leans upon it with folded arms, gazing at Blanche's portrait. Blanche herself appears presently at the study door. When she sees how he is occupied, she closes it softly and steals over to him, watching him intently. He rises from his leaning attitude, and takes the portrait from the easel, holding it out before him at arm's length; then, taking a second look round to reassure himself that nobody is watching him, finds Blanche close upon him. He drops

the portrait and stares at her without the least presence of mind.

Blanche. (*Shrewishly*) Well? So you have come back here. You have had the m e a n- n e s s to come into this house again. (*He flushes and retreats a step. She follows him up remorselessly*) What a poor-spirited creature you must be! Why don't you go? (*Red and wincing, he starts huffily to get his hat from the table; but when he turns to the door with it she deliberately gets in his way, so that he has to stop*) I don't want you to stay. (*For a moment they stand face to face, quite close to one an- other, she provocative, taunting, half defying, half inviting him to advance, in a flush of un- disguised animal excitement. It suddenly flashes on him that all this ferocity is erotic — that she is making love to him. His eye lights up: a cunning expression comes into the corner of his mouth: with a heavy assumption of indifference he walks straight back to his chair, and plants himself in it with his arms folded. She comes down the room after him*) But I forgot: you have found that there is some money to be made here. Lickcheese told you. Y o u , who were so disinterested, so independent, that you could not accept anything from my father! (*At the end of every sentence she waits to see what execution she has done*) I suppose you will try to persuade me that you have come down here on a great philanthropic enterprise — to befriend the poor by having those houses rebuilt, eh? (*Trench maintains his attitude and makes no sign*) Yes, when my father m a k e s you do it. And when Lick- cheese has discovered some way of making it profitable. Oh, I know papa; and I know you. And for the sake of that, you come back here — into the house where you were re- fused — ordered out. (*Trench's face darkens: her eyes gleam as she sees it*) Aha! you remem- ber that. You know it is true: you cannot deny it. (*She sits down, and softens her tone a little as she affects to pity him*) Ah, let me tell you that you cut a poor figure, a v e r y poor figure, Harry. (*At the word "Harry," he relaxes the fold of his arms; and a faint grin of anticipated victory appears on his face*) And you, too, a gentleman! — so highly con- nected! — with such distinguished relations! — so particular as to where your money comes from! I wonder at you. I really wonder at you. I should have thought that if your family brought you nothing else, it might at least have brought you some sense of per- sonal dignity. Perhaps you think you look dignified at present, eh? (*No reply*) Well, I can assure you that you don't: you look most

ridiculous — as foolish as a man could look — you don't know what to say; and you don't know what to do. But after all, I really don't see what anyone c o u l d say in defence of such conduct. (*He looks straight in front of him, and purses up his lips as if whistling. This annoys her; and she becomes affectedly polite*) I am afraid I am in your way, Dr. Trench. (*She rises*) I shall not intrude on you any longer. You seem so perfectly at home that I need make no apology for leaving you to yourself. (*She makes a feint of going to the door; but he does not budge; and she returns and comes behind his chair*) Harry. (*He does not turn. She comes a step nearer*) Harry: I want you to answer me a question. (*Earn- estly, stooping over him*) Look me in the face. (*No reply*) Do you hear? (*Putting her hand on his shoulder*) Look—me—in—the—face. (*He still stares straight in front of him. She suddenly kneels down beside him with her breast against his right shoulder; taking his face in her hands, and twisting it sharply towards her*) Harry: what were you doing with my photo- graph just now, when you thought you were alone? (*His face writhes as he tries hard not to smile. She flings her arms round him, and crushes him in an ecstatic embrace as she adds, with furious tenderness*) How dare you touch anything belonging to me? (*The study door opens and voices are heard*)

Tren. I hear some one coming. (*She regains her chair with a bound, and pushes it back as far as possible*)

Cokane, Lickcheese, and Sartorius come from the study. Sartorius and Lickcheese come to Trench. Cokane crosses to Blanche in his most killing manner.

Cok. How do you do, Miss Sartorius? Nice weather for the return of l'enfant prodigue, eh?

Blanche. Capital, Mr. Cokane. So glad to see you. (*She gives him her hand, which he kisses with gallantry*)

Lick. (*On Trench's left, in a low voice*) Any noos for us, Mr. Trench?

Tren. (*To Sartorius, on his right*) I'll stand in, compensation or no compensation. (*Shakes Sartorius's hand. The parlour maid has just appeared at the door*)

Blanche. Supper is ready, papa.

Cok. Allow me.

> *Exeunt omnes: Blanche on Cokane's arm; Lickcheese jocosely taking Sar- torius on one arm and Trench on the other.*

THE END.

HENRY ARTHUR JONES
1851-1929

The Masqueraders
(1894)

Pinero's shocking and somewhat Ibsenite "new drama" *The Second Mrs. Tanqueray* created a sensation when it was produced at the St. James's Theatre, and the management was eager to follow this success with a play of similar strength. Henry Arthur Jones's *The Masqueraders* was selected. It began its run of a hundred and thirty-nine nights on April 28, 1894.

The Masqueraders is distinctly a new drama, but its plot pattern is derived from the domestic melodrama. The essential conflict of the play resembles the conventional struggle between the wealthy Squire and the poor hero for the heroine; Sir Brice Skene as the villain attempts to possess Dulcie, and David Remon attempts to rescue her from his clutches. But in its details the play is a problem play, for the villain must marry the heroine in order to possess her, and the hero can rescue her from misery only by causing her to break her marriage vows. In the melodrama, right and wrong are clearly defined, and virtue is at last triumphant. But *The Masqueraders* presents (or to an audience of the 1890's presented) two rights and two wrongs: on Sir Brice's side the right of marriage and the wrong of his brutality, and on David's side the right of his unselfish love and the wrong of his attempt to take Dulcie from her lawfully wedded husband. Whatever readers in the twentieth century conclude, the ending of *The Masqueraders* posed a subject for serious discussion in 1894. In the 1870's, given the climate of popular opinion, a playwright would have pleased his audience with a melodramatic ending; Sir Brice might have seen the error of his ways, suffered remorse, and reformed to keep Dulcie at home, or he would have conveniently drunk himself to death or met with a fatal accident to leave Dulcie free to marry David. By the 1920's Dulcie would have felt no shame in leaving her brutal husband. But in the 1890's the question was not decided. It was the decade when Hardy's *Tess of the D'Urbervilles* created a sensation and *Jude the Obscure* shocked readers into angry denunciations. Perhaps to symbolize the tentativeness of any answer to the problem, the action of the play is left incomplete: it is not clear whether David will come out of Africa alive and if he does whether Dulcie will join him.

The play departs from the pattern of melodrama in other ways. It has two great "sensation" scenes — the auction of Dulcie's kiss, with her decision to marry based on what starts as a jest, and the scene in which Sir Brice and David cut cards for Dulcie and her child. In each scene intense personal conflict between the men (as well as Dulcie's inner conflict) replaces acts of violence and the stage machinery for storms, fires, etc.

As a problem play *The Masqueraders* is a serious, satiric study of modern marriage in upper-class life, revealing the hypocrisy of the union when the only tie is a legal form or a religious ritual. It examines three marriages: that of Dulcie and Sir Brice in the center, and those of Monty and Lady Clarice and of Charley and the man she calls "that creature at home" in the background. In this society, marriage is for money, for convenience, and to shield adultery. Monty's proposal to Lady Clarice, based on the supposition that she will inherit a fortune, is utterly cynical, with "No rights, no duties, no self assertion, no quarrels, no jealousy" — and no love. Finally, he escorts both his jealous wife and his mistress to the same ball, one on each arm.

The title *Masqueraders* suggests that a main subject of the play is a dilettante upper class that hides its trifling under masks of persiflage and cynicism. Jones greatly esteemed and often quoted Matthew Arnold, and apparently he shared this author's disdain of the upper class as "barbarians" interested in pleasure, privilege, and display, and the middle class as "Philistines" interested in money and respectability. *The Masqueraders* portrays an idle, frivolous, effete, and cynical aristocracy that has altogether lost any sense of morality or social responsibility, and has both revolted against the stringencies of Philistine morality and adopted the Philistine love of money. These people are not serious in their revolt against the conventions, as radicals were; they sidestep conventions. They have lost faith in everything. Blanchflower foolishly struggles to define a basis for religion: "Oh, but surely there is Something real Somewhere. Oh, yes — surely, surely — we must believe that there is — hum? eh? — a Kind of — eh? — a Sort of a Something — Somewhere, eh?" The disintegration of aristocratic distinctions, not in favor of any ideal of democracy, but as a result of faddist leveling, is evident in the motley crowd assembled at Dulcie's reception: an alcoholic crusader for temperance, a triumphant divorcée, an "impressionist artist, novelist, and general dirty modern dabbler," and a famous astronomer.

Jones's satiric presentation of these characters implies that he himself believes in the virtues they have abandoned. It is evident in his presentation of David Remon that Jones believes in love as a generous, lifelong devotion, but not without passion. David is able to jest as well as the others, but only to comment upon a world which, from the point of view of his scientifically based idealism, has gone wrong. Helen Larondie is obviously Jones's spokesman, and everything she says supports a conservative and even conventional morality. She believes in the sacredness of the marriage tie, no matter what the woman may suffer; she justifies the double standard of sexual morality that excuses men for lapses inexcusable in women; and she believes in old-fashioned duty as a moral imperative. She says that "no nation has ever survived whose women have been immoral. . . . I don't know whether it's a man's duty to be moral. I'm sure it's a woman's." She would have only scorn for

David if he should give up his duty to his fellow scientists for love of Dulcie. It is enlightening to read the radical Bernard Shaw's letter to Jones concerning Helen's (and Jones's) conservatism: "I believe you faked up that atrocious nurse, Dulcie's sister, for the express purpose of infuriating me. . . . Every one of that woman's allusions to duty elicited a howl of rage from me. She morally outrages my tenderest sensibilities." It seems in any rational view (Shaw's, no doubt) that Jones's play makes a convincing case for Dulcie to repudiate her husband and accept David without reservation. But Jones ignored the logic of the situation and rested his conclusion on "instinct," Dulcie's feeling about her wedding ring. Jones's achievement in portraying so fully and fairly a situation that would seem to justify any kind of flight is all the more to be admired since he was personally opposed to separation and divorce.

Jones's reading in science and his creation of David Remon as a scientist no doubt helped him present this rational view. David expresses opinions implicit in scientific reasoning that Jones respected, but did not accept. David could offer idealisms that Jones believed impractical in an imperfect world; a stargazer, devoted to lofty principles, may be careless of the realities that operate on earth. David says, "Your trouble isn't real. This society world of yours isn't a real world," and "I think highly of women; it's a pleasing delusion of mine." David, recognizing that most people think his ideas a little mad, will not compromise. "A man must be mad," he says while still poor, "who drinks the rarest wines when he can get salted beer and doctored gin." Jones, on the other hand, compromises.

The character of Dulcie is likewise complex, and it develops during the play. In the beginning she feels humiliated by her low social position, and her vitality and eagerness make her flighty and mad for pleasure. Perhaps David sees through her caprices to the serious inner self briefly suggested in the first scene with Helen and developed through shame and suffering in her life with her husband. Sir Brice, the villain, is a realistic portrait of a man coarsened beyond redemption by drink, self-indulgence, and a passion for gambling.

Old-fashioned today, Jones's contribution to the new drama in 1894 stated a real problem of the time, and portrayed and criticized a convincingly real world.

THE MASQUERADERS

A Play In Four Acts

by

HENRY ARTHUR JONES

First performed at St. James's Theatre, April 28, 1894.

Cast of Characters

DAVID REMON
SIR BRICE SKENE
MONTAGU LUSHINGTON
EDDIE REMON
THE EARL OF CRANDOVER, *Master of the Crandover Hunt*
HON. PERCY BLANCHFLOWER
SIR WINCHMORE WILLS, M.D.
GEORGE COPELAND
FANCOURT
CARTER
RANDALL
RODNEY
SHARLAND

JIMMY STOKES, *an old huntsman*
BRINKLER, *proprietor of "The Stag"*
THOMSON
DULCIE LARONDIE
HELEN LARONDIE, *her sister*
CHARLEY WISHANGER, *afterwards Lady Shalford*
LADY CLARICE REINDEAN, *Lord Crandover's daughter*
LADY CRANDOVER
GUESTS, DANCERS, FOX-HUNTERS, HOTEL SERVANTS *and* WAITERS

ACT I

The old courtyard of the Stag Hotel and Assembly Rooms at Crandover, roofed in to form a hall. Along right is a bar-counter, surmounted by a glass casement and windows, which open and shut down on to the counter. In the middle of the counter is a lid, which lifts up and forms doorway. At the back are steps leading to the Crandover Assembly Rooms. On the left the large old-fashioned gateway of the Inn. Running all round are the old galleries remaining from coaching times. Plants and banners hung about the hall. On the outside of bar is hung a subscription list, in which the words "Widow and Orphans" and "Dick Ramsden" are dis-

cernible. Dancing in the rooms beyond. Amongst the company are Lord Crandover, Lady Crandover, Lady Clarice Reindean, Charley Wishanger. Montagu Lushington, a modern young man, is coming downstairs.

Lord Cran. (*A jovial English aristocrat of about fifty speaks to Brinkler*) Devilish rum start this of Miss Larondie's, Brinkler.

Brink. (*With a grin*) Yes, my lord.

Lord Cran. Where is she?

Brink. (*Pointing off into the bar*) In the bar there. (*They all look off, and show great interest. Montagu Lushington joins the group*)

Char. (*A very fast, mannish little woman, to Montagu*) Not bad, eh?

Monty. Exquisite. That divine poise of the arm as she draws the handle of the beer machine is really quite priceless.

Lord Cran. Does she bring you much business, Brinkler?

Brink. Well, she's brought me two good customers, my lord.

Lord Cran. Who are they?

Brink. One of them is Sir Brice Skene, my lord. (*Lady Crandover exchanges a look with Lady Clarice*)

Lady Cran. Is Sir Brice often here? (*Lady Clarice is showing interest*)

Brink. He's almost lived here lately, my lady.

Lady Clar. (*To Lady Crandover, aside, bitterly*) What did I tell you?

Lord Cran. Who's the other customer?

Brink. That mad gentleman that lives at Gerard's Heath, Mr. Remon. There he is in the bar now. (*They all look off, and show great interest*)

Monty. That pale individual who is dallying with claret in the corner?

Brink. Yes; that's sixty-nine Mouton Rothschild. I get it specially for him. Fancy drinking Mouton Rothschild!

Char. The man's looking at us.

Sir Brice enters from ball-room, comes down gradually to group.

Lord Cran. He's an astronomer, isn't he?

Brink. I believe he is something in that line, my lord. And he's got a little brother who is likewise touched.

Monty. With the stars, or the barmaid?

Brink. Miss Larondie isn't exactly a barmaid, is she, my lord?

Lord Cran. No; her mother was distantly related to the Skenes. Her father came of a good old French family.

Lady Cran. The girl might have done well for herself. We used to receive her family at the Court and when her father died I interested myself to get her a situation as a governess in a Christian family But she behaved very badly.

Monty. When one is a governess in a Christian family, one is compelled to behave badly for the sake of the higher morality.

Lady Cran. Miss Larondie had thoroughly lost caste. And I should take it as a great favour if Mr. Brinkler would see that she has no chance of — of misconducting herself with — (*Sir Brice has come up, and Lady Crandover stops embarrassed when she sees him*)

Sir B. With whom? Is Miss Larondie about to misconduct herself, Brinkler?

Brink. No, Sir Brice, I trust not.

Sir B. (*To Lady Crandover*) Have you any reason for supposing that Miss Larondie is about to misconduct herself, Lady Crandover?

Lady Cran. (*Embarrassed*) I — I am surprised, Sir Brice —

Sir B. Have you any reason for supposing that Miss Larondie is about to misconduct herself?

Lady Cran. No.

Sir B. (*Politely*) Thank you.

Goes off into the bar. In crossing the bar he has to pass Lady Clarice, he bows to her with extreme politeness, she bites her lips, and returns his bow. Exit Sir Brice into bar.

Lady Clar. (*To her mother, aside*) Oh, I can't bear it!

Lady Cran. Hush!

Lady Clar. He has gone to that girl.

The next dance begins. The stage gradually clears.

Char. Our dance, Monty.

Monty. (*Giving arm*) So your vestal self is dedicate to matrimony and Sir Digby Shalford?

Char. Yes; he's a trifle washed out; but we are frightfully hard up, and you didn't ask me.

Monty. My dear Charley, marriage is the last insult one offers to a woman whom one respects. Love if you please —

Char. Thanks. We'll think about it. By the way, you'll stand a chance with Clarice now Sir Brice has cut her. Her connections would be useful to you.

Monty. What would Crandover settle on her?

Char. Not much. Clarice would tell me. I'll ask her. What would you do it for? A thousand a year?

Monty. (*Reproachfully*) My dear Charley, don't hurt my self-respect.

They go into the ball-room.

Enter Eddie Remon, a delicate boy of about twenty, highly refined, overstrung, unbalanced. He is followed by George Copeland, a bearded, athletic man about forty.

Cope. But what's he doing here?

Eddie. Sun-gazing.

Cope. Sun-gazing?

Eddie. Yes. Look! Here's his sun. She's dragging him through space, and where the devil they're going to, I don't know.

Enter Dulcie Larondie from bar.

Dulcie. (*Speaking off into the outer bar. She has a large key in her hand*) I've forgotten the candle. Sir Brice, would you mind bringing me that candle?

David Remon enters from bar, with the lighted candle in his hand. He is a man of about forty, pale, studious, philosophic-looking. Sir Brice follows quickly, and the two men stand facing each other.

Sir. B. Give me that candle.

David. Miss Larondie — (*Appealing to Dulcie*)

Dulcie. (*Stands coquettishly looking at both of them*) That one shall light me to the cellar who makes himself the most ridiculous over it.

David. (*Coming towards her*) That will be myself.

Sir B. Give me that candle.

Dulcie. Sir Brice, Mr. Remon will make himself far more ridiculous than you.

Sir B. Then let him light you.

> *Exit into bar. Remon is carrying the candle perfectly straight in his hands. Dulcie turns to him.*

Dulcie. You're carrying that candle on one side; you're dropping the grease. (*He looks at her, holds it much on one side, and drops the grease*) That's better. (*She stands a moment or two looking him up and down with comic inspection*) Yes, I think that will do. You look very well. Would you mind waiting here till I come back?

> *Gravely blows out the candle, and exit. David stands there. Pause. Copeland comes behind him, claps him on the shoulder.*

Cope. Davy!

David. (*Turns round, cordially*) My dear fellow! (*Very warm hand-shaking*) You're coming to stay?

Cope. No, to say good-bye. I catch the night mail back, and tomorrow I'm off to Alaska. I'm sick of his nineteenth-century civilisation. I must do a bit of climbing, and get myself re-oxidised.

David. What is it this time?

Cope. Mount Saint Elias, 18,000 feet high, and snow at the sea-level.

Eddie. Davy, your bottle of claret is here in the bar.

David. But Miss Larondie has not come back from the cellar.

Eddie. She came up the other stairs. She's in the bar talking to Sir Brice Skene. (*The band strikes up a very bright dance-tune. Eddie puts his fingers in his ears*) Oh! oh! oh! Those wretched musicians!

Cope. What's the matter?

Eddie. They are playing horribly in tune, as if the world were full of harmony. I must get a tin kettle and put them out.

> *David goes up to the bar, shows intense mortification, conquers it. Exit Eddie into ball-room. David calls "Brinkler."*

Brinkler enters with a bottle and glasses.

David. Brinkler, my claret here. (*Brinkler brings bottle in cradle and two glasses, puts them down on the other side of stage*)

Brink. Mouton Rothschild, sixty-nine.

David. So I'm mad to drink the finest vintages, eh Brinkler? (*Brinkler looks surprised*) I heard you say so.

Brink. Well, it is unusual, sir.

David. You're right. A man must be mad who drinks the rarest wines when he can get salted beer and doctored gin. Still, you must humour me, Brinkler. (*Brinkler seems puzzled*) Though what's the good of climbing Mount Elias, I don't know. (*Turning to Copeland*)

Cope. To get to the top of it.

David. But what's the good of getting to the top of it?

Cope. What's the good of getting to the top of anything? You've spent the last dozen years of your life and nearly blinded yourself to solve the mystery of sun-spots.

David. But sun-spots are practical.

Cope. Practical?

David. Who solves the mystery of sun-spots may show the way to control the future harvests of the world; and who controls the harvests of the world will provide cheaper swipes and smaller beer for Brinkler's grandchildren, eh, Brinkler?

Brink. (*Comes forward*) Sir?

David. I was saying that the elect of the earth, and by the elect of the earth I mean every man who has a vote, may get cheaper swipes when I have solved my problem of sun-spots.

Brink. Sir?

David. Your grandchildren shall be amply provided for, Brinkler. (*Turns to Copeland*) Drink. (*Exit Brinkler, puzzled*) A prosperous voyage and a safe return, old fellow. (*Drinks*) I've drunk to your folly, now drink to mine.

Cope. Tell me all about it, Davy. It is folly, then?

David. No, if folly is happiness, folly is the greatest wisdom.

Cope. You are happy, then?

David. (*Nods*) Yes. And wretched, beyond all telling.

Cope. Why?

David. I shall never win her. She'll never be mine, George. And if she were, — that might be the saddest thing of all.

Cope. How?

David. When the desired one becomes the possessed one, her beauty fades. I love her, George, and I want to keep on loving her. (*Copeland laughs*) Laugh at me! I laugh at myself. I was forty-two last August. You know pretty much what my life has been.

Drink one glass, old boy, to the days when we were twenty-five, and to our old loves.

Cope. (*Drinks*) Our old loves. Your last one, Davy?

David. Ah! She soured me, but she didn't break my heart. And she drove me to my sun-spots. So God bless her! God bless them all! Whatever I've been in practice, George, in theory I've always had the most perfect loyalty to womankind of any man that ever breathed. (*Copeland laughs*) Don't laugh, you rascal! I meant it! I've always kept my reverence for them, and I've always known that some day or the other I should meet one who would make me worship her with the purest devotion a man can feel for a woman.

Cope. And you have met her?

David. (*Nods, looking towards bar*) She's in there, flirting with the choicest blackguard in England.

Cope. You poor dear fool! You always would pay half-a-crown for anything you could get for twopence.

David. Yes, but I always knew what a fool I was. Do you think I don't know what a fool I am now? George, it's not any empress, not any goddess, but just that girl in the bar there that owns me body and soul.

Cope. Pack up your traps and come to Alaska and forget her.

David. (*Hand on his heart*) She's packed herself here, and here she'll lie snug and warm till all grows cold. (*Looking over to bar*) And that blackguard is talking to her!

Cope. Who is he?

David. Sir Brice Skene.

Cope. The racing man?

David. Yes. He's rich. George, if he —

Cope. If he — what?

David. He shook hands with her last night. When his finger-tips touched hers, I felt I could kill him, George. And if he — if he — No, I wrong her! She's a good woman. And yet, damn him, he has twenty thousand a year —

Cope. Is it a question of money?

David. What do you mean?

Cope. I've not a single near relation in the world. My father left me, I suppose, from two to three hundred thousand pounds. (*Holds out hand*) Davy, say the word —

David. No, George.

Cope. Why should you hesitate?

David. I don't want it. I've just enough for my wants. I've only Eddie to provide for. And I've only one extravagance. (*Tapping the bottle*) I love good wine, and plenty — not too much — of it.

Cope. But if you were rich — perhaps she —

David. Thanks, George; I won't buy her.

Cope. You're welcome.

David. I know it.

Cope. By Jove, I've only just time to catch the mail. Good-bye, Davy. (*They stand hand in hand for some moments*) I've left a couple of thousand at Coutts' in your name.

David. I sha'n't use it.

Cope. As you please.

David. How long shall you be away?

Cope. I sha'n't come back till I've stood on Mount Saint Elias. Can I do anything for you?

David. Yes. Tell me the quality of the moonshine on the top.

Cope. The same quality as your moonshine here, and just as real.

David. Is anything real? (*Looking at the fox-hunters and dancers*) I've lived so long alone with only Eddie that the world has grown quite spectral to me. Look at these phantoms! (*Pointing to the fox-hunters and dancers*) Is anything real, George?

Cope. Yes; that two thousand at Coutts'.

David. And friendship. Friendship is real, isn't it? (*Shaking hands*) God bless you, George. I'll come to the station with you.

As he is going off Dulcie enters from bar, Sir Brice Skene following her.

David. (*Sees her*) No! (*Shakes hands*) Don't break your neck over Mount Saint Elias!

Cope. Don't break your heart over a woman!

David. Yes, I shall. After all I'm only playing at life, and so I'll break my heart over her — in play.

Cope. Stick to your sun-spots!

Exit.

Sir B. (*Catching sight of the subscription list*) What a confounded lot of widows and orphans there are in the world!

David. (*Sitting on the other side*) Miss Larondie is an orphan.

Dulcie. Yes, or I shouldn't be here. I wonder why all we superfluous women were sent into the world!

Sir B. (*Leaning on the bar*) You are not superfluous. You are indispensable.

Dulcie. To whom?

Sir B. To me.

Dulcie. (*Makes a profound mock curtsy*) You do me proud. (*Calls to David*) Mr. Remon, can you tell me why I was sent into the world?

David. To be indispensable to Sir Brice Skene.

Sir B. (*Aside to Dulcie*) Why do you talk to that fellow?

Dulcie. (*Aside to Sir Brice*) Oh, he amuses me. I can make such a fool of him, and — I'm so sick of this.

Sir B. I'll send you my new mare on Friday. Come to the meet.

Dulcie. I daren't. What would everybody say?

Sir B. What does it matter? I'll send you the mare.

Dulcie. No. They'd all cut me. Would your sister chaperon me? You know she wouldn't.

Sir B. My dear — you've made an awful mistake.

Dulcie. Don't call me your dear. I won't have it.

Sir B. (*With a little laugh*) My dear, you've made an awful mistake, and there's only one way out of it.

Dulcie. I don't wish to get out of it. Let them laugh at me, and cut me. I can bear it.

Sir B. Don't be a fool. If I were to offer you — (*In a low voice*)

Dulcie. (*Stops him*) No. Pray don't. I sha'n't take it.

Sir B. (*Bending nearer to her*) But if I were to offer you —

David. (*To Sir Brice*) Will you give me those matches, please?

Sir B. Take them.

Enter Jimmy Stokes, an old huntsman in an old hunting suit.

Dulcie. Oh, Jimmy Jimmy Stokes, I'm so glad to see you! How are you, Jimmy Jimmy Stokes?

Jimmy. (*Beaming old fellow of about seventy*) Oh, I'm just tol-lol, miss, for a hold 'un. How's yourself, miss?

Dulcie. Oh, this isn't myself, Jimmy. Myself's dead and buried, and when I come back to life I shall find this queer creature has been playing all sorts of mad pranks in my absence. Sit down, Jimmy Jimmy Stokes, and put a name on it.

Jimmy. Well, just a little wee drop of gin, miss, if I ain't intruding.

Dulcie. Intruding, Jimmy? You ought to be welcome at any meet of the Crandover.

Jimmy. Head whip five-and-thirty years, I was. And thinks I, I'll look in to-night. So I washes myself up, putts on my old whip's coat, and here I be as bold as brass. You see, miss, I be a privileged party, I be. Thank you, miss — Woa, woa, miss — woa!

Sir Brice and David have been sitting at table, looking at each other.

Sir B. You spoke?

David. No. (*The look is continued for some moments*)

Sir B. (*Folds his arms over the table, leans over them to David*) What the devil do you mean?

David. (*Folds his arms over the table so that they meet Sir Brice's, leans over them so that the two men's faces almost touch*) I mean to kill you if you dishonour her.

Sir B. You'll kill me?

David. I'll kill you.

Sir B. I'll have her one way or the other.

David. You're warned. (*Sir Brice rises, goes towards Dulcie, is about to speak to her. David turns round and looks at him. Sir Brice stops, calls out to Dulcie, who is talking over the bar to Jimmy Stokes*)

Sir B. Miss Larondie, I'll send you the mare on Friday.

Dulcie shakes her head, Sir Brice looks at David and exit.

Jimmy. Well, here's luck to you, miss, and I wish I could see you going across the country with the C. H. as you used — that's all the harm I wish you, for you was a sweet, pretty figure on horseback, you was, and you rode straight, you and your father, wire and all — you rode straight.

Dulcie. Don't remind me of old times, Jimmy. (*Turns to David mischievously*) Mr. Remon, it's getting late. Isn't it time you were going?

David. (*Rises*) Good-night.

Dulcie. Good-night. (*As he is passing out to door she calls out to him again*) Mr. Remon — (*David stops*) I've something to say to you.

David. (*Coming to her*) What is it?

Dulcie. (*Tapping her forehead impatiently*) It's gone! Would you mind waiting there till I think what it is?

David. Certainly.

Dulcie. That's so good of you. (*Looks him up and down a little while mischievously*) Can I give you a book while you wait? Here's "Bradshaw," the "Turf Guide," this week's "Sporting Times."

David. I shouldn't understand it. I'll look at you.

Dulcie. Do you understand me?

David. Perfectly.

Dulcie. I don't understand you.

David. You will some day.

The dance has finished, and a crowd of young men dancers, Fancourt, Carter, Randall, Rodney, Sharland, come chattering and laughing to the bar, and shout for drinks together.

Fan. I say, Miss Larondie, I'm dying for a whisky and soda.

Carter. Lemon squash.

Rand. A baby bottle of jump.

Rod. Brandy and soda.

Fan. Don't serve him, Miss Larondie. He's three parts squiffy already.

Rod. Shut up, Fan.

Shar. A gin cocktail, Miss Larondie, and I'll show you how to mix it.

Fan. Don't trust him, miss. He wants to sneak a sample of your spirits for the public analyst.

Rod. Serve me first, Miss Larondie, and I'll give you a guinea for Dick Ramsden's widow. (*General hubbub and clatter*)

Dulcie. Order, order, gentlemen! Jimmy Stokes, take this gentleman's guinea and go round with this list, and see what you can get for poor Dick's family. (*Jimmy takes the subscription list, and is seen to go round with it to several of the bystanders, and talk to them in dumb show*)

Fan. I'll go behind and help you, miss. (*Lifts up the lid of the counter, and tries to push in*)

Rod. (*Pushing him back*) Sling, you animal! I'm going to be underbarmaid here. (*They both push in behind the bar*)

Fan. No, you don't. Now, gents, your orders, and no larking with us poor unprotected females. (*Putting his arm round Dulcie's waist*)

Helen Larondie enters and stands watching Dulcie.

Dulcie. (*Indignantly to Fancourt*) How dare you?

Rod. (*On the other side, puts his arm round her waist — to Fancourt*) How dare you?

Dulcie. (*Disengaging herself indignantly*) Pass out! Do you hear? Pass out! (*Showing them the way out. Sees Helen standing there, shows great shame*) Nell!

Fan. (*Seizes Rodney by the collar and runs him out*) Pass out! Do you hear? Pass out! (*Runs him out of the bar*)

Brink. Gentlemen! Gentlemen! If you please! gentlemen! If you please!

Dulcie. Mr. Brinkler, my sister has come for me. Would you mind waiting on these gentlemen? (*They clamour round Brinkler, repeating their orders for drinks. Dulcie goes to her sister*)

Dulcie. Nell! (*Kisses her*)

Helen. My dear.

Dulcie. Come and talk to me. (*Takes her up to where David is standing. She catches sight of David, who has been watching the scene with a mixture of bitterness and amusement. Seeing David*) Mr. Remon — I had forgotten you.

David. You had such pleasant companions.

Dulcie. I have wasted your time.

David. It's of no value.

Dulcie. But I'm afraid I've made you rather foolish.

David. In a world of fools it's a distinction to play the fool for you. In a world of shadows, what does it matter what part one plays? Good-night.

Dulcie. No, come again.

David. It's nearly closing time.

Dulcie. But we shall be late tonight. Come again by and by.

David. By and by.   *Exit.*

Helen. Who is that?

Dulcie. His name's Remon. He has haunted the place for the last month. He's in love with me. I can make him do any foolish thing I please. (*Brinkler serves the young men with drinks. The music strikes up again, and they gradually go off, leaving the stage with only Dulcie and Helen on it*) Nell, I'm so glad —what makes you come so late?

Helen. (*A soft-voiced, gentle woman of about thirty, in a nurse's dress*) I've just had a telegram to go and nurse a typhoid case at Moorbrow, so I sha'n't see you for a few weeks. You still like it here?

Dulcie. (*Rather defiantly*) Yes. It's livelier than being a governess, and it isn't so horrid as nursing typhoid.

Helen. (*Smiling*) Dear, there's nothing horrid about nursing. It's just like a mother and her baby.

Dulcie. How awful sweet *that* must be. (*Looking at her sister*) How patiently you take our comedown, Nell. Instead of rebelling and hating everybody as I do, you've just gone and nursed all these dirty people and made yourself quite happy over it.

Helen. I've found out the secret of living.

Dulcie. What's that?

Helen. Forget yourself. Deny yourself. Renounce yourself. It's out of the fashion just now. But some day the world will hear that message again.

Dulcie. (*Looking at Helen with admiration*) I wish I was good like you, Nell. No, I don't. I don't want to deny myself, or renounce myself, or forget myself. I want to enjoy myself, and to see life. That's why I screwed up my courage and answered Brinkler's advertisement, and came here.

Helen. And are you enjoying yourself?

Dulcie. (*Defiantly*) Yes, after a fashion. I wish I was a man, or one of those girls upstairs. Why should they have all the pleasure and happiness of life?

Helen. You're sure they have all the pleasure and happiness of life?

Dulcie. At any rate they've got what I

want. Oh, how I long for life! How I could enjoy it! Hark! (*Dance music swells*) Isn't that dance maddening? I must dance! (*Begins*) Oh, Nell, I was made for society! Oh, for London! for pleasure! To be somebody in the world! How I would worship any man who would raise me to a position! And wouldn't I repay him? What parties I'd give! I'd have all London at my feet! I could do it! I know I could! Oh, is there anybody who will take me out of this dead-alive hole and give me the life I was made for? (*Flings herself wildly round, half dancing, and drops her head into Helen's lap sobbing*)

Helen. (*Stroking Dulcie's hair very softly*) My poor Dulcie! I knew you weren't happy here.

Dulcie. I hate it! I hate it! Nell, don't be surprised if I do something desperate before long.

Helen. Dulcie, you'll do nothing wrong. (*Lifting up Dulcie's head, looking keenly at her*)

Dulcie. What do you mean? Nell, you know I wouldn't. Kiss me, ducky. Say you know I wouldn't.

Helen. (*Kisses her*) I don't think you would, but — when I came in and saw those two men —

Dulcie. (*Quickly*) Boys. They meant nothing. One has to put up with a good deal here. Men aren't nice creatures.

Helen. Dulcie, you must come away from this.

Dulcie. Where? What can I do? I wish somebody would marry me. What wouldn't I give to cut Lady Clarice as she cut me tonight!

Helen. Did she cut you?

Dulcie. Yes. She gave me one look — Nell, if she looks at me again like that, I don't care what happens, I shall box her ears.

Helen. Dulcie!

Dulcie. But if she cuts me, Sir Brice has cut her. And he pays me no end of attention.

Helen. You're not growing friendly with Sir Brice?

Dulcie. No — yes — he's always paying me compliments, and asking me to take presents.

Helen. You haven't taken his presents?

Dulcie. No. Don't fear, Nell, I'll take nothing from him except — if he were really fond of me, I'd marry him, Nell.

Helen. No, dear no. He's not a good man.

Dulcie. Nell, there ain't any good men left in the world. The race is extinct. I daresay Sir Brice is as good as the rest, and if he were to ask me I should say "yes." (*Helen shakes her head*) Yes, I should, Nell. And I should make him a good wife, Nell, for there are the makings of a good wife in me. I should say "yes," and oh, wouldn't I like to see Lady Clarice's face when she hears the news.

Helen. I hope he won't ask you, Dulcie.

Dulcie. Stranger things have happened.

Helen. I must be going. I've to watch a fever case to-night.

Dulcie. (*Twining Helen's arms round her neck*) I wish I could have a fever.

Helen. Dulcie!

Dulcie. It would be so lovely to be nursed by you. (*Hugging her*) I shall never love a man as I love you, Nell. But I suppose that's a different kind of love. (*Helen sighs*) What makes you sigh?

Helen. Good-bye, Dulcie.

Dulcie. Good-bye, you dear, nice, soft, warm, comforting thing. You're as good as a boa, or a muff, or a poultice to me. I'll let you out this way. It's nearer for you.

Exeunt Helen and Dulcie through bar.

Sir Brice enters from ball-room, followed by Lady Crandover, Lady Clarice following. Lady Clarice goes and sits down quite apart.

Lady Cran. Sir Brice! (*Sir Brice turns, stops. Lady Crandover somewhat embarrassed*) Do you know what people are saying of you?

Sir B. I haven't an idea. But whatever it is, don't stop them.

Lady Cran. Sir Brice. All through the season you have paid the most marked attention to Clarice.

Sir B. I admire Lady Clarice immensely. I have a very ingenuous nature, and perhaps I allowed it to become too apparent.

Lady Cran. You allowed it to become so apparent that every one in the county supposed as an honourable man —

Sir B. Ah, that's a nice point, isn't it? If Crandover thinks I have behaved dishonourably, the Englishman's three remedies are open to him — he can write a letter to the "Times," or he can bring an action, or — he can horsewhip me. Personally, I'm indifferent which course he takes. Excuse me.

Goes off into the bar.

Lady Cran. (*Enraged and almost in tears, goes to Clarice*) My dear, he's a brute! What an awful life his wife will have!

Lady Clar. Then why did you run after him? Why did you let me encourage him?

Lady Cran. Clarice, he has twenty thousand a year.

Lady Clar. But everybody says he'll run

through it in a few years. He lost fifty thousand on the Leger alone.

Lady Cran. I know. Oh yes, he'll soon get through it. Well, now you've lost him, it's a great comfort to think what a perfect brute he is. You've had a lucky escape.

Dulcie re-enters from bar. Jimmy re-enters with subscription list.

Lady Clar. (*Watching Dulcie*) Yes, but I don't like being thrown aside for that miss there.

Dulcie. What luck, Jimmy? (*Jimmy shakes his head. Dulcie takes the subscription list from him*) Oh, Jimmy Jimmy Stokes, when we keep a Punch and Judy show, I'll never send you round with the hat.

Jimmy. Ah, miss, we know how you could get a peck of money for 'em — don't we, Mr. Fancourt?

Fan. By Jove, yes. Jimmy has made a splendid suggestion, Miss Larondie. The only question is, will you agree to it?

Dulcie. What is it, Jimmy?

Jimmy. You back me up, miss, that's all, will you?

Dulcie. Certainly. Anything to keep Mrs. Ramsden and her chickabiddies out of the workhouse. I always feel, you know, Jimmy, that it was through me that Dick was killed.

Fan. Through you, Miss Larondie?

Dulcie. I was leading across Drubhill. I took the drop into the road. Dick was next behind. His horse stumbled and (*Shudders*) they picked him up dead. (*All the young fellows have crowded around and listen*)

Jimmy. 'Twas me as picked him up, if you remember, miss, and took him home, I did, ah, it's three years ago last February, yes, and I broke the news to his wife, I did, and what's more, I helped to lay Dick out, I did, and I says to his wife, "Don't take on now, you foolish woman," I says, "why," I says, "it might have been *felo-de-se.*" But it were a nasty drop jump, miss, a nasty drop jump.

Dulcie. And if I hadn't taken it, perhaps Dick might have been alive now.

Jimmy. Not he, not he. Dick'd have drunk himself to death before this. He was a royal soul, Dick was. And if you'll only back me up, we'll raise a little fortune for Mrs. Ramsden in no time.

Dulcie. Very well, Jimmy. But what is this plan, eh, Mr. Fancourt?

Fan. Tell her, Jimmy. You started it.

Jimmy. Well, miss, seeing all these young gents here, it struck me as, human nature being what it is, and no getting over it, no offence I hope to anybody, but if you was to offer to sell one, mind you, only one, of your kisses to the highest bidder —

Dulcie. (*Indignantly*) What?

Monty. A very excellent and original suggestion!

Dulcie. The idea! What nonsense!

Fan. Nonsense? I call it a jolly good idea.

Shar. Splendid! By Jove, we'll carry it out too.

Dulcie. Indeed we won't. Jimmy, give me that list. (*Takes the subscription list from Jimmy*) Mr. Fancourt will give me something, I'm sure.

Fan. I should be delighted, but (*Nudging Sharland*) fact is, I've promised Sharland I wouldn't give anything except on the conditions Jimmy Stokes has just laid down.

Dulcie. Mr. Sharland.

Shar. Very sorry, Miss Larondie, but fact is (*Nudging Fancourt*) I've promised Fancourt I wouldn't give anything except on the conditions Jimmy Stokes has laid down. (*Dulcie turns away indignantly, sees Lady Crandover and Lady Clarice, hesitates a moment, then goes somewhat defiantly to them*)

Dulcie. Lady Crandover, may I beg you for a small subscription to Dick Ramsden's widow and children?

Lady Cran. (*Very coolly*) I always leave such things to Lord Crandover. (*Turns away*)

Dulcie. Perhaps Lady Clarice —

Lady Cran. I thought I heard some one propose a way in which you could raise some money.

Sir B. (*Coming from bar*) Raise some money? What's the matter here?

Fan. Jimmy Stokes has just proposed that Miss Larondie should benefit the Dick Ramsden fund by selling a kiss by auction.

Sir B. What does Miss Larondie say?

Dulcie. Impossible!

Monty. Not in the least. If you will allow me, gentlemen, I will constitute myself auctioneer. (*To Dulcie*) I beg you will place yourself entirely in my hands, Miss Larondie. Trust to my tact to bring this affair to a most successful issue. After all, it's not so indelicate as slumming.

Dulcie. No, no!

Monty. Allow me. A rostrum. Rodney, you are my clerk. That wine case. (*A wine case is brought forward from side*) And that barrel, if you please. A hammer. (*A large mallet, such as is used for hammering bungs in beer barrels, is given to him*) Thank you. (*He mounts*) Ladies and gentlemen. (*Chorus of "Hear, hear"*) We must all admit that the methods of raising the wind for all sorts of worthless persons and useless charities stand in need

of entire revision. Fancy fairs, amateur theatricals, tableaux vivants, and such grotesque
futilities have had their day. In the interests
of those long-suffering persons who get up
charity entertainments, and those yet more
long-suffering persons who attend them, it is
high time to inaugurate a new departure.
(*Cries of* "*Hear, hear*") Ladies and gentlemen,
there are three questions I take it which we
ask ourselves when we raise a charitable
subscription. Firstly, how shall we advertise
ourselves, or amuse ourselves, as the case
may be? Secondly, how far shall we be able
to fleece our friends and the public? Thirdly,
is the charity a deserving one? — The only
really vital question of the three is "How
shall we amuse ourselves in the sacred cause
of charity?" (*Cries of* "*Hear, hear*")

Lady Cran. Lushington, stop this nonsense before it goes any further! Do you
hear?

Monty. Ladies and gentlemen, I am in
your hands. Shall I go on? (*Loud cries of*
"*Yes, yes* — Go on, — Go on, Monty —
Go on, Lushington*")

Lady Cran. (*To Lady Clarice*) Now she'll
disgrace herself.

Sir B. (*Having overheard*) What did you
say, Lady Crandover?

Lady Cran. Nothing, Sir Brice.

Sir B. I understood you to say that Miss
Larondie would disgrace herself.

Dulcie. (*With shame*) Oh, Sir Brice, please
let me go!

*David Remon enters. Dulcie going off comes
face to face with him — stops.*

Sir B. No, stay. Don't take any notice of
what has been said.

David. What has been said?

Sir B. What business is it of yours? Miss
Larondie is a connection of my family. Go
on, Lushington — Go on. We'll have this
auction — it's in the cause of charity, isn't
it? Go on!

David. (*To Montagu*) What auction? What
charity?

Monty. (*Soothingly*) Gentlemen, gentlemen, we are taking this far too seriously.
Pray be calm and allow me to proceed. (*Cries
of* "*Hear! — Go on, Monty!*") In an age
when, as all good moralists lament, love is so
often brought into the market, the marriage
market — and other markets — and is sold
to the highest bidder, it would, I am convinced, require a far more alarming outrage
on propriety than that which we are now
about to commit, to cause the now obsolete
and unfashionable blush of shame to mount

into the now obsolete and unfashionable
cheek of modesty. Gentlemen, without further ado I offer for your competition — one
kiss from Miss Larondie. (*Movement on the
part of David. Sir Brice and he stand confronting each other*) One kiss from Miss Larondie.
What shall I say, gentlemen?

Fan. A sovereign.

Monty. A sovereign is offered. I will on
my own account advance ten shillings. Thirty
shillings is offered, gentlemen.

Shar. Thirty-five shillings.

Monty. I cannot take an advance of less
than ten shillings on this lot. Shall I say
two pounds? (*Sharland nods*)

Sir B. A fiver. (*David steps forward towards Sir Brice*)

Monty. Thank you. A fiver. You are trifling, gentlemen.

Fan. Six.

Monty. Six guineas — guineas only. Six
guineas is offered. Gentlemen, if you do not
bid up, in justice to my client I must withdraw the lot.

Shar. Seven.

Sir B. Ten.

Monty. Ten guineas. Gentlemen, only ten
guineas — only ten guineas for this rare
and genuine, this highly desirable —

David. Twenty guineas.

Monty. Twenty guineas. Thank you, sir.
This gentleman sees the quality of the article
I am submitting —

Sir B. Thirty.

Monty. Thirty guineas. Gentlemen, is the
age of chivalry dead? Mr. Fancourt, you are
credited with some small amount of prowess
among helpless ladies —

Shar. Cut in, Fan.

Fan. Thirty-one.

Monty. Cannot take advances of less than
five guineas. Thirty-five guineas. Gentlemen,
will you force me to expatiate further on this
exquisite —

David. Forty.

Sir B. Fifty. (*David and Sir Brice are getting
nearer to each other*)

Lord Cran. Lushington, this is enough.
This is getting beyond a joke.

Monty. Then it's the only thing in life
that ever did, so we'll continue. Bid up,
gentlemen, bid up. I am assured, gentlemen,
by my client, the vendor, that on no account
will this lot ever be duplicated. I am therefore offering you a unique opportunity of
purchasing what I will venture to describe
as the most —

David. Sixty.

Sir B. Seventy.

Lord Cran. Enough — enough! Stop this jest.

Monty. Jest? I presume you are in earnest, gentlemen, about the purchase of this lot?

David. I am.

Sir B. Go on, go on.

Monty. Seventy guineas, seventy guineas. Gentlemen, you have not all done? Mr. Fancourt, faint heart —

Shar. Have another shy, Fan.

Fan. Seventy-five.

Monty. Seventy-five. Going at seventy-five guineas — the only chance; going at seventy-five guineas.

Fan. I say, Bricey, don't let me in.

Sir B. Eighty. (*Looking at David*)

David. Ninety.

Sir B. A hundred. (*Getting close to David*)

David. Two hundred.

Sir B. Three hundred.

Lord Cran. Skene, come away, do you hear? Come away. (*Trying to drag Sir Brice away*)

Sir. B. Let me be. What's the last bidding, Lushington?

Monty. Three hundred guineas.

Sir B. Five.

David. A thousand.

Sir B. Fifteen hundred.

David. Two thousand.

Sir B. Three, and (*Growling*) be damned to you! (*Pause*) Knock it down, Lushington. (*Long pause. David shows disappointment*)

Monty. Three thousand guineas is offered, gentlemen. (*Pause*) No further bid? Going at three thousand. Going, going. (*Knocks it down*) Sir Brice, the lot is yours at three thousand guineas.

Sir B. Brinkler, pens, ink, and paper and a stamp. (*Stepping towards barrel. David comes to him*) You've no further business here.

David. Yes, I think. (*Pens, ink, and paper are brought to Sir Brice; he hastily dashes off the cheque, gives it to Montagu*)

Monty. Thank you. Miss Larondie, a cheque for three thousand guineas. You have secured an annuity for your *protégées.*

Dulcie. (*Refusing the cheque*) No.

Sir. B. Miss Larondie. (*David looks at him*) It will perhaps save any further misconstruction if I tell these ladies and gentlemen that an hour ago I asked you to do me the honour to become my wife. (*General surprise*)

Dulcie. Sir Brice —

Sir B. Will you do me the favour to take that cheque for your charity, and the further favour of becoming Lady Skene? (*Montagu offers the cheque. A pause. Dulcie looks round, looks at Lady Clarice, takes the cheque*)

Dulcie. Thank you, Sir Brice. I shall be very proud. (*David shows quiet despair. Goes to back. Half the guests crowd round Sir Brice and Dulcie, congratulating. The others show surprise, interest, and amazement*)

Lady Cran. (*In a very loud voice*) My carriage at once.

Lord Cran. (*In a low voice to her*) We'd better stay and make the best of it.

Lady Cran. No, my carriage. Come, Clarice.

> *Goes off. A good many of the guests follow her. Exeuent Lady Clarice and Lord Crandover.*

Sir B. (*To Fancourt*) The Crandovers have gone off in a huff. Bet you a tenner they'll dine with me before three months.

Fan. Done!

Sir B. (*To Dulcie*) If you will allow me, I will place you in my sister's care. She's in the ball-room.

Dulcie. (*Looking at her dress*) No, Sir Brice, not yet. I've one of my old evening dresses upstairs. May I put it on?

Sir. B. Yes, if you like. I'll wait for you at the ball-room door.

Dulcie. I won't be a moment. (*Running off upstairs with great excitement and delight*)

Monty. (*To Sir Brice*) Congratulate you heartily, Sir Brice. (*Offering hand*)

Sir B. (*Taking it*) Oh, I suppose it's all right.

Shar. (*To Sir Brice*) Your wooing was charmingly fresh and original, Sir Brice.

Sir B. Think so?

Char. (*To Monty*) What on earth does he want to marry the girl for?

Monty. Somebody has bet him a guinea he wouldn't.

> *Exeunt Charley and Montagu into the ball-room.*

Fan. Bravo, Bricey, my boy! This'll make up to you for losing the Leger.

Sir B. Think so? I'll go and get a smoke outside. *Exit at gates.*

Shar. (*To Fancourt*) Just like Bricey to do a silly fool's trick like this.

Fan. I pity the girl. Bricey will make a sweet thing in husbands.

Shar. By Jove, yes. Her life'll be a regular beno, and no mistake.

> *Exeunt. David is left alone sitting at back.*

Enter Eddie. David drinks and laughs rather bitterly to himself.

Eddie. What's gone wrong, Davy?

David. Miss Larondie is going to marry Sir Brice Skene.

Eddie. Oh, then the solar system is all out of joint! Poor old big brother!

David. I won't feel it, Eddie, I won't feel it.

Eddie. Yes, you will, Davy. Yes, you will. Why weren't you tumbled into Mars, or Jupiter, or Saturn, or into any world but this?

David. Why?

Eddie. This the is very worst world that ever spun round, for a man who has a heart. Look at all the heartless and stupid people; what a paradise this is for them!

David. I'll forget her and plunge into my work. There are millions of new worlds to discover.

Eddie. Yes, but are they all like this? because if they are, what's the use of discovering millions more of them? Oh, Davy, isn't there one perfect world out of all the millions — just one — where everything goes right, and fiddles never play out of tune?

David. There isn't one, Eddie, not one of all the millions. They're all alike.

Eddie. And breaking hearts in all of them? Oh, let's pretend there's just one perfect star somewhere, shall we?

David. Oh, very well; let's pretend there's one in the nebula of Andromeda. It's a long way off, and it does no harm to pretend. Besides, it makes the imbroglio of the universe complete if there is one perfect world somewhere in it. (*Sir Brice enters smoking, throws away his cigarette, looks at David rather insolently, goes into the ball-room*) If he doesn't treat her well — what does it matter? It's all a farce, but if he doesn't treat her well, I feel, Eddie, I could put a murder into the farce, just for fun.

Eddie. Come home, Davy.

David. Let me be, my boy. It's only a pinprick. I shall get over it.

Eddie. I wish I could bear it for you, Davy.

David. That would only mean your heart breaking instead of mine.

Eddie. Don't you think I'd break my heart for you, Davy?

Dulcie. (*Her voice heard off*) Thanks! I can't wait! Sir Brice is waiting for me!

Eddie. Poor old big brother!   *Exit.*

Enter Dulcie down the stairs in evening dress, excited, radiant.

Dulcie. (*Seeing David*) I thought you'd gone. Did you hear? I'm to be Lady Skene. Do I look nice? (*Very excited*) I beg your pardon — I don't know what I'm saying. (*Looks round*) I wish there was a looking-glass here. I wonder where Sir Brice is — I'm to

be Lady Skene — won't you congratulate me?

David. I hope you will be happy

Dulcie. No, congratulate me.

David. I hope you will be happy.

Dulcie. Ah, you think I sha'n't be happy? Then I will, just to spite you!

David. Ah, do spite me and be happy.

Dulcie. (*Fidgeting with her dress*) I'm sure my dress isn't right. Wasn't that a jest about the kiss?

David. A great jest.

Dulcie. You wouldn't have really given two thousand guineas for a kiss from me?

David. (*Nods*) Why not? Sir Brice gave fifty thousand for the pleasure of losing the Leger.

Dulcie. But he stood to win.

David. So did I.

Dulcie. What?

David. The kiss.

Dulcie. But you wouldn't really have given two thousand guineas for it?

David. (*Nods*) I think highly of women. It's a pleasing delusion of mine. Don't disturb it.

Dulcie. (*Looking at him, after a little pause*) You are the strangest creature, but what a splendid friend you'd make! I'm keeping Sir Brice waiting. (*Turns round, sees that the lace on the skirt of her dress is hanging loose*) Look at that lace! What can I do? (*Giving him a pin*) Would you mind pinning that lace on my skirt?

David. (*Takes the pin, kneels, and pins the lace; unseen by Dulcie, kisses the skirt*) Will that do?

Dulcie. Thank you so much. Do I look nice?

He looks up at her imploringly, like a dumb creature; she glances swiftly round to see that they are alone, suddenly bends and kisses him; runs up the ball-room steps. A burst of dance-music.

End of the First Act.

ACT II.

Three years and a half pass between Acts 1 and II. Reception-room at Lady Skene's. A great crowd in farther room. Discover Lady Crandover, Lady Clarice, Charley Wishanger (now Lady Shalford), Montagu, Fancourt, Sharland, and the young men of the first Act. Among the guests in farther room Sir Winchmore Wills and the Hon. Percy Blanchflower.

Lady Cran. It's astounding.

Char. What is?

Lady Cran. The way every one runs after this woman. She's got everybody here again to-night.

Lady Clar. Professor Rawkinson and the Bishop of Malmesbury were fighting to get her an ice.

Char. What is the secret of her popularity?

Monty. Why did you come here to-night?

Char. I? Oh, I came because everybody else comes. Why did you?

Monty. Because everybody else comes. Do we ever have any other reason for going anywhere, admiring anything, saying anything, or doing anything? The secret of getting a crowd to your room is, "*Entice a bell-wether.*" The flock will follow.

Char. Who was the bell-wether to Lady Skene?

Monty. The old Duchess of Norwich.

Lady Cran. I suppose the Duchess knows all about Lady Skene's antecedents?

Monty. What does it matter about anybody's antecedents to-day?

Lady Cran. We must draw the line somewhere.

Monty. On the contrary, my dear Lady Crandover, we must *not* draw the line *anywhere.* We have yet got to learn what democracy means.

Lady Cran. What does democracy mean?

Monty. That there is no line to be drawn, either socially, morally, pecuniarily, politically, religiously, or anywhere.

Lady Clar. How horrid!

Monty. (*Continuing*) Who are the interesting people here to-night? Of course there's a crowd of respectable nonentities — But who are the attractions? Attraction number one: a financier's wife — the most charming woman in the world — gives the very best dinners in London — had an extensive acquaintance amongst the officers at Aldershot fifteen years ago.

The Hon. Percy Blanchflower, a fussy, buzzy, mincing, satirical little creature, with a finicking, feminine manner and gestures, has overheard, comes up to the group.

Blanch. What's this? — eh? — hum? No scandal, I trust?

Monty. No, Blanchflower; no scandal — only the plain, unvarnished truth about all our friends.

Blanch. Ah, then I'll stay and listen. Go on!

Monty. Attraction number two: leading temperance and social purity orator — can move an audience of ten thousand to tears — leads the loosest of lives — and is suspected of having poisoned his wife.

Blanch. But she had a fearful cockney accent. And he's very kind to his aged aunt and pretty niece — eh? — hum? Give him his due.

Monty. My dear Blanchflower, I'm not blaming the man for poisoning his wife. It may have been a necessity of his position; and if she had a cockney accent, it was a noble thing to do. Attraction number three: pretty little lady who has just emerged triumphantly from the Divorce Court without a spot upon her pretty little character. Attraction number four — (*Lady Clarice rejoins the group*)

Blanch. (*Interrupting*) No! No! Skip number four! We know all about her. Attraction number five. And mind, I shall thoroughly scold you all — when Lushington has got through his list.

Monty. (*Proceeding*) Attraction number five: impressionist artist, novelist, and general dirty modern dabbler — is consummately clever — a consistent scoundrel in every relation of life — especially to women — a liar, a cheat, and drunkard — and a great personal friend of my own.

Blanch. Oh, this is too shocking! This is really too shocking!

Lady Clar. You've omitted the chief attraction to-night — our famous astronomer.

Monty. Remon?

Blanch. Of course. Since his great discovery we've only one astronomer in England.

Char. What was his great discovery?

Blanch. Don't know. Some new spots on Venus, I believe.

Monty. No. That she wanted a new belt to hide the manners of her inhabitants, which were distinctly visible through his new large telescope, and if constantly observed would tend to the corruption of London society.

Blanch. You naughty person! You're not to look through that telescope!

Monty. My dear Blanchflower, I have; and I assure you we have nothing to fear. But I tremble for the morals of Venus if they get a telescope as large as Remon's and begin to look at us.

Blanch. Tell me, this friendship of the astronomer with Lady Skene — eh? hum? — quite innocent — eh?

Monty. I have never known any friendship between a man and a married woman that was not innocent. How can it be guilty, unless the woman is ugly?

Lady Clar. Poor dear Lady Skene is fearfully ill-used, I hear. (*Sir Winchmore Wills, a fashionable middle-aged physician, has come up and joined the group*) I've heard that Sir Brice gets drunk and — then — dreadful things happen.

Blanch. But that can't be true — eh? hum? — Sir Winchmore — eh?

Sir W. I have never treated Sir Brice for alcoholism, nor Lady Skene for bruises.

Blanch. No, of course, no — but you've heard — hum? eh?

Sir W. Singularly enough, I have never heard or seen anything in the least discreditable to any one of my patients.

Eddie enters and talks to guests.

Char. I know for a fact Sir Brice came a terrific cropper last week at Epsom, and doesn't know how he stands. (*Eddie is listening attentively*)

Blanch. And — hum — the astronomer — hum? eh? hum? — is there any truth — eh?

Monty. Well, we *know* that our astronomer succeeded a few months ago to an immense fortune left him by a mountaineering friend in Canada. We *know* that Sir Brice neglects his wife and is practically ruined. We *know* that Lady Skene continues her parties, her household, her carriages, and we *know* that our astronomer pays (*Pause*) the greatest attentions to Lady Skene. Of course this doesn't absolutely prove Lady Skene's guilt — yet why should we deprive ourselves of the pleasure of believing and circulating a spicy story about our friends merely because there is only the very slightest foundation for it? (*Eddie rises rather indignantly and comes a little nearer to the group without being noticed by them*)

Blanch. Oh, this is very naughty of us. We are actually talking scandal about our hostess. We ought to be ashamed of ourselves!

Lady Cran. Really, it's time somebody made a stand, or society will be ruined. Here is a woman who was actually a barmaid at a public-house — her name is in everybody's mouth in connection with this astronomer, and yet —

Monty. And yet we crush to her receptions. At least you do, Lady Crandover.

Lady Cran. Oh, we are all to blame for lowering the moral tone of society as we are doing.

Blanch. Oh, my dear Lady Crandover, please, please, please, do not make things unpleasant by dragging in morality. But where is the astronomer? — eh? hum?

Eddie. My brother will be coming by and by. I'll tell him he's wanted here.

> *Exit. Blanchflower looks aghast and stares round at all the rest, who show some slight discomfiture. Fancourt and Sharland join the group.*

Blanch. Dear me! That's the astronomer's brother. Have we said anything? — hum? eh?

Monty. My dear Blanchflower, what does it matter what lies we tell about each other when none of our friends think any the worse of us if they are true!

Blanch. Oh, but it's very wrong to tell lies, very wrong indeed. I've not seen Sir Brice to-night. Where is he? eh?

Fan. Bricey doesn't generally stay very long at his wife's receptions.

Shar. Bricey's latest little hobby is teaching the girls at the Folly Theatre to box.

Fan. Yes. Last Tuesday he was in great force at the Ducks and Drakes Club egging on Betty Vignette to fight Sylvia Vernon.

Shar. Oh, that's coming off — two hundred a side, on Sunday night week.

Fan. (*Cautiously winking at Sharland, in a warning way*) I say, old chap, keep it quiet. I wonder where Bricey is to-night.

Monty. What does it matter whether he is playing baccarat with the pot-boy at the corner, or clandestinely taking his nurse-girl to the Alhambra on the pretence that it is a missionary meeting? We may be quite sure that Bricey is doing something equally vicious, stupid, disreputable, and — original.

Char. (*To Monty*) Come here, you monster. Have you heard the news? (*During the conversation of Charley and Monty the other group put their heads together and whisper*)

Monty. What?

Char. Sir Joseph is going to leave the Marchmoore estates to Clarice.

Monty. (*Glancing at Lady Clarice*) Sure?

Char. Fact. The will is to be signed in a few days. Clarice told me so in confidence.

Monty. Thanks. (*Strolls cautiously up to Lady Clarice, hovers about her till he gets a chance of speaking to her. A general laugh from the group*)

Blanch. (*Who has been in center of group*) Oh, this is very shocking! We are actually talking scandal about our host. And he has his good points. He hasn't strangled his baby, has he, Sir Winchmore?

Sir W. Sir Brice has the greatest consideration for the welfare of his offspring. (*Dulcie comes from other room magnificently dressed, restless, pale, nervous, excited*) He never goes near it. (*An awkward little pause as they see Dulcie. Lady Clarice goes up to her*)

Lady Clar. What a lot of interesting folks you always have, dear. Who is that lady in pale blue?

Dulcie. Mrs. Chalmers.

Lady Clar. The lady who has figured so much in the newspapers lately? What a singular gift you have of attracting all sorts of people, dear.

Dulcie. Have I? That's sometimes a misfortune.

Lady Clar. Yes, it does involve one in undesirable acquaintances and relationships.

Dulcie. Still it must be rather annoying to be without it. (*Goes restlessly to Sir Winchmore. Lady Clarice shows slight mortification. Monty, who has been watching the scene, goes up to her*)

Monty. Lady Clarice, let me give you some supper.

Dulcie. (*Taking Sir Winchmore a little aside*) Sir Winchmore — so kind of you to come. (*In a half whisper*) That sleeping draught's no use — you must send me a stronger one.

Sir W. (*Shakes his head*) Lady Skene —

Dulcie. (*Impetuously*) Yes, yes, please — I must have it — I've not slept for three nights.

Sir W. Lady Skene, let me beg you —

Dulcie. No, no, no, — you must patch me up and keep me going somehow till the end of the season, then you shall do what you like with me.

Sir W. But, Lady Skene —

Dulcie. (*Intense suppressed nervousness*) But — (*Imploringly*) Oh, don't contradict me. — When any one speaks to me I feel I must shriek out "Yah, yah, yah!" (*Blanchflower has overheard the last speech. Dulcie sees that Blanchflower is looking at her, controls herself after an immense effort, puts on society smile. To Blanchflower*) The Bishop was talking to me just now about his mission to convert the West End of London, and I could scarcely keep from shrieking out to him "Yah, yah, yah!" Isn't it strange?

Blanch. Not at all. Clergymen always produce that effect upon me.

Dulcie. (*Turning to Sir Winchmore*) Sir Winchmore, you'll run up to the nursery and see Rosy before you go, won't you?

Sir W. What's the matter?

Dulcie. Nothing, only a little tumble and a bruise. My sister Nell is with her, but you'll just see her?

Sir W. Certainly.

Dulcie. I'm so foolish about her. (*Imploringly*) She is strong and healthy, isn't she?

Sir W. A magnificent child.

Sir Brice has entered through other room. He looks coarser and more dissipated than in First Act, and is more brutalised. There is a slight movement of all the guests away from him. Sharland enters.

Dulcie. (*Not seeing Sir Brice. To Sir Winchmore*) Really? Really?

Sir W. Really. Sir Brice and you may well be proud of her. (*Sir Brice's entrance has caused an awkward pause amongst the guests*) We were talking of your youthful daughter, Sir Brice.

Sir B. I hate brats. (*Another awkward pause*)

Dulcie. (*To cover it, rattles away with forced gaiety*) We shall see you at Ascot, of course, Mr. Blanchflower. — Sir Winchmore, what are these frightful new waters that you are sending all your patients to? — That reminds me, Lady Shalford, how is Sir Digby's gout? (*Slight continued movement of the guests away from Sir Brice*)

Char. Terrible. I pack him off to Aix on Thursday.

Dulcie. (*Same tone*) So sorry he couldn't come to-night.

Char. My dear, I'm very glad, and so I'm sure is everybody who knows him. If Aix doesn't cure him, I shall try something drastic.

Sir B. Serve him as I did my trainer Burstow.

Dulcie. (*Noticing the guests' repulsion, slightly frowns at Sir Brice unobserved by the guests, and goes on speaking to change the subject*) We shall go to Homburg again —

Sir B. (*Speaks her down. To Charley*) Burstow had the gout. I treated him myself. (*Coarse little chuckle*) I gave him a bottle of port, champagne at intervals, and brown brandy *ad lib.* A tombstone now marks Burstow's precise position, which is longitudinal. I wrote his epitaph, but the vicar wouldn't pass it. So the vicar and I have a law-suit on. (*Another coarse little chuckle. Another awkward little pause*)

Dulcie. (*To cover it, continues*) Mr. Fancourt, did you make inquiries about the house-boat for us?

Sir B. We sha'n't go to Henley.

Dulcie. (*To Fancourt*) Then of course you needn't make inquiries.

Fan. But I've arranged it. My brother will be awfully delighted if you'll accept the loan of his for the Henley week. You and Sir Brice will be awfully pleased with it.

Sir B. (*More decidedly*) We shall not go to Henley.

Dulcie. (*Another covered frown at Sir Brice, again controlling herself with immense effort and speaking very calmly*) Will you thank your brother and say we shall not be going. (*Awkward pause. Sir Brice puts his hands in his pockets and yawns. Dulcie engages the group in conversation, and they crowd round her*)

Sir B. Percy, come and have a little game of poker in the smoking-room.

Shar. Very sorry, Bricey, haven't so much as a fiver with me.

Sir B. You can borrow. Can't you borrow, eh?

Shar. Very sorry, dear old chap; never borrow or lend.

    Exit. Sir Brice stands and yawns, looks sulky and vicious, then calls out.

Sir B. Fancourt. (*Fancourt glances but does not come*) Fan — Fan, I say — (*At length Fancourt comes*) We're getting up a little hand at poker just to wind up this infernally dull evening.

Fan. (*Shakes his head and laughs*) Not good enough, Bricey — not good enough.

David Remon enters. At his entrance guests show marked interest, and the conversation stops. Sir Brice watches with a sulky expression. Dulcie shows great pleasure, goes to meet Remon.

Dulcie. I'm so glad you've come. You have so many engagements. (*Shakes hands*)

David. None more pleasing than this.

Blanch. I insist on knowing Mr. Remon — somebody introduce me — introduce me.

Dulcie. Mr. Remon — Mr. Percy Blanch-flower.

Blanch. I'm so delighted to know you. We want to look at Venus through that large telescope of yours.

David. It's in the South of France.

Blanch. I go there every winter. We were talking about your wonderful discoveries — hum? eh? We want to know all about them.

David. Oh, spare me, or rather, your-selves. (*Sir Brice laughs*)

Fan. You seem to have got something good all to yourself, Bricey.

Sir B. Yes, I have. (*Laughs*)

Blanch. (*Aside, to Sir Winchmore*) What is Remon's discovery? eh?

Sir W. Haven't the least idea — some-thing about Saturn, I fancy.

Blanch. (*Buzzes up to Remon*) Your last discovery now — about Saturn, wasn't it — hum? eh?

All through David's conversation with the guests, he adopts the same light frivolous tone throughout, and speaks without the least suggestion of seriousness. This gives a contrast to the scenes with Dulcie.

David. (*Amused, very light and chaffing tone*) About Saturn? Oh yes. My conjecture is that bad folks when they die are sent to Saturn to study current theology, and if at the end of five hundred years they know any-thing about it, their probation is complete. (*General laugh. David turns to group. Sir Brice laughs*)

Fan. What is it, Bricey?

Sir B. Lady Skene is making a howling fuss with all of you to-night. She'll make a howling fuss of another kind next week. I can't stand that astronomer fellow.

Blanch. But do tell us, Lady Skene, what is Mr. Remon's great specialty — hum? eh?

Dulcie. I believe Mr. Remon has devoted a great deal of time to the study of sun-spots.

Blanch. Oh — ah, yes — hum. Now (*To David*) what is the special function of sun-spots — hum? eh? What do they do?

David. (*Still amused, chaffing, mysterious*) I've long had a suspicion that there is a very subtle connection between sun-spots and politics — in fact, I am convinced that the present decadence of political manners and morals is entirely caused by the persistence of a certain sun-spot. As soon as we can re-move it, the natural ingrained honesty and patriotism of our politicians will reassert themselves. (*General laugh*)

Sir B. (*Pushes a little forward with a rather insolent manner to David*) My character is always puzzling me. Can you tell me whether its present development is due to sun-spots?

David. (*Is about to reply rather angrily, is checked by a look from Dulcie, speaks very politely*) You might not think me polite, Sir Brice.

Sir B. (*Persisting*) I should like to have a scientific examination made of my character.

David. (*Still controlling himself*) I fear I should not make a sympathetic operator.

Sir B. (*Still persisting*) But —

Dulcie. (*Who has been watching very ap-prehensively, to Sir Brice*) My dear, Lady Franklin wants to ask you something about a horse for Ascot. She was here a moment ago. (*Looking around, drawing Sir Brice away from the group, who close up round Remon. Dulcie is getting Sir Brice away*) For God's sake keep away from us! (*A guest is just pass-ing, Dulcie turns to her with a forced society smile and manner*) How do you do? What a sweet frock! (*Shakes hands with guest, who passes on*)

Sir B. (*Sulkily*) What's the matter? (*Approaching her*)

Dulcie. Don't go near any one. You smell of brandy. (*All this under breath with great terror and apprehension*)

Sir B. (*Getting a little nearer her*) I rather like the smell of brandy.

Dulcie. (*Terrified, under breath*) Keep away — keep away — if you come a step nearer to me I shall shriek out before everybody. You nearly drove me out of my mind this morning. Oh, for Heaven's sake — do go — do go!

Sir B. Well, as it's infernally slow here I will go — but — you may as well know, there will be no Ascot, no Henley, no Goodwood, no Homburg, no anything. We shall be sold up within a month. (*Dulcie is staggering for a moment*) Ta ta! — my blessing — I'm going to the Club.

> *Exit. Dulcie stands overwhelmed for a moment, tries to pull herself together, staggers a little. David, who has been watching her and Sir Brice, leaves the group and comes to her, speaks with great feeling, very softly, his tone and manner to her in great contrast to his tone and manner with the guests.*

David. Lady Skene, you are in trouble — you are ill.

Dulcie. (*Again with the forced society smile*) No, only the fatigue of the season, and the rooms are so crowded, aren't they?

A group of guests begin little gestures and significant glances and whispers, watching David and Dulcie. Eddie re-enters, and unnoticed looks from one group to the other.

David. I'll tell Sir Winchmore.

Dulcie. No, don't take any notice. If I can only get through this evening! (*With a sudden instinct, appealing to him with great entreaty*) Tell me something that will carry me through this next hour till they have all gone. Give me that sort of medicine!

David. (*With the utmost tenderness and feeling, in a low voice, bending over her. The glances and whispers continue*) Your trouble isn't real. This society world of yours isn't a real world. There's one little star in Andromeda where everything is real. You've wandered down here amongst these shadows when you should have stayed at home.

Dulcie. (*Pleased, lending herself to his suggestions*) Aren't these real men and women?

David. No. They are only masquerading.

Good God, I think we are all masquerading! Look at them! If you touched them with reality they would vanish. And so with your trouble of to-night. Fly back to Andromeda, and you will see what a dream all this is.

Dulcie. How strange! I was half dead a moment ago, and you've made me so well and happy. But you — do you belong to Andromeda, — or to this world? (*Eddie has been watching and comes down nearer to them*)

David. To both. But the little star in Andromeda is my home. I'm only wandering with you amongst these phantoms. (*They have become for the moment quite absorbed. Eddie, who has been watching the whispers and smiles, comes up to them, speaks rather sharply*)

Eddie. Lady Skene — that lamp-shade — (*Pointing off*) Won't it catch fire? (*Taking David's arm, dragging him away*) I want to talk to you, Davy. (*Dulcie turns to manservant, points to the lamp-shade, and gives him directions concerning it*)

David. (*Turns savagely on Eddie, growls*) Why the devil did you come between us?

Eddie. Don't you care for her, Davy?

David. Care for her?

> *Dulcie, having given manservant instructions, goes to guests.*

Eddie. Do you know what these folks are saying? That Sir Brice is ruined, and that you have lately come into a fortune.

David. Well?

Eddie. And that she continues her parties, her dresses, her house, because you — (*Stops, looks at David. David looks around at guests savagely. Stands for a moment or two reflecting, his face then assumes a look of great resolve. Eddie watching him*) I was right to tell you, Davy?

David. (*Shakes Eddie's hand in reply. Another little pause*) Go and tell her, Eddie, that I must see her for a few minutes by and by — to-night — when everybody is gone.

Eddie. What are you going to do, Davy?

David. We'll get away south tomorrow, old boy. The observatory's nearly finished, and — there's no tittle-tattle between the snows and the stars. Go and tell her I must see her, and bring me back her answer.

Eddie. (*To Dulcie*) You've not been down to supper, Lady Skene.

Dulcie. I really don't want any.

Eddie. But I've got a message for you.

Dulcie. A message?

Eddie. From Andromeda.

> *Exeunt Dulcie and Eddie.*

Lady Clar. You are really too dreadful.

Blanch. (*Buzzing round Remon*) That's a charming theory of yours about the effect of sun-spots on morality.

David. Yes. It isn't true, but it's very consoling. That's why I invented it.

Monty. If it's charming and consoling, why should it be true?

David. Why should it? and put everything else out of focus.

Blanch. Out of focus! Ah! I'm afraid you're a dreadful, dreadful pessimist.

David. No; but I'm as willing to play that part as any other, since it's only in jest.

Char. In jest? What do you mean?

David. I have to spend so much time alone amongst the stars, that when I come back into the world I am quite at a loss. I find myself amongst crowds of shadows — very charming shadows they are — playing at money-making, playing at religion, playing at love, at art, at politics, at all sorts of odd games, and so for the time, I join in the game, and pretend to take an interest in it; and a very pleasant game it is, so long as we don't mistake it for reality.

Char. But surely we are realities!

David. With the profoundest respect in the world, Lady Shalford, I cannot bring myself to believe that you are. Still, I won't spoil your game by staying out.

Blanch. (*With a little affected, mincing earnestness*) Oh, but surely, surely there is Something real Somewhere. Oh, yes — surely, surely — we must believe that there is — hum? eh? — a Kind of — eh? — a Sort of a Something — Somewhere, eh?

David. If you like to believe there is a kind of a sort of a something — somewhere — and you find it consoling, I'm as willing to pretend to believe that as anything else.

Blanch. (*Still with the same affected earnestness.*) Oh, but surely, when you look into your own heart — hum? eh? —

David. I always wear a mask over my heart. I never dare look into it.

Monty. I find this world a remarkably comfortable and well-arranged place. I always do exactly as I like. If I want anything I buy it, whether I pay for it or no. If I see a woman I admire I make love to her, whether she belongs to another man or no. If a lie will answer my purpose, I tell it. I can't remember I ever denied myself one single pleasure in life; nor have I ever put myself out to oblige a fellow-creature. I am consistently selfish and I find it pays; I credit everybody else with the same consistent selfishness, and I am never deceived in my estimate of character. These are my principles, and I always act up to them. And I assure you I find this world the pleasantest possible place.

David. A fairy palace! An enchanted spot!

Only take care! While you are dancing, there may be a volcano underneath.

Monty. If there is, surely dancing is the pleasantest preparation for the general burst-up.

Eddie. Davy —

David. (*Goes to him*) Well?

Eddie. She'll see you to-night. Come back here when they've all gone.

Blanch. (*To Monty*) How charmingly frank you are, Monty.

Monty. Why not? We have one supreme merit in this generation — we have ceased to render to virtue the homage of hypocrisy.

David. And our moral evolution is now complete. Good-night!

Exeunt David and Eddie.

Monty. (*Coming down with Lady Clarice*) Of course I know there is something wretchedly philistine and provincial about marriage, but I will take care this aspect of it is never presented to you.

Lady Clar. I wonder what makes marriage so unlovely and so uninteresting?

Monty. The exaggerated notion that prevails of its duties and responsibilities. Once do away with that, and it becomes an ideal state. Lady Clarice, you'd find me the most agreeable partner in the world.

Lady Clar. You'd be like most other husbands, I suppose.

Monty. No; I should be unique. Husbands, as a rule, are foolish, jealous brutes, who insist that men shall have all the rights and women all the duties, — men shall have all the sweets and women all the sours of the marriage state. We would start on an entirely new plan. The sours we would naturally equally avoid, and the sweets, — if there are any, — we would naturally do our best to secure.

Lady Clar. Separately, or together?

Monty. According to our tastes. If you do me the honour to accept me, I pledge you my word I will never have the offensively bad taste to speak of a husband's rights. There shall be no "lord and master" nonsense.

Lady Clar. It sounds very well in theory. I wonder how it would work.

Monty. Let us try. If we succeed we shall solve the vexed question of the age, and make ourselves happy in showing mankind the road to happiness.

Lady Clar. But if we fail?

Monty. We shall have sacrificed ourselves for the benefit of our species. But we can't fail, the plan is perfect.

Lady Clar. If I spoke of rights and duties — if I were jealous —

Monty. Ah! then you would be departing from the plan. Its charm is that it is a patent self-adjusting, self-repairing, safety-valve plan, with double escapement action suited to all climates and dispositions. No rights, no duties, no self-assertion, no quarrels, no jealousy.

Lady Clar. And no love?

Monty. Love is a perverted animal instinct, which is really a great bar to solid happiness in marriage. Believe me, you will like me and respect me in the end for not pretending to any such outworn impulses. You see I am frank.

Lady Clar. You are indeed. (*Looking at him very closely, watching him*) You know — (*Pause*) — my father cannot make any great settlements, and — (*Watching him closely*) I have no expectations.

Monty. (*Stands it without flinching*) So I am aware. I'm frightfully in debt, and I have no expectations. But there is a house in Grosvenor Place — it would suit us exactly.

Lady Clar. (*Watching him*) But — without money?

Monty. I cannot afford to be economical. I have acted on that principle throughout life, and I have always had the very best of everything. I do not see we need change it.

Lady Clar. You are perfectly atrocious — I don't care for you in the least.

Monty. (*With great politeness*) My plan is precisely adapted to such cases.

Lady Cran. Come, Clarice — everybody is going. *Exit.*

Monty. I shall call on Lord Crandover tomorrow. You don't speak. Does silence give consent?

Lady Clar. I can't help your calling.

Exit. Monty stands in slight deliberation. Charley comes out from the conservatory behind him. She has been watching the last part of the scene from the conservatory.

Char. Well?

Monty. Landed, I think. You're sure about Sir Joseph and the estate?

Char. Quite. But it's not to be known yet. I'm a pet, ain't I?

Monty. You are. (*Kisses her hand*)

Char. I must be going. That creature at home will be raising furies.

Monty. When do you pack him to Aix?

Char. Thursday, praise the Lord!

Monty. When shall I call?

Char. Friday?

Monty. What time?

Char. Come to lunch?

Monty. Yes.

Char. Friday at two. (*Exchange looks full of meaning*) Bye-bye.

Monty. Bye-bye.

Char. Oh dear, am I the last? Good-bye, dear. (*Kisses Dulcie*) Monty, come and see me to my carriage.

Monty. Good-bye, Lady Skene.

Dulcie. Good-bye.

Exit Monty and Charley.

(*To Servant*) Thomson, I expect Mr. Remon. Show him in here.

Servant. Yes, my lady. *Exit.*

Helen appears at door, still in nurse's costume.

Helen. (*Peeps in*) They have all gone, dear.

Dulcie. I've got such a fever, Nell. Put your nice cold hand on my forehead. That's right. Hold it tight — tight. Why didn't you dress and come into my party?

Helen. I was so tired and bored at the last, and I wanted to be with Rosy.

Dulcie. She's all right?

Helen. Yes. She was awake a moment ago.

Dulcie. (*Suddenly*) Fetch her! I must see her! Oh, you're right, Nell; it's been a hateful evening, with only one bright spot in it — when he came and whispered something so sweet.

Helen. (*Suddenly*) Dulcie, you're sure of yourself?

Dulcie. I'm sure of him.

Helen. He has never spoken — of — of —

Dulcie. Of love? Never. What does that matter? I know he loves me.

Helen. Dulcie, you shouldn't say that — even to yourself.

Dulcie. Oh, that's all nonsense, Nell; as if there was ever a woman in this world that didn't know when she was loved!

Helen. Dulcie!

Dulcie. (*Provokingly*) He loves me! He loves me! He loves me, and I'm not ashamed of it, and I don't care who knows it. (*Throwing her arms round Helen's neck*) Nell, I'm so happy.

Helen. Why?

Dulcie. He's coming, he's coming. Brice says we are utterly ruined. We're ruined, but I won't feel it to-night. I'll feel it to-morrow. I'll be happy for one minute to-night. He is coming.

Helen. Mr. Remon?

Dulcie. Yes. Don't look shocked, Nell. Listen; this is true. Mr. Remon and I have never said one word to each other that all the world might not have heard. (*Pause*) I'm glad all the world hasn't heard it, though. (*Thomson comes in, announces Mr. Remon. To*

Helen) Go and fetch Rosy. Yes! Yes! (*Exit Helen. David has entered; Servant has gone off. To David*) I'm so glad you've come. I want you to see Rosy. She's awake. You've never seen her. (*All this very excited*)

David. I shall be very pleased. (*Looking at her*)

Dulcie. You're thinking about me.

David. I was thinking that a mother is the most beautiful thing on earth.

Dulcie. Oh, you don't know! You can't imagine! She's over two years old, and I haven't got over remembering that she's mine. Every time I think of her I feel a little catch here in the very middle of my heart, a delicious little stab, as if some angel came behind me and whispered to me, "God has made you a present of ten hundred thousand million pounds all your own." Oh, she makes up to me for everything.

David is approaching her with great tenderness when Helen enters with Rosy, the two-year-old baby, in her arms in nightclothes. Dulcie rushes to Helen.

There! There! You may look at her!

Helen. Hush! She's asleep!

Dulcie. I must kiss her if it kills her! (*Hugging the baby, kisses her, lifts the nightgown, kisses the baby's feet, croons over it — points her finger mockingly at Remon in childlike mockery and laughter*) There! There! There, Mr. Philosopher from Andromeda! You can't say a mother's love isn't real!

David. I never did. It's the one thing that shows what a sham the rest of the world is. That little star in Andromeda is crowded with mothers. They've all been there once in their lives. (*Bends over the baby for a moment*)

Dulcie. (*Excited, feverish*) Nell, Mr. Remon has an odd notion that this world isn't real.

Helen. The cure for that is to earn half-a-crown a day and live on it.

David. Oh yes, I know. Work is real. (*Bends over the baby*)

Dulcie. (*To David*) What are you looking at? (*Scrutinizes him carefully; then suddenly, with savage earnestness, half despair, half entreaty*) She's like *me?* She's like *me!!* (*Crescendo, tigerish, frenzied*) Say she's like *me!!!*

David. (*Very quietly*) She is like *you.* (*Kisses the child reverently*) She is wholly like *you!*

Dulcie. (*Stands absorbed, very quietly*) Take her back again to the nursery, Nell.

Helen. Good-night, Mr. Remon.

David. Good-night. (*Goes towards the door with her*)

Helen. (*To David, smiling*) I've just remembered something else that is real.

David. What's that?

Helen. Duty.

Exit with baby. A summer sunrise shines pink through the conservatory, and lights up the room with summer morning light. David returns to Dulcie, who sits absorbed.

David. Lady Skene, I asked to see you because — it is necessary for me to leave England very soon.

Dulcie. No — no!

David. Yes — yes. I never use the word "honour" about my conduct, because every scamp has used it until it's the most counterfeit word in the language. But I've just learned that if I stay in England I shall injure very deeply a friend of mine, so naturally I'm going away.

Dulcie. But — tell me — (*Pause*) — what —

David. If I stay I cannot continue an honest man. Will you let it rest there?

Dulcie. If you wish —

David. (*After a little pause, with some embarrassment*) I have just heard — I scarcely know how to mention it — that you may be placed in a position of some difficulty.

Dulcie. You mean that Sir Brice is ruined. In one way it's a relief, because at any rate it will break up this life, and I'm so tired of it.

David. Yet you thought you would like it on that night of the Hunt Ball.

Dulcie. Yes. I longed for it. Is life like that all through?

David. Like what?

Dulcie. To long for a thing very much and to find it worthless, and then to long for something else much more — to be sure that this is worth having — to get it, and then to find that that is worthless too. And so on, and so on, and so on?

David. I'm afraid life is very much like that on this particular planet.

Dulcie. Oh, but that would be awful if I found out that — (*Stops*)

David. What?

Dulcie. Nothing. You remember that night of the Hunt Ball?

David. (*Nods*) It was the last time I saw my friend George Copeland. He died in Alaska six months after.

Dulcie. And you went away for over a year.

David. No — only for a few weeks. After Copeland's funeral I went to the Mediterranean to choose a site for my observatory, and I was back in England within less than three months.

Dulcie. But we never saw you till last season. Where were you?

David. When you were in the country, I was there; when you were in town I was in town too. I have never been far away from you. I have kept an account of every time I have seen you for the last three years.

Dulcie. (*Looks at him as if suddenly struck with a thought*) Tell me — where were you two years ago last March?

David. At Gerard's Heath— near you.

Dulcie. (*Suddenly*) Did you — the night Rosy was — I mean the night of the second — it was a dreadful snow-storm —

David. I remember.

Dulcie. One of my nurses said she saw some one in the garden. (*Looks at him*)

David. It was I. Your life was in danger. I passed those two nights outside your window. (*Dulcie with great affection, involuntarily puts her hand on his arm. He raises her hand and is about to kiss it. Helen re-enters. David rises*)

Helen. Sir Brice has just come back and is in the smoking-room downstairs.

Dulcie. (*Turning*) Look! It's morning.

David. Good-bye.

Dulcie. (*Suddenly*) No — I must have another word with you. Wait here a moment. Here is Sir Brice. Nell, take Mr. Remon on to the balcony for a minute or two and wait there with him till Sir Brice has gone upstairs.

Exeunt David and Helen through conservatory and on to balcony.

Sir Brice enters, looking a little flushed and dissipated.

Sir B. (*Staring at Dulcie; after a pause*) Well?

Dulcie. Well?

Sir B. (*Drops into a chair; whistles*) Got rid of your friends?

Dulcie. All except Mr. Remon. He's on the balcony with Nell.

Sir B. Oh! (*Pause. Whistles; takes some change out of his pocket — three shillings and threepence; places the coins very carefully and elaborately in a longitudinal position on the palm of his left hand, arranging the three shillings and the three pennies in a line, whistling carelessly*) That's our net fortune, my girl. (*Holding them up under her face*) That is our precise capital — three shillings and three-pence. (*Whistles*) Not another farthing. And some thousand pounds' worth of debts.

Dulcie. (*Unconcerned*) Indeed.

Sir B. (*With a sudden little burst of brutality — not too marked*) Look here! can't you get some money?

Dulcie. What do you mean?

Sir B. *Get some money!* That's plain English, isn't it?

Dulcie. I don't understand you.

Sir B. This fellow Remon is devilish fond of you. Can't you get some money from him?

Dulcie. Hush! Borrow money from him!

Sir B. (*Suggestively*) You needn't borrow. (*Dulcie looks at him inquiringly*) Now can't you get some? (*Dulcie looks at him for a moment; she raises her fan to strike him; sees David, who has entered from conservatory. Helen stands at conservatory door*)

David. Lady Skene, I have been obliged to overhear what has just been said. To-morrow morning I leave for the South of France, and I shall be quite inaccessible for some years. My bankers will have orders to send you a cheque-book and to honour your signature to any extent that you are likely to require. (*Dulcie makes a protest*) If you please — if you please. As I shall be away from England there cannot be the least slur upon you in accepting it. Miss Larondie, you will be with your sister, always. She will be in your care — always. (*Shakes hands with Helen*) Be very kind to her. Never leave her. Good-bye.

Dulcie. But I — cannot — take —

David. (*Silencing her*) If you please — It is my last request. Good-bye. (*Sir Brice, who has been sitting all the while, listening, rises. David looks at him for half a moment; looks at Dulcie*) Good-bye. *Exit.*

End of the Second Act.

ACT III.

Nine months pass between Acts II and III. Private sitting-room at the Hôtel Prince De Galles, Nice. A rather handsome modern room furnished in French hotel fashion. Two long windows, right, curtained. Door at back. Door left. Small card table down stage, left, with several packs of cards loosely on it. The whole floor round the table strewn with cards. Discover Sir Brice in evening dress seated left of table, aimlessly and mechanically playing with the cards. After a few seconds Dulcie, in dinner dress, enters from door at back, crosses to the window and stands looking out, having taken no notice of Sir Brice. As she enters he leaves off playing with the cards for a moment, looks at her.

Sir B. (*In rather a commanding tone, a little brutal*) Come here. (*Dulcie takes no notice. A little pause. Louder*) D'ye hear? Come here. (*Dulcie comes down to him, does not speak. He looks up at her. Her face is quite blank, looking indifferently in front of her. Sir Brice begins playing with cards again*) I've lost over six hundred pounds. (*Dulcie takes no notice. Sir Brice dashes the pack of cards under his feet, stamps on them*) Damn and damn the cards! (*Dulcie takes no notice. Slight pause. Sir Brice roars out*) The hotel people have sent up their bill again with a request for payment. (*Slight pause. Dulcie goes back to the window, stands there looking out. Pause. Sir Brice roars out furiously*) Why the devil don't you get something for that deafness of yours! (*Suddenly jumps up, goes up to her, seizes her hands, turns her round*) Now look here — (*Hotel Servant enters, with letter on tray. Sir Brice desists. The Hotel Servant brings the letter to Dulcie, who crosses and takes it. Exit Servant. Dulcie opens letter, reads it*) Well? (*Dulcie rings bell*) Well?

Servant enters.

Dulcie. (*In cold equable tone, to Sir Brice*) Mr. Edward Remon wishes to see me. He asks me to excuse his being in fancy dress. He's going to the Opera Ball. Shall I see him here or in the hall?

Sir. B. Here.

Dulcie. (*To Servant*) Show Mr. Remon here.   *Exit Servant.*

Sir B. (*To Dulcie*) Where's his brother, the astronomer?

Dulcie. At his observatory, I suppose. I've not seen him since the night we began to live upon him.

Hotel Servant opens door, announces Mr. Edward Remon. Eddie enters, dressed as Pierrot for the fancy dress ball. Exit Servant.

Eddie. (*All through the Act very excited*) How d'ye do? (*To Dulcie; shakes hands with her. To Sir Brice*) How d'ye do?

Sir B. How d'ye do?

    Looks meaningly at Dulcie and exits left.

Eddie. So good of you to excuse this dress.

Dulcie. Your brother?

Eddie. He's down in the town with me to-night. We've been dining at the Café de Paris. I've taken three glasses of champagne — anything more than a spoonful makes me tipsy, and so, with that and this dress, and our journey to Africa, I'm quite mad to-night.

Dulcie. Africa!

Eddie. We start early to-morrow morning to the deadliest place on the West Coast.

Dulcie. Not your brother?

Eddie. Yes. We're going to watch the transit of Venus, and as there was a jolly lot of fever there all the other astronomers rather funked it. So Davy has fitted out an expedition himself. (*Dulcie shows great concern. Eddie rattles on*) I'm going to have a spree to-night. I've never been drunk in my life, and I thought I should like to try what it's like — because — (*Tossing up a coin*) it's heads we come back alive and prove Davy's theory about sun-spots — and it's tails we leave our bones and all our apparatus out there. It's tails — we're as dead as door-nails. (*Sees Dulcie's pained face*) Lady Skene — I'm so sorry —

Dulcie. We've been three weeks in Nice. Why hasn't your brother come to see me?

Eddie. A mistaken sense of duty. He thinks one ought to do it when it's unpleasant. So do I when I'm in my right clothes, and my right senses, but now I'm half tipsy, and have got a fool's cap on. I can see quite plainly that duty's all moonshine. Duty is doing exactly what one likes, and it's Davy's duty to come to you. And the fool is just breaking his heart for a sight of you. Shall I find him and bring him?

Dulcie. Where is he?

Eddie. He's in the town getting everything ready for to-morrow. Shall I find him?

Dulcie. (*Looking at her watch*) Quarter to eleven. I may be alone in half an hour. Yes, bring him to me here.

Eddie. Hurrah! — *Au revoir.*

Sir Brice appears at the same door, looks after Eddie, who exits, saying "Adieu." Sir Brice shuts door; enters.

Sir B. (*To Dulcie*) Well?

    Dulcie does not reply, goes to her room at back. Sir Brice follows her, the door is closed in his face and a lock is heard to turn. Sir Brice shakes the door handle, kicks the door, looks vicious and spiteful, comes down a step or two, kicks a hassock.

Servant enters, announcing Mr. Lushington. Enter Monty. Sir Brice nods.

Monty. Well, dear chum! (*Looking round at the cards on the floor*) Did you give Fancourt his revenge?

Sir B. Damn the cards.

Monty. By all means. How's Lady Skene?

Sir B. (*Mutters*) —mn Lady Skene.

Monty. By all means.

Sir B. You're married, Lushington —

Monty. I am three months a bride-groom.

Sir B. Why the devil did you get married?

Monty. Because I ascertained that my wife

would have seven thousand a year. Why did you?

Sir B. Because I was a silly fool.

Monty. Well, there couldn't be two better reasons for getting married.

Sir B. (*Furious with his cards*) —mn everything and everybody.

Monty. By all means. And now we've reached finality and are utterly the sport of destiny, will you do me a good turn?

Sir B. What?

Monty. I'm going to take a lady to the Opera Ball, and I fear Lady Clarice will be dull, or I should say *restless*, in my absence. I know you will be going to the Cercle d'Amerique to wreck your farthing chance of eternity at poker.

Sir B. Well?

Monty. It would momentarily reinstate your celestial hopes if you would tell Lady Skene that I'm going to the Club with you, and persuade her to spend the lonely hours of her widow-hood with Lady Clarice in number one-four-three. They will doubtless tear our characters to rags, but that will keep them from the worse mischief of interfering with us.

Sir B. Will you do me a good turn?

Monty. Anything in my power.

Sir B. Lend me a couple of hundred pounds.

Monty. My dear Bricey. If my I.O.U., or my name, or my presence, is good for anything at the Cercle d'Amerique, you're welcome to it.

Sir B. Will you come with me and set me afloat for a quarter of an hour?

Monty. Certainly.

Sir B. I'll ask Lady Skene. (*Goes up to the door at back, raps*) Are you there? (*A little louder*) Are you there?

Monty. Throw in a "my dear," Bricey, or some such trifle. Its effect will be in proportion to its scarcity.

Sir B. My dear! (*Rapping still*) Mr. Lushington has called. (*Rapping*) Do you hear, my love? (*With a grim sneer on the last word. The door is a little opened. Sir Brice forces his way in*) Lady Clarice wants to know if you will go and sit with her while — (*The remainder of sentence is lost by the closing of door after him*)

Lady Clarice enters door, with opera cloak.

Monty. (*Showing surprise, which he instantly checks*) Where so gay and free, my love?

Lady Clar. (*Looking him straight in the face very determinedly*) To the Opera Ball.

Monty. Oh.

Lady Clar. You're going to take that woman.

Monty. I know many *ladies*, but no *women*.

Char. (*Her voice heard outside*) Yes. See if Mr. Lushington is there, and say a lady is waiting for him in the hall — oh, he's in there; I'll go in.

Monty is going. Lady Clarice makes a little movement to intercept him.

Monty. (*In a low voice*) Don't be foolish.

Char. (*Her voice at door, outside*) Aren't you nearly ready, Monty? (*Appears at door, sees Lady Clarice, takes in the situation at a glance, has a slight shock, but instantly recovers herself. Runs to Lady Clarice, brimming with affection*) Darling, are you going too? So pleased! So charmed! How sweet of you! (*Offers to kiss Lady Clarice*)

Lady Clar. (*Indignantly*) How dare you!

Monty. (*Stepping between them*) Hush! (*To Lady Clarice*) What's the use of having a row here, or anywhere? For Heaven's sake, do be a good sensible girl, and don't shatter the happiness of our married life before — before we know where we are. Charley and I are going to the Opera Ball, will you come with us?

Lady Clar. (*Indignantly*) What!

Monty. Or go by yourself. Or go with any one you please. Or go anywhere or do anything in the world you like. Only don't make a scene here.

Lady Clar. My father shall know.

Monty. Very well. Very well. We'll discuss that by and by. But do recognise once and for all the futility of rows. You'd better come with us.

Enter Sir Brice

Lady Clar. Come with you?

Char. (*Begins*) My dear Clarice, I assure you —

Monty. (*Stops Charley with a warning look*) For Heaven's sake, Clarice, whatever we do, do not let us make ourselves ridiculous. (*Monty snatches up Lady Clarice's arm. She reluctantly allows him to do so*) All right, Bricey. Sorry I can't come with you to the Club — but I've persuaded Lady Clarice and Lady Shalford to come to the Opera Ball with me. Bye, bye, dear crony, our love to Lady Skene. Hope you will have as pleasant an evening as we shall — Ta! Ta!

> *Exit with great animation. Lady Clarice holding reluctantly and aloof on one arm, Charley more affectionate on the other. Sir Brice goes to Dulcie's door, throws it wide open, stands back, calls.*

Sir B. Now, will you let us understand each other once for all?

Dulcie enters, looks at him without speaking.

I want some money. This fellow Remon has offered you his purse to any extent. Get a few hundreds for me to go on with.

Dulcie. No.

Sir B. You won't? Then why did you begin to take his money?

Dulcie. Because I was weak, because you bullied me, and because I knew I was welcome.

Sir B. Very good. The same reasons continue. You're weak, I'm a bully, and you're welcome. Aren't you welcome, eh? Aren't you welcome?

Dulcie. I believe I am welcome to every penny he has in the world.

Sir B. He loves you?

Dulcie. Yes.

Sir B. And you love him?

Dulcie. (*Looking straight at Sir Brice very fearlessly and calmly*) With all my heart.

Sir B. And you aren't ashamed to tell me?

Dulcie. Is there anything in your past life that you have taken the trouble to hide from me? Have you ever openly or secretly had an attachment to any living creature that does you as much credit and so little shame as my love for David Remon does to me?

Sir B. All right. Go on loving him. You needn't hesitate. He expects a fair exchange — if he hasn't already got it.

Dulcie. (*Very calmly*) That's a lie, and you know it is.

Sir B. Very well. It's a lie. I don't care one way or the other. Get me some money.

Dulcie. You have had the last farthing that you will ever touch of David Remon's money.

Sir B. All right. (*Jumps up very determinedly*) Then you've seen the last you will see of your child for some years to come.

Dulcie. (*Aroused*) What! you will hit me through my child!

Sir B. I think *my* child's health requires a change for a few years — a different climate from you and myself. We will go upon a little tour by ourselves, shall we? to — where the devil shall we go? I don't care. I shall send Rosy away to-morrow morning. D'ye hear?

Dulcie. I hear.

Sir B. If I don't see you again to-night, get her ready by to-morrow morning.   *Exit.*

Dulcie. (*Stands for a moment or two quiet, then bursts into a fit of ironic laughter*) Nell! (*Goes to the door at back, calls out*) Nell! Nell! Come here!

Helen enters.

Helen. What's the matter?

Dulcie. Nell, old girl, have you got such a thing as a Church Service about you?

Helen. Church Service?

Dulcie. I want you to tell me the end and meaning of marriage. There's something about it in the Church Service, isn't there? I did go through it once, I know, but I've forgotten what it's all about. *What does it mean?*

Helen. Marriage?

Dulcie. Yes. Oh, I know! It's one of Mr. Remon's games.

Helen. Games?

Dulcie. Yes. He says men and women are playing a lot of queer games on earth that they call religion, love, politics, and this and that and the other — marriage must be one, and it's the funniest of them all! It's a two-handed game like — like cribbage, or tossing up. You choose your partner — head's he's a good 'un, then you're in clover; tails he's a bad 'un, then, it's purgatory and inferno for you for the rest of your life, unless you're a man. It's all right if you're a man. The same game as before, choose your partner — heads she's a good 'un, then you're in clover; tails she's a bad 'un, then you cut her, and toss up again and again, until you do get a good 'un. That's the game — that's the game — and it's a splendid game for a man.

Blanchflower, in evening dress, pops in.

Blanch. How d'ye do, Lady Skene? Am I in the way, eh?

Dulcie. Enter! Enter! Enter! You're just in time. Help us solve this mighty question.

Blanch. Something important, eh?

Dulcie. No, only marriage.

Blanch. What about it?

Dulcie. Well — what about it? Give us your opinion. There's something mystical about it, isn't there? Nell, where's that Church Service? Something mystical?

Blanch. Well, yes; and — hum? eh? (*Happy thought*) — something ideal —

Dulcie. Mystical and ideal. Go on, Nell.

Helen. I'd rather not. I don't like to hear you mocking at marriage.

Dulcie. (*Laughing*) Mocking at marriage! Oh, my God! is it women who have married bad men that mock at marriage? Make haste, make haste! (*Dashing her hands on the chair*) Marriage is a mystical, ideal state — isn't there something in the Service about physical? Go on, Nell, go on — help us out. Go on! What have we left out?

Helen. The wife's duty.

Dulcie. Yah. Yah. Yah. (*This is very quiet and calm, with a pause between each Yah, very different from the excited Yah! Yah! Yah! of the Second Act*)

Helen. To her husband to keep her vows. To herself to keep herself pure and stainless, because it is her glory, as it is a man's glory to be brave and honest.

Dulcie. (*Same position, same tone*) Yah. Yah. Yah.

Helen. And to society, to her nation, because no nation has ever survived whose women have been immoral.

Dulcie. (*Suddenly springing up, sitting up upright in the chair*) And the men?

Helen. I don't know whether it's a man's duty to be moral. I'm sure it's a woman's.

Dulcie. Oh, then marriage is a moral state, eh — at least for women, eh, Mr. Blanch-flower?

Blanch. (*Who has shown symptoms of great discomfort through the interview*) Ye — es — decidedly marriage is — or — a — should be a moral state.

Dulcie. (*Jumping up vigorously*) Ah, now we've got it! Now we can go ahead! Marriage is a physical, mystical, ideal, moral game. Oh, I hate these words, moral, ideal. How if it isn't ideal? Suppose it's horribly, horribly real. How if it isn't moral? Suppose it's horribly, horribly immoral! Moral! Moral!! Moral!!! Is there anything under God's sun so immoral, ah — guess it — guess it — as to be married to a man one hates! And you go on plastering it and poulticing it and sugaring it over with "moral" and "ideal" and "respectable," and all those words that men use to cheat themselves with. It isn't moral to be married to a man one hates! It isn't ideal! It isn't mystical! It's hateful! It's martyrdom! (*A long pause*)

Blanch. (*Calm, with a real touch of feeling*) My dear Lady Skene, I won't pretend to offer you advice —

Dulcie. (*Has recovered from her outburst, now speaks in a very calm, indifferent, matter-of-fact tone*) It doesn't matter. You're going to the ball?

Blanch. I was going — but if I can help you in any way — (*Struck with the idea*) My uncle, Canon Butterfield, is here for the winter. He suffers from liver, and has written a book on Socinianism. If you want any spiritual advice, I'm sure you couldn't do better.

Dulcie. What is Socinianism? Is it anything to do with marriage?

Blanch. Well — ah — no. Shall I send him?

Dulcie. No, I won't trouble you. I'll think this out for myself.

Blanch. Well, if you ever do need a clergyman, don't forget my uncle. You can't do better. Or if at any time I can be of any use —

Dulcie. Thank you. Good-night.

Blanch. (*Shaking hands very sympathetically*) Good-bye.   *Exit.*

Dulcie. (*Suddenly*) Nell! (*Helen comes to her*) Take Rosy up at once, dress her, get out of the hotel by the servants' way so that you don't meet Sir Brice — take her over to Beaulieu to the Hôtel des Anglais, and wait there till to-morrow morning. I'll send you a message what to do.

Servant enters, announces Mr. Remon — Mr. Edward Remon. Enter David and Eddie, still in Pierrot's dress. Helen shows some surprise. Exit Servant.

Quick, Nell, do as I tell you.

Helen. (*Looking at David and Eddie*) Promise me —

Dulcie. What?

Helen. You'll take no step till you've seen me.

Dulcie. I promise. Make haste. Come here and tell me when Rosy's ready.

Helen (*Comes to David, shakes hands with him*) You heard her promise.

David. She shall keep it.

    Exit Helen at back.

Eddie. I've brought him, Lady Skene. I'm off to the ball. I'm not so tipsy now as I was, but I'm going to have my fling. It's my only chance of going to the devil. Davy, where shall I meet you?

David. I'll come to the Opera House for you. Wait for me there.

Eddie. Come as soon as you can, won't you? You come too, Lady Skene. You can't think how jolly it is to have no duty and no conscience and no faith and no future, no anything but pleasure and life! Do come! Let's all be fools for once in our lives! Let's be monkeys again! Come on! Come on!

Exit. As soon as he has gone, David and Dulcie, who have been standing on opposite sides of the room, go to each other very calmly. They meet in the middle of the room, take each other's hands. He raises hers to his lips. David's appearance has changed since the last Act; he is more worn and spiritual, a little greyer, very calm at first, an unearthly look in his face. They stand looking at each other for some moments.

Dulcie. You're changed! You're not well!

David. Quite well. So well, I feel no ill can ever happen to me.

Dulcie. Why did you not come to me before?

David. I'd been able to do you a service. I didn't wish you to think that I had any claim on you.

Dulcie. Ah, you shouldn't misunderstand me. I could never misunderstand you like that. I've taken your money. I knew I was welcome, because — if I were rich and you were poor, I would give you all I had.

David. Ah! Take all I have!

Dulcie. Not another farthing.

David. Why not?

Dulcie. I would be proud to owe all my happiness, all my comfort to you. I have been proud these last six months to think that my child's very bread came from you.

David. Ah! (*Coming nearer to her*)

Dulcie. I would only have taken just sufficient for necessaries — but he forced me. I was weak. Now the end has come. I won't waste any more of your money in this (*Pointing to the cards*) and racing, and — I don't know what.

David. Tell it all.

Dulcie. Things can't go on as they are. (*Smiling*) Do you remember the Scotchman who lost his mother-in-law and his aunt and three cousins, all in one epidemic? He said it was "just reedeeclous." Things are "just reedeeclous" with me. (*Laughing*) Sir Brice has threatened to take Rosy away from me.

David. No!

Dulcie. Yes! I'm sending Nell to Beaulieu with her to-night. I don't know what will happen. I don't think I care much. It doesn't matter. Nothing matters. (*Smiling. Then with sudden alarm*) Yes — this journey of yours to Africa. Must you go?

David. I must. I've been waiting for years for this chance. If I succeed, it will crown all my life's work.

Dulcie. But it's dangerous.

David. I take a doctor and drugs. Besides, I bear a charmed life.

Dulcie. But this fever, — Eddie says it is deadly.

David. (*With great calmness, looking away*) It will pass me. But if it kills me, I must go.

Dulcie. No, no, no.

David. Yes, yes, yes. I'm pledged. All my world, the little world that takes an interest in me, is watching me. There's the hope of a great prize. It's my one chance of snatching the poor little laurel-wreath that we mortals call immortality.

Dulcie. But can't you go some other time?

David. I must be at my post, especially as it is a little dangerous, — that makes it the post of honour. I've delayed everything till the last moment that I might be near you till the very end.

Dulcie. The end! Then this is the end? I shall never see you again.

David. Yes. When I return.

Dulcie. (*Shaking her head*) You will not return. (*Looking at him very keenly and closely*) Tell me, in your heart of hearts do you not know that you will never come back? (*David is about to speak*) Ah no — tell me the truth!

David. (*Slowly and fatefully*) I wonder how it is that when one has carefully weeded out all the old superstitions from one's mind, a crop of new superstitions springs up more foolish than the old ones. I've lived up there so long I've grown morbid. I've an attack of the silliest form of superstition — a presentiment.

Dulcie. Ah, I knew it!

David. In six months I shall laugh at it. We will laugh at it together.

Dulcie. (*Determinedly*) You shall not go!

David. I must. I'm working with my comrades all over the world. I've undertaken this part of the work. If I don't carry it out I break faith with them and spoil their work too. All the good fellows who are going with me and sharing in my dangers are waiting for me at Marseilles. I can't leave them in the lurch — I can't — you would not have me do it! Say you wouldn't have me stamp myself a coward, a deserter.

Dulcie. No, no. But I don't want you to go. (*Approaching him*) If I asked you to stay —

David. You will not — (*Going towards her*) You will not (*A little nearer*) ask me to stay. (*She looks at him — gradually they go closer to each other, and his manner changes from a calm, dreamy, fateful tone to a fierce, hoarse, passionate tone*) Do you know what it means if I stay? Dulcie!

Dulcie. You never called me that before.

David. (*Clasping her*) I've never been so near to you. Dulcie! (*With sudden, mad abandonment, clasping her passionately*) Yes, I'll stay! I'll stay! Tell me to stay because — because — you love me.

Dulcie. Stay — because — ah, you know I love you!

David. Eddie's right. Let's be fools to-night. Let's live to-night! I'm hungry for you! Dulcie, tell me once again that you love me.

Dulcie. No — no. Forget it. What have I said? What shall we do?

David. I don't know. What does it matter? We will go to this ball — anything — anywhere! Our lives are in our own hands. Come with me.

Sir Brice enters. He shuts the door, stands against it, his feet a little sprawling, his hands in his pockets, looking at them maliciously. Long pause. Helen enters at the other door. Another pause. She beckons Dulcie.

Helen. Dulcie!

Indicates the inside room. Dulcie goes up to her. Exit Helen. Dulcie at the door looks at the two men. Exit Dulcie. The two men are left alone. Another slight pause. Sir Brice walks very deliberately up to David. The two men stand close to each other for a moment or two.

Sir B. You've come to settle your little account, I suppose?

David. I owe you nothing.

Sir B. But I owe you six thousand pounds. I haven't a penny in the world. I'll cut you for it, double or quits.

David. I don't play cards.

Sir B. You'd better begin. (*Rapping on the table with the cards*)

David. (*Very firmly*) I don't play cards with *you.*

Sir B. And I say you shall.

David. (*Very stern and contemptuous*) I don't play cards with you. (*Going towards door*)

Sir B. You refuse?

David. I refuse.

Sir B. Once for all, will you give me a chance of paying back the six thousand pounds that Lady Skene has borrowed from you? Yes or no?

David. No.

Sir B. No?

David. (*Very emphatically*) No. (*Goes to door, suddenly turns round, comes up to him*) Yes. (*Comes to the table*) I *do* play cards with you. You want my money. Very well. I'll give you a chance of winning all I have in the world.

Sir B. (*After a look of astonishment*) Good. I'm your man. Any game you like, and any stakes.

David. (*Very calm, cold, intense tone all through*) The stakes on my side are some two hundred thousand pounds. The stakes on your side are — your wife and child.

Sir B. (*Taken aback*) My wife and child!

David. Your wife and child. Come — begin! (*Points to the cards*)

Sir B. (*Getting flurried*) My wife and child? (*Puts his hands restlessly through his hair, looks intently at David. Pause*) All right. (*Pause. Cunningly*) I value my wife and child very highly.

David. I value them at all I have in the world. (*Pointing to cards*) Begin!

Sir B. You seem in a hurry.

David. I believe I haven't six months to live. I want to make the most of those six months. If I have more I want to make the most of all the years. Begin!

Sir B. (*Wipes his face with his handkerchief*) This is the first time I've played this game. We'd better arrange conditions.

David. There's only one condition. We play till I'm beggared of every farthing I have, or till you're beggared of them. Sit down!

Sir B. (*Sits down*) Very well. (*Pause*) What game?

David. The shortest.

Sir B. Simple cutting?

David. What you please. Begin!

Sir B. There's no hurry. I mean to have a night's fun out of this.

David. Look at me. Don't trifle with me! I want to have done with you. I want them to have done with you. I want to get them away from you. Quick! I want to know now — now — this very moment — whether they are yours or mine. Begin.

Sir B. (*Shuffles the cards*) All right. What do we cut for?

David. Let one cut settle it.

Sir B. No. It's too much to risk on one throw.

David. One cut. Begin.

Sir B. It's too big. I can't. I like high play, but that's too high for me. (*David remains at table, very calm; does not stir through all the scene; Sir Brice walking about*) No, by Jove! I'll tell you what I'll do. Three cuts out of five. Damn it all! I'm game! Two out of three. By Jove, two out of three! Will that do?

David. So be it! Sit down! Shuffle. (*Sir Brice sits down; begins shuffling the cards. All through the scene he is nervous, excited, hysterical, laughing. David as cold as a statue*)

Sir B. (*Having shuffled*) Now then. Who cuts first? (*The two men stare fixedly at each other*)

Dulcie enters at back.

Dulcie. (*Surprised*) Mr. Remon! No! No! Not that! Not that!

David. (*Coming down, warning her off with a motion of his hand*) If you please. Stand aside for a moment. (*Offers the cards to Sir Brice to cut*)

Sir B. Ace counts lowest.

David. As you will. Cut! (*Sir Brice cuts*)

Sir B. King! By Jove! King! Cut! (*David cuts*) Nine! One to me! By Jove! one to me! (*To Dulcie*) Give us up some of those cards, will you? (*David by a gesture stops her; takes up the pack that Sir Brice has broken and shuffles them*) Shuffle up. By Jove! if I win,—

Dulcie. Mr. Remon, you'll not play any more?

David. (*Very gently*) Stand aside, please.

Sir B. No. Let her shuffle for us. She's in it, isn't she?

Dulcie. What do you mean? What are you playing for?

Sir B. You'd like to know, would you? What are we playing for? I'll tell you. We're playing for you and your child!

Dulcie. (*Suddenly*) What? (*Shows great horror and astonishment*) Mr. Remon! It's not so? It's not so? (*To David*) What are you playing for?

David. He has said. For you and your child. If I win, will you abide by the bargain? (*Very long pause — she looks from one to the other*)

Dulcie. Yes.

David. (*Puts cards on table*) Cut. (*They both shuffle cards*)

Sir B. (*Very excited, laughing, nervous*) You've got to win both now. You know that?

David. I know.

Sir B. (*Cuts*) Ten. Not bad. You've got to beat it. Cut! (*David cuts*) Queen! One each! Now for the final, d'ye hear? This is final. If I win — (*Walking about excitedly; pours out a glass of brandy — drinks*) I'll cut first! No! Damn it all! you cut first! (*Holding cards. David cuts*) Six. (*To David, suddenly*) Suppose I win — you'll pay me? You mean to pay me?

David. I shall pay you every farthing.

Sir B. What security do you give me?

David. My word in the presence of the woman I love.

Sir B. (*Walks about*) Let me be a moment.

David. Cut.

Sir B. (*To Dulcie*) You're anxious, are you? I'm going to win! I mean it! I'm going to win! (*To David*) Now! (*David holds cards; Sir Brice cuts*) My God! I've lost!

David. (*Throws down the card-table; leaps at him; catches hold of him by the throat*) Yes, you've lost! She's mine! (*Gets him down on his knees*) You've cheated me of her all these years! You've cheated me of her love, cheated me of the fatherhood of her child,

you've dragged her down, you've dishonoured her! She's my wife now — my wife and child! Take your oath you'll never lay claim to them again! Swear it! (*Shaking him*)

Sir B. She's yours! Take her! I'll never see her or her child again! I swear it! Take them!

David. Dare to break your word — dare to lay a finger on her or her child — dare to show your face in the home that my love shall give to her — and whatever laws men have made to bind you and her together, I'll break them and rid her of you! D'ye hear? She's mine! She's mine! She's mine! (*Throws Sir Brice back on the floor. To Dulcie*) My wife! My child! Come! You're mine!

David seizes Dulcie in his arms and falls against door. Curtain begins to descend when Sir Brice is thrown down.

End of the Third Act.

ACT IV.

The Observatory on Mount Garidelli in the Maritime Alps, near Nice. A door, right. A large fireplace, with pine cones and pine logs ready laid, above door, right. At the back, seen through a large curtained doorway, is the circular Observatory with large telescope. This room is vaguely seen, the telescope being lighted by a shaft of moonlight at the beginning of the Act. On the left side, slantwise, a large window, with terrace outside, giving scenery of the Maritime Alps. A large armchair above the fireplace. On table and scattered about the room are a number of scientific books and astronomical instruments and apparatus. The window is curtained with Eastern curtains. As curtain rises the whole scene is dark except for the shaft of moonlight that falls on the telescope. Enter David and Dulcie.

David. Come in! Come to your home! My wife!

Dulcie. (*Cold, shuddering*) Ah no — don't call me that — at least not yet.

David. You're shivering! Let me give you some wine. (*Goes to cupboard, brings out bottle and glass, which he fills, places them on table*)

Dulcie. No, no, tell me — (*Goes to him, looks into his face*)

David. (*With great tenderness*) Dulcie! Dulcie! What is it, dear? How cold you are. I'll light the fire. (*Lights fire, which is already* laid with large pine cones and logs and quickly blazes up) I'm your servant now. I've nothing to do all my life but wait on you. We shall soon have a blaze with these pine logs. My servants left me last night. I thought I should have no further use for them. I thought my life here was ended. Ended! My life has only begun this last hour. (Clasping her) Dulcie! Do you know where you are? You are in your home. Take off your hat and cloak, dear. (Gently removes her cloak and puts it on chair) There! (Seats her at the fire in large chair) This is your own hearth, dear, your own fireside. You are my bride! No bride was ever so welcome as you. Poor hands so cold. (Takes her hands in his, rubs them; as he does so, they both at one moment see her wedding-ring. Dulcie withdraws her hand in shame. They look at each other horrified. A pause) Give me your hand. (She holds it out. He takes off the ring, goes to window, draws aside the curtains, opens window, throws away the ring, comes back to her. The dawn outside begins and gradually rises into a full sunrise during progress of Act)

Dulcie. (As he returns to her) Oh, you'll be very kind to me?

David. I have no life, no ambition away from you. The world has gone from me. This journey to Africa — it was the object of my life — it's less than nothing to me now. I've thrown it away, I've forgotten it, because you asked me.

Dulcie. Ah no, you mustn't do that. Oh, I'm selfish to take you from your comrades, from your work. You must go and make this great discovery.

David. I've made the one great discovery there was to make. It's the cunningest of them all. We astronomers have been puzzling all our lives to find out what gravitation is. I've found it out. Gravitation is love. It's love that holds together all this universe. It's love that drives every little atom in space to rush to every other little atom. There's love at the centre of the system. There's love at the centre of all things. No astronomer ever made a discovery equal to that! Dulcie, look at me! What ails you? What are you thinking of?

Dulcie. Nell and Rosy. They'll be here soon.

David. Yes. They can't be long. Don't think of them. Think only of ourselves.

Dulcie. Why wouldn't you come with me to Beaulieu and bring them up here?

David. I was afraid your sister would take you from me. I wanted to have you all to myself. When she comes here I wanted her to find you already in your home.

Dulcie. It's so strange.

David. What is strange?

Dulcie. To be here with you — alone.

David. It's not strange to me. You've been here so often already. In my loneliness I've pictured you here hundreds of times. I at my work in there, you in this chair by the fire, Rosy playing about the floor.

Dulcie. Rosy.

David. She is my child now, as you are my wife. Dulcie, say you know we have done right.

Dulcie. (Distracted) Right! Yes — yes — I suppose so! What else could we do? What else could I do!

David. Say you know we have done right.

Dulcie. Yes — yes — I can't think now. (Returning and throwing her arms round him) I only know I love you.

David. (Clasping her madly) Dulcie, this is your home, this is our wedding day. My bride!

Dulcie. (Tearing herself from him) No, no — not now — not yet! My promise to Nell — I promised her I would take no step till I had seen her.

David. (Pursuing her, fiercely clasping her) You've taken the step. You're mine —

Dulcie. No, no. (Repulsing him again) Let me think. Wait till Nell comes. Ah, don't think I don't love you. There's nothing I wouldn't do or suffer for you. There's not a thought in my heart that isn't yours. Say you know it! Say you know it!

David. I know it. What then? Tell me what's in your heart.

Dulcie. I can't. Can't you guess?

David. Guess — what?

Dulcie. Oh, it was horrible with him. There was no home, no family, no love. It seemed like a blasphemy of home to live with him. But this — I can't tell you how I feel — I don't think any man can understand it. It's only a woman, and not all women — not many women perhaps — but I feel it. I can't get rid of it. To live with you seems more horrible than the other. I cannot! I cannot!

David. (Very calmly, very sweetly, very soothingly) Dearest, you mustn't talk like this. Heaven bear me witness you will come to me as pure as if I took you from your mother's side, as pure as if you had never known any kiss but your sister's. (Attempting to embrace her)

Dulcie. Ah! (Shrinking from him) Don't I tell you, a man can't understand my feelings. (Looks at him half-loving, half-horrified; stands looking at him. A little pause)

David. (*Same soft, tender tone. very persuasive, very low, very sweet*) Dulcie, in a very little while you will grow to think of me as if I were your very husband — as I shall be; and with you, and your sister, and Eddie, and Rosy, we shall make one happy, one united family. (*Approaching her*)

Dulcie. Ah! that's it. I feel —

David. (*Clasping her again*) What?

Dulcie. We can't be a family that way. There's only one way of being a family.

David. And that?

Dulcie. By the marriage and love of husband and wife.

David. It is marriage I offer you. Dulcie, you must see there's no future for you away from me. Say you'll give yourself to me willingly. (*Pause*) I will not take you else. Give yourself to me!

Dulcie. (*After a pause*) I am yours.

David. No. *Give* yourself to me — wholly, freely, willingly.

Dulcie. Oh! don't you see? I would give you myself — a thousand selves if I could. What is there in me that is worth giving, or worth your taking now?

David. Everything, everything. Give yourself to me!

Dulcie. If I give you myself I give you the last four years with me. They are part of me. I shall only feel that I can never get rid of them. I cannot get rid of them. Every time you kiss me I shall see him beside us! I cannot! I cannot! I cannot! I cannot!

Pause. Eddie looks in at window.

Eddie. Ho, ho, Davy! Ho, ho! Here we are!

Dulcie. (*Goes to window, goes up to him*) My sister and Rosy, are they with you?

Eddie. (*Pointing down below*) Quite safe. Here they are. Look alive, Davy! We've no time to waste. I shall be ready in a twinkling. I'm half a fool, and half a wise man just now. In two minutes I shall be in my right senses — or in as many as I've got — and then — (*Passes by*)

David. (*To Dulcie*) Dulcie, your sister is here. Tell her that henceforth you are my wife.

Dulcie. I am your slave, your dog, your anything! Take me if you will — take me! But kill me after. If you don't I shall kill myself.

Helen enters at door, stands for a moment looking at one and then at the other.

Helen. Dulcie. (*Dulcie goes to her, saying, "Nell"*)

Dulcie. Rosy — where is she?

Helen. (*Pointing off*) She's there. (*Dulcie is going. Helen stops her*) Let me look at you. (*Dulcie looks frankly at her. Helen smiles, kisses her*) Go to your baby.

Exit Dulcie. Helen shuts the door after Dulcie.

You've taken her from him? (*David nods*)

Helen. For good and all?

David. For good and all.

Helen. Why have you brought her here?

David. To make her my wife.

Helen. Your wife? That is impossible unless—

David. Unless?

Helen. Unless her husband divorces her and takes her child from her.

David. I've won her from him, her and the child. Don't come between us. Give them to me!

Helen. (*Stops him*) She is not mine to give. She is not yours to take. Your brother tells me you're going on this expedition to Africa this morning.

David. I'm not going.

Helen. Not going? But you have looked forward to it all your life!

David. I've wasted all my life in such dreams and shadows as work and duty. What has it availed me? Now I see one chance of happiness before me, don't take it from me! Give them to me! (*She stops him*) I will have them!

Eddie enters dressed ready to start.

Eddie. Davy, old boy, look alive! The men have got everything on the mules. We've not a moment to waste.

David. I'm not going.

Eddie. Not going? But they are all waiting for us. If we don't go, all the expeditions everywhere will be a failure. Davy, you aren't going to sell them all like a — like a — They'll call you a — well, you fill in the word.

David. I'm not going.

Eddie. But what excuse can we make?

David. Any excuse you like — I've changed my mind.

Helen. (*With quiet sarcasm*) Is that a good excuse for a soldier to make just as he's ordered into a battle?

David. I'm not a soldier.

Helen. Yes, you are. We are all soldiers on this earth, bound to be loyal to every one of our comrades, bound to obey the great rules of life, whether they are easy or hard. Yes, and all the more bound when they are hard, when they may cost us our very life. You'll go — you'll go, and leave her to me and Rosy?

David. I love her! I love her!

Helen. Then save her for her child. Save her to be a good mother to that little helpless creature she has brought into the world, so that when her girl grows up and she has to guide her, she'll not have to say to her child, "You can give yourself to this man, and if you don't like him you can give yourself to another, and to another, and so on. It doesn't matter. It was what I did!"

David. (*Same tone*) I love her! I love her! I love her! You sha'n't reason me out of my happiness!

Helen. (*Stopping him*) I can't reason at all. I can only feel, and I know my instinct is right. I know the woman who gives herself to another man while her husband is alive betrays her sex, and is a bad woman.

David. I love her! I love her! (*Going towards door*)

Helen. (*Stopping him*) Then make your love the best thing in her life, and the best thing in yours. You have loved her so well. You have made so many sacrifices for her. Make this one last sacrifice. Keep her pure for her child.

Eddie. That's God's voice speaking to you now, Davy.

Dulcie enters very quietly, looking off.

Dulcie. (*To David*) She's asleep. Go and look at her.

Exit David. Dulcie is about to follow. Helen stops her.

Helen. Dulcie.

Dulcie. What?

Helen. He's given his word to his comrades. Don't make him play the coward.

David re-enters, much calmer.

David. Miss Larondie, I'll write to you from Marseilles. I have left everything in order for her. If by any chance I should not return —

Dulcie. Ah! (*Goes to him*)

David. Take care of her while I'm away.

Dulcie. But if you do not return?

David. (*Very calm, very bitter, very tender, with a little smile*) Then — we shall have played our parts well in this little puppet-show, shall we not? Don't cry, my dear, why should you? If I were a soldier, you would tell me to go. We shall not be absent from each other long. Don't cry, dear. It's my duty to go, Dulcie. Be brave. Tell me to go.

Dulcie. (*Bows her head*) Go. Go.

David. (*Going from her some steps*) I've played this great game of love like a fool, as men would say. Perhaps I've played the great game of life like a fool, too. If we are sacrificing ourselves for a shadow we are only doing what earth's best creatures have done before us. If duty is reality, we have done right. Right — wrong — duty — they may be all shadows, but my love for you is real. (*Dulcie is sobbing, he comes to her*) Hush! Hush, dear! We shall never know satiety. Our love will never grow stale and commonplace, will it? Dulcie, we've only thrown away the husks. We've kept the immortal part of our love — if there is an immortal part. Look! this is my mother's wedding ring. (*Taking a very thin gold ring from his little finger*) She gave it to me as she was dying. It has never left my finger since. I give it you in exchange for the one I took from you. Give me your hand. (*Dulcie gives it*) With this ring I thee wed. As she that bore me was pure, so I leave you pure, dear. Kiss me once — I've held you sacred! (*She kisses him*) Good-bye. No, stay. (*Pours out a glass of wine, gives it to her*) Drink with me. (*She takes the glass, drinks some of it. He takes it from her, drains it, dashes the glass on the floor, where it is shivered to atoms; he then turns very brightly and gaily to Eddie*) Now Eddie — our work!

Eddie. Ready, big brother!

David. (*To Dulcie*) In six months from now, come to meet me, my wife, and bring our child. Or, it may be a little later — but come and meet me — my wife — a little later.

Dulcie. Where?

David. In that little star in Andromeda. All's real there.

Exeunt Eddie and David through window.

CURTAIN.

If curtain is called up, show a picture of David outside the window, in the full morning sunlight, the mountains covered with snow behind him; Eddie is beside him drawing him away.

THE END.

ARTHUR WING PINERO

1855-1934

The Notorious Mrs. Ebbsmith

(1895)

If, as Henry Arthur Jones asserted, a primary function of the drama is to provoke people seriously to examine and discuss their lives and ideas, then Pinero's *The Second Mrs. Tanqueray* might be considered the most important play of the new drama. The play treated frankly and realistically the double standard of sexual morality, an almost unmentionable subject; it shocked playgoers and set all London talking. Pinero's next play, *The Notorious Mrs. Ebbsmith*, was equally provocative.

Arthur Wing Pinero was born in London on May 24, 1855. His father was a lawyer whose practice so declined during Arthur's childhood that the boy was taken out of school at the age of ten and put to work in his father's office. During his teens, besides his study of the law, Arthur enrolled for night classes in the Birkbeck Institute, chiefly to study elocution; he graduated, performing the role of Hamlet as his final exercise. In these years, as often as he could find the time, he attended Sadler's Wells Theatre, near his home, and increasingly became, as Wilbur Dunkel says, "quite hopelessly stage struck." When Pinero was nineteen his father died, and the young man gave up the idea of becoming a lawyer. He found a place on the stage as "general utility" in W. H. Wyndham's stock company, then performing in Edinburgh. Pinero got to the Globe Theatre in London through a mistake on the part of Wilkie Collins. A dramatization of Collins's novel *Armadale* was scheduled for production, and Collins was looking for actors to fit the parts. In Liverpool he admired the performance of an actor, in the dim light misread the playbill, and checked Pinero's name. Consequently, at the age of twenty, Pinero found himself engaged to act in London. He tried his hand at writing, and in 1877 his first play, *Two Hundred a Year* (a "curtain lifter"), was produced at the Globe. More plays, both melodramas and farces, followed. Pinero married the actress Myra Holme in 1883. His skill in playwriting developed and, in the spirit of the times, in 1889 he wrote a somewhat shocking problem play, *The Profligate*. Unlike Shaw, Pinero had no insistent message; he willingly changed the austere ending of this play at the suggestion of the producer. The rest of his career is that of an increasingly skillful and popular playwright. His contribution to the drama was recognized by King Edward VII, and he was knighted in 1909. Pinero's plays, revolutionary in theme in the 1890's, began to seem somewhat old-fashioned after his *Mid-Channel* of 1909. Younger playwrights outshone him. He died November 23, 1934.

In his apprentice years as a playwright Pinero admired and emulated Tom Robertson and the Bancrofts; his play *Lords and Commons* (1883) was produced by the Bancrofts at the Haymarket. Study of their methods taught Pinero a good deal about stagecraft. In a letter of 1884, Pinero wrote to Sir Squire Bancroft: "It is my opinion, expressed here as it is elsewhere, that the present advanced condition of the English stage — throwing as it does a clear, natural light upon the manners and life of people, where a few years ago there was nothing but mouthing and tinsel — is due to the crusade begun by Mrs. Bancroft and yourself in your little Prince of Wales's Theatre." Like Robertson, Pinero rehearsed a company producing one of his plays and even, like Gilbert, acquired the reputation of a tyrant. Pinero sought to pay his debt to Robertson with the play *Trelawny of the "Wells"* (1898), which dramatized Robertson's life and his contributions to the stage. Pinero's problem plays of the 1890's exhibit some of the austerity and techniques of Ibsen's dramas, but Pinero always denied any significant influence from the Norwegian. Whatever influence may be observed is superimposed upon concepts derived from Robertson and the Bancrofts and developed in Pinero's own experience.

Pinero first departed from the formula for melodrama in *The Money Spinner* of 1880, a play about gamblers and horse racing. His innovation was that all the characters, even the heroine, cheated. Audiences were puzzled, but pleased by the sparkle of the play. Pinero developed skill in writing brisk dialogue in a series of plays called, for the name of the theatre, the Court Farces. One of them, *The Magistrate*, produced in 1885, set a new record with more than three hundred performances. The characteristic of the dialogue was bright naturalness without the puns and other artificialities of stage wit. Pinero's first venture into the problem play was *The Profligate* (1889). Pinero wrote the play (and later published it) as a tragedy growing out of the double standard of sexual morality. It tells the story of a dissipated young man who marries an innocent and trusting girl. The wife becomes a friend of a girl her husband had seduced. Shocked on discovering the facts, the wife leaves home. The husband finds his wife's hiding place and urges her to return. When she is delayed, in remorse and despair he kills himself. This ending seemed to the producer too shocking, and he persuaded Pinero to give the play the happy ending of melodrama: the wife returns just as the husband is about to drink poison, realizes his remorse, and forgives him. The play for the first time presented on the stage a previously forbidden subject while developing the idea that the consequences of past conduct cannot be wished away. The playbill stated this theme in a poem that included these lines:

> You can't turn curds to milk again,
> Nor Now by wishing back to Then;
> And, having tasted stolen honey,
> You can't buy innocence for money.

Also in this play, for the first time, Pinero dropped the soliloquy and the aside, characteristic of the traditional drama since Shakespeare's time and of the melodrama. The success of *The Profligate* determined Pinero to insist upon a realistic ending for his next serious play, no matter what a manager might advise.

The Second Mrs. Tanqueray (1893), treating the similar problem of whether a woman with a shameful past may be restored to social esteem by a respectable marriage, preserves the tragic, logical ending. Even if now old-fashioned in its theme, it is one of the world's great plays. Pinero had trouble finding a manager who would produce the play and an actress who would perform the role of Paula. At last Mrs. Patrick Campbell took the role, and the play was produced at the St. James's Theatre on May 27, 1893. It boldly discusses whether a generous, respectable man can find happiness in marriage with a fallen woman, and whether the woman's past can be buried and forgotten. Pinero's analytic portrayal reaches a negative answer — the conventional answer for the 1890's. Paula discovers that character shaped by conduct determines destiny, that "the future is only the past again, entered through another gate."

Perhaps the success of *The Second Mrs. Tanqueray*, more than any reforming purpose or message, caused Pinero deliberately to choose a shocking and radical subject for his next play, *The Notorious Mrs. Ebbsmith*. The treatment intends utter realism, the repudiation of the last vestige of the domestic melodrama. Perhaps from a twentieth-century point of view, the ending of the play may seem false and sentimental, but the retreat from radicalism has more the ring of Pinero's conviction than of an adherence to the melodramatic formula. Perhaps the Duke of St. Olpherts seems more a profligate type than a real duke, and perhaps Agnes Ebbsmith suggests something less staunch than the actual "new woman" of the period. But these are weaknesses in Pinero's knowledge of his people, rather than echoes of type characters from the melodrama. The play, on the contrary, attacks the dearest convention of domestic melodrama: the prescriptive morality that supported the Victorian home. Agnes Ebbsmith is, from the conventional point of view, a "shameful" woman, but she, the heroine, has arguments to justify and even glorify her conduct.

The play is to be understood as a treatment of an important question in a changing society. Since the time of J. S. Mill's *The Subjection of Women* (1869) the patriarchal family system, with its docile, obedient wife, had been increasingly under attack. By the 1890's woman suffrage, with mass meetings of embattled women and marches on Parliament, was an issue of national importance. (Many of the people who believed in rights for women were also "radicals" who believed in the rights of labor and socialistic reforms of many kinds; the fact that conservatives used the Bible to support the *status quo* to some extent encouraged radicals in agnostic attitudes.) Feminists attacked marriage as a legal bondage that gave the husband the power of a tyrant. The remedy for the woes of marriage might be the kind of union Mrs. Ebbsmith advocates, an equal companionship of minds and purposes without the legal bonds that (under the laws then operative) were nearly unbreakable.

Perhaps to the ordinary playgoer the idea of conjugal companionship without legal marriage suggested the sordid and unprincipled. Agnes Ebbsmith holds the opposite view; she makes her relationship with Lucas Cleeve seem a matter of high principles, and the bondage of the legal tie seem potentially sordid. But the action reveals that ordinary human beings, including Mrs. Ebbsmith, lack the strength to live up to the ideal of free companionship. (The play omits one aspect of the problem: children.) Pinero apparently had no solution for this difficulty. Mrs. Ebbsmith retreats in the direction of religion, though it is not clear how religion may solve the problem she has effectively stated.

To prepare for this ending, Pinero made his radical characters something less than thorough radicals. The "real Lucas Cleeve," as presented by the Duke and by the action, is not the dedicated man Mrs. Ebbsmith believes him to be. And she herself lacks the conviction of which martyrs are made. Pinero based her radicalism upon love for her father, an unhappy marriage, and other emotional experiences — so little upon either theoretical analysis or practical experience that horny-handed workingmen called her "mad Agnes." She had discarded religion simply because prayer had not helped her in time of trouble. She was not a "new woman" of the breed that went to jail for rioting in the House of Commons and, released, rioted again. Perhaps Pinero did not know such women. In any case, the play lacks a firm ending, but provides ample matter for discussion.

For many people, no doubt, the most shocking action in the play was Mrs. Ebbsmith's hurling the Bible into the fire, even though she pulled it out again. It was a strikingly theatrical *tour de force*, more dramatic in its impact upon the audience than the machinery of sensation scenes in the melodrama. And, of course, it illustrated in action and symbol the emotional and impulsive basis of Mrs. Ebbsmith's character.

These comments upon the play raise the question of Pinero's personal beliefs. He was not like Henry Arthur Jones, firmly conservative but determined to present radical views fairly. Other plays, and the comments of his biographers, indicate that Pinero was a liberal, but not a radical. He probably disliked the "new woman" and created Mrs. Ebbsmith with some feeling that she was, in Mr. Fyfe's words, "unladylike, unwomanly, and immoral." But at least, as Mr. Fyfe continues, Pinero, in putting a "feminist with original, independent ideas" on the stage, "was doing a service to the drama. She was a far more real figure than the 'heroines' usual at the time. She and her theories provoked thought. And possibly Pinero was right. In 1895 the time may not have yet come for Agnes to be real up to the end."

THE NOTORIOUS MRS. EBBSMITH

A Drama In Four Acts

by

ARTHUR W. PINERO

First performed at the Garrick Theatre, March 13, 1895.

Cast of Characters

DUKE OF ST. OLPHERTS	ANTONIO POPPI
SIR SANDFORD CLEEVE	AGNES
LUCAS CLEEVE	GERTRUDE THORPE
REV. AMOS WINTERFIELD	SYBIL CLEEVE
SIR GEORGE BRODRICK	NELLA
DR. KIRKE	HEPHZIBAH
FORTUNÉ	

ACT I.

The scene is a room in the Palazzo Arconati, on the Grand Canal, Venice. The room itself is beautiful in its decayed grandeur, but the furniture and hangings are either tawdry and meretricious or avowedly modern. The three windows at the back open on to a narrow, covered balcony, or loggia, and through them can be seen the west side of the canal. Between the recessed double doors, on either side of the room, is a fireplace out of use, and a marble mantelpiece, but a tiled stove is used for a wood fire. Breakfast things are laid on a table. The sun streams into the room. Antonio Poppi and Nella, two Venetian servants, with a touch of the picturesque in their attire, are engaged in clearing the breakfast table.

Nella. (*Turning her head*) Ascolta! (Listen!)

Ant. Una gondola allo scalo. (A gondola at our steps.) (*They open the center window; go out on to the balcony, and look down below*) La Signora Thorpe. (The Signora Thorpe.)

Nella. Con suo fratello. (With her brother.)

Ant. (*Calling*) Buon di, Signor Winterfield! Iddio la benedica! (Good day, Signor

Winterfield! The blessing of God be upon you!)

Nella. (*Calling*) Buon di, Signora! La Madonna l'assista! (Good day, Signora! May the Virgin have you in her keeping!)

Ant. (*Returning to the room*) Noi siamo in ritardo di tutto questa mattina. (We are behindhand with everything this morning.)

Nella. (*Following him*) È vero. (That is true.)

Ant. (*Bustling about*) La stufa! (The stove!)

Nella. (*Throwing wood into the stove*) Che tu sia benedetta per rammentarmelo! Questi Inglesi non si contentono del sole. (Bless you for remembering it! These English are not content with the sun.)

Leaving only a vase of flowers upon the table, they hurry out with the breakfast things. At the same moment, Fortuné, a manservant, enters, showing in Mrs. Thorpe and the Rev. Amos Winterfield. Gertrude Thorpe is a pretty, honest-looking young woman of about seven and twenty. She is in mourning, and has sorrowful eyes, and a complexion that is too delicate; but natural cheerfulness and brightness are seen through all. Amos is about forty — big, burly, gruff; he is untidily dressed, and has a pipe in his hand. Fortuné is carrying a pair of freshly cleaned, tan-coloured boots upon boot-trees.

497

Gert. Now, Fortuné, you ought to have told us downstairs that Dr. Kirke is with Mrs. Cleeve.

Amos. Come away, Gerty. Mrs. Cleeve can't want to be bored with us just now.

For. Mrs. Cleeve give 'er ordares she is always to be bored wiz Madame Thorpe and Mr. Winterfield.

Amos. Ha, ha!

Gert. (*Smiling*) Fortuné!

For. Besides, ze doctares vill go in 'alf a minute, you see.

Gert. Doctors!

Amos. What, is there another doctor with Dr. Kirke?

For. Ze great physician, Sir Brodrick.

Gert. Sir George Brodrick? Amos!

Amos. Doesn't Mr. Cleeve feel so well?

For. Oh, yes. But Mrs. Cleeve 'appen to read in a newspapare zat Sir George Brodrick vas in Florence for ze Pâque — ze Eastare. Sir Brodrick vas Mr. Cleeve's doctare in London, Mrs. Cleeve tell me, so 'e is acquainted wiz Mr. Cleeve's inside.

Amos. Ho, ho!

Gert. Mr. Cleeve's constitution, Fortuné.

For. Excuse, madame. Zerefore Mrs. Cleeve she telegraph for Sir Brodrick to come to Venise.

Amos. To consult with Dr. Kirke, I suppose.

For. (*Listening*) 'Ere is ze doctares.

Dr. Kirke enters, followed by Sir George Brodrick. Kirke is a shabby, snuff-taking old gentleman — blunt, but kind; Sir George, on the contrary, is scrupulously neat in his dress, and has a suave, professional manner. Fortuné withdraws.

Kirke. Good-morning, Mr. Winterfield. (*To Gertrude*) How do you do, my dear? You're getting some colour into your pretty face, I'm glad to see. (*To Sir George*) Mr. Winterfield — Sir George Brodrick. (*Sir George and Amos shake hands. To Sir George*) Mrs. Thorpe. (*Sir George shakes hands with Gertrude*) Sir George and I started life together in London years ago; now he finds me here in Venice — well, we can't all win the race, eh?

Sir G. My dear old friend! (*To Gertrude*) Mr. Cleeve has been telling me, Mrs. Thorpe, how exceedingly kind you and your brother have been to him during his illness.

Gert. Oh, Mr. Cleeve exaggerates our little services.

Amos. I've done nothing.

Gert. Nor I.

Kirke. Now, my dear!

Gert. Dr. Kirke, you weren't in Florence with us; you're only a tale-bearer.

Kirke. Well, I've excellent authority for my story of a young woman who volunteered to share the nursing of an invalid at a time when she herself stood greatly in need of being nursed.

Gert. Nonsense! (*To Sir George*) You know, Amos — my big brother over there — Amos and I struck up an acquaintance with Mr. and Mrs. Cleeve at Florence, at the Hotel d'Italie, and occasionally one of us would give Mr. Cleeve his dose while poor Mrs. Cleeve took a little rest or a drive — but positively that's all.

Kirke. You don't tell us —

Gert. I've nothing more to tell, except that I'm awfully fond of Mrs. Cleeve —

Amos. Oh, if you once get my sister on the subject of Mrs. Cleeve — (*Taking up a newspaper*)

Gert. (*To Sir George*) Yes, I always say that if I were a man searching for a wife, I should be inclined to base my ideal on Mrs. Cleeve.

Sir. G. (*Edging away towards Kirke, with a surprised, uncomfortable smile*) Eh? Really?

Gert. You conceive a different ideal, Sir George?

Sir G. Oh — well —

Gert. Well, Sir George?

Amos. Perhaps Sir George has heard that Mrs. Cleeve holds regrettable opinions on some points. If so, he may feel surprised that a parson's sister —

Gert. Oh, I don't share all Mrs. Cleeve's views, or sympathize with them, of course. But they succeed only in making me sad and sorry. Mrs. Cleeve's opinions don't stop me from loving the gentle, sweet woman; admiring her for her patient, absorbing devotion to her husband; wondering at the beautiful stillness with which she seems to glide through life! —

Amos. (*Putting down the newspaper; to Sir George and Kirke*) I told you so! (*To Gertrude*) Gertrude I'm sure Sir George and Dr. Kirke want to be left together for a few minutes.

Gert. (*Going up to the window*) I'll sun myself on the balcony.

Amos. And I'll go and buy some tobacco. (*To Gertrude*) Don't be long, Gerty. (*Nodding to Sir George and Kirke*) Good-morning.

They return his nod, and he goes out.

Gert. (*On the balcony outside the window to Kirke and Sir George*) Dr. Kirke, I've heard what doctors' consultations consist of. After looking at the pictures you talk about whist. (*She closes the window and sits*)

Kirke. (*Producing his snuff-box*) Ha, ha!

Sir G. Why, this lady and her brother evidently haven't the faintest suspicion of the actual truth, my dear Kirke!

Kirke. (*Taking snuff*) Not the slightest.

Sir G. The woman made a point of being extremely explicit with you, you tell me?

Kirke. Yes; she was plain enough with me. At our first meeting she said, "Doctor, I want you to know so-and-so, and so-and-so, and so-and-so."

Sir G. Really? Well, it certainly isn't fair of Cleeve and his — his associate to trick decent people like Mrs. Thorpe and her brother. Good gracious, the brother is a clergyman too!

Kirke. The rector of some dull hole in the north of England.

Sir G. Really?

Kirke. A bachelor; this Mrs. Thorpe keeps house for him. She's a widow.

Sir G. Really?

Kirke. Widow of a captain in the army. Poor thing! She's lately lost her only child, and can't get over it.

Sir G. Indeed, really, really? . . . But about Cleeve now — he had Roman fever of rather a severe type?

Kirke. In November. And then that fool of a Bickerstaff at Rome allowed the woman to move him to Florence too soon, and there he had a relapse. However, when she brought him on here the man was practically well.

Sir G. The difficulty being to convince him of the fact, eh? A highly strung, emotional creature?

Kirke. You've hit him.

Sir G. I've known him from his childhood. Are you still giving him anything?

Kirke. A little quinine, to humour him.

Sir G. Exactly. (*Looking at his watch*) Where is she, where is she? I've promised to take my wife shopping in the Merceria this morning. By-the-bye, Kirke, — I must talk scandal, I find, — *this* is rather an odd circumstance. Whom do you think I got a bow from as I passed through the hall of the Danieli last night? (*Kirke grunts and shakes his head*) The Duke of St. Olpherts.

Kirke. (*Taking snuff*) Ah! I suppose you're in with a lot of swells now, Brodrick.

Sir G. No, no, you don't understand me. The duke is this young fellow's uncle by marriage. His Grace married a sister of Lady Cleeve's, of Cleeve's mother, you know.

Kirke. Oh! This looks as if the family are trying to put a finger in the pie.

Sir G. The duke may be here by mere chance. Still, as you say, it does look —

(*Lowering his voice as Kirke rises, eyes an opening door*) Who's that?

Kirke. The woman.

Agnes enters. She moves firmly but noiselessly — a placid woman with a sweet, low voice. Her dress is plain to the verge of coarseness; her face, which has little colour, is at the first glance almost wholly unattractive.

Agnes. (*Looking from one to the other*) I thought you would send for me perhaps. (*To Sir George*) What do you say about him?

Kirke. One moment. (*Pointing to the balcony*) Mrs. Thorpe —

Agnes. Excuse me. (*She goes to the window and opens it*)

Gert. O Mrs. Cleeve! (*Entering the room*) Am I in the way?

Agnes. You are never that, dear. Run along to my room; I'll call you in a minute or two. (*Gertrude nods and goes to the door*) Take off your hat and sit with me a little while.

Gert. I'll stay for a bit, but this hat doesn't take off. (*She goes out*)

Agnes. (*To Sir George and Kirke*) Yes?

Sir G. We are glad to be able to give a most favourable report. I may say that Mr. Cleeve has never appeared to be in better health.

Agnes. (*Drawing a deep breath*) He will be very much cheered by what you say.

Sir G. (*Bowing stiffly*) I'm glad —

Agnes. His illness left him with a morbid, irrational impression that he would never be quite his former self again.

Sir G. A nervous man recovering from a scare. I've helped to remove that impression, I believe.

Agnes. Thank you. We have a troublesome, perhaps a hard time before us; we both need all our health and spirits. (*Turning her head, listening*) Lucas?

Lucas enters the room. He is a handsome, intellectual-looking young man of about eight and twenty.

Lucas. (*To Agnes, excitedly*) Have you heard what they say of me?

Agnes. (*Smiling*) Yes.

Lucas. How good of you, Sir George, to break up your little holiday for the sake of an anxious, fidgety fellow. (*To Agnes*) Isn't it?

Agnes. Sir George has rendered us a great service.

Lucas. (*Going to Kirke, brightly*) Yes, and proved how ungrateful I've been to you, doctor.

Kirke. Don't apologize. People who don't

know when they're well are the mainstay of my profession. (*Offering snuff-box*) Here — (*Lucas takes a pinch of snuff, laughingly*)

Agnes. (*In a low voice to Sir George*) He has been terribly hipped at times. (*Taking up the vase of flowers from the table*) Your visit will have made him another man. (*She goes to a table, puts down the vase upon the tray, and commences to cut and arrange the fresh flowers she finds there*)

Lucas. (*Seeing that Agnes is out of hearing*) Excuse me, Kirke — just for one moment. (*To Sir George*) Sir George — (*Kirke joins Agnes*) You still go frequently to Great Cumberland Place?

Sir G. Your mother's gout has been rather stubborn lately.

Lucas. Very likely she and my brother Sandford will get to hear of your visit to me here; in that case you'll be questioned pretty closely, naturally.

Sir G. My position is certainly a little delicate.

Lucas. Oh, you may be perfectly open with my people as to my present mode of life. Only — (*He motions Sir George to be seated; they sit facing each other*) only I want you to hear me declare again plainly (*Looking towards Agnes*) that but for the care and devotion of that good woman over there, but for the solace of that woman's companionship, I should have been dead months ago; I should have died raving in my awful bedroom on the ground-floor of that foul Roman hotel. Malarial fever, of course! Doctors don't admit — do they? — that it is possible for strong men to die of miserable marriages. And yet I was dying in Rome, I truly believe, from *my* bitter, crushing disappointment, from the consciousness of my wretched, irretrievable — (*Fortuné enters carrying Lucas's hat, gloves, overcoat, and silk wrap, and, upon a salver, a bottle of medicine and a glass. Sharply*) Qu'y a-t-il, Fortuné?

For. Sir, you 'ave an appointment.

Lucas. (*Rising*) At the Danieli at eleven. Is it so late? (*Fortuné places the things upon the table. Lucas puts the wrap round his throat. Agnes, who has turned on Fortuné's entrance, goes to Lucas and arranges the wrap for him solicitously*)

Sir G. (*Rising*) I have to meet Lady Brodrick at the Piazzetta. Let me take you in my gondola.

Lucas. Thanks, delighted.

Agnes. (*To Sir George*) I would rather Lucas went in the house gondola: I know its cushions are dry. May he take you to the Piazzetta?

Sir G. (*A little stiffly*) Certainly.

Agnes. (*To Fortuné*) Mettez les coussins dans la gondole.

For. Bien, madame. (*Fortuné goes out. Agnes begins to measure a dose of medicine*)

Sir G. (*To Agnes*) Er — I — ah —

Lucas. (*Putting on his gloves*) Agnes, Sir George —

Agnes. (*Turning to Sir George, the bottle and glass in her hands*) Yes?

Sir G. (*Constrainedly*) We always make a point of acknowledging the importance of nursing as an aid to medical treatment. I — I am sure Mr. Cleeve owes you much in that respect.

Agnes. Thank you.

Sir G. (*To Lucas*) I have to discharge my gondola; you'll find me at the steps, Cleeve. (*Agnes shifts the medicine bottle from one hand to the other so that her right hand may be free, but Sir George simply bows in a formal way and moves towards the door*) You are coming with us, Kirke?

Kirke. Yes.

Sir G. Do you mind seeing that I'm not robbed by my gondolier? (*He goes out*)

Agnes. (*Giving the medicine to Lucas, undisturbed*) Here, dear.

Kirke. (*To Agnes*) May I pop in to-night for my game of chess?

Agnes. Do, doctor; I shall be very pleased.

Kirke. (*Shaking her hand in a marked way*) Thank you. (*He follows Sir George*)

Agnes. (*Looking after him*) Liberal little man. (*She has Lucas's overcoat in her hand; a small pen-and-ink drawing of a woman's head drops from one of the pockets. They pick it up together*) Isn't that the sketch you made of me in Florence?

Lucas. (*Replacing it in the coat pocket*) Yes.

Agnes. You are carrying it about with you?

Lucas. I slipped it into my pocket thinking it might interest the duke.

Agnes. (*Assisting him with his overcoat*) Surely I am too obnoxious in the abstract for your uncle to entertain such a detail as a portrait.

Lucas. It struck me it might serve to correct certain preconceived notions of my people's.

Agnes. Images of a beautiful temptress with peach-blossom cheeks and stained hair?

Lucas. That's what I mean; I assume they suspect a decline of taste on my part of that sort. Good-by, dear.

Agnes. Is this mission of the Duke of St. Olpherts the final attempt to part us, I wonder? (*Angrily, her voice hardening*) Why should they harass and disturb you as they do?

Lucas. (*Kissing her*) Nothing disturbs me now that I *know* I am strong and well. Besides everybody will soon tire of being shocked. Even conventional morality must grow breathless in the chase.

He leaves her. She opens the door and calls.

Agnes. Mrs. Thorpe! I'm alone now. (*She goes to the balcony through the centre window, and looks down below*)

Gertrude enters and joins her.

Gert. How well your husband is looking!

Agnes. Sir George Brodrick pronounces him quite recovered.

Gert. Isn't that splendid! (*Waving her hand and calling*) Buon giorno, Signor Cleeve! Come molto meglio voi state! (*Leaving the balcony, laughing*) Ha, ha! my Italian! (*Agnes waves finally to the gondola below, returns to the room, and slips her arm through Gertrude's*)

Agnes. Two whole days since I've seen you.

Gert. They've been two of my bad days, dear.

Agnes. (*Looking into her face*) All right now?

Gert. Oh, "God's in His heaven" this morning! When the sun's out I feel that my little boy's bed in Ketherick Cemetery is warm and cosy.

Agnes. (*Patting Gertrude's hand*) Ah! —

Gert. The weather's the same all over Europe, according to the papers. Do you think it's really going to settle at last? To me these chilly, showery nights are terrible. You know, I still tuck my child up at night-time, still have my last peep at him before going to my own bed; and it is awful to listen to these cold rains — drip, drip, drip upon that little green coverlet of his! (*She goes and stands by the window silently*)

Agnes. This isn't strong of you, dear Mrs. Thorpe. You mustn't — you mustn't. (*Agnes brings the tray with the cut flowers to the nearer table; calmly and methodically she resumes trimming the stalks*)

Gert. You're quite right. That's over. Now, then, I'm going to gabble for five minutes gaily. (*Settling herself comfortably in an arm-chair*) What jolly flowers you've got there! What have you been doing with yourself! Amos took me to the Caffè Quadri yesterday to late breakfast, to cheer me up. Oh, I've something to say to you! At the Caffè. at the next table to ours, there were three English people — two men and a girl — home from India, I gathered. One of the men was looking out of the window, quizzing the folks

walking in the Piazza, and suddenly he caught sight of your husband. (*Agnes's hands pause in their work*) "I do believe that's Lucas Cleeve," he said. And then the girl had a peep, and said, "Certainly it is." And the man said, "I must find out where he's stopping; if Minerva is with him, you must call." "Who's Minerva?" said the second man. "Minerva is Mrs. Lucas Cleeve," the girl said; "it's a pet-name — he married a chum of mine, a daughter of Sir John Steyning's, a year or so after I went out." (*Rising and coming down*) Excuse me, dear. Do these people really know you and your husband, or were they talking nonsense?

Agnes takes the vase of faded flowers, goes on to the balcony and empties the contents of the vase into the canal. Then she stands by the window, her back towards Gertrude.

Agnes. No; they evidently know Mr. Cleeve.

Gert. Your husband never calls you by that pet-name of yours. Why is it you haven't told me you're a daughter of Admiral Steyning's?

Agnes. Mrs. Thorpe —

Gert. (*Warmly*) Oh, I must say what I mean! I have often pulled myself up short in my gossips with you, conscious of a sort of wall between us. (*Agnes comes slowly from the window*) Somehow, I feel now that you haven't in the least made a friend of me. I'm hurt. It's stupid of me; I can't help it.

Agnes. (*After a moment's pause*) I am not the lady these people were speaking of yesterday.

Gert. Not? —

Agnes. Mr. Cleeve is no longer with his wife; he has left her.

Gert. Left — his wife!

Agnes. Like yourself, I am a widow. I don't know whether you've ever heard my name — Ebbsmith. (*Gertrude stares at her blankly*) I beg your pardon sincerely. I never meant to conceal my true position; such a course is opposed to every principle of mine. But I grew so attached to you in Florence and — well, it was contemptibly weak; I'll never do such a thing again. (*She goes back to the table and commences to refill the vase with the fresh flowers*)

Gert. When you say that Mr. Cleeve has left his wife, I suppose you mean to tell me you have taken her place?

Agnes. Yes, I mean that. (*Gertrude rises and walks to the door*)

Gert. (*At the door*) You knew that I could not speak to you again after hearing this?

Agnes. I thought it almost certain you would not. (*After a moment's irresolution, Gertrude returns, and stands by the settee*)

Gert. I can hardly believe you.

Agnes. I should like you to hear more than just the bare facts.

Gert. (*Drumming on the back of the settee*) Why don't you tell me more?

Agnes. You were going, you know.

Gert. (*Sitting*) I won't go quite like that. Please tell me.

Agnes. (*Calmly*) Well, did you ever read of John Thorold — "Jack Thorold, the demagogue"? (*Gertrude shakes her head*) I daresay not. John Thorold, once a school-master, was my father. In my time he used to write for the two or three so-called inflammatory journals, and hold forth in small lecture halls, occasionally even from the top of a wooden stool in the Park, upon trade and labour questions, division of wealth, and the rest of it. He believed in nothing that people who go to church are credited with believing in, Mrs. Thorpe; his scheme for the re-adjustment of things was Force, his pet doctrine the ultimate healthy healing that follows the surgery of revolution. But to me he was the gentlest creature imaginable; and I was very fond of him, in spite of his — as I then thought — strange ideas. Strange ideas! Hah, many of 'em luckily don't sound quite so irrational to-day!

Gert. (*Under her breath*) Oh! —

Agnes. My home was a wretched one. If dad was violent out of the house, mother was violent enough in it; with her it was rave, sulk, storm, from morning till night; till one day father turned a deaf ear to mother and died in his bed. That was my first intimate experience of the horrible curse that falls upon so many.

Gert. Curse?

Agnes. The curse of unhappy marriage. Though really I'd looked on at little else all my life. Most of our married friends were cursed in a like way; and I remember taking an oath, when I was a mere child, that nothing should ever push me over into the choked-up, seething pit. Fool! When I was nineteen I was gazing like a pet sheep into a man's eyes; and one morning I was married, at St. Andrew's Church in Holburn, to Mr. Ebbsmith, a barrister.

Gert. In church?

Agnes. Yes, in church — in church. In spite of father's unbelief and mother's indifference, at the time I married I was as simple — ay, in my heart as devout — as any girl in a parsonage. The other thing hadn't soaked into me. Whenever I could escape from our stifling rooms at home, and slam the front door behind me, the air blew away uncertainty and scepticism; I seemed only to have to take a long, deep breath to be full of hope and faith. And it was like this till that man married me.

Gert. Of course, I guess your marriage was an unfortunate one.

Agnes. It lasted eight years. For about twelve months he treated me like a woman in a harem, for the rest of the time like a beast of burden. Oh! when I think of it! (*Wiping her brow with her handkerchief*) Phew!

Gert. It changed you?

Agnes. Oh, yes, it changed me.

Gert. You spoke of yourself just now as a widow. He's dead?

Agnes. He died on our wedding-day — the eighth anniversary.

Gert. You were free then — free to begin again.

Agnes. Eh? (*Looking at Gertrude*) Yes, but you don't begin to believe all over again. (*She gathers up the stalks of the flowers from the tray, and, kneeling, crams them into the stove*) However, this is an old story. I'm thirty-three now.

Gert. (*Hesitatingly*) You and Mr. Cleeve?—

Agnes. We've known each other since last November, no longer. Six years of my life unaccounted for, eh? Well, for a couple of years or so I was lecturing.

Gert. Lecturing?

Agnes. Ah, I'd become an out-and-out child of my father by that time — spouting perhaps you'd call it, standing on the identical little platforms he used to speak from, lashing abuses with my tongue as he had done. Oh, and I was fond, too, of warning women.

Gert. Against what?

Agnes. Falling into the pit.

Gert. Marriage?

Agnes. The choked-up, seething pit — until I found my bones almost through my skin, and my voice too weak to travel across a room.

Gert. From what cause?

Agnes. Starvation, my dear. So, after lying in a hospital for a month or two, I took up nursing for a living. Last November I was sent for by Dr. Bickerstaff to go through to Rome to look after a young man who'd broken down there; and who declined to send for his friends. My patient was Mr. Cleeve — (*Taking up the tray*) and that's where his fortunes join mine. (*She crosses the room and puts the tray upon the cabinet*)

Gert. And yet, judging from what that tall girl said yesterday, Mr. Cleeve married quite recently?

Agnes. Less than three years ago. Men don't suffer as patiently as women. In many respects his marriage story is my own reversed — the man in place of the woman. I endured my hell, though; he broke the gates of his.

Gert. I have often seen Mr. Cleeve's name in the papers. His future promised to be brilliant, didn't it?

Agnes. (*Tidying the table, folding the newspapers, etc.*) There's a great career for him still.

Gert. In Parliament — *now?*

Agnes. No; he abandons that and devotes himself to writing. We shall write much together, urging our views on this subject of Marriage. We shall have to be poor, I expect, but we shall be content.

Gert. Content!

Agnes. Quite content. Don't judge us by my one piece of cowardly folly in keeping the truth from you, Mrs. Thorpe. Indeed, it's our great plan to live the life we have mapped out for ourselves, fearlessly, openly; faithful to each other, helpful to each other, for as long as we remain together.

Gert. But tell me — you don't know how I — how I have liked you! — tell me, if Mr. Cleeve's wife divorces him will he marry you?

Agnes. No.

Gert. No!

Agnes. No. I haven't made you quite understand — Lucas and I don't desire to marry, in your sense.

Gert. But you are devoted to each other!

Agnes. Thoroughly.

Gert. What, is that the meaning of "for as long as you are together"! You would go your different ways if ever you found that one of you was making the other unhappy?

Agnes. I do mean that. We remain together only to help, to heal, to console. Why should men and women be so eager to grant to each other the power of wasting life? That is what marriage gives — the right to destroy years and years of life. And the right once given, it *attracts, attracts!* We have both suffered from it. So many rich years of my life have been squandered by it. And out of his life, so much force, energy — spent in battling with the shrew, the termagant he has now fled from; strength never to be replenished, never to be repaid — all wasted, wasted!

Gert. Your legal marriage with him might not bring further miseries.

Agnes. Too late! We have done with Marriage; we distrust it. We are not now among those who regard Marriage as indispensable to union. We have done with it!

Gert. (*Advancing to her*) You know, it would be impossible for me, if I would do so, to deceive my brother as to all this.

Agnes. Why, of course, dear.

Gert. (*Looking at her watch*) Amos must be wondering —

Agnes. Run away, then. (*Gertrude crosses quickly towards the door*)

Gert. (*Retracing a step or two*) Shall I see you? — Oh!

Agnes. (*Shaking her head*) Ah!

Gert. (*Going to her constrainedly*) When Amos and I have talked this over, perhaps — perhaps —

Agnes. No, no, I fear not. Come, my dear friend, (*With a smile*) give me a shake of the hand.

Gert. (*Taking her hand*) What you've told me is dreadful. (*Looking into Agnes's face*) And yet you're not a wicked woman! (*Kissing Agnes*) In case we don't meet again. (*The women separate quickly, looking towards the door as Lucas enters*)

Lucas. (*Shaking hands with Gertrude*) How do you do, Mrs. Thorpe? I've just had a wave of the hand from your brother.

Gert. Where is he?

Lucas. On his back in a gondola, a pipe in his mouth as usual, gazing skywards. (*Going on to the balcony*) He's within hail. (*Gertrude goes quickly to the door, followed by Agnes*) There! by the Palazzo Sforza. (*He re-enters the room; Gertrude has disappeared. Going towards the door*) Let me get hold of him, Mrs. Thorpe.

Agnes. (*Standing before Lucas, quietly*) She knows, Lucas, dear.

Lucas. Does she?

Agnes. She overheard some gossip at the Caffè Quadria yesterday, and began questioning me, so I told her.

Lucas. (*Taking off his coat*) Adieu to them, then, eh?

Agnes. (*Assisting him*) Adieu.

Lucas. I intended to write to the brother directly they had left Venice, to explain.

Agnes. Your describing me as "Mrs. Cleeve" at the hotel in Florence helped to lead us into this; after we move from here, I must always be, frankly, "Mrs. Ebbsmith."

Lucas. These were decent people. You and she had formed quite an attachment.

Agnes. Yes. (*She places his coat, etc., on a chair, then fetches her work-basket from the cabinet*)

Lucas. There's something of the man in your nature, Agnes.

Agnes. I've anathematized my womanhood often enough. (*She sits at the table, taking out her work composedly*)

Lucas. Not that every man possesses the power you have acquired — the power of going through life with compressed lips.

Agnes. (*Looking up smiling*) À propos?

Lucas. These people — this woman you've been so fond of. You see them shrink away with the utmost composure.

Agnes. (*Threading a needle*) You forget, dear, that you and I have prepared ourselves for a good deal of this sort of thing.

Lucas. Certainly, but at the moment —

Agnes. One must take care that the regret lasts no longer than a moment. Have you seen your uncle?

Lucas. A glimpse. He hadn't long risen.

Agnes. He adds sluggishness to other vices, then?

Lucas. (*Lighting a cigarette*) He greeted me through six inches of open door. His toilet has its mysteries.

Agnes. A stormy interview?

Lucas. The reverse. He grasped my hand warmly, declared I looked the picture of health, and said it was evident I had been most admirably nursed.

Agnes. (*Frowning*) That's a strange utterance. But he's an eccentric, isn't he?

Lucas. No man has ever been quite satisfied as to whether his oddities are ingrained or affected.

Agnes. No man. What about women?

Lucas. Ho, they have had opportunities of closer observation.

Agnes. Hah! And they report? —

Lucas. Nothing. They become curiously reticent.

Agnes. (*Scornfully, as she is cutting a thread*) These noblemen!

Lucas. (*Taking a packet of letters from his pocket*) Finally he presented me with these, expressed a hope that he'd see much of me during the week, and dismissed me with a fervent God bless you.

Agnes. (*Surprised*) He remains here then?

Lucas. It seems so.

Agnes. What are those, dear?

Lucas. The duke has made himself the bearer of some letters from friends. I've only glanced at them — reproaches — appeals —

Agnes. Yes, I understand. (*He sits looking through the letters impatiently, then tearing them up and throwing the pieces upon the table*)

Lucas. Lord Warminster — my godfather.

"My dear boy. For God's sake!" — (*Tearing up the letter and reading another*) Sir Charles Littlecote. "Your brilliant future . . . blasted . . . ." (*Another letter*) Lord Froom. "Promise of a useful political career unfulfilled . . . cannot an old friend . . . ?" (*Another letter*) Edith Heytesbury. I didn't notice a woman had honoured me. (*In an undertone*) Edie! — (*Slipping the letter into his pocket and opening another*) Jack Brophy. "Your great career" — Major Leete. "Your career" — (*Destroying the rest of the letters without reading them*) My career! my career! That's the chorus, evidently. Well, there goes my career! (*She lays her work aside and goes to him*)

Agnes. Your career? (*Pointing to the destroyed letters*) True, that one is over. But there's the other, you know — *ours.*

Lucas. (*Touching her hand*) Yes, yes. Still, it's just a little saddening, the saying good-by (*Disturbing the scraps of paper*) to all this.

Agnes. Saddening, dear? Why, this political career of yours — think what it would have been at best! Accident of birth sent you to the wrong side of the House, influence of family would always have kept you there.

Lucas. (*Partly to himself*) But I made my mark. I did make my mark.

Agnes. Supporting the Party that retards; the Party that preserves for the rich, palters with the poor. (*Pointing to the letters again*) Oh, there's not much to mourn for there.

Lucas. Still it was — success.

Agnes. Success!

Lucas. I was talked about, written about, as a Coming Man — *the* Coming Man!

Agnes. How many "coming men" has one known! Where on earth do they all go to?

Lucas. Ah, yes, but I allowed for the failures and carefully set myself to discover the causes of them. And, as I put my finger upon the causes and examined them, I congratulated myself and said, "Well, I haven't *that* weak point in my armour, or *that*"; and, Agnes, at last I was fool enough to imagine I had no weak point, none whatever.

Agnes. It was weak enough to believe that.

Lucas. I couldn't foresee that I was doomed to pay the price all nervous men pay for success; that the greater my success became, the more cancer-like grew the fear of never being able to continue it, to excel it; that the triumph of to-day was always to be the torture of to-morrow! Oh, Agnes, the agony of success to a nervous, sensitive man; the dismal apprehension that fills his life and gives each victory a voice to cry out, "Hear, hear! Bravo, bravo, bravo! but this is to be your last — you'll never overtop it!"

Ha, yes! I soon found out the weak spot in my armour — the need of constant encouragement, constant reminder of my powers; (*Taking her hand*) the need of that subtle sympathy which a sacrificing, unselfish woman alone possesses the secret of. (*Rising*) Well, my very weakness might have been a source of greatness if, three years ago, it had been to such a woman that I had bound myself — a woman of your disposition; instead of to! — Ah! — (*She lays her hand upon his arm soothingly*) Yes, yes, (*Taking her in his arms*) I know I have such a companion now.

Agnes. Yes — now —

Lucas. You must be everything to me, Agnes — a double faculty, as it were. When my confidence in myself is shaken, you must try to keep the consciousness of my poor powers alive in me.

Agnes. I shall not fail you in that, Lucas.

Lucas. And yet, whenever disturbing recollections come uppermost, when I catch myself mourning for those lost opportunities of mine; it is your love that must grant me oblivion — (*Kissing her upon the lips*) your love! (*She makes no response, and, after a pause, gently releases herself and retreats a step or two. His eyes following her*) Agnes, you seem to be changing towards me, growing colder to me. At times you seem to positively shrink from me. I don't understand it. Yesterday I thought I saw you look at me as if I — frightened you!

Agnes. Lucas — Lucas dear, for some weeks, now, I've wanted to say this to you.

Lucas. What?

Agnes. Don't you think that such a union as ours would be much braver, much more truly courageous, if it could but be — be —

Lucas. If it could but be — what?

Agnes. (*Averting her eyes*) Devoid of passion, if passion had no share in it.

Lucas. Surely this comes a little late, Agnes, between you and me.

Agnes. (*Leaning upon the back of a chair, staring before her, and speaking in a low, steady voice*) What has been was inevitable, I suppose. Still, we have hardly yet set foot upon the path we've agreed to follow. It is not too late for us, in our own lives, to put the highest interpretation upon that word — Love. Think of the inner sustaining power it would give us! (*More forcibly*) We agree to go through the world together, preaching the lessons taught us by our experiences. We cry out to all people, "Look at us! Man and woman who are in the bondage of neither law nor ritual! Linked simply by mutual trust! Man and wife, but something better

than man and wife! Friends, but even something better than friends!" I say there is that which is noble, finely defiant, in the future we have mapped out for ourselves, if only — if only —

Lucas. Yes!

Agnes. (*Turning from him*) If only it could be free from passion!

Lucas. (*In a low voice*) Yes, but — is that possible?

Agnes. (*In the same tone, watching him askance, a frightened look in her eyes*) Why not?

Lucas. Young man and woman . . . youth and love . . . ? Scarcely upon this earth, my dear Agnes, such a life as you have pictured.

Agnes. I say it can be, it can be!

Fortuné enters, carrying a letter upon a salver, and a beautiful bouquet of white flowers. He hands the note to Lucas.

Lucas. (*Taking the note, glancing at Agnes*) Eh! (*To Fortuné, pointing to the bouquet*) Qu'avez-vous là?

For. Ah, excuse. (*Presenting the bouquet to Agnes*) Wiz compliment. (*Agnes takes the bouquet wonderingly*) Tell Madame ze Duke of St. Olpherts bring it in person, 'e says.

Lucas. (*Opening the note*) Est-il parti?

For. 'E did not get out of 'is gondola.

Lucas. Bien. (*Fortuné withdraws. Reading the note aloud*) "While brushing my hair, my dear boy, I became possessed of a strong desire to meet the lady with whom you are now improving the shining hour. Why the devil shouldn't I, if I want to! Without prejudice, as my lawyer says, let me turn-up this afternoon and chat pleasantly to her of Shakespeare, also the musical glasses. Pray hand her this flag of truce — I mean my poor bunch of flowers — and believe me yours, with a touch of gout, ST. OLPHERTS." (*Indignantly crushing the note*) Ah!

Agnes. (*Frowning at the flowers*) A taste of the oddities, I suppose!

Lucas. He is simply making sport of us. (*Going on to the balcony, and looking out*) There he is. Damn that smile of his!

Agnes. Where? (*She joins him*)

Lucas. With the two gondoliers.

Agnes. Why — that's a beautiful face! How strange!

Lucas. (*Drawing her back into the room*) Come away. He is looking up at us.

Agnes. Are you sure he sees us?

Lucas. He did.

Agnes. He will want an answer — (*She deliberately flings the bouquet over the balcony into the canal, then returns to the table and picks up her work*)

Lucas. (Looking out again cautiously) He throws his head back and laughs heartily. *(Re-entering the room)* Oh, of course, his policy is to attempt to laugh me out of my resolves. They send him here merely to laugh at me, Agnes, to laugh at me — *(Coming to Agnes angrily)* laugh at me!

Agnes. He must be a man of small resources. *(Threading her needle)* It is so easy to mock.

End of the First Act.

ACT II.

The Scene is the same as that of the previous act. Through the windows some mastheads and flapping sails are seen in the distance. The light is that of late afternoon. Agnes, very plainly dressed, is sitting at the table, industriously copying from a manuscript. After a moment or two, Antonio and Nella enter the room, carrying a dressmaker's box which is corded and labelled.

Nella. Permit us, Signora.

Ant. An enormous box for the Signora.

Agnes. (Turning her head) Eh?

Nella. It has come by the railway —

Ant. (Consulting the label) From Florence.

Agnes. By railway, from Florence?

Nella. (Reading from the label) "Emilia Bardini, Via Rondinelli."

Agnes. Bardini? That's the dressmaker. There must be some mistake. It isn't for me. *(Antonio and Nella carry the box to her animatedly)*

Nella. But look, Signora!

Ant. To the Signora Cleeve!

Nella. Besides, we have paid the railway dues upon it.

Agnes. (Collecting her sheets of paper) Hush, hush! don't trouble me just now. Mettez-là, n'importe où. *(They place the box on another table)*

Nella. The cord would blunt the Signora's scissors. Shall Antonio cut the cord?

Agnes. (Pinning her sheets of paper together) I'll see about it by and by. Laissez-moi!

Nella. (Softly to Antonio) Cut, cut! *(Antonio produces a knife and cuts the cord, whereupon Nella utters a little scream)*

Agnes. (Turning, startled) What is it?

Nella. (Pushing Antonio away) The stupid fellow misunderstood the Signora and has severed the cord.

Agnes. (Rising) It doesn't matter. Be quiet!

Nella. (Removing the lid from the box angrily) And now here is the box open against the Signora's wish! *(Inquisitively pushing aside the paper which covers the contents of the box)* Oh, God, and all the contents exposed! *(When the paper is removed, some beautiful material trimmed with lace, etc., is seen)* Signora, look, look! *(Agnes examines the contents of the box with a puzzled air)* How beautiful!

Lucas enters.

Ant. (To Nella) The master. *(Nella curtsies to Lucas, then withdraws with Antonio)*

Agnes. Lucas, the dressmaker in the Via Rondinelli at Florence — the woman who ran up the little gown I have on now —

Lucas. (With a smile) What of her?

Agnes. This has just come from her. Phuh! What does she mean by sending the showy thing to me?

Lucas. It is my gift to you.

Agnes. (Producing enough of the contents of the box to reveal a very handsome dress) This!

Lucas. I knew Bardini had your measurements; I wrote to her instructing her to make that. I remember Lady Heytesbury in something similar last season.

Agnes. (Examining the dress) A mere strap for the sleeve, and sufficiently décolletée, I should imagine.

Lucas. My dear Agnes, I can't understand your reason for trying to make yourself a plain-looking woman when nature intended you for a pretty one.

Agnes. Pretty!

Lucas. (Looking hard at her) You *are* pretty.

Agnes. Oh, as a girl I may have been *(Disdainfully)* pretty. What good did it do anybody? *(Fingering the dress with aversion)* And when would you have me hang this on my bones?

Lucas. Oh, when we are dining, or —

Agnes. Dining in a public place?

Lucas. Why not look your best in a public place?

Agnes. Look my best! You know, I don't think of this sort of garment in connection with our companionship, Lucas.

Lucas. It is not an extraordinary garment for a lady.

Agnes. Rustle of silk, glare of arms and throat — they belong, in my mind, to such a very different order of things from that we have set up.

Lucas. Shall I appear before you in ill-made clothes, clumsy boots —

Agnes. Why? We are just as we always

have been, since we've been together. I don't tell you that your appearance is beginning to offend.

Lucas. Offend! Agnes, you — you pain me. I simply fail to understand why you should allow our mode of life to condemn you to perpetual slovenliness.

Agnes. Slovenliness!

Lucas. No, no, shabbiness.

Agnes. (*Looking down upon the dress she is wearing*) Shabbiness!

Lucas. (*With a laugh*) Forgive me, dear; I'm forgetting you are wearing a comparatively new afternoon gown.

Agnes. At any rate, I'll make this brighter to-morrow with some trimmings, willingly. (*Pointing to the dressmaker's box*) Then you won't insist on my decking myself out in rags of that kind, eh? There's something in the idea — I needn't explain.

Lucas (*Fretfully*) Insist! I'll not urge you again. (*Pointing to the box*) Get rid of it somehow. Are you copying that manuscript of mine?

Agnes. I had just finished it.

Lucas. Already! (*Taking up her copy*) How beautifully you write! (*Going to her eagerly*) What do you think of my Essay?

Agnes. The subject bristles with truth; it's vital.

Lucas. My method of treating it?

Agnes. Hardly a word out of place.

Lucas. (*Chilled*) *Hardly* a word?

Agnes. Not a word, in fact.

Lucas. No, dear, I daresay your "hardly" is nearer the mark.

Agnes. I assure you it is brilliant, Lucas.

Lucas. What a wretch I am ever to find the smallest fault in you! Shall we dine out to-night?

Agnes. As you wish, dear.

Lucas. At the Grünwald? (*He goes to the table to pick up his manuscript; when his back is turned she looks at her watch quickly*) We'll solemnly toast this, shall we, in Monte-fiascone?

Agnes. (*Eyeing him askance*) You are going out for your chocolate this afternoon as usual, I suppose?

Lucas. Yes; but I'll look through your copy first, so that I can slip it into the post at once. You are not coming out?

Agnes. Not till dinner-time.

Lucas. (*Kissing her on the forehead*) I talked over the points of this (*Tapping the manuscript*) with a man this morning; he praised some of the phrases warmly.

Agnes. A man? (*In an altered tone*) The duke?

Lucas. Er — yes.

Agnes. (*With assumed indifference, replacing the lid on the dressmaker's box*) You have seen him again, to-day, then?

Lucas. We strolled about together for half an hour on the Piazza.

Agnes. (*Replacing the cord round the box*) You — you don't dislike him as much as you did?

Lucas. He's somebody to chat to. I suppose one gets accustomed even to a man one dislikes.

Agnes. (*Almost inaudibly*) I suppose so.

Lucas. As a matter of fact, he has the reputation of being rather a pleasant companion; though I — I confess — I — I don't find him very entertaining.

> He goes out. She stands staring at the door through which he has disappeared. There is a knock at the opposite door.

Agnes. (*Rousing herself*) Fortuné! (*Raising her voice*) Fortuné!

The door opens and Gertrude enters hurriedly.

Gert. Fortuné is complacently smoking a cigarette in the Campo.

Agnes. Mrs. Thorpe!

Gert. (*Breathlessly*) Mr. Cleeve is out, I conclude.

Agnes. No. He is later than usual going out this afternoon.

Gert. (*Irresolutely*) I don't think I'll wait then.

Agnes. But do tell me — you have been crossing the streets to avoid me during the past week — what has made you come to see me now?

Gert. I *would* come. I've given poor Amos the slip; he believes I'm buying beads for the Ketherick school-children.

Agnes. (*Shaking her head*) Ah, Mrs. Thorpe! —

Gert. Of course, it's perfectly brutal to be underhanded. But we're leaving for home to-morrow; I couldn't resist it.

Agnes. (*Coldly*) Perhaps I'm very ungracious —

Gert. (*Taking Agnes's hand*) The fact is, Mrs. Cleeve — oh, what do you wish me to call you?

Agnes. (*Withdrawing her hand*) Well, you're off to-morrow. Agnes will do.

Gert. Thank you. The fact is, it's been a bad week with me — restless, fanciful! And I haven't been able to get you out of my head.

Agnes. I'm sorry.

Gert. Your story, your present life; you,

yourself — such a contradiction to what you profess! — well, it all has a sort of fascination for me.

Agnes. My dear, you're simply not sleeping again. (*Turning away*) You'd better go back to the ammonia Kirke prescribed for you.

Gert. (*Taking a card from her purse, with a little light laugh*) You want to physic me, do you, after worrying my poor brain as you've done? (*Going to her*) "The Rectory, Daleham, Ketherick Moor." Yorkshire, you know. There can be no great harm in your writing to me sometimes.

Agnes. (*Refusing the card*) No; under the circumstances I can't promise that.

Gert. (*Wistfully*) Very well.

Agnes. (*Facing her*) Oh, can't you understand that it can only be — disturbing to both of us for an impulsive, emotional creature like yourself to keep up acquaintanceship with a woman who takes life as I do? We'll drop each other, leave each other alone. (*She walks away, and stands leaning upon the stove, her back towards Gertrude*)

Gert. (*Replacing the card in her purse*) As you please. Picture me, sometimes, in that big, hollow shell of a rectory at Ketherick, strolling about my poor dead little chap's empty room.

Agnes. (*Under her breath*) Oh!

Gert. (*Turning to go*) God bless you.

Agnes. Gertrude! (*With altered manner*) You — you have the trick of making me lonely also. (*Going to Gertrude, taking her hands, and fondling them*) I'm tired of talking to the walls! And your blood is warm to me! Shall I tell you, or not — or not?

Gert. Do tell me.

Agnes. There is a man here, in Venice, who is torturing me — flaying me alive.

Gert. Torturing you?

Agnes. He came here about a week ago; he is trying to separate us.

Gert. You and Mr. Cleeve?

Agnes. Yes.

Gert. You are afraid he will succeed?

Agnes. Succeed! What nonsense you talk!

Gert. What upsets you then?

Agnes. After all, it's difficult to explain — the feeling is so indefinite. It's like — something in the air. This man is influencing us both oddly. Lucas is as near illness again as possible; I can *hear* his nerves vibrating. And I — you know what a fish-like thing I am as a rule — just look at me now, as I'm speaking to you.

Gert. But don't you and Mr. Cleeve — talk to each other?

Agnes. As children do when the lights are put out — of everything but what's uppermost in their minds.

Gert. You have met the man?

Agnes. I intend to meet him.

Gert. Who is he?

Agnes. A relation of Lucas's — the Duke of St. Olpherts.

Gert. He has right on his side then?

Agnes. If you choose to think so.

Gert. (*Deliberately*) Supposing he *does* succeed in taking Mr. Cleeve away from you?

Agnes. (*Staring at Gertrude*) What, *now*, do you mean?

Gert. Yes. (*There is a brief pause; then Agnes walks across the room wiping her brow with her handkerchief*)

Agnes. I tell you, that idea's — preposterous.

Gert. Oh, I can't understand you!

Agnes. You'll respect my confidence?

Gert. Agnes!

Agnes. (*Sitting*) Well, I fancy this man's presence here has simply started me thinking of a time — oh, it may never come! — a time when I may cease to be — necessary to Mr. Cleeve. Do you understand?

Gert. I remember what you told me of your being prepared to grant each other freedom if —

Agnes. Yes, yes — and for the past few days this idea has filled me with a fear of the most humiliating kind.

Gert. What fear?

Agnes. The fear lest, after all my beliefs and protestations, I should eventually find myself loving Lucas in the helpless, common way of women —

Gert. (*Under her breath*) I see.

Agnes. The dread that the moment may arrive some day when, should it be required of me, *I shan't feel myself able to give him up easily.* (*Her head drooping, uttering a low moan*) Oh! —

Lucas, dressed for going out, enters, carrying Agnes's copy of his manuscript, rolled and addressed for the post. Agnes rises.

Agnes. (*To Lucas*) Mrs. Thorpe starts for home to-morrow; she has called to say good-by.

Lucas. (*To Gertrude*) It is very kind. Is your good brother quite well?

Gert. (*Embarrassed*) Thanks, quite.

Lucas. (*Smiling*) I believe I have added to his experience of the obscure corners of Venice, during the past week.

Gert. I — I don't — Why?

Lucas. By so frequently putting him to the inconvenience of avoiding me.

Gert. Oh, Mr. Cleeve, we — I — I —

Lucas. Please tell your brother I asked after him.

Gert. I — I can't; he — doesn't know I've — I've —

Lucas. Ah! really? (*With a bow*) Good-by. (*He goes out, Agnes accompanying him to the door*)

Gert. (*To herself*) Brute! (*To Agnes*) Oh, I suppose Mr. Cleeve has made me look precisely as I feel.

Agnes. How?

Gert. Like people deserve to feel, who do godly, mean things. (*Fortuné appears*)

For. (*To Agnes, significantly*) Mr. Cleeve 'as jus' gone out.

Agnes. Vous savez, n'est-ce pas?

For. (*Glancing at Gertrude*) But Madame is now engage.

Gert. (*To Agnes*) Oh, I am going.

Agnes. (*To Gertrude*) Wait. (*Softly to her*) I want you to hear this little comedy. Fortuné shall repeat my instructions. (*To Fortuné*) Les ordres que je vous ai donnés, répétez-les.

For. (*Speaking in an undertone*) On ze left 'and side of ze Campo —

Agnes. Non, non — tout haut.

For. (*Aloud, with a slight shrug of the shoulders*) On ze left 'and side of ze Campo —

Agnes. Yes.

For. In one of ze doorways — between Fiorentini's and ze leetle lamp shop ze — ze — h'm — ze person.

Agnes. Precisely. Dépêchez-vous. (*Fortuné bows and retires*) Fortuné flatters himself he is engaged in some horrid intrigue. You guess whom I am expecting?

Gert. The duke?

Agnes. (*Ringing a bell*) I've written to him asking him to call upon me this afternoon while Lucas is at Florian's. (*Referring to her watch*) He is to kick his heels about the Campo till I let him know I am alone.

Gert. Will he obey you?

Agnes. A week ago he was curious to see the sort of animal I am. If he holds off now I'll hit upon some other plan. I will come to close quarters with him, if only for five minutes.

Gert. Good-by. (*They embrace, then walk together to the door*) You still refuse my address?

Agnes. You bat! Didn't you see me make a note of it?

Gert. You!

Agnes. (*Her hand on her heart*) Here.

Gert. (*Gratefully*) Ah! (*She goes out*)

Agnes. (*At the open door*) Gertrude!

Gert. (*Outside*) Yes?

Agnes. (*In a low voice*) Remember, in my thoughts I pace that lonely little room of yours with you. (*As if to stop Gertrude from re-entering*) Hush! No, no. (*She closes the door sharply. Nella appears. Pointing to the box on the table*) Portez ce carton dans ma chambre.

Nella. (*Trying to peep into the box as she carries it*) Signora, if you were to wear this magnificent dress! Oh! how much more beautiful you would be!

Agnes. (*Listening*) Sssh! Sssh! (*Nella goes out. Fortuné enters*) Eh, bien?

Fortuné glances over his shoulder. The Duke of St. Olpherts enters; the wreck of a very handsome man, with delicate features, a transparent complexion, a polished manner, and a smooth, weary voice. He limps, walking with the aid of a cane. Fortuné retires.

Agnes. Duke of St. Olpherts?

St. O. (*Bowing*) Mrs. Ebbsmith?

Agnes. Mr. Cleeve would have opposed this rather out-of-the-way proceeding of mine. He doesn't know I have asked you to call on me to-day.

St. O. So I conclude. It gives our meeting a pleasant air of adventure.

Agnes. I shall tell him directly he returns.

St. O. (*Gallantly*) And destroy a cherished secret.

Agnes. You are an invalid; (*Motioning him to be seated*) pray don't stand. (*Sitting*) Your Grace is a man who takes life lightly. It will relieve you to hear that I wish to keep sentiment out of any business we have together.

St. O. I believe I haven't the reputation of being a sentimental man. (*Seating himself*) You send for me, Mrs. Ebbsmith —

Agnes. To tell you I have come to regard the suggestion you were good enough to make a week ago —

St. O. Suggestion?

Agnes. Shakespeare, the musical glasses, you know —

St. O. Oh, yes. Ha! ha!

Agnes. I've come to think it a reasonable one. At the moment I considered it a gross impertinence.

St. O. Written requests are so dependent on a sympathetic reader.

Agnes. That meeting might have saved you time and trouble.

St. O. I grudge neither.

Agnes. It might perhaps have shown your Grace that your view of life is too narrow; that your method of dealing with its problems wants variety; that, in point of fact, your employment upon your present mission is distinctly inappropriate. Our meeting to-day may serve the same purpose.

St. O. My view of life?

Agnes. That all men and women may safely be judged by the standards of the casino and the dancing-garden.

St. O. I have found those standards not altogether untrustworthy. My method — ?

Agnes. To scoff, to sneer, to ridicule.

St. O. Ah! And how much is there, my dear Mrs. Ebbsmith, belonging to humanity that survives being laughed at?

Agnes. More than you credit, duke. For example, I — I think it possible you may not succeed in grinning away the compact between Mr. Cleeve and myself.

St. O. Compact?

Agnes. Between serious man and woman.

St. O. Serious *woman.*

Agnes. Ah, at least you must see that — serious woman. (*Rising, facing him*) You can't fail to realize, even from this slight personal knowledge of me, that you are not dealing just now with some poor, feeble ballet-girl.

St. O. But how well you put it! (*Rising*) And how frank of you to furnish, as it were, a plan of the fortifications to the — the —

Agnes. Why do you stick at "enemy"?

St. O. It's not the word. Opponent! For the moment, perhaps, opponent. I am never an enemy, I hope, where your sex is concerned.

Agnes. No, I am aware that you are not overnice in the bestowal of your patronage — where my sex is concerned.

St. O. You regard my appearance in an affair of morals as a quaint one.

Agnes. Your Grace is beginning to know me.

St. O. Dear lady, you take pride, I hear, in belonging to — The People. You would delight me amazingly by giving me an inkling of the popular notion of my career.

Agnes. (*Walking away*) Excuse me.

St. O. (*Following her*) Please! It would be instructive, perhaps chastening. I entreat.

Agnes. No.

St. O. You are letting sentiment intrude itself. (*Sitting, in pain*) I challenge you.

Agnes. At Eton you were curiously pre-cocious. The head-master, referring to your aptitude with books, prophesied a brilliant future for you; your tutor, alarmed by your attachment to a certain cottage at Ascot which was minus a host, thanked his stars to be rid of you. At Oxford you closed all books, except, of course, betting-books.

St. O. I detected the tendency of the age —

scholarship for the masses. I considered it my turn to be merely intuitively intelligent.

Agnes. You left Oxford a gambler and spendthrift. A year or two in town established you as an amiable, undisguised debauchee. The rest is modern history.

St. O. Complete your sketch. Don't stop at the — rude outline.

Agnes. Your affairs falling into disorder, you promptly married a wealthy woman — the poor, rich lady who has for some years honoured you by being your duchess at a distance. This burlesque of marriage helped to reassure your friends, and actually obtained for you an ornamental appointment for which an over-taxed nation provides a handsome stipend. But, to sum up, you must always remain an irritating source of un-easiness to your own order, as, luckily, you will always be a sharp-edged weapon in the hands of mine.

St. O. (*With a polite smile*) Yours! Ah, to that small, unruly section to which I under-stand you particularly attach yourself. To the —

Agnes. (*With changed manner, flashing eyes, harsh voice, and violent gestures*) The sufferers, the toilers; that great crowd of old and young — old and young stamped by ex-cessive labour and privation all of one pat-tern — whose backs bend under burdens, whose bones ache and grow awry, whose skins, in youth and in age, are wrinkled and yellow; those from whom a fair share of the earth's space and of the light of day is with-held. (*Looking down upon him fiercely*) The half-starved who are bidden to stand with their feet in the kennel to watch gay proces-sions in which you and your kind are borne high. Those who would strip the robes from a dummy aristocracy and cast the broken dolls into the limbo of a nation's discarded toys. Those who — mark me! — are already upon the highway, marching, marching; whose time is coming as surely as yours is going!

St. O. (*Clapping his hands gently*) Bravo! bravo! Really a flash of the old fire. Ad-mirable! (*She walks away to the window with an impatient exclamation*) Your present affaire du cœur does not wholly absorb you then, Mrs. Ebbsmith. Even now the murmur-ings of love have not entirely superseded the thunderous denunciations of — h'm — you once bore a nickname, my dear.

Agnes. (*Turning sharply*) Ho, so you've heard *that*, have you?

St. O. Oh, yes.

Agnes. Mad — Agnes? (*He bows deprecat-*

ingly) We appear to have studied each other's history pretty closely.

St. O. Dear lady, this is not the first time the same roof has covered us.

Agnes. No?

St. O. Five years ago, on a broiling night in July, I joined a party of men who made an excursion from a club-house in St. James's Street to the unsavoury district of St. Luke's.

Agnes. Oh, yes.

St. O. A depressin' building; the Iron Hall, Barker Street — no — Carter Street.

Agnes. Precisely.

St. O. We took our places amongst a handful of frowsy folks who cracked nuts and blasphemed. On the platform stood a gaunt, white-faced young lady resolutely engaged in making up by extravagance of gesture for the deficiencies of an exhausted voice. "There," said one of my companions, "that is the notorious Mrs. Ebbsmith." Upon which a person near us, whom I judged from his air of leaden laziness to be a British working man, blurted out, "Notorious Mrs. Ebbsmith! Mad Agnes! That's the name her sanguinary friends give her — Mad Agnes!" At that moment the eye of the panting oratress caught mine for an instant and you and I first met.

Agnes. (*Passing her hand across her brow, thoughtfully*) Mad — Agnes . . . (*To him, with a grim smile*) We have both been criticised, in our time, pretty sharply, eh, duke?

St. O. Yes. Let that reflection make you more charitable to a poor peer. (*A knock at the door*)

Agnes. Entrez! (*Fortuné and Antonio enter, Antonio carrying tea, etc., upon a tray. To St. Olpherts*) You drink tea — fellow-sufferer? (*He signifies assent. Fortuné places the tray on the table, then withdraws with Antonio. Agnes pours out tea*)

St. O. (*Producing a little box from his waistcoat pocket*) No milk, dear lady. May I be allowed — saccharine? (*She hands him his cup of tea; their eyes meet*)

Agnes. (*Scornfully*) Tell me now — really — why do the Cleeves send a rip like you to do their serious work?

St. O. (*Laughing heartily*) Ha, ha, ha! Rip! ha, ha! Poor solemn family! Oh, set a thief to catch a thief, you know. That, I presume, is their motive.

Agnes. (*Pausing in the act of pouring out tea and staring at him*) What do you mean?

St. O. (*Sipping his tea*) Set a thief to catch a thief. And, by deduction, set one sensualist who, after all, doesn't take the trouble to deceive himself, to rescue another who does.

Agnes. If I understand you, that is an insinuation against Mr. Cleeve.

St. O. Insinuation!

Agnes. (*Looking at him fixedly*) Make yourself clearer.

St. O. You have accused me, Mrs. Ebbsmith, of narrowness of outlook. In the present instance, dear lady, it is *your* judgment which is at fault.

Agnes. Mine?

St. O. It is not I who fall into the error of confounding you with the designing danseuse of commerce; it is, strangely enough, you who have failed in your estimate of Mr. Lucas Cleeve.

Agnes. What is my estimate?

St. O. I pay you the compliment of believing that you have looked upon my nephew as a talented young gentleman whose future was seriously threatened by domestic disorder; a young man of a certain courage and independence, with a share of the brain and spirit of those terrible human pests called reformers; the one young gentleman, in fact, most likely to aid you in advancing your vivacious social and political tenets. You have had such thoughts in your mind?

Agnes. I don't deny it.

St. O. Ah! But what is the real, the actual Lucas Cleeve?

Agnes. Well — what is the real Lucas Cleeve?

St. O. Poor dear fellow! I'll tell you. (*Going to the table to deposit his cup there, while she watches him, her hands tightly clasped, a frightened look in her eyes*) The real Lucas Cleeve. (*Coming back to her*) An egoist. An egoist.

Agnes. An egoist. Yes.

St. O. Possessing ambition without patience, self-esteem without self-confidence.

Agnes. Well?

St. O. Afflicted with a desperate craving for the opium-like drug, adulation; persistently seeking the society of those whose white, pink-tipped fingers fill the pernicious pipe most deftly and delicately. Eh?

Agnes. I didn't — Pray go on.

St. O. Ha, I remember they looked to his marriage to check his dangerous fancy for the flutter of lace, the purr of pretty women. And now— here he is — loose again.

Agnes. (*Suffering*) Oh! —

St. O. In short, in intellect still nothing but a callow boy; in body, nervous, bloodless, hysterical; in morals — an Epicure.

Agnes. Have done! Have done!

St. O. "Epicure" offends you. A vain woman would find consolation in the word.

Agnes. Enough of it! Enough! Enough! (*She turns away, beating her hands together. The light in the room has gradually become subdued; the warm tinge of sunset now colours the scene outside the windows*)

St. O. (*With a shrug of his shoulders*) The real Lucas Cleeve.

Agnes. No, no! untrue! untrue!

Lucas enters. The three remain silent for a moment.

The Duke of St. Olpherts calls in answer to a letter I wrote to him yesterday. I wanted to make his acquaintance. *She goes out.*

Lucas. (*After a brief pause*) By a lucky accident the tables were crowded at Florian's; I might have missed the chance of welcoming you. In God's name, duke, why must you come here?

St. O. (*Fumbling in his pockets for a note*) In God's name? You bring the orthodoxy into this queer firm then, Lucas? (*Handing the note to Lucas*) A peremptory summons.

Lucas. You need not have obeyed it. (*St. Olpherts takes a cigarette from his case and limps away*) I looked about for you just now. I wanted to see you.

St. O. (*Lighting the cigarette*) How fortunate!

Lucas. To tell you that this persecution must come to an end. It has made me desperately wretched for a whole week.

St. O. Persecution?

Lucas. Temptation.

St. O. Dear Lucas, the process of inducing a man to return to his wife isn't generally described as temptation.

Lucas. Ah, I won't hear another word of that proposal. (*St. Olpherts shrugs his shoulders*) I say my people are offering me, through you, a deliberate temptation to be a traitor. To which of these two women — my wife or (*Pointing to the door*) to her — am I really bound now? It may be regrettable, scandalous, but the common rules of right and wrong have ceased to apply here. Finally, duke — and this is my message — I intend to keep faith with the woman who sat by my bedside in Rome, the woman to whom I shouted my miserable story in my delirium, the woman whose calm, resolute voice healed me, hardened me, renewed in me the desire to live.

St. O. Ah! Oh, these modern nurses, in their greys, or browns, and snowy bibs! They have much to answer for, dear Lucas.

Lucas. No, no! Why will you persist, all of you, in regarding this as a mere morbid infatuation bred in the fumes of pastilles? It isn't so! Laugh if you care to! — but this is a meeting of affinities, of the solitary man and the truly sympathetic woman.

St. O. And oh, oh, these sympathetic women!

Lucas. No! Oh, the unsympathetic women! There you have the cause of half the world's misery. The unsympathetic women — you should have loved one of them.

St. O. I daresay I've done that in my time.

Lucas. Love one of these women — I know! — worship her, yield yourself to the intoxicating day-dreams that make the grimy world sweeter than any heaven ever imagined. How your heart leaps with gratitude for your good fortune; how compassionately you regard your unblest fellow-men! What may you not accomplish with such a mate beside you; how high will be your aims, how paltry every obstacle that bars your way to them; how sweet is to be the labour, how divine the rest! Then — you marry her. Marry her, and in six months, if you've pluck enough to do it, lag behind your shooting-party and blow your brains out by accident, at the edge of a turnip-field. You have found out by that time all that there is to look for — the daily diminishing interest in your doings, the poorly assumed attention as you attempt to talk over some plan for the future; then the yawn and, by degrees, the covert sneer, the little sarcasm, and, finally, the frank, open stare of boredom. Ah, duke, when you all carry out your repressive legislation against women of evil lives, don't fail to include in your schedule the Unsympathetic Wives. They are the women whose victims show the sorriest scars; they are the really "bad women" of the world — all the others are snow-white in comparison!

St. O. Yes, you've got a great deal of this in that capital Essay you quoted from this morning. Dear fellow, I admit your home discomforts. But to jump out of that fryingpan into this confounded — what does she call it? — Compact?

Lucas. Compact?

St. O. A vague reference, as I understand, to your joint crusade against the blessed institution of Marriage.

Lucas. (*An alteration in his manner*) Oh — ho, that idea! What — what has she been saying to you?

St. O. Incidentally she pitched into me, dear Lucas; she attacked my moral character. You must have been telling tales.

Lucas. Oh, I — I hope not. Of course, we —

St. O. Yes, yes — a little family gossip, to pass the time while she has been dressing her hair, or — by-the-bye, she doesn't appear to spend much time in dressing her hair.

Lucas. (*Biting his lip*) Really?

St. O. Then she denounced the gilded aristocracy generally. Our day is over; we're broken wooden dolls and are going to be chucked. The old tune, but I enjoyed the novelty of being so near the instrument. I assure you, dear fellow, I was within three feet of her when she deliberately Trafalgar Squared[1] me.

Lucas. (*With an uneasy laugh*) You're the red rag, duke. This spirit of revolt in her — it's ludicrously extravagant; but it will die out in time, when she has become used to being happy and cared for — (*Partly to himself, with clenched hands*) yes, cared for.

St. O. Die out? Bred in the bone, dear Lucas.

Lucas. On some topics she's a mere echo of her father — if you mean that.

St. O. The father — one of these public-park vermin, eh?

Lucas. Dead years ago.

St. O. I once heard her bellowing in a dirty little shed in St. Luke's. I told you?

Lucas. Yes; you've told me.

St. O. I sat there again, it seemed, this afternoon. The orator not quite so lean, perhaps; a little less witch-like, but —

Lucas. She was actually in want of food in those days. Poor girl! (*Partly to himself*) I mean to remind myself of that constantly. Poor girl!

St. O. Girl! Let me see — you're considerably her junior?

Lucas. No, no; a few months perhaps.

St. O. Oh, come!

Lucas. Well, years — two or three.

St. O. The voice remains rather raucous.

Lucas. By God, the voice is sweet.

St. O. Well — considering the wear and tear. Really, my dear fellow, I do believe this — I do believe that if you gowned her respectably —

Lucas. (*Impulsively*) Yes, yes, I say so. I tell her that.

St. O. (*With a smile*) Do you! That's odd now.

Lucas. What a topic! Poor Agnes's dress!

St. O. Your taste used to be rather æsthetic. Even your own wife is one of the smartest women in London.

Lucas. Ha, well, I must contrive to smother these æsthetic tastes of mine.

St. O. It's a pity that other people will retain their sense of the incongruous.

Lucas. (*Snapping his fingers*) Other people! —

St. O. The public.

Lucas. The public?

St. O. Come, you know well enough that unostentatious immodesty is no part of your partner's programme. Of course, you will find yourself by and by in a sort of perpetual public parade with your crack-brained visionary —

Lucas. You shall not speak of her so! You shall not.

St. O. (*Unconcernedly*) Each of you bearing a pole of the soiled banner of Free Union. Free Union for the People! Ho, my dear Lucas!

Lucas. Good heavens, duke, do you imagine, now that I am in sound health and mind again, that I don't see the hideous absurdity of these views of hers!

St. O. Then why the deuce don't you listen a little more patiently to *my* views?

Lucas. No, no. I tell you I intend to keep faith with her, as far as I am able. She's so earnest, so pitiably earnest. If I broke faith with her entirely it would be too damnably cowardly.

St. O. Cowardly?

Lucas. (*Pacing the room agitatedly*) Besides, we shall do well together, after all, I believe — she and I. In the end we shall make concessions to each other and settle down, somewhere abroad, peacefully.

St. O. Hah! And they called you a Coming Man at one time, didn't they?

Lucas. Oh, I — I shall make as fine a career with my pen as that other career would have been. At any rate, I ask you to leave me to it all — to leave me.

Fortuné enters. The shades of evening have now deepened; the glow of sunset comes into the room.

For. I beg your pardon, sir.

Lucas. Well?

For. It is pas' ze time for you to dress for dinner.

Lucas. I'll come. (*Fortuné goes out*)

St. O. When do we next meet, dear fellow?

Lucas. No, no — please not again. (*Nella enters, excitedly*)

Nella. (*Speaking over her shoulder*) Yes, Signora; here is the Signor. (*To Cleeve*) Pardon, Signor. When you see her you'll see how sweet she looks! — (*Agnes's voice is heard*)

---

[1] Trafalgar Square has long been the scene of radical meetings protesting social injustice.

Agnes. (Outside) Am I keeping you waiting, Lucas?

She enters, handsomely gowned, her throat and arms bare, the fashion of her hair roughly altered. She stops abruptly upon seeing St. Olpherts; a strange light comes into her eyes; voice, manner, bearing, all express triumph. The two men stare at her blankly. She appears to be a beautiful woman.

Agnes. (To Nella) Un petit châle noir tricoté — cherchez-le. *(Nella withdraws)* Ah, you are not dressed, Lucas dear.

Lucas. What — what time is it? *(He goes towards the door still staring at Agnes)*

St. O. (Looking at her and speaking in an altered tone) I fear my gossiping has delayed him. You — you dine out?

Agnes. At the Grünwald. Why don't you join us? *(Turning to Lucas lightly)* Persuade him, Lucas. *(Lucas pauses at the door)*

St. O. Er — impossible. Some — friends of mine may arrive to-night. *(Lucas goes out)* I am more than sorry.

Agnes. (Mockingly) Really? You are sure you are not shy of being seen with a notorious woman?

St. O. My dear Mrs. Ebbsmith! —

Agnes. No, I forget — that would be unlike you. *Mad* people scare you, perhaps?

St. O. Ha, ha! don't be too rough.

Agnes. Come, duke, confess — isn't there more sanity in me than you suspected?

St. O. (In a low voice, eyeing her) Much more. I think you are very clever. *(Lucas quietly re-enters the room; he halts upon seeing that St. Olpherts still lingers. — With a wave of the hand to Lucas)* Just off, dear fellow. *(He offers his hand to Agnes; she quickly places hers behind her back)* You — you are charming. *(He walks to the door, then looks round at the pair)* Au 'voir!

Agnes. Au 'voir!   *St. Olpherts goes out.* *(Her head drooping suddenly, her voice hard and dull)* You had better take me to Fulici's before we dine and buy me some gloves.

Lucas. (Coming to her and seizing her hand) Agnes dear!

Agnes. (Releasing herself and sitting with a heavy, almost sullen, look upon her face) Are you satisfied?

Lucas. (By her side) You have delighted me! how sweet you look!

Agnes. Ah —

Lucas. You shall have twenty new gowns now; you shall see the women envying you, the men envying me. Ah, ha! fifty new gowns! you will wear them?

Agnes. Yes.

Lucas. Why, what has brought about this change in you?

Agnes. What!

Lucas. What?

Agnes. I — know —

Lucas. You know.

Agnes. Exactly how you regard me.

Lucas. I don't understand you —

Agnes. Listen. Long ago, in Florence, I began to suspect that we had made a mistake, Lucas. Even there I began to suspect that your nature was not one to allow you to go through life sternly, severely, looking upon me more and more each day as a fellow-worker, and less and less as — a woman. I suspected this — oh, proved it! — but still made myself believe that this companionship of ours would gradually become, in a sense, colder — more temperate, more impassive. *(Beating her brow)* Never! never! Oh, a few minutes ago this man, who means to part us if he can, drew your character, disposition, in a dozen words!

Lucas. You believe *him!* You credit what *he* says of me!

Agnes. I declared it to be untrue. Oh, but —

Lucas. But — but — !

Agnes. (Rising, seizing his arm) The picture he paints of you is not wholly a false one. Sssh! Lucas, hark, attend to me! I resign myself to it all! Dear, I must resign myself to it!

Lucas. Resign yourself? Has life with me become so distasteful?

Agnes. Has it? Think! Why, when I realized the actual conditions of our companionship — why didn't I go on my own way stoically? Why don't I go at this moment?

Lucas. You really *love* me, do you mean — as simple, tender women are content to love? *(She looks at him, nods slowly, then turns away and droops over the table. He raises her and takes her in his arms)* My dear girl! My dear, cold, warm-hearted girl! Ha! You couldn't bear to see me packed up in one of the duke's travelling-boxes and borne back to London, eh? *(She shakes her head; her lips form the word "No")* No fear of that, my — my sweetheart!

Agnes. (Gently pushing him from her) Quick — dress — take me out.

Lucas. You are shivering; go and get your thickest wrap.

Agnes. That heavy brown cloak of mine?

Lucas. Yes.

Agnes. It's an old friend, but — dreadfully *shabby*. You will be ashamed of me again.

Lucas. Ashamed! —

Agnes. I'll write to Bardini about a new one to-morrow. I won't oppose you — I won't repel you any more.

Lucas. Repel me! I only urged you to reveal yourself as what you are — a beautiful woman.

Agnes. Ah! Am I — that?

Lucas. (*Kissing her*) Beautiful — beautiful!

Agnes. (*With a gesture of abandonment*) I — I'm glad.

> *She leaves him and goes out. He looks after her for a moment thoughtfully, then suddenly passes his hands across his brow and opens his arms widely as if casting a burden from him.*

Lucas. Oh! — oh! — (*Turning away alertly*) Fortuné — !

End of the Second Act.

Act III.

The Scene is the same as before, but it is evening, and the lamps are lighted within the room, while outside is bright moonlight. Agnes, dressed as at the end of the preceding Act, is lying upon the settee propped up by pillows. A pretty silk shawl, which she plays with restlessly, is over her shoulders. Her face is pale, but her eyes glitter, and her voice has a bright ring in it. Kirke is seated at a table, writing. Gertrude, without hat or mantle, is standing behind the settee, looking down smilingly upon Agnes.

Kirke. (*Writing*) H'm — (*To Agnes*) Are you often guilty of this sort of thing?

Agnes. (*Laughing*) I've never fainted before in my life; I don't mean to do so again.

Kirke. (*Writing*) Should you alter your mind about that, do select a suitable spot on the next occasion. What was it your head came against?

Gert. A wooden chest, Mr. Cleeve thinks.

Agnes. With beautiful, rusty, iron clamps. (*Putting her hand to her head, and addressing Gertrude*) The price of vanity.

Kirke. Vanity?

Agnes. Lucas was to take me out to dinner. While I was waiting for him to dress I must needs stand and survey my full length in a mirror.

Kirke. (*Glancing at her*) A very excusable proceeding.

Agnes. Suddenly the room sank and left me — so the feeling was — in air.

Kirke. Well, most women can manage to look into their pier-glasses without swooning — eh, Mrs. Thorpe?

Gert. (*Smiling*) How should I know, doctor?

Kirke. (*Blotting his writing*) There. How goes the time?

Gert. Half-past eight.

Kirke. I'll leave this prescription at Mantovani's myself. I can get it made up to-night.

Agnes. (*Taking the prescription out of his hand, playfully*) Let me look.

Kirke. (*Protesting*) Now, now.

Agnes. (*Reading the prescription*) Ha, ha! After all, what humbugs doctors are!

Kirke. You've never heard me deny it.

Agnes. (*Returning the prescription to him*) But I'll swallow it — for the dignity of my old profession. (*She reaches out her hand to take a cigarette*)

Kirke. Don't smoke too many of those things.

Agnes. They never harm me. It's a survival of the time in my life when the cupboard was always empty. (*Striking a match*) Only it had to be stronger tobacco in those days, I can tell you. (*She lights her cigarette*)

Gertrude is assisting Kirke with his overcoat. Lucas enters in evening dress, and looking younger, almost boyish.

Lucas. (*Brightly*) Well?

Kirke. She's to have a cup of good bouillon — Mrs. Thorpe is going to look after that — and anything else she fancies. She's all right. (*Shaking hands with Agnes*) The excitement of putting on that pretty frock — (*Agnes gives a hard little laugh. Shaking hands with Lucas*) I'll look in to-morrow. (*Turning to Gertrude*) Oh, just a word with you, *nurse.* (*Lucas has been bending over Agnes affectionately; he now sits by her, and they talk in undertones; he lights a cigarette from hers. To Gertrude*) There's many a true word, et cetera.

Gert. Excitement?

Kirke. Yes; and that smart gown's connected with it too.

Gert. It is extraordinary to see her like this.

Kirke. Not the same woman.

Gert. No, nor is he quite the same man.

Kirke. How long can you remain with her?

Gert. Till eleven — if you will let my brother know where I am.

Kirke. What, doesn't he know?

Gert. I simply sent word, about an hour ago, that I shouldn't be back to dinner.

Kirke. Very well.

Gert. Look here! I'll get you to tell him the truth.

Kirke. The truth — oh?

Gert. I called here this afternoon, unknown to Amos, to bid her good-by. Then I pottered about, rather miserably, spending money. Coming out of Naya's the photographer's, I tumbled over Mr. Cleeve, who had been looking for you, and he begged me to come round here again after I had done my shopping.

Kirke. I understand.

Gert. Doctor, have you ever seen Amos look dreadfully stern and knit about the brows — like a bishop who is put out?

Kirke. No.

Gert. Then you will.

Kirke. Well, this is a pretty task! — *He goes out. Gertrude comes to Agnes. Lucas rises.*

Gert. I'm going down into the kitchen to see what these people can do in the way of strong soup.

Lucas. You are exceedingly good to us, Mrs. Thorpe. I can't tell you how ashamed I am of my bearishness this afternoon.

Gert. (*Arranging the shawl about Agnes's shoulders*) Hush, please!

Agnes. Are you looking at my shawl? Lucas brought it in with him, as a reward for my coming out of that stupid faint. I — I have always refused to be — spoilt in this way, but now — now —

Lucas. (*Breaking in deliberately*) Pretty work upon it, is there not, Mrs. Thorpe?

Gert. Charming. (*Going to the door which Lucas opens for her*) Thank you.

She passes out. Agnes rises.

Lucas. Oh, my dear girl!

Agnes. (*Throwing her cigarette under the stove*) I'm quite myself again, Lucas dear. Watch me — look! (*Walking, firmly*)

Lucas. No trembling?

Agnes. Not a flutter. (*Watching her open hand*) My hand is absolutely steady. (*He takes her hand and kisses it upon the palm*) Ah! —

Lucas. (*Looking at her hand*) No, it is shaking.

Agnes. Yes when you — when you — oh, Lucas! — (*She sinks into a chair, turning her back upon him, and covering her face with her hands; her shoulders heaving*)

Lucas. (*Going to her*) Agnes, dear!

Agnes. (*Taking out her handkerchief*) Let me — let me —

Lucas. (*Bending over her*) I've never seen you —

Agnes. No; I've never been a crying woman. But some great change has befallen me, I believe. What is it? That swoon — it

wasn't mere faintness, giddiness; it was this change coming over me!

Lucas. You are not unhappy?

Agnes. (*Wiping her eyes*) No, I — I don't think I am. Isn't that strange?

Lucas. My dearest, I'm glad to hear you say that, for you've made me very happy.

Agnes. Because I — ?

Lucas. Because you love me — naturally, that's one great reason.

Agnes. I have always loved you.

Lucas. But never so utterly, so absorbingly, as you confess you do now. Do you fully realize what your confession does? It strikes off the shackles from me, from us — sets us free. (*With a gesture of freedom*) Oh, my dear Agnes, free!

Agnes. (*Staring at him*) Free?

Lucas. Free from the burden of that crazy plan of ours of trumpeting our relations to the world. Forgive me — crazy is the only word for it. Thank heaven, we've at last admitted to each other that we're ordinary man and woman! Of course, I was ill — off my head. I didn't know what I was entering upon. And you, dear — living a pleasureless life, letting your thoughts dwell constantly on old troubles; that is how cranks are made. Now that I'm strong again, body and mind, I can protect you, keep you right. Ha, ha! What were we to pose as? Examples of independence of thought and action! (*Laughing*) Oh, my darling, we'll be independent in thought and action still — but we won't make examples of ourselves, eh?

Agnes. (*Who has been watching him with wide-open eyes*) Do you mean that all idea of our writing together, working together, defending our position, and the positions of such as ourselves, before the world, is to be abandoned?

Lucas. Why, of course.

Agnes. I — I didn't quite mean that.

Lucas. Oh, come, come! We'll furl what my uncle calls the banner of Free Union finally. (*Going to her, and kissing her hair lightly*) For the future, mere man and woman. (*Pacing the room excitedly*) The future! I've settled everything already. The work shall fall wholly on *my* shoulders. My poor girl, you shall enjoy a little rest and pleasure.

Agnes. (*In a low voice*) Rest and pleasure—

Lucas. We'll remain abroad. One can live unobserved abroad, without actually hiding. (*She rises slowly*) We'll find an ideal retreat. No more English tourists prying round us! And there, in some beautiful spot, alone except for your company, I'll work! (*As he paces the room, she walks slowly to and fro, listening, staring before her*) I'll work. My new career! I'll write under a nom de plume. My books, Agnes, shall never ride to popularity on the back of a scandal. Our life! The mornings I must spend by myself, of course, shut up in my room. In the afternoon we will walk together. After dinner you shall hear what I've written in the morning; and then a few turns round our pretty garden, a glance at the stars with my arm about your waist — (*She stops abruptly, a look of horror on her face*) While you whisper to me words of tenderness, words of — (*There is the distant sound of music of mandolin and guitar*) Ah? (*To Agnes*) Keep your shawl over your shoulders. (*Opening the window and stepping out; the music becoming louder*) Some mandolinisti, in a gondola. (*Listening at the window, his head turned from her*) How pretty, Agnes. Now, don't those mere sounds, in such surroundings, give you a sensation of hatred for revolt and turmoil! Don't they conjure up alluringly pictures of peace and pleasure, of golden days and star-lit nights — pictures of beauty and of love?

Agnes. (*Sitting on the settee, staring before her, speaking to herself*) My marriage — the early days of my marriage — all over again!

Lucas. (*Turning to her*) Eh? (*Closing the window, and coming down to her as the music dies away*) Tell me that those sounds thrill you.

Agnes. Lucas —

Lucas. (*Sitting beside her*) Yes?

Agnes. For the first few months of my marriage — (*Breaking off abruptly, and looking into his face wonderingly*) Why, how young you seem to have become; you look quite boyish.

Lucas. (*Laughing*) I believe that this return of our senses will make us both young again.

Agnes. Both? (*With a little shudder*) You know, I'm older than you.

Lucas. Tsch.

Agnes. (*Passing her hand through his hair*) Yes, I shall feel that *now.* (*Stroking his brow tenderly*) Well — so it has come to this.

Lucas. I declare you have colour in your cheeks already.

Agnes. The return of my senses?

Lucas. My dear Agnes, we've both been to the verge of madness, you and I — driven there by our troubles. (*Taking her hand*) Let us agree, in so many words, that we have completely recovered. Shall we?

Agnes. Perhaps mine is a more obstinate case. My enemies called me mad years ago.

Lucas. (*With a wave of the hand*) Ah, but

the future, the future. No more thoughts of reforming unequal laws from public platforms, no more shrieking in obscure magazines. No more beating of bare knuckles against stone walls. Come, say it!

Agnes. (*With an effort*) Go on.

Lucas. (*Looking before him — partly to himself, his voice hardening*) I'll never be mad again — never. (*Throwing his head back*) By heavens! (*To her, in an altered voice*) You don't say it.

Agnes. (*After a pause*) I — I will never be mad again.

Lucas. (*Triumphantly*) Hah! ha, ha! (*She deliberately removes the shawl from about her shoulders and, putting her arms round his neck, draws him to her*) Ah, my dear girl!

Agnes. (*In a whisper with her head on his breast*) Lucas.

Lucas. Yes.

Agnes. Isn't *this* madness?

Lucas. I don't think so.

Agnes. Oh! oh! oh! I believe, to be a woman is to be mad.

Lucas. No, to be a woman trying not to be a woman — *that* is to be mad. (*She draws a long, deep breath, then, sitting away from him, resumes her shawl mechanically*)

Agnes. Now, you promised me to run out to the Capello Nero to get a little food.

Lucas. Oh, I'd rather —

Agnes. (*Rising*) Dearest, you need it.

Lucas (*Rising*) Well — Fortuné shall fetch my hat and coat.

Agnes. Fortuné! Are you going to take *all* my work from me? (*She is walking towards the door; the sound of his voice stops her*)

Lucas. Agnes! (*She returns*) A thousand thoughts have rushed through my brain this last hour or two. I've been thinking — my wife —

Agnes. Yes?

Lucas. My wife — she will soon get tired of her present position. If, by and by, there should be a divorce, there would be nothing to prevent our marrying.

Agnes. Our — marrying!

Lucas. (*Sitting, not looking at her, as if discussing the matter with himself*) It might be to my advantage to settle again in London some day. After all, scandals quickly lose their keen edge. What would you say?

Agnes. Marriage —

Lucas. Ah, remember, we're rational beings for the future. However, we needn't talk about it now.

Agnes. No.

Lucas. Still, I assume you wouldn't oppose it. You would marry me if I wished it?

Agnes. (*In a low voice*) Yes.

Lucas. That's a sensible girl! By Jove, I am hungry! (*He lights a cigarette, as she walks slowly to the door, then throws himself idly back on the settee*)

Agnes. (*To herself, in a whisper*) My old life — my old life coming all over again!

> *She goes out. He lies watching the wreaths of tobacco smoke. After a moment or two, Fortuné enters, closing the door behind him carefully.*

Lucas. Eh?

For. (*After a glance round, dropping his voice*) Ze Duke of Saint Olphert 'e say 'e vould like to speak a meenit alone. (*Lucas rises, with a muttered exclamation of annoyance*)

Lucas. Priez Monsieur le duc d'entrer.

Fortuné goes to the door and opens it. The Duke of St. Olpherts enters; he is in evening dress. Fortuné retires.

St. O. Quite alone?

Lucas. For the moment.

St. O. My excuse to Mrs. Ebbsmith for not dining at the Grünwald — it was a perfectly legitimate one, dear Lucas. I was really expecting visitors.

Lucas. (*Wonderingly*) Yes?

St. O. (*With a little cough and a drawn face*) Oh, I am not so well to-night. Damn these people for troubling me! Damn 'em for keeping me hopping about! Damn 'em for every shoot I feel in my leg. Visitors from England — they've arrived.

Lucas. But what — ?

St. O. I shall die of gout some day, Lucas. Er — your wife is here.

Lucas. Sybil!

St. O. She's come through with your brother. Sandford's a worse prig than ever — and I'm in shockin' pain.

Lucas. This — this is your doing!

St. O. Yes. Damn you, don't keep me standing!

Agnes enters, with Lucas's hat and coat. She stops abruptly on seeing St. Olpherts. — By the settee — playfully, through his pain.

Ah, my dear Mrs. Ebbsmith, how can you have the heart to deceive an invalid, a poor wretch who begs you (*Sitting on the settee*) to allow him to sit down for a moment? (*Agnes deposits the hat and coat*)

Agnes. Deceive?

St. O. My friends arrive, I dine scrappily with them, and hurry to the Grünwald thinking to catch you over your Zabajone. Dear lady, you haven't been *near* the Grünwald.

Agnes. Your women faint sometimes, don't they?

St. O. My — ? (*In pain*) Oh, what *do* you mean?

Agnes. The women in your class of life?

St. O. Faint? oh, yes, when there's occasion for it.

Agnes. I'm hopelessly low-born; I fainted involuntarily.

St. O. (*Moving nearer to her*) Oh, my dear, pray forgive me. You've recovered? (*She nods*) Indisposition agrees with you, evidently. Your colouring to-night is charming. (*Coughing*) You are — delightful — to — look at.

Gertrude enters, carrying a tray on which are a bowl of soup, a small decanter of wine, and accessories. She looks at St. Olpherts unconcernedly, then turns away and places the tray on a table. — Quietly to Agnes.

Not a servant?

Agnes. Oh, no.

St. O. (*Rising promptly*) Good God! I beg your pardon. A friend?

Agnes. Yes.

St. O. (*Looking at Gertrude, critically*) Very nice. (*Still looking at Gertrude, but speaking to Agnes in undertones*) Married or — ? (*Turning to Agnes*) Married or — ? (*Agnes has walked away*)

Gert. (*To Lucas, looking round*) It is draughty at this table.

Lucas. (*Going to the table near the settee and collecting the writing materials*) Here — (*Agnes joins Gertrude*)

St. O. (*Quietly to Lucas*) Lucas — (*Lucas goes to him*) Who's that gal?

Lucas. (*To St. Olpherts*) An hotel acquaintance we made in Florence — Mrs. Thorpe.

St. O. Where's the husband?

Lucas. A widow.

St. O. You might — (*Gertrude advances with the tray*)

Lucas. Mrs. Thorpe, the Duke of St. Olpherts asks me to present you to him. (*Gertrude inclines her head to the Duke. Lucas places the writing materials on another table*)

St. O. (*Limping up to Gertrude and handling the tray*) I beg to be allowed to help you. (*At the table*) The tray here?

Gert. Thank you.

St. O. Ha, how clumsy I am! We think it so gracious of you to look after our poor friend here who is not quite herself to-day. (*To Agnes*) Come along, dear lady — everything is prepared for you. (*To Gertrude*) You are here with — with your mother, I understand.

Gert. My brother.

St. O. Brother. Now, do tell me whether you find your — your little hotel comfortable.

Gert. (*Looking at him steadily*) We don't stay at one.

St. O. Apartments?

Gert. Yes.

St. O. Do you know, dear Mrs. Thorpe, I have always had the very strongest desire to live in lodgings in Venice?

Gert. You should gratify it. Our quarters are rather humble; we are in the Campo San Bartolomeo.

St. O. But how delightful!

Gert. Why not come and see our rooms?

St. O. (*Bowing*) My dear young lady! (*Producing a pencil and writing upon his shirt-cuff*) Campo San Bartolomeo —

Gert. Five — four — nought — two.

St. O. (*Writing*) Five — four — nought — two. Tomorrow afternoon? (*She inclines her head*) Four o'clock?

Gert. Yes; that would give the people ample time to tidy and clear up after us.

St. O. After you — ?

Gert. After our departure. My brother and I leave early to-morrow morning.

St. O. (*After a brief pause, imperturbably*) A thousand thanks. May I impose myself so far upon you as to ask you to tell your landlord to expect me? (*Taking up his hat and stick*) We are allowing this soup to get cold. (*Joining Lucas*) Dear Lucas, you have something to say to me — ?

Lucas. (*Opening the door*) Come into my room.

> *They go out. The two women look at each other significantly.*

Agnes. You're a splendid woman.

Gert. That's rather a bad man, I think. Now, dear — (*She places Agnes on the settee and sets the soup, etc., before her. Agnes eats. — Watching her closely*) So you have succeeded in coming to close quarters, as you expressed it, with him.

Agnes. (*Taciturnly*) Yes.

Gert. His second visit here to-day, I gather?

Agnes. Yes.

Gert. His attitude towards you; his presence here under any circumstances — it's all rather queer.

Agnes. His code of behaviour is peculiarly his own.

Gert. However, are you easier in your mind?

Agnes. (*Quietly, but with intensity*) I shall defeat him. I shall defeat him.

Gert. Defeat him? You will succeed in holding Mr. Cleeve, you mean?

Agnes. Oh, if you put it in that way —

Gert. Oh, come, I remember all you told me this afternoon. (*With disdain*) So it has already arrived, then, at a simple struggle to hold Mr. Cleeve? (*There is a pause. Agnes, without answering, stretches out her hand to the wine. Her hand shakes — she withdraws it helplessly*) What do you want — wine? (*Agnes nods. Gertrude pours out wine and gives her the glass. Agnes drains it eagerly and replaces it*) Agnes —

Agnes. Yes?

Gert. You are dressed very beautifully.

Agnes. Do you think so?

Gert. Don't you know it? Who made you that gown?

Agnes. Bardini.

Gert. I shouldn't have credited the little woman with such excellent ideas.

Agnes. Oh, Lucas gave her the idea when he — when he —

Gert. When he ordered it?

Agnes. Yes.

Gert. Oh, — the whole thing came as a surprise to you?

Agnes. Er — quite.

Gert. I noticed the box this afternoon, when I called.

Agnes. Mr. Cleeve wishes me to appear more like — more like —

Gert. An ordinary smart woman. (*Contemptuously*) Well, you ought to find no difficulty in managing that. You can make yourself very charming, it appears. (*Agnes again reaches out a hand towards the wine. Gertrude pours a very little wine into the wineglass and takes up the glass; Agnes holds out her hand to receive it*) Do you mind my drinking from your glass?

Agnes. (*Staring at her*) No. (*Gertrude empties the glass and then places it in a marked way, on the side of the table furthest from Agnes. — With a little shudder*) Ugh! Ugh! (*Agnes moves away from Gertrude, to the end of the settee, her head bowed, her hands clenched*) I have something to propose. Come home with me to-morrow.

Agnes. (*Raising her head*) Home?

Gert. Ketherick. The very spot for a woman who wants to shut out things. Miles and miles of wild moorland! For company, purple heath and moss-covered granite, in summer; in winter, the moor-fowl and the snow glistening on top of the crags. Oh, and for open-air music, our little church owns the sweetest little peal of old bells! (*Agnes rises, disturbed*) Ah, I can't promise you *their* silence! Indeed, I'm very much afraid that on a still Sunday you can even hear the sound of the organ quite a long distance off. I am the organist when I'm at home. That's Ketherick. Will you come? (*The distant tinkling of mandolin and guitar is again heard*)

Agnes. Listen to that. The mandolinisti! You talk of the sound of your church-organ — and I hear *his* music.

Gert. His music?

Agnes. The music he is fond of; the music that gives him the thoughts that please him, soothe him.

Gert. (*Listening — humming the words of the air, contemptuously*) "Bell' amore deh! porgi l'orecchio, Ad un canto che parte dal cuore. . . ." Love-music!

Agnes. (*In a low voice, staring upon the ground*) Yes, love-music. (*The door leading from Lucas's room opens and St. Olpherts and Lucas are heard talking. Gertrude hastily goes out. Lucas enters; the boyishness of manner has left him — he is pale and excited. — Apprehensively*) What is the matter?

Lucas. My wife is revealing quite a novel phase of character.

Agnes. Your wife — ?

Lucas. The submissive mood. It's right that you should be told, Agnes. She is here, at the Danieli, with my brother Sandford. (*St. Olpherts enters slowly*) Yes, positively. It appears that she has lent herself to a scheme of Sandford's (*Glancing at St. Olpherts*) and of — and of —

St. O. Of Sandford's.

Lucas. (*To Agnes*) A plan of reconciliation. (*To St. Olpherts*) Tell Sybil that the submissive mood comes too late, by a year or so! (*He paces to and fro. Agnes sits, with an expressionless face*)

Agnes. (*Quietly to St. Olpherts*) The "friends" you were expecting, duke?

St. O. (*Meekly*) Yes. (*She smiles at him scornfully*)

Lucas. Agnes, dear, you and I leave here early to-morrow.

Agnes. Very well, Lucas.

Lucas. (*To St. Olpherts*) Duke, will you be the bearer of a note from me to Sandford?

St. O. Certainly.

Lucas. (*Going to the door of his room*) I'll write it at once.

St. O. (*Raising his voice*) You won't see Sandford then, dear Lucas, for a moment or two?

Lucas. No, no; pray excuse me.

He goes out. St. Olpherts advances to Agnes. The sound of the music dies away.

St. O. (*Slipping his cloak off and throwing it upon the head of the settee*) Upon my soul, I think you've routed us!

Agnes. Yes.

St. O. (*Sitting, breaking into a laugh*) Ha, ha! he, he, he! Sir Sandford and Mrs. Cleeve will be so angry. Such a devil of a journey for nothing! Ho! (*Coughing*) Ho, ho, ho!

Agnes. This was to be your grand coup.

St. O. I admit it — I *have* been keeping this in reserve.

Agnes. I see. A further term of cat-and-dog life for Lucas and this lady — but it would have served to dispose of *me*, you fondly imagined. I see.

St. O. I knew your hold on him was weakening. (*She looks at him*) You knew it too. (*She looks away*) He was beginning to find out that a dowdy demagogue is not the cheeriest person to live with. I repeat, you're a dooced clever woman, my dear. (*She rises, with an impatient shake of her body, and walks past him, he following her with his eyes*) And a handsome one, into the bargain.

Agnes. Tsch!

St. O. Tell me, when did you make up your mind to transform yourself?

Agnes. Suddenly, after our interview this afternoon; after what you said —

St. O. Oh! —

Agnes. (*With a little shiver*) An impulse.

St. O. Impulse doesn't account for the possession of those gorgeous trappings.

Agnes. These rags? A surprise gift from Lucas, to-day.

St. O. Really, my dear, I believe I've helped to bring about my own defeat. (*Laughing softly*) Ho, ho, ho! How disgusted the Cleeve family will be! Ha, ha! (*Testily*) Come, why don't you smile — laugh? You can afford to do so! Show your pretty white teeth! Laugh!

Agnes. (*Hysterically*) Ha, ha, ha! Ha!

St. O. (*Grinning*) That's better! (*Pushing the cigarette-box towards him, she takes a cigarette and places it between her lips. He also takes a cigarette gaily. They smoke — she standing, with an elbow resting upon the top of the stove, looking down upon him. As he lights his cigarette*) This isn't explosive, I hope? No nitric and sulphuric acid, with glycerine, eh? (*Eyeing her wonderingly and admiringly*) By Jove! Which is *you*? The shabby, shapeless rebel who entertained me this afternoon, or — (*Kissing the tips of his fingers to her*) or *that*?

Agnes. This — this. (*Seating herself, slowly and thoughtfully, facing the stove, her back turned to him*) My sex has found me out.

St. O. Ha! tsch! (*Between his teeth*) Damn

it, for your sake I almost wish Lucas was a different sort of feller!

Agnes. (*Partly to herself, with intensity*) Nothing matters now — not even that. He's mine. He would have died but for me. I gave him life. He is my child, my husband, my lover, my bread, my daylight — all — everything. Mine, mine.

St. O. (*Rising and limping over to her*) Good luck, my girl.

Agnes. Thanks!

St. O. I'm rather sorry for you. This sort of triumph is short-lived, you know.

Agnes. (*Turning to him*) I know. But I shall fight for every moment that prolongs it. This is my hour.

St. O. Your hour — ?

Agnes. There's only one hour in a woman's life.

St. O. One — ?

Agnes. One supreme hour. Her poor life is like the arch of a crescent; so many years lead up to that hour, so many weary years decline from it. No matter what she may strive for, there is a moment when Circumstance taps her upon the shoulder and says, "Woman, this hour is the best that Earth has to spare you." It may come to her in calm or in tempest, lighted by a steady radiance or by the glitter of evil stars; but however it comes, be it good or evil, *it is her hour* — let her dwell upon every second of it!

St. O. And this little victory of yours — the possession of this man; you think this is the best that earth can spare you? (*She nods, slowly and deliberately, with fixed eyes*) Dear me, how amusin' you women are! And in your dowdy days you had ambitions! (*She looks at him suddenly*) They were of a queer, gunpowder-and-faggot sort — but they were ambitions.

Agnes. (*Starting up*) Oh! — (*Putting her hands to her brows*) Oh! — (*Facing him*) Ambitions! Yes, yes! You're right! Once, long ago, I hoped that my hour would be very different from this. Ambitions! I have seen myself, standing, humbly clad, looking down upon a dense, swaying crowd — a scarlet flag for my background. I have seen the responsive look upon thousands of white, eager, hungry faces, and I've heard the great, hoarse shout of welcome as I have seized my flag and hurried down amongst the people — to be given a place with their leaders! I! With the leaders, the leaders! Yes, that is what I once hoped would be my hour! (*Her voice sinking — weakly*) But this *is* my hour.

St. O. (*After a brief pause*) Well, my dear, when it's over, you'll have the satisfaction of counting the departing footsteps of a ruined man.

Agnes. Ruined — !

St. O. Yes, there's great compensation in that — for women.

Agnes. (*Sitting*) Why do you suggest that he'll be ruined through me? (*Uneasily*) At any rate, he'd ended his old career before we met.

St. O. Pardon me; it's not too late now for him to resume that career. The threads are not quite broken yet.

Agnes. Oh, the scandal in London —

St. O. Would be dispelled by this sham reconciliation with his wife.

Agnes. (*Looking at him*) Sham — ?

St. O. Why, of course. All we desired to arrange was that for the future their household should be conducted strictly à la mode.

Agnes. À la mode?

St. O. (*Behind the settee, looking down upon her*) Mr. Cleeve in one quarter of the house, Mrs. Cleeve in another.

Agnes. Oh, yes.

St. O. A proper aspect to the world, combined with freedom on both sides. It's a more decorous system than the aggressive Free Union you once advocated; and it's much in vogue at my end of the town.

Agnes. Your plan was a little more subtle than I gave you credit for. This was to be your method of getting rid of me!

St. O. No, no. Don't you understand? With regard to yourself, we could have arrived at a compromise.

Agnes. A compromise?

St. O. It would have made us quite happy to see you placed upon a — upon a somewhat different footing.

Agnes. What kind of — footing?

St. O. The suburban villa, the little garden, a couple of discreet servants — everything à la mode. (*There is a brief pause. Then she rises and walks across the room, outwardly calm, but twisting her hands*)

Agnes. Well, you've had Mr. Cleeve's answer to *that*.

St. O. Yes.

Agnes. Which finally disposes of the whole matter — disposes of it —

St. O. Completely. (*Struck by an idea*) Unless *you* — !

Agnes. (*Turning to him*) Unless *I* — !

St. O. Unless you —

Agnes. (*After a moment's pause*) What did Lucas say to you when you — ?

St. O. He said he knew you'd never make that sacrifice for him — (*She pulls herself up rigidly*) So he declined to pain you by asking you to do it.

Agnes. (*Crossing swiftly to the settee and speaking straight into his face*) That's a lie!

St. O. Keep your temper, my dear.

Agnes. (*Passionately*) His love may not last — it won't! — but at this moment he loves me better than that! He wouldn't make a mere light thing of me!

St. O. Wouldn't he! You try him!

Agnes. What!

St. O. You put him to the test!

Agnes. (*With her hands to her brows*) Oh—!

St. O. No, no — don't!

Agnes. (*Faintly*) Why?

St. O. I like you. Damn *him* — you deserve to live your hour!

Lucas enters, with a letter in his hand. Agnes sits.

Lucas. (*Giving St. Olpherts the letter*) Thanks. (*St. Olpherts pockets the letter and picks up his cloak, Lucas assisting him*)

Agnes. (*Outwardly calm*) Oh — Lucas —

Lucas. Yes?

Agnes. The duke has been — has been — telling me —

Lucas. What, dear?

Agnes. The sort of arrangement proposed for your going back to London.

Lucas. Oh, my brother's brilliant idea!

Agnes. Acquiesced in by your wife. (*St. Olpherts strolls away from them*)

Lucas. Certainly; as I anticipated, she has become intensely dissatisfied with her position.

Agnes. And it would be quite possible, it seems, for you to resume your old career?

Lucas. Just barely possible — well, for the moment, quite possible.

Agnes. Quite possible.

Lucas. I haven't, formally, made a sign to my political friends yet. It's a task one leaves to the last. I shall do so now, at once. My people have been busying themselves, it appears, in reporting that I shall return to London directly my health is fully re-established.

Agnes. In the hope? — Oh, yes.

Lucas. Hoping they'd be able to separate us before it was too — too late.

Agnes. Which hope they've now relinquished?

Lucas. Apparently.

Agnes. They're prepared to accept a — a compromise, I hear?

Lucas. Ha, yes!

Agnes. A compromise in my favour?

Lucas. (*Hesitatingly*) They suggest —

Agnes. Yes, yes, I know. After all, your old career was — a success. You made your mark, as you were saying the other day. You did make your mark. (*He walks up and down, restlessly, abstractedly, her eyes following him*) You were generally spoken of, accepted, as a Coming Man. *The* Coming Man, often, wasn't it?

Lucas. (*With an impatient wave of the hand*) That doesn't matter!

Agnes. And now you are giving it up — giving it all up. (*He sits on the settee, resting his elbow on his knee, pushing his hand through his hair*)

Lucas. But — but you believe I shall succeed equally well in this new career of mine?

Agnes. (*Looking at him stonily*) There's the risk, you must remember.

Lucas. Obviously, there's the risk. Why do you say all this to me now?

Agnes. Because *now* is the opportunity to — to go back.

Lucas. (*Scornfully*) Opportunity — ?

Agnes. An excellent one. You're so strong and well now.

Lucas. Thanks to you.

Agnes. (*Staring before her*) Well — I did nurse you carefully, didn't I?

Lucas. But I don't understand you. You are surely not proposing to — to — break with me?

Agnes. No — I — I — I was only thinking that you — you might see something in this suggestion of a compromise. (*Lucas glances at St. Olpherts, whose back is turned to them, but who instinctively looks round, then goes and sits by the window*)

Lucas. (*Looking at her searchingly*) Well, but — you —!

Agnes. (*With assumed indifference*) Oh, I —!

Lucas. You!

Agnes. Lucas, don't — don't make *me* paramount. (*He moves to the end of the settee, showing by a look that he desires her to sit by him. After a moment's hesitation she takes her place beside him*)

Lucas. (*In an undertone*) I do make you paramount, I do. My dear girl, under any circumstances you would still be everything to me — always. (*She nods with a vacant look*) There would have to be this pretence of an establishment of mine — that would have to be faced; the whited sepulchre, the mockery of dinners and receptions and so on. But it would be to you I should fly for sympathy, encouragement, rest.

Agnes. Even if you were ill again — ?

Lucas. Even then, if it were practicable — if it could be — if it —

Agnes. (*Looking him in the face*) Well — ?

Lucas. (*Avoiding her gaze*) Yes, dear?

Agnes. What do you say, then, to asking the duke to give you back that letter to your brother?

Lucas. It wouldn't settle matters, simply destroying that letter. Sandford begs me to go round to the Danieli to-night, to — to —

Agnes. To see him? (*Lucas nods*) And her? (*He shrugs his shoulders*) At what time? Was any time specified?

Lucas. Half-past nine.

Agnes. I — I haven't my watch on.

Lucas. (*Referring to his watch*) Nine twenty-five.

Agnes. You can almost manage it — if you'd like to go.

Lucas. Oh, let them wait a few minutes for me; that won't hurt them.

Agnes. (*Dazed*) Let me see — I did fetch your hat and coat — (*She rises and walks mechanically, stumbling against a chair. Lucas looks up, alarmed; St. Olpherts rises. — Replacing the chair*) It's all right; I didn't notice this. (*Bringing Lucas's hat and coat, and assisting him with the latter*) How long will you be?

Lucas. Not more than half an hour. An hour at the outside.

Agnes. (*Arranging his neck-handkerchief*) Keep this so.

Lucas. Er — if — if I — if we —

Agnes. The duke is waiting. (*Lucas turns away, and joins St. Olpherts*)

Lucas. (*To him, in a low voice*) I am going back to the hotel with you.

St. O. Oh, are you?

The door opens and Fortuné enters, followed by Amos Winterfield. Fortuné retires.

Amos. (*To Lucas, sternly*) Is my sister still here, may I ask? (*Lucas looks to Agnes interrogatively. She inclines her head*) I should like her to know that I am waiting for her. (*Agnes goes out*)

Lucas. (*To Amos*) Pray excuse me.

Amos draws back. St. Olpherts passes out. At the door, Lucas pauses, and bows slightly to Amos, who returns his bow in the same fashion, then Lucas follows St. Olpherts.

Then Gertrude enters, wearing her hat and mantle. Agnes follows; her movements are unsteady, and there is a wild look in her eyes.

Gert. You've come to fetch me, Amos? (*He assents by a nod*)

Amos. (*To Agnes*) I'm sorry to learn from Dr. Kirke that you've been ill. I hope you're better.

Agnes. Thank you, I am quite well. (*Turning away, Gertrude watching her*)

Amos. (*Gruffly*) Are you ready, Gertrude?

Gert. No, dear, not yet. I want you to help me.

Amos. In what way?

Gert. I want you to join me in persuading Mrs. Ebbsmith — *my friend*, Mrs. Ebbsmith — to come to Ketherick with us.

Amos. My dear sister — !

Gert. (*Firmly*) Please, Amos!

Agnes. Stop a moment! Mr. Winterfield, your sister doesn't in the least understand how matters are with me. I am returning to England — but with Mr. Cleeve. (*Recklessly*) Oh, you'd hear of it eventually! He is reconciled to his wife.

Gert. Oh — ! Then, surely, you —

Agnes. No. The reconciliation goes no further than mere outward appearances. (*Turning away*) He relies upon me as much as ever. (*Beating her hands together passionately*) He can't spare me — can't spare me!

Amos. (*In a low voice to Gertrude*) Are you satisfied?

Gert. I suspected something of the kind. (*Going to Agnes, gripping her wrist tightly*) Pull yourself out of the mud! Get up — out of the mud!

Agnes. I have no will to — no desire to!

Gert. You mad thing!

Agnes. (*Releasing herself, facing Gertrude and Amos*) You are only breaking in upon my hour!

Gert. Your hour — ?

Agnes. (*Waving them away*) I ask you to go! to go! (*Gertrude returns to Amos*)

Amos. My dear Gertrude, you see what our position is here. If Mrs. Ebbsmith asks for our help, it is our duty to give it.

Gert. It is especially *my* duty, Amos.

Amos. And I should have thought it especially mine. However, Mrs. Ebbsmith appears to firmly decline our help. And at this point, I confess, I would rather you left it — *you*, at least.

Gert. You would rather *I* left it — I, the virtuous, unsoiled woman! Yes, I am a virtuous woman, Amos; and it strikes you as odd, I suppose — my insisting upon friendship with her. But, look here, both of you! I'll tell you a secret. You never knew it, Amos, my dear; I never allowed anybody to suspect it —

Amos. Never knew — what?

Gert. The sort of married life *mine* was. It didn't last long, but it was dreadful, almost intolerable.

Amos. Gertrude!

Gert. After the first few weeks — weeks, not months! after the first few weeks of it, my husband treated me as cruelly — (*Turning to Agnes*) just as cruelly, I do believe, as your husband treated *you*. (*Amos makes a movement showing consternation*) Wait! Now, then! There was another man — one I loved — one I couldn't help loving! I could have found release with him, perhaps happiness of a kind. I resisted, came through it. They're dead — the two are dead! And here I am, a virtuous, reputable woman; saved by the blessed mercy of Heaven! There, you are not surprised any longer, Amos! (*Pointing to Agnes*) "My friend, Mrs. Ebbsmith!" (*Bursting into tears*) Oh! Oh, if my little boy had been spared to me, he should have grown up tender to women — tender to women! he should, he should — ! (*She sits upon the settee, weeping. There is a short silence*)

Amos. Mrs. Ebbsmith, when I came here to-night I was angry with Gertrude — not altogether, I hope, for being in your company. But I was certainly angry with her for visiting you without my knowledge. I think I sometimes forget that she is eight and twenty, not eighteen. Well, now I offer to delay our journey home for a few days — if you hold out the faintest hope that her companionship is likely to aid you in any way. (*Agnes, standing motionless, makes no response. Amos crosses to her and, as he passes Gertrude, he lets his hand drop over her shoulder; she clasps it, then rises and moves to a chair where she sits, crying silently. — By Agnes's side — in a low voice*) You heard what she said. Saved by the mercy of Heaven.

Agnes. Yes, but she can feel that.

Amos. You felt so once.

Agnes. Once — !

Amos. You have, in years gone by, asked for help upon your knees.

Agnes. It never came.

Amos. Repeat your cry.

Agnes. There would be no answer.

Amos. Repeat it!

Agnes. (*Turning upon him*) If miracles *could* happen! If "help," as you term it, *did* come! Do you know what "help" would mean to *me*?

Amos. What — !

Agnes. It would take the last crumb from me!

Amos. This man's — protection?

Agnes. (*Defiantly*) Yes!

Amos. Oh, Mrs. Ebbsmith — !

Agnes. (*Pointing to the door*) Well, I've asked you both to leave me, haven't I! (*Pointing at Gertrude, who has risen*) The

man *she* loves is dead and gone! She can moralize — ! (*Sitting, beating upon the settee with her hands*) Leave me! (*Amos joins Gertrude*)

Gert. We'll go, Amos. (*He takes from his pocket a small leather-bound book;* [2] *the cover is well-worn and shabby*)

Amos. (*Writing upon the fly-leaf of the book with a pencil*) I am writing our address here, Mrs. Ebbsmith.

Agnes. (*In a hard voice*) I already have it. (*Gertrude glances at the book, over Amos's shoulder, and looks at him wonderingly*)

Amos. (*Laying the book on the settee by Agnes's side*) You might forget it. (*She stares at the book with knitted brows for a moment, then stretches out her hand and opens it*)

Agnes. (*Withdrawing her hand sharply*) No — I don't accept your gift.

Amos. The address of two friends is upon the fly-leaf.

Agnes. I thank both of you — but you shall never be troubled again by me. (*Rising, pointing to the book*) Take that away! (*Sitting, facing the stove, the door of which she opens, replenishing the fire — excitedly*) Mr. Cleeve may be back soon; it would be disagreeable to you all to meet again. (*Gertrude gently pushes Amos aside, and picking up the book from the settee, places it upon the table*)

Gert. (*To Agnes — pointing to the book*) This frightens you. Simple print and paper, so you pretend to regard it — but *it frightens you*. (*With a quick movement, Agnes twists her chair round and faces Gertrude fiercely*) I called you a mad thing just now. A week ago I did think you half-mad — a poor, ill-used creature, a visionary, a moral woman living immorally; yet, in spite of all, a woman to be loved and pitied. But now I'm beginning to think that you're only frail — wanton. Oh, you're not so mad as not to know you're wicked! (*Tapping the book fiercely*) And so this frightens you!

Agnes. You're right! Wanton! That's what I've become! And I'm in my right senses, as you say. I suppose I *was* mad once for a little time, years ago. And do you know what drove me so? (*Striking the book with her fist*) It was *that* — *that!*

Gert. That!

Agnes. I'd trusted in it, clung to it, and it failed me. Never once did it stop my ears to the sound of a curse; when I was beaten it didn't make the blows a whit the lighter; it never healed my bruised flesh, my bruised spirit! Yes, that drove me distracted for a

[2] The book is the Holy Bible.

while; but I'm sane now — *now* it is *you* that are mad, mad to believe! You foolish people, not to know (*Beating her breast and forehead*) that Hell or Heaven is here and here! (*Pointing to the book*) Take it! (*Gertrude turns away and joins Amos, and they walk quickly to the door.* — *Frantically*) I'll not endure the sight of it — !

As they reach the door, Gertrude looks back and sees Agnes hurl the book into the fire. They go out. Agnes starts to her feet and stands motionless for a moment, her head bent, her fingers twisted in her hair. Then she raises her head; the expression of her face has changed to a look of fright and horror. Uttering a loud cry, she hastens to the stove and, thrusting her arm into the fire, drags out the book. Gertrude and Amos re-enter quickly in alarm.

Gert. Agnes — !

They stand looking at Agnes, who is kneeling upon the ground, clutching the charred book.

Act IV.

The Scene is an apartment in the Campo San Bartolomeo. The walls are of plaster; the ceiling is frescoed in cheap modern-Italian fashion. An arch spans the room, at the further end of which is a door leading to Agnes's bedroom; to the left, and behind the support of the arch, is an exit on to a landing, while a nearer door, on the same side, opens into another room. The furniture, and the few objects attached to the walls, are characteristic of a moderate-priced Venetian lodging. Placed about the room, however, are photographs in frames, and pretty knick-knacks personal to Gertrude, and a travelling trunk and bag are also to be seen. The shutters of the two nearer windows are closed; a broad stream of moonlight, coming through the further window, floods the upper part of the room. Hephzibah, a grey-haired north-country-woman dressed as a lady's maid, is collecting the knick-knacks and placing them in the travelling-bag. After a moment or two, Gertrude enters by the further door.

Gert. (*At the partly closed door, speaking into the further room*) I'll come back to you in a little while, Agnes. (*Closing the door and addressing Hephzibah*) How are you getting on, Heppy?

Heph. A'reet, Miss Gerty. I'm puttin' together a' the sma' knick-knacks, to lay them wi' the claes i' th' trunks.

Gert. (*Taking some photographs from the table and bring them to Hephzibah*) We leave here at a quarter to eight in the morning; not a minute later.

Heph. Aye. Will there be much to pack for Mistress Cleeve?

Gert. Nothing at all. Besides her hand-bag, she has only the one box.

Heph. (*Pointing to the trunk*) Nay, nobbut that thing!

Gert. Yes, nobbut that. I packed that for her at the Palazzo.

Heph. Eh, it won't gi' us ower much trouble to maid Mistress Cleeve when we get her hame.

Gert. Heppy, we are not going to call — my friend — "Mrs. Cleeve."

Heph. Nay! what will thee call her?

Gert. I'll tell you — by and by. Remember, she must never, never be reminded of the name.

Heph. Aye, I'll be maist carefu'. Poor leddy! After the way she tended that husband o' hers in Florence neet and day, neet and day!

Gert. The world's full of unhappiness, Heppy.

Heph. The world's full o' husbands. I canna' bide 'em. They're true eneugh when they're ailin' — but a lass can't keep her Jo always sick. Hey, Miss Gerty! Do forgie your auld Heppy!

Gert. For what?

Heph. Why, your own man, so I've heered, ne'er had as much as a bit headache till he caught his fever and died o't.

Gert. No, I never knew Captain Thorpe to complain of an ache or a pain.

Heph. And *he* was a rare, bonny husband to thee, if a' tales be true.

Gert. Yes, Heppy. (*Listening, startled*) Who's this?

Heph. (*Going and looking*) Maister Amos.

Amos enters briskly.

Amos. (*To Gertrude*) How is she?

Gert. (*Assisting him to remove his overcoat*) More as she used to be; so still, so gentle. She's reading.

Amos. (*Looking at her significantly*) Reading?

Gert. Reading. (*He sits humming a tune, while Hephzibah takes off his shoes and gives him his slippers*)

Heph. Eh, Maister Amos, it's good to see thee sae gladsome.

Amos. Home, Heppy, home!

Heph. Aye, hame!

Amos. With our savings!

Heph. Thy savings — !

Amos. Tsch! get on with your packing. (*Hephzibah goes out, carrying the travelling-bag and Amos's shoes. He exchanges the coat he is wearing for a shabby little black jacket which Gertrude brings him*)

Gert. (*Filling Amos's pipe*) Well, dear! Go on!

Amos. Well, I've seen them.

Gert. Them — ?

Amos. The duke and Sir Sandford Cleeve.

Gert. At the hotel?

Amos. I found them sitting together in the hall, smoking, listening to some music.

Gert. Quite contented with the arrangement they believed they had brought about.

Amos. Apparently so. Especially the baronet — a poor, cadaverous creature.

Gert. Where was Mr. Cleeve?

Amos. He had been there, had an interview with his wife, and departed.

Gert. Then by this time he has discovered that Mrs. Ebbsmith has left him?

Amos. I suppose so.

Gert. Well, well! the duke and the cadaverous baronet?

Amos. Oh, I told them I considered it my duty to let them know that the position of affairs had suddenly become altered. (*She puts the pipe in his mouth and strikes a match*) That, in point of fact, Mrs. Ebbsmith had ceased to be an element in their scheme for re-establishing Mr. Cleeve's household.

Gert. (*Holding a light to his pipe*) Did they inquire as to her movements?

Amos. The duke did — guessed we had taken her.

Gert. What did they say to that?

Amos. The baronet asked me whether I was the chaplain of a Home for — [3] (*Angrily*) ah!

Gert. Brute! And then?

Amos. Then they suggested that I ought hardly to leave *them* to make the necessary explanations to their relative, Mr. Lucas Cleeve.

Gert. Yes — well?

Amos. I replied that I fervently hoped I should never set eyes on their relative again.

Gert. (*Gleefully*) Ha!

Amos. But that Mrs. Ebbsmith had left a letter behind her at the Palazzo Arconati, addressed to that gentleman, which I presumed contained as full an explanation as he could desire.

[3] That is, a Home for Fallen Women.

Gert. Oh, Amos — !

Amos. Eh?

Gert. You're mistaken there, dear; it was no letter.

Amos. No letter — ?

Gert. Simply four shakily written words.

Amos. Only four words!

Gert, "My — hour — is — over." (*Hephzibah enters with a card on a little tray. Gertrude reads the card and utters an exclamation. Taking the card — under her breath*) Amos! (*He goes to her; they stare at the card together*)

Amos. (*To Hephzibah*) Certainly.

Hephzibah goes out, then returns with the Duke of St. Olpherts, and retires. St. Olpherts bows graciously to Gertrude, and, more formally, to Amos.

Pray sit down. (*St. Olpherts seats himself on the settee*)

St. O. Oh, my dear sir! If I may use such an expression in your presence — here is the devil to pay!

Amos. (*To St. Olpherts*) You don't mind my pipe? (*St. Olpherts waves a hand pleasantly*) And I don't mind your expression. (*Sitting by the table*) The devil to pay?

St. O. This, I daresay well-intentioned, interference of yours has brought about some very unpleasant results. Mr. Cleeve returns to the Palazzo Arconati and finds that Mrs. Ebbsmith has flown.

Amos. That result, at least, was inevitable.

St. O. Whereupon he hurries back to the Danieli and denounces us all for a set of conspirators.

Amos. Your Grace doesn't complain of the injustice of that charge?

St. O. (*Smilingly*) No, no, I don't complain. But the brother — the wife! Just when they imagined they had bagged the truant — there's the sting!

Gert. Oh, then Mr. Cleeve now refuses to carry out his part of the shameful arrangement?

St. O. Absolutely. (*Rising, taking a chair, and placing it by the settee*) Come into this, dear Mrs. Thorn — !

Amos. Thorpe.

St. O. Come into this! (*Sitting again*) You understand the sort of man we have to deal with in Mr. Cleeve.

Gert. (*Sitting*) A man who prizes a woman when he has lost her.

St. O. Precisely.

Gert. Men don't relish, I suppose, being cast off by women.

St. O. It's an inversion of the picturesque;

the male abandoned is not a pathetic figure. At any rate, our poor Lucas is now raving fidelity to Mrs. Ebbsmith.

Gert. (*Indignantly*) Ah — !

St. O. If you please, he cannot, will not, exist without her. Reputation, fame, fortune, are nothing when weighed against — Mrs. Ebbsmith. And we may go to perdition, so that he recovers — Mrs. Ebbsmith.

Amos. Well — to be plain — you're not asking us to sympathize with Mrs. Cleeve and her brother-in-law over their defeat?

St. O. Certainly not. All I ask, Mr. Winter-field, is that you will raise no obstacle to a meeting between Mrs. Cleeve and — and —

Gert. No! (*St. Olpherts signifies assent; Gertrude makes a movement*)

St. O. (*To her*) Don't go.

Amos. The object of such a meeting?

St. O. Mrs. Cleeve desires to make a direct, personal appeal to Mrs. Ebbsmith.

Gert. Oh, what kind of woman can this Mrs. Cleeve be?

St. O. A woman of character, who sets herself to accomplish a certain task —

Gert. Character!

Amos. Hush, Gerty!

St. O. And who gathers her skirts tightly round her and gently tip-toes into the mire.

Amos. To put it clearly — in order to get her unfaithful husband back to London, Mrs. Cleeve would deliberately employ this weak, unhappy woman as a lure.

St. O. Perhaps Mrs. Cleeve is an unhappy woman.

Gert. What work for a wife!

St. O. Wife — nonsense! She is only married to Cleeve.

Amos. (*Walking up and down*) It is proposed that this meeting should take place — when?

St. O. I have brought Sir Sandford and Mrs. Cleeve with me. (*Pointing toward the outer door*) They are —

Amos. If I decline?

St. O. It's known you leave for Milan at a quarter to nine in the morning; there might be some sort of foolish, inconvenient scene at the station.

Amos. Surely your Grace — ?

St. O. Oh, no, I shall be in bed at that hour. I mean between the women, perhaps — and Mr. Cleeve. (*Going to Amos*) Come, come, sir, you can't abduct Mrs. Ebbsmith — nor can we. Nor must you gag her. (*Amos appears angry and perplexed*) Pray be reasonable. Let her speak out for herself, here, finally, and settle the business. Come, sir, come!

Amos. (*Going to Gertrude, and speaking in a low voice*) Ask her. (*Gertrude goes out*) Cleeve! Where is he while this poor creature's body and soul are being played for? You have told him that she is with us?

St. O. No, *I* haven't.

Amos. He must suspect it.

St. O. Well, candidly, Mr. Winterfield, Mr. Cleeve is just now employed in looking for Mrs. Ebbsmith elsewhere.

Amos. Elsewhere?

St. O. Sir Sandford recognized that, in his brother's present mood, the young man's presence might be prejudicial to the success of these delicate negotiations.

Amos. So some lie has been told him, to keep him out of the way?

St. O. Now, Mr. Winterfield — !

Amos. Good heavens, duke — forgive me for my roughness — you appear to be fouling your hands, all of you, with some relish!

St. O. I must trouble you to address remarks of that nature to Sir Sandford Cleeve. I am no longer a prime mover in the affair; I am simply standing by.

Amos. But how can you "stand by"!

St. O. Confound it, sir — if you will trouble yourself to rescue people — there is a man to be rescued here as well as a woman; a man, by-the-way, who is a — a sort of relative of mine!

Amos. The woman first!

St. O. Not always. You can rescue this woman in a few weeks' time; it can make no difference.

Amos. (*Indignantly*) Ah — !

St. O. Oh, you are angry!

Amos. I beg your pardon. One word! I assure your Grace that I truly believe this wretched woman is at a fatal crisis in her life; I believe that if I lose her now there is every chance of her slipping back into a misery and despair out of which it will be impossible to drag her. Oh, I'll be perfectly open with you! At this moment we — my sister and I — are not sure of her. Her affection for this man may still induce her to sacrifice herself utterly for him; she is still in danger of falling to the lowest depth a woman can attain. Come, duke, don't help these people! And don't "stand by"! Help me and my sister! For God's sake!

St. O. My good Mr. Winterfield, believe me or not, I — I positively like this woman.

Amos. (*Gladly*) Ah!

St. O. She attracts me curiously. And if she wanted assistance —

Amos. Doesn't she?

St. O. Money —

Amos. No, no.

St. O. She should have it. But as for the rest — well —

Amos. Well?

St. O. Well, sir, you must understand me. It is a failure of mine; I can't approach woman — I never could — in the Missionary spirit. (*Gertrude re-enters; the men turn to face her*)

Amos. (*To Gertrude*) Will she — ?

Gert. Yes. (*St. Olpherts limps out of the room, bowing to Gertrude as he passes*) Oh, Amos!

Amos. Are we to lose the poor soul after all, Gerty?

Gert. I — I can't think so — oh, but I'm afraid.

St. Olpherts returns, and Sir Sandford Cleeve enters with Sybil Cleeve. Sandford is a long, lean, old-young man with a pinched face. Sybil is a stately, handsome young woman, beautifully gowned and thickly veiled.

St. O. Mrs. Thorpe — Mr. Winterfield. (*Sandford and Sybil bow distantly to Gertrude and Amos*)

Amos. (*To Sandford and Sybil, indicating the settee*) Will you — ? (*Sybil sits on settee; Sandford takes the chair beside her*) Gertrude— (*Gertrude goes out*)

Sir S. (*Pompously*) Mr. Winterfield, I find myself engaged upon a peculiarly distasteful task.

Amos. I have no hope, Sir Sandford, that you will not have strength to discharge it.

Sir S. We shall object to loftiness of atti-tude on your part, sir. You would do well to reflect that we are seeking to restore a young man to a useful and honourable career.

Amos. You are using very honourable means, Sir Sandford.

Sir S. I shall protest against any perversion of words, Mr. Winterfield —

The door of Agnes's room opens, and Gertrude comes in, then Agnes. The latter is in a rusty, ill-fitting, black, stuff dress; her hair is tightly drawn from her brows; her face is haggard, her eyes are red and sunken. A strip of linen binds her right hand.

St. O. (*Speaking into Sybil's ear*) The lean witch again! The witch of the Iron Hall at St. Luke's!

Sybil. (*In a whisper*) Is *that* the woman?

St. O. You see only one of 'em — there are *two* there. (*Sandford rises as Agnes comes slowly forward, accompanied by Gertrude. Amos joins Gertrude, and they go together into an adjoining room, Gertrude giving Agnes an appealing look*)

Sir S. (*To Agnes*) I — I am Mr. Lucas Cleeve's brother; (*With a motion of the hand towards Sybil*) this is — this is — (*He swal-lows the rest of the announcement, and retires to the back of the room where he stands before the stove. St. Olpherts strolls away and disap-pears*)

Sybil. (*To Agnes, in a hard, dry, disdainful voice*) I beg that you will sit down. (*Agnes sits, mechanically, with an expressionless face*) I — I don't need to be told that this is a very — a very unwomanly proceeding on my part.

Sir S. I can't regard it in that light, under the peculiar circumstances.

Sybil. I'd rather you wouldn't interrupt me, Sandford. (*To Agnes*) But the peculiar circumstances, to borrow my brother-in-law's phrase, are not such as develop sweet-ness and modesty, I suppose.

Sir S. Again I say you wrong yourself there, Sybil —

Sybil. (*Impatiently*) Oh, please let me wrong myself, for a change. (*To Agnes*) When my husband left me, and I heard of his asso-ciation with you, I felt sure that his vanity would soon make an openly irregular life intolerable to him. Vanity is the cause of a great deal of virtue in men; the vainest are those who like to be thought respectable.

Sir S. Really, I must protest — !

Sybil. But Lady Cleeve — the mother — and the rest of the family have not had the patience to wait for the fulfilment of my prophecy. And so I have been forced to undertake this journey.

Sir. S. I demur to the expression "forced," Sybil —

Sybil. Cannot we be left alone? Surely — ! (*Sandford bows stiffly and moves away, follow-ing St. Olpherts*) However — there's this to be said for them, poor people — whatever is done to save my husband's prospects in life must be done *now*. It is no longer possible to play fast and loose with friends and sup-porters — to say nothing of enemies. His future now rests upon a matter of days, hours almost. (*Rising and walking about agi-tatedly*) That is why I am sent here — well, why I *am* here.

Agnes. (*In a low, quavering voice*) What is it you are all asking me to do now?

Sybil. We are asking you to continue to — to exert your influence over him for a little while longer.

Agnes. (*Rising unsteadily*) Ah — ! (*She makes a movement to go, falters, and irreso-lutely sits again*) My influence! mine!

Sybil. (*With a stamp of the foot*) You wouldn't underrate your power if you had seen him, heard him, about an hour ago (*Mockingly*), after he had discovered his bereavement.

Agnes. He will soon forget *me.*

Sybil. Yes, if you don't forsake him.

Agnes. I am going to England, into Yorkshire; according to your showing, that should draw him back.

Sybil. Oh, I've no doubt we shall hear of him — in Yorkshire! You'll find him dangling about your skirts, in Yorkshire!

Agnes. And *he* will find that I am determined, strong.

Sybil. Ultimately he will tire, of course. But when? And what assurance have we that he returns to us when he has wearied of pursuing you? Besides, don't I tell you that we must make sure of him *now?* It's of no use begging us, in a month's time, to patch up home and reputation. It must be *now* — and *you* can end our suspense. Come, hideous as it sounds, this is not much to ask.

Agnes. (*Shrinking from her*) Oh — !

Sybil. Oh, don't regard me as the wife! That's an unnecessary sentiment, I pledge you my word. It's a little late in the day, too, for such considerations. So, come, help us!

Agnes. I will not.

Sybil. He has an old mother —

Agnes. Poor woman!

Sybil. And remember, *you* took him away — !

Agnes. I!

Sybil. Practically you did — with your tender nursing and sweet compassion. Isn't it straining a point — to shirk bringing him back?

Agnes. (*Rising*) I did not take him from you. You — you sent him to me.

Sybil. Ho, yes! that tale has been dinned into your ears often enough, I can quite believe. *I* sent him to you — my coldness, heartlessness, selfishness sent him to you. The unsympathetic wife, eh? Yes, but you didn't put yourself to the trouble of asking for *my* version of the story before you mingled your woes with his. (*Agnes faces her suddenly*) You know him now. Have I been altogether to blame, do you still think? Unsympathetic! Because I've so often had to tighten my lips, and stare blankly over his shoulder, to stop myself from crying out in weariness of his vanity and pettiness? Cruel! Because, occasionally, patience became exhausted at the mere contemplation of a man so thoroughly, greedily self-absorbed? Why, *you* married miserably, the Duke of St. Olpherts tells us! Before you made yourself my husband's champion and protector, why

didn't you let your experience speak a word for *me?* (*Agnes quickly turns away and sits upon the settee, her hands to her brow*) However, I didn't come here to revile you. (*Standing by her*) They say that you're a strange woman — not the sort of woman one generally finds doing such things as you have done; a woman with odd ideas. I hear — oh, I'm willing to believe it! — that there's good in you. (*Agnes breaks into a low peal of hysterical laughter*)

Agnes. Who tells you — that?

Sybil. The duke.

Agnes. Ha, ha, ha! A character — from him! ha, ha, ha!

Sybil. (*Her voice and manner softening*) Well, if there *is* pity in you, help us to get my husband back to London, to his friends, to his old ambitions.

Agnes. Ha, ha, ha, ha! your husband!

Sybil. The word slips out. I swear to you that he and I can never be more to each other than companion figures in a masquerade. The same roof may cover us; but between two wings of a house, as you may know, there often stretches a wide desert. I despise him, he hates me. (*Walking away, her voice breaking*) Only — I did love him once . . . I don't want to see him utterly thrown away — wasted . . . I don't quite want to see that . . . (*Agnes rises and approaches Sybil, fearfully*)

Agnes. (*In a whisper*) Lift your veil for a moment. (*Sybil raises her veil*) Tears — tears — (*With a deep groan*) — Oh — ! (*Sybil turns away*) I — I'll do it . . . I'll go back to the Palazzo . . . at once . . . (*Sybil draws herself up suddenly*) I've wronged you! wronged you! oh, God! oh, God!

> She totters away and goes into her bedroom. For a moment or two Sybil stands still, a look of horror and repulsion upon her face. Then she turns and goes towards the outer door.

Sybil. (*Calling*) Sandford! Sandford! (*Sir Sandford Cleeve and the Duke of St. Olpherts enter*)

Sir S. (*To Sybil*) Well — ?

Sybil. She is going back to the Palazzo.

Sir S. You mean that she consents to — ?

Sybil. (*Stamping her foot*) I mean that she will go back to the Palazzo. (*Sitting and leaning her head upon her hands*) Oh! oh!

Sir S. Need we wait longer, then?

Sybil. These people — these people who are befriending her! Tell them.

Sir S. Really, it can hardly be necessary to consult —

Sybil. (*Fiercely*) I will have them told! I

will have them told! (*Sandford goes to the door of the other room and knocks, returning to Sybil as Gertrude and Amos enter. Sybil draws down her veil*)

Gert. (*Looking round*) Mrs. Ebbsmith — ? Mrs. Ebbsmith — !

Sir S. Er — many matters have been discussed with Mrs. Ebbsmith. Undoubtedly she has, for the moment, considerable influence over my brother. She has consented to exert it, to induce him to return, at once, to London.

Amos. I think I understand you!

Agnes appears at the door of her room dressed in bonnet and cloak.

Gert. Agnes — ! (*Agnes comes forward, stretches out her hand to Gertrude, and throws herself upon the settee*)

Sybil. (*To Sandford, clutching his arm*) Take me away. (*They turn to go*)

Gert. (*To Sybil*) Mrs. Cleeve — ! (*Looking down upon Agnes*) Mrs. Cleeve, we — my brother and I — hoped to save this woman. She was worth saving. You have utterly destroyed her. (*Sybil makes no answer, but walks slowly away with Sandford, then stops and turns abruptly*)

Sybil. (*With a gasp*) Oh — ! No — I will not accept the service of this wretched woman. I loathe myself for doing what I have done. (*Coming to Agnes*) Look up! Look at me! (*Proudly lifting her veil*) I decline your help — I decline it. (*To Gertrude and Amos*) You hear me — you — and you? I unsay all that I've said to her. It's too degrading; I will not have such an act upon my conscience. (*To Agnes*) Understand me! If you rejoin this man I shall consider it a fresh outrage upon me. I hope you will keep with your friends. (*Gertrude holds out her hand to Sybil; Sybil touches it distantly*)

Agnes. (*Clutching at Sybil's skirts*) Forgive me! forgive — !

Sybil. (*Retreating*) Ah, please — ! (*Turning and confronting Sandford*) Tell your mother I have failed. I am not going back to England.

Lucas enters quickly; he and Sybil come face to face. They stand looking at each other for a moment, then she sweeps past him and goes out. Sandford follows her.

Lucas. (*Coming to Agnes*) Agnes — (*To Agnes, in rapid, earnest undertones*) They sent me to the railway station; my brother told me you were likely to leave for Milan tonight. I ought to have guessed sooner that you were in the hands of this meddling parson and his sister. Why has my wife been here — ?

Agnes. (*In a low voice, rocking herself gently to and fro*) Your wife — your wife — !

Lucas. And the others? What scheme is afoot now? Why have you left me? Why didn't you tell me outright that I was putting you to too severe a test? You tempted me, you led me on, to propose that I should patch up my life in that way. (*She rises, with an expressionless face*) But it has had one good result. I know now how much I depend upon you. Oh, I have had it all out with myself, pacing up and down that cursed railway station. (*Laying his hand upon her arm and speaking into her ear*) I don't deceive myself any longer. Agnes, *this* is the great cause of the unhappiness I've experienced of late years — I am not fit for the fight and press of life. I wear no armour; I am too horribly sensitive. My skin bleeds at a touch; even flattery wounds me. Oh, the wretchedness of it! But *you* can be strong — at your weakest, there is a certain strength in you. With you, in time, I feel *I* shall grow stronger. Only I must withdraw from the struggle for a while; you must take me out of it and let me rest — recover breath, as it were. Come! Forgive me for having treated you ungratefully, almost treacherously. To-morrow we will begin our search for our new home. Agnes!

Agnes. I have already found a home.

Lucas. Apart from me, you mean?

Agnes. Apart from you.

Lucas. No, no. You'll not do that!

Agnes. Lucas, this evening, two or three hours ago, you planned out the life we were to lead in the future. We had done with "madness," if you remember; henceforth we were to be "mere man and woman."

Lucas. You agreed —

Agnes. Then. But we hadn't looked at each other clearly then, as mere man and woman. You, the man — what are you? You've confessed —

Lucas. I lack strength; I shall gain it.

Agnes. Never from me — never from me. For what am I? Untrue to myself, as you are untrue to yourself; false to others, as you are false to others; passionate, unstable, like yourself; like yourself, a coward. A coward. *I* — *I* was to lead women! *I* was to show them, in your company, how laws — laws made and laws that are natural — may be set aside or slighted; how men and women may live independent and noble lives without rule, or guidance, or sacrament. *I* was to be the example — the figure set up for others to observe and imitate. But the figure was made of wax — it fell awry at the first hot breath that touched it! You and I! What a partnership it has been! How base and gross and wicked almost from the very beginning! We know each other now thoroughly — how base and wicked it would remain! No, go your way, Lucas, and let me go mine.

Lucas. Where — where are you going?

Agnes. To Ketherick — to think. (*Wringing her hands*) Ah, I have to think, too, now, of the woman I have wronged.

Lucas. Wronged?

Agnes. Your wife; the woman I have wronged, who came here to-night, and — spared me. Oh, go!

Lucas. Not like this, Agnes! not like this!

Agnes. (*Appealingly*) Gertrude! (*Lucas looks round — first at Gertrude, then at Amos — and, with a hard smile upon his face, turns to go. Suddenly Agnes touches his sleeve*) Lucas, when I have learnt to pray again, I will remember you every day of my life.

Lucas. (*Staring at her*) Pray! . . . you! . . . (*She inclines her head twice, slowly; without another word he walks away and goes out.*)

THE END.

Agnes sinks upon the settee; Amos and Gertrude remain, stiffly and silently, in the attitude of people who are waiting for the departure of a disagreeable person)

St. O. (*After watching Lucas's departure*) Now, I wonder whether, if he hurried to his wife at this moment, repentant, and begged her to relent — I wonder whether — whether she would — whether — (*Looking at Amos and Gertrude, a little disconcerted*) — I beg your pardon — you're not interested?

Amos. Frankly, we are not.

St. O. No; other people's affairs *are* tedious. (*Producing his gloves*) Well! A week in Venice — and the weather has been delightful. (*Shaking hands with Gertrude, whose expression remains unchanged*) A pleasant journey! (*Going to Agnes, offering his hand*) Mrs. Ebbsmith — ? (*She lifts her maimed hand*) Ah! An accident? (*She nods*) I'm sorry . . . I . . .

He turns away and goes out, bowing to Amos as he passes.

BIBLIOGRAPHY

Archer, William. *English Dramatists of To-day*. London: Sampson Low, Marston, Searle, and Rivington, 1882.

———. *The Old Drama and the New: An Essay in Re-evaluation*. Boston: Small, Maynard and Co., 1923. (A survey from the Elizabethan period to the twentieth century, with chapters on Victorian plays.)

Ariail, J. M., "Is 'Pippa Passes' a Dramatic Failure?" *Studies in Philology*, XXXVII (1940), 120–129. (A reply to Purcell's interpretation.)

Baker, Henry Barton. *History of the London Stage and Its Famous Players (1576–1903)*. London: George Routledge and Sons, and New York: E. P. Dutton and Co., 1904.

[Bancroft, Sir Squire and Lady.] *Mr. and Mrs. Bancroft on and off the Stage, Written by Themselves*. 2 vols. London: Richard Bentley and Son, 1888. (Third edition. Intimate memories of actors, playwrights, and the revolution in staging at the Prince of Wales's Theatre.)

Bentley, Eric. *Bernard Shaw*. (Revised edition.) New York: New Directions Pub. Corp., 1957.

Brown, Calvin Smith. *The Later English Drama*. New York: A. S. Barnes and Co., 1898.

Chandler, Frank Wadleigh. *Aspects of Modern Drama*. New York and London: The Macmillan Co., 1914. (Analysis of world-dramas from the 1890's to 1914.)

Charlton, H. B. "Browning as Dramatist," *Bulletin of the John Rylands Library*, XXIII (1939), 33–67. (Analysis of the Ottima-Sebald episode in *Pippa Passes*.)

Clinton-Baddeley, Victor Clinton. *The Burlesque Tradition in the English Theatre after 1660*. London: Methuen, 1952.

Cole, John William. *The Life and Theatrical Times of Charles Kean, F. S. A., Including a Summary of the English Stage for the Last Fifty Years*. 2 vols. London: Bentley, 1859.

Coolidge, Archibald C., Jr. "Dickens and the Philosophic Basis of Melodrama," *The Victorian Newsletter*, No. 20 (Fall, 1961), pp. 1–5.

Cordell, Richard A. *Henry Arthur Jones and the Modern Drama*. New York: Ray Long and Richard R. Smith, 1932.

Cunliffe, John W. *Modern English Playwrights: A Short History of the English Drama from 1825*. New York and London: Harper and Brothers, 1927.

Dark, Sidney, and Rowland Grey. *W. S. Gilbert: His Life and Letters*. London: Methuen and Co., and New York: George H. Doran, 1923.

DeVane, William Clyde. *A Browning Handbook*. (Second edition.) New York: Appleton-Century Crofts, Inc., 1955.

Disher, Maurice Willson. *Blood and Thunder: Mid-Victorian Melodrama and Its Origins*. London: Frederick Muller, 1949. (Illustrated.)

———. *Melodrama: Plots that Thrilled*. London: Rockliff, 1954.

Downer, Alan S. "Players and the Painted Stage: Nineteenth Century Acting," *PMLA*, LXI (1946), 522–576.

DuBois, Arthur E. "Robert Browning, Dramatist," *Studies in Philology*, XXXIII (1936), 626–655.

Dunkel, Wilbur Dwight. *Sir Arthur Pinero: A Critical Biography with Letters*. Chicago: University of Chicago Press, 1941.

Evans, Bertrand. *Gothic Drama from Walpole to Shelley*. Berkeley and Los Angeles: University of California Press, 1947.

———. "Manfred's Remorse and Dramatic Tradition," *PMLA*, LXII (1947), 752–773. (Illuminating on the Gothic drama and *Bertram*.)

Filon, Augustin. *The English Stage*. London: John Milne, 1897. (Critical discussions of many Victorian plays.)

Fitzgerald, P. H. *The World Behind the Scenes*. London: Chatto and Windus, 1881.

Forbes-Robertson, Sir Johnston. *A Player under Three Reigns*. Boston: Little, Brown and Co., 1925.

Fyfe, H. Hamilton. *Arthur Wing Pinero, Playwright: A Study*. London: Greening and Co., 1902.

———. *Sir Arthur Pinero's Plays and Players*. London: Ernest Benn, 1930.

Ganzel, Dewey. "Patent Wrongs and Patent Theatres: Drama and the Law in the Early Nineteenth Century," *PMLA*, LXXVI (1961), 384–396.

Hartnoll, Phyllis, ed. *The Oxford Companion to the Theatre*. London: Oxford University Press, 1951. (Reference book: definitions, brief biographies.)

Henderson, Archibald. *Bernard Shaw: Playboy and Prophet*. New York and London: D. Appleton and Co., 1932. (An "authorized" biography and critical study.)

Hopkins, Albert A. *Magic*. New York: Munn and Co., 1898. (Mechanisms for stage effects, illustrated.)

Hudson, Lynton Alfred. *The English Stage, 1850–1950*. London: G. G. Harrap and Co., 1951.

Idman, Niilo. *Charles Robert Maturin: His Life and Works*. London: Constable and Co., 1923.

Irvine, William. *The Universe of G. B. S.* New York, London, Toronto: McGraw-Hill Book Co., 1949. (Analysis of Shaw's plays.)

Jerrold, Blanchard. *The Life and Remains of Douglas Jerrold*. Boston: Ticknor and Fields, 1859.

Jerrold, Walter. *Douglas Jerrold: Dramatist and Wit*. 2 vols. London, New York, Toronto: Hodder and Stoughton, 1914.

Jones, Doris Arthur. *The Life and Letters of Henry Arthur Jones*. London: Victor Gollancz, 1930.

Jones, Henry Arthur. *The Foundations of a National Drama*. London: Chapman and Hall, and New York: George H. Doran, 1913.

———. *The Renascence of the English Drama*. London: Macmillan and Co., 1895.

Lewes, George Henry. *On Actors and the Art of Acting*. New York: Henry Holt and Co., 1878.

Lytton, The Earl of. *The Life of Edward Bulwer, First Lord Lytton*. 2 vols. London: Macmillan and Co., 1913.

Macready, William Charles. *Macready's Reminiscences and Selections from His Diaries and Letters*, ed. Sir Frederick Pollock. 2 vols. New York: Harper and Brothers, 1875.

McCormick, James Patton. "Robert Browning and the Experimental Drama," *PMLA*, LXVIII (1953), 982–989.

Mears, Richard McMath. "Serious Verse Drama in England, 1812–1850," unpublished doctoral dissertation, University of North Carolina, 1954. (A thorough study of the decline of verse drama.)

Meeks, Leslie M. *Sheridan Knowles and the Theatre of His Time*. Bloomington, Ind.: The Principia Press, 1933.

Meisel, Martin. *Shaw and the Nineteenth Century Theater*. Princeton, N. J.: Princeton University Press, 1963.

Morley, Henry. *The Journal of a London Playgoer: 1851–1866*. London: George Routledge and Sons, 1891.

Moses, Montrose J. *Representative British Dramas: Victorian and Modern*. Boston: D. C. Heath and Co., 1918, and Boston: Little, Brown and Co., 1921. (Edition of 1918 contains eleven Victorian plays: James Sheridan Knowles, *Virginius*; Douglas Jerrold,

Black-Ey'd Susan; or, All in the Downs; Sir Edward Bulwer-Lytton, *Richelieu; or, The Conspiracy;* Dion Boucicault, *London Assurance;* Robert Browning, *A Blot in the 'Scutcheon;* Tom Taylor, *The Ticket-of-Leave Man;* T. W. Robertson, *Caste;* W. S. Gilbert, *H. M. S. Pinafore; or, The Lass that Loved a Sailor;* Henry Arthur Jones, *The Masqueraders;* Oscar Wilde, *The Importance of Being Earnest;* and Arthur Wing Pinero, *The Gay Lord Quex.* Edition of 1921 adds Alfred Tennyson, *Becket.*)

Newton, Henry Chance. *Crime and the Drama; or, Dark Deeds Dramatized.* London: Stanley Paul and Co., 1927. (Real crimes and lurid melodramas based upon them.)

Nicoll, Allardyce. *British Drama: An Historical Survey from the Beginnings to the Present Time.* (Fourth edition.) London, Toronto, etc.: George G. Harrap and Co., 1947.

———. *The Development of the Theatre.* London: George G. Harrap and Co., 1927.

———. *A History of Early Nineteenth Century Drama, 1800–1850.* 2 vols. Cambridge, England: Cambridge University Press, 1930. (Standard history and play-lists.)

———. *A History of Late Nineteenth Century Drama, 1850–1900.* 2 vols. Cambridge, England: Cambridge University Press, 1946. (Standard history and play-lists.)

Pearce, Charles E. *Madame Vestris and Her Times.* London: Stanley Paul and Co., 1923.

Pearson, Hesketh. *G. B. S.: A Full Length Portrait.* Garden City, N. Y.: Garden City Publishing Co., 1942.

———. *Gilbert and Sullivan: A Biography.* New York and London: Harper and Brothers, 1935.

———. *Gilbert: His Life and Strife.* London: Methuen, and New York: Harper, 1957.

Pemberton, T. Edgar. *The Life and Writings of T. W. Robertson.* London: Richard Bentley and Son, 1893.

Planché, James Robinson. *The Recollections and Reflections of J. R. Planché. A Professional Autobiography.* 2 vols. London: Tinsley Brothers, 1872.

Pollock, Sir Frederick. *Macready's Reminiscences, and Selections from His Diaries and Letters.* New York: Macmillan and Co., 1875.

Purcell, J. M. "The Dramatic Failure of *Pippa Passes*," *Studies in Philology*, XXXVI (1939), 77–87.

Purnell, Thomas. *Dramatists of the Present Day.* London: Chapman and Hall, 1871.

Qualia, Charles B. "French Dramatic Sources of Bulwer-Lytton's *Richelieu*," *PMLA*, XLII (1927), 177–184.

Reed, Joseph W. "Browning and Macready: The Final Quarrel," *PMLA*, LXXV (1960), 597–603.

Reynolds, Ernest. *Early Victorian Drama (1830–1870).* Cambridge, England: W. Heffer and Sons, 1936.

Rice, Charles. *The London Theatre in the Eighteen-Thirties,* eds. Arthur Colby Sprague and Bertram Shuttleworth. London: The Society for Theatre Research, 1950. (Reviews from the theatrical diary of a playgoer.)

Rowell, George. *Nineteenth Century Plays.* New York and London: Oxford University Press, "The World's Classics" No. 533, 1953. (Contains: Douglas Jerrold, *Black-Ey'd Susan;* Edward Bulwer-Lytton, *Money;* Tom Taylor and Charles Reade, *Masks and Faces;* Dion Boucicault, *The Colleen Bawn;* C. H. Hazlewood, *Lady Audley's Secret;* Tom Taylor, *The Ticket-of-Leave Man;* T. W. Robertson, *Caste;* James Albery, *Two Roses;* Leopold Lewis, *The Bells;* and Sydney Grundy, *A Pair of Spectacles.*)

———. *The Victorian Theatre: A Survey.* London, New York, Toronto: Oxford University Press, 1956.

Savin, Maynard. *Thomas William Robertson: His Plays and Stagecraft.* Providence, R. I.: Brown University Press, 1950.

Sawyer, Newell Wheeler. *The Comedy of Manners from Sheridan to Maugham.* Philadelphia: University of Pennsylvania Press, 1931.

Scholten, Willem. *Charles Robert Maturin: The Terror-Novelist.* Amsterdam: H. J. Paris, 1933.

Scott, Clement. *The Drama of Yesterday and Today.* 2 vols. London: Macmillan and Co., 1899. (Anecdotes and observations of theatres and actors. Illustrated.)

Shaw, George Bernard. *Dramatic Opinions and Essays*. New York: Brentano's, 1910.

————. *Our Theatres in the Nineties*. 3 vols. London: Constable and Co., rev. ed., 1932.

Shattuck, Charles H. *Bulwer and Macready: A Chronicle of the Early Victorian Theatre*. Urbana: University of Illinois Press, 1958. (Details of the growth and structure of *Richelieu*.)

Sherson, Erroll. *London's Lost Theatres of the Nineteenth Century*. London: John Lane, 1925. (Picturesque facts about the minor theatres, actors, and staging. Illustrated.)

Stirling, Edward. *Old Drury Lane: Fifty Years' Recollections of Author, Actor, and Manager*. London: Chatto and Windus, 1881.

Stoakes, J. P. "English Melodrama: Forerunner of Modern Social Drama," *Florida State University Studies*, III (1951), 53–62.

Thorndike, Ashley H. *English Comedy*. New York: The Macmillan Co., 1929. (Four chapters on the Victorian period.)

Tolles, Winton. *Tom Taylor and the Victorian Drama*. New York: Columbia University Press, 1940.

Toynbee, William, ed. *The Diaries of William Charles Macready, 1833–1851*. 2 vols. London: Chapman and Hall, 1912.

Trewin, J. C. *Mr. Macready: A Nineteenth-Century Tragedian and His Theatre*. London: George G. Harrap and Co., 1955.

Vardac, A. Nicholas. *Stage to Screen: Theatrical Method from Garrick to Griffith*. Cambridge, Mass.: Harvard University Press, 1949. (Transition from the melodrama to early moving pictures. Illustrated.)

Waitzkin, Leo. *The Witch of Wych Street: A Study of the Theatrical Reforms of Madame Vestris*. Cambridge, Mass.: Harvard University Press, 1933.

Walsh, Townsend. *The Career of Dion Boucicault*. New York: The Dunlap Society, 1915.

Watson, Ernest Bradlee. *Sheridan to Robertson: A Study of the Nineteenth-Century London Stage*. Cambridge, Mass.: Harvard University Press, 1926.

Wyndham, Henry Saxe. *Annals of the Covent Garden Theatre*. 2 vols. London: Chatto and Windus, 1906.